P9-CRF-018

Second Canadian Edition

Cost Accounting

A Managerial Emphasis

Charles T. Horngren
Stanford University

George Foster
Stanford University

Srikant M. Datar
Stanford University

Howard D. Teall
Wilfrid Laurier University

Prentice Hall Canada Inc.
Scarborough, Ontario

Canadian Cataloguing in Publication Data

Main entry under title:

Cost accounting: a managerial emphasis

2nd Canadian ed.
Includes index.
ISBN 0-13-083250-2

1. Cost accounting. 2. Costs, Industrial. I. Horngren,
Charles T., 1926- .
II. Title: Cost accounting: a managerial approach.

HF5686.C8C67 2000   658.15'4   C99-930372-4

© 2000, 1997 Prentice-Hall Canada Inc., Scarborough,
Ontario
Pearson Education

ALL RIGHTS RESERVED

No part of this book may be reproduced in any form
without permission in writing from the publisher.

Prentice-Hall, Inc., Upper Saddle River, New Jersey
Prentice-Hall International (UK) Limited, London
Prentice-Hall of Australia, Pty. Limited, Sydney
Prentice-Hall Hispanoamericana, S.A., Mexico City
Prentice-Hall of India Private Limited, New Delhi
Prentice-Hall of Japan, Inc., Tokyo
Simon & Schuster Southeast Asia Private Limited, Singapore
Editora Prentice-Hall do Brasil, Ltda., Rio de Janeiro

ISBN 0-13-083250-2

Vice-President and Editorial Director: Patrick Ferrier
Senior Marketing Manager: Ann Byford
Senior Developmental Editor: Lesley Mann
Production Editor: Nicole Mellow
Production Coordinator: Deborah Starks
Copy Editor: Edie Franks
Permissions/Photo Research: Susan Wallace-Cox
Art Direction: Mary Opper
Interior Design: Sputnik Art & Design, Lisa LaPointe
Page Layout: Hermia Chung
Cover Design: David Cheung Design
Cover photo of Halifax harbour: Ron Watts/Firstlight

Original English Language edition published by
Prentice-Hall, Inc., Upper Saddle River, New Jersey
Copyright © 2000, 1997, 1994, 1991, 1987, 1982, 1977,
1972, 1967, 1962

    4 5   04 03 02

Printed and bound in the United States of America.

Visit the Prentice Hall Canada Web site! Send us your
comments, browse our catalogues, and more.
www.phcanada.com. Or reach us through e-mail at
phcinfo_pubcanada@prenhall.com.

Management Accounting Question No. 1
June 1986
Appendix A
Reproduced with permission of The Society of Manage-
ment Accountants of Canada

Comprehensive Question 1
January 1987
Appendix A
Reproduced with permission of The Society of Manage-
ment Accountants of Canada

Management Accounting Question No. 4
June 1987
Appendix A
Reproduced with permission of The Society of Manage-
ment Accountants of Canada

Management Accounting Question No. 1 and No. 2
January 1989
Appendix A
Reproduced with permission of The Society of Manage-
ment Accountants of Canada

Management Accounting Question No. 1 and No. 2
June 1989
Appendix A
Reproduced with permission of The Society of Manage-
ment Accountants of Canada

Uniform Final Examination Questions, 1980 Paper III,
Question 3
Appendix A
Reprinted with permission from The Canadian Institute
of Chartered Accountants, Toronto, Canada. Any
changes to the original material are the sole responsibility of the authors and/or publishers and have not been
reviewed or endorsed by the CICA.

Uniform Final Examination Questions, 1986 Paper III,
Question 3
Appendix A
Reprinted with permission from The Canadian
Institute of Chartered Accountants, Toronto, Canada.
Any changes to the original material are the sole respon-
sibility of the authors and/or publishers and have not
been reviewed or endorsed by the CICA.

Management Accounting 2, Examination and Suggested
Solutions, Questions 2 and 6
December 1992
Appendix A
Reprinted with permission of CGA-Canada

BRIEF CONTENTS

CONTENTS

V

3

COST-VOLUME-PROFIT ANALYSIS   61

4

JOB COSTING   99

5

ACTIVITY-BASED COSTING AND
ACTIVITY-BASED MANAGEMENT   137

8
FLEXIBLE BUDGETS, VARIANCES, AND MANAGEMENT CONTROL: II 257

9
INCOME EFFECTS OF ALTERNATIVE INVENTORY COSTING METHODS 288

PART THREE
COST INFORMATION FOR DECISIONS

10
DETERMINING HOW COSTS BEHAVE   320

11
DECISION MAKING AND RELEVANT INFORMATION   368

24

PERFORMANCE MEASUREMENT, COMPENSATION, AND MULTINATIONAL CONSIDERATIONS   824

PREFACE

Studying cost accounting is one of the best business investments a student can make. Why? Because success in any organization—from the smallest corner store to the largest multinational corporation—requires the use of cost accounting concepts and practices. Cost accounting provides key data to managers for planning and controlling, as well as costing products, services, and customers. Topics covered in this book also are of great value in personal financial management. For example, gaining an understanding of budgeting yields lifelong returns.

The central focus of this book is on how cost accounting helps managers make better decisions. Cost accountants themselves are increasingly becoming integral members of decision-making teams instead of just data providers. To link to this decision-making emphasis, the "different costs for different purposes" theme is used throughout this book. By focusing on basic concepts, analyses, uses, and procedures instead of procedures alone, we recognize cost accounting as a managerial tool for business strategy and implementation, and we also prepare students for the rewards and challenges facing them in the world of professional cost accounting both today and tomorrow.

STRENGTHS OF THE FIRST EDITION RETAINED AND ENHANCED

Reviewers of the first Canadian edition praised the following features, which have been retained and strengthened in the second edition:

- ◆ Exceptionally strong emphasis on managerial uses of cost information
- ◆ Clarity and understandability of the text
- ◆ Excellent balance in integrating modern topics with existing content
- ◆ Emphasis on human behaviour aspects
- ◆ Extensive use of real-world examples
- ◆ Flexibility to teach chapters in different sequences
- ◆ Excellent quantity, quality, and range of assignment material

The first thirteen chapters provide the essence of a one-term (quarter or semester) course. There is ample text and assignment material in the book's twenty-four chapters for a two-term course. This book can be used immediately after the student has had an introductory course in financial accounting. Alternatively, this book can build on an introductory course in managerial accounting.

Deciding on the sequence of chapters in a textbook is a challenge. Every instructor has a favourite way of organizing his or her course. Hence, we present a modular, flexible organization that permits a course to be custom-tailored. *This organization facilitates diverse approaches to teaching and learning.*

As an example of the book's flexibility, consider our treatment of process costing. Process costing is described in Chapter 7. Instructors interested in filling out a student's perspective of costing systems can move directly from job-order costing described in Chapter 4 and Chapter 17 without interruption in the flow of material. Other instructors may want their students to delve into activity-based costing and budgeting and more decision-oriented topics early in the course. These instructors may prefer to postpone discussion of process costing.

CHANGES IN CONTENT AND PEDAGOGY OF THE SECOND CANADIAN EDITION

The pace of change in organizations continues to be rapid. The second edition of *Cost Accounting* reflects changes occurring in the role of cost accounting in organizations and in research on cost accounting. Examples of key additions and changes in the topic areas of the second edition are:

1. *Increased coverage of strategic uses of cost information.* A new chapter (13) on Strategy and Balanced Scorecard discusses the applications of management to strategy, implementation of strategy, and the balanced scorecard to evaluate strategy, reengineering and downsizing, strategic profitability analysis, and productivity measurement.

2. *Activity-based costing (ABC) introduced in a single chapter* (Chapter 5) with explicit linkages to simpler job-costing systems (presented in Chapter 4). New ABC-related material on budgeting (Chapter 6), variance analysis (Chapter 7 and 8), overhead allocation (Chapter 14), and customer-profitability analysis has been added.

3. *Increased attention to decision uses of cost accounting information.* This increase occurs in many topic areas, such as activity-based costing (Chapter 5), variance analysis (Chapter 7 and 8), capacity analysis (Chapter 9), relevant costs and prices (Chapter 10 and 11), and cost allocation (Chapter 14).

4. *Systematic incorporation of new and evolving management thinking* including supply chain analysis (Chapter 1 and 20), theory of constraints (Chapter 19), intangible asset valuation (Chapter 20), and EVA® (Chapter 24).

5. *Consolidation of the treatment of ethics* through addition of new assignments with ethical focus. Examples include problems dealing with ethical challenges with bribery in a global company (Chapter 1), ethics and CVP analysis (Chapter 3), ethics and ABC implementation (Chapter 5), ethics and regression computations (Chapter 10), and ethics and make versus buy (Chapter 11).

6. *Use of margin definitions* to reinforce students' understanding of key terms in the text. Key terms continue to be listed with page references at the end of the chapter for student self-review. The pages on which key terms are defined have been printed in bold in the Subject Index, prompting students to return to the original context when they check definitions in the text.

7. *Increased reference to the Internet*, especially its accounting applications. The new Chapter 6 Concepts in Action box discusses managers' use of Internet resources to fast-track the budgeting process at the T-D Bank. Weblinks in the margins of the text continue to provide quick reference to the sites of key organizations and companies mentioned as examples, while value-added links to articles on accounting topics and related software information have been especially gathered for the second edition. To ensure that all our Weblink information is current, we'll be providing regular updates to the sites under the Destinations button of our Companion Website (see the Supplements description for details).

8. *"Real" years* are used throughout the text, ending such confusing configurations as 20X1.

MAJOR CHANGES IN CONTENT AND SEQUENCE

The overwhelming feedback from instructors and students was for a reduction in length. We have reduced the number of chapters in the second edition to 24 (from 26 in the first edition). This was achieved by consolidating the coverage in two topic areas (cost allocation and inventory management and JIT) from each of two chapters in the first edition to a single chapter in the second edition. One chapter in the first edition (Chapter 2) was eliminated and much of its content incorporated into other chapters. In addition, special attention has been given to streamlining presentations in every chapter of the book as well as providing better and cleaner explanations.

Each chapter was scrutinized by knowledgable critics before a final draft was reached. The result is a book that is more student-friendly and shorter by exactly 100 pages.

Specific major changes in content and in the sequence of individual chapters are:

1. Chapter 2 now covers the basics of job costing methods, using manufacturing as the detailed example followed by examples from the service and merchandising sectors. Chapter 5 is a new chapter on activity-based costing that uses a new illustrative example and draws on material in both Chapter 4 and 5 of the first edition. The same seven-step approach to job costing used in Chapter 4 of the second edition is contained in Chapter 5. Chapter 5 focuses on how ABC modifies the implementation of the basic steps. The cost hierarchy is discussed as an integral part of Chapter 5. These two chapters explain product costing using a single cost-pool system, a departmental costing system, and an ABC system.

2. Chapter 13 is a new chapter that describes the applications of management accounting to strategy. This chapter covers topics on the implementation of strategy using the balanced scorecard, a new method by which accounting information can be used to evaluate strategy, reengineering, and downsizing.

3. Chapters 14 through 24 of the second edition have been restructured to consolidate material in the first edition.

   ◆ Chapter 14 on "Cost Allocation" now consolidates Chapters 13 and 14 of the first edition.
   ◆ Chapter 20 on "Inventory Management, Just-in-Time, and Backflush Costing" now consolidates Chapters 20 and 21 of the first edition.
   ◆ Chapter 13 Appendix ("Productivity Measurement") of the second edition draws on material from Chapter 24 of the first edition.
   ◆ Chapter 16 Appendix ("Mix and Yield Variances for Substitutable Inputs") of the second edition draws on material from Chapter 24 of the first edition.
   ◆ Chapter 17 Appendix ("Operation Costing") draws on material from Chapter 20 of the first edition.

4. Chapter 17 (Process Costing) has been rewritten. The concept of equivalent units and the steps in the various methods of process costing (weighted-average, FIFO, and standard costing) are explained in more detail.

5. Numerical company examples in key chapters have been updated or revised to streamline the exposition and provide better explanations.

ASSIGNMENT MATERIAL

The second edition continues the widely applauded tight linkage between text and assignment material formed in previous editions. We have also significantly expanded the assignment material, provided more structure, and added greater variety.

End-of-chapter assignment material is divided into four groups: Questions, Exercises, Problems, and a Collaborative Learning Problem. *Questions* test students' recall and understanding of key terms and concepts. *Exercises* are short, structured assignments that test basic issues presented in the chapter. *Problems* are longer and more difficult assignments. Each chapter has an ethics-related problem. The *Collaborative Learning Problem* is the last assignment in each chapter. These problems are group assignments that require students to think critically about a particular problem or specific business situation. All in all, 25 percent of the assignments are new for this second edition. We've also expanded our case support. Besides the cases included in Appendix A, we will annually provide new cases in a separate supplement.

ILLUSTRATIONS OF ACTUAL BUSINESSES

Students become highly motivated to learn cost accounting if they can relate the subject matter to the real world. We have spent considerable time interacting with the business community, investigating new uses of cost accounting data and gaining insight into how changes in technology are affecting the roles of cost accounting information. Real-world illustrations are found in many parts of the text.

Concepts in Action Boxes. Found in many chapters, these boxes discuss how cost accounting concepts are applied by individual companies. Examples are drawn from many different countries, including *Canada* (Oetiker in Chapter 5, Ontario Hydro in Chapter 22, and Nortel in Chapter 24), the *United States* (Cummins Engine in Chapter 1, Colorscope in Chapter 4, and Carrier Corporation in Chapter 12), *Indonesia* (Asia-Pacific Rayon in Chapter 8), and the *United Kingdom* (Allied-Signal Skelmersdale in Chapter 19).

These Concept in Action boxes cover a diverse series of industries including computers, electronics, electric utilities, Internet equipment, and manufacturing.

Surveys of Company Practice Boxes. Results from surveys in more than 15 countries are cited in the many Surveys of Company Practices boxes found throughout the book. Examples include:

◆ Activities of a management accountant (Chapter 1)—cites evidence from the United States and Canada.

◆ Management purposes for classifying costs (Chapter 5)—cites evidence from Canada, the United States, Ireland, New Zealand, and the United Kingdom.

◆ Cost allocation bases for manufacturing overhead (Chapter 4)—cites evidence from the United States, Australia, Ireland, Japan, and the United Kingdom.

◆ Activity-based cost information (Chapter 5)—cites evidence from Canada, the United States, Ireland, New Zealand, and the United Kingdom.

◆ Budget practices (Chapter 6)—cites evidence from the United States, Japan, Australia, the United Kingdom, and Holland.

◆ Standard costs (Chapter 7)—cites evidence from United States, Ireland, Japan, Sweden, and the United Kingdom.

◆ Variable costing (Chapter 9)—cites evidence from Canada, the United States, Ireland, Japan, Sweden, and the United Kingdom.

◆ Cost classification (Chapter 10)—cites evidence from the United States, Japan, and Australia.

◆ Pricing practices (Chapter 12)—cites evidence from the United States, Australia, Ireland, Japan, and the United Kingdom.

◆ Purposes of cost allocation (Chapter 14)—cites evidence from Canada, the United States, Australia, and the United Kingdom.

◆ Cost allocation methods (Chapter 15)—cites evidence from the United Kingdom, Australia, and Japan.

◆ Customer profitability analysis (Chapter 16)—cites evidence from the United States, Australia, and the United Kingdom

◆ JIT performance measures (Chapter 20)—cites evidence from Canada, the United States, Ireland, and the United Kingdom.

◆ Capital budgeting practices (Chapter 21)—cites evidence from Canada, the United States, Australia, Ireland, Japan, Scotland, South Korea, and the United Kingdom.

◆ Risk adjustments in capital budgeting (Chapter 22)—cites evidence from Canada, the United States, Australia, the United Kingdom, Taiwan, and Poland.

◆ Transfer pricing practices (Chapter 23)—cites evidence from Canada, the United States, Australia, India, Japan, New Zealand, and the United Kingdom.

◆ Performance measures (Chapter 24)—cites evidence from the United States, Australia, Ireland, Japan, and the United Kingdom.

This extensive survey evidence enables students to see that many of the concepts they are learning are widely used across the globe.

SUPPLEMENTS TO THE SECOND CANADIAN EDITION

A complete package of supplements is available to assist students and instructors in using this book. Supplements available to students include the following:

- *Student Guide and Review Manual.* This learning aid has been extensively revised to enhance students' systematic and effective study of cost accounting. Overviews, learning objectives, and a new detailed chapter prècis provide outstanding pedagogical support. Each chapter also contains multiple choice, true/false, and fill-in-the-blank questions (with answers) for student self-review. An average of three Exercises per chapter are included to test students' application of the material they have studied, while a Featured Exercise provides a more challenging test of students' understanding accounting issues. Preview copies of Chapters 1 to 3 will be made available under the Student Guide button of our Companion Website at **www.prenticehall.ca/horngren** (see below for details). We believe this *Student Guide* will be helpful to students at all levels. 0-13-040128-5

- *Student Solutions Manual.* Designed to enable students to monitor their progress, this supplement contains fully worked-out solutions for all of the even-numbered questions, exercises and problems in the textbook. This supplement may be purchased with the instructor's permission. 0-13-040129-3

Supplements available to instructors include the following:

- *Instructor's Solutions Manual.* In addition to fully worked-out solutions for every question, exercise, and problem in the text, the *Instructor's Solutions Manual* also provides suggested alternative chapter sequences and categorization of assignment material. 0-13-040127-7

- *Solutions Acetates*: In response to concerns about the high environmental and production costs associated with the preparation of acetates, we are offering a special boxed package that contains an unbound copy of the *Instructor's Solutions Manual*, chapter dividers, and a supply of 400 clear acetates. This enables instructors who adopt the text to organize and produce transparencies for the specific solutions that they choose to show in their classrooms. Please contact your Prentice Hall Canada sales representative for ordering information.

- *Instructor's Resource Manual with Case Notes and CBC Video Guide.* This supplement offers a chapter overview, outline, additional examples, alternative means of presenting topics, chapter quiz/demonstration exercises with solutions, and suggested readings. Teaching notes are provided for cases included in the textbook. The CBC Video Guide includes a summary of the content of each of the *Venture* segments included in the Prentice Hall/CBC Video Library, as well as discussion questions and suggested answers. 0-13-040126-9

- *Test Item File.* Quiz and examination materials are included in this valuable supplement. Each chapter contains true/false questions, multiple-choice questions (both quantitative and conceptual), problems, and essay/critical thinking questions. Correct or suggested answers (for essay questions) and page references are included for every question. 0-13-040131-5

- *PH Test Manager*: Utilizing our new Test Manager program, the computerized test bank for *Cost Accounting* offers a comprehensive suite of tools for testing and assessment. Test Manager allows educators to easily create and distribute tests for their courses, either by printing and distributing through traditional methods or by on-line delivery via a Local Area Network (LAN) server. Once you have opened Test Manager, you'll advance effortlessly through a series of folders allowing you to quickly access all available areas of the program. Test Manager has removed the guesswork from your next move by incorporating Screen Wizards that assist you with such tasks as managing question content, managing a portfolio of tests, testing students, and analyzing test results. In addition, this all-new testing package is backed with full technical support, comprehensive on-line help files, a guided tour, and complete written documentation. Available as a CD-ROM for Windows 95. 0-13-040132-3

◆ *Electronic Transparencies in PowerPoint.* For each chapter of the text approximately 20 slides have been prepared in PowerPoint 7.0. The interactive presentation offers helpful graphics that illustrate key figures and concepts from the text, chapter outlines, and additional examples. Also downloadable from the Instructor's area of our Companion Website. 0-13-040134-X

◆ *Prentice Hall/CBC Video Library*: In an exclusive partnership, the CBC and Prentice Hall Canada have worked together to develop an exciting video package consisting of segments from the prestigious series *Venture*. At an average of seven minutes in length, these segments show students issues affecting real Canadian individuals and companies. Teaching notes are provided in *Instructor's Resource Manual with Case Notes and CBC Video Guide*. (Please contact your Prentice Hall sales representative for details. These videos are subject to availability and terms negotiated upon adoption of the text.)

◆ *ON LOCATION! Videos*: Prepared exclusively for Prentice Hall, these videos include interviews with managers and employees illustrating accounting issues at a major North American corporation. Each segment is eight to 10 minutes long. Written summaries with questions are provided in the *Instructor's Resource Manual with Case Notes and CBC Video Guide*. (Please contact your Prentice Hall sales representative for details. These videos are subject to availability and terms negotiated upon adoption of the text.)

Finally, both instructors and students will be sure to benefit the unparalleled Internet support offered by Prentice Hall Canada's accounting websites.

www.prenticehall.ca/horngren

◆ *Companion Website with Online Study Guide*: Our online study guide offers students the perfect platform for quick review and study. Multiple choice, true/false, and fill-in-the-blank questions are offered for each chapter, along with instant feedback and page references to the text to facilitate further review. Every chapter also contains one Exercise (with suggested answer) that covers a key concept from that chapter. The Companion Website also includes Destinations (based on the chapter-specific Weblinks in the margins of the textbook, updated as required), and Accounting's Greatest Hits (Internet links to a wide and comprehensive range of accounting resources; see below for details). Net News and Net Search provide access to Internet news groups and search tools, while the latest news on companies covered in CBC Video Cases can be found under Updates. Additional student support is offered in the *Student Guide and Review Manual* (0-13-040128-5; see the description above for details). For this edition only we've provided a special free preview of Chapters 1 to 3.

Instructors will be interested in our online syllabus builder and the password-protected Instructor's area containing update information and electronic versions of key supplements, including downloadable spreadsheets for selected exercises and problems, and electronic transparencies in PowerPoint. (Instructors who have adopted the text should contact their Prentice Hall sales representative to obtain the password.) See **www.prenticehall.ca/horngren** and explore!

www.prenticehall.ca/
accountingsgreatesthits

◆ *Accounting's Greatest Hits*: Prentice Hall Canada is proud to present the Web sites on the Internet that provide the best accounting information for students, instructors, accountants, researchers, and anyone interested in the latest from the world of accounting. Beginning on Accounting's Greatest Hits home page, you can link to over 80 Web sites that will, in turn, provide links to hundreds more. The accounting sites are grouped into the following broad categories: International, Careers, Firms, Resources, Tax, Software, and Humour. Regular updates to this site ensure that you have access to the newest accounting sites on the Internet, providing accounting information that is as current as possible.

You can access this site by clicking the Accounting's Greatest Hits button on the *Cost Accounting* Companion Website at **www.prenticehall.ca/horngren**, or go straight to **www.prenticehall.ca/accountingsgreatesthits**. Be sure to bookmark this site for future visits. Look for the Accounting's Greatest Hits icon when you need accounting information on the Internet. The icon is your assurance that you have accessed one of the most comprehensive collections of accounting resources available on the web. These are truly Accounting's Greatest Hits!

ACKNOWLEDGMENTS TO THE SECOND CANADIAN EDITION

I would like to acknowledge the assistance I have received from many people. This second Canadian edition is based upon the tenth U.S. edition by Charles Horngren, George Foster and Srikant M. Datar. I appreciate their willingness to share their work with me. Their knowledge and experience has significantly contributed to this book.

I also extend my sincere appreciation to my colleagues at Prentice Hall Canada who have supported me throughout the production of this book. To Pat Ferrier for his recognition of my interest in this subject. To Lesley Mann for her capable editorial assistance in the development of this edition. To Nicole Mellow the Production Editor and Edie Franks, the Copy Editor and, with Carol Fordyce, Proofreader. To Michelle Hodgson and Cam Scholey for their careful technical review. Fran Toepfer of Prentice Hall in Upper Saddle River, New Jersey, has been of inestimable help in co-ordinating the flow of information between the U.S. and Canadian editors, and Anne Graydon provided helpful updates on new developments in the tenth edition.

I am grateful to the School of Business and Economics at Wilfrid Laurier University for providing an environment that supports the development of teaching materials.

I would like to thank the reviewers for their valuable insights and suggestions, especially:

David Cooper, University of Alberta
Craig Emby, Simon Fraser University
Richard Farrar, Conestoga College
Walter Krystia, Ryerson Polytechnic University
R. Murray Lindsay, University of Saskatchewan
Cynthia Simmons, University of Calgary
Shu-Lun Wong, Memorial University of Newfoundland

Finally, I would like to recognize the support of my wife Luanne and my children Katrina, Tanya, Vanessa, and Adam, to whom this book is dedicated.

Comments are most welcome.

Howard D. Teall

Testimonials

As requested, I have read the proof copy of *Cost Accounting*, Second Canadian Edition, for chapters 1-12. I have checked the arithmetic and logic in all of the worked examples and exhibits in that proof as well as ensured that references to those examples and exhibits within the text were accurate.

Michelle Brisebois Hodgson, CGA

As requested, I have read the proof copy of *Cost Accounting*, Second Canadian Edition, for chapters 13-24. I have checked the arithmetic and logic in all of the worked examples and exhibits in that proof as well as ensured that references to those examples and exhibits within the text were accurate.

Cam Scholey, MBA, CMA

ABOUT THE AUTHORS

Charles T. Horngren is the Edmund W. Littlefield Professor of Accounting at Stanford University. A graduate of Marquette University, he received his MBA from Harvard University and his Ph.D. from the University of Chicago. He is also the recipient of honorary doctorates from Marquette University and DePaul University. A Certified Public Accountant, Horngren served on the Accounting Principles Board for six years, the Financial Accounting Standards Board Advisory Council for five years, and the Council of the American Institute of Certified Public Accountants for three years. In addition, he served as a trustee of the Financial Accounting Foundation, which oversees the Financial Accounting Standards Board and the Government Accounting Standards Board for six years.

A member of the American Accounting Association, Horngren has also served as its President and Director of Research. He received the Outstanding Accounting Educator Award in 1973, when the association initiated an annual series of such awards.

The California Certified Public Accountants Foundation gave Horngren its Faculty Excellence Award in 1975 and its Distinguished Professor Award in 1983. He is the first person to have received both awards. In 1985, the American Institute of Certified Public Accountants presented him with its first Outstanding Educator Award. Five years later, he was elected to the Accounting Hall of Fame.

In 1993, Horngren was named Accountant of the Year, Education, by the national professional accounting fraternity, Beta Alpha Psi.

Professor Horngren is a member of the National Association of Accountants, and served on its research planning committee for three years. He was also a member of the Board of Regents, Institute of Management Accounting, which administers the Certified Management Accountant examinations.

Charles T. Horngren, the Consulting Editor for the Prentice Hall Series in Accounting, is the coauthor of six other books published by Prentice Hall: *Principles of Financial and Management Accounting: A Sole Proprietorship Approach* and *Principles of Financial and Management Accounting: A Corporate Approach*, 1994 (with Walter T. Harrison, Jr. and Michael A. Robinson), *Introduction to Financial Accounting*, Seventh Edition, 1999 (with Gary L. Sundem and John Elliott), *Introduction to Management Accounting*, Eleventh Edition, 1999 (with Gary L. Sundem), and *Accounting*, Fourth Edition, 1999 (with Walter T. Harrison, Jr. and Linda Bamber).

George Foster is the Paul L. and Phyllis Wattis Professor of Management at Stanford University. He graduated with a university medal from the University of Sydney and has a Ph.D. from Stanford University. He has been awarded honorary doctorates from the University of Ghent, Belgium, and from the University of Vaasa, Finland. He has received the Outstanding Educator Award from the American Accounting Association.

Foster has received the Distinguished Teaching Award at Stanford University and the Faculty Excellence Award from the California Society of Certified Public Accountants. He has been a Visiting Professor to Mexico for the American Accounting Association.

Research awards Foster has received include the Competitive Manuscript Competition Award of the American Accounting Association, the Notable Contribution to Accounting Literature Award of the American Institute of Certified Public Accountants, and the Citation for Meritorious Contribution to Accounting Literature Award of the Australian Society of Accountants.

He is the author of *Financial Statement Analysis*, published by Prentice Hall. He is coauthor of *Activity-Based Management Consortium Study (APQC and CAM-I)* and *Marketing, Cost Management and Management Accounting (CAM-I)*. He is also coauthor of two monographs published by the American Accounting Association—*Security Analyst Multi-Year Earnings Forecasts and the Capital Market* and *Marketing Microstructure and Capital Market Information Content Research*. Journals publishing his articles include *Abacus, The Accounting Review, Harvard Business Review, Journal of Accounting and Economics, Journal of Accounting Research, Journal of Cost Management, Journal of Management Accounting Research*, and *Management Accounting*.

Foster works actively with many companies, including Apple Computer, ARCO, BHP, Digital Equipment Corp., Exxon, Frito-Lay Corp., Hewlett-Packard, McDonalds Corp., Octel Communications, PepsiCo, Santa Fe Corp., and Wells Fargo. He has also worked closely with Computer Aided Manufacturing-International (CAM-I) in the development of a framework for modern cost management practices. Foster has presented seminars on new developments in cost accounting in North America, Asia, Australia, and Europe.

Srikant M. Datar is Professor of Accounting at Stanford University. A graduate with distinction from the University of Bombay, he received gold medals upon graduation from the Indian Institute of Management, Ahmedabad, and the Institute of Cost and Works Accountants of India. A Chartered Accountant, he holds two master's degrees and a Ph.D. from Stanford University.

Cited by his students as a dedicated and innovative teacher, Datar received the George Leland Bach Award for Excellence in the Classroom at Carnegie Mellon University.

Datar has published his research in various journals, including *The Accounting Review, Journal of Accounting and Economics, Journal of Accounting Research, Contemporary Accounting Research*, and *Management Science*. He has served on the editorial board of several journals and presented his research to corporate executives and academic audiences in North America, Asia, and Europe.

Datar has worked with many corporations, including General Motors, Mellon Bank, Solectron, TRW, and VISA, on field-based projects in management accounting. He is a member of the American Accounting Association and the Institute of Management Accountants.

Howard D. Teall is a Professor in the School of Business and Economics at Wilfrid Laurier University. He is currently serving as Acting Dean of the School of Business and Economics. He received HBA, MBA, and Ph.D. degrees from the School of Business Administration at the University of Western Ontario, and a CA designation while employed with Price Waterhouse.

Professor Teall held previous university positions at the Helsinki School of Economics and Business Administration, INSEAD (the European Institute of Business Administration), the International University of Japan, and the University of Western Ontario.

Professor Teall has published articles in both financial and managerial fields, including research into the impacts of financial disclosures in the oil and gas industry and management control issues. He has recently coauthored the Third Canadian Edition of *Management Accounting* with Charles Horngren, Gary Sundem, and William Stratton and *Introduction to Financial Accounting*, Second Canadian Edition, with Horngren, Gary Sundem and John Elliott.

Professor Teall has provided management training programs and consulting for IBM Canada Ltd., Ontario Hydro, B. F. Goodrich Canada Limited, Petro-Canada, General Motors of Canada Limited, General Motors Corporation, the Federal Business Development Bank, the Canadian Department of Industry, Science, and Technology Canada, the Liquor Control Board of Ontario, the Banff Centre for Management, Polysar Rubber Corporation, Royal Bank of Trinidad and Tobago, and professional qualification programs for Coopers and Lybrand, Deloitte & Touche, the Chartered Accountants Students' Association of Ontario, the Institute of Chartered Accountants of Ontario, the Atlantic Provinces Association of Chartered Accountants, and the Society of Management Accountants.

The Prentice Hall Canada

companion Website...

Your Internet companion to the most exciting, state-of-the-art educational tools on the Web!

The Prentice Hall Canada Companion Website is easy to navigate and is organized to correspond to the chapters in this textbook. The Companion Website is comprised of four distinct, functional features:

1) **Customized Online Resources**

2) **Online Study Guide**

3) **Reference Material**

4) **Communication**

Explore the four areas in this Companion Website. Students and distance learners will discover resources for indepth study, research and communication, empowering them in their quest for greater knowledge and maximizing their potential for success in the course.

A NEW WAY TO DELIVER EDUCATIONAL CONTENT

1) Customized Online Resources

Our Companion Websites provide instructors and students with a range of options to access, view, and exchange content.

- **Syllabus Builder** provides *instructors* with the option to create online classes and construct an online syllabus linked to specific modules in the Companion Website.

- **Mailing lists** enable *instructors* and *students* to receive customized promotional literature.

- **Preferences** enable *students* to customize the sending of results to various recipients, and also to customize how the material is sent, e.g., as html, text, or as an attachment.

- **Help** includes an evaluation of the user's system and a tune-up area that makes updating browsers and plug-ins easier. This new feature will enhance the user's experience with Companion Websites.

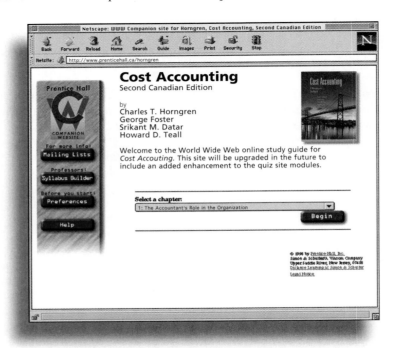

www.prenticehall.ca/horngren

Prentice Hall

COMPANION WEBSITE

2) Online Study Guide

Interactive Study Guide modules form the core of the student learning experience in the Companion Website. These modules are categorized according to their functionality:

- True-False
- Multiple Choice
- Completion

The True-False, Multiple Choice, and Completion modules provide students with the ability to send answers to our grader and receive instant feedback on their progress through our Results Reporter. Answers to the more complex Exercises may be viewed for checking. Page references to the textbook ensure that students take advantage of all resources available to enhance their learning experience.

3) Reference Material

Reference material broadens text coverage with up-to-date resources for learning. **Web Destinations** provides a directory of Web sites relevant to the subject matter in each chapter. **Accounting's Greatest Hits** offers links to a wide range of useful accouting sites. **Net News (Internet Newsgroups)** are a fundamental source of information about a discipline, containing a wealth of brief, opinionated postings. **Net Search** simplifies key term search using Internet search engines.

4) Communication

Companion Websites contain the communication tools necessary to deliver courses in a **Distance Learning** environment. **Message Board** allows users to post messages and check back periodically for responses. **Live Chat** allows users to discuss course topics in real time, and enables professors to host on-line classes.

Communication facilities of Companion Websites provide a key element for distributed learning environments. There are two types of communication facilities currently in use in Companion Websites:

- **Message Board** – this module takes advantage of browser technology providing the users of each Companion Website with a national newsgroup to post and reply to relevant course topics.

- **Live Chat** – enables instructor-led group activities in real time. Using our chat client, instructors can display Website content while students participate in the discussion.

Chapter 1
Objectives
Overview
Multiple Choice
True/False
Completion
Exercise
Destinations
Greatest Hits
Net News
Net Search
Updates
FAQs
Help
Message Board

Companion Websites are currently available for:

- Horngren: Accounting
- Horngren: Management Accounting
- Horngren: Introduction to Financial Accounting
- Slater: College Accounting
- Griffin: Business

Note: CW '99 content will vary slightly from site to site depending on discipline requirements.

The Companion Website can be found at:

www.prenticehall.ca/horngren

PRENTICE HALL CANADA

1870 Birchmount Road
Scarborough, Ontario M1P 2J7

To order:
Call: 1-800-567-3800
Fax: 1-800-263-7733

For samples:
Call: 1-800-850-5813
Fax: (416) 299-2539
E-mail: phcinfo_pubcanada@prenhall.com

1

THE ACCOUNTANT'S ROLE IN THE ORGANIZATION

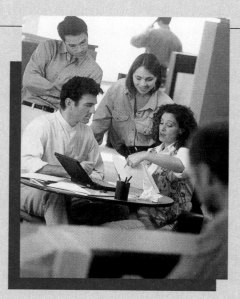

Modern cost management focuses on the use of cost information in management decisions. Today, accountants are an integral part of the management team. By evaluating issues as a team, managers are better able to make effective business decisions.

LEARNING OBJECTIVES

After studying this chapter, you should be able to:

1. Identify five broad purposes of accounting systems
2. Describe cost accounting and its relationship to management accounting and financial accounting
3. Describe the set of business functions in a value chain
4. Understand how accounting can facilitate planning, control, and decision-making
5. Describe the difference between line management and staff management
6. Distinguish between the scorekeeping, attention-directing, and problem-solving functions of the controller
7. Understand the importance of professional ethics to management accountants
8. Describe evolving management themes that are shaping developments in management accounting systems

Canadian Institute of Chartered Accountants
www.cica.ca/new/index.htm

Former accountants currently are senior executives in many large companies, including Coca-Cola, Nike, PepsiCo, Bell Canada, Cadbury Schweppes, and Nissan Motors. Accounting provides a superb training field for executives because it cuts across all facets of the organization. The accountant's duties are intertwined with management planning, control, and decision-making.

The study of modern cost accounting yields numerous insights into both the manager's *and* the accountant's roles in an organization. What types of decisions do managers make? How can accounting help managers make these decisions? This book addresses these questions. In this chapter we look at where the accountant fits in the organization; this will give us a framework for studying the succeeding chapters.

THE MAJOR PURPOSES OF ACCOUNTING SYSTEMS

OBJECTIVE 1

Identify five broad purposes of accounting systems

The accounting system is the principal—and the most credible—quantitative information system in almost every organization. This system should provide information for five broad purposes:

- ◆ **Purpose 1:** *Formulating overall strategies and long-range plans.* This includes new product development and investment in both tangible (equipment) and intangible (brands, patents, or people) assets, and frequently involves special-purpose reports.
- ◆ **Purpose 2:** *Resource allocation decisions such as product and customer emphasis and pricing.* This frequently involves reports on the profitability of products or services, brand categories, customers, distribution channels, and so on.
- ◆ **Purpose 3:** *Cost planning and cost control of operations and activities.* This involves reports on revenues, costs, assets, and the liabilities of divisions, plants, and other areas of responsibility.
- ◆ **Purpose 4:** *Performance measurement and evaluation of people.* This includes comparisons of actual results with planned results. It can be based on financial or nonfinancial measures.
- ◆ **Purpose 5:** *Meeting external regulatory and legal reporting requirements.* Regulations and statutes typically prescribe the accounting methods to be followed here. Consider financial reports that are provided to shareholders who are making decisions to buy, hold, or sell shares in the company. These reports must follow generally accepted accounting principles (GAAP), and are heavily influenced by regulatory bodies such as the Accounting Standards Board in Canada or the Financial Accounting Standards Board in the United States.

Management accounting. Measures and reports financial information as well as other types of information that assist managers in fulfilling the goals of the organization.

Financial accounting. Focuses on external reporting that is guided by generally accepted accounting principles.

Each of the purposes stated here may require a different presentation or reporting method. An ideal database for presentations and reports (sometimes called a data warehouse or infobarn) is very detailed and cuts across business functions. Accountants combine or adjust ("slice or dice") these data to answer the questions from particular internal or external users.

Management Accounting, Financial Accounting, and Cost Accounting

OBJECTIVE 2

Describe cost accounting and its relationship to management accounting and financial accounting

A distinction is often made in practice between management accounting and financial accounting. **Management accounting** measures and reports financial information as well as other types of information that assist managers in fulfilling the goals of the organization. It is thus concerned with purposes 1 to 4. **Financial accounting** focuses on external reporting that is guided by GAAP. It is thus concerned with purpose 5. **Cost accounting** measures and reports financial and other information related to the organization's acquisition or consumption of resources. It provides information for both management accounting and financial accounting.

Cost accounting. Measures and reports financial and other information related to the organization's acquisition or consumption of resources; it provides information for both management accounting and financial accounting.

Financial accounting, as mentioned, is constrained by generally accepted accounting principles. GAAP restrict the set of revenue and cost measurement rules and the types of items that are classified as assets, liabilities, or owners' equity in balance sheets. In contrast, management accounting is not restricted to those accounting principles acceptable for financial reporting. For example, for purposes 3 and 4, a consumer products company may present a particular estimated "value" of a brand name (say, the Coca-Cola brand name) in its *internal* financial reports for marketing managers, although doing so is not in accordance with GAAP.

Do not assume that management accounting focuses exclusively on internal parties. Managers are increasingly sharing accounting information with external parties such as suppliers and customers.

Coca-Cola Corporation
www.cocacola.com

Cost Management and Accounting Systems

A central task of managers is *cost management*. We use **cost management** to describe the actions managers undertake to satisfy customers while continuously reducing and controlling costs. The Toyota Motor Company in a recent annual report noted that:

Cost management. Actions by managers undertaken to satisfy customers while continuously reducing and controlling costs.

> Cost management is . . . for the automobile industry in the 1990s what quality control was in the 1970s and 80s.

Toyota Motor Company
www.toyota.co.jp/e/

An important component of cost management is the recognition that prior management decisions often commit the organization to the subsequent incurrence of costs. Consider the costs of handling materials in a production plant. Decisions about plant layout and the extent of physical movement of materials required for production typically are made before production begins. These decisions greatly influence the level of day-to-day materials-handling costs once production begins.

MODERN COST ACCOUNTING

Managers as Customers of Accounting

Managers around the globe are becoming increasingly aware of the importance of the quality and timeliness of products and services sold to their external customers.

SURVEYS OF COMPANY PRACTICE

"A Day in the Life" of a Management Accountant

What activities do management accountants do? A survey of CMA's found that 10% or more perform the following activities (percentages add across rows):

	Daily	Weekly	Monthly	Quarterly or Annually	Never Perform
Managing the accounting/finance function	64%	14%	11%	5%	6%
Internal consulting	36	32	19	7	6
Accounting systems and financial reporting	18	28	36	9	9
Human resources and personnel reporting	11	23	25	22	19
Financial and economic analysis	10	15	39	24	12

Abilities and skills ranked in terms of importance were: 1. Work ethic, 2. Analytical/problem-solving skills, 3. Interpersonal skills, 4. Listening skills, and 5. Use of computerized spreadsheets.

What changes in the future were projected for management accountants? Work activities projected to become more important were: 1. Long-term strategic planning, 2. Performance evaluation, and 3. Customer and product profitability. The increasing use of information technology in the future was seen as helping management accountants spend a lower percentage of their time on "data collection and financial statement preparation" and a higher percentage on "financial analysis."

Source: Siegel, G., and B. Kulesza, "The Practice Analysis of Management Accounting," *Management Accounting* (Vol. 77, No. 10).

Johnson & Johnson
www.jnj.com

In turn, accountants are becoming increasingly sensitive to the quality and timeliness of accounting information required by managers. For example, a management accounting group at Johnson & Johnson (the manufacturer of many consumer products, such as Band-Aids) has a vision statement that includes the phrases "delight our customers" and "be the best." The success of management accounting depends on whether managers' decisions are improved by the accounting information provided to them.

The Value Chain of Business Functions

OBJECTIVE 3

Describe the set of business functions in a value chain

Value chain. The sequence of business functions in which utility (usefulness) is added to the products or services of an organization.

Design of products, services, or processes. The detailed planning and engineering of products, services, or processes.

Production. The coordination and assembly of resources to produce a product or deliver a service.

Marketing. The manner by which individuals or groups (a) learn about and value the attributes of products or services and (b) purchase those products or services.

Distribution. The mechanism by which products or services are delivered to the customer.

Customer service. The support activities provided to customers.

Throughout this book we organize our look at organizations by using the value chain of the business functions, which appears below as Exhibit 1-1. The **value chain** is the sequence of business functions in which utility (usefulness) is added to the products or services of an organization. These functions are as follows:

◆ **Research and development (R&D).** The generation of, and experimentation with, ideas related to new products, services, or processes

◆ **Design of products, services, or processes**. The detailed planning and engineering of products, services, or processes

◆ **Production**. The coordination and assembly of resources to produce a product or deliver a service

◆ **Marketing**. The manner by which individuals or groups (a) learn about and value the attributes of products or services and (b) purchase those products or services

◆ **Distribution**. The mechanism by which products or services are delivered to the customer

◆ **Customer service**. The support activities provided to customers

Do not interpret Exhibit 1-1 as implying that managers should proceed sequentially through the value chain. There are important gains to be realized (in terms of, say, cost, quality, and the speed with which new products are developed) from having the individual parts of the value chain work concurrently.

Senior managers of an organization (including those from individual parts of the value chain) have the responsibility of deciding on its overall strategy, how resources are to be obtained and used, and how rewards are to be given. This task covers the entire value chain.

Accounting is a major means of helping managers to administer each of the business functions presented in Exhibit 1-1 and to coordinate their activities within the framework of the organization as a whole. This book focuses on how accounting does in fact assist managers in these tasks.

EXHIBIT 1-1
The Value Chain of Business Functions

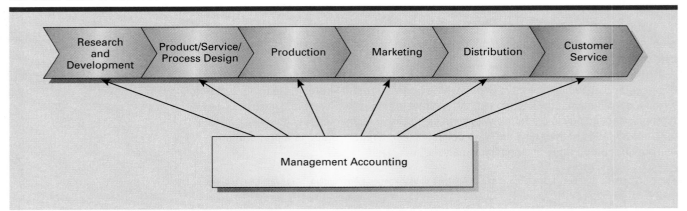

Is Microsoft's management control system better than Novell's? Is Labatt's better than Molson's? This section provides an overview of management control systems, illustrating the role of accounting information.

Microsoft
www.microsoft.com

Planning and Control

There are countless definitions of planning and control. Study the left side of Exhibit 1-2, which uses planning and control at *The Daily Sporting News* (DSN) as an illustration. We define **planning** (the top box) as choosing goals, predicting results under various ways of achieving those goals, and then deciding how to attain the desired goals. For example, one goal of DSN may be to increase operating income. Three main alternatives are considered to achieve this goal:

1. Change the price per newspaper
2. Change the rate per page charged to advertisers
3. Reduce labour costs by having fewer workers at DSN's printing facility

Assume that the publisher, Naomi Crawford, increases advertising rates by 4% to $5,200 per page for March 2000. She budgets advertising revenue to be $4,160,000 ($5,200 × 800 pages predicted to be sold in March 2000). A **budget** is the quantitative expression of a plan of action and an aid to the coordination and implementation of the plan.

Control (the bottom box in Exhibit 1-2) covers both the action that implements the planning decision and the performance evaluation of the personnel and operations. With our DSN example, the action would include communicating the new advertising rate schedule to DSN's marketing sales representatives and advertisers. The performance evaluation provides feedback on the actual results.

During March 2000, DSN sells advertising, sends out invoices, and receives payments. These invoices and receipts are recorded in the accounting system. Exhibit 1-3 shows the March 2000 advertising revenue performance report for DSN.

OBJECTIVE 4

Understand how accounting can facilitate planning, control, and decision-making

Planning. Choosing goals, predicting results under various ways of achieving those goals, and then deciding how to attain the desired goals.

Budget. The quantitative expression of a plan of action and an aid to the coordination and implementation of the plan.

Control. Covers both the action that implements the planning decision and the performance evaluation of the personnel and operations.

EXHIBIT 1-2
How Accounting Facilitates Planning and Control

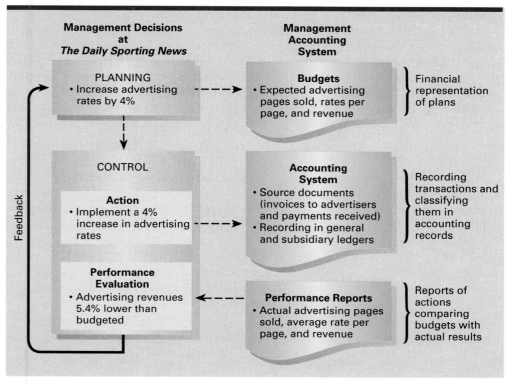

EXHIBIT 1-3
Advertising Revenue Performance Report at *The Daily Sporting News* for March 2000

	Actual Results	Budgeted Amounts	Variance
Advertising pages sold	760	800	40 unfavourable
Average rate per page	$5,080	$5,200	$120 unfavourable
Advertising revenue	$3,860,800	$4,160,000	$299,200 unfavourable

Management by exception. The practice of concentrating on areas that are not operating as expected and placing less attention on areas operating as expected.

Variance. Difference between an actual result and a budgeted amount when that budgeted amount is a financial variable reported by the accounting system.

This report indicates that 760 pages of advertising (40 pages less than the budgeted 800 pages) were sold in March 2000. The average rate per page was $5,080 compared with the budgeted $5,200 rate, yielding actual advertising revenue in March 2000 of $3,860,800. The actual advertising revenue in March 2000 is $299,200 less than the budgeted $4,160,000. Understanding the reasons for any difference between actual results and budgeted results is an important part of **management by exception,** which is the practice of concentrating on areas not operating as expected (such as a cost overrun on a project) and placing less attention on areas operating as expected. The term **variance** in Exhibit 1-3 refers to the difference between the actual results and the budgeted amounts.

The performance report in Exhibit 1-3 could spur investigation. For example, did other newspapers experience a comparable decline in advertising revenue? Did the marketing department make sufficient efforts to convince advertisers that, even with the new rate of $5,200 per page, advertising in the DSN was a good buy? Why was the actual average rate per page $5,080 instead of the budgeted rate of $5,200? Did some sales representatives offer discounted rates? Did a major advertiser threaten to transfer its advertising to another newspaper unless it was given a large rate per page reduction? Answers to these questions could prompt Crawford to take subsequent actions, including, for example, pushing marketing personnel to renew efforts to promote advertising by existing and potential advertisers.

A well-conceived plan includes enough flexibility so that managers can seize opportunities unforeseen at the time the plan is formulated. In no case should control mean that managers cling to a pre-existing plan when unfolding events indicate that actions not encompassed by the original plan would offer the best results to the company.

Planning and control are so strongly intertwined that managers do not spend time drawing artificially rigid distinctions between them. Unless otherwise stated, we use control in its broadest sense to denote the entire management process of both planning and control. For example, instead of referring to a management planning and control system, we will refer to a management control system. Similarly, we will often refer to the control purpose of accounting instead of the awkward planning and control purpose of accounting.

Feedback: A Major Key

Exhibit 1-2 shows a feedback loop from control back to planning. Feedback involves managers examining past performance and systematically exploring alternative ways to improve future performance. It can lead to a variety of responses, including the following:

Canadian Airlines
www.cdnair.ca/

USE OF FEEDBACK	EXAMPLE
◆ Changing goals	◆ Canadian Airlines increases emphasis on cash flow rather than income, after prior liquidity problems.
◆ Searching for alternative means of operating	◆ London University Hospital compares internal processing versus third-party managing (outsourcing) of its accounts receivable operations.

- ◆ Changing methods for making decisions

- ◆ Making predictions

- ◆ Changing operations

- ◆ Changing the reward system

- ◆ Chrysler adopts a team-based new product development process with input from both manufacturing and marketing.

- ◆ British Columbia Telecom incorporates average inflation forecasts for wages when predicting future labour costs.

- ◆ Sony has materials delivered directly to the assembly floor instead of to a storeroom.

- ◆ IBM considers basing its marketing bonuses on the profitability of sales rather than on the dollar amount of sales.

Chrysler Corporation
www.chrysler.com

British Columbia Telecom
www.bctel.ca

Sony
www.sony.com

IBM
www.ibm.com

KEY MANAGEMENT ACCOUNTING GUIDELINES

Three important guidelines help management accountants provide the most value in performing their scorekeeping, attention-directing, and problem-solving functions—employ a cost-benefit approach, give full recognition to behavioural as well as technical considerations, and adopt the different-costs-for-different-purposes theme.

Cost-Benefit Approach

Management accountants continually face resource-allocation decisions, such as whether to purchase a new software package or whether to employ a new associate. A **cost-benefit approach** should be used in these decisions—resources should be spent if they promote decision making that better attains organization goals in relation to the costs of those resources. The perceived net benefits from spending those resources should exceed their perceived expected costs. Although the benefits may take many forms, they can be summarized as the collective set of decisions that will better attain the organization's goals.

Consider the installation of a company's first budgeting system. Previously, the company had probably been using some historical recordkeeping and little formal planning. A major benefit of installing the budgeting system is that it compels managers to plan more formally. They may make a different, more profitable set of decisions than would have been made by using only a historical system. Thus, the expected benefits exceed the expected costs of the new budgeting system. These costs include investments in physical assets, in training people, and in ongoing operating costs of the system.

Cost-benefit approach. Primary criterion for choosing among alternative accounting systems, which is how each system achieves organizational goals in relation to the cost of those systems.

Behavioural and Technical Considerations

The cost-benefit test is the overarching criterion that assists managers in deciding whether, say, to install a proposed budgeting system instead of an existing historical system. Note the human side of why budgeting is used. As was just mentioned, budgets induce a different set of collective decisions because of compelled planning. A management accounting system should have two simultaneous missions for providing information: (a) to help managers make wise economic decisions and (b) to help motivate managers and other employees to aim and strive for goals of the organization. In other words, the technical information by itself might guide managers to wise economic decisions, but it is worthless if managers fail to understand and use it.

Do not underestimate the role of individuals and groups in management planning and control systems. Both accountants and managers should always remember that management systems are not confined exclusively to technical matters such as the type of computer software systems used and the frequency with which reports are prepared. Management is primarily a human activity that should focus on how to help individuals do their jobs better. For example, it is often better for managers to discuss personally with under-performing workers how to improve performance rather than just send those workers a report highlighting their underperformance.

Different Costs for Different Purposes

This book discusses alternative ways to compute costs. A major theme is different costs for different purposes. This is the management accountant's version of the "one shoe does not fit all sizes" notion. A cost concept used for the external reporting purpose need not be the appropriate concept for the internal routine reporting to managers purpose. Consider the advertising costs associated with launching a major new Microsoft product. The product is expected to have a useful life of two years or more. For external reporting to shareholders, advertising costs are fully expensed in the income statement in the year in which they are incurred. This immediate expensing is a requirement of generally accepted accounting principles governing external reporting to shareholders. In contrast, for evaluating management performance (an example of the internal routine reporting purpose), the advertising costs could be capitalized and then written off as expenses over several years. Microsoft could capitalize these advertising costs if it believed this treatment would better represent the performance of the managers launching the new product. In short, immediate period expensing of advertising costs for the external reporting purpose does not imply it is always the "ideal" cost treatment for other purposes of an accounting system.

A management accountant following these guidelines operates within a given organization structure. We now discuss how organization structure affects the reporting responsibilities of a management accountant.

ORGANIZATION STRUCTURE AND THE MANAGEMENT ACCOUNTANT

Line and Staff Relationships

O B J E C T I V E 5

Describe the difference between line management and staff management

Line management. Managers directly responsible for attaining the objectives of the organization.

Staff management. Managers who provide advice and assistance to line management.

Most organizations distinguish between line and staff management. **Line management** is directly responsible for attaining the objectives of the organization. For example, managers of manufacturing divisions may have objectives for a specified amount of operating income plus targets for product quality, safety, and compliance with environmental laws. **Staff management,** such as a management accountant, exists to provide advice and assistance to line management. For example, a plant manager (a line function) may be responsible for investing in new equipment. A plant management accountant (a staff function) may prepare detailed operating cost comparisons for potential pieces of equipment.

Increasingly, organizations are emphasizing the importance of teams in promoting their objectives. These teams often include both line and staff management with the result that the traditional distinctions between line and staff are less clear-cut than they were a decade ago. Line management and staff management designations are best viewed as different ends of a spectrum.

The Chief Financial Officer and the Controller

Chief financial officer (CFO, finance director). The senior officer empowered with overseeing of the financial operations of an organization.

The **chief financial officer (CFO)**—also called the **finance director**—is the senior officer empowered with overseeing the financial operations of an organization. The responsibilities of the CFO vary among organizations, but they almost always encompass the following four areas:

◆ **Controllership** includes providing financial information for both reports to managers and reports to investors.

◆ **Treasury** includes short- and long-term financing, banking, and foreign exchange and derivatives management.

◆ **Tax** includes income taxes, sales taxes, and domestic and international tax planning.

◆ **Internal audit** includes reviewing and analyzing the financial records and other records to attest to the integrity of its financial reports and adherence to the organization's policies and procedures.

In some organizations, the CFO also has responsibility for information systems. In other organizations, an officer of equivalent rank to the CFO—termed *chief information officer*—has responsibility for information systems.

The **controller** is the financial executive primarily responsible for both management accounting and financial accounting. This book focuses on the management accounting function of the controller. The modern controller does not do any controlling in terms of line authority except over his or her own department. Yet the modern concept of controllership maintains that the controller does control in a special sense. That is, by reporting and interpreting relevant data, the controller exerts a force or influence that impels management toward making better-informed decisions.

Exhibit 1-4 presents an organization chart showing the reporting responsibilities of the CFO and the corporate controller at the Clorox Company. Clorox is a leading bleach-producing company and also has major brands in charcoal and salad dressing. The CFO is a staff management function that reports to the most senior line managers (who in turn report to the board of directors). As in most organizations, the corporate controller at Clorox reports to the CFO. Organization charts like that in Exhibit 1-4 show formal reporting relationships. In most organizations, informal relationships also exist that are essential for managers to understand when attempting to implement their decisions.

Controller. The financial executive primarily responsible for both management accounting and financial accounting.

Clorox Company
www.clorox.com

EXHIBIT 1-4
The Clorox Company: Reporting Relationships for the CFO and the Corporate Controller

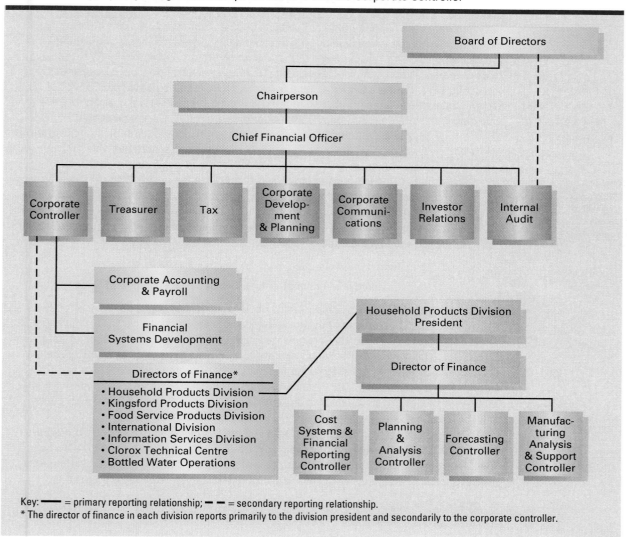

Key: ——— = primary reporting relationship; — — = secondary reporting relationship.
* The director of finance in each division reports primarily to the division president and secondarily to the corporate controller.

OBJECTIVE 6

Distinguish between the scorekeeping, attention-directing, and problem-solving functions of the controller

Scorekeeping. Management accountant's function that involves accumulating data and reporting reliable results to all levels of management.

Attention-directing. Management accountant's function that involves making visible both opportunities and problems on which managers need to focus.

Problem-solving. Management accountant's function that involves comparative analysis to identify the best alternatives in relation to the organization's goals.

Scorekeeping, Attention-Directing, and Problem-Solving Functions

Management accountants perform three important functions—scorekeeping, attention-directing, and problem-solving.

◆ **Scorekeeping.** Accumulating data and reporting reliable results to all levels of management. Examples are the recording of sales, purchases of materials, and payroll payments.

◆ **Attention-directing.** Making visible both opportunities and problems on which managers need to focus. Examples are highlighting rapidly growing markets where the company may be underfunding its investment and highlighting products with higher-than-expected rework rates or customer-return rates. Attention-directing should focus on all opportunities to add value to an organization and not just on cost reduction opportunities.

◆ **Problem-solving.** Comparative analysis to identify the best alternatives in relation to the organization's goals. An example is comparing the financial advantages of leasing a fleet of vehicles rather than owning those vehicles.

CONCEPTS IN ACTION

The Finance Group at Cummins Engine Reinvents Itself

Cummins Engine Company
www.cummins.com

For many years the finance group at Cummins Engine adopted a "we make the rules, you follow them" attitude when dealing with line managers. These managers viewed the finance group as being "preoccupied with transaction processing and not very responsive to user needs." When Cummins faced a sizable increase in competition, it undertook dramatic efforts to "do more with less" and to "work smarter as well as harder." These efforts included the finance group. A Finance Leadership Team (FLT) was formed. Membership included line-manager groups, information-systems people, and members of Cummins' worldwide finance organization. The team's top-priority goal was to ensure that the finance group "make their work more valuable to Cummins Engine."

One initiative adopted was to increase the percentage of resources finance devoted to decision support and to reduce the resources the group spent on transaction processing. Increased attention was paid to "the (accounting department) providing output that its customers deem important." This output included:

◆ Budgets and planning, and

◆ Providing management with readily accessible data for decision support

Cummins compared the costs of its own financial operations for specific transaction activities with those of other companies. For example, representatives from Cummins visited the finance departments of other companies (such as Ford and Hewlett-Packard) and concluded that "best practice" companies averaged a cost of $0.80 per transaction for accounts payable. Cummins estimated its own cost at $3.17. The Finance Leadership Team concluded that major reorganization was necessary at Cummins to move to "best practice." Cummins' entire procurement process, including accounts payable, was centralized into a single location (in Columbus, Indiana). The company had improved the link between existing purchasing systems and accounts payable, both at the employee level and at the information systems level. The result was: "processing costs per invoice rapidly approaching the benchmark of the best-practice company, error rates are down, and user satisfaction is increasing."

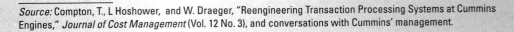

Source: Compton, T., L Hoshower, and W. Draeger, "Reengineering Transaction Processing Systems at Cummins Engines," *Journal of Cost Management* (Vol. 12 No. 3), and conversations with Cummins' management.

Accountants serving the scorekeeping function accumulate data and report the results to all levels of management. Accountants serving this function are responsible for the reliability of the reported information. In this regard, accountants are watchdogs for top management. The scorekeeping function in many organizations requires processing numerous data items (millions of items in some cases). The mechanics of the task should be well understood by those handling it and executed as flawlessly as possible.

Many organizations now have management accountants who concentrate solely on the attention-directing or problem-solving function. The titles of these individuals differ. As shown in Exhibit 1-4, Clorox has special staff positions for "cost systems and financial reporting," "planning and analysis," "forecasting," and "manufacturing analysis and support." The Yoplait Company, the French yogurt company, has staff positions for "operations analysis," "budget analysis and reporting," and "marketing and sales analysis."

Many controllers' departments actively promote their attention-directing and problem-solving abilities to their internal customers in the organization. For example, Swissair's corporate controller's group was reorganized so that each of the 13 staff members in the group was assigned responsibility for assisting an individual Swissair division (such as engineering and maintenance, flight services, and marketing for Europe). Their challenge was to demonstrate to the managers of each division the value of their assistance in areas such as financial analysis, the budgeting process, and cost management.

Article: "Processing Transactions in Accounting Information Systems" by Dave Strothcamp
www.csuohio.edu/accounts/Strothcamp/TOPIC04/index.htm

Yoplait Company
www.yoplait.fr

PROFESSIONAL ETHICS

Ethical Guidelines

Professional accounting organizations representing management accountants exist in many countries. Appendix E discusses professional organizations in Canada, the United States, Australia, Japan, and the United Kingdom. Each of these organizations provides certification programs. For example, the **Society of Management Accountants of Canada (SMAC)**—the largest association of management accountants in Canada—provides a program leading to the **Certified Management Accountant (CMA)** certificate. This certificate signals that the holder has passed the admission criteria and demonstrated the competency of technical knowledge required by the SMAC.

Accountants consistently rank high in public opinion surveys on the ethics exhibited by members of different professions. Professional accounting organizations play an important role in promoting a high standard of ethics. The SMAC has issued a Code of Professional Ethics. Exhibit 1-5 presents the SMAC's guidance on ethical issues.

Typical Ethical Challenges

Ethical issues can confront management accountants in many ways. The following examples are illustrative.

- ◆ **Case A** A management accountant, knowing that reporting a loss for a software division will result in yet another "rightsizing initiative" (a euphemism for layoffs), has concerns about the commercial viability of software for which development costs are currently being capitalized. The division manager argues vehemently that the new product will be a "winner" but has no credible evidence to support the opinion. The last two products from this division have not been successful in the market. The management accountant has many friends in the division and wants to avoid a personal confrontation with the division manager. Should the management accountant require the development to be expensed immediately because of the lack of evidence as to its commercial viability?

- ◆ **Case B** A packaging supplier, bidding for a new contract, offers the management accountant of its customer an all-expenses-paid weekend to the Grey

OBJECTIVE 7

Understand the importance of professional ethics to management accountants

Society of Management Accountants
www.cma-maritimes.com/

Society of Management Accountants of Canada (SMAC). The largest association of management accountants in Canada.

Certified Management Accountant (CMA). The professional designation for management accountants in Canada.

EXHIBIT 1-5
Code of Professional Ethics

All Members shall adhere to the following "Code of Professional Ethics" of the Society:

(a) A Member shall act at all times with

    (i) responsibility for and fidelity to public needs;

    (ii) fairness and loyalty to his associates, clients, and employers; and

    (iii) competence through devotion to high ideals of personal honour and professional integrity;

(b) A Member shall

    (i) maintain at all times independence of thought and action;

    (ii) not express his opinion on financial statements without first assessing his relationship with his client to determine whether he might expect his opinion to be consider independent, objective, and unbiased by one who has knowledge of all the facts; and

    (iii) when preparing financial statements or expressing an opinion on financial statements which are intended to inform management only, disclose all material facts known to him in order not to make such financial statements misleading, acquire sufficient information to warrant an expression of opinion, and report all material misstatements or departures from generally accepted accounting principles;

(c) A Member shall

    (i) not disclose or use any confidential information concerning the affairs of his employer or client unless acting in the course of his duties or except when such information is required to be disclosed in the course of any defence of himself or any associate or employee in any lawsuit or other legal proceeding or against alleged professional misconduct by order of lawful authority or the Board or any committee of the Society in the proper exercise of their duties but only to the extent necessary for such purpose;

    (ii) inform his employer or client of any business connections or interests of which his employer or client would reasonably expect to be informed;

    (iii) not, in the course of exercising his duties on behalf of his employer or client, hold, receive, bargain for, or acquire any fee, remuneration, or benefit without his employer's or client's knowledge and consent; and

    (iv) take all reasonable steps, in arranging any engagement as a consultant, to establish a clear understanding of the scope and objectives of the work before it is commenced and shall furnish the client with an estimate of cost, preferably before the engagement is commenced, but in any event as soon as possible thereafter.

(d) A Member shall

    (i) conduct himself toward other Members with courtesy and good faith;

    (ii) not commit an act discreditable to the profession;

    (iii) not engage in or counsel any business or occupation which, in the opinion of the Society, is incompatible with the professional ethics of a management accountant;

    (iv) not accept any engagement to review the work of another Member for the same employer except with the knowledge of that Member, or except where the connection of that Member with the work has been terminated, unless the Member reviews the work of others as a normal part of his responsibilities;

    (v) not attempt to gain an advantage over other Members by paying or accepting a commission in securing management accounting work;

(vi) uphold the principle of adequate compensation for management accounting work; and

(vii) not act maliciously or in any other way which may adversely reflect on the public or professional reputation or business of another Member.

(e) A Member shall

(i) at all times maintain the standards of competence expressed by the academic and experience requirements for admission to the Society and for continuation as a Member;

(ii) disseminate the knowledge upon which the profession of management accounting is based to others within the profession and generally promote the advancement of the profession;

(iii) undertake only such work as he is competent to perform by virtue of his training and experience and shall, where it would be in the best interests of an employer or client, engage, or advise the employer or client to engage, other specialists;

(iv) expose before the proper tribunals of the Society any incompetent, unethical, illegal, or unfair conduct or practice of a Member which involves the reputation, dignity, or honour of the Society; and

(v) endeavour to ensure that a professional partnership or company with which he is associated as a partner, principal, director, or officer abides by the Code of Professional Ethics and the rules of professional conduct established by the Society.

Source: *Management Accounting Handbook: Bylaw 20* (The Society of Management Accountants of Ontario). Reproduced with permission of The Society of Management Accountants of Ontario.

Cup. The supplier does not mention the new contract when making the invitation. The accountant is not a personal friend of the supplier. He knows operating cost issues are critical in approving the new contract and is concerned that the supplier will ask for details about bids by competing packaging companies.

In each case the management accountant is faced with an ethical challenge. Case A involves competence, objectivity, and integrity, whereas case B involves confidentiality and integrity. Ethical issues are not always black and white. For example, the supplier in case B may have no intention of raising issues associated with the bid. However, the appearance of a conflict of interest in case B is sufficient for many companies to prohibit employees from accepting free "favours" from suppliers.

A survey of 1,500 members of the Australian Society of Accountants found the following to be among the most frequently encountered ethical issues:

1. Proposals by clients or managers for tax evasion
2. Conflicts of interest
3. Proposals to manipulate financial statements
4. Integrity in admitting mistakes made by oneself
5. Coping with superiors' instructions to carry out unethical acts[1]

Most professional accounting organizations around the globe issue statements about professional ethics. While these statements include many of the same issues discussed by the SMAC in Exhibit 1-5, differences do exist in their content. For example, the Chartered Institute of Management Accountants (CIMA) in the United Kingdom identifies four fundamental principles of competency, confidentiality, integrity, and objectivity. A statement by the Institute of Management Accountants in

[1]Leung, P., and B. J. Cooper, "Ethical Dilemmas in Accountancy Practice," *The Australian Accountant*, May 1995.

Common Ethical Dilemmas and Codes of Ethics

Ethical dilemmas occur in many situations. Kirk Hanson, a noted scholar in business ethics, lists the following as most common:

◆ When the boss asks you to do something questionable or unethical

◆ When you have knowledge of the unethical actions of others

◆ When you are tempted to cut corners to meet your performance goals

◆ When you are tempted to oversell your product to close the deal

◆ When disclosing confidential information will greatly help your career or your company

◆ When you are tempted to cover up past underperformance

One survey found 68% of Canadian, 83% of U.S., and 50% of European companies have instituted codes of ethics. In addition to a code of ethics, a survey of Canadian companies found that seven commonly used ethics control mechanisms were primarily designed and implemented by middle or senior management.

Ethics Control Mechanism	A	B	C	Persons* D	E	F	G
Code of ethics	73.3[†]	13.3	10	0	0	3.4	0
Whistle-blowing channels	59.0	17.9	17.9	2.6	0	2.6	0
Ethics reward systems	0	100	0	0	0	0	0
Ethics committee	58.3	33.3	0	0	0	8.4	0
Judiciary board	66.6	16.7	0	16.7	0	0	0
Employee training in ethics	37.5	41.7	8.3	12.5	0	0	0
Corporate governance	60	10	10	10	0	0	10

*A: Senior or executive officers
 B: Middle managers
 C: Controller's department personnel
 D: Other salaried employees
[†] All figures shown as percentages.

E: Hourly employees
F: Persons from outside the organization
G: Other

Source: Hanson, K. O., "Unavoidable Ethical Dilemmas in a Business Career" (Stanford University, 1995); Berenbeim, R. E., *Corporate Ethics Practices* (New York: The Conference Board, 1992), and Irvine, B., and L. Lindsay, "Corporate Ethics and the Controller," *CMA Magazine*, December/January 1994, p.25. Table reprinted with permission from The Society of Management Accountants of Canada.

the United States goes further by providing guidance on the resolution of ethical conflict.

NEWLY EVOLVING MANAGEMENT THEMES AROUND THE GLOBE

OBJECTIVE 8

Describe evolving management themes that are shaping developments in management accounting systems

Management accounting exists to help managers make better decisions. Changes in the way managers operate require re-evaluating the design and operation of the management accounting systems themselves. Exhibit 1-6 presents key themes in the new management approach.

1. **Customer satisfaction is priority one**. This theme is central. Customers are pivotal to the success of an organization. The number of organizations aiming to be "customer-driven" is large and increasing. The organization chart of Furon (a manufacturer of polymer) in Exhibit 1-7 shows how the customer is positioned at the apex of its organizational structure.

EXHIBIT 1-6
Key Themes in the New Management Approach

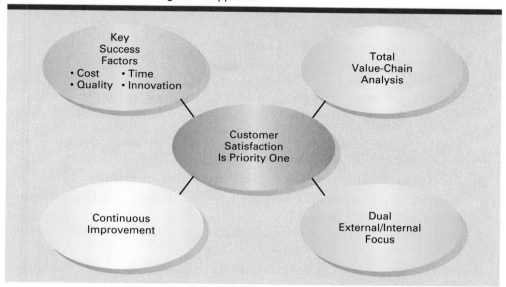

We discuss this theme in Chapter 16 when we look at customer profitability analysis and in Chapter 13 when we address customer feedback in performance measures.

2. **Key success factors.** Customers are demanding ever-improving levels of performance regarding several (or even all) of the following factors:

◆ *Cost.* Organizations are under continuous pressure to reduce the cost of the products or services they sell to their customers.

◆ *Quality.* Customers are expecting higher levels of quality and are less tolerant of low quality than in the past.

◆ *Time.* Time has many components, including the time taken to develop and bring new products to market, the speed with which an organization responds to customer requests, and the reliability with which promised delivery

EXHIBIT 1-7
The Pivotal Position of Customers in the Organization Chart of the Furon Corporation

Furon Corporation
www.furon.com

dates are met. Organizations are under pressure to complete activities faster and to meet promised delivery dates more reliably than in the past in order to increase customer satisfaction.

◆ *Innovation.* There is heightened recognition that a continuing flow of innovative products or services is a prerequisite for the ongoing success of most organizations.

Factors that directly affect customer satisfaction, such as cost, quality, time, and innovative products and services, are termed **key success factors.**

We discuss this theme in Chapter 5 when we address using activity-based costing to guide cost reductions, in Chapter 13 on linking innovation and internal process improvements to customer satisfaction, and in Chapter 19 when we examine cost of quality reports.

3. **Total value-chain analysis**. This theme has two related aspects:

◆ Treating each area of the business functions in Exhibit 1-1 as an essential and valued contributor

◆ Integrating and coordinating the efforts of all business functions in addition to developing the capabilities of each individual business function

Total value-chain or supply chain analysis means focusing on all the business functions related to a product or service from its cradle to its grave ("womb to tomb"), irrespective of whether those functions occur in the same organization or in a set of legally independent organizations. For example, Pepsi-Cola bottlers work with their materials suppliers to reduce materials-handling costs. Similarly, Fujitsu works with the customers of its microchip division to better plan its production scheduling of microchips.

We discuss this theme in Chapter 7 as we look at budgeting, in Chapter 12 when we address target costing, and in Chapter 20 on just-in-time (JIT) and supply chain analysis.

4. **Continuous improvement.** Continuous improvement by competitors creates a never-ending search for higher levels of performance within many organizations. Phrases such as the following capture this theme:

◆ "A journey with no end."

◆ "We are running harder just to stand still."

◆ "If you're not going forward, you're going backward."

Sumitomo Electric Industries, the Japanese manufacturer of electric wires and cables, has daily meetings so that all employees maintain a continuous focus on cost reduction.

We discuss this theme in Chapter 6 on kaizen budgeting, Chapter 7 on continuous improvement standard costs, and Chapter 10 on learning curves.

5. **Dual external/internal focus.** Managers operate in both an external and an internal environment. The external environment includes customers, competitors, shareholders, suppliers, and government bodies. Many organizations now are restructuring the definition of manager responsibilities to give much greater emphasis to the external environment. This greater emphasis increases the likelihood that managers will anticipate external changes and take advantage of such external changes as the introduction of competitors' new products or shifts in customer preferences. The internal environment covers each part of the value chain as well as the coordination of its components.

We discuss this theme in Chapter 7 when we examine benchmarking and in Chapter 23 when we look at market-based transfer pricing.

Over time, the emphasis placed on the five themes in Exhibit 1-6 may change, and new themes may be added. If management accountants are to remain useful to managers, they must keep up to date with changes in the field of management.

Key success factors. Factors that directly affect customer satisfaction such as cost, quality, time, and innovative products and services.

Sumitomo Electric Industries
www.sumitomocorp.co.jp

Quality in Accounting at Motorola

Providing a quality product or service is often defined in terms of consistently meeting or exceeding customers' expectations. Motorola, a $20 billion global company, is a winner of many awards for the quality of its products. The accounting group at Motorola views Motorola managers as its customers and is constantly seeking ways to meet or exceed their expectations. Consider the timeliness of the financial reports. Motorola managers place a premium on receiving timely reports. For many years, monthly results were not available to managers until eight working days after month-end. While an eight-working-day "close period" is faster than that of most companies, managers viewed the provision of more timely reports as very important. The accounting group at Motorola decided to set itself a target of a two-working-day close.

Motorola now requires its six operating groups and its administrative group "to send monthly numbers no later than two working days after month-end in a uniform layout that is compatible with the accounting group's software." As numbers are received, accounting performs real-time checks for "unusual transactions, numbers that don't jibe, and other potentially inaccurate entries." The consolidated financial reports are now provided to senior company executives and board members by noon of the third workday after the month-end.

Motorola managers, with more timely information about business trends, can now make any adjustments at least six working days earlier than before. Moreover, the streamlining undertaken to speed the closing process has resulted in lower costs of monthly closing (a 30% reduction in employees) and a lower errors rate (less than 1,000 errors per 2 million transactions).

Motorola
www.motorola.com

What has been the response of the accounting group to this success? They now have a goal of closing in one-and-one-half days! Motorola has a culture of continuous improvement that is applied to all aspects of its business.

Source: B. Ettorre, "How Motorola Closes Its Books in Two Days," *Management Review,* March 1995, plus discussions with Motorola management.

PROBLEM FOR SELF-STUDY

(Try to solve this problem before examining the solution that follows.)

PROBLEM

The Campbell Soup Company incurs the following costs:

a. Purchase of tomatoes by canning plant for Campbell's tomato soup products.
b. Materials purchased for redesigning Mr. Christie biscuit containers to make biscuits stay fresh longer.
c. Payment to Bates, the advertising agency for the Healthy Request line of soup products.
d. Salaries of food technologists researching feasibility of a Prego pizza sauce that has zero calories.
e. Payment to Safeway for shelf space to display Campbell's food products.
f. Cost of a toll-free telephone line used for customer inquiries about possible taste problems with Campbell's soups.
g. Cost of gloves used by line operators on the Swanson Fiesta breakfast food production line.
h. Cost of hand-held computers used by Maple Leaf Foods delivery staff serving major supermarket accounts.

REQUIRED

Classify each cost item (a) to (h) into a component of the value chain shown in Exhibit 1-1 (p. 4).

SOLUTION
a. Production
b. Design of products, services, or processes
c. Marketing
d. Research and development
e. Marketing
f. Customer service
g. Production
h. Distribution

SUMMARY

The following points are linked to the chapter's learning objectives.

1. Accounting systems provide information for five broad purposes: (a) formulating overall strategies and long-range plans, (b) resource allocation decisions such as product and customer emphasis, (c) cost planning and cost control, (d) performance measurement, and (e) meeting external regulatory and legal reporting obligations.

2. Cost accounting measures and reports financial and other information related to an organization's acquisition or consumption of resources. It is an important component of both management accounting and financial accounting.

3. Managers in all areas of the value chain are customers of accounting information. The business functions in the value chain are research and development; design of products, services, or processes; production; marketing; distribution; and customer service.

4. Accounting helps facilitate planning, control, and decision-making through budgets and other financial benchmarks, its systematic recording of actual results, and its role in performance evaluation.

5. Management accountants and controllers are staff management in most organizations. Staff management exists to provide advice and assistance to line managers, who are directly responsible for attaining the objectives of the organization.

6. In most organizations, management accountants perform scorekeeping, attention-directing, and problem-solving functions. The first function emphasizes the importance of the integrity of information, while the other two emphasize the helper role of the accountant.

7. Management accountants have important ethical responsibilities that are related to competence, confidentiality, integrity, and objectivity.

8. Important management themes that are shaping developments in management accounting systems around the globe include (a) the primacy of customer satisfaction, (b) linking planning and control to key success factors, (c) total value-chain analysis, (d) continuous improvement, and (e) dual external/internal focus.

Each chapter will include this section. Like all technical subjects, accounting contains many terms with precise meanings. Pin down the definitions of new terms when you initially encounter them. The meaning of each of the following terms is explained in this chapter.

attention-directing (p. 10)
budget (p. 5)
Certified Management Accountant
    (CMA) (p. 11)
chief financial officer (CFO) (p. 8)
control (p. 5)
controller (p. 9)
cost accounting (p. 2)
cost-benefit approach (p. 7)
cost management (p. 3)
customer service (p. 4)
design of products, services, or
    processes (p. 4)
distribution (p. 4)
finance director (p. 8)
financial accounting (p. 2)

key success factors (p. 16)
line management (p. 8)
management accounting (p. 2)
management by exception (p. 6)
marketing (p. 4)
planning (p. 5)
problem-solving (p. 10)
production (p. 4)
research and development (R&D) (p. 4)
scorekeeping (p. 10)
Society of Management Accountants of
    Canada (SMAC) (p. 11)
staff management (p. 8)
value chain (p. 4)
variance (p. 6)

ASSIGNMENT MATERIAL

QUESTIONS

1-1 The accounting system should provide information for five broad purposes. Describe them.

1-2 Distinguish between *management accounting* and *financial accounting*.

1-3 "Management accounting should not fit the straitjacket of financial accounting." Explain and give an example.

1-4 Describe the business functions in the value chain.

1-5 Explain the meaning of *cost management*.

1-6 Feedback may be used for a variety of purposes. Identify at least five uses of feedback.

1-7 "Knowledge of technical issues such as computer technology is necessary but not sufficient to becoming a successful accountant." Do you agree? Why?

1-8 Peter Drucker, a noted business observer, made the following comment in an address to management accountants: "I am not saying that you do not need a 'cop on the beat,' you do. . . . But your great challenge is to get across to your associates your ability to identify the opportunities—to identify the wealth-producing characteristics." Do you agree? Explain.

1-9 As a new controller, reply to this comment by a plant manager: "As I see it, our accountants may be needed to keep records for stockholders and Revenue Canada—but I don't want them sticking their noses in my day-to-day operations. I do the best I know how. No pencil-pushing bean counter knows enough about my responsibilities to be of any use to me."

1-10 As used in accounting, what do "SMAC" and "CMA" stand for?

1-11 What organization sets forth the standards of ethical conduct for management accountants in Canada?

1-12 What steps should a management accountant take if established written policies provide insufficient guidance on how to handle an ethical conflict?

1-13 When explaining a motor vehicle market share turnaround, General Motors stated: "We listened to what our customers wanted and acted on what they said. Good things happen when you pay attention to the boss." How might management accountants at General Motors apply this same perspective to their own tasks?

1-14 A leading management observer stated that the most successful companies are those who have an obsession for their customers. Is this statement pertinent to management accountants? Explain.

1-15 Changes in the way managers operate require rethinking the design and operation of management accounting systems. Describe five themes that are affecting both the way managers operate and developments in management accounting.

EXERCISES

1-16 Management accountants and customer focus. A recent Annual Report of Ford Motor Company included the following comment:

> Delivering great value to our customers. That's our passion. Throughout Ford Motor Company we're focused on improving the quality and value of our products, and speeding delivery to market. All our efforts are aimed at exceeding customer expectations. That's the best way to reach and keep customers.

REQUIRED
1. Who are the customers of the management accounting function?
2. How might the Ford Motor Company's credo of "exceeding customer expectations" for its motor vehicles also apply to its management accounting function?

1-17 Purposes of accounting systems. The International Sports Management Group (ISMG) manages and promotes sporting events and sporting personalities. Its managers are currently examining the following reports and accounting statements:
a. Five-year projections for expanding into managing sports television networks for cable television
b. Income statement to be included in a six-month interim report to be sent to investors and filed with the securities regulators
c. Profitability comparison of golf tournaments directed by different managers, each of whom receives a percentage of that tournament's profits
d. Monthly reports of office costs for each of the 14 ISMG offices worldwide
e. Statement showing the revenues ISMG earns from different types of sporting events (for example, golf, motor racing, and tennis)

REQUIRED
Classify the reports in parts (a) to (e) into one of the five major purposes of accounting systems (on p. 2).

1-18 Major purposes of accounting systems. Barnes and Noble is a book retailing company. The majority of its sales are made at its own stores. These stores are often located in shopping malls or in the downtown central business districts of cities. A small but increasing percentage of sales are made via its internet shopping division.

The following five reports were recently prepared by the management accounting group at Barnes and Noble:
1. Annual financial statements included in the Annual Report sent to its stockholders
2. Weekly report to Vice President of Operations for each Barnes and Noble store—includes revenue, gross margin, and operating costs
3. Study for Vice President of New Business Development of the expected revenue and expected costs of the Barnes and Noble Internet Division selling music products (CD's, cassettes, etc.) as well as books
4. Weekly report to book publishers and trade magazines on the sales of the top-ten-selling fiction and non-fiction books at both its own stores and in the Internet Division
5. Report to insurance company on losses Barnes and Noble suffered at its three San Francisco stores resulting from an earthquake

REQUIRED
1. What are the major purposes of accounting systems?
2. Identify a major purpose served by each of the above five reports prepared by Barnes and Noble's management accounting group.
3. For each report, identify both a planning-decision and a control-decision use by a manager (either at Barnes and Noble or another company).

1-19 Value chain and classification of costs, computer company. Apple Computer incurs the following costs:
a. Electricity costs for the plant assembling the Macintosh computer line of products
b. Transportation costs for shipping Macintosh software to a retail chain

c. Payment to David Kelley Designs for design of the Powerbook carrying case

d. Salary of a computer scientist working on the next generation of minicomputers

e. Cost of Apple employees' visit to a major customer to illustrate Apple's ability to interconnect with other computers

f. Purchase of competitors' products for testing against potential future Apple products

g. Payment to a television station for running Apple advertisements

h. Cost of cables purchased from an outside supplier to be used with the Macintosh printer

REQUIRED

Classify each of the cost items in parts (a) to (h) as belonging to a component of the value chain shown in Exhibit 1-1.

1-20 Value chain and classification of costs, pharmaceutical company. Merck, a large pharmaceutical company, incurs the following costs:

a. Cost of redesigning blister packs to make drug containers more tamperproof

b. Cost of videos sent to doctors to promote sales of a new drug

c. Cost of a toll-free telephone line used for customer inquiries about usage, side-effects of drugs, and so on

d. Equipment purchased by a scientist to conduct experiments on drugs yet to be approved by the government

e. Payment to actors on infomercial to be shown on television promoting new hair-growing product for balding men

f. Labour costs of workers in the packaging area of a production facility

g. Bonus paid to a salesperson for exceeding monthly sales quota

h. Cost of Purolator courier service to deliver drugs to hospitals

REQUIRED

Classify each of the cost items in parts (a) to (h) as belonging to a component of the value chain shown in Exhibit 1-1.

1-21 Key management accounting guidelines, integrating management accounting systems. Jeannette Smith is the newly appointed Controller of National Foods, a large food and beverage products company. It has 53 separate European subsidiaries. The company has grown largely by acquisition. Over 30 different companies in Europe have been acquired by National Foods in the last five years. National Foods left each company's management in place with their own internal management structure and accounting systems. Recently, however, several factors have led National Foods to consider adopting a more centralized management style with all subsidiaries using the same management-accounting system. One factor was the demands of several major customers of National Foods to link their own information systems to those of National Foods. Currently this is not possible. A second factor was large unexpected losses at the Polish and Spanish subsidiaries of National Foods.

Smith was hired by National Foods to lead the development of an integrated management accounting system that will be used in each of its subsidiaries. There will be the same recording rules in each subsidiary and the same chart of accounts. The goal is for National Foods to be able to access and analyze simultaneously the data in the management accounting system in each of its subsidiaries.

REQUIRED

1. Describe how each of the following guidelines could be important to Smith in her management accounting system challenges at National Foods:

    a. Cost-benefit approach

    b. Full recognition to behavioural as well as technical considerations

    c. Different costs for different purposes

2. Smith will report to Alex Murphy, the CFO of National Foods. Discuss key areas of Murphy's responsibility.

1-22 Scorekeeping, attention-directing, and problem-solving. For each of the following activities, identify the major function (scorekeeping, attention-directing, or problem-solving) the accountant is performing.

a. Preparing a monthly statement of Australian sales for the IBM marketing vice-president

b. Interpreting differences between actual results and budgeted amounts on a performance report for the customer warranty department of General Electric

c. Preparing a schedule of amortization[2] for forklift trucks in the receiving department of a Hewlett Packard plant in Scotland

---

[2]The term *amortization* is used in this book to be consistent with the *CICA Handbook*. It is synonymous with *depreciation* and *depletion*.

d. Analyzing, for a Mitsubishi international manufacturing manager, the desirability of buying some auto parts made in Korea

e. Interpreting why a Birmingham distribution centre did not adhere to its delivery costs budget

f. Explaining a Xerox shipping department's performance report

g. Preparing, for the manager of production control of a U.S. steel plant, a cost comparison of two computerized manufacturing control systems

h. Preparing a scrap report for the finishing department of a Toyota parts plant

i. Preparing the budget for the maintenance department of Mount Sinai Hospital

j. Analyzing, for a General Motors product designer, the impact on product costs of some new headlight lamps

1-23 Scorekeeping, attention-directing, and problem-solving. For each of the following activities, identify the major function the accountant is performing—scorekeeping, attention-directing, or problem-solving.

a. Interpreting differences between actual results and budgeted amounts on a shipping manager's performance report at a Daewoo distribution centre

b. Preparing a report showing the benefits of leasing motor vehicles versus owning them

c. Preparing adjusting journal entries for amortization on the personnel manager's office equipment at the Bank of Montreal

d. Preparing a customer's monthly statement for a Sears store

e. Processing the weekly payroll for the University of Alberta maintenance department

f. Explaining the product design manager's performance report at a Chrysler division

g. Analyzing the costs of several different ways to blend materials in the foundry of a General Electric plant

h. Tallying sales, by branches, for the sales vice-president of Unilever

i. Analyzing, for the president of CorelDRAW, the impact of a contemplated new product on net income

j. Interpreting why an IBM sales district did not meet its sales quota

1-24 Changes in management and changes in management accounting. A survey on ways organizations are changing their management accounting systems reported the following:

a. Company A now reports a value-chain income statement for each of the brands it sells.

b. Company B now presents in a single report all costs related to achieving high quality levels of its products.

c. Company C now presents estimates of the manufacturing costs of its two most important competitors in its performance reports, in addition to its own internal manufacturing costs.

d. Company D reduces by 1% each month the budgeted labour assembly cost of a product when evaluating the performance of a plant manager.

e. Company E now reports profitability and satisfaction measures (as assessed by a third party) on a customer-by-customer basis.

REQUIRED
Link each of the above changes to one of the key themes in the new management approach outlined in Exhibit 1-6.

PROBLEMS

1-25 Planning and control, feedback. In April 2000, Naomi Campbell, editor of *The Daily Sporting News* (DSN), decides to reduce the price per newspaper from $0.70 in April 2000 to $0.50 starting May 1, 2000. Actual paid circulation in April is 7.5 million (250,000 per day × 30 days). Campbell estimates that the $0.20 price reduction would increase paid circulation in May to 12.4 million (400,000 × 31 days). The actual May circulation turns out to be 13,640,000 (440,000 × 31 days). Assume that one goal of DSN is to increase operating income. The budgeted increase in circulation would enable DSN to charge higher advertising rates in later months of 2000 if those budgeted gains actually occur. The actual price paid in May 2000 was the budgeted $0.50 per newspaper.

REQUIRED
1. Distinguish between planning and control at DSN, giving an example of each.
2. Prepare a newspaper revenue performance report for DSN for May 2000 showing the actual results, budgeted amounts, and the variance.

3. Give two types of action Campbell might take based on feedback on the May 2000 circulation revenue.

1-26 Responsibility for analysis of performance. Karen Phillipson is the new corporate controller of a multinational company that has just overhauled its organizational structure. The company is now decentralized. Each division is under an operating vice-president who, within wide limits, has responsibilities and authority to run the division like a separate company.

Phillipson has a number of bright staff members. One of them, Bob Garrett, is in charge of a newly created performance analysis staff. Garrett and staff members prepare monthly division performance reports for the company president. These reports are division income statements, showing budgeted performance and actual results, and they are accompanied by detailed written explanations and appraisals of variances. In the past, each of Garrett's staff members was responsible for analyzing one division; each consulted with division line and staff executives and became generally acquainted with the division's operations.

After a few months, Bill Whisler, vice-president in charge of Division C, stormed into the controller's office. The gist of his complaint follows:

"Your staff is trying to take over part of my responsibility. They come in, snoop around, ask hundreds of questions, and take up plenty of our time. It's up to me, not you and your detectives, to analyze and explain my division's performance to central headquarters. If you don't stop trying to grab my responsibility, I'll raise the whole issue with the president."

REQUIRED
1. What events or relationships may have led to Whisler's outburst?
2. As Phillipson, how would you answer Whisler's contentions?
3. What alternative actions can Phillipson take to improve future relationships?

1-27 Professional ethics and reporting divisional performance. Marcia Miller is division controller and Tom Maloney is division manager of the Ramses Shoe Company. Miller has line responsibility to Maloney, but she also has staff responsibility to the company controller.

Maloney is under severe pressure to achieve budgeted division income for the year. He has asked Miller to book $200,000 of sales on December 31. The customers' orders are firm, but the shoes are still in the production process. They will be shipped on or about January 4. Maloney said to Miller, "The key event is getting the sales order, not shipping of the shoes. You should support me, not obstruct my reaching division goals."

REQUIRED
1. Describe Miller's ethical responsibilities.
2. What should Miller do if Maloney gives her a direct order to book the sales?

1-28 Planning and control decisions; internet company. WebNews.com is an internet company. It offers subscribers multiple online services ranging from an annotated TV guide to local-area information on restaurants and movie theatres. Recent data for its two main revenue sources are:

Monthly fees from subscribers:

Month/Year	Number of Subscribers	Monthly Fee per Subscriber
June 2000	28,642	$14.95
December 2000	54,813	$19.95
June 2001	58,178	$19.95
December 2001	86,437	$19.95
June 2002	146,581	$19.95

Banner advertising fees from companies advertising on WebNews.com page sites:

Month/Year	Advertising Revenue
June 2000	$ 400,988
December 2000	833,158
June 2001	861,034
December 2001	1,478,072
June 2002	2,916,962

The following decisions were made in the June to October 2002 period:

a. June 2002. Decision to raise the monthly subscription fee from $19.95 per month in June 2002 to $24.95 per month in July 2002. The $19.95 fee first applied in December 2000.

b. June 2002. Decision to inform existing subscribers that the July 2002 subscription fee would be $24.95.

c. July 2002. Decision to upgrade the content of its online services and to offer better internet mail services.

d. October 2002. Demotion of Vice-President–Marketing after significant slowing of subscriber growth in accounts and revenue. Results include:

Month/Year	Number of Subscribers	Monthly Fee per Subscriber
July 2002	128,933	$24.95
August 2002	139,419	$24.95
September 2002	143,131	$24.95

e. October 2002. Decision to reduce the monthly subscription fee from $24.95 per month in September 2002 to $21.95 in October 2002.

REQUIRED

1. Distinguish between planning decisions and control decisions at WebNews.com.
2. Classify each of the (a) to (e) decisions as a planning or a control decision.

1-29 Scorekeeping, attention-directing, and problem-solving; internet company (continuation of 1-28). Management accountants at WebNews.com can play a key role in each of the five decisions described in Problem 1-28. Scorekeeping, attention-directing, and problem-solving are three key functions they can perform.

REQUIRED

1. Distinguish between the scorekeeping, attention-directing, and problem-solving functions of a management accountant at WebNews.com.
2. For each of the five decisions outlined in Problem 1-28, describe a scorekeeping or attention-directing or problem-solving role. Where possible, illustrate the data a management accountant may provide for each decision.

1-30 Software procurement decision, ethics. Jorge Michaels is the Winnipeg-based controller of Mexa Foods, a rapidly growing manufacturer and marketer of Mexican food products. Michaels is currently considering the purchase of a new cost management package for use by each of its six manufacturing plants and its many marketing personnel. Four major competing products are being considered by Michaels.

Horizon 1-2-3 is an aggressive software developer. It views Mexa as a target of opportunity. Every six months Horizon has a three-day user's conference in a Caribbean location. Each conference has substantial time left aside for "rest and recreation." Horizon offers Michaels an all-expenses-paid visit to the upcoming conference in Cancun, Mexico. Michaels accepts the offer believing that it will be very useful to talk to other users of Horizon software. He is especially looking forward to the visit as he has close relatives in the Cancun area.

Prior to leaving, Michaels receives a visit from the president of Mexa. She shows him an anonymous letter sent to her. It argues that Horizon is receiving unfair favourable treatment in the Mexa software decision-making process. The letter specifically mentions Michaels' upcoming "all-expenses-paid trip to Cancun during Winnipeg's deep winter." Michaels is deeply offended. He says he has made no decision and believes he is very capable of making a software choice on the merits of each product. Mexa currently does not have a formal written code of ethics.

REQUIRED

1. Do you think Michaels faces an ethical problem as regards his forthcoming visit to the Horizon user's group meeting? Refer to Exhibit 1-5. Explain.
2. Should Mexa allow executives to attend user's meetings while negotiating with other vendors about a purchase decision? Explain. If yes, what conditions on attending should apply?
3. Would you recommend Mexa develop its own code of ethics to handle situations such as this one? What are the pros and cons of having such a written code?

1-31 Professional ethics and end-of-year games. Janet Taylor is the new division controller of the snack foods division of National Foods. National Foods has reported a minimum 15% growth in annual earnings for each of the past five years. The snack foods division has reported annual earnings growth of over 20% each year in this same period. During the current year, the economy went into a recession. The corporate controller estimates a 10% annual earnings growth rate for National Foods in this year. One month before the December 31 fiscal year-end of the current year, Taylor estimates the snack foods division will report an annual earnings growth of only 8%. Warren Ryan, the snack foods division president, is less than happy, but he says with a wry smile, "Let the end-of-year games begin."

Taylor makes some inquiries and is able to compile the following list of end-of-year games that were more or less accepted by the prior division controller:
a. Deferring routine monthly maintenance in December on packaging equipment by an independent contractor until January of next year
b. Extending the close of the current fiscal year beyond December 31 so that some sales of next year are included in the current year
c. Altering dates of shipping documents of next January's sales to record them as sales in December of the current year
d. Giving salespeople a double bonus to exceed December sales targets
e. Deferring the current period's advertising by reducing the number of television spots run in December and running more than planned in January of next year
f. Deferring the current period's reported advertising costs by having National Food's outside advertising agency delay billing December advertisements until January of next year or having the agency alter invoices to conceal the December date
g. Persuading carriers to accept merchandise for shipment in December of the current year although they normally would not have done so

REQUIRED
1. Why might the snack foods division president want to play the end-of-year games described here?
2. The division controller is deeply troubled and reads the Code of Professional Ethics in Exhibit 1-5. Classify each of the end-of-year games as (i) acceptable or (ii) unacceptable according to that document.
3. What should Taylor do if Ryan suggests that end-of-year games are played in every division of National Foods and that she would greatly harm the snack foods division if she did not play along and paint the rosiest picture possible of the division's results?

COLLABORATIVE LEARNING PROBLEMS

1-32 **Responding to allegations of fraud.** You are the controller of Broad Street Finance (BSF). BSF is an investment banking company that has recently encountered severe financial difficulties and has had to lay off over 200 employees. The only bright spot in this picture is BSF's bond trading division, but you have just received the following anonymous letter:

Dear Sir,

Last year's reported earnings for the bond trading division are fictitious. The top three managers of the division recently received bonuses of over $12 million, based on their share of last year's reported earnings. The head of bond trading has been inventing bond trades that are supposed to be highly profitable. They are not. The division profits are like a deck of cards about to collapse. The head of bond trading cares only about "how much you reportedly made" and nothing about how you made it. The auditors don't understand the complexity of today's bond trading operations. This problem will blow up in your face unless handled quickly and carefully. I am sending a copy of this letter to the Ontario Securities Commission, *The Financial Post*, *Canadian Business*, *The Globe and Mail*, and all members of Broad Street's board of directors.

Sincerely,
Concerned Ex-employee

INSTRUCTIONS
Form groups of three or more students. One is to be the chief financial officer, one the president, and one the chairperson of the board of directors. Other members are on the board of directors.

Develop a group consensus on how you should respond to this letter. Like many firms in the financial services industry, BSF has no formal code of ethics. Should BSF formalize a code of ethics statement?

1-33 Global company, ethical challenges with bribery. Shell Oil Company operates in many parts of the globe. These operations include oil exploration, production, transportation, refining, and marketing. One challenge faced by Shell is how to handle requests for "bribes" and "facilitating payments." The Chairman of Shell's operations recently gave an address where he "claimed that Shell loses valuable business because it refuses to pay bribes. . ."

One form of bribe is a payment to a private bank account that is portrayed as a charitable donation. Shell's Chairman noted that "on occasion it has been suggested to me that Shell's cause would be much helped by a donation to a national cultural or humanitarian fund—which just happens to have a bank account in Switzerland." Another form of a bribe is a payment to an "intermediary" in which a company pays a third party for a "go-between" role that could be more efficiently handled without the third party. The "intermediary" handles the bribery payment plus takes an extra facilitating payment.

The Shell Chairman concluded the address as follows:

> "We do not bribe. We do not sanction any type of illegal payment of any kind anywhere, directly or indirectly, and any employee who is found to have done so will be dismissed and, if possible, prosecuted. The principle employees have to follow is simple: 'Just say no'."

REQUIRED

1. Suppose you are a shareholder of Shell. Would you prefer Shell to pay bribes if it meant "gaining valuable business"?
2. Suppose you are the CFO of Shell. You suspect that one of your overseas subsidiaries is making payments to a local law firm for being an "intermediary" as well as for legal services. This subsidiary also makes payments to several Swiss-based "humanitarian funds" of questionable nature. How would you examine if bribery is occurring? If you discovered it was, what actions would you take?
3. Suppose again you are the CFO of Shell. A major oil discovery by Shell occurs in a country whose political regime is run by a dictator. His extended family has vast business dealings with oil companies. Shell's market capitalization increases by $2 billion when news of the discovery is released. Shell owns the oil leases and is negotiating with the government for construction of an oil refining plant. You are told by the dictator's key advisor that one of the dictator's sons has a company that will have 10% equity in the oil refinery (with no payment) and be actively involved at the director and operating level of the local refining subsidiary. You contact two other oil companies with prior dealings in this country and hear stories about "facilitating payments" and other questionable expenditures. One company called it an "auditor's nightmare." The Board of Directors of Shell has asked you (as CFO) to make a presentation on all financial aspects of the oil refinery project. What ethical issues (with proposed solutions) would you raise in your presentation?

2

AN INTRODUCTION TO COST TERMS AND PURPOSES

Many costing systems have multiple cost objects. Managers at a factory can collect costs for their mass-produced products (such as globes), for the assembly plant, and for customers who have globes custom-assembled at the plant.

LEARNING OBJECTIVES

After studying this chapter, you should be able to:

1. Define and illustrate a cost object
2. Distinguish between direct costs and indirect costs
3. Explain cost drivers, variable costs, and fixed costs
4. Understand why unit costs must be interpreted with caution
5. Distinguish between service sector, merchandising sector, and manufacturing sector companies
6. Differentiate between inventoriable costs and period costs
7. Describe the three categories of inventories commonly found in many manufacturing sector companies
8. Explain how different ways of computing product costs are appropriate for different purposes

This chapter explains several widely recognized cost concepts and terms that will help us demonstrate the multiple purposes of cost accounting systems, which we will stress throughout the book.

Various cost concepts and terms are useful in many contexts, including decision-making in all areas of the value chain. They help managers decide such issues as: How much should we spend for research and development? What is the effect of product design changes on manufacturing costs? Should we replace some production assembly workers with a robot? Should we spend more of the marketing budget on sales promotion coupons and less on advertising? Should we distribute from a central warehouse or from regional warehouses? Should we provide a toll-free number for customer inquiries regarding our products?

COSTS IN GENERAL

OBJECTIVE 1

Define and illustrate a cost object

Cost. Resource sacrificed or forgone to achieve a specific objective.

Cost object. Anything for which a separate measurement of costs is desired.

Cost accumulation. The collection of cost data in some organized way through an accounting system.

Cost assignment. General term that encompasses both (1) tracing accumulated costs to a cost object and (2) allocating accumulated costs to a cost object.

Actual costs. Costs incurred (historical costs), as distinguished from budgeted or forecasted costs.

Cost Objects

Accountants usually define **cost** as a resource sacrificed or forgone to achieve a specific objective. Most people consider costs as monetary amounts (such as dollars, pesos, pounds, or yen) that must be paid to acquire goods and services. For now we can think of costs in this conventional way.

To guide their decisions, managers often want to know how much a certain thing (such as a new product, a machine, a service, or a process) costs. We call this "thing" a **cost object,** which is anything for which a separate measurement of costs is desired. Exhibit 2-1 provides examples of several different types of cost objects.

Cost Accumulation and Cost Assignment

A costing system typically accounts for costs in two basic stages:

◆ **Stage 1.** It *accumulates* costs by some "natural" (often self-descriptive) classification such as materials, labour, fuel, advertising, or shipping.

◆ **Stage 2.** It *assigns* these costs to cost objects.

Cost accumulation is the collection of cost data in some organized way through an accounting system. **Cost assignment** is a general term that encompasses both (1) tracing accumulated costs to a cost object and (2) allocating accumulated costs to a cost object. Costs that are traced to a cost object are direct costs, and costs that are allocated to a cost object are indirect costs. Nearly all accounting systems accumulate **actual costs,** which are the costs incurred (historical costs), as distinguished from budgeted or forecasted costs.

Remember, managers assign costs to designated cost objects to help decision-making. For example, costs may be assigned to a department to facilitate decisions about departmental efficiency. Costs may also be assigned to a product or a customer to facilitate product or customer profitability analysis.

EXHIBIT 2-1
Examples of Cost Objects

Cost Object	Illustration
Product	A ten-speed bicycle
Service	An airline flight from Toronto to London
Project	An airplane assembled by Boeing for Singapore Airlines
Customer	All products purchased by Loblaws (the customer) from General Foods
Brand category	All soft drinks sold by a Pepsi-Cola bottling company with "Pepsi" in their name
Activity	A test to determine the quality level of a television set
Department	A department within a government environmental agency that studies air emissions standards
Program	An athletic program of a university

Cost Tracing and Cost Allocation

A major question concerning costs is whether they have a direct or an indirect relationship to a particular cost object.

OBJECTIVE 2

Distinguish between direct costs and indirect costs

◆ **Direct costs of a cost object** are costs that are related to the particular cost object and that can be *traced* to it in an economically feasible (cost-effective) way.

◆ **Indirect costs of a cost object** are costs that are related to the particular cost object but cannot be traced to it in an economically feasible (cost-effective) way. Indirect costs are *allocated* to the cost object using a cost allocation method.

Take a baseball bat as a cost object. The cost of the piece of wood used to make that bat is a direct cost. Why? Because the amount of wood used in making the bat can easily be traced to the bat. The cost of lighting in the factory where the bat was made is an indirect cost of the bat. Why? Because, although lighting helped in the making of the bat (the workers needed to see), it is not cost-effective to try to determine exactly how much lighting cost was used for a specific bat.

Managers prefer to make decisions on the basis of direct costs rather than indirect costs. Why? Because they know that direct costs are more accurate than indirect costs. In summary, the relationship between these terms is:

Direct costs of a cost object. Costs that are related to the particular cost object and that can be traced to it in an economically feasible way.

Indirect costs of a cost object. Costs that are related to the particular cost object but cannot be traced to it in an economically feasible way.

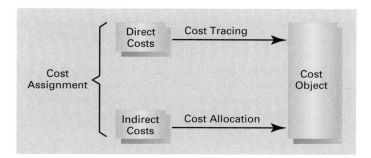

Cost tracing is the assigning of direct costs to the chosen cost object. **Cost allocation** is the assigning of indirect costs to the chosen cost object. *Cost assignment* encompasses both cost tracing and cost allocation.

Cost tracing. The assigning of direct costs to the chosen cost object.

Cost allocation. The assigning of indirect costs to the chosen cost object.

Factors Affecting Direct/Indirect Cost Classifications

Several factors will affect the classification of a cost as direct or indirect:

1. **The materiality of the cost in question.** The higher the cost in question, the more likely is the economic feasibility of tracing that cost to a particular cost object. Consider a mail-order catalogue company. It would probably be economically feasible to trace the courier charges for delivering a package directly to each customer. In contrast, the cost of the invoice paper included in the package sent to the customer is likely to be classified as an indirect cost, because it is not economically feasible to trace the cost of this paper to each customer. The benefits of knowing the exact number of (say) $0.05 worth of paper included in each package typically do not justify the costs of money and time in tracing the costs to each package.

2. **Available information-gathering technology.** Improvements in this area are enabling an increasing percentage of costs to be classified as direct. Bar codes, for example, allow many manufacturing plants to treat certain materials previously classified as indirect costs to be reclassified as direct costs of products. Bar codes can be read into a manufacturing cost file by waving a "wand" in the same quick and efficient way supermarkets now enter the cost of many items purchased by their customers.

3. **Design of operations.** Facility design can impact cost classification. For example, classifying a cost as direct is helped if an organization's facility (or part thereof) is used exclusively for a specific product or specific cost object, such as a particular customer.

4. **Contractual arrangements**. For example, a contract stating that a given component (an Intel Pentium chip) can be used only in a specific product (an IBM PC) makes it easier to classify the component as a direct cost of the product.

This book examines different ways to assign costs to cost objects. For now, be aware that one particular cost may be both direct and indirect. How? *The direct/indirect classification depends on the choice of the cost object.* For example, the salary of an assembly department supervisor may be a direct cost of the assembly department at Ford but an indirect cost of a product such as the Ford Taurus.

Intel Corporation
www.intel.com

COST DRIVERS AND COST MANAGEMENT

OBJECTIVE 3

Explain cost drivers, variable costs, and fixed costs

Value-added activities. Activities that customers perceive as adding value to the products or services they purchase.

Cost driver. Any factor that affects total costs. That is, a change in the level of the cost driver will cause a change in the level of the total cost of a related cost object.

The continuous cost reduction efforts of competitors create a never-ending need for organizations to reduce their own costs. Cost reduction efforts frequently focus on two key areas:

1. Doing only **value-added activities,** that is, those activities that customers perceive as adding value to the products or services they purchase

2. Efficiently managing the use of the cost drivers in those value-added activities

A **cost driver** (also called a *cost generator* or *cost determinant*) is any factor that affects total costs. That is, a change in the level of the cost driver will cause a change in the level of the total cost of a related cost object.

Exhibit 2-2 presents examples of cost drivers in each of the business functions of the value chain. Some cost drivers are financial measures found in accounting systems (such as direct manufacturing labour costs and sales dollars), while others are non-financial variables (such as the number of parts per product and the number of service calls).

EXHIBIT 2-2
Examples of Cost Drivers of Business Functions in the Value Chain

Business Function	Cost Driver
Research and development	◆ Number of research projects ◆ Personnel hours on a project ◆ Technical complexity of projects
Design of products, services, and processes	◆ Number of products in design ◆ Number of parts per product ◆ Number of engineering hours
Production	◆ Number of units produced ◆ Direct manufacturing labour costs ◆ Number of setups ◆ Number of engineering change orders
Marketing	◆ Number of advertisements run ◆ Number of sales personnel ◆ Sales dollars
Distribution	◆ Number of items distributed ◆ Number of customers ◆ Weight of items distributed
Customer service	◆ Number of service calls ◆ Number of products serviced ◆ Hours spent servicing products

Cost management is the set of actions that managers take to satisfy customers while continuously reducing and controlling costs. A caveat on the role of cost drivers in cost management is appropriate. Changes in a particular cost driver do not automatically lead to changes in overall costs. Consider the number of items distributed as a driver of distribution labour costs. Suppose that management reduces the number of items distributed by 25%. This reduction does not automatically translate to a reduction in distribution labour costs. Managers must take steps to reduce distribution labour costs, perhaps by shifting workers out of distribution into other business functions needing additional labour or by laying off some distribution employees. We now discuss the role of cost drivers in describing cost behaviour.

COST BEHAVIOUR PATTERNS: VARIABLE COSTS AND FIXED COSTS

Management accounting systems record the cost of resources acquired and track their subsequent use. Tracing these costs allows managers to see how these costs behave. Let us now consider two basic types of cost behaviour patterns found in many of these systems—variable costs and fixed costs. A **variable cost** is a cost that changes in total in proportion to changes in a cost driver. A **fixed cost** is a cost that does not change in total despite changes in a cost driver.

◆ **Variable costs.** If Ford buys a steering wheel at $60 for each of its Taurus cars, then the total cost of steering wheels should be $60 times the number of cars assembled. This is an example of a variable cost, a cost that changes *in total* in proportion to changes in the cost driver (number of cars). The variable cost per car does not change with the number of cars assembled. Exhibit 2-3 (Panel A) illustrates this variable cost. A second example of a variable cost is a sales commission of 5% of each sales dollar. Exhibit 2-3 (Panel B) shows this variable-cost example.

◆ **Fixed costs.** Ford may incur $20 million in a given year for the leasing and insurance of its Saturn plant. Both are examples of fixed costs, costs that are unchanged in total over a designated range of the cost driver during a given time span. Fixed costs become progressively smaller on a per-unit basis as the cost driver increases. For example, if Ford assembles 10,000 Taurus vehicles at this plant in a year, the fixed cost for leasing and insurance per vehicle is $2,000 ($20 million ÷ 10,000). In contrast, if 50,000 vehicles are assembled, the fixed cost per vehicle becomes $400.

Do not assume that individual cost items are inherently variable or fixed. Consider labour costs. An example of purely variable labour costs is the case where

Variable cost. Cost that changes in total in proportion to changes in a cost driver.

Fixed cost. Cost that does not change in total despite changes in a cost driver.

Ford Canada
www.ford.ca

Business Basics: Understanding Costs
www.lowe.org/data/1/1710.txt

EXHIBIT 2-3
Examples of Variable Costs

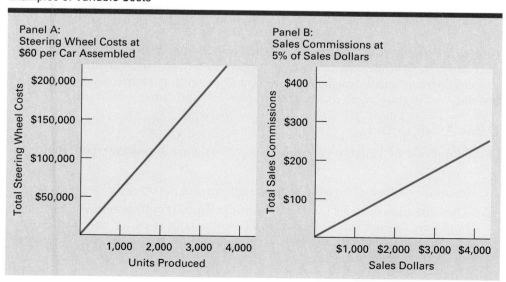

SURVEYS OF COMPANY PRACTICE

Purposes for Distinguishing Between Variable Costs and Fixed Costs

Many chapters in this book illustrate the insights gained from distinguishing between variable costs and fixed costs. One survey* of U.S. companies reported the following ranking of purposes for distinguishing between variable and fixed costs (1 = most important purpose). (The "Relevant Chapters" refer to where each purpose is extensively discussed in this book.)

Rank	Purpose	Relevant Chapters
1 (equal)	Pricing	4, 5, 11, 12 and 13
1 (equal)	Budgeting	6
3	Profitability analysis—existing products	4, 5, 11, 12 and 13
4	Profitability analysis—new products	11, 12 and 13
5	Cost-volume-profit (CVP) analysis	3
6	Variance analysis	7, 8, and 16

Surveys of Australian, Japanese, and U.K. companies provide additional evidence on the ranking by managers of the many purposes for distinguishing between variable costs and fixed costs (1 = most important purpose):[†]

Purpose	Ranking by Companies in Australia	Ranking by Companies in Japan	Ranking by Companies in United Kingdom
Pricing decisions	1	5	1
Budgeting	2	2	3
Making profit plans	3	1	2
Cost reduction	6	3	5 (equal)
CVP analysis	4 (equal)	4	4
Cost-benefit analysis	4 (equal)	6	5 (equal)

These surveys highlight the wide range of decisions for which managers feel that an understanding of cost behaviour is important.

---

*Adapted from Mowen, M., *Accounting for Costs as Fixed and Variable* (National Association of Accountants: Montvale, NJ, 1986)

[†]Blayney, P., and I. Yokoyama, "Comparative Analysis of Japanese and Australian Cost Accounting and Management Practices," (Working Paper, The University of Sydney, Sydney, Australia, 1991)

workers are paid on a piece-unit basis. Some textile workers are paid on a per-shirt-sewn basis. In contrast, labour costs are appropriately classified as fixed when lifetime employment exists or where union conditions severely restrict an organization's flexibility to assign workers to any area that has extra labour requirements.

Major Assumptions

The definitions of variable costs and fixed costs have important underlying assumptions:

1. Costs are defined as variable or fixed with respect to a specific cost object.
2. The time span must be specified. Consider the $20 million rent and insurance Ford pays for its Taurus plant. This amount may be fixed for one year. Beyond that time, the rent and insurance may be renegotiated to be, say, $22 million for a subsequent year.

3. Total costs are linear. That is, when plotted on ordinary graph paper, a total variable-cost or fixed-cost relationship to the cost driver will appear as an unbroken straight line.

4. There is only one cost driver. The influences of other possible cost drivers on total costs are held constant or deemed to be insignificant.

5. Variations in the level of the cost driver are within a relevant range (which we discuss in the next section).

Variable costs and fixed costs are the two most frequently recognized cost behaviour patterns in existing management accounting systems. Additional cost behaviour patterns are discussed in subsequent chapters.

Relevant Range

A **relevant range** is the range of the cost driver in which a specific relationship between cost and driver is valid. A fixed cost is fixed only in relation to a given relevant range (usually wide) of the cost driver and a given time span (usually a particular budget period). Consider the Thomas Transport Company (TTC), which operates two refrigerated trucks that carry agricultural produce to market. Each truck has an annual fixed cost of $40,000 (including an annual insurance cost of $15,000 and an annual registration fee of $8,000) and a variable cost of $1.20 per kilometre of hauling. TTC has chosen kilometres of hauling to be the cost driver. The maximum annual usage of each truck is 120,000 kilometres. In the current year (2000), the predicted combined total hauling of the two trucks is 170,000 kilometres.

Exhibit 2-4 shows how annual fixed costs behave at different levels of kilometres of hauling. Up to 120,000 kilometres, TTC can operate with one truck; from 120,001 to 240,000 kilometres, it can operate with two trucks; and from 240,001 to 360,000, it can operate with three trucks. This pattern would continue as TTC added trucks to its fleet. The bracketed section from 120,001 to 240,000 is the range at which TTC expects the $80,000 to be valid given the predicted 170,000 kilometre usage for 2000.

Fixed costs may change from one year to the next. For example, if the annual registration fee for refrigerated trucks is increased in 2000, the total level of fixed costs will increase (unless offset by a reduction in other fixed items).

Relationships of Types of Costs

We have introduced two major classifications of costs: direct/indirect and variable/fixed. Costs may simultaneously be:

◆ Direct and variable
◆ Direct and fixed

Relevant range. Range of the cost driver in which a specific relationship between cost and driver is valid

EXHIBIT 2-4
Fixed-Cost Behaviour at Thomas Transport Company

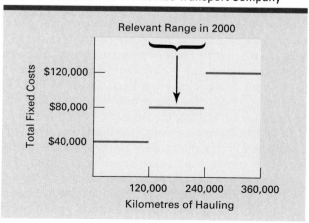

		Assignment of Costs to Cost Object	
		Direct Cost	**Indirect Cost**
Cost Behaviour Pattern	**Variable Cost**	*Cost object*: Assembled automobile *Example*: Tires used in assembly of automobile	*Cost object*: Assembled automobile *Example*: Power costs where power usage is metered only to the plant
	Fixed Cost	*Cost object*: Marketing department *Example*: Annual leasing cost of cars used by sales force representatives	*Cost object*: Marketing department *Example*: Monthly charge by corporate computer centre for marketing's share of corporate computer costs

◆ Indirect and variable

◆ Indirect and fixed

Exhibit 2-5 above presents examples of simultaneous cost classifications with each of the four cost types.

TOTAL COSTS AND UNIT COSTS

Meaning of Unit Costs

OBJECTIVE 4

Understand why unit costs must be interpreted with caution

Unit cost (average cost). Computed by dividing some total cost (the numerator) by some number of units (the denominator).

Accounting systems typically report both total-cost and unit-cost numbers. A **unit cost** (also called an **average cost**) is computed by dividing some total cost by some number of units. Suppose that $980,000 of manufacturing costs were incurred to produce 10,000 units of a finished good. Then the unit cost would be $98:

$$\frac{\text{Total manufacturing costs}}{\text{Number of units manufactured}} = \frac{\$980,000}{10,000} = \$98 \text{ per unit}$$

If 8,000 units are sold and 2,000 units remain in ending inventory, the unit-cost concept helps in the assignment of total costs for the income statement and balance sheet:

Cost of goods sold in the income statement, 8,000 units × $98	$784,000
Ending inventory of finished goods in the balance sheet, 2,000 units × $98	196,000
Total manufacturing costs of 10,000 units	$980,000

Unit costs are found in all areas of the value chain—for example, there are unit costs for product design, sales calls, and customer service calls.

Use Unit Costs Cautiously

Unit costs are averages. As we shall see, they must be interpreted with caution. For decision making, it is best to think in terms of total costs rather than unit costs. Nevertheless, unit-cost numbers are frequently used in many situations. For example, assume the president of a university social club is deciding whether to hire a musical group for an upcoming party. The group charges a fixed fee of $1,000. The president may intuitively compute a unit cost for the group when thinking about an admission price. Given the fixed fee of $1,000, the unit cost is $10 if 100 people attend, $2 if 500 attend, and $1 if 1,000 attend. Note, however, that with a fixed fee of $1,000 the *total cost* is unaffected by the attendance level, while the *unit cost* is a function of the attendance level. In this example, each attendee is considered to be one unit.

Costs are often neither inherently fixed nor inherently variable. Much depends on the specific context. Consider the $1,000 fixed fee that we assumed was to be paid to the musical group. This is but one way the musical group could be paid. Possible payment schedules that might be considered include:

- ◆ **Schedule 1**. $1,000 fixed fee
- ◆ **Schedule 2**. $1 per person attending + $500 fixed fee
- ◆ **Schedule 3**. $2 per person attending

Under schedules 2 and 3, the dollar amount of the payment to the musical group is not known until after the event.

The effects of these three payment schedules on unit costs and total costs for five attendance levels are as follows:

Number of Persons Attending	Schedule 1: $1,000 Fixed Total Cost	Schedule 1: $1,000 Fixed Unit Cost	Schedule 2: $1 per Person + $500 Fixed Total Cost	Schedule 2: $1 per Person + $500 Fixed Unit Cost	Schedule 3: $2 per Person Total Cost	Schedule 3: $2 per Person Unit Cost
50	$1,000	$20	$ 550	$11	$ 100	$2
100	1,000	10	600	6	200	2
250	1,000	4	750	3	500	2
500	1,000	2	1,000	2	1,000	2
1,000	1,000	1	1,500	1.50	2,000	2

The unit cost under schedule 1 is computed by dividing the fixed cost of $1,000 by the attendance level. For schedule 2, the unit cost is computed by first determining the total cost for each attendance level and then dividing that amount by that attendance level. Thus, for 250 people, schedule 2 has a total cost of $750 ($500 + 250 × $1), which gives a unit cost of $3 per person. Schedule 3 has a unit cost of $2 per person for any attendance level, because the musical group is to be paid $2 per person with no fixed payment.

EXHIBIT 2-6
Behaviour of Total Costs and Unit Costs When the Level of the Cost Driver Changes with Illustration of Alternate Payment Schedules for Musical Group

PANEL A: SUMMARY OF KEY RELATIONSHIPS

Cost Behaviour Pattern	Total Costs	Unit Costs
When item is a variable cost	Total costs change with changes in level of cost driver.	Unit costs remain the same with changes in level of cost driver.
When item is a fixed cost	Total costs remain the same with changes in level of cost driver.	Unit costs change with changes in level of cost driver.

PANEL B: PAYMENT IS $2 PER ATTENDEE

All three payment schedules would yield the same unit cost of $2 per person only if 500 people attend. The unit cost is not $2 per person under schedule 1 or schedule 2 for any attendance level except 500 people. Thus, it would be incorrect to use the $2 per person amount in schedule 1 or 2 to predict what the total costs would be for 1,000 people. Consider what occurs if 250 people attend and the group is paid a fixed fee of $1,000. The unit cost is then $4 per person. *While unit costs are often useful, they must be interpreted with extreme caution if they include fixed costs per unit.* When estimating total cost, think of variable costs as an amount per unit and fixed costs as a lump sum total amount.

The key relationships between total costs and unit costs are summarized in Panel A of Exhibit 2-6 on page 35. Panel B illustrates these relationships for schedule 3 where the university social club pays the musical group on a variable basis (cost of $2 per person).

FINANCIAL STATEMENTS AND COST TERMINOLOGY

Financial Statements Samplers
www.providence.edu/acc/jda/
courses/intro1/fssamp.htm

Capitalized costs. Costs that are first recorded as an asset (capitalized) when they are incurred.

Noncapitalized costs. Costs that are recorded as expenses of the accounting period when they are incurred.

We now consider costs included in the income statements or balance sheets of service, merchandising, and manufacturing sector companies. One key distinction of costs is their classification as capitalized or noncapitalized when they are incurred:

◆ **Capitalized costs** are first recorded as an asset (capitalized) when they are incurred. These costs are presumed to provide future benefits to the company. Examples are costs to acquire computer equipment and motor vehicles. These costs are written off to those periods assumed to benefit from their incurrence. For example, the cost of acquiring motor vehicles is written off as an amortization expense that occurs each year of the expected useful life of the vehicle.

◆ **Noncapitalized costs** are recorded as expenses of the accounting period when they are incurred. Examples are salaries paid to marketing personnel and monthly rent paid for administrative offices.

These two categories of costs apply to companies in all three sectors of the economy.

SERVICE SECTOR COMPANIES

OBJECTIVE 5

Distinguish between service sector, merchandising sector, and manufacturing sector companies

Service sector company. Provide services or intangible products to their customers—for example, legal advice, or an audit.

Service sector companies provide services or intangible products to their customers—for example, legal advice or an audit. These companies do not have any inventory of tangible product at the end of an accounting period. Examples include law firms, accounting firms, advertising agencies, and television stations. Labour costs are typically the most significant cost category, often being as high as 70% of total costs.

Exhibit 2-7 (Panel A) presents an income statement for Elliott & Partners, a law firm specializing in personal injury litigation. The customers (clients) of this law firm receive legal advice and representation on their behalf in court and in negotiations. Salaries and wages constitute 67.3% of total operating costs ($970,000 ÷ $1,442,000). The operating cost line items for service companies will include costs from all areas of the value chain (production of services, marketing, and so on). There is not a line item for cost of goods sold in the income statement of Elliott & Partners. Why? Because the business sells only services or intangible products to its customers.

Exhibit 2-7 (Panel B) shows the relationship between capitalized and noncapitalized costs for service sector companies. Capitalized costs include the cost of motor vehicles, computers, and similar equipment purchased by Elliott & Partners. These costs are first capitalized and shown in the balance sheet as assets. They are presumed to provide benefits to the company over several periods. Each period part of the cost of these assets is expensed as amortization—$105,000 in 2000. Noncapitalized costs of Elliott, such as salaries and wages ($970,000) and rent ($180,000), become expenses immediately as incurred and thus are not shown as assets.

EXHIBIT 2-7
Service Sector Income Statement

**PANEL A: ELLIOTT & PARTNERS—INCOME STATEMENT
FOR THE YEAR ENDED DECEMBER 31, 2000**

Revenues		$1,600,000
Costs:		
Salaries and wages	$970,000	
Rent	180,000	
Amortization	105,000	
Other costs	187,000	1,442,000
Operating income		$ 158,000

**PANEL B: ELLIOTT & PARTNERS—RELATIONSHIP OF CAPITALIZED AND
NONCAPITALIZED COSTS**

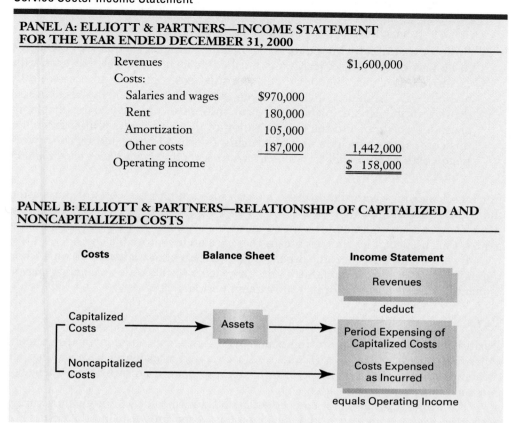

MERCHANDISING AND MANUFACTURING SECTOR COMPANIES

Merchandising sector companies provide tangible products they have previously purchased in the same basic form from suppliers. Merchandise purchased from suppliers but not sold at the end of an accounting period is held as inventory. The merchandising sector includes companies engaged in retailing (such as book stores or department stores), distributing, or wholesaling. **Manufacturing sector companies** provide tangible products that have been converted to a different form from that of the products purchased from suppliers. At the end of an accounting period, a manufacturer has inventory that can include direct materials, work in process, and finished goods.

Merchandising and manufacturing companies differ from service companies in their holding of inventories. The capitalized costs of merchandising and manufacturing companies can be classified as inventoriable costs and period costs.

Inventoriable Costs

Inventoriable costs are all costs of a product that are regarded as an inventory asset when they are incurred and then become cost of goods sold when the product is sold. For manufacturing-sector companies, all manufacturing costs are inventoriable costs. Three terms with widespread use when describing manufacturing costs are direct materials costs, direct manufacturing labour costs, and indirect manufacturing costs.

1. **Direct materials costs** are the acquisition costs of all materials that eventually become part of the cost object ("work in process" or "finished goods"), and that can be exclusively and unambiguously linked to the cost object in an economically feasible way. Acquisition costs of direct materials include freight-in (inward delivery) charges, sales taxes, and custom duties.

OBJECTIVE 6

Differentiate between inventoriable costs and period costs

Merchandising sector company. A company that provides its customers with tangible products it has previously purchased in the same basic form from suppliers.

Manufacturing sector company. A company that provides to its customers tangible products that have been converted to a different form from that of the products purchased from suppliers.

Inventoriable costs. All costs of a product that are regarded as an inventory asset when they are incurred and then become cost of goods sold when the product is sold.

Direct materials costs. The acquisition costs of all materials that eventually become part of the cost object (units finished or in process) and that can be traced to that cost object in an economically feasible way.

Direct manufacturing labour costs. Compensation of all manufacturing labour considered to be specifically identified with the cost object (units finished or in process) and that can be traced to the cost object in an economically feasible way.

Indirect manufacturing costs (manufacturing overhead costs, factory overhead costs). All manufacturing costs considered to be part of the cost object (units finished or in process) but that cannot be individually traced to that cost object in an economically feasible way.

"Elements of the Manufacturing Cost of a Product"
www.danielaero.calpoly.edu/~amdaf/nasa/dfm1.html

Period costs (operating costs). All costs associated with generating revenues, other than cost of goods sold.

2. **Direct manufacturing labour costs** include the compensation of all manufacturing labour that can be exclusively and unambiguously linked to the cost object in an economically feasible way. Examples include wages and fringe benefits paid to machine operators and assembly-line workers.

3. **Indirect manufacturing costs** are all manufacturing costs that are considered to be part of the cost object, units finished or in process, but that cannot be exclusively and unambiguously linked to that cost object in an economically feasible way. Examples include power, supplies, indirect materials, indirect manufacturing labour, plant rent, plant insurance, property taxes on plants, plant depreciation, and the compensation of plant managers. Other terms for this cost category include **manufacturing overhead costs** and **factory overhead costs**. We use *indirect manufacturing costs* and *manufacturing overhead costs* interchangeably in this book.

For merchandising-sector companies, *inventoriable costs* are the costs of purchasing the goods which are resold in their same form. These costs are the costs of the goods themselves and any incoming freight costs for those goods. For service-sector companies, the absence of inventories means there are no inventoriable costs.

Inventoriable costs become expenses (in the form of *cost of goods sold*) only when the units in inventory are sold. Such sales may occur in the same accounting period as manufacture or purchase or in a subsequent period.

Period Costs

Period costs (also called **operating costs**[1]) are all the costs on an income statement other than cost of goods sold. These costs are treated as expenses because they are presumed not to benefit future periods (or because there is no sufficient evidence to conclude that such benefit exists).

For manufacturing-sector companies, period costs include all non-manufacturing costs, for example, research and development costs and distribution costs. For merchandising-sector companies, period costs include all costs not related to the cost of goods purchased for resale in their same form, for example, labour cost of shop floor personnel and marketing costs.

Merchandising Sector Example

Exhibit 2-8 (Panel A) presents the income statement of Prestige Bathrooms, a merchandiser of bathroom fixtures and furnishings (showers, sinks, fixtures, and so on). A merchandiser's cost of goods sold consists of the cost of goods purchased for resale adjusted for changes in the level of merchandise inventory:

$$\begin{array}{c} \text{Beginning} \\ \text{merchandise} \\ \text{inventory} \end{array} + \begin{array}{c} \text{Purchases} \\ \text{of merchandise} \end{array} - \begin{array}{c} \text{Ending} \\ \text{merchandise} \\ \text{inventory} \end{array} = \begin{array}{c} \text{Cost of} \\ \text{goods} \\ \text{sold} \end{array}$$

For Prestige Bathrooms in 2000, the corresponding amounts in Exhibit 2-8 (Panel A) are:

$$\$ 95,000 + \$1,100,000 - \$130,000 = \$1,065,000$$

The $315,000 operating costs of Prestige in Panel A include amortization of noninventory assets as well as costs expensed to the period as incurred (such as the salaries of checkout staff and monthly cost of electricity). Examples of Prestige's operating costs include the costs of designing the showroom, sales personnel, and advertising.

Exhibit 2-8 (Panel B) shows the relationship between inventoriable and period costs for merchandising companies. Merchandise purchased for resale is first shown as an asset; its cost is a capitalized inventoriable cost. As the merchandise is sold, its cost becomes an expense of that period in the form of cost of goods sold. Capitalized noninventoriable costs (such as the costs of fixtures, fittings, and computers) are shown on the balance sheet as assets and then become operating cost line items in

---

[1]The term *operating costs* is sometimes used to include cost of goods sold. In this book, we do not include cost of goods sold in operating costs.

EXHIBIT 2-8
Merchandising Sector Income Statement

PANEL A: PRESTIGE BATHROOMS—INCOME STATEMENT FOR THE YEAR ENDED DECEMBER 31, 2000

Revenues		$1,500,000
Cost of goods sold:		
Beginning merchandise inventory, January 1, 2000	$ 95,000	
Purchases of merchandise	1,100,000	
Cost of goods available for sale	1,195,000	
Ending merchandise inventory, December 31, 2000	130,000	1,065,000
Gross margin (or gross profit)		435,000
Operating costs		315,000
Operating income		$ 120,000

PANEL B: MERCHANDISING COMPANY (RETAILER OR WHOLESALER)

the form of amortization (and other forms of asset write-downs) over the useful life of the asset.

Subsequent chapters examine merchandising sector costs in detail. These costs include cost of goods sold, period expensing of capitalized noninventoriable costs, and costs expensed as incurred (noncapitalized costs).

Manufacturing Sector Example

The manufacturing sector differs from the merchandising sector in that the products sold to customers are converted to a different form from that of the products purchased from suppliers. This distinction results in the manufacturer's having one or more of the following types of inventory:

1. **Direct materials inventory.** Direct materials in stock and awaiting use in the manufacturing process
2. **Work-in-process inventory.** Goods partially worked on but not yet fully completed; also called **work-in-progress inventory**
3. **Finished goods inventory.** Goods fully completed but not yet sold

In this chapter we assume that all manufacturing costs are inventoriable.[2]

---

[2]The term *absorption costing* is used to describe the method in which all manufacturing costs are inventoriable. Chapter 9 further discusses this method and two alternative methods—*variable costing*, in which only variable manufacturing costs are inventoriable, and *throughput costing*, in which only direct materials costs are inventoriable.

OBJECTIVE 7

Describe the three categories of inventories commonly found in many manufacturing sector companies

Direct materials inventory. Direct materials in stock and awaiting use in the manufacturing process.

Work-in-process inventory (work-in-progress inventory). Goods partially worked on but not yet fully completed.

Finished goods inventory. Goods fully completed but not yet sold.

The income statement of a manufacturer, Cellular Products, is shown in Exhibit 2-9 (Panel A). This company manufactures telephone systems for large organizations. Cost of goods sold in a manufacturing company is computed as follows:

$$\begin{array}{c} \text{Beginning} \\ \text{finished goods} \\ \text{inventory} \end{array} + \begin{array}{c} \text{Cost of} \\ \text{goods} \\ \text{manufactured} \end{array} - \begin{array}{c} \text{Ending} \\ \text{finished goods} \\ \text{inventory} \end{array} = \begin{array}{c} \text{Cost of} \\ \text{goods} \\ \text{sold} \end{array}$$

For Cellular Products in 2000, the corresponding amounts (in thousands, Panel A) are:

$$\$22{,}000 + \$104{,}000 - \$18{,}000 = \$108{,}000$$

EXHIBIT 2-9
Income Statement and Schedule of Cost of Goods Manufactured
of Manufacturing Sector Company

PANEL A: CELLULAR PRODUCTS—INCOME STATEMENT FOR THE YEAR ENDED DECEMBER 31, 2000 (IN THOUSANDS)

Revenues		$210,000
Cost of goods sold:		
Beginning finished goods, January 1, 2000	$ 22,000	
Cost of goods manufactured (see Panel B)	104,000	
Cost of goods available for sale	126,000	
Ending finished goods, December 31, 2000	18,000	108,000
Gross margin (or gross profit)		102,000
Operating costs		70,000
Operating income		$ 32,000

PANEL B: CELLULAR PRODUCTS—SCHEDULE OF COST OF GOODS MANUFACTURED* FOR THE YEAR ENDED DECEMBER 31, 2000 (IN THOUSANDS)

Direct materials:		
Beginning inventory, January 1, 2000	$ 11,000	
Purchases of direct materials	73,000	
Cost of direct materials available for use	84,000	
Ending inventory, December 31, 2000	8,000	
Direct materials used		$ 76,000
Direct manufacturing labour		17,750
Indirect manufacturing costs:		
Indirect manufacturing labour	4,000	
Supplies	1,000	
Heat, light, and power	1,750	
Amortization—plant building	1,500	
Amortization—plant equipment	2,500	
Miscellaneous	500	11,250
Manufacturing costs incurred during 2000		105,000
Add: Beginning work-in-process inventory, January 1, 2000		6,000
Total manufacturing costs to account for		111,000
Deduct: Ending work-in-process inventory, December 31, 2000		7,000
Cost of goods manufactured (to income statement)		$104,000

*Note that the term *cost of goods manufactured* refers to the cost of goods brought to completion (finished) during the year, whether they were started before or during the current year. Some of the manufacturing costs incurred during the year are held back as costs of the ending work-in-process inventory; similarly, the costs of the beginning work-in-process inventory become part of the cost of goods manufactured for the year. Note too that this schedule can become a schedule of cost of goods manufactured and sold simply by including the beginning and ending finished goods inventory figures in the supporting schedule rather than directly in the body of the income statement as in Panel A.

Cost of goods manufactured refers to the cost of goods brought to completion, whether they were started before or during the current accounting period. In 2000, these costs amount to $104,000 for Cellular Products (see the schedule of cost of goods manufactured in Panel B of Exhibit 2-9). The manufacturing costs incurred during 2000 ($105,000) is a line item in Panel B. This item refers to the "new" direct manufacturing costs and the "new" manufacturing overhead costs that were incurred during 2000 for all goods worked on during 2000, regardless of whether all those goods were fully completed during this year.

Exhibit 2-10 shows cost relationships for a manufacturing sector company. The manufacturing costs of the finished goods include direct materials, other direct manufacturing costs, and indirect manufacturing costs. All these are capitalized inventoriable costs; they are assigned to work-in-process inventory which, when completed, becomes finished goods inventory until the goods are sold. Capitalized inventoriable costs include the costs of assets that facilitate the manufacturing process and (typically) become part of indirect manufacturing costs in the form of amortization. For example, the costs of the blast furnace of a steel company are first capitalized at the time of construction. These costs subsequently become part of steel inventory costs as amortization on the blast furnace is included in indirect manufacturing costs over the useful life of the blast furnace. Newcomers to cost accounting frequently assume that indirect costs such as rent, telephone, and amortization are always costs of the period in which they are incurred and are unconnected with inventories. However, if these costs are related to manufacturing per se, they are indirect manufacturing costs and are inventoriable. Operating cost items in the income statement in Panel A of Exhibit 2-9 include (1) the expensing of capitalized noninventoriable costs (such as amortization on a fleet of delivery vehicles or amortization on computers purchased for marketing personnel) and (2) the cost of items recorded as an expense as incurred (such as the salaries of customer service representatives).

Manufacturing Costs Classifications

Manufacturing cost accounting systems vary among companies. Some use a three-part classification of manufacturing costs; others use a two-part classification:

THREE-PART CLASSIFICATION	TWO-PART CLASSIFICATION
◆ Direct materials costs	◆ Direct materials costs
◆ Direct manufacturing labour costs	◆ Indirect manufacturing costs
◆ Indirect manufacturing costs	

EXHIBIT 2-10
Relationships of Inventoriable Costs and Period Costs

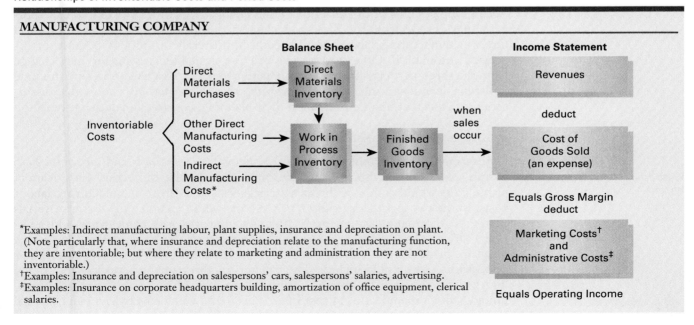

MANUFACTURING COMPANY

*Examples: Indirect manufacturing labour, plant supplies, insurance and depreciation on plant. (Note particularly that, where insurance and depreciation relate to the manufacturing function, they are inventoriable; but where they relate to marketing and administration they are not inventoriable.)
†Examples: Insurance and depreciation on salespersons' cars, salespersons' salaries, advertising.
‡Examples: Insurance on corporate headquarters building, amortization of office equipment, clerical salaries.

Harley-Davidson Eliminates the Direct Manufacturing Labour Cost Category

For many years, Harley-Davidson's Motorcycle Division used a three-part cost classification in its manufacturing facilities—direct materials, direct manufacturing labour, and manufacturing overhead. In the mid-1980s, a task force of Harley-Davidson managers analyzed how its manufacturing product cost structure compared with the administrative costs required to collect, inspect, and report data in its accounting system. It found the following information:

	Manufacturing Product Cost Structure	Administrative Cost Effort
Direct materials	54%	25%
Manufacturing overhead	36	13
Direct manufacturing labour	10	62

The administrative costs associated with tracking direct manufacturing labour as a separate cost category included:

- ◆ Operators' time to fill out labour tickets
- ◆ Supervisors' time to review labour tickets
- ◆ Timekeepers' time to enter the labour data and review the data output reports for errors
- ◆ Cost accountants' time to review the direct labour and variance data

Harley-Davidson Company
www.harley-davidson.com

Harley-Davidson concluded that tracing direct labour to products did not meet a cost-benefit test. Direct labour costs were only 10% of total manufacturing costs but required 62% of the administrative effort used to track all manufacturing costs. The company now includes all manufacturing labour costs as part of manufacturing overhead costs. It uses a two-part classification of direct materials and manufacturing overhead.

Source: Adapted from Turk, "Management Accounting Revitalized: The Harley-Davidson Experience," *Journal of Cost Management,* Winter 1990, and conversations with management.

Accounting systems of organizations often change over time. For example, a company may change from the three-part classification to the two-part classification if direct manufacturing labour costs become immaterial in amount because of increased automation. Other alternatives are also available. A company may change from the three-part classification to one with two direct cost categories and multiple individual manufacturing overhead cost categories. Managers will choose the classification of costs that best helps them in their planning, control, and decision-making.

Prime Costs and Conversion Costs

Two terms used in manufacturing cost systems are *prime costs* and *conversion costs.* **Prime costs** are all direct manufacturing costs. In the three-part classification, prime costs would comprise direct materials costs and direct manufacturing labour costs. In the two-part classification, prime costs would include only direct materials costs. As information-gathering technology improves, companies may add additional direct cost categories. For example, power costs might be metered in specific areas of a plant that are dedicated totally to the assembly of separate products. In this case, prime costs would include direct materials, direct manufacturing labour, and direct metered power. Computer software companies often have a "purchased technology" direct manufacturing cost item. This item, which covers payments to third

Prime costs. All direct manufacturing costs.

parties who develop software algorithms included in a product, would also be included in prime costs. **Conversion costs** are all manufacturing costs other than direct materials costs. These costs are for transforming direct materials into finished goods. In the three-part classification of manufacturing costs, conversion costs would comprise direct manufacturing labour costs and indirect manufacturing costs. In the two-part classification, conversion costs would be only the indirect manufacturing costs.

Conversion costs. All manufacturing costs other than direct materials costs.

The components of prime costs and conversion costs for the three-part and two-part classifications can be summarized as follows:

	Three-Part Classification	Two-Part Classification
Prime costs	Direct materials costs	Direct materials costs
	Direct manufacturing labour costs	
Conversion costs	Direct manufacturing labour costs	Indirect manufacturing costs
	Indirect manufacturing costs	

MEASURING COSTS REQUIRES JUDGMENT

Since differences can exist in the way accounting terms are defined, judgment is frequently required when measuring costs. Care should be taken to define and understand the way costs are measured in an organization or situation in which costs are an issue. We first illustrate this point with respect to labour cost measurement.

Measuring Labour Costs

Manufacturing labour-cost classifications vary among companies, but the following distinctions are generally found:

Direct labour (already defined)

Manufacturing overhead (examples of prominent labour components of this manufacturing overhead follow):

  Indirect labour (compensation)
    Forklift truck operators (internal handling of materials)
    Janitors
    Plant guards
    Rework labour (time spent by direct labourers redoing defective work)
    Overtime premium paid to *all* plant workers
    Idle time
  Managers' salaries
  Payroll fringe costs (for example, health care premiums, pension costs)

All manufacturing labour compensation, other than that for direct labour and managers' salaries, is usually classified as *indirect labour costs*, a major component of manufacturing overhead. The term *indirect labour* is usually divided into many subclassifications. The wages of forklift truck operators are generally not combined with janitors' wages, for example, although both are regarded as indirect labour.

Managers' salaries are usually not classified as part of indirect labour. Instead, the compensation of supervisors, department heads, and all others who are regarded as part of manufacturing management is placed in a separate classification of manufacturing overhead.

Overtime Premium

Costs are classified in a detailed fashion mainly to associate an individual cost with its specific cause or reason for incurrence. Two classes of indirect labour need special mention. **Overtime premium** consists of wages paid to all workers (for both direct labour and indirect labour) in *excess* of their straight-time wage rates. Overtime premium is usually considered a part of overhead. Consider an example from the service sector. George Flexner does home service calls for Sears Appliance Services. He gets $20 per hour for straight-time and gets time and one-half for overtime. His *premium* would be $10 per overtime hour. If he works forty-four hours, including four overtime hours, in one week, his gross earnings would be classified as follows:

Overtime premium. Wages paid to all workers in exess of their straight-time wage rates.

Direct service labour: 44 hours × $20	$880
Overtime premium (manuf. overhead): 4 hours × $10	40
Total earnings for 44 hours	$920

Why is overtime premium of direct labour usually considered an indirect rather than a direct cost? After all, it can usually be traced to specific batches of work. It is generally not considered a direct charge because the scheduling of repair jobs is generally either random or in accordance with overall minimizing of travel times. For example, assume that Jobs 1 through 5 are scheduled for a specific workday of ten hours, including two overtime hours. Each service call (job) requires two hours. Should the job scheduled during hours 9 and 10 be assigned the overtime premium? Or should the premium be prorated over all the jobs? The latter approach does not "penalize"—add to the cost of—a particular batch of work solely because it happened to be worked on during the overtime hours. *Instead, the overtime premium is considered to be attributable to the heavy overall volume of work. Its cost is thus regarded as part of service overhead, which is borne by all repair jobs.*

Sometimes overtime is not random. For example, a special or rush job may clearly be the sole source of the overtime. In such instances, the overtime premium is regarded as a direct cost of the service on that job.

Another sub-classification of indirect labour is the idle time of both direct and indirect manufacturing or service labour. This **idle time** typically represents wages paid for unproductive time caused by lack of orders, machine breakdowns, material shortages, poor scheduling, and the like. For example, if the Sears repair truck broke down for three hours, earnings would be classified as follows:

Direct service labour: 41 hours × $20	$820
Idle time (service overhead): 3 hours × $20	60
Overtime premium (service overhead): 4 hours × $10	40
Total earnings for 44 hours	$920

Benefits of Defining Accounting Terms

We cannot overemphasize the value of obtaining a thorough understanding of the classifications and cost terms introduced in this chapter and later in this book. Managers, accountants, suppliers, and other people will avoid many misunderstandings if they have the same meanings for technical terms.

Consider the classification of manufacturing labour *payroll fringe costs* (for example, employer contributions to employee benefits such as employment insurance, life insurance, health insurance, and pensions). Some companies classify these costs as manufacturing overhead. In other companies, however, the fringe benefits related to direct labour are charged as an additional direct labour cost.

Consider a direct labourer, such as a lathe operator or an assembly line worker, who earns gross wages computed on the basis of a regular wage rate of $20 per hour. This person receives employee fringe benefits (employer contributions to the employee's pension plan, life insurance, health insurance, and so on) totalling $8 per hour. Some companies classify the $20 as direct manufacturing labour cost and the $8 as manufacturing overhead cost. Other companies classify the entire $28 as direct manufacturing labour cost. The latter approach is conceptually preferable, because these payroll fringe benefit costs are a fundamental part of acquiring manufacturing labour services. The magnitude of fringe benefits makes this issue important. Countries where fringe benefit costs are over 30% of wage rates include Italy (105%), France (90%), Germany (86%), the United Kingdom (43%), and the United States (38%).[3]

The problem here is to pinpoint what direct manufacturing labour includes and excludes in a particular situation. Achieving clarity may avoid disputes regarding cost reimbursement contracts, income tax provisions, and labour union matters. For

Idle time. Unproductive time caused by lack of orders, machine breakdowns, material shortages, poor scheduling, and so on.

[3]Salowsky, H., "Labor Costs in Twenty Industrialized Countries, 1970–1991," Institute of the German Economy in Cologne, Germany, 1992.

example, some countries offer substantial income tax savings to companies that locate manufacturing plants there. To qualify, the "direct manufacturing labour" costs of these companies in that country must meet a specified minimum percentage of the total manufacturing costs of their products produced there. What incentive does such an income tax provision give managers to classify fringe benefit costs as direct manufacturing labour or manufacturing overhead? Classifying payroll fringe benefit costs as direct manufacturing labour will increase the percentage of direct manufacturing labour costs, thereby making it easier to qualify for the income tax savings. Consider a company with $8 million of payroll fringe benefit costs (figures are assumed to be in millions):

Method A			Method B		
Direct materials	$ 40	40%	Direct materials	$ 40	40%
Direct manufacturing labour	20	20	Direct manufacturing labour	28	28
Manufacturing overhead	40	40	Manufacturing overhead	32	32
Total manufacturing costs	$100	100%	Total manufacturing costs	$100	100%

Method A classifies payroll fringe benefit costs as part of manufacturing overhead. In contrast, method B classifies payroll fringe benefit costs as part of direct manufacturing labour. If a country sets the minimum percentage of direct manufacturing labour costs at 25%, the company would receive a tax savings using method B, but not using method A. In addition to payroll fringe benefits, other items subject to different possible classifications include compensation for training time, idle time, vacations, sick leave, and extra compensation for overtime. To prevent disputes, contracts and laws should be as specific as feasible regarding definitions and measurements of accounting terms.

THE MANY MEANINGS OF PRODUCT COSTS

An important theme of this book is "different costs for different purposes." This theme can be illustrated with respect to product costing. A **product cost** is the sum of the costs assigned to a product for a specific purpose. Exhibit 2-11 illustrates three different purposes:

1. **Product pricing and product emphasis.** For this purpose, the costs of all those areas of the value chain required to bring a product to a customer should be included.

2. **Contracting with government agencies.** Government agencies frequently provide detailed guidelines on the allowable and nonallowable items in a product

OBJECTIVE 8

Explain how different ways of computing product costs are appropriate for different purposes

Product cost. Sum of the costs assigned to a product for a specific purpose.

EXHIBIT 2-11
Different Product Costs for Different Purposes

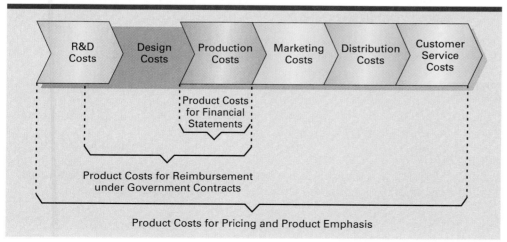

cost amount. For example, some government agencies explicitly exclude marketing costs from reimbursement to contractors and may reimburse only a part of R&D costs. Hence, the bracket in Exhibit 2-11 shows that a specific contract may provide for recovering all design and production costs and part of R&D costs.

3. **Financial statements.** The focus here is on inventoriable costs. For example, under generally accepted accounting principles in manufacturing companies, only manufacturing costs are assigned to products reported in the financial statements.

Exhibit 2-11 illustrates how a product cost amount may include only inventoriable costs in the financial statements, a broader set of costs for reimbursement under a government contract, and a still broader set of costs for pricing and product emphasis.

CLASSIFICATIONS OF COSTS

This chapter has provided many examples of cost classifications that have various purposes. Classifications can be made on the basis of:

1. Business function
   a. Research and development
   b. Design of products, services, and processes
   c. Production
   d. Marketing
   e. Distribution
   f. Customer service
2. Assignment to a cost object
   a. Direct costs
   b. Indirect costs
3. Behaviour pattern in relation to changes in the level of a cost driver
   a. Variable costs
   b. Fixed costs
4. Aggregate or average
   a. Total costs
   b. Unit costs
5. Costs in financial statements
   a. Capitalized costs
      i. Capitalized inventoriable costs
      ii. Capitalized noninventoriable costs
   b. Noncapitalized costs

PROBLEM FOR SELF-STUDY

(Try to solve this problem before examining the solution that follows.)

PROBLEM
Campbell Company is a metal- and wood-cutting manufacturer, selling products to the home construction market. Consider the following data for the year 2000:

Sandpaper	$	2,000
Materials-handling costs		70,000
Lubricants and coolants		5,000
Miscellaneous indirect manufacturing labour		40,000
Direct manufacturing labour		300,000
Direct materials, December 31, 2000		50,000
Direct materials, January 1, 2000		40,000
Finished goods, January 1, 2000		100,000
Finished goods, December 31, 2000		150,000
Work in process, January 1, 2000		10,000
Work in process, December 31, 2000		14,000
Plant leasing costs		54,000
Amortization—plant equipment		36,000
Property taxes on plant equipment		4,000
Fire insurance on plant equipment		3,000
Direct materials purchased		460,000
Revenue		1,360,000
Marketing promotions		60,000
Marketing salaries		100,000
Shipping costs		70,000
Customer service costs		100,000

REQUIRED

1. Prepare an income statement with a separate supporting schedule of cost of goods manufactured. For all manufacturing items, indicate by V or F whether each is basically a variable cost or a fixed cost (where the cost object is a product unit). If in doubt, decide on the basis of whether the total cost will change substantially over a wide range of production output.

2. Suppose that both the direct materials and plant leasing costs are tied to the production of 900,000 units. What is the unit cost for the direct materials assigned to each unit produced? What is the unit cost of the plant leasing costs? Assume that the plant leasing costs are a fixed cost.

3. Repeat the computation in requirement 2 for direct materials and plant leasing costs, assuming that the costs are being predicted for the manufacturing of 1 million units next year. Assume that the implied cost behaviour patterns persist.

4. As a management consultant, explain concisely to the president why the unit costs for direct materials did not change in requirements 2 and 3 but the unit costs for plant leasing costs did.

SOLUTION

1.

CAMPBELL COMPANY
Income Statement for the Year Ended December 31, 2000

Revenue		$1,360,000
Cost of goods sold:		
Beginning finished goods, January 1, 2000	$ 100,000	
Cost of goods manufactured (see below)	960,000	
Cost of goods available for sale	1,060,000	
Ending finished goods, December 31, 2000	150,000	910,000
Gross margin (or gross profit)		450,000
Operating costs:		
Marketing promotions	60,000	
Marketing salaries	100,000	
Distribution costs	70,000	
Customer service costs	100,000	330,000
Operating income		$ 120,000

CAMPBELL COMPANY
Schedule of Cost of Goods Manufactured
for the Year Ended December 31, 2000

Direct materials:

Beginning inventory, January 1, 2000		$ 40,000
Purchases of direct materials		460,000
Cost of direct materials available for use		500,000
Ending inventory, December 31, 2000		50,000
Direct materials used		$450,000 (V)
Direct manufacturing labour		300,000 (V)
Indirect manufacturing costs:		
Sandpaper	$ 2,000 (V)	
Materials-handling cost	70,000 (V)	
Lubricants and coolants	5,000 (V)	
Miscellaneous indirect manufacturing labour	40,000 (V)	
Plant leasing costs	54,000 (F)	
Amortization—plant equipment	36,000 (F)	
Property taxes on plant equipment	4,000 (F)	
Fire insurance on plant equipment	3,000 (F)	214,000
Manufacturing costs incurred during 2000		964,000
Add: Beginning work-in-process inventory, January 1, 2000		10,000
Total manufacturing costs to account for		974,000
Deduct: Ending work-in-process inventory, December 31, 2000		14,000
Cost of goods manufactured (to income statement)		$960,000

2. Direct materials unit cost = Direct materials used ÷ Units produced
= $450,000 ÷ 900,000 = $0.50

Plant leasing unit cost = Plant leasing costs ÷ Units produced
= $54,000 ÷ 900,000 = $0.06

3. The direct materials costs are variable, so they would increase in total from $450,000 to $500,000 (1,000,000 × $0.50). However, their unit costs would be unaffected: $500,000 ÷ 1,000,000 units = $0.50.

In contrast, the plant leasing costs of $54,000 are fixed, so they would not increase in total. However, if the plant leasing costs were assigned to units produced, the unit costs would decline from $0.060 to $0.054: $54,000 ÷ 1,000,000 = $0.054.

4. The explanation would begin with the answer to requirement 3. As a consultant, you should stress that the unitizing (averaging) of costs that have different behaviour patterns can be misleading. A common error is to assume that a total unit cost, which is often a sum of variable unit costs and fixed unit costs, is an indicator that total costs change in a wholly variable way as the level of production output changes. The next chapter demonstrates the necessity for distinguishing between cost behaviour patterns. You must be especially wary about unit fixed costs. Too often, unit fixed costs are erroneously regarded as being indistinguishable from unit variable costs.

SUMMARY

The following points are linked to the chapter's learning objectives.

1. A cost object is anything for which a separate measurement of costs is desired. Examples include a product, service, project, customer, brand category, activity, department, and program.

2. A direct cost of a cost object is any cost that is related to the cost object and can be traced to that cost object in an economically feasible way. Indirect costs are costs that may be direct regarding one cost object and indirect regarding other cost objects. This book uses the term *cost tracing* to describe the assignment of direct costs to a cost object and the term *cost allocation* to describe the assignment of indirect costs to a cost object.

3. A cost driver is any factor that affects costs. Examples include the number of set-ups and direct labour-hours in manufacturing and the number of sales personnel and sales dollars in marketing. A variable cost is a cost that does change in total in proportion to changes in a cost driver. A fixed cost is a cost that does not change in total despite changes in a cost driver.

4. Unit costs of a cost object should be interpreted with caution when they include a fixed cost component. When making total cost estimates, think of variable costs as an amount per unit and fixed costs as a total amount.

5. Service sector companies provide services or intangible products to their customers. In contrast, merchandising and manufacturing sector companies provide tangible products to their customers. Merchandising companies do not change the form of the products they acquire and sell. Manufacturing companies convert materials and other inputs into finished goods for sale. These differences are reflected in both the balance sheets and the income statements of companies in these sectors.

6. Capitalized costs are first recorded as an asset (capitalized) when they are incurred. These costs are presumed to provide future benefits to the company. Noncapitalized costs are recorded as expenses when they are incurred.

7. The three categories of inventory found in many manufacturing sector companies depict stages in the conversion process—direct materials, work in process, and finished goods.

8. Managers may assign different costs to the same cost object depending on their purpose. For example, for financial reporting purposes, the (inventoriable) costs of a product include only manufacturing costs. In contrast, costs from all areas of the value chain can be assigned to a product for decisions on pricing and product emphasis.

TERMS TO LEARN

This chapter contains more basic terms than any other in this book. Do not proceed before you check your understanding of the following terms. You will find definitions of these terms in this chapter.

QUESTIONS

2-1 Define cost object and give three examples.

2-2 Define *cost assignment*, *cost tracing*, and *cost allocation*. How are these terms related?

2-3 Define *direct costs* and *indirect costs*. How are these terms related?

2-4 Why do managers consider direct costs to be more accurate than indirect costs?

2-5 Give three factors that will affect the classification of a cost as direct or indirect.

2-6 Describe two areas that cost reduction efforts frequently focus on.

2-7 What is a *cost driver?* Give one example for each area in the value chain.

2-8 Define *variable cost* and *fixed cost*. Give an example of each.

2-9 What is the *relevant range?* What role does the relevant-range concept play in explaining how costs behave?

2-10 Explain why *unit costs* must often be interpreted with caution.

2-11 Describe how service, merchandising, and manufacturing sector companies differ from each other.

2-12 Do service-sector companies have inventoriable costs? Explain.

2-13 What are the three major categories of the inventoriable costs of a manufactured product?

2-14 Define the following: *direct materials costs, direct manufacturing labour costs, indirect manufacturing costs, prime costs,* and *conversion costs.*

2-15 Define *product costs.* Describe three different purposes for computing product costs.

EXERCISES

2-16 **Total costs and unit costs.** A student association has hired a musical group for a graduation party. The cost will be a fixed amount of $4,000.

REQUIRED

1. Suppose 500 people attend the party. What will be the total cost of the musical group? The unit cost per person?
2. Suppose 2,000 people attend. What will be the total cost of the musical group? The unit cost per person?
3. For prediction of total costs, should the manager of the party use the unit cost in requirement 1? The unit cost in requirement 2? What is the major lesson of this problem?

2-17 **Total costs and unit costs.** Susan Wang is a well-known software engineer. Her speciality is writing software code used in maintaining the security of credit card information. Wang is approached by the Electronic Commerce Group (ECG). They offer to pay her $100,000 for the right to use her code under licence in their e. procurement software package. Wang rejects this offer because it provides her with no additional benefits if the e. procurement package is a runaway success. Both parties eventually agree to a contract in which ECG pays Wang a flat fee of $100,000 for the right to use her code in up to 10,000 packages. If e. procurement sells more than 10,000 packages, Wang receives $8 for each package sold beyond the 10,000 level.

REQUIRED

1. What is the unit cost of ECG for Wang's software code included in its e. procurement package if it sells (a) 2,000, (b) 6,000, (c) 10,000, and (d) 20,000 packages? Comment on the results.
2. For prediction of ECG's total cost of using Wang's software code in e. procurement, which unit cost (if any) of (a) to (d) in requirement 1 would you recommend ECG use? Explain.

2-18 **Computing and interpreting unit manufacturing costs.** Finnish Forest Products (FFP) produces three different paper products at its Vaasa lumber plant—supreme, deluxe, and regular. Each product has its own dedicated production line at the plant. FFP currently uses the following three-part classification for its manufacturing costs—direct materials, direct manufacturing labour, and indirect manufacturing costs. Indirect manufacturing costs are allocated to each product line on the basis of direct manufacturing labour costs on each line. Summary data for the most recent month (July 2000) are (in millions):

	Supreme	Deluxe	Regular
Direct materials costs	$84.0	$54.0	$62.0
Direct manufacturing labour costs	14.0	28.0	8.0
Indirect manufacturing costs	42.0	84.0	24.0
Kilograms produced	80	120	100

REQUIRED

1. Compute the unit manufacturing cost per kilogram for each product produced in July 2000.
2. Suppose that, in August 2000, production was 120 kilograms of Supreme, 160 kilograms of Deluxe, and 180 kilograms of Regular. Why might the July 2000 unit manufacturing cost information be misleading when predicting total manufacturing costs in August 2000?

2-19 Direct and indirect costs, effect of changing the classification of a cost item (continuation of 2-18). Finnish Forest Products (FFP) employs a consultant to help reduce energy costs at its Vaasa plant. Currently, FFP does not trace energy costs to each product line. The energy consultant notes that each production line at the Vaasa plant has multiple energy meters and that tracing of energy costs to each line is possible. Of the $150 million of indirect manufacturing costs in July 2000, $90 million is for energy costs traceable to individual production lines. Using this information, FFP's cost analyst reports the following revised numbers for July 2000 (in millions):

	Supreme	Deluxe	Regular
Direct materials	$84.0	$54.0	$62.0
Direct manufacturing labour	14.0	28.0	8.0
Direct energy costs	39.8	20.7	29.5
Indirect manufacturing costs	16.8	33.6	9.6
Kilograms produced	80	120	100

REQUIRED

1. What is the difference between a direct cost and an indirect cost?
2. Why might FFP's managers prefer energy costs to be traced as a direct cost rather than included as part of indirect manufacturing costs?
3. Compute the revised unit manufacturing cost per kilogram for each product produced in July 2000. Compare these costs with those computed in requirement 1 of Exercise 2-18. Comment on any differences in the unit cost numbers.

2-20 Cost drivers and the value chain. A Johnson & Johnson analyst is preparing a presentation on cost drivers at its pharmaceutical drug subsidiary. Unfortunately, both the list of its business function areas and the accompanying list of representative cost drivers are accidentally randomized. The two lists now on the computer screen are as follows:

BUSINESS FUNCTION AREA	REPRESENTATIVE COST DRIVER
A. Production	1. Minutes of television advertising time on *60 Minutes*
B. Research and development	2. Number of calls to toll-free customer phone line
C. Marketing	3. Hours Tylenol packing line in operation
D. Distribution	4. Number of packages shipped
E. Design of products/processes	5. Hours spent designing tamper-proof bottles
F. Customer service	6. Number of patents filed with government agency

REQUIRED

1. Match each business function area with its representative cost driver.

2. Give a second example of a cost driver for each of the business functions of Johnson & Johnson's pharmaceutical drug subsidiary.

2-21 Cost drivers and the value chain. A Toyota analyst is preparing a presentation on cost drivers. Unfortunately, both the list of its business function areas and the accompanying list of representative cost drivers are accidentally randomized. The two lists now on the computer screen are as follows:

BUSINESS FUNCTION AREA	REPRESENTATIVE COST DRIVER
A. Design of products/processes	1. Number of cars recalled for defective parts
B. Customer service	2. Number of machine assembly hours
C. Marketing	3. Number of research scientists
D. Research and development	4. Hours of computer-aided design (CAD) work
E. Distribution	5. Number of sales personnel
F. Production	6. Weight of cars shipped

REQUIRED

1. Match each business function area with its representative cost driver.
2. Give a second example of a cost driver for each of the business function areas of Toyota.

2-22 Variable costs and fixed costs. Consolidated Minerals (CM) owns the rights to extract minerals from beach sands on Fraser Island. CM has costs in three areas:
   a. Payment to a mining subcontractor who charges $80 per tonne of beach sand mined and returned to the beach (after being processed on the mainland to extract three minerals—ilmenite, rutile, and zircon).
   b. Payment of a government mining and environmental tax of $50 per tonne of beach sand mined.
   c. Payment to a barge operator. This operator charges $150,000 per month to transport batches of beach sand—up to 100 tonnes per batch per day to the mainland and then return to Fraser Island (i.e., 0–100 tonnes per day = $150,000 per month; 101–200 tonnes = $300,000, and so on). Each barge operates 25 days per month. The $150,000 monthly charge must be paid even if less than 100 tonnes are transported on any day and even if Consolidated Minerals requires fewer than 25 days of barge transportation in that month.
   CM is currently mining 180 tonnes of beach minerals per day for 25 days per month.

REQUIRED

1. What is the variable cost per tonne of beach sand mined? What is the fixed cost to CM per month?
2. Plot one graph of the variable costs and another graph of the fixed costs of CM. Your plots should be similar to Exhibits 2-3 and 2-4. Is the concept of relevant range applicable to your plots?
3. What is the unit cost per tonne of beach sand mined (a) if 180 tonnes are mined each day and (b) if 220 tonnes are mined each day? Explain the difference in the unit-cost figures.

2-23 Classification of costs, service sector. Consumer Focus is a marketing research firm that organizes focus groups for consumer product companies. Each focus group has eight individuals who are paid $50 per session to provide comments on new products. These focus groups meet in hotels and are led by a trained independent marketing specialist hired by Consumer Focus. Each specialist is paid a fixed retainer to conduct a minimum number of sessions and a per-session fee of $2,000. A Consumer Focus staff member attends each session to ensure that all the logistical aspects run smoothly.

REQUIRED

Classify each of the following cost items as:
   a. Direct or indirect (D or I) costs with respect to each individual focus group.
   b. Variable or fixed (V or F) costs with respect to how the total costs of Consumer Focus change as the number of focus groups changes. (If in doubt, select the cost type on the basis of whether the total costs will change substantially if a large number of groups are conducted.)

You will have two answers (D or I, and V or F) for each of the following items:

Cost Item	D or I	V or F
A. Payment to individuals in each focus group to provide comments on new products		
B. Annual subscription of Consumer Focus to *Consumer Reports* magazine		
C. Phone calls made by Consumer Focus staff member to confirm individuals will attend a focus group session (records of individual calls are not kept)		
D. Retainer paid to focus group leader to conduct 20 focus groups per year on new medical products		
E. Hotel meals provided to participants in each focus group		
F. Lease payment by Consumer Focus for corporate office		
G. Cost of tapes used to record comments made by individuals in a focus group session (these tapes are sent to the company whose products are being tested)		
H. Gasoline costs of Consumer Focus staff for company-owned vehicles (staff members submit monthly bills with no kilometrage breakdowns)		

2-24 Classification of costs, merchandising sector. Home Entertainment Centre (HEC) operates a large store in Halifax. The store has both a video section and a musical (compact discs, records, and tapes) section. HEC reports revenues for the video section separately from the musical section.

REQUIRED
Classify each of the following cost items as:
a. Direct or indirect (D or I) costs with respect to the video section.
b. Variable or fixed (V or F) costs with respect to how the total costs of the video section change as the number of videos sold changes. (If in doubt, select the cost type on the basis of whether the total costs will change substantially if a large number of videos are sold.)

You will have two answers (D or I; V or F) for each of the following items:

Cost Item	D or I	V or F
A. Annual retainer paid to a video distributor		
B. Electricity costs of HEC store (single bill covers entire store)		
C. Costs of videos purchased for sale to customers		
D. Subscription to *Video Trends* magazine		
E. Leasing of computer software used for financial budgeting at HEC store		
F. Cost of popcorn provided free to all customers of HEC		
G. Fire insurance policy for HEC store		
H. Freight-in costs of videos purchased by HEC		

2-25 Classification of costs, manufacturing sector. The Fremont, California, plant of NUMMI (New United Motor Manufacturing, Inc.), a joint venture of General Motors and Toyota, assembles two types of cars (Corollas and Geo Prisms). A separate assembly line is used for each type of car.

REQUIRED
Classify each of the following cost items as:
a. Direct or indirect (D or I) costs with respect to the type of car assembled (Corolla or Geo Prism).
b. Variable or fixed (V or F) costs with respect to how the total costs of the plant change as the number of cars assembled changes. (If in doubt, select the cost type on the basis of whether the total costs will change substantially if a large number of cars are assembled.)

You will have two answers (D or I, and V or F) for each of the following items:

Cost Item	D or I	V or F
A. Cost of tires used on Geo Prisms		
B. Salary of public relations manager for NUMMI plant		
C. Annual awards dinner for Corolla suppliers		
D. Salary of engineer who monitors design changes on Geo Prism		
E. Freight costs of Corolla engines shipped from Toyota City, Japan, to Fremont, California		
F. Electricity costs for NUMMI plant (single bill covers entire plant)		
G. Wages paid to temporary assembly line workers hired in periods of high production (paid on an hourly basis)		
H. Annual fire insurance policy cost for NUMMI plant		

2-26 **Inventoriable versus period costs.** Each of the following cost items pertains to one of the following companies—General Electric (a manufacturing-sector company), Loblaw (a merchandising-sector company), and Excite (a service-sector company):
a. Perrier mineral water purchased by Loblaw for sale to its customers
b. Electricity used to provide lighting for assembly-line workers at a General Electric refrigerator assembly plant
c. Amortization on computer equipment at Excite used to update directories of Web sites.
d. Electricity used to provide lighting for Loblaw's store aisles
e. Depreciation on computer equipment at General Electric used for quality testing of refrigerator components during the assembly process
f. Salaries of Loblaw marketing personnel planning local-newspaper advertising campaigns
g. Perrier mineral water purchased by Excite for consumption by its software engineers
h. Salaries of Excite marketing personnel selling banner advertising

REQUIRED
1. Distinguish between manufacturing-sector, merchandising-sector, and service-sector companies.
2. Distinguish between inventoriable costs and period costs.
3. Classify each of the (a) to (h) cost items as an inventoriable cost or a period cost. Explain your answers.

2-27 **Computing cost of goods manufactured and cost of goods sold.** Compute cost of goods manufactured and cost of goods sold from the following account balances relating to 2000 (in thousands):

Property tax on plant building	$ 3,000
Marketing, distribution, and customer service costs	37,000
Finished goods inventory, January 1, 2000	27,000
Plant utilities	17,000
Work-in-process inventory, December 31, 2000	26,000
Amortization of plant building	9,000
General and administrative costs (nonplant)	43,000
Direct materials used	87,000
Finished goods inventory, December 31, 2000	34,000
Amortization of plant equipment	11,000
Plant repairs and maintenance	16,000
Work-in-process inventory, January 1, 2000	20,000
Direct manufacturing labour	34,000
Indirect manufacturing labour	23,000
Indirect materials used	11,000
Miscellaneous plant overhead	4,000

PROBLEMS

2-28 Cost of goods manufactured. Consider the following account balances (in thousands) for the Canseco Company:

	Beginning of 2000	End of 2000
Direct materials inventory	$22,000	$26,000
Work-in-process inventory	21,000	20,000
Finished goods inventory	18,000	23,000
Purchases of direct materials		75,000
Direct manufacturing labour		25,000
Indirect manufacturing labour		15,000
Plant insurance		9,000
Amortization—plant building and equipment		11,000
Repairs and maintenance—plant		4,000
Marketing, distribution, and customer service costs		93,000
General and administrative costs		29,000

REQUIRED

1. Prepare a schedule of cost of goods manufactured for 2000.
2. Revenues in 2000 were $300 million. Prepare the 2000 income statement.

2-29 Income statement and schedule of cost of goods manufactured. The Howell Corporation has the following account balances (in millions):

For Specific Date		For Year 2000	
Direct materials, January 1, 2000	$15	Purchases of direct materials	$325
Work in process, January 1, 2000	10	Direct manufacturing labour	100
Finished goods, January 1, 2000	70	Amortization—plant building and equipment	80
Direct materials, December 31, 2000	20		
Work-in-process, December 31, 2000	5	Plant supervisory salaries	5
Finished goods, December 31, 2000	55	Miscellaneous plant overhead	35
		Revenues	950
		Marketing, distribution, and customer service costs	240
		Plant supplies used	10
		Plant utilities	30
		Indirect manufacturing labour	60

REQUIRED

Prepare an income statement and a supporting schedule of cost of goods manufactured for the year ended December 31, 2000. (For additional questions regarding these facts, see the next problem.)

2-30 Interpretation of statements (continuation of 2-29). Refer to the preceding problem.

REQUIRED

1. How would the answer to the preceding problem be modified if you were asked for a schedule of cost of goods manufactured and sold instead of a schedule of cost of goods manufactured? Be specific.
2. Would the sales manager's salary (included in marketing, distribution, and customer service costs) be accounted for differently if the Howell Corporation were a merchandising company instead of a manufacturing company? Using the flow of costs outlined in Exhibit 2-10, describe how the wages of an assembler in the plant would be accounted for in this manufacturing company.
3. Plant supervisory salaries are usually regarded as indirect manufacturing costs. Under what conditions might some of these costs be regarded as direct manufacturing costs? Give an example.
4. Suppose that both the direct materials used and the plant amortization were related to the manufacture of 1 million units of product. What is the unit cost for the direct materials assigned to those units? What is the unit cost for plant building and equipment amortization? Assume that yearly plant amortization is computed on a straight-line basis.

5. Assume that the implied cost behaviour patterns in requirement 4 persist—that is, direct materials costs behave as a variable cost and amortization behaves as a fixed cost. Repeat the computations in requirement 4, assuming that the costs are being predicted for the manufacture of 1.2 million units of product. How would the total costs be affected?

6. As a management accountant, explain concisely to the president why the unit costs differed in requirements 4 and 5.

2-31 Income statement and schedule of cost of goods manufactured. The following items (in millions) pertain to the Chan Corporation:

For Specific Date		For Year 2000	
Work in process, January 1, 2000	$10	Plant utilities	$ 5
Direct materials, December 31, 2000	5	Indirect manufacturing labour	20
Finished goods, December 31, 2000	12	Amortization—plant, building, and equipment	9
Accounts payable, December 31, 2000	20		
Accounts receivable, January 1, 2000	50	Revenues	350
Work in process, December 31, 2000	2	Miscellaneous manufacturing overhead	10
Finished goods, January 1, 2000	40		
Accounts receivable, December 31, 2000	30	Marketing, distribution, and customer service costs	90
Accounts payable, January 1, 2000	40	Purchases of direct materials	80
Direct materials, January 1, 2000	30	Direct manufacturing labour	40
		Plant supplies used	6
		Property taxes on plant	1

Chan's manufacturing cost system uses a three-part classification of manufacturing costs—direct materials, direct manufacturing labour, and indirect manufacturing costs.

REQUIRED

Prepare an income statement and a supporting schedule of cost of goods manufactured. (For additional questions regarding these facts, see the next problem.)

2-32 Interpretation of statements (continuation of 2-31). Refer to the preceding problem.

REQUIRED

1. How would the answer to the preceding problem be modified if you were asked for a schedule of cost of goods manufactured and sold instead of a schedule of cost of goods manufactured? Be specific.

2. Would the sales manager's salary (included in marketing, distribution, and customer service costs) be accounted for any differently if the Chan Corporation were a merchandising company instead of a manufacturing company? Using the flow of costs outlined in Exhibit 2-10, describe how the wages of an assembler in the plant would be accounted for in this manufacturing company.

3. Plant supervisory salaries are usually regarded as indirect manufacturing costs. Under what conditions might some of these costs be regarded as direct manufacturing costs? Give an example.

4. Suppose that both the direct materials used and the plant amortization were related to the manufacture of 1 million units of product. What is the unit cost for the direct materials assigned to those units? What is the unit cost for plant building and equipment amortization? Assume that yearly amortization is computed on a straight-line basis.

5. Assume that the implied cost behaviour patterns in requirement 4 persist. That is, direct materials costs behave as a variable cost and plant amortization behaves as a fixed cost. Repeat the computations in requirement 4, assuming that the costs are being predicted for the manufacture of 1.5 million units of product. How would the total costs be affected?

6. As a management accountant, explain concisely to the president why the unit costs differed in requirements 4 and 5.

2-33 Overtime premium, defining accounting terms. Gwen Benson, Ian Blacklaw, and Eduardo Cabrera are sales representatives for Electronic Manufacturing Inc. (EMI). EMI specializes in low-volume production orders for the research groups of major companies. Each sales representative receives a base salary plus a bonus based on 20% of the actual profit of each order they sell. Prior to this year, the bonus was 5%

of the revenues of each order they sold. Actual profit in the revised system was defined as actual revenue minus actual manufacturing cost. EMI uses a three-part classification of manufacturing costs—direct materials, direct manufacturing labour, and indirect manufacturing costs. Indirect manufacturing costs are determined as 200% of actual direct manufacturing labour cost.

Benson receives a report on an EMI job for BBC Inc. She is dismayed by the low profit on the BBC job. She prided herself on not discounting the price BBC would pay by convincing them of the quality of EMI's work. Benson discussed the issue with Blacklaw and Cabrera. They share with her details of their most recent jobs. Summary data are:

Customer	Westec	La Electricidad	BBC
Sales Representative	Blacklaw	Cabrera	Benson
Revenues	$420	$820	$480
Direct materials	250	410	270
Direct manuf. labour	40	100	60
Indirect manufacturing	80	200	120
Direct labour hours	2 hours	5 hours	2 hours

Benson asks Hans Brunner, EMI's manufacturing manager, to explain the different labour costs charged on the Westec and BBC jobs, given both used 2 direct labour hours. She was told the BBC job was done in overtime and that the actual overtime rate ($30) was 50% higher than the $20 per hour straight-time rate. Benson noted that she brought the BBC order to EMI one week ago and that there was no rush-order on the job. In contrast, the Westec order was a "hot-hot" one with a request it be done by noon the day after the order was received. Brunner said that the "actual cost" he charged to the BBC job was actually paid to the workers on that job.

REQUIRED

1. Using both the straight-time and overtime rates for direct labour, what is the actual profit EMI would report on each of the three jobs?
2. Assume that EMI charges each job for direct labour at the $20 straight-time rate (and that the indirect-manufacturing rate of 200% includes an overtime premium). What would be the revised profit EMI would report on each of the three jobs. Comment on any differences from requirement 1.
3. Discuss the pros and cons of charging the BBC job the $30 labour rate per hour.
4. Why might EMI adopt the 20% profit incentive instead of the prior 5% of revenue incentive? How might EMI define "profit" to reduce possible disagreements with its sales representatives?

2-34 **Finding unknown balances.** An auditor for Revenue Canada is trying to reconstruct some partially destroyed records of two taxpayers. For each of the cases in the accompanying list, find the unknowns designated by capital letters (figures are assumed to be in thousands).

	Case 1	Case 2
Accounts receivable, December 31, 2000	$ 6,000	$ 2,100
Cost of goods sold	A	20,000
Accounts payable, January 1, 2000	3,000	1,700
Accounts payable, December 31, 2000	1,800	1,500
Finished goods inventory, December 31, 2000	B	5,300
Gross margin	11,300	C
Work in process, January 1, 2000	0	800
Work in process, December 31, 2000	0	3,000
Finished goods inventory, January 1, 2000	4,000	4,000
Direct material used	8,000	12,000
Direct manufacturing labour	3,000	5,000
Indirect manufacturing costs	7,000	D
Purchases of direct material	9,000	7,000
Revenues	32,000	31,800
Accounts receivable, January 1, 2000	2,000	1,400

2-35 Fire loss, computing inventory costs. A distraught employee, Guy Arson, put a torch to a manufacturing plant on a blustery February 26. The resulting blaze completely destroyed the plant and its contents. Fortunately, certain accounting records were kept in another building. They revealed the following for the period from January 1, 2000, to February 26, 2000:

Direct materials purchased	$160,000
Work in process, January 1, 2000	$ 34,000
Direct materials, January 1, 2000	$ 16,000
Finished goods, January 1, 2000	$ 30,000
Indirect manufacturing costs	40% of conversion costs
Revenues	$500,000
Direct manufacturing labour	$180,000
Prime costs	$294,000
Gross margin percentage based on sales	20%
Cost of goods available for sale	$450,000

The loss was fully covered by insurance. The insurance company wants to know the historical cost of the inventories as one factor considered when negotiating a settlement.

REQUIRED
Calculate the cost of:
1. Finished goods inventory, February 26, 2000
2. Work-in-process inventory, February 26, 2000
3. Direct materials inventory, February 26, 2000

2-36 Comprehensive problem on unit costs, product costs. Regina Office Equipment manufactures and sells metal shelving. It began operations on January 1, 2000. Costs incurred for 2000 are as follows (V stands for variable; F stands for fixed):

Direct materials used costs	$140,000 V
Direct manufacturing labour costs	30,000 V
Plant energy costs	5,000 V
Indirect manufacturing labour costs	10,000 V
Indirect manufacturing labour costs	16,000 F
Other indirect manufacturing costs	8,000 V
Other indirect manufacturing costs	24,000 F
Marketing, distribution, and customer service costs	122,850 V
Marketing, distribution, and customer service costs	40,000 F
Administrative costs	50,000 F

Variable manufacturing costs are variable with respect to units produced. Variable marketing, distribution, and customer service costs are variable with respect to units sold.

Inventory data are as follows:

	Beginning, January 1, 2000	Ending, December 31, 2000
Direct materials	0 kilograms	2,000 kilograms
Work in process	0 units	0 units
Finished goods	0 units	? units

Production in 2000 was 100,000 units. Two kilograms of direct materials are used to make one unit of finished product.

Revenues in 2000 were $436,800. The selling price per unit and the purchase price per kilogram of direct materials were stable throughout the year. The company's ending inventory of finished goods is carried at the average unit manufacturing costs for 2000. Finished goods inventory, at December 31, 2000, was $20,970.

REQUIRED
1. Direct materials inventory, total cost, December 31, 2000
2. Finished goods inventory, total units, December 31, 2000

3. Selling price per unit, 2000
4. Operating income, 2000. Show your computations.

2-37 Budgeted income statement (continuation of 2-36). Assume management predicts that the selling price per unit and variable cost per unit will be the same in 2001 as in 2000. Fixed manufacturing costs and marketing, distribution, and customer service costs in 2001 are also predicted to be the same as in 2000. Sales in 2001 are forecast to be 122,000 units. The desired ending inventory of finished goods, December 31, 2001, is 12,000 units. Assume zero ending inventories of both direct materials and work in process. The company's ending inventory of finished goods is carried at the average unit manufacturing costs for 2001. The company uses the first-in, first-out inventory method. Management has asked that you prepare a budgeted income statement for 2001.

REQUIRED
1. Units of finished goods produced in 2001
2. Budgeted income statement for 2001

2-38 Revenue and cost recording and classifications, ethics. Canadian Outfitters (C.O.) designs and markets jeans to many retailers and distributors around the globe. Its corporate headquarters is in Montreal, Quebec. Manufacturing is done by a subcontractor (Jeans West) on the island state of Caribe. The Caribe government grants locally owned companies a 20% income tax rebate if the ratio of their domestic labour costs to total costs exceeds 25%. Domestic labour costs are defined as the employment costs of all employees who are citizens of Caribe. Nicola Roberts, the newly appointed controller of C.O., has recently been examining payments made to Jeans West. She observes that Jeans West purchases denim from C.O. ($3 million in 2000). C.O. paid Jeans West $12 million for the jeans manufactured in Caribe in 2000. Based on her industry experience, the $12 million amount is very low. She was told it was "a great deal" for C.O. There is also a sizable payment by C.O. to the Swiss subsidiary of Jeans West ($4.8 million in 2000). Roberts is told by the Jeans West president that this payment is for fabric design work that Jeans West does with C.O. C.O. has included the $4.8 million payment in its own product design cost. The director of product design at C.O. told Roberts it is an "off-statement" item that historically he has no responsibility for nor any say about. To his knowledge, Jeans West uses only C.O. designs with either zero or minimal changes.

Jeans West's domestic labour costs in 2000 were $3.6 million while its total costs were $10 million. Included in this $3.6 million was $1.3 million for labour fringe benefits (for health insurance, etc.). A component of this $1.3 million is $600,000 for life insurance for Jeans West's executives. C.O. helped arrange this life insurance policy. It negotiated with the insurance company managing its own executive life insurance plans to include the Jeans West executives at rates much more favourable than those available in Caribe.

REQUIRED
1. What concerns should Roberts have about the revenue and cost numbers in C.O.'s financial reports?
2. Which (if any) of the concerns in requirement 1 raise ethical issues for Roberts? Explain.
3. What steps should Roberts take to address the ethical issues you identify in requirement 2?

COLLABORATIVE LEARNING PROBLEMS

2-39 Defining cost terms. You are the controller of the Heinz potato processing subsidiary in Ireland. This subsidiary processes potatoes for frozen dinners, fast food restaurants, and other large institutional buyers. Assume that companies setting up manufacturing facilities in Ireland receive an income tax rebate equivalent to the ratio of employment costs of Irish citizens to total manufacturing costs in Ireland. Thus, if the Irish subsidiary has a "pre-rebate" tax bill of $10 million and the ratio of employment costs to total manufacturing costs is 22%, its actual tax bill will be reduced by $2.2 million to $7.8 million.

INSTRUCTIONS
Form groups of two or more students to complete the following requirement.

Develop guidelines as to how Heinz should define costs at its Irish subsidiary. Assume one aim is to minimize the income taxes that Heinz is legitimately required to pay to the Irish government.

2-40 Movie profit sharing, defining terms. Brad Fittler, first-time author of *The Sporting Life*, has just had a meeting with Bill Harrigan, a senior executive of Golden Ventures (GV). GV is a major movie studio with many successes. *The Sporting Life* is a best-selling novel about the personal and professional career of Allan Langer, a recently retired football superstar. Harrigan bubbled with excitement during the meeting. He said the book was the "best thing he had seen in many years" and would make "*Titanic* look like a minor movie." Fittler felt great about a luminary such as Harrigan being so full of praise for a film based on a book that many publishers initially rejected as "not meeting their commercial criteria."

After the meeting, Fittler called Penny Carr, a friend for many years. Carr showed Fittler some extracts from an expose on "Accounting, Hollywood Style"—see the exhibit below. Fittler was dismayed by the Cumulative Distribution Statement. He thought *Bill Goldberg Superstar* was a box-office success and yet it still was over $60 million "in the red."

REQUIRED

You are asked to give advice to Brad Fittler. You should:
a. identify the weaknesses in the Golden Ventures Cumulative Distribution Statement for an author whose payment is 5% of net profits, and
b. propose ways to reduce (or even eliminate) the weaknesses you identify in (a) for a contract for Fittler.

EXHIBIT FOR PROBLEM 2-40

Golden Venture Report on
Bill Goldberg Superstar
Cumulative Distribution Statement (in $millions)
From: July 1, 2000
To: March 31, 2001

1. Gross receipts (a)	$160.295
2. Less distribution fee (b)	56.103
3. Gross after distribution fees	140.192
4. Less distribution expenses (c)	55.063
5. Balance	49.129
6. Less gross participation fees of directors, screen stars, and so on (d)	32.059
7. Balance	17.070
8. Less negative cost (e)	(68.420)
9. Balance	(51.350)
10. Less interest on negative cost (f)	10.786
11. Net profit	$ (62.136)

(a) The studio's revenues from the film to date. All North American theatre screen and television revenues are included. Only 50% of non-North American revenues are included. Only 20% of the gross is included for home video sales. The film's video distributor, Golden Ventures Home Video (100% owned by GV), kept 80% because it was treated as a separate company. Revenues from non-theatre, non-video, and non-television sources are not included.
(b) Distribution fees. Covers overhead costs of running a studio and is a flat percentage (35%) of revenues.
(c) Distribution expenses. The actual costs of putting the movie in theatres, including advertising, printing copies of the film, and transportation.
(d) Gross participation fees of directors, screen stars. The major "talent" on the movie receive 20% of the gross receipts for the first $200 million and 25% thereafter.
(e) Negative cost is the cost of producing everything that is seen onscreen, from film, sets, and up-front fees paid to cast and crew.
(f) Interest on negative cost. The studio views the cost of financing a film as a loan and charges 125% of the prime rate for any negative balance in line 9 as long as the movie "remains in the red."

3
C H A P T E R

COST-VOLUME-PROFIT ANALYSIS

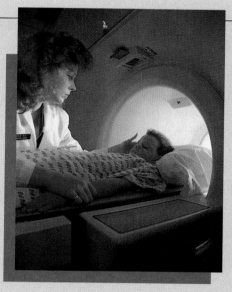

The growing complexity and sophistication of medical testing equipment is increasing the ratio of fixed costs to total costs in many hospitals. Magnetic resonance imaging (MRI) equipment enables hospitals to produce high-quality images without exposing patients to ionizing radiation. Obtaining high utilization for this expensive equipment is essential for hospitals justifying investment in MRI technology.

LEARNING OBJECTIVES

After studying this chapter, you should be able to:

1. Understand basic cost-volume-profit (CVP) assumptions
2. Explain essential features of CVP analysis
3. Determine the breakeven point and target operating income using the equation, contribution margin, and graph methods
4. Incorporate income tax considerations into CVP analysis
5. Explain the use of CVP analysis in decision making, and explain how sensitivity analysis can help managers cope with uncertainty
6. Use CVP analysis to plan costs
7. Apply CVP analysis to a multi-product company
8. Distinguish between contribution margin and gross margin
9. Adapt CVP analysis to multiple cost driver situations

Cost-volume-profit (CVP). Examines the behaviour of total revenues, total costs, and operating income as changes occur in the output level, selling price, variable costs, or fixed costs; a single revenue driver and a single cost driver are used in this analysis.

This chapter examines one of the most basic planning tools available to managers: cost-volume-profit analysis. **Cost-volume-profit (CVP)** analysis examines the behaviour of total revenues, total costs, and operating income as changes occur in the output level, selling price, variable costs, or fixed costs. Managers commonly use CVP as a tool to help them answer such questions as: How will revenues and costs be affected if we sell 1,000 more units? If we raise or lower our selling prices? If we expand business into overseas markets? These questions have a common "what-if" theme. CVP is built on simplifying assumptions about revenue and cost behaviour patterns. By examining various possibilities and alternatives, CVP analysis illustrates various decision outcomes and this serves as a valuable aid in the planning process.

CVP ASSUMPTIONS

OBJECTIVE 1

Understand basic cost-volume-profit (CVP) assumptions

Revenue driver. Any factor that affects revenues.

The CVP analysis is based on the following assumptions:

1. Changes in the level of revenues and costs arise only because of changes in the number of product (or service) units produced or sold—for example, the number of televisions produced or sold by Sony Corporation. Since we assume production equals sales, the number of units is the only *revenue* and *cost driver*. Just as a cost driver is any factor that affects costs, a **revenue driver** is any factor that affects revenues.

2. Total costs can be divided into a fixed component and a component that is variable with respect to the level of output.

3. The behaviour of total revenues and total costs is linear (straight-line) in relation to output units within the relevant range.[1]

4. The unit selling price, unit variable costs, and fixed costs are known. (This assumption is discussed later in the chapter and in the appendix to this chapter.)

5. The analysis either covers a single product or assumes that a given revenue mix of products will remain constant as the level of total units sold changes. (This assumption is also discussed later in the chapter.)

6. All revenues and costs can be added and compared without taking into account the time value of money. (Chapters 22 and 23 relax this assumption.)

Many companies and divisions and plants of companies in industries such as airlines, automobiles, chemicals, plastics, and semiconductors have found the simple CVP relationships to be helpful in strategic and long-range planning decisions as well as decisions about product features and pricing. In other real-world settings, the simple assumptions described above may not hold. For example, predicting total revenues and total costs may require multiple revenue drivers (such as number of sales visits made to customers and number of advertisements placed), and multiple cost drivers (such as number of batches in which units are produced). The basic CVP ideas may still be useful in these situations, but the analysis is more complex. Managers and accountants, however, must always assess whether the simplified CVP relationships generate sufficiently accurate predictions of how total revenues and total costs behave. Managers should consider using a more complicated approach that, for example, considers multiple revenue drivers and cost drivers, and cost functions that are not linear, if doing so will significantly improve their decisions.

---

[1]For example, one set of conditions in which assumption 3 is descriptive includes the following: selling prices are constant within the relevant range; productivity is constant within the relevant range; and costs of production inputs are constant within the relevant range. Under what conditions would assumption 3 not be descriptive? On the revenue side, reductions in the selling price may be necessary to spur sales at higher levels of output. On the cost side, variable costs per unit may decline when output increases as employees learn to handle the process more efficiently. The learning curve is discussed in Chapter 10.

62 | CHAPTER 3

Before explaining the basics of CVP analysis, we must first clarify some terms. As described in Chapter 2,

$$\text{Operating income} = \text{Total revenues from operations} - \text{Cost of goods sold and operating expenses (excluding income taxes)}$$

Net income is **operating income** plus nonoperating revenues (such as interest revenue) minus nonoperating costs (such as interest cost) minus income taxes. For simplicity, throughout this chapter we assume nonoperating revenues and nonoperating costs to be zero. Thus, net income will be computed as:

$$\text{Net income} = \text{Operating income} - \text{Income taxes}$$

Net income. Operating income plus nonoperating revenues (such as interest revenue) minus nonoperating costs (such as interest cost) minus income taxes.

Operating income. Operating income is total revenues from operations minus total costs from operations (excluding income taxes).

ESSENTIALS OF COST-VOLUME-PROFIT (CVP) ANALYSIS

To see how CVP analysis works, consider the following example.

Example: Mary Frost plans to sell Do-All-Software, a home-office software package, at a heavily attended two-day computer convention in Montreal. Mary can purchase this software from a computer software wholesaler at $120 per package with the privilege of returning all unsold units and receiving a full $120 refund per package. The units (packages) will be sold at $200 each. She has already paid $2,000 to Computer Conventions Inc. for the booth rental for the two-day convention. Assume there are no other costs. What profits will Mary make for different quantities of units sold?

OBJECTIVE 2

Explain essential features of CVP analysis

The booth rental costs of $2,000 are fixed costs because they will not change no matter how many units Mary sells. The costs of the package are variable costs because these costs increase in proportion to the number of units sold. For each unit that Mary sells, she incurs a cost of $120 to purchase it. If Mary sells 10 packages, the variable purchase costs are $1,200 ($120 × 10).

Mary can use CVP analysis to examine changes in operating income as a result of selling different quantities of software packages. If Mary sells 2 packages, she will receive revenues of $400 ($200 × 2), incur variable costs of $240 ($120 × 2), and fixed costs of $2,000, and show an operating loss of $1,840 ($400 – $240 –$2,000). If Mary sells 40 packages, she will receive revenues of $8,000 ($200 × 40), incur variable costs of $4,800 ($120 × 40), and the same fixed costs of $2,000, and show an operating income of $1,200 ($8,000 – $4,800 – $2,000). Note that the only numbers that change from selling different quantities of packages are *total revenues* and *total variable costs*. The difference between total revenues and total variable costs is called **contribution margin**. Contribution margin is an effective summary of the reasons why operating income changes as the number of units sold changes. The contribution margin when Mary sells 2 packages is $160 (total revenues, $400, minus total variable costs, $240), and the contribution margin when Mary sells 40 packages is $3,200 (total revenues, $8,000, minus total variable costs, $4,800). Note that contribution margin calculations subtract all variable costs. For instance, if Mary had hired a salesperson to sell Do-All Software at the convention on the basis of a sales commission on each unit sold, variable costs would include the cost of the package plus the sales commission.

Variable Costing and Cost-Volume-Profit Analysis
www.csuohio.edu/accounts/ACT600/Lecture8/index.htm

Contribution margin. Revenues minus all costs of the output (a product or service) that vary with respect to the number of output units.

Contribution margin per unit is a useful tool for calculating contribution margins. The contribution margin per unit is the difference between the *selling price* and the *variable cost per unit*. In the Do-All Software example, the contribution margin per unit = $200 – $120 = $80. Contribution margin can then be calculated as:

$$\text{Contribution margin} = \text{Contribution margin per unit} \times \text{Number of packages sold}$$

For example, when 40 packages are sold, contribution margin = $80 × 40 = $3,200.

Contribution margin is a key concept in CVP analysis. It represents the amount of revenues remaining, after earning back variable costs, that contribute to reimbursing fixed costs. Once fixed costs are fully recovered, the contribution margin contributes to earning operating income. Exhibit 3-1 calculates the contribution margins for different quantities of packages sold and shows how contribution margin recovers fixed costs and generates operating income. The income statement presen-

EXHIBIT 3-1
Contribution Income Statement for Different Quantities of Do-All Software Packages Sold

			Number of Packages Sold		
	0	1	2	25	40
Revenues at $200 per package	$ 0	$ 200	$ 400	$5,000	$8,000
Variable costs at $120 per package	0	120	240	3,000	4,800
Contribution margin at $80 per package	0	80	160	2,000	3,200
Fixed costs	2,000	2,000	2,000	2,000	2,000
Operating income	$(2,000)	$(1,920)	$(1,840)	$ 0	$1,200

Contribution income statement. Income statement that groups line items by cost behaviour pattern to highlight the contribution margin.

tation in Exhibit 3-1 is called a **contribution income statement** because it groups line items by cost-behaviour pattern to highlight the contribution margin. Note that each additional unit sold from 0 to 1 to 2 increases contribution margin by $80, covering more of the fixed costs and reducing the operating loss. If Mary sells 25 packages, the contribution margin equals $2,000 ($80 × 25), exactly reimbursing the fixed costs and resulting in zero operating income. Each package sold beyond 25 packages generates an additional per-unit contribution margin of $80, which adds directly to operating income because fixed costs of $2,000 have already been recovered. For example, if Mary sells 40 units, 15 units more than the break-even point of 25 units, the contribution margin increases by $1,200 ($80 × 15), all of which becomes operating income. Note that, as you move across Exhibit 3-1 from left to right, the increase in contribution margin exactly equals the increase in operating income (or the decrease in operating loss).

Instead of expressing the contribution margin as a per-unit amount, we can also express it as a percentage. **Contribution margin percentage** or **contribution margin ratio** is the contribution margin per unit divided by the selling price.

In our example,

Contribution margin percentage (contribution margin ratio). Contribution margin per unit divided by selling price, or total contribution margin divided by total revenues.

$$\text{Contribution margin percentage} = \frac{\$80}{\$200} = 40\%$$

The contribution margin percentage is the contribution margin achieved per dollar of sales. It indicates that 40% of every dollar of sales (40 cents) will go toward contribution margin.[2]

Mary can calculate the total contribution margin for different sales levels by multiplying the contribution margin percentage and the total revenue dollars shown in Exhibit 3-1, line 1. For example, if Mary sells 25 packages, revenues would be $5,000, and contribution margin would equal 40% × $5,000 = $2,000, exactly offsetting fixed costs.[3] Mary breaks even by selling 25 packages worth $5,000.

THE BREAKEVEN POINT

OBJECTIVE 3

Determine the breakeven point and target operating income using the equation, contribution margin, and graph methods

Breakeven point. Quantity of output at which total revenues and total costs are equal; that is, where the operating income is zero.

The **breakeven point** is that quantity of output at which total revenues equal total costs—that is, where the operating income is zero. Why would managers be interested in the breakeven point? Mainly because they want to avoid operating losses, and the breakeven point tells them what level of sales they must generate to avoid a

[2]Sometimes the contribution margin is expressed as a percentage of variable costs. Suppose this percentage is 25%. We would then have

Variable costs per unit	$100
Add contribution margin per unit	25
Selling price	$125

By definition, contribution margin percentage, as a term, is always expressed as a percentage of selling price. In our example, it equals $25 ÷ $125 or 20%.

[3]Note from Exhibit 3-1 that, given a contribution income statement, contribution margin percentage can also be calculated as total contribution margin divided by total revenues. For example, if 40 packages are sold, contribution margin percentage = $3,200 ÷ $8,000 = 40%.

How a Jobs Bank Agreement Increased GM's Breakeven Point

The breakeven point of an automotive company is greatly affected by the behaviour of manufacturing labour costs. Where manufacturing labour is a fixed cost, the breakeven point will be higher than where it is a variable cost. A 1990 contract between General Motors Corporation (GM) and the United Auto Workers (UAW) resulted in manufacturing labour cost behaving more like a fixed cost than as a variable cost when the level of production declined. In this contract, GM guaranteed $3.3 billion for worker jobs and income guarantees over three years. Provisions of the contract included:

- In the first 36 weeks of a layoff, workers receive [un]employment insurance and supplemental insurance benefits equal to 95% of take-home pay.

- After the 36 weeks of layoff, workers go back on full pay and benefits, either at their old plant or as part of a jobs bank.

This contract was designed, in part, to motivate GM employees to seek new ways to continuously improve quality and reduce costs without their own employment being at risk.

When GM's production output declined in the early 1990s, many workers joined the jobs bank. GM has sought ways to use these workers productively. One proposal was to have their independent supplier companies use GM workers and facilities when manufacturing parts for GM. This proposal was labelled a "strategic insourcing initiative." One commentator noted at the time that the plan met resistance from suppliers who were none too anxious to move into GM's unwanted plants and use GM's highly paid workers.

The result was that GM still had an excessive number of underutilized people who were receiving full pay and benefits. This led to GM's having a higher breakeven point than several of its competitors who did not have similar jobs bank agreements.

Source: Adapted from *The Detroit News,* December 12, 1991, and *Automotive News,* February 1, 1993.

---

loss. This section will continue to use the Do-All Software information to examine three methods for determining the breakeven point: the equation method, the contribution margin method, and the graph method.

The following abbreviations are useful in the subsequent analysis.

- USP = Unit selling price
- UVC = Unit variable costs
- UCM = Unit contribution margin (USP – UVC)
- CM% = Contribution margin percentage (UCM ÷ USP)
- FC = Fixed costs
- Q = Quantity of output units sold (or manufactured)
- OI = Operating income
- TOI = Target operating income
- TNI = Target net income

Equation Method

The first approach for computing the breakeven point is the equation method. Using the terminology in this chapter, the income statement can be expressed in equation form as follows:

$$\text{Revenues} - \text{Variable costs} - \text{Fixed costs} = \text{Operating income}$$
$$(\text{USP} \times Q) - (\text{UVC} \times Q) - \text{FC} = \text{OI} \qquad (1)$$

This equation provides the most general and easy-to-remember approach to any CVP situation. Setting operating income equal to zero in the preceding equation, we obtain:

$$\$200Q - \$120Q - \$2,000 = \$0$$
$$\$80Q = \$2,000$$
$$Q = \$2,000 \div \$80 = 25 \text{ units}$$

If Frost sells fewer than 25 units, she will have a loss; if she sells 25 units, she will break even; and, if she sells more than 25 units, she will make a profit. This breakeven point is expressed in units. It can also be expressed in sales dollars: 25 units × $200 selling price = $5,000.

Contribution Margin Method

A second approach for computing the breakeven point is the contribution margin method, which is simply an algebraic manipulation of the equation method. Contribution margin is equal to revenues minus all costs of the output (a product or service) that vary with respect to the units of output. This method uses the fact that:

$$(\text{USP} \times Q) - (\text{UVC} \times Q) - \text{FC} = \text{OI}$$
$$(\text{USP} - \text{UVC}) \times Q = \text{FC} + \text{OI}$$
$$\text{UCM} \times Q = \text{FC} + \text{OI}$$
$$Q = \frac{\text{FC} + \text{OI}}{\text{UCM}} \qquad (2)$$

At the breakeven point, operating income is, by definition, zero. Setting OI = 0, we obtain:

$$\frac{\text{Breakeven}}{\text{number of units}} = \frac{\text{Fixed costs}}{\text{Unit contribution margin}}$$
$$= \frac{\text{FC}}{\text{UCM}} \qquad (3)$$

The calculations in the equation method and the contribution margin method appear similar because one is merely a restatement of the other. In our example, fixed costs are $2,000 and the unit contribution margin is $80 ($200 − $120). Therefore:

$$\frac{\text{Breakeven}}{\text{number of units}} = \$2,000 \div \$80 = 25 \text{ units}$$

We can also algebraically manipulate equation 3 to calculate breakeven in revenue dollars using the contribution margin percentage. Multiplying both sides of equation 3 by the USP gives

$$\frac{\text{Breakeven in}}{\text{revenue dollars}} = \frac{\text{Breakeven}}{\text{number of units}} \times \text{USP} = \frac{\text{FC} \times \text{USP}}{\text{UCM}}$$

$$= \frac{\frac{\text{FC}}{\text{UCM}}}{\text{USP}} \quad \text{(By dividing both numerator and denominator by USP)}$$

$$= \frac{\text{FC}}{\text{CM\%}} \quad \begin{array}{l}\text{(because contribution margin percentage (CM\%)} \\ \text{equals unit contribution margin (UCM) divided by} \\ \text{unit selling price (USP))}\end{array} \qquad (4)$$

In the Do-All Software example,

$$\text{CM\%} = \frac{\text{UCM}}{\text{USP}} = \frac{\$80}{\$200} = 40\%$$

$$\frac{\text{Breakeven in}}{\text{revenue dollars}} = \frac{\text{FC}}{\text{CM\%}} = \frac{\$2000}{40\%} = \$5,000$$

A contribution income statement groups line items by cost behaviour pattern to highlight the contribution margin. The following such statement confirms the preceding breakeven calculations:

Breakeven Analysis—
EntrepreNet Online
www.enterprise.org/enet/
library/be.html

Breakeven Analysis —The
SOHO Guidebook
www.toolkit.cch.com/text/
p06_7530.asp

Revenues, $200 × 25	$5,000
Variable costs, $120 × 25	3,000
Contribution margin, $80 × 25	2,000
Fixed costs	2,000
Operating income	$ 0

Graph Method

In the graph method, we plot the total costs line and the total revenues line. Their point of intersection is the breakeven point. Exhibit 3-2 illustrates this method for our Do-All example. We need only two points to plot each line if each is assumed to be linear:

1. **Total costs line.** This line is the sum of the fixed costs and the variable costs. Fixed costs are $2,000 at all output levels within the relevant range. To plot fixed costs, measure $2,000 on the vertical axis (point A) and extend a line horizontally. Variable costs are $120 per unit. To plot the total costs line, use as one point the $2,000 fixed costs at 0 output units (point A). Select a second point by choosing any other convenient output level (say, 40 units) and determining the corresponding total costs. The total variable costs at this output level are $4,800 (40 × $120). Fixed costs are $2,000 at all output levels within the relevant range. Hence, total costs at 40 units of output are $6,800, which is point B in Exhibit 3-2. The total costs line is the straight line from point A passing through point B.

2. **Total revenues line.** One convenient starting point is zero revenues at the zero output level, which is point C in Exhibit 3-2. Select a second point by choosing any other convenient output level and determining its total revenues. At 40 units of output, total revenues are $8,000 (40 × $200), which is point D in Exhibit 3-2. The total revenues line is the straight line from point C passing through point D.

The breakeven point is where the total revenues line and the total costs line intersect. At this point, total revenues equal total costs. But Exhibit 3-2 shows the

EXHIBIT 3-2
Cost-Volume-Profit Graph

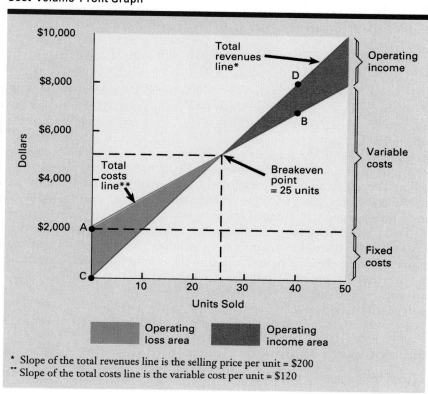

* Slope of the total revenues line is the selling price per unit = $200
** Slope of the total costs line is the variable cost per unit = $120

profit or loss outlook for a wide range of output levels. Many people describe the topics covered in this chapter as *breakeven analysis*. We prefer to use the phrase *cost-volume-profit analysis* to avoid overemphasizing the single point where total revenues equal total costs. Managers want to know how operating income differs at many different output levels.

Target Operating Income

Let us introduce a profit element by asking: How many units must be sold to earn an operating income of $1,200? The equation method provides a straightforward way to answer this question:

$$\text{Let } Q = \text{Number of units sold to earn target operating income}$$
$$\text{Revenues} - \text{Variable costs} - \text{Fixed costs} = \text{Target operating income}$$
$$\$200Q - \$120Q - \$2,000 = \$1,200$$
$$\$80Q = \$2,000 + \$1,200$$
$$\$80Q = \$3,200$$
$$Q = \$3,200 \div \$80 = 40 \text{ units}$$

Alternatively, we could use the contribution margin method. The numerator now consists of fixed costs plus target operating income:

$$Q = \frac{\text{Fixed costs} + \text{Target operating income}}{\text{Unit contribution margin}} = \frac{\text{FC} + \text{TOI}}{\text{UCM}}$$

$$Q = \frac{\$2,000 + \$1,200}{\$80}$$

$$\$80Q = \$3,200$$

$$Q = \$3,200 \div \$80 = 40 \text{ units}$$

Proof:		
	Revenues, $200 × 40	$8,000
	Variable costs, $120 × 40	4,800
	Contribution margin, $80 × 40	3,200
	Fixed costs	2,000
	Operating income	$1,200

The revenue in dollars to earn an operating income of $1,200 can also be calculated directly using the approach of equation 4:

$$\frac{\text{Revenue}}{\text{in dollars}} = \frac{\text{FC} + \text{TOI}}{\text{CM\%}} = \frac{\$2,000 + \$1,200}{0.40} = \frac{\$3,200}{0.40} = \$8,000$$

The graph in Exhibit 3-2, however, is not helpful for answering the question posed at the beginning of this section about how many units Mary must sell to earn an operating income of $1,200. Why not? Because it is not easy to determine the point at which the difference between the total revenues line and the total costs line is $1,200. Recasting Exhibit 3-2 in the form of a profit-volume (PV) graph helps greatly in answering this question. A **PV graph** shows the impact on operating income of changes in the output level. Exhibit 3-3 presents the PV graph for Do-All Software (fixed costs of $2,000, selling price of $200, and variable costs per unit of $120). The PV line can be drawn using two points. One convenient point (X) is the operating loss at zero units sold, which is equal to the fixed costs of $2,000. A second convenient point (Y) is the breakeven point—25 units in our example. The PV line is the straight line from point X passing through point Y. To find the number of units Mary must sell to earn an operating income of $1,200, draw a horizontal line corresponding to $1,200 on the y-axis. At the point where this line intersects the PV line (point A on the graph), draw a vertical line to the x-axis. The vertical line cuts the x-axis at 40 units, indicating that by selling 40 units Mary will generate operating income of $1,200.

PV graph. Shows the impact on operating income of changes in the output level.

Target Net Income and Income Taxes

Thus far, we have ignored the effect of income taxes in our CVP analysis. At times, managers want to know the effect of their decision on income after taxes. CVP cal-

EXHIBIT 3-3
The Profit-Volume Graph

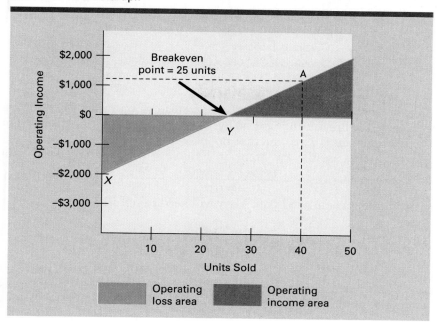

culations for target income must then be stated in terms of target net income instead of target operating income. Net income is operating income minus income taxes. For example, Mary may be interested in knowing the number of units of Do-All Software she must sell to earn a net income of $1,200, assuming an income tax rate of 40%. We modify the target operating income calculations of the previous section to allow for income taxes. Using the equation method:

OBJECTIVE 4

Incorporate income tax considerations into CVP analysis

$$\text{Revenues} - \text{Variable costs} - \text{Fixed costs} = \text{Target operating income}$$

Furthermore,

$$\text{Target net income} = (\text{Target operating income}) - [(\text{Target operating income}) \times (\text{Tax rate})]$$

$$\text{Target net income} = (\text{Target operating income})(1 - \text{Tax rate})$$

$$\text{Target operating income} = \frac{\text{Target net income}}{1 - \text{Tax rate}}$$

Substituting for target operating income, we have:

$$\text{Revenues} - \text{Variable costs} - \text{Fixed costs} = \frac{\text{Target net income}}{1 - \text{Tax rate}}$$

Substituting numbers from our Do-All Software example, we have:

$$\$200Q - \$120Q - \$2,000 = \frac{\$1,200}{1 - 0.40}$$

$$\$200Q - \$120Q - \$2,000 = \$2,000$$

$$\$80Q = \$4,000$$

$$Q = \$4,000 \div \$80 \text{ per unit} = 50 \text{ units}$$

Alternatively, we could use the method of equation 2 and substitute:

$$\text{Target operating income} = \frac{\text{Target net income}}{1 - \text{Tax rate}} , \text{ that is}$$

$$Q = \frac{\text{Fixed costs} + \dfrac{\text{Target net income}}{1 - \text{Tax rate}}}{\text{Unit contribution margin}} = \frac{FC + \dfrac{TNI}{1 - \text{Tax rate}}}{UCM}$$

$$Q = \frac{\$2,000 + \dfrac{\$1,200}{1 - 0.40}}{\$80} = \frac{\$2,000 + \$2,000}{\$80 \text{ per unit}} = 50 \text{ units}$$

Proof:	Revenues, $200 per unit × 50 units	$10,000
	Variable costs, $120 per unit × 50 units	6,000
	Contribution margin	4,000
	Fixed costs	2,000
	Operating income	2,000
	Income taxes, $2,000 × 0.40	800
	Net income	$ 1,200

Focusing the analysis on target net income instead of on target operating income will not change the breakeven point. Why? Because, by definition, operating income at the breakeven point is zero, and thus no income taxes will arise.[4]

Mary can also use the PV graph in Exhibit 3-3. For a target net income of $1,200, $\text{Target operating income} = \dfrac{\text{Target net income}}{1 - \text{Tax rate}} = \dfrac{\$1,200}{1 - 0.40} = \$2,000$. From Exhibit 3-3, to earn operating income of $2,000, Mary will need to sell 50 packages.

USING CVP ANALYSIS IN PLANNING AND DECISION MAKING

OBJECTIVE 5

Explain the use of CVP analysis in decision making, and explain how sensitivity analysis can help managers cope with uncertainty

We have seen how CVP analysis is useful for determining breakeven quantities and the quantities for achieving targeted operating and net incomes. Managers also use CVP analysis to guide other decisions.

Decision to Advertise   Consider again the Do-All Software example. Suppose Mary Frost anticipates selling 40 packages. Exhibit 3-3 indicates that Mary's operating income would be $1,200. Mary is considering placing an advertisement describing the product and its features in the convention brochure. The advertisement will cost $500. This will be a fixed cost because this cost will stay the same regardless of the number of units Mary sells. She anticipates that advertising will increase sales to 45 packages. Should Mary advertise? The following table presents the CVP analysis.

	40 Packages Sold with No Advertising (1)	45 Packages Sold with Advertising (2)	Difference (3) = (2) – (1)
Contribution margin ($80 × 40; $80 × 45)	$3,200	$3,600	$400
Fixed costs	(2,000)	(2,500)	(500)
Operating income	$1,200	$1,100	$(100)

Operating income decreases by $100, so Mary should not advertise. Note that Mary could focus only on the incremental changes and come to the same conclusion: If Mary advertises, contribution margin will increase by $400 ($80 per unit × 5 additional units), and fixed costs will increase by $500, resulting in a $100 decrease in operating income.

Decision to Reduce Selling Price   Having decided not to advertise, Mary is contemplating whether to reduce the selling price of Do-All Software to $175. At this price, she thinks sales will be 50 units. At this quantity, the software wholesaler who supplies Do-All Software will sell the packages to Mary for $115 per package instead of $120. Should Mary reduce the selling price? No, as the following CVP analysis shows.

Expected contribution margin from lowering price to $175, ($175 – $115) × 50 units	$3,000
Expected contribution margin from maintaining price at $200, ($200 – $120) × 40 units	3,200
Increase/(Decrease) in contribution margin from lowering price	$(200)

---

[4]Other types of taxes may affect the breakeven point. For example, a sales tax paid by the seller that is a fixed percentage of revenues can be treated as a variable cost and hence will increase the breakeven point.

Because the fixed costs of $2,000 do not change, decreasing the price will lead to a lower contribution margin and a lower operating income.

Mary can examine other alternatives to increase operating income such as simultaneously increasing advertising costs and lowering prices. In each case, Mary compares the changes in contribution margin (through the effect on selling price, variable costs, and output volume) to the changes in fixed costs and chooses the alternative that gives the highest operating income.

SENSITIVITY ANALYSIS AND UNCERTAINTY

Sensitivity analysis is a what-if technique that examines how a result will change if the original predicted data are not achieved or if an underlying assumption changes. In the context of CVP, sensitivity analysis answers such questions as: What will operating income be if the output level decreases by 5% from the original prediction? What will operating income be if variable costs per unit increase by 10%? The sensitivity to various possible outcomes broadens managers' perspectives as to what might actually occur despite their well-laid plans.

The widespread use of electronic spreadsheets has promoted the use of CVP analysis in many organizations. Using spreadsheets, managers can easily conduct CVP-based sensitivity analyses to examine the effect and interaction of changes in selling prices, unit variable costs, fixed costs, and target operating incomes. Exhibit 3-4 displays a spreadsheet for our Do-All example.[5] Mary can immediately see the revenues that need to be generated to reach particular operating income levels, given alternative levels of fixed costs and variable costs per unit. For example, revenues of $6,000 (30 units at $200 per unit) are required to earn an operating income of $1,000 if fixed costs are $2,000 and variable costs per unit are $100. Mary can also use Exhibit 3-4 to assess whether she wants to sell at the Montreal computer convention if, for example, the booth rental is raised to $3,000 (thus increasing fixed costs to $3,000) or the software supplier raises its price to $140 per unit (thus increasing variable costs to $140 per unit).

One aspect of sensitivity analysis is the **margin of safety,** which is the excess of budgeted revenues over the breakeven revenues. The margin of safety is the answer to the what-if question: If budgeted revenues are above breakeven and drop, how far can they fall below budget before the breakeven point is reached? Such a fall could be due to a competitor's having a better product, poorly executed marketing, and so on. Assume that Mary Frost has fixed costs of $3,000, a selling price of $200, and

Sensitivity analysis. A what-if technique that examines how a result will change if the original predicted data are not achieved or if an underlying assumption changes.

Margin of safety. Excess of budgeted revenues over the breakeven revenues.

EXHIBIT 3-4
Spreadsheet Analysis of CVP Relationships for Do-All Software

Fixed Costs	Variable Costs per Unit	Revenue Dollars Required at $200 Selling Price to Earn Operating Income Of:			
		$0	$1,000	$1,500	$2,000
$2,000	$100	$ 4,000	$ 6,000	$ 7,000	$ 8,000
	120	5,000	7,500	8,750	10,000
	140	6,667	10,000	11,667	13,333
$2,500	$100	$ 5,000	$ 7,000	$ 8,000	$ 9,000
	120	6,250	8,750	10,000	11,250
	140	8,333	11,667	13,333	15,000
$3,000	$100	$ 6,000	$ 8,000	$ 9,000	$10,000
	120	7,500	10,000	11,250	12,500
	140	10,000	13,333	15,000	16,667

[5]Spreadsheet packages such as Excel or Lotus 1-2-3 facilitate sensitivity analyses.

variable costs per unit of $140. For 75 units sold, the budgeted revenues are $15,000 and the budgeted operating income is $1,500. The breakeven point for this set of assumptions is 50 units ($3,000 ÷ $60) or $10,000 ($200 × 50). Hence, the margin of safety is $5,000 ($15,000 − $10,000) or 25 units.

Uncertainty. The possibility that an actual amount will deviate from an expected amount.

Sensitivity analysis is one approach to recognizing **uncertainty,** which is defined here as the possibility that an actual amount will deviate from an expected amount. Another approach is to compute expected values using probability distributions. The appendix to this chapter illustrates this approach.

COST PLANNING AND CVP

Alternative Fixed-Cost/Variable-Cost Structures

OBJECTIVE 6

Use CVP analysis to plan costs

Sensitivity analysis highlights the risks that an existing cost structure poses for an organization. This may lead managers to consider alternative cost structures. CVP helps managers in this task. Consider again Mary and her booth rental agreement with Computer Conventions, Inc. Our original example has Mary paying a $2,000 booth rental fee. Suppose, however, Computer Conventions offers Mary three rental alternatives:

◆ **Option 1.** $2,000 fixed fee

◆ **Option 2.** $1,400 fixed fee plus 5% of the convention revenues from Do-All sales

◆ **Option 3.** 20% of the convention revenues from Do-All sales with no fixed fee

Mary is interested in how her choice of a rental agreement will affect the risks she faces. Exhibit 3-5 presents these options in the CVP format:

◆ **Option 1** exposes her to fixed costs of $2,000 and a breakeven point of 25 units. This option brings $80 additional operating income for each unit sold above 25 units.

◆ **Option 2** exposes her to lower fixed costs of $1,400 and a lower breakeven point of 20 units. There is, however, only $70 in additional operating income for each unit sold above 20 units.

◆ **Option 3** has no fixed costs. Mary makes $40 in additional operating income for each unit sold. This $40 addition to operating income starts from the first unit sold. This option enables Mary to break even if no units are sold.

CVP analysis highlights the different risks and different returns associated with each option. For example, while option 1 has the most downside risk (a $2,000 fixed up-front payment), it also has the highest contribution margin per unit. This $80 contribution margin per unit translates to high upside potential if Mary is able to generate sales above 25 units. By moving from option 1 to option 2, Mary faces less risk (lowers her fixed costs) if demand is low, but she must accept less upside potential (because of the higher variable costs) if demand is high. The choice between options 1, 2, and 3 will be influenced by her confidence in the level of demand for Do-All software and her willingness to risk money.

Operating leverage. Describes the effects that fixed costs have on changes in operating income as changes occur in units sold and hence in contribution margin.

The risk-return tradeoff across alternative cost structures is usefully summarized in a measure called *operating leverage*. **Operating leverage** describes the effects that fixed costs have on changes in operating income as changes occur in units sold and hence in contribution margin. Organizations with a high proportion of fixed costs in their cost structures, as in the case under option 1 in our example, have high operating leverage. As a result, small changes in sales lead to large changes in operating incomes. Consequently, if sales increase, operating incomes increase even more, yielding large returns. If sales decrease, however, operating incomes decline substantially, leading to a greater risk of losses. At any given level of sales, **degree of operating leverage** equals contribution margin divided by operating income.

Degree of operating leverage. Contribution margin divided by operating income.

The table following Exhibit 3-5 shows the degree of operating leverage at sales of 40 units for the three alternative rental options.

EXHIBIT 3-5
CVP Graphs for Alternative Rental Schedules for Do-All Software

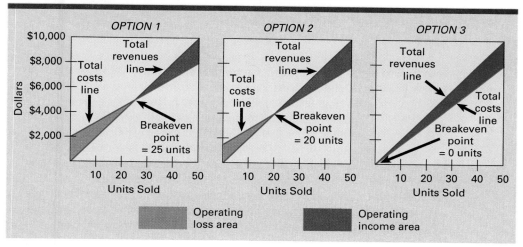

	Option 1	Option 2	Option 3
1. Contribution margin per unit	$80	$70	$40
2. Contribution margin (Row 1 × 40 units)	$3,200	$2,800	$1,600
3. Operating income (from Exhibit 3-5)	$1,200	$1,400	$1,600
4. Degree of operating leverage (Row 2 ÷ Row 3)	$\frac{\$3,200}{\$1,200} = 2.67$	$\frac{\$2,800}{\$1,400} = 2.00$	$\frac{\$1,600}{\$1,600} = 1$

These numbers indicate that, when sales are 40 units, a percentage change in sales and contribution margin will result in 2.67 times that percentage change in operating income for Option 1, but the same percentage change in operating income (as before the change in sales) for Option 3. Consider, for example, a sales increase of 50% from 40 units to 60 units. Contribution margin also increases by 50% under each option. Operating income, however, increases by 2.67 × 50% = 133% from $1,200 to $2,800 in Option 1 but only by 1 × 50% = 50% from $1,600 to $2,400 in Option 3. Knowing the degree of operating leverage at a given level of sales helps managers to calculate quickly the effect of changes in sales on operating incomes.

Effect of Time Horizon

A critical assumption of CVP analysis is that costs can be classified as either variable or fixed. This classification can be affected by the time period being considered. The shorter the time horizon we consider, the higher the percentage of total costs we may view as fixed. Consider Air Canada. Suppose an Air Canada plane will depart from its gate in 30 minutes and there are 20 empty seats. A potential passenger arrives bearing a transferable ticket from a competing airline. What are the variable costs to Air Canada of placing one more passenger in an otherwise empty seat? Variable costs (such as one more meal) would be negligible. Virtually all the costs in that decision situation are fixed. In contrast, suppose Air Canada must decide whether to include another city in its routes. This decision may have a one-year planning horizon. Many more costs would be regarded as variable and fewer as fixed in this decision.

This example underscores the importance of how the time horizon of a decision affects the analysis of cost behaviour. In brief, whether costs are really fixed depends heavily on the relevant range, the length of the time horizon in question, and the specific decision situation.

Revenue mix (sales mix). The relative contribution of quantities of products or services that constitutes total revenues.

EFFECTS OF REVENUE MIX ON INCOME

Revenue mix (also called **sales mix**) is the relative contribution of quantities of products or services that constitutes total revenues. If the mix changes, overall revenue targets may still be achieved. However, the effects on operating income depend

Influencing Cost Structures to Manage the Risk-Return Tradeoff

Emery Air Freight
www.emeryworld.com

Understanding the distinction between fixed and variable costs and its implications for the risk-return tradeoff is also helpful when marketing products. Consider Mueller-Lehmkuhl, a German company that sells snap-on and tack buttons used on blue jeans and other clothing. Mueller-Lehmkuhl also manufactures and sells the machines that attach the buttons to the clothing. For a long period of time Mueller-Lehmkuhl charged very little for the attaching machine and instead recovered its costs (including those of making the attaching machine) by charging a higher price for buttons. From its customers' standpoint, Mueller-Lehmkuhl's strategy converts the fixed costs of the attaching machine into variable costs of buttons, reducing risk. If volumes decline, customers are not saddled with the fixed costs of the attaching machine. Of course, if volumes increase, customers end up paying more overall than they would have had they purchased the attaching machine and paid a lower price for the buttons. Xerox follows a similar strategy by selling copier machines at low margins in exchange for maintenance and supplies (for example, paper and toner) contracts.

Building up too many fixed costs can be hazardous to a company's health. Because fixed costs, unlike variable costs, do not automatically decrease as volumes decline, companies with too many fixed costs can lose a considerable amount of money during lean times. The managers at Emery Air Freight understand this concept well. They prefer to buy cargo space from existing airlines on an as-needed basis (a variable cost structure) rather than purchase their own airplanes (which would produce a fixed cost). As a result, Emery avoids being stuck with costs when business is slow. To avoid losses when their volumes declined in the 1990's, many prominent companies—including IBM, AT&T, and General Motors—had to reduce their fixed costs by closing plants and downsizing their work forces.

As you can tell by the Emery example, managers' decisions influence the mix of fixed and variable costs in a company 's cost structure. In making these decisions, managers use forecasts of the effect on net income at different volume levels to evaluate the risk-return tradeoffs involved in various cost structures.

Source: Mueller-Lehmkuhl GmbH, Harvard Business School Case Number 9–187–048, and conversations with executives.

---

on how the original proportions of lower or higher contribution margin products have shifted.

Suppose Mary in our computer convention example is now budgeting for the next convention. She plans to sell two software products—Do-All and Superword—and budgets the following:

	Do-All	Superword	Total
Units sold	60	30	90
Revenues, $200 and $130 per unit	$12,000	$ 3,900	$15,900
Variable costs, $120 and $90 per unit	7,200	2,700	9,900
Contribution margin, $80 and $40 per unit	$ 4,800	$ 1,200	6,000
Fixed costs			2,000
Operating income			$ 4,000

What is the breakeven point? Unlike the single product (or service) situation, there is not a unique number of units for a multiple-product situation. This number instead depends on the revenue mix. The following approach can be used when it is assumed that the budgeted revenue mix (two units of Do-All sold for each unit of Superword sold) will not change at different levels of total revenue:

$$\text{Let } S = \text{Number of units of Superword to break even}$$
$$2S = \text{Number of units of Do-All to break even}$$
$$\text{Revenues} - \text{Variable costs} - \text{Fixed costs} = \text{Operating income}$$
$$[\$200(2S) + \$130S] - [\$120(2S) + \$90S] - \$2,000 = 0$$
$$\$530S - \$330S = \$2,000$$
$$\$200S = \$2,000$$
$$S = 10$$
$$2S = 20$$

The breakeven point is 30 units when the revenue mix is 20 units of Do-All and 10 units of Superword. The total contribution margin of $2,000 (Do-All $80 × 20 = $1,600 plus Superword $40 × 10 = $400) equals the fixed costs of $2,000 at this mix.

Alternative revenue mixes (in units) that have a contribution margin of $2,000 and thus result in breakeven operations include the following:

Alternative Revenue Mixes (in units)

	1	2	3	4	5	6
Do-All	25	20	15	10	5	0
Superword	0	10	20	30	40	50
Total	25	30	35	40	45	50

Other things being equal, for any given total quantity of units sold, if the mix shifts toward units with higher contribution margins, operating income will be higher. Thus, if the mix shifts toward Do-All (say, to 70% Do-All from 60% Do-All) with a contribution margin of twice that of Superword, Mary's operating income will increase.

CVP ANALYSIS IN SERVICE AND NONPROFIT ORGANIZATIONS

Thus far, our examination of CVP analysis has focused on merchandising companies seeking to make a profit. CVP can be applied readily to decisions by service and nonprofit organizations. The key to applying CVP analysis to these organizations is measuring their output. Examples of output measures in various service and nonprofit industries follow.

Industry	Measure of Output
Airlines	Passenger-miles
Hotels/motels	Room-nights occupied
Hospitals	Patient-days
Universities	Student course credits

Suppose a social welfare agency has a government budget appropriation (revenue) for 2000 of $900,000. This nonprofit agency's major purpose is to assist handicapped people who are seeking employment. On average, the agency supplements each person's income by $5,000 annually. The agency's fixed costs are $270,000. There are no other costs. The agency manager wants to know how many people could be assisted in 2000. We can use CVP analysis here by assuming zero operating income. Let Q be the number of people to be assisted:

$$\text{Revenue} - \text{Variable costs} - \text{Fixed costs} = \$0$$
$$\$900,000 - \$5,000Q - \$270,000 = \$0$$
$$\$5,000Q = \$900,000 - \$270,000$$
$$Q = \$630,000 \div \$5,000 = 126 \text{ people}$$

Suppose the manager is concerned that the total budget appropriation for 2000 will be reduced by 15% to a new amount of $(1 - 0.15) \times \$900{,}000 = \$765{,}000$. The manager wants to know how many handicapped people will be assisted. Assume the same amount of monetary assistance per person:

$$\$765{,}000 - \$5{,}000Q - \$270{,}000 = \$0$$
$$\$5{,}000Q = \$765{,}000 - \$270{,}000$$
$$Q = \$495{,}000 \div \$5{,}000 = 99 \text{ people}$$

Note the following two characteristics of the CVP relationships in this non-profit situation:

1. The percentage drop in service, $(126 - 99) \div 126$, or 21.4%, is more than the 15% reduction in the budget appropriation. Why? Because the existence of $270,000 in fixed costs means that the percentage drop in service exceeds the percentage drop in budget appropriation.

2. If the relationships were graphed, the budget appropriation (revenue) amount would be a straight horizontal line of $765,000. The manager could adjust operations to stay within the reduced appropriation in one or more of three major ways: (a) reduce the number of people assisted, (b) reduce the variable costs (the assistance per person), or (c) reduce the total fixed costs.

CONTRIBUTION MARGIN AND GROSS MARGIN

OBJECTIVE 8

Distinguish between contribution margin and gross margin

Contribution margin is a key concept in this chapter. We now consider how it is related to the gross margin concept discussed in Chapter 2. First some definitions:

$$\text{Contribution margin} = \text{Revenues} - \begin{array}{l}\text{All costs that vary with respect}\\ \text{to number of output units}\end{array}$$

$$\text{Gross margin} = \text{Revenues} - \text{Cost of goods sold}$$

"All costs that vary" refers to variable costs in each of the business functions of the value chain. Cost of goods sold in the merchandising sector is made up of goods purchased for resale. Cost of goods sold in the manufacturing sector consists entirely of manufacturing costs (including fixed manufacturing costs).

Service sector companies can compute a contribution margin figure but not a **gross margin** figure. Service sector companies do not have a cost of goods sold line item in their income statement.

Gross margin. Revenues minus cost of goods sold.

Merchandising Sector

The two areas of difference between contribution margin and gross margin for companies in the merchandising sector are fixed cost of goods sold (such as a fixed annual payment to a supplier to guarantee an exclusive option to purchase merchandise) and variable non–cost of goods sold items (such as a salesperson's commission that is a percentage of sales dollars). Contribution margin is computed after all variable costs have been deducted, whereas gross margin is computed by deducting only cost of goods sold from revenues. The following example (figures assumed to be in thousands) illustrates this difference:

Contribution Margin Format			Gross Margin Format	
Revenues		$200	Revenues	$200
Variable cost of goods sold	$120		Cost of goods sold ($120 + $5)	125
Other variable costs	43	163	Gross margin	75
Contribution margin		37	Operating costs ($43 + $19)	62
Fixed cost of goods sold	5		Operating income	$ 13
Other fixed costs	19	24		
Operating income		$ 13		

Fixed cost of goods sold for a merchandiser include only fixed costs directly related to the purchase of merchandise. The preceding example is a fixed annual payment to a supplier of merchandise. It would not include fixed costs (such as fixed salaries) of the purchasing department. These costs would be included in other fixed costs in the contribution margin format.

Manufacturing Sector

The two areas of difference between contribution margin and gross margin for companies in the manufacturing sector are fixed manufacturing costs and variable nonmanufacturing costs. The following example (figures assumed to be in thousands) illustrates this difference:

Revenues		$1,000	Revenues		$1,000
Variable manufacturing costs	$250		Cost of goods sold ($250 + $160)		410
Variable nonmanufacturing costs	270	520	Gross margin		590
Contribution margin		480	Nonmanufacturing costs ($270 + $138)		408
Fixed manufacturing costs	160		Operating income		$ 182
Fixed nonmanufacturing costs	138	298			
Operating income		$ 182			

Fixed manufacturing costs are not deducted from revenues when computing contribution margin but are deducted when computing gross margin. Cost of goods sold in a manufacturing company includes all and only manufacturing costs. Variable nonmanufacturing costs are deducted from revenues when computing contribution margins but are not deducted when computing gross margins.

Both the contribution margin and the gross margin can be expressed as totals, as amounts per unit, or as percentages. The contribution margin percentage is the total contribution margin divided by revenues. The **variable-cost percentage** is the total variable costs (with respect to units of output) divided by revenues. The contribution margin percentage in our manufacturing sector example is 48% ($480 ÷ $1,000), while the variable-cost percentage is 52% ($520 ÷ $1,000). The **gross margin percentage** is the gross margin divided by revenues—59% ($590 ÷ $1,000) in our manufacturing sector example.

> **Variable-cost percentage.** Total variable costs (with respect to units of output) divided by revenues.
>
> **Gross margin percentage.** Gross margin divided by revenues.

MULTIPLE COST DRIVERS

OBJECTIVE 9

Adapt CVP analysis to multiple cost driver situations

Throughout this chapter we have assumed that the number of units sold is the only revenue and cost driver. In this section, we relax this important assumption and describe how some aspects of CVP analysis can be adapted to the more general case of multiple cost drivers.

Consider again the Do-All Software example. Suppose that Mary will incur a cost of $10 for preparing documents and invoices associated with the sale of Do-All Software. These documents and invoices will need to be prepared for each customer that buys Do-All Software, that is, the cost driver of document-and-invoice-preparation costs is the number of different customers that buy Do-All Software. Mary's operating income can then be expressed as

$$\text{Operating income} = \text{Revenue} - \left(\text{Costs of each Do-All Software package} \times \text{Number of packages sold} - \text{Costs of preparing each document and invoice} \times \text{Number of documents and invoices} \right) - \text{Fixed costs}$$

Assuming that Mary sells 40 packages to 15 customers, then

$$\text{Operating income} = \$200 \times 40 - \$120 \times 40 - \$10 \times 15 - \$2,000$$
$$= \$8,000 - \$4,800 - \$150 - \$2,000 = \$1,050$$

If, instead, Mary sold 40 packages to 40 customers, then

$$\text{Operating income} = (\$200 \times 40) - (\$120 \times 40) - (\$10 \times 40) - \$2,000$$
$$= \$8,000 - \$4,800 - \$400 - \$2,000 = \$800$$

Note that the number of packages sold is not the only determinant of Mary's operating income. For a given number of packages sold, Mary's operating income will be lower if Mary sells Do-All Software to more customers. Mary's cost structure depends on two cost drivers—the number of packages sold and the number of customers.

Just as in the case of multiple products, there is no unique breakeven point when there are multiple cost drivers. For example, Mary will break even if she sells 26 packages to 8 customers or 27 packages to 16 customers:

$$(\$200 \times 26) - (\$120 \times 26) - (\$10 \times 8) - \$2,000 = \$5,200 - \$3,120 - \$80 - \$2,000 = \$0$$
$$(\$200 \times 27) - (\$120 \times 27) - (\$10 \times 16) - \$2,000 = \$5,400 - \$3,240 - \$160 - \$2,000 = \$0$$

This example illustrates that CVP-type analysis can be adapted to multiple cost driver situations. However, in cases involving multiple cost drivers the various simple formulas described earlier in the chapter can no longer be used.

PROBLEM FOR SELF-STUDY

Wembley Travel is a travel agency specializing in flights between Toronto and London. It books passengers on Canadian Airlines. Canadian Airlines charges passengers $900 per round-trip ticket. Until last month, Canadian Airlines paid Wembley a commission of 10% of the ticket price paid by each passenger. This was Wembley's only source of revenues. Wembley's fixed costs are $14,000 per month (for salaries, rent, etc.), and its variable costs are $20 per ticket purchased for a passenger. This $20 includes a $15 per ticket delivery fee paid to Federal Express. (To keep the analysis simple, we assume each round-trip ticket purchased is delivered in a separate package; thus the $15 delivery fee applies to every ticket.)

Canadian Airlines has just announced a revised payment schedule for travel agents. It will now pay travel agents a 10% commission per ticket up to a maximum of $50. Any ticket costing more than $500 receives only a $50 commission, irrespective of the ticket price.

REQUIRED
1. Under the old 10% commission structure, how many round-trip tickets must Wembley sell each month to (a) break even and (b) earn an operating income of $7,000 per month?
2. How does Canadian's revised payment schedule affect your answers to (a) and (b) in requirement 1?
3. Wembley is approached by DHL Express, who offers to charge $9 per ticket delivered. How would accepting this offer affect your answers to (a) and (b) in requirement 2? (Assume the maximum commission is $50 per ticket.) DHL Express offers next-day service, with reliability comparable to Federal Express.

SOLUTION
1. Wembley receives a 10% commission on each ticket—10% × $900 = $90. Thus:

$$USP = \$90$$
$$UVC = \$20$$
$$UCM = \$90 - \$20 = \$70$$
$$FC = \$14,000 \text{ per month}$$

a. $Q = \dfrac{FC}{UCM} = \dfrac{\$14{,}000}{\$70} = 200$ tickets per month

b. When target operating income (TOI) = \$7,000 per month:

$$QT = \frac{FC + TOI}{UCM}$$

$$= \frac{\$14{,}000 + \$7{,}000}{\$70} = \frac{\$21{,}000}{\$70}$$

$$= 300 \text{ tickets per month}$$

2. Wembley receives only \$50 on the \$900 ticket because it exceeds \$500. Thus:

$$USP = \$50$$
$$UVC = \$20$$
$$UCM = \$50 - \$20 = \$30$$
$$FC = \$14{,}000 \text{ per month}$$

a. $Q = \dfrac{\$14{,}000}{\$30} = 467$ tickets (rounded up)

b. $QT = \dfrac{\$21{,}000}{\$30} = 700$ tickets

The \$50 cap on the commission paid per ticket causes the breakeven point to more than double (from 200 to 467), and the tickets sold to yield \$7,000 per month to more than double (from 300 to 700) also. Not surprisingly, travel agents reacted very negatively to the Canadian Airlines proposal to change commission payments.

3. The DHL Express offer reduces the variable cost per ticket from \$20 to \$14 (reflecting the drop in carrier costs from \$15 to \$9).

$$USP = \$50$$
$$UVC = \$14$$
$$UCM = \$50 - \$14 = \$36$$
$$FC = \$14{,}000 \text{ per month}$$

a. $Q = \dfrac{\$14{,}000}{\$36} = 389$ tickets (rounded up)

b. $QT = \dfrac{\$21{,}000}{\$36} = 584$ tickets (rounded up)

The increase in contribution margin decreases both the breakeven point and the number of tickets required to yield the \$7,000 target operating income.

SUMMARY

The following points are linked to the chapter's learning objectives.

1. Using CVP analysis requires simplifying assumptions, including the assumption that costs are either fixed or variable with respect to the number of output units (units manufactured or units sold) and that total sales and total cost relationships are linear.

2. CVP analysis assists managers in understanding the behaviour of total costs, total revenues, and operating income as changes occur in the output level, selling price, variable costs, or fixed costs.

3. The three methods outlined for computing the breakeven point (the quantity of output where total revenues equal total costs) and target operating income are the equation method, the contribution margin method, and the graph method. Each

Review of Cost-Volume-Profit Relationships
darkwing.uoregon.edu/
~nfargher/sesn2.html

CVP Analysis
management.canberra.edu.au/
lectures/accounting/sem972/
unit4146/Lecture_3B.html

method is merely a restatement of the other. Managers often select the method they find easiest to use in their specific situation.

4. Income taxes can be incorporated into CVP analysis by using target net income rather than target operating income in CVP analysis. The breakeven point is unaffected by the presence of income taxes because no income taxes are paid if there is no operating income.

5. When making decisions, managers use CVP analysis to compare contribution margins and fixed costs of the different alternatives. Sensitivity analysis, a "what-if" technique, can systematically examine the effect on operating income and net income of different levels of fixed costs, variable costs per unit, selling prices, and output units.

6. CVP analysis can highlight to managers the downside risk and upside return of alternatives that differ in their fixed costs and variable costs.

7. When CVP analysis is applied to a multiple-product company, it is assumed that there is a constant sales mix of products as the total quantity of units sold changes.

8. Contribution margin is revenues minus all variable costs (through the value chain), while gross margin is revenues minus cost of goods sold.

9. The basic concepts of CVP analysis can be adapted to multiple cost driver situations, but the simple formulae of the single cost driver case can no longer be used.

APPENDIX: DECISION MODELS AND UNCERTAINTY

Managers make predictions and decisions in a world of uncertainty. This appendix explores the characteristics of uncertainty and describes an approach managers can use to cope with it. We also illustrate the additional insights gained when uncertainty is recognized in CVP analysis using data from the Do-All Software example on p. 63.

Coping with Uncertainty[6]

Role of a Decision Model Uncertainty is the possibility that an actual amount will deviate from an expected amount. For example, Mary Frost might forecast sales at 40 units but actual sales may turn out to be 30 units or 60 units. A **decision model** helps managers deal with uncertainty. It is a formal method for making a choice that often involves both quantitative and qualitative analyses. The quantitative analysis usually has the following characteristics:

Decision model. Formal model for making a choice under uncertainty, frequently involving both quantitative and qualitative analysis.

Choice criterion. Objective that can be quantified in a decision model

Events. Possible occurrences in a decision model.

Probability. Likelihood or chance of occurrence of an event.

Outcomes. Predicted consequences of the various possible combinations of actions and events in a decision model.

1. A **choice criterion,** which is an objective that can be quantified. This objective can take many forms. Most often the choice criterion is expressed as a maximization of income or a minimization of cost. The choice criterion provides a basis for choosing the best alternative action.

2. A set of the alternative actions being considered

3. A set of all the relevant **events** that may occur, where an event is a possible occurrence. This set of events should be mutually exclusive and collectively exhaustive. Events are mutually exclusive if they cannot occur at the same time. Events are collectively exhaustive if, taken together, they make up the entire set of possible occurrences (and no other event can occur). Examples are growth or no growth in industry demand, and increase, decrease, or no change in interest rates. Only one event in a set of mutually exclusive and collectively exhaustive events will actually occur.

4. A set of probabilities, where a **probability** is the likelihood or chance of occurrence of an event

5. A set of possible **outcomes** that measure, in terms of the choice criterion, the predicted consequences of the various possible combinations of actions and events

[6]The presentations here draw (in part) from teaching notes prepared by R. Williamson.

EXHIBIT 3-6
A Decision Model and Its Link to Performance Evaluation

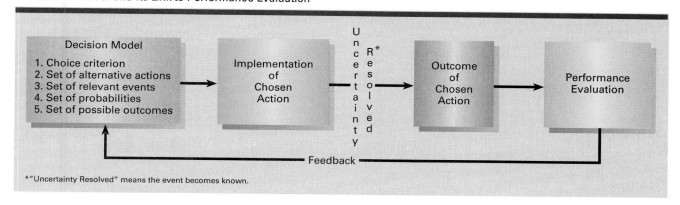

*"Uncertainty Resolved" means the event becomes known.

It is important to distinguish actions from events. Actions are choices made by management—for example, the prices it should charge for the company's products. Events are occurrences that management cannot control—for example, a growing or declining economy. The outcome is the operating income the company makes, which depends both on the action management selects (pricing strategy) and the event that occurs (how the economy performs). Exhibit 3-6 above presents an overview of a decision model, the implementation of the chosen action, its outcome, and subsequent performance evaluation.

Probabilities   Assigning probabilities is a key aspect of the decision model approach to coping with uncertainty. A **probability distribution** describes the likelihood (or probability) of each of the mutually exclusive and collectively exhaustive set of events. The probabilities of these events will add to 1.00, because they are collectively exhaustive. In some cases, there will be much evidence to guide the assignment of probabilities. For example, the probability of obtaining a head in the toss of a fair coin is ½; that of drawing a particular playing card from a standard, well-shuffled deck is 1⁄52. In business, the probability of having a specified percentage of defective units may be assigned with great confidence, on the basis of production experience with thousands of units. In other cases, there will be little evidence supporting estimated probabilities. For example, how many units of a new pharmaceutical product will be sold next year?

The concept of uncertainty can be illustrated by a decision situation facing a book editor. The editor is deciding between publishing a spy novel and publishing a historical novel. Both book proposals require a $200,000 investment at the beginning of the year. (For simplicity here, we ignore the time value of money, which is covered in Chapters 21 and 22.) On the basis of experience, the editor believes that the following probability distribution (assume that the sales life of each book is one year) describes the relative likelihood of cash inflows for the next year:

Proposal A: Spy Novel		Proposal B: Historical Novel	
Probability	Cash Inflows	Probability	Cash Inflows
0.10	$300,000	0.10	$200,000
0.20	350,000	0.25	300,000
0.40	400,000	0.30	400,000
0.20	450,000	0.25	500,000
0.10	500,000	0.10	800,000
1.00		1.00	

Exhibit 3-7 compares the probability distributions graphically.

Expected Value   An **expected value** is a weighted average of the outcomes with the probability of each outcome serving as the weight. Where the outcomes are

Probability distribution. Describes the likelihood (or probability) of each of the mutually exclusive and collectively exhaustive sets of events.

Expected value (expected monetary value). Weighted average of the outcomes of a decision with the probability of each outcome serving as the weight.

COST-VOLUME-PROFIT ANALYSIS | **81**

EXHIBIT 3-7
Decisions under Uncertainty: Comparison of Probability Distributions

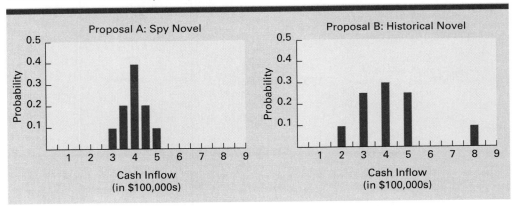

measured in monetary terms, *expected value* is often called **expected monetary value.** The expected monetary value of the cash inflows from the spy novel—denoted $E(a_1)$—is $400,000:

$$E(a_1) = 0.1(\$300,000) + 0.2(\$350,000) + 0.4(\$400,000) + 0.2(\$450,000) + 0.1(\$500,000)$$

$$= \$400,000$$

The expected monetary value of the cash inflows from the historical novel—denoted $E(a_2)$—is $420,000:

$$E(a_2) = 0.1(\$200,000) + 0.25(\$300,000) + 0.3(\$400,000) + 0.25(\$500,000) + 0.1(\$800,000)$$

$$= \$420,000$$

Expected monetary value is widely used as a decision criterion. For a book editor wanting to maximize the expected monetary value, the historical novel is preferable to the spy novel.

To interpret expected value, imagine that the company publishes many historical novels, each with a probability distribution of cash inflows given in proposal B. The expected value of $420,000 is the average cash inflow per novel that the publisher will receive when averaged across all novels. For a specific novel, the cash inflows will be either $200,000, $300,000, $400,000, $500,000, or $800,000. But if the company publishes 100 such novels, it will expect to receive $42 million in total cash inflows, for an average of $420,000 per novel.

Many statisticians and accountants favour presenting the entire probability distribution to the decision maker. Others present information in three categories: optimistic, most likely, and pessimistic. Either presentation reminds the user that uncertainty exists in the decision at hand.

Illustrative Problem

Reconsider Mary and the booth rental alternatives offered by Computer Conventions, Inc. to sell Do-All Software (p. 72):

◆ **Option 1.** $2,000 fixed fee

◆ **Option 2.** $1,400 fixed fee plus 5% of the convention revenues from Do-All sales

◆ **Option 3.** 20% of the convention revenues from Do-All sales (but no fixed fee)

Mary estimates a 0.60 probability that sales will be 40 units and a 0.40 probability that sales will be 70 units. Each Do-All software package will be sold for $200. Mary will purchase the package from a computer software wholesaler at $120 per unit with the privilege of returning all unsold units. Which booth rental alternative should Mary choose?

General Approach to Uncertainty The construction of a decision model consists of five steps that are keyed to the five characteristics described at the beginning of this appendix.[7]

- ◆ **Step 1:** *Identify the choice criterion of the decision maker.* Assume that Mary's choice criterion is to maximize expected net cash inflow at the convention.

- ◆ **Step 2:** *Identify the set of alternative actions under consideration.* The notation for an action is *a*. Mary has three possible actions:

    a_1 = Pay $2,000 fixed fee.

    a_2 = Pay $1,400 fixed fee plus 5% of convention revenues.

    a_3 = Pay 20% of convention revenues (but no fixed fee).

- ◆ **Step 3:** *Identify the set of relevant events that can occur.* Mary's only uncertainty is the number of units of Do-All software that she can sell. Using *x* as the notation for an event:

    x_1 = 40 units

    x_2 = 70 units

- ◆ **Step 4:** *Assign the set of probabilities for the events that can occur.* Mary assesses a 60% chance that she will sell 40 units and a 40% chance that she will sell 70 units. Using $P(x)$ as the notation for the probability of an event, the probabilities are:

    $P(x_1) = 0.60$

    $P(x_2) = 0.40$

- ◆ **Step 5:** *Identify the set of possible outcomes that are dependent on specific actions and events.* The outcomes in this example take the form of six possible net cash flows that are displayed in a decision table in Exhibit 3-8. A **decision table** is a summary of the contemplated actions, events, outcomes, and probabilities of events.

Decision table. Summary of the contemplated actions, events, outcomes, and probabilities of events in a decision.

Mary can now use the information in Exhibit 3-8 to compute the expected net cash inflow of each action as follows:

Pay $2,000 fixed fee: $E(a_1) = 0.60(\$1,200) + 0.40(\$3,600) = \$2,160$

Pay $1,400 fixed fee plus 5% of revenues: $E(a_2) = 0.60(\$1,400) + 0.40(\$3,500) = \$2,240$

Pay 20% of revenues (but no fixed fee): $E(a_3) = 0.60(\$1,600) + 0.40(\$2,800) = \$2,080$

To maximize expected net cash inflows, Mary should select action a_2—that is, contracting to pay Computer Conventions a $1,400 fixed fee plus 5% of convention revenues.

Consider the effect of uncertainty on the preferred action choice. If Mary was certain that she would sell only 40 units of Do-All software, i.e., $P(x_1) = 1$, she would prefer alternative a_3—pay 20% of revenues and no fixed fee. To follow this reasoning, examine Exhibit 3-8. When 40 units are sold, alternative a_3 yields the maximum net cash inflows of $1,600. Because fixed costs are zero, booth rental costs are low when sales are low.

However, if Mary was certain that she would sell 70 units of Do-All software, i.e., $P(x_2) = 1$, she would prefer alternative a_1—pay a $2,000 fixed fee. Exhibit 3-8 indicates that when 70 units are sold, alternative a_1 yields the maximum net cash inflows of $3,600. Rental payments under a_2 and a_3 increase with units sold but are fixed under a_1.

Good Decisions and Good Outcomes Always distinguish between a good decision and a good outcome. One can exist without the other. By definition, uncertainty rules out guaranteeing, after the fact, that the best outcome will always be obtained. It is possible that bad luck will produce unfavourable consequences even when good decisions have been made.

---

[7]For more formal approaches, refer to Eppen, G., F. Gould, and C. Schmidt, *Introductory Management Science*, 4th edition (Prentice Hall, Upper Saddle River, 1994).

EXHIBIT 3-8
Decision Table for Do-All Software

Actions	Probability of Events	
	$x_1 = 40$ units sold $P(x_1) = 0.60$	$x_2 = 70$ units sold $P(x_2) = 0.40$
a_1: Pay \$2,000 fixed fee	\$1,200[l]	\$3,600[m]
a_2: Pay \$1,400 fixed fee plus 5% of convention revenues	\$1,400[n]	\$3,500[p]
a_3: Pay 20% of convention revenues (but no fixed fee)	\$1,600[q]	\$2,800[r]

[l] Net cash flows = (\$200 − \$120)(40) − \$2,000 = \$1,200
[m] Net cash flows = (\$200 − \$120)(70) − \$2,000 = \$3,600
[n] Net cash flows = (\$200 − \$120 − \$10*)(40) − \$1,400 = \$1,400
[p] Net cash flows = (\$200 − \$120 − \$10*)(70) − \$1,400 = \$3,500
[q] Net cash flows = (\$200 − \$120 − \$40**)(40) = \$1,600
[r] Net cash flows = (\$200 − \$120 − \$40**)(70) = \$2,800
* \$10 = 5% of selling price of \$200
**\$40 = 20% of selling price of \$200

Suppose you are offered a one-time-only gamble tossing a fair coin. You will win \$20 if the event is heads, but you will lose \$1 if the event is tails. As a decision maker, you proceed through the logical phases: gathering information, assessing outcomes, and making a choice. You accept the bet. Why? Because the expected value is \$9.50 [0.5(\$20) + 0.5(−\$1)]. The coin is tossed and the event is tails. You lose. From your viewpoint, this was a good decision but a bad outcome.

A decision can be made only on the basis of information available at the time of the decision. Hindsight is flawless, but a bad outcome does not necessarily mean that a bad decision was made. Making a good decision is our best protection against a bad outcome.

▼ TERMS TO LEARN

This chapter contains definitions of the following important terms:

breakeven point (p. 64)
choice criterion (p. 80)
contribution income statement (p. 64)
contribution margin (p. 63)
contribution margin percentage (p. 64)
contribution margin ratio (p. 64)
cost-volume-profit (CVP) (p. 62)
decision model (p. 80)
decision table (p. 83)
degree of operating leverage (p. 72)
events (p. 80)
expected monetary value (p. 81)
expected value (p. 81)
gross margin (p. 76)
gross margin percentage (p. 77)

margin of safety (p. 71)
net income (p. 63)
operating income (p. 63)
operating leverage (p. 72)
outcomes (p. 80)
probability (p. 80)
probability distribution (p. 81)
PV graph (p. 68)
revenue driver (p. 62)
revenue mix (p. 73)
sales mix (p. 73)
sensitivity analysis (p. 71)
uncertainty (p. 72)
variable-cost percentage (p. 77)

▼ ASSIGNMENT MATERIAL

QUESTIONS

Note: To underscore the basic CVP relationships, the assignment material ignores income taxes unless stated otherwise.

3-1 Define cost-volume-profit analysis.

3-2 Describe the assumptions underlying CVP analysis.

3-3 Distinguish between operating income and net income.

3-4 Define *contribution margin, gross margin, contribution margin percentage, variable-cost percentage,* and *margin of safety.*

3-5 Describe three methods that can be used to calculate the breakeven point.

3-6 Why is it more accurate to describe the subject matter of this chapter as CVP analysis rather than as breakeven analysis?

3-7 "CVP is both simple and simplistic. If you want realistic analysis to underpin your decisions, look beyond CVP." Do you agree? Explain.

3-8 How does an increase in the income tax rate affect the breakeven point?

3-9 Describe sensitivity analysis. How has spreadsheet software affected its use?

3-10 Give an example of how a manager can decrease variable costs while increasing fixed costs.

3-11 Give an example of how a manager can increase variable costs while decreasing fixed costs.

3-12 What is operating leverage? How is knowing the degree of operating leverage helpful to managers?

3-13 Give three specific ways units of output are measured in different industries.

3-14 How can a company with multiple products compute its breakeven point?

3-15 "Gross margin is a less useful concept than contribution margin in CVP analysis." Do you agree? Explain.

EXERCISES

3-16 CVP analysis computations. In the following data, fill in the blanks for each of the four independent cases.

Case	Revenues	Variable Costs	Fixed Costs	Total Costs	Operating Income	Contribution Margin Percentage
a	$ —	$500	$ —	$ 800	$1,200	—
b	2,000	—	300	—	200	—
c	1,000	700	—	1,000	—	—
d	1,500	—	300	—	—	40%

3-17 CVP analysis computations. Fill in the blanks for each of the following independent cases.

Case	Selling Price	Variable Costs per Unit	Total Units Sold	Total Contribution Margin	Total Fixed Costs	Operating Income
a	$30	$20	70,000	$ —	$ —	–$15,000
b	25	—	180,000	900,000	800,000	—
c	—	10	150,000	300,000	220,000	—
d	20	14	—	120,000	—	12,000

3-18 CVP analysis, changing revenues and costs. Sunshine Tours is a travel agency specializing in flights between Toronto and Jamaica. It books passengers on Canadian Airlines. Canadian Airlines charges passengers $1,000 per round-trip ticket. Sunshine receives a commission of 8% of the ticket price paid by the passenger. Sunshine's fixed costs are $22,000 per month. Its variable costs are $35 per ticket, including an $18 delivery fee by Emory Express. (Assume each ticket purchased is delivered in a separate package; thus the delivery fee applies to every individual ticket.)

REQUIRED
1. What is the number of tickets Sunshine must sell each month to (a) break even and (b) make a target operating income of $10,000?
2. Assume TNT Express offers to charge Sunshine only $12 per ticket delivered. How would accepting this offer affect your answers to (a) and (b) in requirement 1?

3-19 CVP analysis, changing revenues and costs (continuation of 3-18). Canadian Airlines changes its commission structure to travel agents. Up to a ticket price of $600, the 8% commission applies. For tickets costing $600 or more, there is a fixed commission of $48. Assume Sunshine Tours has fixed costs of $22,000 per month and variable costs of $29 per ticket (including a $12 delivery fee by TNT).

REQUIRED
1. What is the number of Toronto-to-Jamaica round-trip tickets Sunshine must sell each month to (a) break even and (b) make a target operating income of $10,000? Comment on the results.
2. Sunshine tours decides to charge its customers a delivery fee of $5 per ticket. How would this change affect your answers to (a) and (b) in requirement 1? Comment on the results.

3-20 CVP exercises. The Super Donut owns and operates six donut outlets in and around Quebec City. You are given the following corporate budget data for next year:

Revenues	$10,000,000
Fixed costs	1,700,000
Variable costs	8,200,000

Variable costs change with respect to the number of doughnuts sold.

REQUIRED
Compute the budgeted operating income for each of the following deviations from the original budget data. (Consider each case independently.)
1. A 10% increase in contribution margin, holding revenues constant
2. A 10% decrease in contribution margin, holding revenues constant
3. A 5% increase in fixed costs
4. A 5% decrease in fixed costs
5. An 8% increase in units sold
6. An 8% decrease in units sold
7. A 10% increase in fixed costs and 10% increase in units sold
8. A 5% increase in fixed costs and 5% decrease in variable costs

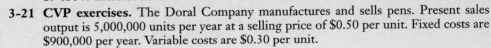 **3-21 CVP exercises.** The Doral Company manufactures and sells pens. Present sales output is 5,000,000 units per year at a selling price of $0.50 per unit. Fixed costs are $900,000 per year. Variable costs are $0.30 per unit.

REQUIRED
(Consider each case separately.)
1. a. What is the present operating income for a year?
   b. What is the present breakeven point in revenues?
Compute the new operating income for each of the following changes:
2. A $0.04 per unit increase in variable costs
3. A 10% increase in fixed costs and a 10% increase in units sold
4. A 20% decrease in fixed costs, a 20% decrease in selling price, a 10% decrease in variable costs per unit, and a 40% increase in units sold
Compute the new breakeven point in units for each of the following changes:
5. A 10% increase in fixed costs
6. A 10% increase in selling price and a $20,000 increase in fixed costs

3-22 CVP, income taxes. The Bratz Company has fixed costs of $300,000 and a variable-cost percentage of 80%. The company earns net income of $84,000 in 2000. The income tax rate is 40%.

REQUIRED
Compute (1) operating income, (2) contribution margin, (3) total revenues, and (4) breakeven revenues.

3-23 CVP, income taxes. The Rapid Meal has two restaurants that are open 24 hours a day. Fixed costs for the two restaurants together total $450,000 per year. Service varies from a cup of coffee to full meals. The average sales cheque for each customer is $8. The average cost of food and other variable costs for each customer is $3.20. The income tax rate is 30%. Target net income is $105,000.

REQUIRED
1. Compute the revenues needed to obtain the target net income.
2. How many sales cheques are needed to earn net income of $105,000? To break even?
3. Compute net income if the number of sales cheques is 150,000.

3-24 CVP, margin of safety. Suppose Lattin Corp's breakeven point is revenues of $1,000,000. Fixed costs are $400,000.

REQUIRED
1. Compute the contribution margin percentage.
2. Compute the selling price if variable costs are $12 per unit.
3. Suppose 80,000 units are sold. Compute the margin of safety.

3-25 Operating leverage. Colour Rugs is holding a 2-week carpet sale at Jerry's Club, a local warehouse store. Colour Rugs plans to sell carpets for $500 each. Colour Rugs will purchase the carpets from a local distributor for $350 each with the privilege of returning any unsold units for a full refund. Jerry's Club has offered Colour Rugs two payment alternatives for the use of space.
◆ Option 1: A fixed payment of $5,000
◆ Option 2: 10% of the total revenues earned during the sale period. Assume Colour Rugs will incur no other costs.

REQUIRED
1. Calculate the breakeven point in units for (a) Option 1 and (b) Option 2.
2. At what level of sales revenue will Colour Rugs earn the same operating income under either option?
3. a. For what range of unit sales will Colour Rugs prefer Option 1?
   b. For what range of unit sales will Colour Rugs prefer Option 2?
4. Calculate the degree of operating leverage at sales of 100 units for the two alternative rental options.
5. Briefly explain and interpret your answer in requirement 4.

3-26 CVP, sensitivity analysis. Hoot Washington is the newly elected charismatic leader of the Western Party. He is the darling of the right-wing media. His "take no prisoners" attitude has left many an opponent on a talk show feeling run over by a Mack truck.

Media Publishers is negotiating to publish *Hoot's Manifesto*, a new book that promises to be an instant bestseller. The fixed costs of producing and marketing the book will be $500,000. The variable costs of producing and marketing will be $4 per book. These costs are before any payments to Hoot. Hoot negotiates an up-front payment of $3 million plus a 15% royalty rate on the net sales price of each book. The net sales price is the listed book store price of $30 minus the margin paid to the book store to sell the book. The normal book store margin of 30% of the listed book store price is expected to apply.

REQUIRED
1. Present a PV graph for Media Publishers.
2. How many copies must Media Publishers sell to (a) break even and (b) earn a target operating profit of $2 million?
3. Examine the sensitivity of the breakeven point to the following changes:
   a. Decreasing the normal bookstore margin to 20% of the listed book store price of $30
   b. Increasing the listed book store price to $40 while keeping the book store margin at 30%.
   Comment on the results.

3-27 CVP, international cost structure differences. Knitwear, Inc. is considering three countries for the sole manufacturing site of its new sweater—Singapore, Thailand, and Canada. All sweaters are to be sold to retail outlets in Canada at $32 per unit. These retail outlets add their own markup when selling to final customers. The three countries differ in their fixed costs and variable costs per sweater.

	Annual Fixed Costs	Variable Manufacturing Costs per Sweater	Variable Marketing and Distribution Costs per Sweater
Singapore	$ 6.5 million	$ 8.00	$11.00
Thailand	4.5 million	5.50	11.50
Canada	12.0 million	13.00	9.00

REQUIRED
1. Compute the breakeven point of Knitwear, Inc. in both (a) units sold and (b) revenues for each of the three countries considered for manufacturing the sweaters.

2. If Knitwear, Inc. sells 800,000 sweaters in 2000, what is the budgeted operating income for each of the three countries considered for manufacturing the sweaters? Comment on the results.

3-28 Revenue mix, new and upgrade customers. Zapo 1-2-3 is a top-selling spreadsheet product. Zapo is about to release Version 5.0. It groups its customers into two groups—new customers and upgrade customers (those who previously purchased Zapo 1-2-3 Version 4.0 or earlier). Although the same physical product is provided to each customer group, sizable differences exist in their selling prices and variable marketing costs:

	New Customers		Upgrade Customers	
Selling price		$210		$120
Variable cost:				
Manufacturing	$25		$25	
Marketing	65	90	15	40

The fixed costs of Zapo 5.0 are $14,000,000.

The planned revenue mix in units is 60% new customers and 40% upgrade customers.

REQUIRED
1. What is the Zapo 1-2-3 Version 5.0 breakeven point in units, assuming that the planned 60/40 mix is maintained?
2. If the mix is maintained, what is the operating income when 200,000 units are sold?
3. Show how the breakeven point in units changes with the following customer mixes:
   a. New 50%/upgrade 50%
   b. New 90%/upgrade 10%
Comment on the results.

3-29 Athletic scholarships, CVP analysis. West University has an annual budget of $5,000,000 for athletic scholarships. Students who receive athletic scholarships do not have to pay tuition, which equals $20,000 per year. Fixed costs of the athletic scholarship program are $1,000,000.

REQUIRED
1. How many athletic scholarships can West University offer each year?
2. Suppose the total budget for the following year is reduced by 20%. Fixed costs are to remain the same. Calculate the number of athletic scholarships that West can offer in the following year.
3. As in requirement 2, assume a budget reduction of 20%. Fixed costs are to remain the same. If West wanted to offer the same number of athletic scholarships as it did in requirement 1, how much reduction in tuition would it be able to offer to each student who receives a scholarship?

3-30 Gross margin and contribution margin. (R. Lambert, adapted) Operating income for Foreman Fork Inc. for the year 2000 on production and sales of 200,000 units was as follows:

Sales	$2,600,000
Cost of goods sold	1,600,000
Gross margin	1,000,000
Marketing and distribution costs	1,150,000
Operating income (loss)	$ (150,000)

Foreman's fixed manufacturing costs were $500,000, and variable marketing and distribution costs were $5 per unit.

REQUIRED
1. Calculate Foreman's variable manufacturing costs per unit in 2000.
2. Calculate Foreman's fixed marketing and distribution costs in 2000.
3. Because Foreman's gross margin per unit is $5 ($1,000,000 ÷ 200,000 units), Sam Hogan, Foreman's president, believes that if Foreman had produced and sold 230,000 units, it would have covered the $1,150,000 of marketing and distribution costs ($1,150,000 ÷ $5 = 230,000) and enabled Foreman to break even for the year. Calculate Foreman's operating income if production and sales equal 230,000 units. Explain briefly why Sam Hogan is wrong.
4. Calculate the breakeven point for the year 2000 in units and dollars.

3-31 CVP Analysis, multiple cost drivers. Susan Wong is a distributor of brass picture frames. During 1999, she plans to purchase frames for $30 each and sell them for $45 each. Susan's fixed costs for 1999 are expected to be $240,000. Susan's only other costs will be variable costs of $60 per shipment for preparing the invoice and delivery documents, organizing the delivery, and following up for collecting cash. The $60 cost will be incurred each time Susan ships an order of picture frames, regardless of the number of picture frames in the order.

REQUIRED

1. Suppose Susan sells 40,000 picture frames in 1,000 shipments in 1999. Calculate Susan's 1999 operating income.
2. Suppose Susan sells 40,000 picture frames in 800 shipments in 1999. Calculate Susan's 1999 operating income.
3. Suppose Susan anticipates making 500 shipments in 1999. How many picture frames must Susan sell to break even in 1999.
4. Calculate another breakeven point for 1999, different from the one described in requirement 3. Explain briefly why Susan has multiple breakeven points.

3-32 Appendix, uncertainty, CVP. Angela King is the Las Vegas promoter for Mike Foreman. King is promoting a new world championship fight for Foreman. The key area of uncertainty is the size of the cable pay-per-view TV market. King will pay Foreman a fixed fee of $2 million and 25% of net cable pay-per-view revenue. Every cable TV home receiving the event pays $29.95, of which King receives $16. King pays Foreman 25% of the $16.

King estimates the following probability distribution for homes purchasing the pay-per-view event:

Demand	Probability
100,000	0.05
200,000	0.10
300,000	0.30
400,000	0.35
500,000	0.15
1,000,000	0.05

REQUIRED

1. What is the expected value of the payment King will make to Foreman?
2. Assume the only uncertainty is over cable TV demand for the fight. King wants to know the breakeven point given her own fixed costs of $1 million and her own variable costs of $2 per home. (Also include King's payments to Foreman in your answer.)

PROBLEMS

3-33 CVP, executive teaching compensation. Brian Smith is an internationally known Canadian professor specializing in consumer marketing. In 1997, Smith and the United Kingdom Business School (UKBS) agreed to conduct a one-day seminar at UKBS for marketing executives. Each executive would pay £260 to attend. The non-speaker-related fixed costs for UKBS conducting the seminar would be:

Advertising in magazines	£4,000
Mailing of brochures	3,000
Administrative labour at UKBS	2,000
Charge for UKBS lecture auditorium	1,000

The variable costs to UKBS for each participant attending the seminar would be:

Meals and drinks	£25
Binders and photocopying	35

The dean at UKBS initially offered Smith its regular compensation package of (a) business class airfare and accommodation (£3,000 maximum) and (b) a £2,000 lecture fee. Smith views the £2,000 lecture fee as providing him no upside potential (that is, no sharing in the potential additional operating income that arises if the seminar is highly attended). He suggests instead that he receive 50% of the operating income to UKBS (if positive) from the one-day seminar and no other payments.

The dean of UKBS quickly agrees to Smith's proposal after confirming that Smith is willing to pay his own airfare and accommodation and deliver the seminar irrespective of the number of executives signed up to attend.

REQUIRED

1. What is UKBS's breakeven point (in number of executives attending) if:
   a. Smith accepts the regular compensation package of £3,000 expenses and a £2,000 lecture fee.
   b. Smith receives 50% of the operating income to UKBS (if positive) from the one-day seminar and no other payments.
   Comment on the results for (a) and (b).
2. Smith gave the one-day seminar at UKBS in 1997 (60 attended), 1998 (90 attended), and 1999 (180 attended). How much was Smith paid by UKBS for the one-day seminar under the 50% of UKBS's operating income compensation plan in (a) 1997, (b) 1998, and (c) 1999? (Assume that the £260 charge per executive attending and UKBS's fixed and variable costs are the same each year.)
3. After the 1999 seminar, the dean at UKBS suggested to Smith that the 50%–50% profit sharing plan was resulting in Smith getting excessive compensation in 1999 and that a more equitable arrangement to UKBS be used in 2000. How should Smith respond to this suggestion?

3-34 CVP, movie production. Royal Rumble Productions has just finished production of *Feature Creatures*, the latest action film directed by Tony Savage and starring Ralph Michaels and Sally Martel. The total production cost to Royal Rumble was $5 million. All the production personnel and actors on *Feature Creatures* received a fixed salary (included in the $5 million) and will have no "residual" (equity interest) in the revenues or operating income from the movie. Media Productions will handle the marketing of *Feature Creatures*. Media agrees to invest a minimum $3 million of its own money in marketing the movie and will be paid 20% of the revenues Royal Rumble itself receives from the box office receipts. Royal Rumble receives 62.5% of the total box office receipts (out of which comes the 20% payment to Media Productions).

REQUIRED

1. What is the breakeven point to Royal Rumble for *Feature Creatures* expressed in terms of (a) revenues received by Royal Rumble and (b) total box office receipts?
2. Assume that, in its first year of release, the box office receipts for *Feature Creatures* total $300 million. What is the operating income to Royal Rumble from the movie in its first year?

3-35 CVP, cost structure differences, movie production (continuation of 3-34). Royal Rumble is negotiating for *Feature Creatures 2*, a sequel to its mega-blockbuster *Feature Creatures*. This negotiation is proving more difficult than for the original movie. The budgeted production cost (excluding payments to the director Savage and the stars Michaels and Martel) for *Feature Creatures 2* is $21 million. The agent negotiating for Savage, Michaels, and Martel proposes either of two contracts:

◆ **Contract A.** Fixed salary component of $15 million for Savage, Michaels, and Martel (combined) with no residual interest in the revenues from *Feature Creatures 2*.

◆ **Contract B.** Fixed salary component of $3 million for Savage, Micheals, and Martel (combined) plus a residual of 15% of the revenues Royal Rumble receives from *Feature Creatures 2*.

Media Productions will market *Feature Creatures 2*. It agrees to invest a minimum of $10 million of its own money. Because of its major role in the success of *Feature Creatures*, Media Productions will now be paid 25% of the revenues Royal Rumble receives from the total box office receipts. Royal Rumble receives 62.5% of the total box office receipts (out of which comes the 25% payment to Media Productions).

REQUIRED

1. What is the breakeven point for Royal Rumble expressed in terms of (a) Revenues received by that company and (b) total box office receipts for *Feature Creatures 2* for contracts A and B? Explain the difference between the breakeven points for contracts A and B.
2. Assume *Feature Creatures 2* achieves the same $300 million in box office revenues as *Feature Creatures*. What is the operating income to Royal Rumble from *Feature Creatures 2* if it accepts contract B? Comment on the difference in operating income between the two films.

3-36 CVP, shoe stores. The Walk Rite Shoe Company operates a chain of shoe stores. The stores sell ten different styles of inexpensive men's shoes with identical unit costs and selling prices. A unit is defined as a pair of shoes. Each store has a store manager who is paid a fixed salary. Individual salespeople receive a fixed salary and a sales commission. Walk Rite is trying to determine the desirability of opening another store, which is expected to have the following revenue and cost relationships:

Unit variable costs per pair:	
Selling price	$30.00
Cost of shoes	$19.50
Sales commissions	1.50
Total variable costs	$21.00

Annual fixed costs:	
Rent	$ 60,000
Salaries	200,000
Advertising	80,000
Other fixed costs	20,000
Total fixed costs	$360,000

REQUIRED

(Consider each question independently.)
1. What is the annual breakeven point in (a) units sold and (b) revenues?
2. If 35,000 units are sold, what will be the store's operating income (loss)?
3. If sales commissions were discontinued for individual salespeople in favour of an $81,000 increase in fixed salaries, what would be the annual breakeven point in (a) units sold and (b) revenues?
4. Refer to the original data. If the store manager were paid $0.30 per unit sold in addition to his current fixed salary, what would be the annual breakeven point in (a) units sold and (b) revenues?
5. Refer to the original data. If the store manager were paid $0.30 per unit commission on each unit sold in excess of the breakeven point, what would be the store's operating income if 50,000 units were sold? (This $0.30 is in addition to both the commission paid to the sales staff and the store manager's fixed salary.)

3-37 CVP, shoe stores. Refer to requirement 3 of 3-36.

REQUIRED
1. Calculate the number of units sold where the operating income under (a) a fixed salary plan and (b) a lower fixed salary and commission plan (for salespeople only) would be equal. Above that number of units sold, one plan would be more profitable than the other; below that number of units sold, the reverse would occur.
2. Compute the operating income or loss under each plan in requirement 1 at sales levels of (a) 50,000 units and (b) 60,000 units.
3. Suppose the target operating income is $168,000. How many units must be sold to reach the target under (a) the fixed salary plan and (b) the lower fixed salary and commission plan?

3-38 Sensitivity and inflation (continuation of 3-37). As president of Walk Rite, you are concerned that inflation may squeeze your profitability. Specifically, you feel committed to the $30 selling price and fear that diluting the quality of the shoes in the face of rising costs would be an unwise marketing move. You expect the cost of shoes to rise by 10% during the coming year. You are tempted to avoid the cost increase by placing a noncancellable order with a large supplier that would provide 50,000 units of the specified quality for each store at $19.50 per unit. (To simplify this analysis, assume that all stores will face identical demands.) These shoes could be acquired and paid for as delivered throughout the year. However, all shoes must be delivered to the stores by the end of the year.

As a shrewd merchandiser, you foresee some risks. If sales were less than 50,000 units, you feel that markdowns of the unsold merchandise would be necessary to sell the goods. You predict that the average selling price of the leftover units would be $18. The regular commission of 5% of revenues would be paid to salespeople.

REQUIRED
1. Suppose that actual sales at $30 for the year are 48,000 units and that you contracted for 50,000 units. What is the operating income for the store?

2. If you had perfect forecasting ability, you would have contracted for 48,000 units rather than 50,000 units. What would the operating income have been if you had ordered 48,000 units?

3. Given actual sales of 48,000 units, by how much would the average cost per unit have had to rise before you would have been indifferent between having the contract for 50,000 units and not having the contract?

3-39 CVP analysis, income taxes, sensitivity. (CMA, adapted) Almo Company manufactures and sells adjustable canopies that attach to motor homes and trailers. For its year 2000 business plan, Almo estimated the following:

Selling price	$400
Variable cost per canopy	$200
Annual fixed costs	$100,000
Net (after-tax) income	$240,000
Tax rate	40%

The May financial statements reported that sales were not meeting expectations. For the first five months of the year, only 350 units had been sold at the established price, with variable costs as planned, and it was clear that the 2000 after-tax profit projection would not be reached unless some action were taken. A management committee presented the following mutually exclusive alternatives to the president.

1. Reduce the selling price by $40. The sales organization forecasts that, with the significantly reduced selling price, 2,700 units can be sold during the remainder of the year. Total fixed and variable unit costs will stay as budgeted.

2. Lower variable costs per unit by $10 through the use of less expensive direct materials and slightly modified manufacturing techniques. The selling price will also be reduced by $30, and sales of 2,200 units for the remainder of the year are forecast.

3. Cut fixed costs by $10,000 and lower the selling price by 5%. Variable costs per unit will be unchanged. Sales of 2,000 units are expected for the remainder of the year.

REQUIRED

1. If no changes are made to the selling price or cost structure, determine the number of units that Almo Company must sell (a) in order to break even, (b) to achieve its net income objective.

2. Determine which alternative Almo should select to achieve its net income objective. Show all calculations.

3-40 Choosing between compensation plans, operating leverage. (CMA, adapted) Marston Corporation manufactures pharmaceutical products that are sold through a network of sales agents. The agents are paid a commission of 18% of sales. The income statement for the year ending December 31, 2000, is as follows:

Marston Corporation
Income Statement for the Year Ending December 31, 2000

Sales		$26,000,000
Cost of goods sold		
Variable	$11,700,000	
Fixed	2,870,000	14,570,000
Gross margin		11,430,000
Selling and marketing expenses		
Commissions	$ 4,680,000	
Fixed costs	3,420,000	8,100,000
Operating income		$ 3,330,000

Marston is considering hiring its own sales staff to replace the network of agents. Marston will pay its sales people a commission of 10% and incur fixed costs of $2,080,000.

REQUIRED

1. Calculate Marston Corporation's breakeven point in sales dollars for the year 2000.

2. Calculate Marston Corporation's breakeven point in sales dollars for the year 2000 if the company has hired its own sales force in 2000 to replace the network of agents.

3. Calculate the degree of operating leverage at sales of $26,000,000 if (a) Marston uses sales agents and (b) Marston employs its own staff. Describe the advantages and disadvantages of each alternative.

4. If Marston increases the commission paid to its sales staff to 15%, keeping all other costs the same, how much revenue (in dollars) would Marston have to generate to earn the same operating income it did in 2000?

3-41 Revenue mix, three products. The Ronowski Company has three product lines of belts, A, B, and C, with contribution margins of $3, $2, and $1 respectively. The president foresees sales of 200,000 units in the coming period, consisting of 20,000 units of A, 100,000 units of B, and 80,000 units of C. The company's fixed costs for the period are $255,000.

REQUIRED

1. What is the company breakeven point in units, assuming that the given revenue mix is maintained?

2. If the mix is maintained, what is the total contribution margin when 200,000 units are sold? What is the operating income?

3. What would operating income become if 20,000 units of A, 80,000 units of B, and 100,000 units of C were sold? What is the new breakeven point in units if these relationships persist in the next period?

3-42 Multi-product breakeven, decision making. Evenkeel Corporation manufactures and sells one product—an infant car seat called Evenflo at a price of $50 per car seat. Variable costs equal $20 per car seat. Fixed costs are $495,000. Evenkeel manufactures Evenflo only after it gets firm orders from its customers. In 2000, it sold 30,000 units of Evenflo. One of Evenkeel's customers, Plaston Corporation, has asked if in 2001 Evenkeel will manufacture a different style of car seat called Ridex. Plaston will pay $25 for each unit of Ridex. The variable costs for Ridex are estimated to be $15 per seat. Fortunately, Evenkeel has enough capacity to manufacture all the units of Evenflo it can sell and the units of Ridex that Plaston wants, and thus will incur no additional fixed costs. Evenkeel estimates it will sell 30,000 units of Evenflo and 20,000 units of Ridex in 2001.

As Andy Minton, the President of Evenkeel, checked the impact of accepting Plaston's offer on the breakeven sales revenues for 2001, he was surprised to find that the dollar sales revenues required to break even using the sales mix for 2001 appeared to increase. He was not sure that his numbers were correct, but if they were, Andy felt inclined to reject Plaston's offer. In any event, he thought it best to seek your advice.

REQUIRED

1. Calculate the breakeven point in units and sales dollars for 2000.

2. Calculate the breakeven point in units and sales dollars for 2001 at the expected sales mix.

3. Explain why the breakeven points in sales dollars calculated in requirements 1 and 2 are different.

4. What would you advise Andy Minton to do? Provide Andy with the support underlying your reasoning.

3-43 Revenue mix, two products. The Goldman Company retails two products, a standard and a deluxe version of a luggage carrier. The budgeted income statement is as follows:

	Standard Carrier	Deluxe Carrier	Total
Units sold	150,000	50,000	200,000
Revenues @ $20 and $30 per unit	$3,000,000	$1,500,000	$4,500,000
Variable costs @ $14 and $18 per unit	2,100,000	900,000	3,000,000
Contribution margins @ $6 and $12 per unit	$ 900,000	$ 600,000	1,500,000
Fixed costs			1,200,000
Operating income			$ 300,000

REQUIRED

1. Compute the breakeven point in units, assuming that the planned revenue mix is maintained.

2. Compute the breakeven point in units (a) if only standard carriers are sold and (b) if only deluxe carriers are sold.

3. Suppose 200,000 units are sold, but only 20,000 are deluxe. Compute the operating income. Compute the breakeven point if these relationships persist in the

next period. Compare your answers with the original plans and the answer in requirement 1. What is the major lesson of this problem?

3-44 CVP analysis, decision making. (M. Rajan, adapted) Tocchet Company manufactures CB1, a citizens' band radio that is sold mainly to truck drivers. The company's plant in Camden has an annual capacity of 50,000 units. Tocchet currently sells 40,000 units at a selling price of $105. It has the following cost structure:

Variable manufacturing costs per unit	$45
Fixed manufacturing costs	$800,000
Variable marketing and distribution costs per unit	$10
Fixed marketing and distribution costs	$600,000

REQUIRED

(Consider each question separately.)
1. Calculate the breakeven volume in units and in dollars.
2. The marketing department indicates that decreasing the selling price to $99 would stimulate sales to 50,000 units. This strategy will require Tocchet to increase its fixed costs, although variable costs per unit will remain the same as before. What is the *maximum* increase in fixed costs for which Tocchet will find it worthwhile to reduce the selling price?
3. The manufacturing department proposes changes in the manufacturing process to add new features to the CB1 product. These changes will increase fixed manufacturing costs by $100,000 and variable manufacturing costs per unit by $2. As its current sales quantity of 40,000 units, what is the *minimum* selling price above which Tocchet will find it worthwhile to add these new features?

3-45 CVP, nonprofit event planning. The American-Canadian Chamber of Commerce is planning its July 4 gala ball. There are two possible plans:
a. Toronto Country Golf Club, which has a fixed rental cost of $2,000 plus a charge of $80 per person for its own catering of meals and serving of drinks and hors d'oeuvres.
b. Toronto Town Hall, which has a fixed rental cost of $6,600. The Chamber of Commerce can hire a caterer for meals and waiters and waitresses to serve drinks and hors d'oeuvres at $60 per person.

The Chamber of Commerce budgets $3,500 in costs for administration and marketing. The band will cost a fixed amount of $2,500. Tickets to this prestige event will be $120 per person. All the drinks served and the prizes given away at the ball will be donated by corporate sponsors.

REQUIRED
1. Compute the breakeven point for each plan in terms of tickets sold.
2. For each plan compute the operating income of the ball (a) if 150 people attend and (b) if 300 people attend. Comment on your results.
3. At what level of tickets sold will the two plans have the same operating income?

3-46 Nonprofit institution. The City of Edmonton, Alberta makes a $400,000 lump sum budget appropriation to an agency to conduct a counselling program for drug addicts for a year. All of the appropriation is to be spent. The variable costs for drug prescriptions average $400 per patient per year. Fixed costs are $150,000.

REQUIRED
1. Compute the number of patients that could be served in a year.
2. Suppose the total budget for the following year is reduced by 10%. Fixed costs are to remain the same. The same level of service to each patient will be maintained. Compute the number of patients that could be served in a year.
3. As in requirement 2, assume a budget reduction of 10%. Fixed costs are to remain the same. The drug counsellor has discretion as to how much in drug prescriptions to give to each patient. She does not want to reduce the number of patients served. On the average, what is the cost of drugs that can be given to each patient? Compute the percentage decline in the annual average cost of drugs per patient.

3-47 CVP, income taxes. (CMA) R. A. Ro and Company, a manufacturer of quality handmade walnut bowls, has experienced a steady growth in sales for the past five years. However, increased competition has led Mr. Ro, the president, to believe that an aggressive marketing campaign will be necessary next year to maintain the company's present growth.

To prepare for next year's marketing campaign, the company's controller has prepared and presented Mr. Ro with the following data for the current year, 2000:

Variable costs (per bowl):

Direct manufacturing labour	$ 8.00
Direct materials	3.25
Variable overhead (manufacturing, marketing distribution, customer service, and administration)	2.50
Total variable costs	$13.75

Fixed costs:

Manufacturing	$ 25,000
Marketing, distribution, and customer service	40,000
Administrative	70,000
Total fixed costs	$135,000
Selling price per bowl	$ 25.00
Expected revenues, 2000 (20,000 units)	$500,000
Income tax rate	40%

REQUIRED

1. What is the projected net income for 2000?
2. What is the breakeven point in units for 2000?
3. Mr. Ro has set the revenue target for 2001 at a level of $550,000 (or 22,000 bowls). He believes an additional marketing cost of $11,250 for advertising in 2001, with all other costs remaining constant, will be necessary to attain the revenue target. What will be the net income for 2001 if the additional $11,250 is spent and the revenue target is met?
4. What will be the breakeven point in revenues for 2001 if the additional $11,250 is spent for advertising?
5. If the additional $11,250 is spent for advertising in 2001, what is the required 2001 revenue for 2001's net income to equal 2000's net income?
6. At a sales level of 22,000 units, what maximum amount can be spent on advertising if a 2001 net income of $60,000 is desired?

3-48 Review of Chapters 2 and 3. For each of the following independent cases, find the unknowns designated by the capital letters.

	Case 1	Case 2
Direct materials used	$ H	$ 40,000
Direct manufacturing labour	30,000	15,000
Variable marketing, distribution, customer service, and administrative costs	K	T
Fixed manufacturing overhead	I	20,000
Fixed marketing, distribution, customer service, and administrative costs	J	10,000
Gross margin	25,000	20,000
Finished goods inventory, January 1, 2000	0	5,000
Finished goods inventory, December 31, 2000	0	5,000
Contribution margin (dollars)	30,000	V
Revenues	100,000	100,000
Direct materials inventory, January 1, 2000	12,000	20,000
Direct materials inventory, December 31, 2000	5,000	W
Variable manufacturing overhead	5,000	X
Work in process, January 1, 2000	0	9,000
Work in process, December 31, 2000	0	9,000
Purchases of direct materials	15,000	50,000
Breakeven point (in dollars)	66,667	Y
Cost of goods manufactured	G	U
Operating income (loss)	L	(5,000)

3-49 Appendix, CVP under uncertainty. (J. Patell) In your new position as supervisor of product introduction, you have to decide on a pricing strategy for a talking doll specialty product with the following cost structure:

Variable costs per unit	$ 50
Fixed costs	$200,000

The dolls are manufactured upon receipt of orders, so the inventory levels are insignificant. Your market research assistant is very enthusiastic about probability models and has presented the results of his price analysis in the following form:

a. If you set the selling price at $100 per unit, the probability distribution of revenues is uniform between $300,000 and $600,000. Under this distribution, there is a 0.50 probability of equalling or exceeding revenues of $450,000.

b. If you lower the selling price to $70 per unit, the distribution remains uniform, but it shifts up to the $600,000–$900,000 range. Under this distribution, there is a 0.50 probability of equalling or exceeding revenues of $750,000.

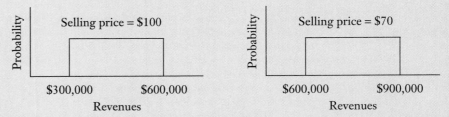

REQUIRED

1. This is your first big contract and, above all, you want to show an operating income. You decide to select the strategy that maximizes the probability of breaking even or earning a positive operating income.
   a. What is the probability of at least breaking even with a selling price of $100 per unit?
   b. What is the probability of at least breaking even with a selling price of $70 per unit?

2. Your assistant suggests that maximum expected operating income might be a better objective to pursue. Which pricing strategy would result in the higher expected operating income? (Use the expected revenues under each pricing strategy when making expected operating income computations.)

3-50 Appendix, CVP under uncertainty. (R. Jaedicke and A. Robichek, adapted) The Jaro Company is considering two new colours for their umbrella products—emerald green and shocking pink. Either can be produced using present facilities. Each product requires an increase in annual fixed costs of $400,000. The products have the same selling price ($10) and the same variable costs per unit ($8).

Management, after studying past experience with similar products, has prepared the following probability distribution:

| | **Probability for:** | |
Event (Units Demanded)	Emerald Green Umbrella	Shocking Pink Umbrella
50,000	0.0	0.1
100,000	0.1	0.1
200,000	0.2	0.1
300,000	0.4	0.2
400,000	0.2	0.4
500,000	0.1	0.1
	1.0	1.0

REQUIRED

1. What is the breakeven point for each product?
2. Which product should be chosen, assuming that the objective is to maximize expected operating income? Why? Show your computations.
3. Suppose management is absolutely certain that 300,000 units of shocking pink will be sold, but it still faces the same uncertainty about the demand for emerald green as outlined in the problem. Which product should be chosen? Why? What benefits are available to management from having the complete probability distribution instead of just an expected value?

3-51 Ethics, CVP, cost analysis. Bob Allen is the controller of the Body Products Division of World Wide Drugs (WWD). It is located in Winnipeg, which is also the headquarters of WWD. Allen is helping develop a proposal for a new product to be called Vital Hair. This product is a cream to be rubbed on the scalp to restore hair growth. Cheryl Kelly, president of the division, and Allen are scheduled to make a presentation to the WWD executive committee on the expected profitability of Vital Hair. The fixed costs associated with the development, production, and marketing of Vital Hair are $20,000,000. Each customer will pay a doctor $80 per monthly treatment, of which $55 is paid to WWD. Allen estimates WWD's variable costs per treatment to be $22. Included in this $22 is $8 for potential product litigation costs. Kelly is livid at Allen for including the $8 estimate. She argues that it is imperative to get the R&D funds approved (and quickly) and that any number that increases the breakeven point reduces the likelihood of the Vital Hair project being approved. She notes that WWD has had few successful lawsuits against it, in contrast to some recent "horrendous" experiences of competitors with breast implant products. Moreover, she is furious that Allen put the $8 amount in writing. "How do we know there will be any litigation problem?" She suggests Allen redo the report excluding the $8 litigation risk cost estimate. "Put it on the chalkboard in the executive committee room, if you insist, but don't put it in the report sent to the committee prior to the meeting. You can personally raise the issue at the executive committee meeting and have a full and frank discussion."

Allen takes Kelly's "advice." He reports a variable cost of $14 per treatment in the proposal. While he feels uneasy about this, he is comforted by the fact that he will flag the $8 amount to the executive committee in his forthcoming oral presentation.

One month later, Kelly walks into Allen's office. She is in a buoyant mood and announces she has just come back from an executive committee meeting that approved the Vital Hair proposal. Allen asks why he was not invited to the meeting. Kelly says the meeting was held in Toronto, and she decided to save the division money by going alone. She then says to Allen that it "was now time to get behind the new venture and help make it the success the committee and her team members believe it will be."

REQUIRED

1. What is the breakeven point (in units of monthly treatments) when WWD's variable costs (a) include the $8 estimate and (b) exclude the $8 estimate for potential product litigation costs?
2. Should Allen have excluded the $8 estimate in his report to the executive committee of WWD? Explain your answer.
3. What should Allen do in response to Kelly's decision to make the Vital Hair presentation on her own?

3-52 Ethics, CVP analysis. Allen Corporation produces a molded plastic casing LX201 for desktop computers. Summary data from its year 2000 income statement are as follows:

Revenues	$5,000,000
Variable costs	3,000,000
Fixed costs	2,160,000
Operating income	$ (160,000)

Jane Woodall, Allen's president, is very concerned about Allen's poor profitability. She asks Max Lemond, production manager, and Lester Bush, controller, to see if there are ways to reduce costs.

After two weeks, Max returns with a proposal to reduce variable costs to 52% of revenues by reducing the expenses Allen currently incurs for safe disposal of wasted plastic. Lester is concerned that this would expose the company to potential environmental liabilities. He tells Max, "We would need to estimate some of these potential future costs and include it in our analysis." "You can't do that," Max replied. "We are not violating any laws. There is some possibility that we may have to incur costs in the future, but if we bring it up now this proposal will not go through because our senior management always assumes these costs to be larger than they are. The market is very tough and we are in danger of shutting down the company. We don't want all our colleagues to lose their jobs. The only reason our competitors are making money is because they are doing exactly what I am proposing."

REQUIRED

1. Calculate Allen's breakeven revenues for the year 2000.
2. Calculate Allen's breakeven revenues if variable costs are 52% of revenues.
3. Calculate Allen's operating income in 2000 if variable costs had been 52% of sales.
4. Given Max Lemond's comments, what should Lester Bush do?

COLLABORATIVE LEARNING PROBLEMS

3-53 Deciding where to produce. (CMA, adapted) The PTO Division of the Galva Manufacturing Company produces the same power take-off units for the farm equipment business in two plants, a newly renovated, automated plant in Peoria, and an older, less automated plant in Moline. The PTO Division expects to produce and sell 192,000 power take-off units during the coming year. The following data are available for the two plants:

	Peoria	Moline
Selling price		$150.00		$150.00
Variable manufacturing cost per unit	$72.00		$88.00	
Fixed manufacturing cost per unit	30.00		15.00	
Sales commission (5% of sales)	7.50		7.50	
Variable marketing and distribution cost per unit	6.50		6.50	
Fixed marketing and distribution cost per unit	19.00		14.50	
Total cost per unit		135.00		131.50
Operating income per unit		$ 15.00		$ 18.50
Production rate per day		400 units		320 units

All unit fixed costs are calculated based on a normal year of 240 working days. When the number of working days exceeds 240, variable manufacturing costs increase by $3.00 per unit in Peoria and $8.00 per unit in Moline. Capacity for each plant is 300 working days.

Wishing to maximize the higher unit profit at Moline, PTO's production manager has decided to manufacture 96,000 units at each plant. This production plan results in Moline operating at capacity (320 units per day x 300 days) and Peoria operating at its normal volume (400 units per day x 240 days). Galva's corporate controller is not happy with this plan as he does not believe it represents optimal usage of PTO's plants.

INSTRUCTIONS
Form groups of two students to complete the following requirements.

REQUIRED
1. Determine the breakeven point for the Peoria and Moline plants in units.
2. Calculate the operating income that would result from the division production manager's plan to produce 96,000 units at each plant.
3. Determine how the production of the 192,000 units should be allocated between Peoria and Moline to maximize operating income for the PTO division. What is the maximum operating income that the PTO division can earn? Show all calculations.

3-54 CVP, theatre planning. *The New York Herald* has just published a stinging criticism of the inflation in theatre ticket prices. The article was titled, "The $75 Price Gouge: Is $100 Next?" This article has increased the concerns of a group planning New York's latest production of *Phantom of the Opera*. It had been planning for a $75 price for all of its seats. The up-front fixed costs to open are $8 million. Production and operating costs are $400,000 per week. The theatre has capacity for 2,000 seats with six performances per week planned. Approximately 100 seats per night are held as complimentary house seats.

INSTRUCTIONS
Form groups of two or more students to complete the following requirements.

REQUIRED
Your group is charged with exploring ways of improving the profitability of the venture and of reducing its breakeven point. Areas you should explore (but are not restricted to) include the following:
a. Increase the number of shows per week. The cast is under contract for up to eight shows a week for a fixed amount that is included in the $400,000.
b. Provide the two star performers (The Phantom and Christine) with a $25,000 weekly salary and a percentage of revenues or operating income instead of the fixed $50,000 per week each is budgeted to receive.
c. Change the single $75 pricing policy. Whereas all seats in the 2,000-person auditorium have unobstructed views, a recent theatre reviewer referred to the back rows of the balcony section as "binocular land."

CHAPTER 4

JOB COSTING

Technology provides the means whereby companies can produce better products at a lower cost. Companies that produce equipment used by manufacturers, such as paper manufacturers, need to understand the latest technological advances in order to provide their customers with the equipment they need to be competitive in today's global markets.

LEARNING OBJECTIVES

After studying this chapter, you should be able to:

1. Describe the building block concept of costing systems
2. Distinguish between job costing and process costing
3. Outline a seven-step approach to job costing
4. Distinguish between actual costing and normal costing
5. Track the flow of costs in a job-costing system
6. Prorate end-of-period under- or overallocated indirect costs using alternative methods
7. Apply variation of normal costing

How much does it cost Ernst & Young to audit Magna International Inc.? How much does it cost Loblaws to sell a six-pack of Pepsi-Cola? How much does it cost the Ford Motor Company to manufacture and sell a Ford Bronco to a dealer? Managers ask these questions for many purposes, including formulating overall strategies, product and service emphasis and pricing, cost control, and meeting external reporting obligations. Chapters 4 and 5 present concepts and techniques that guide the responses to such questions. Chapter 4 presents basic concepts of job costing. Chapter 5 describes applications of activity-based costing.

Before we explore the details of costing systems, three points are worth noting:

1. The cost-benefit approach we discussed in Chapter 1 is essential in designing and choosing costing systems. The costs of elaborate systems, including the costs of educating managers and other personnel, can be quite high. Managers should install a more sophisticated system only if they believe that its benefits will outweigh its costs.

2. Systems should be tailored to the underlying operations, and not vice versa. Any significant change in underlying operations is likely to justify a corresponding change in the accompanying costing systems. The best system design begins with a careful study of how operations are conducted and a resulting determination of which information to gather and report. The worst systems are those that operating managers perceive as misleading or useless.

3. Costing systems accumulate costs to facilitate decisions. Because the types of specific decisions that might need to be made cannot always be foreseen, costing systems are designed to fulfill several general desires that are common among most managers. In this chapter, we will focus on decisions regarding *product costing*. Therefore, we will pay most attention to the part of the costing system that aims to report cost numbers that indicate the manner in which particular cost objects—such as products or services—use the resources of an organization. Managers use product costing information for cost management, planning and control, and inventory valuation.

4. Costing systems are only one source of information for managers. When making decisions, managers combine information on costs with other noncost information, including personal observation of operations and nonfinancial performance measures such as setup times, absentee rates, and number of customer complaints.

BUILDING BLOCK CONCEPT OF COSTING SYSTEMS

OBJECTIVE 1

Describe the building block concept of costing systems

Costing Systems in Service and Merchandising Sectors
management.canberra.edu.au/
lectures/accounting/sem972/
unit4146/lecture_4A.html

We will now review some terms introduced in Chapter 2 that we will use in discussing costing systems:

◆ **Cost object.** Anything for which a separate measurement of costs is desired.
◆ **Direct costs of a cost object.** Costs that are related to the particular cost object and can be traced to it in an economically feasible (cost-effective) way.
◆ **Indirect costs of a cost object.** Costs that are related to the particular cost object but cannot be traced to it in an economically feasible (cost-effective) way. Indirect costs are allocated to the cost object using a cost-allocation method.

The relationships among these three concepts are as follows:

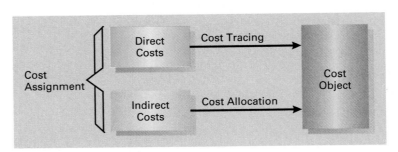

Two concepts not previously defined are also important when discussing costing systems:

◆ **Cost pool.** A grouping of individual cost items. Cost pools can range from the very broad (such as a companywide total-cost pool for telephones and fax machines) to the very narrow (such as the costs of operating a car used by a travelling salesperson).

◆ **Cost allocation base.** A factor that is the common denominator for systematically linking an indirect cost or group of indirect costs to a cost object. A cost allocation base can be financial (such as direct labour costs) or nonfinancial (such as the number of car kilometres travelled). Companies often seek to use the cost driver of the indirect costs as the cost allocation base. For example, the number of kilometres travelled may be used as the base for allocating motor vehicle operating costs among different sales districts.

These five terms constitute the building blocks that we will use to design the costing systems described later in this chapter.

Cost pool. A grouping of individual cost items.

Cost allocation base. A factor that is the common denominator for systematically linking an indirect cost or group of indirect costs to a cost object.

JOB-COSTING AND PROCESS-COSTING SYSTEMS

Companies frequently adopt one of two basic types of costing systems to assign costs to products or services:

◆ **Job-costing system.** In this system, costs are assigned to a distinct unit, batch, or lot of a product or service. A job is a task for which resources are expended in bringing a distinct product or service to market. The product or service is often custom-made, such as an audit by an accounting firm.

◆ **Process-costing system.** In this system, the cost of a product or service is obtained by using broad averages to assign costs to masses of similar units. Frequently, identical items (such as Barbie dolls or roofing nails) are mass-produced for general sale and not for any specific customer.

Exhibit 4-1 presents examples of job and process costing in the service, merchandising, and manufacturing sectors.

These two types of costing systems are best viewed as ends of a continuum:

OBJECTIVE 2

Distinguish between job costing and process costing

Job-costing system. Costing system in which the cost of a product or service is obtained by assigning costs to a distinct unit, batch, or lot of a product or service.

Process-costing system. Costing system in which the cost of a product or service is obtained by using broad averages to assign costs to masses of similar units.

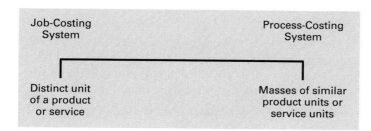

EXHIBIT 4-1

Examples of Job Costing and Process Costing in the Service, Merchandising, and Manufacturing Sectors

	Service Sector	Merchandising Sector	Manufacturing Sector
Job Costing Used	◆ Accounting firm audits ◆ Advertising agency campaigns	◆ Sending a catalogue to a mailing list ◆ Special promotion of a new store product	◆ Aircraft assembly ◆ House construction
Process Costing Used	◆ Deposit processing ◆ Postal delivery (standard items)	◆ Grain dealing ◆ Processing new magazine subscriptions	◆ Oil refining ◆ Beverage production

Most companies have costing systems that are neither pure job costing nor pure process costing. Rather, they combine elements of both job costing and process costing. In this chapter we focus on pure job-costing systems. Chapters 17 and 18 discuss process-costing systems.

JOB COSTING IN MANUFACTURING

OBJECTIVE 3

Outline a seven-step approach to job costing

Papertech Inc.
www.papertek.com

Actual costing. A costing method that traces direct costs to a cost object by using the actual direct cost rate(s) times the actual quantity of the direct cost input(s) and allocates indirect costs on the basis of the actual indirect cost rate(s) times the actual quantity of the cost allocation base.

We illustrate job costing using the example of Robinson Company, which operates at capacity to manufacture and install specialized machinery for the paper-making industry at its Vancouver, British Columbia, plant. In its job-costing system, Robinson accumulates costs incurred on a job in all parts of the value chain—R&D, design, manufacturing, marketing, distribution, and customer service. For simplicity, we focus on Robinson's manufacturing area. To make a machine, Robinson procures some of the components from outside suppliers and makes others itself. A key part of each of Robinson's jobs is assembling and installing the machine at customer sites, integrating it with the customer's other machines and processes, and ensuring its effective functioning. For a real-life example, take a look at the Papertech Web site.

The specific job we will focus on is the manufacture and installation of a small pulp machine for Western Pulp and Paper Company in the year 2000, for a price of $15,000. A key issue for Robinson in determining this price is the cost of doing the job. Knowledge about its own costs helps Robinson to price jobs to make a profit and to make informed estimates of the costs of future jobs.

Consider Robinson's *actual-costing* system, a job-costing system that uses *actual costs* to determine the cost of individual jobs. **Actual costing** is a method of job costing that traces direct costs to a cost object by using the actual direct-cost rate(s) times the actual quantity of the direct-cost input(s) and allocates indirect costs based on the actual indirect-cost rate(s) times the actual quantity of the cost-allocation base.

General Approach to Job Costing

We present a seven-step approach to assigning actual costs to individual jobs. The approach applies equally to job costing in the manufacturing, merchandising, and service sectors.

◆ **Step 1:** *Identify the Chosen Cost Object(s)*   The cost object in this case is the job of manufacturing a pulp machine for the Western Pulp and Paper Company in the year 2000.

◆ **Step 2:** *Identify the Direct Costs for the Cost Object(s)*   Robinson identifies two direct manufacturing cost categories—direct materials and direct manufacturing labour. Direct materials costs for the Western Pulp and Paper Company job are $4,606, while direct manufacturing labour costs are $1,579.

◆ **Step 3:** *Select Cost-Allocation Bases to Use in Allocating Indirect Costs to the Cost Object(s)*   Indirect manufacturing costs are costs that are not identified individually or directly with specific jobs. Yet completing various jobs would be impossible without incurring indirect costs such as supervision, manufacturing engineering, utilities, and repairs. These costs must be allocated to jobs. Different jobs require different quantities of indirect resources. The objective of allocating indirect costs is to measure the underlying usage of indirect resources by individual jobs.

Robinson chooses direct manufacturing labour hours as the only allocation base for linking all indirect manufacturing costs, called *manufacturing overhead costs*, to jobs. Why? Because Robinson believes that direct manufacturing labour costs measure how individual jobs use manufacturing overhead resources, such as salaries paid to supervisors, engineers, production support staff, and quality management staff. There is believed to be a cause-and-effect relationship between the overhead resources demanded and the direct manufacturing labour required by individual jobs. In the year 2000, Robinson records 27,000 actual direct manufacturing labour-hours.

◆ **Step 4:** *Identify the Indirect Costs Associated with Each Cost-Allocation Base*   Because Robinson believes that a single cost-allocation base, direct manufacturing labour hours, is appropriate to allocate indirect manufacturing costs to products, it creates a single cost pool called *manufacturing overhead costs*. This pool represents the indirect costs of the Vancouver Manufacturing Department that are difficult to trace directly to individual jobs. *Actual indirect costs* are often known only at the end of the year. In 2000, actual indirect manufacturing costs total $1,215,000.

◆ **Step 5:** *Compute the Rate per Unit of Each Cost-Allocation Base Used to Allocate Indirect Costs to the Cost Object(s)*   For each cost pool, the *indirect-cost rate* is calculated by dividing total overhead costs in the pool (determined in Step 4) by the total quantity of the cost-allocation base (determined in Step 3). Robinson calculates the allocation rate for its single manufacturing overhead cost pool as follows:

$$\text{Actual indirect-cost rate} = \frac{\text{Actual total costs in indirect-cost pool}}{\text{Actual total quantity of cost-allocation base}}$$

$$= \frac{\$1,215,000}{27,000 \text{ direct manufacturing labour-hours}}$$

$$= \$45 \text{ per direct manufacturing labour-hour}$$

◆ **Step 6:** *Compute the Indirect Costs Allocated to the Cost Object(s)*   The indirect costs of a job are computed by multiplying the actual quantities of the different allocation bases (one for each pool) used to complete a job by their respective indirect cost rates (computed in Step 5). To make the pulp machine, Robinson uses 88 direct manufacturing labour-hours, the cost allocation base for its only indirect cost pool (out of the 27,000 total direct manufacturing labour-hours for the year 2000). Indirect costs allocated to the pulp machine job equal $3,960 (88 hours × $45 per direct manufacturing labour-hour).

◆ **Step 7:** *Determine the Costs of the Cost Object(s) by Adding All Direct and Indirect Costs Assigned to It*   The cost of the pulp machine job for Western Pulp is $10,145.

Direct manufacturing costs		
Direct materials	$4,606	
Direct manufacturing labour	1,579	$6,185
Indirect manufacturing costs		
Manufacturing overhead costs		
($45 × 88 direct manufacturing labour-hours)		3,960
Total manufacturing costs of job		$10,145

Recall that Robinson was paid $15,000 for the job. Thus the actual costing system shows a gross margin of $4,855 ($15,000 − $10,145) or a gross margin percentage of 32.37% ($4,855 ÷ $15,000).

Robinson can use the gross margin and gross margin percentage calculations to compare profitability across various jobs and identify the most profitable types of jobs for its sales force to target. At the same time, Robinson can examine the reasons that some jobs show low profitability. Have direct materials been wasted? Is direct manufacturing labour too high? Are there ways to improve the efficiency with which these jobs are done? Or were these jobs simply mispriced? Job cost analysis provides crucial information for judging performance and making future improvements.

Exhibit 4-2 presents an overview of the Robinson Company job-costing system. This exhibit includes the five building blocks of this chapter—*cost object, cost pool, direct costs of a cost object, indirect costs of a cost object,* and *cost-allocation base.* Costing-system overviews like Exhibit 4-2 are important learning tools. We urge you to sketch one when you need to understand a costing system in manufacturing, service, or merchandising settings. (The symbols in Exhibit 4-2 are used consistently in the costing-system overviews presented in this book. For example, a triangle always

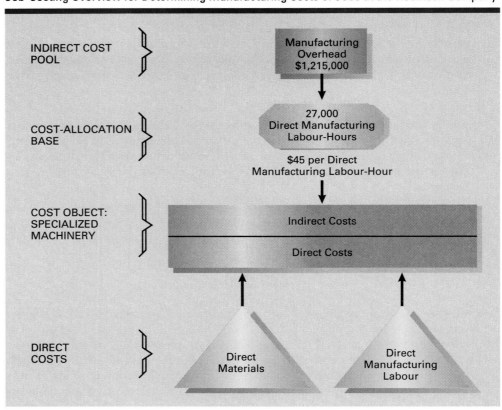

identifies a direct cost.) Note the correspondence between the exhibit diagram and the cost of the pulp-machine job described in Step 7. Exhibit 4-2 shows two direct cost categories (direct materials and direct manufacturing labour) and one indirect cost pool (manufacturing overhead) used to allocate costs. The costs in Step 7 also have three dollar amounts that correspond to the two direct and one indirect cost categories.

Two Major Cost Objects: Products and Departments

As this book emphasizes, all costs are recorded to help individuals make decisions. Cost objects are chosen to aid decision making. The Exhibit 4-2 overview focuses on one major cost object of an accounting system: products. Managers also focus on a second major cost object: **responsibility centres**, which are parts, segments, or subunits of an organization whose managers are accountable for specified sets of activities. Examples are departments, groups of departments, divisions, or geographic territories. The most commonly encountered responsibility centre is a department. Identifying department costs helps managers to control costs they are responsible for. It also enables senior management to judge the performance of subordinates and the performance of subunits of the organization as economic investments. For example, Robinson identifies manufacturing as a critical activity and the Manufacturing Department as an important cost object. The costs of the manufacturing department include all costs of materials, manufacturing labour and other manufacturing costs such as supervision, engineering, and production and quality control. Note that costs such as supervision, engineering, and production and quality control that were considered indirect or overhead costs when costing individual jobs are direct costs of the manufacturing department. Why? Because although these costs are difficult to trace to individual jobs within the manufacturing department in an economically feasible way, they are easily identified with and traced to the manufacturing department itself.

Responsibility centre. A part, segment, or subunit of an organization whose manager is accountable for a specified set of activities.

Cost-Allocation Bases Used for Manufacturing Overhead

How do companies around the world allocate manufacturing overhead costs to products? The percentages in the following table indicate how frequently particular cost-allocation bases are used in management accounting systems in five countries. The reported percentages exceed 100% because many companies surveyed use more than one cost-allocation base.

University of Washington Exercise: Product Cost Estimation, Consumer Electronics
rcs.ee.washington.edu/CE/labs/lab_Coffee.html

	United States*	Australia	Ireland	Japan†	United Kingdom‡
Direct labour-hours	31%	36%	30%	50%	31%
Direct labour-dollars	31	21	22	7	29
Machine-hours	12	19	19	12	27
Direct materials dollars	4	12	10	11	17
Units of production	5	20	28	16	22
Prime cost (%)	—	1	—	21	10
Other	17	—	9	—	—

*Cohen, J., and L. Paquette, "Management Accounting Practices: Perception of Controllers," *Journal of Cost Management* (Fall 1991)

†Blayney, P., and I. Yokoyama, "Comparative Analysis of Japanese and Australian Cost Accounting and Management Practices," (Working Paper, The University of Sydney, Sydney, Australia, 1991)

‡Clarke, P., "Management Accounting Practices and Techniques in Irish Manufacturing Firms," (Working Paper, Trinity College, Dublin, Ireland, 1995)

Source Documents

Robinson's managers and accountants gather information that goes into their cost systems through **source documents**, which are the original records that support journal entries in an accounting system. The key source document in a job-costing system is a **job cost record** (also called a **job cost sheet**), a document that records and accumulates all the costs assigned to a specific job. The job cost record is started as soon as work begins on a particular job. Exhibit 4-3, Panel A, shows the job cost record for the pulp machine ordered by Western Pulp and Paper Company. Source documents also exist for individual items in a job cost record. Consider direct materials. On the basis of the engineering specifications and drawings provided by Western Pulp, a manufacturing engineer orders material from the storeroom. This is done using a basic source document called a **materials requisition record**, which is a form used to charge job cost records and departments for the cost of direct materials used on specific jobs. Exhibit 4-3, Panel B shows a materials requisition record for the Robinson Company. Note how the record specifies the job for which the material is requested (WPP 298), description of the material (Part Number MB 468–A, Metal brackets), the actual quantity (8), the actual price ($14), and the actual total cost ($112). The cost of $112 for Part Number MB 468–A also appears as a cost on the job cost record. Adding the cost of all the materials requisitioned for the pulp machine job gives the actual direct materials costs of $4,606 shown on the job cost sheet.

The accounting for direct manufacturing labour is very similar to that described for direct materials. The basic source document for direct manufacturing labour is a **labour time record**, which is used to charge job cost records and departments for labour time used on specific jobs. Exhibit 4-3, Panel C shows a typical weekly labour time record for a particular employee. Each day the employee records the time spent on individual jobs (in this case WPP 298 and JL 256) as well as the time spent on other tasks such as maintenance of machines or cleaning that are not related to a specific job.

Source documents. The original records that support journal entries in an accounting system.

Job cost record (job cost sheet). Source document that records and accumulates all the costs assigned to a specific job.

Materials requisition record. Form used to charge departments and job cost records for the cost of the materials used on a specific job.

Labour time record. Record used to charge departments and job cost records for labour time used on a specific job.

EXHIBIT 4-3
Source Documents at the Robinson Company: Job Cost Record, Materials Requisition Record, and Labour Time Record

PANEL A:

JOB COST RECORD

JOB NO:	WPP 298		CUSTOMER:	Western Pulp and Paper
Date Started:	Feb.7, 2000		Date Completed:	March 1, 2000
Started:				

DIRECT MATERIALS

Date Received	Materials Requisition No.	Part No.	Quantity Used	Unit Cost	Total Costs
Feb. 7, 2000	2000: 198	MB 468–A	8	$14	$112
Feb. 7, 2000	2000: 199	TB 267–F	12	63	756
					•
					•
					•
Total					$4,606

DIRECT MANUFACTURING LABOUR

Period Covered	Labour Time Record No.	Employee No.	Hours Used	Hourly Rate	Total Costs
Feb. 7–13, 2000	LT 232	551-87-3076	25	$18	$450
Feb. 7–13, 2000	LT 247	287-31-4671	5	19	95
					•
					•
					•
Total					$1,579

MANUFACTURING OVERHEAD*

Date	Cost Pool Category	Allocation Base Dir Manuf.	Allocation Base Units Used	Allocation Base Rate	Total Costs
Dec. 31,2000	Manufacturing	Labour-Hours	88 Hours	$45	$3,960
					•
					•
					•
Total					$3,960
TOTAL JOB COST					$10,145

PANEL B:

MATERIALS REQUISITION RECORD

Materials Requisition Record No:			2000:198	
Job No: WPP 298		Date: Feb. 7, 2000		

Part No.	Part Description	Quantity	Unit Cost	Total Cost
MB468-A	Metal Brackets	8	$14	$112

Issued By: *B. Clyde* Date: Feb. 7, 2000
Received By: *L.Daley* Date: Feb. 7, 2000

PANEL C:

LABOUR TIME RECORD

Labour Time Record No: LT 232

Employee Name: G.L. Cook   Employee No: 551-87-3076

Employee Classification Code: Grade 3 Machinist

Hourly Rate: $18

Week Start: Feb. 7, 2000   Week End: Feb. 13, 2000

Job. No.	M	T	W	Th	F	S	Su	Total
WPP298	4	8	3	6	4	0	0	25
JL256	3	0	4	2	3	0	0	12
Maintenance	1	0	1	0	1	0	0	3
Total	8	8	8	8	8	0	0	40

Supervisor: *R. Stuart*   Date: Feb. 14, 2000

*The Robinson Company uses a single manufacturing overhead cost pool. The use of multiple overhead cost pools would mean multiple entries in the "Manufacturing Overhead" section of its job cost record.

The 25 hours that the employee spends on Job WPP 298 appears on the job cost record in Panel A at a cost of $450 (25 hours × hourly rate of $18 per hour). Similarly the job cost record for job JL 256 will carry a cost of $216 (12 hours × $18 per hour). The three hours of time spent on maintenance and cleaning at $18 per hour, equal to $54, are indirect manufacturing costs because these costs are not traceable to any particular job. These indirect costs are included as part of the manufacturing overhead cost pool that is allocated to jobs using direct manufacturing labour-hours. The total direct manufacturing labour costs of $1,579 for the pulp ma-

Pricing and Efficiency Gains from Job Costing at Colorscope

Colorscope Inc. is a special-effects photography laboratory that designs printed advertisements for companies such as Saatchi & Saatchi, J. Walter Thompson, Walt Disney, and R. H. Macy. Competitive pressures and thin profit margins make understanding costs critical in the pricing decision. Each customer order or job must be estimated individually because the unique end products demand different amounts of Colorscope's resources.

Previously, Colorscope had charged a standard price for all its jobs. Why? Because, regardless of the end result, every customer job goes through five stages—job preparation, scanning, assembly, film developing, and quality control. In the *job preparation* stage the template of the job is created by physically cutting and pasting text, graphics, and photographs and by specifying the layout, font, colour, and shading. The job template is then *scanned* into a computer, where the job is *assembled* using archives of scanned images adjusted for colour and shades. The assembled job is then transferred and *developed* on a large sheet of four-colour film. *Quality control* ensures that the job fully satisfies the customer's specifications. If not, or if the customer's requirements have changed, quality control initiates rework.

Andrew Cha, Colorscope's founder and chief executive, observed large differences in the amount of image-scanning and processing activity required by different jobs as well as varying amounts of rework across jobs. Because the jobs were using different amounts of resources, charging roughly the same standard price for all jobs was making Colorscope lose money on certain jobs. Cha concluded that a job-costing system measuring cost based on the labour hours spent at each operation would give him better information about costs incurred on various jobs. Colorscope's job-costing system now traces direct materials to jobs and allocates all other costs (wages, rent, depreciation, and so on) to jobs using an overhead rate per labour-hour for each operation.

Besides better tracing costs to specific jobs, Colorscope's new job-costing system provided the additional benefit of improving efficiency through process changes. For example, the job-costing system highlighted the significant resources Colorscope had been spending on rework. Colorscope's management discovered that most rework was caused by faulty scanning. These defects were not detected until after the job was completed, by which time significant additional resources had also been incurred on the job. Colorscope implemented process changes to reduce faulty scanning and to test for quality immediately after the scanning stage. Thus, the job-costing system helped Colorscope improve its profitability by pricing jobs better and by improving efficiency and quality.

Colorscope
www.colorscope.com

Source: Colorscope Inc., Harvard Business School Case Number 9–197–040, and discussion with company management.

Explanations of Transactions

The following transaction-by-transaction summary analysis explains how a job costing system serves the twin goals of (1) department responsibility and control and (2) product costing. These transactions track stages (a) through (d):

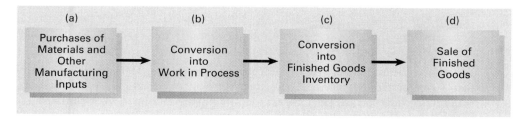

1. **Transaction.** Purchase of materials (direct and indirect), $89,000 on account.

   Analysis. The asset Materials Control is increased. The liability Accounts Payable Control is increased. Both accounts have the word *Control* in their title in the general ledger because they are supported by records in the subsidiary ledger. The subsidiary records for materials at the Robinson Company—called *Materials Records*—maintain a continuous record of additions to, and reductions from, inventory. At a minimum, these records would contain columns for quantity received, issuance to jobs, and balance (see Panel B of Exhibit 4-5, page 110). There is a separate subsidiary materials record for each type of material in the subsidiary ledger. The following journal entry summarizes all the February 2000 entries in the materials subsidiary ledgers:

Journal Entry:	Materials Control	89,000	
	Accounts Payable Control		89,000

   Post to General Ledger:

Materials Control		Accounts Payable Control	
① 89,000			① 89,000

   Materials Control includes all material purchases, whether the items are classified as direct or indirect costs of products.

2. **Transaction.** Materials sent to manufacturing plant floor: direct materials, $81,000, and indirect materials, $4,000.

   Analysis. The accounts Work-in-Process Control and Manufacturing Overhead Control are increased. The account Materials Control is decreased. The assumption is that costs incurred on the work in process "attach" to the work in process, thereby making it a more valuable asset. Responsibility is fixed by using *materials requisitions records* as a basis for charging departments for the materials issued to them. Requisitions are accumulated and posted monthly to the general ledger at the Robinson Company. As direct materials are used, they are charged to individual job records, which are the subsidiary ledger accounts for the Work-in-Process Control account in the general ledger. Indirect materials are charged to individual Manufacturing Department overhead cost records, which make up the subsidiary ledger for Manufacturing Overhead Control at the Robinson Company. The cost of these indirect materials is allocated to individual jobs as a part of the Manufacturing Overhead. The Manufacturing Overhead Control account is the record of the *actual costs* in all the individual overhead categories.

   Each indirect-cost pool in a job-costing system will have its own account in the general ledger. Robinson has only one indirect-cost pool—manufacturing overhead.

Journal Entry:	Work-in-Process Control	81,000	
	Manufacturing Overhead Control	4,000	
	Materials Control		85,000

   Post to General Ledger:

Materials Control			Work-in-Process Control	
① 89,000	② 85,000		② 81,000	

Manufacturing Overhead Control	
② 4,000	

3. **Transaction.** Manufacturing labour wages liability incurred, direct ($39,000) and indirect ($15,000).

   Analysis. The accounts Work-in-Process Control and Manufacturing Overhead Control are increased. Wages Payable Control is also increased. Labour time records are used to trace direct manufacturing labour to Work-in-Process Control (see Panel B of Exhibit 4-5) and to accumulate the indirect manufacturing labour in Manufacturing Overhead Control. The indirect manufacturing labour is, by definition, not being traced to the individual job. Department managers are responsible for making efficient use of available labour.

Journal Entry:

Work-in-Process Control	39,000	
Manufacturing Overhead Control	15,000	
Wages Payable Control		54,000

Post to General Ledger:

Wages Payable Control			Work-in-Process Control		
	③	54,000	②	81,000	
			③	39,000	

Manufacturing Overhead Control		
②	4,000	
③	15,000	

4. **Transaction.** Payment of total manufacturing payroll for the month, $54,000. (For simplicity, payroll withholdings from employees are ignored in this example.)

Analysis. The liability Wages Payable Control is decreased. The asset Cash Control is decreased.

Journal Entry:

Wages Payable Control	54,000	
Cash Control		54,000

Post to General Ledger:

Wages Payable Control				Cash Control		
④	54,000	③	54,000		④	54,000

For convenience here, wages payable for the month is assumed to be completely paid at month-end.

5. **Transaction.** Additional manufacturing overhead costs incurred during the month, $75,000. These costs consist of salaries, $44,000; payables, $11,000; insurance expired, $2,000; and amortization on equipment, $18,000.

Analysis. The indirect cost account of Manufacturing Overhead Control is increased. The liability Accounts Payable Control is increased, the asset Prepaid Insurance Control is decreased, and the asset Equipment is decreased by means of a related contra asset account Accumulated Amortization Control. The detail of these costs is entered in the appropriate columns of the individual manufacturing overhead cost records that make up the subsidiary ledger for Manufacturing Overhead Control. The source documents for these distributions include invoices (for example, a utility bill) and special schedules (for example, an amortization schedule) from the responsible accounting officer.

Journal Entry:

Manufacturing Overhead Control	75,000	
Salaries Payable Control		44,000
Accounts Payable Control		11,000
Accumulated Amortization Control		18,000
Prepaid Insurance Control		2,000

Post to General Ledger:

Salaries Payable Control		
	⑤	44,000

Accounts Payable Control			Manufacturing Overhead Control		
	①	89,000	②	4,000	
	⑤	11,000	③	15,000	
			⑤	75,000	

Accumulated Amortization Control			Prepaid Insurance Control		
	⑤	18,000		⑤	2,000

6. Transaction. Allocation of manufacturing overhead to products, $80,000.

Analysis: The asset Work-in-Process Control is increased. The indirect cost account of Manufacturing Overhead Control is, in effect, decreased by means of its contra account, called Manufacturing Overhead Allocated. **Manufacturing overhead allocated** is the record of manufacturing overhead allocated to individual jobs on the basis of the budgeted rate multiplied by actual units used of the allocation base. It comprises all manufacturing costs that are assigned to a product (or service) using a cost allocation base because they cannot be traced to it in an economically feasible way. The 2000 budgeted overhead rate used by Robinson is $40 per machine-hour. The overhead cost allocated to each job depends on the machine-hours used on that job. The job record for each individual job in the subsidiary ledger will include a debit item for manufacturing overhead allocated. For example, the job cost record for WPP 298 shows Manufacturing Overhead Allocated of $3,520 (88 actual direct manufacturing labour-hours used × budgeted rate of $40). It is assumed that 2,000 machine-hours were used for all jobs, resulting in a total manufacturing overhead allocation of 2,000 × $40 = $80,000.

Note that a subsidiary entry is made for Manufacturing Overhead Allocated when machine-hours are used on a job. These entries are made to the individual job records in the subsidiary ledger. In contrast, subsidiary entries are made for Manufacturing Overhead Control when actual transactions occur during the period.

Manufacturing overhead allocated. All manufacturing costs that are assigned to a product (or service) using a cost allocation base because they cannot be traced to a product (or service) in an economically feasible way.

Journal Entry: Work-in-Process Control   80,000

              Manufacturing Overhead Allocated   80,000

Post to General Ledger:

Manufacturing Overhead Allocated		Work-in-Process Control	
⑥ 80,000	② 81,000		
	③ 39,000		
	⑥ 80,000		

Keep in mind that transactions 5 and 6 are distinct and different. In transaction 5, actual overhead costs incurred throughout the month are debited to Manufacturing Overhead Control account and the subsidiary manufacturing overhead records are *not* to Work-in-Process Control and the individual job cost records. Manufacturing overhead costs are added (debited) to Work-in-Process Control and individual job cost records *only when* manufacturing overhead costs are allocated in transaction 6. At this time, Manufacturing Overhead Control is, in effect, decreased (credited). Under the normal costing system described in our illustration, the budgeted indirect cost rate of $40 per direct manufacturing labour-hour is calculated at the beginning of the year on the basis of predictions of annual manufacturing overhead costs and predictions of the annual quantity of the cost allocation base. Almost certainly, the actual amounts will differ from the predictions.

7. Transaction. Completion and transfer to finished goods of eight individual jobs, $188,800.

Analysis. The asset Finished Goods Control is increased, and the asset Work-in-Process Control is decreased to signify the completion of jobs. The Work in Process records in the subsidiary ledger indicate that the costs of the twelve individual jobs completed in February 2000, equal $188,800.

Journal Entry: Finished Goods Control   188,800

              Work-in-Process Control   188,800

Post to General Ledger:

Work-in-Process Control		Finished Goods Control	
② 81,000	⑦ 188,800	⑦ 188,800	
③ 39,000			
⑥ 80,000			
11,200			

The debit balance of $11,200 in the Work-in-Process Control account represents the total costs of all job cost records (in the subsidiary ledger) that have not been completed.

8. **Transaction.** Cost of Goods Sold, $180,000.

   Analysis. The $180,000 amount represents the cost of goods sold in sales transactions with customers during February 2000. The account Cost of Goods Sold is increased. The asset Finished Goods Control is decreased.

   Journal Entry: Cost of Goods Sold   180,000
                          Finished Goods Control   180,000

   Post to General Ledger:

Finished Goods Control		Cost of Goods Sold	
⑦ 188,800	⑧ 180,000	⑧ 180,000	
8,800			

   The debit balance of $8,800 in Finished Goods Control account represents the costs of all jobs that have been completed and are part of the finished goods records but which have not yet been sold to customers.

   At this point, please pause and review all eight entries in the illustration. Be sure to trace each journal entry, step by step, to the general ledger accounts in the general ledger section in Panel A of Exhibit 4-5.

Accounting for Nonmanufacturing Costs

We have so far concentrated on job costing in the manufacturing function. Manufacturing companies such as Robinson also incur costs in other parts of the value chain—R&D, design, marketing, distribution, and customer service. Robinson Company, for example, incurs costs in the marketing and customer service areas.

9. **Transaction.** Liabilities incurred for the following:

Marketing and Administration Department salaries	$35,000
Advertising costs	10,000
Customer-Service Department salaries	15,000

   Analysis. As described in Chapter 2, for financial accounting these costs are noninventoriable. They should be charged directly as period expenses for February 2000 to be matched against revenues. Unlike manufacturing costs, these costs are not added to work-in-process assets because they do not transform or change a physical product. Robinson would record the following entries.

   Journal Entries: Marketing, Advertising, and Admin. Expense   45,000
                     Customer Service Expense   15,000
                     Salaries Payable Control   50,000
                     Accounts Payable Control   10,000

   Post to General Ledger:

Marketing, Advertising, and Administration Expense		Salaries Payable Control	
⑨ 45,000			⑨ 50,000

Customer-Service Expense		Accounts Payable Control	
⑨ 15,000			⑨ 10,000

10. **Transaction.** Sales, all on account, are $270,000.

    Analysis. The $270,000 represents amounts due from customers for sales made in February 2000.

    Journal entry: Accounts Receivable Control   270,000
                    Revenues   270,000

Accounts Receivable Control		Revenues	
⑩ 270,000		⑩ 270,000	

Nonmanufacturing Costs and Job Costing

Chapter 2 pointed out that companies use product costs for different purposes. The product costs reported as inventoriable costs to shareholders may differ from those reported to tax authorities and may further differ from those reported to managers for guiding pricing and product-mix decisions. We emphasize that even though, as described previously, marketing and customer-service costs are expensed for financial accounting purposes, companies often trace or allocate these costs to individual jobs for pricing, product mix, and cost management decisions.

To identify marketing and customer-service costs of individual jobs, Robinson can use the same basic approach to job costing described earlier in the chapter in the context of jobs. Robinson can then calculate a budgeted indirect-cost rate by dividing budgeted indirect marketing and customer-service costs by the budgeted quantity of the cost allocation base, say, revenues. Robinson can use this rate to allocate indirect costs to jobs. For example, if this rate were $0.15 per dollar of revenue, Robinson would allocate $2,250 to the WPP job (0.15 × $15,000, the revenue from the WPP job). By assigning both manufacturing and nonmanufacturing costs to jobs, Robinson can compare all the resources demanded by different jobs against the revenues earned from them.

BUDGETED INDIRECT COSTS AND END-OF-PERIOD ADJUSTMENTS

OBJECTIVE 6

Prorate end-of-period under- or overallocated indirect costs using alternative methods

Underallocated indirect costs (underapplied indirect costs, underabsorbed indirect costs). Occur when the allocated amount of indirect costs in an accounting period is less than the actual (incurred) amount in that period.

Overallocated indirect costs (overapplied indirect costs, overabsorbed indirect costs). Occurs when the allocated amount of indirect costs in an accounting period is greater than the actual (incurred) amount in that period.

Budgeted indirect cost rates have the advantage of being more timely than actual indirect cost rates. With budgeted rates, indirect costs can be assigned to individual jobs on an ongoing basis rather than waiting until the end of the accounting period when actual costs will be known. However, the disadvantage of budgeted rates is that they likely will be inaccurate, having been made up to 12 months before actual costs are incurred. We now consider adjustments made when the indirect costs allocated differ from the actual indirect costs incurred.

Underallocated indirect costs occur when the allocated amount of indirect costs in an accounting period is less than the actual (incurred) amount in that period. **Overallocated indirect costs** occur when the allocated amount of indirect costs in an accounting period exceeds the actual (incurred) amount in that period.

$$\text{Under- or overallocated indirect costs} = \text{Indirect costs incurred} - \text{Indirect costs allocated}$$

Equivalent terms are **underapplied** (or **overapplied**) **indirect costs** and **underabsorbed** (or **overabsorbed**) **indirect costs**.

The Robinson Company has a single indirect cost pool (Manufacturing Overhead) in its job-costing system. There are two indirect cost accounts in its general ledger that pertain to manufacturing overhead:

◆ **Manufacturing Overhead Control,** which is the record of the *actual* costs in all the individual overhead categories (such as indirect materials, indirect manufacturing labour, power, and rent)

◆ **Manufacturing Overhead Allocated,** which is the record of the manufacturing overhead allocated to individual jobs on the basis of the budgeted rate multiplied by actual machine-hours

Assume the following annual data for the Robinson Company:

Manufacturing Overhead Control		Manufacturing Overhead Allocated	
Bal. Dec. 31, 2000 1,215,000		Bal. Dec. 31, 2000 1,080,000	

The $1,080,000 credit balance in Manufacturing Overhead Allocated results from multiplying the 27,000 actual direct manufacturing labour-hours worked on all the jobs in year 2000 by the budgeted rate of $40 per hour.

The $135,000 difference (a net debit) is an underallocated amount because actual manufacturing overhead costs are greater than the allocated amount. This difference arises from two reasons related to the computation of the $40 budgeted hourly rate:

1. *Numerator reason (indirect costs).* Actual manufacturing overhead costs of $1,215,000 are lower than the budgeted amount of $1,280,000.

2. *Denominator reason (quantity of allocation base).* Actual direct manufacturing labour-hours of 27,000 are lower than the budgeted amount of 32,000 hours.

There are three main approaches to disposing of this $135,000 underallocation of manufacturing overhead caused by Robinson's overestimating indirect costs and the quantity of the cost allocation base. These approaches are (1) the adjusted allocation rate approach, (2) the prorated approach, and (3) the immediate write-off to cost of goods sold approach.

Adjusted Allocation Rate Approach

The adjusted allocation rate approach, in effect, restates all entries in the general ledger by using actual cost rates rather than budgeted cost rates. First, the actual indirect cost rate is computed at the end of each period. Then, every job to which indirect costs were allocated during the period has its amount recomputed using the actual indirect cost rate (rather than the budgeted indirect cost rate). Finally, end-of-period closing entries are made. The result is that every single job cost record—as well as the ending inventory and cost of goods sold accounts—accurately represents actual indirect costs incurred.

The widespread adoption of computerized accounting systems has greatly reduced the cost of using the adjusted allocated rate approach. Consider the Robinson Company example. The actual manufacturing overhead ($1,215,000) exceeds the manufacturing overhead allocated ($1,080,000) by 12.5% [($1,215,000 − $1,080,000) ÷ $1,080,000]. The actual 2000 manufacturing overhead rate is $45 per direct manufacturing labour-hour ($1,215,000 ÷ 27,000) rather than the budgeted $40 per direct manufacturing labour-hour. At year-end, Robinson could increase the year 2000 manufacturing overhead allocated to each job in that year by 12.5% using a single software directive. The directive would affect both the subsidiary ledger and the general ledger.

For example, consider the Western Pulp Machine Job WPP 298. Under normal costing, the manufacturing overhead allocated to the job is $3,520 (88 direct manufacturing labour-hours × the budgeted rate of $40 per hour). Increasing the manufacturing overhead allocated by 12.5% or $440 ($3,520 × 12.5%) means that the new manufacturing overhead allocated to Job WPP 298 equals $3,960 ($3,520 + $440). Recall that under actual costing, manufacturing overhead allocated is also $3,960 (88 manufacturing labour hours × the actual rate of $45 per hour). Making this adjustment for each job on the subsidiary ledger ensures that all $1,215,000 of manufacturing overhead is allocated to jobs.

This approach yields the benefits of both the timeliness of convenience of normal costing and the accuracy of actual costing. Each individual product cost amount and the end-of-year account balances for inventories and cost of goods sold are at actual costs. After-the-fact analysis of actual individual product profitability provides managers with useful insights for future decisions about product pricing and about which products to emphasize. These decisions are improved by having the more accurate actual product-profitability numbers on prior jobs.

Proration Approach

Proration is the spreading of under- or overallocated overhead among ending inventories and cost of goods sold. Consider the Robinson Company where manufacturing

Proration. The spreading of underallocated or overallocated overhead over ending inventories and cost of goods sold.

overhead is allocated on the basis of machine-hours. Materials are not allocated any overhead costs. It is not until materials are put into work in process that machining of them commences. Only the ending work-in-process and finished goods inventories will have an allocated manufacturing overhead component. Hence, in our Robinson example, it is only these two ending inventory accounts (and Cost of Goods Sold) for which end-of-period proration is an issue. Assume the following actual results for Robinson Company in 2000:

BG–PBRAS Proration Based Revenue Accounting system www.bg–aerosoft.com/ pbras.htm

	End-of-Year Balances (before proration)	Manufacturing Overhead Allocated Component of Year-End Balances (before proration)
Work in Process	$ 50,000	$ 16,200
Finished Goods	75,000	31,320
Cost of Goods Sold	2,375,000	1,032,480
	$2,500,000	$1,080,000

How should Robinson prorate all the underallocated $135,000 of manufacturing overhead at the end of year 2000?

Robinson should prorate under- or overallocated amounts from each cost pool on the basis of the total amount of manufacturing overhead allocated (before proration) from the cost pool to the ending balances of Work-in-Process Control, Finished Goods Control, and Cost of Goods Sold. In our Robinson Company example, the $135,000 underallocated overhead is prorated over the three pertinent accounts in proportion to their total amount of manufacturing overhead allocated (before proration) in column 3 in the following table, resulting in the ending balances (after proration) in column 5 at actual costs.

(1)	Account Balance (Before proration) (2)	Indirect Costs Allocated Component in the Balance in Column 2 (3)		Proration of $135,000 Underallocated Manufacturing Overhead (4)	Account Balance (after proration) (5) = (2) + (4)
Work-in-Process	$ 50,000	$ 16,200	(1.5%)	0.015 × $135,000 = $ 2,025	$ 52,025
Finished Goods	75,000	31,320	(2.9%)	0.029 × 135,000 = 3,915	78,915
Cost of Goods Sold	2,375,000	1,032,480	(95.6%)	0.956 × 135,000 = 129,060	2,504,060
	2,500,000	$1,080,000	(100.0%)	$135,000	$2,635,000

Recall that the actual manufacturing overhead ($1,215,000) exceeds the manufacturing overhead allocated ($1,080,000) by 12.5%. The proration amounts in column 4 can also be derived by multiplying the balances in column 3 by 12.5%. For example, the $3,915 proration to Finished Goods is 12.5% × $31,320.
The journal entry to record this proration would be:

Work-in-Process Control	2,025
Finished Goods Control	3,915
Cost of Goods Sold	129,060
Manufacturing Overhead Allocated	1,080,000
Manufacturing Overhead Control	1,215,000

Note that if manufacturing overhead had been overallocated, the Work-in-Process, Finished Goods, and Cost of Goods Sold accounts would be decreased (credited) instead of increased (debited).

This journal entry restates the year 2000 ending balances for Work-in-Process, Finished Goods, and Cost of Goods Sold to what they would have been had actual cost rates rather than budgeted cost rates been used. The proration approach reports the same 2000 ending balances in the general ledger as does the adjusted allocation rate approach.

Some companies use the proration approach but base it on column 2 of the preceding table—that is, the ending balances in Work-in-Process, Finished Goods, and Cost of Goods Sold before proration. It gives the same results as the proration approach only if the proportions of direct costs of manufacturing based on column 3 are constant in the Work-in-Process, Finished Goods, and Cost of Goods Sold accounts. Why? Because, if this were the case, prorating based on total costs is the same as prorating based on allocated overhead costs. It is likely, however, that prorations based on column 2 will not be the same as the more accurate prorations based on column 3. This is true in our example. For instance, work in process is 2% ($50,000 ÷ $2,500,000) of the total of column 2 but 1.5% of the total of column 3. If column 2 were used for proration, work in process would be allocated 2% of $135,000 = $2,700 instead of the $2,025 allocated to it using column 3. Similarly, finished goods would be allocated 3% ($75,000 ÷ $2,500,000) of $135,000 = $4,050, and cost of goods sold would be allocated 95% ($2,375,000 ÷ $2,500,000) of $135,000 = $128,250, instead of $3,915 and $129,060 allocated to these accounts, respectively, using column 3. Proration based on ending balances is frequently justified as being a lower-cost way of approximating the more accurate results based on indirect costs allocated.

Immediate Write-off to Cost of Goods Sold Approach

In this case, the total under- or overallocated overhead is included in this year's Cost of Goods Sold. In our Robinson Company example, the journal entry would be

Cost of Goods Sold	135,000	
Manufacturing Overhead Allocated	1,080,000	
Manufacturing Overhead Control		1,215,000

Robinson's two Manufacturing Overhead accounts are closed out with all the difference between them now included in cost of goods sold. The Cost of Goods Sold account after proration equals $2,510,000, the balance before proration of $2,375,000 plus the underallocated overhead amount of $135,000.

No matter which approach is used, the underallocated overhead is not carried in the overhead accounts beyond the end of the year. That is, the ending balances in Manufacturing Overhead Control and Manufacturing Overhead Allocated are closed to Work-in-Process Control, Finished Goods, or Cost of Goods Sold, and consequently become zero at the end of each year.

Choice among Approaches

In choosing among the approaches, managers should be guided by how the resultant information is to be used. If managers desire to develop the most accurate record of individual job costs for profitability analysis purposes, the adjusted allocation rate approach is preferred. The proration approach does not make any adjustment to individual job cost records. If the purpose is confined to reporting the most accurate inventory and cost of goods sold figures, proration based on the indirect-cost-allocated component of ending balances should be used because it adjusts the balances to what they would have been under actual costing but does not adjust individual job cost records.

The immediate write-off to Cost of Goods Sold is the simplest approach for dealing with under- or overallocated overhead. If the amount of underallocated (or overallocated) overhead is small—in comparison to total operating income, or some other measure of materiality—the approach yields a good approximation to more accurate but more complex approaches. Modern companies are also becoming increasingly conscious of inventory control; thus inventories are lower than they were in earlier years, and Cost of Goods Sold tends to be higher in relation to inventories of Work-in-Process and Finished Goods. Also, the inventory balances of job-costing companies are usually relatively small because goods are often made in response to specific sales orders. Consequently, as is true in our Robinson example, writing off underallocated or overallocated overhead instead of prorating it is unlikely to cause significant distortions in financial statements. For all these reasons, the cost-benefit test would favour the simplest method—immediate write-off to Cost of Goods Sold method—because the more costly attempts at accuracy represented by the other approaches do not appear to provide additional useful information.

MULTIPLE OVERHEAD COST POOLS

The Robinson Company illustration assumed that a single manufacturing overhead cost pool with direct manufacturing labour-hours as the cost allocation base was appropriate for allocating indirect manufacturing costs to jobs. Robinson could have used multiple cost-allocation bases, say, direct manufacturing labour-hours and machine-hours, to allocate indirect costs to jobs. It would do so if Robinson's managers believed that the benefits of the information generated by adding more pools (more accurate costing and pricing of jobs and better ability to manage costs) exceeded the costs of implementing a more complex system. We discuss these issues in more detail in Chapter 5.

To implement a normal costing system with multiple overhead cost pools, Robinson would determine the budgeted total direct manufacturing labour-hours and the budgeted total machine-hours for the year 2000, and identify the associated budgeted indirect total costs for each cost pool. It would then calculate two indirect cost rates, one based on direct manufacturing labour-hours and one based on machine-hours used by various jobs. The General Ledger would contain Overhead Control and Overhead Allocated amounts for each cost pool. End of period adjustments for under- or overallocated indirect costs would then need to be made separately for each cost pool.

VARIATION OF NORMAL COSTING: A SERVICE INDUSTRY EXAMPLE

OBJECTIVE 7

Apply variation of normal costing

As we discussed at the start of this chapter, job costing is very useful in service industries such as accounting and consulting firms, advertising agencies, auto repair shops, and hospitals. In an accounting firm, each audit is a job. The costs of the audit are accumulated on a job cost record, much like the document used by Robinson Company, using the seven-step approach described earlier in the chapter. On the basis of labour time records, direct labour costs of audit partners, audit managers, and audit staff are traced to individual jobs. Other direct costs such as travel, out-of-town meals and lodging, telephone, fax, and copying are also traced to jobs. The costs of secretarial support, head office staff, rent, and depreciation of furniture and equipment are indirect costs because these costs cannot be identified with jobs in an economically feasible way. Indirect costs are allocated to jobs, for example, using a cost allocation base such as professional labour-hours.

In some service, merchandising, and manufacturing organizations, a variation of normal costing is helpful because actual direct-labour costs (the largest component of total cost) are difficult to trace to jobs as they are completed. For example, in our audit illustration, the actual direct-labour costs may include bonuses that are known only at the end of the year (a numerator reason). Also, the hours worked each period might vary significantly, depending on the number of working days each month and the demand from clients (a denominator reason). In these situations, to obtain timely information as a job is completed rather than wait until the end of the year, an organization may choose to use budgeted rates for some direct costs in addition to using budgeted rates for indirect costs. All budgeted rates used are calculated at the start of the accounting period. Recall that normal costing uses actual cost rates for all direct costs and budgeted cost rates only for indirect costs.

The mechanics of using budgeted rates for direct costs are similar to the methods employed when using budgeted rates for indirect costs in normal costing. We illustrate using Lindsay and Associates, a public accounting firm. At the start of the year 2000, Lindsay budgets total direct-labour costs of $14,400,000, total indirect costs of $12,960,000, and total direct (professional) labour-hours of 288,000 for the year. In this case,

$$\text{Budgeted direct labour cost rate} = \frac{\text{Budgeted total direct labour costs}}{\text{Budgeted total direct labour-hours}}$$

$$= \frac{\$14,400,000}{288,000 \text{ hours}} = \$50 \text{ per direct labour-hour}$$

Assuming only one indirect cost pool and total direct labour-hours as the cost allocation base,

$$\text{Budgeted indirect-cost rate} = \frac{\text{Budgeted total costs in indirect-cost pool}}{\text{Budgeted total quantity of cost-allocation base}}$$

$$= \frac{\$12,960,000}{288,000 \text{ hours}} = \$45 \text{ per direct labour-hour}$$

Suppose an audit of Tracy Transport, a client of Lindsay, completed in March 2000, uses 800 direct labour-hours. Lindsay calculates the direct costs of the Tracy Transport audit by multiplying the budgeted direct-cost rate by the actual quantity of the direct-cost input. It allocates indirect costs to the Tracy Transport audit by multiplying the budgeted indirect-cost rate by the actual quantity of the cost-allocation base. Assuming no other direct costs for travel, outsourcing, computer work, etc., the cost of the Tracy Transport audit is:

Direct labour costs, $50 × 800	$40,000
Indirect costs allocated, $45 × 800	36,000
Total	$76,000

At the end of the year, the direct costs traced to jobs using budgeted rates will generally not equal the actual direct costs because the actual and budgeted rates are developed at different points in time using different information. End-of-period adjustments for under- or overallocated direct costs would need to be made in the same way that adjustments were made for under- or overallocated indirect costs.

The Lindsay and Associates example illustrates that all costing systems do not map neatly onto either the actual costing or normal costing system described earlier in the chapter. As another example, engineering consulting firms often have some actual direct costs (cost of making blue prints or fees paid to outside experts), other direct costs traced to jobs using a budgeted rate (professional labour costs), and indirect costs allocated to jobs using a budgeted rate (engineering and office support costs).

MANAGEMENT CONTROL AND TECHNOLOGY

Managers use product-costing information to improve the efficiency of their operations by managing and controlling the materials, labour, and overhead costs used to complete jobs. Modern technology provides the manager with quick and accurate product-cost information that facilitates the management and control of jobs.

Electronic Data Interchange Resources
www.business.auc.dk/edi/

Consider, for example, direct materials that are charged directly to jobs for product-costing purposes. Managers exercise control of these costs well before materials are used on jobs. Through innovative management processes and new technologies such as Electronic Data Interchange (EDI), companies like Robinson can order materials from their suppliers by pushing a few keys on a computer terminal. EDI, an electronic computer link between a company and its suppliers, ensures that the order is transmitted quickly and accurately with minimum paper work and costs. A bar code scanner records the receipt of incoming materials. The computer matches the receipt with the order, prints out a cheque to the supplier, and records the material received in the subsidiary ledger. When a shop floor operator transmits a request for materials through a computer terminal, the computer prepares a material requisition record, instantly recording the issue of materials in the subsidiary ledgers and job-cost records. Each day, the computer adds up the materials requisitions records charged to a particular job or manufacturing department. A performance report is then prepared comparing budgeted and actual costs of direct materials. If desired, direct materials usage might be reported hourly. Information technology allows managers to obtain quick and frequent feedback about the usage of direct materials by jobs and departments.

Similarly, information about manufacturing labour is obtained as employees log into shop-floor terminals and punch in the job number, employee number, and start and end times for different jobs. Using hourly rates stored for each employee, the computer automatically prints out the labour time record and posts the labour costs to individual costs. Information technology also provides managers with instantaneous feedback to control manufacturing overhead, jobs in process, jobs completed, and jobs shipped and installed at customer sites.

PROBLEM FOR SELF-STUDY

Re-examine the Exhibit 4-5 illustration of a job-costing system. Then try to solve the following problem, which requires consideration of many of this chapter's important points in a service sector company.

PROBLEM
You are asked to bring the following incomplete accounts of Endeavor Printing, Inc., up to date through January 31, 2001. Consider the data that appear in the T-accounts as well as the following information in items (a) through (i).

Endeavor's job-costing system, which uses normal costing, has two direct-cost categories (direct materials and direct manufacturing labour) and one indirect-cost pool (manufacturing overhead, which is allocated using direct manufacturing labour costs).

Materials Control		Wages Payable Control	
12-31-2000 Bal. 15,000			1-31-2001 Bal. 3,000

Work-in-Process Control		Manufacturing Overhead Control	
		1-13-2001 Bal. 57,000	

		Manufacturing Overhead Allocated	

Finished Goods Control		Cost of Goods Sold	
12-31-2000 Bal. 20,000			

ADDITIONAL INFORMATION
a. Manufacturing overhead is allocated using a budgeted rate set every December. Management forecasts next year's manufacturing overhead and next year's direct manufacturing labour costs. The budget for 2001 is $400,000 of direct manufacturing labour and $600,000 of manufacturing overhead.
b. The only job unfinished on January 31, 2001, is No. 419, on which direct manufacturing labour costs are $2,000 (125 direct manufacturing labour-hours) and direct materials costs are $8,000.
c. Total materials placed into production during January are $90,000.
d. Cost of goods completed during January is $180,000.
e. Materials inventory as of January 31, 2001, is $20,000.
f. Finished goods inventory as of January 31, 2001, is $15,000.
g. All plant workers earn the same wage rate. Direct manufacturing labour-hours used for January total 2,500. Other labour and supervision labour total $10,000.
h. The gross plant payroll paid in January equals $52,000. Ignore withholdings.
i. All "actual" Manufacturing Department overhead incurred during January has already been posted.

Calculate the following:
1. Materials purchased during January
2. Cost of Goods Sold during January
3. Direct Manufacturing Labour Costs incurred during January
4. Manufacturing Overhead Allocated during January
5. Balance of Wages Payable Control, December 31, 2000
6. Balance of Work-in-Process Control, January 31, 2001
7. Balance of Work-in-Process Control, December 31, 2000
8. Manufacturing Overhead Under- or Overallocated for January 2001

SOLUTION

Amounts from the T-accounts are labelled (T).
1. From Materials Control T-account, Materials purchased: $90,000 (c) + $20,000 (e) – $15,000 (T) = $95,000
2. From Finished Goods Control T-account, Cost of Goods Sold: $20,000 (T) + $180,000 (d) – $15,000 (f) = $185,000
3. Direct manufacturing wage rate: $2,000 (b) ÷ 125 hours (b) = $16 per hour
   Direct manufacturing labour costs: 2,500 hours (g) × $16 = $40,000
4. Manufacturing overhead rate: $600,000 (a) ÷ $400,000 (a) = 150%
   Manufacturing overhead allocated: 150% × $40,000 (see 3) = $60,000
5. From Wages Payable Control T-account, Wages Payable Control, December 31, 2000: $52,000 (h) + $3,000 (T) – $40,000 (see 3) – $10,000 (g) = $5,000
6. Work-in-Process Control, January 31, 2001: $8,000 (b) + $2,000 (b) + 150% of $2,000 (b) = $13,000 (This answer is used in item 7.)
7. From Work-in-Process Control T-account, Work-in-Process Control, December 31, 2000: $180,000 (d) + $13,000 (see 6) – $90,000 (c) – $40,000 (see 3) – $60,000 (see 4) = $3,000
8. Manufacturing overhead overallocated: $60,000 (see 4) – $57,000 (T) = $3,000

Entries in T-accounts are lettered in accordance with the preceding additional information and are numbered in accordance with the requirements.

Materials Control

December 31, 2000 Bal.	(given)	15,000			
	(1)	95,000*		(c)	90,000
January 31, 2001 Bal.	(e)	20,000			

Work-in-Process Control

December 31, 2000 Bal.	(7)	3,000		(d)	180,000
Direct materials	(c)	90,000			
Direct manufacturing labour	(b) (g) (3)	40,000			
Manufacturing overhead allocation	(g) (a) (4)	60,000			
January 31, 2001 Bal.	(b) (6)	13,000			

Finished Goods Control

December 31, 2000 Bal.	(given)	20,000			
	(d)	180,000		(2)	185,000
January 31, 2001 Bal.	(f)	15,000			

Wages Payable Control

	(h)	52,000	December 31, 2000	(5)	5,000
				(g)	40,000
					10,000
			January 31, 2001	(given)	3,000

```
                        Manufacturing Overhead Control
Total January charges  (given)              57,000

                       Manufacturing Overhead Allocated
                                                        (g) (a) (4)        60,000

                              Cost of Goods Sold
                          (f)  (2)   185,000
```

*Can be computed only after all other postings in the account have been found.

SUMMARY

The following points are linked to the chapter's learning objectives.

1. The building blocks of a costing system are cost object, direct costs of a cost object, indirect costs of a cost object, cost pool, and cost-allocation base. Costing-system overview diagrams present these concepts in a systematic way. Costing systems aim to report cost numbers that reflect the way that chosen cost objects (such as products or services) use the resources of an organization.

2. Job-costing systems assign costs to distinct units of a product or service. In contrast, processing systems assign costs to masses of similar or identical units and compute unit costs on an average basis. These two costing systems are best viewed as opposite ends of a continuum. The costing systems of many companies combine some elements of both job costing and process costing.

3. A general approach to job costing involves identifying (a) the job, (b) the direct-cost categories, (c) the cost-allocation bases, (d) the indirect-cost categories, (e) the cost-allocation rates, (f) the allocated indirect costs of a job, and (g) adding all direct and indirect costs of a job.

4. Actual costing and normal costing differ in their use of actual or budgeted indirect cost rates:

	Actual Costing	**Normal Costing**
Direct cost rates	Actual rate(s)	Actual rate(s)
Indirect cost rates	Actual rate(s)	Budgeted rate(s)

Both methods use actual quantities of inputs for tracing direct costs and actual quantities of the allocation base(s) for allocating indirect costs.

5. The transactions in a job-costing system in manufacturing track (a) the acquisition of materials and other manufacturing inputs, (b) their conversion into work in process, (c) their eventual conversion into finished goods, and (d) the sale of finished goods. Each of the (a) to (d) stages in the manufacture/sale cycle is represented by journal entries in the costing system.

6. The theoretically correct alternative to disposing of underallocated or overallocated indirect costs is to prorate that amount on the basis of the total amount of the allocated indirect costs in the ending balances of inventories and cost of goods sold. Many organizations simply write off immaterial amounts to cost of goods sold for the sake of simplicity.

7. In some variations of normal costing, organizations use budgeted rates to assign indirect costs as well as direct labour costs to jobs.

This chapter contains definitions of the following important terms:

actual costing (p. 102)
cost-allocation base (p. 101)
cost pool (p. 101)
job cost record (p. 105)
job cost sheet (p. 105)
job-costing system (p. 101)
labour time record (p. 105)
manufacturing overhead allocated (p. 114)
materials requisition record (p. 105)
normal costing (p. 108)

overabsorbed indirect costs (p. 116)
overallocated indirect costs (p. 116)
overapplied indirect costs (p. 116)
process-costing system (p. 101)
proration (p. 117)
responsibility centre (p. 104)
source documents (p. 105)
underabsorbed indirect costs (p. 116)
underallocated indirect costs (p. 116)
underapplied indirect costs (p. 116)

ASSIGNMENT MATERIAL

QUESTIONS

4-1 Define *cost pool*, *cost tracing*, *cost allocation*, and *cost-allocation base*.

4-2 How does a job-costing system differ from a process-costing system?

4-3 Why might an advertising agency use job costing for an advertising campaign for Pepsi while a bank uses process costing for the cost of chequing account withdrawals?

4-4 Describe the seven steps in job costing.

4-5 What are the two major cost objects that managers focus on?

4-6 Describe three major source documents used in job-costing systems.

4-7 What is the main concern about source documents of job cost records?

4-8 Give two reasons why most organizations use a six-month or annual period rather than a weekly or monthly period to compute budgeted indirect cost rates.

4-9 Distinguish between actual costing and normal costing.

4-10 Describe two ways in which an accounting firm may use job cost information.

4-11 Comment on the following statement, "In a normal costing system, the amounts in Manufacturing Overhead Control account will always equal the amounts in Manufacturing Overhead Allocated account.

4-12 Describe three different debit entries in the Work-in-Process Control general ledger T-account.

4-13 Describe three alternative ways to dispose of under- or overallocated indirect costs.

4-14 When might a company use budgeted costs rather than actual costs to compute direct labour rates?

4-15 Describe briefly why modern technology such as Electronic Data Interchange (EDI) is helpful to managers.

EXERCISES

4-16 Actual costing, normal costing, manufacturing overhead. Destin Products uses a job-costing system with two direct-cost categories (direct materials and direct manufacturing labour) and one manufacturing overhead cost poll. Destin allocates manufacturing overhead costs using direct manufacturing labour costs. Destin provides the following information:

	Budget for year 2001	Actuals for year 2001
Direct manufacturing labour costs	$1,000,000	$980,000
Direct manufacturing overhead costs	$1,750,000	$1,862,000
Direct materials costs	$1,500,000	$1,450,000

REQUIRED

1. Compute the actual and budgeted manufacturing overhead rates for 2001.
2. During March, the cost record for Job 626 contained the following:

Direct materials used	$40,000
Direct manufacturing labour costs	$30,000

Compute the cost of Job 626 using (a) an actual-costing system and (b) a normal-costing system.

3. At the end of 2001, compute the under- or overallocated manufacturing overhead under Destin's normal costing system. Why is there no under- or overallocated overhead under Destin's actual-costing system?
4. Comment briefly on the advantages and disadvantages of actual-costing and normal-costing systems.

4-17 Job costing, normal and actual costing. Anderson Construction assembles residential homes. It uses a job-costing system with two direct-cost categories (direct materials and direct labour) and one indirect-cost pool (assembly support). Direct labour-hours is the allocation base for assembly support costs. In December 2000, Anderson budgets 2001 assembly support costs to be $8,000,000 and 2001 direct labour-hours to be 160,000.

At the end of 2001, Anderson is comparing the costs of several jobs that were started and completed in 2001.

Construction Period	Laguna Model February–June 2001	Mission Model May–October 2001
Direct materials	$106,450	$127,604
Direct labour	$ 36,276	$ 41,410
Direct labour-hours	900	1,010

Direct materials and direct labour are paid for on a contract basis. The costs of each are known when direct materials are used or direct labour-hours are worked. The 2001 actual assembly support costs were $6,888,000 while the actual direct labour-hours were 164,000.

REQUIRED

1. Compute the (a) budgeted and (b) actual indirect cost rate. Why do they differ?
2. What is the job cost of the Laguna Model and the Mission Model using (a) normal costing and (b) actual costing?
3. Why might Anderson Construction prefer normal costing over actual costing?

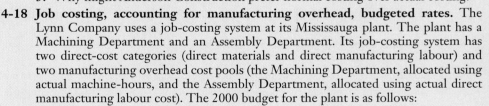

4-18 Job costing, accounting for manufacturing overhead, budgeted rates. The Lynn Company uses a job-costing system at its Mississauga plant. The plant has a Machining Department and an Assembly Department. Its job-costing system has two direct-cost categories (direct materials and direct manufacturing labour) and two manufacturing overhead cost pools (the Machining Department, allocated using actual machine-hours, and the Assembly Department, allocated using actual direct manufacturing labour cost). The 2000 budget for the plant is as follows:

	Machining Department	Assembly Department
Manufacturing overhead	$1,800,000	$3,600,000
Direct manufacturing labour cost	$1,400,000	$2,000,000
Direct manufacturing labour-hours	100,000	200,000
Machine-hours	50,000	200,000

The company uses a budgeted overhead rate for allocating overhead to production orders on a machine-hour basis in Machining and on a direct manufacturing labour cost basis in Assembly.

REQUIRED

1. Present an overview diagram of Lynn's job-costing system. Compute the budgeted manufacturing overhead rate for each department.

2. During February, the cost record for Job 494 contained the following:

	Machining Department	Assembly Department
Direct materials used	$45,000	$70,000
Direct manufacturing labour cost	$14,000	$15,000
Direct manufacturing labour-hours	1,000	1,500
Machine-hours	2,000	1,000

Compute the total manufacturing overhead costs of Job 494.

3. At the end of 2000, the actual manufacturing overhead costs were $2,100,000 in Machining and $3,700,000 in Assembly. Assume that 55,000 actual machine-hours were used in Machining and that actual direct manufacturing labour costs in Assembly were $2,200,000. Compute the over- or underallocated manufacturing overhead for each department.

4-19 Job costing, consulting firm. Taylor & Partners, a consulting firm, has the following condensed budget for 2001:

Revenues		$20,000,000
Total costs:		
Direct costs: Professional labour	$ 5,000,000	
Indirect costs: Audit support	13,000,000	18,000,000
Operating income		$ 2,000,000

Taylor has a single direct-cost category (professional labour) and a single indirect-cost pool (client support). Indirect costs are allocated to jobs on the basis of professional labour costs.

REQUIRED

1. Present an overview diagram of the job-costing system. Compute the 2001 budgeted indirect-cost rate for Taylor & Partners.

2. The markup rate for pricing jobs is intended to produce a 10% operating income-to-revenue margin. Compute the markup rate as a percentage of professional labour costs.

3. Taylor is bidding on a consulting job for Red Rooster, a fast food chain specializing in poultry meats. The budgeted breakdown of professional labour on the job is as follows:

Professional Labour Category	Budgeted Rate per Hour	Budgeted Hours
Director	$200	3
Partner	100	16
Manager	50	40
Assistant	30	160

Compute the budgeted cost of the Red Rooster job. How much will Taylor bid for the job if it is to earn its target operating income-to-revenue margin of 10%?

4-20 Computing indirect cost rates, job costing. Mike Rotundo, the president of Tax Assist, is examining alternative ways to compute indirect cost rates. He collects the following information from the budget for 2000:

◆ Budgeted variable indirect costs: $10 per hour of professional labour time
◆ Budgeted fixed indirect costs: $50,000 per quarter

The budgeted billable professional labour-hours per quarter are:

January–March	20,000 hours
April–June	10,000 hours
July–September	4,000 hours
October–December	6,000 hours

Rotundo pays all tax professionals employed by Tax Assist on an hourly basis ($30 per hour, including all fringe benefits).

Tax Assist's job-costing system has a single direct-cost category (professional labour at $30 per hour) and a single indirect-cost pool (office support that is allocated using professional labour-hours).

Tax Assist charges clients $65 per professional labour-hour.

REQUIRED

1. Compute budgeted indirect cost rates per professional labour-hour using:
   a. Quarterly budgeted billable hours as the denominator
   b. Annual budgeted billable hours as the denominator
2. Compute the operating income for the following four customers using:
   a. Quarterly-based indirect-cost rates
   b. An annual indirect-cost rate
      ◆ Stan Hansen: 10 hours in February
      ◆ Lelani Kai: 6 hours in March and 4 hours in April
      ◆ Ken Patera: 4 hours in June and 6 hours in August
      ◆ Evelyn Stevens: 5 hours in January, 2 hours in September, and 3 hours in November
3. Comment on your results in requirement 2.

4-21 Job costing, journal entries. The University of Toronto Press is wholly owned by the university. It performs the bulk of its work for other university departments, which pay as though the Press were an outside business enterprise. The Press also publishes and maintains a stock of books for general sale. A job-costing system is used to cost each job. There are two direct cost categories (direct materials and direct manufacturing labour) and one indirect-cost pool (manufacturing overhead, allocated on the basis of direct labour costs).

The following data (in thousands) pertain to 2001:

Direct materials and supplies purchased on account	$ 800
Direct materials used	710
Indirect materials issued to various production departments	100
Direct manufacturing labour	1,300
Indirect manufacturing labour incurred by various departments	900
Amortization on building and manufacturing equipment	400
Miscellaneous manufacturing overhead* incurred by various departments (ordinarily would be detailed as repairs, photocopying, utilities, etc.)	550
Manufacturing overhead allocated at 160% of direct manufacturing labour costs	?
Cost of goods manufactured	4,120
Revenues	8,000
Cost of goods sold	4,020
Inventories, December 31, 2000 (not 2001):	
Materials control	100
Work-in-process control	60
Finished goods control	500

*The term *manufacturing overhead* is not used uniformly. Other terms that are often encountered in printing companies include *job overhead* and *shop overhead*.

REQUIRED

1. Present an overview diagram of the job-costing system at the University of Toronto Press.
2. Prepare general journal entries to summarize 2001 transactions. As your final entry, dispose of the year-end over- or underallocated manufacturing overhead as a direct write-off to Cost of Goods Sold. Number your entries. Explanations for each entry may be omitted.
3. Show posted T-accounts for all inventories, Cost of Goods Sold, Manufacturing Overhead Control, and Manufacturing Overhead Allocated.

4-22 Job costing, journal entries, and source documents (continuation of 4-21). For each journal entry in your answer to Exercise 4-21, (a) indicate the source document that would most likely authorize the entry and (b) give a description of the entry in the subsidiary ledgers, if any entry needs to be made there.

4-23 Job costing, journal entries. Donnell Transport assembles prestige mobile homes. Its job-costing system has two direct-cost categories (direct materials and direct manufacturing labour) and one indirect-cost pool (manufacturing overhead allocated at a budgeted $30 per machine-hour in 2001). The following data (in millions) pertain to operations for the year 2001:

Materials control, December 31, 2000	$ 12
Work-in-process control, December 31, 2000	2
Finished goods control, December 31, 2000	6
Materials and supplies purchased on account	150
Direct materials used	145
Indirect materials (supplies) issued to various production departments	10
Direct manufacturing labour	90
Indirect manufacturing labour incurred by various departments	30
Amortization on plant and manufacturing equipment	19
Miscellaneous manufacturing overhead incurred (credit Various Liabilities; ordinarily would be detailed as repairs, utilities, etc.)	9
Manufacturing overhead allocated, 2,100,000 actual machine-hours	?
Cost of goods manufactured	294
Revenues	400
Cost of goods sold	292

REQUIRED

1. Present an overview diagram of Donnell Transport's job-costing system.
2. Prepare general journal entries. Number your entries. Post to T-accounts. What is the ending balance of Work-in-Process Control?
3. Show the journal entry for disposing of over- or underallocated manufacturing overhead directly as a year-end write-off to Cost of Goods Sold. Post the entry to T-accounts.

4-24 Accounting for manufacturing overhead. Consider the following selected cost data for the Hamilton Forging Company for 2000.

Budgeted manufacturing overhead	$7,000,000
Budgeted machine-hours	200,000
Actual manufacturing overhead	$6,800,000
Actual machine-hours	195,000

Hamilton's job-costing system has a single manufacturing overhead cost pool (allocated using a budgeted rate based on actual machine-hours). Any amount of under- or overallocation is immediately written off to cost of goods sold.

REQUIRED

1. Compute the budgeted manufacturing overhead rate.
2. Journalize the allocation of manufacturing overhead.
3. Compute the amount of under- or overallocation of manufacturing overhead. Is the amount significant? Journalize the disposition of this amount on the basis of the ending balances in the relevant accounts.

4-25 Proration of overhead. (Z. Iqbal, adapted) The Zaf Radiator Company uses a single manufacturing overhead cost pool in its job-costing system. It uses a normal-costing system with actual machine hours as the allocation base. The following data are for 2001:

Budgeted manufacturing overhead	$4,800,000
Overhead allocation base	Machine-hours
Budgeted machine-hours	80,000
Manufacturing overhead incurred	$4,900,000
Actual machine-hours	75,000

Machine-hours data and the ending balances (before proration of underallocated or overallocated overhead) are as follows:

	Actual Machine-Hours	2001 End-of-Year Balance
Cost of Goods Sold	60,000	$8,000,000
Finished Goods	11,000	1,250,000
Work in Process	4,000	750,000

REQUIRED

1. Compute the budgeted manufacturing overhead rate for 2001.
2. Compute the under- or overallocated manufacturing overhead of Zaf Radiator in 2001. Prorate this under- or overallocated amount using:
   a. Immediate write-off to Cost of Goods Sold
   b. Proration based on ending balances (before proration) in Work-in-Process, Finished Goods, and Cost of Goods Sold
   c. Proration based on the allocated overhead amount (before proration) in the ending balances of Work-in-Process, Finished Goods, and Cost of Goods Sold
3. Which proration method do you prefer in requirement 3? Explain.

 4-26 Job costing; actual, normal, and variation of normal costing. Chirac & Partners is a Quebec-based public accounting partnership specializing in audit services. Its job-costing system has a single direct-cost category (professional labour) and a single indirect-cost pool (audit support, which contains all the costs in the Audit Support Department). Audit support costs are allocated to individual jobs using actual professional labour-hours. Chirac & Partners employs ten professionals who are involved in their auditing services.

Budgeted and actual amounts for 2001 are as follows:

Budget for 2001

Professional labour compensation	$960,000
Audit support department costs	$720,000
Professional labour-hours billed to clients	16,000 hours

Actual results for 2001

Audit support department costs	$744,000
Professional labour-hours billed to clients	15,500 hours
Actual professional labour-cost rate is $58 per hour.	

REQUIRED

1. Identify the direct-cost rate per professional labour-hour and the indirect-cost rate per professional labour-hour for 2001 under (a) actual costing, (b) normal costing, and (c) variation of normal costing that uses budgeted rates for direct costs.
2. The audit of the Montreal Expos done in 2001 was budgeted to take 110 hours of professional labour time. The actual professional labour time on the audit was 120 hours. Compute the 2001 job cost using (a) actual costing, (b) normal costing, and (c) variation of normal costing that uses budgeted rates for direct costs. Explain any differences.

4-27 Job costing; actual, normal, and variation normal costing. Vista Group provides architectural services for residential and business clients. It employs 25 professionals. Its job-costing system has a single direct-cost category (professional labour) and a single indirect-cost pool (client support, which contains all the costs in the Client Support Department). Client support costs are allocated to individual jobs using actual professional labour-hours.

Budgeted and actual amounts for 2001 are as follows:

Budget for 2001

Professional labour compensation	$4,000,000
Client Support Department costs	$2,600,000
Professional labour-hours billed to clients	40,000 hours

Actual Results for 2001

Client Support Department costs	$2,436,000
Professional labour-hours billed to clients	42,000 hours
Actual professional labour-cost rate is $110 per hour.	

REQUIRED

1. Identify the direct-cost rate per professional labour-hour and the indirect-cost rate per professional labour-hour for 2001 under (a) actual costing, (b) normal costing, and (c) variation normal costing that uses budgeted rates for direct costs.
2. In 2001, the Vista Group designed a new retirement village in Victoria, British Columbia, for Carefree Years, Inc. Vista budgeted to spend 1,500 professional

labour-hours on the project. Actual professional labour-hours spent were 1,720. Compute the job cost of the Carefree Years project using (a) actual costing and (b) normal costing. Explain any differences.

PROBLEMS

4-28 Job costing, accounting for manufacturing overhead, budgeted rates. The Solomon Company uses a job-costing system at its Dover plant. The plant has a Machining Department and a Finishing Department. Its job-costing system has two direct-cost categories (direct materials and direct manufacturing labour) and two manufacturing overhead cost pools (the Machining Department, allocated using actual machine-hours, and the Finishing Department, allocated using actual labour cost). The 2000 budget for the plant is as follows:

	Machining Department	Finishing Department
Manufacturing overhead	$10,000,000	$8,000,000
Direct manufacturing labour cost	$ 900,000	$4,000,000
Direct manufacturing labour-hours	30,000	160,000
Machine-hours	200,000	33,000

REQUIRED

1. Present an overview diagram of Solomon's job-costing system.
2. What is the budgeted overhead rate that should be used in the Machining Department? In the Finishing Department?
3. During the month of January, the cost record for Job 431 shows the following:

	Machining Department	Finishing Department
Direct material used	$14,000	$3,000
Direct manufacturing labour cost	$ 600	$1,250
Direct manufacturing labour-hours	30	50
Machine-hours	130	10

What is the total manufacturing overhead allocated to Job 431?
4. Assuming that Job 431 consisted of 200 units of product, what is the unit product cost of Job 431?
5. Balances at the end of 2000 are as follows:

	Machining Department	Finishing Department
Manufacturing overhead incurred	$11,200,000	$7,900,000
Direct manufacturing labour cost	$ 950,000	$4,100,000
Machine-hours	220,000	32,000

Compute the under- or overallocated manufacturing overhead for each department and for the Dover plant as a whole.
6. Why might Solomon use two different manufacturing overhead cost pools in its job-costing system?

4-29 Job costing, law firm. Keating & Partners is a law firm specializing in labour relations and employee-related work. It employs 25 professionals (5 partners and 20 managers) who work directly with its clients. The average budgeted total compensation per professional for 1999 is $104,000. Each professional is budgeted to have 1,600 billable hours to clients in 1999. Keating is a highly respected firm, and all professionals work for clients to their maximum 1,600 billable hours available. All professional labour costs are included in a single direct cost category and are traced to jobs on a per-hour basis.

All costs of Keating & Partners other than professional labour costs are included in a single indirect-cost pool (legal support) and are allocated to jobs using professional labour-hours as the allocation base. The budgeted level of indirect costs in 1999 is $2.2 million.

REQUIRED

1. Present an overview diagram of Keating's job-costing system.
2. Compute the 1999 budgeted professional labour-hour direct-cost rate.
3. Compute the 1999 budgeted indirect-cost rate per hour of professional labour.
4. Keating & Partners is considering bidding on two jobs:
   a. Litigation work for Richardson, Inc., that requires 100 budgeted hours of professional labour
   b. Labour contract work for Punch, Inc., that requires 150 budgeted hours of professional labour

Prepare a cost estimate for each job.

4-30 Job costing with two direct- and two indirect-cost categories law firm (continuation of 4-29). Keating has just completed a review of its job-costing system. This review included a detailed analysis of how past jobs used the firm's resources and interviews with personnel about what factors drive the level of indirect costs. Management concluded that a system with two direct-cost categories (professional partner labour and professional association labour) and two indirect-cost categories (general support and secretarial support) would yield more accurate job costs. Budgeted information for 1999 related to the two direct-cost categories is as follows:

	Professional Partner Labour	Professional Associate Labour
Number of professionals	5	20
Hours of billable time per professional	1,600 per year	1,600 per year
Total compensation (average per professional)	$200,000	$80,000

Budgeted information for 1999 relating to the two indirect-cost categories is:

	General Support	Secretarial Support
Total costs	$1,800,000	$400,000
Cost allocation base	Professional labour-hours	Partner labour-hours

The budgeted total number of days out of town for all professionals in 1996 is 2,000 days.

REQUIRED

1. Compute the 1999 budgeted direct-cost rates for (a) professional partners and (b) professional associates.
2. Compute the 1999 budgeted indirect-cost rates for (a) general support and (b) secretarial support.
3. Compute the budgeted job costs for the Richardson and Punch jobs, given the following information:

	Richardson, Inc.	Punch, Inc.
Professional partners	60 hours	30 hours
Professional associates	40 hours	120 hours

4. Comment on the results in requirement 3. Why are the job costs different from those computed in Problem 4-29?

4-31 Normal costing, overhead allocation, working backwards. Gibson Company uses a normal costing system with two direct-cost categories—direct materials and direct manufacturing labour—and one indirect-cost category—manufacturing overhead. The following information is obtained from the company's records for 2001.

- Total manufacturing costs $7,500,000
- Cost of goods manufactured   7,275,000
- Manufacturing overhead allocated was 30% of total manufacturing costs
- Manufacturing overhead was allocated to production at a rate of 80% of direct manufacturing labour cost
- The dollar amount of work-in-process inventory on January 1, 2001, was 75% of the dollar amount of work-in-process inventory on December 31, 2001.

REQUIRED

1. What was the total direct labour cost in 2001?
2. What was the total cost of direct materials used in 2001?
3. What was the dollar amount of work-in-process inventory on December 31, 2001?

4-32 Overview of general-ledger relationships. The Blakely Company is a small machine shop that uses highly skilled labour and a job-costing system (using normal costing). The total debits and credits in certain accounts just before year-end are as follows:

	December 30, 1999	
	Total Debits	Total Credits
Materials Control	$100,000	$70,000
Work-in-Process Control	320,000	305,000
Manufacturing Department Overhead Control	85,000	—
Finished Goods Control	325,000	300,000
Cost of Goods Sold	300,000	—
Manufacturing Overhead Allocated	—	90,000

All materials purchased are for direct materials. Note that "total debits" in the inventory accounts would include beginning inventory balances, if any.

The preceding accounts *do not* include the following:

a. The manufacturing labour costs recapitulation for the December 31 working day: direct manufacturing labour, $5,000, and indirect manufacturing labour, $1,000.

b. Miscellaneous manufacturing overhead incurred on December 30 and December 31: $1,000.

ADDITIONAL INFORMATION

◆ Manufacturing overhead has been allocated as a percentage of direct manufacturing labour costs through December 30.
◆ Direct materials purchased during 1999 were $85,000.
◆ There were no returns to suppliers.
◆ Direct manufacturing labour costs during 1999 totalled $150,000, not including the December 31 working day described previously.

REQUIRED

1. Compute the inventories (December 31, 1998) of materials control, work-in-process control, and finished goods control. Show T-accounts.
2. Prepare all adjusting and closing journal entries for the preceding accounts. Assume that all under- or overallocated manufacturing overhead is closed directly to Cost of Goods Sold.
3. Compute the ending inventories (December 31, 1999), after adjustments and closing of materials control, work-in-process control, and finished goods control.

4-33 General ledger relationships, under- and overallocation. (S. Sridhar, adapted) Partially completed T-accounts and additional information for the Needham Company for the year 2000 are presented below. Needham uses a normal costing system.

Materials Control		Work-in-Process Control		Finished Goods Control	
1-1-2000	380,000	1-1-2000 20,000		1-1-2000 10,000	900,000
30,000		Dir. manuf.		940,000	
400,000		labour 360,000			

Manufacturing Overhead Control		Manufacturing Overhead Allocated		Cost of Goods Sold	
540,000					

ADDITIONAL INFORMATION

1. Direct manufacturing labour wage rate was $15 per hour.
2. Manufacturing overhead is allocated at $20 per direct manufacturing labour hour.
3. During the year, sales revenues were $1,090,000, and marketing and distribution expenses were $140,000.

REQUIRED

1. What was the amount of direct materials issued to manufacturing during 2000?
2. What was the amount of manufacturing overhead allocated to jobs during 2000?
3. What was the cost of jobs completed during 2000?
4. What was the balance in work-in-process inventory on December 31, 2000?
5. What was the cost of goods sold before any proration or under- or overallocated overhead?
6. What was the under- or overallocated manufacturing overhead in 2000?

7. Prorate the under- or overallocated manufacturing overhead using
   a. Immediate write-off to Cost of Goods Sold
   b. Proration based on ending balances (before proration) in Work-in-Process, Finished Goods, and Cost of Goods Sold.
8. Using each of the proration methods in requirement 7, calculate Needham's operating income for the year 2000.
9. Which proration method in requirement 7 do you recommend Needham use? Explain your answer briefly.

4-34 General ledger relationships, under- and overallocation, service industry. John Brody and Co. is an engineering consulting firm. Brody uses a variation of a normal-costing system. It charges jobs for blueprints made and fees paid to outside experts at actual costs, professional direct-labour costs at a budgeted direct-labour rate, and engineering support overhead costs (for engineering and office support) at a budgeted indirect-cost rate.

Brody maintains a Jobs-in-Process Control account in its general ledger that accumulates all costs of jobs. As a job is completed, Brody immediately bills the client and transfers the costs of the completed job to the Cost of Jobs Billed account to be matched against the revenues billed to the client. Consequently, unlike manufacturing companies, Brody has no accounts that correspond to Materials Control and Finished Goods Control accounts.

The following data pertain to the year 2001.

Cost of jobs in process on 1-1-2001	$200,000
Direct costs of fees and blueprints (all cash)	$150,000
Actual direct professional labour costs (all cash)	$1,500,000
Direct professional labour allocated at $50 per direct professional labour-hour	?
Actual direct professional labour-hours	29,000
Actual engineering support overhead costs (all cash)	$1,180,000
Engineering support overhead allocated at $0.80 per direct professional labour dollar	?
Cost of jobs billed	$2,500,000
Revenues	$2,800,000

Brody incurs no marketing and business development costs.

REQUIRED
1. Summarize the year 2001 transactions by preparing T-accounts for Jobs-in-Process Control, Cost of Jobs Billed, Direct Professional Labour Control, Direct Professional Labour Allocated, Engineering Support Overhead Control, Engineering Support Overhead Allocated, and Cash Control. As your final entry, dispose of the year-end under- or overallocated account balances as a direct write-off to Cost of Goods Sold.
2. Calculate Brody's operating income for the year 2001.

4-35 Proration of overhead, two indirect cost pools. The Glavine Corporation manufactures precision equipment made to order for the semiconductor industry. Glavine uses two manufacturing overhead cost pools—one for the overhead costs incurred in its highly automated Machining Department and another for overhead costs incurred in its labour-paced Assembly Department. Glavine uses a normal costing system. It allocates Machining Department overhead costs to jobs on the basis of actual machine hours using a budgeted machine-hour overhead rate. It allocates Assembly Department overhead costs to jobs on the basis of actual direct manufacturing labour-hours using a budgeted direct manufacturing labour-hour rate.
The following data are for the year 2000:

	Machining Department	Assembly Department
Budgeted overhead	$6,000,000	$5,000,000
Budgeted machine hours	100,000	
Budgeted direct manufacturing labour-hours		125,000
Actual manufacturing overhead costs	$6,200,000	$4,700,000

Machine-hours and direct manufacturing labour-hours and the ending balances (before proration of underallocated overhead) are as follows:

	Actual Machine-Hours	Actual Direct Manufacturing Labour-Hours	Balance before Proration, December 31, 2000
Cost of Goods Sold	67,500	90,000	$16,000,000
Finished Goods	4,500	4,800	750,000
Work-in-Process	18,000	25,200	3,250,000

REQUIRED

1. Compute the budgeted overhead rates for the year 2000 in the Machining and Assembly Departments.
2. Compute the under- or overallocated overhead in *each* department in 2000. Prorate the under- or overallocated amount in *each* department using:
   a. Immediate write-off to Cost of Goods Sold.
   b. Proration based on ending balances (before proration) in Cost of Goods Sold, Finished Goods, and Work-in-Process.
   c. Proration based on the allocated overhead amount (before proration) in the ending balances of Cost of Goods Sold, Finished Goods, and Work-in-Process.
3. Which proration method do you prefer in requirement 2? Explain.

4-36 Allocation and proration of manufacturing overhead. (SMA, heavily adapted) Nicole Limited is a company that produces machinery to customer order. Its job-costing system (using normal costing) has two direct-cost categories (direct materials and direct manufacturing labour) and one indirect-cost pool (manufacturing overhead, allocated using a budgeted rate based on direct manufacturing labour costs). The budget for 2001 was:

Direct manufacturing labour	$420,000
Manufacturing overhead	$252,000

At the end of 2001, two jobs were incomplete: No. 1768B (total direct manufacturing labour costs were $11,000) and No. 1819C (total direct manufacturing labour costs were $39,000). Machine time totalled 287 hours for No. 1768B and 647 hours for No. 1819C. Direct materials issued to No. 1768B amounted to $22,000. Direct material for No. 1819C came to $42,000.

Total charges to the Manufacturing Overhead Control account for the year were $186,840. Direct manufacturing labour charges made to all jobs were $400,000, representing 20,000 direct manufacturing labour-hours.

There were no beginning inventories. In addition to the ending work in process, the ending finished goods showed a balance of $156,000 (including a direct manufacturing labour cost component of $40,000). Sales for 2001 totalled $2,700,680, cost of goods sold was $1,600,000, and marketing costs were $857,870.

REQUIRED

1. Prepare a detailed schedule showing the ending balances in the inventories and cost of goods sold (before considering any under- or overallocated manufacturing overhead). Show also the manufacturing overhead allocated to these ending balances.
2. Compute the under- or overallocated manufacturing overhead for 2001.
3. Prorate the amount computed in requirement 2 on the basis of:
   a. The ending balances (before proration) of work in process, finished goods, and cost of goods sold
   b. The allocated overhead amount (before proration) in the ending balances of work in process, finished goods, and cost of goods sold
4. Assume that Nicole decides to immediately write off to cost of goods sold any under- or overallocated manufacturing overhead. Will operating income be higher or lower than the operating income that would have resulted from the proration in requirements 3(a) and 3(b)?

4-37 Job costing, contracting, ethics. Jack Halpern is the owner and CEO of Aerospace Comfort, a firm specializing in the manufacture of seats for air transport. He has just received a copy of a letter written to the Auditor General of the Canadian government. He believes it is from an ex-employee of Aerospace.

Dear Sir,

Aerospace Comfort in 2001 manufactured 100 X7 seats for the Canadian Armed Forces. You may be interested to know the following:

1. Direct materials cost billed for the 100 X7 seats was $25,000.
2. Direct manufacturing labour cost billed for 100 X7 seats was $6,000. This cost includes 16 hours of setup labour at $25 per hour, an amount included in the manufacturing overhead cost pool as well. The $6,000 also includes 12 hours of design time at $50 an hour. Design time was explicitly identified as a cost the Armed Forces was not to reimburse.
3. Manufacturing overhead cost billed for 100 X7 seats was $9,000 (150% of direct manufacturing labour costs). This amount includes the 16 hours of setup labour at $25 per hour that is incorrectly included as part of direct manufacturing labour costs.

You may also want to know that over 40% of the direct materials is purchased from Frontier Technology, a company that is 51% owned by Jack Halpern's brother.

For obvious reasons, this letter will not be signed.

c.c: *The Globe and Mail*
Jack Halpern, CEO of Aerospace Comfort

Aerospace Comfort's contract states that the Canadian Armed Forces reimburses Aerospace at 130% of manufacturing costs.

REQUIRED

Assume that the facts in the letter are correct as you answer the following questions.

1. What is the cost amount per X7 seat that Aerospace Comfort billed the Canadian Armed Forces? Assume that the actual direct materials costs are $25,000.
2. What is the amount per X7 seat that Aerospace Comfort should have billed the Canadian Armed Forces? Assume that the actual direct materials costs are $25,000.
3. What should the Canadian Armed Forces do to tighten its procurement procedures to reduce the likelihood of such situations recurring?

COLLABORATIVE LEARNING PROBLEM

4-38 Job costing, accounting for overhead costs, budgeted rates. Jefferson Company is a painting contractor for office and factory buildings. Jefferson uses a normal-costing system to cost each job. Jefferson's normal-costing system has two direct-cost categories (direct materials and direct labour) and one indirect-cost pool called *overhead costs*. Jefferson uses a budgeted overhead rate for allocating overhead costs to jobs on the basis of direct labour costs.

Jefferson provides the following additional information:

1. Budgeted overhead costs for the year 2001	$1,200,000
Budgeted direct labour costs for the year 2001	$1,500,000

2. As of January 31, Job 101 was the only job in process, with direct materials costs of $30,000 and direct labour costs of $50,000.
3. Jobs 102, 103, and 104 were started during February.
4. Direct materials used during February equal $150,000.
5. Direct labour costs for February are $120,000.
6. Actual overhead costs for February are $102,000.
7. The only job still in process at February 28, 2001 was job 104, with direct materials costs of $20,000 and direct labour costs of $40,000.

Jefferson maintains a Jobs in Process Control account in its general ledger. As a job is completed, Jefferson immediately bills the client and transfers the cost of the completed job to the Cost of Jobs Billed account to be matched against the revenues billed to the client. Consequently, unlike manufacturing companies, Jefferson does not have an account that corresponds to Finished Goods Control. Each month, Jefferson closes any under- or overallocated overhead to Cost of Jobs Billed.

INSTRUCTION

Form groups of two students to complete the following requirements.

REQUIRED

1. Calculate the budgeted overhead rate for allocating overhead costs in 2001.
2. Calculate the manufacturing overhead allocated to Job 101 as of January 31, 2001, and the manufacturing overhead allocated to Job 104 as of February 28, 2001.
3. Calculate the under- or overallocated overhead for February 2001.
4. Calculate the Cost of Jobs Billed by Jefferson in February 2001.

ACTIVITY-BASED COSTING AND ACTIVITY-BASED MANAGEMENT

Activity-based costing has been widely adopted in the automotive industry as a means to focus on cost control and efficiency—as illustrated by the Plastim example discussed in this chapter. Through cost reductions, North American manufacturers are able to provide consumers a more competitive price.

LEARNING OBJECTIVES

After studying this chapter, you should be able to:

1. Explain undercosting and overcosting of products
2. Present three guidelines for refining a costing system
3. Distinguish between the traditional and the ABC approaches to designing a costing system
4. Describe a four-part cost hierarchy
5. Cost products or services using activity-based costing (ABC)
6. Use ABC systems for activity-based management (ABM)
7. Compare ABC and department overhead-rate systems
8. Evaluate the costs and benefits of implementing ABC systems

Activity-Based Costing (ABC)
Economic-Value-Added
Website Guide
www.pitt.edu/~roztocki/abc/
abc.htm

Activity Based Costing: ABC
Technologies Inc.
www.abctech.com

Chapter 4 describes a basic job-costing system. In particular, it uses a single cost pool and a single indirect-cost rate to allocate indirect costs to jobs. An important question is "Does using a single indirect-cost rate provide misleading job cost numbers?" The answer depends on whether different jobs, products, and services are relatively alike (identical or at least similar) in the way they consume indirect costs of an organization. If they are alike, as was the case in Chapter 4, then a simple costing system will suffice for job-costing purposes. If they are not alike, a simple costing system will yield inaccurate cost numbers for jobs, products, and services.

As their variety increases, organizations are finding that different products and services place varying demands on resources. The need to measure more accurately how different products and services use organization resources has led companies to refine their costing systems. One of the main forms of cost refinement that companies all around the globe have implemented is activity-based costing (ABC), the focus of this chapter. In this chapter, we describe how ABC systems help companies to make better pricing and product mix decisions and also assist in cost management decisions by improving processes and product designs.

BROAD AVERAGING VIA PEANUT BUTTER COSTING APPROACHES

OBJECTIVE 1

Explain undercosting and overcosting of products

Cost smoothing (peanut butter costing). A costing approach that uses broad averages to assign (spread or smooth out) uniformly the cost of resources to cost objects (such as products, services, or customers) when the individual products, services, or customers in fact use those resources in a nonuniform way.

Product undercosting. Occurs when a product consumes a relatively high level of resources but is reported to have a relatively low total cost.

Product overcosting. Occurs when a product consumes a relatively low level of resources but is reported to have a relatively high total cost.

Product cost cross-subsidization. Costing outcome wherein at least one miscosted product is resulting in the miscosting of other products in the organization.

Companies may use a broad average (for example, a single cost pool) to allocate costs to products. However, they may choose to allocate costs in a nonuniform way. The phrase **cost smoothing** or **peanut butter costing** describes a costing approach that uses broad averages to uniformly assign (spread or smooth out) the cost of resources to cost objects (such as products, services, or customers) when the individual products, services, or customers in fact use those resources in a nonuniform way.

Undercosting and Overcosting

Use of broad averages via a cost smoothing or peanut butter costing approach may lead to undercosting or overcosting of products (services, customers, and so on):

◆ **Product undercosting.** A product consumes a relatively high level of resources but is reported to have a relatively low total cost.

◆ **Product overcosting.** A product consumes a relatively low level of resources but is reported to have a relatively high total cost.

Companies that undercost products may actually make sales that result in losses under the erroneous impression that these sales are profitable. That is, these sales bring in less revenue than the cost of the resources they use. Companies that overcost products run the risk of losing market share to existing or new competitors. Because these products actually cost less than what is reported to management, the company could cut selling prices to maintain or enhance market shares and still make a profit on each sale.

Product Cost Cross-Subsidization

Product cost cross-subsidization means that at least one miscosted product is resulting in the miscosting of other products in the organization. A classic example arises when a cost is uniformly spread (broad-averaged or "peanut-buttered") across multiple users without recognition of their different resource demands. Consider the costing of a restaurant bill for four colleagues who meet once a month to discuss business developments. Each diner orders separate entrees, desserts, and drinks. The restaurant bill for the most recent meeting is as follows:

	Entree	Dessert	Drinks	Total
Emma	$11	$ 0	$ 4	$ 15
James	20	8	14	42
Jessica	15	4	8	27
Matthew	14	4	6	24
Total	$60	$16	$32	$108
Average	$15	$ 4	$ 8	$ 27

The $108 total restaurant bill produces a $27 average cost per dinner. This broad-average costing approach treats each diner the same. Emma would probably object to paying $27, because her actual cost is only $15. Indeed, she ordered the lowest-cost entree, had no dessert, and had the lowest drink bill. When costs are averaged across all four diners, both Emma and Matthew are overcosted, James is undercosted, and Jessica is accurately costed.

The restaurant example is both simple and intuitive. The amount of cost cross-subsidization of each diner can be readily computed given that all cost items can be traced as direct costs to each diner. More complex costing issues arise, however, when there are indirect costs. Then resources are used by two or more individual diners. By definition, indirect costs require allocation—for example, the cost of a bottle of wine shared by two or more diners.

We now examine how costing systems can be refined to reduce the miscosting of jobs, products, or customers.

COSTING SYSTEM AT PLASTIM CORPORATION

Plastim Corporation manufactures lenses for rear (tail) lamps of automobiles. The lens, made from black, red, orange or white plastic, is the part of the lamp visible from the outside. Lenses are made using injection molding. The molding operation consists of injecting molten plastic into a mold to give the lamp its desired shape. The mold is cooled to allow the molten plastic to solidify, and the part is ejected.

Under its contract with Giovanni Motors, a major automobile manufacturer, Plastim makes two types of lenses—a complex lens, CL5, and a simple lens, S3. The complex lens is a large lens with special features such as multicolour molding (where more than one colour is injected into the mold) and complex shapes that wrap around the side of the car. Manufacturing these lenses is more complex because various parts in the mold must align and fit accurately and precisely. The simple lens is smaller and has few special features.

Design, Production, and Distribution Processes

The sequence of steps to design, produce, and distribute lenses, whether simple or complex, is as follows.

1. **Design of products and processes.** Each year Giovanni Motors specifies some modifications to the simple and complex lenses. Plastim's Design Department designs the molds from which the lenses will be made and defines the processes needed (details of the manufacturing operations).

2. **Manufacturing operations.** The lenses are molded, as described earlier, finished, cleaned, and inspected.

3. **Shipping and distribution.** Finished lenses are packed and sent to Giovanni Motors.

Plastim is operating at capacity and incurs very low marketing costs. Because of its high-quality products, Plastim has minimal customer-service costs. Plastim's business environment is very competitive with respect to simple lenses. At a recent meeting, Giovanni's purchasing manager indicated that a new competitor, who makes only simple lenses, was offering to supply the S3 lens to Giovanni at a price of around $53, well below Plastim's price of $63. Unless Plastim lowered its selling price, it would be in jeopardy of losing the Giovanni business for the simple lens, similar to S3, for the upcoming model year. Plastim's management was very concerned about this development. The same competitive pressures did not exist for the complex lens, which Plastim currently sells to Giovanni at a price of $137 per lens.

Plastim's management had various alternatives open to it. Plastim could give up the Giovanni business in simple lenses if it were going to be very unprofitable. It could reduce the price on the simple lens and either accept a lower margin or aggressively seek to reduce costs. But first management needed to understand what it costs to make and sell the S3 and CL5 lenses. To guide its pricing and cost management decisions, Plastim's managers assign all costs, both manufacturing and nonmanufacturing, to the S3 and CL5 lenses. Had the focus been on inventory costing, Plastim would only have assigned manufacturing costs to the lenses.

Existing Single Indirect-Cost Pool System

To cost products, Plastim currently uses a single indirect-cost-pool job-costing system, similar to the system described in Chapter 4. The steps are as follows.

◆ **Step 1:** *Identify the Chosen Cost Objects* The items (jobs) to be costed are the *total* costs of manufacturing and distributing 60,000 simple S3 lenses, and 15,000 complex CL5 lenses. Plastim determines unit costs of each lens by dividing total costs of each model by 60,000 for S3 and 15,000 for CL5.

◆ **Step 2:** *Identify the Direct Costs of the Cost Objects* Plastim identifies the direct costs of the lenses—direct materials and direct manufacturing labour—as follows:

	60,000 Simple Lenses (S3)		15,000 Complex Lenses (CL5)		
	Total (1)	Per Unit (2) = (1) ÷ 60,000	Total (3)	Per Unit (4) = (3) ÷ 15,000	Total (5) = (1) + (3)
Direct materials	$1,125,000	$18.75	$675,000	$45.00	$1,800,000
Direct manufacturing labour	600,000	10.00	195,000	13.00	795,000
Total direct costs	$1,725,000	$28.75	$870,000	$58.00	$2,595,000

◆ **Step 3:** *Select the Cost-Allocation Bases to Use in Allocating Indirect Costs to the Cost Object(s)* Plastim uses direct manufacturing labour-hours as the only allocation base to allocate all indirect costs to S3 and CL5. Most of the indirect costs consist of salaries paid to supervisors, engineers, production support, and maintenance staff that support direct manufacturing labour. In the current year, 2001, Plastim used 39,750 actual direct manufacturing labour-hours.

◆ **Step 4:** *Identify the Indirect Costs Associated with Each Cost-Allocation Base* Plastim groups all indirect costs totalling $2,385,000 into a single overhead cost pool.

◆ **Step 5:** *Compute the Rate per Unit of Each Cost-Allocation Base Used to Allocate Indirect Costs to the Cost Object(s)*

$$\frac{\text{Actual indirect-}}{\text{cost rate}} = \frac{\text{Actual total costs in indirect-cost pool}}{\text{Actual total quantity of cost-allocation base}}$$

$$= \frac{\$2,385,000}{39,750 \text{ hours}} = \$60 \text{ per direct manufacturing labour-hour.}$$

Exhibit 5-1, Panel A shows an overview of Plastim's existing costing system.

◆ **Step 6:** *Compute the Indirect Costs Allocated to the Cost Object(s)* Plastim uses 30,000 total direct manufacturing labour-hours to make the simple S3 lenses and 9,750 direct manufacturing labour-hours to make the complex CL5 lenses. Exhibit 5-1, Panel B shows indirect costs of $1,800,000 ($60 per direct manufacturing labour hour x 30,000) allocated to the simple lens and $585,000 ($60 per direct manufacturing labour hour x 9,750) allocated to the complex lens.

◆ **Step 7:** *Determine the Cost of the Cost Objects by Adding All Direct and Indirect Costs Assigned to Them* Exhibit 5-1, Panel B, presents the product costs for the simple and complex lenses. The direct costs are calculated in Step 2 and the indirect costs in Step 6. Note the correspondence between the costing system overview diagram (Exhibit 5-1, Panel A) and the costs calculated in Step 7. Panel A shows two direct-cost categories and one indirect-cost pool. Hence, the cost of each type of lens in Step 7 (Panel B) has three line items, two for direct costs and one for allocated indirect costs.

PANEL A: OVERVIEW OF PLASTIM'S EXISTING COSTING SYSTEM

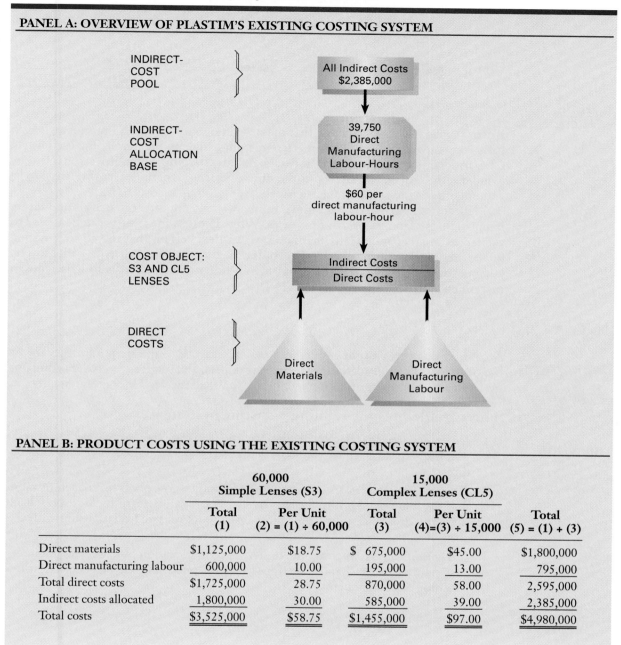

PANEL B: PRODUCT COSTS USING THE EXISTING COSTING SYSTEM

	60,000 Simple Lenses (S3)		15,000 Complex Lenses (CL5)		
	Total (1)	Per Unit (2) = (1) ÷ 60,000	Total (3)	Per Unit (4)=(3) ÷ 15,000	Total (5) = (1) + (3)
Direct materials	$1,125,000	$18.75	$ 675,000	$45.00	$1,800,000
Direct manufacturing labour	600,000	10.00	195,000	13.00	795,000
Total direct costs	$1,725,000	28.75	870,000	58.00	2,595,000
Indirect costs allocated	1,800,000	30.00	585,000	39.00	2,385,000
Total costs	$3,525,000	$58.75	$1,455,000	$97.00	$4,980,000

Plastim's management begins investigating why the S3 lens costs $58.75, well above the $53 price quoted by Plastim's competitor. Are Plastim's technology and processes inefficient in producing and distributing the simple S3 lens? Further analysis indicates that this is not the reason. Plastim has years of experience in manufacturing and distributing lenses like S3. Because Plastim often makes process improvements, management is confident that Plastim's technology and processes for making simple lenses are not inferior to those of its competitors. However, management is less certain about Plastim's capabilities in manufacturing and distributing complex lens. Indeed, Plastim has only recently started making these types of lenses. Management is pleasantly surprised to learn that Giovanni Motors considers the prices of CL5 lenses to be very competitive. Even more puzzling is that, even at these prices, Plastim earns very large margins on the CL5 lenses:

	60,000 Simple Lenses (S3)		15,000 Complex Lenses (CL5)		
	Total (1)	Per Unit (2) = (1) ÷ 60,000	Total (3)	Per Unit (4) = (3) ÷ 15,000	Total (5) = (1) + (3)
Revenues	$3,780,000	$63.00	$2,055,000	$137.00	$5,835,000
Costs	3,525,000	58.75	1,455,000	97.00	4,980,000
Operating income	$ 255,000	$ 4.25	$ 600,000	$ 40.00	$ 855,000
Operating income ÷ Revenues		6.75%		29.20%	

Plastim's managers are surprised that the margins are low on the S3 product where it has strong capabilities, while the margins are quite high on the newer, less-established CL5 product. Since they were not deliberately charging a low price for S3, they wonder if the cost system overcosts the simple S3 lens (assigning excessive costs to it) and undercosts the complex CL5 lens (assigning too little costs to it).

Plastim's management is quite confident about the direct materials and direct manufacturing labour costs of the lenses. Why? Because these costs can be traced to the lenses in an economically feasible way. It is less certain that the costing system effectively measures the overhead resources demanded by each type of lens. The key question, then, is how the system of allocating overhead costs to lenses might be refined.

REFINING A COSTING SYSTEM

OBJECTIVE 2

Present three guidelines for refining a costing system

Refined costing system. Costing system that results in a better measure of the nonuniformity in the use of resources by jobs, products, and customers.

A **refined costing system** results in a better measure of the nonuniformity in the use of an organization's resources by jobs, products, and services. Increased competition and advances in information technology have accelerated these refinements.

Three guidelines for refining a costing system are:

1. *Direct-cost tracing.* Classify as direct costs as many of the total costs as is economically feasible. This guideline reduces the amount of costs classified as indirect.

2. *Indirect-cost pools.* Expand the number of indirect-cost pools until each of these pools is homogeneous. In a *homogeneous cost pool*, all costs in the cost pool have the same or similar cause-and-effect or benefits-received relationship with the cost-allocation base.

3. *Cost-allocation bases.* Identify the preferred cost-allocation base for each indirect-cost pool. In this chapter we focus on the cause-and-effect criterion when choosing allocation bases.

ACTIVITY-BASED COSTING SYSTEMS

OBJECTIVE 3

Distinguish between the traditional and the ABC approaches to designing a costing system

Activity-based costing (ABC). Approach to costing that focuses on activities as the fundamental cost objects. It uses the cost of these activities as the basis for assigning costs to other cost objects such as products, services, or customers.

Activity. An event, task, or unit of work with a specified purpose.

One of the best tools for refining a cost system is *activity-based costing*. **Activity-based costing (ABC)** systems refine costing systems by focusing on individual activities as the fundamental cost objects. An **activity** is an event, task, or unit of work with a specified purpose. Some examples are designing products, setting up machines, operating machines, and distributing products. ABC systems calculate the costs of individual activities and assign costs to cost objects such as products and services on the basis of the activities undertaken to each product or service:

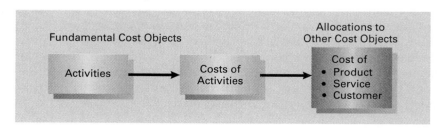

We describe key ideas of an ABC system in the context of our Plastim example. To define activities, Plastim organizes a cross-functional team from design, manufacturing, distribution, and accounting and administration. The team identifies key activities using a flow chart of all the steps and processes needed to design, produce, and distribute lenses.

Plastim's team identifies seven major activities:

1. Design products and processes
2. Set up molding machine to ensure mold is properly held in place and parts are properly aligned before manufacturing starts
3. Operate machines to manufacture lenses
4. Maintain and clean the mold after lenses are manufactured
5. Set up batches of finished lenses for shipment
6. Distribute lenses to customer sites
7. Administer and manage all processes at Plastim

By defining activities and identifying the costs of performing each activity, ABC systems seek a greater level of detail in understanding how an organization uses its resources. As we describe ABC systems, keep in mind three features:

1. ABC systems create smaller cost pools linked to the different activities. Plastim partitions its original single overhead cost pool into seven activity-related cost pools.
2. For each activity-cost pool, a measure of the activity performed serves as the cost-allocation base. For example, Plastim defines setup hours as a measure of setup activity and cubic metres of packages moved as a measure of distribution activity. Because each activity-cost pool pertains to a narrow and focused set of costs (for example, setup and distribution), the cost pools are homogeneous over time, the costs in each cost pool have a cause-and-effect relationship with the cost-allocation base. At Plastim, over the long term, setup hours is a cost driver of setup costs and cubic metres of packages moved is a cost driver of distribution costs.
3. In some cases, costs in a cost pool can be traced directly to products. In the Plastim example, cleaning and maintenance activity consists of salaries and wages paid to workers responsible for cleaning the mold. Following guideline 1 of refining a cost system, these costs can be traced directly to the specific mold used to produce the lens. Direct tracing of costs improves cost accuracy because it makes no assumptions about the cause-and-effect relationship between the cost pool and the cost-allocation base.

The logic of ABC systems is that more finely structured activity cost pools with activity-specific cost-allocation bases, which are cost-drivers of costs in the cost pool, lead to more accurate costing of activities. Allocating costs to products by measuring the cost-allocation bases of different activities used by different products leads to more accurate product costs. In contrast, consider the case when the cause-and-effect relationship between overhead costs and the cost-allocation base(s) is weak, for example, when Plastim uses direct manufacturing labour-hours as the cost-allocation base for all overhead costs, whether in setup or distribution. Direct manufacturing labour-hours do not drive the costs in these activity-cost pools. Consequently, measuring the direct manufacturing labour-hours used by various products does not capture the overhead costs demanded by the different products.

We illustrate the effect of allocating all overhead costs to products using direct manufacturing labour-hours, versus an ABC system with its emphasis on individual activities, by focusing on the setup activity. Setups frequently entail trial runs, fine tuning, and adjustments. Improper setups cause quality problems, such as scratches on the surface of the lens. The resources needed to set up the machines depend on the complexity of the manufacturing operation. Complex lenses require more setup resources than do simple lenses. Furthermore, complex lenses can be produced only in small batches because the mold needs to be cleaned more often. Relative to simple lenses, complex lenses not only use more resources per setup, but also need more frequent setups.

Setup data for the simple S3 lens and the complex CL5 lens are as follows.

		Simple S3 Lens	Complex CL5 Lens	Total
1	Quantity of lenses produced	60,000	15,000	
2	Number of lenses produced per batch	240	50	
3 = (1) ÷ (2)	Number of batches	250	300	
4	Setup time per batch	2 hours	5 hours	
5 = (3) × (4)	Total setup-hours	500 hours	1,500 hours	2,000 hours

Plastim identifies the total costs of setups (consisting mainly of allocated costs of process engineers, supervisors, and setup equipment) as $300,000. The following table shows how setup costs are allocated to the simple and complex lenses using direct manufacturing labour-hours and setup-hours respectively as the allocation bases. The setup cost per direct manufacturing labour-hour equals $7.54717 ($300,000 ÷ 39,750). The setup cost per setup-hour equals $150 ($300,000 ÷ 2,000 setup-hours).

	Simple S3 Lens	Complex CL5 Lens	Total
Cost allocated using direct manufacturing labour-hours			
$7.54717 × 30,000; $7.54717 × 9,750	$226,415	$ 73,585	$300,000
Cost allocated using setup-hours			
$150 × 500; $150 × 1,500	$ 75,000	$225,000	$300,000

Which allocation base should Plastim use? Plastim should allocate setup costs on the basis of setup hours. Why? Because, following guidelines 2 and 3, there is a strong cause-and-effect relationship between setup-related overhead costs and setup-hours, but there is almost no relationship between setup-related overhead costs and direct manufacturing labour-hours. Setup costs depend on the number of batches and the complexity of the setups and hence setup hours drive setup costs. The simple S3 lens attracts more of the setup costs when costs are allocated on the basis of direct manufacturing labour-hours. This occurs because more direct manufacturing labour-hours are needed to produce S3 lenses. However, direct manufacturing-labour time required by the S3 and CL5 lenses bears no relationship to the setup hours demanded by the S3 and CL5 lenses.

Note that setup hours are related to batches (groups) of lenses made, not individual lenses.

An important feature of activity-based costing is its emphasis on highlighting the different levels of activities—for example, individual units of output versus batches of output—when identifying cause-and-effect relationships. As our discussion of setups illustrates, limiting the drivers of costs to only units of output (or cost-allocation bases related to units of output such as direct manufacturing labour-hours) will weaken the cause-and-effect relationship between costs in a cost pool and the cost-allocation base. The *cost hierarchy* distinguishes costs by whether the cost driver is a unit of output (or variables such as machine-hours or direct labour-hours that are a function of units of output), or a *group* of units of a product (such as a batch in the case of setup costs), or the *product itself* (such as the complexity of the model in the case of design costs).

Cost Hierarchies

A **cost hierarchy** is a categorization of costs into different cost pools on the basis of the different types of cost drivers (or cost-allocation bases) or different degrees of difficulty in determining cause-and-effect (or benefits-received) relationships.

ABC systems commonly use a four-part cost hierarchy—output unit-level costs, batch-level costs, product-sustaining costs, and facility-sustaining costs—to

Cost hierarchy. Categorization of costs into different cost pools on the basis of different classes of cost drivers, or different degrees of difficulty in determining cause-and-effect (or benefits received) relationships.

Activity-Based Costing at Oetiker Limited

Oetiker Limited in Alliston, Ontario is part of a worldwide organization founded by Hans Oetiker in Switzerland in 1943. Besides the Alliston plant, there are others in Switzerland, Germany, Spain, France, Austria, and the United States, plus one that recently opened in China. Oetiker's main business is producing hose clamps for applications in a variety of industries. However, Hans Oetiker is a very prolific inventor. Besides his commercial inventions, he is very well known and respected for his charitable work in developing surgical clamps and other mechanical devices for the medical field.

The Alliston business consists of two main parts—the repetitive manufacture of clamps and the production of the machinery used in the repetitive manufacturing operations in all the Oetiker plants. Within repetitive manufacturing at Alliston, three main operations take place: raw materials are converted into a suitable form for stepless clamp manufacture, stepless clamps are produced, and ring clamp work in process (WIP) is produced. Ring clamp WIP is shipped to Oetiker's New Jersey plant to produce the final product, while the majority of the stepless clamps are purchased by a small number of customers in the automotive industry.

The Alliston plant began implementing ABC in October 1993, and the system there has become the standard which will eventually be implemented at all other Oetiker locations. Oetiker started the ABC project in order to determine the costs associated with machinery production, but it quickly became apparent that the plant's two main activities shared many costs, so that it would be more appropriate to examine the whole plant.

Oetiker ABC created an ABC model, which incorporated the basic product, customer, and business-sustaining costs; in addition, it broke down the product activities into materials, machine centre, and product family activities—the key components of Oetiker's product costs.

The Oetiker ABC model has provided management information so that Oetiker now understands the product costs for the approximately 2,000 items it produces and/or distributes, the cost of servicing its customers, and its business-sustaining costs. It also understands the costs involved in each production area.

Oetiker Canada
www.oetiker.com/ca/

Source: Mike Senyshen, "Beyond Product Costing," *CGA Magazine,* May 1996.

---

identify cost-allocation bases that are preferably cost drivers of costs in activity cost pools.

Output unit-level costs are for resources sacrificed on activities performed on each individual unit of product or service. Manufacturing operations costs (such as energy, machine amortization, and repair) that support Plastim's automated molding machines are output unit-level costs. Why? Because the cost of this activity increases with each additional unit of output produced (or machine-hour run).

Suppose that, in our Plastim example, each S3 lens requires 0.15 hours of molding machine time. Then S3 lenses require a total of 9,000 hours of molding machine time (0.15 hours × 60,000 lenses). Similarly, suppose CL5 lenses require 0.25 hours of molding machine time. Then the CL5 lens requires 3,750 molding machine-hours (0.25 hours × 15,000 lenses). The *total* molding machine costs allocated to S3 and CL5 depend on the number of each type of lens produced, regardless of the number of batches in which the lenses are made. Plastim's ABC system uses machine-hours, an output unit-level cost-allocation base, to allocate manufacturing operations costs to products.

Batch-level costs are for resources sacrificed on activities that are related to a group of units of product(s) or service(s) rather than to each individual unit of product

OBJECTIVE 4
Describe a four-part cost hierarchy

Output unit-level costs. The costs of resources sacrificed on activities performed on each individual unit of product or service.

Batch-level costs. The costs of resources sacrificed on activities that are related to a group of units of products or services rather than to each individual unit of product or service.

or service. In the Plastim example, setup costs are batch-level costs. Setup resources are used each time molding machines are set up to produce a batch of lenses. The S3 lens requires 500 setup-hours (2 hours per setup × 250 batches); the CL5 lens requires 1,500 setup-hours (5 hours per setup × 300 batches). The *total* setup costs allocated to S3 and CL5 depend on the total setup-hours required by each type of lens, not on the number of batches of S3 and CL5 produced. Plastim's ABC system uses setup-hours, a batch-level cost-allocation base to allocate setup costs to products.

In companies that purchase many different types of direct materials (Plastim purchases mainly plastic pellets), procurement costs can be significant. Procurement costs include the costs of placing purchase orders, receiving materials, and paying suppliers. These costs are batch-level costs because they are related to the number of purchase orders placed rather than the quantity or value of materials purchased.

Product-sustaining (or **service-sustaining costs**) are resources sacrificed on activities undertaken to support individual products or services. In the Plastim example, design costs are product-sustaining costs. Design costs for each type of lens depend largely on the time spent by designers on designing and modifying the product, mold, and process. These costs are a function of the complexity of the mold, measured by the number of parts in the mold multiplied by the square metre area over which the molten plastic must flow (say, 30 parts × square metre area for the S3 lens, and 70 parts × square metre area for the CL5 lens). The *total* design costs allocated to S3 and CL5 depend on the complexity of the mold, regardless of the number of units or batches in which the units are produced. Design costs cannot be linked in any cause-and-effect way to individual units of products or to individual batches of products. Plastim's ABC system uses parts times square-metre area, a product-sustaining cost-allocation base, to allocate design costs to products. Another example of product-sustaining costs is engineering costs incurred to change product designs, although such changes are infrequent at Plastim.

Facility-sustaining costs are resources sacrificed on activities that cannot be traced to individual products or services but support the organization as a whole. In the Plastim example, the general administration costs (including rent costs and cost of hiring building security) are facility-sustaining costs. It is usually difficult to find good cause-and-effect relationships between these costs and a cost-allocation base. This lack of a cause-and-effect relationship causes some companies not to allocate these costs to products and instead to deduct them from operating income. Other companies, such as Plastim, allocate facility-sustaining costs to products on some basis, for example direct manufacturing labour-hours, because management believes all costs should be allocated to products. Allocating all costs becomes particularly important when management wants to set price on the basis of a cost number that includes all costs.

Product-sustaining costs (service-sustaining costs). The costs of resources sacrificed on activities undertaken to support specific products (or services).

Facility-sustaining costs. The costs of resources sacrificed on activities that cannot be traced to specific products or services but support the organization as a whole.

IMPLEMENTING ACTIVITY-BASED COSTING AT PLASTIM CORPORATION

OBJECTIVE 5

Cost products or services using activity-based costing (ABC)

Now that we understand the basic concepts of ABC, we use it to refine Plastim's existing costing system. We again follow the seven-step approach to costing presented at the start of the chapter and the three guidelines for refining costing systems (increasing direct-cost tracing, creating homogeneous indirect-cost pools, and identifying cost-allocation bases that have a cause-and-effect relationship with costs in the cost pool).

◆ **Step 1:** *Identify the Chosen Cost Objects* The objective is to calculate the *total* costs of designing, manufacturing, and distributing the S3 and CL5 lenses.

◆ **Step 2:** *Identify the Direct Costs of the Cost Objects* Plastim identifies direct materials costs, direct manufacturing labour costs, and mold cleaning and maintenance costs as direct costs of the lenses. In its existing cost system, Plastim had classified mold cleaning and maintenance costs as indirect costs that were allocated to products using direct manufacturing labour-hours. However, these costs can be traced directly to a lens because each type of lens can be produced only from a specific mold. Note that, because mold cleaning and maintenance costs consist of wages paid to workers for cleaning molds after each batch of lenses is run, cleaning and maintenance costs are direct batch-level costs. Complex lenses incur more cleaning and maintenance costs than simple lenses because Plastim runs more batches of complex lenses than of simple lenses and because the molds of complex lenses are harder to clean. Direct manufacturing labour-hours do not capture the demand that complex and simple lenses place on mold cleaning and maintenance resources.

Plastim's direct costs are as follows:

| Description | Cost Hierarchy Category | 60,000 Simple Lenses (S3) | | 15,000 Complex Lenses (CL5) | | Total |
		Total (1)	Per Unit (2) = (1) ÷ 60,000	Total (3)	Per Unit (4) = (3) ÷ 15,000	Total (5) = (1) + (3)
Direct materials	Output-unit	$1,125,000	$18.75	$ 675,000	$45.00	$1,800,000
Direct manuf. labour	Output-unit	600,000	10.00	195,000	13.00	795,000
Cleaning & maintenance	Batch	120,000	2.00	150,000	10.00	270,000
Total direct costs		$1,845,000	$30.75	$1,020,000	$68.00	$2,865,000

◆ **Step 3**: *Select the Cost-Allocation Bases to Use in Allocating Indirect Costs to the Cost Object(s)* Plastim identifies six activities—design, molding-machine setups, manufacturing operations, shipment setup, distribution, and administration—for allocating indirect costs to products. Exhibit 5-2, column 4, shows the cost-allocation base and the quantity of the cost-allocation base for each activity.

The cost-allocation base is pivotal in defining the number of activity pools in an ABC system. For example, rather than define the design activities of product design, process design, and prototyping as separate activities, Plastim defines all these activities as part of a larger design activity. Why? Because the complexity of the mold is an appropriate cost driver for costs incurred in all three design subactivities.

A second consideration in choosing a cost-allocation base is the availability of reliable data and measures. Consider, for example, the problem of choosing a cost-allocation base for the design activity. The driver of design cost, a product-sustaining cost, is the complexity of the mold—more complex molds take more time to design. In its ABC system, Plastim measures complexity in terms of the number of parts in the mold and the surface area of the mold. If these data were difficult to obtain, or if measurement errors were large, Plastim could be forced to use some other measure of complexity, such as the amount of material flowing through the mold. The problem then is that the quantity of material flow may not adequately represent the complexity of the design activity.

◆ **Step 4**: *Identify the Indirect Costs Associated with Each Cost-Allocation Base* In this step, overhead costs incurred by Plastim are assigned to activities on the basis of a cause-and-effect relationship between the costs of an activity and the cost-allocation base for the activity. For example, costs in the distribution-cost pool have a cause-and-effect relationship to cubic metres of packages moved.

Some costs can be directly identified with a particular activity. For example, salaries paid to design engineers are directly identified with the design activity. Other costs need to be allocated across activities. For example, on the basis of interviews or time records, manufacturing engineers and supervisors identify the time spent on design activities, molding machine setup activity, and manufacturing operations. The time spent on these activities serves as a basis for allocating manufacturing engineers' and supervisors' salary costs to various activities. Similarly, other costs are allocated to activity-cost pools using allocation bases that best describe the costs incurred for the different activities. For example, space costs are allocated on the basis of square-metre area used for different activities. However, the allocation base chosen may sometimes be constrained by the availability of reliable data.

EXHIBIT 5-2
Activity-Cost Rates for Indirect-Cost Pools

Activity (1)	Cost Hierarchy Category (2)	(Step 4) Total Costs (3)	(Step 3) Cost Allocation Base (4)	(Step 5) Overhead Allocation Rate (5) = (2) ÷ (4)	Brief explanation of the cause-and-effect relationship that motivates the choice of the allocation base (6)
Design	Product-sustaining	$450,000	100 parts times square-metre area of mold	$4,500 per part times square-metre area of mold	Complex molds (more parts and larger surface area) require greater design department resources.
Setup of molding machines	Batch	$300,000	2,000 setup-hours	$150 per setup-hour	Overhead costs of the setup activity increase as setup-hours increase.
Manufacturing operations	Output unit	$637,500	12,750 molding-machine-hours	$50 per machine-hour	Plastim has mostly automated molding machines. Manufacturing overhead costs support automated molding machines and so increase with molding machine usage.
Shipment setup	Batch	$81,000	200 shipments	$405 per shipment	Costs incurred to prepare batches for shipment increase with the number of shipments
Distribution	Output unit	$391,500	67,500 cubic metres	$5.80 per cubic metre	Overhead costs of the distribution activity increase with cubic metres of packages shipped
Administration	Facility-sustaining	$255,000	39,750 direct manufacturing labour-hours	$6.4151 per direct manufacturing labour-hours	Administration department resources support direct manufacturing labour-hours, so the demand for these resources increases with direct manufacturing labour-hours.

The key point here is that all costs do not fit nicely into activity categories. Often, costs may need to be first allocated to activities before the costs of the activities can be allocated to products.

◆ **Step 5:** *Compute the Rate per Unit of Each Cost-Allocation Base Used to Allocate Indirect Costs to the Cost Object(s)* Exhibit 5-2 summarizes the calculation of the activity-cost rates using the cost-allocation bases selected in Step 3 and the indirect costs of each activity calculated in Step 4. Exhibit 5-3, Panel A, presents an overview of the ABC system.

◆ **Step 6:** *Compute the Indirect Costs Allocated to the Cost Object(s)* Exhibit 5-3 Panel B, shows indirect costs of $1,153,953 allocated to the simple lens and $961,047 allocated to the complex lens. To calculate indirect costs of each lens, the total quantity of the cost-allocation base used for each activity by each type of lens (the data for which is provided by Plastim's operations personnel) is multiplied by the cost-allocation rate calculated in Step 5 (see Exhibit 5-2, column 5). For example, of the 2,000 hours of the setup activity (Exhibit 5-2, column 4), the S3 lens uses 500 setup-hours and the CL5 lens uses 1,500 setup-hours. Hence, the total costs of the setup activity allocated to the S3 lens is $75,000 (500 setup-hours × $150, the setup rate calculated in Exhibit 5-2, column 5) and to the CL5 lens is $225,000 (1,500 setup-hours × $150). The setup cost per unit can then be calculated for the S3 lens as $1.25 ($75,000 ÷ 60,000 units) and for the CL5 lens as $15 ($225,000 ÷ 15,000 units).

◆ **Step 7:** *Determine the Costs of the Cost Objects by Adding All Direct and Indirect Costs Assigned to Them* Exhibit 5-3, Panel B, presents the product costs for the

EXHIBIT 5-3
Product Costs at Plastim Inc. Using Activity-Based Costing

PANEL A: OVERVIEW OF PLASTIM'S ACTIVITY-BASED COSTING SYSTEM

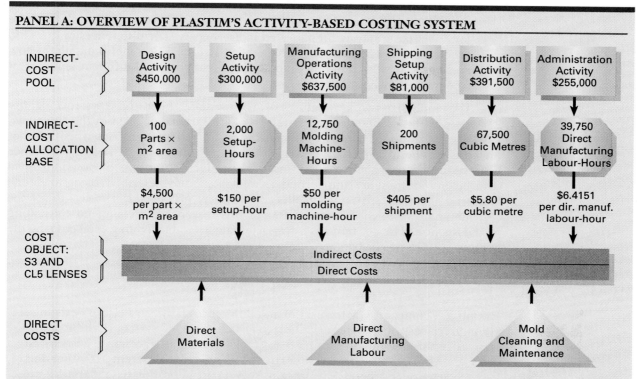

PANEL B: PRODUCT COSTS USING THE ACTIVITY-BASED COST SYSTEM

Description of Cost and the Quantity of Activity Used by Each Type of Lens	60, 000 Simple Lenses (S3)		15,000 Complex Lenses (CL5)		
	Total (1)	Per Unit (2) = (1) ÷ 60,000	Total (3)	Per Unit (4) = (3) ÷ 15,000	Total (5) = (1) + (3)
Direct costs					
Direct materials	$1,125,000	$18.75	$ 675,000	$45.00	$1,800,000
Direct manufacturing labour	600,000	10.00	195,000	13.00	795,000
Direct mold cleaning and maintenance costs	120,000	2.00	150,000	10.00	270,000
Total direct costs	1,845,000	30.75	1,020,000	68.00	2,865,000
Indirect costs					
Design activity costs					
S3: 30 parts × metres² area × $4,500	135,000	2.25			450,000
CL5: 70 parts × metres² area × $4,500			315,000	21.00 }	
Setup activity costs					
S3: 500 setup-hours × $150	75,000	1.25			300,000
CL5: 1,500 setup-hours × $150			225,000	15.00 }	
Manufacturing operations activity costs					
S3: 9,000 molding machine-hours × $50	450,000	7.50			637,500
CL5: 3,750 molding machine-hours × $50			187,500	12.50 }	
Shipping setup activity					
S3: 100 shipments × $405	40,500	0.67			81,000
CL5: 100 shipments × $405			40,500	2.70 }	
Distribution activity					
S3: 45,000 m³ × $5.80	261,000	4.35			391,500
CL5: 22,500 m³ × $5.80			130,500	8.70 }	
Administrative activity					
S3: 30,000 dir. manuf. labour-hours × $6.4151	192,453	3.21			255,000
CL5: 9,750 dir. manuf. labour-hours × $6.4151			62,547	4.17 }	
Total indirect costs	1,153,953	19.23	961,047	64.07	2,115,000
Total costs	$2,998,953	$49.98	$1,981,047	$132.07	$4,980,000

simple and complex lenses. The direct costs are calculated in Step 2 and the indirect costs in Step 6. The activity-based cost system overview in Exhibit 5-3, Panel A, shows three direct-cost categories and six indirect-cost pools. Hence the cost of each type of lens in Exhibit 5-3, Panel B, has nine line items, three for direct costs and six for allocated indirect costs. The differences in the ABC product costs of S3 and CL5 calculated in Exhibit 5-3, Panel B, highlight how these products use different amounts of direct costs and different amounts of resources in each activity area.

We emphasize two key features of ABC systems. First, these systems identify all costs used by products, whether the costs are variable or fixed in the short run. Why? Because the focus of ABC systems is on longer-run decisions when more of the costs can be managed and fewer costs are regarded as fixed and given. Hence ABC systems identify all resources used by products regardless of how individual costs behave in the short run. Second, as we have already described, recognizing the hierarchy of costs is critical when allocating costs to products. It is easiest to use the cost hierarchy to calculate *total* costs. For this reason, we recommend calculating total costs first. The per unit costs are easily calculated by dividing total costs by the number of units produced.

COMPARING ALTERNATIVE COSTING SYSTEMS

Exhibit 5-4 compares key features of and differences between Plastim's existing single indirect-cost pool system (Exhibit 5-1) and the ABC system (Exhibit 5-3). We emphasize three points in Exhibit 5-4: (1) ABC systems trace more costs as direct costs; (2) ABC systems create more cost pools linked to different activities; and (3) for each activity-cost pool, ABC systems seek a cost-allocation base that has a cause-and-effect relationship with costs in the cost pool.

EXHIBIT 5-4
Comparing Alternative Costing Systems

	Existing Single Indirect-Cost Pool System (1)	ABC System (2)	Difference (3) = (2) − (1)
Direct cost categories	2	3	+ 1
	Direct materials	Direct materials	
	Direct manufacturing labour	Direct manufacturing labour	
		Direct cleaning and maintenance labour	
Total direct costs	$2,595,000	$2,865,000	+$270,000
Indirect cost pools	1	6	+ 5
	Single indirect-cost pool allocated using direct manufacturing labour-hours	Design cost pool allocated using parts × square-metre area	
		Molding machine setup cost pool allocated using setup-hours	
		Manufacturing operations cost pool allocated using molding machine-hours	
		Shipment setup cost pool allocated using number of shipment	
		Distribution cost pool allocated using cubic metres of packages shipped	
		Administration cost pool allocated using direct manufacturing labour-hours	
Total indirect costs	$2,385,000	$2,115,000	−$270,000
Total costs assigned to simple (S3) lens	$3,525,000	$2,998,953	−$526,047
Cost per unit of simple (S3) lens	$58.75	$49.98	−$8.77
Total costs assigned to complex (CL5) lens	$1,455,000	$1,981,047	+$526,047
Cost per unit of complex (CL5) lens	$97.00	$132.07	+$35.07

The homogeneous cost pools and the choice of cost-allocation bases, tied to the cost hierarchy, gives Plastim's managers greater confidence in the activity and product cost numbers from the ABC system. Allocating costs to lenses using only an output unit-level allocation base, direct manufacturing labour-hours, as in the existing single indirect-cost pool system overcosts the simple S3 lens and undercosts the complex CL5 lens. The CL5 (S3) lens uses a disproportionately larger (smaller) amount of output unit-level, batch-level, and product-sustaining costs than is represented by the direct manufacturing labour-hour cost-allocation base.

The benefits of ABC systems arise from using ABC information for making better decisions. But these benefits must be traded off against the measurement and implementation costs of these system. We focus on these issues next.

USING ABC SYSTEMS FOR COST MANAGEMENT AND PROFITABILITY IMPROVEMENT

The emphasis of this chapter so far has been on the role of ABC systems in obtaining better activity and product costs. But companies use ABC information for both pricing and cost management decisions. **Activity-based management (ABM)** describes management decisions that use activity-based costing information to improve operations and processes, satisfy customers, and generate profits. In this section, we focus on ABM, including performing activities more efficiently, eliminating activities that do not add value, and improving product design.

Product and pricing decisions. The ABC system gives insight into the cost management structures for making and selling diverse products. As a result, management can make better product and pricing decisions. For example, the ABC system indicates that Plastim can reduce the price of S3 to the $53 range and still make a profit, because the ABC cost of S3 is $49.98. Without the ABC information, Plastim management may have erroneously concluded that it would incur an operating loss on the S3 lens at the $53 price. This incorrect conclusion may have caused Plastim to reduce its business in simple lenses and focus instead on complex lenses, where its existing single indirect-cost pool system indicates it is very profitable.

Focusing on complex lenses would be a mistake. The ABC system indicates that the cost of making the complex lens is much higher ($132.07 versus $97 under Plastim's existing direct manufacturing labour-based costing system). As Plastim's operations staff had thought all along, Plastim has no comparative advantage in making CL5 lenses. At a price of $137 per lens for CL5, the margins look very small. As Plastim reduces prices on simple lenses, it will probably have to negotiate a higher price for the complex lenses.

Cost reduction decisions. Manufacturing and distribution personnel use ABC systems to focus cost reduction efforts. Managers set cost-reduction targets in terms of reducing the cost per unit of the cost-allocation base in different activity areas. For example, the supervisor of the distribution activity area at Plastim could have a performance target of decreasing the distribution cost per cubic metre from $5.80 to $5.40 by reducing distribution labour and warehouse rental costs.

Process decisions. Creating a map of the cost of important activities (activity cost pools) and the factors that cause these costs to be incurred (cost drivers and cost-allocation bases) opens many opportunities for improving efficiency. Management can evaluate whether particular activities can be reduced or eliminated by improving processes. Each of the indirect cost-allocation bases in the ABC system is a nonfinancial variable (number of hours of setup time, cubic metres shipped, and so on). Controlling physical items such as setup hours or cubic metres shipped is often the most fundamental way that operating personnel manage costs. For example, Plastim can reduce distribution costs by packing the lenses in a way that reduces the bulkiness of the shipment.

The following table shows the reduction in distribution costs of the S3 and CL5 lenses as a result of process and efficiency improvements that lower the cost per cubic metre (from $5.80 to $5.40) and the total cubic metres of shipments (from 45,000 to 40,000 for S3 and 22,500 to 20,000 for CL5).

OBJECTIVE 6

Use ABC systems for activity-based management (ABM)

Activity-based management (ABM). Describes management decisions that use activity-based costing information to improve operations and processes, satisfy customers, and generate profits.

MEVATEC ABM Activity-Based Management Home Page www.rpm-abm.com/

	60,000 S3 lenses		15,000 CL5 lenses	
	Total (1)	Per Unit (2) = (1) ÷ 60,000	Total (3)	Per Unit (4) = (3) ÷ 15,000
Distribution cost per unit (from Exhibit 5-3, Panel B)		4.35		8.70
Distribution costs as a result of process improvements				
S3: 40,000 m³ × $5.40	$216,000	$3.60		
CL5: 20,000 m³ × $5.40			$108,000	
		—		$7.20
Savings in distribution cost per unit from process improvements		$0.75		$1.50

Design decisions. Management can identify and evaluate new designs to improve performance by evaluating how product and process designs impact activities and costs. Companies can then work with their customers to evaluate the costs and prices of alternative design choices. For example, creative design decisions that decrease the complexity of the mold reduce costs of design, materials, labour, setups, molding machine operations, and mold cleaning and maintenance.

If Plastim used its existing direct manufacturing labour-hour-based system to choose among alternative designs, which design choices would Plastim favour? Those designs that reduce direct manufacturing labour-hours the most. Why? Because the cost system would erroneously signal that reducing direct manufacturing labour-hours reduces overhead costs. However, as our discussion of ABC systems indicates, direct manufacturing labour-hours has little impact on Plastim's overhead costs.

Planning and managing activities. As was the case with Plastim, most companies implementing ABC systems for the first time analyze actual costs to identify activity-cost pools and activity-cost rates. Many companies then use ABC systems for planning and managing activities. They specify budgeted costs for activities and use budgeted cost rates to cost products using normal-costing systems. At year-end, budgeted and actual costs are compared to provide feedback on how well activities were managed. Adjustment are also made for under- or over-allocated indirect costs for each activity area using the methods described in Chapter 4 (adjusted allocation rate approach, proration, or write-off to cost of goods sold).

ACTIVITY-BASED COSTING AND DEPARTMENT INDIRECT-COSTS RATES

OBJECTIVE 7

Compare ABC and department overhead rate systems

Companies often use costing systems that have features of ABC systems—such as multiple-cost pools and multiple cost-allocation bases—but that do not emphasize individual activities. Many companies calculate separate indirect-cost rates for each department (for example, design, manufacturing, distribution, and so on) or subdepartment (for example, machining and assembly departments within manufacturing) using a cost-allocation base that best represents the usage of resources in that department or subdepartment. Using the same logic that we described for ABC systems, companies prefer using department indirect-cost rates rather than a single company-wide indirect-cost rate when the drivers of costs in each department differ. In this section, we compare ABC systems and department rate costing systems.

Consider again our Plastim illustration. The indirect-cost rate for the design activity is, in fact, a design department indirect-cost rate. Plastim calculates the design activity rate by dividing total design department costs by a measure of the complexity of the mold (the driver of design department costs). Plastim does not find it worthwhile to calculate separate activity rates within the design department. Why? Because the complexity of the mold is an appropriate cost-allocation base for costs incurred for all design activities—the design department costs are homogeneous.

Growing Interest in Activity-Based Costing

Activity-based costing is being implemented by a growing number of companies around the globe.

Among Canadian companies, a survey* indicates that 14% of the interviewed businesses have implemented ABC, and another 15% are now considering changing to it. What attracts Canadian firms to ABC?

More accurate cost information for product pricing	61%
More accurate profit analysis	61
By product	22
By customer	20
By process	24
By department	43
Improved performance measures	43
Improved insight into cost causation	37

The ABC system replaced the existing system for 24% of the Canadian respondents implementing ABC, while it was a supplementary (off-line) system for 76%.

One study[†] of 162 U.S.-based companies (including 29 service sector implementations) reported the following ranking of the primary applications: (1) product/service costing, (2) cost reduction, and (3) process improvement. The rankings for the areas where there were "significant" or "very significant" changes in decisions were (1) pricing strategy, (2) processes, and (3) product mix.

A United Kingdom survey[‡] found that "just under 20% of 251 respondents had adopted ABC." The ranking of the application areas was (1) cost management, (2) performance measurement, (3) product/service pricing, and (4) cost modelling. A New Zealand survey[§] ranked the benefits of ABC as (1) cost management, (2) product/service pricing, and (3) inventory valuation.

A survey[#] of Irish companies that had implemented ABC reported the following percentages for the actual benefits they experienced: (1) more accurate cost information for product costing and pricing (71%), (2) improved cost control and management (66%), (3) improved insight into cost causation (58%), (4) better performance measures (46%), and (5) more accurate customer profitability analysis (25%).

The Canadian survey reported that the two most common implementation problems were difficulties in defining activities and difficulties in selecting cost drivers. Implementation problems in the Irish survey were difficulties in identifying activities and assigning costs to those pools, difficulties in identifying and selecting cost drivers, inadequate computer software, and lack of adequate resources. The two top-ranked problems in the New Zealand survey were (1) difficulties in obtaining reliable data and (2) lack of middle management acceptance.

---

*Adapted from Armitage, H., and R. Nicholson, "Activity-Based Costing: A Survey of Canadian Practice," Supplement to *CMA Magazine* (1993)

[†]APQC/CAM-I, Activity-Based Management Consortium Study (American Productivity and Quality Center/CAM-I, 1995)

[‡]Innes, J., and F. Mitchell, "A Survey of Activity-Based Costing in the U.K.'s Largest Companies," *Management Accounting Research* (June 1995)

[§]Cotton, W. "Activity-Based Costing in New Zealand," (Working Paper, SUNY Genesco, 1993)

[#]Clarke, P. "Management Accounting Practices and Techniques of Irish Manufacturing Firms," (Working Paper Trinity College, Dublin, Ireland, 1995)

In contrast, in the manufacturing (as also in the distribution) department, Plastim identifies two activity-cost pools—setup-cost pool and a manufacturing operations-cost pool—rather than use a single manufacturing department indirect-cost pool. Why? For two reasons. First, each of these activities within manufacturing incurs significant costs and has very different drivers of costs. Second, the S3 and CL5 lenses do not use resources from these two activity areas in the same proportion. For example, CL5 uses 75% (1,500 ÷ 2,000) of the setup hours but only 29.4% (3,750 ÷ 12,750) of the machine hours. Using only machine hours, say, to allocate all manufacturing department costs at Plastim would result in CL5 being undercosted because it would not be charged for the significant setup resources it actually uses.

The preceding discussion suggests that using department indirect-cost rates to allocate costs to products would result in the same product costs as activity-cost rates would if (1) a single activity, for example machining in a manufacturing department, accounts for a sizable fraction of the department's costs or (2) significant costs are incurred on different activities within a department but each activity has the same cost-allocation base or (3) significant costs are incurred on different activities with different cost-allocation bases within a department but different products use resources from the different activity areas in the same proportions.

In many companies, where either of these three conditions hold, a department indirect-cost rate system is often adequate. In companies where these conditions do not hold, department indirect-cost rate systems can be refined using ABC. Emphasizing activities leads to more focused and homogeneous cost pools, and aids in identifying activity-cost-allocation bases that have a better cause-and-effect relationship with the costs in activity-cost pools. But the benefits of an ABC system must be balanced against its costs and limitations.

IMPLEMENTING ABC SYSTEMS

OBJECTIVE 8

Evaluate the costs and benefits of implementing ABC systems

Managers choose the level of detail in their costing systems by evaluating the costs of the system against the benefits that accrue from using these systems to make better decisions. Are there "telltale" signs that indicate when ABC systems are likely to provide the most benefits? We list some signals below:

1. Significant amounts of indirect costs are allocated using only one or two cost pools.
2. All or most costs are identified as output unit-level costs (that is, few costs are described as batch, product-sustaining, or facility-sustaining costs).
3. Products make diverse demands on resources because of differences in volume, process steps, batch size, or complexity.
4. Products that a company is well-suited to make and sell show small profits while products for which a company is less suited to produce and sell show large profits.
5. Complex products appear to be very profitable and simple products appear to be losing money.
6. Operations staff have significant disagreements with the accounting staff about the costs of manufacturing and marketing products and services.

Even if a company decides to implement ABC, it must make important choices about the level of detail. Should it choose many finely-specified activities, cost drivers, and cost pools, or would a few suffice? For example, Plastim could define a different molding machine-hour rate for each different type of molding machine. In making such choices, managers consider the costs and limitations of refining costing systems.

The main costs and limitations of ABC are the measurements necessary to implement the systems. ABC systems require management to estimate costs of activity pools and to identify and measure cost drivers for these pools to serve as cost-allocation bases. Even basic ABC systems require many calculations to determine costs of products and services. These measurements are costly. Activity-cost rates also need to be updated regularly. Very detailed ABC systems are costly to operate and difficult to understand.

In very detailed ABC systems, the allocations necessary to calculate activity costs often result in activity cost pools being measured with error. At times, companies are also forced to use substitute allocation bases for which data are readily available rather than preferred allocation bases. For example, a company might be forced to use the number of loads moved instead of the complexity and distance of different loads moved as the allocation base for material handling costs because the former is easier to track. When measurement errors are large, activity cost information can be misleading. For example, if the cost per load moved decreases, a company may conclude that it has become more efficient in its material handling operations. In fact the lower cost per move may have resulted solely from moving lighter loads over shorter distances.

Managers always trade off the benefits of designing a more detailed and accurate ABC system against the measurement and implementation costs of the system. Improvements in information technology and accompanying declines in technology costs have enabled ABC to be a practical costing system in many organizations. As such trends continue, ABC systems should be better able to meet the cost-benefit test.

ACTIVITY-BASED COSTING IN SERVICE AND MERCHANDISING COMPANIES

Although many of the early examples of ABC originated in manufacturing, it has many applications in the service and merchandising areas. The Plastim example illustrates the application of ABC to a service function, design, and to a merchandising function, distribution. Companies in the banking, insurance, airline, railroad, hospital, accounting, and consulting industries have implemented ABC systems to define profitable product mixes, improve efficiency, and satisfy customers. Similarly, many retail and wholesale companies are working with ABC systems.

Focus on ABC: Activity-Based Management articles
www.icms.net/focusonabm.htm

The general approach to ABC in the service and merchandising areas is very similar to the approach described in this chapter. Costs are desegregated into homogeneous cost pools and classified as output unit-level, batch-level, product- or service-sustaining, and facility-sustaining costs. The cost pools correspond to key activities. Costs are allocated to products or customers using activity drivers or cost-allocation bases that have a cause-and-effect relationship with the costs in the cost pool. Service and merchandising sectors also have to confront the problems of measuring activity-cost pools and identifying and measuring allocation bases.

The Co-operative Bank in the United Kingdom followed this approach when it implemented ABC in its retail bank. It calculated the costs of various activities such as making ATM transactions, opening and closing accounts, administering mortgages, and processing VISA transactions. It then used the activity-cost rates to calculate costs of various products, such as chequing account, mortgage, and VISA card. ABC information helped the Bank to improve its processes and to identify profitable products and customer segments. The Problem for Self-Study describes an application of ABC in the merchandising sector on the following page.

The Co-operative Bank
www.co-operativebank.co.uk

PROBLEM

Family Supermarkets (FS) has decided to increase the size of its St. John's store. It wants information about the profitability of individual product lines: soft drinks, fresh produce, and packaged food.

Operating personnel at FS provide the following data for each product line:

	Soft Drinks	Fresh Produce	Packaged Food
Revenues	$317,400	$840,240	$483,960
Cost of goods sold	240,000	600,000	360,000
Cost of bottles returned	4,800	0	0
Number of purchase orders placed	144	336	144
Number of deliveries received	120	876	264
Hours of shelf-stocking time	216	2,160	1,080
Items sold	50,400	441,600	122,400

FS also provides the following information for the year 2000:

Activity (1)	Description of Activity (2)	Total Costs (3)	Cost Allocation Base (4)
1. Bottle returns	Returning of empty bottles to store	$4,800	Direct tracing to soft drink line
2. Ordering	Placing of orders for purchases	$62,400	624 purchase orders
3. Delivery	Physical delivery and receipt of merchandise	$100,800	1,260 deliveries
4. Self-stocking	Stocking of merchandise on store shelves and ongoing restocking	$69,120	3,456 hours of shelf-stocking time
5. Customer support	Assistance provided to customers, including check out and bagging	$122,880	614,400 items sold

REQUIRED

1. Family Supermarkets currently allocates store support costs (all costs other than cost of goods sold) to product lines on the basis of cost of goods sold of each product line. Calculate the operating income and operating income as a percentage of revenues for each product line.
2. If Family Supermarkets allocates store support costs (all costs other than cost of goods sold) to product lines using an activity-based costing (ABC) system, calculate the operating income and operating income as a percentage of revenues for each product line.
3. Comment on your answers to requirements 1 and 2.

SOLUTION

1. The following table shows the operating income and operating income as a percentage of revenues. All store support costs (that is, costs other than cost of goods sold) are allocated to product lines using cost of goods sold of each product line as the cost-allocation base. Total store support costs equal $360,000 (cost of bottles returned, $4,800 + cost of purchase orders, $62,400 + cost of deliveries, $100,800 + cost of shelf stocking, $69,120 + cost of customer support, $122,880). If cost of goods sold is the cost-allocation base, the allocation rate for store support costs = $360,000 ÷ $1,200,000 = $0.30 per dollar of cost of goods sold. To allocate support costs to each product line, FS multiplies the cost of goods sold of each product line by 0.30. Operating income for each product line is as follows:

	Soft Drinks	Fresh Produce	Packaged Food	Total
Revenues	$317,400	$840,240	$483,960	$1,641,600
Cost of goods sold	240,000	600,000	360,000	1,200,000
Store support cost				
($240,000; $600,000; $360,000): × 0.30	72,000	180,000	108,000	360,000
Total costs	312,000	780,000	468,000	1,560,000
Operating income	$ 5,400	$ 60,240	$ 15,960	$ 81,600
Operating income ÷ Revenues	1.70%	7.17%	3.30%	4.97%

2. Under an ABC system, FS identifies bottle return costs as a direct cost since these costs can be traced easily to the soft drink product line. FS then calculates cost-allocation rates for each activity area (as in Step 5 described in the chapter). The activity rates are as follows:

Activity (1)	Total Costs (2)	Quantity of Cost-Allocation Base (3)	Allocation Rate (4) = (2) ÷ (3)
Ordering	$62,400	624 purchase orders	$100 per purchase order
Delivery	$100,800	1,260 deliveries	$80 per delivery
Shelf-stocking	$69,120	3,456 shelf-stocking-hours	$20 per shelf stocking-hour
Customer support	$122,880	614,400 items sold	$0.20 per item sold

Store support costs for each product line by activity are obtained by multiplying the total quantity of the cost-allocation base for each product line by the activity cost rate. Operating income for each product line is as follows:

	Soft Drinks	Fresh Produce	Packaged Food	Total
Revenues	$317,400	$840,240	$483,960	$1,641,600
Cost of goods sold	240,000	600,000	360,000	1,200,000
Bottle return costs	4,800	0	0	4,800
Ordering costs				
(144; 336; 144) purchase orders × $100	14,400	33,600	14,400	62,400
Delivery costs				
(120; 876; 264) deliveries × $80	9,600	70,080	21,120	100,800
Shelf-stocking costs				
(216; 2,160; 1,080) shelf stocking hours × $20	4,320	43,200	21,600	69,120
Customer support costs				
(50,400; 441,600; 122,400) items sold × $0.20	10,080	88,320	24,480	122,880
Total costs	283,200	835,200	441,600	1,560,000
Operating income	$ 34,200	$ 5,040	$ 42,360	$ 81,600
Operating income ÷ Revenues	10.77%	0.60%	8.75%	4.97%

3. Managers believe the ABC system is more credible than the previous costing system. It distinguishes the different types of activities at FS more precisely. It also tracks more accurately how individual product lines use their resources. Rankings of relative profitability (the percentage of operating income to revenues) of the three product lines under the previous costing system and under the ABC system are as follows:

Previous Costing System		ABC System	
1. Fresh produce	7.17%	1. Soft drinks	10.77%
2. Packaged food	3.30%	2. Packaged food	8.75%
3. Soft drinks	1.70%	3. Fresh produce	0.60%

The percentage of revenues, cost of goods sold, and activity costs for each product line are as follows:

	Soft Drinks	Fresh Produce	Packaged Food
Revenues	19.34%	51.18%	29.48%
Cost of goods sold	20.00	50.00	30.00
Activity Areas:			
Ordering	23.08	53.84	23.08
Delivery	9.53	69.52	20.95
Shelf-stocking	6.25	62.50	31.25
Customer support	8.20	71.88	19.92
Bottle returns	100.00	0	0

Soft drinks consume less of all resources. Soft drinks have fewer deliveries and require less shelf-stocking than does either fresh produce or packaged food. Most major soft-drink suppliers deliver merchandise to the store shelves and stock the shelves themselves. In contrast, the fresh produce area has the most deliveries and consumes a large percentage of shelf-stocking time. It also has the highest number of individual sales items. The previous costing system assumed that each product line used the resources in each activity area in the same ratio as their respective individual cost of goods sold to total cost of goods sold. Clearly, this assumption was inappropriate. The previous costing system was a classic example of broad averaging via cost smoothing.

FS managers can use the ABC information to guide decisions on how to allocate the planned increase in floor space. An increase in the percentage of space allocated to soft drinks is warranted. Note, however, that ABC information should be but one input into decisions about shelf space allocation. FS may have minimum limits on the shelf space allocated to fresh produce because of shoppers' expectations that supermarkets will carry merchandise from this product line.

Pricing decisions can also be made in a more informed way with the ABC information. For example, suppose a competitor announces a 5% reduction in soft-drink prices. Given the 10.77% margin FS currently earns on its soft-drink product line, it has flexibility to reduce prices and still make a profit on this product line. In contrast, the previous costing system erroneously implied that soft drinks only had a 1.70% margin, leaving little room to counter a competitor's pricing initiatives.

SUMMARY

The following points are linked to the chapter's learning objectives.

1. Product undercosting (or overcosting) occurs when a product or service consumes a relatively high (low) level of resource, but is reported to have a relatively low (high) cost. Cost smoothing or peanut butter costing, a common cause of under- or overcosting, is the result of using broad averages that uniformly assign (spread) the cost of resources to products when the individual products use those resources in a nonuniform way. Product-cost cross-subsidization exists when one undercosted (overcosted) product results in at least one other product being overcosted (undercosted).

2. Refining a costing system means making changes that result in cost numbers that better measure the way cost objects (such as products) differentially use the resources of the organization. These changes can require additional direct-cost tracing, the choice of more indirect-cost pools, or the use of different cost-allocation bases.

3. An ABC approach differs from the traditional approach by its fundamental focus on activities. An ABC approach typically results in (a) more indirect-cost pools than the traditional approach, (b) more cost drivers used as cost-allocation bases that are not output unit-level cost drivers, and (c) more frequent use of nonfinancial variables as cost-allocation bases.

4. A cost hierarchy is a categorization of costs into different cost pools on the basis of the different types of cost-allocation bases or different degrees of difficulty in determining cause-and-effect (or benefits-received) relationships. A four-part cost hierarchy consists of output unit-level costs, batch-level costs, product-sustaining or service-sustaining costs, and facility-sustaining costs.

5. In activity-based costing (ABC), costs of activities are used to assign costs to other cost objects such as products or services.

6. Activity-based management (ABM) describes management decisions that use ABC information. ABC systems are used for such management decisions as pricing, product-mix, efficiency improvements, and product and process redesign.

7. Department indirect-cost rate systems approximate ABC systems when the department has a single activity, or a single cost-allocation base for different activities, or when different products use the activities of a department in the same proportions.

8. ABC systems are likely to yield the most benefits when indirect costs are large and products make diverse demands on indirect resources. The main costs are the measurements necessary to implement the system.

▼ TERMS TO LEARN

This chapter contains definitions of the following important terms:

ABC (p. 142)
ABM (p. 151)
activity (p. 142)
activity-based costing (p. 142)
activity-based management (p. 151)
batch-level costs (p. 145)
cost hierarchy (p. 144)
cost smoothing (p. 138)
facility-sustaining cost (p. 146)

output unit-level costs (p. 145)
peanut butter costing (p. 138)
product cost cross-subsidization (p. 138)
product overcosting (p. 138)
product-sustaining costs (p. 146)
product undercosting (p. 138)
refined costing system (p. 142)
service-sustaining costs (p. 146)

▼ ASSIGNMENT MATERIAL

QUESTIONS

5-1 Define cost smoothing, and explain how managers can determine whether it occurs with their costing system.

5-2 Why should managers worry about product over- or undercosting?

5-3 What is costing system refinement? Describe three guidelines for such refinement.

5-4 What is an activity-based approach to designing a costing system?

5-5 Describe four levels of cost hierarchy.

5-6 "The existence of non-output-unit-level costs means that managers should not compute unit product costs on the basis of total manufacturing costs in all levels of the cost hierarchy." Do you agree? Explain.

5-7 What are the key reasons for product cost differences between traditional costing systems and ABC systems?

5-8 Describe four decisions for which ABC information is useful.

5-9 "Department indirect-cost rates are never activity-cost rates." Do you agree? Explain.

5-10 Describe four ways that help indicate when ABC systems are likely to provide the most benefits.

5-11 What are the main costs and limitations of implementing ABC systems?

5-12 "ABC systems apply only to manufacturing companies." Do you agree? Explain.

5-13 "Activity-based costing is the wave of the present and the future. All companies should adopt it." Do you agree? Explain.

5-14 "Increasing the number of indirect-cost pools is guaranteed to sizably increase the accuracy of product or service costs." Do you agree? Why?

5-15 The controller of a retailer has just had a $50,000 request to implement an ABC system quickly turned down. A senior vice-president in rejecting the request noted, "Given a choice, I will always prefer a $50,000 investment in improving things a customer sees or experiences, such as our shelves or our store layout. How does a customer benefit by our spending $50,000 on a supposedly better accounting system?" How should the controller respond?

EXERCISES

5-16 **Cost smoothing or peanut butter costing, cross-subsidization.** For many years, five former classmates—Steve Armstrong, Lola Gonzales, Rex King, Elizabeth Poffo, and Gary Young—have had a reunion dinner at the annual meeting of the Canadian Academic Accounting Association. The bill for the most recent dinner at a Montreal restaurant was broken down as follows:

Diner	Entree	Dessert	Drinks	Total
Armstrong	$27	$8	$24	$59
Gonzales	24	3	0	27
King	21	6	13	40
Poffo	31	6	12	49
Young	15	4	6	25

For at least the last ten dinners, King has put the total restaurant bill on his VISA card. He then mailed the other four a bill for the average cost. They shared the gratuity at the restaurant by paying cash. King continued this practice for the Montreal dinner. However, just before he sent the bill to the other diners, Young phoned him to complain. He was livid at Poffo for ordering the steak and lobster entree ("She always does that!") and at Armstrong for having three glasses of imported champagne ("What's wrong with domestic beer?").

REQUIRED

1. Why is the average cost approach in the context of the reunion dinner an example of peanut butter costing?

2. Compute the average cost to each of the five diners. Who is undercharged and who is overcharged under the average cost approach? Is Young's complaint justified?

3. Give an example of a dining situation where King would find it more difficult to compute the amount of under- or overcosting. How might the behaviour of the diners be affected if each person paid his or her own bill instead of continuing with the average cost approach?

5-17 **Cost hierarchy.** Telecom Inc. manufactures boom boxes (music systems with radio, cassette, and compact disc players) for different well-known companies. The boom boxes differ significantly in their complexity and the batch sizes in which they are manufactured. The following costs were incurred in 1999:

a. Designing processes, drawing process charts, making engineering process changes for products, $800,000

b. Procurement costs of placing purchase orders, receiving materials, and paying suppliers that are related to the number of purchase orders placed, $500,000

c. Direct materials costs, $6,000,000

d. Costs incurred to set up machines each time a different product needs to be manufactured, $600,000

e. Direct manufacturing labour costs, $1,000,000

f. Machine-related overhead costs such as amortization, maintenance, production engineering, $1,100,000. These resources are related to the activity of running the machines.

g. Plant management, plant rent, and insurance, $900,000

REQUIRED

1. Classify each of the preceding costs as output unit-level, batch-level, product-sustaining, or facility-sustaining. Explain your answers.

2. Consider two boom boxes made by Telecom Inc. One boom box is complex to make and made in many batches. The other boom box is simple to make and made in few batches. Suppose that Telecom needs the same number of machine hours to make either boom box. If Telecom allocated all overhead costs using machine hours as the only allocation base, how, if at all, would the boom boxes be miscosted? Briefly explain why.

3. How is the cost hierarchy helpful to Telecom in managing its business?

5-18 Cost hierarchy, ABC, distribution. Sonoma Winery makes two different grades of wine—regular wines and specialty wines. Recently, Sonoma has shown small profits on its regular wines and large profits on its specialty wines. As a result, management is considering getting out of the regular wine business and concentrating on specialty wines. This is a difficult decision because Sonoma had been very profitable in regular wines, its original business. In fact, the profitability of regular wines dipped substantially only after Sonoma got into the specialty wine business. Before making a decision, Sonoma wants to be sure that it understands what it costs to make and sell the regular and specialty wines. This question focuses on costs in the distribution area.

Sonoma distributes the regular wines and the specialty wines through completely different distribution channels. It distributes 120,000 cases of the regular wines through 10 general distributors and 80,000 cases of the specialty wines through 30 specialty distributors. Sonoma incurs $2,130,000 in distribution costs. Under its existing costing system Sonoma allocates distribution costs to products on the basis of cases shipped.

To understand better the demands on its resources in the distribution area, Sonoma identifies three activities and related activity costs:

1. Promotional activity including advertising, antique neon signs, and point-of-sales material at each distributor. Sonoma estimates it incurs $8,000 per distributor.

2. Order handling costs including costs to confirm and input the order into the order-entry system, set aside the correct number of cases, organize shipment and delivery, verify order packing, ensure delivery, send invoices, and follow-up for payments. Sonoma estimates costs of $300 for performing all the activities pertaining to each order. Sonoma's records show that distributors of regular wine placed an average of 10 orders per year, while distributors of specialty wine placed an average of 20 orders per year.

3. Distribution costs of $8 per case for freight.

REQUIRED

1. Calculate the total distribution costs and distribution cost per case for the regular wine and the specialty wine using Sonoma's existing costing system.

2a. For each activity, classify the cost of the activity as an output-unit level, batch-level, product- or service-sustaining, or facility-sustaining cost. Explain your answers.

2b. Calculate the total distribution costs and distribution cost per case for the regular wine and the specialty wine using Sonoma's activity-based costing system.

3. Explain the cost differences and the accuracy of the product costs calculated using the existing and the ABC systems. How might Sonoma's management use the information from the ABC system to manage its business better?

5-19 ABC, cost hierarchy, service. Halifax Test Laboratories does heat testing (HT) and stress testing (ST) on materials. Under its current costing system, Halifax aggregates all operating costs of $1,200,000 into a single overhead cost pool. Halifax calculates a rate per test hour of $15 ($1,200,000 ÷ 80,000 total test-hours). HT uses 50,000 test-hours and ST uses 30,000 test-hours. Gary Celeste, Halifax's controller, believes that there is enough variation in test procedures and cost structures to establish separate costing and billing rates. The market for test services is very competitive, and without this information, any miscosting and mispricing could cause Halifax to lose business. Celeste breaks down Halifax's costs into four activity-cost categories.

1. Direct labour costs, $240,000. These costs can be directly traced to HT, $180,000, and ST, $60,000.

2. Equipment related costs (rent, maintenance, energy, and so on), $400,000. These costs are allocated to HT and ST on the basis of test-hours.
3. Setup costs, $350,000. These costs are allocated to HT and ST on the basis of the number of setup-hours required. HT requires 13,500 setup-hours and ST requires 4,000 setup-hours.
4. Costs of designing tests, $210,000. These costs are allocated to HT and ST on the basis of the time required to design the tests. HT requires 2,800 hours and ST requires 1,400 hours.

REQUIRED

1. Classify each of the activity costs as output-unit-level, batch-level, product- or service-sustaining, or facility-sustaining. Explain your answer.
2. Calculate the cost per test-hour for HT and ST. Explain briefly the reasons why these numbers differ from the $15 per test-hour that Halifax had calculated using its existing costing system.
3. Explain the cost differences and the accuracy of the product costs calculated using the existing and the ABC systems. How might Halifax's management use the cost hierarchy and ABC information to manage its business better?

5-20 Alternative allocation bases for a professional services firm. The Wolfson Group (WG) provides tax advice to multinational firms. WG charges clients for (a) direct professional time (at an hourly rate), and (b) support services (at 30% of the direct professional costs billed). The three professionals in WG and their rates per professional hour are:

Professional	Billing Rate per Hour
Myron Wolfson	$500
Ann Brown	120
John Anderson	80

WG has just prepared the May 1999 bills for two clients. The hours of professional time spent on each client are as follows:

Professional	Hours per Client	
	Winnipeg Dominion	Tokyo Enterprises
Wolfson	15	2
Brown	3	8
Anderson	22	30
Total	40	40

REQUIRED

1. What amounts did WG bill to Winnipeg Dominion and Tokyo Enterprises for May 1999?
2. Suppose support services were billed at $50 per professional labour-hour (instead of 30% of professional labour costs). How would this change affect the amounts WG billed to the two clients for May 1999? Comment on the differences between the amounts billed in requirements 1 and 2.
3. How would you determine whether professional labour costs or professional labour-hours is the more appropriate allocation base for WG's support services?

5-21 Plantwide indirect-cost rates. Automotive Products (AP) designs, manufactures, and sells automotive parts. It has three main operating departments: design, engineering, and production.

♦ There were no returns to suppliers.
♦ *Design*—the design of parts, using state of the art, computer-aided design (CAD) equipment
♦ *Engineering*—the prototyping of parts and testing of their specifications
♦ *Production*—the manufacture of parts

For many years, AP has had long-term contracts with major automobile assembly companies. These contracts have large production runs. AP's costing system allocates variable manufacturing overhead on the basis of machine-hours. Actual variable manufacturing overhead costs for 2001 were $308,600. AP had three contracts in 2001, and its machine-hours used in 2001 were assigned as follows:

United Motors	120
Holden Motors	2,800
Leland Vehicle	1,080
Total	4,000

REQUIRED

1. Compute the plantwide variable manufacturing overhead rate for 2001.
2. Compute the variable manufacturing overhead allocated to each contract in 2001.
3. What conditions must hold for machine-hours to provide an accurate estimate of the variable manufacturing overhead incurred on each individual contract at AP in 2001?

5-22 Department indirect cost rates as activity rates (continuation of 5-21). The controller of Automotive Parts (AP) decides to interview key managers of the Design, Engineering, and Production Departments. Each manager is to indicate the consensus choice among department personnel as to the cost driver of variable manufacturing overhead costs in that department. Summary data are

	2001 Variable Manufacturing Overhead	Cost Driver
Design	$ 39,000	CAD design-hours
Engineering	29,600	Engineering-hours
Production	240,000	Machine-hours
	$308,600	

Details pertaining to usage of these cost drivers for each of the three 2001 contracts are:

Operating Areas	Cost Driver	United Motors	Holden Motors	Leland Vehicle
Design	CAD design-hours	110	200	80
Engineering	Engineering-hours	70	60	240
Production	Machine-hours	120	2,800	1,080

REQUIRED

1. What is the variable manufacturing overhead rate for each department in 2001?
2. What is the variable manufacturing overhead allocated to each contract in 2001 using department variable manufacturing overhead rates?
3. Compare your answer in requirement 2 to that in requirement 2 of Exercise 5-21. Comment on the results.

5-23 ABC, retail product line profitability. Family Supermarkets (FS) found that its ABC analysis (see p. 156) provided important insights. It extends the analysis to cover three more product lines—baked goods, milk and fruit juice, and frozen foods. The revenues, cost of goods sold, store support costs, and activity area usage of the three product lines is as follows:

	Baked Goods	Milk and Fruit Juice	Frozen Products
Financial data:			
Revenues	$57,000	$63,000	$52,000
Cost of goods sold	38,000	47,000	35,000
Store support	11,400	14,100	10,500
Activity area usage (cost driver):			
Ordering (purchase orders)	30	25	13
Delivery (deliveries)	98	36	28
Shelf-stocking (hours)	183	166	24
Customer support (items sold)	15,500	20,500	7,900

There are no bottle returns for any of these three product lines.

REQUIRED

1. Use the previous costing system (support costs allocated to products at the rate of 30% of cost of goods sold) to compute a product line profitability report for FS.

2. Use the ABC system (ordering at $100 per purchase order, delivery at $80 per delivery, shelf-stocking at $20 per hour, and customer support at $0.20 per item sold) to compute a product line profitability report for FS.

3. What new insights does the ABC system in requirement 2 provide to FS managers?

5-24 ABC, product costing at banks, cross-subsidization. First International Bank (FIB) is examining the profitability of its Premier Account, a combined savings and chequing account. Depositors receive a 7% annual interest rate on their average deposit. FIB earns an interest rate spread of 3% (the difference between the rate at which it lends money and the rate it pays depositors) by lending money for residential home loan purposes at 10%. Thus, FIB would gain $60 on the interest spread if a depositor has an average Premier Account balance of $2,000 in 2000 ($2,000 × 3% = $60).

The Premier Account allows depositors unlimited use of services such as deposits, withdrawals, chequing account, and foreign currency drafts. Depositors with Premier Account balances of $1,000 or more receive unlimited free use of services. Depositors with minimum balances of less than $1,000 pay $20 a month service fee for their Premier Account.

FIB recently conducted an activity-based costing study of its services. It assessed the following costs for six individual services. The use of these services in 2000 by three customers is as follows:

	ABC-Based Cost per "Transaction"	Account Usage		
		Robinson	Skerrett	Farrel
Deposit/withdrawal with teller	$ 2.50	40	50	5
Deposit/withdrawal with automatic teller machine	0.80	10	20	16
Deposit/withdrawal on prearranged monthly basis	0.50	0	12	60
Bank cheques written	8.00	9	3	2
Foreign currency drafts	12.00	4	1	6
Inquiries about account balance	1.50	10	18	9
Average Premier Account balance for 2000		$1,100	$800	$25,000

Assume Robinson and Farrel always maintain a balance above $1,000 while Skerrett always had a balance below $1,000 in 2000.

REQUIRED

1. Compute the 2000 profitability of the Robinson, Skerrett, and Farrell Premier Accounts at FIB.

2. What evidence is there of cross-subsidization across Premier Accounts? Why might FIB worry about this cross-subsidization if the Premier Account product offering is profitable as a whole?

3. What changes at FIB would you recommend for its Premier Account?

5-25 ABC, product cost cross-subsidization. PEI Potatoes processes potatoes into potato cuts at its highly automated plant. For many years, it processed potatoes for only the retail consumer market where it had a superb reputation for quality. Recently, it started selling potato cuts to the institutional market that includes hospitals, cafeterias, and university dormitories. Its penetration into the institutional market has been slower than predicted.

PEI's existing costing system has a single direct-cost category (direct materials, which are the raw potatoes) and a single indirect-cost pool (production support). Support costs are allocated on the basis of kilograms of potato cuts processed. Support costs include packaging material. The 1999 total actual costs for producing 1,000,000 kilograms of potato cuts (900,000 for the retail market and 100,000 for the institutional market) are:

Direct materials used	$150,000
Production support	983,000

The existing costing system does not distinguish between potato cuts produced for the retail or the institutional markets.

At the end of 1999, PEI unsuccessfully bid for a large institutional contract. Its bid was reported to be 30% above the winning bid. This came as a shock, as PEI in-

cluded only a minimum profit margin on its bid. Moreover, the PEI plant was widely acknowledged as the most efficient in the industry.

As part of its lost contract bid review process, PEI decided to explore several ways of refining its costing system. First, it identified that $188,000 of the $983,000 pertains to packaging materials that could be traced to individual jobs ($180,000 for retail and $8,000 for institutional). These will now be classified as a direct material. The $150,000 of direct materials used were classified as $135,000 for retail and $15,000 for institutional. Second, it used activity-based costing (ABC) to examine how the two products (retail potato cuts and institutional potato cuts) used the support area differently. The finding was that three activity areas could be distinguished and that different usage occurred in two of these three areas. The indirect cost per kilogram of finished product at each activity area is as follows:

Activity Area	Retail Potato Cuts	Institutional Potato Cuts
Cleaning	$0.120	$0.120
Cutting	0.240	0.150
Packaging	0.480	0.120

There was no beginning or ending amount of any inventory (materials, work in process, or finished goods).

REQUIRED
1. Using the current costing system, what is the cost per kilogram of potato cuts produced by PEI?
2. Using the refined costing system, what is the cost per kilogram of (a) retail market potato cuts and (b) institutional market potato cuts?
3. Comment on the cost differences shown between the two costing systems in requirements 1 and 2. How might PEI use the information in requirement 2 to make better decisions?

5-26 ABC, product cost cross-subsidization (continuation of 5-25). Assume for the following requirements that PEI Potatoes uses information from its activity-cost rates to calculate costs incurred on retail market potato cuts and institutional market potato cuts.

REQUIRED
1. Using the current costing system, what is the cost per kilogram of potato cuts produced by PEI?
2. Using the refined costing system, what is the cost per kilogram of (a) retail market potato cuts, and (b) institutional market potato cuts?
3. Comment on the cost differences shown between the two costing systems in requirement 1 and 2. How might PEI use the information in requirement 2 to make better decisions?

PROBLEMS

5-27 Activity-based job costing system. The Calgary Company manufactures and sells packaging machines. It recently used an activity-based approach to refine the job costing system at its Calgary plant. The resulting job-costing system has one direct cost category (direct materials) and four indirect manufacturing cost pools. These four indirect-cost pools and their allocation bases were chosen by a team of product designers, manufacturing personnel, and marketing personnel:

Indirect-Manufacturing Cost Pool	Cost-Allocation Base	Budgeted Cost-Allocation Rate
1. Materials-handling	Component parts	$ 8 per part
2. Machining	Machine-hours	$ 68 per hour
3. Assembly	Assembly-line-hours	$ 75 per hour
4. Inspection	Inspection-hours	$104 per hour

Cola Supreme recently purchased 50 can-packaging machines from the Calgary Company. Each machine has direct materials costs of $3,000, and requires 50 component parts, 12 machine-hours, 15 assembly-hours, and 4 inspection-hours.

Calgary's prior costing system had one direct cost category (direct materials) and one indirect cost category (manufacturing overhead, allocated using assembly-hours).

REQUIRED

1. Present overview diagrams of the prior job costing system and the refined activity-based job costing system.
2. Compute the unit manufacturing costs (using ABC) of each machine and the total manufacturing cost of the Cola Supreme job.
3. The activity-based job costing system of Calgary has only one manufacturing direct-cost category—direct materials. A competitor of the Calgary Company has two direct-cost categories at its manufacturing plant—direct materials and direct manufacturing labour. Why might Calgary not have a direct manufacturing labour costs category in its job-costing system? Where are the manufacturing labour costs included in the Calgary costing system?
4. What information might members of the team that refined the prior costing system find useful in the activity-based job costing system?

5-28 **Activity-based costing, job costing system.** The Hewlett-Packard (HP) plant in Roseville, California, assembles and tests printed circuit (PC) boards. The job-costing system at this plant has two direct-cost categories (direct materials and direct manufacturing labour) and seven indirect-cost pools. These indirect-cost pools represent the seven activity areas that operating personnel at the plant determined were sufficiently different (in terms of cost behaviour patterns or in terms of individual products being assembled) to warrant separate cost pools. The cost-allocation base chosen for each activity area is the cost driver at that activity area.

Debbie Berlant, a newly appointed marketing manager at HP, attends a training session that describes how an activity-based costing approach has been used to design the Roseville plant's job-costing system. Berlant is provided with the following incomplete information for a specific job (an order for a single PC board, No. A82):

Direct materials	$75	
Direct manufacturing labour	15	$90
Manufacturing overhead (see below)		?
Total manufacturing cost		$?

Manufacturing Overhead Cost Pool	Cost-Allocation Base	Cost-Allocation Rate	Units of Base Used on Job No. A82	Manufacturing Overhead Allocated to Job
1. Axial insertion	Axial insertions	0.08	45	?
2. Dip insertion	Dip insertions	0.25	?	6.00
3. Manual insertion	Manual insertions	?	11	5.50
4. Wave solder	Boards soldered	3.50	?	3.50
5. Backload	Backload insertions	?	6	4.20
6. Test	Budgeted time	90.00	0.25	?
7. Defect analysis	Budgeted time	?	0.10	8.00

REQUIRED

1. Present an overview exhibit of the activity-based job costing system at the Roseville plant.
2. Fill in the blanks (signalled by a question mark) in the cost information provided to Berlant for Job No. A82.
3. Why might manufacturing managers and marketing managers favour this ABC job costing system over the prior costing system, which had the same two direct-cost categories but only a single indirect-cost pool (manufacturing overhead allocated using direct labour cost)?

5-29 **Job costing with single direct-cost category, single indirect-cost pool, law firm.** Wigan Partners is a recently formed law partnership. Ellery Hanley, the managing partner of Wigan Partners, has just finished a tense phone call with Martin Offiah, president of Widnes Coal. Offiah complained about the price Wigan charged for some conveyancing (drawing up property documents) legal work done for Widnes Coal. He requested a breakdown of the charges. He also indicated to Hanley that a competing law firm, Hull & Kingston, was seeking more business with Widnes Coal and that he was going to ask them to bid for a conveyancing job next

month. Offiah ended the phone call by saying that if Wigan bid a price similar to the one charged last month, Wigan would not be hired for next month's job.

Hanley is dismayed by the phone call. He is also puzzled because he believes that conveyancing is an area where Wigan Partners has much expertise and is highly efficient. The Widnes Coal phone call is the bad news of the week. The good news is that yesterday Hanley received a phone call from its only other client (St. Helen's Glass) saying it was very pleased with both the quality of the work (primarily litigation) and the price charged on its most recent case.

Hanley decides to collect data on the Widnes Coal and St. Helen's Glass cases. Wigan Partners uses a cost-based approach to pricing (billing) each legal case. Currently it uses a single direct-cost category (for professional labour time) and a single indirect-cost pool (general support). Indirect costs are allocated to cases on the basis of professional labour-hours per case. The case files show the following:

	Widnes Coal	St. Helen's Glass
Professional labour time	104 hours	96 hours

Professional labour costs at Wigan Partners are $70 an hour. Indirect costs are allocated to cases at $105 an hour. Total indirect costs in the most recent period were $21,000.

REQUIRED

1. Why is it important for Wigan Partners to understand the costs associated with individual cases?
2. Present an overview diagram of the existing job-costing system.
3. Compute the costs of the Widnes Coal and St. Helen's Glass cases.

5-30 Job costing with multiple direct-cost categories, single indirect-cost pool, law firm (continuation of 5-29). Hanley speaks to the other partners about the pricing of the two cases. Several believe that the relative prices charged seem out of line with their intuition. One partner observes that a useful approach to obtaining more accurate job costs is to increase direct-cost tracing.

Hanley asks his assistant to collect details on those costs included in the $21,000 indirect cost pool that can be traced to each individual case. After further analysis, Wigan is able to reclassify $14,000 of the $21,000 as direct costs:

Other Direct Costs	Widnes Coal	St. Helen's Glass
Research support labour	$1,600	$ 3,400
Computer time	500	1,300
Travel and allowances	600	4,400
Telephone/faxes	200	1,000
Photocopying	250	750
Total	$3,150	$10,850

Hanley decides to calculate the costs of each case had Wigan used six direct-cost pools and a single indirect-cost pool. The single indirect-cost pool would have $7,000 of costs and would be allocated to each case using the professional labour-hours base.

REQUIRED

1. Present an overview diagram of the refined job-costing system with its multiple direct cost categories.
2. What is the revised indirect cost-allocation rate per professional labour-hour for Wigan Partners when total indirect costs are $7,000?
3. Compute the costs of the Widnes and St. Helen's cases if Wigan Partners had used its refined costing system with multiple direct-cost categories and one indirect-cost pool.
4. Compare the costs of the Widnes and St. Helen's cases in requirement 3 with those in requirement 3 of Problem 5-29. Comment on the results.

5-31 Job costing with multiple direct-cost categories, multiple indirect-cost pools, law firm (continuation of 5-29 and 5-30). Hanley examines the job-costing approaches in Problems 5-29 and 5-30. He questions the use of a single cost rate for all professional labour of Wigan Partners. Wigan has two classifications of professional staff—partners and managers. Hanley asks his assistant to examine the relative use of partners and managers on the recent Widnes Coal and St. Helen's cases. The

Widnes case used 24 partner-hours and 80 manager-hours. The St. Helen's case used 56 partner-hours and 40 manager-hours.

Hanley decides to examine how the use of separate direct- and indirect-cost pools for partners and managers would have affected the costs of the Widnes and St. Helen's cases. Indirect costs in each cost pool would be allocated on the basis of total hours of that category of professional labour.

The rates per category of professional labour are as follows:

Category of Professional Labour	Direct Cost per Hour	Indirect Cost per Hour
Partner	$100.00	$57.50
Manager	50.00	20.00

These indirect cost rates are based on a total indirect-cost pool of $7,000; $4,600 of this $7,000 is attributable to the activities of partners, and $2,400 is attributable to the activities of managers. (The indirect cost per hour of $57.50 is calculated by dividing $4,600 by 80 partner-hours; the indirect-cost rate of $20 is calculated by dividing $2,400 by 120 manager-hours.)

REQUIRED

1. Present an overview diagram of the refined job-costing system with its multiple direct-cost categories and its multiple indirect-cost pools.
2. Compute the costs of the Widnes and St. Helen's cases with Wigan Partners further refined system, with multiple direct-cost categories and multiple indirect-cost pools.
3. For what decisions might Wigan Partners find it more useful to use this job costing approach rather than the approach in Problems 5-29 or 5-30?

5-32 Activity-based costing, merchandising. Figure Four, Inc. specializes in the distribution of pharmaceutical products. Figure Four buys from pharmaceutical companies and resells to each of three different markets:

a. General supermarket chains
b. Drug store chains
c. "Mom and Pop" single-store pharmacies

Rick Flair, the new controller of Figure Four, reported the following data for August 2000:

	General Supermarket Chains	Drug Store Chains	"Mom and Pop" Single Stores
Average revenue per delivery	$30,900	$10,500	$1,980
Average cost of goods sold per delivery	$30,000	$10,000	$1,800
Number of deliveries	120	300	1,000

For many years, Figure Four has used gross margin percentage [(Revenue – Cost of goods sold) ÷ Revenue] to evaluate the relative profitability of its different groupings of customers (distribution outlets).

Flair recently attended a seminar on activity-based costing and decides to consider using it at Figure Four. Flair meets with all the key managers and many staff members. People generally agree that there are five key activity areas at Figure Four:

Activity Area	Cost Driver
1. Customer purchase order processing	Purchase orders by customers
2. Line item ordering	Line items per purchase order
3. Store delivery	Store deliveries
4. Cartons shipped to stores	Cartons shipped to a store per delivery
5. Shelf-stocking at customer stores	Hours of shelf stocking

Each customer purchase order consists of one or more line items. A line item represents a single product (such as Extra-Strength Tylenol tablets). Each store delivery entails delivery of one or more cartons of products to a customer. Each product is delivered in one or more separate cartons. Figure Four staff stack cartons directly onto display shelves in a store. Currently, there is no charge for this service, and not all customers use Figure Four for this activity.

The August 2000 operating costs (other than cost of goods sold) of Figure Four are $301,080. These operating costs are assigned to the five activity areas. The costs in each area and the amount of the cost drivers units used in that area for August 2000 are as follows:

Activity Area	Total Costs in August 2000	Total Units of Cost Driver Used in August 2000
1. Customer purchase order processing	$ 80,000	2,000 orders
2. Line item ordering	63,840	21,280 line items
3. Store delivery	71,000	1,420 store deliveries
4. Cartons shipped to stores	76,000	76,000 cartons
5. Shelf-stocking at customer stores	10,240	640 hours
	$301,080	

Other data for August 2000 include the following:

	General Supermarket Chains	Drugstore Chains	"Mom and Pop" Single Stores
Total number of orders	140	360	1,500
Average number of line items per order	14	12	10
Total number of store deliveries	120	300	1,000
Average number of cartons shipped per store delivery	300	80	16
Average number of hours of shelf-stocking per store delivery	3.0	0.6	0.1

REQUIRED

1. Compute the August 2000 gross margin percentage for each of its three distribution markets. What is the operating income of Figure Four?
2. Compute the August 2000 per unit cost driver rate for each of the five activity areas.
3. Compute the operating income of each distribution market in August 2000 using the activity-based costing information. Comment on the results. What new insights are available with the activity-based information?
4. Describe four challenges Flair would face in assigning the total August 2000 operating costs of $301,080 to the five activity areas.

5-33 **Plantwide, department, and activity cost rates.** (CGA, adapted) The Sayther Company manufactures and sells two products, A and B. The manufacturing activity is organized in two departments. Manufacturing overhead costs at its Calgary plant are allocated to each product using a plantwide rate of $17 per direct manufacturing labour-hour. This rate is based on budgeted manufacturing overhead of $340,000 and 20,000 budgeted direct manufacturing labour-hours:

Manufacturing Department	Budget Manufacturing Overhead	Budgeted Direct Manufacturing Labour-Hours
1	$240,000	10,000
2	100,000	10,000
Total	$340,000	20,000

The number of direct manufacturing labour-hours required to manufacture each product is:

Manufacturing Department	Product A	Product B
1	4	1
2	1	4
Total	5	5

Per unit costs for the two categories of direct manufacturing costs are:

Direct Manufacturing Costs	Product A	Product B
Direct materials costs	$120	$150
Direct manufacturing labour costs	80	80

At the end of the year, there was no work in process. There were 200 finished units of product A and 600 finished units of product B on hand. Assume that the budgeted production level of the Calgary plant was exactly attained.

Sayther sets the listed selling price of each product by adding 120% to its unit manufacturing costs; that is, if the unit manufacturing costs are $100, the listed selling price is $220 ($100 + $120). This 120% markup is designed to cover costs upstream to manufacturing (for example, product design) and costs downstream from manufacturing (for example, marketing and customer service) as well as to provide an operating income.

REQUIRED

1. What is the manufacturing cost included in the inventory of products A and B if Sayther uses (a) a plantwide overhead rate and (b) department overhead rates?
2. What difference would result in the per unit selling prices of product A and product B from using a plantwide overhead rate instead of department overhead rates?
3. Should Sayther Company prefer plantwide or department manufacturing overhead rates?
4. Under what conditions should Sayther Company further subdivide the department cost pools into activity-cost pools?

5-34 **Plantwide versus department overhead cost rates.** (CMA) The MumsDay Corporation manufactures a complete line of fibreglass attaché cases and suitcases. MumsDay has three manufacturing departments (molding, component, and assembly) and two support departments (maintenance and power).

The sides of the cases are manufactured in the Molding Department. The frames, hinges, locks, and so on are manufactured in the Component Department. The cases are completed in the Assembly Department. Varying amounts of materials, time, and effort are required for each of the various cases. The Maintenance and Power Departments provide services to the three manufacturing departments.

MumsDay has always used a plantwide manufacturing overhead rate. Direct manufacturing labour-hours are used to allocate the overhead to each product. The budgeted rate is calculated by dividing the company's total budgeted manufacturing overhead cost by the total budgeted direct labour-hours to be worked in the three manufacturing departments.

Whit Portlock, manager of Cost Accounting, has recommended that MumsDay use department overhead rates. Portlock has projected operating costs and production levels for the coming year. They are presented (in thousands) by department in the following tables:

	Manufacturing Department		
	Molding	Component	Assembly
Department operating data			
Direct manufacturing labour-hours	500	2,000	1,500
Machine-hours	875	125	
Department costs			
Direct manufacturing materials	$12,400	$30,000	$ 1,250
Direct manufacturing labour	3,500	20,000	12,000
Manufacturing overhead	21,000	16,200	22,600
Total departmental costs	$36,900	$66,200	$35,850
Use of support departments			
Estimated usage of maintenance resources in labour-hours for coming year	90	25	10
Estimated usage of power (in kilowatt-hours) for coming year	360	320	120

Estimated costs of the maintenance department is $4,000 and of the power department is $18,400.

REQUIRED

1. Calculate the plantwide overhead rate for the MumsDay Corporation for the coming year using the same method as used in the past.
2. Whit Portlock has been asked to develop department overhead rates for comparison with the plantwide rate. Follow these steps in developing the department rates:
   a. Allocate the Maintenance Department and Power Department costs to the three manufacturing departments.
   b. Calculate department overhead rates for the three manufacturing departments using a machine-hour allocation base for the Molding Department and a direct manufacturing labour-hour allocation base for the Component and Assembly Departments.
3. Should the MumsDay Corporation use a plantwide rate or department rates to allocate overhead to its products? Explain your answer.

5-35 **ABC, health care.** Uppervale Health Centre runs four programs: (1) alcoholic rehabilitation, (2) drug-addict rehabilitation, (3) children's services, and (4) after-care (counselling and support of patients after release from a mental hospital).

The centre's budget for 1999 follows:

Professional salaries:

6 physicians × $100,000	$600,000	
19 psychologists × $50,000	950,000	
23 nurses × $25,000	575,000	$2,125,000
Medical supplies		300,000
General overhead (administrative salaries, rent, utilities, etc.)		1,275,000
		$3,700,000

Mrs. Muriel Clayton, the director of the Centre, is keen on determining the cost of each program. She has limited funds and feels that this information will help her to budget better and allocate resources more effectively. For example, Clayton needs to decide whether to allocate funds to alcoholic rehabilitation or to drug-addict rehabilitation. Her decision rule is that if the cost to treat a drug-addict patient for a year is more than 15% higher than the cost to treat an alcoholic patient for a year, the alcohol program would receive additional funds.

As a first step, Ms. Clayton, who had earned uniformly high respect from the professional staff, asked the staff to fill out a form indicating the time devoted to each of the four programs. She then allocated costs of medical supplies on the basis of physician-hours spent in each program and general overhead on the basis of direct-labour cost (where direct labour is defined to include the time of doctors, psychologists, and nurses multiplied by the salary rate of each). Clayton compiled the following data describing employee allocations to individual programs:

	Alcohol	Drug	Children	After-care	Total Employees
Physicians		2	4		6
Psychologists	6	4		9	19
Nurses	4	6	4	9	23

Eighty patients are in residence in the alcohol program, each staying about a half-year. Thus, the clinic provided 40 patient-years of service in the alcohol program. Similarly, 100 patients were involved in the drug program for about a half-year each. Thus the clinic provided 50 patient-years of service in the drug program.

Clayton has recently become aware of activity-based costing as a method to refine cost systems. She asks her accountant, Huey Deluth, how she should apply this new technique. Deluth obtains the following information:

1. Consumption of medical supplies depends on the number of patients in each department and the length of their stays (that is, patient-years).
2. General overhead costs consist of:

Rent and clinic maintenance	$200,000
Administrative costs to manage patient charts, food, laundry	800,000
Laboratory services	275,000
Total	$1,275,000

3. Other information about individual departments is:

	Alcohol	Drug	Children	After-care	Total
Square metres of space occupied by each program	9,000	9,000	10,000	12,000	40,000
Patient-years of service	40	50	50	60	200
Number of patients	80	100	200	120	500
Number of laboratory tests	400	1,400	3,000	700	5,500

REQUIRED

1a. Compute indirect-cost rates for medical supplies and general overhead under Clayton's existing costing system.

b. What is the cost of each program and the cost per patient-year of the alcohol and drug programs, using Clayton's existing costing system?

c. Using the existing costing system, would Clayton allocate additional funds to the drug program or to the alcohol program?

2a. Calculate the indirect-cost rates for medical supplies, rent and clinic maintenance, administrative cost rate for patient charts, food, and laundry, and laboratory services, selecting cost-allocation bases that you believe are the most appropriate for allocating indirect-costs to programs.

b. What is the cost of each program and the cost per patient-year of the alcohol and drug programs, using an activity-based costing approach to cost analysis?

c. Using the ABC system, would Clayton allocate additional funds to the drug program or to the alcohol program?

3. Explain the cost differences and the accuracy of program costs calculated using the existing and the ABC system. What other benefits can Uppervale Health Centre obtain by implementing the ABC system?

4. What factors, other than cost, do you think Uppervale Health Centre should consider in allocating resources to its programs?

5-36 Activity-based costing, product cost cross-subsidization. Baker's Delight (BD) has been in the food processing business three years. For its first two years (1999 and 2000), its sole product was raisin cake. All cakes were manufactured and packaged in one-kilogram units. A normal-costing system was used by BD. The two direct-cost categories were direct materials and direct manufacturing labour. The sole indirect manufacturing cost category—manufacturing overhead—was allocated to products using a units-of-production allocation base. BD prices on a cost-plus basis. It currently uses a "cost plus 40% of cost" guideline.

In its third year (2001), BD added a second product—layered carrot cake—that was packaged in one-kilogram units. This product differs from raisin cake in several ways:

◆ More expensive ingredients are used.
◆ More direct manufacturing labour time is required.
◆ More complex manufacturing is required.

In 2001, BD continued to use its existing costing system where a unit of production of either cake was weighted the same.

Direct materials costs in 2001 were $0.60 per kilogram of raisin cake and $0.90 per kilogram of layered carrot cake. Direct manufacturing labour cost in 2001 was $0.14 per kilogram of raisin cake and $0.20 per kilogram of layered carrot cake.

During 2001, BD salespeople reported greater-than-expected sales of layered carrot cake and less-than-expected sales of raisin cake. The budgeted and actual sales volume for 2001 were as follows:

	Budgeted	Actual
Raisin cake	160,000 kilograms	120,000 kilograms
Layered carrot cake	40,000 kilograms	80,000 kilograms

The budgeted manufacturing overhead for 2001 was $210,800.

At the end of 2001, Jonathan Davis, the controller of BD, decided to investigate how use of an activity-based costing system would affect the product cost numbers. After consultation with operating personnel, the single manufacturing overhead cost pool was subdivided into five activity areas. These activity areas, their driver, their 2001 budgeted rate, and the driver units used per kilogram of each cake are as follows:

Activity	Driver	Budgeted 2001 Cost per Driver Unit	Driver Units per Kilogram of Raisin Cake	Driver Units per Kilogram of Layered Carrot Cake
1. Mixing	Labour time	$0.04	5	8
2. Cooking	Oven time	$0.14	2	3
3. Cooling	Cool room time	$0.02	3	5
4. Creaming/icing	Machine time	$0.25	0	3
5. Packaging	Machine time	$0.08	3	7

REQUIRED

1. Compute the 2001 unit product cost of raisin cake and of layered carrot cake with the normal costing system used in the 1999 to 2001 period.
2. Compute the 2001 unit product cost per cake under the activity-based normal costing system.
3. Explain the differences in unit product costs computed in requirements 1 and 2.
4. Describe three uses Baker's Delight might make of the activity-based cost numbers.

5-37 Activity-based job costing. The Schramka Company manufactures a variety of prestige boardroom chairs. Its job-costing system was designed using an activity-based approach. There are two direct-cost categories (direct materials and direct manufacturing labour) and three indirect-cost pools. The three cost pools represent three activity areas at the plant:

Manufacturing Activity Area	Budgeted Costs for 2001	Cost Driver Used as Allocation Base	Cost Allocation Rate
Materials-handling	$ 200,000	Parts	$ 0.25
Cutting	2,160,000	Parts	2.50
Assembly	2,000,000	Direct manufacturing labour-hours	25.00

Two styles of chairs were produced in March, the executive chair and the chairperson chair. Their quantities, direct material costs, and other data for March 2001 are as follows:

	Units Produced	Direct Material Costs	Number of Parts	Direct Manufacturing Labour-Hours
Executive chair	5,000	$600,000	100,000	7,500
Chairperson chair	100	25,000	3,500	500

The direct manufacturing labour rate is $20 per hour. Assume no beginning or ending inventory.

REQUIRED

1. Compute the March 2001 total manufacturing costs and unit costs of the executive chair and the chairperson chair.
2. Suppose that the upstream activities to manufacturing (R&D and design) and the downstream activities (marketing, distribution, and customer service) were analyzed. The unit costs in 2001 were budgeted to be as follows:

	Upstream Activities	Downstream Activities
Executive chair	$ 60	$110
Chairperson chair	146	236

Compute the full product costs per unit of each line of chairs. (Full product costs are the sum of the costs in all business function areas.)

5-38 Activity-based job costing, unit cost comparisons. The Tracy Corporation has a machining facility specializing in jobs for the aircraft components market. The prior job costing system had two direct-cost categories (direct materials and direct manufacturing labour) and a single indirect-cost pool (manufacturing overhead, allocated using direct labour-hours). The indirect-cost allocation rate of the prior system for 2001 would have been $115 per direct manufacturing labour-hour.

Recently, a team with members from product design, manufacturing, and accounting used an activity-based approach to refine its job costing system. The two direct-cost categories were retained. The team decided to replace the single indirect-cost pool with five indirect-cost pools. These five cost pools represent five activity areas at the facility, each with its own supervisor and budget responsibility. Pertinent data are as follows:

Activity Area	Cost Driver Used as Allocation Base	Cost Allocation Rate
Materials-handling	Parts	$ 0.40
Lathe work	Turns	0.20
Milling	Machine-hours	20.00
Grinding	Parts	0.80
Testing	Units tested	15.00

Information-gathering technology has advanced to the point where all the data necessary for budgeting in these five activity areas are automatically collected.

Two representative jobs processed under the new system at the facility in the most recent period had the following characteristics:

	Job 410	Job 411
Direct materials cost per job	$ 9,700	$59,900
Direct manufacturing labour cost per job	$ 750	$11,250
Direct manufacturing labour-hours per job	25	375
Parts per job	500	2,000
Turns per job	20,000	60,000
Machine-hours per job	150	1,050
Units per job	10	200

REQUIRED

1. Compute the per unit manufacturing costs of each job under the prior job costing system.
2. Compute the per unit manufacturing costs of each job under the activity-based job costing system.
3. Compare the per-unit cost figures for Jobs 410 and 411 computed in requirements 1 and 2. Why do the prior and the activity-based costing systems differ in their job cost estimates for each job? Why might these differences be important to the Tracy Corporation?

5-39 **ABC, implementation, ethics.** (CMA, adapted) Applewood Electronics, a division of Elgin Corporation, manufactures two large-screen television models: the Monarch which has been produced since 1995 and sells for $900, and the Regal, a new model introduced in early 1998 which sells for $1,140. Based on the following income statement for the year ended November 30, 1999, senior management at Elgin have decided to concentrate Applewood's marketing resources on the Regal model and begin to phase out the Monarch model.

Applewood Electronics
Income Statement
for the Fiscal Year Ended November 30, 1999

	Monarch	Regal	Total
Sales	$19,800,000	$4,560,000	$24,360,000
Cost of goods sold	12,540,000	3,192,000	15,732,000
Gross margin	7,260,000	1,368,000	8,628,000
Selling and administrative expense	5,830,000	978,000	6,808,000
Operating income	$ 1,430,000	$ 390,000	$ 1,820,000
Units produced and sold	22,000	4,000	
Net income per unit sold	$65.00	$97.50	

Presented below are the unit costs for Monarch and Regal.

	Monarch	Regal
Direct manufacturing materials	$208	$584
Direct labour		
Monarch (1.5 hours × $12)	18	
Regal (3.5 hours × $12)		42
Machine costs[†]		
Monarch (8 hours × $18)	144	
Regal (4 hours × $18)		72
Manufacturing overhead other than machine costs[*]	200	100
Total cost	$570	$798

[†]Machine costs include lease costs of the machine, repairs, and maintenance.
[*]Manufacturing overhead was allocated to machine hours at the rate of $25 per hour.

Applewood's controller, Susan Benzo, is advocating the use of activity-based costing and activity-based management and has gathered the following information about the company's manufacturing overhead costs for the year ended November 30, 1999.

Activity Centre (Cost-Allocation Base)	Total Activity Costs	Units of the Cost-Allocation Base		
		Monarch	Regal	Total
Soldering (number of solder points)	$ 942,000	1,185,000	385,000	1,570,000
Shipments (number of shipments)	860,000	16,200	3,800	20,000
Quality control (number of inspections)	1,240,000	56,200	21,300	77,500
Purchase orders (number of orders)	950,400	80,100	109,980	190,080
Machine power (machine hours)	57,600	176,000	16,000	192,000
Machine setups (number of setups)	750,000	16,000	14,000	30,000
Total manufacturing overhead	$4,800,000			

After completing her analysis, Benzo showed the results to Fred Duval, the Applewood Division President. Duval did not like what he saw. "If you show headquarters this analysis, they are going to ask us to phase out the Regal line, which we have just introduced. This whole costing stuff has been a major problem for us. First Monarch was not profitable and now Regal.

"Looking at the ABC analysis, I see two problems. We do many more activities than the ones you have listed. If you had included all activities, maybe your conclusions would have been different. Second, you used number of setups and number of inspections as allocation bases. The numbers would have been different had you used setup-hours and inspection-hours instead. I know that measurement problems precluded you from using these other cost-allocation bases, but at least you ought to make some adjustments to our current numbers to compensate for these issues. I know you can do better. We can't afford to phase out either product."

Benzo knew her numbers were fairly accurate. On a limited sample, she had calculated the profitability of Regal and Monarch using different allocation bases. The set of activities and activity rates she had chosen resulted in numbers that approximated closely those based on more detailed analyses. She was confident that headquarters, knowing that Monarch was introduced only recently, would not ask Applewood to phase it out. She was also aware that a sizable portion of Duval's bonus was based on division sales. Phasing out either product would adversely affect the bonus. Still, she felt some pressure from Duval to do something.

REQUIRED

1. Using activity-based costing, calculate the profitability of the Regal and Monarch models.
2. Explain briefly why these numbers differ from the profitability of the Regal and Monarch models calculated using Applewood's existing costing system.
3. Comment on Duval's concerns about the accuracy and limitations of ABC.

4. How might Applewood find the ABC information helpful in managing its business?
5. What should Susan Benzo do?

COLLABORATIVE LEARNING PROBLEM

5-40 Activity-based costing, cost hierarchy. (CMA, adapted) Coffee Bean, Inc. (CBI) is a distributor and processor of a variety of different blends of coffee. The company buys coffee beans from around the world and roasts, blends, and packages them for resale. CBI currently offers 15 different coffees to gourmet shops in one-kilogram bags. The major cost is raw materials; however, there is a substantial amount of manufacturing overhead in the predominantly automated roasting and packing process. The company uses relatively little direct labour.

Some of the coffees are very popular and sell in large volumes, while a few of the newer blends have very low volumes. CBI prices its coffee at budgeted cost, including allocated overhead, plus a markup of 30%. If prices for certain coffees are significantly higher than market, the prices are lowered. The company competes primarily on the quality of its products, but customers are price-conscious as well.

Data for the 2001 budget include manufacturing overhead of $3 million, which has been allocated in the existing costing system on the basis of each product's budgeted direct labour cost. The budgeted direct labour cost for 2001 totals $600,000. Purchases and use of materials (mostly coffee beans) are budgeted to total $6 million.

The budgeted direct costs for one-kilogram bags of two of the company's products are:

	Mona Loa	Malaysian
Direct materials	$4.20	$3.20
Direct labour	0.30	0.30

CBI's controller believes the traditional costing system may be providing misleading cost information. She has developed an activity-based analysis of the 2001 budgeted manufacturing overhead costs shown in the following table:

Activity	Cost Allocation	Budgeted Activity	Budgeted Cost
Purchasing	Purchase orders	1,158	$ 579,000
Materials-handling	Setups	1,800	720,000
Quality control	Batches	600	144,000
Roasting	Roasting-hours	96,100	961,000
Blending	Blending-hours	33,600	336,000
Packaging	Packaging-hours	26,000	260,000
Total manufacturing overhead cost			$3,000,000

Data regarding the 2001 production of Mona Loa and Malaysian coffee are presented here. There will be no beginning or ending materials inventory for either of these coffees.

	Mona Loa	Malaysian
Expected sales	100,000 kilograms	2,000 kilograms
Batch size	10,000 kilograms	500 kilograms
Setups	3 per batch	3 per batch
Purchase order size	25,000 kilograms	500 kilograms
Roasting time	1 hour/100 kilograms	1 hour/100 kilograms
Blending time	0.5 hour/100 kilograms	0.5 hour/100 kilograms
Packaging time	0.1 hour/100 kilograms	0.1 hour/100 kilograms

INSTRUCTIONS
Form groups of two or more students to complete the following requirements.

REQUIRED

1. Using Coffee Bean, Inc.'s existing costing approach:
   a. Determine the company's 2001 budgeted manufacturing overhead rate using direct-labour cost as the single allocation base.
   b. Determine the 2001 budgeted costs and selling prices of one kilogram of Mona Loa coffee and one kilogram of Malaysian coffee.
2. Use the controller's activity-based approach to estimate the 2001 budgeted cost for one kilogram of:
   a. Mona Loa coffee
   b. Malaysian coffee

   Allocate all costs to the 100,000 kilograms of Mona Loa and the 2,000 kilograms of Malaysian. Compare the results with those in requirement 1.
3. Discuss how CBI could use a cost hierarchy approach to better understand its cost structure.
4. Examine the implications of your answers to requirements 2 and 3 for CBI's pricing and product emphasis strategy.

PART TWO

6
CHAPTER

MASTER BUDGET AND RESPONSIBILITY ACCOUNTING

Watches are manufactured and sold around the world by leading watch manufacturers. By assigning responsibility and maintaining control through the use of budgets, global manufacturers are able to ensure that cost effeciences are attained despite the complexities of worldwide distribution.

LEARNING OBJECTIVES

After studying this chapter, you should be able to:

1. Define *master budget* and explain its major benefits to an organization
2. Describe major components of the master budget
3. Prepare the operating budget and its supporting budget schedules
4. Describe the uses of computer-based financial planning models
5. Explain kaizen budgeting and its importance for cost management
6. Illustrate an activity-based budgeting approach
7. Describe responsibility centres and responsibility accounting
8. Explain how controllability relates to responsibility accounting

Budgets are one of the most widely used tools for planning and controlling organizations. Surveys show an almost universal use of budgets by medium and large companies in many parts of the globe. Budgeting systems turn managers' perspectives forward. A forward-looking perspective enables managers to be in a better position to exploit opportunities. It also enables them to anticipate problems and take steps to eliminate or reduce their severity. As one observer said, "Few businesses plan to fail, but many of those that flop failed to plan."

This chapter examines budgeting as a planning and coordinating device. Topics covered in prior chapters are widely used in this discussion. By understanding cost behaviour (covered in Chapters 2 and 3), managers can better predict how total budgeted costs are affected by different projected output levels. By understanding cost tracing and cost allocation (covered in Chapters 4 and 5), managers can show how different projected revenue and cost amounts will impact the budgeted income statement and balance sheet.

Chapter 1 described some newly evolving management themes that affect management accounting. Budgets give financial expression to many of these themes. For example, budgets can quantify the planned financial effects of activities aimed at continuous improvement and cost reduction.

The material covered in this chapter is also integral to subsequent chapters. For example, Chapters 7 and 8 examine how the numbers used in budgets assist in evaluating the performance of managers or the business areas where they have responsibility.

MAJOR FEATURES OF BUDGETS

Definition and Role of Budgets

A *budget* is a quantitative expression for a set time period of a proposed future plan of action by management. It can cover both financial and nonfinancial aspects of these plans and acts as a blueprint for the company to follow in the upcoming period. Budgets covering financial aspects quantify management's expectations regarding future income, cash flows, and financial position. Just as individual financial statements are prepared covering past periods, so they can be prepared covering future periods— for example, a budgeted income statement, a budgeted cash flow statement, and a budgeted balance sheet.

Well-managed organizations usually have the following budgeting cycle:

1. Planning the performance of the organization as a whole as well as of its subunits. The entire management team agrees as to what is expected.

2. Providing a frame of reference, a set of specific expectations against which actual results can be compared.

3. Investigating variations from plans. If necessary, corrective action follows investigation.

4. Planning again, considering feedback and changed conditions.

The **master budget** coordinates all the financial projections in the organization's individual budgets in a single, organizationwide set of budgets for a set time period. It embraces the impact of both *operating* decisions and *financing* decisions. Operating decisions centre on the acquisition and use of scarce resources. Financing decisions centre on how to get the funds to acquire resources. This book concentrates on how accounting helps managers make operating decisions, and we emphasize operating budgets in this chapter.

The term *master* in *master budget* refers to its being a comprehensive, organizationwide set of budgets. Consider Seagram Company Ltd. Each of its individual product lines such as Dupont, Time Warner, Seagram Wines, and Tropicana Products has a separate budgeted income statement, a separate budgeted cash flow statement, and so on. The master budgeted income statement for Seagram is a single income statement that combines information from all these many individual budgeted income statements. Similarly, the master budgeted cash flow statement is a single cash

"Master Budget—Introduction" from The International Accounting Network.
caarnet.ntu.edu.sg/anet/education/masterbudget/masterbudget1.html

Master budget. Budget that summarizes the financial projections of all the organization's individual budgets. It describes the financial plans for all value-chain functions.

OBJECTIVE 1

Define *master budget* and explain its major benefits to an organization

DuPont Corporation
www.dupont.com

Nissan Motor Company
www.nissanmotors.com
www.nissan.co.jp

Owens-Corning
www.corning.com

Pro forma statements. Budgeted financial statements of an organization.

flow statement that combines information from all these many individual budgeted cash flow statements.

Terminology

The terminology used to describe budgets varies among organizations. For example, budgeted financial statements are sometimes called **pro forma statements.** The budgeted financial statements of many companies include the budgeted income statement, the budgeted balance sheet, and the budgeted statement of cash flows. Some organizations, such as Hewlett-Packard, refer to budgeting as *targeting.* Indeed, to give a more positive thrust to budgeting, many organizations—for example, the Nissan Motor Company and Owens-Corning—describe the budget as a *profit plan.*

ADVANTAGES OF BUDGETS

Budgets are a major feature of most management control systems. When administered intelligently, budgets (1) compel planning, including the implementation of plans, (2) provide performance criteria, and (3) promote communication and coordination within the organization.

Strategy and Plans

Strategic analysis. Considers how an organization best combines its own capabilities with the opportunities in the marketplace to accomplish its overall objectives.

Budgeting is most useful when done as an integral part of an organization's strategic analysis.[1] **Strategic analysis** considers how an organization best combines its own capabilities with the opportunities in the marketplace to accomplish its overall objectives. It includes consideration of such questions as:

1. What are the overall objectives of the organization?
2. Are the markets for its product local, regional, national, or global? What trends will affect its markets? How is the organization affected by the economy, its industry, and its competitors?
3. What forms of organizational and financial structures serve the organization best?
4. What are the risks of alternative strategies, and what are the organization's contingency plans if its preferred plan fails?

Consider the diagram in Exhibit 6-1. Strategic analysis underlies both long-run and short-run planning. In turn, these plans lead to the formulation of budgets. The arrows in the diagram are pointing in two directions. Why? Because strategy, plans, and budgets are interrelated and affect one another. Budgets provide feedback to managers about the likely effects of their strategic plans. Managers then use this feedback to revise their strategic plans. Apple Computer's strategic decision to reduce the selling prices of its Power Macintosh computer line provides an example of the interrelation between strategic analysis and budgets. By reducing its prices, the company expected to increase the demand for its computers. The budget, however, indicated that, even at the predicted higher sales quantities, Apple would be unable to meet its financial targets. For the strategy to succeed, Apple would need to reduce operating costs by streamlining operations and moving facilities to lower-cost areas. Apple then used cross-functional teams with members from different parts of the value chain to seek major cost reductions.

Apple Computer
www.apple.com

A Framework for Judging Performance

Budgeted performance measures can overcome two key limitations of using past performance as a basis for judging actual results. One limitation is that past results incorporate past miscues and substandard performance. Consider a cellular telephone company (Mobile Communications) examining the 2000 performance of its sales

[1]See Grisold, R. E., "How to Link Strategic Planning with Budgeting," *CMA Magazine,* July–August 1995, for a description of strategic budgeting at Atomic Energy of Canada.

EXHIBIT 6-1
Strategic Analysis in the Formulation of Long-Run and Short-Run Budgets

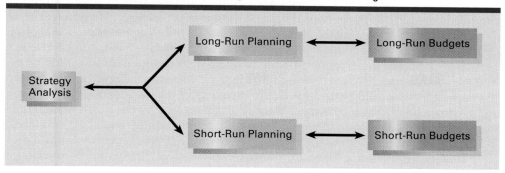

force. Suppose the past performance in 1999 incorporates the efforts of many departed salespeople who left because they did not have an understanding of the marketplace. (As the president of Mobile said, "They could not sell ice cream in a heat wave.") Using the sales record of those departed employees would set the performance bar for new salespeople way too low.

A second limitation of past performance is that the future may be expected to be very different from the past. Consider again our cellular telephone company. Suppose that Mobile Communications had a 20% revenue increase in 2000 compared with a 10% increase in 1999. Does this indicate stellar sales performance? Before saying yes, consider two additional facts. Fact one is that, in November 1999, an industry trade association forecast that, the 2000 growth rate in industry revenues would be 40%. Fact two is that, in 2000, the actual growth rate in industry revenues was 50%. The 20% actual revenue gain in 2000 takes on a negative connotation given these facts, even though it exceeds the 1999 actual growth rate of 10%. Use of the 40% figure as the budgeted rate provides a better way to evaluate the 2000 sales performance than does use of the 1999 actual rate of 10%. A biking analogy is appropriate here. A budgeted industry growth rate of 40% is equivalent to the biker's going downhill on a steep slope. Top management of Mobile Communications expects that good performance will achieve above-average speed compared with other bikers in similar conditions.

Coordination and Communication

Coordination is the meshing and balancing of all factors of production or service and of all the departments and business functions so that the company can meet its objectives. *Communication* is getting those objectives understood and accepted by all departments and functions.

Coordination forces executives to think of relationships among individual operations, departments, and the company as a whole. Coordination implies, for example, that purchasing officers make material purchase plans on the basis of production requirements. Also, production managers plan personnel and machinery needs to produce the number of products necessary to meet revenue forecasts. How does a budget lead to coordination? Consider Snapple Beverage. Production managers who are evaluated on the basis of maximizing output while keeping unit costs per bottle low would prefer long production runs with very few changeovers of flavours. But if the output cannot be sold, Snapple may find itself awash in a costly inventory buildup of Mango Madness. The budget achieves coordination by constraining production managers to produce only what marketing is forecasting it can sell. This may entail doing a changeover from Mango Madness to Lemonade partway into a production shift.

For coordination to succeed, communication is essential. The production manager must know the sales plan. The purchasing manager must know the production plan, and so on. Having a formal document such as the budget is an effective way to communicate a consistent set of plans to the organization as a whole.

Snapple Beverage
www.snapple.com

Management Support and Administration

Budgets help managers, but budgets need help. Top management has the ultimate responsibility for the budgets of the organization they manage. *Management at all levels, however, should understand and support the budget and all aspects of the management control system.* Top management support is especially critical for obtaining active line participation in the formulation of budgets and for successful administration of the budget. If line managers feel that top management does not "believe" in the budget, these managers are unlikely to be active participants in the budget process. Similarly, a top management that always mechanically institutes "across the board" cost reductions (say, a 10% reduction in all areas) in the face of revenue reductions is unlikely to have line managers willing to be "fully honest" in their budget communications.

Budgets should not be administered rigidly. Changing conditions call for changes in plans. A manager may commit to the budget, but a situation might develop where some special repairs or a special advertising program would better serve the interests of the organization. The manager should not defer the repairs or the advertising in order to meet the budget if such actions will hurt the organization in the long run. Attaining the budget should not be an end in itself.

TYPES OF BUDGETS

Time Coverage

The purpose(s) for budgeting should guide the time period chosen for the budget. Consider budgeting for a new Harley-Davidson 500 cc motorcycle. If the purpose is to budget for the total profitability of this new model, a five-year period (or more) may be appropriate (covering design, manufacture, sales, and after-sales support). In contrast, consider budgeting for a Christmas play. If the purpose is to estimate all cash outlays, a six-month period from the planning to staging of the play may be adequate.

The most frequently used budget period is one year. The annual budget is often subdivided by months for the first quarter and by quarters for the remainder of the year. The budgeted data for a year are frequently revised as the year unfolds. For example, at the end of the first quarter, the budget for the next three quarters is changed in light of new information.

Businesses are increasingly using *rolling budgets*. A **rolling budget** is a budget or plan that is always available for a specified future period by adding a month, quarter, or year in the future as the month, quarter, or year just ended is dropped. Thus, a 12-month rolling budget for the March 2000 to February 2001 period becomes a 12-month rolling budget for the April 2000 to March 2001 period the next month, and so on. There is always a 12-month budget in place. Rolling budgets constantly force management to think concretely about the forthcoming 12 months, regardless of the month at hand. The NEC Corporation of Japan has a one-year operating budget that is updated each month. Companies also frequently use rolling budgets when developing five-year budgets for long-run planning. For example, the NEC Corporation also has a five-year budget that is updated each year.

Steps in Developing an Operating Budget

A good way to explain the budgeting process is to walk through the development of an actual budget. We shall use a master budget, because it provides a comprehensive picture of the entire budgeting process at Halifax Engineering, a manufacturer of aircraft replacement parts. Its job costing system for manufacturing costs has two direct-cost categories (direct materials and direct manufacturing labour) and one indirect-cost pool (manufacturing overhead). Manufacturing overhead (both variable and fixed) is allocated to products using direct manufacturing labour-hours as the allocation base.

Exhibit 6-2 shows a simplified diagram of the various parts of the master budget for Halifax Engineering. The master budget summarizes the financial projections of all the organization's individual budgets. The master budget results in a set of related financial statements for a set time period, usually a year. The bulk of Exhibit

---

Rolling budget. Budget or plan that is always available for a specified future period by adding a month, quarter, or year in the future as the month, quarter, or year just ended is dropped.

NEC Corporation
www.nec.com

OBJECTIVE 2

Describe major components of the master budget

EXHIBIT 6-2
Overview of the Master Budget for Halifax Engineering

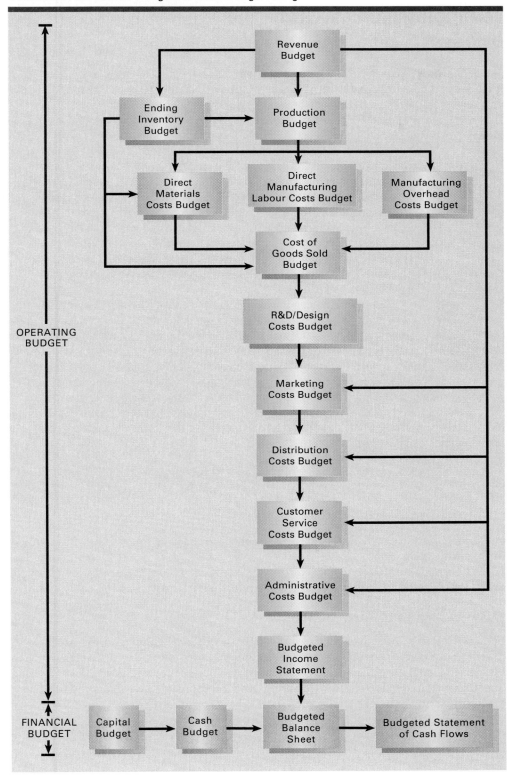

OPERATING
BUDGET

FINANCIAL
BUDGET

Operating budget. The budgeted income statement and its supporting schedules.

Financial budget. That part of the master budget that comprises the capital budget, cash budget, budgeted balance sheet, and budgeted statement of cash flows.

6-2 presents a set of budgets that together is often called the **operating budget,** which includes the budgeted income statement and its supporting budget schedules. The supporting budget schedules cut across different categories of the value chain from R&D to customer service. The **financial budget** is that part of the master budget that comprises the capital budget, cash budget, budgeted balance sheet, and bud-

CONCEPTS IN ACTION

Using Web Technology to Fast-Track the Budgeting Process

The budgeting process for a large-sized company can be a time-consuming and often frustrating process. Different parts of a company may use different (noncompatible) software packages. Moreover, there can be sizable delays between when a division submits a proposed budget revision and when those revisions are integrated into the master budget of the company.

Advances in information technology are greatly assisting managers to improve the budgeting process. For example, the retail bank and discount brokerage division of CLARUS Corporation has a CLARUS Budget software module that is engineered for use over the World Wide Web. This module enables managers in different divisions and in different locations to log on and have instantaneous access to the proposed budgets of other divisions. Managers can access this module from diverse locations. The budget module is linked to other modules (such as human resource budgeting and capital budgeting) so that a total enterprise-wide master budget can be developed online.

Toronto-Dominion Bank proposes to use the CLARUS Budget module as part of a comprehensive integration of the World Wide Web into its business processes. Its controller noted that "in the past we have compiled our business plan using hundreds of spreadsheets, and our analysts have spent a disproportionate amount of their time compiling and verifying data from multiple sources. Implementing a Web-based enterprise-wide budgeting solution will allow our analysts to be proactive in monitoring quarterly results."

CLARUS reports that its Web-based budgeting approach frees the finance department to focus on strategy (not spreadsheets) and increased service levels to employees, and it reduces administrative costs.

TD Bank
www.tdbank.ca

CLARUS
www.claruscorp.com

Source: CLARUS Web site and Hornyak, "Budgeting Made Easy," *Management Accounting.* Vol. LXXX, No. 4 (October 1998), pp. 18–23.

---

geted statement of cash flows. It focuses on the impact of operations and planned capital outlays on cash.

The final master budget is often the result of several iterations. Each of its drafts involves interaction across the various business functions of the value chain.

Basic Data and Requirements

Halifax Engineering is a machine shop that uses skilled labour and metal alloys to manufacture two types of aircraft replacement parts—Regular and Heavy-Duty. Halifax managers are ready to prepare a master budget for the year 2000. To keep our illustration manageable for clarifying basic relationships, we make the following assumptions:

1. The only source of revenues is sales of the two parts. Non-sales-related revenue, such as interest income, is assumed to be zero.

2. Work-in-process inventory is negligible and is ignored.

3. Direct materials inventory and finished goods inventory are costed using the first-in, first-out (FIFO) method.

4. Unit costs of direct materials purchased and finished goods sold remain unchanged throughout the budget year (2000).

5. Variable production costs are variable with respect to direct manufacturing labour-hours. Variable nonproduction costs are variable with respect to rev-

EXHIBIT 6-3

Budgeted Income Statement for Halifax Engineering for the Year Ended December 31, 2000

Revenues	Schedule 1		$3,800,000
Costs:			
Cost of goods sold	Schedule 7		2,444,000
Gross margin			1,356,000
Operating costs:			
R&D/product design costs	Schedule 8	$136,000	
Marketing costs	Schedule 8	200,000	
Distribution costs	Schedule 8	100,000	
Customer service costs	Schedule 8	60,000	
Administration costs	Schedule 8	374,000	870,000
Operating income			$ 486,000

◆ **Step 9:** *Budgeted Income Statement* Schedules 1, 7, and 8 provide the necessary information to complete the budgeted income statement, shown in Exhibit 6-3 above. Of course, more details could be included in the income statement, and then fewer supporting schedules would be prepared.

Top management's strategies for achieving revenue and operating income goals influence the costs planned for the different business functions of the value chain. As strategies change, the budget allocations for different elements of the value chain will also change. For example, a shift in strategy toward emphasizing product development and customer service will result in increased resources being allocated to these parts of the master budget. The actual data resulting from this strategy will be compared to budgeted results. Management can then evaluate whether the focus on product development and customer service has been successful. This feedback is an important input in subsequent plans.

COMPUTER-BASED FINANCIAL PLANNING MODELS

Exhibit 6-1 showed how strategic analysis, planning, and budgeting are interrelated. The value of budgets to managers in their strategic analysis and planning is enhanced by conducting sensitivity analysis. Sensitivity analysis is a what-if technique that examines how a result will change if the original predicted data are not achieved or if an underlying assumption changes. While a hand-held calculator would suffice to do the calculations, commercial software packages are now available for more complex tasks, such as sensitivity analysis for the financial statements found in a master budget. These packages do the calculations for **financial planning models,** which are mathematical representations of the relationships across operating activities, financial activities, and financial statements.

Consider Halifax Engineering. Their financial planning model assumes the following:

◆ Direct materials and direct manufacturing labour costs vary proportionately with the quantities of Regular and Heavy-Duty parts produced.

◆ Variable manufacturing overhead costs vary with direct manufacturing labour-hours.

◆ Variable nonmanufacturing costs vary with revenue dollars.

◆ Target ending inventories remain unchanged.

Exhibit 6-4 presents the budgeted operating income for three what-if scenarios for Halifax Engineering:

◆ **Scenario 1.** A 3% decrease in the selling price of the Regular part and a 3% decrease in the selling price of the Heavy-Duty part.

Financial planning models. Mathematical representations of the relationships among all operating activities, financial activities, and financial statements.

EXHIBIT 6-4
Effect of Changes in Budget Assumptions on Budgeted Income for Halifax Engineering

What-If Scenario	Key Assumptions						Budgeted Operating Income	
	Units Sold		Selling Price		Direct Materials Cost*			
	Regular	Heavy-Duty	Regular	Heavy-Duty	111 Alloy	112 Alloy	Dollars	Change from Master Budget
Master budget	5,000	1,000	$600	$800	$7.00	$10.00	$486,000	—
Scenario 1	5,000	1,000	582	776	7.00	10.00	386,250	21% decrease
Scenario 2	4,800	960	600	800	7.00	10.00	438,273	10% decrease
Scenario 3	5,000	1,000	600	800	7.35	10.50	448,380	8% decrease

*Per kilogram.

◆ **Scenario 2.** A 4% decrease in units sold of the Regular part and a 4% decrease in units sold of the Heavy-Duty part.

◆ **Scenario 3.** A 5% increase in the price per kilogram of 111 alloy and a 5% increase in the price per kilogram of 112 alloy.

Exhibit 6-4 indicates that, relative to the master budget, budgeted operating income decreases by 21% under scenario 1, by 10% under scenario 2, and by 8% under scenario 3. Managers can use this information to plan actions that they may need to take if faced with these scenarios.

SURVEYS OF COMPANY PRACTICE

Budget Practices Around the Globe

Surveys of companies in the United States, Japan, Australia, the United Kingdom, and Holland indicate some interesting similarities and differences in budgeting practices across countries. The use of master budgets is widespread in all countries. Differences arise with respect to other dimensions of budgeting. U.S. managers prefer more participation and regard return on investment as the most important budget goal. In comparison, Japanese managers prefer less participation and regard sales revenues as the most important budget goal.

	United States	Japan	Australia	United Kingdom	Holland
1. Percentage of firms that prepare a complete master budget	91%	93%	95%	100%	100%
2. Percentage of firms reporting division manager participation in budget committee discussions	78%	67%	—	—	82%
3. Ranking of the most important budget goals for division managers (1 = most important)					
Return on investment	1	3	—	—	—
Operating income	2	2	—	—	—
Sales revenues	3	1	—	—	—

Source: Adapted from Asada, T., J. Bailes, and M. Amano, "An Empirical Study of Japanese and American Budget Planning and Control Systems," (Working Paper, Tsukuba University and Oregon State University, 1989) Blayney, P., and I. Yokoyama, "Comparative Analysis of Japanese and Australian Cost Accounting and Management Practices," (Working Paper, The University of Sydney, Sydney, Australia, 1991) and de With E., and E. Ijskes, "Current Budgeting Practices in Dutch Companies." (Working Paper, Vrije Uniersiteit, 1992, Amsterdam, Netherlands)

Chapter 1 noted how continuous improvement is one of the key issues facing management today. The Japanese use the term *kaizen* for continuous improvement. **Kaizen budgeting** is a budgetary approach that explicitly incorporates continuous improvement during the budget period into the resultant budget numbers.[3]

Consider our Halifax Engineering example in schedule 4. The 2000 budget assumes that it will take 4.0 and 6.0 manufacturing labour-hours respectively for each Regular and Heavy-Duty aircraft part. A kaizen budgeting approach would incorporate continuous reduction in these manufacturing labour-hour requirements during 2000. Assume Halifax budgets the following labour-hour amounts:

OBJECTIVE 5

Explain kaizen budgeting and its importance for cost management

Kaizen budgeting. Budgetary approach that explicitly incorporates continuous improvement during the budget period into the resultant budget numbers.

	Budgeted Amounts (labour-hours)	
	Regular	Heavy-Duty
January–March 2000	4.00	6.00
April–June 2000	3.90	5.85
July–September 2000	3.80	5.70
October–December 2000	3.70	5.55

Unless Halifax meets these continuous improvement goals, unfavourable variances will be reported. Note that, in the Halifax budget, the implications of these direct labour-hour reductions would extend to reductions in variable manufacturing overhead costs, given that direct manufacturing labour-hours is the driver of these costs.

Kaizen at Citizen Watch

Citizen Watch is the world's largest manufacturer of watches. The assembly areas at its plants are highly automated. Component part costs for each watch are a sizable percentage of the unit cost of each watch. A central part of Citizen's cost management system is kaizen budgeting. All parts of the entire production area, including component suppliers, are required to seek out cost reduction opportunities continually. For example, at its Tokyo plant, it budgets that all external suppliers will have a steady cost reduction of 3% per annum. Suppliers who exceed this 3% target retain for at least one year any cost reductions that they achieve in excess of this 3% level. Suppliers who do not attain the 3% target receive the "assistance" of Citizen engineers in the following year.[4]

Chapters 4 and 5 explained how activity-based costing systems can lead to improved decision-making. Activity-based costing principles extend to budgeting. **Activity-based budgeting** focuses on the cost of activities necessary to produce and sell products and services. It separates indirect costs into separate homogeneous activity cost pools. Management uses the cause-and-effect criterion to identify the cost drivers for each of these indirect cost pools.

OBJECTIVE 6

Illustrate an activity-based budgeting approach

Activity-based budgeting. Approach to budgeting that focuses on the costs of activities necessary to produce and sell products and services.

Four key steps in activity-based budgeting are:

1. Determine the budgeted costs of performing each unit of activity at each activity area.
2. Determine the demand for each individual activity based on budgeted, production, new product development, and so on.
3. Compute the costs of performing each activity.
4. Describe the budget as costs of performing various activities (rather than budgeted costs of functional or conventional value-chain spending categories).

An activity-based budgeting approach is facilitated by adopting activity-based costing as described in Chapters 4 and 5.

[3]For an overview of Japanese management accounting, see Cooper, R., "Japanese Cost Management Practices," *CMA Magazine*, October 1994.

[4]See Cooper, R., "Citizen Watch Company, Ltd.: Cost Reduction for Mature Products," Harvard Business School, Case No. 9-194-033.

EXHIBIT 6-5
Activity-Based Budget for R&D/Product Design Costs of Bradford Aerospace:
January to December 1999

Activity Area	Budgeted Usage of Driver	Budgeted Rate per Cost Driver	Budgeted Costs
Computer-aided design	200 hours	$80	$16,000
Manual design	70 hours	50	3,500
Prototype development	80 hours	60	4,800
Testing	280 hours	40	11,200
Procurement	120 orders*	25	3,000
Total			$38,500

*Purchase orders.

Consider activity-based budgeting for the R&D/product design parts of the value chain at Bradford Aerospace. Four activity areas and their cost drivers have been identified. The budgeted 1999 rates for the costs in each activity area are as follows:

Activity	Cost Driver/ Budgeted Cost Rate
Computer aided design (CAD)—using computer software to design aircraft parts	CAD hours, $80 per hour
Manual design—manually designing aircraft parts	Manual design hours, $50 per hour
Prototype development—building actual versions of aircraft parts	Prototyping hours, $60 per hour
Testing—examining how new aircraft parts "perform" in different operating conditions	Testing hours, $40 per hour
Procurement—purchasing supplies and component parts	Purchase orders, $25 per purchase order

Exhibit 6-5 (above) presents the activity-based budget for January to December 1999. Bradford budgets usage of the cost driver in each activity area on the basis of budgeted production and new product development. This budgeted usage of the cost driver for each activity is multiplied by the respective budgeted costs rate per activity to obtain the budgeted activity costs. The budgeted total costs for R&D/product design is the sum of the budgeted costs of the individual activities in that part of the value chain.

The activity-based budget in Exhibit 6-5 is for one part of Bradford's value chain. In many cases, the same activity will appear in more than one part of the value chain. For example, procurement activities such as purchase ordering and supplier payment are found in most areas of the value chain. Companies using activity-based budgeting may choose to present their budgets at either the individual value-chain level or at some more basic activity level such as procurement by combining budgeted procurement costs from different parts of the value chain.

A survey of U.K. managers reported the following ranking of the benefits from activity-based budgeting: (1) ability to set more realistic budgets, (2) better identification of resource needs, (3) linking of costs to outputs, (4) clearer linking of costs with staff responsibilities, and (5) identification of budgetary slack.[5]

BUDGETING AND RESPONSIBILITY ACCOUNTING

Organizational Structure and Responsibility

Organizational structure. The arrangement of lines of responsibility within the entity.

Organizational structure is an arrangement of lines of responsibility within the entity. A company such as Petro-Canada may be organized primarily by business function:

[5]Innes, J., and F. Mitchell, "A Survey of Activity-Based Costing in the U.K.'s Largest Companies," *Management Accounting Research*, Vol. 6, pp. 137–53.

exploration, refining, and marketing. Another company such as Procter & Gamble, a household products giant, may be organized by product or brand line. The managers of the individual divisions (toothpaste, soap, and so on) would each have decision-making authority concerning all the business functions (manufacturing, marketing, and so on) within that division.

To attain the goals described in the master budget, an organization must coordinate the efforts of all its employees—from the top executive through all levels of management to every supervised worker. Coordinating the organization's efforts means assigning responsibility to managers who are accountable for their actions in planning and controlling human and physical resources. Management is essentially a human activity. Budgets exist not for their own sake, but to help managers.

Each manager, regardless of level, is in charge of a responsibility centre. A *responsibility centre* is a part, segment, or subunit of an organization whose manager is accountable for a specified set of activities. The higher the manager's level, the broader the responsibility centre he or she manages and, generally, the larger the number of subordinates who report to him or her. **Responsibility accounting** is a system that measures the plans (by budgets) and actions (by actual results) of each responsibility centre. Four major types of responsibility centres are:

1. **Cost centre**. Manager accountable for costs only
2. **Revenue centre**. Manager accountable for revenues only
3. **Profit centre**. Manager accountable for revenues and costs
4. **Investment centre**. Manager accountable for investments, revenues, and costs

The Maintenance Department of a Delta hotel could be a cost centre if the maintenance manager is responsible only for costs. Hence, the budget would emphasize costs. The sales department of the hotel could be a revenue centre if the sales manager is responsible only for revenues. Here the budget would emphasize revenues. The hotel manager could be in charge of a profit centre if the hotel manager is accountable for both revenues and costs. Here the budget would emphasize both revenues and costs. The regional manager responsible for investments in new hotel projects and for revenues and costs could be in charge of an investment centre; revenues, costs, and the investment base would be emphasized in the budget for this manager.

Responsibility accounting affects behaviour. Consider the following incident:

The Sales Department requests a rush production run. The plant scheduler argues that it will disrupt his production and will cost a substantial though not clearly determined amount of money. The answer coming from sales is, "Do you want to take the responsibility of losing the X Company as a customer?" Of course, the production scheduler does not want to take such a responsibility and he gives up, but not before a heavy exchange of arguments and the accumulation of a substantial backlog of ill feeling. The controller proposes an innovative solution. He analyzes the payroll in the Assembly Department to determine the costs involved in getting out rush orders. This information eliminates the cause for argument. Henceforth, any rush order is accepted by the production scheduler, "no questions asked." The extra costs are duly recorded and charged to the Sales Department.

As a result, the tension created by rush orders disappears, and, somehow, the number of rush orders requested by the Sales Department is progressively reduced to an insignificant level.[6]

The responsibility accounting approach traces costs to either (1) the individual who has the best knowledge about why the costs arose or (2) the activity that caused the costs. In this incident, the cause was the sales activity, and the resulting costs were charged to the sales department. If rush orders occur regularly, the sales department might have a budget for such costs, and the department's actual performance would then be compared against the budget.

[6]Villers, R., "Control and Freedom in a Decentralized Company," *Harvard Business Review*, Vol. 32, No. 2, p. 95.

OBJECTIVE 7

Describe responsibility centres and responsibility accounting

Responsibility accounting. System that measures the plans (by budgets) and actions (by actual results) of each responsibility centre.

Cost centre. A responsibility centre in which a manager is accountable for costs only.

Revenue centre. A responsibility centre in which a manager is accountable for revenues only.

Profit centre. A responsibility centre in which a manager is accountable for revenues and costs.

Investment centre. A responsibility centre in which a manager is accountable for investments, revenues, and costs.

Feedback and Fixing Blame

Budgets coupled with responsibility accounting provide systematic help for managers, particularly if managers interpret the feedback carefully. Managers, accountants, and students of management accounting repeatedly tend to "play the blame game"—using variances (the difference between the actual results and the budgeted results) appearing in the responsibility accounting system to pinpoint fault for operating problems. In looking at variances, managers should focus on whom they should ask and not on whom they should blame. Variances only suggest questions or direct attention to persons who should have the relevant information. Nevertheless, variances, properly used, can be helpful in evaluating managers' performances.

RESPONSIBILITY AND CONTROLLABILITY

Definition of Controllability

OBJECTIVE 8

Explain how controllability relates to responsibility accounting

Controllability. The degree of influence that a specific manager has over costs, revenues, or other items in question.

Controllable cost. Any cost that is primarily subject to the influence of a given manager of a given responsibility centre for a given time span.

Controllability is the degree of influence that a specific manager has over costs, revenues, or other items in question. A **controllable cost** is any cost that is primarily subject to the influence of a given manager of a given responsibility centre for a given time span. A responsibility accounting system could either exclude all uncontrollable costs from a manager's performance report or segregate such costs from the controllable costs. For example, a machining supervisor's performance report might be confined to quantities (not costs) of direct materials, direct manufacturing labour, power, and supplies.

In practice, controllability is difficult to pinpoint:

1. Few costs are clearly under the sole influence of one manager. For example, costs of direct materials may be influenced by a purchasing manager, but such costs also depend on market conditions beyond the manager's control. Quantities used may be influenced by a production manager, but quantities used also depend on the quality of materials purchased. Moreover, managers often work in teams. How can individual responsibility be evaluated in a team decision?

2. With a long enough time span, all costs will come under somebody's control. However, most performance reports focus on periods of a year or less. A current manager may have inherited problems and inefficiencies from his or her predecessor. For example, present managers may have to work under undesirable contracts with suppliers or labour unions that were negotiated by their predecessors. How can we separate what the current manager actually controls from the results of decisions made by others? Exactly what is the current manager accountable for? Answers to such questions may not be clear-cut.

Senior managers differ in how they embrace the controllability notion when evaluating those reporting to them. For example, a newly appointed president took his management team on a cruise and commented, "I expect everybody to meet their budget targets no matter what happens, and those who don't should stand a little closer to the railing." Other presidents believe that a more risk-sharing approach with managers is preferable where noncontrollable factors are taken into account when making judgments about the performance of managers who miss their budgets.

Emphasis on Information and Behaviour

Managers should avoid overemphasizing controllability. Responsibility accounting is more far-reaching. It focuses on *information* and *knowledge*, not control. The key question is: Who is the best informed? To put it another way: Who is the person who can tell us the most about the specific item in question, regardless of that person's ability to exert personal control? For instance, purchasing managers may be held accountable for total purchase costs, not because of their ability to affect market prices, but because of their ability to predict uncontrollable prices and explain uncontrollable price changes. Similarly, managers at a Tim Horton's store may be held responsible for operating income of their units, even though they do not fully control selling prices or the costs for many food items, and have minimal flexibility as to items to sell or their ingredients. Why? Because unit managers are in the best position to explain variances between their actual operating income and their budgeted operating income.

Performance reports for responsibility centres may also include uncontrollable items because this approach could change behaviour in the directions top management desires. For example, some companies have changed the accountability of a cost centre to a profit centre. Why? Because the manager will probably behave differently. A cost centre manager may emphasize production efficiency and de-emphasize the pleas of sales personnel for faster service and rush orders. In a profit centre, the manager is responsible for both costs and revenues. Thus, even though the manager still has no control over sales personnel, the manager will now more likely weigh the impact of his or her decisions on costs and revenues, rather than solely on costs.

HUMAN ASPECTS OF BUDGETING

Why did we cover two major topics, master budgets and responsibility accounting, in the same chapter? Primarily to emphasize that human factors are crucial parts of budgeting. Too often, students study budgeting as though it were a mechanical tool.

The budgeting techniques themselves are free of emotion; however, their administration requires education, persuasion, and intelligent interpretation. Many managers regard budgets negatively. To them, the word *budget* is about as popular as, say, *downsizing, layoff,* or *strike.* Top managers must convince their subordinates that the budget is a positive tool designed to help them choose and reach goals. But budgets are not cure-alls. They are not remedies for weak management talent, faulty organization, or a poor accounting system.

BUDGETING: A DISCIPLINE IN TRANSITION

Many areas of management accounting are subject to ongoing debate. Budgeting is no exception. Advocates of new proposals invariably include criticisms of so-called "traditional budgeting." These criticisms are often exaggerations of "current worst practice." Exhibit 6-6 summarizes six proposals designed to improve traditional budgeting systems. Few of the negative features cited in the left-hand column are new; they have long been singled out for criticism. Indeed, prior sections of this chapter have mentioned the importance of avoiding many of these problems. Nonetheless, major changes that address these problems are currently being examined by managers.

EXHIBIT 6-6
Criticisms of Traditional Budgeting and Proposals for Change

Criticism of Traditional Budgeting	Proposal for Change
Excessive reliance on extrapolating past trends	Link budgeting explicitly to strategy.
Making across-the-board fixed percentage cuts when early iterations of a budget provide "unacceptable results"	Use activity-based budgeting to guide areas for cost reduction.
Examining individual functional areas as if they are independent (so-called "silos," to use a farming analogy)	Explicitly adopt a cross-functional approach where interdependencies across business function areas of the value chain are recognized.
Myopically overemphasizing a fixed time horizon such as a year. Viewing annual cost targets as key task to be accomplished	Tailor the budget cycle to the purpose of budgeting. Events beyond current period are recognized as important when evaluating current actions. Value creation is given paramount importance.
Being preoccupied with financial aspects of events in the budget period	Balance financial aspects with nonfinancial (such as quality and time) aspects.
Not using budgets to evaluate performance until end of budget period	Signal to all employees the need for continuous improvement of performance (such as revenue enhancement and cost reduction) within the budget period.

Source: Adapted from *"Advanced Budgeting Study Group Report* for CAM-I," *Management Accounting* (U.K.: December 1994).

Before trying to solve the following problem, review the illustration of the master budget, page 183.

PROBLEM
Prepare a budgeted income statement, including all necessary detailed supporting budget schedules. Use the data given in the illustration of the master budget to prepare your own budget schedules. (See the "Basic Data and Requirements" section on pp. 184–186.)

SUMMARY

The following points are linked to the chapter's learning objectives.

1. The master budget summarizes the financial projections of all the organization's budgets and plans. It expresses management's comprehensive operating and financial plans—the formalized outline of the organization's financial objectives and their means of attainment. Budgets are tools that by themselves are neither good nor bad. How managers administer budgets is the key to their value. When administered wisely, budgets compel management planning, provide definite expectations that are an appropriate framework for judging subsequent performance, and promote communication and coordination among the various subunits of the organization.

2. Two major parts of the master budget are the operating budget, which is the budgeted income statement and its supporting budget schedules, and the financial budget, which comprises the capital budget, cash budget, budgeted balance sheet, and budgeted statement of cash flows.

3. The foundation for the operating budget is generally the revenue budget. The supporting budget schedules are geared to the revenue budget, which could include the following: production budget, direct materials usage budget, direct materials purchases budget, direct manufacturing labour budget, manufacturing overhead costs budget, ending inventory budget, cost of goods sold budget, R&D/design budget, marketing budget, distribution budget, customer service budget, and administrative costs budget. The operating budget ends with the budgeted income statement.

4. Computer-based financial planning models are mathematical statements of the relationships among operating activities, financial activities, and other factors that affect the budget. These models allow management to conduct what-if (sensitivity) analyses of the effects on the master budget of changes in the original predicted data or changes in budget assumptions.

5. Kaizen budgeting captures the continuous improvement notion that is a key management concern. Costs in kaizen budgeting are based on future improvements that are yet to be implemented rather than on current practices or methods.

6. Activity-based budgeting focuses on the costs of activities necessary to produce and sell products and services. It is inherently linked to activity-based costing, but differs in its emphasis on future costs and future usage of activity areas.

7. A responsibility centre is a part, segment, or subunit of an organization whose manager is accountable for a specified set of activities. Four major types of responsibility centres are cost centres, revenue centres, profit centres, and investment centres. Responsibility accounting systems measure the plans (by budgets) and actions (by actual results) of each responsibility centre.

8. Controllable costs are costs that are primarily subject to the influence of a given manager of a given responsibility centre for a given time span. Performance reports of responsibility centre managers, however, often include costs, revenues, and investments that the managers cannot control. Responsibility accounting associates financial items with managers on the basis of which manager has the most knowledge and information about the specific items, regardless of the manager's ability to exercise full control. The important question is who should be asked, not who should be blamed.

APPENDIX: THE CASH BUDGET

The major illustration in this chapter features the operating budget. The other major part of the master budget is the financial budget, which includes the capital budget, cash budget, budgeted balance sheet, and budgeted statement of cash flows. This appendix focuses on the cash budget and the budgeted balance sheet. Capital budgeting is covered in Chapters 21 and 22; coverage of the budgeted statement of cash flows is beyond the scope of this book.

Suppose Halifax Engineering in our chapter illustration had the balance sheet for the year ended December 31, 1999, shown in Exhibit 6-7. The budgeted cash flows for 2000 are as follows:

	Quarters			
	1	2	3	4
Collections from customers	$913,700	$984,600	$976,500	$918,400
Disbursements:				
Direct materials	314,360	283,700	227,880	213,800
Payroll	557,520	432,080	409,680	400,720
Income taxes	50,000	46,986	46,986	46,986
Other costs	184,000	156,000	151,000	149,000
Machinery purchase	—	—	—	35,080

The quarterly data are based on the cash effects of the operations formulated in schedules 1 to 8 in the chapter, but the details of that formulation are not shown here in order to keep the illustration relatively brief and focused.

EXHIBIT 6-7
Balance Sheet for Halifax Engineering for the Year Ended December 31, 1999

Assets		
Current assets:		
Cash	$ 30,000	
Accounts receivable	400,000	
Direct materials	109,000	
Finished goods	64,600	$ 603,600
Property, plant, and equipment:		
Land	200,000	
Building and equipment	2,200,000	
Accumulated amortization	(690,000)	1,710,000
Total		$2,313,600

Liabilities and Stockholders' Equity		
Current liabilities:		
Accounts payable	$ 150,000	
Income taxes payable	50,000	$ 200,000
Stockholders' equity:		
Common stock, no-par, 25,000 shares outstanding	350,000	
Retained earnings	1,763,600	2,113,600
Total		$2,313,600

The company wants to maintain a $35,000 minimum cash balance at the end of each quarter. The company can borrow or repay money in multiples of $1,000 at an interest rate of 12% per year. Management does not want to borrow any more cash than is necessary and wants to repay as promptly as possible. By special arrangement, interest is computed and paid when the principal is repaid. Assume that borrowing takes place at the beginning and repayment at the end of the quarters in question. Interest is computed to the nearest dollar.

Suppose an accountant at Halifax Engineering is given the preceding data and the other data contained in the budgets in the chapter. He is instructed as follows:

1. Prepare a cash budget, that is, prepare a statement of cash receipts and disbursements by quarters, including details of borrowing, repayment, and interest expense.

2. Prepare a budgeted balance sheet.

3. Prepare a budgeted income statement, including the effects of interest expense and income taxes. Assume that income taxes for 2000 (at a tax rate of 40%) are $187,944.

Preparation of Budgets

Cash budget. Schedule of expected cash receipts and disbursements.

1. The **cash budget** (Exhibit 6-8) is a schedule of expected cash receipts and disbursements. It predicts the effects on the cash position at the given level of operations. Exhibit 6-8 presents the cash budget by quarters to show the impact of cash flow timing on bank loans and their repayment. In practice, monthly—and sometimes weekly—cash budgets are very helpful for cash planning and

EXHIBIT 6-8
Cash Budget for Halifax Engineering for the Year Ended December 31, 2000

	Quarters				Year as a Whole
	1	2	3	4	
Cash balance, beginning	$ 30,000	$ 35,820	$ 35,934	$ 35,188	$ 30,000
Add: Receipts:					
Collections from customers	913,700	984,600	976,500	918,400	3,793,200
Total cash available for needs: (a)	943,700	1,020,420	1,012,434	953,588	3,823,200
Deduct: Disbursements:					
Direct materials	314,360	283,700	227,880	213,800	1,039,740
Payroll	557,520	432,080	409,680	400,720	1,800,000
Income taxes	50,000	46,986	46,986	46,986	190,958
Other costs	184,000	156,000	151,000	149,000	640,000
Machinery purchase	0	0	0	35,080	35,080
Total disbursements: (b)	1,105,880	918,766	835,546	845,586	3,705,778
Minimum cash balance desired	35,000	35,000	35,000	35,000	35,000
Total cash needed: (c)	1,140,880	953,766	870,546	880,586	3,740,778
Cash excess (deficiency): (a) – (c)*	$ (197,180)	$ 66,654	$ 141,888	$ 73,002	$ 82,422
Financing:					
Borrowing (at beginning)	$ 198,000	$ 0	$ 0	$ 0	$ 198,000
Repayment (at end)	—	(62,000)	(130,000)	(6,000)	(198,000)
Interest (at 12% per year)†	—	(3,720)	(11,700)	(720)	(16,140)
Total effects of financing: (d)	$ 198,000	$ (65,720)	$ (141,700)	$ (6,720)	$ (16,140)
Cash balance, ending: (a) – (b) + (d)	$ 35,820	$ 35,934	$ 35,188	$101,282	$ 101,282

*Excess of total cash available over total cash needed before current financing
†Note that the interest payments pertain only to the amount of principal being repaid at the end of a given quarter. The specific computations regarding interest are $62,000 × 0.12 × ¾ = $3,720; $130,000 × 0.12 × ¾ = $11,700; and $6,000 × 0.12 × ¼ = $720. Also note that *amortization does not require a cash outlay.*

control. Cash budgets help avoid unnecessary idle cash and unexpected cash deficiencies. Cash balances are kept in line with needs. Ordinarily, the cash budget has the following main sections:

a. The beginning cash balance plus cash receipts equals the total cash available before financing. Cash receipts depend on collections of accounts receivable, cash sales, and miscellaneous recurring sources such as rental or royalty receipts. Information on the prospective collectibility of accounts receivable is needed for accurate predictions. Key factors include bad debt (uncollectible accounts) experience and average time lag between sales and collections.

b. Cash disbursements include the following items:

   i. *Direct materials purchases.* Depends on credit terms extended by suppliers and bill-paying patterns of the buyer.

   ii. *Direct labour and other wage and salary outlays.* Depends on payroll dates.

   iii. *Other costs.* Depends on timing and credit terms. *Be sure to note that amortization does not require a cash outlay.*

   iv. *Other disbursements.* Outlays for property, plant, and equipment, and for long-term investments

c. Financing requirements depend on how the total cash available for needs, keyed as (a) in Exhibit 6-8, compares with the total cash needed, keyed as (c). Total cash needed includes total disbursements, keyed as (b), plus the minimum ending cash balance desired. The financing plans will depend on the relationship between total cash available for needs and total cash needed. If there is excess cash, loans may be repaid or temporary investments made. The outlays for interest expense are usually shown in this section of the cash budget.

d. The ending cash balance. The total effect of the financing decisions on the cash budget, keyed as (d) in Exhibit 6-8, may be positive (borrowing) or negative (repayment), and the ending cash balance is (a) − (b) + (d).

   The cash budget in Exhibit 6-8 shows the pattern of short-term "self-liquidating cash loans." Seasonal peaks of production or sales often result in heavy cash disbursements for purchases, payroll, and other operating outlays as the products are produced and sold. Cash receipts from customers typically lag behind sales. The loan is *self-liquidating* in the sense that the borrowed money is used to acquire resources that are combined for sale, and the proceeds from sales are used to repay the loan. This **self-liquidating cycle**—sometimes called the **working capital cycle, cash cycle,** or **operating cycle**—is the movement from cash to inventories to receivables and back to cash.

> **Self-liquidating cycle (cash cycle, operating cycle, working capital cycle).** The movement of cash to inventories to receivables and back to cash.

2. The budgeted balance sheet is presented in Exhibit 6-9. Each item is projected in the light of the details of the business plan as expressed in all the previous budget schedules. For example, the ending balance of accounts receivable of $406,800 is computed by adding the budgeted revenues of $3,800,000 (from schedule 1) to the beginning balance of $400,000 (given) and subtracting cash receipts of $3,793,200 (given in Exhibit 6-8).

3. The budgeted income statement is presented in Exhibit 6-10. It is merely the budgeted operating income statement in Exhibit 6-3 expanded to include interest expense and income taxes.

For simplicity, the cash receipts and disbursements were given explicitly in this illustration. Frequently, there are lags between the items reported on the accrual basis of accounting in an income statement and their related cash receipts and disbursements. In the Halifax Engineering example, collections from customers are derived under two assumptions: (1) In any month, 10% of sales are cash sales and 90% of sales are on credit, and (2) Half the total credit sales are collected in each of the two months subsequent to the sale, as the following table shows.

	May	June	July	August	September	Cash Collections in Third Quarter as a Whole
Monthly revenue budget for Halifax (given):						
Credit sales, 90%	$307,800	$307,800	$280,800	$280,800	$280,800	
Cash sales, 10%	34,200	34,200	31,200	31,200	31,200	
Total revenues	$342,000	$342,000	$312,000	$312,000	$312,000	
Cash collections from:						
Cash sales this month			$ 31,200	$ 31,200	$ 31,200	
Credit sales last month			153,900*	140,400‡	140,400$	
Credit sales two months ago			153,900†	153,900*	140,400‡	
Total collections			$339,000	$325,500	$312,000	$976,500

*$0.50 \times \$307,800$ (June sales) = $153,900.
†$0.50 \times \$307,800$ (May sales) = $153,900.
‡$0.50 \times \$280,800$ (July sales) = $140,400.
$$0.50 \times \$280,800$ (August sales) = $140,400.

EXHIBIT 6-9
Halifax Engineering: Budgeted Balance Sheet for the Year Ended December 31, 2000

Assets

Current assets:

Cash (from Exhibit 6-8)		$ 101,282	
Accounts receivable (1)		406,800	
Direct materials (2)		76,000	
Finished goods (2)		448,600	$1,032,682
Property, plant, and equipment:			
Land (3)		200,000	
Building and equipment (4)	$2,235,080		
Accumulated amortization (5)	(920,000)	1,315,080	1,515,080
Total			$2,547,762

Liabilities and Stockholders' Equity

Current liabilities:

Accounts payable (6)		$ 105,260	
Income taxes payable (7)		46,986	$ 152,246
Stockholders' equity:			
Common stock, no-par, 25,000 shares outstanding (8)		350,000	
Retained earnings (9)		2,045,516	2,395,516
Total			$2,547,762

Notes:
Beginning balances are used as the starting point for most of the following computations:
(1) $400,000 + $3,800,000 revenues – $3,793,200 receipts (Exhibit 6-8) = $406,800.
(2) From schedule 6B, p.190
(3) From beginning balance sheet, Exhibit 6-7
(4) $2,200,000 + $35,080 purchases = $2,235,080.
(5) $690,000 + $230,000 amortization from schedule 5, p. 189.
(6) $150,000 + $995,000 (schedule 3B) – $1,039,740 (Exhibit 6-8) = $105,260.

There are no wages payable.
(7) $50,000 + $187,944 current year – $190,958 payment = $46,986.
(8) From beginning balance sheet.
(9) $1,763,600 + $281,916 net income per Exhibit 6-10 = $2,045,516.

EXHIBIT 6-10
Budgeted Income Statement for Halifax Engineering for the Year Ended December 31, 2000

Revenues	Schedule 1		$3,800,000
Costs:			
Cost of goods sold	Schedule 7		2,444,000
Gross margin			1,356,000
Operating costs:			
R&D/product design costs	Schedule 8	$136,000	
Marketing costs	Schedule 8	200,000	
Distribution costs	Schedule 8	100,000	
Customer service costs	Schedule 8	60,000	
Administration costs	Schedule 8	374,000	870,000
Operating income			486,000
Interest expense	Exhibit 6-8		16,140
Income before income taxes			469,860
Income taxes	Given		187,944
Net income			$ 281,916

Of course, such schedules of cash collections depend on credit terms, collection histories, and expected bad debts. Similar schedules can be prepared for operating costs and their related cash disbursements.

TERMS TO LEARN

The chapter contains definitions of the following important terms:

activity-based budgeting   (p. 193)
budgetary slack   (p. 187)
cash budget   (p. 200)
cash cycle   (p. 201)
controllability   (p. 196)
controllable cost   (p. 196)
cost centre   (p. 195)
financial budget   (p. 183)
financial planning models   (p. 191)
investment centre   (p. 195)
kaizen budgeting   (p. 193)
master budget   (p. 179)
operating budget   (p. 183)

operating cycle   (p. 201)
organizational structure   (p. 194)
padding   (p. 187)
pro forma statements   (p. 180)
profit centre   (p. 195)
responsibility accounting   (p. 195)
responsibility centre   (p. 195)
revenue centre   (p. 195)
rolling budget   (p. 182)
self-liquidating cycle   (p. 201)
strategic analysis   (p. 180)
working capital cycle   (p. 201)

ASSIGNMENT MATERIAL

QUESTIONS

6-1 Define *master budget*.

6-2 What are the elements of the budgeting cycle?

6-3 "Strategy, plans, and budgets are unrelated to one another." Do you agree? Explain.

6-4 "Budgeted performance is a better criterion than past performance for judging managers." Do you agree? Explain.

6-5 "Production and marketing are like oil and water. They just don't mix." How can a budget assist in reducing traditional battles between these two areas?

6-6 How might a company benefit by sharing its own internal budget information with other companies?

6-7 "Budgets meet the cost-benefit test. They force managers to act differently." Do you agree? Explain.

6-8 Define *rolling budget*. Give an example.

6-9 Outline the steps in preparing an operating budget.

6-10 "The revenue budget is the cornerstone for budgeting." Why?

6-11 How can use of sensitivity analysis increase the benefits of budgeting?

6-12 Why is cash budgeting pivotal to a startup company?

6-13 Define *kaizen budgeting*.

6-14 Describe how non-output-based cost drivers can be incorporated into budgeting.

6-15 Explain how the choice of the responsibility centre type (cost, revenue, profit, or investment) affects budgeting.

EXERCISES

6-16 Production budget (in units), fill in the missing numbers. The following (in units) is taken from the production budget for three models of fax machines in October 2001:

	Model 101	Model 201	Model 301
1. Beginning finished goods inventory	11	8	?
2. Target ending finished goods inventory	?	6	33
3. Budgeted production	?	?	855
4. Budgeted sales	180	?	867
5. Total required units (2 + 4)	194	199	?

REQUIRED

Fill in the missing numbers.

6-17 Sales and production budget. The Mendez Company expects 2002 sales of 100,000 units of serving trays. Mendez' beginning inventory for 2002 is 7,000 trays; target ending inventory, 11,000 trays.

REQUIRED

Compute the number of trays budgeted for production in 2002.

6-18 Direct materials budget. The London Wines Company produces wine. The company expects to produce 1.5 million two-litre bottles of Chablis in 2000. London purchases empty glass bottles from an outside vendor. Its target ending inventory of such bottles is 50,000; its beginning inventory is 20,000. For simplicity, ignore breakage.

REQUIRED

Compute the number of bottles to be purchased in 2000.

6-19 Budgeting material purchases. The Mahoney Company has prepared a sales budget of 42,000 finished units for a three-month period. The company has an inventory of 22,000 units of finished goods on hand at December 31 and has a target finished goods inventory of 24,000 units at the end of the succeeding quarter.

It takes three litres of direct materials to make one unit of finished product. The company has an inventory of 90,000 litres of direct materials at December 31 and has a target ending inventory of 110,000 litres.

REQUIRED

How many litres of direct materials should be purchased during the three months ending March 31?

6-20 Sales and production budget. Purity, Inc., bottles and distributes mineral water from the company's natural springs in Northern Ontario. Purity markets its product in 1-litre disposable plastic bottles and in 16-litre reusable plastic containers.

REQUIRED

1. For the year 2001, Purity marketing managers project monthly sales of 400,000 1-litre and 100,000 16-litre units. Average selling prices are estimated at $0.25

per 1-litre unit and $1.50 per 16-litre unit. Prepare a revenue budget for Purity, Inc., for the year ending December 31, 2001.

2. Purity begins 2001 with 900,000 1-litre units in inventory (that is, beginning inventory). The VP of Operations requests that 1-litre ending inventory on December 31, 2001, be no less than 600,000 units. Based on sales projections as budgeted above, what is the minimum number of 1-litre units Purity must produce during 2001?

3. The VP of Operations requests that ending inventory of 16-litre units on December 31, 2001, be 200,000 units. If the production budget calls for Purity to produce 1,300,000 16-litre units during 2001, what is the beginning inventory of 16-litre units on January 1, 2001?

6-21 Budgeting revenue, cost of goods sold, and gross margin. Janet Grossman operates the Centrum Gift Shop. She expects cash sales of $10,000 for October, $11,000 for November, and $16,000 for December. Grossman expects credit card sales of $7,000 during October and $8,000 and $12,000 respectively during November and December. Sales returns and allowances can be ignored. Credit card companies like VISA and MasterCard charge 4% on credit card sales, so Centrum net sales will be 96%. Cost of goods sold averages 40% of net sales.

REQUIRED

Grossman asks you to prepare a schedule of budgeted revenue, cost of goods sold, and gross margin for each month of the last quarter. She also wants you to show totals for the quarter.

6-22 Revenue, production, and purchases budget. The Suzuki Company in Japan has a division that manufactures two-wheel motorcycles. Its budgeted sales for Model G in 2002 is 800,000 units. Suzuki's target ending inventory is 100,000 units, and its beginning inventory is 120,000 units. The company's budgeted selling price to its distributors and dealers is 400,000 yen (¥) per motorcycle.

Suzuki buys all its wheels from an outside supplier. No defective wheels are accepted. (Suzuki's needs for extra wheels for replacement parts are ordered by a separate division of the company.) The company's target ending inventory is 30,000 wheels, and its beginning inventory is 20,000 wheels. The budgeted purchase price is ¥16,000 per wheel.

REQUIRED

1. Compute the budgeted revenue in yen.
2. Compute the number of motorcycles to be produced.
3. Compute the budgeted purchases of wheels in units and in yen.

6-23 Budget for production and direct manufacturing labour. (CMA, adapted) The Roletter Company makes and sells artistic frames for pictures of weddings, graduations, and other special events. Bob Anderson, controller, is responsible for preparing Roletter's master budget and has accumulated the following information for 2000:

	2000				
	January	**February**	**March**	**April**	**May**
Estimated sales in units	10,000	12,000	8,000	9,000	9,000
Selling price	$54.00	$51.50	$51.50	$51.50	$51.50
Direct manufacturing labour-hours per unit	2.0	2.0	1.5	1.5	1.5
Wage per direct manufacturing labour-hour	$10.00	$10.00	$10.00	$11.00	$11.00

Besides wages, direct manufacturing labour-related costs include pension contributions of $0.50 per hour, worker's compensation insurance of $0.15 per hour, employee medical insurance of $0.40 per hour, and employment insurance. Assume that as of January 1, 2000, the employment insurance rates are 7.5% of wages for employers and 7.5% of wages for employees. The cost of employee benefits paid by Roletter for its employees is treated as a direct manufacturing labour cost.

Roletter has a labour contract that calls for a wage increase to $11.00 per hour on April 1, 2000. New labour-saving machinery has been installed and will be fully operational by March 1, 2000.

Roletter expects to have 16,000 frames on hand on December 31, 1999, and has a policy of carrying an end-of-month inventory of 100% of the following month's sales plus 50% of the second following month's sales.

REQUIRED

Prepare a production budget and a direct manufacturing labour budget for the Ro-letter Company by month and for the first quarter of 2000. Both budgets may be combined in one schedule. The direct manufacturing labour budget should include labour-hours and show the detail for each labour cost category.

6-24 Activity-based budgeting. Family Supermarkets (FS) is preparing its activity-based budget for January 2000 for its operating costs (that is, its costs for goods other than those purchased for resale). Its current concern is with its four activity areas (which are also indirect cost categories in its product profitability reporting system):

a. **Ordering.** Covers purchasing activities. The cost driver is the number of purchase orders.

b. **Delivery.** Covers the physical delivery and receipt of merchandise. The cost driver is the number of deliveries.

c. **Shelf stacking.** Covers the stacking of merchandise on store shelves and the on-going restacking before sale.

d. **Customer support.** Covers assistance provided to customers, including check-out and bagging.

Assume FS has only three product areas—soft drinks, fresh produce, and packaged food. The budgeted usage of each cost driver in these three areas of the store and the January 2000 budgeted cost driver rates are as follows:

	Cost Driver Rates		January 2000 Budgeted Amount of Driver Used		
Activity Area and Driver	**1999 Actual Rate**	**January 2000 Budgeted Rate**	**Soft Drinks**	**Fresh Produce**	**Packaged Food**
Ordering (per purchase order)	$100	$90	14	24	14
Delivery (per delivery)	$80	$82	12	62	19
Shelf stacking (per hour)	$20	$21	16	172	94
Customer support (per item sold)	$0.20	$0.18	4,600	34,200	10,750

REQUIRED

1. What is the total budgeted cost for each activity area in January 2000?
2. What advantages might FS gain by using an activity-based budgeting approach rather than an approach for budgeting operating costs based on a budgeted percentage of the budgeted cost of goods sold?

6-25 Kaizen approach to activity-based budgeting (continuation of 6-24). Family Supermarkets (FS) has a kaizen (continuous improvement) approach to budgeting monthly activity area costs for each month of 2000. February's budgeted cost driver rate is 0.998 times the budgeted January 2000 rate. March's budgeted cost driver rate is 0.998 times the budgeted February 2000 rate, and so on. Assume that March 2000 has the same budgeted amount of cost drivers used as did January 2000.

REQUIRED

1. What is the total budgeted cost for each activity area in March 2000?
2. What are the benefits for FS in adopting a kaizen budgeting approach? What are the limitations?

6-26 Budgeting and behaviour. (CMA, adapted) Many managers claim that budgets are impractical because companies experience so many uncertainties. However, it is very probable that a firm's competitors are using budgets as indispensable management tools. A major objective of budgeting is to substitute deliberate, well-conceived business judgment for accidental success or failure in enterprise management. Implicit in this objective is the confidence that a competent management team can plan for, manage, and control in large measure the relevant variables that dominate the life of a business. Managers must grapple with uncertainties, regardless of whether or not they have a budget.

REQUIRED

1. Describe at least three benefits, other than improved cost control, that an organization can expect to realize from the implementation of budgeting.
2. Because a reliable prediction of sales is critical to the planning process, describe at least two factors that should be considered when preparing sales forecasts.

6-27 Appendix, cash flow analysis. (CMA, adapted) TabComp Inc. is a retail distributor for MZB-33 computer hardware and related software and support services. TabComp prepares annual sales forecasts, of which the first six months for 2000 are presented as follows:

TabComp Inc.
Sales Forecast
Six Months—2000

	Hardware Sales		Software Sales and Support	Total Sales
	Units	Dollars		
January	130	$ 390,000	$160,000	$ 550,000
February	120	360,000	140,000	500,000
March	110	330,000	150,000	480,000
April	90	270,000	130,000	400,000
May	100	300,000	125,000	425,000
June	125	375,000	225,000	600,000
Total	675	$2,025,000	$930,000	$2,955,000

Cash sales account for 25% of TabComp's total sales, 30% of the total sales are paid by bank credit card, and the remaining 45% are on open account (TabComp's own charge accounts). The cash and bank credit card sales are received in the month of the sale. Bank credit card sales are subject to a 4% discount deducted at the time of the daily deposit. The cash receipts for sales on open account are 70% in the month following the sales, 28% in the second month following the sale, and the remaining are estimated to be uncollectible.

TabComp's month-end inventory requirements for computer hardware units are 30% of the next month's sales. A one-month lead time is required for delivery from the manufacturer. Thus, orders for computer hardware units are placed on the 25th of each month to assure that they will be in the store by the first day of the month needed. The computer hardware units are purchased under terms of n/45, measured from the time the units are delivered to TabComp. TabComp's purchase price for the computer units is 60% of the selling price.

REQUIRED

1. Calculate the cash that TabComp can expect to collect during April 2000. Be sure to show all of your calculations.
2. TabComp is determining the MZB-33 computer hardware units that will be ordered on January 25, 2000.
   a. Determine the projected number of computer hardware units that will be ordered.
   b. Calculate the dollar value of the order that TabComp will place for these computer hardware units.
   c. In which month will TabComp pay for these computer hardware units?
3. As part of the annual budget process, TabComp prepares a cash budget by month for the entire year. Explain why a company such as TabComp prepares a cash budget by month for the entire year.

PROBLEMS

6-28 Budget schedules for manufacturer. Sierra Furniture is an elite desk manufacturer. It manufactures two products:
- ◆ **Executive desks.** 3' × 5' oak desks
- ◆ **Chairperson desks.** 6' × 4' red oak desks

The budgeted direct cost inputs for each product in 2000 are as follows:

	Executive Line	Chairperson Line
Direct materials:		
Oak top	16 square feet	—
Red oak top	—	25 square feet
Oak legs	4 legs	—
Red oak legs	—	4 legs
Direct manufacturing labour	3 hours	5 hours

Unit data pertaining to the direct materials for March 2000 are as follows:

Actual Beginning Direct Materials Inventory
(March 1, 2000)

	Product	
	Executive Line	**Chairperson Line**
Oak top	320 square feet	—
Red oak top	—	150 square feet
Oak legs	100 legs	—
Red oak legs	—	40 legs

Target Ending Direct Materials Inventory
(March 31, 2000)

	Product	
	Executive Line	**Chairperson Line**
Oak top	192 square feet	—
Red oak top	—	200 square feet
Oak legs	80 legs	—
Red oak legs	—	44 legs

Unit cost data for direct cost inputs pertaining to February 2000 and March 2000 are:

	February 2000 (Actual)	March 2000 (Budgeted)
Oak top (per square foot)	$18	$20
Red oak top (per square foot)	23	25
Oak legs (per leg)	11	12
Red oak legs (per leg)	17	18
Manufacturing labour cost per hour	30	30

Manufacturing overhead (both variable and fixed) is allocated to each desk on the basis of budgeted direct manufacturing labour-hours per desk. The budgeted variable manufacturing overhead rate for March 2000 is $35 per direct manufacturing labour-hour. The budgeted fixed manufacturing overhead for March 2000 is $42,500. Both variable and fixed manufacturing overhead costs are allocated to each unit of finished goods.

Data relating to finished goods inventory for March 2000 are:

	Executive Line	Chairperson Line
Beginning inventory	20 units	5 units
Beginning inventory in dollars (cost)	$10,480	$4,850
Target ending inventory	30 units	15 units

Budgeted sales for March 2000 are 740 units of the Executive Line and 390 units of the Chairperson Line. The budgeted selling prices per unit in March 2000 are $1,020 for an Executive Line desk and $1,600 for a Chairperson Line desk.

Assume the following in your answer:

a. Work-in-process inventories are negligible and ignored.

b. Direct materials inventory and finished goods inventory are costed using the FIFO method.

c. Unit costs of direct materials purchased and finished goods are constant in March 2000.

REQUIRED

Prepare the following budgets for March 2000:

1. Revenue budget
2. Production budget in units

3. Direct materials usage budget and direct materials purchases budget
4. Direct manufacturing labour budget
5. Manufacturing overhead budget
6. Ending inventory budget
7. Cost of goods sold budget

6-29 Continuous improvement, budgeting (continuation of 6-28). Sierra Furniture decides to incorporate continuous improvement into its budgeting process. Describe four areas where Sierra could incorporate continuous improvement into the budget schedules in Problem 6-28. Be explicit as to how the incorporation would occur.

6-30 Sensitivity analysis and changing budget assumptions. Choco Chip produces two brands of chocolate chip cookies—Chippo, a cookie rich in chocolate, and Choco, a less sumptuous production for the more weight conscious. Choco Chip's cookies are produced from two ingredients–chocolate chips and cookie dough. Chippo is 50% chips and 50% dough, whereas Choco is 25% chips and 75% dough.

Cookie packages of either brand weigh one kilogram. Choco Chips's master budget projects sales of 500,000 packages of Choco and 500,000 packages of Chippo in 2000. According to the master budget for 2000, estimated average selling prices are $3.00 per package (both brands). An industry analyst forecasts 2000 ingredients costs as follows: one kilogram of industrial grade chocolate will cost $2.00, and one kilogram of industrial grade cookie dough will cost $1.00. Assume Choco Chip incurs no other costs in the production of their cookies.

REQUIRED

1. Use the preceding information to calculate Choco Chip's budgeted operating income and gross margins for 2000.
2. In August 2000, Choco Chips' VP of Marketing is fired after overestimating sales for the first half of 2000 by more than 50%. Choco Chip's CEO re-evaluates the marketing plans for 2000 and believes Chippo cookies can average only $2.60 a package. However, he thinks Choco cookies will average at least $3.20 per package. Based on these new estimates, recalculate budgeted operating income and gross margins. Calculate the percentage change in the budgeted operating income relative to your initial estimate in requirement 1.
3. The original sales quantity estimates allowed for the new production line to begin operations on January 1, 2000. However, engineering reports the new line will become operational only during the second quarter. Based on this new knowledge, the CEO trims sales estimates of Chippos to 400,000. Using the initial $3.00 price per package, recalculate the budgeted operating income. Calculate the percentage change from the initial estimate in requirement 1.
4. A war in South America had led to an increase in cocoa prices. As a result, your resident economist re-estimates 2000 chocolate prices at $4.00 a kilogram. Using the initial estimates for quantities and prices (that is, 500,000 packages of each brand at $3.00 per package) recalculate the budgeted operating income and the percentage change from your original estimate in requirement 1.

6-31 Revenue and production budgets. (CPA, adapted) The Scarborough Corporation manufactures and sells two products, Thingone and Thingtwo. In July 2000, Scarborough's Budget Department gathered the following data in order to prepare budgets for 2001:

2001 Projected Sales

Product	Units	Price
Thingone	60,000	$165
Thingtwo	40,000	$250

2001 Inventories in Units

Product	Expected January 1, 2001	Target December 31, 2001
Thingone	20,000	25,000
Thingtwo	8,000	9,000

To produce one unit of Thingone and Thingtwo, the following direct materials are used:

Direct Material	Unit	Amount Used per Unit	
		Thingone	Thingtwo
A	Kilograms	4	5
B	Kilograms	2	3
C	Each	0	1

Projected data for 2001 with respect to direct materials are as follows:

Direct Material	Anticipated Purchase Price	Expected Inventories January 1, 2001	Target Inventories December 31, 2001
A	$12	32,000 kilograms	36,000 kilograms
B	$5	29,000 kilograms	32,000 kilograms
C	$3	6,000 units	7,000 units

Projected direct manufacturing labour requirements and rates for 2001 are as follows:

Product	Hours per Unit	Rate per Hour
Thingone	2	$12
Thingtwo	3	$16

Manufacturing overhead is allocated at the rate of $20 per direct manufacturing labour-hour.

REQUIRED

Based on the preceding projections and budget requirements for Thingone and Thingtwo, prepare the following budgets for 2001:
1. Revenue budget (in dollars)
2. Production budget (in units)
3. Direct materials purchases budget (in quantities)
4. Direct materials purchases budget (in dollars)
5. Direct manufacturing labour budget (in dollars)
6. Budgeted finished goods inventory at December 31, 2001 (in dollars)

6-32 **Budgeted income statement.** (CMA, adapted) The Easecom Company is a manufacturer of videoconferencing products. Regular units are manufactured to meet marketing projections, and specialized units are made after an order is received. Maintaining the videoconferencing equipment is an important area of customer satisfaction. With the recent downturn in the computer industry, the videoconferencing equipment segment has suffered, leading to a decline in Easecom's financial performance. The following income statement shows results for the year 2000:

Income Statement for the Easecom Company
for the Year Ended December 31, 2000
(in thousands)

Revenues:		
Equipment	$6,000	
Maintenance contracts	1,800	
Total revenues		$7,800
Cost of goods sold		4,600
Gross margin		3,200
Operating costs:		
Marketing	600	
Distribution	150	
Customer maintenance	1,000	
Administration	900	
Total operating costs		2,650
Operating income		$ 550

Easecom's management team is in the process of preparing the 2001 budget and is studying the following information:

a. Selling prices of equipment are expected to increase by 10% as the economic recovery begins. The selling price of each maintenance contract is unchanged from 2000.

b. Equipment sales in units are expected to increase by 6%, with a corresponding 6% growth in units of maintenance contracts.

c. The cost of each unit sold is expected to increase by 3% to pay for the necessary technology and quality improvements.

d. Marketing costs are expected to increase by $250,000, but administration costs are expected to be held at 2000 levels.

e. Distribution costs vary in proportion to the number of units of equipment sold.

f. Two maintenance technicians are to be added at a total cost of $130,000, which covers wages and related travel costs. The objective is to improve customer service and shorten response time.

g. There is no beginning or ending inventory of equipment.

REQUIRED
Prepare a budgeted income statement for 2001.

6-33 Operating budget. Slopes Inc. manufactures and sells snowboards. Slopes manufactures a single model, the Pipex. In the summer of 2000, Slope's accountant gathered the following data in order to prepare budgets for 2001.

Materials and labour requirements

Direct materials

Wood	5 board-feet per snowboard
Fibreglass	6 yards per snowboard
Direct labour	5 hours per snowboard

Slopes' CEO expects to sell 1,000 snowboards during 2001 at an estimated retail price of $450 per board. Further, he expects 2001 beginning inventory to be 100 boards, and would like to end 2001 with 200 snowboards in stock.

Direct material inventories

	Beginning Inventory 1-1-2001	Ending Inventory 12-31-2001
Wood	2,000	1,500
Fibreglass	1,000	2,000

The beginning inventory of wood was purchased at $28 per board foot and fibreglass was purchased at $4.80 per yard. Prices have now risen to $30 per board foot and $5 per yard of fibreglass. Variable manufacturing overhead is allocated at the rate of $7.00 per direct manufacturing labour-hour. Fixed manufacturing overhead costs are budgeted at $66,000 for 2001. Variable marketing costs are allocated at the rate of $250 per sales visit, and the marketing plan calls for 30 sales visits during 2001. Finally, fixed nonmanufacturing costs are budgeted at $30,000 for 2001.

REQUIRED
Based on the data and projections supplied by Slopes' managers,

1. Prepare the 2001 revenue budget (in dollars).
2. Prepare the 2001 production budget (in units).
3. Prepare direct materials usage and purchases budgets for 2001.
4. Prepare a direct manufacturing labour budget for 2001.
5. Prepare a manufacturing overhead budget for 2001.
6. What is the budgeted manufacturing overhead rate?
7. What is the budgeted manufacturing overhead cost per output unit?
8. Calculate the cost of a snowboard manufactured in 2001.
9. Prepare an ending inventory budget for 2001.
10. Prepare a cost-of-goods-sold budget for 2001.
    (Opening finished goods inventory is $37,480.)
11. Prepare the budgeted income statement for Slopes Inc. for 2001.

6-34 Cash budgeting. Retail outlets purchase snowboards from Slopes, Inc., throughout the year. However, in anticipation of late summer and early fall purchases, outlets ramp up inventories from May through August. Outlets are billed when boards are ordered. Invoices are payable within 60 days. From past experience, Slopes' accountant projects 20% of invoices are paid in the month invoiced, 50% are paid in the following month, and 30% of invoices are paid two months past the month of invoice. The average selling price per snowboard is $450.

To meet demand, Slopes increases production from April through July. The snowboards are produced a month prior to their projected sale. Materials are purchased in the month of production and paid for during the following month (terms are invoice date plus 30 days). During this period there is no production to inventory, and no materials are purchased for inventory.

Direct labour and manufacturing overhead are paid monthly. Variable manufacturing overhead is incurred at the rate of $7 per direct manufacturing labour hour. Variable marketing costs are driven by the number of sales visits. However, there are no sales visits during the months studied. Slopes, Inc., also incurs fixed manufacturing overhead costs of $5500 per month and fixed nonmanufacturing overhead costs of $2500 per month.

Projected Sales

May	80 units
June	120 units
July	200 units
August	100 units
September	60 units
October	40 units

Materials and Labour Utilization and Cost

	Units per Board	Price per Unit	Unit
Wood	5	$30	Board feet
Fibreglass	6	5	Yard
Direct labour	5	25	Hour

On September 1, 2000, Slopes had a cash crunch and borrowed $30,000 on a 6% 1-year note with interest payable monthly. The note is due October 1, 2001. Using the preceding information, you must determine whether Slopes will be in a position to pay off this short-term debt properly.

REQUIRED

1. Prepare a cash budget for the months of July through September, 2001, assuming an opening cash balance of zero. Show supporting schedules for the calculation of receivables and payables.
2. Will Slopes be in a position to pay off the $30,000 1-year note on October 1, 2001? If not, what actions would you recommend to Slopes' management?
3. Suppose Slopes is interested in maintaining a minimum cash balance of $10,000. Does the company manage to maintain such a balance during all three months analyzed? If not, suggest a suitable cash management strategy.

6-35 **Responsibility of purchasing agent.** (Adapted from a description by R. Villers) Mark Richards is the purchasing agent for the Hart Manufacturing Company. Kent Sampson is head of the Production Planning and Control Department. Every six months, Sampson gives Richards a general purchasing program. Richards gets specifications from the Engineering Department. He then selects suppliers and negotiates prices. When he took this job, Richards was informed very clearly that he bore responsibility for meeting the general purchasing program once he accepted it from Sampson.

During week 24, Richards was advised that Part No. 1234—a critical part—would be needed for assembly on Tuesday morning of week 32. He found that the regular supplier could not deliver. He called everywhere and finally found a supplier in the Midwest, and accepted the commitment.

He followed up by mail. Yes, the supplier assured him, the part would be ready. The matter was so important that on Thursday of week 31, Richards checked by phone. Yes, the shipment had left in time. Richards was reassured and did not check further. But on Tuesday of week 32, the part had not arrived. Inquiry revealed that the shipment had been misdirected by the railroad and was still in Winnipeg.

REQUIRED

What department should bear the costs of time lost in the plant? Why? As purchasing agent, do you think it fair that such costs be charged to your department?

6-36 Fixing responsibility. (Adapted from a description by H. Bierman, Jr.) The city of Mountainvale hired its first city manager four years ago. She favoured a "management by objectives" philosophy and accordingly set up many profit responsibility centres, including a sanitation department, a utility department, and a repair shop.

For many months, the sanitation manager had been complaining to the utility manager about wires being too low at one point in the road. There was barely clearance for large sanitation trucks. The sanitation manager asked the repair shop to make changes in the clearance. The repair shop manager asked, "Should I charge the sanitation or the utility department for the $2,000 cost of making the adjustment?" Both departments refused to accept the charge, so the repair department refused to do the work.

Late one day, the top of a sanitation truck caught the wires and ripped them down. The repair department made an emergency repair at a cost of $2,600. Moreover, the city lost $1,000 of utility revenues (net of variable costs) because of the disruption of service.

Investigation disclosed that the sanitation truck had failed to clamp down its top properly. The extra two inches of height caused the wire to be caught.

Both the sanitation manager and the utility manager argued strenuously about who should bear the $2,600 cost. Moreover, the utility manager demanded reimbursement from the sanitation department of the $1,000 of lost utility income.

REQUIRED

As the city controller in charge of the responsibility accounting system, how would you favour accounting for these costs? Specifically, what would you do next? What is the proper role of responsibility accounting in fixing the blame for this situation?

6-37 Traditional budgeting and its critics. Critics of traditional budgeting often make their points in a colourful way. Consider the following comments by the CEO of a multinational with revenues over $30 billion and over 200,000 employees.

We set "stretch" goals for our people. Stretch means that we try for huge gains while having no idea how to get there—but our people figure out ways to get there. To reach these stretch goals, it takes an atmosphere where a goal doesn't become part of the old-fashioned budget. The budget is the bane of the corporate world. It never should have existed. A budget is this: If you make it, you generally get a pat on the back and a few bucks. If you miss it, you get a stick in the eye—or worse.

Making a budget is an exercise in minimization. You're always trying to get the lowest out of people, because everyone is negotiating to get a lower number.

If I worked for you, you would come charging into the boardroom and say, "I need four! We'd haggle all day, me making presentations, with 50 charts, saying the right number is two. In the end we'd settle on three. We'd go home and tell our families that we had a helluva day at the office. And what did we do? We ended up minimizing our activity. We weren't dreaming, reaching. I was trying to get the lowest budget number I could sell you. It's all backward.

REQUIRED

1. Do you agree that "The budget is the bane of the corporate world. It never should have existed"? Explain.
2. Assume you are the CEO of a television station. Your marketing manager shows you the preceding extract and suggests that you "dispense with the annual budget ritual." How would you respond?

6-38 Comprehensive review of budgeting. British Beverages bottles two soft drinks under licence to Cadbury Schweppes at its Manchester plant. Bottling at this plant is a highly repetitive, automated process. Empty bottles are removed from their carton, placed on a conveyor, and cleaned, rinsed, dried, filled, capped, and heated (to reduce condensation). All inventory is in direct materials and finished goods at the end of each working day. There is no work-in-process inventory.

The two soft drinks bottled by British Beverages are lemonade and diet lemonade. The syrup for both soft drinks is purchased from Cadbury Schweppes. Syrup for the regular brand contains a higher sugar content than the syrup for the diet brand.

British Beverages uses a lot size of 1,000 cases as the unit of analysis in its budgeting. (Each case contains 24 bottles.) Direct materials are expressed in terms of lots, where one lot of direct materials is the input necessary to yield one lot (1,000 cases) of beverage. In 2000, the following purchase prices are forecast for direct materials:

	Lemonade	Diet Lemonade
Syrup	$1,200 per lot	$1,100 per lot
Containers (bottles, caps, etc.)	$1,000 per lot	$1,000 per lot
Packaging	$800 per lot	$800 per lot

The two soft drinks are bottled using the same equipment. The equipment is sanitized daily, but it is rinsed only when a switch is made during the day between diet lemonade and lemonade. Diet lemonade is always bottled first each day to reduce the risk of sugar contamination. The only difference in the bottling process for the two soft drinks is the syrup.

Summary data used in developing budgets for 2000 are as follows:

a. Sales
   ◆ Lemonade, 1,080 lots at $9,000 selling price per lot
   ◆ Diet lemonade, 540 lots at $8,500 selling price per lot
b. Beginning (January 1, 2000) inventory of direct materials
   ◆ Syrup for lemonade, 80 lots at $1,100 purchase price per lot
   ◆ Syrup for diet lemonade, 70 lots at $1,000 purchase price per lot
   ◆ Containers, 200 lots at $950 purchase price per lot
   ◆ Packaging, 400 lots at $900 purchase price per lot
c. Beginning (January 1, 2000) inventory of finished goods
   ◆ Lemonade, 100 lots at $5,300 per lot
   ◆ Diet lemonade, 50 lots at $5,200 per lot
d. Target ending (December 31, 2000) inventory of direct materials
   ◆ Syrup for lemonade, 30 lots
   ◆ Syrup for diet lemonade, 20 lots
   ◆ Containers, 100 lots
   ◆ Packaging, 200 lots
e. Target ending (December 31, 2000) inventory of finished goods
   ◆ Lemonade, 20 lots
   ◆ Diet lemonade, 10 lots
f. Each lot requires 20 direct manufacturing labour-hours at the 2000 budgeted rate of $25 per hour. Indirect manufacturing labour costs are included in the manufacturing overhead forecast.
g. Variable manufacturing overhead is forecast to be $600 per hour of bottling time; bottling time is the time the filling equipment is in operation. It takes two hours to bottle one lot of lemonade and two hours to bottle one lot of diet lemonade.
   Fixed manufacturing overhead is forecast to be $1,200,000 for 2000.
h. Hours of budgeted bottling time is the sole allocation base for all fixed manufacturing overhead.
i. Administration costs are forecast to be 10% of the cost of goods manufactured for 2000. Marketing costs are forecast to be 12% of dollar sales for 2000. Distribution costs are forecast to be 8% of dollar sales for 2000.

REQUIRED
Assume British Beverages uses the first-in, first-out method for costing all inventories. On the basis of the preceding data, prepare the following budgets for 2000:
   1. Revenue budget (in dollars)
   2. Production budget (in units)
   3. Direct materials usage budget (in units and dollars)
   4. Direct materials purchases budget (in units and dollars)
   5. Direct manufacturing labour budget
   6. Manufacturing overhead costs budget
   7. Ending finished goods inventory budget
   8. Cost of goods sold budget
   9. Marketing costs budget
   10. Distribution costs budget
   11. Administration costs budget
   12. Budgeted income statement

6-39 **Appendix, cash budgeting for distributor.** (CMA) Alpha-Tech, a rapidly growing distributor of electronic components, is formulating its plans for 2000. Carol Jones, the firm's marketing director, has completed the revenue budget presented here.

Alpha-Tech
2000 Budgeted Revenues
(in thousands)

Month	Revenues	Month	Revenues
January	$ 9,000	July	$15,000
February	10,000	August	15,000
March	9,000	September	16,000
April	11,500	October	16,000
May	12,500	November	15,000
June	14,000	December	17,000

Phillip Smith, an accountant in the planning and budgeting department, is responsible for preparing the cash flow projection. The following information will be used in preparing the cash flow projection:

a. Alpha-Tech's excellent record in accounts receivable collection is expected to continue: 60% of billings are collected the month after the sale and the remaining 40% two months after.

b. The purchase of electronic components is Alpha-Tech's largest expenditure and is estimated to be 40% of revenues. Alpha-Tech receives 70% of the parts one month prior to sale and 30% during the month of sale.

c. Historically, 75% of accounts payable have been paid one month after receipt of the purchased components, and the remaining 25% paid two months after receipt.

d. Hourly wages and fringe benefits, estimated to be 30% of the current month's revenues, are paid in the month incurred.

e. General and administrative expenses are projected to be $15,620,000 for the year. The breakdown of these expenses is as follows:

2000 Budgeted General and Administrative Costs
(in thousands)

Salaries and fringe benefits	$ 3,200
Promotion	3,800
Property taxes	1,360
Insurance	2,000
Utilities	1,800
Amortization	3,460
Total	$15,620

All expenditures are paid uniformly throughout the year, except the property taxes, which are paid at the end of each quarter in four equal instalments.

f. Income tax payments are made at the beginning of each calendar quarter based on the income of the prior quarter. Alpha-Tech is subject to an effective income tax rate of 40%. Alpha-Tech's operating income for the first quarter of 2000 is projected to be $3,200,000. The company pays 100% of the estimated tax payment.

g. Alpha-Tech maintains a minimum cash balance of $500,000. If the cash balance is less than $500,000 at the end of each month, the company borrows amounts necessary to maintain this balance. All amounts borrowed are repaid out of subsequent positive cash flow. The projected April 1, 2000 opening balance is $500,000.

h. Alpha-Tech has no short-term debt as of April 1, 2000.

i. Alpha-Tech uses a calendar year for both financial reporting and tax purposes.

REQUIRED

1. Prepare a cash budget for Alpha-Tech by month for the second quarter of 2000. Ignore any interest expense associated with borrowing.

2. Discuss why cash budgeting is important for Alpha-Tech.

6-40 **Cash budgeting.** On December 1, 2000, the Itami Wholesale Company is attempting to project cash receipts and disbursements through January 31, 2001. On this latter date, a note will be payable in the amount of $100,000. This amount was borrowed in September to carry the company through the seasonal peak in November and December.

The trial balance on December 1 shows in part the following information:

Cash	$ 10,000	
Accounts receivable	280,000	
Allowance for bad debts		$15,800
Inventory	87,500	
Accounts payable		92,000

Sales terms call for a 2% discount if payment is made within the first ten days of the month after purchase; after that, the full amount is due by the end of the month after purchase. Experience has shown that 70% of the billings will be collected within the discount period, 20% by the end of the month after purchase, 8% in the following month, and that 2% will be uncollectible. There are no cash sales.

The average selling price of the company's products is $100 per unit. Actual and projected sales are:

October actual	$ 180,000
November actual	250,000
December estimated	300,000
January estimated	150,000
February estimated	120,000
Total estimated for year ended June 30, 2001	1,500,000

All purchases are payable within 15 days. Thus approximately 50% of the purchases in a month are due and payable in the next month. The average unit purchase cost is $70. Target ending inventories are 500 units plus 25% of the next month's unit sales.

Total budgeted marketing, distribution, and customer service costs for the year are $400,000. Of this amount, $150,000 is considered fixed (and includes amortization of $30,000). The remainder varies with sales. Both fixed and variable marketing, distribution, and customer service costs are paid as incurred.

REQUIRED
Prepare a cash budget for December and January. Supply supporting schedules for collections of receivables, payments for merchandise, and marketing, distribution, and customer service costs.

6-41 **Comprehensive budget; fill in schedules.** The following information is for the Newport Stationery Store.

Balance Sheet Information as of September 30

Current assets:	
Cash	$ 12,000
Accounts receivable	10,000
Inventory	63,600
Equipment, net	100,000
Liabilities as of September 30	None

Recent and Anticipated Sales

September	$40,000
October	48,000
November	60,000
December	80,000
January	36,000

◆ **Credit sales.** Sales are 75% for cash and 25% on credit. Assume that credit accounts are all collected within 30 days from sale. The accounts receivable on September 30 are the result of the credit sales for September (25% of $40,000).

Gross margin averages 30% of sales. Newport treats cash discounts on purchases in the income statement as "other income."

◆ **Operating costs.** Salaries and wages average 15% of monthly sales; rent, 5%; other operating costs, excluding amortization, 4%. Assume that these costs are disbursed each month. Amortization is $1,000 per month.

◆ **Purchases.** Newport keeps a minimum inventory of $30,000. The policy is to purchase additional inventory each month in the amount necessary to provide for the following month's sales. Terms on purchases are 2/10, n/30: a 2% discount is available if the payment is made within ten days after purchase; no discount is available if payment is made beyond ten days after purchase; and the full amount is due within thirty days. Assume that payments are made in the month of purchase and that all discounts are taken.

◆ **Light fixtures.** The expenditures for light fixtures are $600 in October and $400 in November. These amounts are to be capitalized.

Assume that a minimum cash balance of $8,000 must be maintained. Assume also that all borrowing is effective at the beginning of the month and all repayments are made at the end of the month of repayment. Loans are repaid when sufficient cash is available. Interest is paid only at the time of repaying principal. The interest rate is 18% per year. Management does not want to borrow any more cash than is necessary and wants to repay as soon as cash is available.

REQUIRED

1. On the basis of the preceding facts, complete schedule A.
2. Complete schedule B. Note that purchases are 70% of next month's sales.
3. Complete schedule C.
4. Complete schedule D.
5. Complete schedule E.
6. Complete schedule F (assume that borrowings must be made in multiples of $1,000).
7. What do you think is the most logical type of loan needed by Newport? Explain your reasoning.
8. Prepare a budgeted income statement for the fourth quarter and a budgeted balance sheet as of December 31. Ignore income taxes.
9. Some simplifications have been introduced in this problem. What complicating factors would be met in a typical business situation?

Schedule A
Budgeted Monthly Cash Receipts

Item	September	October	November	December
Total sales	$40,000	$48,000	$60,000	$80,000
Credit sales	10,000	12,000		
Cash sales				
Receipts:				
Cash sales		$36,000		
Collections on accounts receivable		10,000		
Total		$46,000		

Schedule B
Budgeted Monthly Cash Disbursements for Purchases

Item	October	November	December	4th Quarter
Purchases	$42,000			
Deduct: 2% cash discount	840			
Disbursements	$41,160			

Schedule C
Budgeted Monthly Cash Disbursements for Operating Costs

Item	October	November	December	4th Quarter
Salaries and wages	$ 7,200			
Rent	2,400			
Other cash operating costs	1,920			
Total	$11,520			

Schedule D
Budgeted Total Monthly Cash Disbursements

Item	October	November	December	4th Quarter
Purchases	$41,160			
Cash operating costs	11,520			
Light fixtures	600			
Total	$53,280			

Schedule E
Budgeted Cash Receipts and Disbursements

Item	October	November	December	4th Quarter
Receipts	$46,000			
Disbursements	53,280			
Net cash increase (decrease)	$(7,280)			

Schedule F
Financing Required

Item	October	November	December	Total
Beginning cash balance	$12,000			
Net cash increase				
Net cash decrease	7,280			
Cash position before borrowing	4,720			
Minimum cash balance required	8,000			
Excess/deficiency	(3,280)			
Borrowing required	4,000			
Interest payments				
Borrowing repaid				
Ending cash balance	$ 8,720			
Total	$53,280			

6-42 Budgetary slack and ethics. (CMA) Marge Atkins, the budget manager at the Norton Company, a manufacturer of infant furniture and carriages, is working on the 2000 annual budget. In discussions with Scott Ford, the sales manager, Atkins discovers that Ford's sales projections are lower than what Ford believes are actually achievable. When Atkins asked Ford about this, Ford said, "Well, we don't want to fall short of the sales projections, so we generally give ourselves a little breathing room by lowering the sales projections anywhere from 5 to 10%." Atkins also finds that Pete Granger, the production manager, makes similar adjustments. He pads budgeted costs, adding 10% to estimated costs.

REQUIRED

As a management accountant, should Marge Atkins take the position that the behaviour described by Scott Ford and Pete Granger is unethical? Refer to the Code of Professional Ethics described in Chapter 1.

COLLABORATIVE LEARNING PROBLEM

6-43 Athletics department of a university, budget revision options. Gary Connolly is the athletics director of Pacific University (PU). He has been director for over ten years. PU is a men's football and basketball powerhouse. The women's athletics program, however, has had less success. Last year, the women's basketball team finally had more wins than losses.

Connolly has just had a meeting with Laura Reddy, the newly appointed president of PU. It did not go well. Reddy and Connolly discussed what she called "Draft I" of the 2000 athletics department budget. He had believed it was the final draft. Reddy expressed four grave concerns about Draft I in particular and about the PU athletics program in general:

◆ **Concern 1.** The athletics department was budgeting a loss of over $3 million in 2000. Given the tight fiscal position of the university, this was unacceptable. A budgeted loss of $1 million was the most she would tolerate for 2000. Draft II of the 2000 budget was due in two weeks' time. By 2001, the athletics department had to operate with a balanced budget. She told Connolly this was nonnegotiable.

◆ **Concern 2.** The low allocation of money to the women's athletics program. *Frontline*, a tabloid television show, recently ran a program titled "It's a Man's World at the Pacific University Athletics Program." Reddy said Connolly was treating woman athletes as "third-class citizens."

◆ **Concern 3.** The low academic performance of the men's football athletes, many of whom had full scholarships. She noted that the local TV news recently ran an interview with three football-team students, none of whom "exemplified the high academic credentials she wanted Pacific to showcase to the world." She called one student "incoherent" and another "incapable of stringing sentences together."

◆ **Concern 4.** The outrageous salary paid to Bill Madden, the football coach. She noted it was twice that of the highest-paid academic on campus, a Nobel Prize winner! Moreover, Madden received other payments from his "Football the Pacific Way" summer program for high school students.

Exhibit 6-11 is a summary of the Draft I athletics department budget for 2000.

INSTRUCTIONS

Form groups of two or more students to complete the following requirement.

REQUIRED

Your group is to prepare Draft II of the athletics department's 2000 budget. This draft will form the basis of a half-day meeting Connolly will have with key officials of the athletics department.

EXHIBIT 6-11
Pacific University 2000 Athletics Department Budget (in millions)

Revenues:		
Men's athletics programs	$10.350	
Women's athletics programs	0.780	
Other (endowment income, gifts)	3.400	$14.530
Costs:		
Men's athletics programs	$11.040	
Women's athletics programs	2.800	
Other (not assigned to programs)	3.700	17.540
Operating income		$ (3.010)

Men's Athletics Programs

	Football	Basketball	Swimming	Other	Total
Revenues	$8.600	$1.500	$0.100	$0.150	$10.350
Costs	7.400	2.700	0.300	0.640	11.040
Full student scholarships	37	21	6	4	68

Women's Athletic Programs

	Basketball	Swimming	Other	Total
Revenues	$0.600	$0.080	$0.100	$0.780
Costs	1.800	0.200	0.800	2.800
Full student scholarships	11	4	2	17

7

FLEXIBLE BUDGETS, VARIANCES, AND MANAGEMENT CONTROL: I

The manufacturers of pantyhose use large quantities of elastic fibres, such as Dorlastan sold by Bayer A.G. Customers of Bayer are restructuring their procurement relationships with Bayer to reduce the total costs of their elastic fibre and other manufacturing inputs.

LEARNING OBJECTIVES

After studying this chapter, you should be able to:

1. Describe the difference between a static budget and a flexible budget

2. Develop a flexible budget and compute flexible-budget and sales-volume variances

3. Explain why standard costs are often used in variance analysis

4. Compute the price and efficiency variances for direct cost input categories

5. Explain why purchasing performance measures should focus on more factors than just price variances for inputs

6. Describe how the continuous improvement theme can be integrated into variance analysis

7. Describe benchmarking and how it can be used by managers in cost management

We have learned that managers quantify their plans in the form of budgets. This chapter focuses on how flexible budgets and variances can play a key role in management planning and control. Recall from Chapter 1 that feedback enables managers to compare the actual results with the planned performance. Flexible budgets and variances help managers gain insights into why the actual results differ from the planned performance. It is this insight into "why" that makes the topics covered in this chapter and the next important ones to master.

Each *variance* we compute is the difference between an actual result and a budgeted amount. The budgeted amount is a **benchmark;** that is, it is a point of reference from which comparisons may be made. Companies choose various benchmarks, including:

1. Financial variables reported in a company's own accounting system (such as Ford's manufacturing cost for a Bronco wagon)
2. Financial variables not reported in a company's own accounting system (such as when Ford uses the estimated cost Toyota incurs to manufacture a 4 Runner wagon as the benchmark for evaluating the cost competitiveness of its Bronco product line)
3. Nonfinancial variables (such as Ford's assembly line defect rate)

This chapter emphasizes financial benchmarks reported in a company's own accounting system. Benchmarks related to items 2 and 3 above are discussed but covered in less detail.

Organizations differ widely in how they compute and label the budgeted amounts they report in their own accounting system. Some organizations rely heavily on past results when developing budgeted amounts. Other organizations conduct detailed engineering or time-and-motion studies when developing budgeted amounts. The term *standard* is frequently used when such studies underlie the budgeted amounts. A **standard** is a carefully predetermined amount; it is usually expressed on a per-unit basis. In practice, there is not a precise dividing line between a *budgeted amount* and a *standard amount*. We use *budgeted amount* as the more general term, because some budgeted amounts may not be carefully predetermined amounts. However, all of the variances we discuss can be computed using standard amounts or budgeted amounts.

Benchmark. Point of reference from which comparisons may be made.

Honeywell Solutions for Industry
www.honeywell.com/industry/

Variance Management Class—
Robert Luttman & Associates
www.tiac.net/users/rllutman/
VMS/Week1/index.htm

Standard. Carefully predetermined amount; usually expressed on a per-unit basis.

Static budget. Budget that is based on one level of output; when variances are computed at the end of the period, no adjustment is made to the budgeted amounts.

STATIC BUDGETS AND FLEXIBLE BUDGETS

This chapter illustrates both static budgets and flexible budgets. A **static budget** is a budget that is based on one level of output; it is not adjusted or altered after it is set, regardless of ensuing changes in actual output (or actual revenue and cost drivers). A **flexible budget** is adjusted in accordance with ensuing changes in actual output (or actual revenue and cost drivers). As we shall see, a flexible budget enables managers to compute a richer set of variances than does a static budget. A **favourable variance**—denoted F in the exhibits—is a variance that increases operating income relative to the budgeted amount. An **unfavourable variance**—denoted U—is a variance that decreases operating income relative to the budgeted amount.

Budgets, both static and flexible, can differ in their level of detail. Increasingly, organizations are developing approaches to budgeting that report summary figures with the capability to display more detailed breakdowns of these figures on a computer screen. In this book, the term *Level* followed by a number denotes the amount of detail indicated by the variance(s) isolated. Level 0 reports the least detail, Level 1 offers more information, and so on.

Accounting System at Webb

The example of the Webb Company illustrates static budgets and flexible budgets. Webb manufactures and sells a single product, a distinctive jacket that requires many materials, tailoring, and hand operations. Sales are made to independent clothing stores and retail chains. Webb sets budgeted revenues (budgeted selling price × budgeted

OBJECTIVE 1

Describe the difference between a static budget and a flexible budget

Flexible budget. A budget developed using budgeted revenues or cost amounts; when variances are computed, the budgeted amounts are adjusted (flexed) to recognize the actual level of output and the actual quantities of the revenue and cost drivers.

Favourable variance. Variance that increases operating income relative to the budgeted amount. Denoted "F."

Unfavourable variance. Variance that decreases operating income relative to the budgeted amount. Denoted "U."

units sold) on the basis of input from its marketing personnel and an analysis of general and industry economic conditions.

The costing system at Webb includes both manufacturing costs and marketing costs. There are direct and indirect costs in each category:

	Direct Costs	Indirect Costs
Manufacturing	Direct materials	Variable manufacturing overhead
	Direct manufacturing labour	Fixed manufacturing overhead
Marketing	Direct marketing labour	Variable marketing overhead
		Fixed marketing overhead

Webb's manufacturing costs include direct materials (all variable), direct manufacturing labour (all variable), and manufacturing overhead (both variable and fixed). Its marketing costs (which include distribution and customer service costs as well as advertising costs) are made up of direct marketing labour (primarily distribution personnel, which are all variable) and marketing overhead (both variable and fixed). The cost driver for direct materials, direct manufacturing labour, and variable manufacturing overhead is the *number of units manufactured*. The cost driver for direct marketing labour and variable marketing overhead is the *number of units sold*. The revenue driver is the *number of units sold*. The relevant range for the $180 selling price per jacket and for the cost drivers in both manufacturing and marketing is from 8,000 to 16,000 units. All costs at Webb are either driven by output units or are fixed. We make this simplifying assumption to highlight the basic approach to flexible budgeting.

STATIC-BUDGET VARIANCES

The actual results and the static budget amounts of Webb for April 2000 are as follows:

	Actual Results	Static Budget Amounts
Units sold	10,000	12,000
Revenues	$1,850,000	$2,160,000
Variable costs	1,120,000	1,188,000
Fixed costs	705,000	710,000
Operating income	25,000	262,000

Exhibit 7-1 presents the Level 0 and Level 1 variance analyses for April 2000. Level 0 gives the least detailed comparison of the actual and budgeted operating income. The unfavourable variance of $237,000 is simply the result of subtracting the budgeted operating income of $262,000 from the actual operating income of $25,000:

$$\text{Static budget variance of operating income} = \text{Actual results} - \text{Static budget amount}$$

$$= \$25,000 - \$262,000$$

$$= \$237,000 \text{ U}$$

This variance is often called a *static-budget variance* because the number used for the budgeted amount ($262,000) is taken from a static budget.

Level 1 analysis in Exhibit 7-1 provides managers with more detailed information on the static-budget variance of operating income of $237,000 U. The additional information added in Level 1 pertains to revenues, variable costs, and fixed costs. The budgeted contribution margin percentage of 45.0% ($972,000 ÷ $2,160,000) decreases to 39.5% ($730,000 ÷ $1,850,000) for the actual results.

While Level 1 contains more information than Level 0, additional insights into the causes of variances can be gained by incorporating a flexible budget into the computation of variances.

EXHIBIT 7-1

Static-Budget-Based Variance Analysis for the Webb Company for April 2000

LEVEL 0 ANALYSIS

Actual operating income	$ 25,000 F*
Budgeted operating income	262,000 F
Static budget variance of operating income	$237,000 U

LEVEL 1 ANALYSIS

	Actual Results (1)	Static-Budget Variances (2) = (1) – (3)	Static Budget (3)
Units sold	10,000	2,000 U	12,000
Revenues	$1,850,000	$310,000 U	$2,160,000
Variable costs	1,120,000	68,000 F	1,188,000
Contribution margin	730,000	242,000 U	972,000
Fixed costs	705,000	5,000 F	710,000
Operating income	$ 25,000	$237,000 U	$ 262,000

$237,000 U
Total static-budget variance

*F = favourable effect on operating income; U = unfavourable effect on operating income.

STEPS IN DEVELOPING A FLEXIBLE BUDGET

Webb's five-step approach to developing a flexible budget is relatively straightforward, given the assumption that all costs are either variable with respect to output units or fixed. The five steps are as follows:

◆ **Step 1:** *Determine the budgeted selling price per unit, the budgeted variable costs per unit, and the budgeted fixed costs.* Each output unit (a jacket) has a budgeted selling price of $180. The budgeted variable cost is $99 per jacket. Column 2 of Exhibit 7-2 has a breakdown of this $99 amount. The budgeted fixed costs total $710,000 ($276,000 manufacturing and $434,000 marketing).

◆ **Step 2:** *Determine the actual quantity of the revenue driver.* Webb's revenue driver is the number of units sold. In April 2000, Webb sold 10,000 jackets.

◆ **Step 3:** *Determine the flexible budget for revenue on the basis of budgeted unit revenue and the actual quantity of the revenue driver.*

Flexible budget revenues = $180 × 10,000
= $1,800,000

◆ **Step 4:** *Determine the actual quantity of the cost driver(s).* Webb's cost driver for manufacturing costs is units produced. The cost driver for marketing costs is units sold. In April 2000, Webb produced and sold 10,000 jackets.

◆ **Step 5:** *Determine the flexible budget for costs on the basis of the budgeted unit variable costs and fixed costs and the actual quantity of the cost driver(s).*

Flexible budget variable costs:
Manufacturing = $88 × 10,000 = $880,000
Marketing = $11 × 10,000 = 110,000
$990,000

Flexible budget fixed costs:
Manufacturing = $276,000
Marketing = 434,000
$710,000

OBJECTIVE 2

Develop a flexible budget and compute flexible-budget and sales-volume variances

EXHIBIT 7-2
Flexible Budget Data for the Webb Company for April 2000

Line Item (1)	Budgeted Cost Amount per Unit (2)	Flexible Budget Amounts for Alternative Levels of Output Units Sold			Actual Results for 10,000 Units (6)
		10,000 (3)	12,000 (4)	15,000 (5)	
Revenue	$180	$1,800,000	$2,160,000	$2,700,000	$1,850,000
Variable costs:					
Direct materials	60	600,000	720,000	900,000	688,200
Direct manufacturing labour	16	160,000	192,000	240,000	198,000
Direct marketing labour	6	60,000	72,000	90,000	57,600
Variable manufacturing overhead	12	120,000	144,000	180,000	130,500
Variable marketing overhead	5	50,000	60,000	75,000	45,700
Total variable costs	99	990,000	1,188,000	1,485,000	1,120,000
Contribution margin	$ 81	810,000	972,000	1,215,000	730,000
Fixed costs:					
Manufacturing overhead		276,000	276,000	276,000	285,000
Marketing overhead	——	434,000	434,000	434,000	420,000
Total fixed costs		710,000	710,000	710,000	705,000
Total costs	——	1,700,000	1,898,000	2,195,000	1,825,000
Operating income		$ 100,000	$ 262,000	$ 505,000	$ 25,000

These five steps enable Webb to move to a Level 2 variance analysis, which helps them better explore reasons for the $237,000 unfavourable static budget variance of operating income. Exhibit 7-2 shows the flexible budget for 10,000 units (column 3) as well as for 12,000 and 15,000 units (columns 4 and 5).

FLEXIBLE-BUDGET VARIANCES AND SALES-VOLUME VARIANCES

OBJECTIVE 3

Explain why standard costs are often used in variance analysis

Flexible-budget variance. Difference between the actual result and the flexible budget amount for the actual output achieved.

Sales-volume variance. Difference between the flexible budget amount and the static budget amount; unit selling prices, unit variable costs, and fixed costs are held constant.

Exhibit 7-3 presents the Level 2 flexible-budget-based variance analysis for Webb. Note that the $237,000 unfavourable static-budget variance of operating income is now split into two categories—a flexible-budget variance and a sales-volume variance. The **flexible-budget variance** is the difference between the actual results and the flexible-budget amount for the actual levels of the revenue and cost drivers. The **sales-volume variance** is the difference between the flexible-budget amount and the static-budget amount; unit selling prices, unit variable costs, and fixed costs are held constant. Knowing these variances helps managers better explain the static-budget variance of $237,000 U.

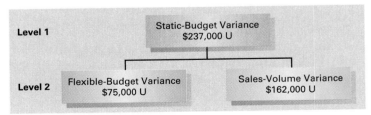

Flexible-Budget Variances

The first three columns of Exhibit 7-3 compare the actual results with the flexible-budget amounts. Flexible-budget variances are reported in column 2 for four line items in the income statement:

$$\text{Flexible-budget variance} = \text{Actual results} - \text{Flexible-budget amount}$$

EXHIBIT 7-3
Flexible-Budget-Based Variance Analysis for the Webb Company for April 2000

LEVEL 2 ANALYSIS

	Actual Results (1)	Flexible-Budget Variances (2) = (1) – (3)	Flexible Budget (3)	Sales-Volume Variances (4) = (3) – (5)	Static Budget (5)
Units sold	10,000	0	10,000	2,000 U	12,000
Revenues	$1,850,000	$ 50,000 F*	$1,800,000	$360,000 U	$2,160,000
Variable costs	1,120,000	130,000 U	990,000	198,000 F	1,188,000
Contribution margin	730,000	80,000 U	810,000	162,000 U	972,000
Fixed costs	705,000	5,000 F	710,000	0	710,000
Operating income	$ 25,000	$ 75,000 U	$ 100,000	$162,000 U	$ 262,000

$ 75,000 U
Total flexible-budget variance

$162,000 U
Total sales-volume variance

$237,000 U
Total static-budget variance

*F = favourable effect on operating income; U = unfavourable effect on operating income.

For the operating income line item, the flexible-budget variance is $75,000 U ($25,000 – $100,000). This variance arises because the actual selling price, unit variable costs, and fixed costs differ from the budgeted amounts. The actual and budgeted unit amounts for the selling price and variable costs are as follows:

	Actual Unit Amount	Budgeted Unit Amount
Selling price	$185	$180
Variable cost	112	99

The actual fixed cost of $705,000 is $5,000 less than the budgeted $710,000 amount.

The flexible-budget variance pertaining to revenues is often called a **selling-price variance**, because it arises solely from differences between the actual selling price and the budgeted selling price:

Selling-price variance. Flexible budget variance that pertains to revenues; arises solely from differences between the actual selling price and the budgeted selling price.

$$\text{Selling-price variance} = \left(\begin{array}{c} \text{Actual} \\ \text{selling price} \end{array} - \begin{array}{c} \text{Budgeted} \\ \text{selling price} \end{array} \right) \times \begin{array}{c} \text{Actual} \\ \text{units sold} \end{array}$$

$$= (\$185 - \$180) \times 10,000$$

$$= \$50,000 \text{ F}$$

Webb has a favourable selling-price variance because the actual selling price exceeds the budgeted amount (by $5). Marketing managers typically are best-informed as to why this selling price difference arose.

Sales-Volume Variances

The flexible-budget amounts in column 3 of Exhibit 7-3 and the static-budget amount in column 5 are both computed using the budgeted selling prices and budgeted costs. This variance is labelled the "sales-volume variance," because in many contexts the number of units sold is both the revenue driver and the cost driver. For the operating income line item:

$$\begin{array}{ccc} \text{Sales-volume} \\ \text{variance} \end{array} = \begin{array}{c} \text{Flexible-budget} \\ \text{amount} \end{array} - \begin{array}{c} \text{Static-budget} \\ \text{amount} \end{array}$$

$$= \$100,000 - \$262,000$$

$$= \$162,000 \text{ U}$$

In our Webb example, this sales-volume variance in operating income arises solely because Webb sold 10,000 units, which was 2,000 less than the budgeted 12,000 units.

PRICE VARIANCES AND EFFICIENCY VARIANCES FOR INPUTS

The flexible-budget variance (Level 2) captures the difference between the actual results and the flexible budget. The sources of this variance (as regards costs) are the individual differences between actual and budgeted prices or quantities for inputs. The next two variances we discuss—price variances and efficiency variances for inputs—analyze such differences. This information helps managers to better understand past performance and to plan for future performance. We call this a Level 3 analysis, as it takes a more detailed analysis of the Level 2 variances.

Price variance (input-price variance, rate variance). The difference between actual price and budgeted price multiplied by the actual quantity of input in question.

Efficiency variance (input-efficiency variances, usage variance). The difference between the actual quantity of input used (such as square metres of materials) and the budgeted quantity of input that should have been used, multiplied by the budgeted price.

A **price variance** is the difference between the actual price and the budgeted price multiplied by the actual quantity of input in question (such as direct materials purchased or used). *Price variances* are sometimes called **input-price variances** or **rate variances** (especially when those variances are for direct labour). An **efficiency variance** is the difference between the actual quantity of input used (such as yards of cloth in direct materials) and the budgeted quantity of input that should have been used, multiplied by the budgeted price. *Efficiency variances* are sometimes called **input-efficiency variances** or **usage variances**.

The relationship of these two variances to those we have already discussed for Webb is as follows:

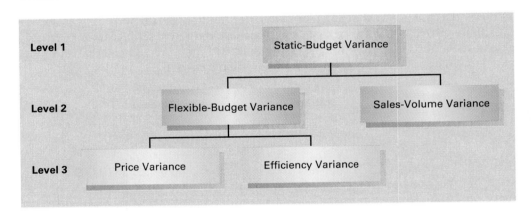

OBJECTIVE 4

Compute the price and efficiency variances for direct cost input categories

Obtaining Budgeted Input Prices and Input Quantities

Webb's two main sources of information about budgeted input prices and budgeted input quantities are:

1. **Actual input data from past periods.** Most companies have past data on actual input prices and actual input quantities. These past amounts could be used for the budgeted amounts in a flexible budget. Past data are typically available at a relatively low cost. The limitations of using this source are (a) past data include past inefficiencies and (b) past data do not incorporate any expected changes planned to occur in the budget period.

2. **Standards developed by Webb.** A standard is a carefully predetermined amount; it is usually expressed on a per-unit basis. Webb uses time-and-motion and engineering studies to determine its standard amounts. For example, it conducts a detailed breakdown of the steps in making a jacket. Each step is then assigned a standard time based on work by a skilled operator using equipment

operating in an efficient manner. The advantages of using standard amounts are that (a) they can exclude past inefficiencies and (b) they can take into account expected changes in the budget period. An example of (a) is a supplier making dramatic improvements in its ability to consistently meet Webb's demanding quality requirements for the cloth material used to make jackets. An example of (b) is the acquisition of new loom machines that operate at a faster speed and that enable work to be done with lower reject rates.

Webb has developed standard inputs and standard costs for each of its variable cost items. A **standard input** is a carefully predetermined quantity of inputs (such as pounds of materials or hours of labour time) required for one unit of output. A **standard cost** is a carefully predetermined cost. Standard costs can relate to units of inputs or units of outputs. Webb's budgeted cost for each variable cost item is computed using the following formula:

$$\text{Standard inputs allowed for one output unit} \times \text{Standard cost per input unit}$$

And the variable cost items are:

◆ **Direct materials.** 2 square metres of cloth input allowed per output unit (jacket) manufactured, at $30 standard cost per square metre

$$\text{Standard cost} = 2 \times \$30 = \$60 \text{ per output unit manufactured}$$

◆ **Direct manufacturing labour.** 0.80 manufacturing labour-hours of input allowed per output unit manufactured, at $20 standard cost per hour

$$\text{Standard cost} = 0.80 \times \$20 = \$16 \text{ per output unit manufactured}$$

◆ **Direct marketing labour.** 0.25 marketing labour-hours of input allowed per output unit sold, at $24 standard cost per hour

$$\text{Standard cost} = 0.25 \times \$24 = \$6 \text{ per output unit sold}$$

◆ **Variable manufacturing overhead.** Allocated on the basis of 1.20 machine-hours per output unit manufactured, at $10 standard cost per machine-hour

$$\text{Standard cost} = 1.20 \times \$10 = \$12 \text{ per output unit manufactured}$$

◆ **Variable marketing overhead.** Allocated on the basis of 0.125 direct marketing labour-hours per output unit sold, at $40 standard cost per hour

$$\text{Standard cost} = 0.125 \times \$40 = \$5 \text{ per output unit sold}$$

Standard input. Carefully predetermined quantity of inputs (such as pounds of materials or hours of labour time) required for one unit of output.

Standard cost. Carefully predetermined cost. Standard costs can relate to units of inputs or units of outputs.

These standard cost computations explain how Webb developed the numbers in column 2 of Exhibit 7-2.

The breakdown of the flexible-budget variance into its price and efficiency components is important when evaluating individual managers. At Webb, the production manager is responsible for the efficiency variance, while the purchasing manager is responsible for the price variance. This separate computation of the price variance enables the efficiency variance to be computed using budgeted input prices. Thus, judgments about efficiency (the quantity of inputs used to produce a given level of output) are not affected by whether actual input prices differ from budgeted input prices. A word of caution, however, is appropriate. As will be discussed in the following text, the causes of price and efficiency variances can be interrelated. For this reason, do not interpret these variances in isolation from each other.

An Illustration of Price and Efficiency Variances for Inputs

Consider Webb's three direct cost categories. The actual cost for each of these three categories is:

Direct materials purchased and used:

Direct materials costs	$688,200
Square metres of cloth input purchased and used	22,200
Actual price per yard	$31

Direct manufacturing labour:

Direct manufacturing labour costs	$198,000
Manufacturing labour-hours of input	9,000
Actual price per hour	$22

Direct marketing labour:

Direct marketing labour costs	$57,600
Marketing labour-hours of input	2,304
Actual price per hour	$25

SURVEYS OF COMPANY PRACTICE

The Widespread Use of Standard Costs

Surveys of company practice around the globe report widespread use of standard costs by manufacturers. The following data are representative of surveys conducted in five countries:

Country	Respondents Using Standard Costs in Their Accounting System (%)
United States*	86
Ireland[†]	84
United Kingdom[††]	76
Sweden[≈]	73
Japan[#]	65

*Cornick, M., W. Cooper, and S. Wilson, "How Do Companies Analyze Overhead," *Management Accounting* (June 1988)

[†]Clarke, P.," Management Accounting Practices and Techniques in Irish Manufacturing Firms, " (Working Paper, Trinity College, Dublin, Ireland, 1995)

[††]Drury, C., S. Braund, P. Osborne, and M. Tayles, A Survey of Management Accounting Practices in UK Manufacturing Companies, (London, U.K.: Chartered Association of Certified Accountants, 1993)

[≈]Ask, U., and C. Ax, "Trends in the Development of Product Costing Practices and Techniques—A Survey of the Swedish Manufacturing Industry, " (Working Paper, Gothenburg School of Economics, Gothenburg, Sweden, 1992)

[#]Scarbrough, P., A. Nanni, and M. Sakurai, "Japanese Management Accounting Practices and the Effects of Assembly and Process Automation," *Management Accounting Research* (March 1991)

The Irish survey reported that standard costs were most frequently used for direct materials (84%), then direct labour (69%), and then manufacturing overhead (59%). The standard costs were most frequently revised on an annual basis (55%).

What explains the popularity of standard costs? Companies based in four countries report the following reasons (ranked 1 for most important, 4 for least important) for using standard costs:

Reason*	United States	Canada	Japan	United Kingdom
Cost management	1	1	1	2
Price-making and price policy	2	3	2	1
Budgetary planning and control	3	2	3	3
Financial statement preparation	4	4	4	4

*Inoue, S., "A Comparative Study of Recent Development of Cost Management Problems in U.S.A., U.K., Canada, and Japan," *Kagawa University Economic Review* (June 1988)

The materials price and efficiency variances discussed in this chapter illustrate the use of standard costs in promoting cost management.

For simplicity, we assume here that direct materials used is equal to direct materials purchased.

The actual results and the flexible-budget amounts for each category of direct costs for the 10,000 actual output units in April 2000 are:

	Actual Results	Flexible Budget		Flexible-Budget Variances
Direct materials	$688,200	$600,000	(10,000 × $60)	$ 88,200 U
Direct manufacturing labour	198,000	160,000	(10,000 × $16)	38,000 U
Direct marketing labour	57,600	60,000	(10,000 × $6)	2,400 F
Total	$943,800	$820,000		$123,800 U

We now use this Webb Company data to illustrate the input price and input-efficiency variances. Consider first the input-price variances.

Price Variances

The formula for computing a price variance is:

$$\text{Price variance} = \left(\begin{array}{c} \text{Actual price} \\ \text{of input} \end{array} - \begin{array}{c} \text{Budgeted price} \\ \text{of input} \end{array} \right) \times \begin{array}{c} \text{Actual quantity} \\ \text{of input} \end{array}$$

Price variances for each of Webb's three direct cost categories are:

Direct Cost Category	(Actual Price of Input − Budgeted Price of Input)	×	Actual Quantity of Input	=	Input-Price Variance
Direct materials	($31 − $30)	×	22,200	=	$22,200 U
Direct manufacturing labour	($22 − $20)	×	9,000	=	18,000 U
Direct marketing labour	($25 − $24)	×	2,304	=	2,304 U

All three price variances are unfavourable (they reduce operating income) because the actual price of each direct cost input exceeds the budgeted price; that is, Webb incurred more cost per input unit than was budgeted.

Always consider a broad range of possible causes for price variances. For example, Webb's unfavourable direct materials price variance could be due to one or more of the following reasons:

◆ Webb's purchasing manager negotiated less skillfully than was assumed in the budget.

◆ Webb's purchasing manager bought in smaller lot sizes than budgeted, even though quantity discounts were available for the larger lot sizes.

◆ Materials prices unexpectedly increased because of disruptive weather conditions.

◆ Budgeted purchase prices for Webb's materials were set without careful analysis of the market.

Webb's response to a materials price variance will be vitally affected by the presumed cause of the variable. Assume it decides an unfavourable variance is due to poor negotiating by its purchasing officer. Webb may decide to invest more in training this officer in negotiations, or it may decide to hire a more skillful purchasing officer.

When interpreting materials price variances, Webb's managers should consider any change in the relationship with the company's suppliers. For example, assume that Webb moves to a long-term relationship with a single supplier of material. Webb and the supplier agree to a single purchase price per unit for all material purchases in the next six months. It is likely that price variances will be minimal for this material because all purchases will be made from this supplier.

Efficiency Variances

Consider now the efficiency variance. Computation of efficiency variances requires measurement of inputs for a given level of output. For any actual level of output, the efficiency variance is the difference between the input that was actually used and the input that should have been used to achieve that actual output, holding input price constant:

$$\text{Efficiency variance} = \left(\begin{array}{c} \text{Actual quantity} \\ \text{of input used} \end{array} - \begin{array}{c} \text{Budgeted quantity of input allowed} \\ \text{for actual output units achieved} \end{array} \right) \times \begin{array}{c} \text{Budgeted price} \\ \text{of input} \end{array}$$

The idea here is that an organization is inefficient if it uses more inputs than budgeted for the actual output units achieved, and it is efficient if it uses less inputs than budgeted for the actual output units achieved.

The efficiency variances for each of Webb's direct cost categories are:

Direct Cost Category	(Actual Input Used − Budgeted Input Allowed for Actual Output Units) ×	Budgeted Price of Input	= Efficiency Variance
Direct materials	[22,200 metres − (10,000 units × 2.00 metres)] ×	$30	
	(22,200 metres − 20,000 metres) ×	$30	= $66,000 U
Direct manufacturing labour	[9,000 hours − (10,000 units × 0.80 hours)] ×	$20	
	(9,000 hours − 8,000 hours) ×	$20	= $20,000 U
Direct marketing labour	[2,304 hours − (10,000 units × 0.25 hours)] ×	$24	
	(2,304 hours − 2,500 hours) ×	$24	= $ 4,704 F

The two manufacturing-efficiency variances (direct materials and direct manufacturing labour) are both unfavourable because more input was used than was budgeted, resulting in a decrease in operating income. The marketing-efficiency variance is favourable because less input was used than was budgeted, resulting in an increase in operating income.

As with price variances, Webb's managers need to consider a broad range of possible reasons for efficiency variances arising. For example, Webb's unfavourable direct-manufacturing labour variance could be due to one or more of the following reasons:

◆ Webb's personnel manager hired underskilled workers.

◆ Webb's production scheduler inefficiently scheduled work, resulting in more direct manufacturing labour time per jacket.

◆ Webb's maintenance department did not properly maintain machines, resulting in more direct manufacturing labour time per jacket.

◆ Budgeted time standards were set without careful analysis of the operating conditions and the employees' skills.

Suppose Webb determines that the unfavourable variance is due to poor machine maintenance. It may decide to have a team consisting of plant machine engineers and machine operators develop a maintenance schedule so that, in the future, jackets can be sewn in shorter times.

Presentation of Price and Efficiency Variances for Inputs

Note how the sum of the price variance and the efficiency variance equals the flexible budget variance:

	Price Variance	+	Efficiency Variance	=	Flexible Budget Variance
Direct materials	$22,200 U		$66,000 U		$88,200 U
Direct manufacturing labour	18,000 U		20,000 U		38,000 U
Direct marketing labour	2,304 U		4,704 F		2,400 F

Exhibit 7-4 illustrates a convenient way to integrate the actual and budgeted input information used to compute the price and efficiency variances for direct materials. This exhibit assumes that materials purchased equals materials used.

EXHIBIT 7-4
Columnar Presentation of Variance Analysis: Direct Materials Costs for the Webb Company for April 2000

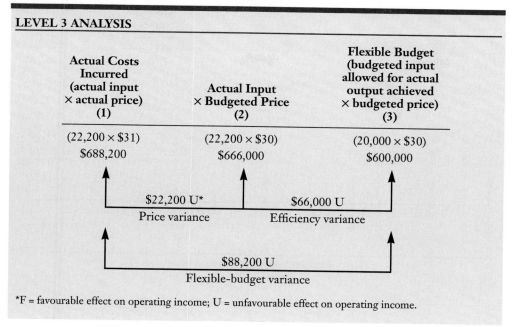

LEVEL 3 ANALYSIS

Actual Costs Incurred (actual input × actual price) (1)	Actual Input × Budgeted Price (2)	Flexible Budget (budgeted input allowed for actual output achieved × budgeted price) (3)
(22,200 × $31)	(22,200 × $30)	(20,000 × $30)
$688,200	$666,000	$600,000

$22,200 U* $66,000 U
Price variance   Efficiency variance

$88,200 U
Flexible-budget variance

*F = favourable effect on operating income; U = unfavourable effect on operating income.

Overview of Variance Analysis

Exhibit 7-5 presents a comprehensive road-map of where we have been. The Level 0 and Level 1 analyses are reproductions of Exhibit 7-1. Level 2 is a reproduction of Exhibit 7-3. We have just discussed price and efficiency variances, which are Level 3.

Some managers refer to proceeding through successively more detailed data as "drilling-down" (or "peeling the onion"). The growing use of online data collection is increasing the number of databases that have this drill-down capability.

EXHIBIT 7-5
Overview of Variance Analysis for the Webb Company for April 2000

LEVEL 0 ANALYSIS

Actual operating income	$ 25,000
Budgeted operating income	262,000
Static-budget variance of operating income	$237,000 U*

LEVEL 1 ANALYSIS

	Actual Results (1)	Static-Budget Variances (2) = (1) − (3)	Static Budget (3)
Units sold	10,000	2,000 U	12,000
Revenues	$1,850,000	$310,000 U	$2,160,000
Variable costs	1,120,000	68,000 F	1,188,000
Contribution margin	730,000	242,000 U	972,000
Fixed costs	705,000	5,000 F	710,000
Operating income	$ 25,000	$237,000 U	$ 262,000

$237,000 U
Total static-budget variance

LEVEL 2 ANALYSIS

	Actual Results (1)	Flexible-Budget Variances (2) = (1) − (3)	Flexible Budget (3)	Sales-Volume Variances (4) = (3) − (5)	Static Budget (5)
Units sold	10,000	0	10,000	2,000 U	12,000
Revenues (sales)	$1,850,000	$ 50,000 F	$1,800,000	$360,000 U	$2,160,000
Variable costs	1,120,000	130,000 U	990,000	198,000 F	1,188,000
Contribution margin	730,000	80,000 U	810,000	162,000 U	972,000
Fixed costs	705,000	5,000 F	710,000	0	710,000
Operating income	$ 25,000	$ 75,000 U	$ 100,000	$162,000 U	$ 262,000

$ 75,000 U ← Total flexible-budget variance

$162,000 U ← Total sales-volume variance

$237,000 ← Total static-budget variance

LEVEL 3 ANALYSIS

Revenue Variances by Customers		Cost Variances		Sales-Volume Variances
Retail chains	$ 0 F	Price Variance	Efficiency Variance	Sales quantity variances
Independent stores	50,000 F			Sales mix variances (covered in Chapter 16)
Sales price variances	50,000 F	Direct materials $22,200 U	$66,000 U	
		Direct manufacturing labour 18,000 U	20,000 U	
		Direct marketing labour 2,304 U	4,704 F	

(Chapter 8 contains further discussion of Level 3 cost variance analysis.)

*F = favourable effect on operating income; U = unfavourable effect on operating income.

PERFORMANCE MEASUREMENT USING VARIANCES

Effectiveness and Efficiency

OBJECTIVE 5

Explain why purchasing performance measures should focus on more factors than just price variances for inputs

A key use of variance analysis is in performance evaluation. Two attributes of performance are commonly measured:

◆ **Effectiveness**. The degree to which a predetermined objective or target is met

◆ **Efficiency**. The relative amount of inputs used to achieve a given level of output

Effectiveness. The degree to which a predetermined objective or target is met.

Efficiency. The relative amount of inputs used to achieve a given level of output.

Be careful to understand the cause(s) of a variance before using it as a performance measure. Assume that a Webb purchasing manager has just negotiated a deal that results in a favourable price variance for materials. The deal could have achieved a favourable variance for any or all of three reasons:

1. The purchasing manager bargained effectively with suppliers.
2. The purchasing manager accepted lower-quality materials at a lower price.
3. The purchasing manager secured a discount for buying in bulk. However, she bought higher quantities than necessary for the short run, which resulted in excessive inventories.

If the purchasing manager's performance is evaluated solely on materials price variances, then only reason 1 will be considered acceptable, and the evaluation will be positive. Reasons 2 and 3 will be considered unacceptable, and will likely cause the company to incur additional costs, such as higher materials scrap costs and higher storage costs respectively.

Performance measures increasingly focus on reducing the total costs of the company as a whole. Such a focus is central to the total value-chain analysis theme in the new management approach. In the purchasing manager example, the company may ultimately lose more money because of reasons 2 and 3 than it gains from reason 1. Conversely, manufacturing costs may be deliberately increased (for example, because higher costs are paid for better materials or more direct manufacturing labour time) in order to obtain better product quality. In turn, the costs of the better product quality may be more than offset by reductions in customer-service costs.

If any single performance measure (for example, a labour efficiency cost variance or a consumer rating report) receives excessive emphasis, managers tend to make decisions that will maximize their own reported performance in terms of that single performance measure. Such actions may conflict with the organization's overall goals. This faulty perspective on performance arises because top management has designed a performance measurement and reward system that does not adequately emphasize total organization objectives.

The Concepts in Action box on Parker-Hannifin later in this chapter shows the innovative approach of one company to monitoring variables in addition to purchase price when evaluating the performance of the materials procurement function.

Parker-Hannifin
www.parker.com

Multiple Causes of Variances

Often the causes of variances are interrelated. For example, an unfavourable materials efficiency variance can be related to a favourable materials price efficiency variance because a purchasing officer purchased lower-priced lower-quality materials. It is always best to consider possible interdependencies among variances and not to interpret variances in isolation from each other. In some cases, the causes of variances are in different parts of the value chain in one organization or in other organizations. Consider an unfavourable materials efficiency variance in the production area of Webb. Possible causes of this variance across the value chain of the organization are:

  (i) poor design of products or processes,
 (ii) poor work in the manufacturing area,
(iii) inadequate training of the labour force,
 (iv) inappropriate assignment of labour or machines to specific jobs, and
  (v) congestion due to scheduling a large number of rush orders required by Webb marketing representatives.

An even broader perspective is to consider actions taken in the supply chain of an organization. A *supply chain* is the flow of goods, services, and information from cradle to grave (womb to tomb) of a product or service. The supply chain of Webb (the manufacturer) includes:

Webb Company

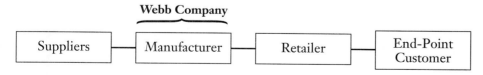

For example, actions taken by Webb's suppliers could cause unfavourable material efficiency variances at Webb:

(vi) Webb's suppliers do not manufacture cloth materials of uniformly high quality.

This list of six possible causes is far from exhaustive. However, it does indicate that the cause of a variance in one part of the value chain (production in our example) can be due to actions taken in other parts of the value chain (for example, product design, or marketing) and in other organizations. Note how improvements in early stages of the supply chain or value chain can sizably reduce the magnitudes of variances in subsequent stages.

The most important task in variance analysis is to understand why variances arise and then to use that knowledge to promote learning and continuous improvement. For instance, in our list of examples above, we may seek improvements in product design, in the commitment of the manufacturing labour force to do the job right the first time, in the activities undertaken by suppliers to provide high-quality materials, and so on. Variance analysis should not be a tool to "play the blame game" (that is, for every unfavourable variance a person is sought to blame or even punish). Rather, it should be an essential ingredient that helps promote learning in the organization.

Top management should recognize that this learning/continuous improvement use of variance analysis can be undermined if it places excessive (obsessive) emphasis on meeting individual variance targets. For example, managers may engage in "padding" of the standard input quantities or input prices so that their targets are more easily attained. "Padded" numbers in a budget, however, mean that management underperformance potentially is rewarded and less learning and less improvement potentially occur.

When to Investigate Variances

When should variances be investigated? Frequently, managers base their answer on subjective judgments, or rules of thumb. For critical items, a small variance may prompt follow-up. For other items, a minimum dollar variance or a certain percentage of variance from budget may prompt investigations. Of course, a 4% variance in direct materials costs of $1 million may deserve more attention than a 20% variance in repair costs of $10,000. Therefore, rules such as "investigate all variances exceeding $5,000 or 25% of budgeted cost, whichever is lower" are common. Variance analysis is subject to the same cost-benefit test as all other phases of a management control system.

Management accounting systems have traditionally implied that a standard is a single acceptable measure. Practically, managers realize that the standard is a band or range of possible acceptable outcomes. Consequently, they expect variances to vary within some normal limits. A variance within this band is deemed to be from an in-control process and calls for no corrective action by managers.

OBJECTIVE 6

Describe how the continuous improvement theme can be integrated into variance analysis

Continuous improvement budgeted costs. Budgeted cost that is successively reduced over succeeding time periods.

Continuous Improvement

Continuous improvement is one of the evolving management themes highlighted in this book. See Exhibit 1-6 and the discussion of kaizen budgeting in Chapter 6. Using **continuous improvement budgeted costs** is yet another way to control variances. This is a budgeted cost that is successively reduced over succeeding time periods. The budgeted direct materials cost for each jacket that Webb Company manufactured in April 2000 is $60 per unit. The budgeted cost used in variance analysis for subsequent periods could be based on a targeted 1% reduction each period:

Month	Prior Month's Budgeted Amount	Reduction in Budgeted Amount	Revised Budgeted Amount
April 2000	—	—	$60.00
May 2000	$60.00	$0.600 (0.01 × $60.00)	59.40
June 2000	59.40	0.594 (0.01 × $59.40)	58.81
July 2000	58.81	0.588 (0.01 × $58.81)	58.22

The source of the 1% reduction in budgeted direct materials costs could be efficiency improvements or price reductions. By using continuous improvement budgeted costs, an organization signals the importance of constantly seeking ways to reduce total costs. For example, managers could avoid unfavourable materials efficiency variances by continuously reducing materials waste.

Products in the initial months of their production may have higher budgeted improvement rates than those that have been in production for, say, three years. Im-

Total Costs of Materials Ownership at Parker-Hannifin

At Parker-Hannifin's Compumotor Division, materials costs are over 50% of the total manufacturing costs. P-H has developed a supplier cost model that recognizes that the total cost of materials includes many items in addition to materials purchase costs. This model is used to guide supplier selection decisions and in ongoing cost management of materials-related costs. The supplier cost ratio is the ratio of nonpurchase costs of materials to total supplier costs. P-H uses this supplier cost ratio to examine the performance of each supplier over time. It also uses the ratio to make comparisons across suppliers. P-H can use its model to examine the cause of any change in the supplier cost ratio over time. In Acme's supplier cost ratio, for example, a change could be due to an increase in receiving errors. P-H shares this model with its suppliers so that both the purchaser and the supplier can jointly seek out cost improvements to make the relationship a more productive one for each party. A hypothetical report for a hypothetical supplier (Acme Components) is as follows:

Supplier Metric	Output Measure	Number of Output Measures	Cost per Activity	Total Cost
Ordering:				
Automatic purchase	Flat monthly rate	0	$10	$ 0
Manual purchase	Number of purchase orders	22	2	44
Commodity complexity	Categories, 1–4 rating	1	16	16
Receiving inspection	Rate per hour	6	10	60
Receiving errors	Number of supplier errors	2	25	50
Payment method:				
Automatic voucher	Number of vouchers	0	1	0
Manual	Number of vouchers	16	3	48
Inventory carrying	Average balance × capital costs			940
1. Total nonpurchase costs				1,158
2. Purchase costs				23,842
3. Total supplier costs (1 + 2)				$25,000
Supplier cost ratio (1 ÷ 3)				4.632%

Source: Presentation by Parker-Hannifin at 1995 CAM-I meeting, plus discussion with P-H executives.

provement opportunities may be much easier to identify when products have just started in production. Once the easy opportunities have been identified ("the low-hanging fruit picked"), much more ingenuity may be required to identify successive improvement opportunities.

Financial and Nonfinancial Performance Measures

Almost all organizations use a combination of financial and nonfinancial performance measures rather than relying exclusively on either type. Consider our Webb Company illustration. In its cutting room, fabric is laid out and cut into pieces, which are then matched together and assembled. Control is often exercised at the cutting room level by focusing on nonfinancial measures such as the number of square metres of cloth used to produce 1,000 jackets or the percentage of jackets started and completed without requiring any rework. Production managers at Webb also will likely use financial measures to evaluate the overall cost efficiency with

The Decision to Investigate Variances

A survey of U.S. managers reported the following approaches to investigating direct materials and direct labour variances:

Approach	Direct Materials (%)	Direct Labour (%)
All variances investigated	6.9	5.3
Variances over prescribed dollar limits investigated	34.8	31.0
Variances over prescribed percentage limits investigated	12.2	14.1
Statistical procedures used to select cases for investigation	0.9	0.0 0.9
Variances never investigated	0.0	0.9
Judgment used to decide if investigation is needed	45.2	47.8
	100.0%	100.0%

Investigating all variances may be justified if the cost of the process being out of control is extremely high. An example is the manufacture of a door lock for a space shuttle.

Source: Gaumnitz, B., and F. Kollaritsch, "Manufacturing Variances: Current Practice and Trends," *Journal of Cost Management* (Spring 1991)

which operations are being run and to help guide decisions about, say, changing the mix of inputs used in manufacturing jackets. Financial measures are often critical in an organization because they summarize the economic impact of diverse physical activities in a way managers readily understand. Moreover, managers are often evaluated on results compared with financial measures.

IMPACT OF INVENTORIES

Our Webb Company illustration assumed the following:

1. All units are manufactured and sold in the same accounting period. There are no work-in-process or finished goods inventories at either the beginning or the end of the accounting period.

2. All direct materials are purchased and used in the same accounting period. There is no direct materials inventory at either the beginning or the end of the period.

Both assumptions can be relaxed without changing the key concepts introduced in this chapter. However, changes in the computation or interpretation of variances would be required when beginning or ending inventories exist.

Suppose direct materials are purchased some time prior to their use and that direct materials inventories exist at the beginning or end of the accounting period. Managers typically want to pinpoint variances at the earliest possible time so that their decisions can be best informed by the variances. For direct materials price variances, the purchase date will almost always be the earliest possible time to isolate them. As a result, many organizations compute direct materials price variances using the quantities purchased in an accounting period. The Problem for Self-Study at the end of this chapter illustrates how to use two different times (purchase time and use time) to pinpoint direct materials variances.

AN ILLUSTRATION OF JOURNAL ENTRIES USING STANDARD COSTS

Control Feature of Standard Costs

We will now illustrate journal entries when standard costs are used. For illustrative purposes, we will focus on direct materials and direct manufacturing labour.

We will continue with the data in the Webb Company illustration with one exception. Assume that during April 2000 Webb purchases 25,000 square metres of materials. Recall that the actual quantity used is 22,200 metres and that the standard quantity allowed for the actual output achieved is 20,000 metres. The actual purchase price was $31 per square metre, while the standard price was $30.

Note that in each of the following entries, unfavourable variances are always debits and favourable variances are always credits.

◆ **Entry 1(a).** Isolate the direct-materials-price variance at the time of purchase by debiting Materials Control at standard prices. This is the earliest date possible to isolate this variance.

1. a. Materials Control		
(25,000 metres × $30)	$750,000	
Direct-Materials-Price Variance		
(25,000 metres × $1)	25,000	
Accounts Payable Control		
(25,000 metres × $31)		775,000
To record direct materials purchased.		

◆ **Entry 1(b).** Isolate the direct-materials-efficiency variance at the time of usage by debiting Work-in-Process Control at standard input quantities allowed for actual output units achieved at standard input prices.

1. b. Work-in-Process Control		
(20,000 metres × $30)	$600,000	
Direct-Materials-Efficiency Variance		
(2,200 metres × $30)	66,000	
Materials Control		
(22,200 metres × $30)		666,000
To record direct materials used.		

◆ **Entry 2.** Isolate the direct-manufacturing labour price and efficiency variances at the time this labour is used by debiting Work-in-Process Control at standard quantities allowed for actual output units achieved at standard input prices. Note that Wages Payable Control measures the payroll liability and hence is always at actual wage rates.

2. Work-in-Process Control		
(8,000 hours × $20)	$160,000	
Direct-Manufacturing-Labour-Price-Variance		
(9,000 hours × $2)	18,000	
Direct-Manufacturing-Labour-Efficiency Variance		
(1,000 hours × $20)	20,000	
Wages Payable Control		
(9,000 hours × $22)		198,000
To record liability for direct manufacturing labour costs.		

A major advantage of this standard costing system is its emphasis on the control feature of standard costs. All variances are isolated at the earliest possible time, when managers can make informed decisions based on those variances.

End-of-Period Adjustments

Chapter 5 discussed two main approaches to recognizing the under- or overallocated manufacturing overhead at the end of a period:

◆ The adjusted allocation rate approach, which adjusts every job cost record for the difference between the allocated and actual indirect cost amounts

◆ The proration approach, which makes adjustments to one or more of the following end-of-period account balances: materials, work in process, finished goods, and cost of goods sold

Price and efficiency variances can also be disposed of using these same two approaches.

FLEXIBLE BUDGETING AND ACTIVITY-BASED COSTING

Activity-based costing systems focus on individual activities as the fundamental cost objects. The Levels 1 to 3 variance analysis framework can be used to gain insight into costs at each individual activity. Consider Kitchen Inc., which assembles a diverse range of electrical kitchen products at its Winnipeg plant. A comparison of the actual results for 2000 with the static budget shows the following for its purchasing activity area:

	Actual Results	Static Budget
1. Number of purchase orders made	40,000	50,000
2. Labour-hours of procurement officers	4,000 hours	8,000 hours
3. Total labour cost	$100,000	$192,000
4. Labour-hours per purchase order (2 ÷ 1)	0.10 hours	0.16 hours
5. Labour cost per hour (3 ÷ 2)	$25	$24
6. Labour cost per invoice (3 ÷ 1)	$2.50	$3.84

The budgeted number of purchase orders for 2000 was a management estimate based on the expected volume of output at the plant for each product, the number of different suppliers for each separate component part purchased, the number of different parts in each product, and the delivery schedules of the suppliers. The budgeted time for each purchase order was based on a time-and-motion study of the steps taken in placing a purchase order. The $24 labour rate was based on the existing labour agreement at the start of 2000.

The static-budget variance (Level 1) for procurement labour costs in 2000 is:

$$\text{Static-budget variance} = \text{Actual results} - \text{Static-budget amount}$$
$$= \$100,000 - \$192,000$$
$$= \$92,000 \text{ F}$$

This Level 1 variance can be subdivided using the flexible budget for 2000. The flexible budget is based on budgeted inputs (0.16 hours per purchase order at $24 per hour) times the actual output in 2000:

$$(0.16 \times \$24) \times 40,000 = \$153,600$$

The Level 2 variances are:

$$\text{Flexible-budget variance} = \text{Actual results} - \text{Flexible-budget amount}$$
$$= \$100,000 - \$153,600$$
$$= \$53,600 \text{ F}$$

$$\text{Sales-volume variance} = \text{Flexible-budget amount} - \text{Static-budget amount}$$
$$= \$153,600 - \$192,000$$
$$= \$38,400 \text{ F}$$

Moving to Level 3, we can further subdivide the flexible-budget variance into its price and efficiency components:

$$\begin{matrix} \text{Price} \\ \text{variance} \end{matrix} = \left(\begin{matrix} \text{Actual price} \\ \text{of input} \end{matrix} - \begin{matrix} \text{Budgeted price} \\ \text{of input} \end{matrix} \right) \times \begin{matrix} \text{Actual quantity} \\ \text{of input} \end{matrix}$$
$$= (\$25 - \$24) \times 4,000$$
$$= \$4,000 \text{ U}$$

$$\text{Efficiency variance} = \left(\begin{array}{c} \text{Actual quantity} \\ \text{of input} \end{array} - \begin{array}{c} \text{Budgeted quantity of input} \\ \text{allowed for actual output} \end{array} \right) \times \begin{array}{c} \text{Budgeted price} \\ \text{of input} \end{array}$$

$$= [4,000 - (0.16 \times 40,000)] \times \$24$$
$$= (4,000 - 6,400) \times \$24$$
$$= \$57,600 \text{ F}$$

Kitchen Inc. used the above Levels 1 to 3 variances to investigate their causes:

(a) The sales-volume variance of $38,400 F highlights the effect of the number of purchase orders being 40,000 rather the budgeted 50,000. Management determined that this reduction was primarily due to a decrease in the number of suppliers and a decrease in the number of component parts per product compared with that assumed in the static budget.

(b) The efficiency variance of $57,600 F arises from the reduction in labour time from 9.6 minutes (0.16 hours) to 6.0 minutes (0.10 hours) per purchase order. This reduction arose from Kitchen Inc. restructuring its procurement operations to use internet-based purchasing where possible.

(c) The price variance of $4,000 U was due to the increase in the labour rate from $24 per hour in the static budget to an actual rate of $25 per hour. During 2000, the labour agreement was renegotiated to reflect an increase in technical skills of procurement personnel.

BENCHMARKING AND VARIANCE ANALYSIS

The budgeted amounts in the variance formulas discussed in this chapter are *benchmarks* (points of reference from which comparisons may be made). The term **benchmarking** is often used to refer to the continuous process of measuring products, services, and activities against the best levels of performance. These best levels of performance may be found in the organization using internal benchmarking information or by using external benchmarks from competing organizations or from other organizations having similar processes. Many consulting firms now offer benchmarking services. Here we discuss information provided by one such service and then note how the variance computations discussed in this chapter can incorporate this information.

Market Insights (MI), based in San Francisco, analyzes cost information submitted by hospitals to various U.S. regulatory bodies. MI develops benchmark reports that show how the cost level at one hospital compares with that at numerous other U.S. hospitals. Reports can be prepared at the total hospital level (for example, cost per patient-day) or at a specific diagnostic group level (for example, cardiology, orthopedics, or gynecology cost per patient).

Exhibit 7-6 illustrates an MI report for a client hospital. Panel A shows that the client hospital's cost per case is 10% above the average for comparable hospitals. Panel B shows an extract of an MI report at the diagnostic group level. This report shows that the client hospital has a cost per stroke patient of $33,700 compared with a market average among all hospitals of $31,300. The cost level at this client hospital is well above that of many hospitals. Cost benchmark reports are attention-directing in nature. An individual hospital administrator may well be able to justify an above-average cost level by documenting above-average quality levels or revenue levels. However, in many cases, hospitals with above-average costs have no documentable superiority in their service quality levels, success in surgery operations, or revenue per patient day.

Exhibit 7-6 highlights how hospitals can differ sizably on costs. An administrator of a hospital with above-average costs potentially has much to learn from administrators at hospitals with below-average costs. Be cautious, however, in using benchmark reports such as Exhibit 7-6. The reliability of individual hospital cost data used in benchmark reports varies widely. Many hospitals have not invested heavily in refining their cost accounting systems. In addition, cost figures for individual diagnostic groups require numerous cost allocations, which also vary widely in reliability.

Benchmarking. The continuous process of measuring products, services, or activities against the best levels of performance.

PANEL A: COST COMPARISONS AT HOSPITAL LEVEL

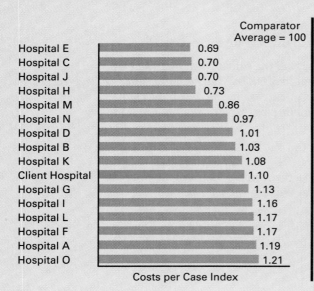

Comparator Average = 100

Hospital	Costs per Case Index
Hospital E	0.69
Hospital C	0.70
Hospital J	0.70
Hospital H	0.73
Hospital M	0.86
Hospital N	0.97
Hospital D	1.01
Hospital B	1.03
Hospital K	1.08
Client Hospital	1.10
Hospital G	1.13
Hospital I	1.16
Hospital L	1.17
Hospital F	1.17
Hospital A	1.19
Hospital O	1.21

Costs per Case Index

HOW TO READ THIS CHART:

This chart shows the client hospital's relative-case costs performance versus that of comparator hospitals. The client hospital is benchmarked with the average-case costs of its peers at the DRG level.

EXAMPLE:

On an overall costs per case basis, after adjusting for case mix, the client hospital's cost is 10% higher than the comparator group average. There are nine hospitals that have lower overall case costs than the client hospital.

PANEL B: COST COMPARISONS AT DIAGNOSTIC GROUP LEVEL*

Diagnostic Group	Client Hospital	Market Average	25th Percentile	Average of Lowest Cost Quartile (0–25th)
Stroke	$33,700	$31,300	$21,900	$20,500
Respiratory disorders	66,800	53,700	44,400	38,400
Simple pneumonia	37,100	29,500	23,300	22,000
Heart catheterization	24,800	21,200	20,100	17,100

*The cost amounts refer to the insurance premium per month that an insuree would have to pay to the client hospital.
Source: Market Insights (San Francisco, California).

Cost reports like Exhibit 7-6 provide an external benchmark that forces the administrator to ask *why* cost levels differ between hospitals and *how* best practices can be transferred from the more efficient to the less efficient hospitals.

Evaluating the overall performance of a hospital or hospital personnel requires analyzing other factors in addition to costs. These factors include the perceived quality of service to patients; the success rate of operations (for example, how many patients with strokes survive?); and the morale of the doctors, nurses, and other staff. In many cases, however, cost factors have been given too little weighting in the past, in part because of the lack of reliable information on cost relationships in this sector of the economy.

Benchmark reports based on the costs of other companies can be developed for many activities and products. For example, the Webb Company could estimate (possibly with the aid of consultants) the materials cost of the jackets manufactured by its competitors. The materials cost estimate of the lowest-cost competitor could be used as the budgeted amounts in its variance computations. An unfavourable materials-efficiency variance would signal that Webb has a higher materials cost than "best cost practice" in its industry. The magnitude of the cost difference would be of great interest to Webb. It could prompt Webb to do an extensive search into how to bring its own cost structure in line with that of the lowest in the industry.

WorldWide Benchmarking
Resource Guide
www.well.com/user/benchmar/
tbnhome.html

*Benchmarking for Quality
Management and Technology
An International Journal*
www.mcb.co.uk/bqmt.htm

PROBLEM

The O'Shea Company manufactures ceramic vases. It uses its standard costing system when developing its flexible budget amounts. In April 2000, 2,000 finished units were produced. The following information is related to its two direct manufacturing cost categories of direct materials and direct manufacturing labour.

Direct materials used were 4,400 kilograms. The standard direct materials input allowed for one output unit is two kilograms at $15 per kilogram, and 6,000 kilograms of materials were purchased at $16.50 per kilogram, a total of $99,000.

Actual direct manufacturing labour-hours were 3,250 at a total cost of $40,300. Standard manufacturing labour time allowed is 1.5 hours per output unit, and the standard direct manufacturing labour cost is $12 per hour.

REQUIRED

1. Calculate the direct materials price and efficiency variances and the direct manufacturing labour price and efficiency variances. The direct materials price variance will be based on a flexible budget for actual quantities purchased, but the efficiency variance will be based on a flexible budget for actual quantities used.
2. Prepare journal entries for a standard-costing system that isolates variances as early as feasible.

SOLUTION

1. Exhibit 7-7 shows how the columnar presentation of variances introduced in Exhibit 7-4 can be adjusted for the difference in timing between the purchase and use of materials. In particular, note the two sets of computations in column 2 for direct materials. The $90,000 pertains to the direct materials purchased; the $66,000 pertains to the direct materials used.

2.

Materials Control		
(6,000 kilograms × $15)	$90,000	
Direct Materials Price Variance		
(6,000 kilograms × $1.50)	9,000	
Accounts Payable Control		
(6,000 kilograms × $16.50)		$99,000
Work-in-Process Control		
(4,000 kilograms × $15)	$60,000	
Direct Materials Efficiency Variance		
(400 kilograms × $15)	6,000	
Materials Control		
(4,400 kilograms × $15)		$66,000
Work-in-Process Control		
(3,000 hours × $12)	$36,000	
Direct Manufacturing Labour Price Variance		
(3,250 hours × $0.40)	1,300	
Direct Manufacturing Labour Efficiency Variance		
(250 hours × $12)	3,000	
Wages Payable Control		
(3,250 hours × $12.40)		$40,300

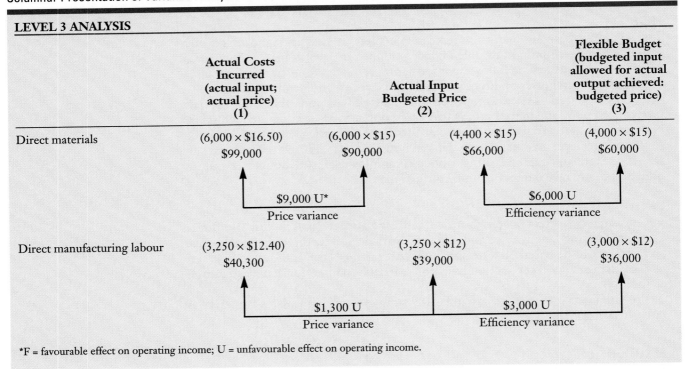

SUMMARY

The following points are linked to the chapter's learning objectives.

1. A static budget is a budget that is based on one level of output; when variances are computed at the end of the accounting period, no adjustments are made to the amounts in the static budget. A flexible budget is a budget that is developed using budgeted revenue or cost amounts; when variances are computed, the budgeted amounts are adjusted (flexed) to recognize the actual level of output and the actual quantities of the revenue and cost drivers. Flexible budgets help managers gain more insight into the causes of variances than do static budgets.

2. A five-step procedure can be used to develop a flexible budget. Where all costs are either variable with respect to output units or fixed, these five steps require only information about budgeted selling price, budgeted variable cost per output unit, budgeted fixed costs, and the actual quantity of output units achieved.

3. Standard costs are used to develop a static budget which can be compared with the actual results to compute the static budget variance. The static-budget variance can be broken into a flexible-budget variance (the difference between the actual result and the flexible-budget amount) and a sales-volume variance. The sales-volume variance arises because the actual output units differ from the budgeted output units.

4. Budgeted input prices and input quantities can be developed from past data (with or without adjustments) or by developing standards based on time-and-motion studies, engineering studies, and so on. There is much diversity in practice as to how budgeted amounts are obtained.

5. The computation of price variances and efficiency variances helps managers gain insight into two different (but not independent) aspects of performance. Price variances focus on the difference between actual and budgeted input prices. Efficiency variances focus on the difference between actual inputs used and the budgeted inputs allowed for the actual output achieved.

6. Price variances capture only one aspect of a manager's performance. Other aspects include the quality of the inputs the manager purchases and his or her ability to get suppliers to deliver on time.

7. Managers can use continuous improvement budgeted costs in their accounting system to highlight to all employees the importance of continuously seeking ways to reduce total costs.

8. Benchmarking is the continuous process of measuring products, services, and activities against the best levels of performance. Benchmarking enables companies to use the best levels of performance within their organizations or by competitors or other external companies, to gauge the performance of their own managers.

▼ TERMS TO LEARN

This chapter contains definitions of the following important terms:

benchmark (p. 221)	input-price variance (p. 226)
benchmarking (p. 239)	price variance (p. 226)
continuous improvement budgeted cost (p. 234)	rate variance (p. 226)
effectiveness (p. 232)	sales-volume variance (p. 224)
efficiency (p. 232)	selling-price variance (p. 225)
efficiency variance (p. 226)	standard (p. 221)
favourable variance (p. 221)	standard cost (p. 227)
flexible budget (p. 221)	standard input (p. 227)
flexible-budget variance (p. 224)	static budget (p. 221)
input-efficiency variance (p. 226)	unfavourable variance (p. 221)
	usage variance (p. 226)

▼ ASSIGNMENT MATERIAL

QUESTIONS

7-1 What is the relationship between *management by exception* and *variance analysis*?

7-2 What are two possible sources of information a company might use to compute the *budgeted amount* in variance analysis?

7-3 Distinguish between a *favourable variance* and an *unfavourable variance*.

7-4 What is the key difference between a *static budget* and a *flexible budget*?

7-5 Why might managers find a Level 2 flexible-budget analysis more informative than a Level 1 static-budget analysis?

7-6 Describe the steps in developing a flexible budget.

7-7 List four reasons for using standard costs.

7-8 How might a manager gain insight into the causes of a flexible-budget variance for direct materials?

7-9 List three causes of a favourable materials-price variance.

7-10 Describe why direct-materials-price and direct-materials-efficiency variances may be computed with reference to different points in time.

7-11 How might the continuous improvement theme be incorporated into the process of setting budgeted costs?

7-12 Why might an analyst examining variances in the production area look beyond that business function for explanations of those variances?

7-13 Comment on the following statement made by a plant supervisor: "Meetings with my plant accountant are frustrating. All he wants to do is pin the blame for the many variances he reports."

7-14 How can variances be used to analyze costs in individual activity areas?

7-15 "Benchmarking against other companies enables a company to identify the lowest-cost producer which should become the performance measure for the next year." Do you agree?

EXERCISES

7-16 Flexible budget. Brabham Enterprises manufactures tires for the Formula I motor racing circuit. For August 2000, Brabham budgeted to manufacture and sell 3,000 tires at a variable cost of $74 per tire and a total fixed cost of $54,000. The budgeted selling price was $110 per tire. Actual results in August 2000 were 2,800 tires manufactured and sold at a selling price of $112 per tire. The actual total variable costs were $229,600, and the actual total fixed costs were $50,000.

REQUIRED

1. Prepare a performance report (akin to Exhibit 7-3) that uses a flexible budget and a static budget.
2. Comment on the results in requirement 1.

7-17 Flexible budget. The budgeted prices for direct materials, direct manufacturing labour, and direct marketing (distribution) labour per attaché case are $40, $8, and $12 respectively. The president is pleased with the following performance report:

	Actual Costs	Static Budget	Variance
Direct materials	$364,000	$400,000	$36,000 F
Direct manufacturing labour	78,000	80,000	2,000 F
Direct marketing (distribution) labour	110,000	120,000	10,000 F

REQUIRED

Actual output was 8,800 attaché cases. Is the president's pleasure justified? Prepare a revised performance report that uses a flexible budget and a static budget. Assume all three direct-cost items are variable costs.

7-18 Flexible budget. The Virtual Candy Company sells sweets in bulk over the Web. Virtual Candy's budgeted operating income for the year ended December 31, 2000, was $3,150,000. As a result of continued explosive growth on the Web, actual operating income totalled $6,556,000.

REQUIRED

1. Calculate the total static-budget variances.
2. Flexible-budget operating income was $6,930,000. Calculate the total flexible-budget and total sales-volume variance.
3. Comment on the total flexible-budget variance in the light of Virtual Candy's explosive growth.

7-19 Price and efficiency variances. Peterson Foods manufactures pumpkin scones. For January 2000, it budgeted to purchase and use 15,000 kilograms of pumpkin at $0.89 a kilogram; budgeted output was 60,000 scones. Actual purchase and use for January 2000 was 16,000 kilograms at $0.82 a kilogram; actual output was 60,800 scones.

REQUIRED

1. Compute the flexible-budget variance.
2. Compute the price and efficiency variances.
3. Comment on the results in requirements 1 and 2.

7-20 Materials and manufacturing-labour variances. Consider the following data collected for Great Homes, Inc.:

	Direct Materials	Direct Manufacturing Labour
Costs incurred: Actual inputs × actual prices	$200,000	$90,000
Actual inputs × standard prices	214,000	86,000
Standard inputs allowed for actual outputs × standard prices	225,000	80,000

REQUIRED

Compute the price, efficiency, and flexible-budget variances for direct materials and direct manufacturing labour.

7-21 Price and efficiency variances. CellOne, a cellular phone service reseller, contracts with major cellular operators for airtime in bulk and then resells service to retail customers. CellOne budgeted to sell 7,800,000 minutes in the month ended March 31, 2000. Actual minutes sold totalled only 7,500,000. Because of fluctuations in hourly usage, CellOne "overbuys" airtime from cellular operators. CellOne plans to buy 10% more airtime than they plan to sell—for example, CellOne's budgets called for the purchase of 8,580,000 minutes based on the plan to sell 7,800,000 minutes. We refer to purchased airtime as direct materials.

CellOne's budgets purchased airtime to cost 4.5 cents per minute. Actual purchased airtime in 2000 averaged 5 cents per minute. CellOne incurs direct labour costs from the employment of technicians. One hour of technical support is required for every 5,000 minutes of airtime sold. In practice, only 1,600 hours of technical support were used. Technical support was planned at $60 per hour. Actual technical support costs averaged $62 per hour.

REQUIRED
1. Calculate the flexible-budget variance.
2. Calculate the price and efficiency variances for materials and labour.

7-22 Comprehensive variance analysis. Pacific Furniture is an elite desk manufacturer. At the start of May 2000, the following budgeted unit amounts (based on a standard costing system) related to its manufacture of executive desks (made out of oak):
◆ Direct materials:
16 square metres of oak per desk
$20 per square metre
◆ Direct manufacturing labour:
3 hours per desk
$30 per direct manufacturing labour-hour

Budgeted production for May 2000 was 700 executive desks. There were no beginning inventories of direct materials or finished goods on May 1, 2000. Work in process is minimal.

Actual results for May 2000 are as follows:

◆ Direct materials purchased (12,640 square metres) $259,120
◆ Direct materials used (11,850 square metres)   ?
◆ Direct manufacturing labour (2,325 hours at $31 per hour)   ?

Actual production in May 2000 is 750 executive desk units. A constant purchase price for oak wood existed in May 2000.

REQUIRED
1. Prepare a detailed flexible-budget variance analysis for May 2000 covering direct materials and direct manufacturing labour.
2. Give two explanations for each of the variances you compute in requirement 1.

7-23 Flexible budgets, variance analysis. You have been hired as a consultant by Mary Flanagan, the president of a small manufacturing company that makes automobile parts. Flanagan is an excellent engineer, but she has been frustrated by working with inadequate cost data.

You helped install flexible budgeting and standard costs for Flanagan's company. She has now asked you to consider the following data for May and recommend how variances might be computed and presented in performance reports:

Static budget in output units	20,000
Actual output units produced and sold	23,000
Budgeted selling price per output unit	$40
Budgeted variable costs per output unit	$25
Budgeted total fixed costs per month	$200,000
Actual revenue	$874,000
Actual variable costs	$630,000
Favourable variance in fixed costs	$5,000

Flanagan is disappointed in the May data. Although output units sold exceeded expectations, operating income did not. Assume that there was no beginning or ending inventory.

REQUIRED
1. You decide to present Flanagan with alternative ways to analyze variances so that she can decide what level of detail she prefers. The reporting system can then be

designed accordingly. Prepare an analysis similar to Levels 1 and 2 in Exhibit 7-5.

2. What are some likely causes for the variances you report in requirement 1?

7-24 Flexible budget preparation and analysis. Bank Management Printers, Inc., produces luxury chequebooks with three cheques and stubs per page. Each chequebook is designed for an individual customer and is ordered through the customer's bank. The company's operating budget for September 2000 included these data:

Number of chequebooks	15,000
Selling price per book	$20
Variable costs per book	$8
Total fixed costs for the month	$145,000

The actual results for September 2000 were:

Number of chequebooks produced and sold	12,000
Average selling price per book	$21
Variable costs per book	$7
Total fixed costs for the month	$150,000

The executive vice-president of the company observed that the operating income for September was much less than anticipated, despite a higher-than-budgeted selling price and a lower-than-budgeted variable cost per unit. You have been asked to provide explanations for the disappointing September results.

Bank Management develops its flexible budget on the basis of budgeted revenue per output unit and variable costs per output unit without a detailed analysis of budgeted inputs.

REQUIRED

1. Prepare a Level 1 analysis of the September performance.
2. Prepare a Level 2 analysis of the September performance.
3. Why might Bank Management find the Level 2 analysis more informative than the Level 1 analysis? Explain your answer.

7-25 Flexible budget, working backward. The Specialty Balls Company designs and manufactures ball bearings for extreme performance machinery. The accompanying table is a partially complete variance analysis of Specialty Balls budgeted and actual results from sales of platinum balls for the year ended December 31, 2000.

Variance Analysis for Specialty Balls for 2000, Incomplete

	Actual Results (1)	Flexible-Budget Variances (2) = (1) – (3)	Flexible Budget (3)	Sales-Volume Variances (4) = (3) – (5)	Static Budget (5)
Units sold	650,000				600,000
Revenues (sales)	$3,575,000				$2,100,000
Variable costs	2,575,000				1,200,000
Contribution margin	1,000,000				900,000
Fixed costs	700,000				600,000
Operating income	$ 300,000				$ 300,000

Total flexible-budget variance Total sales-volume variance

Total static-budget variance

REQUIRED

1. Complete the variance analysis. Calculate all the required variances. If your work is accurate, you will find that the total static-budget variance is $0 (zero).
2. What are the actual and budgeted prices per unit? What are the actual and budgeted costs per unit?

3. Specialty Balls' CEO was delighted with the lack of a static-budget variance. Was his reaction appropriate? Review the variances you have calculated and discuss possible causes and potential problems.

7-26 Flexible-budget variances for finance function activities. Sam Chase is the chief financial officer of Flowers.net, an internet company that enables customers to order home deliveries of flowers by accessing its website. Flowers.net has a network of florists ("strategic partners") who do the physical delivery of flowers. Flowers.net has a group of representatives that continually visit florists and nurseries. This group monitors product and service quality and explores new products or new partners.

Chase is concerned with the efficiency and effectiveness of the finance function at Flowers.net. He collects the following information for five finance activities in 2000:

Finance Activity	Output Measure	2000 Budgeted Total Cost of Process	2000 Budgeted Total # of Outputs	2000 Actual Cost of Process	2000 Actual Total # of Outputs
Payables	# of invoices	$580,000	200,000	$594,020	212,150
Receivables	# of remittances	639,000	900,000	711,504	948,672
Travel and expense	# of expense reports	15,200	2,000	13,986	1,890
Fixed assets	# of assets tracked	2,950	500	3,836	548
Payroll	# of paycheques	27,600	9,200	26,502	9,465

The budgeted amounts are based on an analysis of costs in past periods at Flowers.net.

REQUIRED

1. Prepare a flexible-budget-based report explaining differences between budgeted and actual costs for each of the five finance processes in 2000. Comment on the results.
2. Why might the variances computed in requirement 1 pertain to efficiency but not to effectiveness?
3. How might Chase monitor the efficiency of the five finance processes in this question?

7-27 Finance function activities, benchmarking (continuation of 7-26). Sam Chase, CFO of Flowers.net, receives a brochure from The Hackett Group, a consulting firm specializing in benchmarking. He asks the Hackett Group to provide benchmark data from its recent study of the finance function at over 100 retail companies (both traditional retail and internet-based retail). Hackett's "world-class" cost benchmarks (based on the lowest-cost company for that activity) for Flowers.net's five finance activities are:

Finance Activity	World-Class Cost Performance
Payables	$0.71 per invoice
Receivables	$0.10 per remittance
Travel and expense	$1.58 per expense report
Fixed assets	$1.20 per asset tracked
Payroll	$0.95 per paycheque

REQUIRED

1. What new insights might arise the concerning the use of the budgeted amounts in Question 7-26, using Hackett benchmark data?
2. Assume you are in charge of travel and expense report processing. What concerns might you have with Sam Chase using the Hackett $1.58 per expense report benchmark as the key measure to evaluate your performance next period.

7-28 Price and efficiency variances, journal entries. Chemical, Inc., has set up the following standards per finished output unit for direct materials and direct manufacturing labour.

◆ Direct materials: 10 kilograms at $3 per kilogram $30
◆ Direct manufacturing labour: 0.5 hour at $20 per hour   10

The number of finished output units budgeted for March 2000 was 10,000; 9,810 units were actually produced.

Actual results in March 2000 were:

Direct materials: 98,073 kilograms used

Direct manufacturing labour: 4,900 hours $102,900

Assume that there was no beginning inventory of either direct materials or finished units.

During the month, materials purchases amounted to 100,000 kilograms, at a total cost of $310,000. Price variances are isolated upon purchase. Efficiency variances are isolated at the time of usage.

REQUIRED

1. Compute the March 2000 price and efficiency variances of direct materials and direct manufacturing labour. Comment on these variances.
2. Prepare journal entries to record the variances in requirement 1.
3. Why might Chemical, Inc., calculate materials price variances and materials efficiency variances with reference to different points in time?

7-29 Continuous improvement (continuation of 7-28). Chemical, Inc., adopts a continuous improvement approach to setting monthly standards' costs. Assume the direct materials standard quantity input of ten kilograms per output unit and the direct manufacturing labour quantity input of 0.5 hours per output unit pertain to January 2000. The standard amounts for February 2000 are 0.997 of the January standard amount. The standard amounts for March 2000 are 0.997 of the February standard amount. Assume the same information for March 2000 as in Exercise 7-28 except for these revised standard amounts.

REQUIRED

1. Compute the March 2000 standard quantity input amounts per output unit for direct materials and direct manufacturing labour.
2. Compute the March 2000 price and efficiency variances of direct materials and direct manufacturing labour.

7-30 Materials and manufacturing labour variances, standard costs. Consider the following selected data regarding the manufacture of a line of upholstered chairs:

	Standards per Chair
Direct materials	2 square metres of input at $10 per square metre
Direct manufacturing labour	0.5 hour of input at $20 per hour

The following data were compiled regarding actual performance: actual output units (chairs) produced, 20,000; square metres of input purchased and used, 37,000; price per square metre, $10.20; direct manufacturing labour costs, $176,400; actual hours of input, 9,000; labour price per hour, $19.60.

REQUIRED

1. Show your computations on the price and efficiency variances for direct materials and for direct manufacturing labour. Give a plausible explanation of why the variances occurred.
2. Suppose 60,000 square metres of materials were purchased (at $10.20 per square metre) even though only 37,000 square metres were used. Suppose further that variances are identified with their most likely control point; accordingly, direct-materials-price variances are isolated and traced to the purchasing department rather than to the production department. Compute the price and efficiency variances under this approach.

7-31 Journal entries and T-accounts (continuation of 7-30). Prepare journal entries and post them to T-accounts for all transactions in Exercise 7-30, including requirement 2. Summarize in three sentences how these journal entries differ from the normal costing entries described in Chapter 5.

7-32 Flexible budget (continuation of 7-30). Suppose the static budget was for 24,000 units of output. The general manager is thrilled about the following report:

	Actual Results	Static Budget	Variance
Direct materials	$377,400	$480,000	$102,600 F
Direct manufacturing labour	176,400	240,000	63,600 F

REQUIRED

Is the manager's glee warranted? Prepare a report that provides a more detailed explanation of why the static budget was not achieved. Actual output was 20,000 units.

PROBLEMS

7-33 Flexible budget preparation, service sector. Meridian Finance helps prospective homeowners of substantial means to find low-cost financing and assists existing homeowners in refinancing their current loans at lower interest rates. Meridian works only for customers with excellent borrowing capacity. Hence, Meridian is able to obtain a loan for every customer with whom it decides to work.

Meridian charges clients ½% of the loan amount it arranges. In 1998, the average loan amount per customer was $199,000. In 2000, the average loan amount was $200,210. In its 2000 flexible budgeting system, Meridian assumes the average loan amount will be $200,000. Budgeted cost data per loan application for 2000 are:

◆ Professional labour: 6 budgeted hours at a budgeted rate of $40 per hour
◆ Loan filing fees: budgeted at $100 per loan application
◆ Credit-worthiness checks: budgeted at $120 per loan application
◆ Courier mailings: budgeted at $50 per loan application

Office support (the costs of leases, secretarial workers, and others) is budgeted to be $31,000 per month. Meridian Finance views this amount as a fixed cost.

REQUIRED

1. Prepare a static budget for November 2000 assuming 90 loan applications.
2. Actual loan applications in November 2000 were 120. Other actual data for November 2000 were:

◆ Professional labour: 7.2 hours per loan application at $42 per hour
◆ Loan filing fees: $100 per loan application
◆ Credit-worthiness checks: $125 per loan application
◆ Courier mailings: $54 per loan application

Office support costs for November 2000 were $33,500. The average loan amount for November 2000 was $224,000. Meridian received its ½% fee on all loans. Prepare a Level 2 variance analysis of Meridian Finance for November 2000. Meridian's output measure in its flexible budgeting system is the number of loan applications.

7-34 Professional labour efficiency and effectiveness (continuation of 7-33). Meridian Finance is analyzing the efficiency and effectiveness of its professional labour staff.

REQUIRED

1. Compute professional-labour price and efficiency variances for November 2000. (Compute labour price on a per-hour basis.)
2. What factors would you consider in evaluating the effectiveness of professional labour in November 2000?

7-35 Direct materials variances, long-term agreement with supplier. Yamazaki Mazak manufactures large-scale machining systems that are sold to other industrial companies. Each machining system has a sizable direct materials cost, consisting primarily of the purchase price for a metal compound. For its Montreal, Quebec, manufacturing facility, Mazak has a long-term contract with Fuji Metals. Fuji will supply to Mazak up to 2,400 kilograms of metal per month at a fixed purchase price of $120 per kilogram for each month in 2000. For purchases above 2,400 kilograms in any month, Mazak renegotiates the price for the additional amount with Fuji Metals (or another supplier). The standard price per kilogram is $120 for each month in the January to December 2000 period.

Production data, direct materials actual usage in dollars, and direct materials actual price per kilogram for the January to May 2000 period, are:

	Number of Machining Systems Produced	Total Actual Direct Materials Usage	Average Actual Direct Materials Purchase Price per Kilogram of Metal
January	10	$242,400	$120
February	12	286,560	120
March	18	442,260	126
April	16	395,264	128
May	11	253,440	120

The average actual direct materials purchase price is for all units purchased in that month. Assume that (a) the direct materials purchased in each month are all used in that month and (b) each machining system is started and completed in the same month.

The Montreal facility is one of three plants that Mazak operates to manufacture large-scale machining systems. The other plants are in Worcester, U.K., and Tokyo, Japan.

REQUIRED

1. Assume that Mazak's standard materials input per machining system is 198 kilograms of metal. Compute the direct materials price variance and direct materials efficiency variance for each month of the January to May 2000 period.
2. How does the signing of a long-term agreement with a supplier—an agreement that includes a fixed-purchase-price clause—affect the interpretation of a materials price variance?

7-36 Flexible and static budgets, service company. Avanti Transportation Company executives have had trouble interpreting operating performance for a number of years. The company has used a budget based on detailed expectations for the forthcoming quarter. For example, the condensed performance report for a Western branch for the most recent quarter was as follows:

	Actual Result	Budget	Variance
Revenue	$9,500,000	$10,000,000	$500,000 U*
Variable costs:			
Fuel	986,000	1,000,000	14,000 F
Repairs and maintenance	98,000	100,000	2,000 F
Supplies and miscellaneous	196,000	200,000	4,000 F
Variable labour payroll	5,500,000	5,700,000	200,000 F
Total variable costs†	6,780,000	7,000,000	220,000 F
Fixed costs:			
Supervision	200,000	200,000	0
Rent	200,000	200,000	0
Amortization	1,600,000	1,600,000	0
Other fixed costs	200,000	200,000	0
Total fixed costs	2,200,000	2,200,000	0
Total costs	8,980,000	9,200,000	220,000 F
Operating income	$ 520,000	$ 800,000	$280,000 U

*U = unfavourable; F = favourable.
†For purposes of this analysis, assume that all these variable costs are purely variable (in relation to revenue dollars). Also assume that the prices and mix of services sold remain unchanged.

Although the branch manager was upset about the unfavourable revenue variance, he was happy that his cost performance was favourable; otherwise his operating income would have been even lower. His immediate superior, the vice-president for operations, was totally unhappy and remarked:

> I can see some merit in comparing actual performance with budgeted performance, because we can see whether actual revenue coincided with our best guess for budget purposes. But I can't see how this performance report helps us evaluate the cost control performance of the branch manager.

REQUIRED

1. Prepare a columnar flexible budget for Avanti at revenue levels of $9 million, $10 million, and $11 million. Use the format of Exhibit 7-2. Assume that the prices and mix of products sold are equal to the budgeted prices and mix.
2. Express the flexible budget for costs in formula form.
3. Prepare a condensed contribution format income statement showing the static-budget, sales-volume, and flexible-budget variances. Use the format of Exhibit 7-3.

7-37 Direct materials and manufacturing labour variances, solving unknowns. (CPA, adapted) On May 1, 2000, the Bovar Company began the manufacture of a new paging machine known as Dandy. The company installed a standard costing system to account for manufacturing costs. The standard costs for a unit of Dandy are as follows:

Direct materials (3 kilograms at $5 per kilogram)	$15.00
Direct manufacturing labour (0.5 hour at $20 per hour)	10.00
Manufacturing overhead (75% of direct manufacturing labour costs)	7.50
	$32.50

The following data were obtained from Bovar's records for the month of May:

	Debit	Credit
Revenues		$125,000
Accounts payable control (for May's purchases of direct materials)		68,250
Direct materials price variance	$3,250	
Direct materials efficiency variance	2,500	
Direct-manufacturing-labour-price variance	1,900	
Direct-manufacturing-labour-efficiency variance		2,000

Actual production in May was 4,000 units of Dandy, and actual sales in May were 2,500 units. The amount shown for direct-materials-price variance applies to materials purchased during May. There was no beginning inventory of materials on May 1, 2000.

REQUIRED

Compute each of the following items for Bovar for the month of May. Show your computations.

1. Standard direct manufacturing labour-hours allowed for actual output achieved
2. Actual direct manufacturing labour-hours worked
3. Actual direct manufacturing labour wage rate
4. Standard quantity of direct materials allowed (in kilograms)
5. Actual quantity of direct materials used (in kilograms)
6. Actual quantity of direct materials purchased (in kilograms)
7. Actual direct materials price per kilogram

7-38 **Benchmarking, hospital cost comparisons.** Julie Smith is the newly appointed president of Provincial University. Provincial University Hospital (PUH) is a major problem for her, because it is running large deficits. Sam Horn, the chairman of the hospital, tells Smith that he and his staff have cut costs to the bare bone. Any further cost cutting, he argues, would destroy the culture of the hospital. He also argues that the use of detailed cost studies is totally inappropriate for a medical institution because of (a) the inability to have well-defined relationships between inputs and outputs and (b) the problem of even defining what is a good output for a hospital. He notes that he is "fed up with people equating continuous improvement at PUH with continued cost reduction. This is only a cost accountant's view of the world. Our top priority is to help doctors save lives and to help people recover their health."

Smith hears about a new benchmark cost analysis service offered by Market Insights. She asks Horn to hire Market Insights to provide a benchmark cost report that pertains to PUH. Horn is not enthusiastic about doing so, but he complies with her request. The report includes the following:

a. Aggregate Hospital Cost Comparison
(average = 1.00)

Hospital E	0.69
Hospital C	0.70
Hospital J	0.70
⋮	⋮
Hospital A	1.19
Provincial University Hospital	1.20
Hospital O	1.21

b.

Diagnostic Group Cost Comparison

Diagnostic Group	Provincial University Hospital	Market Average	25th Percentile	Average of Best Quartile (0–25th)
Angina, chest pain	$23,000	$20,500	$17,300	$15,300
Asthma, bronchitis	15,400	13,100	10,400	9,000
Skin disorders, cellulitis	9,600	9,200	6,500	5,800
Renal failure and dialysis	7,600	5,500	4,200	3,600
Diabetes	6,700	5,100	3,700	3,100
Gastroenteritis	12,000	18,500	16,000	12,800

REQUIRED

1. Do you agree with Horn that the use of detailed cost studies at PUH is totally inappropriate? Explain your answer and comment on Horn's reasoning.
2. What inferences do you draw from the MI benchmark cost report on PUH?
3. What use might Smith make of the MI benchmark cost report?
4. What criticisms might you anticipate Horn would make of the MI benchmark cost report?
5. What factors other than cost might Smith consider in evaluating Horn's performance and that of PUH?

7-39 Comprehensive variance analysis. (CMA, adapted) Aunt Molly's Old Fashioned Cookies bakes cookies for a chain of U.K. retail stores. The company's best-selling cookie is chocolate nut supreme, which is marketed as a gourmet cookie and regularly sells for $8 per pound. The standard cost per pound of chocolate nut supreme, based on Aunt Molly's normal monthly production of 400,000 pounds, is calculated as follows:

Cost Item	Quantity	Standard Unit Costs	Total Cost
Direct materials:			
Cookie mix	10 ounces	$ 0.02 per ounce	$0.20
Milk chocolate	5 ounces	0.15 per ounce	0.75
Almonds	1 ounce	0.50 per ounce	0.50
			$1.45
Direct labour:*			
Mixing	1 minute	$14.40 per hour	$0.24
Baking	2 minutes	18.00 per hour	0.60
			$0.84

*Direct labour rates include employee benefits.

Aunt Molly's management accountant, Karen Blair, prepares monthly budget reports based on these standard costs. Presented here is April's report, which compares budgeted and actual performance.

Performance Report
April 2000

	Budget	Actual	Variance
Units (in pounds)*	400,000	450,000	50,000 F
Revenue	$3,200,000	$3,555,000	$355,000 F
Direct material	580,000	865,000	285,000 U
Direct labour	336,000	348,000	12,000 U

*Units produced and sold

Usage Report
April 2000

Cost Item	Quantity	Actual Cost
Direct materials:		
Cookie mix	4,650,000 ounces	$ 93,000
Milk chocolate	2,660,000 ounces	532,000
Almonds	480,000 ounces	240,000
Direct labour:		
Mixing	450,000 minutes	108,000
Baking	800,000 minutes	240,000

REQUIRED
1. Compute the following variances
   a. Selling-price variance
   b. Material-price variance
   c. Material-efficiency variance
   d. Labour-price variance
   e. Labour-efficiency variance
2. What explanations might exist for the variances in requirement 1?

7-40 Comprehensive variance analysis responsibility issues. (CMA, adapted) Horizons Unlimited manufactures a full line of well-known sunglass frames and lenses. Horizons uses a standard cost system to set attainable standards for direct materials, labour, and overhead costs. Standards have been reviewed and revised annually, as necessary. Departmental managers, whose evaluations and bonuses are affected by their department's performance, have been held responsible to explain variances in their departmental performance reports.

Recently, the manufacturing variances in the Visionaire prestige line of sunglasses have caused some concern. For no apparent reason, unfavourable material and labour variances have increased. At the monthly staff meeting, Jim Denton, manager of the Visionaire line, will be expected to explain his variances and suggest ways of improving performance. The performance report for 2000 that Denton will be asked to explain is presented below.

	Actual Results	Static Budget Amounts
Units sold	4,850	5,000
Revenues	$397,700	$400,000
Variable manufacturing costs	234,643	216,000
Fixed manufacturing costs	72,265	75,000
Gross margin	90,792	109,000

Denton collected the following information:
a. The standard variable manufacturing costs in 2000 is comprised of three items:

Direct materials: Frames. Static budgeted cost of $33,000. The standard input (in grams) for 2000 is 3.00 grams per unit.

Direct materials: Lenses. Static budgeted costs of $93,000. The standard input (in grams) for 2000 is 6.00 grams per unit.

Direct manufacturing labour. Static budgeted costs of $90,000. The standard input (in hours) for 2000 is 1.20 hours per unit.

Assume there are no indirect manufacturing costs.

b. The actual variable manufacturing costs in 2000 were:

Direct materials: Frames. Actual costs of $37,248. Actual grams used per frame was 3.20 grams per unit.

Direct materials: Lenses. Actual costs of $100,492. Actual grams used per frame was 7.00 grams per unit.

Direct manufacturing labour. Actual costs of $96,903. The actual labour rate was $14.80 per hour.

REQUIRED

1. Prepare a manufacturing performance analysis report that includes:
   a. Selling-price variance
   b. Sales-volume variance and flexible-budget variance for
      ◆ revenues
      ◆ variable manufacturing costs
      ◆ fixed manufacturing costs
      ◆ gross margin
   c. Price and efficiency variances for
      ◆ total direct materials
      ◆ direct materials: lenses
      ◆ direct manufacturing labour
2. Give three possible explanations for each of the three price and efficiency variances at Horizons in requirement 1 (c).

7-41 Continuous improvement (continuation of 7-40). Horizon receives a suggestion that continuous improvement standard costs be used and updated monthly. Consider monthly revisions in 2000 for the three variable manufacturing cost items.

REQUIRED

1. Assume the data in Problem 7-40 is the December 1999 standard. The January 2000 standard is 0.995 times the December 1999 standard. The February 2000 standard is 0.995 times the January 2000 standard. Using the data from Question 7-40, what is the standard for the direct materials usage for each variable cost item in January and February 2000?
2. What are the pros and cons of using the approach in (a) as the primary approach to drive the cost competitiveness of Horizon?

7-42 Variance analysis, solve for unknowns. Homerun Headgear manufactures and distributes baseball caps to ballparks and other sports venues. Homerun's budget for 2000 forecasts sales of 600,000 caps. However, only 500,000 caps were sold. Based on the data provided in the table below, calculate the missing numbers and complete the analysis.

Variance Analysis for Homerun Headgear for 2000, Incomplete

	Actual Results (1)	Flexible-Budget Variances (2) = (1) – (3)	Flexible Budget (3)	Sales-Volume Variances (4) = (3) – (5)	Static Budget (5)
Units sold	500,000	___	___	___	600,000
Revenues (sales)	$5,000,000	___	___	___	$4,800,000
Variable costs	1,400,000	___	___	___	1,800,000
Contribution margin	___	1,100,000 F	___	500,000U	___
Fixed costs	1,150,000	___	1,000,000	___	1,000,000
Operating income	___	___	___	___	___

Total flexible-budget variance   Total sales-volume variance

Total static-budget variance

REQUIRED

1. Calculate the budgeted and actual unit sales price.
2. Assuming that the driver for variable costs is units sold, what are the budgeted and actual variable costs per unit?
3. What is Homerun's 2000 flexible-budget operating income?
4. What is the total flexible-budget variance?
5. What is the total sales-volume variance?
6. What is the total static-budget variance?

7-43 Procurement costs, variance analysis, ethics. Rick Daley is the manager of the athletic shoe division of Raider Products. Raider is a European-based company that has just purchased Fastfoot, a leading European shoe company. Fastfoot has long-term production contracts with suppliers in two East European countries, Hergovia and Tanistan. Daley receives a request from Kevin Neal, president of Raider Products. Daley and his controller, Brooke Mullins, are to make a presentation to the next board of directors' meeting on the cost competitiveness of its Fastfoot subsidiary. This should include budgeted and actual procurement costs for 2000 at its Hergovia and Tanistan supply sources.

Mullins decides to visit the two supply operations. The budgeted average procurement cost for 2000 was $12 per pair of shoes. This includes payments to the shoe manufacturer and all other payments to conduct business in each country. Mullins reports the following to Daley:

◆ **Hergovia.** Total 2000 procurement costs for 250,000 pairs of shoes was $3,325,000. Payment to the shoe manufacturer was $2,650,000. Very few receipts exist for the remaining $675,000. Kickback payments are viewed as common in Hergovia.

◆ **Tanistan.** Total 2000 procurement costs for 900,000 pairs of shoes was $10,485,000. Payment to the shoe manufacturer was $8,640,000. Receipts exist for $705,000 of the other costs, but Mullins is skeptical of their validity. Kickback payments are a "way of business" in Tanistan.

At both the Hergovia and Tanistan plants, Mullins is disturbed by the employment of young children (many of them under 15 years). She is told that all major shoe-producing companies have similar low-cost employment practices in both countries.

Daley is uncomfortable about the upcoming presentation to the board of directors. He was a leading advocate of the acquisition. A recent business magazine reported that the Fastfoot acquisition would make Raider Products the global low-cost producer in its market lines. The stock price of Raider Products jumped 21% the day the Fastfoot acquisition was announced. Mullins likewise is widely identified as a proponent of the acquisition. She is seen as a rising star due for promotion to a division management post in the near future.

REQUIRED

1. What summary procurement cost variances could be reported to the board of directors of Raider Shoes?
2. What ethical issues do (a) Daley and (b) Mullins face when preparing and making a report to the board of directors?
3. How should Mullins address the issues you identify in requirement 2?

7-44 Comprehensive variance analysis review. FlexMem, Inc., manufactures 120 Mb diskettes that are compatible with a popular portable storage device. FlexMem sells diskettes wholesale to computer retail chains and direct marketing organizations that resell the diskettes as a house brand. The diskettes retail for an average of $8 per unit, and compete with well-known brands that retail for between $10 and $12 per diskette.

FlexMem's CFO has provided you with the following budgeted standards for the month of February, 2000:

Budgeted average wholesale selling price per unit	$ 4.00
Total direct material standard cost per diskette	$ 0.85
Direct manufacturing labour	
Direct manufacturing labour standard cost per hour	$ 15.00
Average labour productivity rate (diskettes per hour)	300
Direct marketing cost per unit	$ 0.30
Total fixed overhead	$900,000

The VP of Marketing forecasts sales of 1,500,000 units for the month.

On March 7th, the VP of Planning and Control meets with the executive committee to discuss February results. He reports as follows:

◆ Unit sales totalled 80% of plan.
◆ Actual average selling price declined to $3.70.
◆ Productivity dropped to 250 diskettes/hour; however, because of favourable market conditions, the actual price per unit dropped to $0.80.
◆ Fixed costs came in $30,000 below plan.

REQUIRED

As the senior financial analyst, you are asked to calculate the following:

1. Static-budget and actual operating income
2. Total static-budget variance
3. Flexible-budget operating income
4. Total flexible-budget variance
5. Total sales-volume variance
6. Price and efficiency variances
7. What is the material-price variance? Labour-price variance?
8. What is the material-efficiency variance? Labour-efficiency variance?

COLLABORATIVE LEARNING PROBLEM

7-45 **Price and efficiency variances, problems in standard-setting, benchmarking.** NorthWest Fashions manufactures shirts for retail chains. Jorge Rivera, the controller, is becoming increasingly disenchanted with NorthWest's six-month-old standard costing system. The budgeted amounts for both its direct materials and direct manufacturing labour are drawn from its standard costing system. The budgeted and actual amounts for July 2000 were:

	Budgeted	Actual
Shirts manufactured	4,000	4,488
Direct materials cost	$20,000	$20,196
Direct materials units used (rolls of cloth)	400	408
Direct manufacturing labour costs	$18,000	$18,462
Direct manufacturing labour-hours	1,000	1,020

There was no beginning or ending inventory of materials.

Rivera observes that in the past six months he has rarely seen an unfavourable variance of any magnitude. The standard costing system is based on a study of the operations conducted by an independent consultant. Rivera decides to play detective and makes some unobtrusive observations of the work force at the plant. He notes that, even at their current output levels, the workers seem to have a lot of time to discuss baseball, sitcoms, and the local hot fishing spots.

At a recent industry conference on "Benchmarking and Competitiveness," Mary Blanchard, the controller of Winston Fabrics, told Rivera that Winston had employed the same independent consultant to design a standard costing system. However, the company dismissed him after two weeks, because Winston employees quickly became aware of the consultant observing their work.

At the industry conference, Rivera participated in seminars on "benchmarking for the fabric industry." A consultant for the Benchmarking Clearing House showed how she could develop six-month benchmark reports on the estimated costs of NorthWest's major competitors. She indicated that she was already examining the estimated cost of shirts manufactured by the four largest importers into Canada. These importers had taken much business from NorthWest in recent years. This information would soon be available by subscribing to the Benchmarking Clearing House monthly service.

INSTRUCTIONS

Form groups of two or more students to complete the following requirements.

REQUIRED

1. Compute the price and efficiency variances of NorthWest Fashions for direct materials and direct manufacturing labour in July 2000.
2. Describe the types of actions the employees at Winston Fabrics may have taken to reduce the accuracy of the standards set by the independent consultant. Why would employees take those actions? Is this behaviour ethical?
3. Describe how NorthWest might use information from the Benchmarking Clearing House when computing the variances in requirement 1.
4. Discuss the pros and cons of NorthWest using the Benchmarking Clearing House information to increase its cost-competitiveness.

CHAPTER 8

FLEXIBLE BUDGETS, VARIANCES, AND MANAGEMENT CONTROL: II

The planning and control of indirect costs is pivotal in organizations with high investments in plant, equipment, and operating systems. Rank Hovis' flour milling and blending facilities at Manchester, U.K., uses high levels of computer-operated machinery in its operations.

LEARNING OBJECTIVES

After studying this chapter, you should be able to:

1. Explain the similarities in the planning of variable overhead costs and the planning of fixed overhead costs
2. Explain the computation and meaning of spending and efficiency variances for variable overhead
3. Compute the budgeted fixed overhead rate
4. Explain why the production-volume variance may not be a good measure of the opportunity cost of unused capacity
5. Explain how variance analysis can provide an integrated overview of overhead-cost variances
6. Explain the differing roles of cost-allocation bases for fixed manufacturing overhead when (a) planning and controlling and (b) inventory costing
7. Prepare journal entries for variable and fixed overhead variances
8. Explain why managers frequently use both financial and nonfinancial variables to plan and control overhead costs

Cost Variance Analysis
www.swcollege.com/vircomm/
gita/gita19-4.html

A Primer on Job Costing—
Walker Mowers
www.walkermowers.com/vollo/
vollo_f.html

Overhead or indirect costs are a major cost area for many organizations. Chemical, paper, steel, and telecommunications companies, for example, incur sizable costs to construct and maintain their physical plant and equipment and other aspects of their infrastructure. Such costs are included in the indirect costs of the individual products or services they produce and sell. This chapter covers methods of planning and controlling overhead costs, allocating these costs to products, and analyzing overhead variances.

Please proceed slowly as you study this chapter. Trace the data to the analysis in a systematic way. In particular, note how fixed manufacturing overhead is accounted for in one way for the planning and control purpose and in a different way for the inventory costing purpose.

PLANNING OF VARIABLE AND FIXED OVERHEAD COSTS

OBJECTIVE 1

Explain the similarities in the planning of variable overhead costs and the planning of fixed overhead costs

We continue the Chapter 7 analysis of the Webb Company. Chapter 7 illustrated how a static-budget variance can be divided into a flexible-budget variance and a sales-volume variance. This chapter focuses on understanding flexible-budget variances for overhead costs and their causes.

Webb's cost structure illustrates why it views the planning of overhead costs as important. The following percentages of total static-budget costs (see column 4 of Exhibit 7-2) are based on Webb's budget for 12,000 output units for April 2000:

	Variable Overhead Costs	Fixed Overhead Costs	Total Overhead Costs
Manufacturing	7.59%	14.54%	22.13%
Marketing	3.16	22.87	26.03
Total	10.75%	37.41%	48.16%

Total overhead costs amount to almost half (48.16%) of Webb's total budgeted costs at 12,000 output units for April 2000. Clearly, Webb can greatly improve its profitability by effective planning of its overhead costs, both variable and fixed.

Planning Variable Overhead Costs

Among Webb's variable manufacturing overhead costs are energy, engineering support, indirect materials, and indirect manufacturing labour. Effective planning of variable overhead costs involves undertaking only value-added variable overhead activities and then managing the cost drivers of those activities in the most efficient way. A **value-added cost** is one that, if eliminated, would reduce the value customers obtain from using the product or service. A **non-value-added cost** is one that, if eliminated, would not reduce the value customers obtain from using the product or service. Consider the cost of sewing needles used in the sewing of jackets manufactured by Webb. Sewing is an essential element of manufacturing a jacket. Hence, costs associated with sewing (for example, sewing needles) would be classified as adding value. In contrast, consider the cost of a warehouse that stores rolls of cloth to be used in case of an emergency (if, say, a supplier fails to meet the delivery schedule). A jacket sewn from cloth stored in a warehouse is no different from a jacket sewn from cloth delivered by a supplier directly to the production floor. Hence, costs associated with warehousing are likely viewed as "non-value-adding." There is a continuum between value-added costs and non-value-added costs. Many overhead cost items are in a gray, uncertain area between value-adding and non-value-adding costs.

Planning Fixed Overhead Costs

Effective planning of fixed overhead costs includes undertaking only value-added fixed overhead activities and then determining the appropriate level for those activities. Webb examples in manufacturing include amortization or leasing costs on plant and equipment, some administrative costs (for example, the plant manager's salary),

Value-added cost. A cost that, if eliminated, would reduce the value customers obtain from using the product or service.

Non-value-added cost. A cost that, if eliminated, would not reduce the value customers obtain from using the product or service.

Manufacturing Overhead Allocation Bases and Rates in the Electronics Industry

Manufacturing overhead costs are the second most important category of manufacturing costs for electronics companies such as Apple Computer, Hewlett-Packard, Hitachi, Philips, Siemens, and Toshiba. Two frequently used allocation bases for manufacturing overhead costs in this industry are direct manufacturing labour dollars (or hours) and direct materials dollars. Many individual companies use both allocation bases (and, in addition, other bases such as hours of equipment testing). Individual segments of this industry differ in their overhead rates, in part because of differences in their cost structures. The following industry data for four segments of the electronics industry are drawn from companies that are members of the American Electronics Association. The four segments are as follows:

◆ **Components.** Includes capacitors, amplifiers, oscillators, and wire and cable

◆ **Computers.** Includes mainframes, minicomputers, and microcomputers

◆ **Peripherals.** Includes disc drives, printers, and keyboards

◆ **Instruments.** Includes test, analytical, and scientific equipment and medical instruments

Hewlett-Packard
www.hp.com

Hitachi
www.hitachi.com
www.hitachi.co.jp

Philips
www.philips.com

Toshiba
www.toshiba.com

	Components	Computers	Peripherals	Instruments
Cost Structure				
Revenues	100.0%	100.0%	100.0%	100.0%
Research and development costs	6.3%	11.4%	8.4%	9.6%
Manufacturing costs:				
Materials and subcontracts	28.3%	36.5%	40.2%	28.6%
Direct manufacturing labour	10.6	2.8	3.2	4.3
Manufacturing overhead	22.6	10.3	12.2	17.0
Total manufacturing costs	61.5	49.6	55.6	49.9
Marketing costs	12.4	17.9	15.9	20.5
General and administrative costs	11.9	7.8	9.6	11.4
Other costs, taxes, and profits	7.9	13.3	10.5	8.6
	100.0%	100.0%	100.0%	100.0%
Average Manufacturing Overhead Rates				
Allocation base is direct manufacturing labour dollars	214.5%	440.0%	277.0%	262.0%
Allocation base is materials dollars	17.0%	15.5%	12.5%	15.0%

The ratio of manufacturing overhead costs to direct manufacturing labour costs ranges from 3.95 for companies manufacturing instruments (17.0% ÷ 4.3%) to 2.13 for companies manufacturing components (22.6% ÷ 10.6%). Clearly, planning and controlling manufacturing overhead costs is a high priority for managers in the electronics industry.

Source: American Electronics Association, *Operating Ratios Survey 1993-94,* (Santa Clara, CA: American Electronics Association, 1993)

and property taxes. Frequently, the most critical issue is how much plant and equipment to acquire. Consider Webb's leasing of weaving machines, each of which has a fixed cost per year. Failure to lease sufficient machine capacity will result in an inability to meet demand and thus in lost sales of jackets. In contrast, if Webb greatly overestimates demand, it will incur additional fixed leasing costs on machines that are not fully utilized during the year.

    At the start of an accounting period, management will likely have made most of the key decisions that determine the level of fixed overhead costs to be incurred. In contrast, day-to-day, ongoing management decisions play a larger role in determining the level of variable overhead costs incurred in that period.

Webb Company Data

The Webb Company summary information for April 2000 that we will use in this chapter is as follows:

Overhead Category	Actual Results	Flexible Budget Amount (for 10,000 output units)	Static Budget Amount (for 12,000 output units)
Variable manufacturing overhead	$130,500	$120,000	$144,000
Fixed manufacturing overhead	285,000	276,000	276,000
Variable marketing overhead	45,700	50,000	60,000
Fixed marketing overhead	420,000	434,000	434,000

DEVELOPING BUDGETED VARIABLE OVERHEAD RATES

Webb uses a three-step approach when developing its variable overhead rate:

◆ **Step 1:** *Identify the costs to include in the variable overhead cost pool(s).* Webb groups all of its variable manufacturing overhead costs in a single cost pool. Costs in this pool include energy, engineering support, indirect materials, and indirect manufacturing labour.

◆ **Step 2:** *Select the cost-allocation base(s).* Webb's operating managers believe that machine-hours are an important driver of variable manufacturing overhead costs and decided to use this measure as the cost allocation base.

◆ **Step 3:** *Estimate the budgeted variable overhead rate(s).* Several approaches can be used in this step. One approach is to adjust the past actual variable overhead cost rate per unit of the allocation base—for example, an adjustment to take into account expected inflation. A second approach is to use standard costing.

Webb uses the standard costing approach to develop its April 2000 budgeted variable overhead cost rate of $30 per machine-hour and also its budgeted machine-hour rate of 0.40 hours per actual output unit. These input amounts are used to compute the budgeted variable manufacturing overhead rate per unit:

$$\text{Budgeted inputs allowed per output unit} \times \text{Budgeted costs per input unit} = 0.40 \times \$30$$
$$= \$12 \text{ per output unit}$$

VARIABLE OVERHEAD COST VARIANCES

We now illustrate how the budgeted variable manufacturing overhead rate is used in computing Webb's variable manufacturing overhead cost variances. The following data are for April 2000:

Cost Item/Allocation Base	Actual Results	Flexible Budget Amount (for 10,000 output units)	Static Budget Amount (for 12,000 output units)
1. Variable manufacturing overhead costs	$130,500	$120,000	$144,000
2. Variable manufacturing overhead costs per machine-hour (1 ÷ 5)	29	30	30
3. Variable manufacturing overhead costs per output unit (1 ÷ 4)	13.05	12	12
4. Output units (jackets)	10,000	10,000	12,000
5. Machine-hours	4,500	4,000	4,800

Static Budget and Flexible Budget Analyses

The Level 1 static-budget variance for variable manufacturing overhead cost is shown in Exhibit 8-1:

$$\begin{aligned}\text{Variable overhead} \atop \text{static budget variance} &= {\text{Actual} \atop \text{results}} - {\text{Static budget} \atop \text{amount}}\\ &= \$130,500 - \$144,000\\ &= \$13,500 \text{ F}\end{aligned}$$

Additional insight into the ability of Webb's managers to control variable manufacturing overhead can be gained by moving to the Level 2 flexible budget analysis, also shown in Exhibit 8-1. The budgeted amounts in Level 2 recognize that 10,000 output units were produced instead of the budgeted 12,000 output units. The April 2000 flexible budget for variable manufacturing overhead is $120,000 $(0.4 \times 10,000 \times \$30)$.

The variable manufacturing overhead sales volume variance arises solely because the actual number of output units sold by Webb differs from the budgeted number of output units sold.

EXHIBIT 8-1
Static and Flexible Budget Analysis of Variable Manufacturing Overhead Costs for the Webb Company for April 2000

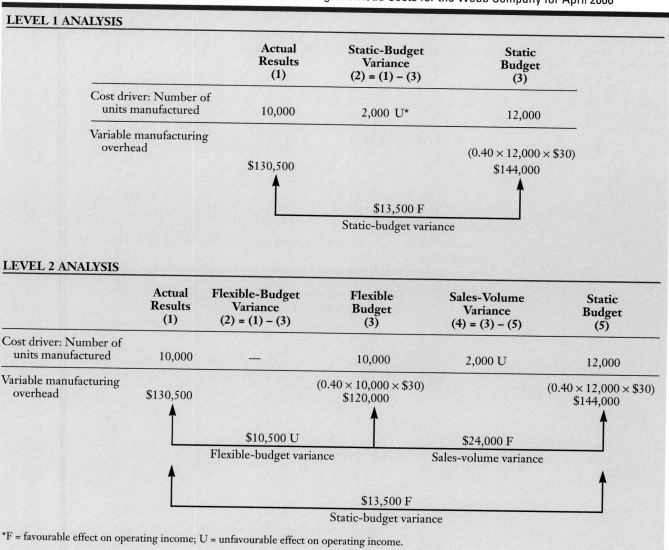

LEVEL 1 ANALYSIS

	Actual Results (1)	Static-Budget Variance (2) = (1) – (3)	Static Budget (3)
Cost driver: Number of units manufactured	10,000	2,000 U*	12,000
Variable manufacturing overhead	$130,500		(0.40 × 12,000 × $30) $144,000

$13,500 F
Static-budget variance

LEVEL 2 ANALYSIS

	Actual Results (1)	Flexible-Budget Variance (2) = (1) – (3)	Flexible Budget (3)	Sales-Volume Variance (4) = (3) – (5)	Static Budget (5)
Cost driver: Number of units manufactured	10,000	—	10,000	2,000 U	12,000
Variable manufacturing overhead	$130,500		(0.40 × 10,000 × $30) $120,000		(0.40 × 12,000 × $30) $144,000

$10,500 U
Flexible-budget variance

$24,000 F
Sales-volume variance

$13,500 F
Static-budget variance

*F = favourable effect on operating income; U = unfavourable effect on operating income.

$$\frac{\text{Variable overhead}}{\text{sales volume variance}} = \frac{\text{Flexible budget}}{\text{amount}} - \frac{\text{Static budget}}{\text{amount}}$$

$$= \$120,000 - \$144,000$$

$$= \$24,000 \text{ F}$$

The variable manufacturing overhead flexible budget variance arises because Webb's actual variable manufacturing overhead cost differs from that budgeted for the actual output units sold:

$$\frac{\text{Variable overhead}}{\text{flexible budget variance}} = \frac{\text{Actual}}{\text{results}} - \frac{\text{Flexible budget}}{\text{amount}}$$

$$= \$130,500 - \$120,000$$

$$= \$10,500 \text{ U}$$

This $10,500 unfavourable flexible-budget variance shows that Webb's actual variable manufacturing overhead exceeded the flexible budget amount by $10,500 for the 10,000 jackets actually produced in April 2000.

We now discuss how managers can gain additional insight by splitting the Level 2 variable manufacturing overhead flexible-budget variance into its Level 3 efficiency and price (labelled *spending* when dealing with overhead) variances. Exhibit 8-2 is the columnar presentation of these Level 3 efficiency and spending variances.

Variable Overhead Efficiency Variance

Variable overhead efficiency variance. The difference between the actual and budgeted quantities of the variable overhead cost allocation base allowed for the actual output units achieved times the budgeted variable overhead cost allocation rate.

The **variable overhead efficiency variance** measures the efficiency with which the cost allocation base is used. The formula is:

$$\frac{\text{Variable overhead}}{\text{efficiency variance}} = \left(\begin{array}{c} \text{Actual units of} \\ \text{variable overhead cost} \\ \text{allocation base used} \\ \text{for actual output units} \\ \text{achieved} \end{array} - \begin{array}{c} \text{Budgeted units of} \\ \text{variable overhead cost} \\ \text{allocation base allowed} \\ \text{for actual output units} \\ \text{achieved} \end{array} \right) \times \begin{array}{c} \text{Budgeted} \\ \text{variable overhead} \\ \text{cost allocation rate} \end{array}$$

$$= [4,500 - (10,000 \times 0.40)] \times \$30$$

$$= (4,500 - 4,000) \times \$30 = 500 \times \$30$$

$$= \$15,000 \text{ U}$$

EXHIBIT 8-2
Columnar Presentation of Variance Analysis: Variable Manufacturing Overhead for the Webb Company

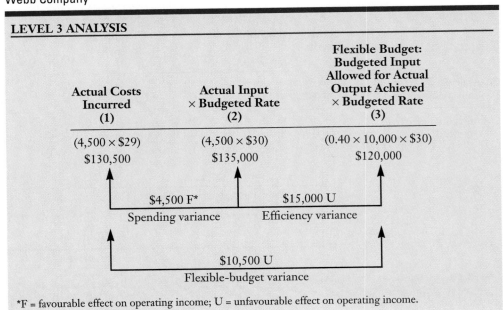

LEVEL 3 ANALYSIS		
Actual Costs Incurred (1)	**Actual Input × Budgeted Rate** (2)	**Flexible Budget: Budgeted Input Allowed for Actual Output Achieved × Budgeted Rate** (3)
(4,500 × $29)	(4,500 × $30)	(0.40 × 10,000 × $30)
$130,500	$135,000	$120,000

$4,500 F* — Spending variance

$15,000 U — Efficiency variance

$10,500 U — Flexible-budget variance

*F = favourable effect on operating income; U = unfavourable effect on operating income.

The variable overhead efficiency variance is computed similarly to the efficiency variance described in Chapter 7 (p. 242) for direct cost items. But the interpretation of the Chapter 7 efficiency variances differs. In Chapter 7, input efficiency variances for direct cost items are based on differences between actual inputs used and the budgeted inputs allowed for actual outputs achieved. Here, efficiency variances for variable overhead costs are based on the efficiency with which the *cost-allocation base* is used. Webb's unfavourable variable overhead efficiency variance of $15,000 means that actual machine-hours (the cost allocation base) were higher than the budgeted machine-hours allowed to manufacture 10,000 jackets. Possible causes of this higher-than-budgeted machine-hour usage include the following:

◆ Webb's workers were less skillful in the use of machines than budgeted.
◆ Webb's production scheduler inefficiently scheduled jobs, resulting in higher-than-budgeted machine usage.
◆ Webb's machines were not maintained in good operating condition.
◆ Budgeted machine time standards were set without careful analysis of the operating conditions.

Management's response to this $15,000 unfavourable variance would be guided by which cause(s) best describe(s) the April 2000 results.

The use of cotton thread for sewing jackets illustrates the difference between the efficiency variance for direct-cost inputs and the efficiency variance for variable-overhead cost categories. If Webb classifies cotton thread as a direct-cost item, the direct materials efficiency variance will indicate whether more or less cotton thread per jacket is used than was budgeted for the actual output achieved. In contrast, if Webb classifies cotton thread as an indirect-cost item, the variable manufacturing overhead efficiency variance will indicate whether Webb used more or fewer machine-hours (the cost allocation base for variable manufacturing overhead) than were budgeted for the actual output achieved. Any variation in cotton thread usage other than that budgeted to vary with respect to machine-hours will be shown in the variable manufacturing overhead spending variance.

Variable Overhead Spending Variance

The **variable overhead spending variance** is the difference between the actual amount of variable overhead incurred and the budgeted amount allowed for the actual quantity of the variable overhead allocation base used for the actual output units achieved. The formula for the variable overhead spending variance is:

$$\begin{pmatrix} \text{Variable overhead} \\ \text{spending variance} \end{pmatrix} = \begin{pmatrix} \text{Actual variable} \\ \text{overhead cost} \\ \text{per unit of cost} \\ \text{allocation base} \end{pmatrix} - \begin{pmatrix} \text{Budgeted variable} \\ \text{overhead cost per} \\ \text{unit of cost} \\ \text{allocation base} \end{pmatrix} \times \begin{pmatrix} \text{Actual quantity of variable} \\ \text{overhead cost allocation} \\ \text{base used for actual output} \\ \text{units achieved} \end{pmatrix}$$

$$= (\$29 - \$30) \times 4,500$$
$$= -\$1 \times 4,500 = \$4,500 \text{ F}$$

Webb operated in April 2000 with a lower-than-budgeted variable overhead cost per machine-hour. Hence, there is a favourable variable overhead spending variance.

The variable overhead spending variance is computed similarly to the price variance described in Chapter 7 (p. 241) for direct cost items such as direct materials. Do not assume, however, that the causes of these two variances are the same. Two main causes could explain a variable overhead spending variance of $4,500 F at Webb:

◆ **Cause A.** The actual prices of individual items included in variable overhead differ from their budgeted prices—for example, the April 2000 purchase price of energy, indirect materials, or indirect manufacturing labour was less than the budget price.
◆ **Cause B.** The actual usage of individual items included in variable overhead differs from the budgeted usage—for example, the budgeted usage of energy, indirect materials, or indirect manufacturing labour was less than the usage

Variable overhead spending variance. The difference between the actual amount of variable overhead incurred and the budgeted amount allowed for the actual quantity of the variable overhead allocation base used for the actual output units achieved.

assumed in setting the $30 budgeted variable manufacturing overhead rate per machine-hour.

Cause A has implications for the purchasing area of Webb. Cause B has implications for the production area of Webb. Distinguishing between these two causes for a variable overhead spending variance requires detailed information about the budgeted prices and the budgeted quantities of the individual line items in the variable overhead cost pool.

The following is a summary of the variable manufacturing overhead variances computed in this section:

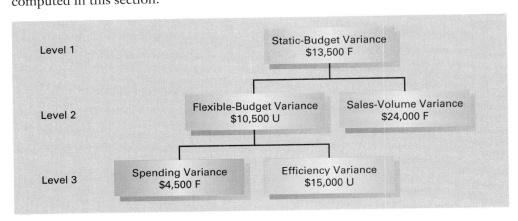

The key cause of Webb's unfavourable flexible budget variance is that the actual use of machine-hours is higher than budgeted.

DEVELOPING BUDGETED FIXED OVERHEAD RATES

OBJECTIVE 3

Compute the budgeted fixed overhead rate

Fixed overhead costs are, by definition, a lump sum that does not change in total despite changes in a cost driver. While total fixed costs are frequently included in flexible budgets, they remain the same total amount within the relevant range regardless of the output level chosen to "flex" the variable costs and revenues. The four steps in developing Webb Company's budgeted fixed overhead rate are as follows:

◆ **Step 1:** *Choose the time period used to compute the budget.* As with variable overhead rates, the budget period is typically twelve months. Chapter 4 provides three reasons for using annual overhead rates rather than, say, monthly rates— reducing the influence of seasonality, reducing the effect of the varying number of days in a month, and preventing management time from being tied up in monthly budget rate setting.

◆ **Step 2:** *Identify the costs in the fixed overhead cost pool(s).* This is the numerator of the budgeted rate computation. For Webb, fixed manufacturing overhead costs include depreciation, plant leasing costs, property taxes, plant manager's salary, and some administrative costs, all of which are included in a single cost pool. Webb's budget is $276,000 for April 2000.

Denominator level (production denominator level, production denominator volume). Quantity of the allocation base used to allocate fixed overhead costs to a cost object.

◆ **Step 3:** *Estimate the budgeted quantity of the allocation base(s).* This is the denominator of the budgeted rate computation. It is termed the **denominator level.** Webb uses machine-hours as its allocation base. It budgets to manufacture 12,000 jackets in April 2000. The budgeted machine-hours to manufacture 12,000 jackets is 4,800 (12,000 × 0.40 budgeted machine-hours per output unit).

◆ **Step 4:** *Compute the budgeted fixed overhead rate(s).*

$$\text{Budgeted fixed overhead rate per unit of allocation base} = \frac{\text{Budgeted fixed overhead costs}}{\text{Budgeted quantity of allocation base units}}$$

$$= \frac{\$276,000}{4,800 \text{ machine-hours}}$$

$$= \$57.50 \text{ per machine-hour}$$

In manufacturing settings, the denominator level is commonly termed the **production denominator level** or the **production denominator volume.**

FIXED OVERHEAD COST VARIANCES

The Level 1 static-budget variance for Webb's fixed manufacturing overhead is $9,000 U:

$$\frac{\text{Fixed overhead}}{\text{static-budget variance}} = \frac{\text{Actual}}{\text{results}} - \frac{\text{Static budget}}{\text{amount}}$$

$$= \$285,000 - \$276,000$$

$$= \$9,000 \text{ U}$$

The actual results for fixed manufacturing overhead are in Exhibit 7-2. The static budget amount for fixed manufacturing overhead is based on 12,000 output units. Given that it is for a fixed cost, this same $276,000 would be the budgeted amount for all output levels in the relevant range. There is no "flexing" of fixed costs.

The formula for the fixed manufacturing overhead flexible budget variance is as follows:

$$\frac{\text{Fixed overhead}}{\text{flexible-budget variance}} = \frac{\text{Actual}}{\text{results}} - \frac{\text{Flexible budget}}{\text{amount}}$$

$$= \$285,000 - \$276,000$$

$$= \$9,000 \text{ U}$$

The fixed overhead flexible-budget variance is the same as the fixed overhead static-budget variance. Why? Because there is no "flexing" of fixed costs. For Level 3 analysis (decomposing the flexible-budget variance into its efficiency and spending components), all of the flexible-budget variance is attributed to the spending variance because this is precisely why this variance arises for fixed costs.

The $9,000 unfavourable variance simply means that Webb spent more on fixed manufacturing overhead in April 2000 than it budgeted.

A summary of the Levels 1, 2, and 3 variance analyses for Webb's fixed manufacturing overhead in April 2000 is as follows:

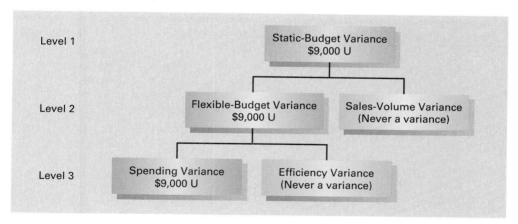

There is never a sales-volume variance in Level 2 for fixed overhead costs. Why? Because budgeted fixed costs are, by definition, unaffected by sales volume changes. Similarly, there is never an efficiency variance in Level 3 for fixed overhead costs. After all, a manager cannot be more or less efficient in dealing with a given amount of fixed costs.

PRODUCTION-VOLUME VARIANCE

The variances discussed so far in this chapter are presented in Exhibit 8-3: Panel A for variable costs and the first three columns of Panel B for fixed costs. We now discuss a new variance for fixed overhead costs (shown on the right-hand side of Exhibit 8-3,

Panel B). The **production-volume variance** is the difference between budgeted fixed overhead and the fixed overhead allocated. Fixed overhead is allocated based on the fixed overhead rate times the quantity of the fixed overhead allocation base for the actual output units achieved. Other terms for this variance include **denominator-level variance** and **output-level overhead variance.**

The formula for the production volume variance, expressed in terms of allocation base units (machine-hours for Webb), is:

$$\begin{array}{l}\text{Production-} \\ \text{volume} \\ \text{variance}\end{array} = \begin{array}{l}\text{Budgeted} \\ \text{fixed} \\ \text{overhead}\end{array} - \left(\begin{array}{l}\text{Fixed overhead allocated using} \\ \text{budgeted input allowed for} \\ \text{actual output units achieved}\end{array} \times \begin{array}{l}\text{Budgeted fixed} \\ \text{overhead rate}\end{array}\right)$$

$$= \$276{,}000 - (0.40 \times 10{,}000 \times \$57.50)$$

$$= \$276{,}000 - (4{,}000 \times \$57.50)$$

$$= \$276{,}000 - \$230{,}000$$

$$= \$46{,}000 \text{ U}$$

The amount used for budgeted fixed overhead will be the same lump sum shown in the static budget and also in any flexible budget within the relevant range. Fixed overhead costs allocated is the sum of the individual fixed overhead costs allocated to each of the products manufactured during the accounting period.

Panel A of Exhibit 8-3 does not have the column 4 shown for Panel B. Why? Because column 4 does not apply to variable overhead costs. The amount of variable overhead allocated is always the same as the flexible budget amount.

Interpreting the Production-Volume Variance

The production volume variance arises whenever actual production differs from the denominator level used to calculate the budgeted fixed overhead rate. We compute this rate because inventory costing and some types of contracts require fixed overhead costs to be expressed on a unit-of-output basis. The production volume variance

EXHIBIT 8-3
Variance Analysis: Variable and Fixed Manufacturing Overhead for the Webb Company

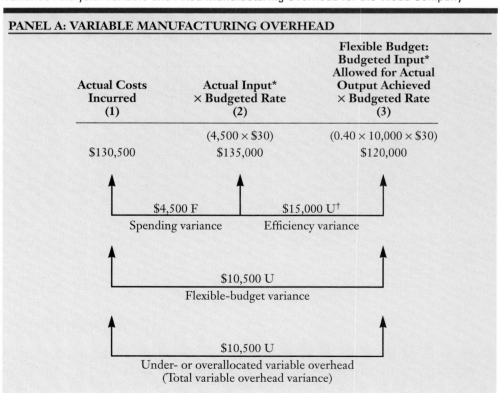

EXHIBIT 8-3 *continued*

PANEL B: FIXED MANUFACTURING OVERHEAD

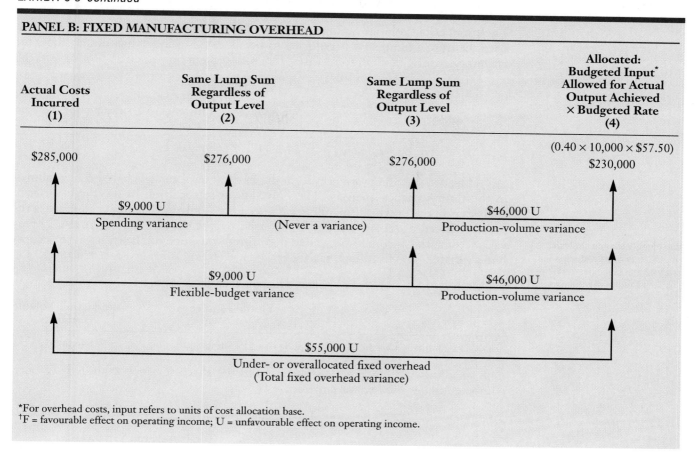

Actual Costs Incurred (1)	Same Lump Sum Regardless of Output Level (2)	Same Lump Sum Regardless of Output Level (3)	Allocated: Budgeted Input* Allowed for Actual Output Achieved × Budgeted Rate (4)
$285,000	$276,000	$276,000	(0.40 × 10,000 × $57.50) $230,000

$9,000 U   Spending variance   (Never a variance) $46,000 U   Production-volume variance

$9,000 U   Flexible-budget variance $46,000 U   Production-volume variance

$55,000 U   Under- or overallocated fixed overhead (Total fixed overhead variance)

*For overhead costs, input refers to units of cost allocation base.
†F = favourable effect on operating income; U = unfavourable effect on operating income.

results from "unitizing" fixed costs. Be careful not to attribute much economic significance to this variance. The most common misinterpretation is to assume this variance measures the economic cost of producing and selling 10,000 units rather than the 12,000 budgeted for April. This assumption does not consider why Webb sold only 10,000 units. Assume that a new competitor had gained market share by pricing below what Webb charged its customers. To sell the budgeted 12,000 units, Webb may have had to reduce its own selling price on all 12,000 units. Suppose it decided that selling 10,000 units at a higher price yielded higher operating income than selling 12,000 units at a lower price. The production volume variance does not take into account such information. Hence, it would be misleading to interpret the $46,000 unfavourable amount as Webb's economic cost of selling 2,000 units fewer than the budgeted quantity of 12,000 units for April.

INTEGRATED ANALYSIS OF OVERHEAD-COST VARIANCES

Exhibit 8-3 illustrates the four variances explained in this chapter. When all four variances are presented, it is called a four-variance analysis.

Four-Variance Analysis

	Spending Variance	Efficiency Variance	Production-Volume Variance
Variable Manufacturing Overhead	$4,500 F	$15,000 U	(Never a variance)
Fixed Manufacturing Overhead	$9,000 U	(Never a variance)	$46,000 U

The four variances in this presentation are the two variable manufacturing overhead variances and the two fixed manufacturing overhead variances. Note also that two areas show "Never a variance." Why? The efficiency variance pertains only

OBJECTIVE 5

Explain how variance analysis can provide an integrated overview of overhead-cost variances

to variable manufacturing overhead. There can be no efficiency for fixed manufacturing overhead because this amount is a lump sum regardless of the output level. The production-volume variance pertains only to fixed manufacturing overhead. It arises because a lump sum is required to be allocated to individual output units for inventory costing (and, in some cases, for contract reimbursement).

Three-Variance Analysis

	Spending Variance	Efficiency Variance	Production-Volume Variance
Total Manufacturing Overhead	$4,500 U	$15,000 U	$46,000 U

The two spending variances from the four-variance analysis have been combined in the three-variance analysis. The only loss of information in the three-variance analysis is in the overhead spending variance area—only one spending variance is reported instead of separate variable and fixed overhead spending variances. Three-variance analysis is sometimes called **combined-variance analysis,** because it combines variable- and fixed-cost variances when reporting overhead cost variances.

Combined-variance analysis. Approach to overhead-variance analysis that combines variable-cost and fixed-cost variances.

Two-Variance Analysis

	Flexible-Budget Variance	Production-Volume Variance
Total Manufacturing Overhead	$19,500 U	$46,000 U

The spending and efficiency variances from the three-variance analysis have been combined under the two-variance analysis.

One-Variance Analysis

	Total Overhead Variance
Total Manufacturing Overhead	$65,500 U

The single variance of $65,500 U in one-variance analysis is the sum of the flexible-budget variance and the production-volume variance under two-variance analysis. Using figures from Exhibit 8-3, the total overhead variance is the difference between the total actual manufacturing overhead incurred ($130,500 + $285,000 = $415,500) and the manufacturing overhead allocated to the actual output units produced ($120,000 + $230,000 = $350,000). The $65,500 unfavourable total manufacturing overhead variance for the Webb Company in April 2000 is largely the result of the $46,000 unfavourable production-volume variance. Using the four-variance analysis presentation, the next-largest amount (after the $46,000) is the $15,000 unfavourable variable overhead efficiency variance. This variance arises from the additional 500 machine-hours used in April 2000 above the 4,000 machine-hours allowed to manufacture the 10,000 jackets. The two spending variances ($4,500 F and $9,000 U) partially offset each other.

The variances in Webb's four-variance analysis are not necessarily independent of each other. For example, Webb may purchase lower-quality machine fluids (giving rise to a favourable spending variance); this results in a slower operating speed for the machines than was budgeted (giving rise to an unfavourable efficiency variance).

OVERHEAD-COST VARIANCES IN NONMANUFACTURING SETTINGS

Our Webb Company example examines variable and fixed manufacturing overhead costs. Under generally accepted accounting principles, both variable and fixed manufacturing overhead costs are inventoriable costs for financial reporting purposes. In contrast, the overhead costs of nonmanufacturing areas of the value chain (such as R&D and marketing) are not inventoriable costs under generally accepted accounting principles; they either are capitalized noninventoriable costs or are immediately expensed to the period in which they are incurred. Should the overhead costs of nonmanufacturing areas be examined using the variance analysis framework discussed in this chapter?

Variable cost information pertaining to nonmanufacturing as well as manufacturing costs is used for pricing decisions and for decisions about which products to emphasize. Variance analysis of all variable overhead costs is important when analyzing such decisions. For example, managers in industries with high distribution costs may invest in accounting systems that give reliable and timely information on spending and efficiency variances for variable distribution costs.

Variance analysis of fixed nonmanufacturing overhead costs is important where a company is doing work on a full-actual-cost-plus basis—that is, where it is reimbursed for its full actual costs plus an additional percentage of those costs. Here, information on these variances enables more accurate estimates of actual costs to be computed. In many other cases, however, managers do not conduct detailed variance analysis of fixed nonmanufacturing costs. Most believe little information is gained by computing spending or efficiency variances for these fixed nonmanufacturing costs.

DIFFERENT PURPOSES OF MANUFACTURING OVERHEAD COST ANALYSIS

Different types of cost analysis may be appropriate for different purposes. Consider the planning and control purpose and the inventory costing for financial reporting purpose. Panel A of Exhibit 8-4 depicts variable manufacturing overhead for each purpose; Panel B depicts fixed manufacturing overhead for each purpose.

OBJECTIVE 6

Explain the differing roles of cost allocation bases for fixed manufacturing overhead when (a) planning and controlling and (b) inventory costing

Variable Manufacturing Overhead Costs

Webb's variable manufacturing overhead is shown in Panel A of Exhibit 8-4 as being variable, with respect to output units (jackets) produced, for both the planning and control purpose (graph 1) and the inventory costing purpose (graph 2). The greater the number of output units manufactured, the higher will be the budgeted total variable manufacturing overhead costs and the total variable manufacturing overhead costs allocated to output units.

Graph 1 of Exhibit 8-4 presents an overall picture of how total variable overhead might behave. Of course, variable overhead consists of many items, including energy costs, repairs, indirect labour, and so on. Managers help control variable overhead costs by budgeting each line item and then investigating possible causes for any significant variances.

Fixed Manufacturing Overhead Costs

Panel B of Exhibit 8-4 (graph 3) shows that, for the planning and control purpose, fixed overhead costs do not change in the 8,000-to-16,000-unit output range. Consider a monthly leasing cost of $20,000 for a building under a three-year leasing agreement. Managers control this fixed leasing cost at the time the lease is signed. During any month in the leasing period, management can do little to change this $20,000 lump sum payment. Contrast this description of fixed overhead with how these costs are depicted for the inventory costing purpose, graph 4 of Panel B. Under generally accepted accounting principles, fixed manufacturing costs are capitalized as part of inventory on a unit-of-output basis. Every output unit that Webb manufactures will increase the fixed overhead allocated to products by $23 ($57.50 per machine-hour × 0.40 machine-hours per output unit). Managers should not use this unitization of fixed manufacturing overhead costs for their planning and control.

The denominator level in each graph in Exhibit 8-4 is expressed in output units produced. Alternatively, we could also have expressed this denominator in terms of input units. For Webb, machine-hours would be the chosen denominator, as this is the allocation base for both variable and fixed manufacturing overhead costs.

EXHIBIT 8-4
Behaviour of Variable and Fixed Manufacturing Overhead Costs for Planning and Control and for Inventory Costing

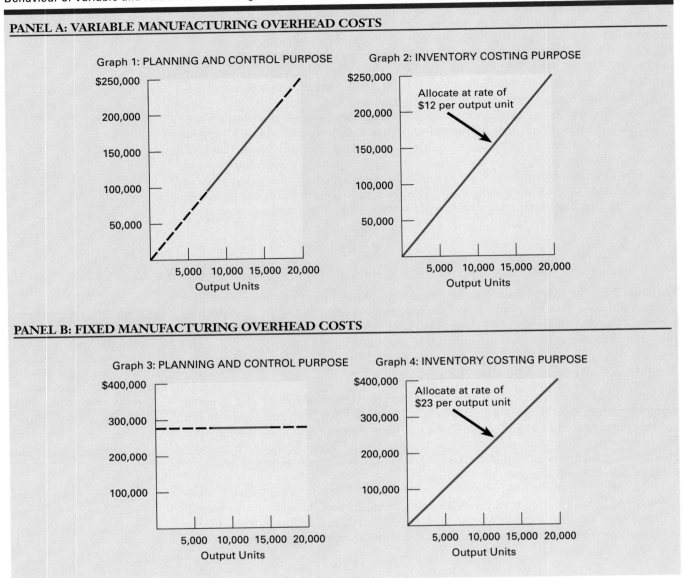

PANEL A: VARIABLE MANUFACTURING OVERHEAD COSTS

Graph 1: PLANNING AND CONTROL PURPOSE

Graph 2: INVENTORY COSTING PURPOSE
Allocate at rate of $12 per output unit

PANEL B: FIXED MANUFACTURING OVERHEAD COSTS

Graph 3: PLANNING AND CONTROL PURPOSE

Graph 4: INVENTORY COSTING PURPOSE
Allocate at rate of $23 per output unit

JOURNAL ENTRIES FOR OVERHEAD COSTS AND VARIANCES

Recording Overhead Costs

OBJECTIVE 7

Prepare journal entries for variable and fixed overhead variances

Previously, in the Robinson Company job costing example, a single manufacturing overhead control account was used. This chapter illustrates separate variable and fixed manufacturing overhead control accounts. Each overhead control account requires its own overhead allocated account.

Consider the following journal entries for the Webb Company. Recall that for April 2000:

	Actual Results	Flexible Budget Amount (10,000 units)	Allocated Amount
Variable manufacturing overhead	$130,500	$120,000*	$120,000*
Fixed manufacturing overhead	285,000	276,000†	230,000‡

*0.40 × 10,000 × $30 = $120,000.
†$276,000 is the budgeted fixed manufacturing overhead.
‡0.40 × 10,000 × $57.50 = $230,000.

The budgeted variable overhead rate is $30 per machine-hour. The denominator level for fixed manufacturing overhead is 4,800 machine-hours of input with a budgeted rate of $57.50 per machine-hour. Webb uses four-variance analysis.

During the accounting period, actual variable overhead and actual fixed overhead costs are accumulated in separate control accounts. As each unit is manufactured, the budgeted variable and fixed overhead rates are used to record the amounts in the respective overhead allocated accounts.

Entries for variable manufacturing overhead for April 2000 are:

1. Variable Manufacturing Overhead Control   130,500
     Accounts Payable Control and other accounts   130,500
     To record actual variable manufacturing overhead costs incurred.

2. Work-in-Process Control   120,000
     Variable Manufacturing Overhead Allocated   120,000
     To record variable manufacturing overhead cost allocated
     (0.40 × 10,000 × $30).

3. Variable Manufacturing Overhead Allocated   120,000
     Variable Manufacturing Overhead Efficiency Variance   15,000
     Variable Manufacturing Overhead Control   130,500
     Variable Manufacturing Overhead Spending Variance   4,500
     To isolate variances for the accounting period.

Entries for fixed manufacturing overhead are:

1. Fixed Manufacturing Overhead Control   285,000
     Wages Payable, Accumulated Amortization, etc.   285,000
     To record actual fixed overhead costs incurred.

2. Work-in-Process Control   230,000
     Fixed Manufacturing Overhead Allocated   230,000
     To record fixed manufacturing overhead costs allocated
     (0.40 × 10,000 × $57.50).

3. Fixed Manufacturing Overhead Allocated   230,000
     Fixed Manufacturing Overhead Spending Variance   9,000
     Fixed Manufacturing Production Volume Variance   46,000
     Fixed Manufacturing Overhead Control   285,000
     To isolate variances for the accounting period.

The end-of-period adjustments for these variances are now discussed.

Overhead Variances and End-of-Period Adjustments

Chapter 4 outlined the adjusted allocation rate approach and the proration approach to handling the end-of-period difference between manufacturing overhead incurred and manufacturing overhead allocated. Consider Webb's variable manufacturing overhead. The budgeted rate was $30 per machine-hour. The actual rate is $29 per machine-hour.

Under the adjusted allocation rate approach, Webb would adjust the job record of every job worked on during the year. This adjustment, in effect, would entail using the actual rate per machine-hour of $29 instead of the budgeted rate of $30. Then, Webb would accordingly recompute the ending inventory and cost of goods sold for the accounting period. This approach has several benefits. Individual job records are restated to show actual costs accurately. Also, ending inventory and cost of goods sold would accurately show actual variable overhead incurred. A similar approach could be used to restate the fixed manufacturing overhead in job records. Providing all accounting records are on compatible computer systems, the adjusted allocation rate approach can often be done in a low-cost, timely manner.

The proration approach is used where managers view the adjusted allocation rate approach as not being cost-effective. The three main options for disposing of variances under this approach are:

◆ Proration based on the allocated overhead amount (before proration) in the ending balances of Inventory and Cost of Goods Sold

◆ Proration based on total ending balances (before proration) in Inventory and Cost of Goods Sold

◆ Immediate write-off to Cost of Goods Sold

Webb could use any one of these options when prorating the $10,500 of underallocated variable manufacturing overhead (and the $55,000 of underallocated fixed manufacturing overhead).

FINANCIAL AND NONFINANCIAL PERFORMANCE MEASURES

OBJECTIVE 8

Explain why managers frequently use both financial and nonfinancial variables to plan and control overhead costs

The overhead variances discussed in this chapter are examples of financial performance measures. Managers also find that nonfinancial measures provide useful information. Examples of such measures that Webb would likely find useful in planning and controlling its overhead costs are:

1. Actual indirect materials usage in metres per machine-hour, compared with budgeted indirect materials usage in metres per machine-hour

2. Actual energy usage per machine-hour, compared with budgeted energy usage per machine-hour

3. Actual machining time per job, compared with budgeted machining time per job

CONCEPTS IN ACTION

Standard Costing and Daily Income Statements at Asia-Pacific Rayon

Asia-Pacific Rayon (APR) manufactures rayon fibre at its Indonesian plant. Its output is sold on the export market to companies in China, Malaysia, Pakistan, and South Korea, as well as to Indonesian spinning-mills. APR receives export-market inquiries on a daily basis. Potential customers can differ greatly in terms of the size of the order, the price paid, and the related cost of manufacture and distribution. Some large customers enter the market unpredictably, buy large quantities, and require large discounts. To help in negotiations over the price and terms of new business with potential customers, APR uses a standard costing system. This system is also central to ARP's innovative daily income statement. The owner of APR has developed this daily income-reporting system to remain continually updated on the profit implications of the ever-changing mix of jobs being produced at negotiated terms that can vary dramatically across customers.

The daily income statement includes net revenues, cost of goods sold, operating expenses, and allocated costs. Net revenues are selling prices less variable selling expenses (such as freight, commissions, and discounts). The materials, labour, and plant operating costs are based on a standard costing system. These standards are prepared and updated every month on the basis of new information, including that month's actual performance. APR allocates budgeted overhead costs on the basis of budgeted production volume. The overhead costs allocated include fixed selling, general, and administrative costs, and interest costs, as well as fixed manufacturing overhead costs.

APR's use of a daily income statement is relatively unusual. Although many companies track costs for key items on a daily basis, few report a daily income statement. Managers at APR believe this statement increases the profit consciousness of the company. The Chief Executive Officer (located away from the production facility) uses the statement to monitor the performance of the top operating managers. For example, the profit implications of equipment breakdowns at the plant are highlighted quickly in a daily income statement. Variances for each of its cost categories are computed monthly. These variances are an integral part of the performance measures the CEO uses to evaluate key operating personnel.

Source: Case by L. Lakshmanan and R. Ramarian, "Asia-Pacific Rayon Company."

These performance measures, like the variances discussed in this chapter, are best viewed as attention-directors, not problem-solvers. These performance measures would probably be reported on the manufacturing floor on a daily, or even hourly, basis. The manufacturing overhead variances we discussed in this chapter capture the financial effects of items such as 1, 2, and 3, which in many cases first appear as nonfinancial performance "flags."

Both financial and nonfinancial performance measures are key inputs when evaluating the performance of managers. Exclusive reliance on either one is nearly always simplistic.

VARIANCE ANALYSIS FOR ACTIVITY AREAS

The Webb Company example focused on variance analysis where the output measure is units of product manufactured. This same variance analysis framework can be used to analyze variances at individual activity areas. Recall from Chapter 5 that activity analysis is a building block when designing and operating an activity-based costing system.

The Problem for Self-Study illustrates variance analysis for the testing activity area of a semiconductor manufacturing facility. The output measure at this activity area is the number of tests conducted. While each test takes the same time, products differ in the number of tests conducted. Semiconductor chips produced for military and aerospace customers often require a larger number of tests than do chips produced for (say) personal computer manufacturers. Over time, the number of total tests conducted at this activity area will be a function of both the total number of products produced at the plant and the mix of customers with differing testing requirements.

PROBLEM FOR SELF-STUDY

Dragon Semiconductor, a manufacturer of semiconductor chips, is analyzing the variable and fixed costs in its testing activity area. Mark Coyne, the manager of the testing area, has been asked to explain why the actual activity area cost of $4,758,000 in 2000 differs from the static budget amount of $4,800,000 at the start of 2000.

Coyne collects data on (i) the number of tests done (the output measure in this activity area), (ii) testing hours (the cost driver for variable costs), and (iii) the variable and fixed activity area costs. Both variable and fixed costs are allocated to products tested on the basis of standard hours of test time per product. Each semiconductor test has the same standard test time. Coyne uses the data collected to develop the following summary:

	Actual Results	Flexible Budget Amount (for 310,000 tests)	Static Budget Amount (for 320,000 tests)
1. Output units (tests)	310,000	310,000	320,000
2. Testing hours	77,500	93,000	96,000
3. Testing hours per test: (2 ÷ 1)	0.25	0.30	0.30
4. Variable testing activity area costs	$1,472,500	$1,860,000	$1,920,000
5. Variable testing activity area costs per testing hour: (4 ÷ 2)	$19.00	$20.00	$20.00
6. Variable testing activity area costs per test: (4 ÷ 1)	$4.75	$6.00	$6.00
7. Fixed testing activity area costs	$3,286,000	$2,880,000	$2,880,000
8. Fixed testing activity area costs per testing hour: (7 ÷ 2)	$42.40	$30.97 (approx.)	$30.00
9. Fixed testing activity area costs per test (7 ÷ 1)	$10.60	$9.29 (approx.)	$9.00

REQUIRED

1. Reconcile the $4,758,500 actual activity costs for 2000 with the static-budget amount of $4,800,000.
2. Reconcile the $4,758,500 actual activity costs for 2000 with the testing area standard costs allocated to products tested in 2000.

SOLUTION

1. Exhibit 8-5 reports the variance analysis of Dragon's testing activity area. A summary reconciliation between actual activity costs of $4,758,500 and the static-budget amount of $4,800,000 is:

	Actual costs incurred	=	Static budget	+	End of period variances	
Variable activity costs	$1,472,500 = $1,920,000 − $447,500 F				Sales-volume var.	$ 60,000 F
					Spending var.	77,500 F
					Efficiency var.	310,000 F
						$447,500 F
Fixed activity costs	$3,286,000 = $2,880,000 + 406,000 U				Spending var.	$406,000 U
Total activity costs	$4,758,500 = $4,800,000 − $41,500 F					

There are two large offsetting variances:

(i) The $310,000 favourable efficiency variance and the $77,500 favourable spending variance for variable testing activity costs—the actual average time for a test was 0.25 hours compared with the budgeted 0.30 hours.

(ii) The $406,000 unfavourable spending variance for fixed testing activity costs.

Dragon should examine possible interdependencies across these variances. For example, did the testing area lease more expensive testing equipment (with higher fixed costs)? Did the new equipment reduce the time required to test the electrical and other performance specifications of each semiconductor chip?

2. Each product unit tested in Dragon's testing area will be allocated the following two standard cost amounts:

◆ Variable activity cost of $6.00 per test
◆ Fixed activity cost of $9.00 per test

During 2000, Dragon made 310,000 tests. The testing area total standard costs allocated to products tested in 2000 were:

Variable activity area costs allocated	$1,860,000	(310,000 × $6.00)
Fixed activity area costs allocated	2,790,000	(310,000 × $9.00)
Total activity area costs allocated	$4,650,000	

The data in Exhibit 8-5 can be used to reconcile the actual testing area costs of $4,758,500 and the testing area standard costs allocated to products of $4,650,000:

	Actual Costs Incurred	=	Standard Cost Amounts Allocated during Period	+	End of Period Variance	
Variable activity costs	$1,472,500 = $1,860,000 − $387,500 F				Spending var.	$ 77,500 F
					Efficiency var.	310,000 F
						$387,500 F

Fixed activity costs	$3,286,500 = $2,790,000 − $496,000 U	Spending var. Prodn. vol. var.	$406,500 U 90,000 U
			$496,000 U
Total activity costs	$4,758,500 = $4,650,000+$108,500 U		

EXHIBIT 8-5
Static-Budget and Flexible-Budget Analysis of Variable and Fixed Testing Activity Area Costs for Dragon Semiconductor Company for 2000

LEVEL 1 ANALYSIS

	Actual Costs Incurred (1)	Static-Budget Variance (2) = (1) − (3)	Static Budget (3)
Number of tests conducted	310,000	310,000	320,000
Variable activity area costs	$1,472,500	$447,500 F	$1,920,000
Fixed activity area costs	3,286,000	406,000 U	2,880,000
Total activity area costs	$4,758,500	$41,500 F	$4,800,000

$41,500 F
Static-budget variance

LEVEL 2 ANALYSIS

	Actual Costs Incurred (1)	Flexible-Budget Variance (2) = (1) − (3)	Flexible Budget (3)	Sales-Volume Variance (4) = (3) − (5)	Static Budget (5)
Number of tests conducted	310,000		310,000	10,000	320,000
Variable activity area costs	$1,472,500	$387,500 F	$1,860,000	$60,000 F	$1,920,000
Fixed activity area costs	3,286,000	406,000 U	2,880,000	0	2,880,000
Total activity area costs	$4,758,500	$ 18,500 U	$4,740,000	$60,000 F	$4,800,000

$18,500 U
Flexible-budget variance

$60,000 F
Sales-volume variance

$41,500 F
Static-budget variance

LEVEL 3 ANALYSIS   Variable Activity Area Costs

Actual Costs Incurred (1)	Actual Inputs Budgeted Rate (2)	Flexible Budget: Budgeted Input Allowed for Actual Output Achieved × Budgeted Rate (3)
(77,500 × $19.00)	(77,500 × $20)	(0.3 × 310,000 × $20.00)
$1,472,500	**$1,550,000**	**$1,860,000**

$77,500 F
Spending variance

$310,000 F
Efficiency variance

$387,500 F
Flexible-budget variance

EXHIBIT 8-5   *continued*

LEVEL 3 ANALYSIS   Fixed Activity Area Costs

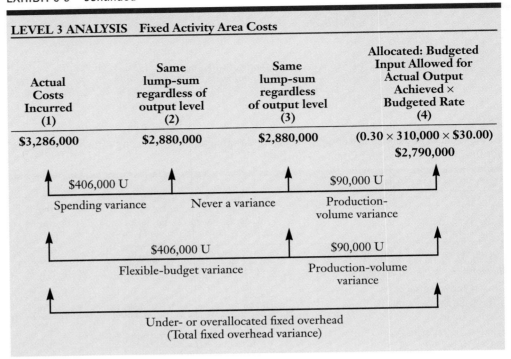

Actual Costs Incurred (1)	Same lump-sum regardless of output level (2)	Same lump-sum regardless of output level (3)	Allocated: Budgeted Input Allowed for Actual Output Achieved × Budgeted Rate (4)
$3,286,000	$2,880,000	$2,880,000	(0.30 × 310,000 × $30.00) $2,790,000

$406,000 U — Spending variance

Never a variance

$90,000 U — Production-volume variance

$406,000 U — Flexible-budget variance

$90,000 U — Production-volume variance

Under- or overallocated fixed overhead
(Total fixed overhead variance)

SUMMARY

The following points are linked to the chapter's learning objectives.

1. Planning of variable overhead costs involves undertaking only value-added variable cost activities and then efficiently managing the cost drivers of those activities. Planning of fixed overhead costs includes undertaking only value-added fixed cost activities and then determining the appropriate level of those activities, given the expected demand and the level of uncertainty pertaining to that demand.

2. When the flexible budget for variable overhead is developed, a spending variance and an efficiency variance can be computed. The variable overhead spending variance is the difference between the actual amount of variable overhead incurred and the budgeted amount that is allowed for the actual quantity of the variable overhead allocation base used for the actual output units achieved. The variable overhead efficiency variance measures the efficiency with which the cost-allocation base is used; this is a different type of efficiency variance than that calculated in Chapter 7 for direct-cost items, such as direct materials.

3. The budgeted fixed overhead rate is calculated by dividing the budgeted fixed overhead costs by the budgeted quantity of allocation base units. This rate is calculated for inventory costing and, in some cases, for contract reimbursement.

4. Production-volume variances are rarely a good measure of the opportunity cost of unused capacity. For example, the plant capacity level may exceed the budgeted level; hence, some unused capacity may not be included in the denominator. Moreover, the production-volume variance focuses only on costs. It does not take into account any price changes necessary to spur extra demand that would in turn make use of any idle capacity.

5. A four-variance analysis presents spending and efficiency variances for variable overhead costs and spending- and production-volume variances for fixed overhead costs. By analyzing these four variances together, managers can consider possible interrelationships among them. These variances collectively measure differences between actual and budgeted amounts for output level, selling prices, variable costs, and fixed costs.

6. For planning and control, fixed manufacturing overhead is a lump sum that is unaffected by the budgeted quantity of the fixed overhead allocation base. In contrast, for inventory costing the unitized fixed manufacturing overhead rate will be affected by the budgeted quantity of the fixed overhead allocation base.

7. The separate analysis of variable and fixed overhead costs requires the use of separate variable and fixed overhead control accounts and separate variable and fixed overhead allocated accounts. At the end of each accounting period, any variances for variable or fixed overhead costs can be disposed of as illustrated in Chapter 5.

8. Managers use both financial and nonfinancial measures to plan and control overhead costs. In many cases, overhead variances initially appear as nonfinancial measures. Expressing these measures in financial terms can highlight the relative importance of different types of nonfinancial performance gaps.

▼ TERMS TO LEARN

This chapter contains definitions of the following important terms:

combined-variance analysis (p. 268)
denominator level (p. 264)
denominator-level variance (p. 266)
non-value-added cost (p. 258)
output-level overhead variance (p. 266)
production denominator level (p. 264)

production denominator volume (p. 264)
production-volume variance (p. 266)
value-added cost (p. 258)
variable overhead efficiency variance (p. 262)
variable overhead spending variance (p. 263)

▼ ASSIGNMENT MATERIAL

QUESTIONS

8-1 What are the steps in planning variable overhead costs?

8-2 How does the planning of fixed overhead costs differ from the planning of variable overhead costs?

8-3 How does a standard costing system differ from an actual costing system?

8-4 What are the steps in developing a budgeted variable overhead cost rate?

8-5 The spending variance for variable manufacturing overhead is affected by several factors. Explain.

8-6 Assume variable manufacturing overhead is allocated using machine-hours. Give three possible reasons for a $25,000 favourable variable overhead efficiency variance.

8-7 Describe the difference between a direct materials efficiency variance and a variable manufacturing overhead efficiency variance.

8-8 What are the steps in developing a budgeted fixed overhead rate?

8-9 Why is the flexible-budget variance the same amount as the spending variance for fixed manufacturing overhead?

8-10 Explain how four-variance analysis differs from one-, two-, and three-variance analysis.

8-11 What variances might explain how actual overhead costs differ from the overhead costs in the static budget?

8-12 What variances might explain how actual overhead costs differ from the standard overhead costs allocated during the period?

8-13 "Overhead variances should be viewed as interdependent rather than independent." Give an example.

8-14 Explain how the analysis of fixed overhead costs differs for (a) planning and control on the one hand and (b) inventory costing for financial reporting on the other.

8-15 How can the Levels 1 to 3 variance analysis approach be used in control of costs in activity areas?

EXERCISES

8-16 Variable manufacturing overhead, variance analysis. Esquire Clothing is a manufacturer of designer suits. The cost of each suit is the sum of three variable costs (direct material costs, direct manufacturing labour costs, and manufacturing overhead costs) and one fixed cost category (manufacturing overhead costs). Variable manufacturing overhead cost is allocated to each suit on the basis of budgeted direct manufacturing labour-hours per suit. For June 2000, each suit is budgeted to take four labour-hours. Budgeted variable manufacturing overhead costs per labour-hour is $12. The budgeted number of suits to be manufactured in June 2000 is 1,040.

Actual variable manufacturing overhead costs in June 2000 were $52,164 for 1,080 suits started and completed. There was no beginning or ending inventory of suits. Actual direct manufacturing labour-hours for June were 4,536.

REQUIRED
1. Compute the static-budget variance, the flexible-budget variance, and the sales-volume variance for variable manufacturing overhead.
2. Comment on the results.

8-17 Fixed manufacturing overhead, variance analysis (continuation of 8-16). Esquire Clothing allocates fixed manufacturing overhead to each suit using budgeted direct manufacturing labour-hours per suit. Data pertaining to fixed manufacturing overhead costs for June 2000 are: budgeted, $62,400, and actual, $63,916.

REQUIRED
1. Compute the spending variance and the flexible-budget variance for fixed manufacturing overhead. Comment on these results.
2. Compute the production volume variance for June 2000. What inferences can Esquire Clothing draw from this variance?

8-18 Variable manufacturing overhead variance analysis. The French Bread Company bakes baguettes for distribution to upscale grocery stores. The company has two direct-cost categories, direct materials and direct manufacturing labour. Variable manufacturing overhead is allocated to products on the basis of standard direct manufacturing labour-hours. Baguettes are baked in batches of 100 loaves. Following is some pertinent data for the French Bread Company:

Direct manufacturing labour use	2.00 hours per batch
Variable manufacturing overhead	$10.00 per direct labour hour

The French Bread Company recorded the following additional data for the year ended December 31, 2000:

Planned (budgeted) output	3,200,000 baguettes
Actual production	2,800,000 baguettes
Direct manufacturing labour	50,400 hours
Actual variable MOH	$680,400

REQUIRED
1. What is the denominator used for allocating manufacturing overhead (i.e., how many direct manufacturing labour hours is French Bread budgeting for)?
2. Prepare a complete analysis of variable manufacturing overhead (Levels 1 through 3). Use the exhibits in this chapter for reference.
3. Discuss the variances you have calculated. Posit possible explanations for these variances.

8-19 Fixed manufacturing overhead variance analysis. The French Bread Company bakes baguettes for distribution to upscale grocery stores. The company has two direct-cost categories, direct materials and direct manufacturing labour. Fixed manufacturing overhead is allocated to products on the basis of standard direct manufacturing labours. Baguettes are baked in batches of 100 loaves. Following is some pertinent data for the French Bread Company:

Direct manufacturing labour use	2.00 hours per batch
Fixed manufacturing overhead	$4.00 per direct labour hour

The French Bread Company recorded the following additional data for the year ended December 31, 2000:

Planned (budgeted) output	3,200,000 baguettes
Actual production	2,800,000 baguettes
Direct manufacturing labour	50,400 hours
Actual fixed MOH	$272,000

REQUIRED

1. Prepare a complete variance analysis of fixed manufacturing overhead cost.
2. Is fixed overhead under- or overallocated? By how much?
3. Comment on your results. Discuss the various variances and explain what may be driving them.

8-20 **Manufacturing overhead, variance analysis.** Zyton assembles its CardioX product at its Scottsdale plant. Manufacturing overhead (both variable and fixed) is allocated to each CardioX unit using budgeted assembly time hours. Budgeted assembly time per CardioX product is two hours. The budgeted variable manufacturing overhead cost per assembly time hour is $40. The budgeted number of CardioX units to be assembled in March 2000 is 8,000. Budgeted fixed manufacturing overhead costs are $480,000.

Actual variable manufacturing overhead costs for March 2000 were $610,500 for 7,400 units actually assembled. Actual assembly-time-hours were 16,280. Actual fixed manufacturing overhead costs were $503,420.

REQUIRED

1. Conduct a four-variance analysis (Exhibit 8-3) for Zyton's Scottsdale plant.
2. Comment on the results in requirement 1.
3. How does the planning and control of variable manufacturing overhead costs differ from that of fixed manufacturing overhead costs?

8-21 **Spending and efficiency overhead variances, service sector.** Meals on Wheels (MOW) operates a home meal delivery service. It has agreements with 20 restaurants to pick up and deliver meals to customers who phone or fax in orders. MOW is currently examining its overhead costs for May 2000.

Variable overhead costs for May 2000 were budgeted at $2 per hour of home delivery time. Fixed overhead costs were budgeted at $24,000. The budgeted number of home deliveries in May 2000 was 8,000. Delivery time, the allocation base for variable and fixed overhead costs, is budgeted to be 0.80 hour per delivery.

Actual results for May 2000 were:

Variable overhead	$14,174
Fixed overhead	$27,600
Number of home deliveries	7,460
Hours of delivery time	5,595

Customers are charged $12 per delivery. The delivery driver is paid $7 per delivery. MOW receives a 10% commission on the meal costs that the restaurants charge the customers who use MOW.

REQUIRED

1. Compute spending and efficiency variances for MOW's variable and fixed overhead in May 2000. Comment on the results.
2. How might MOW manage its variable overhead costs differently from the way it manages its fixed overhead costs?

8-22 **Spending and efficiency overhead variances, distribution.** Package Postal Service (PPS) operates a parcel delivery service. PPS's costing system has one direct cost category (delivery driver payments) and two overhead categories—variable delivery overhead and fixed delivery overhead. In 2000 it charged retail companies and mail-order catalogue companies $15 per delivery. Delivery drivers in 2000 were contracted at $5 per delivery. Variable delivery overhead for September 2000 was budgeted at $2 per hour of delivery time. Budgeted fixed delivery overhead in September 2000 was $120,000. PPS budgeted 100,000 deliveries for September 2000. Delivery time, the allocation base for variable and fixed overhead costs, is budgeted to be 0.25 hours per delivery.

Actual results for September 2000 were:

Variable delivery overhead	$ 60,000
Fixed delivery overhead	$128,400
Number of deliveries	96,000
Hours of delivery time	28,800

REQUIRED

1. Compute the spending and efficiency variances for PPS's variable delivery overhead costs in September 2000. Compute the spending and production volume variances for PPS's fixed delivery overhead costs in September 2000. Comment on the results.
2. What problems PPS face in managing (a) its direct costs, (b) its variable delivery overhead costs, and (c) its fixed delivery overhead costs.

8-23 Four-variance analysis, fill in the blanks. Use the given manufacturing overhead data to fill in the blanks.

	Variable	Fixed
Actual costs incurred	$11,900	$6,000
Allocated to products	9,000	4,500
Flexible budget: Budgeted input allowed for actual output achieved × budgeted rate	9,000	5,000
Actual input × budgeted rate	10,000	5,000

Use F for favourable and U for unfavourable:

	Variable	Fixed
1. Spending variance	$_____	$_____
2. Efficiency variance	_____	_____
3. Production-volume variance	_____	_____
4. Flexible-budget variance	_____	_____
5. Underallocated (overallocated) manuf. overhead	_____	_____

8-24 Straightforward four-variance overhead analysis. The Lopez Company uses a standard cost system in its manufacturing plant for auto parts. Its standard cost of an auto part, based on a denominator level of 4,000 output units per year, included six machine-hours of variable manufacturing overhead at $8 per hour and six machine-hours of fixed manufacturing overhead at $15 per hour. Actual output achieved was 4,400 units. Variable manufacturing overhead incurred was $245,000. Fixed manufacturing overhead incurred was $373,000. Actual incurred machine-hours were 28,400.

REQUIRED

1. Prepare an analysis of all variable manufacturing overhead and fixed manufacturing overhead variances, using the four-variance analysis (p. 283).
2. Prepare journal entries using the four-variance analysis.
3. Describe how individual variable manufacturing overhead items are controlled from day to day. Also, describe how individual fixed manufacturing overhead items are controlled.

8-25 Straightforward coverage of manufacturing overhead, standard cost system. The Singapore division of a Canadian telecommunications company uses a standard cost system for its machine-based production of telephone equipment. Data regarding production during June are:

Variable manufacturing overhead costs incurred	$155,100
Variable manufacturing overhead costs allocated (per standard machine-hour allowed for actual output achieved)	$12
Fixed manufacturing overhead costs incurred	$401,000
Fixed manufacturing overhead budgeted	$390,000
Denominator level in machine-hours	13,000
Standard machine-hours allowed per unit of output	0.30
Units of output	41,000
Actual machine-hours used	13,300
Ending work-in-process inventory	0

1. Prepare an analysis of all manufacturing overhead variances. Use the four-variance analysis framework illustrated in Exhibit 8-3.
2. Prepare journal entries for manufacturing overhead without explanations.
3. Describe how individual variable manufacturing overhead items are controlled from day to day. Also, describe how individual fixed manufacturing overhead items are controlled.

8-26 Total overhead, three-variance analysis. The Atlantic Canada Air Force Base has an extensive repair facility for jet engines. It developed standard costing and flexible budgets to account for this activity. Budgeted variable overhead at a level of 8,000 standard monthly direct labour-hours was $64,000; budgeted total overhead at 10,000 standard direct labour-hours was $197,600. The standard cost allocated to repair output included a total overhead rate of 120% of standard direct labour cost.

Total overhead incurred for October was $249,000. Direct labor costs incurred were $202,440. The direct labour price variance was $9,640 U. The direct labour flexible-budget variance was $14,440 U. The standard labour price was $16 per hour. The production-volume variance was $14,000 F.

REQUIRED

1. Compute the direct labour efficiency variance and the spending, efficiency, and production volume variances for overhead. Also, compute the denominator level.
2. Describe how individual variable manufacturing overhead items are controlled from day to day. Also, describe how individual fixed manufacturing overhead items are controlled.

8-27 Four-variance analysis, working backwards. Lookmeup.com is striving to become a Web portal. The site allows surfers to find anything they wish to look up—be it a person, a site, a company, or news article—through one interactive and easy-to-use interface. Most of Lookmeup.com's operating overhead is due to internet connection costs. Lookmeup.com faces both fixed and variable internet connection charges. Following is the four-variance analysis of Lookmeup.com's operations overhead:

	Spending Variance	Efficiency Variance	Production- Volume Variance
Variable Operating Overhead	$37,000 F	$24,000 F	Never a variance
Fixed Operating Overhead	$14,000 U	Never a variance	$17,000 U

REQUIRED

1. For total operating overhead, compute the following:
   a. Spending variance
   b. Efficiency variance
   c. Production-volume variance
   d. Flexible-budget variance
   e. Total overhead variance
   Arrange your results in a suitable format for presenting three-variance, two-variance, and one-variance analyses.
2. If Lookmeup.com's total actual operating overhead was $420,000, what was the operating overhead allocated to actual output units provided?
3. Can you say whether fixed operating overhead was under- or overallocated? If so, by what amount?
4. Are Lookmeup.com's different variances in the four-variance analysis above necessarily independent? Explain and provide an example.

8-28 Comprehensive review of Chapters 7 and 8, static budget. *The Monthly Herald* budgets to produce 300,000 copies of its monthly newspaper for August 2000. It is budgeted to run 15,000,000 print pages in August with 50 print pages per newspaper. Actual production in August 2000 was 320,000 copies with 17,280,000 print pages run. Each paper was only 50 print pages, but quality problems with paper led to many pages being unusable.

Variable costs comprise direct materials, direct labour, and variable indirect costs. Variable and fixed indirect costs are allocated to each copy on the basis of print pages. The driver for all variable costs is the number of print pages. Data pertaining to August 2000 are:

	Budgeted	Actual
Direct materials	$180,000	$224,640
Direct labour costs	45,000	50,112
Variable indirect costs	60,000	63,936
Fixed indirect costs	90,000	97,000

Data pertaining to revenues for *The Monthly Herald* in August 2000 are:

	Budgeted	Actual
Circulation revenue	$140,000	$154,000
Advertising revenue	360,000	394,600

The Monthly Herald sells for $0.50 per copy in 2000. No change from this budgeted price of $0.50 per copy occurred in August 2000. The actual direct labour rate in August 2000 was $29 per hour. Actual and budgeted pages produced per direct labour-hour in August 2000 was 10,000 print pages. Copies produced but not sold have no value. Advertising revenue covers payments from all advertising sources.

REQUIRED
1. Present a static-budget variance (Level 1) report for *The Monthly Herald*.
2. Comment on the results in requirement 1.

8-29 Comprehensive review of Chapters 7 and 8, flexible budget (continuation of 8-28).

REQUIRED
1. Prepare a comprehensive set of variances for each of the four categories of cost of *The Monthly Herald*.
2. Comment on the results in requirement 1. What extra insights are available with a flexible-budget analysis over that of a static-budget analysis?

PROBLEMS

8-30 Comprehensive variance analysis. FlatScreen manufactures flat-panel LCD displays. The displays are sold to major PC manufacturers. Following is some manufacturing overhead data for FlatScreen for the year ended December 31, 2000:

	Actual	Flexible Budget	Allocated Amount
Variable manufacturing overhead	$1,532,160	$1,536,000	$1,536,000
Fixed manufacturing overhead	$7,004,160	$6,961,920	$7,526,400

FlatScreen's budget was based on the assumption that 17,760 units (panels) will be manufactured during 2000. The planned allocation rate was two machine hours per unit. FlatScreen uses machine hours as the cost driver. Actual number of machine hours used during 2000 was 36,480. The budgeted variable manufacturing overhead costs equal $1,420,800.

REQUIRED
Compute the following quantities (you should be able to do so in the prescribed order):
1. Budgeted number of machine hours planned
2. Budgeted fixed manufacturing overhead costs per machine hour
3. Budgeted variable manufacturing overhead costs per machine hour
4. Budgeted number of machine hours allowed for actual output achieved
5. Actual number of output units
6. Actual number of machine hours used per panel
7. Allocated amount for fixed manufacturing overhead (check)

8-31 Journal entries (Continuation of 8-30).
1. Prepare appropriate journal entries for variable and fixed manufacturing overhead (you will need to calculate the various variances to accomplish this).
2. Overhead variances may be used to reconcile the cost-of-goods-sold account at the end of the fiscal year. Cost-of-goods-sold (COGS) is then entered on the income statement. Show how COGS is reconciled through journal entries.

8-32 Graphs and overhead variances. The Carvelli Company is a manufacturer of housewares. In its job-costing system, manufacturing overhead (both variable and fixed) is allocated to products on the basis of budgeted machine-hours. The budgeted amounts are taken from Carvelli's standard-costing system. The budget for 2000 included:

Variable manufacturing overhead	$9 per machine-hour
Fixed manufacturing overhead	$72,000,000
Denominator level	4,000,000 machine-hours

REQUIRED

1. Prepare four graphs, two for variable manufacturing overhead and two for fixed manufacturing overhead. Each pair of graphs should display how total manufacturing overhead costs of Carvelli will be depicted for the purpose of (a) planning and control and (b) inventory costing.
2. Suppose that 3,500,000 machine-hours were allowed for actual output achieved in 2000, but 3,800,000 machine-hours were used. Actual manufacturing overhead was: variable, $36,100,000; fixed, $72,200,000. Compute (a) variable manufacturing overhead spending and efficiency variances and (b) the fixed manufacturing overhead spending and production-volume variances. Use the columnar presentation illustrated in Exhibit 8-2.
3. What is the amount of the under- or overallocated variable manufacturing overhead? Of the under- or overallocated fixed manufacturing overhead? Why are the flexible-budget variance and the under- or overallocated overhead amount always the same for variable manufacturing overhead but rarely the same for fixed manufacturing overhead?
4. Suppose the denominator level was 3,000,000 rather than 4,000,000 machine-hours. What variances in requirement 2 would be affected? Recompute them.

8-33 Journal entries (continuation of 8-32). Refer to requirement 2. Consider variable manufacturing overhead and then fixed manufacturing overhead. Prepare the journal entries for (a) the incurrence of overhead, (b) the allocation of overhead, and (c) the isolation and closing of overhead variances to Cost of Goods Sold for the year.

8-34 Variance analysis for an activity area. CellOne is a cellular phone service reseller, contracting with major cellular operators for airtime in bulk and then reselling service to retail customers. Having adopted an ABC system last year, CellOne has defined the following activity areas—contracting, marketing, technical service, and customer service.

The technical service area has one major cost driver—technical support hours. One hour of technical support is budgeted for every 5,000 minutes of airtime sold. For the month ended August 31, 2000, CellOne budgeted to sell 6,850,000 minutes; however, actual minutes sold totalled 7,350,000. During the month of August 2000, 1,500 actual technical support hours were logged. Some additional data:

	Actual	Budget
Variable technical service activity costs	$31,500	$32,880
Fixed technical service activity costs	$67,500	$69,870

Further, you are told that budgeted input allowed for actual output achieved totalled 1,470 hours of technical support.

REQUIRED

1. What is the actual variable technical service activity area cost per technical service hour? Budgeted cost per hour?
2. What is the allocated fixed technical service area overhead?
3. Calculate the spending variance, the efficiency variance, and the flexible-budget variance for variable overhead costs. Explain these variances based on the data provided.
4. Has CellOne management under- or overallocated fixed overhead for August 2000? Show how you calculate the under/overallocation.

8-35 Four-variance analysis, find the unknowns. Consider each of the following situations—cases A, B, and C—independently. Data refer to operations of April 2000. For each situation, assume a standard cost system. Also assume the use of a flexible budget for control of variable and fixed manufacturing overhead based on machine-hours.

	Cases		
	A	**B**	**C**
1. Fixed manufacturing overhead incurred	$10,600	—	$12,000
2. Variable manufacturing overhead incurred	7,000	—	—
3. Denominator level in machine-hours	500	—	1,100
4. Standard machine-hours allowed for actual output achieved	—	$650	—
Flexible budget data:			
5. Fixed manufacturing overhead	—	—	—
6. Variable manufacturing overhead (per standard machine-hour)	—	8.50	5.00
7. Budgeted fixed manufacturing overhead	10,000	—	11,000
8. Budgeted variable manufacturing overhead*	—	—	—
9. Total budgeted manufacturing overhead*	—	12,525	—
Additional data:			
10. Standard variable manufacturing overhead allocated	7,500	—	—
11. Standard fixed manufacturing overhead allocated	10,000	—	—
12. Production, volume variance	—	500 U	500 F
13. Variable manufacturing overhead spending variance	950 F	0	350 U
14. Variable manufacturing overhead efficiency variance	—	0	100 U
15. Fixed manufacturing overhead spending variance	—	300 F	—
16. Actual machine-hours used	—	—	—

*For standard machine-hours allowed for actual output achieved.

REQUIRED

Fill in the blanks under each case. (*Hint:* Prepare a worksheet similar to that in Exhibit 8-3. Fill in the knowns and then solve for the unknowns.)

8-36 Working backward from given variances. The Mancusco Company uses a flexible budget and standard costs to aid planning and control of its manufacturing operations. Its normal costing system for manufacturing has two direct cost categories (direct materials and direct manufacturing labour—both variable) and two indirect cost categories (variable manufacturing overhead and fixed manufacturing overhead, both allocated using direct manufacturing labour-hours).

At the 40,000 budgeted direct manufacturing labour-hour level for August, budgeted direct manufacturing labour is $800,000, budgeted variable manufacturing overhead is $480,000, and budgeted fixed manufacturing overhead is $640,000. The following actual results are for August:

Direct materials price variance (based on purchases)	$176,000 F
Direct materials efficiency variance	69,000 U
Direct manufacturing labour costs incurred	522,750
Variable manufacturing overhead flexible budget variance	10,350 U
Variable manufacturing overhead efficiency variance	18,000 U
Fixed manufacturing overhead incurred	597,460
Fixed manufacturing overhead spending variance	42,540 F

The standard cost per kilogram of direct materials is $11.50. The standard allowance is three kilograms of direct materials for each unit of product. Thirty thousand units of product were produced during August. There was no beginning inventory of direct materials. There was no beginning or ending work in process. In August, the direct materials price variance was $1.10 per kilogram.

In July, labour troubles caused a major slowdown in the pace of production, resulting in an unfavourable direct manufacturing labour efficiency variance of $45,000. There was no manufacturing labour price variance. These troubles persisted into August. Some workers quit. Their replacements had to be hired at higher rates, which had to be extended to all workers. The actual average wage rate in August exceeded the standard average wage rate by $0.50.

REQUIRED

1. Compute the following for August:
   a. Total kilograms of direct materials purchased
   b. Total number of kilograms of excess direct materials used
   c. Variable manufacturing overhead spending variance
   d. Total number of actual hours of direct manufacturing labour-hours used
   e. Total number of standard direct manufacturing labour-hours allowed for the units produced
   f. Production-volume variance
2. Describe how Mancuso's control of variable manufacturing overhead items differs from its control of fixed manufacturing overhead items.

8-37 Flexible budgets, four-variance analysis. (CMA, adapted) Nolton Products uses a standard costing system. It allocates manufacturing overhead (both variable and fixed) to products on the basis of standard direct manufacturing labour-hours (DLH). Nolton develops its manufacturing overhead rate from the current annual budget. The manufacturing overhead budget for 2000 is based on budgeted output of 720,000 units requiring 3,600,000 direct manufacturing labour-hours. The company is able to schedule production uniformly throughout the year.

A total of 66,000 output units requiring 315,000 direct labour-hours was produced during May 2000. Manufacturing overhead (MOH) costs incurred for May amounted to $375,000. The actual costs as compared with the annual budget and $\frac{1}{12}$ of the annual budget are shown below.

Annual Manufacturing Overhead Budget 2000

	Total Amount	Per Output Unit	Per DLH Input Unit	Monthly MOH Budget May 2000	Actual MOH Costs for May 2000
Variable MOH:					
Indirect manufacturing labour	$ 900,000	$1.25	$0.25	$ 75,000	$ 75,000
Supplies	1,224,000	1.70	0.34	102,000	111,000
Fixed MOH:					
Supervision	648,000	0.90	0.18	54,000	51,000
Utilities	540,000	0.75	0.15	45,000	54,000
Amortization	1,008,000	1.40	0.28	84,000	84,000
Total	$4,320,000	$6.00	$1.20	$360,000	$375,000

REQUIRED

Calculate the following amounts for Nolton Products for May 2000:
1. Total manufacturing overhead costs allocated
2. Variable manufacturing overhead spending variance
3. Fixed manufacturing overhead spending variance
4. Variable manufacturing overhead efficiency variance
5. Production-volume variance
Be sure to identify each variance as favourable (F) or unfavourable (U).

8-38 Review of Chapters 7 and 8, three-variance analysis. (CPA, adapted) The Beal Manufacturing Company's job costing system has two direct cost categories, direct materials and direct manufacturing labour. Manufacturing overhead (both variable and fixed) is allocated to products on the basis of standard direct manufacturing labour-hours (DLH). At the beginning of 2000, Beal adopted the following standards for its manufacturing costs:

	Input	Cost per Output Unit
Direct materials	3 kilograms at $5 per kilogram	$ 15
Direct manufacturing labour	5 hours at $15 per hour	75
Manufacturing overhead:		
Variable	$6 per DLH	30
Fixed	$8 per DLH	40
Standard manufacturing cost per output unit		$160

The denominator level for total manufacturing overhead per month in 2000 is 40,000 direct manufacturing labour-hours. Beal's flexible budget for January 2000 was based on this denominator level. The records for January indicate the following:

Direct materials purchased	25,000 kilograms at $5.20 per kilogram
Direct materials used	23,100 kilograms
Direct manufacturing labour	40,100 hours, at $14.60 per hour
Total actual manufacturing overhead (variable and fixed)	$600,000
Actual production	7,800 output units

REQUIRED
1. Prepare a schedule of total standard manufacturing costs for the 7,800 output units in January, 2000.
2. For the month of January 2000, compute the following variances, indicating whether each is favourable (F) or unfavourable (U):
   a. Direct materials price variance, based on purchases
   b. Direct materials efficiency variance
   c. Direct manufacturing labour price variance
   d. Direct manufacturing labour efficiency variance
   e. Total manufacturing overhead spending variance
   f. Variable manufacturing overhead efficiency variance
   g. Production-volume variance

8-39 **Variance analysis for ABC.** Starport manufactures and launches space stations. The stations are custom-made according to specifications furnished by the ordering party. Starport has adopted an ABC system, and has defined activity areas as follows: design, prototyping, testing, fabrication, launching, and assembly. In what follows, we focus on the launching activity area.

Starport launches space station components into orbit from a base located on a remote island in the Pacific Ocean. Components are assembled in orbit according to the custom designs. Starport sells unused capacity in its launch facilities to launch other companies' products into orbit and beyond. The launching activity area has both variable and fixed costs. You are presented with the following data for the year ended December 31, 2000:

	Actual	Budget
Launches	265	250
Launch hours	5,300	5,500
Variable launch activity area costs (millions)	$ 371	$ 374
Fixed launch activity area costs (millions)	$1,643	$1,694

REQUIRED
1. Complete the numbers in the following table. The calculations will assist you in answering requirement 2.
2. Prepare an analysis of Starport's 2000 launching activity area costs.
3. Analyze your results. Provide explanations for the variances you calculate.

ABC Variance Analysis—Calculation of Key Information

	Actual Results	Flexible Budget Amount	Static Budget Amount
1. Output units (tests)	265		250
2. Launching hours	5,300		5,500
3. Launching hours per test (2 ÷ 1)			
4. Variable launch activity area costs	$371,000,000		$374,000,000
5. Variable launch activity area costs per testing hour (4 ÷ 2)			
6. Variable launch activity area costs per test (4 ÷ 1)			
7. Fixed launch activity area costs	$1,643,000,000		$1,694,000,000
8. Fixed launch activity area costs per testing hour (7 ÷ 2)			
9. Fixed launch activity area costs per test (7 ÷ 1)			

COLLABORATIVE LEARNING PROBLEM

8-40 Hospital overhead variances, four-variance analysis. The Sharon Hospital, a large metropolitan health care complex, has had difficulty controlling its accounts receivable. Bills for patients, various government agencies, and private insurance companies have frequently been inaccurate and late. This situation has led to intolerable levels of bad debts and investments in receivables.

With the participation of the billing department, a set of standard costs and standard amounts was developed for 2000. These standard costs can be used in a flexible budget with separate variable cost and fixed cost categories. The output unit is defined to be a single bill.

The accountant of Sharon Hospital provides you with the following for April 2000:

Variable overhead costs, allowance per standard hour	$10
Fixed overhead flexible budget variance	$200 F
Total budgeted overhead costs for the bills prepared	$22,500
Production volume variance	$900 F
Variable cost spending variance	$2,000 U
Variable cost efficiency variance	$2,000 F
Standard hours allowed for the bills prepared	1,800 labour-hours

REQUIRED

1. Actual hours of input used
2. Fixed overhead budget
3. Fixed overhead allocated
4. Budgeted fixed overhead rate per hour
5. Denominator level in hours

8-41 Standard setting, benchmarking, ethics. Ira Stone, the president of Sharon Hospital, has a meeting with the Medical Economics Group (MEG). MEG is a consulting firm in the health services sector. It reports that Sharon's billing operations are grossly inefficient. Its standard costing per bill is above 90% of the 130 hospitals MEG tracks in its benchmarking database.

Stone suspects the billing group deliberately "padded" its standard costs and standard amounts. Despite large investment in new information systems, the standards for 2000 were not below actual results for 1999. Stone does not want to institute a witch hunt, but he does want to eliminate the fat in Sharon's cost structure.

REQUIRED

1. How might Sharon's billing operations group have "padded" its standard costs and standard amounts? Why might they do this padding?
2. What steps should Stone take to "reduce the fat" in the overhead costs of the billing operations at Sharon Hospital?

9

INCOME EFFECTS OF ALTERNATIVE INVENTORY COSTING METHODS

The bottling lines at the Salem, New Hampshire, 7-Up bottling plant can operate at varying degrees of speed. Management considers these different operating speeds, as well as demand factors, when determining the denominator level to use in setting fixed overhead cost rates.

LEARNING OBJECTIVES

After studying this chapter, you should be able to:

1. Identify the fundamental feature that distinguishes variable costing from absorption costing
2. Prepare income statements using absorption costing and variable costing
3. Explain differences in operating income under absorption costing and variable costing
4. Understand how absorption costing influences performance evaluation decisions
5. Differentiate throughput costing from variable costing and absorption costing
6. Describe the various denominator-level concepts that can be used in absorption costing
7. Explain how the choice of denominator level affects reported operating income and inventory costs

The reported income number captures the attention of managers in a way few other numbers do. Consider three examples:

◆ Planning decisions typically include an analysis of how the considered options affect future reported income.

◆ Increases in reported income is the object of many decisions related to cost reduction.

◆ Reported income is a key number in the performance evaluation of managers.

The reported income number of manufacturing companies is affected by cost accounting choices related to inventories. In this chapter we examine two such choices:

1. **Inventory costing choices.** The choices here relate to the costs which are to be recorded as inventory assets when they are incurred. We discuss three alternatives: variable costing, absorption costing, and throughput costing.

2. **Denominator-level choices.** The choices here relate to the preselected level of the cost allocation base used to set budgeted fixed manufacturing cost rates. We discuss four alternatives: theoretical capacity, practical capacity, normal utilization, and master budget utilization.

Alternative Inventory Costing Methods
www.canberra.edu.au/cwis/faculty/Management/Lectures/962/Unit3880/Lecture_6.html

Report on a Review of Inventory Management Practices in the Federal Government
www.tbs-sct.gc.ca/tb/materiel/invman/inmp01e.html

◆ PART ONE: INVENTORY COSTING METHODS

The two most commonly encountered methods of costing inventories are variable costing and absorption costing. We discuss these two first and then cover throughput costing.

VARIABLE COSTING AND ABSORPTION COSTING

These two methods differ in only one conceptual respect: whether fixed manufacturing costs (both direct and indirect) are inventoriable costs. Recall that *inventoriable costs* for a manufacturing company are costs associated with the acquisition and conversion of materials and all other manufacturing inputs into goods for sale; these costs are first recorded as an asset and then subsequently become an expense when the goods are sold.

Variable costing is a method of inventory costing in which all variable manufacturing costs are included as inventoriable costs. All fixed manufacturing costs are excluded from inventoriable costs; they are costs of the period in which they are incurred. **Absorption costing** is a method of inventory costing in which all variable manufacturing costs and all fixed manufacturing costs are included as inventoriable costs. That is, inventory "absorbs" all manufacturing costs. Throughout this chapter, to emphasize underlying concepts, we assume that the chosen denominator level for computing the variable and fixed manufacturing overhead allocation rates is a production output-related variable. Examples include direct labour-hours, direct machine-hours, and units of production output.

We will use the Radius Company, which manufactures specialty clothing belts, to illustrate the difference between variable costing and absorption costing.[1] Radius uses a normal costing system. That is, its direct costs are traced to products using actual prices and the actual inputs used, and its indirect (overhead) costs are allocated using budgeted indirect cost rate(s) times actual inputs used. The allocation base for all indirect manufacturing costs is units produced. The allocation base for all variable indirect marketing costs is units sold. (Only manufacturing costs are included in inventoriable costs.)

OBJECTIVE 1

Identify the fundamental feature that distinguishes variable costing from absorption costing

Variable costing (direct costing). Inventory costing method in which all variable manufacturing costs are included as inventoriable costs. All fixed manufacturing costs are excluded from inventoriable costs; they are costs of the period in which they are incurred.

Absorption costing. Inventory costing method in which all variable manufacturing costs and all fixed manufacturing costs are included as inventoriable costs.

[1]The variable versus absorption costing choice is but one of several pertaining to inventory costing. For example, decisions related to cost flows (FIFO, LIFO, weighted-average, and so on) must also be made.

To keep our focus on variable versus absorption costing issues, we assume the following for 2000:

◆ The budgeted number and actual number of units produced are equal (1,100,000 units).

◆ The budgeted number and actual number of units sold are equal (1,000,000 units).

◆ The budgeted and actual fixed costs are equal.

◆ Work in process is minimal.

◆ There is no beginning inventory on January 1, 2000.

◆ All variable costs are driven by an output-unit-related variable. (We assume, for example, batch-level and product-sustaining costs are zero.)

With 2000 production of 1,100,000 units and sales of 1,000,000 units, the ending inventory on December 31, 2000, is 100,000 units.

The per unit and total actual costs for 2000 are:

	Per Unit	Total Costs
Variable costs:		
Direct materials	$3.50	$3,850,000
Direct manufacturing labour	1.60	1,760,000
Indirect manufacturing costs	0.90	990,000
Manufacturing costs	6.00	6,600,000
Direct marketing costs	0.80	800,000
Indirect marketing costs	1.60	1,600,000
Marketing costs	2.40	2,400,000
Total variable costs	$8.40	$9,000,000
Fixed costs:		
Direct manufacturing costs	$0.30	$ 330,000
Indirect manufacturing costs	1.70	1,870,000
Manufacturing costs	2.00	2,200,000
Direct marketing costs	2.10	2,100,000
Indirect marketing costs	3.40	3,400,000
Marketing costs	5.50	5,500,000
Total fixed costs	$7.50	$7,700,000

The heart of the difference between variable and absorption costing for financial reporting is accounting for fixed manufacturing costs:

		Direct	Indirect
Same under Both Methods	} Variable	Direct manufacturing cost	Indirect manufacturing
Differs under the Two Methods	} Fixed	Direct manufacturing cost	Indirect manufacturing

For inventory valuation under both methods, all variable manufacturing costs (both direct and indirect) are capitalizable costs. That is, they are first recorded as an asset when they are incurred. Under variable costing, fixed manufacturing costs (both direct and indirect) are deducted as a period cost in the period in which they are incurred. Examples of variable direct manufacturing costs are direct materials and direct manufacturing labour. An example of a fixed direct manufacturing cost is the annual lease cost of a machine dedicated exclusively to the assembly of a single product. The annual lease cost of a building in which multiple products are assembled illustrates a fixed indirect manufacturing cost. Under absorption costing, fixed manufacturing costs are initially capitalized as an inventoriable cost. They then become expenses in the form of cost of goods sold when sales occur. The unit inventoriable costs for Radius under the two methods are:

	Variable Costing		Absorption Costing	
Variable manufacturing costs:				
Direct materials	$3.50		$3.50	
Direct manufacturing labour	1.60		1.60	
Indirect manufacturing costs	0.90	6.00	0.90	6.00
Fixed manufacturing costs:				
Direct manufacturing costs			0.30	
Indirect manufacturing costs			1.70	2.00
Total inventoriable costs		$6.00		$8.00

OBJECTIVE 2

Prepare income statements using absorption costing and variable costing

Exhibit 9-1 presents the variable costing and absorption costing income statements for the Radius Company in 2000. The variable costing income statement uses the contribution approach format introduced in Chapter 3. The absorption costing income statement uses the gross margin format introduced in Chapter 2. Why these differences in format? The distinction between variable and fixed costs is central to variable costing; the contribution format highlights this distinction. The distinction between manufacturing and nonmanufacturing costs is central to absorption costing; the gross margin format highlights this distinction. Many companies using absorption costing do not make any distinction between variable and fixed costs in their accounting system.

Trace the fixed manufacturing costs of $2,200,000 in Exhibit 9-1. The income statement under variable costing deducts the $2,200,000 lump sum as a period cost in 2000. In contrast, the income statement under absorption costing regards each finished unit as absorbing $2 of fixed manufacturing costs. Under absorption costing the $2,200,000 is initially capitalized as an inventoriable cost in 2000. Given the preceding data for Radius, $2,000,000 subsequently becomes an expense in 2000, and $200,000 remains an asset—part of ending finished goods inventory, 100,000 units × $2—at December 31, 2000. The variable manufacturing costs are accounted for in the same way in both income statements in Exhibit 9-1.

Never overlook the heart of the matter. The difference between variable costing and absorption costing centres on accounting for fixed manufacturing costs. If inventory levels change, operating income will differ between the two methods because of the difference in accounting for fixed manufacturing overhead. Compare sales of 900,000, 1,000,000, and 1,100,000 units by the Radius Company in 2000. Fixed manufacturing costs would be included in the 2000 expense as follows:

	Fixed Manufacturing Costs Treated as an Expense in 2000
Variable costing, where:	
◆ Sales are 900,000, 1,000,000, or 1,100,000 units	$2,200,000
Absorption costing, where:	
◆ Sales are 900,000 units, $400,000 (200,000 × $2) held back in inventory	$1,800,000
◆ Sales are 1,000,000 units, $200,000 (100,000 × $2) held back in inventory	$2,000,000
◆ Sales are 1,100,000 units, $0 held back in inventory	$2,200,000

Some companies use the term **direct costing** to describe the inventory costing method we call *variable costing*. This is an unfortunate choice of term for two reasons: (1) Variable costing does not include all direct costs as inventoriable costs. Only direct variable manufacturing costs are included. Any direct fixed manufacturing costs and any direct nonmanufacturing costs (such as marketing) are excluded from inventoriable costs. (2) Variable costing includes as inventoriable costs not only direct manufacturing costs, but also some indirect costs (variable indirect manufacturing costs).

Direct costing (variable costing). Inventory costing method in which all variable manufacturing costs are included as inventoriable costs. All fixed manufacturing costs are excluded from inventoriable costs; they are costs of the period in which they are incurred.

EXHIBIT 9-1

Comparison of Variable Costing and Absorption Costing Income Statements for the Year Ended December 31, 2000, for the Radius Company (in thousands)

PANEL A: VARIABLE COSTING

Revenues: $17 × 1,000,000 units		$17,000
Variable costs:		
Beginning inventory	$ 0	
Variable cost of goods manufactured: $6 × 1,100,000	6,600	
Cost of goods available for sale	6,600	
Ending inventory: $6 × 100,000	600	
Variable manufacturing cost of goods sold	6,000	
Variable marketing costs	2,400	
Adjustment for variable cost variances	0	
Total variable costs		8,400
Contribution margin		8,600
Fixed costs:		
Fixed manufacturing costs	2,200	
Fixed marketing costs	5,500	
Adjustment for fixed cost variances	0	
Total fixed costs		7,700
Operating income		$ 900

PANEL B: ABSORPTION COSTING

Revenues: $17 × 1,000,000 units		$17,000
Cost of goods sold:		
Beginning inventory	$ 0	
Variable manufacturing costs: $6 × 1,100,000	6,600	
Fixed manufacturing costs: $2 × 1,100,000	2,200	
Cost of goods available for sale	8,800	
Ending inventory: $8 × 100,000	800	
Adjustment for manufacturing variances	0	
Cost of goods sold		8,000
Gross margin		9,000
Marketing costs:		
Variable marketing costs	2,400	
Fixed marketing costs	5,500	
Adjustment for marketing variances	0	
Total marketing costs		7,900
Operating income		$ 1,100

COMPARISON OF STANDARD VARIABLE COSTING AND STANDARD ABSORPTION COSTING

Our next example explores the implications of accounting for fixed manufacturing costs in more detail. The Stassen Company manufactures and markets telescopes. It uses a standard costing system for both its manufacturing and its marketing costs.[2] It began business on January 1, 2000, and it is now March 2000. The president asks

[2]For ease of exposition, we assume that the Stassen Company uses a standard costing system for all its operating costs—that is, it uses standards for both variable and fixed costs in both its manufacturing and marketing.

you to prepare comparative income statements for January 2000 and February 2000. The following simplified data in units are available:

Unit Data	January 2000	February 2000
Beginning inventory	0	200
Production	600	650
Sales	400	750
Ending inventory	200	100

Other Data	
Selling price	$99
Standard variable manufacturing costs per unit produced	$20
Standard variable marketing costs per unit sold	$19
Standard fixed manufacturing costs per month	$12,800
Standard fixed marketing costs per month	$10,400
Budgeted denominator level of production per month	800 output units

The standard variable manufacturing costs per unit of $20 includes $11 for direct materials. For simplicity, we assume all fixed manufacturing costs are indirect product costs.

We assume work in process is minimal. There were no beginning or ending inventories of materials. On January 1, 2000, there was no beginning inventory of finished goods. In order to highlight the effect of the production volume variance, we assume there were no price, efficiency, or spending variances for any costs in either January or February of 2000. The standard fixed manufacturing cost per unit is $16 ($12,800 ÷ 800). Thus the key standard cost data per unit are:

Variable costs:	
Standard variable manufacturing costs	$20
Standard variable marketing costs	19
Total variable costs	$39
Manufacturing costs:	
Standard variable manufacturing costs	$20
Standard fixed manufacturing costs	16
Total manufacturing costs	$36

Stassen expenses all variances to cost of goods sold in the accounting period in which they occur.

Assume that managers at Stassen receive a bonus based on reported monthly income. The following points illustrate how the choice between variable and absorption costing will affect Stassen's reported monthly income and hence the bonuses their managers will receive.

Comparative Income Statements

Exhibit 9-2 contains the comparative income statements under variable costing (Panel A) and absorption costing (Panel B) for the Stassen Company in January 2000 and February 2000. The operating income numbers are:

	January 2000	February 2000
1. Absorption costing	$4,000	$20,200
2. Variable costing	800	21,800
3. Difference (1) – (2)	$3,200	$ (1,600)

In Panel A, Variable Costing, all variable cost line items are at standard cost except the adjustment for variances. This item would include all price, spending, and efficiency variances related to variable cost items (which are zero in our Stassen

EXHIBIT 9-2
Stassen Company: Comparison of Variable Costing and Absorption Costing Income Statements for January 2000 and February 2000

PANEL A: VARIABLE COSTING

	January 2000	February 2000
Revenue*	$39,600	$74,250
Variable costs:		
Beginning inventory	0	4,000
Variable cost of goods manufactured†	12,000	13,000
Cost of goods available for sale	12,000	17,000
Ending inventory‡	4,000	2,000
Variable manufacturing cost of goods sold	8,000	15,000
Variable marketing costs ≈	7,600	14,250
Total variable costs (at standard)	15,600	29,250
Contribution margin (at standard)	24,000	45,000
Adjustment for variable cost variances	0	0
Contribution margin	24,000	45,000
Fixed costs:		
Fixed manufacturing costs	12,800	12,800
Fixed marketing costs	10,400	10,400
Total fixed costs (at standard)	23,200	23,200
Adjustment for fixed cost variances	0	0
Total fixed costs	23,200	23,200
Operating income	$ 800	$21,800

*400 × $99 = $39,600; 750 × $99 = $74,250.
†600 × $20 = $12,000; 650 × $20 = $13,000.
‡200 × $20 = $4,000; 100 × $20 = $2,000.
≈400 × $19 = $7,600; 750 × $19 = $14,250

PANEL B: ABSORPTION COSTING

	January 2000	February 2000
Revenue*	$39,600	$74,250
Cost of goods sold:		
Beginning inventory	0	7,200
Variable manufacturing costs†	12,000	13,000
Fixed manufacturing costs‡	9,600	10,400
Cost of goods available for sale	21,600	30,600
Ending inventory ≈	7,200	3,600
Total cost of goods sold (at standard)	14,400	27,000
Gross margin (at standard costs)	25,200	47,250
Adjustment for manufacturing variances#	3,200 U	2,400 U
Gross margin	22,000	44,850
Marketing costs:		
Variable marketing costs‖	7,600	14,250
Fixed marketing costs	10,400	10,400
Total marketing (at standard)	18,000	24,650
Adjustment for marketing variances	0	0
Total marketing	18,000	24,650
Operating income	$ 4,000	$20,200

*400 × $99 = $39,600; 750 × $99 = $74,250.
†600 × $20 = $12,000; 650 × $20 = $13,000.
‡600 × $16 = $9,600; 650 × $16 = $10,400.
≈200 × ($20 + $16) = $7,200; 100 × ($20 + $16) = $3,600.
#January, 2000 has $3,200 unfavourable (U) production volume variance (600 – 800) × $16 = $3,200 unfavourable. February, 2000 has $2,400 unfavourable production volume variance (650 – 800) × $16.00 = $2,400 unfavourable.
‖400 × $19 = $7,600; 750 × $19 = $14,250

example). In Panel B, Absorption Costing, all cost of goods sold line items are at standard cost except the adjustment for variances. This item would include all manufacturing cost variances—price, spending, efficiency, and production volume variances. Only the production volume variance is nonzero in our Stassen example.

Keep the following points in mind about absorption costing as you study Panel B of Exhibit 9-2:

1. The inventoriable costs are $36 per unit, not $20, because fixed manufacturing costs ($16) as well as variable manufacturing costs ($20), are assigned to each unit of product.

2. The $16 fixed manufacturing costs rate was based on a denominator level of 800 units per month ($12,800 ÷ 800 = $16). Whenever *production* (not sales) deviates from the denominator level, a production-volume variance arises. The amount of the variance is $16 multiplied by the difference between the actual level of production and the denominator level.

3. The production-volume variance, which relates to fixed manufacturing overhead, exists only under absorption costing and not under variable costing. All other variances exist under both absorption costing and variable costing.

4. The absorption costing income statement classifies costs primarily by *business function*, such as manufacturing and marketing. In contrast, the variable costing income statement features *cost behaviour* (variable or fixed) as the basis of classification. Absorption costing income statements need not differentiate between the variable and fixed costs. Exhibit 9-2 does make this differentiation for the Stassen Company in order to highlight how individual line items are classified differently under variable and absorption costing formats.

Explaining Differences in Operating Income

If the inventory level increases during an accounting period, variable costing will generally report less operating income than absorption costing; when the inventory level decreases, variable costing will generally report more operating income than absorption costing. These differences in operating income are due solely to moving fixed manufacturing costs into inventories as inventories increase, and out of inventories as they decrease.

The difference between operating income under absorption costing and variable costing can be computed by formula 1, which is illustrated with Exhibit 9-2 data:[3]

OBJECTIVE 3

Explain differences in operating income under absorption costing and variable costing

Formula 1

$$\begin{pmatrix} \text{Absorption costing} \\ \text{operating} \\ \text{income} \end{pmatrix} - \begin{pmatrix} \text{Variable costing} \\ \text{operating} \\ \text{income} \end{pmatrix} = \begin{pmatrix} \text{Fixed manufacturing} \\ \text{costs in} \\ \text{ending inventory} \end{pmatrix} - \begin{pmatrix} \text{Fixed manufacturing} \\ \text{costs in} \\ \text{beginning inventory} \end{pmatrix}$$

January 2000 $4,000 - $800 = (200 \times $16) - (0 \times $16)$

$$\$3,200 = \$3,200$$

February 2000 $20,200 - $21,800 = (100 \times $16) - (200 \times $16)$

$$-\$1,600 = -\$1,600$$

Fixed manufacturing costs in ending inventory are a current-period expense under variable costing that absorption costing defers to future periods.

Two alternative formulas can be used if we assume that all manufacturing variances are written off as period costs, that no change occurs in work-in-process inventory, and that no change occurs in the budgeted fixed manufacturing overhead rate between accounting periods:

[3]This formula assumes that the amounts used for beginning and ending inventory are after proration of manufacturing overhead variances.

Formula 2

$$\begin{pmatrix} \text{Absorption costing} \\ \text{operating} \\ \text{income} \end{pmatrix} - \begin{pmatrix} \text{Variable costing} \\ \text{operating} \\ \text{income} \end{pmatrix} = \begin{pmatrix} \text{Units} \\ \text{produced} - \text{Units} \\ \text{sold} \end{pmatrix} \times \begin{pmatrix} \text{Budgeted fixed} \\ \text{manufacturing} \\ \text{cost rate} \end{pmatrix}$$

January 2000 $\qquad \$4,000 - \$800 = (600 - 400) \times \$16$

$\$3,200 = \$3,200$

February 2000 $\qquad \$20,200 - \$21,800 = (650 - 750) \times \$16$

$-\$1,600 = -\$1,600$

Formula 3

$$\begin{pmatrix} \text{Absorption costing} \\ \text{operating} \\ \text{income} \end{pmatrix} - \begin{pmatrix} \text{Variable costing} \\ \text{operating} \\ \text{income} \end{pmatrix} = \begin{pmatrix} \text{Ending} \\ \text{inventory} - \text{Beginning} \\ \text{in units} - \text{inventory} \\ \text{in units} \end{pmatrix} \times \begin{pmatrix} \text{Budgeted fixed} \\ \text{manufacturing} \\ \text{cost rate} \end{pmatrix}$$

January 2000 $\qquad \$4,000 - \$800 = (200 - 0) \times \$16$

$\$3,200 = \$3,200$

February 2000 $\qquad \$20,200 - \$21,800 = (100 - 200) \times \$16$

$-\$1,600 = -\$1,600$

Effect of Sales and Production on Operating Income

The period-to-period change in operating income under variable costing is driven solely by changes in the unit level of sales, given a constant contribution margin per unit. Consider for Stassen the variable costing operating income in February 2000 versus that in January 2000:

$$\frac{\text{Change in}}{\text{operating income}} = \frac{\text{Contribution}}{\text{margin}} \times \frac{\text{Change in unit}}{\text{sales level}}$$

$$\$21,800 - \$800 = (\$99 - \$39) \times (750 - 400)$$

$$\$21,000 = \$60 \times 350$$

$$\$21,000 = \$21,000$$

Note that under variable costing, Stassen managers cannot increase operating income (and hence their bonuses) by producing for inventory.

Under absorption costing, however, period-to-period change in operating income is driven by variations in *both* the unit level of sales and the unit level of production. Exhibit 9-3 illustrates this point. The exhibit shows how absorption costing operating income for February 2000 changes as the production level in February 2000 changes. This exhibit assumes that all variances (including the production-volume variance) are written off to cost of goods sold at the end of each accounting period. The beginning inventory in February 2000 of 200 units and the February sales of 750 units are unchanged. Exhibit 9-3 shows that production of only 550 units meets February 2000 sales of 750. Operating income at this production level is $18,600. By producing more than 550 units in February 2000, Stassen increases absorption costing operating income. Each unit in February 2000 ending inventory will increase February operating income by $16. For example, if 800 units are produced, ending inventory will be 250 units and operating income will be $22,600. This amount is $4,000 more than what operating income is with zero ending inventory (250 units × $16 = $4,000) on February 28, 2000. Recall that Stassen's managers receive a bonus based on monthly operating income. Absorption costing enables them to increase operating income (and hence their bonuses) by producing for inventory.

Exhibit 9-4 compares the key differences between variable and absorption costing.

EXHIBIT 9-3

Stassen Company: Effect on Absorption Costing Operating Income of Different Production Levels Holding the Unit Sales Level Constant—Data for February 2000 with Sales of 750 Units

	February 2000 Production Level				
	550	650	700	800	850
Unit data:					
Beginning inventory	200	200	200	200	200
Production	550	650	700	800	850
Goods available for sale	750	850	900	1,000	1,050
Sales	750	750	750	750	750
Ending inventory	0	100	150	250	300
Income statement:					
Revenues	$74,250	$74,250	$74,250	$74,250	$74,250
Beginning inventory	7,200	7,200	7,200	7,200	7,200
Variable manufacturing costs*	11,000	13,000	14,000	16,000	17,000
Fixed manufacturing costs†	8,800	10,400	11,200	12,800	13,600
Cost of goods available for sale	27,000	30,600	32,400	36,000	37,800
Ending inventory‡	0	3,600	5,400	9,000	10,800
Cost of goods sold (at standard cost)	27,000	27,000	27,000	27,000	27,000
Adjustment for manufacturing variances≈	4,000 U	2,400 U	1,600 U	0	800 F
Total cost of goods sold	31,000	29,400	28,600	27,000	26,200
Gross margin	43,250	44,850	45,650	47,250	48,050
Total marketing and administrative costs	24,650	24,650	24,650	24,650	24,650
Operating income	$18,600	$20,200	$21,000	$22,600	$23,400

*$20 per unit.
†Assigned at $16 per unit.
‡$36 per unit.
≈(Production in units − 800) × $16. All written off to cost of goods sold at end of the accounting period.

PERFORMANCE MEASURES AND ABSORPTION COSTING

Undesirable Buildups of Inventories

Absorption costing enables managers to increase operating income in the short run by increasing the production schedule independent of customer demand for products. Exhibit 9-3 showed how a Stassen manager could increase February 2000 operating income from $18,600 to $22,600 by producing an additional 250 units for inventory. Such an increase in the production schedule can increase the costs of doing business without any attendant increase in sales. For example, a manager whose performance is evaluated on the basis of absorption costing income may increase production at the end of a review period solely to increase reported income. Each additional unit produced absorbs fixed manufacturing costs that would otherwise have been written off as a cost of the period.

The undesirable effects of such an increase in production may be sizable, and they can arise in several ways, as the following examples show:

1. A plant manager may switch production to those orders that absorb the highest amount of fixed manufacturing costs, irrespective of the customer demand for these products (called "cherry picking" the production line). Some difficult-to-manufacture items may be delayed, resulting in failure to meet promised customer delivery dates.

2. A plant manager may accept a particular order to increase production even though another plant in the same company is better suited to handle that order.

OBJECTIVE 4

Understand how absorption costing influences performance evaluation decisions

INCOME EFFECTS OF
ALTERNATIVE INVENTORY
COSTING METHODS

EXHIBIT 9-4
Comparative Income Effects of Variable Costing and Absorption Costing

Question	Variable Costing	Absorption Costing	Comment
Are fixed manufacturing costs inventoried?	No	Yes	Basic theoretical question when these costs should be expensed as period costs
Is there a production-volume variance?	No	Yes	Choice of denominator level affects measurement of operating income under absorption costing only.
How are the other variances treated?	Same	Same	Highlights that the basic difference is the accounting for fixed manufacturing costs, not the accounting for any variable manufacturing costs.
Are classifications between variable and fixed costs routinely made?	Yes	Not always	Absorption costing can be easily modified to obtain subclassifications for variable and fixed costs, if desired (for example, see Exhibit 9-1, Panel B).
How do changes in unit inventory levels affect operating income?			
Production = sales	Equal	Equal	Differences are attributable to the timing of when fixed manufacturing costs become period costs.
Production > sales	Lower*	Higher†	
Production < sales	Higher	Lower	
What are the effects on CVP relationships?	Driven by unit sales level	Driven by unit sales level and unit production level	Management control benefit: Effects of changes in production level on operating income are easier to understand under variable costing.

*That is, lower operating income than under absorption costing.
†That is, higher operating income than under variable costing.

3. To meet increased production, a manager may defer maintenance beyond the current accounting period. Although operating income may increase now, future operating income will probably decrease because of increased repairs and less efficient equipment.

Early criticisms of absorption costing concentrated on whether fixed manufacturing overhead qualified as an asset under generally accepted accounting principles. However, current criticisms of absorption costing have increasingly emphasized its potentially undesirable incentives for managers. Indeed, one critic labels absorption costing as "one of the black holes of cost accounting," in part because it may induce managers to make decisions "against the long-run interests" of the company.

Proposals for Revising Performance Evaluation

Critics of absorption costing have made a variety of proposals for revising how managers are evaluated. Their proposals include the following:

1. **Change the accounting system.** As discussed previously in this chapter, both variable and throughput costing reduce the incentives of managers to build up inventory. An alternative approach is to incorporate into the accounting system a carrying charge for managers who tie up funds in inventory. The higher the amount of inventory held, the higher the inventory holding charge.

2. **Change the time period used to evaluate performance.** Critics of absorption costing give examples where managers take actions that maximize quarterly or annual income at the potential expense of long-run income. By evaluating performance over a three-to-five-year period, the incentive to take short-run actions that reduce long-term income is lessened.

Variable versus Absorption Costing: A Company President's Perspective

To understand properly the difference between variable cost accounting and absorption cost accounting to today's manufacturers, the individual must understand that the environment in which the manufacturer operates and the concerns of the manager of such an operation have changed with time.

Priorities are now product quality, which includes all aspects of design, service, and price. A common definition of quality is "that which the customer wants, at a competitive price."

The accounting system must provide the correct data to make informed decisions about these quality issues. The absorption costing system was developed by accountants whose objective was to match revenue and expenses for financial statement presentation. It was developed during times of high setup costs and long runs of identical products. There is no mention in these objectives of customer or quality.

Consider the environment in which decisions are presently being made:

◆ **The whole world is the market and the whole world is the competitor.** This market cares only about product quality. Competitors are interested only in what they can do better than the competition. Manufacturers must ensure that no such opportunity exists or they will lose competitive position.

◆ **Niche marketing.** Meaning specific products aimed at particular markets or market segments. Customer needs do vary, which means the manufacturer must be in a position to make decisions continuously as to the costs associated with making the changes requested and required by the individual customer.

◆ **Flexible manufacturing.** Being capable of setting up quickly and changing or modifying products quickly to meet the demands of the niche market

◆ **Continuous improvement.** Everyone in the operation, from the President to the floor sweeper, must continuously strive to find better methods to do what they do. If they do not do so, they can be assured that a competitor somewhere will be doing such, and the organization will lose competitive advantage.

Randy White
President, Arriscraft
Corporation

None of the above refers to short-term profit presentation, financial statement ratios, or current share prices—the issues around which absorption costing was developed.

Since managers are now looking at numerous customized orders and specialized markets, their decisions in this environment cannot be made on the basis of an arbitrary allocation of overhead costs.

Rather, the managers must know what costs will vary with any particular decision and how the costs will vary with volume. The manager must look at the price that can be obtained for the product in question and at the contribution margin generated by that product during the plant time absorbed to produce the product. The manager must investigate the overheads to ensure that in fact these will not vary as a result of taking a particular order (or entering a particular market). The manager must compare the value of that order against other possible orders that cannot be accepted because they would require the same production time slot.

The manager can then consider all aspects of an order (or market segment) and its effect on the overall marketing plans of the organization, including such subjective items as corporate image and market share and the long-term effect on customers and markets.

A manager who follows this procedure will be in a position to truly maximize real profits. Real profits are the cash generated over time, not the short-term results reported in audited financial statements in any particular year.

Variable costs are important not only to managers but at all levels of the manufacturing organization. The people on the floor are involved in making recommendations and improvements in the organization. As such, they have access to and are using costs to calculate the return on investment of proposed improvements. Such decisions must be made on the basis of cash flow, not financial statement profit and loss. Only variable costing systems provide the correct information.

Absorption costing is meant to match revenue with costs. If used by managers to make operating decisions about quality or competitive position, it will distort the decisions. These are the decisions that affect the customers and the markets. It must be understood that the key to the success of the manufacturer is the customer; it is not an accountant's view of profit and loss.

The absorption costing system adds nothing of value to the manager's operating decisions—therefore, nothing of value to the product or the customer. If the important decisions within the company are being based upon variable costs, does it not follow that eventually the outside investor will want to make decisions on a similar basis? Perhaps absorption costing will go the way of the large, inflexible manufacturer and the dinosaur.

Source: Written by Randy White, President, Arriscraft Corporation.

Company Usage of Variable Costing

Surveys of company practice in many countries report that approximately 30% to 50% of companies use variable costing in their internal accounting systems:

	Canada*	United States*	Australia[†]	Japan[†]	Sweden[‡]	United Kingdom[†]
Variable costing used	48%	31%	33%	31%	42%	52%
Absorption costing used	52	65	}67	}69	}58	}48
Other	0	4				

A survey of Irish companies[~] reported predominant use of absorption costing. Only 19% of respondents used variable costing as the primary format in their internal reports to top management. A further 31% used it as a supplementary format in their internal reports. Surveys to date have not examined usage of throughput costing.

Many companies use some version of variable costing for internal reporting but use absorption costing for external reporting or tax reporting. How do companies using some version of variable costing treat fixed manufacturing overhead (MOH) in their internal reporting systems?

	Australia[†]	Japan[†]	United Kingdom[†]
Prorate fixed MOH to inventory/ cost of goods sold at period-end	41%	39%	25%
Use variable costing for monthly costing, and convert to absorption costing once a year	11	8	4
Use both variable costing and absorption costing as dual systems	23	33	31
Treat fixed MOH as a period cost	25	3	35
Other	0	17	4

The most common problem reported by companies using variable costing was the difficulty of classifying costs into fixed or variable categories.

*Adapted from Inoue, S., "A Comparative Study of Recent Development of Cost Management Problems in U.S.A., U.K., Canada, and Japan," *Kagawa University Economic Review* (June 1988)
[†]Adapted from Blayney, P., and I. Yokoyama, "Comparative Analysis of Japanese and Australian Cost Accounting and Management Practices, " (Working Paper, The University of Sydney, Sydney, Australia, 1991)
[‡]Adapted from Ask, U., and C. Ax, "Trends in the Development of Product Costing Practices and Techniques—A Survey of the Swedish Manufacturing Industry, " (Working Paper, Gothenburg School of Economics, Gothenburg, Sweden, 1992)
[~]Adapted from Clarke, P., "Management Accounting Practices and Techniques in Irish Manufacturing Firms, " (Working Paper, Trinity College, Dublin, Ireland, 1995)

3. Include nonfinancial as well as financial variables in the measures used to evaluate performance. Companies currently are using nonfinancial variables, such as the following, to monitor managers' performance in key areas:

a. $\dfrac{\text{Ending inventory in units this period}}{\text{Ending inventory in units last period}}$

b. $\dfrac{\text{Sales in units this period}}{\text{Ending inventory in units this period}}$

Any buildup of inventory at the end of the year would be signalled by tracking the month-to-month behaviour of these two nonfinancial inventory measures. Where a company manufactures or sells several products, the two measures could be reported on a product-by-product basis.

THROUGHPUT COSTING

Some critics of existing costing systems maintain that even variable costing promotes an excessive amount of costs being inventoried. They argue that only direct materials are "truly variable" and propose the use of throughput costing instead. **Throughput costing** (also called **super-variable costing**) treats all costs except those related to variable direct materials as costs of the period in which they are incurred; only variable direct materials costs are inventoriable. This method is a very recent proposal and currently is not yet widely used.

Exhibit 9-5 is the throughput costing income statement for the Stassen Company. Compare the operating income amounts reported with those for absorption and variable costing:

Throughput costing (super-variable costing). Inventory costing method that treats all costs except those related to variable direct materials as costs of the accounting period in which they are incurred; only variable direct materials costs are inventoriable.

EXHIBIT 9-5
Throughput Costing for Stassen Company

	January 2000	February 2000
Unit Data:		
Production	600	650
Sales	400	750
Income statement:		
Revenues*	$39,600	$74,250
Variable direct materials costs:		
Beginning inventory	0	2,200
Direct materials in goods manufactured†	6,600	7,150
Cost of goods available for sale	6,600	9,350
Ending inventory‡	2,200	1,100
Direct materials costs (at standard)	4,400	8,250
Adjustment for direct materials variances	0	0
Total variable direct materials costs	4,400	8,250
Throughput contribution~	35,200	66,000
Other costs:		
Manufacturing#	18,200	18,650
Marketing‖	18,000	24,650
Adjustment for variances	0	0
Total other costs	36,200	43,300
Operating income	$ (1,000)	$22,700

*$400 \times \$99 = \$39,600; 750 \times \$99 = \$74,250$.
†$600 \times \$11 = \$6,600; 650 \times \$11 = \$7,150$.
‡$200 \times \$11 = \$2,200; 100 \times \$11 = \$1,100$.
~Throughput contribution is the difference between revenues and variable direct materials costs.
#$(600 \times \$9) + \$12,800 = \$18,200; (650 \times \$9) + \$12,800 = \$18,650$.
‖$(400 \times \$19) + \$10,400 = \$18,000; (750 \times \$19) + \$10,400 = \$24,650$.

	Absorption Costing	Variable Costing	Throughput Costing
January 2000	$ 4,000	$ 800	$ (1,000)
February 2000	20,200	21,800	22,700

Only the $11 direct materials cost per unit is inventoriable under throughput costing (compared with $36 for absorption costing and $20 for variable costing). Where production exceeds sales (as in January 2000), throughput costing results in the largest amount of costs being expensed to the current period. Throughput contribution in Exhibit 9-5 is revenues minus all variable direct materials costs.

Advocates of throughput costing maintain there is reduced incentive for building up excess inventories vis-à-vis the case when variable or (especially) absorption costing is used. Reducing inventory levels means less funds are tied up in inventory and hence there are more funds available to invest in productive outlets. Moreover, reducing inventory levels typically means reducing inventory spoilage and obsolescence costs.

CAPSULE COMPARISON OF INVENTORY COSTING METHODS

Variable costing, absorption costing, or throughput costing may be combined with actual, normal, or standard costing. Exhibit 9-6 presents a capsule comparison of a job costing record under nine alternative inventory costing systems:

Variable Costing	Absorption Costing	Throughput Costing
1. Actual costing	4. Actual costing	7. Actual costing
2. Normal costing	5. Normal costing	8. Normal costing
3. Standard costing	6. Standard costing	9. Standard costing

The data in Exhibit 9-6 represent the debits to job costing account(s) (that is, the amounts assigned to product) under alternative inventory costing systems.

EXHIBIT 9-6
Capsule Comparison of Alternative Inventory Costing Systems

	Actual Costing	Normal Costing	Standard Costing
Variable Direct Materials Costs	Actual prices × Actual inputs used	Actual prices × Actual inputs used	Standard prices × Standard inputs allowed for actual output achieved
Variable Direct Conversion Costs*	Actual prices × Actual inputs used	Actual prices × Actual inputs used	Standard prices × Standard inputs allowed for actual output achieved
Variable Indirect Manufacturing Costs	Actual variable indirect rates × Actual inputs used	Budgeted variable indirect rates × Actual inputs used	Standard variable indirect rates × Standard inputs allowed for actual output achieved
Fixed Direct Manufacturing Costs	Actual prices × Actual inputs used	Actual prices × Actual inputs used	Standard prices × Standard inputs allowed for actual output achieved
Fixed Indirect Manufacturing Costs	Actual fixed indirect rates × Actual inputs used	Budgeted fixed indirect rates × Actual inputs used	Standard fixed indirect rates × Standard inputs allowed for actual output achieved

(Bracket labels at left, from innermost to outermost: Throughput Costing, Variable Costing, Absorption Costing)

*Conversion costs are all manufacturing costs minus direct materials costs.

Variable costing has been a controversial subject among accountants—not so much because there is disagreement about the need for delineating between variable and fixed costs for management planning and control, but because there is a question about using variable costing for *external* reporting. Those favouring variable costing for external reporting maintain that the fixed portion of manufacturing costs is more closely related to the capacity to produce than to the production of specific units. Supporters of absorption costing maintain that inventories should carry a fixed manufacturing cost component. Why? Since both variable and fixed manufacturing costs are necessary to produce goods, both types of costs should be inventoriable, regardless of their having different behaviour patterns.

Absorption costing (or variants close to it) is the method most commonly used for the external regulatory purpose of accounting systems. For example, for reporting to the Ontario Securities Commission, generally accepted accounting principles as stated in the *CICA Handbook* must be followed. Thus, all manufacturing costs plus some product overhead must be included as inventoriable costs. Overhead costs must be allocated between those costs related to manufacturing activities (inventoriable costs) and those not related to manufacturing activities. For external reporting to shareholders, companies around the globe tend to follow the generally accepted accounting principle that all manufacturing overhead is inventoriable.

Throughput costing is not permitted for the external regulatory purpose of accounting systems if it results in materially different numbers to those reported by absorption costing. Advocates of throughput costing emphasize the internal purposes of management accounting data.

◆ PART TWO: DENOMINATOR-LEVEL CONCEPTS AND ABSORPTION COSTING

Now we examine how alternative denominator-level concepts affect fixed manufacturing overhead rates and operating income under absorption costing. Reported cost numbers can be sizably affected by the choice of a denominator level. This can be important in many contexts, such as pricing and contracting based on reported cost numbers.

ALTERNATIVE DENOMINATOR-LEVEL CONCEPTS

We use an iced tea bottling plant to illustrate several alternative denominator-level concepts. The Bushells Company produces bottles of iced tea. The variable manufacturing costs of each bottle are $0.35. The fixed monthly manufacturing costs of the bottling plant are $50,000. Bushells uses absorption costing for its monthly internal reporting system and for financial reporting to shareholders. Bushells could use any one of at least four different denominator-level concepts for computing the fixed manufacturing overhead rate—theoretical capacity, practical capacity, normal utilization, and master budget utilization. Whichever the denominator-level concept, Bushells defines its denominator in output units (bottles of iced tea).

OBJECTIVE 6

Describe the various denominator-level concepts that can be used in absorption costing

Theoretical Capacity and Practical Capacity

The term *capacity* means constraint, an upper limit. **Theoretical capacity** is the denominator-level concept that is based on the production of output at full efficiency for all of the time. Bushells can produce 2,400 bottles an hour when the bottling lines are operating at full speed. There is a maximum of two eight-hour shifts per day because of a labour union agreement. Thus, the theoretical monthly capacity would be:

2,400 per hour × 16 hours × 30 days = 1,152,000 bottles

Theoretical capacity is theoretical in the sense that it does not allow for any plant maintenance, any interruptions because of bottle breakages on the filling lines, or a host of other factors. While it is a rare plant that is able to operate at theoretical capacity, it can represent a goal or target level of usage.

Theoretical capacity. The denominator-level concept based on the production of output at maximum efficiency for all of the time.

Practical capacity. The denominator-level concept that reduces theoretical capacity for unavoidable operating interruptions such as scheduled maintenance time, shutdowns for holidays and other days, and so on.

Managing Design Capacity in an Uncertain World
www.cadence.com/features/designCap.html

Practical capacity is the denominator-level concept that reduces theoretical capacity for unavoidable operating interruptions such as scheduled maintenance time, shutdowns for holidays and other days, and so on. Assume that the practical hourly production rate is 2,000 bottles an hour and that the plant can operate 25 days a month. The practical monthly capacity is thus:

$$\text{2,000 per hour} \times 16 \text{ hours} \times 25 \text{ days} = 800,000 \text{ bottles}$$

Engineering, economic, and human factors are important to consider when estimating theoretical or practical capacity. Engineers at the Bushells plant can provide input on the technical capabilities of machines for filling bottles. In some cases, however, an increase in capacity may be technically possible but not economically sound. For example, the labour union may actually permit a third shift per day but only at unusually high wage rates that clearly do not make financial sense in the iced tea market. Human safety factors, such as increased injury risk when the line operates at faster speeds, are also important to consider.

Normal Utilization and Master Budget Utilization

Both theoretical capacity and practical capacity measure the denominator level in terms of what a plant can supply. In contrast, normal utilization and master-budget utilization measure the denominator level in terms of demand for the output of the plant. In many cases, budgeted demand is well below the supply available (productive capacity).

Normal utilization. The denominator-level concept based on the level of capacity utilization that satisfies average customer demand over a period (say two or three years) that includes seasonal, cyclical, or other trend factors.

Master budget utilization. The denominator-level concept based on the anticipated level of capacity utilization for the coming budget period.

Normal utilization is the denominator-level concept based on the level of capacity utilization that satisfies average customer demand over a period (say, of two to three years) that includes seasonal, cyclical, or other trend factors. **Master budget utilization** is the denominator-level concept based on the anticipated level of capacity utilization for the next budget period. These two denominator levels can differ—for example, when an industry has cyclical periods of high and low demand or when management believes that the budgeted production for the coming period is unrepresentative of "long-term" demand.

Consider our Bushells example of iced tea production. The master budget for 2000 is based on production of 400,000 bottles per month. Hence the master budget denominator level is 400,000 bottles. However, Bushells' senior management believes that over the next one to three years the normal monthly production level will be 500,000 bottles. These people view the 2000 budgeted production level of 400,000 bottles to be "abnormally" low. Why? A major competitor has been sharply reducing its iced tea selling prices and has also been spending enormous amounts on advertising. Bushells expects that the lower prices and advertising blitz will be a short-run phenomenon and that in 2001 the market share it has lost to this competitor will be regained.

A major reason for choosing master budget utilization over normal utilization is the difficulty of forecasting normal utilization in many industries with long-run cyclical patterns. For example, many Canadian steel companies in the 1980s believed that they were in a downturn of the demand cycle and that there would be an upturn shortly. Unfortunately, the cycle did not turn up for years. A similar problem occurs when estimating "normal" demand. Some marketing managers are prone to overestimating their ability to regain lost market share. Their estimate of "normal" demand for their product may be based on an overly optimistic outlook ("anticipating roses when all that exists are thorns").

EFFECT ON FINANCIAL STATEMENTS

OBJECTIVE 7

Explain how the choice of denominator level affects reported operating income and inventory costs

Bushells has budgeted fixed manufacturing costs of $50,000 per month. Assume that actual costs are also $50,000. To keep this example simple, we assume all fixed manufacturing costs are indirect. The budgeted fixed manufacturing overhead rates in May 2000 for the four alternative denominator-level concepts discussed are:

Denominator-Level Concept (1)	Budgeted Fixed Manufacturing Overhead per Month (2)	Budgeted Denominator Level (in bottles) (3)	Budgeted Fixed Manufacturing Overhead Cost Rate (4) = (2) ÷ (3)
Theoretical capacity	$50,000	1,152,000	$0.0434
Practical capacity	50,000	800,000	0.0625
Normal utilization	50,000	500,000	0.1000
Master budget utilization	50,000	400,000	0.1250

The budgeted fixed manufacturing overhead rate based on master budget utilization ($0.1250) is more than 180% above the rate based on theoretical capacity ($0.0434).

Assume now that Bushells' actual production in May 2000 is 460,000 bottles of iced tea. Actual sales are 420,000 bottles. Also assume no beginning inventory on May 1, 2000, and no price, spending, or efficiency variances in manufacturing for May 2000. The manufacturing plant sells bottles of iced tea to another division for $0.50 per bottle. Its only costs are variable manufacturing costs of $0.35 per bottle and $50,000 per month for fixed manufacturing overhead. Bushells writes off all variances to cost of goods sold on a monthly basis.

The budgeted manufacturing costs per bottle of iced tea for each denominator-level concept are the sum of $0.35 in variable manufacturing costs and the budgeted fixed manufacturing overhead costs (shown from the preceding table).

Denominator-Level Concept (1)	Variable Manufacturing Costs (2)	Budgeted Fixed Manufacturing Overhead Cost Rate (3)	Total Manufacturing Costs (4) = (2) + (3)
Theoretical capacity	$0.3500	$0.0434	$0.3934
Practical capacity	0.3500	0.0625	0.4125
Normal utilization	0.3500	0.1000	0.4500
Master budget utilization	0.3500	0.1250	0.4750

Each denominator-level concept will result in a different production-volume variance.

$$\text{Production-volume variance} = \left(\begin{array}{c} \text{Denominator} \\ \text{level in} \\ \text{output units} \end{array} - \begin{array}{c} \text{Actual} \\ \text{output units} \end{array} \right) \times \begin{array}{c} \text{Budgeted fixed} \\ \text{manufacturing overhead} \\ \text{rate per output unit} \end{array}$$

Theoretical capacity = (1,152,000 − 460,000) × $0.0434

= $30,033 U (rounded up)

Practical capacity = (800,000 − 460,000) × $0.0625

= $21,250 U

Normal utilization = (500,000 − 460,000) × $0.1000

= $4,000 U

Master budget utilization = (400,000 − 460,000) × $0.1250

= $7,500 F

Exhibit 9-7 shows how the choice of a denominator affects Bushells' operating income for May 2000. Using the master budget denominator results in assigning the highest amount of fixed manufacturing overhead costs per bottle to the 40,000 bottles in ending inventory. Accordingly, operating income is highest using the master budget utilization denominator. Recall that Bushells had no beginning inventory on May 1, 2000, production in May of 460,000 bottles, and sales in May of 420,000 bottles. Hence, the ending inventory on May 31 is 40,000 bottles. The differences between the operating income for the four denominator-level concepts in Exhibit 9-7 are due to different amounts of fixed manufacturing overhead being inventoried:

EXHIBIT 9-7
Bushells Company: Income Statement Effects of Alternative Denominator-Level Concepts for May 2000

	Theoretical Capacity	Practical Capacity	Normal Utilization	Master Budget Utilization
Sales, $0.50 × 420,000	$210,000	$210,000	$210,000	$210,000
Cost of goods sold:				
Beginning inventory	0	0	0	0
Variable manufacturing costs*	161,000	161,000	161,000	161,000
Fixed manufacturing overhead costs†	19,964	28,750	46,000	57,500
Cost of goods available for sale	180,964	189,750	207,000	218,500
Ending inventory‡	15,736	16,500	18,000	19,000
Total COGS (at standard costs)	165,228	173,250	189,000	199,500
Adjustment for manufacturing variances≈	30,033 U	21,250 U	4,000 U	7,500 F
Total COGS	195,261	194,500	193,000	192,000
Gross margin	14,739	15,500	17,000	18,000
Marketing costs	10,000	10,000	10,000	10,000
Operating income	$ 4,739	$ 5,500	$ 7,000	$ 8,000

*$0.35 × 460,000 = $161,000.
†Fixed manufacturing overhead costs:
   $0.0434 × 460,000 = $19,964
   $0.0625 × 460,000 = $28,750
   $0.1000 × 460,000 = $46,000
   $0.1250 × 460,000 = $57,500
‡Ending inventory costs:
   ($0.3500 + $0.0434) × (460,000 − 420,000) = $15,736
   ($0.3500 + $0.0625) × (460,000 − 420,000) = $16,500
   ($0.3500 + $0.1000) × (460,000 − 420,000) = $18,000
   ($0.3500 + $0.1250) × (460,000 − 420,000) = $19,000
≈The only variance for Bushells in May 2000 is the production-volume variance.
See text (p. 305) for the computations.

Denominator-Level Concept	Fixed Manufacturing Overhead in May 31, 2000 Inventory
Theoretical capacity	40,000 × $0.0434 = $1,736
Practical capacity	40,000 × 0.0625 = 2,500
Normal utilization	40,000 × 0.1000 = 4,000
Master budget utilization	40,000 × 0.1250 = 5,000

Thus, in Exhibit 9-7 the difference in operating income between the master budget utilization concept and the normal utilization concept of $1,000 ($8,000 – $7,000) is due to the difference in fixed manufacturing overhead inventoried ($5,000 – $4,000).

There is no requirement that Canadian companies use the same denominator-level concept for internal reporting, financial reporting, and income tax purposes. Nevertheless, the costs of recordkeeping and the desire for simplicity often lead companies to choose the same denominator level for internal reporting and tax purposes. Income tax rulings by Revenue Canada effectively prohibit use of the theoretical capacity or practical capacity denominator-level concepts. Both these concepts typically result in companies taking writeoffs of fixed manufacturing overhead as tax deductions more quickly than desired by Revenue Canada. Revenue Canada requires companies to use the master budget denominator level (along with full proration of variances between inventories and cost of goods sold) for income tax reporting.

PROBLEM

Suppose that the Bushells Company in our example is computing the operating income for May 2001. This month is identical to May 2000, the results of which are in Exhibit 9-7, except that master budget utilization for 2001 is 600,000 bottles per month instead of 400,000 bottles. There was no beginning inventory on May 1, 2001, and no variances other than the production-volume variance. Bushells writes off this variance to cost of goods sold on a monthly basis.

REQUIRED

How would the results in Exhibit 9-7 for Bushells Company be different if the month is May 2001 rather than May 2000? Show your computations.

SOLUTION

The only change in the Exhibit 9-7 results will be for the master budget utilization level. The budgeted fixed manufacturing overhead cost rate in May 2001 is:

$$\frac{\$50,000}{600,000 \text{ bottles}} = \$0.0833 \text{ per bottle}$$

The manufacturing cost per bottle becomes $0.4333 ($0.3500 + $0.0833). In turn, the production volume variance for May 2001 becomes:

$$(600,000 - 460,000) \times (\$0.0833) = \$11,662 \text{ U}$$

The income statement for May 2001 is now:

Revenues	$210,000
Cost of goods sold:	
Beginning inventory	0
Variable manufacturing costs: $0.35 × 460,000	161,000
Fixed manufacturing costs: $0.0833 × 460,000	38,318
Cost of goods available for sale	199,318
Ending inventory: $0.4333 × (460,000 − 420,000)	17,332
Total cost of goods sold (at standard costs)	181,986
Adjustment for variances	11,662 U
Total cost of goods sold	193,648
Gross margin	16,352
Marketing costs	10,000
Operating income	$ 6,352

The higher denominator level in the 2001 master budget means that lower fixed manufacturing overhead costs are inventoried in May 2001 than in May 2000, given identical sales and production levels.

SUMMARY

The following points are linked to this chapter's learning objectives.

1. Variable costing and absorption costing differ in only one respect—how to account for fixed manufacturing overhead costs. Under variable costing, fixed manufacturing overhead costs are excluded from inventoriable costs and are a cost of the period in which they are incurred. Under absorption costs, these costs are inventoriable and become expenses only when a sale occurs.

2. The variable costing income statement is based on the contribution margin format. The absorption costing income statement is based on the gross margin format.

3. Under variable costing, reported operating income is driven by variations in unit sales levels. Under absorption costing, reported operating income is driven by variations in unit production levels as well as by variations in unit sales levels.

4. There is only one breakeven point with a variable costing income statement. In contrast, there can be multiple breakeven points with an absorption costing income statement because there are multiple combinations of fixed costs, unit contribution margin, unit sales, unit production, and the denominator level that yield an operating income of zero.

5. Throughput costing treats all costs except those related to variable direct materials as costs of the period in which they are incurred. It results in a lower percentage of manufacturing costs being inventoried than does either variable or absorption costing.

6. Managers can increase operating income when absorption costing is used by producing for inventory even when there is no immediate demand for the extra production. Critics of absorption costing label this as the major negative consequence of treating fixed manufacturing overhead as an inventoriable cost. Such negative consequences can be mitigated by using nonfinancial as well as financial variables for performance evaluation.

7. The denominator level chosen for fixed manufacturing overhead can greatly affect reported inventory and operating income amounts. In some cases it can also affect pricing and contract reimbursement. Denominator levels focusing on the capacity of a plant to supply product are theoretical capacity and practical capacity. Denominator levels focusing on the demand for the products a plant can manufacture are normal utilization and master budget utilization.

8. The smaller the denominator level chosen, the higher will be the fixed manufacturing overhead cost per output unit that is inventoriable. Revenue Canada's requirement that the master budget utilization concept be used typically results in higher operating income amounts being reported compared with the operating income reported using the practical capacity or theoretical capacity denominator-level concepts.

TERMS TO LEARN

This chapter contains definitions of the following important terms:

absorption costing (p. 289)
direct costing (p. 291)
master budget utilization (p. 304)
normal utilization (p. 304)
practical capacity (p. 304)

super-variable costing (p. 301)
theoretical capacity (p. 303)
throughput costing (p. 301)
variable costing (p. 289)

ASSIGNMENT MATERIAL

QUESTIONS

9-1 "Differences in operating income between variable and absorption costing are due solely to accounting for fixed costs." Do you agree? Explain.

9-2 Why is the term *direct costing* a misnomer?

9-3 "The term *variable costing* could be improved by calling it *variable manufacturing costing*." Do you agree? Why?

9-4 Explain the main conceptual issue under variable and absorption costing regarding the proper timing for the release of fixed manufacturing overhead as expense.

9-5 "Companies that make no variable cost/fixed cost distinctions must use absorption costing and those that do make variable cost/fixed cost distinctions must use variable costing." Do you agree? Explain.

9-6 "The main trouble with variable costing is that it ignores the increasing importance of fixed costs in modern manufacturing." Do you agree? Why?

9-7 Give an example of how, under absorption costing, operating income could fall even though the unit sales level rises.

9-8 What are the factors that affect the breakeven point under variable costing?

9-9 What are the factors that affect the breakeven point under absorption costing?

9-10 Why might *throughput costing* be also called *super-variable costing?*

9-11 Critics of absorption costing have increasingly emphasized its potential for promoting undesirable incentives for managers. Give an example.

9-12 What are two ways of reducing the negative aspects associated with using absorption costing to evaluate the performance of a plant manager?

9-13 What is the costing method most frequently used by companies in their internal accounting system—throughput costing, variable costing, or absorption costing?

9-14 Which denominator-level concepts emphasize what a plant can supply? Which denominator-level concepts emphasize what customers demand for products produced by a plant?

9-15 Name one reason why many companies prefer the master budget utilization-level concept rather than the normal utilization-level concept.

EXERCISES

9-16 Variable and absorption costing, explaining operating income differences. Nascar Motors assembles and sells motor vehicles. It uses an actual costing system, in which unit costs are calculated on a monthly basis. Data relating to April and May of 2000 are:

	April	May
Unit data:		
Beginning inventory	0	150
Production	500	400
Sales	350	520
Variable cost data:		
Manufacturing costs per unit produced	$ 10,000	$ 10,000
Marketing costs per unit sold	3,000	3,000
Fixed cost data:		
Manufacturing costs	$2,000,000	$2,000,000
Marketing costs	600,000	600,000

The selling price per motor vehicle is $24,000.

REQUIRED

1. Present income statements for Nascar Motors in April and May of 2000 under (a) variable costing and (b) absorption costing.
2. Explain any differences between (a) and (b) for April and May.

9-17 Throughput costing (continuation of 9-16). The unit variable manufacturing costs of Nascar Motors are:

	April	May
Direct materials	$6,700	$6,700
Direct manufacturing labour	1,500	1,500
Manufacturing overhead	1,800	1,800

REQUIRED

1. Present income statements for Nascar Motors in April and May of 2000 under throughput costing.
2. Contrast the results in requirement 1 with those in requirement 1 of Exercise 9-16.
3. Give one motivation for Nascar Motors to adopt throughput costing.

9-18 Variable and absorption costing, explaining operating income differences. BigScreen Corporation manufactures and sells 50-inch television sets. It uses an actual costing system, in which unit costs are calculated on a monthly basis. Data relating to January, February, and March of 2000 are:

	January	February	March
Unit data:			
Beginning inventory	0	300	300
Production	1,000	800	1,250
Sales	700	800	1,500
Variable cost data:			
Manufacturing costs per unit produced	$900	$900	$900
Marketing costs per unit sold	600	600	600
Fixed cost data:			
Manufacturing costs	$400,000	$400,000	$400,000
Marketing costs	140,000	140,000	140,000

The selling price per unit is $2,500.

REQUIRED

1. Present income statements for BigScreen in January, February, and March of 2000 under (a) variable costing and (b) absorption costing.
2. Explain any differences between (a) and (b) for January, February, and March.

9-19 Throughput costing (continuation of 9-18). The unit variable manufacturing costs of BigScreen Corporation are:

	January	February	March
Direct materials	$500	$500	$500
Direct manufacturing labour	100	100	100
Manufacturing overhead	300	300	300
	$900	$900	$900

REQUIRED

1. Present income statements for BigScreen in January, February, and March of 2000 under throughput costing.
2. Contrast the results in requirement 1 with those in requirement 1 of Exercise 9-18.
3. Give one motivation for BigScreen to adopt throughput costing.

9-20 Absorption and variable costing. (CMA) Osawa, Inc. planned and actually manufactured 200,000 units of its single product in 2000, its first year of operation. Variable manufacturing costs were $20 per unit produced. Variable marketing and administrative costs were $10 per unit sold. Planned and actual fixed manufacturing costs were $600,000. Planned and actual marketing and administrative costs totalled $400,000 in 2000. Osawa sold 120,000 units of product in 2000 at a selling price of $40 per unit.

REQUIRED

1. Osawa's 2000 operating income using absorption costing is (a) $440,000, (b) $200,000, (c) $600,000, (d) $840,000, (e) none of these.
2. Osawa's 2000 operating income using variable costing is (a) $800,000, (b) $440,000, (c) $200,000, (d) $600,000, (e) none of these.

9-21 Comparison of actual costing methods. The Rehe Company sells its razors at $3 per unit. The company uses a first-in, first-out actual costing system. A new fixed manufacturing overhead allocation rate is computed each year by dividing the actual fixed manufacturing overhead cost by the actual production units. The following simplified data are related to its first two years of operation:

	Year 1	Year 2
Unit data:		
Sales	1,000	1,200
Production	1,400	1,000
Cost:		
Variable manufacturing	$ 700	$ 500
Fixed manufacturing	700	700
Variable marketing and administration	1,000	1,200
Fixed marketing and administration	400	400

REQUIRED

1. Prepare income statements based on (a) variable costing and (b) absorption costing for each year.

2. Prepare a reconciliation and explanation of the difference in the operating income for each year resulting from the use of absorption costing and variable costing.

3. Critics have claimed that a widely used accounting system has led to undesirable buildups of inventory levels.

   a. Is variable costing or absorption costing more likely to lead to such buildups? Why?

   b. What can be done to counteract undesirable inventory buildups?

9-22 Income statements. (SMA) The Mass Company manufactures and sells a single product. The following data cover the two latest years of operations:

	2000	2001
Unit data:		
Sales	25,000	25,000
Beginning inventory	1,000	1,000
Ending inventory	1,000	5,000
Selling price per unit	$40	$40
Cost data:		
Standard fixed costs:		
Manufacturing overhead	$120,000	$120,000
Marketing and administrative	$190,000	$190,000
Standard variable costs per unit:		
Direct materials	$10.50	
Direct manufacturing labour	$9.50	
Manufacturing overhead	$4.00	
Marketing and administrative	$1.20	

The denominator level is 30,000 output units per year. The Mass Company's accounting records produce variable costing information, and year-end adjustments are made to produce external reports showing absorption costing information. All variances are charged to cost of goods sold.

REQUIRED

1. Prepare two income statements for 2001, one under variable costing and one under absorption costing.

2. Explain briefly why the operating income figures computed in requirement 1 agree or do not agree.

3. Give two advantages and two disadvantages of using variable costing for internal reporting.

PROBLEMS

9-23 Variable costing versus absorption costing. The Mavis Company uses an absorption costing system based on standard costs. Total variable manufacturing costs, including direct materials costs, were $3 per unit; the standard production rate was ten units per machine-hour. Total budgeted and actual fixed manufacturing overhead costs were $420,000. Fixed manufacturing overhead was allocated at $7 per machine-hour ($420,000 ÷ 60,000 machine-hours of denominator level). The selling price is $5 per unit. Variable marketing and administrative costs, which are driven by units sold, were $1 per unit. Fixed marketing and administrative costs were $120,000. Beginning inventory in 2000 was 30,000 units; ending inventory was 40,000 units. Sales in 2000 were 540,000 units. The same standard unit costs persisted throughout 1999 and 2000. For simplicity, assume that there were no price, spending, or efficiency variances.

REQUIRED

1. Prepare an income statement for 2000 assuming that all under- or overallocated overhead is written off directly at year-end as an adjustment to cost of goods sold.

2. The president has heard about variable costing. She asks you to recast the 2000 statement as it would appear under variable costing. Explain the difference in operating income as calculated in requirements 1 and 2.

3. Graph how fixed manufacturing overhead is accounted for under absorption costing. There will be two lines, one for the budgeted fixed overhead (which is equal to the actual fixed manufacturing overhead in this case) and one for the fixed overhead allocated. Show how the over- or underallocated manufacturing overhead might be indicated on the graph.

9-24 Breakeven under absorption costing (continuation of 9-23).

REQUIRED

1. Compute the breakeven point in units under variable costing.

2. Compute the breakeven point in units under absorption costing.

3. Suppose that production was exactly equal to the denominator level, but no units were sold. Fixed manufacturing costs are unaffected. Assume, however, that all marketing and administrative costs were avoided. Compute operating income under (a) variable costing and (b) absorption costing. Explain the difference between your answers.

9-25 Alternative denominator-level concepts. Lucky Lager recently purchased a brewing plant from a bankrupt company. It was constructed only two years ago. The plant has budgeted fixed manufacturing overhead of $42 million ($3.5 million each month) in 2000. Paul Vautin, the controller of the brewery, must decide on the denominator-level concept to use in its absorption costing system for 2000. The options available to him are:

A. Theoretical capacity: 600 barrels an hour for 24 hours a day × 365 days = 5,256,000 barrels

B. Practical capacity: 500 barrels an hour for 20 hours a day × 350 days = 3,500,000 barrels

C. Normal utilization for 2000: 400 barrels an hour for 20 hours a day × 350 days = 2,800,000 barrels

D. Master budget utilization for 2000 (separate rates computed for each half-year):
  ◆ January to June 2000 budget—320 barrels an hour for 20 hours a day × 175 days = 1,120,000 barrels
  ◆ July to December 2000 budget—480 barrels an hour for 20 hours a day × 175 days = 1,680,000 barrels

Variable standard manufacturing costs per barrel are $45 (variable direct materials, $32; variable manufacturing labour, $6; and variable manufacturing overhead, $7). The brewery "sells" its output to the sales division of Lucky Lager at a budgeted price of $68 per barrel.

REQUIRED

1. Compute the budgeted fixed manufacturing overhead rate using each of the four denominator-level concepts for (a) beer produced in March 2000 and (b) beer produced in September 2000. Explain why any differences arise.

2. Explain why the theoretical capacity and practical capacity concepts are different.

3. Which denominator-level concept would the plant manager of the brewery prefer when senior management of Lucky Lager is judging plant manager performance during 2000? Explain.

9-26 Operating income effects of alternative denominator-level concepts (continuation of 9-25). In 2000, the brewery of Lucky Lager showed these results:

Unit data in barrels:	
Beginning inventory, January 1, 2000	0
Production	2,600,000
Ending inventory, December 31, 2000	200,000

The brewery had actual costs of:

Cost data:	
Variable manufacturing	$120,380,000
Fixed manufacturing overhead	$ 40,632,000

The sales division of Lucky Lager purchased 2,400,000 barrels in 2000 at the $68 per barrel rate.

All manufacturing variances are written off to cost of goods sold in the period in which they are incurred.

REQUIRED

1. Compute the operating income of the brewery using the following: (a) theoretical capacity, (b) practical capacity, and (c) normal utilization denominator-level concepts. Explain any differences between (a), (b), and (c).

2. What denominator-level concept would Lucky Lager prefer for income tax reporting? Explain.

3. Explain the ways in which Revenue Canada might restrict the flexibility of a company like Lucky Lager, which uses absorption costing, to reduce its reported taxable income.

9-27 Standard absorption, variable and throughput costing. (CMA) The Byrd Company is a manufacturer of appliances for both residential and commercial use. The company's accounting and financial reporting system is primarily designed to meet external reporting requirements in accordance with generally accepted accounting principles. For inventory costing purposes, Byrd uses the absorption costing method in conjunction with a standard costing system. Normal utilization is used as the denominator level. Costs are allocated to products on a units produced basis. The denominator of fixed manufacturing costs is normal utilization in production units. Relevant information on Byrd's steam cooker appliance is provided below for the last two years.

Unit Data	2000	2001
Beginning inventory	900	1,400
Production	2,000	400
Sales	1,500	1,700
Normal utilization	2,000	2,000

The standard costs for this product are the same in 1999, 2000, and 2001:

Financial Data	2000	2001
Selling price per unit	$ 100	$ 100
Standard variable direct manufacturing costs per unit*	40	40
Standard variable indirect manufacturing cost per unit	15	15
Variable marketing costs per unit sold	1	1
Total budgeted (and actual) fixed manufacturing costs	10,000	10,000
Total fixed marketing costs	3,000	3,000
Net unfavourable variance[†] pertaining to variable manufacturing costs	1,000	1,000

*Standard variable direct materials costs are $23 per unit.
[†]All variances are written off to cost of goods sold in the period incurred.

Currently, Byrd evaluates the performance of its product-line managers and calculates the bonus on the basis of operating income computed on an absorption costing basis. It has been suggested that the use of variable costing for internal reporting purposes would more accurately reflect the performance of each product-line manager.

REQUIRED

1. Calculate the Byrd Company's operating income on its steam cooker appliance line for 2000 and 2001 using (a) absorption costing, (b) variable costing, and (c) throughput costing.

2. Discuss the features of variable costing that allow it to reflect the performance of Byrd's product-line managers more accurately. Be sure to include in your discussion how absorption costing may influence a product-line manager's behaviour differently from the way variable costing would.

3. What are the pros and cons of adopting throughput costing?

9-28 The All-Fixed Company in 2000. (R. Marple, adapted) It is the end of 2000. The All-Fixed Company began operations in January 1999. The company is so named because it has no variable costs. All its costs are fixed; they do not vary with output.

All-Fixed is located on the bank of a river and has its own hydroelectric plant to supply power, light, and heat. The company manufactures a synthetic fertilizer from air and river water and sells its product at a price that is not expected to change. It has a small staff of employees, all hired on a fixed annual salary. The output of the plant can be increased or decreased by adjusting a few dials on a control panel.

The following are data regarding the operations of the All-Fixed Company:

	1999	2000*
Sales (units)	10,000	10,000
Production (units)	20,000	—
Selling price per tonne	$30	$30
Costs (all fixed):		
Manufacturing	$280,000	$280,000
Marketing and administrative	$40,000	$40,000

*Management adopted the policy, effective January 1, 2000, of producing only as much product as was needed to fill sales orders. During 2000, sales were the same as for 1999 and were filled entirely from inventory at the start of 2000.

REQUIRED

1. Prepare income statements with one column for 1999, one column for 2000, and one column for the two years together, using (a) variable costing and (b) absorption costing.
2. What is the breakeven point under (a) variable costing and (b) absorption costing?
3. What inventory costs would be carried on the balance sheets at December 31, 1999 and 2000, under each method?
4. Assume that the performance of the top manager of the company is evaluated and rewarded largely on the basis of reported operating income. Which costing method would the manager prefer? Why?

9-29 The Semi-Fixed Company in 2000. The Semi-Fixed Company began operations in 1999 and differs from the All-Fixed Company (described in Problem 9-28) in only one respect: it has both variable and fixed manufacturing costs. Its variable manufacturing costs are $7 per tonne, and its fixed manufacturing costs are $140,000 per year. The denominator level is 20,000 tonnes per year.

REQUIRED

1. Using the same data as in Problem 9-28 except for the change in manufacturing cost behaviour, prepare income statements with adjacent columns for 1999, 2000, and the two years together, under (a) variable costing and (b) absorption costing.
2. Why did the Semi-Fixed Company have operating income for the two-year period when the All-Fixed Company in Problem 9-28 suffered an operating loss?
3. What inventory costs would be carried on the balance sheets at December 31, 1999 and 2000, under each method?
4. Assume that the performance of the top manager of the company is evaluated and rewarded largely on the basis of reported operating income. Which costing method would the manager prefer? Why?

9-30 Comparison of variable costing and absorption costing. Consider the following data:

Hinkle Company
Income Statements for the Year Ended December 31, 2000

	Variable Costing	Absorption Costing
Revenues	$7,000,000	$7,000,000
Costs of goods sold (at standard)	3,660,000	4,575,000
Fixed manufacturing overhead	1,000,000	—
Manufacturing variances (all unfavourable):		
Direct materials price and efficiency	50,000	50,000
Direct manufacturing labour price and efficiency	60,000	60,000
Variable manufacturing overhead spending and efficiency	30,000	30,000

Fixed manufacturing overhead:			
Spending		100,000	100,000
Production volume		—	400,000
Total marketing costs (all fixed)		1,000,000	1,000,000
Total administrative costs (all fixed)		500,000	500,000
Total costs		6,400,000	6,715,000
Operating income		$ 600,000	$ 285,000

The inventories, carried at standard costs, were:

	Variable Costing	Absorption Costing
December 31, 1999	$1,320,000	$1,650,000
December 31, 2000	60,000	75,000

REQUIRED

1. Tim Hinkle, president of the Hinkle Company, has asked you to explain why the operating income for 2000 is less than for 1999, even though sales have increased 40% over last year. What will you tell him?
2. At what percentage of denominator level was the plant operating during 2000?
3. Prepare a numerical reconciliation and explanation of the difference between the operating incomes under absorption costing and variable costing.
4. Critics have claimed that a widely used accounting system has led to undesirable buildups of inventory levels.
   a. Is variable costing or absorption costing more likely to lead to such buildups? Why?
   b. What can be done to counteract undesirable inventory buildups?

9-31 **Inventory costing and management planning.** It is November 30, 2000. Consider the income statement (shown below) for the operations of Industrial Products, Inc., for January through November, 2000.

Production in the past three months has been 100 units monthly. Practical capacity is 125 units monthly. To retain a stable nucleus of key employees, management never schedules monthly production at less than 40 units.

Maximum available storage space for inventory is regarded as 200 units. The sales outlook for the next four months is 70 units monthly. Inventory is never to be less than 50 units.

Industrial Products, Inc.
Income Statement for 11 Months Ended November 30, 2000

	Units		Dollars
Revenues @ $1,000	1,000		$1,000,000
Cost of goods sold:			
Beginning inventory, December 31, 1999, @ $800	50	$ 40,000	
Manufacturing costs @ $800, including $600 per unit for fixed manufacturing overhead	1,100	880,000	
Total standard cost of goods available for sale	1,150	920,000	
Ending inventory, November 30, 2000, @ $800	150	120,000	
Standard cost of goods sold*	1,000		800,000
Gross margin			200,000
Marketing, distribution and customer service costs:			
Variable, 1,000 units @ $50		50,000	
Fixed, @ $10,000 monthly		110,000	160,000
Operating income			$ 40,000

*There are no variances for the 11-month period considered as a whole.

The company uses a standard absorption costing system. The denominator production level is 1,200 units annually. All variances are disposed of at year-end as an adjustment to cost of goods sold.

REQUIRED
1. The division manager is given an annual bonus that is geared to operating income. Assume that the manager wants to maximize the company's operating income for 2000. How many units should the manager schedule for production in December? Note that you do not have to (nor should you) compute the operating income for 2000 in this or in subsequent parts of this problem.
2. Assume that standard variable costing is in use rather than standard absorption costing. Would variable costing operating income for 2000 be higher, lower, or the same as standard absorption costing income, assuming that production for December is 80 units and sales are 70 units? Why?
3. If standard variable costing were used, what production schedule should the division manager set? Why?
4. Assume that the manager is interested in maximizing his performance over the long run and that performance is being judged on the basis of net income. Assume that the company's income tax rate will be substantially reduced in 2001 and that the year-end write-offs of variances are acceptable for income tax purposes. Assume that standard absorption costing is used. How many units should be scheduled for production in December? Why?
5. Assume that the total production and total sales for 2000 and 2001, taken together, will be unchanged by the specific decision in requirement 4. Assume also that the standards will be unchanged in 2001. Suppose the decision in requirement 4 is to schedule 50 units instead of an originally scheduled 120 units. By how much will operating income in 2001 be affected by the decision to schedule 50 units in December 2000? (That is, how much operating income is shifted from 2000 to 2001?)

9-32 **Some additional requirements for Problem 9-31; absorption costing and output -level variances.**

REQUIRED
1. What operating income will be reported for 2000 as a whole, assuming that the implied cost behaviour patterns will continue in December as they did in January through November and assuming without regard to your answer to requirement 1 in Problem 9-31 that production for December is 80 units and sales are 70 units?
2. Assume the same conditions as in requirement 1 except that a monthly denominator level of 125 units (practical capacity) was used in setting fixed manufacturing overhead rates for inventory costing throughout 2000. What production volume variance would be reported for 2000?

9-33 **Effects of denominator-level concept choice.** The Wong Company installed standard costs and a flexible budget on January 1, 2000. The president had been pondering how fixed manufacturing overhead should be allocated to products. Machine-hours had been chosen as the allocation base. Her remaining uncertainty was the denominator-level concept for machine-hours. She decided to wait for the first month's results before making a final choice of what denominator-level concept should be used from that day forward.

In January 2000, the actual units of output had a standard of 70,000 machine-hours allowed. If the company used practical capacity as the denominator-level concept, the fixed manufacturing overhead spending variance would be $10,000, unfavourable, and the production volume variance would be $36,000, unfavourable. If the company used normal utilization as the denominator-level concept, the production volume variance would be $20,000, favourable. Budgeted fixed manufacturing overhead was $120,000 for the month.

REQUIRED
1. Compute the denominator level, assuming that the normal utilization concept is chosen.
2. Compute the denominator level, assuming that the practical capacity concept is chosen.
3. Suppose you are the executive vice-president. You want to maximize your 2000 bonus, which depends on 2000 operating income. Assume that the production volume variance is charged or credited to income at year-end. Which denominator-level concept would you favour? Why?

9-34 Variable and absorption costing and breakeven points. Shasta Hills, a winery in British Columbia, manufactures a premium white cabernet and sells primarily to distributors. Wine is sold in cases of one dozen bottles. In the year ended December 31, 2000, Shasta Hills sold 242,400 cases at an average selling price of $94 per case. The following additional data are for Shasta Hills for the year ended December 31, 2000 (assume constant unit costs and no price, spending, or efficiency variances):

Beginning inventory, January 1, 2000	32,600	cases
Ending inventory, December 31, 2000	24,800	cases
Fixed manufacturing overhead	$3,753,600	
Fixed operating costs	$6,568,000	
Variable costs per case		
Direct materials		
Grapes	$16	per case
Bottles, corks, and crates	$10	per case
Direct labour		
Bottling	$6	per case
Winemaking	$14	per case
Aging	$2	per case

On December 31, 2000, the unit costs per case for closing inventory are $46 for variable costing and $61 for absorption costing.

REQUIRED

1. Calculate cases of production for Shasta Hills in 2000.
2. Find the breakeven point (number of cases) in 2000:
   a. under variable costing
   b. under absorption costing
3. Grape prices are expected to increase 25% in 2001. Assuming all other data remain constant, what is the minimum number of cases Shasta Hills must sell in 2001 to break even? Calculate the breakeven point:
   a. under variable costing
   b. under absorption costing
4. Assume the owners of Shasta Hills want to increase 2001 operating income 10% over 2000 levels. Using the same data as in requirement 3, recalculate the target quantity of cases under variable and absorption costing.

9-35 Absorption costing, standard costs, management ethics. Industrial Engineering Company (IEC) is a multinational business selling metal products used in the assembly of many cars, trucks, and planes. IEC has over fifty manufacturing divisions worldwide and is listed on the Toronto Stock Exchange. IEC has consistently reported annual earnings growth rates of 15% or more for each of the last ten years.

Division managers at IEC receive an annual bonus of 30% of their annual salary if the plant operating income increases 15% or more over the previous years operating income. Division managers who increase operating income more than 10% but less than 15% receive a bonus of 5% of their annual salary. Division managers who do not achieve a 10% increase in operating income receive no bonus. Instead, they receive a visit from the IEC corporate consulting team.

Bob Wood is manager of the Mississauga, Ontario, division, which manufactures crankshafts for sale to automobile manufacturers. Wood has just received a 30% bonus for 2000. Mary Easson, head of the IEC corporate consulting team, is less than impressed by Wood's performance. She suspects him of producing for inventory and collects the following information on the Mississauga division for 2000:

Unit data in crankshafts:	
Beginning inventory	0
Production	480,000
Ending inventory	30,000
Sales	450,000
Selling price per unit	$66

Cost data:

Standard variable costs per crankshaft:

Direct materials	$20
Direct manufacturing labour	5
Manufacturing overhead	12
Variable marketing	4

Standard fixed costs:

Manufacturing overhead	$9,000,000
Marketing	1,000,000

Manufacturing overhead is allocated to each crankshaft on the basis of standard machine-hours. Each crankshaft has a standard machining time of 30 minutes. The denominator level in 2000 was the master budget utilization for the Mississauga plant, 500,000 crankshafts. A standard absorption costing system is used for each IEC plant. All variances are recorded as a cost of the period in which they are incurred.

All auto companies require suppliers to deliver on a just-in-time basis (that is, just before the crankshafts are required for assembly). The last four months of 2000 saw a reduction in the orders auto companies placed for crankshafts.

The price, spending, and efficiency manufacturing variances for 2000 were $300,000, unfavourable. The total marketing variances were $156,000, favourable (variable $130,000 favourable and fixed $26,000 favourable).

Operating income for the Mississauga division in 1999 was $1,427,010.

REQUIRED

1. Compute the absorption costing operating income for the Mississauga division in 2000.
2. Why might Easson believe that in 2000 Wood engaged in behaviour not in the best interests of IEC? How might Wood respond to any charges Easson might make about producing for inventory?
3. Is the problem Easson raised likely to be eliminated by her talking to Wood about management ethics? Explain.

9-36 Absorption costing, management ethics (continuation of 9-35). Mary Easson decides to undertake a systematic investigation of how the combination of the existing division manager bonus plan and absorption costing may be causing division managers to make decisions not in the best interests of Industrial Engineering Company (IEC). She will first visit the Morristown division of IEC, which manufactures more than 100 different metal products.

REQUIRED

1. Name three types of behaviour that Easson should look for that would suggest problems for IEC with the existing bonus plan and accounting system.
2. What possible changes might Easson consider if her investigation produces widespread evidence of systematic poor decision-making by division managers at IEC?

COLLABORATIVE LEARNING PROBLEM

9-37 Absorption, variable, and throughput costing. The Waterloo, Ontario, plant of Maple Leaf Motors assembles the Icarus motor vehicle. The standard unit manufacturing cost per vehicle in 2000 is:

Direct materials	$6,000
Direct manufacturing labour	1,800
Variable manufacturing overhead	2,000
Fixed manufacturing overhead	?

The Waterloo plant is highly automated. Maximum productive capacity per month is 4,000 vehicles. Variable manufacturing overhead is allocated to vehicles on the basis of assembly time on the line. The standard assembly time per vehicle is 20 hours. Fixed manufacturing overhead in 2000 is allocated on the basis of the standard assembly time for the budgeted normal utilization of the plant. In 2000, the budgeted normal utilization is 3,000 vehicles per month. The budgeted monthly fixed manufacturing overhead is $7,500,000.

On January 1, 2000, there is zero beginning inventory of Icarus vehicles. The actual unit production and sales figures for the first three months of 2000 are:

	January	February	March
Production	3,200	2,400	3,800
Sales	2,000	2,900	3,200

Assume no direct-materials variances, no direct manufacturing labour variances, and no manufacturing overhead spending or efficiency variances in the first three months of 2000.

Pierre Rougeau, a vice-president of Maple Leaf Motors, is the manager of the Waterloo plant. His compensation includes a monthly bonus that is 0.5% of monthly operating income. Operating income is calculated using absorption costing. Maple Leaf Motors reports monthly absorption costing income statements. Each month an adjustment to cost of goods sold is made for the total manufacturing variances occurring in that month.

The Waterloo plant "sells" each Icarus to Maple Leaf's marketing subsidiary at $16,000 per vehicle. No marketing costs are incurred by the Waterloo plant.

INSTRUCTIONS

Form groups of two or more students to complete the following requirements.

REQUIRED

1. Compute (a) the unit fixed manufacturing overhead cost and (b) the unit total manufacturing cost.
2. Compute the monthly operating income for January, February, and March under absorption costing. What bonus is paid each month to Rougeau?
3. How much would the use of variable costing change the bonus paid each month to Rougeau if the same 0.5% figure is applied to variable costing operating income?
4. Explain the differences in the bonuses paid each month to Rougeau in requirements 2 and 3.
5. How much would the use of throughput costing change the bonus paid each month to Rougeau if the same 0.5% figure is applied to throughput costing operating income?
6. Describe different approaches Maple Leaf Motors could use to reduce the dysfunctional aspects associated with absorption costing at its Waterloo plant.

PART THREE

10

CHAPTER

DETERMINING HOW COSTS BEHAVE

Speedboat assembly companies report reductions in unit variable costs as the number of speedboats assembled increases because of learning curve effects. Regal Marine has observed such learning curve effects when assembling boats at its plant.

LEARNING OBJECTIVES

After studying this chapter, you should be able to:

1. Explain the two assumptions frequently used in cost behaviour estimation
2. Describe linear cost functions and three common ways in which they behave
3. Recognize various approaches to cost estimation
4. Outline six steps in estimating a cost function on the basis of current or past cost relationships
5. Describe three criteria to evaluate and choose cost drivers
6. Explain and give examples of nonlinear cost functions
7. Distinguish between the cumulative average time learning model and incremental unit time learning model
8. Understand data problems encountered in estimating cost functions

This chapter focuses on how to determine cost behaviour—that is, on understanding how costs change with changes in activity levels, units of products produced, and so on. Knowing how costs vary by identifying the drivers of costs and by distinguishing fixed from variable costs is frequently the key to making good management decisions. Many managerial functions, such as planning and control, rely on knowing how costs will behave. For example, consider the questions: What price should we charge? Should we make the item or buy it? What effect will a 20% increase in units sold have on operating income? Decisions in the control area, such as the interpretation of some variances, similarly rely heavily on knowledge of cost behaviour. Determining and understanding how costs behave are among the most important functions of the cost accountant.

GENERAL ISSUES IN ESTIMATING COST FUNCTIONS

Basic Assumptions and Examples of Cost Functions

A cost function is a mathematical function describing cost behaviour patterns—how costs change with changes in the cost driver. Cost functions can be plotted on graph paper by measuring the cost driver on the x-axis and the corresponding amount of total costs on the y-axis.

Two assumptions are frequently made when estimating cost functions:

1. Variations in the total costs of a cost object are explained by variations in a single cost driver.

2. Cost behaviour is adequately approximated by a *linear cost function* of the cost driver within the relevant range. A **linear cost function** is a cost function where, within the relevant range, the graph of total costs versus a single cost driver forms a straight line.

We use these assumptions throughout much of this chapter. Later sections give examples of nonlinear cost behaviour patterns in which the plot of the relationship between the cost driver and total costs is not a straight line. The last section in the appendix to this chapter describes how changes in two or more cost drivers can explain changes in the level of total costs. We illustrate cost functions in the context of negotiations between Cannon Services and World Wide Communications (WWC) for exclusive use of a telephone line between New York and Paris. WWC offers Cannon Services three alternative cost structures.

◆ **Alternative 1.** $5 per minute of phone use. As we saw in Chapter 2, this is a *strictly variable cost* for Cannon Services. The number of phone minutes used is the cost driver; that is, the number of phone minutes used is the factor whose change causes a change in total costs.

Graph 1 in Exhibit 10-1 presents the *strictly variable* or *proportionately variable* cost. Total costs (measured along the vertical y-axis) change in proportion to the number of phone minutes used (measured along the horizontal x-axis) within the relevant range. The *relevant range*, described in Chapter 2, is the range of the cost driver where the relationship between total costs and the driver is valid. There are no fixed costs. Every additional minute adds $5 to total costs. Graph 1 of Exhibit 10-1 illustrates the $5 **slope coefficient**, the amount by which total costs change for a unit change in the cost driver within the relevant range.

We can write the cost function in graph 1 of Exhibit 10-1 as:

$$y = \$5X$$

where X measures the number of phone minutes used and y measures the total costs of the phone minutes determined from the cost function.

◆ **Alternative 2.** $10,000 per month. Under this alternative, Cannon Services has a fixed cost of $10,000. Graph 2 in Exhibit 10-1 presents the *fixed cost*. The total costs will be $10,000 per month regardless of the number of phone minutes used. (We use the same cost driver, the number of phone minutes used, to compare cost behaviour patterns under various alternatives.)

OBJECTIVE 1

Explain the two assumptions frequently used in cost behaviour estimation

OBJECTIVE 2

Describe linear cost functions and three common ways in which they behave

Linear cost function. Cost function in which the graph of total costs versus a single cost driver forms a straight line within the relevant range.

Slope coefficient. Coefficient term in a cost estimation model indicates how much total costs change for each unit change in the cost driver within the relevant range.

EXHIBIT 10-1
Examples of Linear Cost Functions

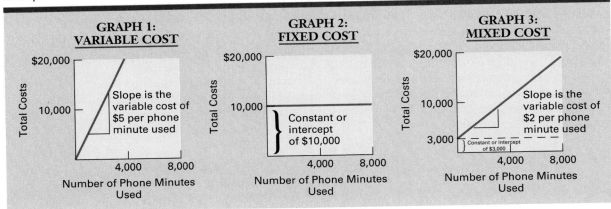

Graph 2 in Exhibit 10-1 refers to the fixed cost of $10,000 as a **constant** or **intercept,** the component of total costs that, within the relevant range, does not vary with changes in the level of the cost driver. Under alternative 2, the constant or intercept accounts for all the costs, since there are no variable costs. The slope is zero.

We can write the cost function in graph 2 of Exhibit 10-1 as:

$$y = \$10,000$$

showing that total costs will be $10,000, regardless of the number of phone minutes used by Cannon Services.

◆ **Alternative 3.** $3,000 per month plus $2 per minute of phone use. This is an example of a *mixed* cost. A **mixed cost** (or **semivariable cost**) is a cost that has both fixed and variable elements. Graph 3 in Exhibit 10-1 presents the mixed cost. It has one component that is fixed regardless of the number of phone minutes used ($3,000 per month) and another component that is variable with respect to the number of phone minutes used ($2 per minute of phone use). In this example, the constant or intercept is $3,000 and the slope coefficient is $2.

We can write the cost function in Graph 3 of Exhibit 10-1 as:

$$y = \$3,000 + \$2X$$

In the case of mixed costs, the total costs in the relevant range increase as the number of phone minutes used increases in the relevant range. *However, total costs do not change in proportion to the change in the number of phone minutes used in the relevant range.* For example, when 4,000 phone minutes are used, the total costs are [$3,000 + ($2 × 4,000)] = $11,000, but when 8,000 phone minutes are used, the total costs are [$3,000 + ($2 × 8,000)] = $19,000. Although the number of phone minutes used has doubled, the total costs have increased to only 1.73 ($19,000 ÷ $11,000) times the original costs.

Understanding cost behaviour patterns is a crucial input in choosing between the alternatives. Suppose Cannon Services expects to use at least 4,000 phone minutes per month. Its costs for 4,000 phone minutes under the three alternatives would be: alternative 1, $20,000 ($5 × 4,000); alternative 2, $10,000; alternative 3, $11,000 [$3,000 + ($2 × 4,000)]. Alternative 2 is the least costly. Moreover, if Cannon used more than 4,000 phone minutes, alternatives 1 and 3 would be even more costly than alternative 2. Cannon would prefer alternative 2.

Basic Terms

Note two features of the cost functions in the Cannon Services/WWC example. For specificity, consider graph 3.

1. Variations in a *single* cost driver (number of phone minutes used) explain variations in total costs.

2. The cost functions are linear; that is, the plot of total costs versus phone minutes used is a straight line. Because graph 3 is a straight line, the only information we need to draw graph 3 is the constant or intercept term ($3,000) and the slope coefficient ($2 per phone minute used). These two pieces of information describe total costs for the entire relevant range of the number of phone minutes used. That is, within the relevant range, linear cost functions (in the single cost driver case) can be described by a single constant or intercept (called *a*) and a single slope coefficient (called *b*). We write the linear cost function as:

$$y = a + bX$$

Under alternative 1, *a* = $0 and *b* = $5 per phone minute used; under alternative 2, *a* = $10,000, *b* = $0 per phone minute used; and under alternative 3, *a* = $3,000, *b* = $2 per phone minute used.

The Cannon Services/WWC example illustrates variable, fixed, and mixed cost functions using information about future cost structures proposed to Cannon by WWC. Often, however, cost functions are estimated from past cost data. **Cost estimation** is the attempt to measure *past* cost relationships between total costs and the drivers of those costs. For example, managers could use cost estimation to understand what causes marketing costs to change from year to year (the number of cars sold or the number of new models introduced), and its fixed and variable cost components. Managers are interested in estimating past cost behaviour patterns primarily because these estimates can help them make more accurate **cost predictions,** or forecasts, about future costs. Better cost predictions help managers make more informed planning and control decisions, such as the marketing costs budget for next year.

Cost estimation. The measurement of past cost relationships.

Cost prediction. Forecast of future costs.

Chapter 2 outlined three other specifications necessary to classify costs into their variable and fixed cost components. We review them briefly here.

♦ **Choice of cost object.**   A particular cost item could be variable with respect to one cost object and fixed with respect to another. For example, annual van registration and licence costs would be a variable cost with respect to the number of vans owned and operated by SuperShuttle, an airport transportation company, but registration and licence costs for a particular van are a fixed cost with respect to the number of miles that the van covered during the year.

♦ **Time span.**   *Whether a cost is variable or fixed with respect to a particular driver depends on the time span considered in the decision situation. The longer the time span, other things being equal, the more likely it is that the cost will be variable.* For example, inspection salaries and costs at the Bombardier Company are typically fixed in the short run with respect to hours of inspection activity. But in the long run, Bombardier's total inspection costs will vary with the inspection time required: more inspectors will be hired if more inspection is needed, while some inspectors will be reassigned to other tasks if less inspection is needed.

♦ **Relevant range.**   Accountants and managers use linear cost functions to approximate the relation of total costs to cost drivers within a relevant range. Exhibit 10-2 plots the relationship over several years between total direct

EXHIBIT 10-2
Linearity Within Relevant Range

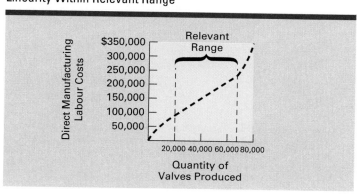

manufacturing labour costs and the number of valves produced each year by AMC, Inc. at its Cleveland plant. Costs are nonlinear outside the relevant range. In this case, nonlinearities occur when the valve output is low because of inefficiencies in using manufacturing labour. Nonlinearities occur at very high levels of production because of greater congestion in the plant and the need for more coordination.

THE CAUSE-AND-EFFECT CRITERION IN CHOOSING COST DRIVERS

The most important issue in estimating a cost function is to determine whether a cause-and-effect relationship exists between the cost driver and the resulting costs. The cause-and-effect relationship might arise in several ways.

1. It may be due to a physical relationship between costs and the cost driver. An example of a physical relationship is when units of production is used as the cost driver of materials costs. To produce more units requires more materials, which results in higher materials costs.

2. Cause and effect can arise from a contractual arrangement, as in the Cannon Services example described earlier, where the number of phone minutes used is the cost driver of the telephone line costs.

SURVEYS OF COMPANY PRACTICE

International Comparison of Cost Classification by Companies

Organizations differ in classifying individual costs. A variable cost item in one organization can be a fixed cost item in another organization. Consider labour costs. Home construction companies often classify labour cost as a variable cost. These companies rapidly adjust their labour force in response to changes in the demand for housing construction. In contrast, oil refining companies often classify labour cost as a fixed cost. The labour force is stable even when sizable changes occur in the volume or type of oil products refined.

Surveys indicate significant differences in the percentage of companies in various countries classifying individual cost categories as variable, fixed, or mixed. A lower percentage of U.S. and Australian companies treat labour costs as a fixed cost compared with Japanese companies.

Cost Category	U.S. Companies			Japanese Companies			Australian Companies		
	Variable	Mixed	Fixed	Variable	Mixed	Fixed	Variable	Mixed	Fixed
Production labour	86%	6%	8%	52%	5%	43%	70%	20%	10%
Setup labour	60	25	15	44	6	50	45	33	22
Materials-handling labour	48	34	18	23	16	61	40	30	30
Quality control labour	34	36	30	13	12	75	21	27	52
Tooling	32	35	33	31	26	43	25	28	47
Energy	26	45	29	42	31	27	—	—	—
Building occupancy	1	6	93	0	0	100	—	—	—
Amortization	1	7	92	0	0	100	—	—	—

Source: Adapted from the NAA Tokyo Affiliate, "Management Accounting in the Advanced Manufacturing Surrounding: Comparative Study on Survey in Japan and U.S.A.," (Tokyo, Japan, 1988) and Joye, M., and P. Blayney, "Cost and Management Accounting Practices in Australian Manufacturing Companies: Survey Results," (Accounting Research Centre, The University of Sydney, 1991)

3. Cause and effect can be implicitly established by logic and knowledge of operations. An example is when number of component parts is used as a cost driver of design costs. It seems intuitively clear that a complex product design with many component parts that must fit together precisely will incur higher design costs than a simple product with few parts.

Be careful not to interpret a high correlation, or connection, between two variables to mean that either variable causes the other. A high correlation between two variables, u and v, indicates merely that the two variables move together. It is possible that u may cause v; v may cause u; u and v may interact; both may be affected by a third variable z; or the correlation may be due to chance. No conclusions about cause and effect are warranted by high correlations. For example, higher production generally results in higher materials costs and higher labour costs. Materials costs and labour costs are highly correlated, but neither causes the other.

Consider another example. Over the past 28 years, the New York Stock Exchange Index has almost always increased during the year in which an original National Football League team (such as the San Francisco 49ers) has won the Super Bowl, and almost always decreased in the year in which an original American Football League team (such as the Miami Dolphins) has won.[1] There is, however, no plausible cause-and-effect explanation for this high correlation.

Only a true cause-and-effect relationship, not merely correlation, establishes an economically plausible relationship between costs and their cost drivers. Economic plausibility gives the analyst confidence that the estimated relationship will appear again and again in other similar sets of data. Establishing economic plausibility is a vital aspect of cost estimation.

COST ESTIMATION APPROACHES

There are four approaches to cost estimation:

1. Industrial engineering method
2. Conference method
3. Account analysis method
4. Quantitative analysis of current or past cost relationships

These approaches differ in the costs of conducting the analysis, the assumptions they make, and the evidence they provide about the accuracy of the estimated cost function. They are not mutually exclusive. Many organizations use a combination of these approaches.

Industrial Engineering Method

The **industrial engineering method,** also called the **work measurement method,** estimates cost functions by analyzing the relationship between inputs and outputs in physical terms. This method has its roots in studies and techniques developed by Frank and Lillian Gilbreth in the early twentieth century. Consider, for example, a carpet manufacturer that uses inputs of cotton, wool, dyes, direct labour, machine time, and power. Production output is square metres of carpet. Time-and-motion studies analyze the time and materials required to perform the various operations to produce the carpet. For example, a time-and-motion study may conclude that to produce 20 square metres of carpet requires two bales of cotton and eleven litres of dye. Standards and budgets transform these physical input and output measures into costs. The result is an estimated cost function relating total manufacturing costs to the cost driver, square metres of carpet.

The industrial engineering method can be very time-consuming. Some government contracts mandate its use. Many organizations, however, find it too costly

OBJECTIVE 3

Recognize various approaches to cost estimation

BC Research Inc.: Ergonomics & Human Factors
www.bcr.bc.ca/ergonomics/default.htm

Industrial engineering method (work measurement method). Approach to cost estimation that first analyzes the relationship between inputs and outputs in physical terms.

Lillian Gilbreth
www.greatwomen.org/glbrth.htm

[1]Granelli, J. and T. Petruno, "You Can Take Heart from the January Gain or You Can Punt," *Los Angeles Times,* February 1, 1993.

Co-operative Bank
www.co-operativebank.co.uk

VISA
www.visa.com

Conference method. Approach to cost estimation that develops cost estimates on the basis of analysis and opinions gathered from various departments of an organization.

for analyzing their entire cost structure. More frequently, organizations use this approach for direct cost categories such as materials and labour but not for indirect cost categories such as manufacturing overhead. Physical relationships between inputs and outputs may be difficult to specify for individual overhead cost items.

Conference Method

The **conference method** estimates cost functions on the basis of analysis and opinions about costs and their drivers gathered from various departments of an organization (purchasing, process engineering, manufacturing, employee relations, and so on). The Co-operative Bank in the United Kingdom has a cost estimating department that develops cost functions for its retail banking products (current account, VISA cards, mortgages, and so on) on the basis of a consensus of estimates from the relevant departments. The Bank uses this information to price products, to adjust its product mix to the products that are most profitable, and to monitor and measure cost improvements over time.

The conference method allows cost functions and cost estimates to be developed quickly. The pooling of expert knowledge from each value-chain area gives the conference method credibility. The accuracy of the cost estimates largely depends on the care and detail taken by the people providing the inputs.[2]

Account Analysis Method

Account analysis method. Approach to cost estimation that classifies cost accounts in the ledger as variable, fixed, or mixed with respect to the cost driver. Typically, qualitative rather than quantitative analysis is used in making these classification

The **account analysis method** estimates cost functions by classifying cost accounts in the ledger as variable, fixed, or mixed with respect to the identified cost driver. Typically, managers use qualitative rather than quantitative analysis when making these cost classification decisions. The account analysis approach is widely used.[3]

Consider indirect manufacturing labour costs for a small production area (or cell) at Elegant Rugs, which weaves carpets for homes and offices and uses state-of-the-art automated weaving machines. These costs include maintenance, quality control, and setup costs for the machines. During the most recent 12-week period, Elegant Rugs worked the machines in the cell for a total of 862 hours and incurred total indirect manufacturing labour costs of $12,501. Management wants the cost analyst to use the account analysis method to estimate a linear cost function for indirect manufacturing labour costs with machine-hours as the cost driver.

The cost analyst decides to separate total indirect manufacturing labour costs ($12,501) into costs that are fixed ($2,157) and costs that are variable ($10,344) with respect to the number of machine-hours worked. Variable costs per machine hour are $10,344 \div 862 = 12. The general cost equation, $y = a + bX$, is: indirect manufacturing labour costs = $2,157 + ($12 \times$ number of machine-hours). The indirect manufacturing labour cost per machine-hour is $12,501 \div 862 = 14.50.

Management at Elegant Rugs can use the cost function to estimate the indirect manufacturing labour costs of using 950 machine-hours to produce carpet in the next 12-week period. Using the cost function, estimated costs = $2,157 + (950 \times 12)$ = $13,557$. The indirect manufacturing labour costs per machine-hour decrease to $13,557 \div 950 = 14.27, as fixed costs are spread over a greater number of units.

Organizations differ with respect to the care taken in implementing account analysis. In some organizations, individuals thoroughly knowledgeable about the operations make the cost classification decisions. For example, manufacturing personnel may classify costs such as machine lubricants and materials-handling labour, while marketing personnel may classify costs such as advertising brochures and sales salaries. In other organizations, only cursory analysis is conducted, sometimes by individuals with limited knowledge of operations, before cost classification decisions are made. Clearly, the former approach would provide more reliable cost classifications, and hence estimates of the fixed and variable components of the cost, than the

---

[2]The conference method is further described in W. Winchell, *Realistic Cost Estimating for Manufacturing*, 2nd ed. (Dearborn, Mich.: Society for Manufacturing Engineers, 1991).

[3]Survey evidence appears in M. M. Mowen, *Accounting for Costs as Fixed and Variable* (Montvale, N.J.: National Association of Accountants, 1986).

EXHIBIT 10-3
Weekly Indirect Manufacturing Labour Costs, Machine-Hours, and Direct Manufacturing
Labour-Hours for Elegant Rugs

Week	Indirect Manufacturing Labour Costs (1)	Machine-Hours (2)	Direct Manufacturing Labour-Hours (3)
1	$1,190	68	30
2	1,211	88	35
3	1,004	62	36
4	917	72	20
5	770	60	47
6	1,456	96	45
7	1,180	78	44
8	710	46	38
9	1,316	82	70
10	1,032	94	30
11	752	68	29
12	963	48	38

latter. Supplementing the account analysis method by the conference method improves its credibility.

Quantitative Analyses of Cost Relationships

Quantitative analyses of cost relationships are formal methods to fit linear cost functions to past data observations. Columns 1 and 2 of Exhibit 10-3 above break down the $12,501 of total indirect manufacturing labour costs and the 862 total machine-hours for the most recent 12-week period into weekly data. Note that the data are paired. For example, week 12 shows indirect manufacturing labour costs of $963 and 48 machine-hours. The next section uses the data in Exhibit 10-3 to illustrate two different quantitative ways to estimate a cost function: the high-low method and regression analysis.

STEPS IN ESTIMATING A COST FUNCTION

There are six steps in estimating a cost function on the basis of an analysis of current or past cost relationships: (1) choose the dependent variable (the variable to be predicted, which is some type of cost); (2) identify the cost driver(s) (independent variable[s]); (3) collect data on the dependent variable and the cost driver(s); (4) plot the data; (5) estimate the cost function; and (6) evaluate the estimated cost function. As we discussed earlier in this chapter, choosing a cost driver is not always straightforward. Frequently, the cost analyst will cycle through these steps several times trying alternative economically plausible cost drivers to see which cost driver best fits the data.

◆ **Step 1:** *Choose the dependent variable.* Choice of the **dependent variable** (the cost variable to be predicted) will depend on the purpose for estimating a cost function. For example, if the purpose is to determine indirect manufacturing costs for a production line, then the dependent variable should incorporate all costs that are classified as indirect with respect to the production line.

◆ **Step 2:** *Identify the cost driver(s).* The chosen cost driver should have an economically plausible relationship with the dependent variable and be accurately measurable. Ideally, all the individual items included in the dependent variable should have the same cost driver(s). Where a single relationship does not exist, the cost analyst should investigate the possibility of estimating more than one cost function.

OBJECTIVE 4

Outline six steps in estimating a cost function on the basis of current or past cost relationships

Dependent variable. The cost variable to be predicted in a cost estimation or prediction model.

Consider several types of fringe benefits paid to employees and their cost drivers:

Fringe Benefit	Cost Driver
Health benefits	Number of employees
Cafeteria meals	Number of employees
Pension benefits	Salaries of employees
Life insurance	Salaries of employees

The costs of health benefits and cafeteria meals can be combined into one cost pool, because they both have the same cost driver, number of employees. Pension benefits and life insurance costs have a different cost driver, salaries of employees, and hence should not be combined with health benefits and cafeteria meals. Instead, they should be combined in a separate cost pool and estimated using salaries of employees receiving the benefits as the cost driver.

◆ **Step 3:** *Collect data on the dependent variable and the cost driver(s).* This step is usually the most difficult one in cost analysis. Cost analysts obtain data from company documents, from interviews with managers, and through special studies. These data may be time series data or cross-sectional data. *Time series data* pertain to the same entity (organization, plant, activity area, and so on) over a sequence of past time periods. Weekly observations of indirect manufacturing labour costs and machine-hours in the Elegant Rugs illustration are an example of time series data. The ideal time series database would contain numerous observations for a firm whose operations have not been affected by economic or technological change. Stable technology ensures that data collected in the estimation period represent the same underlying relationship between the dependent variable and the cost driver(s). Moreover, the time periods (for example, daily, weekly, or monthly) used to measure the dependent variable and the cost driver(s) should be identical. *Cross-sectional data* pertain to different entities for the same time period. For example, studies of personnel costs and loans processed at 50 individual branches of a bank during March would produce cross-sectional data for March. A later section of this chapter describes problems that arise in data collection.

◆ **Step 4:** *Plot the data.* This step is important. The saying "A picture is worth a thousand words" conveys the benefits of plotting the data. The general relation between the dependent variable and the cost driver can readily be observed in a plot of the data. Moreover, the plot highlights extreme observations that analysts should check. Was there an error in recording the data or an unusual event, such as a labour strike, that makes these observations unrepresentative of the normal relationship between the dependent variable and the cost driver? Plotting the data can also provide insight into whether the relation is approximately linear and what the relevant range of the cost function is.

Exhibit 10-4 plots the weekly data from columns 1 and 2 of Exhibit 10-3. There is strong visual evidence of a positive relation between indirect manufacturing labour costs and machine-hours (that is, when machine-hours go up, so do costs). There do not appear to be any extreme observations in Exhibit 10-4. The relevant range is from 46 to 96 machine-hours per week.

◆ **Step 5:** *Estimate the cost function.* We show how to estimate the cost function for our Elegant Rugs data using the high-low method and regression analysis.

◆ **Step 6:** *Evaluate the estimated cost function.* We describe criteria for evaluating a cost function after illustrating the high-low method and regression analysis.

High-low method. Method used to estimate a cost function that entails using only the highest and lowest observed values of the cost driver within the relevant range.

High-Low Method

Managers, at times, use very simple methods to estimate cost functions. An example is the **high-low method,** which entails using only the highest and lowest observed values of the *cost driver* within the relevant range. The line connecting these two points becomes the estimated cost function.

EXHIBIT 10-4
Plot of Weekly Indirect Manufacturing Labour Costs and Machine-Hours for Elegant Rugs

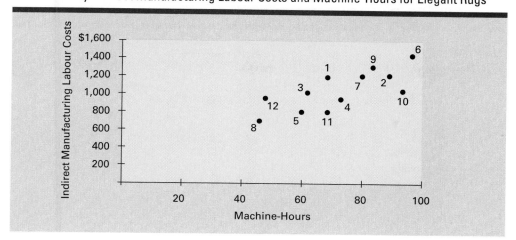

We illustrate the high-low method using data from Exhibit 10-3.

	Machine-Hours	Indirect Manufacturing Labour Costs
Highest observation of cost driver (week 6)	96	$1,456
Lowest observation of cost driver (week 8)	46	710
Difference	50	$ 746

$$\text{Slope coefficient } b = \frac{\text{Difference between costs associated with highest and lowest observations of the cost driver}}{\text{Difference between highest and lowest observations of the cost driver}}$$

$$= \$746 \div 50 = \$14.92 \text{ per machine-hour}$$

To compute the constant, we can use either the highest or the lowest observation of the cost driver. The two calculations yield the same answer (because the solution technique solves two linear equations with two unknowns, the slope coefficient and the constant).

$$y = a + bX, \qquad a = y - bX$$

At the highest observation of the cost driver:

$$\text{Constant } a = \$1,456 - (\$14.92 \times 96) = \$23.68$$

At the lowest observation of the cost driver:

$$\text{Constant } a = \$710 - (\$14.92 \times 46) = \$23.68$$

Therefore, the high-low estimate of the cost function is::

$$y = a + bX$$
$$= \$23.68 + (\$14.92 \times \text{machine-hours})$$

The bottom line in Exhibit 10-5 shows the estimated cost function using the high-low method. The estimated cost function is a straight line joining the observations with the highest and lowest values of the cost driver (machine-hours). The constant, or intercept, term does not serve as an estimate of the fixed costs of Elegant Rugs if no machines were run. Why? Because running no machines and shutting down the plant is outside the relevant range. The intercept term is the constant component of the equation that provides the best (linear) approximation of how a cost behaves within the relevant range.

Suppose indirect manufacturing labour costs in week 6 were $1,280 instead of $1,456 while 96 machine-hours were worked. In this case, the highest observation of the cost driver (machine-hours of 96 in week 6) will not coincide with the next highest

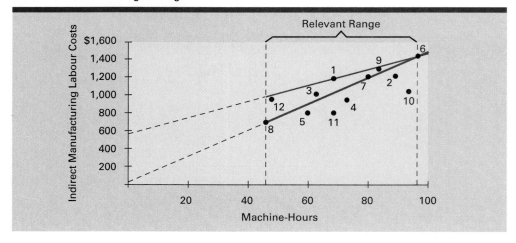

observation of the dependent variable (costs of $1,316 in week 9). Given that causality runs from the cost driver to the dependent variable in a cost function, choosing the highest and lowest observation of the cost driver is appropriate. The high-low method would estimate the new cost function still using data from weeks 6 and 8.

There is an obvious danger of relying on only two observations. Suppose that because of certain provisions in the labour contract that guarantee certain minimum payments, indirect manufacturing labour costs in week 8 were $1,000 instead of $710 when only 46 machine-hours were worked. The top line in Exhibit 10-5 shows the revised estimated cost function using the high-low method. It lies above the data. In this case, picking the highest and lowest observations for the machine-hours variable can result in an estimated cost function that poorly describes the underlying (linear) cost relationship between indirect manufacturing labour costs and machine-hours.

Sometimes the high-low method is modified so that the two observations chosen are a representative high and a representative low. The reason is that management wants to avoid having extreme observations, which arise from abnormal events, affect the cost function. Even with such a modification, this method ignores information from all but two observations when estimating the cost function.

Regression Analysis Method

Regression analysis. Statistical model that measures the average amount of change in the dependent variable that is associated with a unit change in one or more independent variables.

Simple regression. Regression model that uses only one independent variable to estimate the dependent variable.

Multiple regression. Regression model that uses more than one independent variable to estimate the dependent variable.

Unlike the high-low method, regression analysis uses all available data to estimate the cost function. **Regression analysis** is a statistical method that measures the *average* amount of change in the dependent variable that is associated with a unit change in one or more independent variables. In the Elegant Rugs example, the dependent variable is total indirect manufacturing labour costs. The independent variable, or cost driver, is machine-hours. **Simple regression** analysis estimates the relationship between the dependent variable and one independent variable; **multiple regression** analysis estimates the relationship between the dependent variable and multiple independent variables.

We emphasize the interpretation and use of output from computer software programs for regression analysis and so only present detailed computations for deriving the regression line in this chapter's appendix. Commonly available programs (for example, SPSS, SAS, Lotus, and Excel) on mainframes and personal computers calculate almost all the statistics referred to in this chapter.

Exhibit 10-6 shows the line developed using regression analysis that best fits the data in columns 1 and 2 of Exhibit 10-3. The estimated cost function is:

$$y = \$300.98 + \$10.31X$$

where y is the predicted indirect manufacturing labour costs for any level of machine-hours (X). The constant, or intercept, term of the regression a is $300.98, and the slope coefficient b is $10.31 per machine-hour.

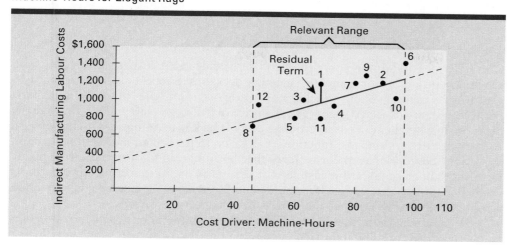

How do we derive the regression equation and regression line in Exhibit 10-6? We use the least-squares technique. We draw the regression line to minimize the sum of the squared vertical distances from the data points (the various points on the graph) to the regression line. Vertical differences measure distance between actual cost and the estimated cost for each observation. The difference between actual and predicted cost is called the **residual term** (also called **disturbance term** and **error term**). The smaller the residual terms, the better the fit between predicted costs and actual cost observations. Goodness of fit indicates the strength of the relationship between the cost driver and costs. The regression line in Exhibit 10-6 rises reasonably steeply from left to right. The positive slope of this line indicates that, on average, indirect manufacturing labour costs increase as machine-hours increase.

> **Residual term (disturbance term, error term).** The difference between the actual and the predicted amount of a dependent variable (such as a cost) in a regression model.

The vertical dashed lines in Exhibit 10-6 indicate the relevant range. As discussed previously, the estimated cost function applies only to cost driver levels *within the relevant range*, not to cost driver levels outside the relevant range.

The estimate of the slope coefficient b indicates that the average indirect manufacturing labour costs vary at the rate of $10.31 for every machine-hour within the relevant range. Management can use this equation when budgeting for future indirect manufacturing labour costs. For instance, if 90 machine-hours are budgeted for the upcoming week, the predicted indirect manufacturing labour costs would be:

$$y = \$300.98 + (\$10.31 \times 90) = \$1,228.88$$

Compare the regression equation with the high-low equation in the preceding section, which was $23.68 + $14.92 per machine-hour. For 90 machine-hours, the predicted cost based on the high-low equation is $23.68 + ($14.92 × 90) = $1,366.48. Suppose that for three weeks over the next 12-week period, Elegant Rugs runs its machines for 90 hours each week. Assume average indirect manufacturing labour costs for those three weeks is $1,300. On the basis of high-low prediction of $1,366.48, Elegant Rugs would conclude it has performed well. But comparing the $1,300 performance with the $1,228.88 prediction of the regression model tells a different story, and would probably prompt Elegant Rugs to search for ways to improve its cost performance.

Intelligent application of regression analysis requires knowledge of both operations and cost accounting. Consider the costs to maintain and repair metal-cutting machines at Helix Corporation, a manufacturer of filing cabinets. Helix schedules repairs and maintenance when production is at a low level to avoid having to take machines out of service when they are needed most. A plot and regression analysis of the monthly data will then show high repair costs in months of low production and low repair costs in months of high production. The engineering link between units of production and repair costs, however, is usually clear-cut. Over time there is a cause-and-effect relation: the higher the level of production, the higher the repair costs. To estimate the relation correctly, a thoughtful analyst will recognize that repair costs will tend to lag behind periods of high production, and use *lagged* production as the cost driver.

EVALUATING AND CHOOSING COST DRIVERS

OBJECTIVE 5

Describe three criteria to evaluate and choose cost drivers

Correctly identifying the cost driver and separating fixed costs from variable costs are important inputs for many management decisions. Suppose management at Elegant Rugs is thinking of introducing a new style of carpet. Sales of 650 square metres of this carpet are expected each week at a price of $12 per square metre. To make this decision, management needs to estimate costs. The key to doing so is identifying the correct cost drivers and cost functions. Consider, in particular, indirect manufacturing labour costs. Management believes that both machine-hours and direct manufacturing labour-hours are plausible cost drivers of indirect manufacturing labour costs. It estimates that 72 machine-hours and 21 direct manufacturing labour-hours would be required to produce the square metres of carpet it needs.

What guidance do the different cost estimation methods provide for choosing among cost drivers? The industrial engineering method relies on analyzing physical relationships between costs and cost drivers, which are difficult to specify in this case. The conference method and the account analysis method use subjective assessments to choose a cost driver and to estimate the fixed and variable components of the cost function. In these cases, management must go with its best judgment. Management cannot use these methods to test and try alternative cost drivers. The major advantage of quantitative methods is that managers can use these methods to evaluate different cost drivers. We illustrate how using the regression analysis approach.

Suppose Elegant Rugs wants to evaluate whether direct manufacturing labour-hours is a better cost driver than machine-hours for indirect manufacturing labour costs. The cost analyst at Elegant Rugs inputs the data in columns 1 and 3 of Exhibit 10-3 into a computer program and estimates the cost function:

$$y = \$744.67 + \$7.72X$$

Exhibit 10-7 shows the plot for indirect manufacturing labour costs and direct manufacturing labour-hours, and the regression line that best fits the data.

Which cost driver should Elegant Rugs choose? We consider three of the most important criteria:

1. **Economic plausibility.** Both cost drivers are economically plausible. However, in the state-of-the-art, highly automated production environment of Elegant Rugs, costs are likely to be more closely related to machine-hours than to direct manufacturing labour-hours.

2. **Goodness of fit.** Compare Exhibits 10-6 and 10-7. The vertical differences between actual and predicted costs are much smaller for machine-hours than for direct manufacturing labour-hours—machine-hours has a stronger relationship with indirect manufacturing labour costs.

3. **Slope of regression line.** Again compare Exhibits 10-6 and 10-7. The machine-hours regression line has a relatively steep slope while the direct manufacturing labour hours regression line is relatively flat (small slope). A relatively flat regression line indicates a weak or no relationship between indirect manufacturing labour costs and direct manufacturing labour-hours, since, on average, changes in direct manufacturing labour-hours appear to have a minimal effect on indirect manufacturing labour costs.

Elegant Rugs should choose machine-hours as the cost driver and use the cost function $y = \$300.98 + (\$10.31 \times$ machine-hours$)$ to predict future indirect manufacturing labour costs. Using this model, Elegant Rugs would predict costs of $y = \$300.98 + (\$10.31 \times 72) = \$1,043.30$. Had it used direct manufacturing labour-hours as the cost driver, it would have incorrectly predicted costs of $\$744.67 + (\$7.72 \times 21) = \$906.79$. If Elegant Rugs systematically underestimates costs and chooses incorrect cost drivers for other indirect costs as well, it

EXHIBIT 10-7

Regression Model for Weekly Indirect Manufacturing Labour Costs and Direct
Manufacturing Labour-Hours for Elegant Rugs

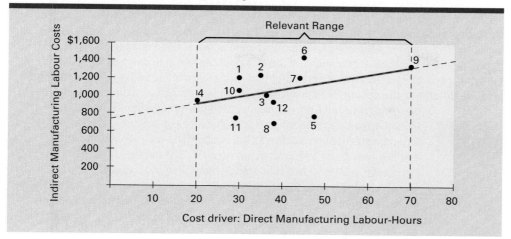

would conclude that the costs of manufacturing the new style of carpet are quite low and essentially fixed (the regression line is relatively flat). But the actual costs driven by machine-hours would prove to be much higher. Without identifying the correct cost drivers, management would be misled into believing the new style of carpets are more profitable than they actually are.

Incorrectly estimating the cost function will also have repercussions for cost management and cost control. Suppose direct manufacturing labour-hours was used as the cost driver, and actual indirect manufacturing labour costs were $970. Actual costs would then be higher than the predicted costs of $906.79. Management would feel compelled to find ways to cut costs. In fact, on the basis of the preferred machine-hour cost driver, the plant has actual costs lower than the predicted amount ($1,043.30)—a performance that management should seek to replicate, not change.

NONLINEARITY AND COST FUNCTIONS

In practice, cost functions are not always linear. A **nonlinear cost function** is a cost function where, within the relevant range, the graph of total costs versus a single cost driver does not form a straight line. Exhibit 10-2 graphically illustrated a cost function that is nonlinear over the range from 0 to 80,000 valves produced. Consider another example. Economies of scale in advertising may enable an advertising agency to double the number of advertisements for less than double the costs. Even direct materials costs are not always linear variable costs. Consider quantity discounts on direct materials purchases. As shown in Exhibit 10-8, the total direct materials costs rise, but they rise more slowly as the cost driver increases because of quantity discounts. The cost function in Exhibit 10-8 has $b = \$25$ for 1 to 1,000 units purchased; $b = \$15$ for 1,001 to 2,000 units purchased; and $b = \$10$ for 2,000 or more units purchased ($a = \$0$ for all ranges of the units purchased). The cost per unit falls at each price break; that is, the cost per unit decreases with larger orders.

Step cost functions are also examples of nonlinear cost functions. A **step cost function** is a cost function in which the cost is constant over various ranges of the cost driver, but the cost increases by discrete amounts (that is, in steps) as the cost driver moves from one range to the next. The graph in Exhibit 10-9 on page 335 shows a *step variable cost function*, a step cost function in which cost is constant over narrow ranges of the cost driver in each relevant range. Exhibit 10-9 shows the relationship between setup costs and units of production. The pattern is a step cost function because setup costs are incurred only when each production batch is started. This step pattern behaviour also occurs when inputs such as production scheduling,

OBJECTIVE 6

Explain and give examples of nonlinear cost functions

Nonlinear cost function. Cost function in which the graph of total costs versus a single cost driver does not form a straight line within the relevant range.

Step cost function. A cost function in which the cost is constant over various ranges of the cost driver, but the cost increases by discrete amounts (that is, in steps) as the cost driver moves from one range to the next.

Activity-Based Costing and Cost Estimation

Cost estimation in activity-based costing (ABC) systems blends the various methods presented in this chapter. ABC systems exploit managers' knowledge of operations via in-depth interviews (as well as company records) to identify key activities and the cost drivers and costs of each activity at the output unit level, batch level, and product-sustaining level. To determine the cost of an activity, ABC systems often rely on expert analyses and opinions gathered from operating personnel (the conference method). For example, loan department staff at the Co-operative Bank in the United Kingdom subjectively estimates the costs of the loan processing activity and the cost driver of loan processing costs (the number of loans processed, a batch-level cost driver, rather than the value of the loans, an output-unit-level cost driver), to derive the cost of processing a loan. ABC systems sometimes use input-output relationships (the industrial engineering method) to identify cost drivers and the cost of an activity. For example, John Deere and Company uses work measurement methods to identify a batch-level cost driver (the number of standard loads moved) and the cost per load moved within its components plant.

John Deere and Company
www.deere.com

Caterpillar Tractor
www.caterpillar.com

In complex, manufacturing environments, multiple cost drivers are necessary for accurate product costing. Consider heavy equipment manufacturer Caterpillar Tractor's method of identifying the cost driver for receiving costs in its ABC system. Three plausible cost drivers were the weight of parts received, the number of parts received, or the number of shipments received. The weight of parts and number of parts are output-unit-level cost drivers, while the number of shipments is a batch-level cost driver. Caterpillar uses the weight of parts as the basis for cost assignment because a regression analysis showed that it is the primary driver of the costs of receiving material. Caterpillar also uses a variety of other cost drivers in assigning costs to its products.

Source: Based on the Co-operative Bank, Harvard Business School Case No. N9-195-196, John Deere Component Works (A), Harvard Business School Case 9-187-107, and discussions with the company managements.

product design labour, and process engineering labour are acquired in discrete quantities but used in fractional quantities. As shown in Exhibit 10-9, management often approximates step variable costs with a variable cost function.

The graph in Exhibit 10-10 shows a *step fixed cost function* for Crofton Steel, a company that operates large heat treatment furnaces to harden steel parts. The main

EXHIBIT 10-8
Effects of Quantity Discounts on Slope of Direct Materials Cost Function

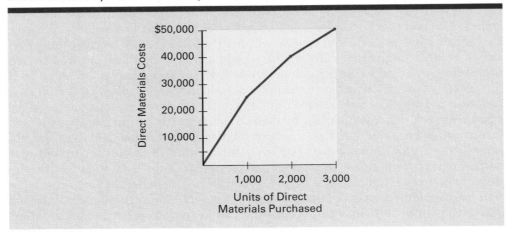

EXHIBIT 10-9
Step Variable Cost Function

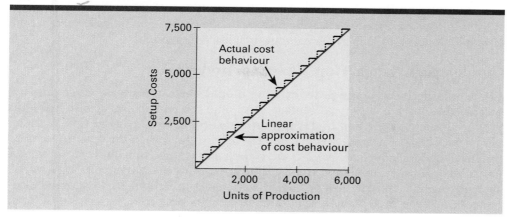

difference relative to Exhibit 10-9 is that the cost in a step fixed cost function is constant over large ranges of the cost driver in each relevant range. The ranges indicate the number of furnaces being used (each furnace costing $300,000). The cost changes from one range to the next higher range when the hours of furnace time demanded require the use of another furnace. The relevant range indicates that the company expects to operate with two furnaces at a cost of $600,000. Management considers the cost of operating furnaces as a fixed cost within the relevant range of operation.

LEARNING CURVES AND NONLINEAR COST FUNCTIONS

Learning curves also result in cost functions being nonlinear. A **learning curve** is a function that shows how labour-hours per unit decline as units of production increase and workers learn and become better at what they do. Managers use learning curves to predict how labour-hours (or labour costs) will change as more units are produced.

The aircraft assembly industry first documented the effect that learning has on efficiency. As workers become more familiar with their tasks, their efficiency improves. Managers learn how to improve the scheduling of work shifts. Plant operators learn how best to operate the facility. Unit costs decrease as productivity increases, which means that the unit-cost function behaves nonlinearly.

Managers are now extending the learning curve notion to include other cost areas in the value chain, such as marketing, distribution, and customer service. The

Learning curve. Function that shows how labour-hours per unit decline as units of production increase.

EXHIBIT 10-10
Step Fixed Cost Function

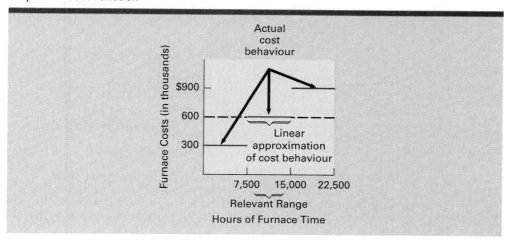

term *experience curve* describes this broader application of the learning curve. An **experience curve** is a function that shows how full product costs per unit (including manufacturing, marketing, distribution, and so on) decline as units of output increase.

We now describe two learning curve models: the cumulative average time learning model and the incremental unit time learning model.[4]

Experience curve. Function that shows how full product costs per unit (including manufacturing, distribution, marketing, and so on) decline as units of output increase.

OBJECTIVE 7

Distinguish between the cumulative average time learning model and incremental unit time learning model

Cumulative Average Time Learning Model

In the **cumulative average time learning model,** the cumulative average time per unit declines by a constant percentage each time the cumulative quantity of units produced doubles. Exhibit 10-11 illustrates the cumulative average time learning model with an 80% learning curve. The 80% means that when the quantity of units produced is doubled from X to $2X$, the cumulative average time *per unit* for the $2X$ units is 80% of the cumulative average time *per unit* for the X units. In other words, average time per unit has dropped by 20%. Graph 1 in Exhibit 10-11 shows the cumulative average time *per unit* as a function of units produced. Graph 2 in Exhibit 10-11 shows the cumulative *total* labour-hours as a function of units produced. The data points underlying Exhibit 10-11, and the details of their calculation, are presented in Exhibit 10-12. To obtain the cumulative total time, multiply the cumulative average time per unit by the cumulative number of units produced. For example, to produce four cumulative units would require 256 labour-hours (4×64).

Cumulative average time learning model. Learning curve model in which the cumulative average time per unit declines by a constant percentage each time the cumulative quantity of units produced is doubled.

Incremental Unit Time Learning Model

In the **incremental unit time learning model**, the incremental unit time (the time needed to produce the last unit) declines by a constant percentage each time the cumulative quantity of units produced doubles. Exhibit 10-13 illustrates the incremental unit time learning model with an 80% learning curve. The 80% here means that when the quantity of units produced is doubled from X to $2X$, the time needed to produce the *last unit* at the $2X$ production level is 80% of the time needed to produce the *last unit* at the X production level. Graph 1 in Exhibit 10-13 shows the cumulative average time *per unit* as a function of cumulative units produced. Graph 2 in Exhibit 10-13 shows the cumulative *total* labour-hours as a function of units produced. The data points underlying Exhibit 10-13, and the details of their calculation, are presented in Exhibit 10-14. We obtain the cumulative total time by summing the individual unit times. For example, to produce four cumulative units would require 314.21 labour-hours ($100.00 + 80.00 + 70.21 + 64.00$).

The incremental unit time model predicts that a higher cumulative total time is required to produce two or more units than does the cumulative average time model,

Incremental unit time learning model. Learning curve model in which the incremental unit time (the time needed to produce the last unit) declines by a constant percentage each time the cumulative quantity of units produced is doubled.

EXHIBIT 10-11
Plots for Cumulative Average Time Learning Model

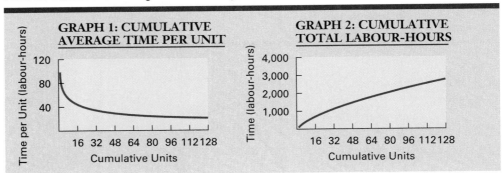

[4]For further discussion, see J. Chen and R. Manes, "Distinguishing the Two Forms of the Constant Percentage Learning Curve Model," *Contemporary Accounting Research*, Spring 1985, pp. 242–252. See also the Northern Aerospace Manufacturing case study in A. A. Atkinson, *Cost Estimation in Management Accounting—Six Case Studies* (Hamilton, Ontario: Society of Management Accountants of Canada, 1987).

EXHIBIT 10-12
Cumulative Average Time Learning Model

Cumulative Number of Units (1)	Cumulative Average Time per Unit (y): Labour-Hours (2)	Cumulative Total Time: Labour-Hours (3) = (1) × (2)	Individual Unit Time for Xth Unit: Labour-Hours (4)
1	100.00	100.00	100.00
2	80.00 (100 × 0.8)	160.00	60.00
3	70.21	210.63	50.63
4	64.00 (80 × 0.8)	256.00	45.37
5	59.57	297.85	41.85
6	56.17	337.02	39.17
7	53.45	374.15	37.13
8	51.20 (64 × 0.8)	409.60	35.45
•	•	•	•
•	•	•	•
•	•	•	•
16	40.96 (51.2 × 0.8)	655.36	28.06

Note: The mathematical relationship underlying the cumulative average-time learning model is:

$$y = p X^q$$

where:

y = cumulative average time (labour-hours) per unit
X = cumulative number of units produced
p = time (labour-hours) required to produce the first unit
q = rate of learning

The value of q is calculated as:

$$q = \frac{\ln (\% \text{ learning})}{\ln 2}$$

For an 80% learning curve:

$$q = \frac{-0.2231}{0.6931} = -0.3219$$

As an illustration, when $X = 3$, $p = 100$, and $q = -0.3219$:

$$y = 100 \times 3^{-0.3219} = 70.21 \text{ labour-hours}$$

The cumulative total time when $X = 3$ is $70.21 \times 3 = 210.63$ labour-hours.
   The individual unit times in column 4 are calculated using the data in column 3. For example, the individual unit time of 50.63 labour-hours for the third unit is calculated as $210.63 - 160.00$.

assuming the same learning rate for the two models (compare results in Exhibit 10-12 with results in Exhibit 10-14). For example, to produce four cumulative units, the 80% incremental unit time learning model predicts 314.21 labour-hours versus 256.00 labour-hours predicted by the 80% cumulative average time learning model.

EXHIBIT 10-13
Plots for Incremental Unit Time Learning Model

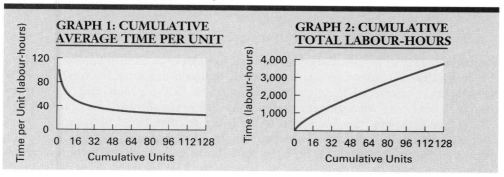

GRAPH 1: CUMULATIVE AVERAGE TIME PER UNIT

GRAPH 2: CUMULATIVE TOTAL LABOUR-HOURS

EXHIBIT 10-14
Incremental Unit Time Learning Model

Cumulative Number of Units (1)	Individual Unit Time for Xth Unit (m): Labour-Hours (2)	Cumulative Total Time: Labour-Hours (3)	Cumulative Average Time per Unit: Labour-Hours (4) = (3) ÷ (1)
1	100.00	100.00	100.00
2	80.00 (100 × 0.8)	180.00	90.00
3	70.21	250.21	83.40
4	64.00 (80 × 0.8)	314.21	78.55
5	59.57	373.78	74.76
6	56.17	429.95	71.66
7	53.45	483.40	69.06
8	51.20 (64 × 0.8)	534.60	66.82
•	•	•	•
•	•	•	•
•	•	•	•
16	40.96 (51.2 × 0.8)	892.00	55.75

Note: The mathematical relationship underlying the incremental unit time learning model is:

$$m = pX^q$$

where:

m = time (labour-hours) taken to produce the last single unit
X = cumulative number of units produced
p = time (labour-hours) required to produce the first unit
q = rate of learning

The value of q is calculated as:

$$q = \frac{\ln (\% \text{ learning})}{\ln 2}$$

For an 80% learning curve:

$$q = \frac{-0.2231}{0.6931} = -0.3219$$

As an illustration, when $X = 3$, $p = 100$, and $q = -0.3219$:

$$m = 100 \times 3^{-0.3219} = 70.21 \text{ labour-hours}$$

The cumulative total time when $X = 3$ is $100 + 80 + 70.21 = 250.21$ labour-hours.

Which of these two models is preferable? The one that more accurately approximates the behaviour of manufacturing labour-hour usage as production levels increase is better. The choice can be decided only on a case-by-case basis. Engineers, plant managers, and workers are good sources of information on the amount and type of learning actually occurring as production increases. Plotting this information is helpful in selecting the appropriate model.

The Problem for Self-Study that follows the next section illustrates the cumulative average time learning model and the incremental unit time learning model in a job-costing situation.

Setting Prices, Budgets, and Standards

Predictions of costs should allow for learning. Consider the data in Exhibit 10-12 for the cumulative average time learning model. Suppose the variable costs subject to learning effects consist of direct manufacturing labour ($20 per hour) and related overhead ($30 per hour). Management should predict the costs shown in Exhibit 10-15.

These data show that the effects of the learning curve could have a major influence on decisions. For example, a company might set an extremely low selling price on its product in order to generate high demand. As the company's production increases to meet this growing demand, costs per unit drop. The company rides the product

EXHIBIT 10-15
Predicting Costs Using Learning Curves

Cumulative Number of Units	Cumulative Total Labour-Hours*	Cumulative Costs	Additions to Cumulative Costs
1	100.00	$ 5,000 (100.00 × $50)	$ 5,000
2	160.00	8,000 (160.00 × $50)	3,000
4	256.00	12,800 (256.00 × $50)	4,800
8	409.60	20,480 (409.60 × $50)	7,680
16	655.36	32,768 (655.36 × $50)	12,288

*Based on the cumulative average time learning model. See Exhibit 10-12 for the computation of these amounts.

down the learning curve as it establishes a higher market share. Although the company may have earned little on its first unit sold—it may actually have lost money—the company earns more profit per unit as output increases.

Alternatively, subject to legal and other considerations, the company might set a low price on just the final eight units. After all, the labour and related overhead costs per unit are predicted to be only $12,288 for these final eight units ($32,768 − $20,480). The per-unit costs of $1,536 on these final eight units ($12,288 ÷ 8) are much lower than the $5,000 costs per unit of the first unit produced.

Many companies incorporate learning curve effects when evaluating performance. For example, the Nissan Motor Company sets assembly labour efficiency standards for new models of cars after taking into account the learning that will occur as more units are produced.

The learning curve models examined in Exhibits 10-11 to 10-14 assume that learning is driven by a single variable (production output). Other models of learning have been developed by companies such as Analog Devices and Yokogawa Hewlett-Packard that focus on how quality (rather than manufacturing labour-hours) will change over time (rather than as more units are produced). Some recent studies suggest that factors other than production output—such as job rotation and organizing workers into teams—contribute to learning that improves quality.

Analog Devices
www.analog.com

DATA COLLECTION AND ADJUSTMENT ISSUES

The ideal database for estimating cost functions quantitatively has two characteristics:

OBJECTIVE 8

Understand data problems encountered in estimating cost functions

1. It contains numerous reliably measured observations of the cost driver(s) and the dependent variable. Errors in measuring the costs and cost driver(s) are particularly serious. They result in inaccurate estimates of the effect of the cost driver(s) on costs.

2. It considers many values for the cost driver over a wide range. Using only a few values that are grouped closely together considers too small a segment of the relevant range and reduces the confidence in the estimates obtained.

Unfortunately, cost analysts typically do not have the advantage of working with a database having both characteristics. This section outlines some frequently encountered data problems, and steps the analyst can take to overcome them.

1. The time period for measuring the dependent variable (for example, indirect manufacturing labour costs) does not properly match the period for measuring the cost driver(s). This problem often arises when accounting records are not kept on an accrual basis. Consider a cost function with machine lubricant costs as the dependent variable and machine-hours as the cost driver. Assume that the lubricant is purchased sporadically and stored for later use. Records maintained on a cash basis will indicate no lubricant consumption in many months and sizable lubricant consumption in other months. This is an obviously inaccurate

picture of what is actually taking place. The analyst should use accrual accounting to measure consumption of machine lubricants to better match costs with the cost driver in this example.

2. Fixed costs are allocated as if they are variable. For example, costs such as amortization, insurance, or rent may be allocated to products to calculate costs per unit of output. *The danger is to regard these costs as variable rather than as fixed. They seem to be variable because of the allocation methods used.* To avoid this problem, the analyst should distinguish carefully between fixed and variable costs, and not treat allocated fixed costs per unit as a variable cost.

3. Data are either not available for all observations or are not uniformly reliable. Missing cost observations often arise from a failure to record a cost or from classifying a cost incorrectly. Data on cost drivers often originate outside the internal accounting system. For example, the accounting department may get data on testing times for medical instruments from the company's manufacturing department and data on the number of items shipped to customers from the distribution department. The reliability of such data varies greatly among organizations. In some systems, data are still recorded manually rather than electronically. Manually recorded data typically have a higher percentage of missing observations and erroneously entered observations than electronically entered data. To minimize this problem, the cost analyst should design data collection reports that regularly and routinely obtain the required data, and should follow up immediately whenever data is missing.

4. Extreme values of observations occur from errors in recording costs (for example, a misplaced decimal point); from nonrepresentative time periods (for example, from a period in which a major machine breakdown occurred or from a period in which delay in delivery of materials from an international supplier curtailed production); or from observations being outside the relevant range. Analysts should adjust or eliminate unusual observations before estimating a cost relationship; otherwise, an incorrect estimate would result.

5. There is no homogeneous relationship between the individual cost items in the dependent variable pool and the cost driver. A homogeneous relationship exists when each activity whose costs are included in the dependent variable has the same cost driver. Consider materials procurement overhead costs. This overhead cost account can include a diverse set of activities (for example, new vendor negotiations, materials ordering, incoming inspection, and materials-handling). If each activity has the same cost driver, the homogeneous relationship principle suggests that a single cost function can be estimated for the entire cost pool. Where the cost driver for each activity is different, separate cost functions, each with its own cost driver, would be estimated for each activity.

6. The relationship between cost and the cost driver is not stationary; that is, the underlying process that generated the observations has not remained stable over time. For example, the relationship between manufacturing overhead costs and machine-hours is unlikely to be stationary if the data covers a period in which new technology was introduced. One way to test if the relationship is stationary in this case is to split the sample into two parts and estimate separate cost relationships for the before- and after-technology-change periods. Then, if the estimated coefficients for the two periods are similar, the analyst can pool all the data together to estimate a single cost relationship. Pooling data provides a larger data set for the estimation, which increases the confidence in the cost predictions being made.

7. Inflation has affected the dependent variable, the cost driver, or both. For example, inflation may cause costs to change even when there is no change in the cost driver. To study the underlying cause-and-effect relationship between the cost driver and costs, the analyst should remove purely inflationary price effects from the data.

In many cases, a cost analyst must expend much effort to reduce the effect of these problems before estimating a cost function on the basis of past data.

PROBLEM

The Helicopter Division of Aerospatiale is examining helicopter assembly costs at its plant in Marseilles, France. It has received an initial order for eight of its new land surveying helicopters. Aerospatiale can adopt one of two methods of assembling the helicopters:

	Labour-Intensive Assembly Method	Machine-Intensive Assembly Method
Direct materials costs per helicopter	$40,000	$36,000
Direct assembly labour time for first helicopter	2,000 labour-hours	800 labour-hours
Learning curve for assembly labour time per helicopter	85% cumulative average time*	90% incremental unit time†
Direct assembly labour costs	$30 per hour	$30 per hour
Equipment-related indirect manufacturing costs	$12 per direct assembly labour-hour	$45 per direct assembly labour-hour
Materials-handling-related indirect manufacturing costs	50% of direct materials costs	50% of direct materials costs

*An 85% learning curve is expressed mathematically as $q = -0.2345$.
†A 90% learning curve is expressed mathematically as $q = -0.1520$.

REQUIRED

1. How many direct assembly labour-hours are required to assemble the first eight helicopters under (a) the labour-intensive method and (b) the machine-intensive method?
2. What is the cost of assembling the first eight helicopters under (a) the labour-intensive method and (b) the machine-intensive method?

SOLUTION

1. a. Labour-intensive assembly method based on cumulative average-time learning model (85% learning):

Cumulative Number of Units (1)	Cumulative Average Time per Unit (y): Labour-Hours (2)	Cumulative Total Time: Labour-Hours (3) = (1) × (2)	Individual Unit Time for Xth Unit: Labour-Hours (4)
1	2,000	2,000	2,000
2	1,700 (2,000 × 0.85)	3,400	1,400
3	1,546	4,638	1,238
4	1,445 (1,700 × 0.85)	5,780	1,142
5	1,371	6,855	1,075
6	1,314	7,884	1,029
7	1,267	8,869	985
8	1,228.25 (1,445 × 0.85)	9,826	957

The cumulative average time per unit for the Xth unit in column 2 is calculated as $y = pX^q$; see Exhibit 10-12. For example, when $X = 3$, $y = 2{,}000 \times 3^{-0.2345} = 1{,}546$ labour-hours.

1. b. Machine-intensive assembly method based on incremental unit time learning model (90% learning).

Cumulative Number of Units (1)	Individual Unit Time for Xth Unit (m): Labour-Hours (2)	Cumulative Total Time: Labour-Hours (3)	Cumulative Average Time per Unit: Labour-Hours (4) = (3) ÷ (1)
1	800	800	800
2	720 (800 × 0.9)	1,520	760
3	677	2,197	732
4	648 (720 × 0.9)	2,845	711
5	626	3,471	694
6	609	4,080	680
7	595	4,675	668
8	583 (648 × 0.9)	5,258	657

The individual unit time for the Xth unit in column 2 is calculated as $m = pX^q$; see Exhibit 10-14. For example, when $X = 3$, $m = 800 \times 3^{-0.1520} = 677$ labour-hours.

2. Costs of assembling the first eight helicopters are:

	Labour-Intensive Assembly Method	Machine-Intensive Assembly Method
Direct materials: 8 × $40,000; 8 × $36,000	$320,000	$288,000
Direct assembly labour: 9,826 × $30; 5,258 × $30	294,780	157,740
Indirect manufacturing costs: Equipment-related: 9,826 × $12; 5,258 × $45	117,912	236,610
Materials-handling-related: 0.50 × $320,000; 0.50 × $288,000	160,000	144,000
Total assembly costs	$892,692	$826,350

The machine-intensive method has assembly costs that are $66,342 lower than the labour-intensive method ($892,692 − $826,350).

SUMMARY

The following points are linked to the chapter's learning objectives.

1. Two assumptions frequently made in cost-behaviour estimation are (a) that changes in total costs can be explained by changes in the level of a single cost driver and (b) that cost behaviour can adequately be approximated by a linear function of the cost driver within the relevant range.

2. A linear cost function is a cost function where, within the relevant range, the graph of total costs versus a single cost driver forms a straight line. Linear cost functions can be described by a single constant a, which represents the estimate of the total cost component that does not vary with changes in the level of the cost driver, and a slope coefficient b, which represents the estimate of the amount by which total costs change for each unit change in the level of the cost driver. Three types of linear cost functions are variable, fixed, and mixed (or semivariable).

3. Four broad approaches to estimating cost functions are the industrial engineering method, the conference method, the account analysis method, and quantitative analysis of cost relationships (the high-low method and regression analysis method). Regression analysis is a systematic approach to estimating a cost function on the basis of identified cost drivers. Ideally, the cost analyst applies more than one approach; each approach serves as a check on the others.

4. The six steps in estimating a cost function on the basis of an analysis of current or past cost relationships are (a) choose the dependent variable, (b) identify the cost driver(s), (c) collect data on the dependent variable and the cost driver(s), (d) plot the data, (e) estimate the cost function, and (f) evaluate the estimated cost function. In most situations, the cost analyst will cycle through these steps several times before identifying an acceptable cost function.

5. Three criteria for evaluating and choosing cost drivers are (a) economic plausibility, (b) goodness of fit, and (c) the slope of the regression line.

6. A nonlinear cost function is a cost function where, within the relevant range, the graph of total costs versus a single cost driver does not form a straight line. Nonlinear costs can arise because of economies of scale, quantity discounts, step cost functions, and learning curve effects.

7. The learning curve is an example of a nonlinear cost function. Labour-hours per unit decline as units of production increase. In the cumulative average time learning model, the cumulative average time per unit declines by a constant percentage each time the cumulative quantity of units produced doubles. In the incremental unit time learning model, the incremental unit time (the time needed to produce the last unit) declines by a constant percentage each time the cumulative quantity of units produced doubles.

8. The most difficult task in cost estimation is collecting high-quality, reliably measured data on the dependent variable and the cost driver(s). Common problems include missing data, extreme values of observations, changes in technology, and distortions resulting from inflation.

APPENDIX: REGRESSION ANALYSIS

This appendix describes formulas for estimating the regression equation and several commonly used statistics. We use the data for Elegant Rugs presented in Exhibit 10-3. The appendix also discusses goodness of fit, significance of independent variables, and specification analysis of estimation assumptions for regression analysis.

Estimating the Regression Line

The least-squares technique for estimating the regression line minimizes the sum of the squares of the vertical deviations (distances) from the data points to the estimated regression line.

The object is to find the values of a and b in the predicting equation $y = a + bX$, where y is the predicted cost value as distinguished from the observed cost value, which we denote by Y. We wish to find the numerical values of a and b that minimize $\Sigma(Y-y)^2$. This calculation is accomplished by using two equations, usually called the *normal equations:*

$$\Sigma Y = na + b(\Sigma X)$$

$$\Sigma XY = a(\Sigma X) + b(\Sigma X^2)$$

where n is the number of data points; ΣX and ΣY are respectively the sums of the given X and Y values; ΣX^2 is the sum of squares of the X values; and ΣXY is the sum of the amounts obtained by multiplying each of the given X values by the associated observed Y value.

Exhibit 10-16 shows the calculations required for obtaining the line that best fits the data of indirect manufacturing labour costs and machine-hours for Elegant Rugs. Substituting into the two normal equations simultaneously, we obtain:

$$12{,}501 = 12a + 862b$$

and
$$928{,}716 = 862a + 64{,}900b$$

The solution is $a = \$300.98$ and $b = \$10.31$, which can be obtained by direct substitution if the normal equations are re-expressed symbolically as follows:

EXHIBIT 10-16
Computation for Least-Squares Regression between Indirect Manufacturing Labour Costs and Machine-Hours for Elegant Rugs

Week (1)	Machine-Hours* X (2)	Indirect Manufacturing Labour Costs* Y (3)	X^2 (4)	XY (5)	y (6)	Variance of Y $(Y-\bar{Y})^2$ (7)	Unexplained Variance $(Y-y)^2$ (8)	Variance of X $(X-\bar{X})^2$ (9)
1	68	1,190	4,624	80,920	1,002.06	21,978	35,321	15
2	88	1,211	7,744	106,568	1,208.26	28,646	8	261
3	62	1,004	3,844	62,248	940.20	1,425	4,070	97
4	72	917	5,184	66,024	1,043.30	15,563	15,952	0
5	60	770	3,600	46,200	919.58	73,848	22,374	140
6	96	1,456	9,216	139,776	1,290.74	171,603	27,311	584
7	78	1,180	6,084	92,040	1,105.16	19,113	5,601	38
8	46	710	2,116	32,660	775.24	110,058	4,256	667
9	82	1,316	6,724	107,912	1,146.40	75,213	28,764	103
10	94	1,032	8,836	97,008	1,270.12	95	56,701	491
11	68	752	4,624	51,136	1,002.06	83,955	62,530	15
12	48	963	2,304	46,224	795.86	6,202	27,936	568
Total	862	12,501	64,900	928,716	$\approx$12,501	607,699	290,824	2,979

*Same data as in columns 1 and 2 of Exhibit 10-3.

$$a = \frac{(\Sigma Y)(\Sigma X^2) - (\Sigma X)(\Sigma XY)}{n(\Sigma X^2) - (\Sigma X)(\Sigma X)} \quad \text{and} \quad b = \frac{n(\Sigma XY) - (\Sigma X)(\Sigma Y)}{n(\Sigma X^2) - (\Sigma X)(\Sigma X)}$$

For our illustration, we now have:

$$a = \frac{(12,501)(64,900) - (862)(928,716)}{12(64,900) - (862)(862)} = \$300.98$$

$$b = \frac{12(928,716) - (862)(12,501)}{12(64,900) - (862)(862)} = \$10.31$$

Placing the amounts for a and b in the equation of the least-squares line, we have:

$$y = \$300.98 + \$10.31X$$

where y is the predicted indirect manufacturing labour costs for any specified number of machine-hours within the relevant range. Generally, these computations are done using software packages such as SPSS, SAS, Lotus, and Excel.

Goodness of Fit

Coefficient of determination, r^2
Measures the percentage of variation in a dependent variable explained by one or more independent variables.

Goodness of fit measures how well the predicted values, y, based on the cost driver, X, match actual cost observations, Y. The regression analysis method computes a formal measure of goodness of fit, called the coefficient of determination. The **coefficient of determination, r^2**, measures the percentage of variation in Y explained by X (the independent variable). The coefficient of determination (r^2) indicates the proportion of the variance of Y, $(Y-\bar{Y})^2 \div n$, that is explained by the independent variable X (where $\bar{Y} = \Sigma Y \div n$). It is more convenient to express the coefficient of determination as 1 minus the proportion of total variance that is *not* explained by the independent variable. The unexplained variance arises because of differences between the actual values of Y and the predicted values of y:

$$r^2 = 1 - \frac{\text{Unexplained variation}}{\text{Total variation}} = 1 - \frac{\Sigma(Y-y)^2}{\Sigma(Y-\bar{Y})^2}$$

From Exhibit 10-16, $\Sigma Y = 12{,}501$ and $\bar{Y} = 12{,}501 \div 12 = 1{,}041.75$. Therefore, to obtain the total variation:

$$\Sigma(Y - \bar{Y})^2 = (1{,}190 - 1{,}041.75)^2 + (1{,}211 - 1{,}041.75)^2 + \cdots + (963 - 1{,}041.75)^2$$
$$= 607{,}699$$

Each value of X generates a prediction, y. For example, in week 1, $y = \$300.98 + (\$10.31 \times 68) = \$1{,}002.06$. Therefore, to obtain the unexplained variation:

$$\Sigma(Y - y)^2 = (1{,}190 - 1{,}002.06)^2 + (1{,}211 - 1{,}208.26)^2 + \cdots + (963 - 795.86)^2$$
$$= 35{,}321 + 8 + \cdots + 27{,}936 = 290{,}824$$
$$r^2 = 1 - \frac{290{,}824}{607{,}699} = 0.52$$

The calculations indicate that r^2 increases as the predicted values, y, more closely approximate the actual observations, Y. The range of r^2 is from 0 (implying no explanatory power) to 1 (implying perfect explanatory power). When $r^2 = 1$, the predicted cost values exactly equal actual cost values; that is, the independent variable X has perfectly explained variations in actual costs, Y. Generally, an r^2 of 0.30 or higher passes the goodness-of-fit test. Do not rely exclusively on goodness of fit. It can lead to the indiscriminate inclusion of independent variables that increase r^2 but have no economic plausibility as cost driver(s). Goodness of fit has meaning only if the relationship between costs and the drivers is economically plausible.

Significance of Independent Variables

A key question that managers ask is: Do changes in the economically plausible independent variable result in significant changes in the dependent variable, or, alternatively, is the slope b of the regression line significant? Recall, for example, that in the regression of machine-hours on indirect manufacturing labour costs in the Elegant Rugs illustration, b is estimated from a sample of 12 observations. The estimate, b, is subject to random factors, as are all sample statistics. That is, a different sample of 12 data points will give a different estimate of b. The **standard error of the estimated coefficient** indicates how much the estimated value, b, is likely to be affected by random factors. The t-value of the b coefficient measures how large the value of the estimated coefficient is relative to its standard error. A t-value with an absolute value greater than 2.00 suggests that the b coefficient is significantly different from zero.[5] In other words, a relationship exists between the independent variable and the dependent variable that cannot be attributed to chance alone.

Standard error of the estimated coefficient. Regression statistic that indicates how much the estimated value is likely to be affected by random factors.

Exhibit 10-17 presents a convenient format for summarizing the regression results for indirect manufacturing labour costs and machine-hours. The t-value for the slope coefficient, b, is $\$10.31 \div \$3.12 = 3.30$, which exceeds the benchmark of 2.00. Therefore, the coefficient of the machine-hours variable is significantly different from zero. The probability is low (less than 5%) that random factors could have

---

[5]The benchmark for inferring that a b coefficient is significantly different from zero is a function of the degrees of freedom in a regression. The benchmark of 2.00 assumes a sample size of 60 observations. The number of degrees of freedom is calculated as the sample size minus the number of a and b parameters estimated in the regression. For a simple regression, the benchmark values for the t-values are:

Sample Size	Benchmark*
12	$\lvert t \rvert > 2.23$
15	$\lvert t \rvert > 2.16$
20	$\lvert t \rvert > 2.10$
30	$\lvert t \rvert > 2.05$
60	$\lvert t \rvert > 2.00$

*$\lvert t \rvert$ denotes the absolute value of the t-value.

For simplicity, we use a cutoff t-value of 2.00 throughout this chapter.

EXHIBIT 10-17

Simple Regression Results with Indirect Manufacturing Labour Costs as Dependent Variable and Machine-Hours as Independent Variable for Elegant Rugs

Variable	Coefficient (1)	Standard Error (2)	t-Value (3) = (1) ÷ (2)
Constant	$300.98	$229.75	1.31
Independent variable 1: machine-hours	$ 10.31	$ 3.12	3.30

$r^2 = 0.52$; Durbin-Watson statistic = 2.05.

caused the coefficient, b, to be positive. Alternatively, we can restate our conclusion in terms of a "confidence interval"—there is less than a 5% chance that the true value of the machine-hours coefficient lies outside the range $10.31 \pm (2.00 \times \$3.12)$ or $10.31 \pm \$6.24$, or from $4.07 and $16.55. Therefore, we can conclude that changes in machine-hours do affect indirect manufacturing labour costs. Similarly, using data from Exhibit 10-17, the t-value for the constant term, a, is $300.98 ÷ $229.76 = 1.31, which is less than 2.00. This value indicates that, within the relevant range, the constant term is not significantly different from zero.

Specification Analysis of Estimation Assumptions

Specification analysis. Testing of the assumptions of regression analysis.

Specification analysis is the testing of the assumptions of regression analysis. If the assumptions of (1) linearity within the relevant range, (2) constant variance of residuals, (3) independence of residuals, and (4) normality of residuals hold, the simplest regression procedures give reliable estimates of unknown coefficient values. This section provides a brief overview of specification analysis. When these assumptions are not satisfied, more complex regression procedures are necessary to obtain the best estimates.[6]

1. Linearity within the relevant range. A common assumption is that a linear relationship exists between the independent variable X and the dependent variable Y within the relevant range. If a linear regression model is used to estimate a fundamentally nonlinear relationship, however, the coefficient estimates obtained will be inaccurate.

Where there is only one independent variable, the easiest way to check for linearity is by studying the data on a scatter diagram, a step that often is unwisely skipped. Exhibit 10-6 presented a scatter diagram for the indirect manufacturing labour costs and machine-hours variables of Elegant Rugs shown in Exhibit 10-3. The scatter diagram revealed that linearity appears to be a reasonable assumption for these data.

The learning curve models discussed on pages 335–339 are examples of nonlinear cost functions; costs increase when the level of production increases, but by lesser amounts than would occur with a linear cost function. In this case, the analyst should estimate a nonlinear cost function that explicitly incorporates learning effects.

2. Constant variance of residuals. The vertical deviation of the *observed* value, Y, from the regression line estimate, y, is called the *residual term, disturbance term,* or *error term, $u = Y - y$.* The assumption of constant variance implies that the residual terms are unaffected by the level of the independent variable. The assumption also implies that there is a uniform scatter, or dispersion, of the data points about the regression line. The scatter diagram is the easiest way to check for *constant variance.* This assumption holds for Panel A of Exhibit 10-18 but not for Panel B. Constant variance is also known as *homoscedasticity.* Violation of this assumption is called *heteroscedasticity.*

---

[6]For details see, for example, C. J. Watson, P. Billingsley, D. J. Croft, and D. V. Huntsberger, *Statistics for Management and Economics,* 5th ed. (Needham Heights: Allyn and Bacon, 1993), and W. H. Greene, *Econometric Analysis,* 2nd ed. (New York: Macmillan, 1993).

EXHIBIT 10-18
Constant Variance of Residuals Assumption

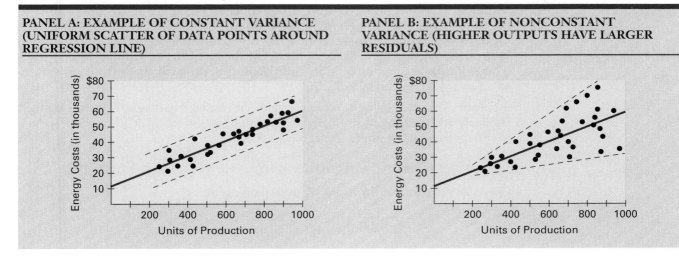

PANEL A: EXAMPLE OF CONSTANT VARIANCE (UNIFORM SCATTER OF DATA POINTS AROUND REGRESSION LINE)

PANEL B: EXAMPLE OF NONCONSTANT VARIANCE (HIGHER OUTPUTS HAVE LARGER RESIDUALS)

Heteroscedasticity does not affect the accuracy of the regression estimates, a and b. It does, however, reduce the reliability of the estimates of the standard errors, and thus affects the precision with which inferences can be drawn.

3. Independence of residuals. The assumption of the independence of residuals is that the residual term for any one observation is not related to the residual term for any other observation. The problem of *serial correlation* in the residuals (also called *autocorrelation*) arises when the residuals are not independent. Serial correlation means that there is a systematic pattern in the sequence of residuals such that the residual in observation n conveys information about the residuals in observation $n + 1$, $n + 2$, and so on. In time series data, inflation is a common cause of autocorrelation because it causes costs (and hence residuals) to be related over time. Autocorrelation can also occur in cross-sectional data, as, for example, in Exhibit 10-19. The scatter diagram helps in identifying autocorrelation. Autocorrelation does not exist in Panel A of Exhibit 10-19 but does exist in Panel B. Observe the systematic pattern of the residuals in Panel B—positive residuals for extreme quantities of direct materials used and negative residuals for moderate quantities of direct materials used. No such systematic pattern prevails for Panel A.

Like nonconstant variance in residuals, serial correlation does not affect the accuracy of the regression estimates, a and b. It does, however, affect the standard

EXHIBIT 10-19
Independence of Residuals Assumption

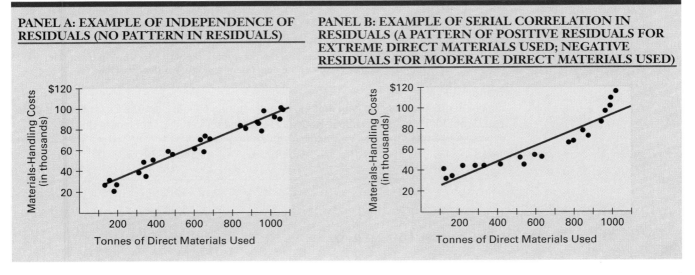

PANEL A: EXAMPLE OF INDEPENDENCE OF RESIDUALS (NO PATTERN IN RESIDUALS)

PANEL B: EXAMPLE OF SERIAL CORRELATION IN RESIDUALS (A PATTERN OF POSITIVE RESIDUALS FOR EXTREME DIRECT MATERIALS USED; NEGATIVE RESIDUALS FOR MODERATE DIRECT MATERIALS USED)

errors of the coefficients, which in turn affect the precision with which inferences about the population parameters can be drawn from the regression estimates.

The Durbin-Watson statistic is one measure of serial correlation in the estimated residuals. For samples of 10 to 20 observations, a Durbin-Watson statistic in the 1.10 to 2.90 range suggests that the residuals are independent. The Durbin-Watson statistic for the regression results of Elegant Rugs in Exhibit 10-17 is 2.05. Therefore, an assumption of independence in the estimated residuals seems reasonable for this regression model.

4. Normality of residuals. The normality of residuals assumption means that the residuals are distributed normally around the regression line. This assumption is necessary for making inferences about y, a, and b.

Using Regression Output to Choose between Cost Functions

Consider the two cost functions we described earlier:

$$y = a + (b \times \text{machine-hours})$$
$$y = a + (b \times \text{direct manufacturing labour-hours})$$

Exhibits 10-6 and 10-7 presented plots of the data for the two regressions. Exhibit 10-17 reported regression results for the cost function using machine-hours as the independent variable. Exhibit 10-20 presents comparable regression results for the cost function using direct manufacturing labour-hours as the independent variable.

On the basis of the material in this appendix, which regression is better? Exhibit 10-21 compares these two cost functions in a systematic way. For several criteria, the cost function based on machine-hours is preferable to the cost function based on direct manufacturing labour-hours. The economic plausibility criterion is especially important.

Do not always assume that any one cost function will perfectly satisfy all the criteria in Exhibit 10-21. A cost analyst must often make a choice between "imperfect" cost functions, in the sense that the data of any particular cost function will not perfectly meet one or more of the assumptions underlying regression analysis.

Multiple Regression and Cost Hierarchies

In some cases, a satisfactory estimation of a cost function may be based on only one independent variable, such as machine-hours. In many cases, however, basing the estimation on more than one independent variable is more economically plausible and improves accuracy. The most widely used equations to express relationships between two or more independent variables and a dependent variable are linear in the form:

$$Y = a + b_1 X_1 + b_2 X_2 + \cdots + u$$

where:

Y = cost variable to be predicted

$X_1, X_2, \ldots$ = independent variables on which the prediction is to be based

$a, b_1, b_2, \ldots$ = estimated coefficients of the regression model

u = residual term that includes the net effect of other factors not in the model and measurement errors in the dependent and independent variables

EXHIBIT 10-20

Simple Regression Results with Indirect Manufacturing Labour Costs as Dependent Variable and Direct Manufacturing Labour-Hours as Independent Variable for Elegant Rugs

Variable	Coefficient (1)	Standard Error (2)	t-Value (3) = (1) ÷ (2)
Constant	$744.67	$217.61	3.42
Independent variable 1: direct manufacturing labour-hours	$ 7.72	$ 5.40	1.43

$r^2 = 0.17$; Durbin-Watson statistic = 2.26.

EXHIBIT 10-21

Comparison of Alternative Cost Functions for Indirect Manufacturing Labour Costs
Estimated with Simple Regression for Elegant Rugs

Criterion	Cost Function 1: Machine-Hours as Independent Variable	Cost Function 2: Direct Manufacturing Labour-Hours as Independent Variable
Economic plausibility	A positive relationship between indirect manufacturing labour costs (technical support labour) and machine-hours is economically plausible in a highly automated plant.	A positive relationship between indirect manufacturing labour costs and direct manufacturing labour-hours is economically plausible, but less so than machine-hours in a highly automated plant on a week-to-week basis.
Goodness of fit	$r^2 = 0.52$ Excellent goodness of fit	$r^2 = 0.17$ Poor goodness of fit
Significance of independent variable(s)	The t-value of 3.30 is significant.	The t-value of 1.43 is not significant.
Specification analysis of estimation assumptions	Plot of the data indicates that assumptions of linearity, constant variance, independence of residuals, and normality of residuals hold, but inferences drawn from only 12 observations are not reliable; Durbin-Watson statistic = 2.05.	Plot of the data indicates that assumptions of linearity, constant variance, independence of residuals, and normality of residuals hold, but inferences drawn from only 12 observations are not reliable; Durbin-Watson statistic = 2.26.

Example: Consider the Elegant Rugs data in Exhibit 10-22. Indirect manufacturing labour costs include sizable costs incurred for setup and changeover costs when production on one carpet batch is stopped and production on another batch is started. Management believes that, in addition to machine-hours (an output-unit-level cost driver), indirect manufacturing labour costs are also affected by the number of different batches of carpets produced during each week (a batch-level driver). Elegant Rugs estimates the relation between two independent variables, machine-hours and number of separate carpet jobs worked on during the week, and indirect manufacturing labour costs.

Exhibit 10-23 presents results for the following multiple regression model, using data in columns 1, 2, and 4 of Exhibit 10-22:

$$y = \$42.58 + \$7.60X_1 + \$37.77X_2$$

EXHIBIT 10-22

Weekly Indirect Manufacturing Labour Costs, Machine-Hours, Direct Manufacturing
Labour-Hours, and Number of Production Batches for Elegant Rugs

Week	Indirect Manufacturing Labour Costs (1)	Machine-Hours (2)	Direct Manufacturing Labour-Hours (3)	Number of Production Batches (4)
1	$1,190	68	30	12
2	1,211	88	35	15
3	1,004	62	36	13
4	917	72	20	11
5	770	60	47	10
6	1,456	96	45	12
7	1,180	78	44	17
8	710	46	38	7
9	1,316	82	70	14
10	1,032	94	30	12
11	752	68	29	7
12	963	48	38	14

EXHIBIT 10-23

Multiple Regression Results with Indirect Manufacturing Labour Costs and Two Independent Variables (Machine-Hours and Production Batches) for Elegant Rugs

Variable	Coefficient (1)	Standard Error (2)	t-Value (3) = (1) ÷ (2)
Constant	$42.58	$213.91	0.20
Independent variable 1: machine-hours	$ 7.60	$ 2.77	2.74
Independent variable 2: production batches	$37.77	$ 15.25	2.48

$r^2 = 0.72$; Durbin-Watson statistic $= 2.49$.

where X_1 is the number of machine-hours and X_2 is the number of production batches. It is economically plausible that both machine-hours and production batches would help explain variations in indirect manufacturing labour costs at Elegant Rugs. The r^2 of 0.52 for the simple regression using machine-hours (Exhibit 10-17) increases to 0.72 with the multiple regression in Exhibit 10-23. The t-values suggest that the independent variable coefficients of both machine-hours and production batches are significantly different from zero ($t = 2.74$ for the coefficient on machine-hours, and $t = 2.48$ for the coefficient on production batches). The multiple regression model in Exhibit 10-23 satisfies both economic and statistical criteria, and it explains much greater variation in indirect manufacturing labour costs than does the simple regression model using only machine-hours as the independent variable. The information in Exhibit 10-23 indicates that both machine-hours and production batches are important cost drivers of monthly indirect manufacturing labour costs at Elegant Rugs.

In Exhibit 10-23, the slope coefficients—$7.60 for machine-hours and $37.77 for production batches—measure the change in indirect manufacturing labour costs associated with a unit change in an independent variable (assuming that the other independent variable is held constant). For example, indirect manufacturing labour costs increase by $37.77 when one more production batch is added, assuming that the number of machine-hours is held constant.

An alternative approach would create two separate cost pools—one for costs tied to machine-hours and another for costs tied to production batches. Elegant Rugs would then estimate the relationship between the cost driver and overhead costs separately for each cost pool. The difficult task under that approach would be properly dividing overhead costs into the two cost pools.

Multicollinearity

Multicollinearity. Exists when two or more independent variables in a regression model are highly correlated.

A major concern that arises with multiple regression is multicollinearity. **Multicollinearity** exists when two or more independent variables are highly correlated with each other. Generally, users of regression analysis believe that a coefficient of correlation between independent variables greater than 0.70 indicates multicollinearity. Multicollinearity increases the standard errors of the coefficients of the individual variables. The result is that there is greater uncertainty about the underlying value of the coefficients of the individual independent variables. That is, variables that are economically and statistically significant will appear insignificant.

The coefficients of correlation between the potential independent variables for Elegant Rugs in Exhibit 10-22 are:

Pairwise Combinations	Coefficient of Correlation
Machine-hours and direct manufacturing labour-hours	0.12
Machine-hours and production batches	0.40
Direct manufacturing labour-hours and production batches	0.31

These results indicate that multiple regressions using any pair of the independent variables in Exhibit 10-23 are not likely to encounter multicollinearity problems.

If severe multicollinearity exists, try to obtain new data that does not suffer from multicollinearity problems. Do not drop an independent variable (cost driver) that should be included in a model because it is correlated with another independent variable. Omitting such a variable will cause the estimated coefficient of the independent variable included in the model to be biased away from its true value.

TERMS TO LEARN

This chapter contains definitions of the following important terms:

account analysis method (p. 326)
coefficient of determination, r^2 (p. 344)
conference method (p. 326)
constant (p. 322)
cost estimation (p. 323)
cost predictions (p. 323)
cumulative average time learning model (p. 336)
dependent variable (p. 327)
disturbance term (p. 331)
error term (p. 331)
experience curve (p. 336)
high-low method (p. 328)
incremental unit time learning model (p. 336)
industrial engineering method (p. 325)
intercept (p. 322)

learning curve (p. 335)
linear cost function (p. 321)
mixed cost (p. 322)
multicollinearity (p. 350)
multiple regression (p. 330)
nonlinear cost function (p. 333)
regression analysis (p. 330)
residual term (p. 331)
semivariable cost (p. 322)
simple regression (p. 330)
slope coefficient (p. 321)
specification analysis (p. 346)
standard error of the estimated coefficient (p. 345)
step cost function (p. 333)
work measurement method (p. 325)

ASSIGNMENT MATERIAL

QUESTIONS

10-1 What two assumptions are frequently made when estimating a cost function?

10-2 Describe three alternative linear cost functions.

10-3 What is the difference between a linear and a nonlinear cost function? Give an example of each type of cost function.

10-4 "High correlation between two variables means that one is the cause and the other is the effect." Do you agree? Explain.

10-5 Name four approaches to estimating a cost function.

10-6 Describe the conference method for estimating a cost function. What are two advantages of this method?

10-7 Describe the account analysis method for estimating a cost function.

10-8 List the six steps in estimating a cost function on the basis of an analysis of current or past cost relationships. Which step is typically the most difficult for a cost analyst?

10-9 When using the high-low method, should you base the high and low observations on the dependent variable or on the cost driver?

10-10 Describe three criteria for evaluating cost functions and choosing cost drivers.

10-11 Define *learning curve*. Outline two models that can be used when incorporating learning into the estimation of cost functions.

10-12 Discuss four frequently encountered problems when collecting cost data on variables included in a cost function.

10-13 What are the four key assumptions examined in specification analysis in the case of simple regression?

10-14 "All the independent variables in a cost function estimated with regression analysis are cost drivers." Do you agree? Explain.

10-15 "Multicollinearity exists when the dependent variable and the independent variable are highly correlated." Do you agree? Explain.

EXERCISES

10-16 Estimating a cost function. The controller of the Ijiri Company wants you to estimate a cost function from the following two observations in a general ledger account called Maintenance:

Month	Machine-Hours	Maintenance Costs Incurred
January	4,000	$3,000
February	7,000	3,900

REQUIRED
1. Estimate the cost function for maintenance.
2. Can the constant in the cost function be used as an estimate of fixed maintenance cost per month? Explain.

10-17 Identifying variable, fixed, and mixed cost functions. The Pacific Corporation operates car rental agencies at over 20 airports. Customers can choose from one of three contracts for car rentals of one day or less:
◆ **Contract 1.** $50 for the day
◆ **Contract 2.** $30 for the day plus $0.20 per kilometre travelled
◆ **Contract 3.** $1 per kilometre travelled

REQUIRED
1. Present separate plots for each of the three contracts, with costs on the vertical axis and kilometres travelled on the horizontal axis.
2. Describe each contract as a linear cost function of the form $y = a + bX$.
3. Describe each contract as a variable, fixed, or mixed cost function.

10-18 Various cost-behaviour patterns. (CPA, adapted) Select the graph that matches the numbered manufacturing cost data. Indicate by letter which of the graphs best fits each of the situations or items described.

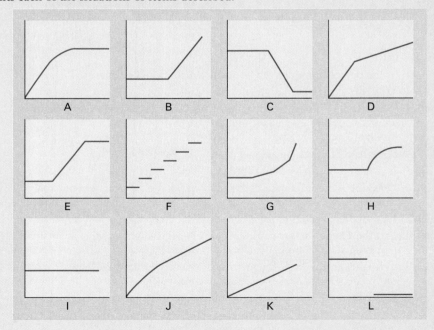

The vertical axes of the graphs represent *total* dollars of cost, and the horizontal axes represent production output during a calendar year. In each case, the zero point of dollars and production is at the intersection of the two axes. The graphs may be used more than once.

1. Annual amortization of equipment, where the amount of amortization charged is computed by the machine-hours method.
2. Electricity bill—a flat fixed charge, plus a variable cost after a certain number of kilowatt-hours are used, where the quantity of kilowatt-hours used varies proportionately with quantity of production output.
3. City water bill, which is computed as follows:

First 1,000,000 litres or less	$1,000 flat fee
Next 10,000 litres	$0.003 per litre used
Next 10,000 litres	$0.006 per litre used
Next 10,000 litres	$0.009 per litre used
And so on	And so on

The litres of water used vary proportionately with the quantity of production output.

4. Cost of lubricant for machines, where cost per unit decreases with each kilogram of lubricant used (for example, if one kilogram is used, the cost is $10; if two kilograms are used, the cost is $19.98; if three kilograms are used, the cost is $29.94) with a minimum cost per kilogram of $9.20.
5. Annual amortization of equipment, where the amount is computed by the straight-line method. When the amortization rate was established, it was anticipated that the obsolescence factor would be greater than the wear-and-tear factor.
6. Rent on a manufacturing plant donated by the city, where the agreement calls for a fixed fee payment unless 200,000 labour-hours are worked, in which case no rent need be paid.
7. Salaries of repair personnel, where one person is needed for every 1,000 machine-hours or less (that is, 0 to 1,000 hours requires one person, 1,001 to 2,000 hours requires two people, etc.).
8. Cost of direct materials used (assume no quantity discounts).
9. Rent on a manufacturing plant donated by the county, where the agreement calls for rent of $100,000 reduced by $1 for each direct manufacturing labour-hour worked in excess of 200,000 hours, but a minimum rental fee of $20,000 must be paid.

10-19 Matching graphs with descriptions of cost behaviour. (D. Green) Given below are a number of charts, each indicating some relationship between cost and a cost driver. No attempt has been made to draw these charts to any particular scale; the absolute numbers on each axis may be closely or widely spaced.

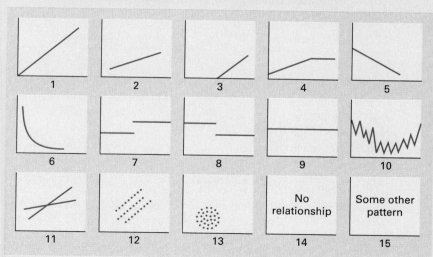

Indicate by number which one of the charts best fits each of the situations or items described. Each situation or item is independent of all the others; all factors not stated are assumed to be irrelevant. Some charts will be used more than once; some may not apply to any of the situations. Note that category 14, "No relationship," is not the same as 15, "Some other pattern."

If the horizontal axis represents the production output over the year and the vertical axis represents *total cost* or *revenue*, indicate the one best pattern or relationship for:

1. Direct materials costs
2. Supervisors' salaries
3. A breakeven chart
4. Mixed costs—for example, fixed electrical power *demand* charge plus variable usage rate
5. Amortization of plant, computed on a straight-line basis
6. Data supporting the use of a variable cost rate, such as manufacturing labour cost of $14 per unit produced
7. Incentive bonus plan that pays managers $0.10 for every unit produced above some level of production
8. Interest charges on money borrowed at a fixed rate of interest to finance the acquisition of a plant, before any payments on principal

10-20 Account analysis method. Lorenzo operates a brushless car wash. Incoming cars are put on an automatic, continuously moving conveyor belt. Cars are washed as the conveyor belt carries the car from the start station to the finish station. After the car moves off the conveyor belt, the car is dried manually. Workers then clean and vacuum the inside of the car. Workers are managed by a single supervisor. Lorenzo serviced 80,000 cars in 2000. Lorenzo reports the following costs for 2000.

Account Description	Costs
Car wash labour	$240,000
Soap, cloth, and supplies	32,000
Water	28,000
Power to move conveyor belt	72,000
Amortization	64,000
Supervision	30,000
Cashier	16,000

REQUIRED
1. Classify each account as variable or fixed with respect to cars washed. Explain.
2. Lorenzo expects to wash 90,000 cars in 2001. Use the cost classification you developed in requirement 1 to estimate Lorenzo's total costs in 2001.
3. Calculate the average cost of washing a car in 2000 and 2001. (Use the expected 90,000 car wash level for 2001.)

10-21 Account analysis method. Gower, Inc., a manufacturer of plastic products, reports the following manufacturing costs and account analysis classification for the year ended December 31, 2000.

Account	Classification	Amount
Direct materials	All variable	$300,000
Direct manufacturing labour	All variable	225,000
Power	All variable	37,500
Supervision labour	20% variable	56,250
Materials-handling labour	50% variable	60,000
Maintenance labour	40% variable	75,000
Amortization	0% variable	95,000
Rent, property taxes, and administration	0% variable	100,000

Gower, Inc., produced 75,000 units of product in 2000. Gower's management is estimating costs for 2001on the basis of 2000 numbers. The following additional information is available for 2001:
a. Direct materials prices in 2001 are expected to increase by 5% compared with 2000.
b. Under the terms of the labour contract, direct manufacturing labour wage rates are expected to increase by 10% in 2001 compared with 2000.
c. Power rates and wage rates for supervision, materials-handling, and maintenance are not expected to change from 2000 to 2001.
d. Amortization costs are expected to increase by 5%, and rent, property taxes, and administration costs are expected to increase by 7%.
e. Gower, Inc., expects to manufacture and sell 80,000 units in 2001.

1. Prepare a schedule of variable, fixed, and total manufacturing costs for each account category in 2001. Estimate total manufacturing costs for 2001.
2. Calculate Gower's total manufacturing cost per unit in 2000 and estimate total manufacturing cost per unit in 2001.
3. How can you get better estimates of fixed and variable costs? Why would these better estimates be useful to Gower?

10-22 Estimating a cost function, high-low method. Laurie Daley is examining customer service costs in the Southern Region of Capitol Products. Capitol Products has over 200 separate electrical products that are sold with a six-month guarantee of full repair or replacement with a new product. When a product is returned by a customer, a service report is made. This service report includes details of the problem and the time and cost of resolving the problem.

Weekly data for the most recent ten-week period are:

Week	Customer Service Department Costs	Number of Service Reports
1	$13,845	201
2	20,624	276
3	12,941	122
4	18,452	386
5	14,843	274
6	21,890	436
7	16,831	321
8	21,429	328
9	18,267	243
10	16,832	161

REQUIRED

1. Plot the relationship between customer service costs and number of service reports. Is the relationship economically plausible?
2. Use the high-low method to compute the cost function, relating customer service costs to the number of service reports.
3. What variables, in addition to number of service reports, might be cost drivers of monthly customer service costs of Capitol Products?

10-23 Linear cost approximation. Terry Lawler, managing director of the Winnipeg Consulting Group, is examining how overhead costs behave with variations in monthly professional labour-hours billed to clients. Assume the following historical data:

Total Overhead Costs	Professional Labour-Hours Billed to Clients
$340,000	3,000
400,000	4,000
435,000	5,000
477,000	6,000
529,000	7,000
587,000	8,000

REQUIRED

1. Compute the linear cost function, relating total overhead cost to professional labour-hours, using the representative observations of 4,000 and 7,000 hours. Plot the linear cost function. Does the constant component of the cost function represent the fixed overhead costs of the Winnipeg Consulting Group? Why?
2. What would be the predicted total overhead costs for (a) 5,000 hours and (b) 8,000 hours using the cost function estimated in requirement 1? Plot the predicted costs and actual costs for 5,000 and 8,000 hours.
3. Lawler had a chance to accept a special job that would have boosted professional labour-hours from 4,000 to 5,000 hours. Suppose Lawler, guided by the linear cost function, rejected this job because it would have brought a total increase in contribution margin of $38,000, before deducting the predicted increase in total overhead cost, $43,000. What is the total contribution margin actually forgone?

10-24 Cost-volume-profit and regression analysis. Oxbow Corporation manufactures a children's bicycle, model CT8. It currently makes the bicycle frame in-house. During 2000, it manufactured 30,000 frames at a total cost of $900,000. Ryan Corporation has offered to supply as many frames as Oxbow wants at a cost of $28.50 per frame. Oxbow anticipates needing 36,000 frames each year for the next few years.

REQUIRED

1. **a.** What is the average cost of manufacturing a bicycle frame in 2000? How does it compare with Ryan's offer?
   b. Can Oxbow use the answer in requirement **1.a.** to determine the cost of manufacturing 36,000 bicycle frames? Explain your answer.
2. Oxbow's cost analyst uses annual data for the past eight years to estimate the following regression equation with total manufacturing costs of the bicycle frame as the dependent variable and number of bicycle frames as the independent variable

$$y = \$432,000 \times \$15X$$

   During the years used to estimate the regression equation, the production of bicycle frames had varied from 28,000 to 36,000. Using this equation, estimate how much it would cost Oxbow to manufacture 36,000 bicycle frames. How much more costly or less costly is it than acquiring the frames from Ryan?
3. What other information would you need in order to be confident that the equation in requirement 2 accurately predicts the cost of manufacturing bicycle frames.

10-25 Regression analysis, service company. (CMA, adapted) Bob Jones owns a catering company that prepares banquets and parties for both individual and business functions throughout the year. Jones's business is seasonal, with a heavy schedule during the summer months and the year-end holidays and a light schedule at other times. During peak periods there are extra costs.

One of the major events Jones's customers request is a cocktail party. He offers a standard cocktail party and has developed the following cost structure on a per-person basis.

Food and beverages	$15
Labour (0.5 hour × $10 per hour)	5
Overhead (0.5 hour × $14 per hour)	7
Total costs per person	$27

Jones is quite certain about his estimates of the food, beverages, and labour costs but is not as comfortable with the overhead estimate. This estimate was based on the actual data for the past 12 months presented here. These data indicate that overhead expenses vary with the direct labour-hours expended. The $14 estimate was determined by dividing total overhead expended for the 12 months by total labour-hours.

Month	Labour-Hours	Overhead Costs
January	2,500	$ 55,000
February	2,700	59,000
March	3,000	60,000
April	4,200	64,000
May	4,500	67,000
June	5,500	71,000
July	6,500	74,000
August	7,500	77,000
September	7,000	75,000
October	4,500	68,000
November	3,100	62,000
December	6,500	73,000
Total	57,500	$805,000

Jones has recently become aware of regression analysis. He estimated the following regression equation with overhead costs as the dependent variable and labour-hours as the independent variable:

$$y = \$48,271 + \$3.93X$$

1. Plot the relationship between overhead costs and labour-hours. Draw the regression line and evaluate it using the criteria of economic plausibility, goodness of fit, and slope of the regression line.
2. Using data from the regression analysis, find the variable cost per person for a cocktail party.
3. Bob Jones has been asked to prepare a bid for a 200-person cocktail party to be given next month. Determine the minimum bid price that Jones would be willing to submit to earn a positive contribution margin.

10-26 Regression analysis, activity-based costing, choosing cost drivers. Jill Flaherty has been collecting data over the last year in an effort to understand the cost drivers of distribution costs at Waterloo Corporation, a manufacturer of brass door handles. Distribution costs include the costs of organizing different shipments as well as physically handling and moving packaged units. Flaherty believes that, because the product is heavy, number of units moved will impact distribution costs significantly but she is not certain that this is the case. Flaherty collects the following monthly data for the past 12 months.

Month	Distribution Costs	Number of Packaged Units Moved	Number of Shipments Made
January	$28,000	51,000	200
February	20,000	43,000	210
March	17,000	28,000	185
April	32,000	67,000	315
May	40,000	73,000	335
June	24,000	54,000	225
July	22,000	37,000	190
August	35,000	72,000	390
September	42,000	71,000	280
October	23,000	56,000	360
November	33,000	52,000	380
December	22,000	45,000	270
Total	$338,000	649,000	3,340

Flaherty estimates the following regression equations

$$y = \$1,349 + (\$0.496 \times \text{Number of packaged units moved})$$
$$y = \$10,417 + (\$63.77 \times \text{Number of shipments made})$$

REQUIRED

1. Present plots of the monthly data and the regression lines underlying each of the following cost functions:
   a. Distribution costs = $a + (b \times \text{Number of packaged units moved})$
   b. Distribution costs = $a + (b \times \text{Number of shipments made})$
      Which cost driver for support overhead costs would you choose? Explain your answer briefly.
2. Flaherty anticipates moving 40,000 units in 220 shipments next month. Using the cost function you chose in requirement 1, what distribution costs should Flaherty budget?
3. If Flaherty chose the wrong cost function—the cost function other than the one you chose in requirement 1—and 40,000 units were moved in 220 shipments, would you expect actual costs to be lower than, to be greater than, or to closely approximate the predictions made using the "wrong" cost driver and cost function. Explain your answer briefly and any other implications of choosing the "wrong" cost driver and cost function.

10-27 Learning curve, cumulative average-time learning curve. Global Defence manufactures radar systems. It has just completed the manufacture of its first newly designed system, RS-32. It took 3,000 direct manufacturing labour-hours (DMLH) to produce this one unit. Global believes that a 90% cumulative average time learning model for direct manufacturing labour-hours applies to RS-32. (A 90% learning curve implies $q = -0.1520$.) The variable costs of producing RS-32 are:

Direct materials costs	$80,000 per RS-32
Direct manufacturing labour costs	$25 per DMLH
Variable manufacturing overhead costs	$15 per DMLH

REQUIRED

Calculate the total variable costs of producing two, four, and eight units.

10-28 Learning curve, incremental unit time learning curve. Assume the same information for Global Defence as in Exercise 10-27 except that Global Defence uses a 90% incremental unit-time learning curve as a basis for forecasting direct manufacturing labour-hours. (A 90% learning curve implies $q = -0.1520$.)

REQUIRED

1. Calculate the total variable costs of producing two, three, and four units.
2. If you solved Exercise 10-27, compare your cost predictions in the two exercises for two and four units. Why are the predictions different?

10-29 Organizing data, high-low method. Ken Howard, financial analyst at JVR Corporation, a manufacturer of precision parts, is examining the behaviour of quarterly maintenance costs for budgeting purposes. Howard collects data on machine-hours worked and maintenance costs for the past 13 quarters. The data are as follows:

Quarter	Machine-Hours	Maintenance Costs
1	90,000	$235,000
2	110,000	185,000
3	100,000	220,000
4	120,000	200,000
5	85,000	240,000
6	105,000	170,000
7	95,000	215,000
8	115,000	195,000
9	95,000	235,000
10	115,000	190,000
11	105,000	225,000
12	125,000	180,000
13	90,000	250,000

REQUIRED

1 a. Present plots of the quarterly data underlying the cost function: Maintenance costs = $a + (b \times$ Machine-hours).
   b. Estimate the cost function for the data represented by the plots in requirement **1.a.** using the high-low method.
   c. How well does the cost function fit the data?
2 a. Construct a table and present plots of the quarterly data relating machine-hours in a quarter (t, say) to maintenance costs in the following quarter (t + 1). That is, plot machine-hours in quarter 1 against maintenance costs in quarter 2, machine-hours in quarter 2 against maintenance costs in quarter 3, and so on.
   b. Estimate the cost function for the data represented by the plots in requirement **2.a.** using the high-low method.
   c. How well does the cost function fit the data?
3. Howard anticipates that JVR will operate machines for 90,000 hours in quarter 14. Calculate the predicted maintenance costs in quarter 14 using the cost functions estimated in requirements **1.b.** and **2.b.** What maintenance costs should Howard budget for quarter 14? Explain your answer briefly.

10-30 High-low versus regression method. (CIMA, heavily adapted) Anna Martinez, the financial manager at the Casa Real restaurant, is working with Jan Brown, the marketing manager, to establish if there is any relationship between newspaper advertising and sales revenue at the restaurant. They obtain the following monthly data for the past 10 months.

Month	Revenues	Advertising Expense
March	$50,000	$2,000
April	70,000	3,000
May	55,000	1,500
June	65,000	3,500
July	55,000	1,000
August	65,000	2,000
September	45,000	1,500
October	80,000	4,000
November	55,000	2,500
December	60,000	2,500

They estimate the following regression equation

$y = 39,502 + (8.723 \times \text{Advertising Expense})$, where y is the monthly revenue

REQUIRED

1. Plot the relationship between advertising expense and revenues.
2. Draw the regression line and evaluate it using the criteria of economic plausibility, goodness of fit, and slope of the regression line.
3. Use the high-low method to compute the cost function, relating advertising expense and revenues.
4. Using (a) the regression equation and (b) the high-low equation, what is the increase in revenues for each $1,000 spent on advertising within the relevant range.
5. Should Martinez and Brown use the cost function estimated from the regression method or the high-low method to predict the effect of advertising on revenues? Explain briefly.

10-31 Regression analysis, activity-based costing, choosing cost drivers. Larry Chu, the plant controller at Rohan Plastics, has been concerned about correctly identifying cost drivers ever since the plant began implementing activity-based costing a year or so ago. Correctly identifying cost drivers is important for bidding on and pricing of jobs and for managing costs within the plant.

Choosing the cost drivers for support overhead has been a particular problem. Rohan has eliminated many job categories, so indirect support consists of skilled staff responsible for the efficient functioning of all aspects (setup, production, maintenance, and quality control) of the plastic injection-molding facility. In talking to the support staff, Chu has the impression that they spend a good portion of their time ensuring that the equipment is set up correctly and checking that the first units of production in each batch are of good quality.

Chu has collected the following monthly data for the past 12 months:

Month	Support Overhead	Machine-Hours	Number of Batches
January	$ 57,000	2,000	106
February	41,000	2,400	128
March	33,000	1,850	147
April	44,000	2,100	159
May	46,000	3,600	162
June	48,000	2,250	174
July	66,000	3,800	264
August	44,000	2,700	216
September	63,000	2,850	249
October	66,000	3,300	219
November	81,000	3,750	303
December	84,000	2,250	309
Total	$673,000	32,850	2,436

Chu estimates the following regression equations:

$$y = \$28{,}089 + (\$10.23 \times \text{Machine-hours})$$

$$\text{and} \quad y = \$16{,}031 + (\$197.30 \times \text{Number of batches})$$

where y is the monthly support overhead.

REQUIRED

1. Present plots of the monthly data and the regression lines underlying each of the following cost functions:
   a. Support overhead costs $= a + (b \times \text{machine-hours})$
   b. Support overhead costs $= a + (b \times \text{number of batches})$
   Which cost driver for support overhead costs would you choose?
2. Chu anticipates 2,600 machine-hours and 300 batches will be run next month. Using the cost driver you chose in requirement 1, what support overhead costs should Chu budget?
3. a. Chu adds 20% to costs as a first cut for determining target revenues (and hence prices). Costs other than support overhead are expected to equal $125,000 next month. Compare the target revenue numbers obtained if (i) machine-hours and (ii) number of batches is used as the cost driver. Discuss what would happen if Chu picked the "wrong" cost driver—the cost driver other than the one you chose in requirement 1—to set target revenues and prices.
   b. Describe any other implications of choosing the "wrong" cost driver and cost function.

PROBLEMS

10-32 Cost estimation, cumulative average time learning curve. The Nautilus Company, which is under contract to the Armed Forces, assembles troop deployment boats. As part of its research program, it completes the assembly of the first of a new model (PT109) of deployment boats. The Armed Forces is impressed with the PT109. It requests that Nautilus submit a proposal on the cost of producing another seven PT109s.

The accounting department at Nautilus reports the following cost information for the first PT109 assembled by Nautilus:

Direct materials	$100,000
Direct manufacturing labour (10,000 labour-hours × $30)	300,000
Tooling cost*	50,000
Variable manufacturing overhead[†]	200,000
Other manufacturing overhead[‡]	75,000
	$725,000

*Tooling can be reused at no extra cost, since all of its cost has been assigned to the first deployment boat.
[†]Variable overhead incurred is directly affected by direct manufacturing labour-hours; a rate of $20 per hour is used for purposes of bidding on contracts.
[‡]Other overhead is allocated at a flat rate of 25% of direct manufacturing labour costs for purposes of bidding on contracts.

Nautilus uses an 85% cumulative average time learning curve as a basis for forecasting direct manufacturing labour-hours on its assembling operations. (An 85% learning curve implies $q = -0.2345$.)

REQUIRED

1. Prepare a prediction of the total costs for producing the seven PT109s for the Armed Forces. (Nautilus will keep the first deployment boat assembled, costed at $725,000, as a demonstration model for other potential customers.)
2. What is the difference between (a) the predicted total costs for producing the seven PT109s in requirement 1 and (b) the predicted total costs for producing the seven PT109s assuming that there is no learning curve for direct manufacturing labour? (That is, for (b) assume a linear function for direct labour-hours and units produced.)

10-33 Cost estimation, incremental unit time learning curve. Assume the same information for the Nautilus Company as that in requirement 1 of Problem 10-32 with one exception, that Nautilus uses an 85% incremental unit time learning curve as a basis for forecasting direct manufacturing labour-hours on its assembling operations. (An 85% learning curve implies $q = -0.2345$.)

REQUIRED

1. Prepare a prediction of the total expected costs for producing the seven PT109s for the Armed Forces.
2. If you solved requirement 1 of Problem 10-32, compare your cost prediction there with the one you made here. Why are the predictions different?

10-34 Promotion of a new product, simple and multiple regression analysis. (Chapter Appendix, S. Stickel, adapted) "What does all this mean. All I really want to know is whether I should advertise or not, and where?" said Rick Savalas, the sales manager of Cleanhair Products Inc. Rick has asked for your help to understand the results of regression analyses that have been prepared by his assistants for a new product, Glowbright, that Cleanhair Products recently introduced. The notation used is as follows:

y estimated sales of Glowbright

X_1 dollars incurred on discount coupons placed in magazines

X_2 dollars spent on advertising Glowbright on television

Standard errors of the coefficients (not t-statistics) are in parentheses.

1. $y = \$381,000 + \$3.98\ X_1$ $r^2 = 0.47$
   ($1.73)
2. $y = \$467,000 + \$4.23\ X_2$ $r^2 = 0.53$
   ($1.86)
3. $y = \$752,300 + \$0.87\ X_1 + \$0.91\ X_2$ $r^2 = 0.88$
   ($0.79)   ($0.99)

REQUIRED

1. For each of the regressions, perform a statistical test and indicate whether or not sales are affected by discount coupons and television advertising.
2. Contrast the multiple regression results (equation 3) with the simple regression results (equations 1 and 2) in terms of the statistical tests that you performed in requirement 1. Suggest a possible explanation for any differences in the results of the statistical tests.
3. Interpret the $3.98, the $4.23, the $0.87, and the $0.91 coefficients in the regression equations. Specifically, explain briefly what the coefficients imply about whether and how Rick should advertise?

10-35 Evaluating alternative simple regression models, not for profit. (Chapter Appendix) Kathy Hanks, executive assistant to the president of Eastern University, is concerned about the overhead costs at her university. Cost pressures are severe, so controlling and reducing overhead is very important. Hanks believes overhead costs incurred are generally a function of the number of different academic programs (including different specializations, degrees, and majors) that the university has and the number of enrolled students. Both have grown significantly over the years. She collects the following data:

Year	Overhead Costs (in thousands)	Number of Academic Programs	Number of Enrolled Students
1	$13,500	29	3,400
2	19,200	36	5,000
3	16,800	49	2,600
4	20,100	53	4,700
5	19,500	54	3,900
6	23,100	58	4,900
7	23,700	88	5,700
8	20,100	72	3,900
9	22,800	83	3,500
10	29,700	73	3,700
11	31,200	101	5,600
12	38,100	103	7,600

She finds the following results for two separate simple regression models:

◆ **Regression 1.** Overhead costs = $a + (b \times$ number of academic programs)

Variable	Coefficient	Standard Error	*t*-Value
Constant	$7,127.75	$3,335.34	2.14
Independent variable 1: number of academic programs	$ 240.64	$ 47.33	5.08

$r^2 = 0.72$; Durbin-Watson statistic = 1.81.

◆ **Regression 2.** Overhead costs = $a + (b \times$ number of enrolled students)

Variable	Coefficient	Standard Error	*t*-Value
Constant	$5,991.75	$5,067.88	1.18
Independent variable 1: number of enrolled students	$ 3.78	$ 1.07	3.53

$r^2 = 0.55$; Durbin-Watson statistic = 0.77.

REQUIRED
1. Plot the relationship between overhead costs and each of the following variables: (a) number of academic programs and (b) number of enrolled students.
2. Compare and evaluate the two simple regression models estimated by Hanks. Use the comparison format employed in Exhibit 10-21.
3. What insights do the analyses provide about controlling and reducing overhead costs at the University?

10-36 Evaluating multiple regression models, not for profit (continuation of Problem 10-35). (Chapter Appendix)

REQUIRED
1. Given your findings in Problem 10-35, should Hanks use multiple regression analysis to better understand the cost drivers of overhead costs? Explain your answer.
2. Hanks decides that the simple regression analysis in Problem 10-35 should be extended to a multiple regression analysis. She finds the following result:

◆ **Regression 3.** Overhead costs = $a + (b_1 \times$ number of academic programs) $+ (b_2 \times$ number of enrolled students)

Variable	Coefficient	Standard Error	*t*-Value
Constant	$2,779.62	$3,620.05	0.77
Independent variable 1: number of academic programs	$ 178.37	$ 51.54	3.46
Independent variable 2: number of enrolled students	$ 1.87	$ 0.92	2.03

$r^2 = 0.81$; Durbin-Watson statistic = 1.84.

The coefficient of correlation between number of academic programs and number of students is 0.60. Use the format in Exhibit 10-21 to evaluate the multiple regression model. (Assume linearity, and constant variance and normality of residuals.) Should Hanks choose the multiple regression model over the two simple regression models of Problem 10-35?
3. How might the president of Eastern University use these regression results to manage overhead costs?

10-37 Purchasing department cost drivers, activity-based costing, simple regression analysis. (Chapter Appendix) Fashion Flair operates a chain of ten retail department stores. Each department store makes its own purchasing decisions. Barry Lee, assistant to the president of Fashion Flair, is interested in better understanding the drivers of purchasing department costs. For many years, Fashion Flair has allocated purchasing department costs to products on the basis of the dollar value of merchandise purchased. An item costing $100 is allocated ten times as much overhead costs associated with the purchasing department as an item costing $10 is allocated.

Lee recently attended a seminar titled "Cost Drivers in the Retail Industry." In a presentation at the seminar, Couture Fabrics, a leading competitor that has implemented activity-based costing, reported the number of purchase orders and the number of suppliers to be the two most important cost drivers of purchasing department costs. The dollar value of merchandise purchased on each purchase order was not found to be a significant cost driver by Couture Fabrics. Lee interviewed several members of the purchasing department at the Fashion Flair store in Victoria. These people told Lee that they believed that Couture Fabrics' conclusions also applied to their purchasing department.

Lee collects the following data for the most recent year for the ten retail department stores of Fashion Flair:

Department Store	Purchasing Department Costs (PDC)	Dollar Value of Merchandise Purchased (MP$)	Number of Purchase Orders (no. of POs)	Number of Suppliers (no. of Ss)
Saskatoon	$1,523,000	$ 68,315,000	4,357	132
Chicago	1,100,000	33,456,000	2,550	222
Victoria	547,000	121,160,000	1,433	11
Miami	2,049,000	119,566,000	5,944	190
New York	1,056,000	33,505,000	2,793	23
Calgary	529,000	29,854,000	1,327	33
Seattle	1,538,000	102,875,000	7,586	104
St. Louis	1,754,000	38,674,000	3,617	119
Toronto	1,612,000	139,312,000	1,707	208
Vancouver	1,257,000	130,944,000	4,731	201

Lee decides to use simple regression analysis to examine whether one or more of three variables (the last three columns in the table) are cost drivers of purchasing department costs. Summary results for these regressions are as follows:

◆ **Regression 1.** PDC $= a + (b \times$ MP$)$

Variable	Coefficient	Standard Error	t-Value
Constant	$1,039,061	$343,439	3.03
Independent variable 1: MP$	0.0031	0.0037	0.84

$r^2 = 0.08$; Durbin-Watson statistic $= 2.41$.

◆ **Regression 2.** PDC $= a + (b \times$ no. of POs$)$

Variable	Coefficient	Standard Error	t-Value
Constant	$730,716	$265,419	2.75
Independent variable 1: no. of POs	$ 156.97	$ 64.69	2.43

$r^2 = 0.42$; Durbin-Watson statistic $= 1.98$.

◆ **Regression 3.** PDC $= a + (b \times$ no. of Ss$)$

Variable	Coefficient	Standard Error	t-Value
Constant	$814,862	$247,821	3.29
Independent variable 1: no. of Ss	$ 3,875	$ 1,697	2.28

$r^2 = 0.39$; Durbin-Watson statistic $= 1.97$.

REQUIRED
1. Compare and evaluate the three simple regression models estimated by Lee. Graph each one. Also, use the format employed in Exhibit 10-21 to evaluate the information.
2. Do the regression results support the Couture Fabrics presentation about purchasing department cost drivers? Which of these cost drivers would you recommend in designing an activity-based cost system?
3. How might Lee gain additional evidence on drivers of purchasing department costs at each store of Fashion Flair?

10-38 Purchasing department cost drivers, multiple regression analysis (continuation of 10-37). (Chapter Appendix) Barry Lee decides that the simple regression analysis reported in Problem 10-37 could be extended to a multiple regression analysis. He finds the following results for several multiple regressions:

◆ **Regression 4.** PDC = $a + (b_1 \times$ no. of POs$) + (b_2 \times$ no. of Ss$)$

Variable	Coefficient	Standard Error	t-Value
Constant	$485,384	$257,477	1.89
Independent variable 1: no. of POs	$ 123.22	$ 57.69	2.14
Independent variable 2: no. of Ss	$ 2,952	$ 1,476	2.00

$r^2 = 0.63$; Durbin-Watson statistic = 1.90.

◆ **Regression 5.** PDC = $a + (b_1 \times$ no. of POs$) + (b_2 \times$ no. of Ss$) + (b_3 \times$ MP$\$)$

Variable	Coefficient	Standard Error	t-Value
Constant	$494,684	$310,205	1.59
Independent variable 1: no. of POs	$ 124.05	$ 63.49	1.95
Independent variable 2: no. of Ss	$ 2,984	$ 1,622	1.84
Independent variable 3: MP$	−0.0002	0.0030	−0.07

$r^2 = 0.63$; Durbin-Watson statistic = 1.90.

The coefficients of correlation between pairwise combinations of the variables are:

	PDC	MP$	No. of POs
MP$	0.29		
No. of POs	0.65	0.27	
No. of Ss	0.63	0.34	0.29

REQUIRED

1. Evaluate regression 4 using the economic plausibility, goodness of fit, significance of independent variables, and specification analysis criteria. Compare regression 4 with regressions 2 and 3 in Problem 10-37. Which model would you recommend that Lee use? Why?
2. Compare regression 5 with regression 4. Which model would you recommend that Lee use? Why?
3. Lee estimates the following data for the Saskatoon store for next year: dollar value of merchandise purchased, $75,000,000; number of purchase orders, 3,900; number of suppliers, 110. How much should Lee budget for purchasing department costs for the Saskatoon store for next year?
4. What difficulties may arise in multiple regressions that do not arise in simple regressions? Is there evidence of such difficulties in either of the multiple regressions presented in this problem?
5. Give two examples of decisions where the regression results reported here (and in Problem 10-37) could be informative.

10-39 **Regression computations, ethics.** (Chapter Appendix) Cambridge Engineering manufactures small electric motors. Data on manufacturing labour costs and units produced for the last four quarters are as follows:

Quarter	Manufacturing Labour Costs	Units Produced
1	$176,000	9,000
2	174,000	10,000
3	165,000	9,000
4	205,000	12,000
Total	$720,000	40,000

Peter Smith, the manufacturing manager, is evaluated on how labour costs in a quarter compare with labour costs in the previous four quarters. In the recently concluded Quarter 5, Cambridge Engineering produced 12,000 motors and incurred manufacturing labour costs of $208,000. Smith is very happy with the results. Over the previous four quarters, the average manufacturing labour cost per unit are $18 ($720,000 ÷ 40,000 units) resulting in a benchmark for Quarter 5 of $18 × 12,000 = $216,000. Just as Smith is thinking about what he might do with the bonus, Allison Hart, the plant controller, knocks on Smith's door.

Allison Hart:	I am sorry that we couldn't beat the benchmark over the last four quarters. We certainly gave it our best shot.
Peter Smith:	What do you mean we didn't beat the benchmark. Here are the numbers I just calculated. Against a benchmark of $216,000, we achieved $208,000.
Allison Hart:	No, that's not how the calculations are done. Some of the labour costs are fixed and others vary with production. My analysis here first separates out the fixed from the variable components. My calculations then show that our Quarter 5 performance was worse than the previous four quarters.
Peter Smith:	Please review your calculations. I am sure you can report better numbers than that. This regression approach you are using is subject to estimation error. You should make some adjustment for that. If we don't show senior management that we are succeeding in reducing labour costs, they might shut us down because they do not believe that we can be competitive. I am sure that no one in this plant wants that to happen.

REQUIRED

1. Verify, either by using the actual formulae given in the Appendix, or by using a regression routine on a computer, that the regression equation is given by

$$y = \$65,000 + (\$11.50 \times \text{Units produced})$$

with an $r^2 = 0.88$.

2. What is the benchmark for Quarter 5 that Allison Hart had calculated?
3. Why is there a difference between the benchmark calculated by Peter Smith and the benchmark calculated in requirement 2? Which benchmark do you prefer? Explain your answer.
4. Identify the steps that Allison Hart should follow in attempting to resolve the situation created by Peter Smith's comment about adjusting the benchmark.

10-40 Data analysis and ethics. Comdex Electronics makes videocassette recorders (VCRs). Sales of VCRs have been very steady over the past ten years. Helen Gibbs, the manager of the department that makes the head mechanism for the VCR, is keen on introducing robots into the department to improve VCR quality. To obtain funding, Gibbs knows that she will need to justify the investment in terms of labour cost savings. Gibbs estimates average annual labour costs in the department of $1,200,000 over the past ten years. Labour costs over the past three years have averaged $800,000. If robots are introduced, labour costs would decrease to $550,000 per year. Average savings in labour costs of at least $400,000 per year are needed to justify the investment in robots. Gibbs uses the $1,200,000 number in her analysis. She then asks Joan Hansen, the management accountant, to review her calculations before she submits the robot proposal to senior management.

Hansen has a problem with Gibbs's analysis. She feels that by using a long time period of ten years, Gibbs was able to show larger labour cost savings than was justified. Hansen knew that Gibbs would be unhappy with these findings.

Hansen also felt that the robot investment was good for the company. She tried to redo the analysis in a way that might show larger cost savings, even though she knew that the assumptions she was using were not appropriate. Nothing she tried could change the conclusion that the cost savings were not large enough to justify the investment in robots. Gibbs is upset when she sees Hansen's report. She tells Hansen, "Try something else. I am sure you can come up with a set of assumptions under which this investment can be justified. You and I both know this is a good investment for the company to make. Quality is essential if we are to compete."

REQUIRED

1. Calculate the labour cost savings if Gibbs uses average labour costs incurred (a) over the past ten years and (b) over the past three years. Does it make a difference in terms of justifying the robot investment?
2. Why do you think the average labour costs over the past ten years differ significantly from the average labour costs over the past three years?
3. Explain whether Joan Hansen's initial attempts to redo the data analysis to justify the robot investment were ethical.
4. Identify the steps that Joan Hansen should follow in attempting to resolve this situation.

COLLABORATIVE LEARNING PROBLEM

10-41 High-low method, alternative regression functions, accrual accounting adjustments. Trevor Kennedy, the cost analyst at a can manufacturing plant of United Packaging, is seeking to examine the relationship between total engineering support costs reported in the plant records and machine-hours. These costs have two components: (1) labour (which is paid monthly) and (2) materials and parts (which are purchased from an outside vendor every three months). After further discussion with the operating manager, Kennedy discovers that the materials and parts numbers reported in the monthly records are on an "as purchased" basis and not on an "as used" or accrual accounting basis. By examining materials and parts usage records, Kennedy is able to restate the materials and parts costs to an "as used" basis. (No restatement of the labour costs was necessary.) The reported and restated costs are as follows:

Month	Labour: Reported Costs (1)	Materials and Parts: Reported Costs (2)	Materials and Parts: Restated Costs (3)	Total Engineering Support: Reported Costs (4) = (1) + (2)	Total Engineering Support: Restated Costs (5) = (1) + (3)	Machine-Hours (6)
March	$347	$847	$182	$1,194	$529	30
April	521	0	411	521	932	63
May	398	0	268	398	666	49
June	355	961	228	1,316	583	38
July	473	0	348	473	821	57
August	617	0	349	617	966	73
September	245	821	125	1,066	370	19
October	487	0	364	487	851	53
November	431	0	290	431	721	42

The regression results, when total engineering support reported costs (column 4) are used as the dependent variable, are:

◆ **Regression 1.** Engineering support reported costs = $a + (b \times$ machine-hours)

Variable	Coefficient	Standard Error	t-Value
Constant	$1,393.20	$305.68	4.56
Independent variable 1: machine-hours	$ −14.23	$ 6.15	−2.31

$r^2 = 0.43$; Durbin-Watson statistic = 2.26.

The regression results, when total engineering support restated costs (column 5) are used as the dependent variable, are:

◆ **Regression 2.** Engineering support restated costs = $a + (b \times$ machine-hours)

Variable	Coefficient	Standard Error	t-Value
Constant	$176.38	$53.99	3.27
Independent variable 1: machine-hours	$ 11.44	$ 1.08	10.59

$r^2 = 0.94$; Durbin-Watson statistic = 1.31.

INSTRUCTIONS
Form groups of two or more students to complete the following requirements.

REQUIRED
1. Present a plot of the data for the cost function relating the *reported costs* for total engineering support to machine-hours. Present a plot of the data for the cost function relating the *restated costs* for total engineering support to machine-hours. Comment on the plots.
2. Compute estimates of the cost functions ($y = a + bX$) for reported engineering support costs and machine-hours and restated engineering support costs and machine-hours using the high-low method.
3. Contrast and evaluate the cost function estimated with regression using restated data for materials and parts with the cost function estimated with regression using the data reported in the plant records. Use the comparison format employed in Exhibit 10-19.

4. Of all the cost functions estimated in requirements 2 and 3, which one would you choose to best represent the relationship between engineering support costs and machine-hours? Why?

5. Kennedy expects 50 machine-hours to be worked in December. What engineering support costs should Kennedy budget for December?

6. What problems might Kennedy encounter when restating the materials and parts costs recorded to an "as used" or accrual accounting basis?

7. Why is it important for Kennedy to pick the correct cost function? That is, illustrate two potential problems Kennedy could run into, by choosing a cost function other than the one you chose in requirement 4.

CHAPTER 11

DECISION MAKING AND RELEVANT INFORMATION

Grocery stores, such as Loblaws, must decide how to allocate limited shelf space among different products. An analysis of relevant revenues, relevant costs, and contribution margin per unit of the limited resource is useful in making informed decisions.

LEARNING OBJECTIVES

After studying this chapter, you should be able to:

1. Describe a five-step sequence in the decision process
2. Differentiate relevant costs and revenues from irrelevant costs and revenues in any decision situation
3. Distinguish between quantitative factors and qualitative factors in decisions
4. Indicate two ways in which per-unit cost data can mislead decision-makers
5. Identify two common pitfalls in relevant-cost analysis
6. Describe the opportunity cost concept; explain why it is used in decision-making
7. Describe the key concept in choosing which among multiple products to produce when there are capacity constraints
8. Discuss the key issue managers must consider when adding or dropping customers and segments
9. Explain why the book value of equipment is irrelevant in equipment replacement decisions
10. Explain how conflicts can arise between the decision model used by a manager and the performance model used to evaluate the manager

Working with managers to make decisions is one of the main functions of the management accountant and an important thrust of this book. The use of accounting information for decision making has been a consistent theme in earlier chapters. In this chapter, we focus on decisions such as accepting or rejecting a one-time-only special order, insourcing or outsourcing products or services, and replacing or keeping equipment. We especially stress the importance of distinguishing between relevant and irrelevant items in making these decisions.

INFORMATION AND THE DECISION PROCESS

Each manager has a method, often called a decision model, for deciding among different courses of action. A *decision model* is a formal method for making a choice, frequently involving quantitative analysis. Accountants serve as technical experts supplying managers with relevant data to guide their decisions.

Predictions and Models

Consider a decision that Home Appliances, a manufacturer of vacuum cleaners, faces: Should it rearrange a manufacturing assembly line to reduce manufacturing labour costs? For simplicity, assume that the only alternatives are "do not rearrange" and "rearrange." The rearrangement will eliminate all manual handling of materials. The current manufacturing line uses 20 workers—15 workers operate machines, and 5 workers handle materials. Each worker puts in 2,000 hours annually. The rearrangement is predicted to cost $90,000. The predicted production output of 25,000 units for the next year will be unaffected by the decision. Also unaffected by the decision are the predicted selling price per unit of $250, direct materials costs per unit of $50, other manufacturing overhead of $750,000, and marketing costs of $2,000,000. The cost driver is units of production.

To make the decision, management proceeds in a sequence of steps. The first step is to gather more information about manufacturing labour costs. The historical manufacturing labour rate of $14 per hour is the starting point for predicting total manufacturing labour costs under both alternatives. The manufacturing labour rate is expected to increase to $16 per hour following a recently negotiated increase in employee benefits.

The second step is to predict future costs under the two alternatives. Predicted manufacturing labour costs under the "do not rearrange" alternative are 20 workers × 2,000 hours × $16 per hour = $640,000. Predicted manufacturing labour costs under the "rearrange" alternative are 15 workers × 2,000 hours × $16 per hour = $480,000. Predicted costs of rearrangement are $90,000.

As the third step, Home Appliances' management compares the predicted savings from eliminating materials-handling labour costs (5 workers × 2,000 hours × $16 per hour) = $160,000 to the costs of rearrangement of $90,000. It also takes into account other qualitative considerations such as the effect that reducing the number of workers will have on employee morale. After weighing the costs and benefits, management chooses the "rearrange" alternative. Management next implements the decision in the fourth step by rearranging the manufacturing assembly line.

Models and Feedback

As the fifth and final step, management gathers information about the actual results of the plant rearrangement to evaluate performance and to provide feedback. Actual results show that the new manufacturing labour costs are $550,000 (because of, say, lower-than-expected manufacturing labour productivity) rather than the predicted $480,000. This feedback may lead to better implementation through, for example, a change in supervisory behaviour, employee training, or personnel so that the $480,000 target is achieved in subsequent periods. However, the feedback may convince the decision-maker that the prediction method, rather than the implementation, was faulty. Perhaps the prediction method for similar decisions in the future should be modified to allow for worker training or learning time.

Decision-Making in Operations Management—Nicholls State University
server.nich.edu/~wshell/mgt368/368-l1b.html

AICPA Reference Sources For Preparing Financial Models
www.aicpa.org/members/div/mcs/refs/fnclmdls.htm

OBJECTIVE 1

Describe a five-step sequence in the decision process

EXHIBIT 11-1
Accounting Information and the Decision Process

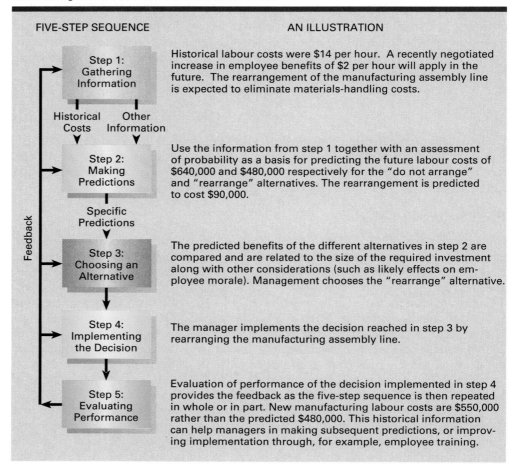

FIVE-STEP SEQUENCE	AN ILLUSTRATION
Step 1: Gathering Information	Historical labour costs were $14 per hour. A recently negotiated increase in employee benefits of $2 per hour will apply in the future. The rearrangement of the manufacturing assembly line is expected to eliminate materials-handling costs.
Historical Costs ∨ Other Information ∨	
Step 2: Making Predictions	Use the information from step 1 together with an assessment of probability as a basis for predicting the future labour costs of $640,000 and $480,000 respectively for the "do not arrange" and "rearrange" alternatives. The rearrangement is predicted to cost $90,000.
Specific Predictions ∨	
Step 3: Choosing an Alternative	The predicted benefits of the different alternatives in step 2 are compared and are related to the size of the required investment along with other considerations (such as likely effects on employee morale). Management chooses the "rearrange" alternative.
Step 4: Implementing the Decision	The manager implements the decision reached in step 3 by rearranging the manufacturing assembly line.
Step 5: Evaluating Performance	Evaluation of performance of the decision implemented in step 4 provides the feedback as the five-step sequence is then repeated in whole or in part. New manufacturing labour costs are $550,000 rather than the predicted $480,000. This historical information can help managers in making subsequent predictions, or improving implementation through, for example, employee training.

Feedback

Exhibit 11-1 above summarizes the five-step decision process that we just described—gathering information, making predictions, choosing an alternative, implementing the decision, and evaluating actual performance to provide feedback. The feedback, in turn, might affect future predictions, the prediction method itself, the decision model, or the implementation.

THE MEANING OF RELEVANCE

Relevant Costs and Relevant Revenues

O B J E C T I V E   2

Differentiate relevant costs and revenues from irrelevant costs and revenues in any decision situation

Relevant costs. Expected future costs that differ across alternative courses of action.

Relevant revenues. Expected future revenues that differ across alternative courses of action.

The most important decision-making concepts in this chapter are relevant costs and relevant revenues. **Relevant costs** are those *expected future costs* that differ between alternative courses of action. The two key aspects to this definition are that the costs must occur in the future and that they must differ between the alternative courses of action. We focus on the future because *every decision deals with the future*—whether it be 20 seconds ahead (the decision to adjust a dial) or 20 years ahead (the decision to plant and harvest pine trees). The function of decision-making is to select courses of action for the future. *Nothing can be done to alter the past*. Also, the future costs must differ among the alternatives, because if they do not there will be no difference in costs no matter what decision is made. Likewise, **relevant revenues** are those expected future revenues that differ between alternative courses of action.

In Exhibit 11-2, the $640,000 and $480,000 manufacturing labour costs are relevant costs—they are expected future costs that differ between the two alternatives. The past manufacturing labour rate of $14 per hour and total past manufacturing labour costs of $560,000 (2,000 hours × 20 workers × $14 per hour) are not relevant,

EXHIBIT 11-2

Determining Relevant Revenues and Relevant Costs for Home Appliances

	All Data		Relevant Data	
	Alternative 1: Do Not Rearrange	Alternative 2: Rearrange	Alternative 1: Do Not Rearrange	Alternative 2: Rearrange
Revenues*	$6,250,000	$6,250,000	—	—
			—	—
Costs:				
Direct materials†	1,250,000	1,250,000	—	—
Manufacturing labour	640,000‡	480,000$	$ 640,000‡	$ 480,000$
Manufacturing overhead	750,000	750,000	—	—
Marketing	2,000,000	2,000,000	—	—
Rearrangement costs	—	90,000	—	90,000
Total costs	4,640,000	4,570,000	640,000	570,000
Operating income	$1,610,000	$1,680,000	$(640,000)	$(570,000)

$70,000 difference $70,000 difference

*25,000 × $250 = $6,250,000.   ‡20 × 2,000 × $16 = $640,000
†25,000 × $50 = $1,250,000. $15 × 2,000 × $16 = $480,000.

even though they may play a role in preparing the $640,000 and $480,000 labour cost predictions. *Although they may be a useful basis for making informed judgments for predicting expected future costs, historical costs in themselves are irrelevant to a decision.* Why? Because they deal strictly with the past, not the future.

Exhibit 11-2 presents the quantitative data underlying the choice between the "do not rearrange" and the "rearrange" alternatives. The first two columns present *all data*. The last two columns present only relevant costs or revenues. The revenues, direct materials, manufacturing overhead, and marketing items can be ignored. Why? Because although they are expected future costs, they do not differ between the alternatives. They are thus irrelevant. The data in Exhibit 11-2 indicate that rearranging the production line will increase next year's predicted operating income by $70,000. Note that we reach the same conclusion whether we use all data or include only the relevant data in the analysis. By confining the analysis to only the relevant data, managers can clear away related but irrelevant data that might confuse them.

The difference in total cost between two alternatives is a **differential** or **net relevant cost.** The differential cost between alternatives 1 and 2 in Exhibit 11-2 is $70,000.

Differential cost (net relevant cost). Difference in total cost between two alternatives.

Qualitative and Quantitative Relevant Information

We divide the consequences of alternatives into two broad categories: *quantitative and qualitative.* **Quantitative factors** are outcomes that are measured in numerical terms. Some quantitative factors are financial—that is, they can be easily expressed in financial terms. Examples include the costs of direct materials, direct manufacturing labour, and marketing. Other quantitative factors are nonfinancial—that is, they can be measured numerically, but they are not expressed in financial terms. Reduction in product development time for a manufacturing company and the percentage of on-time flight arrivals for an airline company are examples of quantitative, nonfinancial factors. **Qualitative factors** are outcomes that cannot be measured in numerical terms. Employee morale is an example.

Cost analysis generally emphasizes quantitative factors that can be expressed in financial terms. But just because qualitative factors and nonfinancial quantitative factors cannot be easily measured in financial terms does not make them unimportant. Managers must at times give more weight to qualitative or nonfinancial quantitative factors. For example, Home Appliances may find that it can purchase a part from an

OBJECTIVE 3

Distinguish between quantitative factors and qualitative factors in decisions

Quantitative factors. Outcomes that are measured in numerical terms.

Qualitative factors. Outcomes that cannot be measured in numerical terms.

outside supplier at a price that is lower than what it costs to manufacture the part in-house. Home Appliances may still choose to make the part in-house because it feels that the supplier is unlikely to meet the demanding delivery schedule—a quantitative nonfinancial factor—and because purchasing the part from outside may adversely affect employee morale—a qualitative factor. Trading off nonfinancial and financial considerations, however, is seldom easy.

AN ILLUSTRATION OF RELEVANCE: CHOOSING OUTPUT LEVELS

Managers often make decisions that affect output levels. For example, managers must choose whether to introduce a new product or sell more units of an existing product. When changes in output levels occur, managers are interested in the effect they have on the organization and on operating income. Why? Because maximizing organizational objectives (typically, operating income in our illustrations) also increases managers' rewards.

One-Time-Only Special Orders

Management sometimes faces the decision of accepting or rejecting one-time-only special orders when there is idle production capacity and where the order has no long-run implications. We assume that all costs can be classified as either variable with respect to a single driver (units of output) or fixed. The following example illustrates how focusing on revenues, variable costs, and contribution margins can provide key information for decisions about the choice of output level. The example also indicates how reliance on unit-cost numbers calculated after allocating fixed costs can mislead managers about the effect that increasing output has on operating income.

Example: Fancy Fabrics manufactures quality bath towels at its highly automated Cambridge, Ontario, plant. The plant has a production capacity of 48,000 towels each month. Current monthly production is 30,000 towels. Retail department stores account for all existing sales. Expected results for the coming month (August) are shown in Exhibit 11-3. (Note that these amounts are predictions.) The manufacturing costs per unit of $12 consist of direct materials $6 (all variable), direct manufacturing labour $2 ($0.50 of which is variable), and manufacturing overhead $4 ($1 of which is variable). The marketing costs per unit are $7 ($5 of which is variable). Fancy Fabrics has no R&D costs or product design costs. Marketing costs include distribution costs and customer service costs.

A luxury hotel chain offers to buy 5,000 towels per month at $11 a towel for each of the next three months. No subsequent sales to this customer are anticipated. No marketing costs will be necessary for the 5,000-unit one-time-only special order. The acceptance of this special order is not expected to affect the selling price or the quantity of towels sold to regular customers. Should Fancy Fabrics accept the hotel chain's offer?

Exhibit 11-3 presents data in an absorption costing format: fixed manufacturing costs are included as product costs (see Chapter 9). The manufacturing cost per unit is $12 ($7.50 of which is variable and $4.50 of which is fixed), which is above the $11 price offered by the hotel chain. Using the $12 absorption cost as a guide in decision-making, a manager might reject the offer.

EXHIBIT 11-3
Budgeted Income Statement for August, Absorption Costing Format for Fancy Fabrics

	Total	Per Unit
Sales (30,000 towels × $20)	$600,000	$20
Cost of goods sold	360,000	12
Gross margin (gross profit)	240,000	8
Marketing costs	210,000	7
Operating income	$ 30,000	$ 1

Exhibit 11-4 presents data in a contribution income statement format. The relevant costs are the expected future costs that differ between the alternatives—the variable manufacturing costs of $37,500 ($7.50 per unit × 5,000 units). The fixed manufacturing costs and all marketing costs (including variable marketing costs) are irrelevant in this case; they will not change in total whether or not the special order is accepted. Therefore, the only relevant items here are sales revenues and variable manufacturing costs. Given the $11 relevant revenue per unit (the special-order price) and the $7.50 relevant costs per unit, Fancy Fabrics would gain an additional $17,500 [($11 − $7.50) × 5,000] in operating income per month by accepting the special order. In this example, comparisons based on either total amounts or relevant amounts (Exhibit 11-4) avoid the misleading implication of the absorption cost per unit (Exhibit 11-3).

The additional costs of $7.50 per unit that Fancy Fabrics will incur if it accepts the special order for 5,000 towels are sometimes called incremental costs, outlay costs, or out-of-pocket costs. **Incremental, outlay,** or **out-of-pocket costs** are additional costs to obtain an additional quantity, over and above existing or planned quantities, of a cost object. Fancy Fabrics could avoid these costs if it did not accept the special order. Fancy Fabrics incurs no incremental fixed manufacturing costs if it accepts the special order; those costs will not change whether or not the special order is accepted. Fixed manufacturing costs do not change because the analysis in Exhibit 11-4 assumes that the 5,000-towel special order will use already acquired capacity that will otherwise remain idle for each of the next three months.

The assumption of no long-run implications is crucial in the analysis we present for the one-time-only special order decision. Suppose, for example, that Fancy Fabrics is concerned that the retail department stores (its regular customers) will demand a lower price if it sells towels at $11 a towel to the luxury hotel chain. In this case, the analysis of the luxury hotel chain order must be modified to consider both

Incremental costs (outlay costs, out-of-pocket costs). Additional costs to obtain an additional quantity over and above existing or planned quantities of a cost object.

EXHIBIT 11-4

Comparative Income Statements for August, Contribution Income Statement Format for Fancy Fabrics

	Without One-Time-Only Special Order, 30,000 Units		With One-Time-Only Special Order, 35,000 Units	Difference, 5,000 Units
	Per Unit	Total	Total	Total
Sales	$20.00	$600,000	$655,000	$55,000‡
Variable costs:				
Manufacturing	7.50*	225,000	262,500	37,500§
Marketing	5.00	150,000	150,000	— #
Total variable costs	12.50	375,000	412,500	37,500
Contribution margin	7.50	225,000	242,500	17,500
Fixed costs:				
Manufacturing	4.50†	135,000	135,000	— ‖
Marketing	2.00	60,000	60,000	— ‖
Total fixed costs	6.50	195,000	195,000	—
Operating income	$ 1.00	$ 30,000	$ 47,500	$17,500

*Variable manufacturing costs = direct materials, $6 + direct manufacturing labour, $0.50 + manufacturing overhead, $1 = $7.50.
†Fixed manufacturing costs = direct manufacturing labour, $1.50 + manufacturing overhead, $3 = $4.50.
‡5,000 × $11.00 = $55,000.
§5,000 × $7.50 = $37,500.
#No variable marketing costs would be incurred for the 5,000-unit one-time-only special order.
‖Fixed manufacturing costs and fixed marketing costs are also unaffected by the special order.

the short-term benefits from accepting the order and the long-term consequences on Fancy Fabrics' business and profitability.

OBJECTIVE 4

Indicate two ways in which per-unit cost data can mislead decision-makers

How Unit Costs Can Mislead

Unit-cost data can often help in the cost analysis. Nevertheless, they can also mislead decision makers in two major ways:

1. **When irrelevant costs are included.** Consider the $4.50 per unit allocation of fixed direct manufacturing labour and manufacturing overhead costs in the one-time-only special-order decision for Fancy Fabrics (see Exhibit 11-4). This $4.50 per unit cost is irrelevant given the assumptions of our example and therefore should be excluded.

2. **When unit costs at different output levels are compared.** Generally, use total costs rather than unit costs. Then, if desired, the total costs can be unitized. Machinery sales personnel, for example, may brag about the low unit costs of using their new machines. However, they sometimes neglect to say that the unit costs are based on outputs far in excess of their prospective customer's current or anticipated production levels. Consider, for example, a new machine that costs $100,000, is capable of producing 100,000 units over its useful life, and has a zero terminal disposal price. The salesperson may represent the machine-related costs per unit to be $1. This amount is incorrect if the company anticipates a total demand of, say, only 50,000 units over the useful life of the machine (unit cost would be $100,000 ÷ 50,000 = $2). Unitizing fixed costs over different production levels can be particularly misleading.

OBJECTIVE 5

Identify two common pitfalls in relevant-cost analysis

Pitfalls in Relevant-Cost Analysis

One pitfall in relevant-cost analysis is to assume that all variable costs are relevant. In the Fancy Fabrics example, the marketing costs of $5 per unit are variable but not relevant. Why? Because for the special-order decision Fancy Fabrics incurs no extra marketing costs.

A second pitfall is to assume that all fixed costs are irrelevant. Consider fixed manufacturing costs. In our example, we assume that the extra production of 5,000 towels per month does not affect fixed manufacturing costs. That is, we assume that the relevant range is at least from 30,000 to 35,000 towels per month. In some cases, however, the extra 5,000 towels might increase fixed manufacturing costs. Assume that Fancy Fabrics would have to run three shifts of 16,000 towels per shift to achieve full capacity of 48,000 towels per month. Increasing the monthly production from 30,000 to 35,000 would require a partial third shift, because two shifts alone could produce only 32,000 towels. This extra shift would probably increase fixed manufacturing costs, thereby making any partial additional fixed manufacturing costs relevant for this decision.

The best way to avoid these two pitfalls is to focus first and foremost on the relevance concept. Always require each item included in the analysis *both* (1) to be an expected future revenue or cost and (2) to differ between the alternatives.

Confusing Terminology

Business function costs. The sum of all the costs in a particular business function.

Full product costs. The sum of all the costs in all the business functions: R&D, design, production, marketing, distribution, and customer service.

Many different terms are used to describe the costs of specific products and services. Exhibit 11-5 presents several different unit-cost numbers using the data from column 1 of Exhibit 11-4. **Business function costs** are the sum of all the costs (variable costs and fixed costs) in a particular business function in the value chain. For example, manufacturing costs are $12 per unit, and marketing costs are $7 per unit. For inventory costing purposes, absorption costs are often used as a synonym for manufacturing costs.

Full product costs refer to the sum of all the costs in all the business functions in the value chain (R&D, design, production, marketing, distribution, and customer service). Full product costs in Exhibit 11-5 are $19 per unit.

Managers use terms such as *business function costs* and *full product costs* differently. In a given situation, be sure to understand their exact meanings.

EXHIBIT 11-5

Variety of Cost Terms for Fancy Fabrics* Using Unit-Cost Data from Exhibit 11-4

	Variable Product Costs	Fixed Product Costs	Manufacturing (Absorption) Costs	Marketing Costs	Full Product Costs
Variable manufacturing costs	$ 7.50		$ 7.50		$ 7.50
Variable marketing costs	5.00			$5.00	5.00
Fixed manufacturing costs		$ 4.50	4.50		4.50
Fixed marketing costs		2.00		2.00	2.00
	$12.50	$ 6.50	$12.00†	$7.00†	$19.00

*In this example, marketing costs include distribution costs and customer service costs, and there are no R&D or product design costs.
†Business function costs.

OUTSOURCING AND MAKE/BUY DECISIONS

We now consider the decision of whether a company should make a part or buy it. As in the previous section, we retain the assumption of idle capacity.

Outsourcing and Idle Facilities

Outsourcing is the process of purchasing goods and services from outside vendors rather than producing the same goods or providing the same services within the organization, which is called **insourcing.** For example, Kodak prefers to manufacture its own films (insourcing) but has IBM do its data processing (outsourcing). Toyota relies on outside vendors to supply some parts and components but chooses to manufacture other parts internally. In making decisions about outsourcing and insourcing, cost is a major factor.

Decisions about whether a producer of goods or services will insource or outsource are also called **make/buy decisions.** Sometimes qualitative factors dictate management's make/buy decision. For example, Dell Computers must buy the Pentium chip for its personal computers from Intel because it does not have the know-how and technology to make the chip itself. Sometimes a company may prefer to make the product in-house to retain control of the product and technology. For example, in order to safeguard Coca-Cola's formula, the company does not outsource the manufacture of its concentrate. What are the most important factors in the make/buy decision? Surveys of company practices indicate they are quality, dependability of supplies, and cost.

Example: In the El Cerrito Company example described here, assume that financial factors predominate in the make/buy decision. The question we address is: What financial factors are relevant?

The El Cerrito Company manufactures thermostats for home and industrial use. Thermostats consist of relays, switches, and valves. El Cerrito makes its own switches. Columns 1 and 2 of the following table report the current costs for its heavy-duty switch (HDS) based on an analysis of its various manufacturing activities. Purchasing, receiving, and setup activities occur each time a batch of HDS is made. El Cerrito produces the 10,000 units of HDS in 25 batches of 400 units each. The cost driver for mixed overhead costs is number of batches. Mixed overhead costs of purchasing, receiving, and setup consist of fixed costs of $5,000 plus variable costs of $500 per batch giving total costs of $5,000 + 25 × $500 = $17,500. El Cerrito only commences production after it receives a firm customer order. El Cerrito's customers are pressuring the company to supply thermostats in smaller batch sizes. El Cerrito anticipates that next year the 10,000 units of HDS will be manufactured in 50 batches of 200 units each. Through continuous improvement, El Cerrito expects to reduce purchasing, receiving, and setup costs to $300 per batch. No other changes in fixed costs or unit variable costs are anticipated.

Outsourcing. Process of purchasing goods and services from outside vendors rather than producing the same goods or providing the same services within the firm.

Insourcing. Process of producing goods or providing services within the firm rather than purchasing those same goods or services from outside vendors.

Make/buy decisions. Decisions about whether a producer of goods or services will produce goods or services within the firm or purchase them from outside vendors.

Dell Computers
www.dell.com

	Total Current Costs of Producing 10,000 Units (1)	Current Cost per Unit (2) = (1) ÷ 10,000	Expected Total Costs of Producing 10,000 Units Next Year (3)	Expected Cost per Unit (4) = (3) ÷ 10,000
Direct materials	$ 80,000	$ 8.00	$ 80,000	$ 8
Direct manufacturing labour	10,000	1.00	10,000	1
Variable manufacturing overhead costs for power and utilities	40,000	4.00	40,000	4
Mixed overhead costs of purchasing, receiving, and setups	17,500	1.75	20,000	2
Fixed overhead costs of plant amortization, insurance, and administration	30,000	3.00	30,000	3
Total manufacturing costs	$177,500	$17.75	$180,000	$18

Another manufacturer offers to sell El Cerrito 10,000 units of HDS next year for $16 per unit on whatever delivery schedule El Cerrito wants. Should El Cerrito make or buy the part?

Columns 3 and 4 of the preceding table indicate the expected total costs and the expected per-unit cost of producing 10,000 units of HDS next year. Direct materials, direct manufacturing labour, and variable manufacturing overhead costs that vary with units produced are not expected to change, since El Cerrito plans to continue to produce 10,000 units next year at the same variable costs per unit as this year. The costs of purchasing, receiving, and setups are expected to increase even though there is no expected change in the total production quantity. Why? Because these costs vary with the number of batches started, not the quantity of production. Expected total purchasing, receiving, and setup costs = $5,000 + 50 batches × the cost per batch of $300 = $5,000 + $15,000 = $20,000. El Cerrito expects fixed overhead costs to remain the same. The expected manufacturing cost per unit equals $18. At this cost, it seems that the company should buy HDS from the outside supplier because making the part appears to be more costly than the $16 per unit to buy it. A make/buy decision, however, is rarely obvious. A key question for management is: What is the difference in relevant costs between the alternatives?

For the moment, suppose the capacity now used to make HDS will become idle if HDS is purchased. Assume that the $5,000 in fixed clerical salaries to support setup, receiving, and purchasing will not be incurred if the manufacture of HDS is completely shut down. Further suppose that the $30,000 in plant amortization, insurance, and administration costs represent fixed manufacturing overhead that will not vary regardless of the decision made.

Exhibit 11-6 presents the relevant cost computations. El Cerrito saves $10,000 by making HDS rather than buying it from the outside supplier. Alternatively stated, purchasing HDS costs $160,000 but saves only $150,000 in manufacturing costs. Making HDS is thus the preferred alternative. Exhibit 11-6 excludes the $30,000 of plant amortization, insurance, and administration costs under both the make and the buy alternative. Why? Because these costs are irrelevant; they do not differ between the two alternatives. Alternatively, the $30,000 could be included under both alternatives, since the $30,000 will continue to be incurred whether HDS is bought or made. Exhibit 11-6 includes the $20,000 of purchasing, receiving, and setup costs under the make alternative but not under the buy alternative. Why? Because buying HDS and not having to manufacture it saves both the variable costs per batch and the avoidable fixed costs. The $20,000 of costs differ between the alternatives and hence are relevant to the make/buy decision.

The figures in Exhibit 11-6 are valid only if the released facilities remain idle. If the component part is bought from the outside supplier, the released facilities can potentially be used for other, more profitable purposes. More generally, then, the choice in our example is not fundamentally whether to make or buy; it is how best to use available facilities.

EXHIBIT 11-6
Relevant (Incremental) Items for Make/Buy Decision for HDS at the El Cerrito Company

Relevant Items	Total Relevant Costs		Per-Unit Relevant Costs	
	Make	Buy	Make	Buy
Outside purchase of parts		$160,000		$16
Direct materials	$ 80,000		$ 8	
Direct manufacturing labour	10,000		1	
Variable manufacturing overhead	40,000		4	
Fixed purchasing, receiving, and setup overhead*	20,000		2	
Total relevant costs	$150,000	$160,000	$15	$16
Difference in favour of making HDS	$10,000		$1	

*Alternatively, the $30,000 of amortization, plant insurance, and plant administration costs could be included under both alternatives. These would be irrelevant to the decision.

The use of otherwise idle resources can often increase profitability. For example, consider the machine repair plant of Beijing Engineering, where the decision was whether to drop or keep a product. *The China Daily* noted that workers were "busy producing electric plaster spraying machines" even though the unit cost exceeded the selling price. According to the prevailing method of calculating its cost, each sprayer costs 1,230 yuan to make. However, each sprayer sells for only 985 yuan, resulting in a loss of 245 yuan per sprayer. Still, to meet market demand, the plant continues to produce sprayers. Workers and machines would otherwise be idle, and the plant would still have to pay 759 yuan even if no sprayers were made. In the short run, the production of sprayers, even at a loss, actually helps cut the company's operating loss.

Strategic and Qualitative Factors

Several strategic and qualitative factors affect the outsourcing decision. For example, El Cerrito may prefer to manufacture HDS in-house to retain more control over the design, quality, reliability, and delivery schedules of the switches it uses in its thermostats. Conversely, despite the cost advantages documented in Exhibit 11-6, El Cerrito may prefer to outsource, become a smaller and leaner organization, and focus on areas of its core competencies—the manufacture and sale of thermostats. As an example of focus, advertising companies, like J. Walter Thompson, only do the creative and planning aspects of advertising (their core competencies) and outsource production activities such as film, photographs, and illustrations.

Of course, outsourcing is not without its risks. As a company's dependence on its suppliers increases, suppliers could increase prices and let quality and delivery performance slip. To minimize these risks, companies generally enter into long-term contracts with their suppliers that specify costs, quality, and delivery schedules. Intelligent managers will build close partnerships or alliances with a few key suppliers, teaming with suppliers on design and manufacturing decisions and building a culture and commitment for quality and timely delivery. Toyota goes so far as to send its own engineers to improve suppliers' processes. Companies such as Ford, Hyundai, Panasonic, and Sony have found that suppliers that are allowed to gain expertise and grow have researched and developed innovative new products, met demands for increased quantities, maintained quality and on-time delivery, and lowered costs—actions that the companies themselves would not have had the competencies to achieve. The following Concepts In Action box describes how Volkswagen has outsourced the entire manufacturing of its trucks and buses at its Resende, Brazil, plant to its suppliers.

VW Takes Outsourcing to the Limit

Volkswagen's (VW's) bus and truck plant in Resende, Brazil, is a virtual plant: VW has completely outsourced manufacturing to a team of carefully selected supplier-partners in a radical experiment in production operations. At Resende, VW is transformed from manufacturer to general contractor, overseeing assembly operations performed by seven German, US, Brazilian, and Japanese components suppliers, with not one VW employee so much as turning a screw. Only 200 of the total 1,000 Resende workers are actual VW employees.

When designing the Resende plant, VW asked suppliers to bid for the opportunity to own one of seven major modules required to build a car, such as axles and brakes, and engine and transmission. Suppliers have invested $50 million to build, equip, and stock their areas. VW's contract with suppliers is for 10- to 15-year periods with the conditions that suppliers must achieve specified cost and performance targets and maintain cutting-edge technologies.

The plant is divided into seven zones, demarcated by yellow floor stripes. Within the boundaries of its zone, each supplier assembles its component from sub-components sourced from 400 minor suppliers. In parallel with sub-component assembly, final assembly occurs as the chassis (the vehicle platform) passes through the zones, and each company adds its respective component-module until the finished VW rolls off the line. Following each vehicle through the line is a single VW employee—a master craftsman assigned to track the vehicle and solve problems on the spot. Suppliers are paid for each completed vehicle that passes final inspection.

Despite representing seven different companies, the suppliers operate as a tightly integrated team, wearing the same uniforms and receiving the same pay. The assembly line is highly cross-functional, with representatives from each supplier meeting each morning to plan the day's production, and each evening to address issues and solve any problems. Each supplier has visibility of the entire production process, which stimulates ideas for simplification, streamlining, and product and process changes.

The specialization and superior component knowledge of each supplier, combined with the close interaction among suppliers, improves quality and efficiency. Co-location of the major component and final assemblies improves production flow and compresses total assembly time. It also simplifies logistics and reduces material handling, production control, manufacturing engineering, and coordination costs.

Although the plant remains in startup mode, preliminary results look promising. Resende employs 800 manufacturing workers instead of 2,500 at a comparable older VW plant. The time to assemble a truck has been reduced from 52 hours to 35 hours. These improvements have enabled VW to quickly earn a 19% share in the Brazilian truck market, and a 23% share in the bus market.

Source: Schemo, D. J., "Is VW's New Plant Lean, or Just Mean," *New York Times,* November 19, 1996; Friedland, J., "VW Puts Suppliers on Production Line," *Wall Street Journal,* Feb 15, 1996; Goering, L., "Revolution at Plant X," *Chicago Tribune,* April 13, 1997.

OPPORTUNITY COSTS, OUTSOURCING, AND CAPACITY CONSTRAINTS

OBJECTIVE 6

Describe the opportunity cost concept; explain why it is used in decision-making

Reconsider the El Cerrito Company example where we assumed that the capacity currently used to make HDS became idle if the parts were purchased. Suppose instead that El Cerrito has alternative uses for the extra capacity. The best available alternative is for El Cerrito to use the capacity to produce 5,000 units each year of a regular switch (RS) that the Terrence Corporation wants. John Marquez, the accountant at El Cerrito, estimates the following future revenues and future costs if RS is manufactured and sold:

Expected additional future revenues	$80,000
Expected additional future costs:	
Direct materials	$30,000
Direct manufacturing labour	5,000
Variable overhead (power, utilities)	15,000
Purchasing, receiving, and setup overheads	5,000
Total expected additional future costs	55,000
Expected additional operating income	$25,000

Since El Cerrito cannot make both HDS and RS, the three alternatives available to management are as follows:

1. Make HDS and do not make RS for Terrence.
2. Buy HDS and do not make RS for Terrence.
3. Buy HDS and use excess capacity to make and sell RS to Terrence.

Exhibit 11-7, Panel A, summarizes the "total alternatives" approach—the incremental expected future costs and expected future revenues for *all* alternatives. Buying HDS and using the excess capacity to make RS and sell it to Terrence is the preferred alternative. The incremental costs of buying HDS from an outside supplier are more than the incremental costs of making HDS in-house ($160,000 to buy versus $150,000 to make). But the capacity freed up by buying HDS from the outside supplier enables El Cerrito to gain $25,000 in operating income (expected additional future revenues of $80,000 minus expected additional future costs of $55,000) by making RS and selling to Terrence. The total relevant costs of buying HDS (and making and selling RS) is $160,000 – $25,000 = $135,000.

EXHIBIT 11-7

Total Alternatives Approach and Opportunity Costs Approach to Make/Buy Decisions for El Cerrito

PANEL A: TOTAL ALTERNATIVES APPROACH TO MAKE/BUY DECISIONS

	Choices for El Cerrito		
Relevant Items	Make HDS and Do Not Make RS	Buy HDS and Do Not Make RS	Buy HDS and Make RS
Total incremental costs of making/buying HDS (from Exhibit 11-6)	$150,000	$160,000	$160,000
Excess of future revenues over future costs from RS	0	0	(25,000)
Total relevant costs	$150,000	$160,000	$135,000

PANEL B: OPPORTUNITY COSTS APPROACH TO MAKE/BUY DECISIONS

	Choices for El Cerrito	
Relevant Items	Make HDS	Buy HDS
Total incremental costs of making/buying HDS (from Exhibit 11-6)	$150,000	$160,000
Opportunity cost: profit contribution forgone because capacity cannot be used to make RS, the next-best alternative	25,000	0
Total relevant costs	$175,000	$160,000
Difference in favour of buying HDS	$15,000	

Outsourcing Information Technology in Nova Scotia

In a government office building in Halifax, dozens of employees process hundreds of thousands of vehicle registrations, medical claims, phone bills, and paycheques in a state-of-the-art data centre. The technology needs of these workers were once provided by the Nova Scotia government and Maritime Telegraph and Telephone Co. Ltd. (MT&T). But in a move designed to slim down the bureaucracy and concentrate on core services, the government and the utility decided to farm out their data processing to SHL Systemhouse Inc. of Ottawa. Now Systemhouse manages the facility that housed these workers and all technology related employees work directly for Systemhouse.

The centralized data centre is an information factory. The government and MT&T have signed a major multimillion dollar deal to hand over their data processing to Systemhouse. Systemhouse pays the Nova Scotia government a fixed fee per year to lease the office space. With Systemhouse's expertise and economies of scale it can do the job better—and at lower cost. Government officials say the deal will save taxpayers millions of dollars over the life of the contract. In addition to mainframe computing services, Systemhouse also provides LAN management and enterprise help desk services from a network operating centre giving Systemhouse the ability to remotely manage clients' LAN and network environments.

Like the Nova Scotia government and MT&T, more and more managers are contracting outsiders to run their data processing and even selective information technology operations. While executives cite a raft of reasons, cost savings are at the heart of the trend. For many years, information technology has promised much but delivered only partially on those promises—sometimes at high cost. The move toward outsourcing these services marks a serious effort by managers to demand cost limits and get results from their information technology operations. It's a trend that industry watchers say will soon take hold of the information technology sector—and lead to quicker development of new data services.

Source: Andrew Safer (Freelance Writer/Communications Consultant, Halifax, Nova Scotia), "Revenge on the Nerds," *Canadian Business,* October 1992.

Opportunity cost. The contribution to income that is forgone (rejected) by not using a limited resource in its best alternative use.

Deciding to use a resource in a particular way causes a manager to give up the opportunity to use the resource in alternative ways. The lost opportunity is a cost that the manager must take into account when making a decision. **Opportunity cost** is the contribution to income that is forgone (rejected) by not using a limited resource in its next-best alternative use.

Exhibit 11-7, Panel B, displays the opportunity costs approach for analyzing the alternatives faced by El Cerrito. Management focuses on the two alternatives before it—whether to make or buy HDS. It does not explicitly include RS in the analysis. Focus first on the Make HDS column and ask: What are all the costs of choosing this alternative? Certainly, El Cerrito incurs $150,000 of incremental costs to make HDS. But is this the entire cost? No, because by using limited manufacturing resources to make HDS El Cerrito gives up the opportunity to earn $25,000 from not using these resources to make RS. Therefore, the relevant costs of making HDS are the incremental costs of $150,000 plus the opportunity cost of $25,000. Next consider the buy alternative. The incremental costs are $160,000. The opportunity cost is zero, because choosing this alternative does not require the use of a limited resource—El Cerrito's manufacturing capacity is still available to make and sell RS. Panel B leads management to the same conclusion as Panel A does—buying HDS is the preferred alternative by an amount of $15,000.

Panels A and B of Exhibit 11-7 describe two consistent approaches to decision making with capacity constraints. The total alternatives approach in Panel A includes only incremental costs and benefits and no opportunity costs. Why? Because the incremental benefit from making RS when HDS is bought is explicitly considered under the alternatives. Panel B does not explicitly consider the incremental benefits from selling RS. Instead, it factors in the forgone benefit as a cost of the make alternative. Panel B highlights the idea that when capacity is constrained relevant costs equal the incremental costs plus the opportunity cost.

Opportunity costs are seldom incorporated into formal financial accounting reports, because these costs do not entail cash receipts or disbursements. Accountants usually confine their systematic recording to costs that require cash disbursements currently or in the near future. Historical recordkeeping is limited to alternatives selected rather than those rejected, because, once rejected, there are no transactions to record. For example, if El Cerrito makes HDS, it would not make RS, and it would not record any accounting entries for RS. Yet the opportunity cost of making HDS, which equals the profit contribution that El Cerrito forgoes by not making RS, is a crucial input into the make/buy decision. Consider again Exhibit 11-7, Panel B. On the basis of incremental costs alone, the costs systematically recorded in the accounting system, it is less costly for El Cerrito to make rather than buy HDS. Recognizing the opportunity cost of $25,000 leads to a different conclusion. It is preferable to buy HDS.

Suppose El Cerrito has sufficient excess capacity to make RS (and indeed any other part) even if it makes HDS. Under this assumption, the opportunity cost of making HDS is zero. Why? Because El Cerrito gives up nothing even if it chooses to manufacture HDS. It follows from Panel B (substituting opportunity costs equal to zero) that, under these conditions, El Cerrito would prefer to make HDS.

Our analysis emphasizes purely quantitative considerations. The final decision, however, should consider qualitative factors as well. For example, before deciding to buy HDS from an outside supplier, El Cerrito management will consider such qualitative factors as the supplier's reputation for quality and the supplier's dependability for on-time delivery.

Carrying Costs of Inventory

The notion of opportunity cost can also be illustrated for the Garvey Corporation's direct materials purchase order decision. Garvey has enough cash to pay for whatever quantity of direct materials it buys.

Annual estimated direct materials requirements for the year	120,000 kilograms
Cost per kilogram for purchase orders below 120,000 kilograms	$10
Cost per kilogram for purchase orders equal to or greater than 120,000 kilograms; $10 minus 2% discount	$9.80
Alternatives under consideration:	
A. Buy 120,000 kilograms at start of year	
B. Buy 10,000 kilograms per month	
Average investment in inventory:	
A. (120,000 kilograms × $9.80) ÷ 2*	$588,000
B. (10,000 kilograms × $10.00) ÷ 2*	$50,000
Annual interest rate for investment in government bonds	6%

*The example assumes that the direct materials purchased will be used up uniformly at the rate of 10,000 kilograms per month. If direct materials are purchased at the start of the year (month), the average investment in inventory during the year is the cost of the inventory at the beginning of the year (month) plus the cost of inventory at the end of the year (month) divided by 2.

The following table presents the two alternatives. The opportunity cost of holding inventory is the income forgone from not investing this money elsewhere. These opportunity costs would not be recorded in the accounting system, because they are not incremental or outlay costs. Column 3 indicates that, consistent with the trends toward holding smaller inventories as in JIT systems, purchasing 10,000 kilograms per month is preferred relative to purchasing 120,000 kilograms at the beginning of the year, because the lower opportunity cost of holding smaller inventory exceeds the higher purchase cost. If other incremental benefits of holding lower inventory such as lower insurance, materials handling, storage, obsolescence, and breakage costs were considered, alternative B would be preferred even more.

	Alternative A: Purchase 120,000 Kilograms at Beginning of Year (1)	Alternative B: Purchase 10,000 Kilograms at Beginning of Each Month (2)	Difference (3) = (1) - (2)
Annual purchase (incremental) costs (120,000 × $9.80; 120,000 × $10)	$1,176,000	$1,200,000	$(24,000)
Annual interest income that could be earned if investment in inventory were invested in government bonds (opportunity cost) (6% × $588,000; 6% × $50,000)	35,280	3,000	32,280
Relevant costs	$1,211,280	$1,203,000	$ 8,280

PRODUCT MIX DECISIONS UNDER CAPACITY CONSTRAINTS

OBJECTIVE 7

Describe the key concept in choosing which among multiple products to produce when there are capacity constraints

General Mills
jobs.genmills.com/1_0.htm

Companies with capacity constraints, such as El Cerrito, must also often decide which products to make and in what quantities. When a multiple-product plant operates at full capacity, managers must often make decisions regarding which products to emphasize. These decisions frequently have a short-run focus. For example, General Mills must continually adapt the mix of its different products to short-run fluctuations in materials costs, selling prices, and demand. Throughout this section, we assume that, as short-run changes in product mix occur, the only costs that change are those that, are variable with respect to the number of units produced (and sold).

Analysis of individual product contribution margins provides insight into the product mix that maximizes operating income. Consider Power Engines, a company that manufactures engines for a broad range of commercial and consumer products. At its Calgary, Alberta, plant, it assembles two engines—a snowmobile engine and a boat engine. Information on these products is as follows:

	Snowmobile Engine	Boat Engine
Selling price	$800	$1,000
Variable costs per unit	560	625
Contribution margin per unit	$240	$ 375
Contribution margin ratio	30%	37.5%

At first glance, boat engines appear more profitable than snowmobile engines. The product to be emphasized, however, is not necessarily the product with the higher individual contribution margin per unit or contribution margin percentage. Rather, managers should aim for the *highest contribution margin per unit of the constraining factor*—that is, the scarce, limiting, or critical factor. The constraining factor restricts or limits the production or sale of a given product. (See also Chapter 19 on the theory of constraints.)

Assume that only 600 machine-hours are available daily for assembling engines. Additional capacity cannot be obtained in the short run. Power Engines can sell as many engines as it produces. The constraining factor, then, is machine-hours. It takes two machine-hours to produce one snowmobile engine and five machine-hours to produce one boat engine.

	Snowmobile Engine	Boat Engine
Contribution margin per engine	$240	$375
Machine-hours required to produce one engine	2 machine-hours	5 machine-hours
Contribution margin per machine-hour (240 ÷ 2; 375 ÷ 5)	$120	$75
Total contribution margin for 600 machine-hours ($120 × 600; $75 × 600)	$72,000	$45,000

Producing snowmobile engines contributes more margin per machine-hour, which is the constraining factor in this example. Therefore, choosing to emphasize snowmobile engines is the correct decision. Other constraints in manufacturing settings can be the availability of direct materials, components, or skilled labour, as well as financial and sales considerations. In a retail department store, the constraining factor may be linear metres of display space. The greatest possible contribution margin per unit of the constraining factor yields the maximum operating income.

As you can imagine, in many cases a manufacturer or retailer must meet the challenge of trying to maximize total operating income for a variety of products, each with more than one constraining factor. The problem of formulating the most profitable production schedules and the most profitable product mix is essentially that of maximizing the total contribution margin in the face of many constraints. Optimization techniques, such as the linear programming technique discussed in the appendix to this chapter, help solve these complicated problems.

CUSTOMER PROFITABILITY, ACTIVITY-BASED COSTING, AND RELEVANT COSTS

In addition to making choices among products, companies must often decide about whether they should add some customers and drop others. This section illustrates relevant-revenue and relevant-cost analysis when different cost drivers are identified for different activities in activity-based costing. The cost object in our example is customers. The analysis focuses on customer profitability at Allied West, the west coast sales office of Allied Furniture, a wholesaler of specialized furniture.

Allied West supplies furniture to three local retailers, Vogel, Brenner, and Wisk. Exhibit 11-8 presents representative revenues and costs of Allied West by customers for the year 2000. Additional information on Allied West's costs for different activities at various levels of the cost hierarchy is as follows:

OBJECTIVE 8

Discuss the key issue managers must consider when adding or dropping customers and segments

1. Materials-handling labour costs vary with the number of units of furniture shipped to customers.

2. Different areas of the warehouse stock furniture for different customers. Materials-handling equipment in an area and amortization costs on the equipment are identified with individual customer accounts. Any equipment not used remains idle. The equipment has a one-year useful life and zero disposal price.

3. Allied West allocates rent to each customer account on the basis of the amount of warehouse space occupied by the products to be shipped to that customer.

4. Marketing costs vary with the number of sales visits made to customers.

EXHIBIT 11-8
Customer Profitability Analysis for Allied West

	Vogel	Brenner	Wisk	Total
Sales	$500,000	$300,000	$400,000	$1,200,000
Cost of goods sold	370,000	220,000	330,000	920,000
Materials-handling labour	41,000	18,000	33,000	92,000
Materials-handling equipment cost written off as amortization	10,000	6,000	8,000	24,000
Rent	14,000	8,000	14,000	36,000
Marketing support	11,000	9,000	10,000	30,000
Purchase orders and delivery processing	13,000	7,000	12,000	32,000
General administration	20,000	12,000	16,000	48,000
Total operating costs	479,000	280,000	423,000	1,182,000
Operating income	$ 21,000	$ 20,000	$ (23,000)	$ 18,000

5. Purchase order costs vary with the number of purchase orders received; delivery processing costs vary with the number of shipments made.

6. Allied West allocates fixed general administration costs to customers on the basis of dollar sales made to each customer.

Relevant-Cost Analysis of Dropping a Customer

Exhibit 11-8 indicates a loss of $23,000 on sales to Wisk. Allied West's manager believes this loss occurred because Wisk places many low-volume orders with Allied, resulting in high purchase order, delivery processing, materials-handling, and marketing activity. Allied West is considering several possible actions with respect to the Wisk account—reducing its own costs of supporting Wisk by becoming more efficient, cutting back on some of the services it offers Wisk, charging Wisk higher prices, or dropping the Wisk account. The following analysis focuses on the operating income effect of dropping the Wisk account.

The key question is: What are the relevant costs and relevant revenues? The following information about the effect of reducing various activities related to the Wisk account is available.

1. Dropping the Wisk account will save cost of goods sold, materials-handling labour, marketing support, purchase order, and delivery processing costs incurred on the Wisk account.

2. Dropping the Wisk account will mean that the warehouse space currently occupied by products for Wisk and the materials-handling equipment used to move them will become idle.

3. Dropping the Wisk account will have no effect on fixed general administration costs.

Exhibit 11-9 presents the relevant-cost computations. Allied West's operating income will be $15,000 lower if it drops the Wisk account, so Allied decides to keep the Wisk account. The last column in Exhibit 11-9 shows that the cost savings from dropping the Wisk account, $385,000, is not enough to offset the loss of $400,000 in revenue. The key reason is that amortization, rent, and general administration costs will not decrease if the Wisk account is dropped.

Now suppose that if Allied drops the Wisk account it could lease the extra warehouse space to the Sanchez Corporation, which has offered $20,000 per year for

EXHIBIT 11-9
Relevant-Cost Analysis for Allied West Dropping the Wisk Account

| | Amount of Total Revenues and Total Costs | | Difference: Incremental (Loss in Revenue) and Savings in Costs from Dropping Wisk Account |
	Keep Wisk Account	Drop Wisk Account	
Sales	$1,200,000	$800,000	$(400,000)
Cost of goods sold	920,000	590,000	330,000
Materials-handling labour	92,000	59,000	33,000
Materials-handling equipment cost written off as amortization	24,000	24,000	0
Rent	36,000	36,000	0
Marketing support	30,000	20,000	10,000
Purchase orders and delivery processing	32,000	20,000	12,000
General administration	48,000	48,000	0
Total operating costs	1,182,000	797,000	385,000
Operating income (loss)	$ 18,000	$ 3,000	$ (15,000)

EXHIBIT 11-10
Relevant-Cost Analysis for Adding the Loral Account

	Amount of Total Revenues and Total Costs		Difference: Incremental Revenue and (Incremental Costs) from Adding Loral Account
	Do Not Add Loral Account	Add Loral Account	
Sales	$1,200,000	$1,600,000	$400,000
Cost of goods sold (variable)	920,000	1,250,000	(330,000)
Materials-handling labour	92,000	125,000	(33,000)
Materials-handling equipment cost written off as depreciation	24,000	32,000	(8,000)
Rent	36,000	36,000	0
Marketing support	30,000	40,000	(10,000)
Purchase orders and delivery processing	32,000	44,000	(12,000)
General administration	48,000	48,000	0
Total operating costs	1,182,000	1,575,000	393,000
Operating income	$ 18,000	$ 25,000	$ 7,000

it. Then the $20,000 that Allied would receive would be the opportunity cost of continuing to use the warehouse to service Wisk. Allied would gain $5,000 by dropping the Wisk account ($20,000 from lease revenue minus lost operating income of $15,000). Before reaching a final decision, however, Allied must examine whether Wisk can be made more profitable so that supplying products to Wisk earns more than the $20,000 from leasing to Sanchez. Allied must also consider qualitative factors such as the effect of the decision on Allied's reputation for developing stable, long-run business relationships.

Relevant-Cost Analysis of Adding a Customer

Suppose that in addition to Vogel, Brenner, and Wisk, Allied is evaluating the profitability of adding a fourth customer, Loral. Allied is already paying rent of $36,000 for the warehouse and is incurring general administration costs of $48,000. These costs will not change if Loral is added as a customer. Loral is a customer with a profile much like Wisk's. Suppose Allied predicts other revenues and costs of doing business with Loral to be the same as those described under the Wisk column of Exhibit 11-8. Should Allied add Loral as a customer? Exhibit 11-10 shows incremental revenues exceed incremental costs by $7,000. Allied would prefer to add Loral as a customer. The key point is that the cost of acquiring new equipment to support the Loral order (written off as amortization of $8,000 in Exhibit 11-10) is included as a relevant cost. Why? Because this cost can be avoided if Allied decides not to do business with Loral. Note the critical distinction here. Amortization cost is irrelevant in deciding whether to drop Wisk as a customer (because it is a past cost), but the purchase cost of the new equipment that will then be written off as amortization in the future is relevant in deciding whether to add Loral as a new customer.

IRRELEVANCE OF PAST COSTS AND EQUIPMENT REPLACEMENT DECISIONS

The illustrations in this chapter have shown that expected future costs that do not differ among alternatives are irrelevant. Now we return to the idea that all past costs are irrelevant.

   Consider an example of equipment replacement. The irrelevant cost illustrated here is the **book value** (original cost minus accumulated amortization) of the existing equipment. Assume that the Tormart Company is considering replacing a metal-cutting machine for aircraft parts with a more technically advanced model. The new

Book value. The original cost minus accumulated amortization of an asset.

machine has an automatic quality-testing capability and is more efficient than the old machine. The new machine, however, has a shorter life. The Tormart Company uses the straight-line amortization method. Sales from aircraft parts ($1.1 million per year) will be unaffected by the replacement decision. Summary data on the existing machine and the replacement machine are as follows:

	Existing Machine	Replacement Machine
Original cost	$1,000,000	$600,000
Useful life in years	5 years	2 years
Current age in years	3 years	0 years
Useful life remaining in years	2 years	2 years
Accumulated amortization	$600,000	Not acquired yet
Book value	$400,000	Not acquired yet
Current disposal price (in cash)	$40,000	Not acquired yet
Terminal disposal price (in cash two years from now)	$0	$0
Annual operating costs (maintenance, energy, repairs, coolants, and so on)	$800,000	$460,000

To focus on the main concept of relevance, we ignore the time value of money in this illustration.

Exhibit 11-11 presents a cost comparison of the two machines. Some managers would not replace the old machine because it would entail recognizing a $360,000 "loss on disposal" ($400,000 book value minus $40,000 current disposal price); retention would allow spreading the $400,000 book value over the next two years in the form of "amortization expense" (a term more appealing than "loss on disposal").

We can apply our definition of relevance to four commonly encountered items in equipment replacement decisions such as the one facing Tormart Company:

1. **Book value of old machine.** Irrelevant, because it is a past (historical) cost. All past costs are "down the drain." Nothing can change what has already been spent or what has already happened.

2. **Current disposal price of old machine.** Relevant, because it is an expected future cash inflow that differs between alternatives.

3. **Gain or loss on disposal.** This is the algebraic difference between items 1 and 2. It is a meaningless combination blurring the distinction between the

EXHIBIT 11-11
Cost Comparison—Replacement of Machinery, Including Relevant and Irrelevant Items for the Tormart Company

	Two Years Together		
	Keep	Replace	Difference
Sales	$2,200,000	$2,200,000	—
Operating costs:			
Cash operating costs	1,600,000	920,000	$680,000
Old machine book value:			
Periodic writeoff as amortization	400,000	—	—
or Lump sum writeoff	—	400,000*	
Current disposal price of old machine	—	(40,000)*	40,000
New machine cost, written off periodically as amortization	—	600,000	(600,000)
Total operating costs	2,000,000	1,880,000	120,000
Operating income	$ 200,000	$ 320,000	$120,000

*In a formal income statement, these two items would be combined as "loss on disposal of machine" of $360,000.

EXHIBIT 11-12

Cost Comparison—Replacement of Machinery, Relevant Items Only for the Tormart Company

	Two Years Together		
	Keep	Replace	Difference
Cash operating costs	$1,600,000	$ 920,000	$680,000
Current disposal price of old machine	—	(40,000)	40,000
New machine, written off periodically as amortization	—	600,000	(600,000)
Total relevant costs	$1,600,000	$1,480,000	$120,000

irrelevant book value and the relevant disposal price. Each item should be considered separately.

4. **Cost of new machine.** Relevant, because it is an expected future cash outflow that will differ between alternatives.

Exhibit 11-11 should clarify these four assertions. The difference column in Exhibit 11-11 shows that the book value of the old machine is not an element of difference between alternatives and could be completely ignored for decision-making purposes. No matter what the timing of the charge against revenue, the amount charged is still $400,000 regardless of the alternative chosen because it is a past (historical) cost. Note that the advantage of replacing is $120,000 for the two years together.

In either event, the unamortized cost will be written off with the same ultimate effect on operating income. The $400,000 enters into the income statement either as a $400,000 offset against the $40,000 proceeds to obtain the $360,000 loss on disposal in the current year or as $200,000 amortization in each of the next two years. But how it appears in the income statement is irrelevant to the replacement decision. In contrast, the $600,000 cost of the new machine is relevant because it can be avoided by deciding not to replace.

Past costs that are unavoidable because they cannot be changed, no matter what action is taken, are sometimes described as **sunk costs.** In our example, old equipment has a book value of $400,000 and a current disposal price of $40,000. What are the sunk costs in this case? The entire $400,000 is sunk and down the drain because it represents an outlay made in the past that cannot be changed. Thus, past costs and sunk costs are synonyms.

Exhibit 11-12 above concentrates on relevant items only. Note that the same answer (the $120,000 net difference) will be obtained even though the book value is completely omitted from the calculations. The only relevant items are the cash operating costs, the disposal price of the old machine, and the cost of the new machine (represented as amortization in Exhibit 11-12).

Decision-makers vary in their preference between the formats presented in Exhibits 11-11 and 11-12. Some prefer the format used in Exhibit 11-11, because it illustrates why some items are irrelevant to the decision. Other managers prefer the format used in Exhibit 11-12, because it is concise.

Sunk costs. Past costs that are unavoidable because they cannot be changed no matter what action is taken.

DECISIONS AND PERFORMANCE EVALUATION

Consider our equipment replacement example in light of the five-step sequence in Exhibit 11-1.

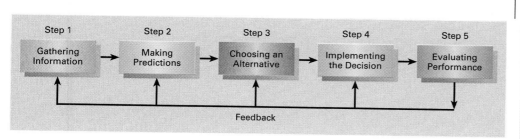

Step 1	Step 2	Step 3	Step 4	Step 5
Gathering Information	Making Predictions	Choosing an Alternative	Implementing the Decision	Evaluating Performance

Feedback

OBJECTIVE 10

Explain how conflicts can arise between the decision model used by a manager and the performance model used to evaluate the manager

If the decision model (step 3) demands choosing the alternative that will minimize total costs over the life span of the equipment, then the analysis in Exhibits 11-11 and 11-12 dictates replacing rather than keeping. In the real world, however, would the manager replace? The answer depends on the manager's perceptions of whether the decision model is consistent with the performance evaluation model (step 5). The performance evaluation model describes the basis on which the manager's performance is judged.

Managers tend to favour the alternative that makes their performance look best. If the performance evaluation model conflicts with the decision model, the performance evaluation model often prevails in influencing a manager's behaviour. For example, the decision model in Exhibit 11-11, on the basis of a relevant cost analysis over the life of the two machines, favours replacing the machine. But if the manager's promotion or bonus hinges on the first year's operating income performance under accrual accounting, the manager's temptation *not* to replace will be overwhelming. Why? Because the accrual accounting model for measuring performance will show a higher first-year operating income if the old machine is kept than if it is replaced (as the following table shows):

	First-Year Results: Accrual Accounting			
	Keep		**Replace**	
Sales		$1,100,000		$1,100,000
Operating costs:				
Cash operating costs	$800,000		$460,000	
Amortization	200,000		300,000	
Loss on disposal	—		360,000	
Total operating costs		1,000,000		1,120,000
Operating income		$ 100,000		$ (20,000)

Even if top management's goals are long-run (and consistent with the decision model), the subordinate manager's concern is more likely to be short-run if his or her evaluation is based on short-run measures such as operating income.

Resolving the conflict between the decision model and the performance evaluation model is frequently a baffling problem in practice. In theory, resolving the difficulty seems obvious—merely design consistent models. Consider our replacement example. Year-by-year effects on operating income of replacement can be budgeted over the planning horizon of two years. The manager would be evaluated on the understanding that the first year would be expected to be poor, the next year much better.

The practical difficulty is that accounting systems rarely track each decision separately. Performance evaluation focuses on responsibility centres for a specific time period, not on projects or individual items of equipment for their entire useful lives. Therefore, the impacts of many different decisions are combined in a single performance report. Top management, through the reporting system, is rarely aware of particular desirable alternatives that were not chosen by subordinate managers.

Consider another conflict between the decision model and the performance evaluation model. Suppose a manager buys a particular machine only to discover that a better machine could have been purchased in its place. The decision model may suggest replacing the existing machine with the better machine, but the manager may be reluctant to do so. Why? Because replacing the machine so soon after its purchase may reflect badly on the manager's capabilities and performance. If the manager's superiors have no knowledge of the better machine, the manager may prefer to keep, rather than replace, the existing machine.

PROBLEM

Wally Lewis is manager of the engineering development division of Goldcoast Products, Inc. Lewis has just received a proposal signed by all ten of his engineers to replace the existing mainframe computing system with ten workstations. Lewis is not enthusiastic about the proposal.

Summary data on the mainframe and workstation machines are as follows:

	Mainframe	Workstations
Original cost	$300,000	$135,000
Useful life in years	5 years	3 years
Current age in years	2 years	0 years
Useful life remaining in years	3 years	3 years
Accumulated amortization	$120,000	Not acquired yet
Current book value	$180,000	Not acquired yet
Current disposal price (in cash)	$95,000	Not acquired yet
Terminal disposal price (in cash three years from now)	$0	$0
Annual computer-related cash operating costs	$40,000	$10,000
Annual revenues	$1,000,000	$1,000,000
Annual non-computer-related operating costs	$880,000	$880,000

Lewis's annual bonus includes a component based on division operating income. He has a promotion possibility next year that would make him a group vice-president of Goldcoast Products.

REQUIRED

1. Compare the costs of the mainframe and workstation options. Consider the cumulative results for the three years together, ignoring the time value of money.
2. Why might Lewis be reluctant to purchase the ten workstations?

SOLUTION

1. The following table considers all cost items when comparing future costs of the mainframe and workstation options:

	Three Years Together		
All Items	Mainframe	Workstations	Difference
Revenues	$3,000,000	$3,000,000	—
Operating costs:			
Non-computer-related operating costs	2,640,000	2,640,000	—
Computer-related cash operating costs	120,000	30,000	$ 90,000
Mainframe book value:			
Periodic writeoff as amortization	180,000	—	
or Lump sum writeoff	—	180,000	
Current disposal price of mainframe	—	(95,000)	95,000
Workstations, written off periodically as amortization		135,000	(135,000)
Total operating costs	2,940,000	2,890,000	50,000
Operating income	$ 60,000	$ 110,000	$ 50,000

Alternatively, the analysis could focus on only those items in the preceding table that differ across the alternatives.

Relevant Items	Mainframe	Three Years Together Workstations	Difference
Computer-related cash operating costs	$120,000	$ 30,000	$ 90,000
Current disposal price of mainframe	—	(95,000)	95,000
Workstations, written off periodically as amortization	—	135,000	(135,000)
Total relevant costs	$120,000	$ 70,000	$ 50,000

The analysis suggests that it is cost-effective to replace the mainframe with the workstations.

2. The accrual accounting operating incomes for the first year under the "keep mainframe" versus the "buy workstations" alternatives are as follows:

	Keep Mainframe		Buy Workstations	
Revenues		$1,000,000		$1,000,000
Operating costs:				
Non-computer-related operating costs	$880,000		$880,000	
Computer-related cash operating costs	40,000		10,000	
Amortization	60,000		45,000	
Loss on disposal of mainframe	—		85,000*	
Total operating costs		980,000		1,020,000
Operating income		$ 20,000		$ (20,000)

*85,000 = book value of mainframe, $180,000 – current disposal price, $95,000.

Lewis would probably react negatively to the expected operating loss of $20,000 if the workstations are replaced as compared to an operating income of $20,000 if the mainframe is kept. The decision would eliminate the component of his bonus based on operating income. He might also perceive the $20,000 operating loss as reducing his chances of being promoted to a group vice-president.

SUMMARY

The following points are linked to the chapter's learning objectives.

1. The five steps in a decision process are (a) obtaining information, (b) making predictions, (c) building decision models, (d) implementing decisions, and (e) evaluating performance.

2. To be relevant to a particular decision, a revenue or cost must meet two criteria: (a) it must be an expected future revenue or cost and (b) it must differ among alternative courses of action.

3. The consequences of alternative actions can be quantitative and qualitative. Quantitative factors are outcomes that are measured in numerical terms. Some quantitative factors can be easily expressed in financial terms; others cannot. Qualitative factors, such as employee morale, cannot be measured in numerical terms. Due consideration must be given to both financial and nonfinancial factors in making decisions.

4. Unit-cost data can mislead decision-makers in two major ways: (a) when costs that are irrelevant to a particular decision are included in unit costs and (b) when unit costs that are computed at different output levels are used to choose between alternatives. Unitized fixed costs are often erroneously interpreted as if they behave like unit variable costs. Generally, use total costs rather than unit costs in relevant-cost analysis.

5. There are two common pitfalls in relevant-cost analysis: (a) assuming all variable costs are relevant and (b) assuming all fixed costs are irrelevant.

6. Opportunity cost is the maximum available contribution to income that is forgone (rejected) by not using a limited resource in its next-best alternative use. The idea of an opportunity cost arises when there are multiple uses for resources and some alternatives are not selected. Opportunity cost is included in decision-making because it represents the best alternative way in which an organization may have used its resources had it not made the decision it did.

7. In choosing between multiple products when resource capacity is constrained, managers should emphasize the product that yields the highest contribution margin per unit of the constraining or limiting factor.

8. Managers should ignore allocated overhead costs when making decisions about dropping customers and sales offices. They should focus instead on the differential total costs between alternatives.

9. Past revenues and costs, though irrelevant for decision-making, can be useful in predicting future relevant revenues and relevant costs. Expected future revenues and costs are the only revenues and costs relevant in any decision model. The book value of existing equipment in equipment replacement decisions represents past (historical) cost and therefore is irrelevant.

10. Top management faces a persistent challenge—that is, making sure that the performance evaluation model is consistent with the decision model. A common inconsistency is to tell subordinate managers to take a multiple-year view in their decision-making but then judge their performance only on the basis of the current year's operating income.

"Chainsaw Al's Encore"— TIME.com, November 11, 1996 cgi.pathfinder.com/time/ magazine/archive/1996/dom/ 961111/business.chainsaw _als_en53.html

'Chainsaw Al' fires back— cnnfn.com, July 8, 1998 www.cnnfn.com/hotstories/ busunu/9807/08/dunlap_intv/ index-txt.htm

'Chainsaw Al' aide fired— cnnfn.com, July 18, 1998 www.cnnfn.com/hotstories/ companies/9806/18/sunbeam/ index.htm

"Audit: 'Chainsaw Al' Turnaround a Myth" seattletimes.com, October 21, 1998 www.seattletimes.com/news/ business/html98/altbeam_ 102198.html

APPENDIX: LINEAR PROGRAMMING

Linear programming (LP) is an optimization technique used to maximize total contribution margin (the objective function), given multiple constraints. LP models typically assume that all costs can be classified as either variable or fixed with respect to a single driver (units of output). LP models also require certain other linear assumptions to hold. When these assumptions fail, other decision models should be considered.[1]

Consider the Power Engines example described earlier in the chapter. Suppose that both the snowmobile and boat engines must be tested on a very expensive machine before they are shipped to customers. The available testing machine time is limited. Production data are as follows:

Department	Available Daily Capacity in Hours	Use of Capacity in Hours per Unit of Product		Daily Maximum Production in Units	
		Snowmobile Engine	Boat Engine	Snowmobile Engine	Boat Engine
Assembly	600 machine-hours	2.0	5.0	300*	120
Testing	120 testing-hours	1.0	0.5	120	240

*For example, 600 machine-hours ÷ 2.0 machine-hours per snowmobile engine = 300, the maximum number of snowmobile engines that the assembly department can make if it works exclusively on snowmobile engines.

Exhibit 11-13 summarizes these and other relevant data. Note that snowmobile engines have a contribution margin of $240 and that boat engines have a contribution margin of $375. Material shortages for boat engines will limit production to 110 boat engines per day. How many engines of each type should be produced daily to maximize operating income?

---

[1]Other decision models are described in G. Eppen, F. Gould, and C. Schmidt, *Quantitative Concepts for Management* (Englewood Cliffs, N.J.: Prentice-Hall, 1991); and S. Nahmias, *Production and Operations Analysis* (Homewood, Ill.: Irwin, 1993).

Steps in Solving an LP Problem

We use the data in Exhibit 11-13 to illustrate the three steps in solving an LP problem. Throughout this discussion, S equals the number of units of snowmobiles produced and B equals the number of units of boat engines produced.

Objective function. Expresses the objective to be maximized (for example, operating income) or minimized (for example, operating costs) in a decision model, for example, a linear programming model.

◆ **Step 1:** *Determine the objective.* The **objective function** of a linear program expresses the objective or goal to be maximized (for example, operating income) or minimized (for example, operating costs). In our example, the objective is to find the combination of products that maximizes total contribution margin in the short run. Fixed costs remain the same regardless of the product mix chosen and are therefore irrelevant. The linear function expressing the objective for the total contribution margin (TCM) is:

$$\text{TCM} = \$240S + \$375B$$

Constraint. A mathematical inequality or equality that must be satisfied by the variables in a mathematical model.

◆ **Step 2:** *Specify the constraints.* A **constraint** is a mathematical inequality or equality that must be satisfied by the variables in a mathematical model. The following linear inequalities depict the relationships in our example:

Assembly department constraint	$2S + 5B \leq 600$
Testing department constraint	$1S + 0.5B \leq 120$
Material shortage constraint for boat engines	$B \leq 110$
Negative production is impossible	$S \geq 0$ and $B \geq 0$

The coefficients of the constraints are often called *technical coefficients*. For example, in the assembly department, the technical coefficient is two machine-hours for snowmobile engines and five machine-hours for boat engines.

The three solid lines on the graph in Exhibit 11-14 show the existing constraints for assembly and testing and the material shortage constraint.[2] The feasible alternatives are those combinations of quantities of snowmobile engines and boat engines that satisfy all the constraining factors. The shaded "Area of feasible solutions" in Exhibit 11-14 shows the boundaries of those product combinations that are feasible, or technically possible.

◆ **Step 3:** *Compute the optimal solution.* We present two approaches for finding the optimal solution: the trial-and-error approach and the graphic approach. These approaches are easy to use in our example, because there are only two variables in the objective function and a small number of constraints. An understanding of these two approaches provides insight into LP modelling. In most real-world LP applications, however, managers use computer software packages to calculate the optimal solution.[3]

EXHIBIT 11-13
Operating Data for Power Engines

Product	Department Capacity (per Day) in Product Units		Selling Price	Variable Cost per Unit	Contribution Margin per Unit
	Assembly	Testing			
Only snowmobile engines	300	120	$ 800	$560	$240
Only boat engines	120	240	$1,000	$625	$375

[2] As an example of how the lines are plotted in Exhibit 11-14, use equal signs instead of inequality signs and assume for the assembly department that $B = 0$; then $S = 300$ (600 machine-hours ÷ 2 machine-hours per snowmobile engine). Assume that $S = 0$; then $B = 120$ (600 machine-hours ÷ 5 machine-hours per boat engine). Connect those two points with a straight line.

[3] Although the trial-and-error and graphic approaches can be useful for two or possibly three variables, they are impractical when many variables exist. Standard computer software packages rely on the *simplex method*, an interactive step-by-step procedure for determining the optimal solution to an LP problem. It starts with a specific feasible solution and then tests it by substitution to see whether the result can be improved. These substitutions continue until no further improvement is possible and the optimal solution is obtained.

EXHIBIT 11-14
Linear Programming—Graphic Solution for Power Engines

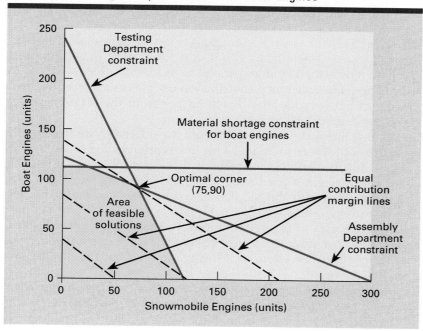

Trial-and-Error Approach The optimal solution can be found by trial and error, by working with coordinates of the corners of the area of feasible solutions. The approach is simple.

First, select any set of corner points and compute the total contribution margin. Five corner points appear in Exhibit 11-14. It is helpful to use simultaneous equations to obtain the exact graph coordinates. To illustrate, the point $(S = 75, B = 90)$ can be derived by solving the two pertinent constraint inequalities as simultaneous equations:

$$2S + 5B = 600 \qquad (1)$$
$$1S + 0.5B = 120 \qquad (2)$$

Multiplying (2) by 2.0, we get $\qquad 2S + 1B = 240 \qquad (3)$

Subtracting (3) from (1) $\qquad\qquad 4B = 360$

Therefore $\qquad\qquad B = 360 \div 4 = 90$

Substituting for B in (2) $\qquad 1S + 0.5(90) = 120$

$$S = 120 - 45 = 75$$

Given $S = 75$ and $B = 90$, TCM = $240(75) + $375(90) = $51,750.

Second, move from corner point to corner point, computing the total contribution margin at each corner point. The total contribution margin at each corner point is as follows:

Trial	Corner Point (S, B)	Snowmobile Engines (S)	Boat Engines (B)	Total Contribution Margin
1	(0, 0)	0	0	$240(0) + $375(0) = $ 0
2	(0, 110)	0	110	$240(0) + $375(110) = 41,250
3	(25, 110)	25	110	$240(25) + $375(110) = 47,250
4	(75, 90)	75	90	$240(75) + $375(90) = 51,750*
5	(120, 0)	120	0	$240(120) + $375(0) = 28,800

*Indicates the optimal solution.

The optimal product mix is the mix that yields the highest total contribution—75 snowmobile engines and 90 boat engines.

Graphic Approach   Consider all possible combinations that will produce an equal total contribution margin of, say, $12,000. That is:

$$\$240S + \$375B = \$12,000$$

This set of $12,000 contribution margins is a straight dashed line in Exhibit 11-14 through ($S = 50$, $B = 0$) and ($S = 0$, $B = 32$). Other equal total contribution margins can be represented by lines parallel to this one. In Exhibit 11-14, we show three dashed lines. The equal total contribution margins increase as the lines get farther from the origin because lines drawn farther from the origin represent more sales of both snowmobile and boat engines.

The optimal line is the one farthest from the origin but still passing through a point in the area of feasible solutions. This line represents the highest contribution margin. The optimal solution is the point at the corner ($S = 75$, $B = 90$). This solution will become apparent if you put a ruler on the graph and move it outward from the origin and parallel with the $12,000 line. The idea is to move the ruler as far away from the origin as possible (that is, to increase the total contribution margin) without leaving the area of feasible solutions. In general, the optimal solution in a maximization problem lies at the corner where the dashed line intersects an extreme point of the area of feasible solutions. Moving the ruler out any further puts it outside the feasible region.

The key to the optimal solution is exchanging a given contribution margin per unit of scarce resource for some other contribution margin per unit of scarce resource. Examine Exhibit 11-14 and consider moving from corner ($S = 25$, $B = 110$) to corner ($S = 75$, $B = 90$). In the assembly department, each machine-hour devoted to 1 unit of boat engines (B) may be given up (sacrificed or traded) for 2.5 units of snowmobile engines (S) (5 hours required for 1 boat engine ÷ 2 hours required for 1 snowmobile engine). Will this exchange add to profitability? Yes, as shown here:

Total contribution margin at ($S = 25$, $B = 110$): $240 × 25 + $375 × 110		$47,250
Added contribution margin from product S by moving to corner ($S = 75$, $B = 90$): $(75 - 25) × $240	$12,000	
Lost contribution margin from product B by moving to corner ($S = 75$, $B = 90$): $(110 - 90) × $375	7,500	
Net additional contribution margin		4,500
Total contribution margin at ($S = 75$, $B = 90$): $240 × 75 + $375 × 90		$51,750

As we move from corner ($S = 25$, $B = 110$) to corner ($S = 75$, $B = 90$), we are contending with the assembly department constraint. In this department, there is a net advantage of trading 1 unit of B for 2.5 units of S. At corner ($S = 25$, $B = 110$), the testing department constraint comes into effect. Should we move to corner ($S = 120$, $B = 0$) along the testing department constraint? No. An analysis (not presented) similar to the one here will show that such a move is not worthwhile.

Sensitivity Analysis

What are the implications of uncertainty about the accounting or technical coefficients used in the LP model? Changes in coefficients affect the slope of the objective function (the equal contribution margin lines) or the area of feasible solutions. Consider how a change in the contribution margin of snowmobile engines from $240 to $300 per unit might affect the optimal solution. Assume the contribution margin for boat engines remains unchanged at $375 per unit. The revised objective function will be:

$$TCM = \$300S + \$375B$$

Using the trial-and-error approach, calculate the total contribution margin for each of the five corner points described in the table on p. 393. The optimal solution is still ($S = 75$, $B = 90$).

Now suppose the contribution margin of snowmobile engines is lower than $240 per unit. By repeating the preceding steps, you will find that the optimal solution will not change so long as the contribution margin of the snowmobile engine does not fall below $150. *Big changes in the contribution margin per unit of snowmobile engines have no effect on the optimal solution.*

What happens if the contribution margin falls below $150? The optimal solution will then shift to the corner ($S = 25$, $B = 110$). Snowmobile engines now generate so little contribution margin per unit that Power Engines will choose to shift its mix in favour of boat engines.

▼ TERMS TO LEARN

This chapter contains definitions of the following important terms:

book value (p. 385)	opportunity cost (p. 380)
business function costs (p. 374)	outlay costs (p. 373)
constraint (p. 392)	out-of-pocket costs (p. 373)
differential cost (p. 371)	outsourcing (p. 375)
full product costs (p. 374)	qualitative factors (p. 371)
incremental costs (p. 373)	quantitative factors (p. 371)
insourcing (p. 375)	relevant costs (p. 370)
make/buy decisions (p. 375)	relevant revenues (p. 370)
net relevant cost (p. 371)	sunk costs (p. 387)
objective function (p. 392)	

▼ ASSIGNMENT MATERIAL

QUESTIONS

11-1 Outline the five-step sequence in a decision process.

11-2 Define *relevant cost*. Why are historical costs irrelevant?

11-3 "All future costs are relevant." Do you agree? Why?

11-4 Distinguish between *quantitative* and *qualitative* factors in decision-making.

11-5 Describe two ways in which unit-cost data can mislead a decision-maker.

11-6 "Variable costs are always relevant, and fixed costs are always irrelevant." Do you agree? Why?

11-7 "A component part should be purchased whenever the purchase price is less than its total unit manufacturing cost." Do you agree? Why?

11-8 Define *opportunity cost.*

11-9 "Managers should always buy inventory in quantities that result in the lowest purchase cost per unit." Do you agree? Why?

11-10 "Management should always maximize sales of the product with the highest contribution margin per unit." Do you agree? Why?

11-11 "A customer, branch, or business segment that shows negative operating income should be shut down." Do you agree? Explain briefly.

11-12 "Cost written off as amortization is always irrelevant." Do you agree? Why?

11-13 "Managers will always choose the alternative that maximizes operating income or minimizes costs in the decision model." Do you agree? Why?

11-14 Describe the three steps in solving a linear programming problem.

11-15 How might the optimal solution of a linear programming problem be determined?

EXERCISES

11-16 Disposal of assets.

1. A company has an inventory of 1,000 assorted parts for a line of missiles that has been discontinued. The inventory cost is $80,000. The parts can be either (a)

remachined at total additional costs of $30,000 and then sold for $35,000 or (b) sold as scrap for $2,000. Which action should be taken?

2. A truck, costing $100,000 and uninsured, is wrecked its first day in use. It can be either (a) disposed of for $10,000 cash and replaced with a similar truck costing $102,000 or (b) rebuilt for $85,000 and thus be brand-new as far as operating characteristics and looks are concerned. What should be done?

11-17 The careening personal computer. (W. A. Paton) An employee in the accounting department of a certain business was moving a personal computer from one room to another. As he came alongside an open stairway, he slipped and let the computer get away from him. It went careening down the stairs with a great racket and wound up at the bottom, completely wrecked. Hearing the crash, the office manager came rushing out and turned rather pale when he saw what had happened. "Someone tell me quickly," the manager yelled, "if that is one of our fully amortized items." A check of the accounting records showed that the smashed computer was, indeed, one of those items that had been written off. "Thank God!" said the manager.

REQUIRED
Explain and comment on the point of this anecdote.

11-18 Multiple choice. (CPA) Choose the best answer.
1. The Woody Company manufactures slippers and sells them at $10 a pair. Variable manufacturing costs are $4.50 a pair, and allocated fixed manufacturing costs are $1.50 a pair. The company has enough idle capacity available to accept a one-time-only special order of 20,000 pairs of slippers at $6 a pair. Woody will not incur any marketing costs as a result of the special order. What would the effect on operating income be if the special order could be accepted without affecting normal sales? (a) $0, (b) $30,000 increase, (c) $90,000 increase, (d) $120,000 increase.

2. The Reno Company manufactures Part No. 498 for use in its production line. The manufacturing costs per unit for 20,000 units of Part No. 498 are as follows:

Direct materials	$ 6
Direct manufacturing labour	30
Variable manufacturing overhead	12
Fixed manufacturing overhead allocated	16
	$64

The Tray Company has offered to sell 20,000 units of Part No. 498 to Reno for $60 per unit. Reno will make the decision to buy the part from Tray if there is an overall savings of at least $25,000 for Reno. If Reno accepts Tray's offer, $9 per unit of the fixed overhead allocated would be totally eliminated. Furthermore, Reno has determined that the released facilities could be used to save relevant costs in the manufacture of Part No. 575. For Reno to have an overall savings of $25,000, the amount of relevant costs that would have to be saved by using the released facilities in the manufacture of Part No. 575 would be (a) $80,000, (b) $85,000, (c) $125,000, (d) $140,000.

11-19 Special order, activity-based costing. (CMA, adapted) The Award Plus Company manufactures medals for winners of athletic events and other contests. Its manufacturing plant has the capacity to produce 10,000 medals each month; current production and sales are 7,500 medals per month. The company normally charges $150 per medal. Cost information for the current activity level is as follows:

Variable costs that vary with units produced:	
Direct materials	$ 262,500
Direct manufacturing labour	300,000
Variable costs (for setups, materials-handling, quality control, and so on) that vary with number of batches, 150 batches × $500 per batch	75,000
Fixed manufacturing costs	275,000
Fixed marketing costs	175,000
Total costs	$1,087,500

Award Plus has just received a special one-time-only order for 2,500 medals at $100 per medal. Award Plus makes medals for its existing customers in batch sizes of 50 medals (150 batches × 50 medals per batch = 7,500 medals). The special order requires Award Plus to make the medals in 25 batches of 100 each.

REQUIRED

1. Should Award Plus accept this special order? Why? Explain briefly.
2. Suppose plant capacity was only 9,000 medals instead of 10,000 medals each month. The special order must either be taken in full or rejected totally. Should Award Plus accept the special order?
3. As in requirement 1, assume that monthly capacity is 10,000 medals. Award Plus is concerned that if it accepts the special order, its existing customers will immediately demand a price discount of $10 in the month in which the special order is being filled. They would argue that Award Plus's capacity costs are now being spread over more units, and that existing customers should get the benefit of these lower costs. Should Award Plus accept the special order under these conditions? Show all calculations.

11-20 **Make versus buy, activity-based costing.** The Svenson Corporation manufactures cellular modems. It manufactures its own cellular modem circuit boards (CMCB), an important part of the cellular modem. It reports the following cost information about the costs of making CMCBs in 2000 and the expected costs in 2001:

	Current Costs in 2000	Expected Costs in 2001
Variable manufacturing costs:		
Direct materials costs per CMCB	$ 180	$ 170
Direct manufacturing labour costs per CMCB	50	45
Variable manufacturing costs per batch for setups, materials-handling, and quality control	1,600	1,500
Fixed manufacturing costs:		
Fixed manufacturing overhead costs that can be avoided if CMCBs are not made	320,000	320,000
Fixed manufacturing overhead costs of plant amortization, insurance, and administration that cannot be avoided even if CMCBs are not made	800,000	800,000

Svenson manufactured 8,000 CMCBs in 2000 in 40 batches of 200 each. In 2001, Svenson anticipates needing 10,000 CMCBs. The CMCBs would be needed in 80 batches of 125 each.

The Minton Corporation has approached Svenson about supplying CMCBs to Svenson in 2001 at $300 per CMCB on whatever delivery schedule Svenson wants.

REQUIRED

1. Calculate the total expected manufacturing (absorption) cost per unit of making CMCBs in 2001.
2. Suppose the capacity currently used to make CMCBs will become idle if Svenson purchases CMCBs from Minton. Should Svenson make CMCBs or buy them from Minton?
3. Now suppose that, if Svenson purchases CMCBs from Minton, its best alternative use of the capacity currently used to make CMCBs is to make and sell special circuit boards (CB3s) to the Essex Corporation. Svenson estimates the following incremental revenues and costs from CB3s:

Total expected incremental future revenues	$2,000,000
Total expected incremental future costs	$2,150,000

Should Svenson make CMCBs or buy them from Minton?

11-21 **Which bases to close, relevant-cost analysis, opportunity costs.** The Department of National Defence has the difficult decision of deciding which military bases to close down. Military and political factors obviously matter, but cost savings are also an important factor. Consider two naval bases—one in Vancouver, British Columbia, and one in Halifax, Nova Scotia. National Defence has decided that it needs only one of those two bases permanently, so one must be shut down. The decision regarding which base to shut down will be made on cost considerations alone. The following information is available:

a. The Vancouver base was built at a cost of $10 million. The operating costs of the base are $400 million per year. The base is built on land owned by National Defence, so it pays nothing for the use of the property. If the base is closed, the land will be sold to developers for $500 million.

b. The Halifax base was built at a cost of $15 million on land leased by National Defence from private citizens. National Defence can choose to lease the land permanently for an annual lease payment of $3 million per year. If it decides to keep the Halifax base open, National Defence plans to invest $60 million in a fixed income note, which at 5% interest will earn the $3 million the government needs for the lease payments. The land and buildings will immediately revert to the owner if the base is closed. The operating costs of the base, excluding lease payments, are $300 million per year.

c. If the Vancouver base is closed down, National Defence will have to transfer some personnel to the Halifax facility. As a result, the yearly operating costs at Halifax will increase by $100 million per year. If the Halifax facility is closed down, no extra costs will be incurred to operate the Vancouver facility.

REQUIRED

The British Columbia delegation argues that it is cheaper to close down the Halifax base, for two reasons: (1) it would save $100 million per year in additional costs required to operate the Halifax base and (2) it would save $3 million dollars per year in lease payments. (Recall that the Vancouver base requires no cash payments for use of the land because the land is owned by National Defence.) Do you agree with the British Columbia delegation's arguments and conclusions? In your answer, identify and explain all costs that you consider relevant and all costs that you consider irrelevant for the base-closing decision.

11-22 Inventory decision, opportunity cost. Lawnox, a manufacturer of lawn mowers, predicts that 240,000 spark plugs will have to be purchased during the next year. The manufacturer estimates that 20,000 spark plugs will be required each month. A supplier quotes a price of $8 per spark plug. The supplier also offers a special discount option: if all 240,000 spark plugs are purchased at the start of the year, a discount of 5% off the $8 price will be given. Lawnox can invest its cash at 8% per year. It costs Lawnox $200 to place each purchase order.

REQUIRED

1. What is the opportunity cost of interest forgone from purchasing all 240,000 units at the start of the year instead of in 12 monthly purchases of 20,000 units per order?

2. Would this opportunity cost ordinarily be recorded in the accounting system? Why?

3. Should Lawnox purchase 240,000 units at the start of the year or 20,000 units each month?

11-23 Relevant costs, contribution margin, product emphasis. The Beach Comber is a takeout food store at a popular beach resort. Susan Sexton, owner of the Beach Comber, is deciding how much shelf space to devote to four different drinks. Pertinent data on these four drinks are as follows:

	Cola	Lemonade	Punch	Natural Orange Juice
Selling price per case	$18.00	$19.20	$26.40	$38.40
Variable costs per case	$13.50	$15.20	$20.10	$30.20
Cases sold per metre of shelf space per day	25	24	4	5

Sexton has a maximum front shelf space of 12 metres to devote to the four drinks. She wants a minimum of 1 metre and a maximum of 6 metres of front shelf space for each drink.

REQUIRED

1. What is the contribution margin per case of each type of drink?

2. A coworker of Sexton's recommends that she maximize the shelf space devoted to those drinks with the highest contribution margin per case. Evaluate this recommendation.

3. What shelf space allocation for the four drinks would you recommend for the Beach Comber?

11-24 Selection of most profitable product. Body-Builders, Inc., produces two basic types of weightlifting equipment, Model 9 and Model 14. Pertinent data are as follows:

	Per Unit	
	Model 9	**Model 14**
Sales price	$100.00	$70.00
Costs:		
Direct materials	$ 28.00	$13.00
Direct manufacturing labour	15.00	25.00
Variable manufacturing overhead*	25.00	12.50
Fixed manufacturing overhead*	10.00	5.00
Marketing costs (all variable)	14.00	10.00
Total costs	$ 92.00	$65.50
Operating income	$ 8.00	$ 4.50

*Allocated on the basis of machine-hours.

The weightlifting craze is such that enough of either Model 9 or Model 14 can be sold to keep the plant operating at full capacity. The two products are processed through the same production departments.

REQUIRED

Which product should be produced? If both should be produced, indicate the proportions of each. Briefly explain your answer.

11-25 Closing and opening stores. Sanchez Corporation runs two convenience stores in Regina and Saskatoon. Operating income for each store in 2000 follows:

	Regina Store	**Saskatoon Store**
Revenues	$1,070,000	$860,000
Operating costs		
Cost of goods sold	750,000	660,000
Lease rent (renewable each year)	90,000	75,000
Labour costs (paid on an hourly basis)	42,000	42,000
Amortization of equipment	25,000	22,000
Utilities (electricity, heating)	43,000	46,000
Allocated corporate overhead	50,000	40,000
Total operating costs	1,000,000	885,000
Operating income	$ 70,000	$ (25,000)

The equipment has a remaining useful life of one year and zero disposal price. In a senior management meeting, Maria Lopez, the management accountant at Sanchez Corporation, makes the following comment, "Sanchez can increase its profitability by closing down the Saskatoon store or by adding more stores like it."

REQUIRED

Answer the following questions referring to the preceding data.
1. Calculate Sanchez's operating income if it closes down the Saskatoon store. By closing down the store, Sanchez can reduce overall corporate overhead costs by $43,000. Is Maria Lopez correct?
2. Calculate Sanchez's operating income if it opens another store with revenues and costs identical to the Saskatoon store (including a cost of $22,000 to acquire equipment with a one-year useful life and zero disposal price). Opening this store will increase corporate overhead costs by $4,000. Is Maria Lopez correct?

11-26 Customer profitability, choosing customers. Broadway Printers operates a printing press with a monthly capacity of 2,000 machine-hours. Broadway has two main customers, Taylor Corporation and Kelly Corporation. Data on each customer for January follow:

	Taylor Corporation	Kelly Corporation	Total
Revenues	$120,000	$80,000	$200,000
Variable costs	42,000	48,000	90,000
Fixed costs (allocated on the basis of revenues)	60,000	40,000	100,000
Total operating costs	102,000	88,000	190,000
Operating income	$ 18,000	$ (8,000)	$ 10,000
Machine-hours required	1,500 hours	500 hours	2,000 hours

Each of the following requirements refers only to the preceding data; there is *no connection* between the requirements.

REQUIRED

1. Should Broadway drop the Kelly Corporation business? If Broadway drops the Kelly Corporation business, its total fixed costs will decrease by 20%.

2. Kelly Corporation indicates that it wants Broadway to do an *additional* $80,000 worth of printing jobs during February. These jobs are identical to the existing business Broadway did for Kelly in January in terms of variable costs and machine-hours required. Broadway anticipates that the business from Taylor Corporation in February would be the same as that in January. Broadway can choose to accept as much of the Taylor and Kelly business for February as it wants. Assume that total fixed costs for February will be the same as the fixed costs in January. What should Broadway do? What will Broadway's operating income be in February?

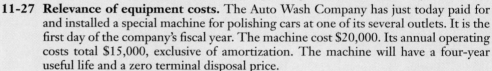

11-27 Relevance of equipment costs. The Auto Wash Company has just today paid for and installed a special machine for polishing cars at one of its several outlets. It is the first day of the company's fiscal year. The machine cost $20,000. Its annual operating costs total $15,000, exclusive of amortization. The machine will have a four-year useful life and a zero terminal disposal price.

After the machine has been used for a day, a machine salesperson offers a different machine that promises to do the same job at a yearly operating cost of $9,000, exclusive of amortization. The new machine will cost $24,000 cash, installed. The "old" machine is unique and can be sold outright for only $10,000, minus $2,000 removal cost. The new machine, like the old one, will have a four-year useful life and zero terminal disposal price.

Sales, all in cash, will be $150,000 annually, and other cash costs will be $110,000 annually, regardless of this decision.

For simplicity, ignore income taxes, interest, and present value considerations.

REQUIRED

1. (a) Prepare a statement of cash receipts and disbursements for each of the four years under both alternatives. What is the cumulative difference in cash flow for the four years taken together? (b) Prepare income statements for each of the four years under both alternatives. Assume straight-line amortization. What is the cumulative difference in operating income for the four years taken together? (c) What are the irrelevant items in your presentations in requirements (a) and (b)? Why are they irrelevant?

2. Suppose the cost of the "old" machine was $1 million rather than $20,000. Nevertheless, the old machine can be sold outright for only $10,000, minus $2,000 removal cost. Would the net differences in requirements 1 and 2 change? Explain.

3. "To avoid a loss, we should keep the old machine." What is the role of book value in decisions about replacement of machines?

11-28 Equipment upgrade versus replacement. (A. Spero, adapted) The Pacifica Corporation makes steel table lamps. It is considering either upgrading its existing production line or replacing it. The production equipment was purchased two years ago for $600,000. It has an expected useful life of five years and a terminal disposal price of $0, and is amortized on a straight-line basis at the rate of $120,000 per year. It has a current book value of $360,000 and a current disposal price of $90,000. The following table presents expected costs under the upgrade and replace alternatives:

	Upgrade	Replace
Expected one-time-only capital costs	$300,000	$750,000
Variable manufacturing costs per unit	$12	$9
Expected production and sales per year	60,000 units	60,000 units
Selling price per unit	$25	$25

The expected useful life after the machine is upgraded or replaced is three years, and the expected terminal disposal price is $0. If the machine is upgraded, the $300,000 would be added to the current book value of $360,000 and amortized on a straight-line basis. The new equipment, if purchased, would also be amortized on a straight-line basis.

For simplicity, ignore income taxes, interest, and present value considerations.

REQUIRED

1. Should Pacifica upgrade its production line or replace it?
2. (a) Now suppose the capital expenditure needed to replace the production line is not known. All other data are as given previously. What is the maximum price that Pacifica would be willing to pay for the new line to prefer replacing the existing line over upgrading it? (b) Assume that the capital expenditure needed to replace the production line is $750,000. Now suppose the expected production and sales quantity is not known. For what production and sales quantity would Pacifica prefer to (i) replace the line, (ii) upgrade the line?
3. Consider again the basic information given in this exercise. Suppose John Azinger, the manager of the Pacifica Corporation, is evaluated on operating income. The upcoming year's operating income is crucial to Azinger's bonus. What alternative would Azinger choose?

PROBLEMS

11-29 Special-order decision. The Modern Packing Corporation (MPC) specializes in the manufacture of one-litre plastic bottles. The plastic molding machines are capable of producing 100 bottles per hour. The firm estimates that the variable cost of producing a plastic bottle is 25 cents. The bottles are sold for 55 cents each.

Management has been approached by a local toy company that would like the firm to produce a molded plastic toy for them. The toy company is willing to pay $3 per unit for the toy. The unit variable cost to manufacture the toy will be $2.40. In addition, MPC would have to incur a cost of $20,000 to construct the mold required exclusively for this order. Because the toy uses more plastic and is of a more intricate shape than a bottle, a molding machine can produce only 40 units per hour. The customer wants 100,000 units. Assume that MPC has a total capacity of 10,000 machine-hours available during the period in which the toy company wants delivery of the toys. The firm's fixed costs, *excluding* the costs to construct the toy mold, during the same period will be $200,000.

REQUIRED

1. Suppose the demand for its bottles is 750,000 units, and the special toy order has to be either taken in full or rejected totally. Should MPC accept the special toy order? Explain your answer.
2. Suppose the demand for its bottles is 850,000 units, and the special toy order has to be either taken in full or rejected totally. Should MPC accept the special toy order? Explain your answer.
3. Suppose the demand for its bottles is 850,000 units, and MPC can accept any quantity of the special toy order. How many bottles and toys should it manufacture?
4. Suppose the demand for its bottles is 900,000 units, and the special toy order has to be either taken in full or rejected totally. Should MPC accept the special toy order? Explain your answer.
5. Suppose the demand for its bottles is 900,000 units, and MPC can accept any quantity of the special toy order. How many bottles and toys should it manufacture?
6. Suppose the demand for its bottles is 950,000 units, and MPC can accept any quantity of the special toy order. How many bottles and toys should it manufacture?
7. The management has located a firm that has just entered the molded plastic business. This firm has considerable excess capacity and more efficient molding machines, and is willing to subcontract the toy job, or any portion of it, for $2.80 per unit. It will construct its own toy mold. Suppose the demand for its bottles is 900,000 units, and MPC can accept any quantity of the special toy order. How many bottles and toys should MPC manufacture? How many toys should it subcontract out?

11-30 Product mix, relevant costs. (N. Melumad, adapted) Pendleton Engineering makes cutting tools for metal working operations. It makes two types of tools, R3, a regular cutting tool, and HP6, a high-precision cutting tool. R3 is manufactured on a regular machine but HP6 must be worked on both the regular machine and a high-precision machine. The following information is available.

	R3	HP6
Selling price	$100	$150
Variable manufacturing costs per unit	$60	$100
Variable marketing costs per unit	$15	$35
Budgeted total fixed overhead costs	$350,000	$550,000
Hours required to produce 1 unit on the regular machine	1	0.5

The following additional information is available:

a. Pendleton faces a capacity constraint on the regular machine of 50,000 hours per year.

b. Pendleton has no capacity constraint on the high-precision machine.

c. Of the $550,000 budgeted fixed overhead costs of HP6, $300,000 is for lease payments for the high-precision machine. This cost is charged entirely to HP6 because Pendleton uses the machine exclusively to produce HP6. The leasing agreement for the high-precision machine can be cancelled at any time without penalties.

d. All other fixed overhead costs cannot be changed.

REQUIRED

1. What product mix—that is how many units of R3 and HP6—will maximize Pendleton's operating income?

2. Suppose Pendleton can increase the annual capacity of regular machines by 15,000 hours at a cost of $150,000? Should Pendleton increase the capacity of regular machines? By how much will Pendleton's operating income increase?

3. Suppose that the capacity of the regular machine has been increased to 65,000 hours. Pendleton has been approached by Carter Corporation to supply 20,000 units of another cutting tool S3 for $120 per unit. S3 is exactly like R3 except that its variable manufacturing costs are $70 per unit. What product mix should Pendleton choose to maximize operating income?

11-31 Discontinuing a product line, selling more product. The Northern Furniture Division of Grossman Corporation makes and sells tables and beds. The following revenue and cost information from the divisions activity-based costing system is available:

	4,000 Tables	5,000 Beds	Total
Revenues ($125 × 4,000; $200 × 5,000)	$500,000	$1,000,000	$1,500,000
Variable direct materials and direct manufacturing labour costs ($75 × 4,000; $105 × 5,000)	300,000	525,000	825,000
Amortization on equipment used exclusively by each product line	68,000	92,000	160,000
Marketing and distribution costs			
$40,000 (fixed) + $750 per shipment × 40 shipments	70,000		205,000
$60,000 (fixed) + $750 per shipment × 100 shipments		135,000	
Fixed general administration costs of the division allocated to product lines on the basis of revenues	90,000	180,000	270,000
Allocated corporate-office costs allocated to product lines on the basis of revenues	20,000	40,000	60,000
Total costs	548,000	972,000	1,520,000
Operating income (loss)	$(48,000)	$28,000	$(20,000)

a. Equipment has a remaining useful life of one year and zero disposal price. Any equipment not used remains idle.

b. Fixed marketing and distribution costs of a product line can be avoided if the line is discontinued.

c. Fixed general administration costs of the division and corporate-office costs will not change if sales of individual product lines are increased or decreased, or if product lines are added or dropped.

REQUIRED

1. Should the Furniture Division discontinue the tables product line assuming the released facilities remain idle? Show all calculations.
2. Should the Furniture Division sell 4,000 more tables? Assume that to do so the division would have to acquire equipment costing $68,000 with a one year useful life. Assume further that the fixed marketing and distribution costs will not change but that the number of shipments will double. Show all calculations.

11-32 Opportunity cost. (H. Schaefer) The Wolverine Corporation is working at full production capacity producing 10,000 units of a unique product, Rosebo. Manufacturing costs per unit for Rosebo are as follows:

Direct materials	$ 2
Direct manufacturing labour	3
Manufacturing overhead	5
	$10

The unit manufacturing overhead cost is based on a variable cost per unit of $2 and fixed costs of $30,000 (at full capacity of 10,000 units). The selling costs, all variable, are $4 per unit, and the selling price is $20 per unit.

A customer, the Windsor Company, has asked Wolverine to produce 2,000 units of Orangebo, a modification of Rosebo. Orangebo would require the same manufacturing processes as Rosebo. The Windsor Company has offered to pay Wolverine $15 for a unit of Orangebo and half the selling costs per unit.

REQUIRED

1. What is the opportunity cost to Wolverine of producing the 2,000 units of Orangebo? (Assume that no overtime is worked.)
2. The Buckeye Corporation has offered to produce 2,000 units of Rosebo for Wolverine so that Wolverine may accept the Orangebo offer. That is, if Wolverine accepts the Buckeye offer, Wolverine would manufacture 8,000 units of Rosebo and 2,000 units of Orangebo and purchase 2,000 units of Rosebo from Buckeye. Buckeye would charge Wolverine $14 per unit to manufacture Rosebo. Should Wolverine accept the Buckeye offer? (Support your conclusions with specific analysis.)
3. Suppose Wolverine had been working at less than full capacity, producing 8,000 units of Rosebo at the time the Orangebo offer was made. What is the minimum price Wolverine should accept for Orangebo under these conditions? (Ignore the previous $15 unit price.)

11-33 Contribution approach, relevant costs. Air Pacific owns a single jet aircraft and operates between Vancouver and the Hawaiian Islands. Flights leave Vancouver on Mondays and Thursdays and depart from Hawaii on Wednesdays and Saturdays. Air Pacific cannot offer any more flights between Vancouver and Hawaii. Only tourist-class seats are available on its planes. An analyst has collected the following information:

Seating capacity per plane	360 passengers
Average number of passengers per flight	200 passengers
Flights per week	4 flights
Flights per year	208 flights
Average one-way fare	$500
Variable fuel costs	$14,000 per flight
Food and beverage service cost (no charge to passenger)	$20 per passenger
Commission to travel agents paid by Air Pacific (all tickets are booked by travel agents)	8% of fare
Fixed annual lease costs allocated to each flight	$53,000 per flight
Fixed ground services (maintenance, check-in, baggage handling) cost allocated to each flight	$7,000 per flight
Fixed flight crew salaries allocated to each flight	$4,000 per flight

For simplicity, assume that fuel costs are unaffected by the actual number of passengers on a flight.

REQUIRED

1. What is the operating income that Air Pacific makes on each one-way flight between Vancouver and Hawaii?
2. The market research department of Air Pacific indicates that lowering the average one-way fare to $480 will increase the average number of passengers per flight to 212. Should Air Pacific lower its fare?
3. Travel International, a tour operator, approaches Air Pacific on the possibility of chartering (renting out) its jet aircraft twice each month, first to take Travel International's tourists from Vancouver to Hawaii and then to bring the tourists back from Hawaii to Vancouver. If Air Pacific accepts Travel International's offer, Air Pacific will be able to offer only 184 (208 − 24) of its own flights each year. The terms of the charter are as follows: (a) For each one-way flight, Travel International will pay Air Pacific $75,000 to charter the plane and to use its flight crew and ground service staff; (b) Travel International will pay for fuel costs; and (c) Travel International will pay for all food costs. On purely financial considerations, should Air Pacific accept Travel International's offer? What other factors should Air Pacific consider in deciding whether or not to charter its plane to Travel International?

11-34 Make or buy, unknown level of volume. (A. Atkinson) Oxford Engineering manufactures small engines. The engines are sold to manufacturers who install them in such products as lawn mowers. The company currently manufactures all the parts used in these engines but is considering a proposal from an external supplier who wishes to supply the starter assembly used in these engines.

The starter assembly is currently manufactured in Division 3 of Oxford Engineering. The costs relating to Division 3 for the past 12 months were as follows:

Direct materials	$200,000
Direct manufacturing labour	150,000
Manufacturing overhead	400,000
Total	$750,000

Over the past year, Division 3 manufactured 150,000 starter assemblies; the average cost for the starter assembly is computed as $5 ($750,000 ÷ 150,000).

Further analysis of manufacturing overhead revealed the following information. Of the total manufacturing overhead reported, only 25% is considered variable. Of the fixed portion, $150,000 is an allocation of general overhead that would remain unchanged for the company as a whole if production of the starter assembly is discontinued. A further $100,000 of the fixed overhead is avoidable if self-manufacture of the starter assembly is discontinued. The balance of the current fixed overhead, $50,000, is the division manager's salary. If self-manufacture of the starter assembly is discontinued, the manager of Division 3 will be transferred to Division 2 at the same salary. This move will allow the company to save the $40,000 salary that would otherwise be paid to attract an outsider to this position.

REQUIRED

1. Tidnish Electronics, a reliable supplier, has offered to supply starter assembly units at $4 per unit. Since this price is less than the current average cost of $5 per unit, the vice-president of manufacturing is eager to accept this offer. Should the outside offer be accepted? (*Hint:* Production output in the coming year may be different from production output in the last year.)
2. How, if at all, would your response to requirement 1 change if the company could use the vacated plant space for storage and, in so doing, avoid $50,000 of outside storage charges currently incurred? Why is this information relevant or irrelevant?

11-35 Make or buy, activity-based costing, opportunity costs. (N. Melumad and S. Reichelstein, adapted) The Ace Bicycle Company produces bicycles. This year's expected production is 10,000 units. Currently, Ace makes the chains for its bicycles. Ace's accountant reports the following costs for making the 10,000 bicycle chains:

	Costs per Unit	Costs for 10,000 Units
Direct materials	$4.00	$ 40,000
Direct labour	2.00	20,000
Variable manufacturing overhead (power and utilities)	1.50	15,000
Inspection, setup, materials-handling		2,000
Machine rent		3,000
Allocated fixed costs of plant administration, taxes, and insurance		30,000
Total costs		$110,000

Ace has received an offer from an outside vendor to supply any number of chains Ace requires at $8.20 per chain. The following additional information is available:

a. Inspection, setup, and materials-handling costs vary with the number of batches in which the chains are produced. Ace produces chains in batch sizes of 1,000 units. Ace estimates that it will produce the 10,000 units in ten batches.

b. Ace rents the machine used to make the chains. If Ace buys all its chains from the outside vendor, it does not need to pay rent on this machine.

REQUIRED

1. Assume that, if Ace purchases the chains from the outside supplier, the facility where the chains are currently made will remain idle. Should Ace accept the outside supplier's offer at the anticipated production (and sales) volume of 10,000 units?

2. For this question, assume that if the chains are purchased outside, the facilities where the chains are currently made will be used to upgrade the bicycles by adding mud flaps and reflectors. As a consequence, the selling price on bicycles will be raised by $20. The variable per-unit cost of the upgrade would be $18, and additional tooling costs of $16,000 would be incurred. Should Ace make or buy the chains, assuming that 10,000 units are produced (and sold)?

3. The sales manager at Ace is concerned that the estimate of 10,000 units may be high and believes that only 6,200 units will be sold. Production will be cut back, and this opens up work space, which can be used to add the mud flaps and reflectors whether Ace goes outside for the chains or makes them in-house. At this lower output, Ace will produce the chains in eight batches of 775 units each. Should Ace purchase the chains from the outside vendor?

11-36 **Relevant cost of materials.** The Hernandez Corporation is bidding on a new construction contract, here called Contract No. 1. If the bid is accepted, work will begin in a few days, on January 1, 2000. Contract No. 1 requires a special cement. Hernandez has already purchased 10,000 kilograms of the special cement for $20,000. The current purchase cost of the cement is $2.40 per kilogram. The company could sell the cement now for $1.60 per kilogram after all selling costs.

Hernandez will also bid on Contract No. 2 one month from now. If Contract No. 1 is not landed, the special cement will be available for Contract No. 2. If Contract No. 1 is landed, Hernandez will need to buy 10,000 kilograms of another grade of cement for $2.10 per kilogram to fulfill Contract No. 2.

If it is not used in either of these two ways, the special cement would be of no use to the company and would be sold a little more than a month from now for $1.50 per kilogram after all selling costs.

The president of Hernandez, Julio Gomez, is puzzled about the appropriate total cost of the special cement to be used in bidding on Contract No. 1. Competition is intense and markups are very thin, so determining the relevant material costs when bidding on Contract No. 1 is crucial.

REQUIRED

1. Suppose Gomez is certain that Hernandez will land Contract No. 2; what (relevant) cost figure should Gomez use for the special cement when bidding on Contract No. 1?

2. This part requires knowledge of the material on decision making under uncertainty in the appendix to Chapter 3. Suppose Gomez estimates a probability of 0.7 that Hernandez will land Contract No. 2. What (relevant) cost figure should Gomez use for the special cement when bidding on Contract No. 1?

3. Suppose Hernandez could sell the special cement now for $2.30 per kilogram after all selling costs (instead of $1.60 per kilogram described in paragraph 1). Suppose Gomez is certain that Hernandez will land Contract No. 2. What (relevant) cost figure should Gomez use for the special cement when preparing a bid on Contract No. 1?

11-37 Discontinuing a product line, selling more product, activity-based costing. Home Furnishings makes bookshelves, tables, and beds. The following sales and cost information is available about the profitability of each of these lines:

	Bookshelves	Tables	Beds	Total
Revenues	$750,000	$500,000	$1,000,000	$2,250,000
Direct materials	300,000	220,000	400,000	920,000
Direct manufacturing labour	75,000	60,000	80,000	215,000
Setups and materials-handling	45,000	40,000	60,000	145,000
Amortization on tools and fixtures	50,000	48,000	72,000	170,000
Marketing and distribution	75,000	60,000	120,000	255,000
General administration and facilities	150,000	100,000	200,000	450,000
Total costs	695,000	528,000	932,000	2,155,000
Operating income (loss)	$ 55,000	$ (28,000)	$ 68,000	$ 95,000

Home Furnishings uses an activity-based cost system to assign costs to products. The following additional information is available:
a. Direct materials and direct manufacturing labour costs vary with the number of units of products manufactured.
b. Setups and materials-handling costs vary with the number of batches made.
c. Tools and fixtures have one-year lives and zero disposal prices.
d. Of the total marketing and distribution costs, $112,500 are fixed costs allocated to product lines on the basis of sales revenue. Fixed marketing and distribution costs allocated to a product line can be avoided if the line is discontinued. The remaining marketing costs vary with the number of shipments made.
e. General administration and facilities costs are fixed costs that will not change if sales of individual product lines are increased or decreased or if product lines are added or dropped. These costs are allocated to product lines on the basis of sales revenues.

REQUIRED
In answering the following requirements, assume that prices of the various products do not change.
1. Should Home Furnishings discontinue the tables product line assuming the released facilities remain idle? Assume Home Furnishings has already acquired the tools and fixtures it needs to manufacture tables.
2. Suppose that if Home Furnishings discontinues the tables product line, the released facilities could be used to sell beds worth an additional $250,000. This would require Home Furnishings to purchase tools and fixtures for $4,000. Assume that there will be no change in either the number of batches in which beds are made or the number of shipments.
   a. On the basis of your calculations, should Home Furnishings discontinue the tables product line?
   b. What is the opportunity cost of continuing the tables product line?
   c. What other factors should Home Furnishings consider before making a decision?
3. What would be the effect on operating income if Home Furnishings could double its sales of tables? Assume that, at the higher sales, both the number of batches and the number of shipments would be three times and purchases of tools and fixtures would be twice the current levels.

11-38 Considering three alternatives. (CMA) The Auer Company had just completed an order for a special machine from the Jay Company when the Jay Company declared bankruptcy, defaulted on the order, and forfeited the 10% deposit paid on the selling price of $72,500. Auer's manufacturing manager identified the costs already incurred in the production of the special machine for Jay as follows:

Direct materials used		$16,600
Direct manufacturing labour incurred		21,400
Overhead allocated:		
Manufacturing:		
Variable	$10,700	
Fixed	5,350	16,050
Fixed marketing and administration		5,405
Total costs		$59,455

Another company, the Kaytell Corporation, would be interested in buying the special machine if it is reworked to Kaytell's specifications. Auer offered to sell the reworked machine to Kaytell as a special order for a net price (price minus cash discount, if any) of $68,400. Kaytell has agreed to pay the net price when it takes delivery in two months. The additional traceable costs to rework the machine to Kaytell's specifications are as follows:

Direct materials	$ 6,200
Direct manufacturing labour	4,200
	$10,400

A second alternative available to Auer is to convert the special machine to the standard model. The standard model lists for $62,500. The additional incremental costs to convert the special machine to the standard model are:

Direct materials	$2,850
Direct manufacturing labour	3,300
	$6,150

A third alternative for the Auer Company is to sell, as a special order, the machine as is (that is, without modification) for a net price of $52,000. However, the potential buyer of the unmodified machine does not want it for 60 days. The buyer offers a $7,000 down payment with final payment upon delivery.

The following additional information is available regarding Auer's operations:

◆ The sales commission rate is 2% on sales of standard models and 3% on special orders. All sales commissions are calculated on net selling price (that is, list price minus cash discount, if any).

◆ Normal credit terms for sales of standard models are 2/10, n/30 (2/10 means a discount of 2% is given if payment is made within 10 days; n/30 means full amount is due within 30 days). Customers take the discounts except in rare instances. Credit terms for special orders are negotiated with the customer.

◆ The allocation rates for manufacturing overhead and the fixed marketing and administrative costs are:

Manufacturing:	
Variable	50% of direct manufacturing labour costs
Fixed	25% of direct manufacturing labour costs
Marketing and administration:	
Fixed	10% of the total of direct materials, direct manufacturing labour costs, and manufacturing overhead costs

◆ Normal time required for rework is one month.
◆ A surcharge of 5% of the selling price is placed on all customer requests for minor modifications of standard models.
◆ Auer normally sells a sufficient number of standard models for the company to operate at a volume in excess of the breakeven point.

Auer does not consider the time value of money in their analyses of special orders whenever the time period is less than one year, because the effect is not significant.

REQUIRED

1. Determine the dollar contribution that each of the three alternatives will add to the Auer Company's operating income.

2. If Kaytell makes Auer a counteroffer, what is the lowest price Auer should accept from Kaytell for the reworked machine? Explain your answer.
3. Discuss the influence that fixed manufacturing overhead costs should have on the selling prices Auer quotes for special orders when (a) the firm is operating at or below the breakeven point and (b) the firm's special orders constitute efficient utilization of unused capacity above the breakeven point.

11-39 Multiple choice, comprehensive problem on relevant costs. The following are the Class Company's *unit* costs of manufacturing and marketing a high-style pen at a level of 20,000 units per month:

Manufacturing costs:	
Direct materials	$1.00
Direct manufacturing labour	1.20
Variable manufacturing indirect costs	0.80
Fixed manufacturing indirect costs	0.50
Marketing costs:	
Variable	1.50
Fixed	0.90

REQUIRED

The following situations refer only to the preceding data; there is no connection between the situations. Unless stated otherwise, assume a regular selling price of $6 per unit.

Choose the best answer to each of the seven questions. Support each answer with summarized computations.

1. In an inventory of 10,000 units of the high-style pen presented on the balance sheet, the unit cost used is (a) $3, (b) $3.50, (c) $5, (d) $2.20, (e) $5.90.
2. The pen is usually produced and sold at the rate of 240,000 units per year (an average of 20,000 per month). The selling price is $6 per unit, which yields total annual sales of $1,440,000. Total costs are $1,416,000, and operating income is $24,000, or $0.10 per unit. Market research estimates that unit sales could be increased by 10% if prices were cut to $5.80. Assuming the implied cost behaviour patterns to be correct, this action, if taken, would:
   a. Decrease operating income by a net of $7,200
   b. Decrease operating income by $0.20 per unit ($48,000) but increase operating income by 10% of sales ($144,000) for a net increase of $96,000
   c. Decrease unit fixed costs by 10%, or $0.14, per unit, and thus decrease operating income by $0.06 ($0.20 − $0.14) per unit
   d. Increase unit sales to 264,000 units, which at the $5.80 price would give total sales of $1,531,200; costs at $5.90 per unit for 264,000 units would be $1,557,600; and a loss of $26,400 would result
   e. None of these
3. A cost contract with the government for 5,000 units of the pens calls for the reimbursement of all manufacturing costs plus a fixed fee of $1,000. No variable marketing costs are incurred on the government contract. You are required to compare the following two alternatives:

Sales Each Month To:	Alternative A	Alternative B
Regular customers	15,000 units	15,000 units
Government	0 units	5,000 units

Operating income under alternative B is greater than that under alternative A by (a) $1,000, (b) $2,500, (c) $3,500, (d) $300, (e) none of these.
4. Assume the same data with respect to the government contract as in requirement 3 except that the two alternatives to be compared are:

Sales Each Month To:	Alternative A	Alternative B
Regular customers	20,000 units	15,000 units
Government	0 units	5,000 units

Operating income under alternative B relative to that under alternative A is (a) $4,000 less, (b) $3,000 greater, (c) $6,500 less, (d) $500 greater, (e) none of these.
5. The company wants to enter a foreign market in which price competition is keen. The company seeks a one-time-only special order for 10,000 units on a

minimum-unit-price basis. It expects that shipping costs for this order will amount to only $0.75 per unit, but the fixed costs of obtaining the contract will be $4,000. The company incurs no variable marketing costs other than shipping costs. Domestic business will be unaffected. The selling price to break even is (a) $3.50, (b) $4.15, (c) $4.25, (d) $3, (e) $5.

6. The company has an inventory of 1,000 units of pens that must be sold immediately at reduced prices. Otherwise, the inventory will be worthless. The unit cost that is relevant for establishing the minimum selling price is (a) $4.50, (b) $4, (c) $3, (d) $5.90, (e) $1.50.

7. A proposal is received from an outside supplier who will make and ship these high-style pens directly to the Class Company's customers as sales orders are forwarded from Class's sales staff. Class's fixed marketing costs will be unaffected, but its variable marketing costs will be slashed by 20%. Class's plant will be idle, but its fixed manufacturing overhead will continue at 50% of present levels. How much per unit would the company be able to pay the supplier without decreasing operating income? (a) $4.75, (b) $3.95, (c) $2.95, (d) $5.35, (e) none of these.

11-40 Make or buy (continuation of 11-39). Assume that, as in requirement 7 of Problem 11-39, a proposal is received from an outside supplier who will make and ship high-style pens directly to the Class Company's customers as sales orders are forwarded from Class's sales staff. If the supplier's offer is accepted, the present plant facilities will be used to make a new pen whose unit costs will be:

Variable manufacturing costs	$5.00
Fixed manufacturing costs	1.00
Variable marketing costs	2.00
Fixed marketing costs for the new pen	0.50

Total fixed manufacturing overhead will be unchanged from the original level given at the beginning of Problem 11-39. Fixed marketing costs for the new pens are over and above the fixed marketing costs incurred for marketing the high-style pens at the beginning of Problem 11-39. The new pen will sell for $9. The minimum desired operating income on the two pens taken together is $50,000 per year.

REQUIRED
What is the maximum purchase cost per unit that the Class Company should be willing to pay for subcontracting the production of the high-style pens?

11-41 Optimal production plan, computer manufacturer. (Chapter Appendix) Information Technology, Inc., assembles and sells two products: printers and desktop computers. Customers can purchase either (a) a computer or (b) a computer plus a printer. The printers are *not* sold without the computer. The result is that the quantity of printers sold is equal to or less than the quantity of desktop computers sold. The contribution margins are $200 per printer and $100 per computer.

Each printer requires six hours' assembly time on production line 1 and ten hours' assembly time on production line 2. Each computer requires four hours' assembly time on production line 1 only. (Many of the components of each computer are preassembled by external vendors.) Production line 1 has 24 hours of available time per day. Production line 2 has 20 hours of available time per day.

Let X represent units of printers and Y represent units of desktop computers. The production manager must decide on the optimal mix of printers and computers to manufacture.

REQUIRED
1. Express the production manager's problem in an LP format.
2. Which combination of printers and computers will maximize the operating income of Information Technology? Use both the trial-and-error and the graphic approach.

11-42 Optimal sales mix for a retailer, sensitivity analysis. (Chapter Appendix) Always Open, Inc., operates a chain of food stores open 24 hours a day. Each store has a standard 40,000 square metres of floor space available for merchandise. Merchandise is grouped in two categories: grocery products and dairy products. Always Open requires each store to devote a minimum of 10,000 square metres to grocery products and a minimum of 8,000 square metres to dairy products. Within these restrictions, each store manager can choose the mix of products to carry.

The manager of the Winnipeg store estimates the following weekly contribution margins per square metre: grocery products, $10; dairy products, $3.

REQUIRED

1. Formulate the decision facing the store manager as an LP model. Use G to represent square metres of floor space for grocery products and D to represent square metres of floor space for dairy products.
2. Why might Always Open set minimum bounds on the floor space devoted to each line of products?
3. Compute the optimal mix of grocery products and dairy products for the Winnipeg store.
4. Will the optimal mix determined in requirement 3 change if the contribution margins per square metre change to grocery products, $8, and dairy products, $5?

11-43 Make versus buy, ethics. (CMA, adapted) Lynn Hardt, a management accountant with the Paibec Corporation, is evaluating whether a component, MTR-2000, should continue to be manufactured by Paibec or purchased from Marley Company, an outside supplier. Marley has submitted a bid to manufacture and supply the 32,000 units of MTR-2000 that Paibec will need for 2000 at a unit price of $17.30 to be delivered according to Paibec's production specifications and needs. While the contract price of $17.30 is only applicable in 2000, Marley is interested in entering into a long-term arrangement beyond 2000.

Hardt has gathered the following information regarding Paibec's annual cost to manufacture 30,000 units of MTR-2000 in 1999.

Direct materials	$195,000
Direct manufacturing labour costs	120,000
Plant space rental costs	84,000
Equipment leasing costs	36,000
Other manufacturing overhead costs	225,000
Total manufacturing costs	$660,000

Hardt has collected the following additional information related to manufacturing MTR-2000.

◆ Direct materials used in the production of MTR-2000 are expected to increase eight percent in 1999.
◆ Paibec's direct manufacturing labour contract calls for a five-percent increase in 2000.
◆ Paibec can withdraw from the plant space rental agreement without any penalty. Paibec will have no need for this space if MTR-2000 is not manufactured.
◆ The equipment lease can be terminated by paying $6,000.
◆ Forty percent of the other manufacturing overhead is considered variable. Variable overhead changes with the number of units produced. The rate per unit is not expected to change in 2000. The fixed manufacturing overhead costs are not expected to change whether or not MTR-2000 is manufactured.

John Porter, plant manager at Paibec Corporation, is concerned that Hardt's analysis may lead to the closing down of the MTR-2000 line. Porter indicates to Hardt that the current performance of the plant can be significantly improved upon and that the price increases she is assuming are unlikely to occur. Hence, the analysis should be done assuming costs will be considerably below current levels. Hardt knows that Porter is concerned about outsourcing MTR-2000 because it will mean that some of his close friends will be laid off. Furthermore, Porter had played a key role in convincing management to produce MTR-2000 in-house.

Hardt believes that it is unlikely that the plant will achieve the lower costs Porter describes. She is very confident about the accuracy of the information she has collected, but she is unhappy about laying off employees.

REQUIRED

1. On the basis of the information Hardt has obtained, should Paibec make MTR-2000 or buy it? Show all calculations.
2. What other factors should Paibec consider before making a decision?
3. What should Lynn Hardt do in response to John Porter's comments?

11-44 Ethics and relevant costs. The Pastel Company must reach a make/buy decision with respect to a high-volume, easily made metal tool, RG1. Sean Gray, the cost analyst, estimates the following costs and production information for the 50,000 units of RG1 that are expected to be put into production.

Total direct materials costs	$600,000
Direct manufacturing labour costs (all variable)	$200,000
Manufacturing overhead costs (all fixed)	$400,000
Good units of RG1 manufactured and sold	40,000 units
Units of RG1 scrapped for zero revenue	10,000 units

York Corporation has offered to supply as many units of RG1 as Pastel needs for $21 per unit. If Pastel buys RG1 from York instead of manufacturing it in-house, Pastel would be able to save $239,500 of the $400,000 fixed manufacturing overhead costs. (There is no alternative use for the capacity currently used to make RG1.)

Gray shows his analysis to Jim Berry, the controller. Berry does not like what he sees. He asks Gray to review all his assumptions and calculations with the comment, "The yield assumptions you made are very low. I think this plant can achieve much better quality than we have in the past. Better quality will reduce our costs and make them competitive with the outside purchase price." Gray knows that Berry is very concerned about purchasing RG1 from an outside supplier because it will mean that some of his close friends who work on the RG1 line will be laid off. Berry had played a key role in convincing management to produce RG1 in-house.

Gray rechecks his calculations. He believes it is unlikely that the plant can achieve the quality levels it would take for the make alternative to be superior to the buy alternative.

REQUIRED

1. On the basis of the information Gray obtains, should Pastel make or buy RG1?
2. For what levels of scrap would the make alternative be preferred to purchasing from outside?
3. Evaluate whether Jim Berry's suggestion to Gray to review his estimates is unethical. Will it be unethical for Gray to change his analysis to support the make alternative? What steps should Gray take next?

COLLABORATIVE LEARNING PROBLEMS

11-45 Optimal product mix. (CMA, adapted) OmniSport's Plastics Department is currently manufacturing 5,000 pairs of skates annually, making full use of its machine capacity. Presented below are the selling price and costs associated with OmniSport's skates.

Selling price per pair of skates		$98
Costs per pair of skates		
Molded plastic	$8	
Other direct materials	12	
Variable machine operating costs ($16 per hour)	24	
Manufacturing overhead costs	18	
Marketing and administrative costs	15	77
Operating income per pair of skates		$21

OmniSport believes it could sell 8,000 pairs of skates annually if it had sufficient manufacturing capacity. Colcott, Inc., a steady supplier of quality products, has agreed to provide 6,000 pairs of skates per year at a price of $75 per pair delivered to OmniSport's facility.

Jack Petrone, OmniSport's product manager, has suggested that the company can make better use of its Plastics Department by manufacturing snowboard bindings. Petrone believes that OmniSport could expect to sell 12,000 snowboard bindings annually at a price of $60 per binding. Petrone's estimate of the costs to manufacture the bindings is presented below.

Selling price per snowboard binding		$60
Costs per snowboard binding		
Molded plastic	$16	
Other direct materials	4	
Variable machine operating costs ($16 per hour)	8	
Manufacturing overhead costs	6	
Marketing and administrative costs	14	48
Operating income per snowboard binding		$12

Other information pertinent to OmniSport's operations is presented below.

◆ An allocated $6 fixed overhead cost per unit is included in the marketing and administrative cost for all of the purchased and manufactured products. Total fixed and variable marketing and administrative costs for the purchased skates would be $10 per pair.

◆ In the Plastics Department, OmniSport uses machine hours as the allocation base for other manufacturing overhead costs. The fixed manufacturing overhead component of these costs for the current year is the $30,000 of fixed plantwide manufacturing overhead that has been allocated to the Plastics Department.

INSTRUCTIONS

Form groups of two students to complete the following requirement.

REQUIRED

Which product or products should OmniSport manufacture and/or purchase to maximize operating income. Show all calculations.

11-46 **Relevant costs, opportunity costs.** Larry Miller, the general manager of Basil Software, scheduled a meeting on June 2, 2000 with Sally Shields, sales manager, Andy Ashby, accountant, and Ellen Eisner, software operations manager, to discuss the development and release of Basil Software's new version of its spreadsheet package, Easyspread 2.0. It is only a question of time before other software firms have a package that matches Easyspread 2.0. Sally Shields, the sales manager, could hardly control her enthusiasm for the new product.

Sally Shields: This product is exactly what the market has been waiting for. We should not delay, by even a single day, the introduction of this product. Let's make July 1, 2000, the sales release date.

Ellen Eisner: I don't disagree with Sally's assessment of the market potential for this product, but I have a problem. The threatened strike by our printers caused us to purchase large quantities of user's manuals for Easyspread 1.0. We don't like to store the manuals separately, so we also got extra diskettes duplicated. The manuals and diskettes were then packaged and shrink-wrapped. We are currently holding 60,000 completed packages, which equals the expected sales for July, August, and September 2000 of Easyspread 1.0. I think we should make October 1, 2000, the expected release date of Easyspread 2.0. This date would enable us to sell all of our inventory of Easyspread 1.0.

Larry Miller: Sally, do you see any problem with Ellen's suggestion? Our inventory of Easyspread 1.0 seems rather large for us to ignore. If we introduce Easyspread 2.0 on July 1, what would we do with the inventory of Easyspread 1.0 that we currently hold?

Sally Shields: We currently sell Easyspread 1.0 to our wholesalers and distributors for $150 each. The additional optimization features in Easyspread 2.0 mean that we should be able to sell Easyspread 2.0 to our distributors for about $185. We should not ignore the higher profit margins from Easyspread 2.0. It is true, though, that each time we sell one unit of Easyspread 2.0, we forgo the sale of one unit of Easyspread 1.0. Since the expected demand for Easyspread 2.0 is at least as large as the demand for Easyspread 1.0, we may have to throw away the existing inventory of Easyspread 1.0 once we introduce Easyspread 2.0.

Larry Miller: Andy, you've heard what Sally and Ellen have to say. I would like you to do a detailed analysis of the alternatives, and let me know within a week what you come up with. We need to make a decision on this one way or another, and we need to do so soon.

When Ashby returned to his office, he pulled out the cost records he had developed for Easyspread 1.0 and Easyspread 2.0. The unit costs for the two products could be summarized as follows:

	Easyspread 1.0	Easyspread 2.0
Manuals, diskettes	$ 20	$ 25
Development costs	75	105
Marketing and administration costs	25	30
Total cost per unit	$120	$160

The following additional facts are available:

a. Basil contracts with outside vendors to print manuals and duplicate diskettes.

b. Development costs are allocated on the basis of the total costs of developing the software and the anticipated unit sales over the life of the software.

c. Marketing and administration costs are fixed costs in 2000, incurred to support all activities of Basil Software. Marketing and administration costs are allocated to products on the basis of the budgeted revenues from each of the products. The preceding unit costs assume Easyspread 2.0 will be introduced on July 1, 2000.

INSTRUCTIONS

Form groups of three students to complete the following requirements. To answer requirement 2, each student should play the role of one of Larry Miller, Sally Shields, and Ellen Eisner.

REQUIRED

1. On the basis of financial considerations only, is Basil Software better off introducing Easyspread 2.0 immediately instead of waiting? Explain your conclusion, clearly identifying relevant and irrelevant costs.

2. What other factors might Sally Shields and Ellen Eisner raise? What factors might Larry Miller consider important?

12 CHAPTER

PRICING DECISIONS, PRODUCT PROFITABILITY DECISIONS, AND COST MANAGEMENT

Computer component manufacturers recognize that the key to managing manufacturing costs is at the product design stage before costs get locked in. Tatung at its Taipei plant uses multi-function teams to design new colour monitors that both satisfy customers on quality and are competitive on cost.

LEARNING OBJECTIVES

After studying this chapter, you should be able to:

1. Discuss the three major influences on pricing decisions

2. Distinguish between short-run and long-run pricing decisions

3. Describe the target-costing approach to pricing

4. Distinguish between cost incurrence and locked-in costs

5. Describe the cost-plus approach to pricing

6. Describe two pricing practices in which noncost reasons are important when setting price

7. Explain how life cycle product budgeting and costing assist in pricing decisions

8. Explain the effects of competition laws on pricing

Pricing decisions are decisions that managers make about what to charge for the products and services they deliver. For brevity, we use the term *pricing decision* in this chapter to include decisions about the profitability of products. These decisions impact the revenues a company earns, which must exceed total costs if profits are to be achieved. Consequently, determining product costs is important for pricing decisions. There is, however, no single way of computing a product cost that is universally relevant for all pricing decisions. Why? Because pricing decisions differ greatly in both their time horizons and their contexts. We emphasize how an understanding of cost behaviour patterns and cost drivers can lead to better pricing decisions and also apply the relevant-revenue and relevant-cost framework described in Chapter 11.

Economic theory indicates that companies acting optimally should produce and sell units until the marginal revenue (the additional revenue from selling an additional unit based on the demand for a product) equals the marginal or variable cost (the additional cost of supplying an additional unit). The market price is the price that creates a demand for these optimal numbers of units. This chapter describes how managers evaluate demand at different prices, manage their costs to influence supply, and earn a profit.

Journal of Economic Theory
www.apnet.com/www/journal/
et.htm

MAJOR INFLUENCES ON PRICING

There are three major influences on pricing decisions: customers, competitors, and costs.

OBJECTIVE 1

Discuss the three major influences on pricing decisions

◆ **Customers.** Managers must always examine pricing problems through the eyes of their customers. A price increase may cause customers to reject a company's product and choose a competing or substitute product.

◆ **Competitors.** Competitors' reactions influence pricing decisions. At one extreme, a rival's prices and products may force a business to lower its prices to be competitive. At the other extreme, a business without a rival in a given situation can set higher prices. A business with knowledge of its rival's technology, plant capacity, and operating policies is able to estimate its rival's costs, which is valuable information in setting competitive prices.

Competitor analysis takes different forms. Many companies, including Ford, General Motors, Nutrasweet, PPG Industries, and Raychem have established departments to search out information on their competitors' financial performance, patents, technologies, revenue and cost structures, and strategic alliances. Competitors themselves and their customers, suppliers, and former employees are important sources of information. Another form of obtaining information is via reverse engineering—a process of analyzing and tearing apart competitors' products—to incorporate the best features, materials, and technology in a company's own designs.

Competition spans international borders. For example, when companies have excess capacity in their domestic markets, they often take an aggressive pricing policy in their export markets. Today, managers often take a global viewpoint, and it is increasingly common for them to consider both domestic and international rivals in making pricing decisions.

Nutrasweet
www.nutrasweetkelco.com

PPG Industries
www.ppg.com

Raychem
www.raychem.com

◆ **Costs.** Companies price products to exceed the costs of making them. The study of cost behaviour patterns gives insight into the income that results from different combinations of price and output quantities sold for a particular product.

Economic theory and surveys of how executives make pricing decisions reveal that companies weigh customers, competitors, and costs differently. Companies selling commodity-type products in highly competitive markets must accept the price determined by market forces. For example, sellers of wheat, rice, and soybeans have many competitors, each offering the identical product at the same price. The market sets the price, but cost data can help these sellers to decide, say, on the output level that best meets a company's particular objective.

In less competitive markets, managers have some discretion in setting prices. The pricing decision depends on how much customers value the product, the pricing strategies of competitors, and the costs of the product. The price of a product or service is the outcome of the interaction between *demand* for the product or service and its *supply*. Customers influence prices through their effect on demand. Costs influence prices because they affect supply. Competitors offer alternative or substitute products and so affect demand and price.

Chapter 1 described customer satisfaction, continuous improvement, and the dual internal/external focus as important, newly evolving themes in management. Pricing is an area where many of these themes explicitly come together. For example, charging lower prices for high-quality products is important for customer satisfaction, an external focus. But when prices are lower, costs must be reduced as well. Continuous improvement, an internal focus, is the key to keeping costs down.

PRODUCT COST CATEGORIES AND TIME HORIZON

OBJECTIVE 2

Distinguish between short-run and long-run pricing decisions

When reducing costs, a company must consider costs in all six value-chain business functions, from R&D to customer service. In computing the costs within these functions that are relevant in a pricing decision, the time horizon of the decision is critical. Most pricing decisions are either short-run or long-run. Short-run decisions include (1) pricing for a one-time-only special order with no long-term implications and (2) adjusting product mix and output volume in a competitive market. The time horizon used to compute those costs that differ among the alternatives for short-run decisions is typically six months or less but sometimes as long as a year. Long-run decisions include pricing a product in a major market where price setting has considerable leeway. A time horizon of a year or longer is used when computing relevant costs for these long-run decisions. Many pricing decisions have both short-run and long-run implications. We next examine short-run pricing decisions.

COSTING AND PRICING FOR THE SHORT RUN

A One-Time-Only Special Order

Consider a one-time-only special order from a customer to supply products for the next four months. Acceptance or rejection of the order will not affect the revenues (units sold or the selling price per unit) from existing sales outlets. The customer is unlikely to place any future sales orders.

Example: The National Tea Corporation (NTC) operates a plant with a monthly capacity of 1 million cases (each case consisting of 200 cans) of iced tea. Current production and sales are 600,000 cases per month. The selling price is $90 per case. The costs of R&D and of product and process design at NTC are negligible. Customer-service costs are also small and are included in marketing costs. All variable costs vary with respect to output units (cases), and production is equal to sales. The variable cost per case and the fixed cost per case (based on a production quantity of 600,000 cases per month) are as follows:

	Variable Cost per Case	Fixed Cost per Case	Variable and Fixed Cost per Case
Manufacturing costs:			
Direct materials costs	$ 7	—	$ 7
Packaging costs	18	—	18
Direct manufacturing labour costs	4	—	4
Manufacturing overhead costs	6	$13	19
Manufacturing costs	35	13	48
Marketing costs	5	16	21
Distribution costs	9	8	17
Full product costs	$49	$37	$86

Variable manufacturing overhead of $6 per case is the cost of power and utilities. Details of the fixed manufacturing overhead costs and their per-case unitized costs (based on a production quantity of 600,000 cases per month) are as follows:

	Total Fixed Manufacturing Overhead Costs	Fixed Manufacturing Overhead Cost per Case
Amortization and production support costs	$3,000,000	$ 5
Materials procurement costs	600,000	1
Salaries paid for process changeover	1,800,000	3
Product and process engineering costs	2,400,000	4
Total fixed manufacturing overhead costs	$7,800,000	$13

Canadian Tea (CT) is constructing a new plant to make iced tea in Toronto. The plant will not open for four months. CT's management, however, wants to start selling 250,000 cases of iced tea each month for the next four months in Canada. CT has asked NTC and two other companies to bid on this special order. From a manufacturing cost viewpoint, the iced tea to be made for CT is identical to that currently made by NTC.

If NTC makes the extra 250,000 cases, the existing total fixed manufacturing overhead ($7,800,000 per month) would continue to be incurred. In addition, NTC would incur a further $300,000 in fixed manufacturing overhead costs (materials procurement costs of $100,000 and process changeover costs of $200,000) each month. No additional costs will be required for R&D, design, marketing, distribution, or customer service. The 250,000 cases will be marketed by CT in Canada, where NTC does not sell its iced tea.

A vice-president of CT notifies each potential bidder that a bid above $45 per case will probably be noncompetitive. NTC knows that one of its competitors, with a highly efficient plant, has sizable idle capacity and will definitely bid for the contract. What price should NTC bid for the 250,000-case contract?

To compute the relevant costs for the bidding price decision, NTC systematically analyzes the costs in each business function of the value chain. In this example, only manufacturing costs are relevant. All other costs in the value chain will be unaffected if the special order is accepted, so they are irrelevant.

Exhibit 12-1 presents an analysis of the relevant costs. They include all manufacturing costs that will change in total if the special order is obtained: all direct and indirect variable manufacturing costs plus materials procurement costs and process changeover salaries related to the special order. *Existing* fixed manufacturing overhead costs are irrelevant. Why? Because these costs will not change if the special order is accepted. But the *additional* materials procurement and process changeover salaries of $300,000 per month for the special order are relevant, because these additional fixed manufacturing costs will be incurred only if the special order is accepted.

EXHIBIT 12-1
Monthly Relevant Costs for NTC: The 250,000-Case One-Time-Only Special Order

Direct materials (250,000 cases × $7)		$1,750,000
Packaging (250,000 cases × $18)		4,500,000
Direct manufacturing labour (250,000 cases × $4)		1,000,000
Variable manufacturing overhead (250,000 × $6)		1,500,000
Fixed manufacturing overhead:		
Materials procurement	$100,000	
Salaries paid for process changeover	200,000	
Total fixed manufacturing overhead		300,000
Total relevant costs		$9,050,000

Per case relevant costs: $9,050,000 ÷ 250,000 cases = $36.20

Exhibit 12-1 shows the total relevant costs of $9,050,000 per month (or $36.20 per case) for the 250,000-case special order. Any bid above $36.20 per case will improve NTC's profitability. For example, a successful bid of $40 per case, well under CT's ceiling of $45 per case, will add $950,000 to NTC's monthly operating income: 250,000 × ($40 − $36.20) = $950,000. Note again how unit costs can mislead. The table on p. 416 reports total manufacturing costs to be $48 per case. The $48 cost might erroneously suggest that a bid of $45 per case for the Canadian Tea special order will result in NTC sustaining a $3 per case loss on the contract. Why erroneous? Because total manufacturing cost per case includes $13 of fixed manufacturing cost per case that will not be incurred on the 250,000-case special order. These costs are hence irrelevant for the special-order bid.

Cost data, though key information in NTC's decision on the price to bid, are not the only inputs. NTC must also consider business rivals and their likely bids. For example, if NTC knows that its under-capacity rival plans to bid $39 per case, NTC will bid $38 per case instead of $40 per case.

COSTING AND PRICING FOR THE LONG RUN

Bechtel Corporation
www.bechtel.com

Many pricing decisions are made for the long run. Buyers—whether a person buying a box of Corn Flakes, a construction company, such as Bechtel Corporation, buying a fleet of tractors, or General Foods Corporation buying audit services—prefer stable prices over an extended time horizon. A stable price reduces the need for continuous monitoring of suppliers' prices. Greater price stability also improves planning and builds long-run buyer-seller relationships.

Calculating Product Costs

Obtaining accurate product cost information is essential to a manager making a pricing decision. In industries such as oil and gas and mining, competitive forces set the price for a product, and knowledge of long-run product costs can guide decisions about entering or remaining in the market. In other industries such as specialized machines, appliances, and automobiles, managers have some control over the price charged for a product, and long-run product costs can be used as a base for setting that price.

Consider the Astel Computer Corporation. Astel manufactures two brands of personal computers (PCs)—Deskpoint and Provalue. Deskpoint is Astel's top-of-the-line product, a Pentium-chip-based PC sold through computer dealers to large organizations and government accounts. Our analysis focuses on pricing Provalue, a less powerful 486 DX-chip-based machine sold through catalogues and mass merchandisers to individual consumers and small organizations.

The manufacturing costs of Provalue are calculated using the activity-based costing (ABC) approach described in Chapters 4 and 5. Astel has three direct manufacturing cost categories (direct materials, direct manufacturing labour, and direct machining costs) and three indirect manufacturing cost pools (ordering and receiving, testing and inspection, and rework) in its accounting system. Astel treats machining costs as a direct cost of Provalue because it is manufactured on machines that are used for no other products. The following table summarizes the activity cost pools, the cost driver for each activity, and the cost per unit of cost driver which Astel uses to allocate manufacturing overhead costs to products.

Manufacturing Activity	Description of Activity	Cost Driver	Cost per Unit of Cost Driver
1. Ordering and receiving	Placing orders, receiving, and paying for components	Number of orders	$80 per order
2. Testing and inspection	Testing components and final product	Testing-hours	$2 per testing-hour
3. Rework	Correcting and fixing errors and defects	Units reworked	$100 per unit reworked

Astel uses a long-run time horizon to price Provalue. Over this horizon, Astel's management views direct materials costs and direct manufacturing labour costs as variable with respect to the units of Provalue produced, and manufacturing overhead costs as variable with respect to their chosen cost drivers. For example, ordering and receiving costs vary with the number of orders. Staff members responsible for placing orders can be reassigned or laid off in the long run if fewer orders need to be placed. Direct machining costs (rent paid on leased machines) do not vary over this time horizon for the relevant range of production; they are fixed long-run costs.

Astel has no beginning or ending inventory of Provalue in 2000 and manufactures and sells 150,000 units. How does Astel calculate Provalue's manufacturing costs? It uses the following information, which indicates the resources used to manufacture Provalue in 2000:

1. Direct materials costs per unit of Provalue are $460.
2. Direct manufacturing labour costs per unit of Provalue are $64.
3. Direct fixed costs of machines used exclusively for the manufacture of Provalue are $11,400,000.
4. Number of orders placed to purchase components required for the manufacture of Provalue is 22,500. (We assume for simplicity that Provalue has 450 components supplied by different suppliers, and that 50 orders are placed for each component to match Provalue's production schedule.)
5. Number of testing-hours used for Provalue is 4,500,000 (150,000 Provalue units are tested for 30 hours per unit).
6. Number of units of Provalue reworked during the year is 12,000 (8% of the 150,000 units manufactured).

The detailed calculations underlying each of these numbers are shown in Exhibit 12-2. This exhibit indicates that the total costs of manufacturing Provalue are $102 million, and the manufacturing cost per unit of Provalue is $680. Manufacturing, however, is just one business function in the value chain. For setting long-run prices and for managing costs, Astel determines the full product costs of Provalue.

For brevity, we do not present any detailed analyses or calculations for the other value-chain functions. Astel chooses cost drivers and cost pools in each value-chain

EXHIBIT 12-2
Manufacturing Costs of Provalue in 2000 Based on an Activity Analysis

	Total Manufacturing Costs for 150,000 Units (1)	Manufacturing Cost per Unit (2) = (1) ÷ 150,000
Direct manufacturing costs:		
Direct materials costs (150,000 units × $460)	$ 69,000,000	$460
Direct manufacturing labour costs (150,000 units × $64)	9,600,000	64
Direct machining costs (fixed costs of $11,400,000)	11,400,000	76
Direct manufacturing costs	90,000,000	600
Manufacturing overhead costs:		
Ordering and receiving costs (22,500 orders × $80)	1,800,000	12
Testing and inspection costs (4,500,000 hours × $2)	9,000,000	60
Rework costs (12,000 units × $100)	1,200,000	8
Manufacturing overhead costs	12,000,000	80
Total manufacturing costs	$102,000,000	$680

function to measure the cause-and-effect relationship between the activities and costs within each activity's cost pool. Costs are allocated to Provalue on the basis of the quantity of cost driver units that Provalue requires. Exhibit 12-3 summarizes the product operating income statement for Provalue for the year 2000 based on an activity analysis of costs in all value-chain functions (supporting calculations for non-manufacturing value-chain functions are not given). Astel earned $15 million from Provalue, or $100 per unit sold. We next consider the role of costs in long-run pricing decisions.

Alternative Long-Run Pricing Approaches

The starting point for pricing decisions can be:

1. Market-based
2. Cost-based (also called cost-plus)

The market-based approach to pricing *starts* by asking: Given what our customers want and how our competitors will react to what we do, what price should we charge? The cost-based approach to pricing *starts* by asking: What does it cost us to make this product, and hence what price should we charge that will recoup our costs and produce a desired profit? Both approaches consider customers, competitors, and costs. Only their starting points differ.

In very competitive markets (for example, oil and gas and airlines) the market-based approach is logical. The items produced or services provided by one company are very similar to those produced or provided by others, so companies have no influence over the prices to charge. In other industries, where there is more product differentiation (for example, automobiles, management consulting, and legal services) firms have some discretion over prices, products, and services. Companies choose prices and product and service features on the basis of anticipated customer and competitor reactions. A final decision on price, product, and service is made after evaluating these external influences on pricing along with the costs to produce and sell the product.

EXHIBIT 12-3

Product Profitability of Provalue in 2000 Based on Value-Chain Activity Analysis

	Total for 150,000 Units (1)	Per Unit (2) = (1) ÷ 150,000
Revenues	$150,000,000	$1,000
Cost of goods sold* (from Exhibit 12-2):		
Direct materials costs	69,000,000	460
Direct manufacturing labour costs	9,600,000	64
Direct machining costs	11,400,000	76
Manufacturing overhead costs	12,000,000	80
Cost of goods sold	102,000,000	680
Operating costs:		
R&D costs	5,400,000	36
Design costs of products and processes	6,000,000	40
Marketing costs	15,000,000	100
Distribution costs	3,600,000	24
Customer service costs	3,000,000	20
Operating costs	33,000,000	220
Full product costs	135,000,000	900
Operating income	$ 15,000,000	$ 100

*Cost of goods sold = total manufacturing costs, since there is no beginning or ending inventory of Provalue in 2000.

Under the cost-plus approach, price is first computed on the basis of the costs to produce and sell a product. Typically, a markup, representing a reasonable return, is added to cost. Often, the price is then modified on the basis of anticipated customer reaction to alternative price levels and the prices charged by competitors for similar products. In short, market forces dictate the eventual size of the markup and thus the final price.

TARGET COSTING FOR TARGET PRICING

An important form of market-based price is the *target price*. A **target price** is the estimated price for a product (or service) that potential customers will be willing to pay. This estimate is based on an understanding of customers' perceived value for a product and competitors' responses. A **target operating income per unit** is the operating income that a company wants to earn on each unit of a product (or service) sold. The target price leads to a *target cost*. A **target cost per unit** is the estimated long-run cost per unit of a product (or service) that, when sold at the target price, enables the company to achieve the target operating income per unit. Target cost per unit is derived by subtracting the target operating income per unit from the target price.

What relevant costs should we include in the target cost calculations? *All* costs, both variable and fixed. Why? Because in the long run, a company's prices and revenues must recover all its costs. If not, the company's best alternative is to shut down. Relative to the shutting-down alternative, all costs, whether fixed or variable, are relevant.

Target cost per unit is often lower than the existing full product cost per unit. To achieve the target cost per unit and the target operating income per unit, the organization must improve its products and processes. Target costing is widely used among different industries around the world. Ford, General Motors, Mercedes, Toyota, and Daihatsu in the automobile industry, Matsushita, Panasonic, and Sharp in the electronics industry, and Compaq and Toshiba in the personal computer industry are examples of companies that use target pricing and target costing.

Implementing Target Pricing and Target Costing

Developing target prices and target costs requires the following four steps:

◆ **Step 1.** Develop a product that satisfies the needs of potential customers.

◆ **Step 2.** Choose a *target price* based on customers' perceived value for the product and the prices competitors charge, and a *target operating income per unit.*

◆ **Step 3.** Derive a *target cost per unit* by subtracting the target operating income per unit from the target price.

◆ **Step 4.** Perform *value engineering* to achieve target costs. **Value engineering** is a systematic evaluation of all aspects of the value-chain business functions, with the objective of reducing costs while satisfying customer needs. Value engineering can result in improvements in product designs, changes in materials specifications, or modifications in process methods.

We illustrate the four steps for target pricing and target costing using the Astel Computer's example introduced earlier in the chapter.

◆ **Step 1:** *Product planning for Provalue.* Astel is in the process of planning design modifications for Provalue. Astel is very concerned about severe price competition from several competitors.

◆ **Step 2:** *Target price of Provalue.* Astel expects its competitors to lower the prices of PCs that compete against Provalue by 15%. Astel's management believes that it must respond aggressively by reducing Provalue's price by 20%, from $1,000 per unit to $800 per unit. At this lower price, Astel's marketing manager forecasts an increase in annual sales from 150,000 to 200,000 units.

◆ **Step 3:** *Target cost per unit of Provalue.* Astel's management wants a 10% target operating income on sales revenues.

OBJECTIVE 3

Describe the target-costing approach to pricing

Target price. Estimated price for a product (or service) that potential customers will be willing to pay

Target operating income per unit. Operating income that a company wants to earn on each unit of a product (or service) sold.

Target cost per unit. Estimated long-run cost per unit of a product (or service) that when sold at the target price enables the company to achieve the targeted income per unit. Derived by subtracting the target operating income per unit from the target price.

Mercedes Benz
www.mercedes-net.com

Daihatsu
www.infoweb.or.jp/DAIHATSU

Matsushita
Panasonic Corporation
www.panasonic.com

Sharp
www.sharp-usa.com
www.sharp.co.jp

Compaq
www.compaq.com

Value engineering. Systematic evaluation of all aspects of the value-chain business functions, with the objective of reducing costs while satisfying customer needs.

Total target sales revenues	= $800 × 200,000 units = $160,000,000
Total target operating income	= 10% × $160,000,000 = $16,000,000
Target operating income per unit	= $16,000,000 ÷ 200,000 units = $80 per unit
Target cost per unit	= Target price − target operating income per unit
	= $800 − $80 = $720
Total current costs of Provalue	= $135,000,000 (from Exhibit 12-3)
Current cost per unit of Provalue	= $135,000,000 ÷ 150,000 units = $900 per unit

The target cost per unit of $720 is substantially lower than Provalue's existing unit cost of $900. The goal is to find ways to reduce the cost per unit of Provalue by $180, from $900 to $720. The challenge in step 4 is to achieve the target cost through value engineering.

◆ **Step 4:** *Value engineering for Provalue.* An important element of Astel's value engineering is determining the kind of low-end PC that will meet the needs of potential customers. For example, the existing Provalue design accommodates various upgrades that can make the PC run faster and perform calculations more quickly. It also comes with special audio features. An essential first step in the value engineering process is to determine whether potential customers are willing to pay the price for these features. Customer feedback indicates that customers do not value Provalue's extra features. They want Astel to redesign Provalue into a no-frills PC and sell it at a much lower price. Value engineering at Astel then proceeds with cross-functional teams consisting of marketing managers, product designers, manufacturing engineers, and production supervisors making suggestions for design improvements and process modifications. Cost accountants estimate the savings in costs that would result from the proposed changes.

Managers often find the distinction between value-added and non-value-added activities and costs introduced in Chapter 2 useful in value engineering. A *value-added cost* is a cost that customers perceive as adding value, or utility (usefulness), to a product or service. Determining value-added costs requires identifying attributes that customers perceive to be important. For Provalue, these attributes include the PC's features and its price. Activities undertaken within the company (such as the manufacturing line) influence the attributes that customers value. Astel assesses whether each activity adds value or not. Activities and the costs of these activities do not always fall neatly into value-added or non-value-added categories. Some costs fall in the gray area in between, and include both value-added and nonvalue-added components. The following examples are drawn from classifications made by operating personnel at a General Electric medical equipment assembly plant:

Category	Examples
Value-added costs	Costs of assembly, design, tools, and machinery
Non-value-added costs	Costs of rework, expediting, special delivery, and obsolete inventory
Gray area	Costs of testing, materials movement, and ordering

In the Provalue example, direct materials, direct manufacturing labour, and machining costs are value-added costs; ordering and testing costs fall in the gray area (customers perceive some portion of but not all of these costs as necessary for adding value); while rework costs are non-value-added costs.

Value engineering seeks to reduce or eliminate non-value-added activities and hence non-value-added costs by reducing the cost drivers of the non-value-added activities. For example, to reduce rework costs, Astel must reduce rework-hours. Value engineering also focuses on achieving greater efficiency in value-added activities to reduce value-added costs. For example, to reduce direct manufacturing labour costs, Astel must reduce the time it takes to make Provalue. But how should Astel reduce rework time and direct manufacturing labour time? We focus on these issues next.

General Electric
www.ge.com

Achieving Target Costs Using Activity-Based Management at Carrier Corporation*

Carrier Corporation, a subsidiary of United Technologies' Company, is the largest manufacturer of air-conditioning and heating products in the United States. Although known for the high quality of its products, Carrier operates in a highly competitive market, so it must also keep its prices comparatively low. A key to keeping prices low is keeping costs low, thus Carrier establishes target costs for its products. It forms cross-functional teams drawn from the marketing, design, manufacturing, engineering, and accounting functions, and uses activity-based costing to evaluate and monitor its progress in achieving target costs.

Carrier has undertaken multiple initiatives to reach its target-costing goals, focused heavily on reducing the complexity of its operations.

1. **Product design.** Employing value-engineering techniques, Carrier's product design teams work with manufacturing to introduce product designs that use cost-effective manufacturing processes. For example, one new product at Carrier's McMinville plant required three design attempts before meeting its target cost. Designers had to reduce the number of parts required to make the product from 160 to 60, thereby reducing the costs of ordering, materials handling, coordination, and inspection.
2. **Just-in-time (JIT) production.** Carrier has implemented JIT production methods to reduce costs of materials and work-in-process inventories, as well as materials handling costs.
3. **Parts Standardization.** Carrier's parts standardization program aims to reduce the number of components and manufacturing processes. For example, the plant currently maintains 280 different circuit breakers and 580 different fasteners. Carrier's goal—to eliminate over 50% of these components. Carrier uses an activity-based costing system (with its distinctions of output-unit level, batch-level, product-sustaining and facility-sustaining costs) to estimate savings in direct and indirect costs from using a common component in place of three existing components.
4. **Strategic outsourcing.** Using activity-based costing data, Carrier evaluates components it should make in-house and those it should outsource. For example, Carrier's decision to purchase pre-painted sheet metal rather than paint the sheet metal itself reduced materials handling, inspection, inventory holding, and environment costs and improved quality.

*Adapted from D.W. Swenson, "Managing Costs Through Complexity Reduction at Carrier Corporation," *Management Accounting* (April 1998).

Cost Incurrence and Locked-In Costs

Two key concepts in value engineering and in managing value-added and non-value-added costs are *cost incurrence* and *locked-in costs*. **Cost incurrence** occurs when a resource is sacrificed or used up. Costing systems emphasize cost incurrence. They recognize and record costs only when costs are incurred. Astel's costing system, for example, recognizes the direct materials costs of Provalue as each unit of Provalue is assembled and sold. But Provalue's direct materials costs per unit are determined much earlier when designers finalize the components that will go into Provalue. Direct materials costs per unit of Provalue are *locked in* (or *designed in*) at the product design stage. **Locked-in costs (designed-in costs)** are those costs that have not yet been incurred but that will be incurred in the future on the basis of decisions that have already been made.

Why is it important to distinguish between when costs are locked in and when costs are incurred? Because it is difficult to alter or reduce costs that have already

OBJECTIVE 4

Distinguish between cost incurrence and locked-in costs

Cost incurrence. Occurs when a resource is sacrificed or used up.

Locked-in costs (designed-in costs). Costs that have not yet been incurred but that will be incurred in the future on the basis of decisions that have already been made.

been locked in. For example, if Astel experiences quality problems during manufacturing, its ability to improve quality and reduce scrap may be limited by Provalue's design. Scrap costs are incurred during manufacturing, but they may be locked in by a faulty design. Similarly, in the software industry, costs of producing software are often locked in at the design and analysis stage. Costly and difficult-to-fix errors that appear during coding and testing are frequently locked in by bad designs.

Other examples of how Astel's design decisions affect costs include the following:

1. Design decisions influence direct materials costs through the choices of printed circuit boards and add-on features used in Provalue. Better designs also reduce both product failures in the plant and the time it takes to rework defective products.

2. Designing Provalue so that it is easy to manufacture and easy to assemble decreases direct manufacturing labour costs. For example, designing Provalue so that various parts snap-fit together (rather than having various parts soldered together) saves manufacturing labour time.

3. Designing Provalue with fewer components reduces ordering and materials handling costs.

4. Simplifying the Provalue design decreases the time required for testing and inspection.

5. Designing Provalue to reduce the need for repairs as well as the time it takes to service and repair Provalue at customer sites reduces customer service costs.

Exhibit 12-4 illustrates how the locked-in cost curve and the cost-incurrence curve might appear in the case of Provalue. (The numbers underlying the graph are assumed.) The bottom curve plots the cumulative costs per unit incurred in different business functions. The top curve plots the cumulative costs locked in. Both curves deal with the same total cumulative costs per unit. The graph emphasizes the wide divergence between the time when costs are locked in and the time when those costs are incurred. In our example, once the product and processes are designed, more than 86% (say, $780 \div $900) of the unit costs of Provalue are locked in when only about 8% (say, $76 \div $900) of the unit costs are actually incurred. For example, at the end of the design stage, costs such as direct materials; direct manufacturing

EXHIBIT 12-4
Pattern of Cost Incurrence and Locked-In Costs for Provalue

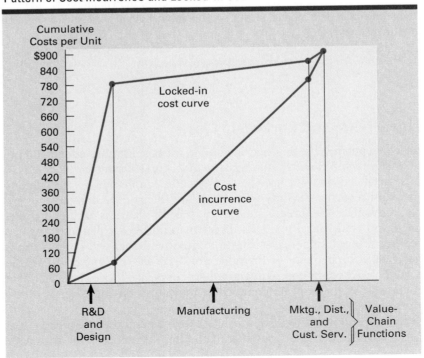

labour; direct machining; and many manufacturing, marketing, distribution, and customer service overheads are all locked in. To reduce total costs, Astel must act to modify the design before costs get locked in.

We caution that it is not always the case that costs are locked in early in the design stage as was the case with Provalue. In some industries, such as mining, costs are locked in and incurred at about the same time. When costs are not locked in early, cost reduction activities can be successful right up to the time that costs are incurred. In these industries, the key to lowering costs is improved operational efficiency and productivity rather than better design.

ACHIEVING THE TARGET COST PER UNIT FOR PROVALUE

Astel's value engineering teams focus their cost reduction efforts on analyzing the Provalue design. Their goal? To design a high-quality, highly reliable machine with fewer features that meets customers' price expectations and achieves target cost.

Provalue is discontinued. In its place, Astel introduces Provalue II. Provalue II has fewer components than does Provalue and is easier to manufacture and test. The following tables compare the direct costs and the manufacturing overhead costs and cost drivers of Provalue and Provalue II. In place of the 150,000 Provalue units manufactured and sold in 2000, Astel expects to make and sell 200,000 Provalue II units in 2001.

DIRECT COSTS

	Costs per Unit		
Cost Category	Provalue	Provalue II	Explanation of Costs for Provalue II
1. Direct materials	$460	$385	The Provalue II design will use a simplified main printed circuit board, fewer components, and no audio features.
2. Direct manufacturing labour	$ 64	$ 53	Provalue II will require less assembly time.
3. Direct machining costs	$ 76	$ 57	Machining costs are fixed at $11,400,000. Astel can use the machine capacity to produce 200,000 units of Provalue II. The new design will enable Astel to manufacture each unit of Provalue II in less time than a unit of Provalue. Direct machining costs per unit of Provalue II will equal $57 ($11,400,000 ÷ 200,000).

MANUFACTURING OVERHEAD COSTS

Cost Driver	Quantity of Cost Driver		Explanation for Quantity of Cost Driver Used by Provalue II
	Provalue*	Provalue II	
1. Number of orders	22,500	21,250	Astel will place 50 orders for each of the 425 components in Provalue II. Total orders for Provalue II will equal 21,250 (425 × 50).
2. Testing-hours	4,500,000	3,000,000	Provalue II is easier to test and will require 15 testing-hours per unit. Total number of expected testing-hours will equal 3,000,000 (15 × 200,000).
3. Units reworked	12,000	13,000	Provalue II will have a lower rework rate of 6.5%, because it is easier to manufacture. Total units reworked will equal 13,000 (6.5% × 200,000).

*From Exhibit 12-2.

Note that value engineering activities reduce both value-added and non-value-added costs. For example, direct manufacturing labour cost per unit, a value-added cost, is reduced by designing a product that requires fewer direct manufacturing labour-hours (the cost driver for direct manufacturing labour costs). Rework cost per unit, a non-value-added cost, is reduced by simplifying the design to reduce defects during manufacturing and hence rework-hours (the cost driver for rework costs).

Exhibit 12-5 presents the target manufacturing costs of Provalue II, assuming no change in the cost per unit of the cost drivers. (The Problem for Self-Study considers

EXHIBIT 12-5
Target Manufacturing Costs of Provalue II

	Provalue II		Provalue
	Estimated Manufacturing Costs for 200,000 Units (1)	Estimated Manufacturing Costs per Unit (2) = (1) ÷ 200,000	Manufacturing Costs per Unit (Exhibit 12-2, Column 2) (3)
Direct manufacturing costs:			
Direct materials costs (200,000 units × $385)	$ 77,000,000	$385.00	$460.00
Direct manufacturing labour costs (200,000 units × $53)	10,600,000	53.00	64.00
Direct machining costs (fixed costs of $11,400,000)	11,400,000	57.00	76.00
Direct manufacturing costs	99,000,000	495.00	600.00
Manufacturing overhead costs:			
Ordering and receiving costs (21,250 orders × $80)	1,700,000	8.50	12.00
Testing and inspection costs (3,000,000 hours × $2)	6,000,000	30.00	60.00
Rework costs (13,000 units × $100)	1,300,000	6.50	8.00
Manufacturing overhead costs	9,000,000	45.00	80.00
Total manufacturing costs	$108,000,000	$540.00	$680.00

changes in the cost per unit of the cost drivers.) For comparison, Exhibit 12-5 also reproduces the manufacturing costs per unit of Provalue from Exhibit 12-2. Exhibit 12-5 shows that the new design is expected to reduce the manufacturing cost per unit by $140 to $540 from $680. A similar analysis (not presented) estimates the expected effect of the new design on costs in other value-chain business functions. Exhibit 12-6 shows that the estimated full product cost per unit equals $720—the

EXHIBIT 12-6
Target Product Profitability of Provalue II in 2001

	Total for 200,000 Units (1)	Per Unit (2) = (1) ÷ 200,000
Revenues	$160,000,000	$800
Cost of goods sold* (from Exhibit 12-5):		
Direct materials costs	77,000,000	385
Direct manufacturing labour costs	10,600,000	53
Direct machining costs	11,400,000	57
Manufacturing overhead costs	9,000,000	45
Cost of goods sold	108,000,000	540
Operating costs:		
R&D costs	4,000,000	20
Design of products and processes costs	6,000,000	30
Marketing costs	18,000,000	90
Distribution costs	5,000,000	25
Customer service costs	3,000,000	15
Operating costs	36,000,000	180
Full product costs	144,000,000	720
Operating income	$ 16,000,000	$ 80

*Cost of goods sold = total manufacturing costs (since we assume no beginning or ending inventory for Provalue II in 2001).

target cost per unit for Provalue II. Astel's goal is to sell Provalue II at the target price, achieve target cost, and earn the target operating income.[1]

As illustrated in the last section, Astel uses an external market-based approach in its long-run pricing decisions. An alternative approach is to determine a cost-based price. Managers can turn to numerous pricing formulas based on cost. The general formula for setting a price adds a markup to the cost base:

OBJECTIVE 5

Describe the cost-plus approach to pricing

Cost base	$X
Markup component	Y
Prospective selling price	$X + Y

Cost-Plus Target Rate of Return on Investment

Consider a cost-based pricing formula that Astel could use for Provalue II. Assume that Astel's engineers have redesigned Provalue into Provalue II as described earlier and that Astel uses a 12% markup on the full product cost per unit in developing the prospective selling price.

Cost base (full product cost per unit, from Exhibit 12-6)	$720.00
Markup component (12% × $720)	86.40
Prospective selling price	$806.40

How is the markup percentage of 12% determined? One approach is to choose a markup to earn a *target rate of return on investment*. The **target rate of return on investment** is the target operating income that an organization must earn divided by invested capital. Invested capital can be defined in many ways. In this chapter, we define it as total assets (long-term or fixed assets plus current assets). Companies usually specify the target rate of return required on investments. Suppose Astel's (pretax) target rate of return on investment is 18%. Assume that the capital investment needed for Provalue II is $96 million. The target operating income that Astel must earn from Provalue II can then be calculated as follows:

Target rate of return on investment. The target operating income that an organization must earn divided by invested capital.

Invested capital	$96,000,000
Target rate of return on investment	18%
Total target operating income (18% × $96,000,000)	$17,280,000
Target operating income per unit of Provalue II ($17,280,000 ÷ 200,000 units)	$ 86.40

The calculation indicates that Astel would like to earn a target operating income of $86.40 on each unit of Provalue II. What markup does this return amount to? Expressed as a percentage of the full product cost per unit of $720, the markup is equal to 12% ($86.40 ÷ $720). Do not confuse the 18% target rate of return on investment with the 12% markup percentage. The 18% target rate of return on investment expresses Astel's expected operating income as a percentage of investment. The 12% markup expresses operating income per unit as a percentage of the full product cost per unit. Astel first calculates the target rate of return on investment, and then determines the markup percentage.

Companies sometimes find it difficult to determine the capital invested to support a product. Computing invested capital requires allocations of investments in equipment and buildings (used for design, production, marketing, distribution, and customer service) to individual products—a difficult and sometimes arbitrary task. Some companies therefore prefer to use alternative cost bases and markup percentages that do not require calculations of invested capital to set price.

[1]For a description of target pricing, target costing, and value engineering in the automobile industry, see R. Cooper, "Nissan Motor Company, Ltd.: Target Costing System," Harvard Business School Case N9-194-040.

Alternative Cost-Plus Methods

We illustrate these alternatives using the Astel example. Exhibit 12-7 separates the cost per unit for each value-chain business function into its variable and fixed components (without providing details of the calculations). The following table illustrates some alternative cost bases and markup percentages.

Cost Base	Estimated Cost per Unit of Provalue II (1)	Markup Percentage (2)	Markup Component for Provalue II (3) = (1) × (2)	Prospective Selling Price for Provalue II (4) = (1) + (3)
Variable manufacturing costs	$483.00	65%	$313.95	$796.95
Variable product costs	547.00	45	246.15	793.15
Manufacturing function costs	540.00	50	270.00	810.00
Full product cost	720.00	12	86.40	806.40

To illustrate the markup calculations, we have assumed (but not derived) the markup percentages in the table. The different cost bases and markup percentages that we use in the table give prospective selling prices that are relatively close to one another. In practice, a company will choose a cost base that it regards as reliable, and a markup percentage on the basis of its experience in pricing products to recover its costs and earn a desired return on investment. For example, a company may choose a full product cost base if it is unsure about variable and fixed cost distinctions.

The markup percentages in the table vary a great deal, from a high of 65% on variable manufacturing costs to a low of 12% on full product costs. Why? Because the markup based on variable manufacturing costs takes into account the need to earn a profit, and to recoup fixed manufacturing costs and other business function costs such as R&D, marketing, and distribution. The greater these costs relative to variable manufacturing costs, the higher the markup percentage. The markup percentage on full product costs is much lower. Why? Because full product costs already include all costs incurred to sell the product. The precise markup percentage also depends on the competitiveness of the product market. Markups and profit margins tend to be lower the more competitive the market.

Surveys indicate that most managers use full product costs (see the Surveys of Company Practice on page 430)—that is, they include both fixed costs per unit and variable costs per unit in the cost base when making their pricing decisions. The

EXHIBIT 12-7
Estimated Cost Structure for Provalue II

Business Function	Variable Cost per Unit	Fixed Cost per Unit*	Business Function Cost per Unit
R&D	$ 8.00	$ 12.00	$ 20.00
Design of product/process	10.00	20.00	30.00
Manufacturing	483.00	57.00	540.00
Marketing	25.00	65.00	90.00
Distribution	15.00	10.00	25.00
Customer service	6.00	9.00	15.00
Product costs	$547.00	$173.00	$720.00
	↑ Variable product cost per unit	↑ Fixed product cost per unit	↑ Full product cost per unit

*Based on budgeted annual production of 200,000 units.

advantages cited for including fixed costs per unit for pricing decisions include the following:

1. **Full product cost recovery.** For long-run pricing decisions, full product costs inform managers of the bare minimum costs they need to recover to continue in business rather than shut down. Using variable costs as a base does not give managers this information. There is then a temptation to engage in excessive long-run price cutting as long as prices give a positive contribution margin. Long-run price cutting, however, may result in long-run revenues being less than long-run (full product) costs, resulting in the company going out of business.

2. **Price stability.** Managers believe that full-cost formula pricing promotes price stability, because it limits the ability of managers to cut prices. Managers prefer price stability because it facilitates planning.

3. **Simplicity.** A full-cost formula for pricing does not require a detailed analysis of cost behaviour patterns to separate costs into fixed and variable components for each product. Calculating variable costs for each product is expensive and prone to errors. For these reasons, many managers believe that full-cost formula pricing meets the cost-benefit test.

Including unit fixed costs when pricing is not without its problems. Allocating fixed costs to products can be somewhat arbitrary. Calculating fixed cost per unit requires an estimate of expected future sales quantities. If actual sales fall short of this estimate, the actual full product cost per unit could exceed price.

Cost-Plus Pricing and Target Pricing

The selling prices computed under cost-plus pricing are *prospective* prices. For example, suppose Astel's initial product design results in a $750 cost for Provalue II. Assuming a 12% markup, Astel sets a prospective price of $840 [$750 + (12% × $750)]. Since the personal computer market is reasonably competitive, customer and competitor reactions to this price may force Astel to reduce the markup percentage, and the price to $800. Alternatively, Astel may redesign Provalue II to reduce cost to $720 per unit, as in our example, and achieve a markup of $80 per unit. The eventual design and cost-plus price balance the conflicting tensions among costs, markup, and customer reactions.

The target pricing approach eliminates the need to go back and forth among cost-plus prospective prices, customer reactions, and design and cost modifications. Instead, the target pricing approach first determines product characteristics and price on the basis of customer preferences and competitor responses. The target price then serves to focus and motivate managers to achieve the target cost to earn the target operating income. Sometimes the target cost is not achieved. Managers must then redesign the product, adjust the price, or work with a smaller margin.

Suppliers who provide relatively unique products and services—accountants and management consultants, for example—frequently use cost-plus pricing. Professional service firms set prices on the basis of hourly cost-plus billing rates of partners, managers, and associates. These prices are, however, reduced in competitive situations. Professional service firms also consider a multi-year client perspective when choosing prices. Chartered accountants, for example, may charge a client a low price initially and higher prices later.

Refined cost driver and cost information play an important role in both cost-plus pricing and target costing and pricing. The identification of cost drivers is critical as managers do value engineering to *cost down* their products—to reduce the cost of a product while still satisfying customer expectations.

CONSIDERATIONS OTHER THAN COSTS IN PRICING DECISIONS

Consider the prices airlines charge for a round-trip flight from Toronto to Calgary. A coach-class ticket for the flight is $400 if the passenger stays in Calgary over a Saturday night. It is $1,500 if the passenger returns without staying over a Saturday night. Can this price difference be explained by the difference in the cost to the airlines of

Differences in Pricing Practices and Cost Management Methods in Various Countries

Surveys* of financial officers of the largest industrial companies in several countries indicate similarities and differences in pricing practices across the globe. The use of cost-based pricing appears to be more prevalent in the United States than in Ireland, Japan, and the United Kingdom.

Some Japanese survey data indicate that market-based target pricing practices vary considerably across industries. While a majority of Japanese companies in assembly-type operations (for example, electronics and automobiles) use target costing for pricing, it is far less prevalent in Japanese process-type industries (for example, chemicals, oil, and steel). Japanese companies use value engineering more frequently and involve designers more often when estimating costs. When costs are used for pricing decisions, the pattern is consistent—overwhelmingly, companies across the globe use full costs rather than variable costs.

Ranking of Factors Primarily Used to Price Products
(1 is most important)

	United States	Japan	Ireland	United Kingdom
Market-based	2	1	1	1
Cost-based	1	2	2	2

Use of Value Engineering and Designers in Cost Management

	Australia	Japan	United Kingdom
Percentage of companies that use value engineering or analysis for cost reduction	24	58	29
Percentage of companies in which designers are involved in estimating costs	25	46	32

Ranking of Cost Methods Used in Pricing Decisions
(1 is most important)

	United States	United Kingdom	Ireland
Full-product-cost-based	1	1	1
Variable-cost-based	2	2	2

*Adapted from Management Accounting Research Group, "Investigation into the Actual State of Target Costing, Corporate Accounting," (Working Paper, Kobe University, Japan, May 1992); Blayney, P., and I. Yokoyama, "Comparative Analysis of Japanese and Australian Cost Accounting and Management Practices," (Working Paper, The University of Sydney, Sydney, Australia, 1991); Grant, Thornton, *Survey of American Manufacturers*, (New York: Grant Thornton, 1992); Cornick, M., W. Cooper, and S. Wilson, "How do Companies Analyze Overhead," *Management Accounting* (June 1998); Mills, R., and C. Sweeting, "Pricing Decisions in Practice: How Are They Made in U.K. Manufacturing and Service Companies?" (London, U.K.: Chartered Institute of Management Accountants, Occasional Paper, 1988); Drury, C., S. Braund, P. Osborne, and M. Tayles, A Survey of Management Accounting Practices in UK Manufacturing Companies, (London, U.K.: Chartered Association of Certified Accountants, 1993)

OBJECTIVE 6

Describe two pricing practices in which noncost reasons are important when setting price

these round-trip flights? No, it costs the airline the same amount of money to transport the passenger from Toronto to Calgary and back regardless of whether the passenger stays in Calgary over a Saturday night. How then can we explain this difference in price? We must recognize the potential for price discrimination.

Price discrimination is the practice of charging some customers a higher price than is charged to other customers. How does price discrimination work in our airline example? The demand for airline tickets comes from two main sources: business travellers and pleasure travellers. Business travellers need to travel in order to conduct business on behalf of their companies. They generally travel to their destinations and return home within the same week immediately after completing their work, because time is very important to them. These aspects make business travellers' demand for air travel relatively insensitive to prices. The insensitivity of demand to price changes is called *demand inelasticity*. Airlines can charge business travellers higher fares because the higher fares have little effect on demand and earn higher operating income for the airlines.

Pleasure travellers have a less pressing need to return home during the week—in fact, they generally prefer to spend weekends at their destinations. Since they pay for their tickets themselves, they are much more sensitive to price than the business traveller (demand is more price-elastic). For pleasure travellers, it is profitable for the airlines to keep fares low to stimulate demand. Requiring a Saturday night stay distinguishes between the two customer segments. The airline company price-discriminates between the two market segments to take advantage of the different sensitivities to prices exhibited by the business and pleasure travellers. Price differences exist even though there is no cost difference in serving the two segments.

Price discrimination. Practice of charging some customers a higher price than is charged to other customers.

In addition to price discrimination, pricing decisions also consider other non-cost considerations such as capacity constraints. **Peak-load pricing** is the practice of charging a higher price for the same product or service when demand approaches physical capacity limits. That is, the prices charged during busy periods (when loads on the system are high) are greater than the prices charged when slack or excess capacity is available. Peak-load pricing can be found in the telephone, telecommunication, hotel, car rental, and electric utility industries. The following are the daily rental rates charged by the Discount Car Rental in June 1996 for mid-sized cars rented at Pearson International Airport:

Peak-load pricing. Practice of charging a higher price for the same product or service when demand approaches physical capacity limits.

Weekdays (Monday through Thursday)	$42 per day
Weekends (Friday through Sunday)	$38 per day

Discount's incremental costs of renting a car are the same whether the car is rented on a weekday or a weekend. What then explains the difference in prices? We offer two separate, but related, explanations. One explanation is that there is a greater demand for cars during weekdays because of business activity. Faced with capacity limits, Discount raises rental rates to levels that the market will bear.

A second explanation is that the rental rates are a form of price discrimination. During weekdays, the demand for cars comes largely from business travellers who need to rent cars to conduct their business and who are relatively insensitive to prices. Charging higher rental rates during weekdays is profitable because it has little effect on demand. In contrast, the demand for weekend rentals comes largely from nonbusiness or pleasure travellers who are more price-sensitive. Lower rates stimulate demand from these individuals and increase Discount's operating income. Under either explanation, the pricing decision is not driven by cost considerations.

Product life cycle. Spans the time from initial R&D to the time at which support to customers is withdrawn.

Life cycle budgeting. Budgeting that incorporates the revenues and costs attributable to each product from its initial R&D to its final customer servicing and support in the marketplace.

LIFE CYCLE PRODUCT BUDGETING AND COSTING

The **product life cycle** spans the time from initial R&D to the time at which support to customers is withdrawn. For motor vehicles, this time span may range from five to ten years. For some pharmaceutical products, the time span may be three to five years. For fashion clothing products, the time span may be less than one year.

Using **life cycle budgeting,** managers estimate the revenues and costs attributable to each product from its initial R&D to its final customer servicing and support in the marketplace. **Life cycle costing** tracks and accumulates the actual costs attributable to each product from start to finish. The terms "cradle-to-grave costing" and "womb-to-tomb costing" convey the sense of fully capturing all costs associated with the product.

OBJECTIVE 7

Explain how life cycle product budgeting and costing assist in pricing decisions

Life cycle costing. System that tracks and accumulates the actual costs attributable to each product from start to finish

Life Cycle Budgeting and Pricing Decisions

Life cycle budgeted costs can provide important information for pricing decisions. For some products, the development period is relatively long, and many costs are incurred prior to manufacturing. Consider Insight, Inc., a computer software company developing a new accounting package, General Ledger. Assume the following budgeted amounts for General Ledger over a six-year product life cycle:

	Years 1 and 2
R&D costs	$240,000
Design costs	160,000

Years 3 to 6

	One-Time Setup Costs	Costs per Package
Production costs	$100,000	$25
Marketing costs	70,000	24
Distribution costs	50,000	16
Customer service costs	80,000	30

To be profitable, Insight must generate revenues to cover costs in all six business functions. A product life cycle budget highlights the importance of setting prices and budgeting revenues to recover costs in *all* the value-chain business functions rather than costs in only some of the functions (such as production). The life cycle budget also indicates the costs to be incurred over the life of the product. Exhibit 12-8 presents the life cycle budget for General Ledger.

Three combinations of the selling price per package and predicted demand are shown. The high nonproduction costs at Insight are readily apparent in Exhibit 12-8. For example, R&D and product design costs constitute over 30% of total costs for each of the three combinations of selling price and predicted sales quantity. Insight should put a premium on having as accurate a set of revenue and cost predictions for General Ledger as possible, given the high percentage of total life cycle costs incurred before any production begins and before any revenue is received.

Exhibit 12-8 assumes that the selling price per package is the same over the entire life cycle. For strategic reasons, however, Insight may choose to "skim the market" by charging higher prices to customers eager to try General Ledger when it first

EXHIBIT 12-8
Budgeted Life Cycle Revenues and Costs for General Ledger Software Package of Insight, Inc.*

	Alternative Selling Price/ Sales Quantity Combinations		
	1	2	3
Selling price per package	$400	$480	$600
Sales quantity in units	5,000	4,000	2,500
Life cycle revenues ($400 × 5,000; $480 × 4,000; $600 × 2,500)	$2,000,000	$1,920,000	$1,500,000
Life cycle costs:			
R&D costs	240,000	240,000	240,000
Design costs of product/process	160,000	160,000	160,000
Production costs:			
$100,000 + ($25 × 5,000); $100,000 + ($25 × 4,000); $100,000 + ($25 × 2,500)	225,000	200,000	162,500
Marketing costs:			
$70,000 + ($24 × 5,000); $70,000 + ($24 × 4,000); $70,000 + ($24 × 2,500)	190,000	166,000	130,000
Distribution costs:			
$50,000 + ($16 × 5,000); $50,000 + ($16 × 4,000); $50,000 + ($16 × 2,500)	130,000	114,000	90,000
Customer service costs:			
$80,000 + ($30 × 5,000); $80,000 + ($30 × 4,000); $80,000 + ($30 × 2,500)	230,000	200,000	155,000
Total life cycle costs	1,175,000	1,080,000	937,500
Life cycle operating income	$ 825,000	$ 840,000	$ 562,500

*This exhibit does not take into consideration the time value of money when computing life cycle revenues or life cycle costs. Chapters 22 and 23 outline how this important factor can be incorporated into such calculations.

comes out, and lower prices to customers who are willing to wait. The life cycle budget will then express this strategy.

Developing Life Cycle Reports

Most accounting systems emphasize reporting on a calendar basis—monthly, quarterly, and annually. In contrast, product life cycle reporting does not have this calendar-based focus. Consider the life spans of four Insight products:

	Year 1	Year 2	Year 3	Year 4	Year 5	Year 6
General Ledger package						
Law package						
Payroll package						
Engineering package						

Each product spans more than one calendar year.

Developing life cycle reports for each product requires tracking costs and revenues on a product-by-product basis over several calendar periods. For example, the R&D costs included in a product life cycle cost report are often incurred in different calendar years. When R&D costs are tracked over the entire life cycle, the total magnitude of these costs for each individual product can be computed and analyzed.

A product life cycle reporting format offers at least three important benefits:

1. The full set of revenues and costs associated with each product becomes visible. Manufacturing costs are highly visible in most accounting systems. However, the costs associated with upstream areas (for example, R&D) and downstream areas (for example, customer service) are frequently less visible on a product-by-product basis.

2. Differences between products in the percentage of their total costs incurred at early stages in the life cycle are highlighted. The higher this percentage, the more important it is for managers to develop, as early as possible, accurate predictions of the revenues for that product.

3. Interrelationships among business function cost categories are highlighted. For example, companies that cut back their R&D and product design costs may experience major increases in customer service costs in subsequent years. Those costs arise because products fail to meet promised quality-performance levels. A life cycle revenue and cost report prevents such causally related changes among business function costs from being hidden (buried) as they are in calendar income statements.

Life cycle costs further reinforce the importance of locked-in costs, target costing, and value engineering in pricing and cost management. For products with long life cycles, a very small fraction of the total life cycle costs are actually incurred at the time when costs are locked in. But locked-in costs will determine how costs will be incurred over several years. Automobile companies combine target costing with life cycle budgeting. For example, Chrysler, Ford, General Motors, Mercedes, Nissan, and Toyota determine target prices and target costs for their car models on the basis of estimated costs and revenues over a multi-year horizon.

Management of environmental costs provides another example of life cycle budgeting. The enactment of strict environmental laws has introduced tougher environmental standards and increased the penalties and fines for polluting the air and contaminating subsurface soil and groundwater. Environmental costs are often locked in at the product and process design stage itself. To avoid these environmental liabilities, companies design products, processes, and procedures to prevent and reduce pollution over the product's life cycle. The computer manufacturers Compaq and Apple, for example, have recently introduced costly recycling programs to ensure that nickel-cadmium batteries (used to run laptop computers) are disposed of in an environmentally safe way at the end of the product's life.

A different notion of life cycle costs is customer life cycle costs. **Customer life cycle costs** focus on the total costs to a customer of acquiring and using a product or service until it is replaced. Customer life cycle costs for a car, for example, include the cost of the car itself plus the costs of operating and maintaining the car minus the disposal price of the car. Customer life cycle costs can be an important consideration in the pricing decision. The Ford Motor Company's goal is to design cars that require minimal maintenance for 150,000 kilometres. Ford expects to charge a higher price and/or gain a greater market share by selling these cars.

Customer life cycle costs. Focuses on the total costs to a customer of acquiring and using a product or service until it is replaced.

EFFECTS OF CANADIAN COMPETITION LAW ON PRICING[2]

OBJECTIVE 8

Explain the effects of competition laws on pricing

Pricing practices in most industries are governed by the Competition Act (the Act). The purpose of the legislation and its predecessors is to "protect the specific public interest in free competition."[3] This concept is founded on the belief that unrestricted competition improves the performance of industries as a whole, and protects the public from unfair pricing practices. Each of the sections discussed below creates criminal offences for contravening the Act.

Under section 50(1)(a) of the Act, a manufacturer cannot price-discriminate between two customers if the intent is to lessen or prevent competition between customers. Four key sections of the price discrimination laws are: (1) they apply to manufacturers and not service providers; (2) price discrimination is permissible if differences in prices can be justified by differences in costs; (3) price discrimination is illegal only if the intent is to discriminate between competitors; and (4) it is not an offence to discriminate in pricing, unless doing so is part of a practice of discrimination.[4]

To comply with section 50(1)(c) of the Act, pricing must not be predatory. Section 50(1) of the Act states that a business engages in **predatory pricing** when it sells products at unreasonably low prices which either tend to substantially lessen competition or were designed to have that effect.

However, it is difficult to state with certainty what the legal thresholds are, as only three cases have ever been decided under this section.[5] In the light of the lack of judicial consideration, and to further clarify matters, the Director of Investigation and Research (the Director) released the *Predatory Pricing Enforcement Guidelines* (the *Guidelines*) on May 21, 1992. In these *Guidelines* the Director defined predatory pricing as "a situation where a dominant firm charges low prices over a long enough period of time so as to drive a competitor from the market or deter others from entering and raises prices to recoup its losses."[6] According to these *Guidelines*, the predator must account for more than 35% of the market and be able to sustain a pricing increase for more than two years after the period of low pricing in order for its actions to be considered predatory pricing.

In determining whether pricing is "unreasonably low," courts draw a distinction between pricing a product above average variable cost and below. It is likely that as long as a product is sold above average variable cost (even if below average total cost), and it cannot be established that the accused would have made a greater total contribution to overhead by raising prices, a court will not find the price "unreasonably low."

Predatory pricing. Occurs when a company deliberately prices below its costs in an effort to drive out competitors and restrict supply and then raises prices rather than enlarge demand or meet competition.

Competition Act C-34
canada.justice.gc.ca/STABLE/
EN/Laws/Chap/C/C-34.html

Competition Bureau - Industry Canada
strategis.ic.gc.ca/SSG/
ct01250e.html

---

[2]This section is provided with assistance from Russell Hoffman, LL.B., MBA.

[3]See *Weidman v. Schragge* (1912), 20 CCC 177 at 147, where the Supreme Court of Canada first considered the rationale for regulating trades and industries.

[4]Although a "practice" is not specifically defined, more than one sale is likely required. Further, it should be noted that, in order to contravene this section of the Act, a practice of price discrimination does not have to actually have an adverse affect on competition.

[5]Although the Supreme Court of Canada has never considered a case under this section, the most recent of these cases, *R. v. Hoffmann-La Roche Ltd.* (1980), 28 O.R. (2d) 164, was affirmed by the Ontario Court of Appeal in 1981 @ 125 D.L.R. (3d) 607 (C.A.).

[6]Director of Investigation and Research, "Executive Summary," *Predatory Pricing Enforcement Guidelines* (Ottawa: Consumer and Corporate Affairs Canada, 1992).

In a 1981 case, *R. v. Consumers Glass Co.*,[7] the accused, which sold small plastic lids prior to 1975, had faced reduced demand for its products. When the accused's competition cut prices by 2% to 3%, it responded by cutting prices by 16% and then a further 5%, which still enabled the accused to cover its average variable costs but not its total costs. The Court held that "it is better for a manufacturer to produce and sell at a loss, than to cease production and suffer the loss of having to bear all the fixed overhead."[8] The Court went on to hold that there was no evidence of predatory pricing, as the accused had lowered its price to retain market share, and maximize its contribution to fixed overhead.

In contrast, pricing below average variable costs will only be tolerated by the courts in limited circumstances. In *R. v. Hoffmann-La Roche Ltd.*[9] the Ontario Court of Appeal affirmed the trial judge's decision of an "unreasonably low" price. In this trial it was held that a pharmaceutical firm that chose to combat new competition in the hospital market by giving away valium was "selling" its products at an unreasonably low price. The year-long valium giveaways were in response to the new competitor's price reductions of 25% to 50% of the accused's price. The Court stated that in determining the reasonableness or unreasonableness of a particular price it will "take into account all the economic costs, which include the direct production costs as well as any potential future savings or benefits."[10] This will include looking at benefits which derive to related markets, or future markets.

The trial judge then went on to state that the court should look to four general considerations in determining whether the actual price is unreasonably low. Firstly, the difference between the average variable cost and the sale price is important, as the greater the reduction in price the more likely it is that it will be seen as unreasonable. Secondly, the length of time during which sales take place at the questionable price is significant; the longer the "deal" continues the more unreasonable the price becomes. Thirdly, the circumstances of the price cut should be considered; defensive price-cutting may be justifiable where offensive price-cutting is not. Lastly, consideration must be given to any accruals of external or long-term benefits to the seller which result from pricing below costs.[11]

Managers and accountants who are concerned with their conformance to the competition laws would be prudent to have a system that incorporates the following procedures:

1. Collect data in a manner that permits relatively easy compilation of variable costs.

2. Keep detailed records of variable costs for all value-chain business functions and review all proposed prices below variable costs in advance, with a presumption of claims of predatory intent.

Closely related to predatory pricing is dumping. Under Canadian laws, **dumping** occurs when a non-Canadian company sells goods in Canada at a price below the market value in the country of its creation or receives a government subsidy, and this action materially injures or threatens to materially injure an industry in Canada. If dumping is proven, under section 42(I)(c)(ii) of the Special Import Measures Act (SIMA) the Canadian International Trade Tribunal (the Tribunal) has the power to impose a countervailing duty on the goods in order to prevent the recurrence of the material injury.

Cases related to dumping have occurred in the agricultural and automotive industries. In 1990, the Supreme Court of Canada considered an appeal of the Tribunal's decision that the subsidization of corn imports from the United States had caused, was causing, and would likely cause material injury to the production of like goods in Canada. The Supreme Court held that the Tribunal's decision was final in

Dumping. Under Canadian laws, occurs when a non-Canadian company sells a product in Canada at a price below the market value in the country of its creation, and this action materially injures or threatens to materially injure an industry in Canada.

---

[7](1981), 33 O.R. (2d) 228 (H.C.).

[8]Id. at 238.

[9]See n. 5 *supra*.

[10]*R. v. Hoffmann-La Roche Ltd.*, p. 199.

[11]*R. v. Hoffmann-La Roche Ltd.*, pp. 200–204.

this case and that decisions are generally final unless the Tribunal acts outside the scope of its mandate, or its interpretation of the SIMA is patently unreasonable.[12]

Collusive pricing. Companies in an industry conspiring in their pricing and output decisions to achieve a price above the competitive price.

Another violation of the Act is collusive pricing. **Collusive pricing** occurs when companies in an industry conspire in their pricing and output decisions to achieve a price above the competition price. Section 45 of the Act makes it a criminal offence to conspire, agree, or combine with another person to prevent, lessen, or restrain competition unduly. Collusive pricing violates the Act because an agreement with respect to pricing and output levels prevents competition between the companies in an industry.

PROBLEM FOR SELF-STUDY

PROBLEM
Consider again the Astel Computer example described earlier. Astel's marketing manager realizes that a further reduction in price is necessary to sell 200,000 units of Provalue II. To maintain a target profitability of $16 million, or $80 per unit on Provalue II (the same figure shown in Exhibit 12-6), Astel will need to reduce costs of Provalue II by $6 million or $30 per unit. The new version is called Modified Provalue II. Astel targets a reduction of $4 million or $20 per unit in manufacturing costs, and the rest in marketing, distribution, and customer service costs. The cross-functional team assigned to this task proposes the following changes in the manufacture of Modified Provalue II:

1. Purchase some subassembled components that combine the functions performed by individual components. This change will not affect Modified Provalue II's quality or performance but will reduce direct materials costs from $385 to $375 per unit.

2. Re-engineer processes to reduce ordering and receiving costs per order from $80 to $60. Using component subassemblies will reduce the number of purchased components in Modified Provalue II from 425 to 400. As in the chapter example, Astel will place 50 orders per year for each component.

3. Reduce the labour and power required per hour of testing. This will decrease testing and inspection costs for Modified Provalue II from $2 to $1.70 per testing-hour. Under the new proposal, each Modified Provalue II will be tested for 14 hours rather than 15 hours.

4. Develop new rework procedures that will reduce the rework cost of Modified Provalue II from $100 to $80 for each of the 13,000 units (6.5% of 200,000) expected to be reworked.

No changes are proposed in direct manufacturing labour costs per unit and in total machining costs.

REQUIRED
Will the proposed changes achieve Astel's targeted reduction of $4 million (or $20 per unit) in manufacturing costs? Show your computations.

SOLUTION
Exhibit 12-9 presents the manufacturing costs for Modified Provalue II. The proposed changes will reduce manufacturing costs from $108 million or $540 per unit (see Exhibit 12-5) to $104 million or $520 per unit (Exhibit 12-9), and will thus achieve the target reduction of $4 million or $20 per unit.

[12]See *American Farm Bureau Federation v. Canadian Import Tribunal* (1990), 74 D.L.R. (4th) 449.

EXHIBIT 12-9
Target Manufacturing Costs of Modified Provalue II in 2001

	Estimated Manufacturing Costs for 200,000 Units (1)	Estimated Manufacturing Cost per Unit (2) = (1) ÷ 200,000
Direct manufacturing costs:		
Direct materials costs (200,000 units × $375)	$ 75,000,000	$375.00
Direct manufacturing labour costs (200,000 units × $53)	10,600,000	53.00
Direct machining costs (fixed costs of $11,400,000)	11,400,000	57.00
Direct manufacturing costs	97,000,000	485.00
Manufacturing overhead costs:		
Ordering and receiving costs (20,000* orders × $60)	1,200,000	6.00
Testing and inspection costs (2,800,000† hours × $1.70)	4,760,000	23.80
Rework costs (13,000 units × $80)	1,040,000	5.20
Manufacturing overhead costs	7,000,000	35.00
Total manufacturing costs	$104,000,000	$520.00

*400 components × 50 orders per component = 20,000 orders.
†200,000 units × 14 testing-hours per unit = 2,800,000 testing-hours.

SUMMARY

The following points are linked to the chapter's learning objectives.

1. Three major influences on pricing decisions are customers, competitors, and costs.

2. Short-run pricing decisions focus on a period of a year or less and have no long-run implications. Long-run pricing decisions focus on a product in a major market with a time horizon of longer than one year. The time horizon appropriate to a decision on pricing dictates which costs are relevant.

3. One approach to pricing is to use a target price. Target price is the estimated price that potential customers are willing to pay for a product (or service). A target operating profit per unit is subtracted from the target price to determine the target cost per unit. The target cost per unit is the estimated long-run cost of a product (or service) that when sold enables the firm to achieve the targeted income. The challenge for the organization is to make the cost improvements necessary through value engineering methods to achieve the target cost.

4. Cost incurrence arises when resources are actually sacrificed or used up. Locked-in costs refer to costs that have not yet been incurred but which, on the basis of decisions that have already been made, will be incurred in the future.

5. The cost-plus approach to pricing chooses prospective prices by using a general formula that adds a markup to a cost base. Many different costs (such as full product costs or manufacturing costs) can serve as the cost base in applying the cost-plus formula. Prices are then modified on the basis of customers' reactions and competitors' responses.

6. Price discrimination is the practice of charging some customers a higher price than is charged to other customers. Peak-load pricing is the practice of charging a higher price for the same product or service when demand approaches physical capacity limits. Under price discrimination and peak-load pricing, prices differ among market segments even though the outlay costs of providing the product or service are approximately the same.

7. Life cycle budgeting and life cycle costing estimate, track, and accumulate the costs (and revenues) attributable to each product from its initial R&D to its final customer service and support in the marketplace. Life cycle costing offers three important benefits: (a) the full set of costs associated with each product becomes visible, (b) differences among products in the percentage of their total costs incurred at early

Rolls-Royce: Profit and Loss Account
www.rolls-royce.com/compi/compi009.htm

stages in the life cycle are highlighted, and (c) interrelationships between value-chain business function costs are emphasized. Companies choose prices to maximize the profits earned over a product's life cycle.

8. To comply with competition laws, a company must not engage in predatory pricing, dumping, or collusive pricing, which lessens competition or puts another company at a competitive disadvantage.

▼ TERMS TO LEARN

This chapter contains definitions of the following important terms:

collusive pricing (p. 436)	predatory pricing (p. 434)
cost incurrence (p. 423)	price discrimination (p. 430)
customer life cycle costs (p. 434)	product life cycle (p. 431)
designed-in costs (p. 423)	target cost per unit (p. 421)
dumping (p. 435)	target operating income per unit (p. 421)
life cycle budgeting (p. 441)	target price (p. 421)
life cycle costing (p. 441)	target rate of return on investment
locked-in costs (p. 423)	(p. 427)
peak-load pricing (p. 431)	value engineering (p. 421)

▼ ASSIGNMENT MATERIAL

QUESTIONS

12-1 What are the three major influences on pricing decisions?

12-2 "The relevant costs for pricing decisions are full product costs." Comment.

12-3 Give two examples of pricing decisions with a short-run focus.

12-4 How is activity-based costing useful for pricing decisions?

12-5 Describe two alternative approaches to long-run pricing decisions.

12-6 What is a *target cost per unit?*

12-7 Describe *value engineering* and its role in target costing.

12-8 Give two examples each of a *value-added cost* and a *non-value-added cost.*

12-9 "It is not important for a firm to distinguish between cost incurrence and locked-in costs." Do you agree? Explain.

12-10 What is *cost-plus pricing?*

12-11 Describe three alternative cost-plus methods.

12-12 Give two examples where the difference in the costs of two products or services is much smaller than the difference in their prices.

12-13 What is *life cycle budgeting?*

12-14 What are three benefits of using a product life cycle reporting format?

12-15 Define *predatory pricing, dumping,* and *collusive pricing.*

EXERCISES

12-16 Relevant-cost approach to pricing decisions, special order. The following financial data apply to the videotape production plant of the Dill Company for October 2000:

	Budgeted Manufacturing Costs per Videotape
Direct materials	$1.50
Direct manufacturing labour	0.80
Variable manufacturing overhead	0.70
Fixed manufacturing overhead	1.00
Total manufacturing costs	$4.00

Variable manufacturing overhead varies with respect to units produced. Fixed manufacturing overhead of $1 per tape is based on budgeted fixed manufacturing overhead of $150,000 per month and budgeted production of 150,000 tapes per month. The Dill Company sells each tape for $5.

Marketing costs have two components:
◆ Variable marketing costs (sales commissions) of 5% of dollar sales
◆ Fixed monthly costs of $65,000

During October 2000, Lyn Randell, a Dill Company salesperson, asked the president for permission to sell 1,000 tapes at $3.80 per tape to a customer not in its normal marketing channels. The president refused this special order on the grounds that the order would show a loss because the selling price was below the total budgeted manufacturing cost.

REQUIRED
1. What would have been the effect on monthly operating income of accepting the special order?
2. Comment on the president's "below manufacturing costs" reasoning for rejecting the special order.
3. What factors would you recommend that the president consider when deciding whether to accept or reject the special order?

12-17 Relevant-cost approach to short-run pricing decisions. The Tectronics Company is an electronics business with eight product lines. Income data for one of the products (XT-107) for the month just ended (June 2001) are as follows:

Sales, 200,000 units at average price of $100		$20,000,000
Variable costs:		
Direct materials at $35 per unit	$7,000,000	
Direct manufacturing labour at $10 per unit	2,000,000	
Variable manufacturing overhead at $5 per unit	1,000,000	
Sales commissions at 15% of sales	3,000,000	
Other variable costs at $5 per unit	1,000,000	
Total variable costs		14,000,000
Contribution margin		6,000,000
Fixed costs		5,000,000
Operating income		$ 1,000,000

Abrams, Inc., an instruments company, has a problem with its preferred supplier of XT-107 component products. This supplier has had a three-week labour strike and will not be able to supply Abrams with 3,000 units next month. Abrams approaches the sales representative, Sarah Holtz, of the Tectronics Company about providing 3,000 units of XT-107 at a price of $80 per unit. Holtz informs the XT-107 product manager, Jim McMahon, that she would accept a flat commission of $6,000 rather than the usual 15% if this special order were accepted. Tectronics has the capacity to produce 300,000 units of XT-107 each month, but demand has not exceeded 200,000 units in any month in the last year.

REQUIRED
1. If the 3,000-unit order from Abrams is accepted, what will be the effect on monthly operating income? (Assume the same cost structure as occurred in June 2001.)
2. McMahon ponders whether to accept the 3,000-unit special order. He is afraid of the precedent that might be set by cutting the price. He says, "The price is below our full cost of $95 per unit. I think we should quote a full price, or Abrams will expect favoured treatment again and again if we continue to do business with them." Do you agree with McMahon? Explain.

12-18 Short-run pricing, capacity constraints. Boutique Chemicals makes a specialized chemical product, Bolzene, from a specially imported material, Pyrone. To make 1 kilogram of Bolzene requires 1.5 kilograms of Pyrone. Bolzene has a contribution margin of $6 per kilogram. Boutique has just received a request to manufacture 3,000 kilograms of Seltium that also requires Pyrone as the material input. Boutique calculates the following costs of making 1 kilogram of Seltium:

Pyrone (2 kilograms × $4 per kilogram)	$ 8
Direct manufacturing labour	4
Variable manufacturing overhead costs	3
Fixed manufacturing overhead costs allocated	5
Total manufacturing costs	$20

Boutique has adequate excess plant capacity to make Seltium.

REQUIRED

1. Suppose Boutique has adequate Pyrone available to make Seltium. What is the minimum price per kilogram that Boutique should charge to manufacture Seltium?
2. Now suppose Pyrone is in short supply. The Pyrone used to make Seltium will reduce the Bolzene that Boutique can make and sell. What is the minimum price per kilogram that Boutique should charge to manufacture Seltium?

12-19 Value-added, non-value-added costs. The Marino Repair Shop repairs and services machine tools. A summary of its costs (by activity) for 2000 is as follows:

a. Materials and labour for servicing machine tools	$800,000
b. Rework costs	75,000
c. Expediting costs caused by work delays	60,000
d. Materials-handling costs	50,000
e. Materials procurement and inspection costs	35,000
f. Preventive maintenance of equipment	15,000
g. Breakdown maintenance of equipment	55,000

REQUIRED

1. Classify each of the seven costs as value-added, non-value-added, or in the gray area in between.
2. For any costs classified in the gray area, assume 65% of the costs are value-added and 35% are non-value-added. How much of the total costs are value-added and how much are non-value-added?
3. Marino is considering the following changes at the shop: (a) introducing quality improvement programs whose net effect will be to reduce rework and expediting costs by 75% and materials and labour costs by 5%, (b) working with suppliers to reduce materials procurement and inspection costs by 20% and materials-handling costs by 25%, and (c) increasing preventive maintenance costs by 50% to reduce breakdown maintenance costs by 40%. What effect would each of these programs have on value-added costs, non-value-added costs, and total costs? Comment briefly.

12–20 Target operating income, value-added cost, service company. Carasco Associates is a small structural-design firm that prepares architectural drawings that focus on structural safety for various clients. The architectural plans are then submitted to local government departments for approval. Carasco's income statement for 2000 follows:

Revenues	$680,000
Salaries of professional staff (8,000 hours × $50 per hour)	400,000
Travel	18,000
Administration and support	160,000
Total costs	578,000
Operating income	$102,000

An analysis of the percentage of time spent by professional staff on various activities is as follows:

Doing calculations and preparing drawings for clients	75%
Checking calculations and drawings	4%
Correcting drawings	7%
Making changes in response to client requests	6%
Making corrections required by government officials before they give their approval	8%
Total	100%

Further assume that administration and support costs vary with professional labour-hours.

REQUIRED

1. How much of the total costs in 2000 are value-added, nonvalue-added, or in the gray area in between. Explain your answers briefly. What actions can Carasco take to reduce its costs?
2. If Carasco can eliminate all corrections and proportionately reduce professional labour-hours, how much will Carasco's operating income be?
3. Carasco would like to double operating income in 2001. Carasco can take on as much business as it can get done but it cannot add more professional staff. By how much will Carasco be able to increase its operating income if all corrections are eliminated and the time saved is used to increase revenues proportionately? Assume travel expenses for 2001 will remain at $18,000.

12-21 Target prices, target costs, activity-based costing systems. Snappy Tiles is a small distributor of marble tiles. Snappy identifies its three major activities and cost pools as ordering, receiving and storage, and shipping, and reports the following details for 2000:

Activity	Cost Driver	Quantity of Cost Driver	Cost per Unit of Cost Driver
1. Placing and paying for orders of marble tiles	Number of orders	500	$50 per order
2. Receiving and storage	Number of loads moved	4,000	$30 per load
3. Shipping of marble tiles to retailers	Number of shipments	1,500	$40 per shipment

Snappy buys 250,000 marble tiles at an average cost of $3 per tile and sells them to retailers at an average price of $4 per tile. Fixed costs are $40,000.

REQUIRED

1. Calculate Snappy's operating income for 2000.
2. For 2001, retailers are demanding a 5% discount off the 2000 price. Snappy's suppliers are only willing to give a 4% discount. Snappy expects to sell the same quantity of marble tiles in 2001 as it did in 2000. If all other costs and cost driver information remain the same, what will Snappy's operating income be in 2001?
3. Suppose further that Snappy decides to make changes in its ordering and receiving and storing practices. By placing long-term orders with its key suppliers, it expects to reduce the number of orders to 200 and the cost per order to $25 per order. By redesigning the layout of the warehouse and reconfiguring the crates in which the marble tiles are moved, Snappy expects to reduce the number of loads moved to 3,125 and the cost per load moved to $28. Will Snappy achieve its target operating income of $0.30 per tile in 2001? Show your calculations.

12-22 Cost-plus target return on investment pricing. John Beck is the managing partner of a partnership that has just finished building a 60-room motel. Beck anticipates that he will rent these rooms for 16,000 nights next year (or 16,000 room-nights). All rooms are similar and will rent for the same price. Beck estimates the following operating costs for next year:

Variable operating costs	$3 per room-night
Fixed costs:	
Salaries and wages	$175,000
Maintenance of building and pool	37,000
Other operating and administration costs	140,000
Total fixed costs	$352,000

The capital invested in the motel is $960,000. The partnership's target return on investment is 25%. Beck expects demand for rooms to be about uniform throughout the year. He plans to price the rooms at cost plus a markup to earn the target return on investment.

REQUIRED

1. What price should Beck charge for a room-night? What is the markup over the full cost of a room-night?

2. Beck's market research indicates that if the price of a room-night determined in requirement 1 was reduced by 10%, the expected number of room-nights Beck could rent would increase by 10%. Should Beck make the 10% cut?

12-23 Cost-plus and target pricing. (S. Sridhar, adapted) Waterford, Inc., manufactures and sells 15,000 units of a raft RF17 in 2000. The full cost per unit is $200. Waterford earns a 20% return on an investment of $1,800,000 in 2000.

REQUIRED

1. Calculate the selling price of RF17 in 2000. Calculate the markup percentage on the full cost per unit of RF17 in 2000.
2. If the markup percentage on variable costs per unit is 40%, calculate the variable cost per unit of RF17 in 2000.
3. Calculate Waterford's operating income if it sold 13,500 units of RF17 at a price of $230 per unit in 2000. Assume no change in total fixed costs for 2000.
4. In response to competitive pressures, Waterford must reduce the price of RF17 to $210 in 2001, in order to achieve sales of 15,000 units. Waterford plans to reduce its investment to $1,650,000. If Waterford wants to maintain a 20% return on investment, what is the target cost per unit in 2001?

12-24 Target costs, effect of product-design changes on product costs. Medical Instruments manufactures many products. To compute manufacturing costs, it uses an accounting system with one direct-cost category (direct materials) and three indirect-cost categories:

1. Batch-related setup, production order, and material-handling costs, all of which vary with the number of batches.
2. Manufacturing operations costs that vary with machine-hours.
3. Costs of engineering changes that vary with the number of engineering changes made. In response to competitive pressures, product designers at Medical Instruments have employed value-engineering methods to reduce manufacturing costs. Actual information for 2000 and budgeted information for 2001 follow:

	Actuals for 2000	Budgeted for 2001
Total setup, production-order, and material-handling costs	$7,200,000	$7,500,000
Total number of batches	900	1,000
Total manufacturing operations costs	$12,100,000	$12,500,000
Total quantity of machine-hours worked	220,000	250,000
Total costs of engineering changes	$2,640,000	$2,000,000
Total number of engineering changes	220	200

The management of Medical Instruments wants to evaluate whether value engineering has succeeded in reducing the target cost per unit of one of its products, HJ6, by 12%. Actual data for 2000 and budgeted data for 2001 for HJ6 follow:

	Actuals for 2000	Budgeted for 2001
Units of HJ6 produced	3,500	4,000
Direct materials cost per unit of HJ6	$1,200	$1,100
Total number of batches required to produce HJ6	70	80
Total machine-hours required to produce HJ6	21,000	22,000
Number of engineering changes	15	10

REQUIRED

1. Calculate the actual manufacturing cost per unit of HF6 in 2000.
2. Calculate the estimated manufacturing cost per unit of HF6 in 2001.
3. Did Medical Instruments achieve the target cost per unit for HF6?
4. Comment briefly on how Medical Instruments was able to reduce the estimated cost per unit of HF6 in 2001.

12-25 Considerations other than cost in pricing. Examples of prices charged by Bell Canada for long-distance telephone calls within Canada at different times of the day and week are as follows:

Peak period (8 a.m. to 6 p.m., Monday through Friday)			Basic rate	
Evenings (6 p.m. to 11 p.m., Monday through Friday)			35% savings	
Nights and weekends			60% savings	

REQUIRED

1. Are there differences in incremental or outlay costs per minute for Bell Canada for telephone calls made during peak hours compared with telephone calls made at other times of the day?
2. Why do you think Bell Canada charges different prices for telephone calls made during peak hours compared with telephone calls made at other times of the day?

12-26 Life cycle product costing, product emphasis. Decision Support Systems (DSS) is examining the profitability and pricing policies of its software division. The DSS software division develops software packages for engineers. DSS has collected data on three of its more recent packages:

- ◆ **EE-46.** Package for electrical engineers
- ◆ **ME-83.** Package for mechanical engineers
- ◆ **IE-17.** Package for industrial engineers

Summary details on each package over their two-year "cradle-to-grave" product lives are as follows:

Package	Selling Price	Number of Units Sold Year 1	Number of Units Sold Year 2
EE-46	$250	2,000	8,000
ME-83	300	2,000	3,000
IE-17	200	5,000	3,000

Assume that no inventory remains on hand at the end of year 2.

DSS is deciding which product lines to emphasize in its software division. In the past two years, the profitability of this division has been mediocre. DSS is particularly concerned with the increase in R&D costs in several of its divisions. An analyst in the software division pointed out that, for one of its most recent packages (IE-17), major efforts had been made to cut back R&D costs.

Last week Nancy Sullivan, the software division manager, attended a seminar on product life cycle management. The topic of life cycle reporting was discussed. Sullivan decides to use this approach in her own division. She collects the following life cycle revenue and cost information for the EE-46, ME-83, and IE-17 packages:

	EE-46 Year 1	EE-46 Year 2	ME-83 Year 1	ME-83 Year 2	IE-17 Year 1	IE-17 Year 2
Revenues	$500,000	$2,000,000	$600,000	$900,000	$1,000,000	$600,000
Costs:						
R&D	700,000	0	450,000	0	240,000	0
Design of product	185,000	15,000	110,000	10,000	80,000	16,000
Manufacturing	75,000	225,000	105,000	105,000	143,000	65,000
Marketing	140,000	360,000	120,000	150,000	240,000	208,000
Distribution	15,000	60,000	24,000	36,000	60,000	36,000
Customer service	50,000	325,000	45,000	105,000	220,000	388,000

REQUIRED

1. How does a product life cycle income statement differ from an income statement that is calendar-based? What are the benefits of using a product life cycle reporting format?
2. Present a product life cycle income statement for each software package. Which package is the most profitable, and which is the least profitable?
3. How do the three software packages differ in their cost structure (the percentage of total costs in each cost category)?

PROBLEMS

12-27 Pricing of hotel rooms on weekends. Paul Diamond is the owner of the Galaxy chain of four-star prestige hotels. These hotels are in Chicago, London, Los Angeles, Montreal, New York, Seattle, Tokyo, and Vancouver. Diamond is currently struggling to set weekend rates for the Vancouver hotel (the Vancouver Galaxy). From Sunday through Thursday, the Galaxy has an average occupancy rate of 90%. On Friday and Saturday nights, however, average occupancy declines to less than 30%. Galaxy's major customers are business travellers who stay mainly Sunday through Thursday.

The current room rate at the Galaxy is $150 a night for single occupancy and $180 a night for double occupancy. These rates apply seven nights a week. For many years, Diamond has resisted having rates for Friday and Saturday nights that are different from those for the remainder of the week. Diamond has long believed that price reductions convey a "nonprestige" impression to his guests. The Vancouver Galaxy highly values its reputation for treating its guests as "royalty."

Most room costs at the Galaxy are fixed on a short-stay (per-night) basis. Diamond estimates the variable costs of servicing each room to be $20 a night per single occupancy and $22 a night per double occupancy.

Many prestige hotels in Vancouver offer special weekend rate reductions (Friday and/or Saturday) of up to 50% of their Sunday-through-Thursday rates. These weekend rates also include additional items such as a breakfast for two, a bottle of champagne, and discounted theatre tickets.

REQUIRED

1. Would you recommend that Diamond reduce room rates at the Vancouver Galaxy on Friday and Saturday nights? What factors should be considered in his decision?
2. In six months' time, the Grey Cup is to be held in Vancouver. Diamond observes that several four-star prestige hotels have already advertised a Friday-through-Sunday rate for Grey Cup weekend of $300 a night. Should Diamond charge extra for the Grey Cup weekend? Explain.

12-28 Relevant-cost approach to pricing decisions. Stardom, Inc., cans peaches for sale to food distributors. All costs are classified as either manufacturing or marketing. Stardom prepares monthly budgets. The March 2000 budgeted absorption costing income statement is as follows:

Revenues (1,000 crates × $100 a crate)	$100,000	100%
Cost of goods sold	60,000	60
Gross margin	40,000	40
Marketing costs	30,000	30
Operating income	$ 10,000	10%

Normal markup percentage:
  $40,000 ÷ $60,000 = 66.7% of absorption cost

Monthly costs are classified as fixed or variable (with respect to the cans produced for manufacturing costs and with respect to the cans sold for marketing costs):

	Fixed	Variable
Manufacturing	$20,000	$40,000
Marketing	16,000	14,000

Stardom has the capacity to can 1,500 crates per month. The relevant range in which monthly fixed manufacturing costs will be "fixed" is from 500 to 1,500 crates per month.

REQUIRED

1. Calculate the normal markup percentage based on total variable costs.
2. Assume that a new customer approaches Stardom to buy 200 crates at $55 per crate. The customer does not require additional marketing effort. Additional manufacturing costs of $2,000 (for special packaging) will be required. Stardom believes that this is a one-time-only special order, because the customer is discontinuing business in six weeks' time. Stardom is reluctant to accept this 200-crate special order because the $55 per crate price is below the $60 per crate absorption cost. Do you agree with this reasoning? Explain.

3. Assume that the new customer decides to remain in business. How would this longevity affect your willingness to accept the $55 per crate offer? Explain.

12-29 Cost-plus pricing. (CMA, adapted) Hall Company specializes in packaging bulk drugs. Wyant Memorial Hospital has asked Hall to bid on the packaging of one million doses of medication at full cost plus a return on full cost of no more than 9% after income taxes. Wyant defines cost as including all variable costs of performing the service, a reasonable amount of fixed overhead, and incremental administrative costs. The hospital will supply all packaging materials and ingredients. Wyant has indicated that any bid over $0.07 per dose will be rejected.

Don Greenway, Director of Cost Accounting, has accumulated the following information prior to the preparation of the bid:

Variable direct manufacturing labour costs	$16.00 per direct manufacturing labour-hour
Variable overhead costs	$6.00 per direct manufacturing labour-hour
Fixed overhead costs	$30.00 per direct manufacturing labour-hour
Incremental administrative costs	$5,000 for the order
Production rate	1,000 doses per direct manufacturing labour-hour

Hall Company is subject to an income tax rate of 40%.

REQUIRED

1. Calculate the minimum price per dose that Hall could bid for the Wyant job without changing Hall's net income.
2. Calculate Hall's bid price per dose using the full cost criterion and the maximum allowable return specified by Wyant.
3. Without considering your answer to requirement 2, assume that the price per dose that Hall calculated using the cost-plus criterion specified by Wyant is greater than the maximum bid of $0.07 per dose allowed by Wyant. Discuss the factors that Hall should before deciding whether or not to submit a bid at the maximum price of $0.07 per dose.

12-30 Cost-plus and market-based pricing. Construction Temps, a large labour contractor, supplies contract labour to building construction companies. For 2000, Construction Temps has budgeted to supply 80,000 hours of contract labour. Its variable cost is $12 per hour and its fixed costs are $240,000. Roger Mason, the general manager, has proposed a cost-plus approach for pricing labour at full cost plus 20%.

REQUIRED

1. Calculate the price per hour that Construction Temps should charge on the basis of Mason's proposal.
2. Sheila Woods, the marketing manager, has supplied the following information on demand levels at different prices:

Price per Hour	Demand (Hours)
$16	120,000
17	100,000
18	80,000
19	70,000
20	60,000

Construction Temps can meet any of these demand levels. Fixed costs will remain unchanged for all the preceding demand levels. On the basis of this additional information, what price per hour should Construction Temps charge?
3. Comment on your answers to requirements 1 and 2. Why are they the same or not the same?

12-31 Airline pricing, considerations other than cost in pricing. Air North is about to introduce a daily round-trip flight from Toronto to Vancouver. Air North offers only one class of seats—Comfort Class, which allows more leg room for passengers—on all its flights. No other airline offers this kind of seat. Air North is in the process of determining how it should price its round-trip tickets. The following information is available:

Seating capacity per plane	360
Maximum demand for seats on any flight	300
Food and beverage service cost for a round trip (no charge to passenger)	$40 per passenger
Commission to travel agents paid by Air North on each ticket booked on Air North (assume all of Air North's tickets are booked by travel agents)	8% of fare
Fuel costs for a round-trip flight	$24,000
Fixed annual lease costs allocated to a round-trip flight	$100,000
Fixed ground services (maintenance, check-in, baggage handling) costs allocated to a round-trip flight	$10,000
Fixed flight crew salaries allocated to a round-trip flight	$8,000

For simplicity, assume that fuel costs are not affected by the actual number of passengers on a flight.

The market research group at Air North segments the market into business and pleasure travellers and provides the following information on the effect of two different prices on the estimated number of seats sold:

	Price Charged	Number of Seats Expected to Be Sold
Business travellers	$500	200
	$2,000	190
Pleasure travellers	$500	100
	$2,000	20

Assume these prices are the only choices available to Air North. The market research team offers one additional fact. Pleasure travellers start their travel in one week, spend at least one weekend at their destination, and return in some following week. Business travellers usually start and complete their travel within the week. They do not stay over weekends.

REQUIRED
1. If you could charge different prices to business travellers and pleasure travellers, would you? Show all your computations.
2. Explain the key factor (or factors) that drives your answer in requirement 1.
3. How might Air North implement price discrimination? That is, what scheme could the airline devise so that business travellers pay the price the airline would like business travellers to pay, and pleasure travellers pay the price the airline would like pleasure travellers to pay?

12-32 **Target prices, target costs, value engineering, cost incurrence, locked-in cost, activity-based costing.** Cutler Electronics makes a radiocassette player, CE100, which has 80 components. Cutler sells 7,000 units each month for $70 each. The costs of manufacturing CE100 are $45 per unit, or $315,000 per month. Monthly manufacturing costs incurred are as follows:

Direct materials costs	$182,000
Direct manufacturing labour costs	28,000
Machining costs (fixed)	31,500
Testing costs	35,000
Rework costs	14,000
Ordering costs	3,360
Engineering costs (fixed)	21,140
Total manufacturing costs	$315,000

Cutler's management identifies the activity cost pools, the cost drivers for each activity, and the cost per unit of cost driver for each overhead cost pool as follows:

Manufacturing Activity	Description of Activity	Cost Driver	Cost per Unit of Cost Driver
1. Machining costs	Machining components	Fixed costs	No cost driver
2. Testing costs	Testing components and final product (each unit of CE100 is tested individually)	Testing-hours	$2 per testing-hour
3. Rework costs	Correcting and fixing errors and defects	Units of CE100 reworked	$20 per unit
4. Ordering costs	Ordering of components	Number of orders	$21 per order
5. Engineering costs	Designing and managing of products and process	Fixed costs	No cost driver

Over a long-run time horizon, Cutler's management views direct materials costs and direct manufacturing labour costs as variable with respect to the units of CE100 manufactured. Each of the overhead costs described in the preceding table varies, as described, with the chosen cost drivers.

The following additional information describes the existing design:
a. Testing and inspection time per unit is 2.5 hours.
b. Ten % of the CE100s manufactured are reworked.
c. Cutler places two orders with each component supplier each month. Each component is supplied by a different supplier. It takes one hour to place an order.

To respond to competitive pressures, Cutler must reduce its price to $62 per unit and reduce its costs by $8 per unit. No additional sales are anticipated at this lower price. However, Cutler stands to lose significant sales if it does not cut its price. Manufacturing has been asked to reduce its costs by $6 per unit. Improvements in manufacturing efficiency are expected to yield net savings of $1.50 per radiocassette player, but that is not enough. The chief engineer has proposed a new modular design that reduces the number of components to 50 and also simplifies testing. The newly designed radiocassette player, called "New CE100," will replace CE100.

The expected effects of the new design are as follows:
a. Direct materials costs for New CE100 are expected to be lower by $2.20 per unit.
b. Direct manufacturing labour costs for New CE100 are expected to be lower by $0.50 per unit.
c. Machining time required to manufacture New CE100 is expected to be 20% less. It currently takes one hour to manufacture 1 unit of CE100.
d. Time required for testing New CE100 is expected to be lower by 20%.
e. Rework is expected to decline to 4% of New CE100s manufactured.
Assume that the cost per unit of the cost driver for CE100 continues to apply to New CE100.

REQUIRED
1. Calculate Cutler's manufacturing cost per unit of New CE100.
2. Will the new design achieve the per-unit cost reduction targets that have been set for the manufacturing costs of New CE 100?
3. The problem describes two strategies to reduce costs: (a) improving manufacturing efficiency and (b) modifying the design. Which strategy has a bigger impact on costs? Why? Explain briefly.

12-33 **Product costs, activity-based costing systems.** Executive Power (EP) manufactures and sells computers and computer peripherals to several nationwide retail chains. John Farnham is the manager of the printer division. Its two largest selling printers are P-41 and P-63.

The manufacturing cost of each printer is calculated using EP's activity-based costing system. EP has one direct manufacturing cost category (direct materials) and the following five indirect manufacturing cost pools:

Indirect Manufacturing Cost Pool	Allocation Base	Allocation Rate
1. Materials-handling	Number of parts	$1.20 per part
2. Assembly management	Hours of assembly time	$40 per hour of assembly time
3. Machine insertion of parts	Number of machine-inserted parts	$0.70 per machine-inserted part
4. Manual insertion of parts	Number of manually inserted part	$2.10 per manually inserted part
5. Quality testing	Hours of quality testing time	$25 per testing-hour

Product characteristics of P-41 and P-63 are as follows:

	P-41	P-63
Direct materials costs	$407.50	$292.10
Number of parts	85 parts	46 parts
Hours of assembly time	3.2 hours	1.9 hours
Number of machine-inserted parts	49 parts	31 parts
Number of manually inserted parts	36 parts	15 parts
Hours of quality testing	1.4 hours	1.1 hours

REQUIRED

What is the manufacturing cost of P-41? Of P-63?

12-34 Target cost, activity-based costing systems (continuation of 12-33). Assume all the information in Problem 12-33. Farnham has just received some bad news. A foreign competitor has introduced products very similar to P-41 and P-63. Given their announced selling prices, Farnham estimates the P-41 clone to have a manufacturing cost of approximately $680 and the P-63 clone to have a manufacturing cost of approximately $390. He calls a meeting of product designers and manufacturing personnel at the printer division. They all agree to have the $680 and $390 figures become target costs for redesigned versions of EP's P-41 and P-63, respectively. Product designers examine alternative ways of designing printers with comparable performance but lower cost. They come up with the following revised designs for P-41 and P-63 (termed P-41 REV and P-63 REV, respectively):

	P-41 REV	P-63 REV
Direct materials costs	$381.20	$263.10
Number of parts	71 parts	39 parts
Hours of assembly time	2.1 hours	1.6 hours
Number of machine-inserted parts	59 parts	29 parts
Number of manually inserted parts	12 parts	10 parts
Hours of quality testing	1.2 hours	0.9 hours

REQUIRED

1. What is a target cost per unit?
2. Using the activity-based costing system outlined in Problem 12-33, compute the manufacturing costs of P-41 REV and P-63 REV. How do they compare with the $680 and $390 target costs per unit?
3. Explain the differences between P-41 and P-41 REV and between P-63 and P-63 REV.
4. Assume now that John Farnham has achieved major cost reductions in one of the activity areas. As a consequence, the allocation rate in the assembly management activity area will be reduced from $40 to $28 per assembly-hour. How will this activity-area cost reduction affect the manufacturing costs of P-41 REV and P-63 REV? Comment on the results.

12-35 Life cycle product costing, activity-based costing. Destin Products makes digital watches. Destin is preparing a product life cycle budget for a new watch, MX3. Development on the new watch with features such as a calculator and a daily diary is to start shortly. Destin expects the watch to have a product life cycle of three years. Estimates about MX3 are as follows:

	Year 1	Year 2	Year 3
Units manufactured and sold	50,000	200,000	150,000
Price per watch	$45	$40	$35
R&D and design costs	$900,000	$100,000	—
Manufacturing:			
Variable cost per watch	$16	$15	$15
Variable cost per batch	$700	$600	$600
Watches per batch	400	500	500
Fixed costs	$600,000	$600,000	$600,000

Marketing:

Variable cost per watch	$3.60	$3.20	$2.80
Fixed costs	$400,000	$300,000	$300,000

Distribution:

Variable cost per watch	$1	$1	$1
Variable cost per batch	$120	$120	$100
Watches per batch	200	160	120
Fixed costs	$240,000	$240,000	$240,000
Customer service costs per watch	$2	$1.50	$1.50

Ignore the time value of money in your answers.

REQUIRED

1. Calculate the budgeted life cycle operating income for the new watch.
2. What percentage of the budgeted product life cycle costs will be incurred at the end of the R&D and design stages?
3. An analysis reveals that 80% of the total product life cycle costs of the new watch will be locked in at the end of the R&D and design stages. What implications would this finding have on managing MX3's costs?
4. Destin's Market Research Department estimates that reducing MX3's price by $3 each year will increase sales by 10% each year. If sales increase by 10%, Destin plans to increase manufacturing and distribution batch sizes by 10% as well. Assume that all variable costs per watch, variable costs per batch, and fixed costs will remain the same. Should Destin reduce MX3's price by $3?

12-36 Ethics and pricing. Baker, Inc., manufactures ball bearings. Baker is preparing to submit a bid for a new ball bearings order. Greg Lazarus, controller of the Bearings Division of Baker, Inc., has asked John Decker, the cost analyst, to prepare the bid. Baker determines price on the basis of full product costs plus a markup of 10%. Lazarus tells Decker that he is keen on winning the bid and that the price he calculates should be competitive.

Decker prepares the following costs for the bid:

Direct materials costs	$40,000
Direct manufacturing labour costs	10,000
Design and parts administration overhead costs	4,000
Production order overhead costs	5,000
Setup overhead costs	5,500
Materials-handling overhead costs	6,500
General and administration overhead costs	9,000

All direct costs and 30% of overhead costs are incremental costs of the order.

Lazarus reviews the numbers and says, "As usual, your costs are way too high. You have allocated a lot of overhead costs to this job. You know our fixed overhead is not going to change if we win this order and manufacture the bearings. Ever since we installed this new activity-based costing system, we never seem to be able to come up with reasonable product and job costs. Rework your numbers. You have got to make the costs lower."

On returning to his office, Decker rechecks his numbers. He knows that Lazarus wants this order because the additional revenue from the order would lead to a big bonus for Lazarus and the senior division managers. Decker wonders if he can adjust the costs downward. He knows that if he does not come up with a lower bid, Lazarus will be very upset.

REQUIRED

1. Using Baker's pricing policy and based on Decker's estimates, what price should Baker bid for the ball bearings order?
2. Calculate the incremental costs of the ball bearings order. Why do you think Baker uses full product costs rather than incremental costs in his pricing decisions?
3. Evaluate whether Lazarus's suggestion to Decker to use lower cost numbers is unethical. Will it be unethical for Decker to change his analysis so that a lower price can be bid? What steps should Decker take to resolve this situation?

COLLABORATIVE LEARNING PROBLEM

12-37 Target prices, target costs, value engineering. Avery, Inc., manufactures two component parts for the television industry:

◆ **Tvez.** Annual production and sales of 50,000 units at a selling price of $40.60 per unit

◆ **Premia.** Annual production and sales of 25,000 units at a selling price of $60 per unit

Avery includes all R&D and design costs in engineering costs. Assume that Avery has no marketing, distribution, or customer service costs.

The direct and overhead costs incurred by Avery on Tvez and Premia are described as follows:

	Tvez	Premia	Total
Direct materials costs (variable)	$850,000	$600,000	$1,450,000
Direct manufacturing labour costs (variable)	300,000	200,000	500,000
Direct machining costs (fixed)	150,000	100,000	250,000
Manufacturing overhead costs:			
Machine setup costs			86,250
Testing costs			487,500
Engineering costs			450,000
Manufacturing overhead costs			1,023,750
Total costs			$3,223,750

Avery's management identifies the following activity cost pools, cost drivers for each activity, and the costs per unit of cost driver for each overhead cost pool:

Manufacturing Activity	Description of Activity	Cost Driver	Cost per Unit of Cost Driver
1. Setup	Preparing machine to manufacture a new batch of products	Setup-hours	$25 per setup-hour
2. Testing	Testing components and final product (Avery tests each unit of Tvez and Premia individually.)	Testing-hours	$2 per testing-hour
3. Engineering	Designing products and processes and ensuring their smooth functioning	Complexity of product and process	Costs assigned to products by special study

Over a long-run time horizon, Avery's management views direct materials costs and direct manufacturing labour costs as variable with respect to the units of Tvez and Premia produced. Direct machining costs for each product do not vary over this time horizon and are fixed long-run costs. Overhead costs vary with respect to their chosen cost drivers. For example, setup costs vary with the number of setup-hours. Additional information is as follows:

	Tvez	Premia
1. Production batch sizes	500 units	200 units
2. Setup time per batch	12 hours	18 hours
3. Testing and inspection time per unit of product produced	2.5 hours	4.75 hours
4. Engineering costs incurred on each product	$170,000	$280,000

Avery is facing competitive pressure to reduce the price of Tvez and has set a target price of $34.80, well below its current price of $40.60. The challenge for Avery is to reduce the cost of Tvez. Avery's engineers have proposed a new product design and process improvements for the "New Tvez" to replace Tvez. The new design would improve product quality, and reduce scrap and waste. The reduction in prices will not enable Avery to increase its current sales. (However, if Avery does not reduce prices, it will lose sales.)

The expected effects of the new design relative to Tvez are as follows:

1. Direct materials costs for New Tvez are expected to decrease by $2.00 per unit.
2. Direct manufacturing labour costs for New Tvez are expected to decrease by $0.50 per unit.
3. Time required for testing each unit of New Tvez is expected to be reduced by 0.5 hours.
4. Machining time required to make New Tvez is expected to decrease by 20 minutes. It currently takes one hour to manufacture one unit of Tvez. The machines are dedicated to the production of New Tvez.
5. New Tvez will take seven setup-hours for each setup.
6. Engineering costs are unchanged.

Assume that the batch sizes are the same for New Tvez as for Tvez. If Avery requires additional resources to implement the new design, it can acquire these additional resources in the quantities needed. Further assume the costs per unit of cost driver for the New Tvez are the same as those described for Tvez.

INSTRUCTIONS

Form groups of two students to complete the following requirements.

REQUIRED

1. Develop full product costs per unit for Tvez and Premia, using an activity-based product costing approach.
2. What is the markup on the full product cost per unit for Tvez?
3. What is Avery's target cost per unit for New Tvez if it is to maintain the same markup percentage on the full product cost per unit as it had for Tvez?
4. Will the New Tvez design achieve the cost reduction targets that Avery has set?
5. What price would Avery charge for New Tvez if it used the same markup percentage on the full product cost per unit for New Tvez as it did for Tvez?
6. What price should Avery charge for New Tvez, and what next steps should Avery take regarding New Tvez?

13

STRATEGY, BALANCED SCORECARD, AND STRATEGIC PROFITABILITY ANALYSIS

The drive to be world-class producers of products, such as Motorola and microchips, requires that companies think strategically and establish performance measurement systems that assess their success in achieving their strategic goals. Performance measures commonly include a balance of both financial and nonfinancial elements of the strategic plan.

LEARNING OBJECTIVES

After studying this chapter, you should be able to:

1. Recognize which of two generic strategies a company is using

2. Identify key aspects of reengineering

3. Present the four perspectives of the balanced scorecard

4. Analyze changes in operating income to evaluate strategy

5. Distinguish between engineered and discretionary costs

6. Identify and manage unused capacity

The focus of much of the earlier chapters is on managing operations. In this chapter, we explore the use of management accounting information in the implementation and evaluation of an organization's strategy. Strategy is at the core of any business. It drives the operations of a company and guides managers' short-run and long-run decisions. In this chapter, we describe the balanced scorecard approach to implementing strategy and present ways to analyze operating income for purposes of evaluating strategy. We also show how management accounting information helps strategic initiatives, such as productivity improvement, reengineering, and downsizing. We start, however, by discussing what strategy is.

WHAT IS STRATEGY?

Strategy describes how an organization matches its own capabilities with the opportunities in the marketplace to accomplish its overall objectives. In formulating its strategy, an organization must thoroughly understand the industry in which it operates. Industry analysis focuses on five forces: (a) competitors, (b) potential entrants into the market, (c) substitute products, (d) bargaining power of customers, and (e) bargaining power of input suppliers.[1] The collective effect of these forces shapes an organization's profit potential. In general, profit potential decreases with greater competition, stronger potential entrants, products that are similar, and tougher customers and suppliers.

We illustrate these five forces using the example of Chipset Inc., a manufacturer of linear integrated circuit devices (LICD's) used in modems and communication networks. Chipset produces a single specialized product, CX1. This standard, high-performance microchip can be used in multiple applications that require instant processing of real-time data. CX1 was designed with extensive inputs from key customers.

Competitors. Chipset has many growth opportunities, but it also faces significant competition from many small competitors. Companies in the industry have high fixed costs. There is steady pressure to utilize capacity fully; in turn, there is ceaseless pressure on selling prices. Reducing prices of products is critical for industry growth because it allows LICD's to be incorporated into mass-market modems. CX1 enjoys a reputation of having slightly superior product features relative to competitive products, but competition is severe along the dimensions of price, timely delivery, and quality. Quality is important because LICD failure disrupts the communication network.

Potential entrants into the market. This is not an attractive industry for new entrants. Competition keeps profit margins small, and significant capital is needed to set up a new manufacturing facility. Companies that have already been making LICD's are further down the learning curve and hence are likely to have lower costs. Existing companies also have the advantage of close relationships with customers.

Equivalent products. Chipset uses a technology that allows its customers to use CX1 flexibly to best meet their needs. The flexible design of CX1, and the fact that it is closely integrated into end-products made by Chipset's customers, reduces the potential for equivalent products or new technologies to replace CX1 during the next few years. This risk is reduced even further if Chipset continuously improves CX1's design and processes to decrease costs.

Bargaining power of customers. Customers have bargaining power because each buys large quantities of product. Customers can also obtain microchips from other potential suppliers. Signing a contract to deliver microchips is very important to Chipset. Recognizing this fact, customers negotiate hard to keep prices down.

[1] M. Porter, *Competitive Strategy*, Free Press, 1980; M. Porter, *Competitive Advantage*, Free Press, 1985; M. Porter, "What is Strategy?," *Harvard Business Review*, November-December 1996.

OBJECTIVE 1

Recognize which of two generic strategies a company is using

Strategy. The matching of an organization's capabilities with opportunities in the marketplace in order to accomplish its overall objectives.

Accounting Technology Strategies software www.accts.com

Bargaining power of input suppliers. Chipset purchases high-quality materials such as silicon wafers, pins for connectivity, and plastic or ceramic packaging from its suppliers. Chipset also requires skilled engineers, technicians and manufacturing labour. Materials suppliers and employees have some bargaining power to demand higher prices and wages.

In summary, strong competition and the bargaining powers of customers and suppliers put significant pressure on prices. Chipset can respond to these challenges by adopting one of two basic strategies, differentiating its product or achieving cost leadership.

Product differentiation is an organization's ability to offer products or services that are perceived by its customers as being superior and unique relative to those of its competitors. For example, Hewlett Packard has successfully differentiated its products in the electronics industry, as have Merck in the pharmaceutical industry and Coca-Cola in the soft drinks industry. Through innovative product research and development, and by developing processes that bring products to market rapidly, each of these companies has been able to provide better and differentiated products. This differentiation increases brand loyalty and the prices that customers are willing to pay.

Cost leadership is an organization's ability to achieve low costs relative to competitors through productivity and efficiency improvements, elimination of waste, and tight cost control. Some cost leaders in their respective industries are Home Depot (building products), Texas Instruments (consumer electronics), and Magna (automotive parts). These companies all provide products and services that are similar to, not differentiated from, those of their competitors, but at a lower cost to the customer. Lower selling prices—rather than unique products or services—provide a competitive advantage for these cost leaders.

What strategy should Chipset follow? CX1 is already somewhat differentiated from competing products. Differentiating CX1 further will be costly but it may allow Chipset to charge a higher price. Conversely, reducing the cost of manufacturing and selling CX1 will allow Chipset to reduce the price of CX1 and spur growth. The CX1 technology allows Chipset's customers to achieve different performance levels by simply altering the number of CX1 units in their products. This solution is more cost effective than designing new customized microchips for different applications. Customers want Chipset to keep the current design of CX1 but to lower its price. Chipset's current engineering talent is also more oriented toward making product and process improvements than in creatively designing brand new products and technologies. Chipset concludes that it should pursue a cost leadership strategy. Of course, successful cost leadership generally would increase Chipset's market share and help the company to grow.

To be successful, a company must both formulate an effective strategy and implement it vigorously. In the next section, we focus on the balanced scorecard as a tool for implementing strategy.

Product differentiation. An organization's ability to offer products or services that are perceived by its customers as superior and unique relative to those of its competitors.

Cost leadership. An organization's ability to achieve low costs relative to competitors through productivity and efficiency improvements, elimination of waste, and tight cost control.

Merck
www.merck.com

Home Depot
www.homedepot.com

Texas Instruments
www.ti.com

IMPLEMENTATION OF STRATEGY AND THE BALANCED SCORECARD

Consistent with the score-keeping function, the management accountant has an important role to play in the implementation of strategy. This role takes the form of designing reports to help managers track progress in implementing strategy. Many organizations have introduced a balanced scorecard approach to manage the implementation of their strategies.

The Balanced Scorecard

The **balanced scorecard** translates an organization's mission and strategy into a comprehensive set of performance measures that provides the framework for implementing its strategy.[2] The balanced scorecard does not focus solely on achieving financial objectives. It also highlights the nonfinancial objectives that an organization must achieve in order to meet its financial objectives. The scorecard measures

Balanced scorecard. The translation of an organization's mission and strategy into a comprehensive set of performance measures that provide the framework for implementing its strategy.

[2]See R. S. Kaplan and D. P. Norton, "The Balanced Scorecard." Harvard Business School Press, 1996.

an organization's performance from four key perspectives: (1) financial, (2) customer, (3) internal business processes, and (4) learning and growth. A company's strategy influences the measures used in each of these perspectives.

The balanced scorecard gets its name from the attempt to balance financial and nonfinancial performance measures to evaluate both short-run and long-run performance in a single report. Consequently, the balanced scorecard reduces managers' emphasis on short-run financial performance, such as quarterly earnings. Why? Because the nonfinancial and operational indicators measure fundamental changes that a company is making. The financial benefits of these changes may not be captured in short-run earnings, but strong improvements in nonfinancial measures signal the prospect of creating economic value in the future. For example, an increase in customer satisfaction signals higher sales and income in the future. By balancing the mix of financial and nonfinancial measures, the balanced scorecard focuses management's attention on both short-run and long-run performance.

Shortly we will illustrate the four perspectives of the balanced scorecard using the Chipset example. To understand the measures Chipset uses to monitor progress under each perspective, it is important to recognize key elements of Chipset's cost leadership strategy—improve quality and reengineer processes. As a result of these initiatives, Chipset plans to reduce costs and downsize and eliminate capacity in excess of that needed to support future growth. However, it does not want to make deep cuts in personnel that would adversely affect employee morale and hinder future growth.

Quality Improvement and Reengineering at Chipset

One key element of Chipset's strategy to reduce costs is improving quality (that is reducing defects and improving yields in its manufacturing process). To improve quality, Chipset needs to obtain real-time data about manufacturing process parameters and to implement advanced process control methods. The goal is to ensure that process parameters such as temperature and pressure are maintained within tight ranges. Chipset must also train its front-line workers in quality management techniques to help them identify and resolve defects and problems. Following this training, Chipset needs to empower its workforce to make timely decisions and continuously improve the process.

Another key element of Chipset's strategy to reduce costs is reengineering its order delivery process. **Reengineering** is the fundamental rethinking and redesign of business processes to achieve improvements in critical measures of performance such as cost, quality, service, speed, and customer satisfaction.[3] To illustrate the concept of reengineering, we examine the order delivery system at Chipset Inc. in 1999. Chipset's salespersons work with customers to identify and plan customer needs. A copy of each purchase order received from a customer is sent to manufacturing where a production scheduler begins the planning for manufacturing the order. Frequently, there is a long waiting time before production begins. After manufacturing is complete, the CX1 chips are sent to the shipping department, which matches the quantities of CX1 to be shipped against customer purchase orders. Often, the completed CX1 chips are held in inventory until a truck is available for shipment to the customer. If the quantity shipped does not match the number of chips requested by the customer, a special shipment is scheduled. The shipping documents are sent to the billing department for issuing of invoices. Special staff in the accounting department follows up with customers for payments.

Chipset discovered that the many transfers across departments (sales, manufacturing, shipping, billing, and accounting) to satisfy a customer order slowed down the process and created delays. A multi-function team from the various departments has reengineered the order delivery process for 2000. Its goal is to make the entire organization more customer-focused and reduce delays by eliminating the number

The Balanced Scorecard Institute
www.balancedscorecard.org

The Balanced Scorecard Technology Council
www.balancedscorecard.com

OBJECTIVE 2

Identify key aspects of reengineering

Reengineering. The fundamental rethinking and redesign of business processes to achieve improvements in critical measures of performance.

---

[3]See M. Hammer and J. Champy, "*Reengineering the Corporation: A Manifesto for Business Revolution*," NY: Harper, 1993; Ruhli, Treichler, and Schmidt, "From Business Reengineering to Management Reengineering—A European Study," *Management International Review*, 1995, p. 361-71; G. Hall, J. Rosenthal, and J. Wade, "How to Make Reengineering Really Work," *Harvard Business Review*, November-December 1993, pp. 119-131.

The BMA Group: Balanced
Scorecard and Performance
Measurement—Australian
Consulting Firm
www.bma.com.au

AT&T Canada
www.attcanada.com

Cigna Insurance
www.cigna.com

Ford of Canada
www.ford.ca

Siemens Nixdorf
www.sni.ca

of interdepartment transfers. Under the new system, a customer relationship manager is responsible for the entire customer relationship. Chipset has entered into long-term contracts with customers that specify quantities and prices. The customer relationship manager will work closely with the customer and with manufacturing to specify delivery schedules for CX1 one month in advance. The schedule of customer orders will be sent electronically to manufacturing. Completed chips will be shipped directly from the manufacturing plant to customer sites. Each shipment will automatically trigger an invoice that will be sent electronically to the customer.

The experiences of many companies, such as AT&T, Banca di America e di Italia (BAI), Cigna Insurance, Ford Motor, Hewlett Packard, and Siemens Nixdorf, indicate that the benefits from reengineering are the most significant when it cuts across functional lines to focus on an entire business process (as in the Chipset example). Reengineering only the shipping or invoicing activity at Chipset rather than the entire order delivery process would not be particularly beneficial. Successful reengineering efforts involve changing roles and responsibilities, eliminating unnecessary activities and tasks, using information technology, and developing employee skills. Chipset's balanced scorecard for 2000 must track Chipset's progress in reengineering the order delivery process from both a nonfinancial and financial perspective.

The Four Perspectives of the Balanced Scorecard

OBJECTIVE 3

Present the four perspectives
of the balanced scorecard

Exhibit 13-1 presents Chipset's balanced scorecard. It highlights the four key perspectives of performance—financial, customer, internal business processes, and learning and growth. At the beginning of the year 2000, Chipset specifies the objectives, measures, initiatives to achieve the objectives, and target performance (the first four columns of Exhibit 13-1). The target performance levels for nonfinancial measures are based on competitor benchmarks. They indicate the performance levels necessary to meet customer needs, compete effectively and achieve financial goals. The fifth column, which describes actual performance, is completed at the end of the year 2000. This column shows how well Chipset has performed relative to its target performance.

Financial perspective. This perspective evaluates the profitability of the strategy. Because cost reduction relative to competitors and growth are Chipset's key strategic initiatives, the financial perspective focuses on how much of operating income and return on capital employed results from reducing costs and selling more units of CX1.

Customer perspective. This perspective identifies the targeted market segments and measures the company's success in these segments. To monitor its growth objectives, Chipset uses measures such as market share in the communication networks segment, number of new customers, and customer satisfaction.

Internal business process perspective. This perspective focuses on internal operations that further both the customer perspective by creating value for customers and the financial perspective by increasing shareholder wealth. Chipset determines internal business process improvement targets after benchmarking against key competitors. As we discussed in Chapter 12, there are different sources of competitor cost analysis–published financial statements, prevailing prices, customers, suppliers, former employees, industry experts, and financial analysts. Chipset also physically takes apart competitors' products to compare them with its own designs. This activity also helps Chipset estimate competitors' costs. The internal business process perspective comprises three principal sub-processes:

1. **The innovation process:** Creating products, services, and processes that will meet the needs of customers. At Chipset, the key to lowering costs and promoting growth is improving the technology of manufacturing.
2. **The operations process:** Producing and delivering existing products and services to customers. Chipset's key strategic initiatives are (a) improving manufacturing quality, (b) reducing delivery time to customers and (c) meeting specified delivery dates.

EXHIBIT 13-1

The Balanced Scorecard for Chipset Inc. for the year 2000

Objectives	Measures	Initiatives	Target Performance	Actual Performance
Financial Perspective				
Increase shareholder value	Operating income from productivity gain	Manage costs & unused capacity	$2,000,000	$2,100,000
	Operating income from growth	Build strong customer relationships	$3,000,000	$3,420,000
	Revenue growth	Build strong customer relationships	6%	6.48%[1]
Customer Perspective				
Increase market share	Market share in communication networks segment	Identify future needs of customers	6%	7%
	New customers	Identify target new customer segments	5	6[2]
Increase customer satisfaction	Customer satisfaction survey	Increase customer focus of sales organization	90% of customers give top two ratings	87% of customers give top two ratings
Internal Business Process Perspective				
Improve manufacturing capability	Percentage of processes with advanced controls	Organize R&D/manufacturing teams to implement advanced controls	75%	75%
Improve manufacturing quality and productivity	Yield	Identify root causes of problems and improve quality	78%	79.3%[3]
Reduce delivery time to customers	Order delivery time	Reengineer order delivery process	30 days	30 days
Meet specified delivery dates	On-time delivery	Reengineer order delivery process	92%	90%
Learning and Growth Perspective				
Develop process skill	Percentage of employees trained in process and quality management	Employee training programs	90%	92%
Empower workforce	Percentage of front-line workers empowered to manage processes	Have supervisors act as coaches rather than decision makers	85%	90%
Align employee and organization goals	Employee satisfaction survey	Employee participation and suggestions program to build teamwork	80% of employees give top two ratings	88% of employees give top two ratings
Enhance information system capabilities	Percentage of manufacturing processes with real-time feedback	Improve off-line data gathering	80%	80%
Improve manufacturing processes	Number of major improvements in process controls	Organize R&D/manufacturing teams to study processes	5	5

[1](Revenues in 2000 − Revenues in 1999) ÷ Revenues in 1999 = ($28,750,000 − $27,000,000) ÷ $27,000,000 = 6.48%
[2]Customers increased from 40 to 46 in the year 2000.
[3]Yield = Units of CX1 produced ÷ Units of CX1 started × 100 = 1,150,000 ÷ 1,450,000 × 100 = 79.3%

3. Post-sales service: Providing service and support to the customer after the sale or delivery of a product or service. Chipset's sales staff works closely with customers to monitor and understand how well product features of CX1 match customer needs.

Learning and growth perspective. This perspective identifies the capabilities in which the organization must excel to achieve superior internal processes that create value for customers and shareholders. Chipset's learning and growth perspective emphasizes three capabilities (1) employee capabilities measured using employee education and skill levels, surveys of employee satisfaction, employee turnover (fraction of employees who have left the company annually), and employee productivity; (2) information system capabilities measured by percentage of front-line employees that have on-line access to customer information, and percentage of business processes with real-time feedback; and (3) motivation and empowerment measured by number of suggestions per employee, percentage of suggestions implemented, and percentage of compensation based on individual and team incentives.

The arrows in Exhibit 13-1 indicate how gains in the learning and growth perspective lead to improvements in internal business processes which, in turn, lead to higher customer satisfaction and market share and, finally, to superior financial performance. Note how key elements of Chipset's strategy implementation—empowering workers, training, information systems, quality and process improvements, reengineering, and customer focus—filter through the scorecard. These initiatives have been successful from a financial perspective in 2000. Chipset has earned significant operating income from its cost leadership strategy that has also translated into growth.

Aligning the Balanced Scorecard to Strategy

Different strategies call for different scorecards. Suppose that Visilog, another company in the microchip industry, follows a product differentiation strategy by designing custom chips for the communication networks business. Visilog designs its scorecard to fit its strategy. For example, in the financial perspective, Visilog evaluates how much of its operating income comes from charging premium prices for its products. In the customer perspective, Visilog measures the percentage of its revenues from new products (and new customers). In the internal business process perspective, Visilog measures the development of advanced manufacturing capabilities to produce custom chips. In the learning and growth perspective, Visilog measures new product development time. Of course, Visilog uses some of the measures described in the balanced scorecard in Exhibit 13-1. For example, revenue growth, customer satisfaction ratings, order delivery time, on-time delivery, percentage of front-line workers empowered to manage processes, and employee satisfaction ratings, are important measures under the new strategy. The key point, though, is to align the balanced scorecard to company strategy.[4]

Exhibit 13-2 presents some common balanced scorecard measures that companies have used.

Features of a Good Balanced Scorecard

A good balanced scorecard design has several features:

1. It tells the story of a company's strategy by articulating a sequence of cause-and-effect relationships. For example, because Chipset's goal is to be a low-cost producer and to emphasize growth, the balanced scorecard describes the specific objectives and measures in the learning and growth perspective that lead to improvements in internal business processes. These, in turn, lead to increased

---

[4]For simplicity, we have presented the balanced scorecard in the context of companies that have followed either a cost leadership or a product differentiation strategy. Of course, a company may have some products for which cost leadership is critical and other products for which product differentiation is important. The company will then develop separate scorecards to implement the different product strategies. In still other contexts, product differentiation may be of primary importance but some cost leadership must also be achieved. The balanced scorecard measures would then link to this strategy.

EXHIBIT 13-2
Frequently Cited Balanced Scorecard Measures

◆ *Financial Perspective*

Operating income, revenue growth, revenues from new products, gross margin percentage, cost reductions in key areas, economic value added[a] (EVA®), return on investment.[a]

◆ *Customer Perspective*

Market share, customer satisfaction, customer retention percentage, time taken to fulfill customers requests.

◆ *Internal Business Process Perspective*

Innovation Process: Manufacturing capabilities, number of new products or services, new product development times, and number of new patents.

Operations Process: Yield, defect rates, time taken to deliver product to customers, percentage of one-time deliveries, average time taken to manufacture orders, setup time, manufacturing downtime.

Post-sales Service: Time taken to replace or repair defective products, hours of customer training for using the product.

◆ *Learning and Growth Perspective*

Employee education and skill levels, employee satisfaction scores, employee turnover rates, information system availability, percentage of processes with advanced controls, percentage of employee suggestions implemented, percentage of compensation based on individual and team incentives.

[a]These measures are described in Chapter 24.

customer satisfaction and market share, as well as higher operating income and shareholder value. Each measure in the scorecard is part of a cause-and-effect chain, a linkage from strategy formulation to financial outcomes.

2. It helps to communicate the strategy to all members of the organization by translating the strategy into a coherent and linked set of understandable and measurable operational targets. Guided by the scorecard, managers and employees take actions and make decisions that aim to achieve the company's strategy. To focus these actions, some companies, such as Mobil and Citibank, have pushed down and developed scorecards at the division and department levels.

3. In for-profit companies, the balanced scorecard places strong emphasis on financial objectives and measures.[5] Managers sometimes tend to focus too much on innovation, quality, and customer satisfaction as ends in themselves even if they do not lead to tangible payoffs. A balanced scorecard emphasizes nonfinancial measures as a part of a program to achieve future financial performance. When financial and nonfinancial performance measures are properly linked, many of the nonfinancial measures serve as leading indicators of future financial performance. In the Chipset example, the improvements in nonfinancial factors have, in fact, led to improvements in financial factors.

4. The scorecard limits the number of measures used by identifying only the most critical ones. Avoiding a proliferation of measures focuses management's attention on those that are key to the implementation of strategy.

5. The scorecard highlights suboptimal tradeoffs that managers may make when they fail to consider operational and financial measures together. For example, a company for which innovation is a key strategy could achieve superior short-run financial performance by reducing money spent on R&D. A good balanced scorecard would signal that the short-run financial performance may have been achieved by taking actions that hurt future financial performance because a leading indicator of that performance, R&D spending and R&D output, has declined.

[5]Not-for-profit organizations have other primary objectives such as number of people served and development goals reached.

Pitfalls When Implementing a Balanced Scorecard

Pitfalls to avoid when implementing a balanced scorecard include:

1. Don't assume the cause-and-effect linkages to be precise. They are merely hypotheses. A critical challenge is to identify the strength and speed of the causal linkages among the nonfinancial and financial measures. Hence, an organization must gather evidence of these linkages over time. With experience, organizations should alter their scorecards to include those nonfinancial objectives and measures that are the best leading indicators of subsequent financial performance (a lagging indicator). Committing to evolve the scorecard over time avoids the paralysis associated with trying to design the "perfect" scorecard at the outset.

2. Don't seek improvements across all measures all the time. This approach may be inappropriate because trade-offs may need to be made across various strategic goals. For example, emphasizing quality and on-time performance beyond a point may not be worthwhile—improving these objectives may be inconsistent with profit maximization.

3. Don't use only objective measures on the scorecard. Chipset's scorecard includes both objective measures (such as operating income from cost leadership, market share and manufacturing yield), as well as subjective measures (such as customer and employee satisfaction surveys). When using subjective measures, management must trade off the benefits of the richer information these measures provide against the imprecision of and the potential for manipulating these measures.

4. Don't fail to consider both costs and benefits of initiatives such as spending on information technology and research and development before including these objectives in the scorecard. Otherwise management may focus the organization on measures that will not result in overall financial benefits.

5. Don't ignore nonfinancial measures when evaluating managers and employees. Managers tend to focus on what their performance is measured by. Excluding nonfinancial measures when evaluating performance will reduce the significance and importance that managers give to nonfinancial scorecard measures.

EVALUATING THE SUCCESS OF A STRATEGY

To evaluate how successful it has been in implementing its strategy, Chipset compares the target and actual performance columns of its balanced scorecard in Exhibit 13-1. This comparison indicates that Chipset met most of the targets it had set on the basis of competitor benchmarks. Meeting the targets suggests that the strategic initiatives that Chipset had identified and measured for learning and growth resulted in improvements in internal business processes, customer measures, and financial performance. The financial measures show that Chipset achieved targeted cost savings and growth. The key question is, how does Chipset isolate operating income from specific sources such as cost savings and growth instead of focusing on the change in total operating income?

Some companies might be tempted to guage the success of their strategies by measuring the change in their operating incomes from one year to the next, but this approach is inadequate. For example, operating income can increase simply because entire markets are expanding, not because a specific strategy has been successful. Also, changes in operating income might be caused by factors outside the strategy. For example, a company such as Chipset that has chosen a cost leadership strategy may find that operating income increases have instead been caused incidentally by, say, some degree of product differentiation. Company managers and accountants need to evaluate the success of a strategy on the basis of whether the sources of operating income increases are the result of implementing the chosen strategy.

To use operating income numbers to evaluate the success of a strategy, a company needs to isolate the operating income due to cost leadership from the operating income due to product differentiation. Of course, successful cost leadership or product differentiation generally increases market share and helps a company to grow. To evaluate the success of a company's strategy, we subdivide changes in operating income into components that can be identified with growth, product differentiation, and cost leadership. Subdividing the change in operating income to evaluate the success of a company's strategy is similar to variance analysis discussed in Chapters 7 and 8. The focus here, however, is on comparing actual operating performance over two different time periods and explicitly linking it to strategic choices. A company is considered to be successful in implementing its strategy when the amounts of the product differentiation, cost leadership, and growth components align closely with its strategy.

STRATEGIC ANALYSIS OF OPERATING INCOME

The following simplified example illustrates how operating income changes between two years can be divided into components that can describe how successful a company has been with regard to cost leadership, product differentiation, and growth.[6] Chipset presents the following data for the years 1999 and 2000.

OBJECTIVE 4

Analyze changes in operating income to evaluate strategy

	1999	2000
1. Good units of CX1 produced and sold	1,000,000	1,150,000
2. Defective units of CX1 produced and disposed of a zero net disposal price	500,000	300,000
3. Selling price	$27	$25
4. Direct materials (square centimetres of silicon wafer)	3,000,000	2,900,000
5. Direct materials cost per square centimetre	$1.40	$1.50
6. Manufacturing capacity	1,875,000 units	1,750,000 units
7. Total manufacturing conversion costs	$11,250,000	$10,850,000
8. Manufacturing conversion costs per unit of capacity (Row 7 ÷ Row 6)	$6	$6.20
9. Selling and customer service capacity	60 customers	55 customers
10. Total selling and customer service costs	$4,800,000	$4,400,000
11. Cost per customer of selling and customer service capacity (Row 10 ÷ Row 9)	$80,000	$80,000
12. R&D employees	40	39
13. Total R&D costs	$4,000,000	$3,900,000
14. R&D costs per employee (Row 12 ÷ Row 11)	$100,000	$100,000

Chipset provides the following additional information.

1. Manufacturing conversion costs for each year depend on production capacity defined in terms of the number of units of CX1 that can be produced. Such costs do not vary with the actual quantity of CX1 units produced. Because direct manufacturing labour costs are small (and tied to capacity), Chipset includes these costs and other manufacturing costs as part of manufacturing conversion costs rather than as a separate cost category. To reduce manufacturing conversion costs, management would have to reduce capacity by selling some of the manufacturing equipment and laying off some manufacturing personnel.

2. Most of Chipset's marketing costs are costs of selling chips to customers. Selling and customer service costs for each year depend on the number of customers that the selling and customer service functions are designed to support. They do not vary with the actual number of customers Chipset sells to in each year. Chipset had 40 customers in 1999 and 46 customers in 2000. To reduce selling and customer service costs, Chipset management would have to lay off selling and customer service staff.

[6]For other details, see R. Banker, S. Datar and R. Kaplan, "Productivity Measurement and Management Accounting," *Journal of Accounting, Auditing and Finance* (1989, pp. 528-554).

3. At the start of each year, management uses its discretion to determine the amount of R&D to be done. The amount of R&D is independent of the actual quantity of CX1 produced or the number of customers to whom CX1 is sold.

4. The investment base and asset structure are not materially different in the years 1999 and 2000.

Operating income for each year is as follows.

	1999	2000
Revenues ($27 × 1,000,000; $25 × 1,150,000)	$27,000,000	$28,750,000
Costs		
Direct materials costs ($1.40 × 3,000,000; $1.50 × 2,900,000)	4,200,000	4,350,000
Manufacturing conversion costs ($6 × 1,875,000; $6.20 × 1,750,000)	11,250,000	10,850,000
Selling and customer-service costs ($80,000 × 60; $80,000 × 55)	4,800,000	4,400,000
R&D costs	4,000,000	3,900,000
Total costs	24,250,000	23,500,000
Operating income	$ 2,750,000	$ 5,250,000
Increase in operating income		$2,500,000

Our goal is to evaluate how much of this $2,500,000 increase in operating income was caused by the successful implementation of the company's strategy. To do so, we examine three main analysis components: growth, price recovery, and productivity.

The **growth component** measures the change in operating income attributable solely to an increase in the quantity of output sold between 1999 and 2000. That is, it measures the increase in revenues minus the increase in costs from selling more units of CX1. The calculations for the growth component are similar to the sales-volume variance in Chapter 7.

The **price-recovery component** measures the change in operating income attributable solely to changes in Chipset's profit margins between 1999 and 2000. The calculations for the price-recovery component are similar to the selling-price variance and input price variances for materials, labour, and overhead calculated in Chapters 7 and 8. The price-recovery component measures the amount by which output price increases outstrip input price increases. A company that has successfully pursued a strategy of product differentiation will be able to increase its output price faster than the increase in its input prices, boosting profit margins and operating income—it will show a large positive price-recovery component.

The **productivity component** measures the reduction in costs attributable to a reduction in the quantity of inputs used in 2000 relative to the quantity of inputs that would have been used in 1999 to produce the year 2000 output. The calculations for the productivity component are similar to the efficiency variances calculated in Chapter 7. The productivity component measures the amount by which companies earn operating income by using inputs productively to lower costs even when prices for their products are not increasing. A company that has successfully pursued a strategy of cost leadership will be able to produce a given quantity of output with fewer inputs—it will show a large positive productivity component. Given Chipset's strategy of cost leadership, we expect the increase in operating income to be attributable to the productivity and growth components but not price recovery.

We now examine the three components in detail.

The Growth Component

The growth component measures the increase in revenues minus the increase in costs from selling more units of CX1 in 2000 (1,150,000 units) compared to 1999 (1,000,000 units), assuming nothing else has changed. That is, the output prices, input prices, efficiencies, and capacities of 1999 are assumed to continue into 2000.

Growth component. The measurement of the change in operating income attributable solely to an increase in the quantity of output sold.

Price-recovery component. The measurement of the amount by which output price increases outstrip input price increases.

Productivity component. The measurement of the amount by which companies earn operating income by using inputs to lower costs even when prices for their products are not increasing.

Revenue Effect of Growth

$$\begin{pmatrix} \text{Revenue effect} \\ \text{of growth} \\ \text{component} \end{pmatrix} = \begin{pmatrix} \text{Actual units of output} \\ \text{sold in 2000} \end{pmatrix} - \begin{pmatrix} \text{Actual units of output} \\ \text{sold in 1999} \end{pmatrix} \times \begin{matrix} \text{Output price} \\ \text{in 1999} \end{matrix}$$

$$= (1{,}150{,}000 - 1{,}000{,}000) \times \$27 = \$4{,}050{,}000 \text{ F}$$

This component is favourable (F) because it increases operating income. Decreases in operating income are unfavourable (U).

Note that we keep the 1999 price of CX1 unchanged and focus only on the increase in output sold between 1999 and 2000. Why? Because the objective of the revenue effect of the growth component is to isolate the increase in revenues between 1999 and 2000 due solely to the change in the quantity sold, *assuming* the 1999 selling price continues into 2000.

Cost Effect of Growth. Of course, to produce the higher output sold in 2000, more inputs would be needed. The cost increase from growth measures the amount by which costs in 2000 would have increased (1) if the relationship between inputs and outputs that existed in 1999 continued in 2000, and (2) if prices of inputs in 1999 continued in 2000.

$$\begin{pmatrix} \text{Cost effect} \\ \text{of growth} \\ \text{component} \end{pmatrix} = \begin{pmatrix} \text{Actual units of input or capacity} \\ \text{that would have been used to} \\ \text{produce year 2000 output} \\ \text{assuming the same input-output} \\ \text{relationship that existed in 1999} \end{pmatrix} - \begin{pmatrix} \text{Actual units of input} \\ \text{capacity to produce} \\ \text{1999 output} \end{pmatrix} \times \begin{matrix} \text{Input} \\ \text{prices} \\ \text{in 1999} \end{matrix}$$

We use 1999 input-output relationships and 1999 input prices because the goal is to isolate the increase in costs caused solely by the growth in the units of CX1 sold between 1999 and 2000. The actual units of input or capacity to produce 1999 output is given in the basic data for Chipset on p. 461. A brief explanation follows of the individual calculations for the actual units of input or capacity that would have been used to produce year 2000 output, assuming the same input-output relationship that existed in 1999.

◆ *Direct materials.* To produce 1,150,000 units of CX1 in 2000 compared to the 1,000,000 units produced in 1999 (15% more), Chipset would require a proportionate increase in the 3,000,000 square centimetres of direct materials used in 1999. That is, the quantity of direct materials that would be required equals 3,450,000 square centimetres ($3{,}000{,}000 \times \frac{1{,}150{,}000}{1{,}000{,}000}$).

◆ *Manufacturing conversion costs.* For simplicity, our example assumes manufacturing conversion costs are fixed costs at any given level of capacity. Chipset has 1,875,000 units of manufacturing capacity in 1999 at a cost of $11,250,000. To produce the higher year 2000 output of 1,150,000 units of CX1 in 1999, assuming the same input-output relationship that existed in 1999, Chipset would need to use 1,725,000 units of this capacity. Therefore, Chipset would not need any additional capacity. To see this point, recall that to produce 1,000,000 good units of CX1, Chipset actually processed 1,500,000 units of CX1 in 1999 (of which 500,000 units were defective). To produce 15% more units in 1999, assuming the same input-output (defect-rate) relationship as in 1999, Chipset would be required to process, $1{,}500{,}000 \times 1.15$ (the growth factor) = 1,725,000 units.

◆ *Selling and customer-service costs.* Selling and customer service costs are fixed costs at any given level of capacity. These costs do not change as a result of producing and selling more units of CX1 because the selling and customer service capacity of 60 customers in 1999 is large enough to support both the 40 customers in 1999 and the 46 customers in 2000.

◆ *R&D costs.* R&D costs are fixed costs unless management uses its discretion to change the level of costs. The R&D costs incurred in 1999 do not change as result of producing and selling more units of CX1 in 2000 because R&D costs are adequate to support the higher output of CX1. R&D costs do not depend on either the quantity of CX1 produced or the number of customers to whom CX1 is sold.

The cost effects of growth component are:

Direct materials costs	$(3,450,000 - 3,000,000) \times \$1.40$	$= \$630,000$ U
Manuf. conversion costs	$(1,875,000 - 1,875,000) \times \$6$	$= 0$
Selling and customer-service costs	$(60 - 60) \times \$80,000$	$= 0$
R&D costs	$(40 - 40) \times \$100,000$	$= 0$
Cost effects of growth component		$\$630,000$ U

In summary, the net increase in operating income as a result of growth equals:

Revenue effect of growth component	$\$4,050,000$ F
Cost effect of growth component	$630,000$ U
Increase in operating income due to growth component	$\$3,420,000$ F

The Price-Recovery Component

The price recovery component of operating income measures the change in revenues and the change in costs to produce the 1,150,000 units of CX1 manufactured in 2000 as a result of the change in the prices of CX1 and the change in the prices of inputs required to make CX1, assuming that the relationship between inputs and outputs that existed in 1999 continued in 2000.

Revenue Effect of Price Recovery

$$\begin{array}{c} \text{Revenue effect} \\ \text{of product differentiation} \\ \text{component} \end{array} = \left(\begin{array}{c} \text{Output price} \\ \text{in 2000} \end{array} - \begin{array}{c} \text{Output price} \\ \text{in 1999} \end{array} \right) \times \begin{array}{c} \text{Actual units of} \\ \text{output sold} \\ \text{in 2000} \end{array}$$

$$= (\$25 - \$27) \times 1,150,000 = \$2,300,000 \text{ U}$$

Note that the calculation focuses on the decrease in the price of CX1 between 1999 and 2000. Why? Because the objective of the revenue effect of price recovery is to isolate the change in revenues between 1999 and 2000 due solely to the change in selling prices.

Cost Effect of Price Recovery

$$\begin{array}{c} \text{Cost effect} \\ \text{of product} \\ \text{differentiation} \\ \text{component} \end{array} = \left(\begin{array}{c} \text{Input prices} \\ \text{in year 2000} \end{array} - \begin{array}{c} \text{Input prices} \\ \text{in year 1999} \end{array} \right) \times \begin{array}{c} \text{Actual units of inputs/capacity} \\ \text{that would have been used to} \\ \text{produce year 2000 output} \\ \text{assuming the same input-output} \\ \text{relationship that existed in 1999} \end{array}$$

Direct materials costs	$(\$1.50 - \$1.40) \times 3,450,000$	$= \$345,000$ U
Manufacturing conversion costs	$(\$6.20 - \$6.00) \times 1,875,000$	$= 375,000$ U
Selling, and customer-service costs	$(\$80,000 - \$80,000) \times 60$	$= 0$
R&D costs	$(\$100,000 - \$100,000) \times 40$	$= 0$
Total cost effect of price-recovery component		$\$720,000$ U

Note that the quantity of inputs that would have been needed to produce the output in year 2000 (assuming the relationship between inputs and outputs that existed in 1999 continued in 2000), has already been determined when calculating the cost effects of growth. The calculation focuses on the change in costs caused solely by the change in the prices of inputs between 1999 and 2000.

In summary, the net decrease in operating income attributable to price recovery (measured by the change in output prices relative to the change in input prices) is

Revenue effect of price-recovery component	$\$2,300,000$ U
Cost effect of price-recovery component	$720,000$ U
Decrease in operating income due to price-recovery component	$\$3,020,000$ U

The price-recovery analysis indicates that, even as the prices of its inputs increased, Chipset could not pass these increases on to its customers via higher prices of CX1.

The Productivity Component

The productivity component of operating income compares how costs have decreased as a result of using fewer inputs, a better mix of inputs, and less capacity to produce year 2000 output, assuming year 2000 input prices.

$$\begin{pmatrix} \text{Productivity/} \\ \text{cost leadership} \\ \text{component} \end{pmatrix} = \begin{pmatrix} \text{Actual units of} \\ \text{input/capacity to} \\ \text{produce year} \\ \text{2000 input} \end{pmatrix} - \begin{pmatrix} \text{Actual units of inputs/capacity that} \\ \text{would have been used to produce} \\ \text{year 2000 output assuming the} \\ \text{same input–output relationship that} \\ \text{existed in 1999} \end{pmatrix} \times \begin{pmatrix} \text{Year} \\ \text{2000} \\ \text{prices} \end{pmatrix}$$

Note that the calculations use year 2000 prices and year 2000 output. Why? Because the objective of the productivity component is to isolate the change in costs between 1999 and 2000 caused solely by the change in the quantities, mix, and capacities of inputs.

The actual units of capacity that would have been used to produce year 2000 output, assuming the same input-output relationship that existed in 1999, have already been calculated and explained when computing the growth component (p. 464). The actual units of inputs or capacity to produce year 2000 output is given in the basic data for Chipset on p. 461.

The productivity component of cost changes is:

Direct materials costs	$(2,900,000 - 3,450,000) \times \$1.50$ =	$825,000 F
Manufacturing conversion costs	$(1,750,000 - 1,875,000) \times \$6.20$ =	775,000 F
Selling and customer-service costs	$(55 - 60) \times \$80,000$ =	400,000 F
R&D costs	$(39 - 40) \times \$100,000$ =	100,000 F
Increase in operating income due to productivity component		$2,100,000 F

We comment briefly on the individual items of the productivity component.

- *Direct materials.* As indicated earlier, at the 1999 quality levels, Chipset would have required 3,450,000 $(3,000,000 \times \frac{1,150,000}{1,000,000})$ square centimetres of silicon wafers to produce 1,150,000 good units of CX1 in 2000. As a result of improvements in quality and yield, Chipset processes 2,900,000 square centimetres of silicon wafers or the equivalent of 1,450,000 $(2,900,000 \div 2)$ units of CX1.

- *Manufacturing conversion costs* are fixed costs that change only if management takes actions to alter manufacturing capacity. Because of the reengineered processes and quality improvements, Chipset needs to put into process only 1,450,000 units to produce 1,150,000 good units of CX1 in the year 2000. In 1999, Chipset had the capacity to process 1,875,000 units. To reduce costs, Chipset's management decreases capacity to 1,750,000 units of CX1, by selling some old equipment and laying off some workers.

- *Selling and customer-service costs* are fixed costs that change only if management takes actions to alter selling and customer-service capacity. Chipset has 46 customers in the year 2000. It started 2000 with a selling and customer-service capability for 60 customers. Although Chipset may add more customers, the goal of reengineering the order-delivery process is to enter into long-term contracts to increase sales to existing customers. To reduce costs, Chipset's management decreases capacity to 55 customers by not replacing marketing personnel that retired or quit.

- *R&D costs* are also fixed costs that change only if management takes actions to reduce the number of R&D employees. Chipset has 39 research engineers in the year 2000. It started 2000 with 40 engineers. Chipset's management did not replace the engineer who quit during the year.

The productivity component indicates that Chipset was able to increase operating income by improving quality and productivity, eliminating capacity, and reducing costs. The Appendix to the chapter examines partial and total factor productivity changes between 1999 and 2000 and describes how the management accountant can obtain a deeper understanding of Chipset's cost leadership strategy.

Exhibit 13-3 summarizes the growth, price recovery and productivity components of the changes in operating income. At a basic level, companies that have been successful at cost leadership will show large favourable productivity and growth components; companies that have successfully differentiated their products will show large favorable price-recovery and growth components. In Chipset's case productivity contributed $2,100,000 to the increase in operating income and growth contributed $3,420,000. Operating income suffered because Chipset was unable to pass along increases in input prices. Had Chipset been able to differentiate its product, the price effects may have been less unfavourable.

Further Analysis of Growth, Price-Recovery, and Productivity Components

As in all variance and profit analysis, the thoughtful analyst will want to analyze the sources of operating income more closely. For instance, in the Chipset example, growth may have been helped by an increase in industry market size. Therefore, at least a part of the increase in operating income may be attributable to favorable economic conditions in the industry rather than to any successful implementation of strategy. Some of the growth may also have come as a result of a management decision at Chipset to take advantage of its productivity gains by cutting prices. In this case, the increase in operating income from cost leadership equals the productivity gain plus any increase in operating income from growth in market share attributable to productivity improvements minus any decrease in operating income from a strategic decision to lower prices.

To illustrate these ideas, consider again the Chipset example and the following additional information.

◆ The market growth rate in the industry is 10%. That is, of the 150,000 (1,150,000 − 1,000,000) units of increase in sales of CX1 between 1999 and 2000, 100,000 (10% × 1,000,000) units are due to an increase in industry market size (which Chipset would have benefited from regardless of its productivity gains) and the remaining 50,000 units are due to an increase in market share.

◆ Of the $2 decrease in the selling price of CX1, $1.25 is due to a general decline in the market prices of chips in the industry. The further decrease of $0.75 is the result of a management decision to lower prices to take advantage of its productivity gains, which increased market share by 50,000 units.

Chipset would compute the increase in operating income from cost leadership as follows:

Productivity component	$2,100,000 F
Decrease in price of CX1 ($0.75 × 1,150,000 units)	862,500 U
Growth in market share due to productivity improvement and lower prices	
$3,420,000 (from Exh. 13-3, col. 2) × $\dfrac{50,000 \text{ units}}{150,000 \text{ units}}$	1,140,000 F
Change in operating income due to cost leadership	$2,377,500 F

Further suppose that the growth in market size was the result of a decrease in industry-wide market prices. Then the effect on Chipset's operating income from industry-wide effects rather than specific strategic actions is:

Change in operating income due to growth in industry market size	
(3,420,000 (Exh. 13-3, Col. 2) × $\dfrac{100,000}{150,000}$	$2,280,000 F
Change in operating income due to decline in industry-wide selling prices	
$1.25 × 1,150,000	1,437,500 U
Effect on operating income of industry-wide factors	$ 842,500 F

EXHIBIT 13-3
Strategic Analysis of Profitability

	Income Statement Amounts in 1999 (1)	Revenue and Cost Effects of Growth Component in 2000 (2)	Revenue and Cost Effects of Price-Recovery Component in 2000 (3)	Cost Effect of Productivity Component in 2000 (4)	Income Statement Amounts in 2000 (5) = (1)+(2)+(3)+(4)
Revenues	$27,000,000	$4,050,000 F	$2,300,000 U	—	$28,750,000
Costs	24,250,000	630,000 U	720,000 U	$2,100,000 F	23,500,000
Operating income	$ 2,750,000	$3,420,000 F	$3,020,000 U	$2,100,000 F	$ 5,250,000

$2,500,000 F

Change in operating income

CONCEPTS IN ACTION

Linking Performance to Strategy at Chrysler Corporation

Chrysler Corporation's impressive profits in recent years have come despite steep reductions in the selling prices of its products. Chrysler, like many of its competitors in the automotive market, offers "manufacturer rebates" (price discounts) to spur sales. For example, in the second quarter that ended on June 30, 1998, Chrysler offered price discounts of $1,485 per car sold to entice buyers, 50% higher than the $980 average price discount that Chrysler gave in 1997. As news of these higher price discounts in 1998 reached investors and analysts, they expected Chrysler's operating incomes to decrease. But Chrysler easily surpassed Wall Street's expectations. How? Through productivity gains that resulted in lower costs. Chrysler passed on these cost savings to its customers in the form of lower prices in return for higher sales and an increase in its North American market share from 15.5% in 1997 to 16.1% in the first half of 1998.

Chrysler Corporation
www.daimlerchrysler.com

Chrysler's goal is to cut costs by $1.5 billion in 1998. By the middle of 1998, Chrysler had already cut costs by about $800 million. Improvements in efficiency and productivity reduced engineered costs of direct materials and manufacturing labour, as well as indirect manufacturing costs by hundreds of millions of dollars. Chrysler also cut discretionary costs such as advertising.

Chrysler's strategic analysis of operating income for 1998 indicates that operating income increases were due largely to successful implementation of its cost leadership strategy. Cost leadership, however, is not the key strategy in all of Chrysler's businesses. Chrysler is an innovative product differentiator in the minivan and sports utility vehicle (SUV) market. It "invented" the minivan and has a very strong presence in the SUV market. Its Dodge Caravan and Plymouth Voyager minivans and its Dodge Durango, Jeep, and Jeep Cherokee SUVs enjoy high margins because customers are willing to pay premium prices for these innovative products.

Chrysler emphasizes both financial and nonfinancial measures. For example, the company regularly monitors nonfinancial measures of customer satisfaction, customer preferences, delivery times, quality, defects and yields, new product development time, and employee capability, skills, and satisfaction. These nonfinancial measures span the four perspectives—financial, customer, internal business process, and learning and growth—of the balanced scorecard.

Source: Adapted from B.J. Feder, "Chrysler Posts Strong Second Quarter Earnings," The New York Times, July 14, 1998 and conversations with Chrysler executives.

Lacking a differentiated product, Chipset is unable to pass along increases in input prices to its customers. The effect of product differentiation on operating income is:

Increase in market prices of inputs (cost effect of price recovery) $720,000 U

The change in operating income between 1999 and 2000 can then be summarized as:

Change due to cost leadership	$2,377,500 F
Change due to industry-wide factors	842,500 F
Change due to product differentiation	720,000 U
Change in operating income	$2,500,000 F

Under different assumptions of how changes in prices affect the quantity of CX1 sold, the analyst will attribute different amounts to the different strategies. The important point, though, is that, consistent with its cost leadership strategy, the productivity gains of $2,100,000 Chipset made in 2000 were key to the operating income increases in 2000.

DOWNSIZING AND THE MANAGEMENT OF CAPACITY

OBJECTIVE 5

Distinguish between engineered and discretionary costs

As we saw in our discussion of the productivity component, fixed costs are tied to capacity. Unlike variable costs, fixed costs do not change automatically with changes in the level of the cost driver (such as units started into production in the case of manufacturing overhead costs). How then can managers reduce capacity-based fixed costs? The key is in understanding and managing unused capacity. To understand unused capacity, managers find it useful to classify costs into *engineered* and *discretionary* categories.

Engineered costs. Costs that result from a clear cause-and-effect relationship between output (or cost driver) and the (direct or indirect) resources used to produce that output.

Engineered costs result specifically from a clear cause-and-effect relationship between output (or cost driver) and the (direct or indirect) resources used to produce that output. In the Chipset example, direct materials costs are an example of direct engineered costs. Manufacturing conversion costs are an example of indirect engineered costs. Consider the year 2000. The output of 1,150,000 units of CX1 and the efficiency with which inputs are converted into outputs result in 1,450,000 units of CX1 started into production. Manufacturing conversion resources needed and used to process 1,450,000 units of CX1 equal $8,990,000 ($6.20 × 1,450,000), assuming that the cost of resources used increases proportionately with the number of units started. Of course, total manufacturing conversion costs are higher ($10,850,000) because they are related to the manufacturing capacity of 1,750,000 units ($6.20 × 1,750,000 = $10,850,000). These costs are fixed in the short run but, over time, there is a clear cause-and-effect relationship between output, manufacturing capacity required, and manufacturing conversion costs needed. Thus, engineered costs can be variable or fixed in the short-run. Selling and customer-service cost is also an example of an engineered cost that is fixed in the short run. There is, however, a clear cause-and-effect relationship between selling and customer-service resources used and the number of customers served.

Discretionary costs. Costs that have no clearly measurable cause-and-effect relationship between output and resources used, and they arise from periodic decisions regarding the maximum amount of costs to be incurred.

Discretionary costs have two important features: (1) they arise from periodic (usually yearly) decisions regarding the maximum amount to be incurred, and (2) they have no clearly measurable cause-and-effect relationship between output and resources used. There is often a delay between the acquisition of a resource and its eventual use. Examples of discretionary costs include advertising, executive training, R&D, health care, and corporate staff department costs such as legal, human resources, and public relations. The most noteworthy aspect of discretionary costs is that managers are seldom confident that the "correct" amounts are being spent. The founder of Lever Brothers, an international consumer-products company, once noted, "Half the money I spend on advertising is wasted; the trouble is, I don't know which half." In the Chipset example, R&D costs are discretionary costs because there is no measurable cause-and-effect relationship between output of 1,150,000 units produced and R&D resources needed or used.[7]

Relationships between Inputs and Outputs

Engineered costs differ from discretionary costs along two key dimensions: the type of process and the level of uncertainty. Engineered costs pertain to processes that are detailed, physically observable, and repetitive, such as manufacturing or customer service activities. In contrast, discretionary costs are associated with processes that are sometimes called *black boxes*, because they are less precise and not well understood.

Uncertainty refers to the possibility that an actual amount will deviate from an expected amount. The higher the level of uncertainty about the relationship between resources used and outputs, the less likely a cause-and-effect relationship will exist, leading the cost to be classified as a discretionary cost. R&D costs have an uncertain effect on output because other factors such as overall market conditions, competitors' R&D investments, and new product introductions also affect the level of output produced. In contrast, there is a low level of uncertainty about the effect of output on manufacturing conversion resources used because other factors do not affect this relationship. Uncertainty is greater in the case of discretionary costs such as R&D because, in most cases, R&D resources are committed well before any output is produced. Exhibit 13-4 summarizes these key distinctions between engineered and discretionary costs.

Identifying Unused Capacity for Engineered and Discretionary Overhead Costs

How does the distinction between engineered and discretionary costs help a manager to understand and manage unused capacity? Actually, the different types of costs have very different relationships to capacity. Consider first the engineered manufacturing conversion costs. Chipset management indicates that manufacturing capacity can be added or reduced in increments of 125,000 units. Adding capacity, however, takes time. Manufacturing conversion costs are a step function as shown in Exhibit 13-5. Each step represents increments of 125,000 units of capacity at a cost of $775,000. At each step, manufacturing conversion costs are fixed. For example,

EXHIBIT 13-4
Differences Between Engineered and Discretionary Costs

	Engineered Costs	**Discretionary Costs**
1. Process or activity	a. Detailed and physically observable	a. Black box (knowledge of process is sketchy or unavailable)
	b. Repetitive	b. Nonrepetitive or nonroutine
2. Level of uncertainty	Moderate or small (for example, shipping or manufacturing settings)	Large (for example, R&D or advertising settings)

Source: This exhibit is a modification of one suggested by H. Itami.

[7]Managers also describe some costs as **infrastructure costs**, costs that arise from having property, plant and equipment, and a functioning organization. Examples are amortization, long-run lease rental, and the acquisition of long-run technical capabilities. These costs are generally fixed costs, because they are committed to and acquired before they are used. Infrastructure costs can be engineered or discretionary. For instance, manufacturing overhead costs incurred at Chipset to acquire manufacturing capacity is an infrastructure cost that is an example of an engineered cost. In the long run, there is a clear cause-and-effect relationship between output and lease rental costs needed to produce that output. R&D costs incurred to acquire technical capability is an infrastructure cost that is an example of a discretionary cost. There is no clear cause-and-effect relationship between output and R&D costs incurred.

Infrastructure costs. Costs that arise from having property, plant and equipment, and a functioning organization.

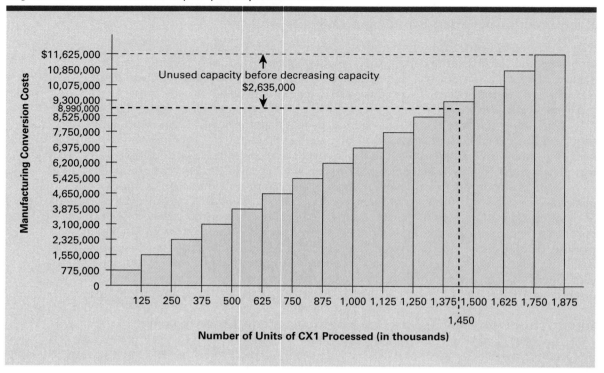

manufacturing conversion costs are fixed at $9,300,000 if Chipset wants enough capacity to process between 1,375,000 and 1,500,000 units.

At the start of the year 2000, Chipset has capacity to process 1,875,000 units. Quality and productivity improvements made during 2000 enable Chipset to produce 1,150,000 units of CX1 by processing 1,450,000 units. Chipset calculates its unused manufacturing capacity as 425,000 (1,875,000 – 1,450,000) units for 2000, which corresponds to manufacturing conversion costs of $2,635,000 ($6.20 × 425,000 units). As shown in Exhibit 13-5, this unused capacity of $2,635,000 can also be calculated as $11,625,000 (manufacturing overhead costs for 1,875,000 units) minus $8,990,000 ($6.20 × 1,450,000, the manufacturing resources used to process 1,450,000 units).

The absence of a cause-and-effect relationship makes identifying unused capacity for discretionary costs much more difficult. Management cannot determine the R&D resources used for the actual output produced to compare R&D capacity against. Consequently, they cannot compute unused capacity as they did in the case of the engineered manufacturing conversion costs.

Managing Unused Capacity

OBJECTIVE 6

Identify and manage unused capacity

Downsizing (rightsizing). An integrated approach to configure processes, products, and people to match costs to the activities needed to be performed to operate effeciently and effectively in the present and future.

What actions can Chipset management take when it identifies unused capacity? In general, it has two options. It can attempt to eliminate the unused capacity, or it can attempt to use the unused capacity to grow revenues.

In recent years, many companies have tried to *downsize* in an attempt to eliminate their unused capacity. **Downsizing** (also called **rightsizing**) is an integrated approach to configure processes, products, and people to match costs to the activities needed to be performed to operate efficiently and effectively in the present and future. Companies such as Bell Canada, Canadian Airlines, General Motors, IBM, and Molson's have downsized to focus on their core businesses and have instituted organization changes to increase efficiency, reduce costs, and improve quality. Downsizing often means eliminating jobs, which can have an adverse effect on employee morale and the culture of the organization. It is important that downsizing be done in the context of the organization's overall strategy, and by retaining individuals with key management, leadership, and technical skills.

Consider Chipset's options with respect to its unused manufacturing capacity. Because it needs to process 1,450,000 units in 2000, it could potentially reduce capacity to 1,500,000 units (recall that manufacturing conversion capacity can be added or reduced only in increments of 125,000 units) resulting in cost savings of $2,325,000 [(1,875,000 – 1,500,000 × $6.20]. Chipset's strategy, however, is not only to cut costs but also to grow its business. So Chipset only reduces its manufacturing capacity by 125,000 units from 1,875,000 units to 1,750,000 units, saving $775,000 ($6.20 × 125,000). It retains some unused capacity for future growth. By avoiding deep cuts in capacity, it also maintains the morale of its skilled and capable work force. The success of this strategy will depend on Chipset achieving the future growth it has projected.

Chipset makes similar decisions with respect to the engineered selling and customer-service costs. At the start of 2000, Chipset has the capacity to serve 60 customers. Chipset currently has 46 customers, resulting in unused service capacity of 14 customers, which corresponds to $1,120,000 ($80,000 × 14) in selling and customer-service costs. (Recall that it costs $80,000 to support each customer.) Chipset could potentially reduce selling and customer-service capacity by 10 customers. However, because the company anticipates adding 9 more customers in the near future, it decides only to reduce its selling and customer-service capability from 60 to 55 customers realizing savings of $400,000 ($80,000 × 5). Chipset's goal is to align its selling and customer-service capabilities of 55 customers with its manufacturing capacity of 1,750,000 units.

Because identifying unused capacity for discretionary costs is difficult, downsizing or otherwise managing this unused capacity is also difficult. Chipset's management uses judgment and discretion to reduce R&D costs by $100,000 in 2000. Its rationale is to cut R&D costs without significantly affecting the output of the R&D activity. Deeper cuts in R&D costs, however, could harm the business by slowing down critically needed product and process improvements. The key is to balance the need for cost reductions without compromising quality, continuous improvement, and future growth.

Following a strategy of product differentiation, Westwood Corporation makes a high-end kitchen range hood, KE8. Westwood presents the following data for the years 1999 and 2000.

	1999	2000
1. Units of KE8 produced and sold	40,000	42,000
2. Selling price	$100	$110
3. Direct materials (square metres)	120,000	123,000
4. Direct materials costs per square metre	$10	$11
5. Manufacturing capacity for KE8	50,000 units	50,000 units
6. Total manufacturing conversion costs	$1,000,000	$1,110,000
7. Manufacturing conversion costs per unit of capacity (Row 6 ÷ Row 5)	$20	$22
8. Selling and customer-service capacity	30 customers	29 customers
9. Total selling and customer-service costs	$720,000	$725,000
10. Cost per customer of selling and customer-service capacity (Row 9 ÷ Row 8)	$24,000	$25,000

Westwood produces no defective units but it wants to reduce direct materials usage per unit of KE8 in 2000. Manufacturing conversion costs in each year depend on production capacity defined in terms of KE8 units that can be produced. Selling and customer-service costs depend on the number of customers that the customer and service functions are designed to support. Westwood has 23 customers in 1999 and 25 customers in 2000. The industry market size for high-end kitchen range hoods increased 5% from 1999 to 2000.

REQUIRED

1. Describe briefly key elements that you would include in Westwood's balanced scorecard.
2. Calculate the growth, price-recovery, and productivity components of changes in operating income between 1999 and 2000.
3. Without doing any more calculations, explain in a few sentences whether Westwood was successful in implementing its strategy.

SOLUTION

1. Key elements that Westwood should include in its balanced scorecard are:

   ◆ *Financial perspective* Operating income growth from charging higher margins on KE8.

   ◆ *Customer perspective* Market share in high-end kitchen range market, and customer satisfaction.

   ◆ *Internal business perspective* Manufacturing quality, order delivery time, on-time delivery, and new product features added.

   ◆ *Learning and growth perspective* Development time for designing new products and improving manufacturing processes.

2. Operating income for each year is as follows:

	1999	2000
Revenues ($100 × 40,000; $110 × 42,000)	$4,000,000	$4,620,000
Costs		
Direct materials costs ($10 × 120,000; $11 × 123,000)	1,200,000	1,353,000
Manufacturing conversion costs ($20 × 50,000; $22 × 50,000)	1,000,000	1,100,000
Selling & cust.-serv. costs ($24,000 × 30; $25,000 × 29)	720,000	725,000
Total costs	2,920,000	3,178,000
Operating income	$1,080,000	$1,442,000
Change in operating income	$362,000 F	

The Growth Component

$$\begin{pmatrix} \text{Revenue effect} \\ \text{of growth} \\ \text{component} \end{pmatrix} = \begin{pmatrix} \text{Actual units} \\ \text{of output sold} \\ \text{in 2000} \end{pmatrix} - \begin{pmatrix} \text{Actual units} \\ \text{of output sold in} \\ 1999 \end{pmatrix} \times \begin{pmatrix} 1999 \\ \text{output} \\ \text{price} \end{pmatrix}$$

$$= (42,000 - 40,000) \times \$100 \times \$200,000 \text{ F}$$

$$\begin{pmatrix} \text{Cost effect} \\ \text{of growth} \\ \text{component} \end{pmatrix} = \begin{pmatrix} \text{Actual units of input/capacity} \\ \text{that would have been used to} \\ \text{produce year 2000 output} \\ \text{assuming the same input-output} \\ \text{relationship that existed in 1999} \end{pmatrix} - \begin{pmatrix} \text{Actual units of} \\ \text{input/capacity to} \\ \text{produce 1999} \\ \text{output} \end{pmatrix} \times \begin{pmatrix} \text{Year} \\ 1999 \\ \text{prices} \end{pmatrix}$$

Direct materials costs that would be required in 2000 to produce 42,000 units instead of the 40,000 units produced in 1999, assuming the 1999 input-output relationship continued into 2000, equal 126,000 square metres ($\frac{120,000}{40,000} \times 42,000$). Manufacturing conversion costs and selling and customer-service costs will not change since adequate capacity exists in 1999 to support year 2000 output and customers.

The cost effects of growth component are:

Direct materials costs	(126,000 − 120,000)	×	$10	= $60,000 U
Manuf. conversion costs	(50,000 − 50,000)	×	$20	= 0
Selling & cust.-serv. costs	(30 − 30)	×	$25,000	= 0
Cost effect of growth component				$60,000 U

In summary, the net increase in operating income as a result of the growth component equals:

Revenue effect of growth component	$200,000 F
Cost effect of growth component	60,000 U
Increase in operating income due to growth component	$140,000 F

The Price-Recovery Component

$$\text{Revenue effect of product differentiation component} = \left(\begin{array}{c} \text{Output price} \\ \text{in 2000} \end{array} - \begin{array}{c} \text{Output price} \\ \text{in 1999} \end{array} \right) \times \begin{array}{c} \text{Actual units of} \\ \text{output sold} \\ \text{in 2000} \end{array}$$

$$= (\$110 - \$100) \times 42,000 = \$420,000 \text{ F}$$

$$\text{Cost effect of product differentiation} = \left(\begin{array}{c} \text{Input price} \\ \text{in year 2000} \end{array} - \begin{array}{c} \text{Input price} \\ \text{in year 1999} \end{array} \right) \times \begin{array}{c} \text{Actual units of input/capacity that} \\ \text{would have been used to produce} \\ \text{year 2000 output assuming the} \\ \text{same input–output relationship} \\ \text{that existed in 1999} \end{array}$$

Direct materials costs	($11 – $10) × 126,000 =	$126,000 U
Manuf. conversion costs	($22 – $20) × 50,000 =	100,000 U
Selling & cust.-serv. costs	($25,000 – $24,000) × 30 =	30,000 U
Total cost effect of price-recovery component		$256,000 U

In summary, the net increase in operating income as a result of the price-recovery component equals:

Revenue effect of price-recovery component	$420,000 F
Cost effect of price-recovery component	256,000 U
Increase in operating income due to price-recovery component	$164,000 F

The Productivity Component

$$\text{Productivity/ cost leadership component} = \left(\begin{array}{c} \text{Actual units of} \\ \text{input/capacity to} \\ \text{produce year} \\ \text{2000 output} \end{array} - \begin{array}{c} \text{Actual units of inputs/} \\ \text{capacity that would have been} \\ \text{used to produce year 2000} \\ \text{output assuming the same} \\ \text{input–output relationship} \\ \text{that existed in 1999} \end{array} \right) \times \begin{array}{c} \text{Year} \\ \text{2000} \\ \text{prices} \end{array}$$

The productivity component of cost changes are:

Direct materials costs	(123,000 – 126,000) × $11 =	$33,000 F
Manuf. conversion costs	(50,000 – 50,000) × $20 =	0
Selling & cust.- serv. costs	(29 – 30) × $25,000 =	25,000 F
Increase in operating income due to productivity component		$58,000 F

The change in operating income between 1999 and 2000 can be analyzed as follows:

	Income Statement Amounts in 1999 (1)	Revenue and Cost Effects of Growth Component in 2000 (2)	Revenue and Cost Effects of Price-Recovery Component in 2000 (3)	Cost Effect of Productivity Component in 2000 (4)	Income Statement Amounts in 2000 (5) = (1)+(2)+(3)+(4)
Revenues	$4,000,000	$200,000 F	$420,000 F	—	$4,620,000
Costs	2,920,000	60,000 U	256,000 U	$58,000 F	3,178,000
Operating income	$1,080,000	$140,000 F	$164,000 F	$58,000 F	$1,442,000

$362,000 F

Change in operating income

3. The analysis of operating income indicates that Westwood was successful in implementing its product differentiation strategy. The company was able to continue to charge a premium price for KE8. Westwood was also able to earn additional operating income from improving its productivity. The growth in units (from 40,000 to 42,000) was attributable entirely to the 5% increase in market size rather than Westwood's product differentiation strategy.

SUMMARY

The following points are linked to this chapter's learning objectives.

1. Two generic strategies that organizations use are product differentiation and cost leadership. Product differentiation refers to offering products and services that are perceived by customers as being superior and unique. Cost leadership is achieving low costs relative to competitors and thus having lower prices.

2. Reengineering is the fundamental rethinking of business processes, such as order delivery, to improve critical performance measures such as cost, quality or customer satisfaction.

3. The balanced scorecard translates an organization's mission and strategy into a comprehensive set of performance measures that provides the framework for a strategic measurement and management system. The scorecard measures performance from four key perspectives (1) financial, (2) customer satisfaction, (3) internal business processes, and (4) learning and growth.

4. To evaluate the success of its strategy, a company can subdivide the change in operating income into growth, price-recovery and productivity components. The growth component measures the increase in revenues over costs from selling more units, assuming no changes in prices, efficiencies or capacities. The price-recovery component measures changes in revenues and changes in costs as a result solely of changes in the prices of outputs and inputs. The productivity component measures the decrease in costs from using fewer inputs and from reducing capacity. A company is considered to be successful in implementing its strategy when the changes in operating income align closely with its strategy.

5. Engineered costs result specifically from a clear cause-and-effect relationship between output and the resources needed to produce that output. Discretionary costs arise from periodic (usually yearly) decisions regarding the maximum amount to be incurred. They are not tied to a clear cause-and-effect relationship between inputs and outputs.

6. Identifying unused capacity is easier for engineered costs than for discretionary costs. Downsizing is an approach to managing unused capacity by matching costs to the activities that need to be performed.

APPENDIX: PRODUCTIVITY MEASUREMENT

Productivity. The measurement of the relationship between actual inputs used and actual outputs produced.

Partial productivity. The comparison of quantity of output produced with the quantity of an individual input used.

Productivity measures the relationship between actual inputs used (both quantities and costs) and actual outputs produced. The lower the inputs for a given quantity of outputs or the higher the outputs for a given quantity of inputs, the higher the level of productivity. Measuring productivity improvements over time highlight the specific input-output relationships that contribute to cost leadership.

Partial Productivity Measures

Partial productivity, the most frequently used productivity measure, compares the quantity of output produced with the quantity of an individual input used. In its most common form, partial productivity is expressed as a ratio:

$$\text{Partial productivity} = \frac{\text{Quantity of output produced}}{\text{Quantity of input used}}$$

The higher the ratio, the greater the productivity.

Consider direct materials productivity at Chipset in the year 2000.

$$\begin{aligned}\text{Direct materials} \atop \text{partial productivity} &= \frac{\text{Quantity of CX1 units produced during 2000}}{\text{Direct materials quantity used to produce CX1 in 2000}}\\[2mm]
&= \frac{1{,}150{,}000 \text{ units of CX1}}{2{,}900{,}000 \text{ cm}^2 \text{ of direct materials}}\\[2mm]
&= 0.40 \text{ units of CX1 per cm}^2 \text{ of direct materials}\end{aligned}$$

Note that the direct materials partial productivity ignores Chipset's other inputs, manufacturing conversion, selling and customer service, and R&D. Partial productivity measures gain meaning when comparisons are made that examine productivity changes over time, either across several facilities, or relative to a benchmark. Exhibit 13-6 presents partial productivity measures for Chipset's various inputs for 1999 and 2000 using information from the productivity calculations on p. 465. These measures compare the actual inputs used in the year 2000 to produce 1,150,000 units of CX1 with the inputs that would have been used in 2000 had the input-output relationship from 1999 continued in 2000.

Evaluating Changes in Partial Productivities

It is important to distinguish between the partial productivity effects of variable and fixed cost components. Why? Because for variable cost elements, such as direct materials, productivity improvements automatically result in using fewer input resources. For example, Chipset's improvements in direct materials productivity in 2000 resulted in 2,900,000 cm^2 of direct materials being acquired and used rather than the 3,450,000 cm^2 that would have been required to produce 1,150,000 units of output in 2000 at the 1999 productivity level. On the other hand, for fixed cost elements such as manufacturing conversion costs, using less of the available fixed capacity resources will not lead automatically to lowering the cost of these resources. To improve, partial productivity in these cases, management must take actions to release workers or reduce capacity. These actions are often more difficult to implement and, as in Exhibit 13-6, result in lower partial productivity gains for fixed-cost categories than for variable-cost categories.

Consider, for example, manufacturing conversion partial productivity. At the 1999 productivity levels, Chipset would need to start 1,725,000 units of CX1 to produce 1,150,000 units. Chipset has manufacturing capacity of 1,875,000 units. Efficiency improvements in 2000 result in Chipset having to start 1,450,000 units in 2000. Reducing the number of units started into production, however, does not

EXHIBIT 13-6
Comparing Chipset's Partial Productivities in 1999 and 2000

Input (1)	Partial Productivity in 2000 (2)	Partial Productivity in 1999 (3)	Percentage Change from 1999 to 2000 (4)
Direct materials	$\frac{1{,}150{,}000}{2{,}900{,}000} = 0.40$	$\frac{1{,}150{,}000}{3{,}450{,}000} = 0.337$	$\frac{0.40 - 0.33}{0.33} = 21.2\%$
Manufacturing conversion	$\frac{1{,}150{,}000}{1{,}750{,}000} = 0.66$	$\frac{1{,}150{,}000}{1{,}875{,}000} = 0.61$	$\frac{0.66 - 0.61}{0.61} = 8.2\%$
Selling and customer service	$\frac{1{,}150{,}000}{55} = 20{,}909$	$\frac{1{,}150{,}000}{60} = 19{,}167$	$\frac{20{,}909 - 19{,}167}{19{,}167} = 9.1\%$
R&D	$\frac{1{,}150{,}000}{39} = 29{,}487$	$\frac{1{,}150{,}000}{40} = 28{,}750$	$\frac{29{,}487 - 28{,}750}{28{,}750} = 2.56\%$

automatically lead to a decrease in manufacturing capacity. Partial productivity increases because Chipset's managers take actions to release workers and reduce manufacturing capacity to 1,750,000 units.

A major advantage of partial productivity measures is that they focus on a single input. As a result, they are simple to calculate and easily understood by operations personnel. Managers and operators examine these numbers to understand the reasons underlying productivity changes from one period to the next. For example, Chipset's managers will evaluate whether the lower defect rates (that resulted in management being able to reduce capacity and increase manufacturing conversion partial productivity from 1999 to 2000) was caused by better training of workers, lower absenteeism, lower labour turnover, better incentives, improved methods, or substitution of materials for labour. Isolating the relevant factors is important because it helps Chipset implement and sustain these practices in the future. Chipset can then set targets for gains in manufacturing conversion productivity and monitor planned productivity improvements.

For all their advantages, partial productivity measures also have some serious drawbacks. Because partial productivity focuses on only one input at a time rather than on all inputs simultaneously, it does not allow managers to evaluate the effect of input substitutions on overall productivity. For example, manufacturing conversion partial productivity may increase from one period to the next while direct materials partial productivity may decrease. Partial productivity measures cannot evaluate whether the increase in manufacturing conversion partial productivity offsets the decrease in direct materials partial productivity. Total factor productivity (TFP) or total productivity is a technique for measuring productivity that considers all inputs simultaneously.

TOTAL FACTOR PRODUCTIVITY

Total factor productivity (TFP). The ratio of the quantity of output produced to the costs of all inputs used, where the inputs are combined on the bases of current period prices.

Total factor productivity (TFP) is the ratio of the quantity of output produced to the costs of all inputs used, where the inputs are combined on the basis of current period prices.

$$\text{Total factor productivity} = \frac{\text{Quantity of output produced}}{\text{Costs of all inputs used}}$$

TFP considers all inputs simultaneously and also considers the trade-offs across inputs based on current input prices. Do not be tempted to think of all productivity measures as physical measures lacking financial content—how many units of output are produced per unit of input. Total factor productivity is intricately tied to minimizing total cost—a financial objective. We next measure changes in TFP at Chipset from 1999 to 2000.

Calculating and Comparing Total Factor Productivity

We first calculate Chipset's TFP in 2000, using 2000 prices and 1,150,000 units of output produced (using information from the first column of the productivity component calculations on p. 465).

$$\begin{aligned}
\frac{\text{Total factor productivity}}{\text{for 2000 using 2000 prices}} &= \frac{\text{Quantity of output produced in 2000}}{\text{Costs of inputs used in 2000 based on 2000 prices}} \\[6pt]
&= \frac{1,150,000}{2,900,000 \times \$1.50 + 1,750,000 \times \$6.20 + 55 \times \$80,000 + 39 \times \$100,000} \\[6pt]
&= \frac{1,150,000}{23,500,000} \\[6pt]
&= 0.048936 \text{ units of output per dollar of input}
\end{aligned}$$

By itself, the 2000 TFP of 0.048936 units of CX1 per dollar of input is not particularly helpful. We need something to compare the 2000 TFP against. One alternative is to compare TFPs of other similar companies in 2000. However, finding similar companies and obtaining accurate comparable data are often difficult. Companies therefore usually compare their own TFP over time. In the Chipset example, we use as a benchmark, TFP calculated using the inputs that Chipset would have used in 1999 to produce 1,150,000 units of CX1 at 2000 prices (that is, we use the costs calculated from the second column in the productivity component calculations on p. 465). Why do we use 2000 prices? Because using the current year's (2000) prices in both calculations controls for input price differences and focuses the analysis on the adjustments the manager made in the quantities of inputs in response to changes in prices.

$$\begin{aligned}\frac{\text{Benchmark}}{\text{TFP}} &= \frac{\text{Quantity of output produced in 2000}}{\begin{array}{c}\text{Costs of inputs that would have been used}\\ \text{in 1999 to produce 2000 output}\end{array}}\\[2mm] &= \frac{1,150,000}{3,450,000 \times \$1.50 + 1,875,000 \times \$6.20 + 60 \times \$80,000 + 40 \times \$100,000}\\[2mm] &= \frac{1,150,000}{25,600,000}\\[2mm] &= 0.044922 \text{ units of output per dollar of inputs}\end{aligned}$$

Using year 2000 prices, total factor productivity increased 8.94% [(0.048936 − 0.044922 ÷ 0.044922] from 1999 to 2000. Note that the 8.94% increase in TFP equals the $2,100,000 gain (Exhibit 13-3 column 4) divided by the $23,500,000 of actual costs incurred in 2000 (Exhibit 13-3, column 5). Total factor productivity increased because Chipset produced more output per dollar of input in 2000 relative to 1999, measured in both years using 2000 prices. The gain in TFP occurs because Chipset increases the partial productivities of individual inputs and, consistent with its strategy, seeks the least expensive combination of inputs to produce CX1. Note that TFP increases cannot be due to differences in input prices because we used year 2000 prices to evaluate both the inputs that Chipset would have used in 1999 to produce 1,150,000 units of CX1, and the inputs actually used in 2000.

Using Both Partial and Total Factor Productivity Measures

A major advantage of TFP is that it measures the combined productivity of all inputs used to produce output. Therefore, it explicitly considers gains from using fewer physical inputs as well as substitution among inputs. Managers can analyze these numbers to understand the reasons for changes in TFP. For example, Chipset's managers will try to evaluate whether the increase in TFP from 1999 to 2000 was due to better human resource management practices, higher quality of materials, or improved manufacturing methods. Chipset will adopt the most successful practices and use TFP measures to implement and evaluate strategy by setting targets and monitoring trends.

Many companies such as Monsanto, a manufacturer of fibers, Behlen Manufacturing, a steel fabricator, and Motorola, a microchip manufacturer, use both partial productivity and total factor productivity to evaluate performance. *Partial productivity and TFP measures work best together because the strengths of one are the weaknesses of the other.*

Although TFP measures are comprehensive, operations personnel find financial TFP measures more difficult to understand and less useful than physical partial productivity measures in performing their tasks. Physical measures of manufacturing labour partial productivity, for example, provide direct feedback to workers about output produced per labour-hour worked by focusing on factors within the workers' control. Manufacturing labour partial productivity also has the advantage that it can be easily compared across time periods because it uses physical inputs rather than inputs that are weighted by the prices prevailing in different periods. Workers, therefore, often prefer to tie productivity-based bonuses to gains in manufacturing labour partial productivity. Unfortunately, this situation creates incentives for workers to substitute materials (and capital) for labour, which improves their own productivity measure while possibly decreasing overall productivity of the company as measured by TFP. To overcome the possible incentive problems of partial productivity measures, some companies—for example, TRW, Eaton, and Whirlpool—explicitly adjust bonuses based on manufacturing labour partial productivity for the effects of other factors such as investments in new equipment and higher levels of scrap. That is, they combine partial productivity with TFP-like measures.

This chapter contains definitions of the following important terms:

balanced scorecard (p. 454)	price-recovery component (p. 462)
cost leadership (p. 454)	product differentiation (p. 454)
discretionary costs (p. 468)	productivity (p. 474)
downsizing (p. 470)	productivity component (p. 462)
engineered costs (p. 468)	reengineering (p. 455)
growth component (p. 462)	rightsizing (p. 470)
infrastructure costs (p. 469)	strategy (p. 453)
partial productivity (p. 474)	total factor productivity (TFP) (p. 476)

▼ ASSIGNMENT MATERIAL

QUESTIONS

13-1 Define strategy.

13-2 Describe the five key forces when analyzing an industry.

13-3 Describe two generic strategies.

13-4 What are the four key perspectives in the balanced scorecard?

13-5 What is reengineering?

13-6 Describe three features of a good balanced scorecard.

13-7 What are three important pitfalls to avoid when implementing a balanced scorecard?

13-8 Describe three key components in doing a strategic analysis of operating income?

13-9 How can an analyst incorporate marketwide factors and the interrelationships between the growth, price-recovery and productivity components into a strategic analysis of operating income?

13-10 How does an engineered cost differ from a discretionary cost?

13-11 "The distinction between engineered and discretionary costs is irrelevant when identifying unused capacity." Do you agree? Comment briefly.

13-12 What is downsizing?

13-13 What is a partial productivity measure?

13-14 What is total factor productivity?

13-15 "We are already measuring total factor productivity. Measuring partial productivities would be of no value." Do you agree? Comment briefly.

EXERCISES

13-16 Balanced scorecard. La Quinta Corporation manufactures corrugated cardboard boxes. It competes and plans to grow by producing high quality boxes at a low cost that are delivered to customers in a timely manner. There are many other manufacturers who produce similar boxes. La Quinta believes that continuously improving its manufacturing processes and having satisfied employees are critical to implementing its strategy in 2001.

REQUIRED

1. Is La Quinta's 2001 strategy, one of product differentiation or cost leadership? Explain briefly.

2. Indicate two measures you would expect to see under each perspective on La Quinta's balanced scorecard for 2001. Explain your answer briefly.

13-17 Analysis of growth, price-recovery and productivity components (continuation of 13-16). An analysis of La Quinta's operating income changes between 2000 and 2001 shows the following:

The industry market size for corrugated boxes did not grow in 2001, input prices did not change, and La Quinta reduced the price of its boxes in line with the market.

Operating income for 2000		$1,600,000
Add growth component		10,000
Deduct price-recovery component		(50,000)
Add productivity component		180,000
Operating income for 2001		$1,740,000

REQUIRED

1. Was La Quinta's gain in operating income in 2001 consistent with the strategy you identified in requirement 1 of Exercise 13-16?
2. Explain the productivity component. In general, does it represent savings in only variable costs, only fixed costs, or both variable and fixed costs?

13-18 Strategy, balanced scorecard. Meredith Corporation makes a special-purpose machine D4H used in the textile industry. Meredith has designed the D4H machine for 2000 to be distinct from its competitors. It has been generally regarded as a superior machine. Meredith presents the following data for the years 1999 and 2000.

	1999	2000
1. Units of D4H produced and sold	200	210
2. Selling price	$40,000	$42,000
3. Direct materials (kilograms)	300,000	310,000
4. Direct materials cost per kilogram	$8	$8.50
5. Manufacturing capacity in units of D4H	250	250
6. Total manufacturing conversion costs	$2,000,000	$2,025,000
7. Manufacturing conversion costs per unit of capacity	$8,000	$8,100
8. Selling and customer-service capacity	100 customers	100 customers
9. Total selling and customer-service costs	$1,000,000	$990,000
10. Selling and customer-service capacity cost per customer	$10,000	$9,900
11. Design staff	12	12
12. Total design costs	$1,200,000	$1,212,000
13. Design costs per employee	$100,000	$101,000

Meredith produces no defective machines, but it wants to reduce direct materials usage per D4H machine in 2000. Manufacturing conversion costs in each year depend on production capacity defined in terms of D4H units that can be produced, not the actual units of D4H produced. Selling and customer-service costs depend on the number of customers that Meredith can support, not the actual number of customers Meredith serves. Meredith has 75 customers in 1999 and 80 customers in 2000. At the start of each year, management uses its discretion to determine the number of design staff for the year. The design staff and costs have no direct relationship with the quantity of D4H produced or the number of customers to whom D4H is sold.

REQUIRED

1. Is Meredith's strategy one of product differentiation or cost leadership? Explain briefly.
2. Describe briefly key elements that you would include in Meredith's balanced scorecard and the reasons for doing so.

13-19 Strategic analysis of operating income. Refer to the information in Exercise 13-18.

REQUIRED

1. Calculate the operating income of Meredith Corporation in 1999 and 2000.
2. Calculate the growth, price-recovery, and productivity components of changes in operating income between 1999 and 2000.
3. Comment on your answer in requirement 2. What do these components indicate?

13-20 Analysis of growth, price-recovery, and productivity components (continuation of 13-19). Suppose that between 1999 and 2000 the market for Meredith's special-purpose machines grew at 3%, and that industry-wide selling prices increased by 2.5%.

REQUIRED

Calculate how much of the change in operating income between 1999 and 2000 is due to industry-wide factors, cost leadership, and product differentiation. How successful has Meredith been in implementing its strategy?

13-21 Identifying and managing unused capacity. Refer to the Meredith Corporation information in Exercise 13-18.

REQUIRED
1. Where possible, calculate the amount and cost of unused capacity for (a) manufacturing, (b) selling and customer-service, and (c) design in the year 2000. If you could not calculate the amount and cost of unused capacity, indicate why not.
2. Suppose Meredith can add or reduce its manufacturing capacity in increments of 30 units. What is the maximum amount of costs that Meredith could save by downsizing manufacturing capacity?
3. Meredith, in fact, does not eliminate any of its unused manufacturing capacity. Why might Meredith not downsize?

13-22 Strategy, balanced scorecard, service company. Snyder Corporation is a small, information systems consulting firm that specializes in helping companies implement sales management software. The market for Snyder's products is very competitive. To compete, Snyder must deliver quality service at a low cost. Snyder bills clients in terms of units of work performed, which depends on the size and complexity of the sales management system. Snyder presents the following data for the years 1999 and 2000.

	1999	2000
1. Units of work performed	60	70
2. Selling price	$50,000	$48,000
3. Software implementation labour-hours	30,000	32,000
4. Cost per software implementation labour-hour	$60	$63
5. Software implementation support capacity (in units of work)	90	90
6. Total cost of software implementation support	$360,000	$369,000
7. Software implementation support capacity cost per unit of work	$4,000	$4,100
8. Number of employees doing software development	3	3
9. Total software development costs	$375,000	$390,000
10. Software development costs per employee	$125,000	$130,000

Software implementation labour-hour costs are variable costs. Software implementation support costs for each year depend on the software implementation support capacity (defined in terms of units of work) that Snyder chooses to maintain each year. It does not vary with the actual units of work performed each year. At the start of each year, management uses its discretion to determine the number of software development employees. The software development staff and costs have no direct relationship with the number of units of work performed.

REQUIRED
1. Is Snyder Corporation's strategy one of product differentiation or cost leadership?
2. Describe briefly key elements that you would include in Snyder's balanced scorecard and your reasons for doing so.

13-23 Strategic analysis of operating income. Refer to the information in Exercise 13-22.

REQUIRED
1. Calculate the operating income of Snyder Corporation in 1999 and 2000.
2. Calculate the growth, price-recovery, and productivity components of changes in operating income between 1999 and 2000.
3. Comment on your answer in requirement 2. What do these components indicate?

13-24 Analysis of growth, price-recovery and productivity components (continuation of 13-23). Suppose that between 1999 and 2000 the market for implementing sales management software increased by 5%, and that industry-wide selling prices decreased by 1%.

REQUIRED
Calculate how much of the change in operating income between 1999 and 2000 is due to industry-wide factors, cost leadership, and product differentiation. How successful has Snyder been in implementing its strategy?

13-25 Identifying and managing unused capacity. Refer to the Snyder Corporation information in Exercise 13-22.

1. Where possible, calculate the amount and cost of unused capacity for (a) software implementation support and (b) software development in the year 2000. If you could not calculate the amount and cost of unused capacity, indicate why not.
2. Suppose Snyder can add or reduce its software implementation support capacity in increments of 15 units. What is the maximum amount of costs that Snyder could save by downsizing software implementation support capacity?
3. Snyder, in fact, does not eliminate any of its unused software implementation support capacity. Why might Snyder not downsize?

PROBLEMS

13-26 Balanced scorecard. Caltex Inc. refines gasoline and sells it through its own Caltex Gas Stations. On the basis of market research, Caltex determines that 60% of its customers (medium to high income individuals) are willing to pay a higher price for its gas if the gas stations can provide excellent customer service such as a clean facility, a convenience store, friendly employees, quick turnaround, the ability to pay by credit card, and high octane premium fuel. Market-wide prices for inputs and outputs and the market size did not change in 2001. Caltex's balanced scorecard for the year 2001 follows. For brevity, the initiatives taken under each objective are omitted.

Objectives	Measures	Target Performance	Actual Performance
Financial Perspective			
Increase shareholder value	Operating income changes from price recovery	$90,000,000	$95,000,000
	Operating income changes from growth	$65,000,000	$67,000,000
Customer Perspective			
Increase market share	Market share of total gasoline market	10%	9.8%
Internal Business Process Perspective			
Improve gasoline quality	Quality index	94 points	95 points
Improve refinery performance	Refinery reliability index (%)	91%	91%
Ensure gasoline availability	Product availability index (%)	99%	100%
Learning and Growth Perspective			
Increase refinery process capability	Percentage of refinery processes with advanced controls	88%	90%

REQUIRED

1. Was Caltex successful in implementing its strategy in 2001? Explain your answer.
2. Would you have included some measure of employee satisfaction and employee training in the learning and growth perspective? Are these objectives critical to Caltex for implementing its strategy? Why or why not? Explain briefly.
3. Explain how Caltex did not achieve its target market share in the total gasoline market but still exceeded its financial targets. Is "market share of total gasoline market" the correct measure of market share? Explain briefly.
4. Is there a clear cause-and-effect linkage between improvements in the measures in the internal business process perspective and the measures in the customer perspective? That is, would you add other measures to the internal business process perspective or the customer perspective? Why or why not? Explain briefly.
5. Do you agree with Caltex's decision not to include measures of changes in operating income from productivity improvements under the financial perspective of the balanced scorecard? Explain briefly.

13-27 Balanced scorecard. Lee Corporation manufactures various types of colour laser printers in a highly automated facility with high fixed costs. The market for laser printers is competitive. The various colour laser printers on the market are comparable in terms of features and price. Lee believes that satisfying customers with products of high quality at low costs is key to achieving its target profitability. For 2001, Lee plans to achieve higher quality and lower costs by improving yields and reducing defects in its manufacturing operations. Lee will train workers and encourage and empower them to take the necessary actions. Currently, a significant amount of Lee's capacity is used to produce products that are defective and cannot be sold. Lee expects that higher yields will reduce the capacity that Lee needs to use to manufacture products. Lee does not anticipate that improving manufacturing will automatically lead to lower costs because Lee has high fixed costs. Lee plans to lay off workers and sell equipment to reduce some of the unused capacity and use the rest of the capacity to produce and sell more of its current products or improved models of its current products. Selling more products will result in lower fixed costs per unit of product.

Market prices for inputs and outputs and market size did not change in 2001. Lee's balanced scorecard for the just-completed accounting year 2001 follows. For brevity, the initiatives taken under each objective are omitted.

Objectives	Measures	Target Performance	Actual Performance
Financial Perspective			
Increase shareholder value	Operating income changes from productivity	$1,000,000	$400,000
	Operating income changes from growth	$1,500,000	$600,000
Customer Perspective			
Increase market share	Market-share in colour laser printers	5%	4.2%
Internal Business Process Perspective			
Improve manufacturing quality	Yield	82%	85%
Reduce delivery time to customers	Order delivery time	25 days	22 days
Learning and Growth Perspective			
Develop process skills	Percentage of employees trained in process and quality management	90%	92%
Enhance information system capabilities	Percentage of manufacturing processes with real-time feedback	85%	87%

REQUIRED
1. Was Lee successful in implementing its strategy in 2001? Explain.
2. Is Lee Corporation's balanced scorecard useful in helping Lee understand why it did not reach its target market share in 2001? If it is, explain why. If it is not, explain what other measures you might want to add under the customer perspective and why.
3. Would you have included some measure of employee satisfaction in the learning and growth perspective and new product development in the internal business process perspective? That is, do you think employee satisfaction and development of new products are critical to Lee for implementing its strategy? Why or why not? Explain briefly.
4. What problems, if any, do you see in Lee improving quality and significantly downsizing to eliminate unused capacity?

13-28 Analysis of growth, price-recovery and productivity components. Halsey and Company sells women's clothing. Halsey's strategy is to offer a wide selection of clothes and excellent customer service, and to charge a premium price. Halsey presents the following data for the years 2001 and 2002. For simplicity, assume that each customer purchases one piece of clothing.

	2001	2002
1. Pieces of clothing purchased and sold	40,000	40,000
2. Average selling price	$60	$59
3. Average cost per piece of clothing	$40	$41
4. Selling and customer-service capacity	51,000 customers	43,000 customers
5. Selling and customer-service costs	$357,000	$296,700
6. Selling and customer-service capacity cost per customer	$7	$6.90
7. Purchasing and administrative capacity measured by the number of distinct clothing designs purchased	980	850
8. Purchasing and administrative costs	$245,000	$204,000
9. Purchasing and administrative capacity cost per distinct design	$250	$240

Total selling and customer-service costs depend on the number of customers that Halsey has created capacity to support, not the actual number of customers that Halsey serves. Total purchasing and administrative costs depend on purchasing and administrative capacity that Halsey has created (defined in terms of the number of distinct clothing designs that Halsey can purchase and administer). Purchasing and administration costs do not depend on the actual number of clothing pieces purchased. Halsey purchased 930 distinct designs in 2001 and 820 distinct designs in 2002.

Marketwide prices for clothes and the market size was unchanged in 2001 and 2002. At the start of 2002, Halsey planned to increase operating income by 10% over the operating income in 2001.

REQUIRED

1. Is Halsey's strategy one of product differentiation or cost leadership?
2. Calculate Halsley's operating income in 2001 and 2002.
3. Calculate the growth, price-recovery, and productive components of changes in operating income between 2001 and 2002.
4. Does the strategic analysis of operating income indicate Halsey was successful in implementing its strategy in 2002? Explain.

13-29 Analysis of growth, price-recovery, and productivity components. Winchester Corporation manufactures special ball bearings. In 2002, it plans to grow and increase operating income by capitalizing on its reputation for manufacturing a product that is superior to its customers. An analysis of Winchester's operating income changes between 2001 and 2002 shows the following:

Operating income for 2001	$3,450,000
Add growth component	300,000
Add price-recovery component	400,000
Add productivity component	350,000
Operating income for 2002	$4,500,000

Further analysis of these components indicates that the entire growth component is accounted for by an increase in the market size for ball bearings in 2002 and that 90% of the price-recovery component is accounted for by an increase in the market prices of ball bearings in 2002. Input prices did not change from 2001 to 2002.

REQUIRED

1. Is Winchester's 2002 strategy one of product differentiation or cost leadership? Explain briefly.
2. Was Winchester's gain in operating income in 2002 consistent with the strategy you identified in requirement 1? Explain briefly.

13-30 Engineered and discretionary overhead costs, unused capacity, repairs and maintenance. Rowland Corporation manufactures gears using turning machines. In 2001 Rowland's turning machines operated for 80,000 hours. Rowland employed four workers in its repairs and maintenance area to fix and repair machines that have broken down or are functioning improperly. In 2001, each repairs and maintenance person was paid a fixed annual salary of $40,000 for 250 days of work at eight hours per day. During 2001, the workers spent 6,000 hours on repairs and maintenance.

REQUIRED

1. Do you think repairs and maintenance costs at Rowland Corporation are engineered costs or discretionary costs? Explain your answer.
2. Assume repairs and maintenance costs are engineered costs. Calculate the cost of unused repairs and maintenance capacity in 2001. Would you recommend that Rowland downsize its repairs and maintenance capacity? Explain your answer briefly.
3. Assume repairs and maintenance costs are discretionary costs. Calculate the cost of unused repairs and maintenance capacity in 2001.

13-31 Engineered and discretionary overhead costs, unused capacity, customer help-desk. Cable Galore, a large cable television operator, had 750,000 subscribers in 1999. Cable Galore employs five customer-help-desk representatives to respond to customer questions and problems. During 1999, each customer-help-desk representative worked eight hours per day for 250 days at a fixed annual salary of $36,000. Cable Galore received 45,000 telephone calls from its customers in 1999. Each call took an average of 10 minutes.

REQUIRED

1. Do you think customer-help-desk costs at Cable Galore are engineered costs or discretionary costs? Explain your answer.
2. Calculate the cost of unused customer-help-desk capacity in 1999 under each of the following two assumptions: (a) customer-help-desk costs are engineered costs and (b) customer-help-desk costs are discretionary costs.
3. Assume that Cable Galore had 900,000 subscribers in 2000 and that the 1999 percentage of telephone calls received to total subscribers continued into 2000. Customer-help-desk capacity in 2000 was the same as it was in 1999. Calculate the cost of unused customer-help-desk capacity in 2000 under each of the following two assumptions: (a) customer-service costs are engineered costs and (b) customer-service costs are discretionary costs.

13-32 Partial productivity measurement (Chapter Appendix). Berkshire Corporation makes small steel parts. Berkshire management has some ability to substitute direct materials for direct manufacturing labour. If workers cut the steel carefully, Berkshire can manufacture more parts out of a metal sheet, but this will require more direct manufacturing labour-hours. Alternatively, Berkshire can use fewer direct manufacturing labour-hours if it is willing to tolerate a larger quantity of direct materials waste. Berkshire operates in a very competitive market. Its strategy is to produce a quality product at a low cost. Berkeshire produces no defective products. It reports the following data for the last two years of operations:

	2001	2002
Output units	375,000	525,000
Direct material used, in kilograms	450,000	610,000
Direct material cost per kilogram	$1.20	$1.25
Direct manufacturing labour-hours used	7,500	9,500
Wages per hour	$20	$25
Manufacturing capacity in output units	600,000	582,000
Manufacturing capacity-related fixed costs	$1,038,000	$1,018,500
Fixed manufacturing costs per unit of capacity	$1.73	$1.75

REQUIRED

1. Compute the partial productivity ratios for 2001 and 2002.
2. On the basis of the partial productivity ratios alone, can you conclude whether and by how much productivity improved overall in 2002 relative to 2001? Explain.
3. How might the management of Berkshire Corporation use the partial productivity analysis?

13-33 Total factor productivity (continuation of 13-32). Use the data given for Berkshire Corporation in Problem 13-32.

REQUIRED

1. Compute Berkshire Corporation's total factor productivity in 2002.
2. Compare Berkshire Corporation's total factor productivity performance in 2002 relative to 2001.

3. What does total factor productivity tell you that partial productivity measures do not?

13-34 Balanced scorecard, ethics. John Emburey, Division manager of the Household Product Division, a maker of kitchen dishwashers, had just seen the balanced scorecard for his division for 2001. He immediately called Patricia Conley, the management accountant for the division into his office for a meeting. "I think the employee satisfaction and customer satisfaction numbers are way too low. These numbers are based on a random sample of subjective assessments made by individual managers and customer representatives. My own experience indicates that we are doing well on both these dimensions. Until we do a formal survey of employees and customers sometime next year, I think we are doing a disservice to ourselves and this company by reporting such low scores for employee and customer satisfaction. These scores will be an embarrassment for us at the division managers' meeting next month. We need to get these numbers up."

Patricia knew that the employee and customer satisfaction scores were subjective but the procedure she had used was identical to the procedures she had used in the past. She believed the scores represented the unhappiness of employees with the latest work rules and the unhappiness of customers with missed delivery dates. She also knew that these problems would be corrected in time.

REQUIRED
1. Do you think that Household Products Division should include subjective measures of employee satisfaction and customer satisfaction in its balanced scorecard? Explain.
2. What should Patricia Conley do?

COLLABORATIVE LEARNING PROBLEM

13-35 Downsizing. (CMA, adapted) Mayfair Corporation currently subsidizes cafeteria services for its 200 employees. Mayfair is in the process of reviewing the cafeteria services as cost cutting measures are needed throughout the organization to keep the prices of its products competitive. Two alternatives are being evaluated: downsize the cafeteria staff and offer a reduced menu or contract with an outside vendor.

The current cafeteria operation has four employees with a combined annual salary of $110,000 plus additional employee benefits at 25% of salary. The cafeteria operates 250 days each year, and the costs for utilities and equipment maintenance average $30,000 annually. The daily sales include 100 entrées at $4.00 each, 80 sandwiches or salads at an average price of $3.00 each, plus an additional $200 for beverages and desserts. The cost of all cafeteria supplies is 60% of revenues.

The plan for downsizing the current operation envisions retaining two of the current employees whose combined base annual salaries total $65,000. An entrée would no longer be offered, and prices of the remaining items would be increased slightly. Under this arrangement, Mayfair expects daily sales of 150 sandwiches or salads at a higher average price of $3.60. The additional revenue for beverages and desserts is expected to increase to $230 each day. Because of the elimination of the entrée, the cost of all cafeteria supplies is expected to drop to 50% of revenues. All other conditions of operation would remain the same. Mayfair is willing to continue to subsidize this reduced operation but will not spend more than 20% of the current subsidy.

A proposal has been received from Wilco Foods, an outside vendor who is willing to supply cafeteria services. Wilco has proposed to pay Mayfair $1,000 per month for use of the cafeteria and utilities. Mayfair would be expected to cover equipment repair costs. In addition, Wilco would pay Mayfair 4% of all revenues received above the breakeven point; this payment would be made at the end of the year. All other costs incurred by Wilco to supply the cafeteria services are variable and equal 75% of revenues. Wilco plans to charge $5.00 for an entrée, and the average price for the sandwich or salad would be $4.00. All other daily sales are expected to average $300. Wilco expects daily sales of 66 entrées and 94 sandwiches or salads.

INSTRUCTIONS
Form groups of two students to complete the following requirements.

REQUIRED
1. Determine if the plan for downsizing the current cafeteria operation would be acceptable to Mayfair Corporation. Show all calculations.
2. Is the Wilco Foods proposal more advantageous to Mayfair Corporation than the downsizing plan? Show all calculations.

PART FOUR

14

COST ALLOCATION

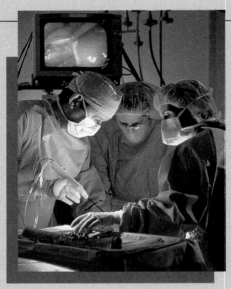

The increasing use of sophisticated medical technology, such as new laparoscopic instruments, is leading to much concern about medical costs. Hospital administrators are now examining how different cost allocation approaches can better prompt doctors to balance cost factors with health considerations in their patient decisions.

LEARNING OBJECTIVES

After studying this chapter, you should be able to:

1. Outline four purposes for allocating costs to cost objects
2. Describe alternative criteria used to guide decisions related to cost allocations
3. Discuss key decisions faced when collecting costs in indirect cost pools
4. Describe how the single-rate cost allocation method differs from the dual-rate method
5. Explain how the choice of budgeted versus actual allocation rates changes the risks managers face
6. Distinguish between direct allocation, step-down, and reciprocal methods of allocating support department costs
7. Make decisions that draw on the allocation of common costs using either the stand-alone or incremental methods
8. Explain the importance of explicit agreement between parties when reimbursement is based on costs incurred

Cost allocation is an inescapable problem in nearly every organization and in nearly every facet of accounting. How should the airline costs of a recruiting trip from Winnipeg to Montreal to Halifax and then return to Winnipeg be allocated among the prospective employers in Montreal and Halifax? How should university costs be allocated among undergraduate programs, graduate programs, and research? How should the costs of expensive medical equipment, facilities, and staff be allocated in a hospital? How should manufacturing overhead be allocated to individual products in a multiple-product company such as Procter & Gamble?

Finding answers to cost allocation questions is difficult. The answers are seldom clearly right or clearly wrong. Nevertheless, in this chapter, we will try to obtain some insight into cost allocation and to understand the dimensions of the questions, even if the answers seem elusive. Regardless of your profession, you will undoubtedly be faced with many cost allocation questions in your career.

Procter & Gamble
www.pg.com

PURPOSES OF COST ALLOCATION

Indirect costs often comprise a sizable percentage of the costs assigned to cost objects such as products, distribution channels, and customers. Exhibit 14-1 illustrates four possible purposes for allocating indirect costs to such cost objects:

1. To provide information for economic decisions
2. To motivate managers and employees
3. To justify costs or compute reimbursement
4. To measure income and assets for reporting to external parties

The allocation of one particular cost need not satisfy all purposes simultaneously. Consider the salary of an aerospace scientist in a central research department of Boeing or Airbus. This salary cost may be allocated as part of central research costs to satisfy purpose 1 (economic decisions); it may or may not be allocated to satisfy purpose 2 (motivation); it may or may not be allocated to a government contract to justify a cost to be reimbursed to satisfy purpose 3 (cost reimbursement); and it must not be allocated (under generally accepted accounting principles) to inventory to satisfy purpose 4 (income and asset measurement).

OBJECTIVE 1

Outline four purposes for allocating costs to cost objects

Airbus
www.airbus.com

"A Model for Cost Allocation and Pricing in the Internet" by David D. Clark—MIT March, 1995
www.press.umich.edu/jep/works/ClarkModel.html

EXHIBIT 14-1
Purposes of Cost Allocation

Purpose	Illustrations
1. To provide information for economic decisions	◆ To decide whether to add a new airline flight ◆ To decide whether to make a component part of a television set or to purchase it from another manufacturer ◆ To decide on the selling price for a customized product or service
2. To motivate managers and employees	◆ To encourage the design of products that are simpler to manufacture or less costly to service ◆ To encourage sales representatives to push high-margin products or services
3. To justify costs or compute reimbursement	◆ To cost products at a "fair" price, often done with government defence contracts ◆ To compute reimbursement for a consulting firm that is paid a percentage of the cost savings resulting from the implementation of its recommendations
4. To measure income and assets for meeting external regulatory and legal reporting obligations	◆ To cost inventories for financial reporting to stockholders, bondholders, and so on (under generally accepted accounting principles, inventoriable costs include manufacturing costs but exclude R&D, marketing, distribution, and customer service costs) ◆ To cost inventories for reporting to tax authorities

Different costs are appropriate for different purposes. Consider product costs of the following business functions in the value chain:

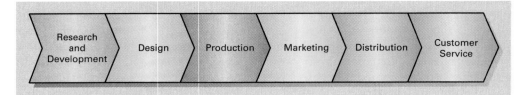

The same combination of costs in these six business functions typically will not satisfy each of the four purposes in Exhibit 14-1. For the economic decision purpose (for example, product pricing), the costs in all six functions should be included. For the motivation purpose, costs from more than one function are often included to emphasize to managers how costs in different functions are related to each other. For example, some Japanese companies require product designers to incorporate costs further down the chain than design (such as distribution and customer service, as well as manufacturing) into their product cost estimates. The aim is to focus attention on how different product design options affect the total costs of the organization. For the cost reimbursement purpose, the particular contract will often stipulate whether all six of the business functions or only a subset of them are to be reimbursed. For instance, cost reimbursement rules governing government contracts may explicitly exclude marketing costs. For the purpose of income and asset measurement for reporting to external parties, inventoriable costs under generally accepted accounting principles include only manufacturing costs (and product design costs in some cases). In Canada, research costs are expensed to the accounting period in which they are incurred, while development costs may be capitalized and charged to future periods.

CRITERIA FOR GUIDING COST ALLOCATION DECISIONS

The Role of Dominant Criteria

OBJECTIVE 2

Describe alternative criteria used to guide decisions related to cost allocations

Exhibit 14-2 presents four criteria used to guide decisions related to cost allocations. These decisions include both the number of indirect cost pools and the cost allo-

EXHIBIT 14-2
Criteria for Guiding Cost Allocation Decisions

1. **Cause and effect.** Using this criterion, managers identify the variable or variables that cause resources to be consumed. For example, managers may use hours of testing as the variable when allocating the costs of a quality testing area to products. Cost allocations based on the cause-and-effect criterion are likely to be the most credible to operating personnel.

2. **Benefits received.** Using this criterion, managers identify the beneficiaries of the outputs of the cost object. The costs of the cost object are allocated among the beneficiaries in proportion to the benefits each receives. For example, consider a corporatewide advertising program that promotes the general image of the corporation rather than any individual product. The costs of this program may be allocated on the basis of division sales; the higher the sales, the higher the division's allocated cost of the advertising program. The rationale behind this allocation is the belief that divisions with higher sales levels apparently benefited from the advertising more than did divisions with lower sales levels and therefore ought to be allocated more of the advertising costs.

3. **Fairness or equity.** This criterion is often cited in government contracts when cost allocations are the basis for establishing a price satisfactory to the government and its supplier. The cost allocation here is viewed as a "reasonable" or "fair" means of establishing a selling price in the minds of the contracting parties. For most allocation decisions, fairness is a lofty objective rather than an operational criterion.

4. **Ability to bear.** This criterion advocates allocating costs in proportion to the cost object's ability to bear them. An example is the allocation of corporate executive salaries on the basis of divisional operating income; the presumption is that the more profitable divisions have a greater ability to absorb corporate headquarters' costs.

cation base for each indirect cost pool. Managers must first choose the primary purpose for a particular cost allocation and then select the appropriate criterion to implement the allocation. This book emphasizes the superiority of the cause-and-effect and benefits-received criteria, especially when the purpose for cost allocation is related to economic decisions or motivation.

For government contract purposes the fairness criterion may be more relevant. For example, the Department of National Defence requires facilities to full-cost their services in any proposal to offer unused capacity for sale. While it would be financially beneficial to sell any unused capacity of a facility as long as the price exceeds

SURVEYS OF COMPANY PRACTICE

Why Allocate Corporate and Other Support Costs to Divisions and Departments?

Extensive survey evidence exists on the reasons why managers allocate corporate and other support costs to divisions and departments.

Canadian executives[*] cited the following objectives, ranked in order of importance:

1. To determine costs

2. To evaluate profit centres

3. To fix accountability

4. To allocate costs per usage

5. To promote more effective resource usage

6. To foster cost awareness

These executives encountered the following difficulties in implementing their cost allocation programs: making the allocations results in losses being reported, friction arises among managers, market prices are unstable, allocations are perceived as arbitrary, usage is hard to monitor, agreement on the allocation method is difficult to obtain, and the allocation process is time-consuming.

A survey[†] of U.S. managers revealed the following purposes, ranked by frequency:

1. To remind profit centre managers that indirect costs exist and that profit centre earnings must be adequate to cover some share of those costs

2. To encourage the use of central services that would otherwise be underutilized

3. To stimulate profit centre managers to put pressure on central managers to control service costs

A similar survey was conducted among Australian[‡] and U.K.[§] managers. The two sets of managers gave the same ranking of the following reasons for allocating corporate costs to divisions (in order of importance):

1. To acknowledge that divisions would incur such costs if they were independent units or if the services were not provided centrally

2. To make division managers aware that central costs exist

3. To stimulate divisional managers to put pressure on central support managers to control costs

4. To stimulate divisional managers to economize in usage of central services.

[*]Atkinson, A., *Intrafirm Cost and Resource Allocations: Theory and Practice*, (Hamilton, Canada: Society of Management Accountants of Canada and Canadian Academic Accounting Association Research Monograph, 1987)

[†]Fremgen, J., and S. Liao, *The Allocation of Corporate Indirect Costs* (New York: National Association of Accountants, 1981)

[‡]Ramadan, S., "The Rationale for Cost Allocation: A Study of U.K. Divisionalised Companies," *Accounting and Business Research* (Winter 1989)

[§]Dean, G., M. Joye, and P. Blayney, *Strategic Management Accounting Survey*, (Sydney, Australia: The University of Sydney, 1991)

the incremental cost, the government does not want to be seen as competing unfairly in the private sector. Thus the price must cover all costs including allocations of overhead costs.

The feasibility of using an individual criterion in Exhibit 14-2 varies according to the context of the cost allocation. Consider using the cause-and-effect criterion for allocating indirect costs to individual products in a multiple-product company. Where the indirect costs are variable and each product is assembled sequentially, the cause-and-effect criterion can guide the choice of a cost allocation base. In contrast, where the indirect costs are fixed and two or more products are jointly assembled, it is not possible to identify specific cause-and-effect relationships between work on an individual product and the total costs incurred.

THE COST-BENEFIT APPROACH

Many companies place great importance on cost-benefit considerations when designing their cost allocation systems. Companies incur costs not only in gathering data, but also in taking the time necessary to educate management about the chosen system. The more sophisticated the system, in general, the higher these education costs.

The costs of designing and implementing sophisticated cost allocation systems are highly visible, and most companies work to reduce them. In contrast, the benefits from using a well-designed cost allocation system—being able to make better-informed make/buy decisions, pricing decisions, cost control decisions, and so on—are difficult to measure and are frequently less visible. Still, designers of cost allocation systems should consider these benefits as well as costs.

Spurred by rapid reductions in the costs of collecting and processing information, organizations today are moving toward more detailed cost allocation systems. Many companies have now developed manufacturing or distribution overhead costing systems that use more than ten different cost allocation bases. Also, some businesses have state-of-the-art information technology already in place for operating their plants or distribution networks. Applying this existing technology to the development and operation of a cost allocation system is less expensive—and thus more inviting—than starting up such a system from scratch.

COST ALLOCATION AND COSTING SYSTEMS

We will use Computer Horizons to illustrate how costs incurred in different parts of an organization can be assigned and then reassigned when costing products, services, customers, or contracts. Computer Horizons has two manufacturing divisions. The MicroComputer Division manufactures its Plum, Plum Laptop, and Super Plum products. The Plum and Plum Laptop are assembled at its St. Louis, Birmingham, and Singapore plants. The Super Plum is assembled at its Vancouver plant. The Peripheral Equipment Division manufactures printers, cables, and other items used with its computer products. It has plants in St. Louis and Toronto.

Exhibit 14-3 presents an overview of the costing system at the St. Louis assembly plant of the MicroComputer Division. This plant assembles the Plum line and the Laptop Plum line. The area within the box in Exhibit 14-3 shows a costing system overview for the Model A version of the Plum. This costing overview is similar to that presented in earlier chapters.

The product costing overviews presented in earlier chapters (and, indeed, in this chapter) are typically only parts of larger costing systems. This larger costing system can be for a plant, a division, or even a whole company with multiple plants and divisions in many countries. Computer Horizons has manufacturing plants located in Canada, the United States, Mexico, Singapore, and the United Kingdom. It has marketing operations in more than 20 countries. Every month it consolidates accounting information from each of its operations to use in its planning and control decisions. A detailed costing overview of this companywide system would be sizably more complex than that in Exhibit 14-3.

Cost Allocations and Inspection Costs at Volkswagen Canada

The reason accountants can assess costs a lot more accurately this way is that ABC allows them to break down overheads and allocate them to the right products. The revelations can be startling. Take a 1991 ABC pilot project undertaken in the die-cast engine parts area of the Volkswagen Canada Inc. plant in Barrie, Ontario. Volkswagen was ripe for ABC: it made about 25 engine parts ranging from mass-produced gear housings to highly specialized camshaft-bearing caps. The cost analysis turned up numerous profit laggards. "A lot of them came out negative," says George Waddell, a cost account who led the project team. "The whole die-cast operation was profitable then, but that was because maybe five or six of those parts were making a lot of money and covering (for) the ones that were losing money."

How can this happen? Consider one of the not-so-profitable parts: an engine mounting bracket. Random samples of most parts pass through an X-ray machine to check for structural defects that could cause them to break. But a snapped engine-mounting bracket could be a safety hazard. So Volkswagen was X-raying every single bracket to guard against a flawed one slipping through. In fact, X-raying these brackets took up about 80% of machine time. Under the ABC system, when the pool of inspection costs was divided up according to the proportion of X-ray inspections devoted to the various parts, engine brackets carried 80% of the load. Compare that to the old system of costing, where all 25 die-cast engine parts carried a share of inspection costs as one of the overheads. A labour-intensive gear housing that didn't pass through the comprehensive X-ray process got socked with a disproportionate share of overhead. Based on its share of inspections, it should have attracted, say, 5% of these costs—instead of the 50% it might have attracted on the basis of invested labour-hours.

Management is only as good as the information behind it. In Volkswagen's case, knowing the high cost of inspection spurred a decision not to inspect so many brackets. Workers now X-ray 25 from each bin. They only inspect the rest if they find a reject in the sample. ABC analysis has now moved on to Volkswagen's wheel department, where an automated work flow system of looping conveyors has given way to manual trolleys. "The ABC study confirmed that conveyor breakdowns were costing us a lot of downtime," says financial analyst Jim Gurowka. "We found that short spurts get through the system faster than with a continuous conveyor."

Volkswagen America
www.vw.com

The ABC Authority
www.abctech.com

Source: J. Southerst, "Suddenly, It All Makes Sense," *Canadian Business*, March 1994. Reprinted by permission of *Canadian Business Magazine*. © 1994.

The costing system for the St. Louis plant portrayed in Exhibit 14-3 highlights two important points. First, it highlights how there are multiple cost objects in most costing systems. Examples at the St. Louis plant include the Plant Maintenance Department, the Plum Assembly Department, the Laptop Plum Assembly Department, and the separate products in the Plum Assembly Department—for example, Plum Models A, B, and C. Note, however, that Exhibit 14-3 presents only a small subset of the separate cost objects at the St. Louis plant. Other examples include the Procurement Department, the Energy Department, and the various Plum Laptop products.

Exhibit 14-3 also highlights how an individual cost item can be simultaneously a direct cost of one cost object and an indirect cost of another cost object. Consider the salary of the Plant Maintenance Department manager. This salary is a direct cost

EXHIBIT 14-3
Cost Tracing and Cost Allocation at the St. Louis Assembly Plant of Computer Horizons

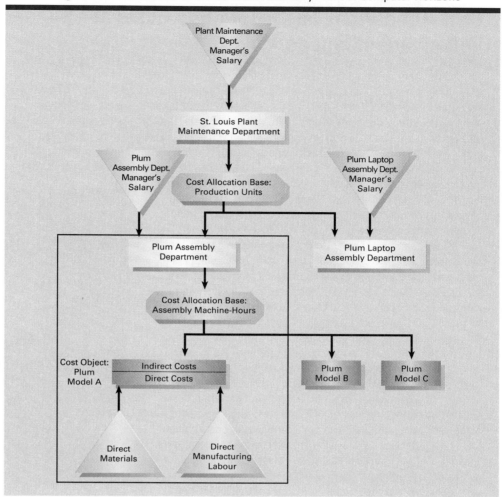

traced to the Plant Maintenance Department. Computer Horizons then allocates the costs of this department to the two Assembly Departments at the St. Louis plant using units produced as the allocation base. In turn, the costs of the two Assembly Departments are allocated to individual products, such as the Plum Model A, using assembly machine-hours as the allocation base. Thus, the salary of the Plant Maintenance Department manager is both an indirect cost of each computer assembled at the plant and a direct cost of the Plant Maintenance Department.

INDIRECT COST POOLS AND COST ALLOCATION

The indirect costs of products assembled at the manufacturing plants of Computer Horizons include (1) costs incurred at corporate headquarters and (2) costs incurred at the manufacturing plants. Exhibit 14-4 illustrates cost pools at both levels.

OBJECTIVE 3

Discuss key decisions faced when collecting costs in indirect cost pools

Choices Related to Indirect Costs

Computer Horizons has several key choices to make when accumulating and subsequently allocating the indirect costs to products of the MicroComputer Division:

◆ Which cost categories from Corporate Headquarters and the other divisions should be included in the indirect costs of the MicroComputer Division? Should all of the corporate headquarters cost pools in Exhibit 14-4 be allocated, or should only a subset of them be allocated? For example, some companies exclude corporate public relations from any corporate cost allocations to

EXHIBIT 14-4
Indirect Cost Pools (When the Cost Object Is an Individual Product) of Computer Horizons

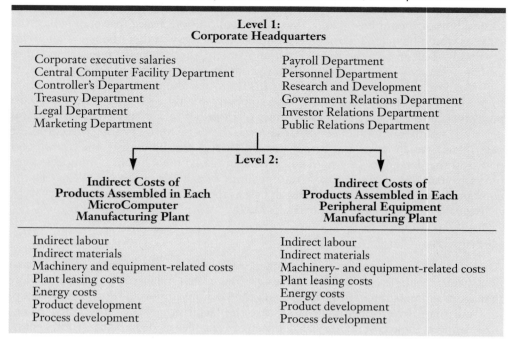

Level 1:
Corporate Headquarters

Corporate executive salaries
Central Computer Facility Department
Controller's Department
Treasury Department
Legal Department
Marketing Department

Payroll Department
Personnel Department
Research and Development
Government Relations Department
Investor Relations Department
Public Relations Department

Level 2:

Indirect Costs of
Products Assembled in Each
MicroComputer
Manufacturing Plant

Indirect labour
Indirect materials
Machinery and equipment-related costs
Plant leasing costs
Energy costs
Product development
Process development

Indirect Costs of
Products Assembled in Each
Peripheral Equipment
Manufacturing Plant

Indirect labour
Indirect materials
Machinery- and equipment-related costs
Plant leasing costs
Energy costs
Product development
Process development

the divisions; division managers have little say in corporate public relations decisions and would object to allocations as "taxation without representation."

◆ How many cost pools should be used when allocating corporate costs to the MicroComputer Division? A *cost pool* is a grouping of individual cost items. One extreme is to aggregate all corporate costs into a single cost pool. The other extreme is to have numerous individual corporate cost pools. The concept of homogeneity (described in the following section) is important in making this decision.

◆ Which allocation base should be used for each of the corporate cost pools when allocating corporate costs to the MicroComputer Division? Examples include the following:

Cost Pool	Possible Allocation Bases
Corporate executive salaries	Sales; assets employed; operating income
Treasury Department	Sales; assets employed; estimated time or usage
Legal Department	Estimated time or usage; sales; assets employed
Marketing Department	Sales; number of sales personnel
Payroll Department	Number of employees; payroll dollars
Personnel Department	Number of employees; payroll dollars; number of new hires

◆ Which allocation base should be used when allocating the indirect cost pools at each manufacturing plant to the products assembled in those plants? Examples include number of parts assembled in each product, direct manufacturing labour-hours, machining-hours, and testing-hours.

These allocation bases for both corporate and plant indirect costs are illustrative only. Managers' choices of allocation bases depend on the purpose served by the cost allocation (see Exhibit 14-1), the criteria used to guide the cost allocation (see Exhibit 14-2), and the costs of implementing the different allocation bases.

Homogeneity of Cost Pools

A **homogeneous cost pool** is one in which all the activities whose costs are included in the pool have the same or a similar cause-and-effect relationship or benefits-

Homogeneous cost pool. A cost pool in which all the activities whose costs are included in the pool have the same or a similar cause-and-effect relationship or benefits-received relationship between the cost allocator and the costs of the activity.

received relationship between the cost allocator and the costs of the activity. Why is homogeneity important? Because using homogeneous indirect cost pools enables more accurate product, service, and customer costs to be obtained. A consequence of using a homogeneous cost pool is that the cost allocations using that pool will be the same as would be made if costs of each individual activity in that pool were allocated separately. The greater the degree of homogeneity, the fewer cost pools required to explain accurately the differences in how products use resources of the organization.

Assume that Computer Horizons wishes to use the cause-and-effect criterion to guide cost allocation decisions. The company should aggregate only those cost pools that have the same cause-and-effect relationship to the cost object. For example, if the number of employees in a division is the cause for incurring both corporate payroll department costs and corporate personnel department costs, the payroll cost pool and the personnel cost pool could be aggregated before determining the combined payroll and personnel cost rate per unit of the allocation base. That is, the combined rate per unit of the allocation base is the same as the sum of the rates if the individual cost pools were allocated separately.

Recognizing More Cost Pools

A variety of factors may prompt managers to consider recognizing multiple cost pools where a single cost pool is currently being used. One factor is the views of line managers and personnel. For example, do they believe important differences exist in how costs are driven or how products use the facilities not currently being recognized using a single cost pool? A second factor is changes made in plant layout, general operations, and so on such that all products do not use the facility in an equivalent way. A third factor is changes in the diversity of products (or services) produced or in the way those products use the resources in the cost pool. A fourth factor is the changes in information-gathering technology. Improvements in this technology are expanding the ability to develop multiple cost pools.

Allowability of Costs in Cost Pools

A given cost item or amount may be included or excluded from a cost pool depending on the purpose at hand. Consider a consulting firm whose purpose is to price jobs for (1) a commercial client and (2) a government client. When pricing for a commercial client, the consulting firm may include the cost of beer and wine at meals that have a clear business-related rationale. In contrast, when billing the government under a contract, the contract may state that no cost amount for any alcoholic beverage is permitted to enter the cost pools from which costs are allocated to the government.

ALLOCATING COSTS FROM ONE DEPARTMENT TO ANOTHER

In many cases, the costs of a department will include costs allocated from other departments. Three key issues that arise when allocating costs from one department to another are (1) whether to use a single-rate method or a dual-rate method, (2) whether to use budgeted rates or actual rates, and (3) whether to use budgeted quantities or actual quantities.

Single-Rate and Dual-Rate Methods

Single-rate cost allocation method. Allocation method that pools all costs in one cost pool and allocates them to cost objects using the same rate per unit of the single allocation base.

Dual-rate cost allocation method. Allocation method that first classifies costs in one cost pool into two subpools (typically into a variable cost subpool and a fixed-cost subpool). Each subpool has a different allocation rate or a different allocation base.

A **single-rate cost allocation method** pools all costs in one cost pool and allocates them to cost objects using the same rate per unit of the single allocation base. There is no distinction between costs in the cost pool in terms of cost variability (such as fixed-costs versus variable costs). A **dual-rate cost allocation method** first classifies costs in one cost pool into two subpools (typically into a variable-cost subpool and a fixed-cost subpool). Each subpool has a different allocation rate or a different allocation base.

Consider the Central Computer Department at the corporate headquarters of Computer Horizons (shown in Exhibit 14-4). For simplicity, assume that the only users of this facility are the MicroComputer Division and the Peripheral Equipment Division. The following data apply to the coming budget year:

OBJECTIVE 4

Describe how the single-rate cost allocation method differs from the dual-rate method

Fixed costs of operating the facility	$300,000 per year
Total capacity available	1,500 hours
Budgeted long-term usage (quantity) in hours:	
MicroComputer Division	800
Peripheral Equipment Division	400
Total	1,200
Budgeted variable costs per hour in the 1,000- to 1,500-hour relevant range	$200 per hour used

Under the single-rate method, the costs of the Central Computer Department (assuming budgeted usage is the allocation base and budgeted rates are used) would be allocated as follows:

Total cost pool: $300,000 + (1,200 budgeted hours × $200)	$540,000 per year
Budgeted usage	1,200 hours
Budgeted total rate per hour rate: $540,000 ÷ 1,200 hours	$450 per hour used
Allocation rate for MicroComputer Division	$450 per hour used
Allocation rate for Peripheral Equipment Division	$450 per hour used

The rate of $450 per hour differs sizably from the $200 budgeted variable cost per hour. The $450 rate includes an allocated amount of $250 per hour ($300,000 ÷ 1,200 hours) for the fixed costs of operating the facility. These fixed costs will be incurred whether the computer runs its 1,500-hour capacity, its 1,200-hour budgeted usage, or even, say, only 600 hours' usage.

Using the $450 per hour single-rate method (combined with the budgeted usage allocation base) transforms what is a fixed cost to the Central Computer Department (and to Computer Horizons) into a variable cost to users of that facility. This approach could lead internal users to purchase computer time outside the company. Consider an external vendor that charges less than $450 per hour but more than $200 per hour. A division of Computer Horizons that uses this vendor rather than the Central Computer Department may decrease its own division costs, but the overall costs to Computer Horizons are increased. For example, suppose the MicroComputer Division uses an external vendor that charges $360 per hour when the Central Computer Department has excess capacity. In the short run, Computer Horizons incurs an extra $160 per hour, because this external vendor is used ($360 external purchase price per hour minus the $200 internal variable costs per hour) instead of its own Central Computer Department.

When the dual-rate method is used, allocation bases for each different subcost pool must be chosen. Assume that the budgeted rates are used. The allocation quantities chosen are budgeted usage for fixed costs and actual usage for variable costs. The total budgeted usage of 1,200 hours comprises 800 hours for the MicroComputer Division and 400 hours for the Peripheral Equipment Division. The costs allocated to the MicroComputer Division would be as follows:

Fixed-cost function (800 hours ÷ 1,200 hours) × $300,000	$200,000 per year
Variable-cost function	$200 per hour used

The costs allocated to the Peripheral Equipment Division would be:

Fixed-cost function: (400 hours ÷ 1,200 hours) × $300,000	$100,000 per year
Variable-cost function	$200 per hour used

Assume now that during the coming year the MicroComputer Division actually uses 900 hours but the Peripheral Equipment Division uses only 300 hours. The costs allocated to these two divisions would be computed as follows.

Under the Single-Rate Method

MicroComputer Division	$900 \times \$450 = \$405,000$
Peripheral Equipment Division	$300 \times \$450 = \$135,000$

Under the Dual-Rate Method

MicroComputer Division	$\$200,000 + (900 \times \$200) = \$380,000$
Peripheral Equipment Division	$\$100,000 + (300 \times \$200) = \$160,000$

One obvious benefit of using the single-rate method is the low cost of implementation. It avoids the often-expensive analysis necessary to classify the individual cost items of a department into fixed and variable categories. However, a single-rate method may lead divisions to take actions that appear to be in their own best interests but are not in the best interests of the organization as a whole.

An important benefit of the dual-rate method is that it signals to division managers how variable costs and fixed costs behave differently. This important information could steer division managers into making decisions that benefit the corporation as well as each division. For example, it would signal that using a third-party computer provider who charges more than $200 per hour could result in Computer Horizons being worse off than if it had used its own Central Computer Department, which has a variable cost of $200 per hour.

OBJECTIVE 5

Explain how the choice of budgeted versus actual allocation rates changes the risks managers face

Budgeted Versus Actual Rates

The decision on whether to use budgeted cost rates or actual cost rates affects the level of uncertainty user departments face. Budgeted rates let the user departments know the cost rates they will be charged in advance. Users are then better equipped to determine the amount of the service to request and—if the option exists—whether to use the internal department source or an external vendor. In contrast, when actual rates are used, the user department will not know the rates charged until the end of the period.

Budgeted rates also help motivate the manager of the support department (for example, the Central Computer Department) to improve efficiency. During the budget period, the support department, not the user departments, bears the risk of any unfavourable cost variances. Why? Because the user department does not pay for any costs that exceed the budgeted rates. The manager of the support department would likely view this as a con of using budgeted rates, especially when unfavourable cost variances occur because of price increases outside the department's control.

Some organizations recognize that it may not always be best to impose all the risks of variances from budgeted amounts completely on the support department (as when costs are allocated using budgeted rates) or completely on the user departments (as when costs are allocated using actual rates). For example, the two departments may agree to share the risk (through an explicit formula) of a large, uncontrollable increase in the price of materials used by the support department.

Budgeted Versus Actual Usage Allocation Bases

The choice between actual usage and budgeted usage for allocating department fixed costs also can affect a manager's behaviour. Consider the budget of $300,000 fixed costs at the Central Computer Department of Computer Horizons. Assume that actual and budgeted fixed costs are equal. Assume also that the actual usage by the MicroComputer Division is always equal to the budgeted usage. We now look at the effect on allocating the $300,000 in total fixed costs when actual usage by the Peripheral Equipment Division equals (case 1), is greater than (case 2), and is less than (case 3) than the budgeted usage. Recall that the budgeted usage is 800 hours for the MicroComputer Division and 400 hours for the Peripheral Equipment Division. Exhibit 14-5 presents the allocation of total fixed costs of $300,000 to each division for these three cases.

In case 1, the fixed-cost allocation equals the expected amount. In case 2, the fixed-cost allocation is $40,000 less to the MicroComputer Division than expected ($160,000 vs. $200,000). In case 3, the fixed-cost allocation is $40,000 more than expected ($240,000 vs. $200,000). Consider case 3. Why is there an increase of $40,000

EXHIBIT 14-5
Effect of Variations in Actual Usage on Departmental Cost Allocations

Case	Actual Usage		Budgeted Usage as Allocation Base		Actual Usage as Allocation Base	
	MicroComputer Division	Peripheral Equipment Division	MicroComputer Division	Peripheral Equipment Division	MicroComputer Division	Peripheral Equipment Division
1	800 hours	400 hours	$200,000*	$100,000†	$200,000*	$100,000†
2	800 hours	700 hours	$200,000*	$100,000†	$160,000‡	$140,000‖
3	800 hours	200 hours	$200,000*	$100,000†	$240,000§	$ 60,000#

$* \dfrac{800}{(800 + 400)} \times \$300,000$ $† \dfrac{400}{(800 + 400)} \times \$300,000$ $‡ \dfrac{800}{(800 + 700)} \times \$300,000$

$§ \dfrac{800}{(800 + 200)} \times \$300,000$ $‖ \dfrac{700}{(800 + 700)} \times \$300,000$ $\# \dfrac{200}{(800 + 200)} \times \$300,000$

even though the MicroComputer Division's actual and budgeted usage are exactly equal? Because the fixed costs are spread over fewer hours of usage. Variations in usage in another division will affect the fixed costs allocated to the MicroComputer Division when fixed costs are allocated on the basis of actual usage. When actual usage is the allocation base, user divisions will not know how much cost is allocated to them until the end of the budget period.

When budgeted usage is the allocation base, user divisions will know their allocated costs in advance. This information helps the user divisions with both short-run and long-run planning. The main justification given for the use of budgeted usage to allocate fixed costs relates to long-run planning. Organizations commit to infrastructure costs (such as the fixed costs of a support department) on the basis of a long-run planning horizon; the use of budgeted usage to allocate these fixed costs is consistent with this long-run horizon.

If fixed costs are allocated on the basis of estimated long-run use, some managers may be tempted to underestimate their planned usage. In this way, they will bear a lower fraction of the total costs (assuming all other managers do *not* similarly underestimate). Some organizations offer rewards in the form of salary increases and promotions to managers who make accurate forecasts of long-run usage. (This is the carrot approach.) Alternatively, some organizations impose cost penalties for underpredicting long-run usage. For instance, a higher cost rate may be charged after a division exceeds its budgeted usage. (This is the stick approach.)

ALLOCATING COSTS OF SUPPORT DEPARTMENTS

Operating Departments and Support Departments

Many organizations distinguish between operating departments and support departments. An **operating department** (also called a **production department** in manufacturing companies) adds value to a product or service that is observable by a customer. A **support department** (also called a **service department**) provides the services that maintain other internal departments (operating departments and other support departments) in the organization. Support departments at Computer Horizons include the Legal Department and the Personnel Department at corporate headquarters.

Support departments create special accounting problems when they provide reciprocal support to each other as well as support to operating departments. An example of reciprocal support at Computer Horizons would be the Legal Department providing services to the Personnel Department (such as advice on compliance with labour laws) and the Personnel Department providing support to the Legal Department (such as advice about the hiring of attorneys and secretaries). To obtain accu-

Operating department (production department). A department that adds value to a product or service that is observable by a customer.

Support department (service department). A department that provides the services that maintain other internal departments (operating departments and other support departments) in the organization.

rate product, service, and customer costs at Computer Horizons requires inclusion of support department costs as well as operating department costs. This section illustrates alternative ways to recognize support department costs. More accurate support department cost allocations results in more accurate product, service, and customer costs.

Be cautious here for several reasons. First, organizations differ in the departments located at the corporate and division levels. Some departments located at corporate headquarters of Computer Horizons (for example, R&D) are located at the division level in other organizations. Second, organizations differ in their definitions of *operating department* and *support department*. Always try to ascertain the precise meaning of these terms when analyzing data that include allocations of operating department costs and support department costs. Third, organizations differ in the percentage of total support costs allocated using the methods described in this section. Some companies allocate all support department costs using one of the methods outlined in this section. Other companies only allocate *indirect* support department costs using these methods, with all *direct* support costs traced to the appropriate operating department.

Support Department Cost Allocation Methods

OBJECTIVE 6

Distinguish between direct allocation, step-down, and reciprocal methods of allocating support department costs

We now examine three methods of allocating the costs of support departments: *direct*, *step-down*, and *reciprocal*. To focus on concepts, we use the single-rate method to allocate the costs of each support department. The Problem for Self-Study at the end of this chapter illustrates the use of the dual-rate method for allocating support department costs.

Consider Castleford Engineering, which manufactures engines used in electric power generating plants. Castleford has two support departments and two operating departments in its manufacturing facility:

Support Departments	Operating Departments
Plant maintenance	Machining
Information systems	Assembly

Costs are accumulated in each department for planning and control purposes. For inventory costing, however, the support department costs of Castleford must be allocated to the operating departments. The data for our example are listed in Exhibit 14-6. The percentages in this table can be illustrated by reference to the Plant Maintenance Department. This support department provides a total of 8,000 hours of support work: 20% (1,600 ÷ 8,000) goes to the Information Systems support department; 30% (2,400 ÷ 8,000) to the Machining Department; and 50% (4,000 ÷ 8,000) to the Assembly Department.

EXHIBIT 14-6
Data for Allocating Support Department Costs at Castleford Engineering for 2000

	Support Departments		Operating Departments		
	Plant Maintenance	Information Systems	Machining	Assembly	Total
Budgeted manufacturing overhead costs before any interdepartment cost allocations	$600,000	$116,000	$400,000	$200,000	$1,316,000
Support work furnished:					
By Plant Maintenance:					
Budgeted labour-hours	—	1,600	2,400	4,000	8,000
Percentage	—	20%	30%	50%	100%
By Information Systems:					
Budgeted computer time	200	—	1,600	200	2,000
Percentage	10%	—	80%	10%	100%

Direct Allocation Method The **direct allocation method** (often called the **direct method**) is the most widely used method of allocating support department costs. This method allocates each support department's costs directly to the operating departments. Exhibit 14-7 illustrates this method using the data in Exhibit 14-6. Note how this method ignores both the 1,600 hours of support time rendered by the Plant Maintenance Department to the Information Systems Department and the 200 hours of support time rendered by Information Systems to Plant Maintenance. The base used to allocate Plant Maintenance is the budgeted total maintenance labour-hours worked in the operating departments: 2,400 + 4,000 = 6,400 hours. This amount excludes the 1,600 hours of support time provided by Plant Maintenance to Information Systems. Similarly, the base used for allocation of Information Systems costs is 1,600 + 200 = 1,800 hours of computer time, which excludes the 200 hours of support time provided by Information Systems to Plant Maintenance.

The benefit of the direct method is its simplicity. There is no need to predict the usage of support department resources by other support departments.

Step-Down Allocation Method Some organizations use the **step-down allocation method** (sometimes called the **step allocation method**, or **sequential allocation method**), which allows for *partial* recognition of the services rendered by support departments to other support departments. This method requires the support departments to be ranked (sequenced) in the order in which the step-down allocation is to proceed. The costs in the first-ranked support department are allocated to the other support departments and to the operating departments. The costs in the second-ranked department are allocated to those support departments not yet allocated

Direct allocation method (direct method). Method of support cost allocation that ignores any service rendered by one support department to another; it allocates each support department's total costs directly to the operating departments.

Step-down allocation method (step allocation method, sequential allocation method). Method of support cost allocation that allows for partial recognition of services rendered by support departments to other support departments.

EXHIBIT 14-7
Direct Method of Allocating Support Department Costs for 2000 at Castleford Engineering

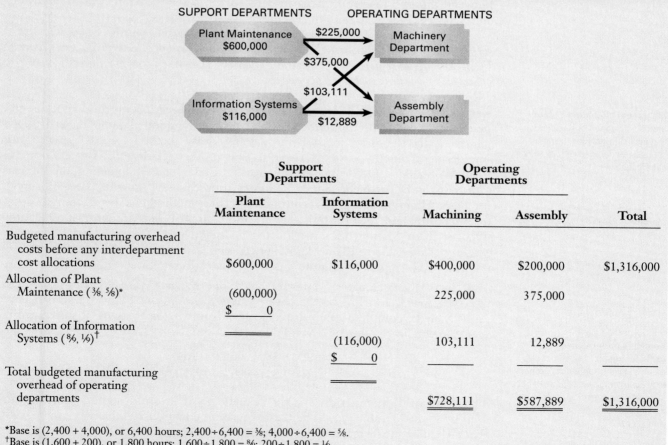

	Support Departments		Operating Departments		
	Plant Maintenance	Information Systems	Machining	Assembly	Total
Budgeted manufacturing overhead costs before any interdepartment cost allocations	$600,000	$116,000	$400,000	$200,000	$1,316,000
Allocation of Plant Maintenance (3/8, 5/8)*	(600,000)		225,000	375,000	
	$ 0				
Allocation of Information Systems (8/9, 1/9)†		(116,000)	103,111	12,889	
		$ 0			
Total budgeted manufacturing overhead of operating departments			$728,111	$587,889	$1,316,000

*Base is (2,400 + 4,000), or 6,400 hours; 2,400÷6,400 = 3/8; 4,000÷6,400 = 5/8.
†Base is (1,600 + 200), or 1,800 hours; 1,600÷1,800 = 8/9; 200÷1,800 = 1/9.

and to the operating departments. This procedure is followed until the costs in the last-ranked support department have been allocated to the operating departments. Two ways to determine the sequence to allocate support department costs are as follows:

◆ **Approach A.** Rank support departments on the percentage of the support department's total support provided to other support departments. The support department with the highest percentage is allocated first. The support department with the lowest percentage is allocated last. In our Castleford Engineering example, the chosen order would be:

	Percentage of Total Service Provided to Other Support Departments
1. Plant Maintenance	20%
2. Information Systems	10%

◆ **Approach B.** Rank support departments on the total dollars of service provided to other support departments. In our Castleford Engineering example, the chosen order would be:

	Dollar Amount of Total Service Provided to Other Support Departments
1. Plant Maintenance (0.20 × $600,000)	$120,000
2. Information Systems (0.10 × $116,000)	11,600

Exhibit 14-8 shows the step-down method where the Plant Maintenance costs of $600,000 are allocated first; $120,000 is allocated to Information Systems (20% of $600,000); $180,000 to Machining (30% of $600,000); and $300,000 to Assembly (50% of $600,000). The costs in Information Systems now total $236,000 ($116,000 + $120,000 from the first-round allocation). This $236,000 amount is then allocated between the two operating departments—$209,778 ($\frac{8}{9}$ × $236,000) to Machining and $26,222 ($\frac{1}{9}$ × $236,000) to Assembly.

Under the step-down method, once a support department's costs have been allocated, no subsequent support department costs are allocated or circulated back to it. Thus, once the Plant Maintenance department costs are allocated, they receive no further allocation from other (lower-ranked) support departments.

Reciprocal allocation method. Method of support cost allocation that explicitly includes the mutual services rendered among all support departments.

Reciprocal Allocation Method   The **reciprocal allocation method** allocates costs by explicitly including the mutual services provided among all support departments. Theoretically, the direct method and the step-down method are less accurate when support departments provide services to one another reciprocally. For example, the Plant Maintenance Department maintains all the computer equipment in the Information Systems Department. Similarly, Information Systems provides database support for Plant Maintenance. The reciprocal allocation method enables us to incorporate interdepartmental relationships *fully* into the support department cost allocations. That is, Plant Maintenance is allocated to Information Systems, and Information Systems is allocated to Plant Maintenance; each is allocated to the operating departments as well. Implementing the reciprocal allocation method requires three steps.

◆ **Step 1:** *Express support department costs and reciprocal relationships in linear equation form.*   Let PM be the *complete reciprocated costs* of Plant Maintenance and IS be the complete reciprocated costs of Information Systems. We then express the data in Exhibit 14-6 as follows:

$$PM = \$600,000 + 0.1IS \quad (1)$$
$$IS = \$116,000 + 0.2PM \quad (2)$$

Complete reciprocated cost (artifical costs). The actual cost incurred by the service department plus a part of the costs of the other support departments that provide services to it; always larger than the actual cost.

The 0.1IS term in equation 1 is the percentage of the Information Systems work used by Plant Maintenance. The 0.2PM term in equation 2 is the percentage of the Plant Maintenance work used by Information Systems.

By **complete reciprocated cost** in equations 1 and 2, we mean the actual costs incurred by a support department plus a part of the costs of the other support

EXHIBIT 14-8
Step-Down Method of Allocating Support Department Costs for 2000 at Castleford Engineering

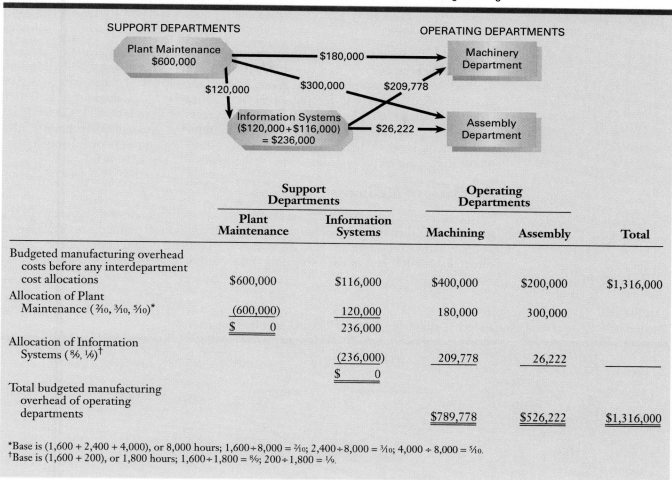

	Support Departments		Operating Departments		
	Plant Maintenance	Information Systems	Machining	Assembly	Total
Budgeted manufacturing overhead costs before any interdepartment cost allocations	$600,000	$116,000	$400,000	$200,000	$1,316,000
Allocation of Plant Maintenance ($\frac{2}{10}$, $\frac{3}{10}$, $\frac{5}{10}$)*	(600,000)	120,000	180,000	300,000	
	$ 0	236,000			
Allocation of Information Systems ($\frac{8}{9}$, $\frac{1}{9}$)†		(236,000)	209,778	26,222	
		$ 0			
Total budgeted manufacturing overhead of operating departments			$789,778	$526,222	$1,316,000

*Base is (1,600 + 2,400 + 4,000), or 8,000 hours; 1,600÷8,000 = $\frac{2}{10}$; 2,400÷8,000 = $\frac{3}{10}$; 4,000 ÷ 8,000 = $\frac{5}{10}$.
†Base is (1,600 + 200), or 1,800 hours; 1,600÷1,800 = $\frac{8}{9}$; 200÷1,800 = $\frac{1}{9}$.

departments that provide service to it. This complete reciprocated costs figure is sometimes called the **artificial costs** of the support department; it is always larger than the actual costs.

◆ **Step 2:** *Solve the system of simultaneous equations to obtain the complete reciprocated costs of each support department.* Where there are two support departments, the following substitution approach can be used. Substituting equation 2 into equation 1:

$$PM = \$600,000 + [0.1(\$116,000 + 0.2PM)]$$
$$PM = \$600,000 + \$11,600 + 0.02PM$$
$$0.98PM = \$611,600$$
$$PM = \$624,082$$

Substituting into equation 2:

$$IS = \$116,000 + 0.2(\$624,082) = \$240,816$$

Where there are more than two support departments with reciprocal relationships, computer programs can be used to calculate the complete reciprocated costs of each support department.

◆ **Step 3:** *Allocate the complete reciprocated costs of each support department to all other departments (both support and operating departments) on the basis of the usage proportions (based on total units of service provided to all departments).* Consider the Information Systems Department, which has a complete reciprocated cost of $240,816. This amount would be allocated as follows:

To Plant Maintenance ($\frac{1}{10} \times \$240,816$)	=	$ 24,082
To Machining ($\frac{8}{10} \times \$240,816$)	=	192,653
To Assembly ($\frac{1}{10} \times \$240,816$)	=	24,082
Total		$240,817

Exhibit 14-9 presents summary data pertaining to the reciprocal method.

One source of confusion to some managers using the reciprocal cost allocation method is why the complete reciprocated costs of the support departments $864,898 ($624,082 and $240,816 in Exhibit 14-9) exceed their budgeted amount of $716,000 ($600,000 and $116,000 in Exhibit 14-6). The excess of $148,898 ($24,082 for Plant Maintenance and $124,816 for Information Systems) is the total costs that are allocated among support departments. The total costs allocated to the operating departments under the reciprocal allocation method are still only $716,000.

Overview of Methods

Assume that the total budgeted overhead costs of each operating department in the example in Exhibits 14-7 to 14-9 are allocated to individual products on the basis of budgeted machine-hours for the Machining Department (4,000 hours) and budgeted direct labour-hours for the Assembly Department (3,000 hours). The budgeted

EXHIBIT 14-9
Reciprocal Method of Allocating Support Department Costs for 2000 at Castleford Engineering

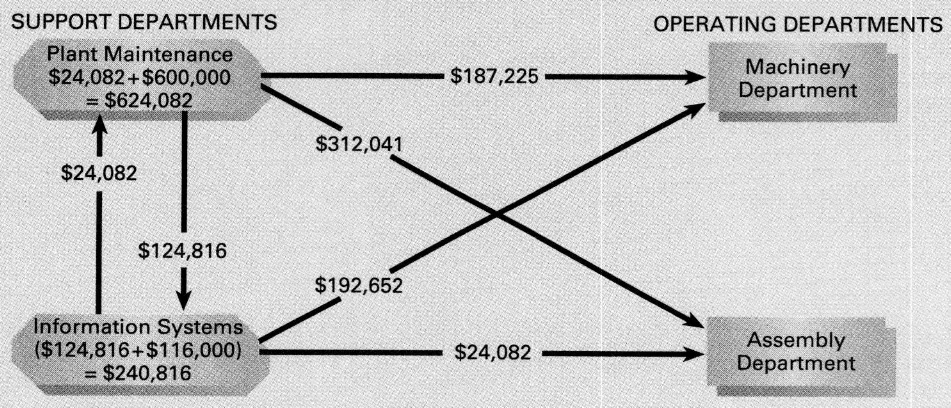

	Support Departments		Operating Departments		
	Plant Maintenance	Information Systems	Machining	Assembly	Total
Budgeted manufacturing overhead costs before any interdepartment cost allocations	$600,000	$116,000	$400,000	$200,000	$1,316,000
Allocation of Plant Maintenance ($\frac{2}{10}$, $\frac{3}{10}$, $\frac{5}{10}$)*	(624,082)	124,816	187,225	312,041	
Allocation of Information Systems ($\frac{1}{10}$, $\frac{8}{10}$, $\frac{1}{10}$)†	24,082	(240,816)	192,652	24,082	
	$ 0	$ 0			
Total budgeted manufacturing overhead of operating departments			$779,877	$536,123	$1,316,000

*Base is (1,600 + 2,400 + 4,000), or 8,000 hours; 1,600÷8,000 = $\frac{2}{10}$; 2,400÷8,000 = $\frac{3}{10}$; 4,000÷8,000 = $\frac{5}{10}$.
†Base is (200 + 1,600 + 200), or 2,000 hours; 200÷2,000 = $\frac{1}{10}$; 1,600÷2,000 = $\frac{8}{10}$; 200÷2,000 = $\frac{1}{10}$.

overhead allocation rates associated with each support department allocation method (rounded to the nearest dollar) are:

Support Department Cost Allocation Method	Total Budgeted Costs After Support		Overhead Allocation of All Department Costs	Budgeted Overhead Rate per Hour for Product Costing Purposes	
	Machining	Assembly		Machining (4,000 machine-hours)	Assembly (3,000 labour-hours)
Direct	$728,111	$587,889		$182	$196
Step-down	789,778	526,222		197	175
Reciprocal	779,877	536,123		195	179

These differences in budgeted overhead rates with alternative support department cost allocation methods can be important to managers. For example, consider a cost reimbursement contract that uses 100 machine-hours and 15 assembly labour-hours. The support department costs allocated to this contract would be:

Direct	$21,140	$182 × 100 + $196 × 15
Step-down	22,325	$197 × 100 + $175 × 15
Reciprocal	22,185	$195 × 100 + $179 × 15

Use of the step-down method would result in the highest cost reimbursement to the contractor.

The reciprocal method, while conceptually preferable, is not widely used. The advantage of the direct and step-down methods is that they are relatively simple to compute and understand. However, with the ready availability of computer software to solve sets of simultaneous equations, the extra costs of using the reciprocal method will, in most cases, be minimal. The more likely roadblocks to the reciprocal method being widely adopted are (1) many managers find it difficult to understand and (2) the numbers obtained by using the reciprocal method differ little, in some cases, from those obtained by using the direct or step-down method.

ALLOCATING COMMON COSTS

We next consider two methods used to allocate common costs. A **common cost** is a cost of operating a facility, operation, activity, or like cost object that is shared by two or more users. Consider Jason Stevens, a senior student in Winnipeg who has been invited to an interview with an employer in Montreal. The round-trip Winnipeg-Montreal airfare is $1,200. A week prior to leaving, Stevens is also invited to an interview with an employer in Halifax. The round-trip Winnipeg-Halifax fare is $800. Stevens decides to combine the two recruiting steps into a Winnipeg-Montreal-Halifax trip that will cost $1,500 in airfare. The $1,500 is a common cost that benefits both employers. Two methods for allocating this common cost between the two potential employers are now discussed: the stand-alone method and the incremental method.

Stand-Alone Cost Allocation Method

The **stand-alone cost allocation method** uses information pertaining to each cost object as a separate operating entity to determine the cost allocation weights. For the airfare common cost of $1,500, information about the separate (stand-alone) return airfares ($1,200 and $800) is used to determine the allocation weights:

Halifax employer: $\frac{\$1,200}{\$1,200 + \$800} \times \$1,500 = 0.60 \times \$1,500 = \$900$

Montreal employer: $\frac{\$800}{\$800 + \$1,200} \times \$1,500 = 0.40 \times \$1,500 = \$600$

Advocates of this method often emphasize an equity or fairness rationale. That is, fairness occurs because each employer bears a proportionate share of total costs in relation to their individual stand-alone costs.

OBJECTIVE 7

Make decisions that draw on the allocation of common costs using either the stand-alone or incremental methods

Common cost. The cost of operating a facility, operation, activity area, or like cost object that is shared by two or more users.

Stand-alone cost allocation method. Cost allocation method that allocates the common cost on the basis of each user's percentage of the total of the individual stand-alone costs.

Allocation of Support Department Costs

Use of the direct method of allocating support department costs is widespread. Systematic surveys of support department cost allocation methods are available for Australia, Japan, and the United Kingdom.

Support Department Cost Allocation Method	Australia	Japan	United Kingdom
1. Direct method	43%	58%	64%
2. Step-down method	3	27	6
3. Reciprocal method	5	10	14
4. Other method	15	1	8
5. Not allocated	34	4	8
	100%	100%	100%

Source: Blayney, P., and I. Yokoyama, "Comparative Analysis of Japanese and Australian Cost Accounting Management Practices," (Working Paper, The University of Sydney, Sydney, Australia, 1991)

Incremental Cost Allocation Method

Incremental cost allocation method. Cost allocation method requiring that one user be viewed as the primary party and the second user be viewed as the incremental party.

The **incremental cost allocation method** ranks the individual cost objects and then uses this ranking to allocate costs among those cost objects. The first-ranked cost object is termed the *primary party* and is allocated costs up to its cost as a stand-alone entity. The second-ranked cost object is termed the *incremental party* and is allocated the additional cost that arises from there being two users instead of only the primary user. If there are more than two parties, the nonprimary parties will need to be ranked.

Consider Jason Stevens and his $1,500 airfare cost. Assume that the Montreal employer is viewed as the primary party. Stevens' rationale was that he had already committed to go to Montreal. The cost allocations would then be:

Party	Costs Allocated	Costs Remaining to Be Allocated to Other Parties
Montreal (primary)	$1,200	$300 ($1,500 − $1,200)
Halifax (incremental)	300	0

The Montreal employer is allocated the full Winnipeg-Montreal airfare. The nonallocated part of the total airfare is allocated to the Halifax employer. Had the Halifax employer been chosen as the primary party, the cost allocations would have been Halifax, $800 (the stand-alone Winnipeg-Halifax return airfare) and Montreal, $700 ($1,500 − $800). Where there are more than two parties, this method requires them to be ranked and the common costs allocated to those parties in the ranked sequence.

Under the incremental method, the primary party typically receives the highest allocation of the common costs. Not surprisingly, most users in common cost situations propose themselves as the incremental party. In some cases, the incremental party is a newly formed "organization" such as a new product line or a new sales territory. Chances for its short-term survival may be enhanced if it bears a relatively low allocation of common costs.

A caution is appropriate here as regards Stevens' cost allocation options. His chosen method must be acceptable to each prospective employer. Indeed, some prospective employers may have guidelines that recruiting candidates must follow. For example, the Montreal employer may have a policy that the maximum reimbursable airfare is a seven-day advance booking price in economy class. If this amount is less than the amount that Stevens would receive under (say) the stand-alone method, then the employer's upper-limit guideline would govern how much could be allocated to that interviewer. Stevens should obtain approval before he purchases his ticket as to what cost allocation method(s) each potential employer views as acceptable.

Disputes over how to allocate common costs are often encountered. The final section of this chapter discusses the role of cost data in contracting. This is also an area where disputes about cost allocation frequently arise.

COST ALLOCATIONS AND CONTRACTS

Many commercial contracts include clauses that require the use of cost accounting information. Examples include:

OBJECTIVE 8

Explain the importance of explicit agreement between parties when reimbursement is based on costs incurred

1. A contract between the Department of National Defence and a company designing and assembling a new fighter plane. The price paid for the plane is based on the contractor's costs plus a preset fixed fee.
2. A research contract between a university and a government agency. The university is reimbursed its direct costs plus an overhead rate that is a percentage of direct costs.
3. A contract between an energy-consulting firm and a hospital. The consulting firm receives a fixed fee plus a share of the energy-cost savings arising from the consulting firm's recommendations.

Contract disputes arise with some regularity, often with respect to cost allocation. The areas of dispute between the contracting parties can be reduced by making the "rules of the game" explicit and in writing at the time the contract is signed. Such "rules of the game" include the definition of cost items allowed, the permissible cost-allocation bases, and how differences between budgeted and actual costs are to be handled.

Contracting

There are two main approaches to reimbursing costs as determined by a contract.

1. The *contractor is paid a set price without analysis of actual contract cost data.* This approach is used, for example, where there is competitive bidding, where there is adequate price competition, or where there is an established catalog with prices quoted for items sold in substantial quantities to the general public.
2. The *contractor is paid after analysis of actual contract cost data.* In some cases, the contract will explicitly state that reimbursement is based on actual allowable costs plus a set fee. This arrangement is a cost-plus contract.

Fairness of Pricing

When uncertainty is high, as in many defence contracts involving new weapons and equipment, contracts are rarely subject to competitive bidding. Why? Because no contractor is willing to assume all the risk. Hence, market-based fixed-price setting fails to attract a contractor, or the resulting price is too outrageously high for the government. So the government assumes a major share of the risks. It negotiates contracts by using costs as a substitute for selling prices as ordinarily set by suppliers in open markets. In this contracting arena, a cost allocation may be difficult to defend on the basis of any cause-and-effect reasoning. Nonetheless, the contracting parties may still view it as a "reasonable" or "fair" means to help establish a selling price. Some costs become "allowable," but others are "unallowable". An **allowable cost** is a cost that the contract parties agree to include in the costs to be reimbursed. Some contracts specify how allowable costs are to be determined. For example, only economy-class airfares may be allowable in a contract. Other contracts identify cost categories that are nonallowable. For example, the costs of lobbying activities and the costs of alcoholic beverages are not allowable costs on some contracts.

Allowable cost. Cost that the parties to a contract agree to include in the costs to be reimbursed.

PROBLEM

This problem illustrates how support department cost allocation methods can be used in a setting different from that of the manufacturing example examined earlier in the chapter (Exhibits 14-6 to 14-9). In this problem, the costs of central corporate support departments are allocated to operating divisions. The corporate departments provide services to each other as well as to the operating divisions. Also, this problem illustrates the use of the dual-rate method of allocating support department costs. (The dual-rate method can also be used in manufacturing support department cost allocations.)

Computer Horizons budgets the following amounts for its two central corporate support departments (Legal and Personnel) in supporting each other and the two manufacturing divisions—the MicroComputer Division (MCD) and the Peripheral Equipment Division (PED):

To Be Supplied By:	Budgeted Capacity				
	Legal	Personnel	MCD	PED	Total
Legal (hours)	—	250	1,500	750	2,500
Legal (percentages)	—	10%	60%	30%	100%
Personnel (hours)	2,500	—	22,500	25,000	50,000
Personnel (percentages)	5%	—	45%	50%	100%

Details on actual usage are as follows:

To Be Supplied By:	Actual Usage By:				
	Legal	Personnel	MCD	PED	Total
Legal (hours)	—	400	400	1,200	2,000
Legal (percentages)	—	20%	20%	60%	100%
Personnel (hours)	2,000	—	26,600	11,400	40,000
Personnel (percentages)	5%	—	66.5%	28.5%	100%

The actual costs were:

	Fixed	Variable
Legal	$360,000	$200,000
Personnel	$475,000	$600,000

Fixed costs are allocated on the basis of budgeted capacity. Variable costs are allocated on the basis of actual usage.

REQUIRED

What support department costs for Legal and Personnel will be allocated to MCD and PED using (a) the direct method, (b) the step-down method (allocating the Legal Department costs first), and (c) the reciprocal method?

SOLUTION

Exhibit 14-10 presents the computations for allocating the fixed and variable support department costs. A summary of these costs is as follows:

	MicroComputer Division	Peripheral Equipment Division
A. Direct method:		
Fixed costs	$465,000	$370,000
Variable costs	470,000	330,000
	$935,000	$700,000
B. Step-down method:		
Fixed costs	$458,053	$376,947
Variable costs	488,000	312,000
	$946,053	$688,947

C. Reciprocal method:

Fixed costs	$462,513	$372,487
Variable costs	476,364	323,636
	$938,877	$696,123

The simultaneous equations for the reciprocal method are:

Fixed Costs
$L = \$360,000 + 0.05P$
$P = \$475,000 + 0.10L$
$L = \$360,000 + 0.05(\$475,000 + 0.10L) = \$385,678$
$P = \$475,000 + 0.10(\$385,678) = \$513,568$

Variable Costs
$L = \$200,000 + 0.05P$
$P = \$600,000 + 0.20L$
$L = \$200,000 + 0.05(\$600,000 + 0.20L) = \$232,323$
$P = \$600,000 + 0.20(\$232,323) = \$646,465$

EXHIBIT 14-10

Alternative Methods of Allocating Corporate Support Department Costs to Operating Divisions of Computer Horizons: Dual-Rate Method

Allocation Method	Corporate Support Department		Manufacturing Divisions	
	Legal	Personnel	MCD	PED
A. Direct Method				
Fixed costs:	$360,000	$475,000		
Legal (⁶⁄₉, ³⁄₉)	(360,000)		$240,000	$120,000
Personnel ($^{225}/_{475}$, $^{250}/_{475}$)	$ 0	(475,000)	225,000	250,000
		$ 0	$465,000	$370,000
Variable costs:	$200,000	$600,000		
Legal (0.25, 0.75)	(200,000)		$ 50,000	$150,000
Personnel (0.7, 0.3)	$ 0	(600,000)	420,000	180,000
		$ 0	$470,000	$330,000
B. Step-Down Method				
(Legal Department first)				
Fixed costs:	$360,000	$475,000		
Legal (0.10, 0.60, 0.30)	(360,000)	36,000	$216,000	$108,000
Personnel ($^{225}/_{475}$, $^{250}/_{475}$)	$ 0	(511,000)	242,053	268,947
		$ 0	$458,053	$376,947
Variable costs:	$200,000	$600,000		
Legal (0.20, 0.20, 0.60)	(200,000)	40,000	$ 40,000	$120,000
Personnel (0.05, 0.45, 0.50)	$ 0	(640,000)	448,000	192,000
		$ 0	$488,000	$312,000
C. Reciprocal Method				
Fixed costs:	$360,000	$475,000		
Legal (0.10, 0.60, 0.30)	(385,678)	(38,568)	$231,407	$115,703
Personnel (0.05, 0.45, 0.50)	25,678	513,568	231,106	256,784
	$ 0	$ 0	$462,513	$372,487
Variable costs:	$200,000	$600,000		
Legal (0.20, 0.20, 0.60)	(232,323)	46,465	$ 46,465	$139,393
Personnel (0.05, 0.665, 0.285)	32,323	(646,465)	429,899	184,243
	$ 0	$ 0	$476,364	$323,636

SUMMARY

The following points are linked to the chapter's learning objectives.

1. A *cost object* is anything for which a separate measurement of costs is desired. Costing systems in organizations have multiple cost objects (departments, products, services, and customers) meaning many individual costs are allocated and reallocated several times before becoming an indirect cost of a specific cost object.

2. The four possible purposes of cost allocation are to provide information for economic decisions, to motivate managers and employees, to justify costs or compute reimbursement, and to measure income and assets for meeting external regulatory and legal reporting obligations. Different cost allocations may be appropriate depending on the specific purpose.

3. The cause-and-effect and the benefits-received criteria guide most decisions related to cost allocations. Other criteria found in practice include fairness or equity and ability to bear.

4. A cost pool is a grouping of individual cost items. Two key decisions related to indirect cost pools are the number of indirect cost pools and the allowability of individual cost items to be included in those cost pools.

5. A single-rate cost allocation method pools all costs in one cost pool and allocates them to cost objects using the same rate per unit of the single allocation base. In the dual-rate method, costs are grouped in two separate cost pools, each of which has a different allocation rate and which may have a different allocation base.

6. When cost allocations are made using budgeted rates, managers of divisions to which costs are allocated face no uncertainty about the rates to be used in that period. In contrast, when actual rates are used for cost allocation, managers do not know the rates to be used until the end of the accounting period.

7. The three main methods of allocating support department costs to operating departments are the direct, step-down, and reciprocal. The last is conceptually preferable, but the direct and step-down methods are more widely used. The direct method ignores any reciprocal support among support departments; the step-down method allows for partial recognition; the reciprocal method provides full recognition of support among support departments.

8. Common costs are the costs of operating a facility, operation, or activity area that are shared by two or more users. The stand-alone cost allocation method uses information pertaining to each operating entity to determine how to allocate the common costs. The incremental cost allocation method ranks cost objects and allocates common costs first to the primary cost object and then to the other remaining (incremental) cost objects.

9. Contract disputes over amounts to be paid often can be reduced by making the cost assignment rules as explicit as possible (and in writing). These rules should include details such as the allowable cost items, the acceptable cost-allocation bases, and how differences between budgeted and actual costs are to be handled.

This chapter ontains definitions of the following important terms:

allowable cost (p. 505)
artificial costs (p. 501)
common cost (p. 503)
complete reciprocated cost (p. 500)
direct allocation method (p. 499)
direct method (p. 499)
dual-rate cost allocation method (p. 494)
homogeneous cost pool (p. 493)
incremental cost allocation method (p. 501)
operating department (p. 497)

production department (p. 497)
reciprocal allocation method (p. 500)
sequential allocation method (p. 499)
service department (p. 497)
single-rate cost allocation method (p. 494)
stand-alone cost allocation method (p. 503)
step allocation method (p. 499)
step-down allocation method (p. 499)
support department (p. 497)

QUESTIONS

14-1 "I am going to focus on the customers of my business and leave cost allocation issues to my accountant." Do you agree with this comment by a division president?

14-2 How can an individual cost item, such as the salary of a plant security guard, be both a direct cost and an indirect cost at the same time?

14-3 A given cost may be allocated for one or more purposes. List four purposes.

14-4 What criteria might be used to guide cost allocation decisions? Which are the dominant criteria?

14-5 Identify six reasons why Canadian executives allocate costs to divisions and departments.

14-6 How do cost-benefit considerations affect choices by a company about the allocation of indirect costs to products, services, or customers?

14-7 Name three decisions managers face when designing the cost allocation component of an accounting system.

14-8 Give examples of bases used to allocate corporate cost pools to the operating divisions of an organization.

14-9 Why might a manager prefer that budgeted rather than actual indirect cost allocation rates be used for costs being allocated to her department from another department?

14-10 "To ensure unbiased cost allocations, fixed indirect costs should be allocated on the basis of estimated long-run use by user department managers." Do you agree? Why?

14-11 Distinguish among the three methods of allocating the costs of service departments to production departments.

14-12 What is the theoretically most defensible method for allocating service department costs?

14-13 Distinguish between two methods of allocating common costs.

14-14 What is one key way to reduce cost allocation disputes arising with government contracts?

EXERCISES

14-15 Cost allocation in hospitals, alternative allocation criteria. Dave Meltzer went to Lake Louise for his annual winter vacation. Unfortunately, he suffered a severe break in his ankle while skiing and had to spend two days at the Foothills Hospital. Meltzer's insurance company received a $4,800 bill for his two-day stay. One item that caught Meltzer's eye was an $11.52 charge for a roll of cotton. Meltzer was a salesman for Johnson & Johnson and knew that the cost to the hospital of the roll of cotton would be in the $2.20 to $3 range. He asked for a breakdown of how the $11.52 charge was derived. The accounting office of the hospital sent him the following information:

a. Invoiced cost of cotton roll	$ 2.40
b. Processing of paperwork for purchase	0.60
c. Supplies room management fee	0.70
d. Operating-room and patient-room handling charge	1.60
e. Administrative hospital costs	1.10
f. Research-related recoupment	0.60
g. Malpractice insurance costs	1.20
h. Cost of treating uninsured patients	2.72
i. Profit component	0.60
Total	$11.52

Meltzer believes the overhead charge is obscene. He comments, "There was nothing I could do about it. When they come in and dab your stitches, it's not as if you can say, 'Keep your cotton roll. I brought my own.'"

REQUIRED

1. Compute the overhead rate Foothills Hospital charged on the cotton roll.
2. What criteria might Foothills use to justify allocation of each of the overhead items (b) through (i) in the preceding list? Examine each item separately, and use the allocation criteria listed in Exhibit 14-2 in your answer.
3. What should Meltzer do about the $11.52 charge for the cotton roll?

14-16 Single-rate versus dual-rate cost allocation methods. (W. Crum, adapted) The Ontario Company has a power plant designed and built to serve its three factories. Data for 2000 are as follows:

	Usage in Kilowatt-Hours	
Factory	**Budget**	**Actual**
Mississauga	100,000	80,000
Cambridge	60,000	120,000
Burlington	40,000	40,000

Actual fixed costs of the power plant were $1 million in 2000; actual variable costs, $2 million.

REQUIRED

1. Compute the amount of power costs that would be allocated to Cambridge using a single-rate method for both budgeted and actual usage.
2. Compute the amount of power costs that would be allocated to Cambridge using a dual-rate method for both budgeted and actual usage.

14-17 Single-rate versus dual-rate allocation methods, support department. The power plant that services all manufacturing departments of West Engineering has a budget for the coming year. This budget has been expressed in the following terms on a monthly basis:

Manufacturing Departments	Needed at Practical Capacity Production Level* (kilowatt-hours)	Average Expected Monthly Usage (kilowatt-hours)
Rockford	10,000	8,000
Peoria	20,000	9,000
Hammond	12,000	7,000
Kankakee	8,000	6,000
Totals	50,000	30,000

*This factor was the most influential in planning the size of the power plant.

The expected monthly costs for operating the department during the budget year are $15,000: $6,000 variable and $9,000 fixed.

REQUIRED

1. Assume that a single cost pool is used for the power plant costs. What dollar amounts will be allocated to each manufacturing department? Use (a) practical capacity and (b) average expected monthly usage as the allocation bases.
2. Assume a dual-rate method; separate cost pools for the variable and fixed costs are used. Variable costs are allocated on the basis of expected monthly usage.

Fixed costs are allocated on the basis of practical capacity. What dollar amounts will be allocated to each manufacturing department? Why might you prefer the dual-rate method?

14-18 Cost allocation to divisions. Rembrandt Hotel and Casino is situated in Ontario. The complex includes a 300-room hotel, a casino, and a restaurant. As Rembrandt's new controller, you are asked to recommend the basis use for allocating fixed overhead costs to the three divisions in 2000. You are presented with the following income statement for the year 2000.

	Hotel	Restaurant	Casino
Revenue	$16,425,000	$5,256,000	$12,340,000
Direct costs	9,819,260	3,749,172	4,248,768
Segment margin	6,605,740	1,506,828	8,055,232

You are also given the following data on the three segments

	Hotel	Restaurant	Casino
Square Metres	80,000	16,000	64,000
# of Employees	200	50	250

You may choose to allocate costs based on direct costs, square metrage (floor space), or the number of employees. Total fixed overhead for 2000 was $14,550,000.

REQUIRED
1. Calculate segment margins in percentage terms prior to allocating fixed overhead costs.
2. Allocate indirect costs to the three divisions using each of the three allocation basis suggested. Calculate segment margins in dollar and percentage terms.
3. Discuss the results. What is your preferred base for allocating indirect costs to the divisions?
4. Would you recommend shutting any of the three divisions (and possibly reallocating resources to other divisions) as a result of your analysis? If so, which division would you close, and why?

14-19 Single-rate cost allocation method, budgeted versus actual costs and quantities. Fruit Juice, Inc. processes orange juice at its East Miami plant and grapefruit juice at its West Miami plant. It purchases oranges and grapefruit from growers' cooperatives in the Orlando area. It owns its own trucking fleet. It takes the same mileage to go to each Miami plant from Orlando. The trucking fleet is run as a cost centre. Each Miami plant is billed for the direct costs and the indirect costs of each return trip.

The trucking fleet costs include direct costs (labour costs of drivers, fuel, and toll charges) and indirect costs. Indirect costs include wear and tear on tires and the vehicle, leasing costs, insurance, and state registration fees.

At the start of 2000, the Orange Juice Division budgeted for 150 Orlando to East Miami truck trips while the Grapefruit Juice Division budgeted for 100 Orlando to West Miami truck trips. On the basis of these 250 budgeted trips, the Trucking Fleet Division budgeted trucking fleet indirect costs of $575,000. The following actual results occurred for 2000:

Trucking fleet indirect costs	$645,000
Trips to East Miami plant	200
Trips to West Miami plant	100

The Trucking Fleet Division uses a single-rate method when allocating indirect trucking costs. The costs charged to each plant equal this rate times the actual number of trips made.

REQUIRED
1. What is the indirect cost rate per truck trip when (a) budgeted costs and budgeted quantities (trips) are used and (b) actual costs and actual quantities (trips) are used?
2. From the viewpoint of the Orange Juice Division, what are the effects of using budgeted costs/quantities rather than actual costs/quantities?

14-20 Dual-rate cost allocation method, budgeted versus actual costs and quantities (continuation of 14-19). Fruit Juice, Inc. decides to examine the effect of using a dual-rate method for allocating indirect trucking costs to each truck trip. At the start of 2000, the budgeted indirect costs were:

Variable indirect costs per trip	$1,500
Fixed indirect costs	$200,000

The actual results for the 300 round trips made in 2000 were:

Variable indirect costs	$465,000
Fixed indirect costs	180,000
	$645,000

Assume all other information to be the same as in Exercise 14-19.

REQUIRED
1. What is the indirect cost per truck trip with a dual-rate method when (a) variable indirect costs are allocated using the budgeted variable indirect rate times actual trips made and (b) fixed indirect costs are allocated using the budgeted fixed indirect cost rate times budgeted trips to be made?
2. Compare the results for requirement 1 with that in requirements 1(a) and (b) for Exercise 14-19. From the viewpoint of the Orange Juice Division, what are the effects of using a dual-rate method rather than a single-rate method?

14-21 Contracting, cost allocations. Sprout Consulting has been working with Gemini Widgets to improve the widget production process. In the year ended December 31, 2000, Gemini produced and sold 450,000 widgets at $5.60 per widget. Variable costs were $2.80 per widget, and total fixed manufacturing costs were $1,350,000.

As a result of Sprout's analysis, Gemini has been able to produce 12% more widgets in 2001. Gemini has also been able to reduce fixed costs by 25% and variable costs by 10%. The average selling price remained constant from 2000 to 2001.

Sprout's contract was as follows:
◆ a $50,000 fixed fee
◆ 10% of the costs saved on production of up to 450,000 widgets
◆ $0.10 on every widget produced over and above the year 2000 quantity of 450,000 regardless of any cost savings being achieved.

REQUIRED
1. Was Gemini Widgets profitable in 2000? What was Gemini's net income (loss)?
2. Calculate Gemini's budgeted fixed cost per widget in 2000. What did you use for the budgeted denominator level? What was the total cost per widget?
3. Repeat requirements 1 and 2 for 2001.
4. What is Sprout's total remuneration for this assessment? (Assume this has already been included in 2001 fixed costs.

14-22 Allocation of common costs. Sam, Sarah, and Tony are members of the Toronto Fire Department. They share a penthouse apartment that has a lounge room with the latest 50″ TV. Tony owns the apartment, its furniture, and the 50″ TV. He can subscribe to a cable television company that has the following packages available:

Package	Rate per Month
A. Basic news	$32
B. Premium movies	25
C. Premium sports	30
D. Basic news and premium movies	50
E. Basic news and premium sports	54
F. Premium movies and premium sports	48
G. Basic news, premium movies, and premium sports	70

Sam is a TV news junkie, has average interest in movies and zero interest in sports ("They're overpaid jocks"). Sarah is a movie buff, likes sports, and avoids the news ("It's all depressing anyway"). Tony is into sports in a big way, has average interest in news, and zero interest in movies ("He always falls asleep before the end"). They all agree that the purchase of the $70 total package is a "win-win-win" situation.

Each works on a different eight-hour shift at the fire station, so conflicts in viewing are minimal.

REQUIRED

1. What criteria might be used to guide the choice about how to allocate the $70 monthly cable fee between Sam, Sarah, and Tony?
2. Outline two methods of allocating the $70 among Sam, Sarah, and Tony.

14-23 Allocation of travel costs. Joan Ernst, a graduating senior at a university in Vancouver, received an invitation to visit a prospective employer in Halifax. A few days later, she received an invitation from a prospective employer in Toronto. She decided to combine her visits, travelling from Vancouver to Halifax, Halifax to Toronto, and Toronto to Vancouver.

Ernst received job offers from both companies. Upon her return, she decided to accept the offer in Toronto. She was puzzled about how to allocate her travel costs between the two employers. She gathered the following data:

Regular Round-Trip Fares with No Stopovers

Vancouver to Halifax	$1,400
Vancouver to Toronto	$1,100

Ernst paid $1,800 for her three-leg flight (Vancouver to Halifax, Halifax to Toronto, Toronto to Vancouver). In addition, she paid $30 for a limousine from her home to Vancouver Airport and another $30 for a limousine from Vancouver Airport to her home when she returned.

REQUIRED

1. How should Ernst allocate the $1,800 airfare between the employers in Halifax and Toronto? Show the actual amounts you would allocate, and give reasons for your allocations.
2. Repeat requirement 1 for the $60 limousine charges at the Vancouver end of her travels.

14-24 Support department cost allocation; direct and step-down methods. Phoenix Consulting provides outsourcing services and advice to both government and corporate clients. For costing purposes, Phoenix classifies its departments into two support departments (Administrative/Human Resources and Information Systems) and two operating departments (Government Consulting and Corporate Consulting). For the first quarter of 2000, Phoenix incurs the following costs in its four departments:

Administrative/Human Resources (A/H)	$600,000
Information Systems (IS)	$2,400,000
Government Consulting (GOVT)	$8,756,000
Corporate Consulting (CORP)	$12,452,000

The actual level of support relationships between the four departments for the first quarter of 2000 was:

	Used By:			
Supplied By:	**A/HR**	**IS**	**GOVT**	**CORP**
A/HR	—	25%	40%	35%
IS	10%	—	30%	60%

The Administrative/Human Resource support percentages are based on head count. The Information Systems support percentages are based on actual hours of computer time used.

REQUIRED

1. Allocate the two support department costs to the two operating departments using the following methods.
   a. Direct method
   b. Step-down method (allocate Administrative/Human Resources first)
   c. Step-down method (allocate Information Systems first)
2. Compare and explain differences in the support department costs allocated to each operating department.

3. What criteria could determine the sequence for allocating support departments using the step-down method? What criterion should Phoenix use if government consulting jobs require the step-down method?

14-25 Support department cost allocation, reciprocal method (continuation of 14-24). Assume the same facts as in Exercise 14-24.

REQUIRED
1. Allocate the two support department costs to the two operating departments using the reciprocal method.
2. Compare and explain differences in requirement 1 with those in requirement 1 of Exercise 14-24. Which method do you prefer?

14-26 Support department cost allocation. (CMA) Computer Information Services is a computer software consulting company. Its three major functional areas are computer programming, information systems consulting, and software training. Carol Birch, a pricing analyst in the Accounting Department, must develop total costs for the functional areas. These costs will guide pricing for new contracts. In computing these costs, Birch is considering two different methods of allocating support department costs—the direct method and the step-down method. Birch assembled the following data on budgeted costs from its two support departments, the Information Systems Department and the Facilities Department.

	Support Departments		Operating Departments			
	Information Systems	Facilities	Computer Programming	Consulting	Software Training	Total
Budgeted costs	$50,000	$25,000	$75,000	$110,000	$85,000	$345,000
Information Systems (hours)	—	300	1,200	600	900	3,000
Facilities (thousands of square metres)	200	—	400	600	800	2,000

REQUIRED
1. Allocate the support department costs in Information Systems and Facilities using (a) the direct method and (b) the step-down method (Information Systems first).
2. Explain to Birch any differences between the methods. Which method should she use?

14-27 Direct and step-down allocation. e-books is an online book retailer. The company has four departments. The two revenue producing departments are corporate sales and consumer sales. The two support departments are administrative (human resources, accounting, and so on), and information systems (IS). Each of the sales departments conducts merchandising and marketing operations independently.

The following data for the month of September 2000 will assist you in allocating costs to the different departments:

	Revenue	# of Employees	Processing Time Used
Corporate Sales	$1,334,200	42	1920
Consumer Sales	$667,100	28	1600
Administrative	–	14	320
IS	–	21	1120

Costs incurred in each of the four departments for the month of September 2000 are as follows:

Corporate Sales	$998,270
Consumer Sales	489,860
Administrative	72,700
Information Systems	234,400

REQUIRED
1. Allocate the support department costs to the revenue-producing departments using the direct method.

2. Develop appropriate overhead allocation rates for the four departments. Rank the support departments on the dollar amount of services rended to other support departments (using September departmental costs). Use this ranking and your overhead rates to allocate support costs based on the step-down allocation method.

3. Could you have ranked the support departments differently? If so, how else could you rank the support departments? Had you done so in this problem, would the allocations have changed?

14-28 Reciprocal cost allocation (continuation of 14-27). Consider e-books again. The controller reads a widely used text that states that "the reciprocal method is conceptually the most defensible." He seeks your assistance.

REQUIRED

1. Describe the key features of the reciprocal cost allocation method.
2. Allocate the support department costs (administrative and information systems) to the two revenue-producing departments using the reciprocal allocation method.
3. Under what conditions is the reciprocal method more accurate than the direct and step-down methods? In the case presented in this problem, which method would you recommend? Why?

PROBLEMS

14-29 Allocation of central corporate costs to divisions. Dusty Rhodes, the corporate controller of the Richfield Oil Company, is about to make a presentation to the senior corporate executives and the top managers of its four divisions. These divisions are:

a. Oil and Gas Upstream (the exploration, production, and transportation of oil and gas)
b. Oil and Gas Downstream (the refining and marketing of oil and gas)
c. Chemical Products
d. Copper Mining

Under the existing internal accounting system, costs incurred at central corporate headquarters are collected in a single pool and allocated to each division on the basis of the actual revenues of each division. The central corporate costs (in millions) for the most recent year are as follows:

Interest on debt	$2,000
Corporate salaries	100
Accounting and control	100
General marketing	100
Legal	100
R&D	200
Public affairs	208
Personnel and payroll	192
	$3,000

"Public affairs" includes the public relations staff, the lobbyists, and the sizable donations Richfield makes to numerous charities and nonprofit institutions.

Summary data (in millions) related to the four divisions for the most recent year are as follows:

	Oil and Gas Upstream	Oil and Gas Downstream	Chemical Products	Copper Mining	Total
Revenue	$7,000	$16,000	$4,000	$3,000	$30,000
Operating costs	$3,000	$15,000	$3,800	$3,200	$25,000
Operating income	$4,000	$1,000	$200	$(200)	$5,000
Identifiable assets	$14,000	$6,000	$3,000	$2,000	$25,000
Number of employees	9,000	12,000	6,000	3,000	30,000

The top managers of each division share in a divisional income bonus pool. Divisional income is defined as operating income less allocated central corporate costs.

Rhodes is about to propose a change in the method used to allocate central corporate costs. He favours collecting these costs in four separate pools:

♦ **Cost pool 1.** Allocated using identifiable assets of division
  Cost Item: Interest on debt
♦ **Cost pool 2.** Allocated using revenue of division
  Cost Items: Corporate salaries, accounting and control, general marketing, legal, R&D
♦ **Cost pool 3.** Allocated using operating income (if positive) of division, with only divisions with positive operating income included in the allocation base
  Cost Item: Public affairs
♦ **Cost pool 4.** Allocated using number of employees in division
  Cost Item: Personnel and payroll

REQUIRED

1. What purposes might be served by the allocation of central corporate costs to each division at Richfield Oil?
2. Compute the divisional income of each of the four divisions when central corporate costs are allocated using revenue of each division.
3. Compute the divisional income of each of the four divisions when central corporate costs are allocated through the four cost pools.
4. What are the strengths and weaknesses of Rhodes' proposal relative to the existing single-pool method?

14-30 Division managers' reactions to the allocation of central corporate costs to divisions (continuation of 14-29). Dusty Rhodes presents his proposal for the use of four separate cost pools to allocate central corporate costs to the divisions. The comments of the top managers of each of the four divisions include the following:

a. By the top manager of the Oil and Gas Upstream Division: "The multiple-pool method of Rhodes is absurd. We are the only division generating a substantial positive cash flow, and this is ignored in the proposed (and indeed the existing) system. We could pay off any debt very quickly if we were not a cash cow for the rest of the dog divisions in Richfield Oil."

b. By the top manager of the Oil and Gas Downstream Division: "Rhodes' proposal is the first sign that the money we spend in the accounting and control function at corporate headquarters is justified. The proposal is fair and equitable."

c. By the top manager of the Chemical Products Division: "I oppose any cost allocation method. Last year I was the only major player in the chemical industry to show a positive operating income. We are operating at the bare-bones level. Last year I saved $300,000 by making everyone travel economy class. This policy created a lot of dissatisfaction, but we finally managed to get it accepted. Then at the end of the year we get a charge of $400 million for corporate central costs. What's the point of our division economy drives when they get swamped by allocations of corporate fat?"

d. By the top manager of Copper Mining Division: "I should probably get concerned, but frankly I view it all as bookkeeping entries. If we were in the black, certain aspects would really infuriate me. For instance, why should corporate R&D costs be allocated to the Copper Division? The only research corporate does for us is how to best prepare our division for divestiture."

REQUIRED

How should Rhodes respond to these comments?

14-31 Cost allocation, monthly reports (CMA, revised). Bulldog Inc. is a large manufacturing company that runs its own electrical power plant from the excess steam produced in its manufacturing process. Power is provided to two production departments—Department A and Department B. The capacity of the power plant was originally determined by the expected peak demands of the two production departments. The expected average usage and peak demands are, respectively, 60 percent and 66,000,000 kilowatt hours (kwh) for Department A and 40 percent and 44,000,000 for Department B.

The budgeted monthly costs of producing power, based on normal usage of 100,000,000 kwh, are $30,000,000 in fixed costs and $7,500,000 in variable costs. For the month of November, the actual kwh used was 60,000,000 by Department A and 20,000,000 by Department B. Actual fixed costs were $30,000,000, and actual variable costs were $7,500,000.

Terry Lamb, the controller, prepared the following monthly report:

Bulldog Inc.
Monthly Allocation Report
November 2000

Power plant usage		80,000,000 kwh
Actual costs:		
Fixed		$30,000,000
Variable		7,500,000
Total		$37,500,000
Rate per kwh	($37,500,000 ÷ 80,000,000 kwh)	$0.46875
Allocations:		
To Department A	(60,000,000 kwh × $0.46875)	$28,125,000
To Department B	(20,000,000 kwh × $0.46875)	9,375,000
Total allocated		$37,500,000

Lamb fully allocated all power plant costs on the basis of actual kwh used by each production department. This report will be submitted to the two production department operating managers.

REQUIRED

1. Discuss at least two problems with the monthly allocation report prepared by Lamb for November 2000 at Bulldog Inc.
2. Prepare a revised monthly allocation report for November 2000 using a flexible budget approach.
3. Discuss the behavioural implications of Lamb's monthly allocation report for November 2000 on the production managers of Department B at Bulldog Inc.

14-32 Cost allocation downward demand spiral. Diversified Inc. is an industrial conglomerate operating in Western Canada. The conglomerate runs 14 companies in a diverse range of businesses from its corporate headquarters in Vancouver. Diversified Inc. also runs a cleaning and maintenance company, Clean Shop Inc., from headquarters in Calgary. Clean Shop provides cleaning and maintenance services to all of Diversified's facilities.

Clean Shop has the capacity to clean and maintain 5,000,000 square metres (m^2) on a daily basis. Total square metrage for all of Diversified's facilities as of September 1, 2000, is 2,250,000 m^2 (assume this is average square metrage for 2000 in what follows). Bubba Smith, Clean Shop's CEO, prepares the 2001 budget based on growth estimates from corporate headquarters. Bubba estimates an average 2,500,000 m^2 will be cleaned and maintained daily during 2001. Facilities are operational 360 days a year.

For the six months ended June 30, 2000, Clean Shop incurred total costs of $64,800,000. Fixed costs were $16,200,000. Bubba budgets fixed costs of $36,000,000 for 2001. Variable costs are projected to remain at 2000 levels. Bubba figures out what he will charge the subsidiary companies in 2001 (per square metre). He learns that, on average, competitors are charging $0.14 per square metre for similar jobs.

As the year 2000 draws to a close, Johnson Almighty, CEO of Diversified, announces that all of Diversified's units will operate as profit centres beginning January 1, 2001. Towards the end of December, Bubba learns that six of the 14 companies have decided to employ external third-party cleaning and maintenance services. The six companies account for 40% of projected 2001 square metrage.

REQUIRED

1. What were Clean Shop's variable costs per square metre in the first half of 2000? What are fixed costs allocated per square metre?
2. Before Almighty's announcement, and assuming Bubba does not plan on margins, how much (per square metre) does Bubba plan to charge the subsidiary companies in 2001? Is this rate competitive? (using estimated square metres in the denomination level)
3. Using the cost allocation techniques studied in this chapter, what accounting change could Bubba make to come up with a competitive rate?

4. Consider Almighty's announcement. How much must Bubba charge the remaining companies per square metre to break even? How much will Clean Shop lose if Bubba does not change the rate per square metre as calculated in requirement 2? By how much would Bubba have to reduce capacity at Clean Shop to make the business competitive *and* break even? (Assume that any reduction in capacity will bring about a proportional reduction in fixed costs.)

5. Why was 2000 capacity at Clean Shop more than double Diversified's needs? Was Bubba operating in the best interests of Diversified? Explain how surplus capacity at Clean Shop may have affected Diversified's bottom line. What were the underlying accounting practices that allowed such negligence to occur?

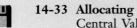

14-33 Allocating costs of support departments; step-down and direct methods. The Central Valley Company has prepared departmental overhead budgets for normal volume levels before allocations, as follows:

Support departments:		
Building and grounds	$10,000	
Personnel	1,000	
General factory administration	26,090	
Cafeteria (subsidy for operating loss)	1,640	
Storeroom	2,670	
Total support departments		$ 41,400
Operating departments:		
Machining	$34,700	
Assembly	48,900	
Total operating departments		83,600
Total for both departments		$125,000

Management has decided that the most sensible inventory costs are achieved by using individual departmental overhead rates. These rates are developed after appropriate support department costs are allocated to operating departments. Bases for allocation are to be selected from the following:

Department	Manufacturing Labour-Hours	Direct Number of Employees	Square Metres of Floor Space Occupied	Manufacturing Labour-Hours	Total Number of Requisitions
Building and grounds	0	0	0	0	0
Personnel*	0	0	2,000	0	0
General plant administration	0	35	7,000	0	0
Cafeteria	0	10	4,000	1,000	0
Storeroom	0	5	7,000	1,000	0
Machining	5,000	50	30,000	8,000	2,000
Assembly	15,000	100	50,000	17,000	1,000
Total	20,000	200	100,000	27,000	3,000

*Basis used is number of employees.

REQUIRED

1. Using a worksheet, allocate support department costs by the step-down method. Develop overhead rates per direct manufacturing labour-hour for machining and assembly. Allocate the support departments in the order given in this problem. Use the allocation base for each support department you think is most appropriate.

2. Using the direct method, rework requirement 1.

3. Based on the following information about two jobs, determine the total overhead costs for each job by using rates developed in requirements 1 and 2.

Direct Manufacturing Labour-Hours

	Machining	Assembly
Job 88	18	2
Job 89	3	17

14-34 Support department cost allocations; single-department cost pools; direct, step-down, and reciprocal methods. The Manes Company has two products. Product 1 is manufactured entirely in Department X. Product 2 is manufactured entirely in Department Y. To produce these two products, the Manes Company has two support departments: A (a materials-handling department) and B (a power-generating department).

An analysis of the work done by Departments A and B in a typical period is as follows:

	Used By:			
Supplied By:	**A**	**B**	**X**	**Y**
A	—	100	250	150
B	500	—	100	400

The work done in Department A is measured by the direct labour-hours of materials-handling time. The work done in Department B is measured by the kilowatt-hours of power.

The budgeted costs of the support departments for the coming year are:

	Department A	**Department B**
Variable indirect labour and indirect materials costs	$ 70,000	$10,000
Supervision	10,000	10,000
Amortization	20,000	20,000
	$100,000	$40,000
	+ Power costs	+ Materials-handling costs

The budgeted costs of the operating departments for the coming year are $1,500,000 for Department X and $800,000 for Department Y.

Supervisory costs are salary costs. Amortization in B is the straight-line amortization of power-generation equipment in its nineteenth year of an estimated 25-year useful life; it is old but well-maintained equipment.

REQUIRED
1. What are the allocations of costs of support Departments A and B to operating Departments X and Y using the direct method, two different sequences of the step-down method, and the reciprocal method of reallocation?
2. The power company has offered to supply all the power needed by the Manes Company and to provide all the services of the present Power Department. The cost of this service will be $40 per kilowatt-hour of power. Should Manes accept? Explain.

14-35 Allocating costs of support departments; dual rates; direct, step-down, and reciprocal methods. Magnum T.A., Inc. specializes in the assembly and installation of high-quality security systems for the home and business segments of the market. The four departments at its highly automated state-of-the-art assembly plant are as follows:

Service Departments	Assembly Departments
Engineering Support	Home Security Systems
Information Systems Support	Business Security Systems

The budgeted level of service relationships at the start of the year was:

	Used By:			
Supplied By:	**Engineering Support**	**Information Systems Support**	**Home Security Systems**	**Business Security Systems**
Engineering Support	—	0.10	0.40	0.50
Information Systems Support	0.20	—	0.30	0.50

The actual level of service relationships for the year was:

		Used By:		
Supplied By:	Engineering Support	Information Systems Support	Home Security Systems	Business Security Systems
Engineering Support	—	0.15	0.30	0.55
Information Systems Support	0.25	—	0.15	0.60

Magnum collects fixed costs and variable costs of each department in separate cost pools. The actual costs (in thousands) in each pool for the year were:

	Fixed-Cost Pool	Variable-Cost Pool
Engineering Support	$2,700	$8,500
Information Systems Support	8,000	3,750

Fixed costs are allocated on the basis of the budgeted level of service. Variable costs are allocated on the basis of the actual level of service.

The support department costs allocated to each assembly department are allocated to products on the basis of units assembled. The units assembled in each department during the year were:

Home Security Systems	7,950 units
Business Security Systems	3,750 units

REQUIRED

1. Allocate the support department costs to the assembly departments using a dual-rate system and (a) the direct method, (b) the step-down method (allocate Information Systems Support first), (c) the step-down method (allocate Engineering Support first), and (d) the reciprocal method. Present results in a format similar to that of Exhibit 14-10.
2. Compare the support department costs allocated to each Home Security Systems unit assembled and each Business Security Systems unit assembled under (a), (b), (c), and (d) in requirement 1.
3. What factors might explain the very limited adoption of the reciprocal method by many organizations?

14-36 Division cost allocation, R&D, ethics. World Semiconductor (WS) has eight divisions. It has a central R&D group in Waterloo that conducts contract research for each of these eight divisions. At the start of each year, each division estimates the hours of research scientist time at the Waterloo group it will use in the coming year. These estimates are summed for WS as a whole. Each division is charged for budgeted overhead costs incurred at the Waterloo facility on the basis of its relative budgeted percentage use of research scientist time in the coming year. Central R&D bears the risk of any overruns on overhead costs during the year. Each division also pays (in 2000) the Waterloo facility $100 per hour of research scientist time and the actual costs of any materials used on the project.

Toni Goodwin is the controller of the Applied Semiconductor Division (ASD), which is based in Regina, Saskatchewan. She notes that in the first nine months of 2000, ASD was charged $12.597 million for contract research at the Waterloo facility:

Research scientist time	$ 2,564,000
Materials and other direct charges	2,883,000
Overhead cost charge (22% of $32,500,000)	7,150,000
	$12,597,000

The $32,500,000 amount represents WS's budgeted overhead costs for the first nine months of 2000.

It is now time to prepare the 2001 budget. Goodwin estimates that ASD will have a 2001 budget of 30,000 hours of research scientist time at the Waterloo facility. This estimate is based on detailed interviews she has had with operating managers at ASD and on a recent ASD retreat, at which the strategy and operations for 2001 were finalized. Roy Masters, the new president of ASD, is less than pleased with the 30,000 budget number. Goodwin and Masters have the following conversation.

Goodwin: But Roy, you were at the retreat where we all signed off on the 30,000 number.

Masters: I was there, but I think "signed off" is too strong a phrase. By all means use the 30,000 number in our internal planning and budgeting at ASD. However, I want you to tell Waterloo that we are budgeting for only 25,000 hours in 2001.

Goodwin: But . . .

Masters: But nothing, Toni. Everyone plays games in this company. This is the fourth division of World Semiconductor I have worked in. I know for a fact that in all my three prior divisions, we deliberately understated budgeted usage of research scientists to the Waterloo people at the start of each year. Anyway, Waterloo always artificially inflates its estimate of overhead costs for the coming year. They do it every year. Anyone who thinks this is a level playing field is more naive than my dog.

Goodwin: Roy, I have to think about this.

Masters: Don't think too long, Toni. I want the senior managers on my team to be team players. The issue you face, Toni, is whether you want to remain on the team.

REQUIRED

1. Why might Masters want Goodwin to report 25,000 budgeted hours rather than 30,000 budgeted hours to Waterloo?
2. What steps might Waterloo take to reduce WS divisions' understating their budgeted usage of Waterloo research scientist time?
3. What should Goodwin do?

COLLABORATIVE LEARNING PROBLEM

14-37 Cost allocation, pricing decisions. (CMA adapted) Best Test Laboratories began as a one-man operation 25 years ago to evaluate the reaction of materials to extreme increases in temperature. Much of the company's early growth was attributable to government contracts to test the properties of weapons, transportation equipment, and clothing for use in arid desert regions.

Recent growth has come from diversification and expansion into commercial markets. Environmental testing at Best Test now includes:

Heat testing	(HTT)
Air turbulence testing	(ATT)
Stress testing	(SST)
Arctic condition testing	(ACT)
Aquatic testing	(AQT)

Currently, all of the budgeted operating costs are collected in a common overhead pool. All of the estimated testing hours are also collected in a common pool. One rate per test hour is used for all five types of testing. This hourly rate is marked up by 45 percent in order to recover administrative expenses, taxes, and profit in the sales price.

Rich Shaw, Best Test's controller, believes that there is enough variation in the test procedures and cost structure to establish separate costing and billing rates. He also believes that the inflexible rate structure currently being used is inadequate in today's competitive environment. After analyzing the following data, he has recommended that new rates be put into effect at the beginning of Best Test's fiscal year.

The budgeting total test laboratory costs for the coming year are as follows:

Test pool labour (10 employees)	$420,000
Supervision	72,000
Equipment amortization	178,460
Heat	170,000
Electricity	124,000
Water	74,000
Set-up	58,000
Indirect materials	104,000
Operating supplies	62,000
Total test lab cost	$1,262,460
Total estimated test hours	106,000

Shaw has determined the resource usage by test type in the chart shown below.

	HTT	ATT	SST	ACT	AQT
Test pool labour employees	3	2	2	1	2
Supervision	40%	15%	15%	15%	15%
Amortization	$48,230	$22,000	$39,230	$32,000	$37,000
Heat	50%	5%	5%	30%	10%
Electricity	30%	10%	10%	40%	10%
Water	—	—	20%	20%	60%
Set-up	20%	15%	30%	15%	20%
Indirect materials	15%	15%	30%	20%	20%
Operating supplies	10%	10%	25%	20%	35%
Test hours	29,680	12,720	27,560	22,260	13,780
Competitors' hourly billing rates	$17.50	$19.00	$15.50	$16.00	$20.00

REQUIRED

1. Compute the common pool hourly cost and hourly billing rate for Best Test Laboratories.
2. Compute the five separate costs for Best Test Laboratories.
3. Discuss what effect the new costing method will have on the pricing structure for each of the five test types given the competitor's hourly billing rates.
4. In general, identify at least three other internal or external determinants of pricing structure.

15

CHAPTER

COST ALLOCATION: JOINT PRODUCTS AND BYPRODUCTS

Joint cost issues often arise in extractive industries, such as petroleum, where hydrocarbons are processed to yield crude oil, gas, and raw liquefied petroleum gas simultaneously.

LEARNING OBJECTIVES

After studying this chapter, you should be able to:

1. Identify the splitoff point(s) in a joint cost situation

2. Distinguish between joint products and byproducts

3. Provide several reasons for allocating joint costs to individual products

4. Allocate joint costs using several different methods

5. Identify the criterion used to support market-based joint cost allocation methods

6. Describe the irrelevance of joint costs in deciding to sell or further process

7. Account for byproducts using two different methods

Prior chapters have emphasized costing for either single-product companies or companies in which individual products are separately produced. We now consider costing for the more complex case where two or more products are simultaneously produced with each other. This chapter examines methods for allocating joint costs to products and services. Some of the topics discussed in this chapter are related to issues already covered in Chapter 14. Before reading on, be sure you are comfortable with pages 487–492 of Chapter 14.

MEANING OF TERMS

OBJECTIVE 1

Identify the splitoff point(s) in a joint cost situation

OBJECTIVE 2

Distinguish between joint products and byproducts

Joint cost. Cost of a single process that yields multiple products simultaneously.

Splitoff point. Juncture in the process when one or more products in a joint cost setting become separately identifiable.

Separable costs. Costs incurred beyond the splitoff point that are assignable to one or more individual products.

Product. Any output sold to a customer that has a positive sales value (or an output used internally that enables an organization to avoid incurring costs).

Joint products. Products from a joint process that have relatively high sales value and are not separately identifiable as individual products until the splitoff point.

Main product. The one product with a relatively high sales value resulting from a process yielding two or more products.

Byproduct. Product from a joint process that has a low sales value compared with the sales value of the main or joint product(s).

Scrap. Product that has a minimal (frequently zero) sales value.

A **joint cost** is the cost of a single process that yields multiple products simultaneously. Consider a single process that yields two or more products (or services) simultaneously. The distillation of coal, for example, gives us coke, gas, and other products. The cost of this distillation process would be called a joint cost. The juncture in the process when one or more products in a joint cost setting become separately identifiable is called the **splitoff point.** An example is the point where coal becomes coke, gas, and other products. **Separable costs** are costs incurred beyond the splitoff point that are assignable to one or more individual products. At or beyond the splitoff point, decisions relating to sale or further processing of individual products can be made independently of decisions about other products.

Various terms have arisen in conjunction with production processes. A **product** is any output that has a positive sales value (or an output that enables an organization to avoid incurring costs). **Joint products** all have relatively high sales value but are not separately identifiable as individual products until the splitoff point. When a single process yielding two or more products yields only one product with a relatively high sales value, that product is termed a **main product.** A **byproduct** has a low sales value compared with the sales value of the main or joint product(s). **Scrap** has a minimal sales value. The classification of products as main, joint, byproduct, or scrap can change over time, especially for products (such as tin) whose market price can increase or decrease by, say, 30% or more in any one year.

Exhibit 15-1 shows the relationship between the terms defined in the preceding paragraph. Be careful. These distinctions are not firm in practice. The variety of terminology and accounting practice is bewildering. Always gain an understanding of the terms as used by the particular organization with which you are dealing.

Industries abound in which single processes simultaneously yield two or more products. Exhibit 15-2 presents examples of joint cost situations in diverse industries. In each example in Exhibit 15-2, no individual product can be produced without the accompanying products appearing, although sometimes the proportions can be varied. A poultry farm cannot kill a turkey wing; it has to kill a whole turkey, which yields breasts, thighs, drumsticks, digest, feathermeal, and poultrymeal in addition to wings. In this example, the focus is on building up costs of individual products as disassembly occurs. This focus contrasts with that of prior chapters that emphasize building up costs of individual products as assembly occurs.

In some joint cost settings, the number of outputs produced exceed the number of products. This situation can occur where an output, produced as an inherent part

EXHIBIT 15-1
Classification of Products of a Joint Production Process

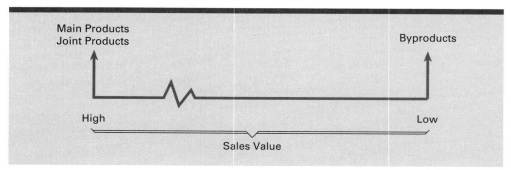

EXHIBIT 15-2
Examples of Joint Cost Situations

Industry	Separable Products at the Splitoff Point
Agriculture	
Lamb	Lamb cuts, tripe, hides, bones, fat
Raw milk	Cream, liquid skim
Turkey farm	Breasts, wings, thighs, drumsticks, digest, feathermeal, and poultrymeal
Extractive Industries	
Coal	Coke, gas, benzole, tar, ammonia
Copper ore	Copper, silver, lead, zinc
Petroleum	Crude oil, gas, raw LPG
Salt	Hydrogen, chlorine, caustic soda
Chemical Industries	
Raw LPG (liquefied petroleum gas)	Butane, ethane, propane
Semiconductor Industry	
Fabrication of silicon wafer chips	Memory chips of different quality (as to capacity), speed, life expectancy, and temperature tolerance

of the joint production process, is recycled without any value being added by its production. For example, the offshore processing of hydrocarbons to yield oil and gas also yields water as an output, which is recycled back into the ocean. Similarly, the processing of mineral ore to yield gold and silver also yields dirt as an output, which is recycled back into the ground. The water and dirt in these examples typically are not classified as products, but they are outputs. No entries are made in the accounting system to record their processing. The physical quantity of these outputs can be large relative to the physical quantity of outputs that are recorded in the accounting system as products. It is only those outputs that have a positive sales value that are typically labelled products.

WHY ALLOCATE JOINT COSTS?

There are many contexts that require the allocation of joint costs to individual products or services. Examples include:

1. Inventory costing and cost-of-goods-sold computations for external financial statements and reports for income tax authorities.

2. Inventory costing and cost-of-goods-sold computations for internal financial reporting. Such reports are used in division profitability analysis when determining compensation for division managers.

3. Cost reimbursement under contracts when only a portion of a business's products or services is sold or delivered to a single customer (such as a government agency).

4. Customer profitability analysis where individual customers purchase varying combinations of joint products or byproducts as well as other products of the company.

5. Insurance settlement computations when damage claims made by businesses with joint products, main products, or byproducts are based on cost information.

6. Rate regulation when one or more of the jointly produced products or services are subject to price regulation.[1]

OBJECTIVE 3

Provide several reasons for allocating joint costs to individual products

"What are Joint Costs, and Why Are We Concerned About Them?" National Charities Information Bureau speech www.give.org/artwggjc.cfm

[1] See J. Crespi and J. Harris, "Joint Cost Allocation Under the Natural Gas Act: An Historical Review," *Journal of Extractive Industries Accounting*, Vol. 2, No. 2, pp. 133–142.

APPROACHES TO ALLOCATING JOINT COSTS

OBJECTIVE 4

Allocate joint costs using
several different methods

These six areas are illustrative rather than exhaustive. Their wide-ranging natures illustrate why it is important to master methods for allocating joint costs.

There are two basic approaches to allocating joint costs:

◆ **Approach 1:** *Allocate costs using market-based data (for example, revenues).* Three methods that can be used in applying this approach are:
   ◆ The sales value at splitoff method
   ◆ The estimated net realizable value (NRV) method
   ◆ The constant gross margin percentage NRV method
◆ **Approach 2:** *Allocate costs using physical-measure-based data such as weight or volume.*

In prior chapters we have emphasized both the cause-and-effect and the benefits-received criterion (see Exhibit 14-2) for guiding cost allocation decisions. In joint cost settings, it is not feasible to use the cause-and-effect criterion to guide individual product cost allocations. Joint costs, by definition, cannot be the subject of cause-and-effect analysis at the individual-product level. The cause-and-effect relationship exists only at the joint process level. The benefits-received criterion leads to a preference for methods under approach 1. Revenues, in general, are a better indicator of benefits received than are physical measures such as weight or volume.

In the simplest situation, the joint products are sold at the splitoff point without further processing. We use this case first (termed Example 1) to illustrate the sales value at splitoff method and the physical measures method using volume as the metric. Then we consider situations involving further processing beyond the splitoff point (termed Example 2) to illustrate the estimated NRV method and the constant gross margin percent NRV method.

To highlight each joint cost example, we make extensive use of exhibits in this chapter. We use the following notation:

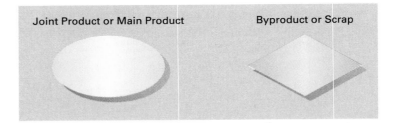

To enable comparisons across the methods, we report for each method individual gross margin percentages for individual products.

Example 1: Farmers Dairy purchases raw milk from individual farms and processes it up to the splitoff point, where two products (cream and liquid skim) are obtained. These two products are sold to an independent company, which markets and distributes them to supermarkets and other retail outlets.

Exhibit 15-3 presents an overview of the basic relationships in this example. Summary data for May 2000 are as follows:

◆ **Raw milk processed:** 110 four-litre containers (110 four-litre containers of raw milk yield 100 four-litre containers of good product with a ten-container shrinkage)

	Production	Sales
◆ **Cream:**	25 containers	20 containers at $8 per container
◆ **Liquid skim:**	75 containers	30 containers at $4 per container

EXHIBIT 15-3
Farmers Dairy: Example 1 Overview

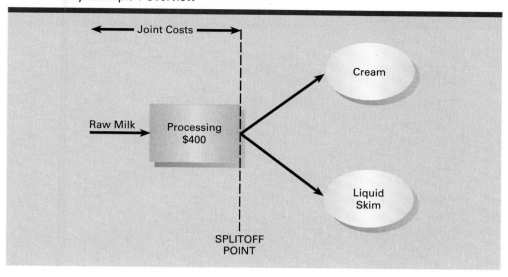

◆ **Inventories:**

	Beginning Inventory	Ending Inventory
Raw milk	0 containers	0 containers
Cream	0 containers	5 containers
Liquid skim	0 containers	45 containers

◆ Cost of purchasing 110 containers of raw milk and processing it up to the splitoff point to yield 25 containers of cream and 75 containers of liquid skim: $400

How much of the joint costs of $400 should be allocated to the ending inventory of 5 containers of cream and 45 containers of liquid skim? The joint production costs of $400 cannot be uniquely identified with or traced to either product. Why? Because the products themselves were not separated before the splitoff point. The joint cost allocation methods we now discuss can be used for costing the inventory of cream and liquid skim as well as determining cost of goods sold.

Sales Value at Splitoff Method

The **sales value at splitoff method** allocates joint costs on the basis of the relative sales value at the splitoff point of the total production in the accounting period of each product. In Example 1, the sales value at splitoff of the May 2000 production is $200 for cream and $300 for liquid skim. We then assign a weighting to each product, which is a percentage of total sales value. Using this weighting, we allocate the joint costs to the individual products:

Sales value at splitoff method. Joint cost allocation method that allocates joint costs on the basis of the relative sales value at the splitoff point of the total production in the accounting period of each product.

	Cream	Liquid Skim	Total
1. Sales value at splitoff point (cream, 25 containers × $8; liquid skim, 75 containers × $4)	$200	$300	$500
2. Weighting ($200 ÷ $500; $300 ÷ $500)	0.40	0.60	
3. Joint costs allocated (cream, 0.40 × $400; liquid skim, 0.60 × $400)	$160	$240	$400
4. Joint production costs per container (cream, $160 ÷ 25 containers; liquid skim, $240 ÷ 75 containers)	$6.40	$3.20	

Note that this method uses the sales value of the *entire production* of the accounting period. The joint costs were incurred on all units produced and not just those sold.

EXHIBIT 15-4
Farmers Dairy Product Line Income Statement for May 2000: Joint Costs Allocated Using Sales Value at Splitoff Method

	Cream	Liquid Skim	Total
Sales (cream, 20 containers × $8; liquid skim, 30 containers × $4)	$160	$120	$280
Joint costs:			
Production costs (cream, 0.4 × $400; liquid skim, 0.6 × $400)	160	240	400
Deduct: Ending inventory (cream, 5 containers × $6.40; liquid skim, 45 containers × $3.20)	32	144	176
Cost of goods sold	128	96	224
Gross margin	$ 32	$ 24	$ 56
Gross margin percentage	20%	20%	20%

Exhibit 15-4 above presents the product line income statement, using the sales value at splitoff method of joint cost allocation. Use of this method has enabled us to obtain individual product costs and gross margins. Both cream and liquid skim have gross-margin percentages of 20%.[2]

The sales value at splitoff point method exemplifies the benefits-received criterion of cost allocation. Costs are allocated to products in proportion to their ability to contribute revenue. This method is both straightforward and intuitive. The cost-allocation base (sales value at splitoff) is expressed in terms of a common denominator (dollars) that is systematically recorded in the accounting system and well understood by all parties.

Physical Measure Method

Physical measure method. Joint cost allocation method that allocates joint costs on the basis of their relative proportions at the splitoff point, using a common physical measure such as weight or volume of the total production of each product.

The **physical measure method** allocates joint costs on the basis of their relative proportions at the splitoff point, using a common physical measure such as weight or volume of the total production of each product. In Example 1, the $400 joint costs produced 25 four-litre containers of cream and 75 four-litre containers of liquid skim. Joint costs using these quantities are allocated as follows:

	Cream	Liquid Skim	Total
1. Physical measure of production (four-litre containers)	25	75	100
2. Weighting (25 containers ÷ 100 containers; 75 containers ÷ 100 containers)	0.25	0.75	
3. Joint costs allocated (cream, 0.25 × $400; liquid skim, 0.75 × $400)	$100	$300	$400
4. Joint production costs per container (cream, $100 ÷ 25 containers; liquid skim, $300 ÷ 75 containers)	$4	$4	

Exhibit 15-5 presents the product line income statement using this method of joint cost allocation. The gross margin percentages are 50% for cream and 0% for liquid skim.

The physical weights used for allocating joint costs may have no relationship to the revenue-producing power of the individual products. Using the benefits-received criterion, the physical measure method is less preferred than the sales value at splitoff method. Consider a mine that extracts ore containing gold, silver, and

[2]The equality of the gross margin percentages for the two products is a mechanical result reached with the sales value at splitoff method when there are no beginning inventories and all products are sold at the splitoff point.

EXHIBIT 15-5
Farmers Dairy Product Line Income Statement for May 2000: Joint Costs Allocated Using Physical Measure Method

	Cream	Liquid Skim	Total
Sales (cream, 20 containers × $8; liquid skim, 30 containers × $4)	$160	$120	$280
Joint costs:			
Production costs (cream, 0.25 × $400; liquid skim, 0.75 × $400)	100	300	400
Deduct: Ending inventory (cream, 5 containers × $4; liquid skim, 45 containers × $4)	20	180	200
Cost of goods sold	80	120	200
Gross margin	$ 80	$ 0	$ 80
Gross margin percentage	50%	0%	28.6%

lead. Use of a common physical measure (tonnes) would result in almost all the costs being allocated to the product that weighs the most—lead, which has the lowest revenue-producing power. As a second example, if the joint cost of a hog were assigned to its various products on the basis of weight, centre-cut pork chops would have the same cost per kilogram as pigs' feet, lard, bacon, bones, and so forth. In a product line income statement, the pork products that have a high sales value per kilogram (for example, centre-cut pork chops) would show a fabulous "profit," and products that have a low sales value per kilogram (for example, bones) would show consistent losses.

Obtaining comparable physical measures for all products is not always straightforward. Consider oil and gas joint cost settings, where oil is a liquid and gas is a vapour. A standard physical measure, the British thermal unit (BTU), is often used here. However, this physical measure can vary with the temperature of the gas. Technical personnel outside of accounting may be required when using some physical measures in joint cost allocation situations.

Example 2: Assume the same situation as in Example 1 except that both cream and liquid skim can be processed further:

◆ **Cream → butter cream.** 25 four-litre containers of cream are further processed to yield 20 four-litre containers of butter cream at additional processing (separable) costs of $280. Butter cream is sold for $25 per container.

◆ **Liquid skim → condensed milk.** 75 four-litre containers of liquid skim are further processed to yield 50 four-litre containers of condensed milk at additional processing costs of $520. Condensed milk is sold for $22 per container.

Sales during the accounting period were 12 containers of butter cream and 45 containers of condensed milk. Exhibit 15-6 presents an overview of the basic relationships. Inventory information is as follows:

	Beginning Inventory	Ending Inventory
Raw milk	0 containers	0 containers
Cream	0 containers	0 containers
Liquid skim	0 containers	0 containers
Butter cream	0 containers	8 containers
Condensed milk	0 containers	5 containers

Example 2 will be used to illustrate the estimated NRV method and the constant gross margin percentage NRV method.

EXHIBIT 15-6
Farmers Dairy: Example 2 Overview

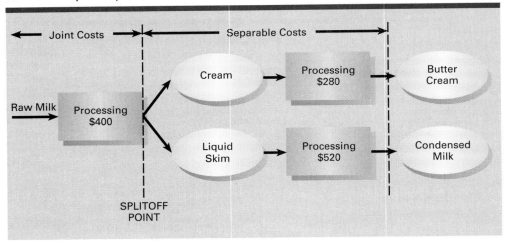

Estimated Net Realizable Value (NRV) Method

**Estimated net realizable value
(NRV) method.** Joint cost allocation method that allocates joint
costs on the basis of the relative
estimated net realizable value
(expected final sales value in the
ordinary course of business minus
the expected separable costs of
production and marketing of the
total production of the period).

The **estimated net realizable value (NRV) method** allocates joint costs on the basis
of the *relative estimated net realizable value* (expected final sales value in the ordinary
course of business minus the expected separable costs of production and marketing of
the total production of the period). Joint costs would be allocated as follows:

	Butter Cream	Condensed Milk	Total
1. Expected final sales value of production (butter cream, 20 containers × $25; condensed milk, 50 containers × $22)	$ 500	$1,100	$1,600
2. Deduct: Expected separable costs to complete and sell	280	520	800
3. Estimated net realizable value at splitoff point	$ 220	$ 580	$ 800
4. Weighting ($220 ÷ $800; $580 ÷ $800)	0.275	0.725	
5. Joint costs allocated (butter cream, 0.275 × $400; condensed milk, 0.725 × $400)	$ 110	$ 290	$ 400
6. Production costs per container (butter cream, ($110 + $280) ÷ 20 containers; condensed milk, ($290 + $520) ÷ 50 containers)	$19.50	$16.20	

Exhibit 15-7 presents the product line income statement using the estimated NRV
method. The gross margin percentages are 22.0% for butter cream and 26.4% for
condensed milk.

Estimating the net realizable value of each product at the splitoff point requires
information about the subsequent processing steps to be taken (and their expected
separable costs).[3] In some plants, such as in petrochemicals, there may be many possible subsequent steps. Companies may frequently change further processing to exploit fluctuations in the separable costs of each processing stage or in the selling
prices of individual products. Under the estimated NRV method, each such change
would affect the joint cost allocation percentages. (In practice, a set of standard subsequent steps is assumed at the start of the accounting period when using the estimated NRV method.)

The sales value at splitoff method is less complex than the estimated NRV
method, as it does not require knowledge of the subsequent steps in processing.

---

[3]The estimated NRV method is clear-cut when there is only one splitoff point. When there are
multiple splitoff points, however, additional allocations may be required if processes subsequent
to the initial splitoff point remerge with each other to create a second joint cost situation.

EXHIBIT 15-7

Farmers Dairy Product Line Income Statement for May 2000: Joint Costs Allocated Using Estimated NRV Method

	Butter Cream	Condensed Milk	Total
Sales (butter cream, 12 containers × $25; condensed milk, 45 containers × $22)	$300	$990	$1,290
Cost of goods sold:			
Joint costs (butter cream, 0.275 × $400; condensed milk, 0.725 × $400)	110	290	400
Separable processing costs	280	520	800
Cost of goods available for sale	390	810	1,200
Deduct: Ending inventory (butter cream, 8 containers × $19.50; condensed milk, 5 containers × $16.20)	156	81	237
Cost of goods sold	234	729	963
Gross margin	$ 66	$261	$ 327
Gross margin percentage	22.0%	26.4%	25.3%

However, it is not always feasible to use the sales value at splitoff method. Why? Because there may not be any market prices at the splitoff point for one or more individual products. Market prices may not first appear until after processing beyond the splitoff point has occurred.

Constant Gross Margin Percentage NRV Method

The **constant gross margin percentage NRV method** allocates joint costs in such a way that the overall gross margin percentage is identical for all the individual products. This method entails three steps:

Constant gross margin percentage NRV method. Joint cost allocation method that allocates joint costs in such a way that the overall gross margin percentage is identical for all the individual products.

◆ **Step 1.** Compute the overall gross margin percentage.

◆ **Step 2.** Use the overall gross margin percentage and deduct the gross margin from the final sales values to obtain the total costs that each product should bear.

◆ **Step 3.** Deduct the expected separable costs from the total costs to obtain the joint-cost allocation.

Exhibit 15-8 presents these three steps for allocating the $400 joint costs between butter cream and condensed milk. To determine the joint cost allocation, Exhibit 15-8 uses the expected final sales value of the *total production* of the period ($1,600) and *not* the actual sales of the period. The joint costs allocated to each product need not always be positive under this method. Some products may receive negative allocations of joint costs to bring their gross margin percentages up to the overall company average. The overall gross margin percentage is 25%. A product line income statement for the constant gross margin percentage NRV method is presented in Exhibit 15-9.

The tenuous assumption underlying the constant gross margin percentage NRV method is that all the products have the same ratio of cost to sales value. A constant ratio of cost to sales value across products is rarely seen in companies that produce multiple products but have no joint costs.

Comparison of Methods

Which method of allocating joint costs should be chosen? Because the costs are joint in nature, managers cannot use the cause-and-effect criterion in making this choice. Managers cannot be sure what causes what cost when examining joint costs. The benefits-received criterion leads to a preference for the sales value at splitoff point

O B J E C T I V E   5

Identify the criterion used to support market-based joint cost allocation methods

EXHIBIT 15-8
Farmers Dairy for May 2000: Joint Costs Allocated Using Constant Gross Margin Percentage NRV Method

	Butter Cream	Condensed Milk	Total
Step 1			
Expected final sales value of production: (20 containers × $25) + (50 containers × $22)		$1,600	
Deduct: Joint and separable costs ($400 + $280 + $520)		1,200	
Gross margin		$ 400	
Gross margin percentage ($400 ÷ $1,600)		25%	
Step 2			
Expected final sales value of production (butter cream, 20 containers × $25; condensed milk, 50 containers × $22)	$500	$1,100	$1,600
Deduct: Gross margin, using overall gross margin percentage (25%)	125	275	400
Cost of goods sold	375	825	1,200
Step 3			
Deduct: Separable costs to complete and sell	280	520	800
Joint costs allocated	$ 95	$ 305	$ 400

method (or other related revenue or market-based methods). Additional benefits of this method include:

1. **No anticipation of subsequent management decisions.** The sales value at splitoff method does not presuppose an exact number of subsequent steps undertaken for further processing.
2. **Availability of a meaningful common denominator to compute the weighing factors.** The denominator of the sales value at splitoff method (dollars) is a meaningful one. In contrast, the physical measure method may lack a

EXHIBIT 15-9
Farmers Dairy Product Line Income Statement for May 2000: Joint Costs Allocated Using Constant Gross Margin Percentage NRV Method

	Butter Cream	Condensed Milk	Total
Sales (butter cream, 12 containers × $25; condensed milk, 45 containers × $22)	$300.0	$990.0	$1,290.0
Cost of goods sold:			
Joint costs (from Exhibit 15-8)	95.0	305.0	400.0
Separable costs to complete and sell	280.0	520.0	800.0
Cost of goods available for sale	375.0	825.0	1,200.0
Deduct: Ending inventory (butter cream, 8 × $18.75*; condensed milk, 5 × $16.50[†])	150.0	82.5	232.5
Cost of goods sold	225.0	742.5	967.5
Gross margin	$ 75.0	$247.5	$ 322.5
Gross margin percentage	25%	25%	25%

*$375 ÷ 20 containers = $18.75.
[†]$825 ÷ 50 containers = $16.50.

Chicken Processing: Costing on the Disassembly Line

Chicken processing operations provide many examples where joint and byproduct costing issues can arise. Each chicken is killed and then "disassembled" into many products. Every effort is made to obtain revenue from each disassembled item.

White breast meat, the highest-revenue-generating product, is obtained from the front end of the bird. Dark meat is obtained from the back end of the bird. Other edible products include chicken wings, giblets, and kidneys. There are many non-edible products, including feathers and blood, head, feet, and intestines. The non-edible products have a diverse set of uses. Poultry feathers are used in bedding and sporting goods; poultry leftover parts such as bones, beaks, and feet are ground into livestock pellets and fertilizer; and poultry fat is used in animal feed and pet food.

Poultry companies use individual product cost information for several purposes. One purpose is in customer profitability analysis. Customers (such as supermarkets and fast food restaurants) differ greatly in the mix of products purchased. Individual product cost data enable companies to determine differences in individual customer profitability. A subset of products is placed into frozen storage, which creates a demand for individual product cost information for inventory valuation.

Companies differ in how they cost individual products. One classifies white breast meat as the single main product in its costing system. All other products are classified as byproducts. Market selling prices of the many byproducts are used to reduce the chicken processing costs that are allocated to the main product. The white breast meat is often further processed into many individual products (such as trimmed chicken and marinated chicken). The separable cost of this further processing is added to the cost per kilogram of deboned white breast meat to obtain the cost of further processed products.

Another company classifies any product sold to a retail outlet as a joint product. Such products include breast fillets, half breasts, drummettes, thighs, and whole legs. All other products are classified as byproducts. Revenue from byproducts is offset against the chicken processing cost before that cost is allocated among the joint products. The average selling prices of products sold to its retail outlets are used to allocate the net chicken processing cost among the individual joint products. The distribution costs of transporting the chicken products from the processing plants to retail outlets are not taken into account when determining the joint cost allocation weights.

Source: Adapted from conversations with executives of the two companies.

---

meaningful common denominator for all the separable products (for example, when some products are liquids and other products are solids).

3. **Simplicity.** The sales value at splitoff method is simple. In contrast, the estimated NRV method can be very complex in operations with multiple products and multiple splitoff points. The total sales value at splitoff is unaffected by any change in the production process after the splitoff point.

The purpose of the joint cost allocation is important. Consider rate regulation. Market-based measures are difficult to use in this context. It is circular to use selling prices as a basis for setting prices (rates) and at the same time use selling prices to allocate the costs on which prices (rates) are based. Physical measures represent one joint cost allocation approach available in rate regulation.

All of the preceding methods of allocating joint costs to individual products are subject to criticism. As a result, some companies refrain from joint cost allocation entirely. Instead, they carry all inventories at estimated net realizable value. Income on each product is recognized when production is completed. Industries that use variations of this approach include meat packing, canning, and mining.

Accountants ordinarily criticize carrying inventories at estimated net realizable values. Why? Because income is recognized *before* sales are made. Partly in response to this criticism, some companies using this no-allocation approach carry their inventories at estimated net realizable values minus a normal profit margin.

Exhibit 15-10 presents the product line income statement with no allocation of joint costs for Example 2. The separable costs are assigned first, which highlights for managers the cause-and-effect relationship between individual products and the costs incurred on them. The joint costs are not allocated to butter cream and condensed milk as individual products.

SURVEYS OF COMPANY PRACTICE

Joint Cost Allocation Methods Used by U.K. Companies

Systematic survey evidence on company use of joint cost allocation methods is available for Australia, Japan, and the United Kingdom. The reported percentage use by companies exceeds 100% because some companies use more than one method.

	Australia	Japan	United Kingdom
Physical measure method	60%	45%	76%
Sales value method	6	28	5
Negotiated basis	10	10	19
Not allocated	8	0	10
Other	27	10	14

The most detailed study reports joint cost allocation methods used by chemical and oil refining companies in the United Kingdom.

Type of Company	Predominant Joint Cost Allocation Method Used
Petrochemicals	Sales value at splitoff or estimated NRV
Coal processing	Physical measure
Coal chemicals	Physical measure
Oil refining	No allocation of joint cost

The authors of the survey noted that it was considered by the majority of oil refineries that the complex nature of the process involved and the vast number of joint product outputs made it impossible to establish any meaningful cost apportionment between products. In addition, market prices for many partly processed products at one or more of the splitoff points are typically not available.

Source: Adapted from Blayney, P., and I. Yokoyama, "Comparative Analysis of Japanese and Australian Cost Accounting Management Practices," (Working Paper, The University of Sydney, Sydney, Australia, 1991) and Slater, K., and C. Wooten, *A Study of Joint and By-Product Costing in the UK* (London, U.K.: Institute of Cost and Management Accountants, 1984)

EXHIBIT 15-10

EXHIBIT 15-10
Farmers Dairy Product Line Income Statement for May 2000: No Allocation of Joint Costs

	Butter Cream	Condensed Milk	Total
Produced and sold (butter cream, 12 containers × $25; condensed milk, 45 containers × $22)	$300	$ 990	$1,290
Produced but not sold (butter cream, 8 containers × $25; condensed milk, 5 containers × $22)	200	110	310
Total sales value of production	500	$1,100	1,600
Separable costs	280	520	800
Contribution to joint costs and operating income	$220	$ 580	800
Joint costs			400
Gross margin			$ 400
Gross margin percentage			25%

IRRELEVANCE OF JOINT COSTS FOR DECISION-MAKING

No technique for allocating joint product costs should guide management decisions regarding whether a product should be sold at the splitoff point or processed beyond splitoff. When a product is an inevitable result of a joint process, the decision to further process should not be influenced either by the size of the total joint costs or by the portion of the joint costs allocated to particular products. Instead, managers should use the relevant cost concepts introduced in Chapter 11.

OBJECTIVE 6

Describe the irrelevance of joint costs in deciding to sell or further process

Sell or Further Process

The decision to incur additional costs beyond splitoff should be based on the incremental operating income attainable beyond the splitoff point. Example 2 assumed that it was profitable for both cream and liquid skim to be further processed into butter cream and condensed milk respectively. The incremental analysis for these decisions to further process is as follows:

Further Processing Cream into Butter Cream

Incremental revenue ($500 – $200)	$300
Incremental processing costs	280
Incremental operating income	$ 20

Further Processing Liquid Skim into Condensed Milk

Incremental revenue ($1,100 – $300)	$800
Incremental processing costs	520
Incremental operating income	$280

The amount of joint costs incurred up to splitoff ($400)—and how it is allocated—is irrelevant in deciding whether to process further cream or liquid skim. Why? Because the joint costs of $400 are the same whether or not further processing is done.

Incremental costs are those costs that differ between the alternatives being considered (such as sell or process further). Do not assume that all separable costs in our joint-cost allocations for product-costing purposes are always incremental costs. For example, some separable costs may be allocated costs that do not differ between the specific alternatives being considered.

Joint Cost Allocation and Performance Evaluation

The potential conflict between the cost concepts used for decision making and those used for evaluating the performance of managers is a key theme of this book. If managers make process (and process or sell) decisions using an incremental revenue/incremental cost approach, the resulting budgeted product-line income statement using any of the three methods under the market-based approach (sales value at splitoff, estimated NRV, and constant gross-margin percentage NRV) will all show each individual product budgeted to have a positive (or zero) operating income. In contrast, allocating joint costs using a physical measure can show a manager being responsible for one or more products budgeted to have losses even though the company has higher operating income by producing those products in a joint-product setting.

Consider again our Example 1 (Farmers' Dairy) with the following change. The selling price per container of liquid skim is now $3.80 rather than $4.00. This change would not affect the joint costs allocated and the cost of goods computed using the physical measure method (see Exhibit 15-5). However, it would affect the revenues of the liquid skim product. The revised product-line income statement for May 2000 using the physical measure method is:

	Cream	Liquid Skim	Total
Revenues (cream 20 × $8, liquid skim 30 × $3.80)	$160	$114	$274
Cost of goods sold	80	120	200
Gross margin	$ 80	$ (6)	$ 74

Note that the liquid skim product has a negative gross margin of $6. A manager evaluated on the basis of product by product gross margin information may be reluctant to process the raw milk into cream and liquid skim to avoid having to explain why liquid skim is being produced at a negative gross margin. Use of a market-based joint cost allocation method will not put a manager in this situation.

ACCOUNTING FOR BYPRODUCTS

OBJECTIVE 7

Account for byproducts using two different methods

Processes that yield joint products often also yield what are frequently referred to as byproducts—products that have relatively low sales value compared with the sales value of the main or joint product(s). We now discuss accounting for byproducts. To simplify the discussion, consider a two-product example consisting of a main product and a byproduct.

Example 4: The Meatworks Group processes meat from slaughterhouses. One of its departments cuts lamb shoulders and generates two products:

◆ Shoulder meat (the main product)—sold for $60 per pack
◆ Hock meat (the byproduct)—sold for $4 per pack

Both products are sold at the splitoff point without further processing, as Exhibit 15-11 shows. Data (number of packs) for this department in July 2000 are as follows:

	Production	Sales	Beginning Inventory	Ending Inventory
Shoulder meat	500	400	0	100
Hock meat	100	30	0	70

Total manufacturing costs of these products were $25,000 (comprising $15,000 for direct materials and $10,000 for conversion costs).

Two byproduct accounting methods will be presented. Method A (the production byproduct method) recognizes byproducts in the financial statements at the time their production is completed. Method B (the sale byproduct method) delays recognition of byproducts until the time of their sale. Recognition of byproducts at the time of production is conceptually correct. Where recognition at the time of sales occurs in practice, it is usually rationalized on the grounds that the dollar amounts of byproducts are immaterial. Exhibit 15-12 presents the income statement of the Meatworks Group under both methods.

EXHIBIT 15-11
Meatworks Group: Example 4 Overview

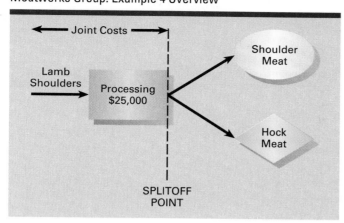

Method A: Byproducts Recognized at Time Production is Completed

This method recognizes the byproduct in the financial statements–the 100 packs of hock meat–in the month it is produced (July 2000). The estimated net realizable value from the byproduct is offset against the costs of the main (or joint) products. The following journal entries illustrate this method:

1. Work in Progress   15,000
       Accounts Payable   15,000
    To record direct materials purchased and used in production during July.

2. Work in Progress   10,000
       Various accounts   10,000
    To record conversion costs in the joint process during July; examples include energy, manufacturing supplies, all manufacturing labour, and plant amortization.

3. Byproduct Inventory   400
    Finished goods: Shoulder Meat ($25,000 – $400)   24,600
       Work in Process ($15,000 + $10,000)   25,000
    To record cost of goods completed during July.

4a. Cost of Goods Sold (400/500 × $24,600)   19,680
       Finished Goods: Shoulder Meat   19,680
    To record the cost of the main product sold during July.

4b. Cash or Accounts Receivable (400 × $60)   24,000
       Revenues: Shoulder Meat   24,000
    To record the sale of the main product during July.

5. Cash or Accounts Receivable (30 × $4)   120
       Byproduct Inventory: Hock Meat   120
    To record the sale of the byproduct during July.

This method reports the byproduct inventories of hock meat on the balance sheet at their $4 per pack selling price.

One variant of this method would be to report byproduct inventory at its estimated net realizable value reduced by a normal profit margin. When the byproduct inventory is sold in a subsequent period, the income statement would match the selling price with the "net" selling price reported for the byproduct inventory.

Method B: Byproducts Recognized at Time of Sale

This method makes no journal entries until sale of the byproduct occurs. Revenues of the byproduct are reported as a revenue item in the income statement at the time

EXHIBIT 15-12

Income Statement of Meatworks Group for July 2000

When byproducts recognized in financial statements	Byproduct Accounting Method	
	Method A	**Method B**
	At Production	**At Sale**
Revenues		
Main product: shoulder meat (400 × $60)	$24,000	$24,000
Byproduct: hock meat (30 × $4)	–	120
Total revenues	24,000	24,120
Cost of goods sold		
Total manufacturing costs	25,000	25,000
Deduct byproduct revenue (100 × $4)	400	–
Net manufacturing costs	24,600	25,000
Deduct main product inventory*	4,920	5,000
Cost of goods sold	19,680	20,000
Gross margin	$ 4,320	$ 4,120
Gross-margin percentage	18.00%	17.08%
Inventoriable costs (end of period);		
Main product: Should meat	$4,920	$5,000
Byproduct: Hock meat (70 × $4)[†]	280	0

*(100 ÷ 500) × net manufacturing costs = (100 ÷ 500) × $24,600 = $4,920
[†]Recorded at selling prices

of sale. In the Meatworks Group example, byproduct revenues in July 2000 would be $120 (30 × $4) because only 30 packs of the hock meat are sold in July. The journal entries would be:

1. and 2.	Same as for Method A.		
3.	Finished Goods: Shoulder Meat	25,000	
	Work in Process		25,000
	To record cost of goods completed during July.		
4a.	Cost of Goods Sold (400/500 × $25,000)	20,000	
	Finished Goods: Shoulder Meat		20,000
	To record the cost of the main product sold during July.		
4b.	Same as for Method A.		
5.	Cash or Accounts Receivable	120	
	Revenues: Hock Meat		120
	To record the sale of the byproduct during July.		

Method B is rationalized in practice primarily on grounds that the dollar amounts of byproducts are immaterial. However, this method permits managers to "manage" reported earnings by timing when they sell byproducts. Managers may stockpile byproducts so that they have the flexibility to give revenues a "boost" at opportune times.

Joint Cost Allocation In The Oil Patch

The petroleum industry is one of the largest industries in the world. It also provides a classic example of an industry with joint costs. Petroleum mining and processing starts with hydrocarbons being extracted from either onshore or offshore fields. Oil refineries process (disassemble) hydrocarbons into multiple products such as crude oil, gas, and raw LPG (liquefied petroleum gas). The LPG is often further processed into butane, ethane and propane. How should the joint refining costs be allocated to the separate marketable products produced at the refinery? These costs include the costs of hydrocarbons put into the refinery and the processing costs at the refinery.

One survey focused on the joint cost allocation method chosen by refiners for external reporting purposes:

Market-based measures	
• Net realizable value	46%
• Other	20
Physical-based measures	
• Volume (barrels, gallons or cubic feet)	27
• Mass (weight or molecular mass)	2
Other	5
	100%

Market-based measures are the preferred joint cost allocation, with the net realizable value method the predominant choice. The most common other market-based measure reported in the survey was a variation of the net realizable value method in which the final sales value of each product is used as the allocation base without any deduction for the expected separable costs of production and marketing. This variation illustrates how companies may make their own adjustment to the basic methods described in this chapter, often on the grounds of a perceived cost-benefit basis.

Source: Adapted from Koester, R. J., and D. J. Barnett, "Petroleum Refinery Joint Cost Allocation" (Working Paper, California State University, Dominguez Hills, 1996)

PROBLEM

Inorganic Chemicals purchases salt and processes it into more refined products such as caustic soda, chlorine, and PVC (polyvinyl chloride). In the most recent month (July), Inorganic Chemicals purchased salt for $40,000. Conversion costs of $60,000 were incurred up to the splitoff point, at which time two salable products were produced: caustic soda and chlorine. Chlorine can be further processed into PVC. The July production and sales information are as follows:

	Production	Sales	Sales Price per Tonne
Caustic soda	1,200 tonnes	1,200 tonnes	$ 50
Chlorine	800 tonnes		
PVC	500 tonnes	500 tonnes	$200

All 800 tonnes of chlorine were further processed, at an incremental cost of $20,000, to yield 500 tonnes of PVC. There were no byproducts or scrap from this further processing of chlorine. There were no beginning or ending inventories of caustic soda, chlorine, or PVC in July.

There is an active market for chlorine. Inorganic Chemicals could have sold all its July production of chlorine at $75 a tonne.

1. Calculate how the joint costs of $100,000 would be allocated between caustic soda and chlorine under each of the following methods: (a) sales value at splitoff, (b) physical measure (tonnes), and (c) estimated net realizable value.
2. What is the gross margin percentage of (a) caustic soda and (b) PVC under the three methods cited in requirement 1?
3. Lifetime Swimming Pool Products offers to purchase 800 tonnes of chlorine in August at $75 a tonne. This sale would mean that no PVC would be produced in August. How would accepting this offer affect August operating income?

SOLUTION

1. a. Sales value at splitoff method:

	Caustic Soda	Chlorine	Total
1. Sales value at splitoff (caustic, 1,200 × $50; chlorine, 800 × $75)	$60,000	$60,000	$120,000
2. Weighting ($60,000 ÷ $120,000; $60,000 ÷ $120,000)	0.5	0.5	
3. Joint costs allocated (caustic, 0.5 × $100,000; chlorine, 0.5 × $100,000)	$50,000	$50,000	$100,000

b. Physical measure method:

	Caustic Soda	Chlorine	Total
1. Physical measure (tonnes)	1,200	800	2,000
2. Weighting (1,200 ÷ 2,000; 800 ÷ 2,000)	0.6	0.4	
3. Joint costs allocated (caustic, 0.6 × $100,000; chlorine, 0.4 × $100,000)	$60,000	$40,000	$100,000

c. Estimated NRV method:

	Caustic Soda	Chlorine	Total
1. Expected final sales value of production (caustic, 1,200 × $50; PVC from chlorine, 500 × $200)	$60,000	$100,000	$160,000
2. Expected separable costs		20,000	20,000
3. Estimated NRV at splitoff point	$60,000	$ 80,000	$140,000
4. Weighting ($60,000 ÷ $140,000; $80,000 ÷ $140,000)	$\frac{3}{7}$	$\frac{4}{7}$	
5. Joint costs allocated (caustic, $\frac{3}{7}$ × $100,000; chlorine, $\frac{4}{7}$ × $100,000)	$42,857	$ 57,143	$100,000

2. a. Caustic soda:

	Sales Value at Splitoff Point	Physical Measure	Estimated Net Realizable Value
Sales	$60,000	$60,000	$60,000
Joint costs	50,000	60,000	42,857
Gross margin	$10,000	$ 0	$17,143
Gross margin percentage	16.67%	0%	28.57%

b. PVC:

	Sales Value at Splitoff Point	Physical Measure	Estimated Net Realizable Value
Sales	$100,000	$100,000	$100,000
Joint costs	50,000	40,000	57,143
Separable costs	20,000	20,000	20,000
Gross margin	$ 30,000	$ 40,000	$ 22,857
Gross margin percentage	30.00%	40.00%	22.86%

3. Incremental revenue from further processing of chlorine into PVC:

$(500 \times \$200) - (800 \times \$75)$	$40,000
Incremental costs of further processing chlorine into PVC	20,000
Incremental operating income from further processing	$20,000

The operating income of Inorganic Chemicals would be reduced by $20,000 if it sold 800 tonnes of chlorine to Lifetime Swimming Pool Products instead of further processing the chlorine into PVC for sale.

The following points are linked to the chapter's learning objectives.

1. A joint cost is the cost of a single process that yields multiple products. The *splitoff point* is the juncture in the process when the products become separately identifiable.

2. Joint products have relatively high sales value and are not separately identifiable as individual products until the splitoff point. A byproduct has a low sales value compared with the sales value of a joint product. Individual products can change from being a byproduct or a joint product when their market prices move sizably in one direction.

3. The purposes for allocating joint costs to products include inventory costing for external financial reporting, internal financial reporting, cost reimbursement under contracts, customer profitability analysis, insurance settlements, and rate regulation.

4. The accounting methods available for allocating joint costs include using market selling price (either sales value at splitoff or estimated net realizable value) or using a physical measure. Choosing not to allocate is also an option.

5. The benefits-received criterion leads to a preference for revenue or market-based methods such as the sales value at splitoff point method. Additional pros of this method include not anticipating subsequent management decisions on further processing, using a meaningful common denominator, and being simple.

6. The incremental cost analysis emphasized elsewhere in this book applies equally to joint cost situations. No techniques for allocating joint product costs should guide decisions about whether a product should be sold at the splitoff point or processed beyond splitoff, because joint costs are irrelevant.

7. Byproduct accounting is an area where there is much inconsistency in practice and where some methods used are justified on the basis of expediency rather than theoretical soundness. Byproducts can be recognized at production or at the point of sale. Byproduct revenues can appear as a separate revenue item or an offset to other costs.

This chapter contains definitions of the following important terms:

byproduct (p. 524)
constant gross margin percentage
   NRV method (p. 531)
estimated net realizable value (NRV)
   method (p. 530)
joint cost (p. 524)
joint products (p. 524)
main product (p. 524)

physical measure method (p. 528)
product (p. 524)
sales value at splitoff method (p. 527)
scrap (p. 524)
separable costs (p. 524)
splitoff point (p. 524)

ASSIGNMENT MATERIAL

QUESTIONS

15-1 Give two examples of industries in which joint costs are found. For each example, what are the individual products at or beyond the splitoff point?

15-2 What is a joint cost?

15-3 Distinguish between a joint product and a byproduct.

15-4 Why might the number of products in a joint cost setting differ from the number of outputs? Give an example.

15-5 Provide three reasons for allocating joint costs to individual products or services.

15-6 Why does the sales value at splitoff method use the sales value of the total production in the accounting period and not just the sales value of the products sold?

15-7 Describe a situation where the sales value at splitoff method cannot be used but the estimated NRV method can be used for joint cost allocation.

15-8 Distinguish between the sales value at splitoff method and the estimated NRV method.

15-9 Give two limitations of the physical measure method of joint cost allocation.

15-10 How might a company simplify its use of the estimated NRV method when the final selling prices can vary sizably in an accounting period and management makes frequent changes to the point at which it sells individual products?

15-11 Why is the constant gross-margin percentage NRV method sometimes called a "joint cost and a profit allocation" method?

15-12 "Managers must decide whether a product should be sold at splitoff or processed further. The sales value at splitoff method of joint cost allocation is the best method for generating the information managers need." Do you agree? Why?

15-13 "Managers should consider only additional revenues and separable costs when making decisions about selling now or processing further." Do you agree? Why?

15-14 Describe two major methods to account for byproducts.

15-15 Why might managers with a monthly bonus payment based on attaining a target operating income prefer a byproduct accounting method that recognizes byproducts at the time of sale rather than production?

EXERCISES

15-16 Joint cost allocation, insurance settlement. Chicken Little grows and processes chickens. Each chicken is disassembled into five main parts. Information pertaining to production in July 2000 is as follows:

Parts	Kilograms of Product	Wholesale Selling Price per Kilogram at End of Production Line
Breasts	100	$1.10
Wings	20	0.40
Thighs	40	0.70
Bones	80	0.20
Feathers	10	0.10

Joint costs of production in July 2000 were $100.

A special shipment of 20 kilograms of breasts and 10 kilograms of wings has been destroyed in a fire. Chicken Little's insurance policy provides for reimbursement for the cost of the items destroyed. The insurance company permits Chicken Little to use a joint cost allocation method. The splitoff point is assumed to be at the end of the production line.

REQUIRED

1. Compute the cost of the special shipment destroyed using (a) the sales value at splitoff point method and (b) the physical measure method using pounds of finished product.
2. Which joint cost allocation method would you recommend that Chicken Little use?

15-17 Joint products and byproducts (continuation of 15-16). Chicken Little is computing the ending inventory values for its July 31, 2000 balance sheet. Ending inventory amounts on July 31 are 10 kilograms of breasts, 4 kilograms of wings, 3 kilograms of thighs, 5 kilograms of bones, and 2 kilograms of feathers.

Chicken Little's management wants to use the sales value at splitoff point method. However, they want you to explore the effect of ending inventory values of classifying one or more products as a byproduct rather than a joint or main product.

REQUIRED

1. Assume Chicken Little classifies all five products as joint products. What are the ending inventory values of each product on July 31, 2000?
2. Assume Chicken Little uses a byproduct method that recognizes byproducts in the financial statements at the time production is completed. The total revenues to be received from the sale of byproducts produced that period is offset against the joint cost of production of the joint products. What are the ending inventory values for each joint and byproduct on July 31, 2000 assuming breasts and thighs are the joint products and wings, bones, and feathers are byproducts.
3. Repeat requirement 2 using the byproduct method that recognizes byproducts in financial statements (as a revenue item) at the time of their sale.
4. Comment on differences in the results in requirements 1, 2, and 3.

15-18 Estimated net realizable value method. Illawara, Inc. produces two joint products, cooking oil and soap oil, from a single vegetable oil refining process. In July 2000, the joint costs of this process were $24,000,000. Separable processing costs beyond the splitoff point were cooking oil, $30,000,000; and soap oil, $7,500,000. Cooking oil sells for $50 per drum. Soap oil sells for $25 per drum. Illawara produced and sold 1,000,000 drums of cooking oil and 500,000 drums of soap oil. There are no beginning or ending inventories of cooking oil or soap oil.

REQUIRED

Allocate the $24,000,000 joint costs using the estimated NRV method.

15-19 Joint cost allocation, process further. The Sinclair Refining Company (SRC) is a 100%-owned subsidiary of Sinclair Oil & Gas. SRC operates a refinery that processes hydrocarbons sold to it by the Sinclair Production Company, another 100%-owned subsidiary of Sinclair Oil & Gas. SRC's refinery has three outputs from its processing of hydrocarbons—crude oil, natural gas liquids, and gas. The first two outputs are liquids, while gas is a vapour. However, gas can be expressed as a liquid equivalent using a standard industry conversion factor. For costing purposes, SRC assumes all three outputs are jointly produced until a single splitoff point where each output separately appears and is then further processed individually.

For August, 2000, the following data (in millions) apply:

- **Crude oil.** 150 barrels produced and sold at $18 per barrel. Separable costs beyond the splitoff point are $175.
- **Natural gas liquids.** 50 barrels produced and sold at $15 per barrel. Separable costs beyond the splitoff point are $105.
- **Gas.** 800 equivalent barrels produced and sold at $1.30 per equivalent barrel. Separable costs beyond the splitoff point are $210.

SRC paid the Sinclair Production Company $1,400 for hydrocarbons delivered to it from its offshore platform in August 2000. The cost of operating the refinery in August up to the splitoff point was $400, including $100 of gas charges from Deadhorse Utilities, an independent utility company. Deadhorse signed a long-term contract with SRC several years ago when gas prices were much lower than in 2000.

A new federal law has recently been passed that taxes crude oil at 30% of operating income. No new tax is to be paid on natural gas liquid or natural gas. Starting in August 2000, SRC must report a separate product line income statement for crude oil. One challenge facing SRC is how to allocate the joint cost of producing the three separate salable outputs. Assume no beginning or ending inventory.

REQUIRED
1. Draw an exhibit showing the joint cost situation for SRC.
2. Allocate the August 2000 joint cost among the three salable products using (a) the physical measures method and (b) the estimated NRV method. Compute the operating income for each product using each of these methods.
3. Discuss the pros and cons of each method for Sinclair product emphasis decisions.

15-20 Joint cost allocation, physical measures method (continuation of 15-19). Assume that SRC is not able to sell its gas output. The refinery is located in a remote area and a terrorist group has just destroyed major sections of the gas pipeline used to transport the gas to market. The pipeline that carries the crude oil and natural gas liquid is still operational. The Sinclair Production Company must now reinject the gas into the offshore field. The costs of the hydrocarbons to SRC will not be reduced, but Sinclair Production (not SRC) will bear the cost of gas reinjection. No separable costs of gas production beyond the splitoff point will now be incurred.

REQUIRED
1. Assume that the same data for all three outputs for August 2000 apply to the new set of facts. Show the operating income for each salable product using the estimated NRV method of joint cost allocation.
2. Assume the taxation authorities argue that, for crude oil income tax determination, the physical measures method should be used to allocate joint costs and that all outputs (including gas, whether sold or reinjected) should be used in deciding the cost allocation weights. Do you agree with this argument? Explain your position.

15-21 Alternative methods of joint cost allocation, ending inventories. The Darl Company operates a simple chemical process to reduce a single material into three separate items, here referred to as X, Y, and Z. All three end products are separated simultaneously at a single splitoff point.

Products X and Y are ready for sale immediately upon splitoff without further processing or any other additional costs. Product Z, however, is processed further before being sold. There is no available market price for Z at the splitoff point.

The selling prices quoted below have not changed for three years, and no changes are foreseen for the coming year. During 2000, the selling prices of the items and the total amounts sold were as follows:

- **X.** 120 tonnes sold for $1,500 per tonne
- **Y.** 340 tonnes sold for $1,000 per tonne
- **Z.** 475 tonnes sold for $700 per tonne

The total joint manufacturing costs for the year were $400,000. An additional $200,000 was spent in order to finish product Z.

There were no beginning inventories of X, Y, or Z. At the end of the year, the following inventories of completed units were on hand: X, 180 tonnes; Y, 60 tonnes; Z, 25 tonnes. There was no beginning or ending work in process.

REQUIRED
1. What will be the cost of inventories of X, Y, and Z for balance sheet purposes and what will be the cost of goods sold for income statement purposes as of December 31, 2000, using (a) the estimated NRV method of joint cost allocation and (b) the constant gross margin percentage NRV method of joint cost allocation?
2. Compare the gross margin percentages for X, Y, and Z using the two methods given in requirement 1.

15-22 Net realizable value cost allocation method, further process decision. (W. Crum) The Tuscania Company crushes and refines mineral ore into three products in a joint cost operation. Costs and production for 2000 were as follows:

- **Department 1,** at initial joint costs of $420,000, produces 20,000 kilograms of Alco, 60,000 kilograms of Devo, 100,000 kilograms of Holo.
- **Department 2** processes Alco further at a cost of $100,000.
- **Department 3** processes Devo further at a cost of $200,000.

Results for 2000 are:
- **Alco.** 20,000 kilograms completed; 19,000 kilograms sold for $20 per kilogram; ending inventory, 1,000 kilograms.

- ◆ **Devo.** 60,000 kilograms completed; 59,000 kilograms sold for $6 per kilogram; ending inventory, 1,000 kilograms.
- ◆ **Holo.** 100,000 kilograms completed; 99,000 kilograms sold for $1 per kilogram; ending inventory, 1,000 kilograms; Holo required no further processing.

REQUIRED

1. Use the estimated NRV method to allocate the joint costs of the three products. Compute the total costs and unit costs of ending inventories.
2. Compute the individual gross margin percentages of the three products.
3. Suppose Tuscania receives an offer to sell all of its Devo product for a price of $2 per kilogram at the splitoff point before going through Department 3, just as it comes off the production line in Department 1. Using last year's figures, would Tuscania be better off by selling Devo that way or processing it through Department 3 and selling it? Show computations to support your answer. Disregard all other factors not mentioned in the problem.

15-23 Process further or sell, joint-cost allocation. (R. Capettini) Henley Company produces three joint products, A, B and C, from a single joint process with a fixed cost of $5,000 and a variable cost of $2.00 per input unit. Each of the products can be either processed further or, at the split-off point, it (1) can be sold or (2) must be disposed of at a cost. Out of each input unit, Henley Company produces 1 unit of A, 3 units of B, and 2 units of C. Selling and administrative costs are $14,000.

REQUIRED

1. Given the table below, for each product, should Henley Company process the product further or dispose of it (or sell it) at the splitoff point if Henley Company inputs 5,000 units? Show, for each product, how much better off Henley would be if it followed your advice versus making the alternative decision. Assume that if Henley does not further process a product, it does not incur any of the further processing costs.

Product	Selling Price Per Unit at Splitoff Point	Cost Per Unit To Dispose of Product at Splitoff Point	Further Processing Costs		Selling Price Per Unit After Further Processing
			Fixed	Variable Per Unit	
A	–	$0.20	$ 6,000	$0.90	$1.50
B	$0.50	–	1,000	1.00	1.50
C	–	0.90	10,000	1.10	5.40

2. What is Henley Company's gross margin at the 5,000 unit input level?

15-24 Process further or sell, byproduct. (CMA adapted) Newcastle Mining Company (NMC) produces and sells bulk raw coal to other coal companies and exporters. NMC mines and stockpiles the coal; it is then passed through a one-step crushing process before being loaded onto river barges for shipment to customers. The annual output of ten million tonnes, which is expected to remain stable, has an average cost of $20 per tonne with an average selling price of $27 per tonne.

Management is currently evaluating the possibility of further processing the coal by sizing and cleaning in order to expand markets and enhance product revenues. Management has rejected the possibility of constructing a large sizing and cleaning plant because it would require a significant long-term capital investment.

Bill Rolland, controller of NMC, has asked Amy Kimbell, mining engineer, to develop cost and revenue projections for further processing the coal through a variety of contractual arrangements. After extensive discussions with vendors and contractors, Kimbell has prepared the following projections of incremental costs of sizing and cleaning NMC's annual output.

Newcastle Mining Company
Sizing and Cleaning Processes

	Incremental Costs
Direct labour	$600,000 per year
Supervisory personnel	100,000 per year
Heavy equipment rental, operating, and maintenance costs	25,000 per month
Contract sizing and cleaning	3.50 per tonne
Outbound rail freight (per 60-tonne rail car)	240 per car

In addition to the preceding cost information, market samples obtained by Kimbell have shown that electrical utilities enter into contracts for sized and cleaned coal similar to that mined by Newcastle at an expected average price of $36 per tonne.

Kimbell has learned that 5% of the raw bulk output that enters the sizing and cleaning process will be lost as a primary product. Normally, 75% of this product loss can be salvaged as coal fines. These are small pieces ranging from dust-like particles up to pieces five centimetres in diameter. Coal fines are too small for use by electrical utilities but are frequently sold to steel manufacturers for use in blast furnaces.

Unfortunately, the price for coal fines frequently fluctuates between $14 and $24 per tonne (F.O.B. shipping point), and the timing of market volume is erratic. While companies generally sell all their coal fines during a year, it is not unusual to stockpile this product for several months before making any significant sales.

REQUIRED

1. Prepare an analysis to show whether it would be more profitable for Newcastle Mining Company to continue to sell the raw bulk coal or to process it further through sizing and cleaning. (Note: Ignore any value related to the coal fines in your analysis.)

2. **a.** Taking into consideration any potential value to the coal fines, prepare an analysis to show if the coal fines would affect the results of your analysis prepared in requirement 1.

   b. What other factors should be considered in evaluating a sell-or-process-further decision?

15-25 Accounting for a main product and a byproduct. (Cheatham and Green, adapted) Bill Dundee is the owner and operator of Western Bottling, a bulk soft drink producer. A single production process yields two bulk soft drinks, Rainbow Dew (the main product) and Resi-Dew (the byproduct). Both products are fully processed at the splitoff point, and there are no separable costs.

Summary data for September 2000 are as follows:
◆ Cost of soft drink operations = $120,000
◆ Production and sales data:

	Production (in litres)	Sales (in litres)	Selling Price per Litre
Main product (Rainbow Dew)	10,000	8,000	$20
Byproduct (Resi-Dew)	2,000	1,400	2

There were no beginning inventories on September 1, 2000. The following is an overview of operations:

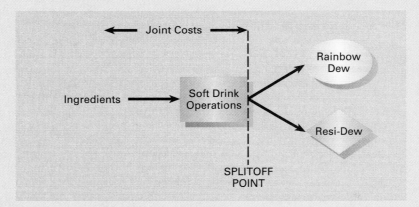

REQUIRED

1. What is the gross margin for Western Bottling under methods A, B, C, and D of byproduct accounting?

2. What are the inventory amounts reported in the balance sheet on September 30, 2000, for Rainbow Dew and Resi-Dew under each of the four methods of byproduct accounting cited in requirement 1?

3. Which method would you recommend Western Bottling use? Explain.

15-26 Joint costs and byproducts. (W. Crum) The Caldwell Company processes an ore in Department 1, out of which come three products, L, W, and X. Product L is processed further through Department 2. Product W is sold without further processing. Product X is considered a byproduct and is processed further through Department 3. Costs in Department 1 are $800,000 in total; Department 2 costs are $100,000; and Department 3 costs are $50,000. Processing 600,000 kilograms in Department 1 results in 50,000 kilograms of product L, 300,000 kilograms of product W, and 100,000 kilograms of product X.

Product L sells for $10 per kilogram, Product W sells for $2 per kilogram, and Product X sells for $3 per kilogram. The company wants to make a gross margin of 10% of sales on product X and also allow 25% for marketing costs on product X.

REQUIRED

1. Compute unit costs per kilogram for products L, W, and X, treating X as a byproduct. Use the estimated NRV method for allocating joint costs. Deduct the estimated NRV of the byproduct produced from the joint cost of products L and W.
2. Compute unit costs per kilogram for products L, W, and X, treating all three as joint products and allocating costs by the estimated NRV method.

PROBLEMS

15-27 Alternative methods of joint-cost allocation, product-mix decision. Pacific Lumber processes lumber products for sale to lumber wholesalers. Its most popular line is oak products. Oak tree growers sell Pacific Lumber whole trees. These trees are jointly processed up to the splitoff point at which raw select oak, raw white oak, and raw knotty oak become separable products. Each of these raw products is then separately further processed by Pacific Lumber into finished products (select oak, white oak, and knotty oak) that are sold to lumber wholesalers. Data for August 2000 are:

a. Joint processing costs (including cost of oak trees) $300,000
b. Separable product at splitoff point
   ◆ Raw select oak   30,000 board feet
   ◆ Raw white oak   50,000 board feet
   ◆ Raw knotty oak   20,000 board feet
c. Final product produced and sold
   ◆ Select oak   25,000 board feet at $16 per board foot
   ◆ White oak   40,000 board feet at $9 per board foot
   ◆ Knotty oak 15,000 board feet at $7 per board foot
d. Separable processing costs
   ◆ For select oak $60,000
   ◆ For white oak $90,000
   ◆ For knotty oak $15,000

There is an active market for raw oak products. Selling prices available in August 2000 were raw select oak ($8 per board foot), raw white oak ($4 per board foot), and raw knotty oak ($3 per board foot).

There were no beginning or ending inventories for August 2000.

REQUIRED

1. Allocate the joint costs to the three products using:
   a. sales value at splitoff method
   b. physical measures method
   c. estimated net realizable value method.
2. Assume that not all final product produced in August 2000 was sold. Ending inventory for August 2000 was select oak (1,000 board feet), white oak (2,000 board feet), and knotty oak (500 board feet). What would be the ending inventory values in the August 30 balance sheet under each product for each of the three methods in requirement 1?
3. Is Pacific Lumber maximizing its total August 2000 operating income by fully processing each raw oak product into its finished product form? Show computations.

15-28 Alternative methods of joint cost allocation, product mix decisions. The Sunshine Oil Company buys crude vegetable oil. Refining this oil results in four products at the splitoff point: A, B, C, and D. Product C is fully processed at the splitoff point. Products A, B, and D can be individually further refined into Super A, Super B, and Super D. In the most recent month (December), the output at the splitoff point was:

Product A	300,000 litres
Product B	100,000 litres
Product C	50,000 litres
Product D	50,000 litres

The joint cost of purchasing the crude vegetable oil and processing it was $100,000.

Sunshine had no beginning or ending inventories. Sales of product C in December were $50,000. Total output of products A, B, and D was further refined and then sold. Data related to December are as follows:

	Separable Processing Costs to Make Super Products	Sales
Super A	$200,000	$300,000
Super B	80,000	100,000
Super D	90,000	120,000

Sunshine had the option of selling products A, B, and D at the splitoff point. This alternative would have yielded the following sales for the December production:

Product A	$50,000
Product B	30,000
Product D	70,000

REQUIRED

1. What is the gross margin percentage for each product sold in December, using the following methods for allocating the $100,000 joint costs: (a) sales value at splitoff, (b) physical measure, and (c) estimated NRV?
2. Could Sunshine have increased its December operating income by making different decisions about the further refining of products A, B, or D? Show the effect on operating income of any changes you recommend.

15-29 **Comparison of alternative joint cost allocation methods, further process decision, chocolate products.** Roundtree Chocolates manufactures and distributes chocolate products. It purchases cocoa beans and processes them into two intermediate products:
◆ Chocolate powder liquor base
◆ Milk chocolate liquor base

These two intermediary products become separately identifiable at a single splitoff point. Every 500 kilograms of cocoa beans yields 20 four-litre containers of chocolate powder liquor base and 30 four-litre containers of milk chocolate liquor base.

The chocolate powder liquor base is further processed into chocolate powder. Every 20 containers of chocolate powder liquor base yields 200 kilograms of chocolate powder. The milk chocolate liquor base is further processed into milk chocolate. Every 30 containers of milk chocolate liquor base yields 340 kilograms of milk chocolate.

The following is an overview of the manufacturing operations at Roundtree Chocolates:

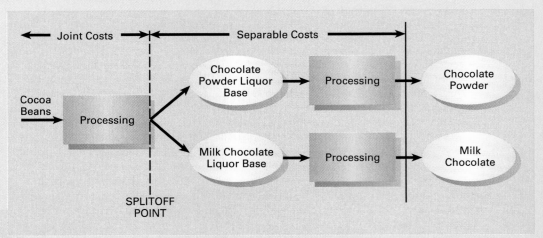

Production and sales data for August 2000 are as follows:
- Cocoa beans processed, 5,000 kilograms
- Costs of processing cocoa beans to splitoff point (including purchase of beans) = $10,000

	Production	Sales	Unit Selling Price
Chocolate powder	2,000 kilograms	2,000 kilograms	$4 per kilogram
Milk chocolate	3,400 kilograms	3,400 kilograms	$5 per kilogram

The August 2000 separable costs of processing chocolate powder liquor base into chocolate powder are $4,250. The August 2000 separable costs of processing milk chocolate liquor base into milk chocolate are $8,750.

Roundtree fully processes both of its intermediate products into chocolate powder or milk chocolate. There is an active market for these intermediate products. In August 2000, Roundtree could have sold chocolate powder liquor base for $21 a container and milk chocolate liquor base for $26 a container.

REQUIRED

1. Calculate how the joint costs of $10,000 would be allocated between chocolate powder liquor base and milk chocolate liquor base under each of the following methods: (a) sales value at splitoff, (b) physical measure (containers), (c) estimated NRV, and (d) constant gross margin percentage NRV.
2. What is the gross margin percentage of chocolate powder liquor base and milk chocolate liquor base under methods (a), (b), (c), and (d) in requirement 1?
3. Could Roundtree Chocolates have increased its operating income by a change in its decision to fully process both of its intermediate products?

15-30 **Joint-cost allocation, process further or sell.** (CMA adapted) Sonimad Sawmill Inc. (SSI) purchases logs from independent timber contractors and processes the logs into three types of lumber products.

1. Studs for residential building (e.g., walls, ceilings).
2. Decorative pieces (e.g., fireplace mantels, beams for cathedral ceilings).
3. Posts used as support braces (e.g., mine support braces, braces for exterior fences around ranch properties).

These products are the result of a joint sawmill process that involves removal of bark from the logs, cutting the logs into a workable size (ranging from 8 to 16 feet in length), and then cutting the individual products from the logs, depending upon the type of wood (pine, oak, walnut, or maple) and the size (diameter) of the log.

The joint process results in the following costs and output of products for a typical month.

Joint production costs	
Direct materials (rough timber logs)	$ 500,000
Debarking (labour and overhead)	50,000
Sizing (labour and overhead)	200,000
Product cutting (labour and overhead)	250,000
Total joint costs	$1,000,000

Product yield and average sales value on a per unit basis from the joint process are as follows:

Product	Monthly Output of Materials at Splitoff Point	Fully Processed Selling Price
Studs	75,000 units	$ 8
Decorative pieces	5,000 units	100
Posts	20,000 units	20

The studs are sold as rough-cut lumber after emerging from the sawmill operation without further processing by SSI. Also, the posts require no further processing beyond the splitoff point. The decorative pieces must be planed and further sized after emerging from the sawmill. This additional processing costs $100,000 per month and normally results in a loss of 10% of the units entering the process. Without this planing and sizing process, there is still an active intermediate market for the unfinished decorative pieces where the selling price averages $60 per unit.

REQUIRED

1. Based on the information given for Sonimad Sawmill Inc., allocate the joint processing costs of $1,000,000 to each of the three product lines using the
   a. sales value at splitoff method.
   b. physical measures method using volume in units.
   c. estimated net realizable value method.

2. Prepare an analysis for Sonimad Sawmill Inc. to compare processing the decorative pieces further as they presently do, with selling them as a rough-cut product immediately at split-off.

3. Assume Sonimad Sawmill Inc. announced that in six months it will sell the rough-cut product at splitoff due to increasing competitive pressure. Identify at least three types of likely behaviour that will be demonstrated by the skilled labour the planing and sizing process as a result of this announcement. Include in your discussion how this behaviour could be improved by management.

15-31 Joint and byproducts, estimated net realizable value method. (CPA) The Harrison Corporation produces three products—Alpha, Beta, and Gamma. Alpha and Gamma are joint products, and Beta is a byproduct of Alpha. No joint costs are to be allocated to the byproduct. The production processes for a given year are as follows:

a. In Department 1, 110,000 kilograms of direct material, Rho, are processed at a total cost of $120,000. After processing in Department 1, 60% of the units are transferred to Department 2, and 40% of the units (now Gamma) are transferred to Department 3.

b. In Department 2, the material is further processed at a total additional cost of $38,000. Seventy percent of the units (now Alpha) are transferred to Department 4, and 30% emerge as Beta, the byproduct, to be sold at $1.20 per kilogram. Separable marketing costs for Beta are $8,100.

c. In Department 4, Alpha is processed at a total additional cost of $23,660. After this processing, Alpha is ready for sale at $5 per kilogram.

d. In Department 3, Gamma is processed at a total additional cost of $165,000. In this department, a normal loss of units of Gamma occurs, which equals 10% of the good output of Gamma. The remaining good output of Gamma is then sold for $12 per kilogram.

REQUIRED

1. Prepare a schedule showing the allocation of the $120,000 joint costs between Alpha and Gamma using the estimated NRV method. The estimated NRV of Beta should be treated as an addition to the sales value of Alpha.

2. Independently of your answer to requirement 1, assume that $102,000 of total joint costs were appropriately allocated to Alpha. Assume also that there were 48,000 kilograms of Alpha and 20,000 kilograms of Beta available to sell. Prepare an income statement through gross margin for Alpha using the following facts:
   a. During the year, sales of Alpha were 80% of the kilograms available for sale. There was no beginning inventory.
   b. The estimated NRV of Beta available for sale is to be deducted from the cost of producing Alpha. The ending inventory of Alpha is to be based on the net costs of production.
   c. All other cost and selling price data are listed in (a) to (d).

15-32 Estimated net realizable value method, byproducts. (CMA, adapted) The Princess Corporation grows, processes, packages, and sells three joint apple products: (a) sliced apples that are used in frozen pies, (b) applesauce, and (c) apple juice. The outside skin of the apple, processed as animal feed, is treated as a byproduct. Princess uses the estimated NRV method to allocate costs of the joint process to its joint products. The byproduct is inventoried at its selling price when produced; the net realizable value of the byproduct is used to reduce the joint production costs before the splitoff point. Details of Princess production process are presented here:

◆ The apples are washed and the outside skin is removed in the Cutting Department. The apples are then cored and trimmed for slicing. The three joint products and the byproduct are recognizable after processing in the Cutting Department. Each product is then transferred to a separate department for final processing.

◆ The trimmed apples are forwarded to the Slicing Department, where they are sliced and frozen. Any juice generated during the slicing operation is frozen with the slices.

◆ The pieces of apple trimmed from the fruit are processed into applesauce in the Crushing Department. The juice generated during this operation is used in the applesauce.

◆ The core and any surplus apple pieces generated from the Cutting Department are pulverized into a liquid in the Juicing Department. There is a loss equal to 8% of the weight of the good output produced in this department.

◆ The outside skin is chopped into animal feed and packaged in the Feed Department. It can be kept in cold storage until needed.

A total of 270,000 kilograms of apples were entered into the Cutting Department during November. The following schedule shows the costs incurred in each department, the proportion by weight transferred to the four final processing departments, and the selling price of each end product.

Processing Data and Costs, November 2000

Department	Costs Incurred	Proportion of Product by Weight Transferred to Departments	Selling Price per Kilogram of Final Product
Cutting	$60,000		
Slicing	11,280	33%	$0.80
Crushing	8,550	30	0.55
Juicing	3,000	27	0.40
Feed	700	10	0.10
Total	$83,530	100%	$1.85

REQUIRED

1. The Princess Corporation uses the estimated NRV method to determine inventory cost of its joint products; byproducts are reported on the balance sheet at their selling price when produced. For the month of November 2000, calculate the following:

   a. The output for apple slices, applesauce, apple juice, and animal feed, in kilograms.

   b. The estimated NRV at the splitoff point for each of the three joint products.

   c. The amount of the cost of the Cutting Department assigned to each of the three joint products and the amount assigned to the byproduct in accordance with corporate policy.

   d. The gross margins in dollars for each of the three joint products.

2. Comment on the significance to management of the gross margin dollar information by joint product for planning and control purposes, as opposed to inventory costing purposes.

15-33 **Joint product/byproduct distinctions, ethics (continuation of 15-32).** The Princess Corporation classifies animal feed as a byproduct. The byproduct is inventoried at its selling price when produced; the net realizable value of the product is used to reduce the joint production costs before the splitoff point. Prior to 2000, Princess classified both apple juice and animal feed as byproducts. These byproducts were not recognized in the accounting system until sold. Revenues from their sale were treated as a revenue item at the time of sale.

The Princess Corporation uses a "management by objectives" basis to compensate its managers. Every six months, managers are given "stretch" operating-income-to-revenue ratio targets. They receive no bonus if the target is not met and a fixed amount if the target is met or exceeded.

REQUIRED

1. Assume that Princess managers aim to maximize their bonuses over time. What byproduct method (the pre-2000 method or the 2000 method) would the manager prefer?

2. How might a controller gain insight into whether the manager of the Apple Products division is "abusing" the accounting system in an effort to maximize his or her bonus?

3. Describe an accounting system for the Princess Corporation that would reduce "gaming" behaviour by managers with respect to accounting rules for byproducts.

COLLABORATIVE LEARNING PROBLEM

15-34 Joint cost allocation, process further or sell byproducts. (CMA) The Goodson Pharmaceutical Company manufactures three joint products from a joint process: Altox, Lorex, and Hycol. Data regarding these products for the fiscal year ended May 31, 2000 are as follows:

	Altox	Lorex	Hycol
Units produced	170,000	500,000	330,000
Selling price per unit at splitoff	$3.50	—	$2
Separable costs	—	$1,400,000	—
Final selling price per unit	—	$5	—

The joint production cost up to the splitoff point where Altox, Lorex, and Hycol become separable products is $1,800,000 (which includes the $17,500 disposal costs for Dorzine as described below).

The president of Goodson, Arlene Franklin, is reviewing an opportunity to change the way in which these three products are processed and sold. Proposed changes for each product are as follows:

♦ Altox is currently sold at the splitoff point to a manufacturer of vitamins. Altox can also be refined for use as a medication to treat high blood pressure; however, this additional processing would cause a loss of 20,000 units of Altox. The separable costs to further process Altox are estimated to be $250,000 annually. The final product would sell for $5.50 per unit.

♦ Lorex is currently processed further after the splitoff point and sold by Goodson as a cold remedy. The company has received an offer from another pharmaceutical company to purchase Lorex at the splitoff point for $2.25 per unit.

♦ Hycol is an oil produced from the joint process and is currently sold at the splitoff point to a cosmetics manufacturer. Goodson's research department has suggested that the company process this product further and sell it as an ointment to relieve muscle pain. The additional processing would cost $75,000 annually and would result in 25% more units of product. The final product would be sold for $1.80 per unit.

The joint process currently used by Goodson also produces 50,000 units of Dorzine, a hazardous chemical waste product. The company pays $0.35 per unit to dispose of the Dorzine properly. Dietriech Mills, Inc. is interested in using the Dorzine as a solvent; however, Goodson would have to refine the Dorzine at an annual cost of $43,000. Dietriech would purchase all the refined Dorzine produced by Goodson and is willing to pay $0.75 for each unit.

INSTRUCTIONS

Form groups of two or more students to complete the following requirements.

REQUIRED

1. Allocate the $1,800,000 joint production cost to Altox, Lorex, and Hycol using the estimated NRV method.
2. Identify which of the three joint products Goodson should sell at the splitoff point in the future and which of the three main products the company should process further in order to maximize profits. Support your decisions with appropriate calculations.
3. Assume that Goodson has decided to refine the waste product Dorzine for sale to Dietriech Mills, Inc., and will treat Dorzine as a byproduct of the joint process in the future.
   a. Evaluate whether Goodson made the correct decision regarding Dorzine. Support your answer with appropriate calculations.
   b. Explain whether the decision to treat Dorzine as a byproduct will affect the decisions reached in requirement 2.

REVENUES, SALES VARIANCES, AND CUSTOMER PROFITABILITY ANALYSIS

The revenues of most large carbonated soft drink companies—such as Cott, Coca-Cola, Pepsi-Cola, and Schweppes—come from many countries. Revenue analysis that highlights sales mix, sales quantity, market size, and market share is a key input to decisions regarding product and country emphasis.

LEARNING OBJECTIVES

After studying this chapter, you should be able to:

1. Give examples of the bundling of products that give rise to revenue allocation issues
2. Allocate the revenues of a bundled package to the individual products in that package
3. Provide additional information about the sales-volume variance by calculating the sales-mix and sales-quantity variances
4. Provide additional information about the sales-quantity variance by calculating the market-share and market-size variances
5. Explain what information is pivotal to the reliability of market-share and market-size variances
6. Discuss why revenues can differ across customers purchasing the same product
7. Prepare a customer-profitability report
8. Apply the concept of cost hierarchy to customer costing

In prior chapters we have highlighted how a detailed understanding of costs is essential when making decisions related to, say, products, services, customers, or departments. We have also highlighted the importance of costs in managing company operations. The other half of the profit equation—revenues—is equally important. Companies that prosper make revenue planning and revenue analysis top priorities for their managers.

This chapter covers three revenue-related topics. Part One on Revenue Allocation examines how challenging revenue allocation issues arise with the now commonly used practice of selling multiple products or services as a single bundle for a single price. Part Two on Sales Variances highlights how the tools outlined in Chapter 7 can be used to analyze the variances of companies with revenues from multiple products. The Appendix shows how the framework outlined in Part Two of this chapter helps analyze cost variances for a company with substitutable inputs. Part Three on Customer Profitability Analysis explores topics related to customer revenues and customer costs. Having a customer focus is a key theme underlying many planning and control decisions of managers. Part Three highlights several ways management accountants can help managers better focus on their customers.

◆ PART ONE: REVENUE ALLOCATION

REVENUES AND BUNDLED PRODUCTS

OBJECTIVE 1

Give examples of the bundling of products that give rise to revenue allocation issues

Revenue allocation. The assigning of revenues that are related, but not traceable to, individual products (services, customers, etc.) in an economically feasible (cost-effective) way. A revenue allocation base is used to make this assignment.

Bundled product. A package of two or more products or services, sold for a single price, whose individual components may be sold as separate items, each with their stand-alone prices.

"Intergovernmental Revenue Allocation Theory and Practice: Application to Nepal" by Roy Kelly
www.law.harvard.edu/
Programs/itp/1008abst.html

Revenues are inflows of assets (almost always cash or accounts receivable) received for products or services provided to customers. Just as costs can be allocated to specific products, customers, and the like, so can revenues. **Revenue allocation** occurs when revenues, related but not traceable to individual products (services, customers, and so on), are assigned to those individual products. Revenue tracing results in a more accurate assignment of revenues to products than does revenue allocation. Just as with cost data, more accurate information is believed to result in better decisions.

The Superhighway Group, a computer software company, will be used to illustrate the issues discussed. Superhighway develops, sells, and supports three software packages:

1. **WordMaster.** Current version is WordMaster 5.0, which was released 36 months ago. WordMaster was the company's initial product.

2. **SpreadMaster.** Current version is SpreadMaster 3.0, which was released 18 months ago.

3. **FinanceMaster.** Current version is FinanceMaster 2.0. This product, the company's most recent, has been its most successful. The 2.0 version was released 6 months ago.

Superhighway sells these three products individually and also sells them as bundled products. A **bundled product** is a package of two or more products or services, sold for a single price, where the individual components of the bundle may also be sold as separate items, each with their own stand-alone prices. The single price for the bundled product is typically less than the sum of the prices of two or more products if purchased separately. For example, banks often provide their customers with a bundle of services from different departments (chequing, security deposit, and investment advisory) for a single fee. A resort hotel may offer, for a single amount, a weekend package that includes services from its lodging (the room), food (the restaurant), and recreational (golfing) divisions. Where individual department or division managers have revenue or profit responsibilities, the issue thus becomes how to allocate the single bundled revenue amount among the individual products in that bundle.

Superhighway encounters revenue allocation decisions with its bundled product sales (termed "suite sales"). Here, two or more of the software products are sold as a single package. Managers at Superhighway are keenly interested in individual-product profitability figures. There are separate managers for each product who are responsible for the operating income of that product. Moreover, its Software Department engineers are organized on a product-by-product basis and receive a percentage of product profitability as part of their bonus.

REVENUE ALLOCATION METHODS

How should Superhighway allocate suite revenues to individual products? Information pertaining to its three suite sales and the stand-alone prices of its individual products is as follows:

OBJECTIVE 2

Allocate the revenues of a bundled package to the individual products in that package

Suites	Stand-Alone Sales Price			Suite Sales Price
	WordMaster	**SpreadMaster**	**FinanceMaster**	
Word and Spread	$250	$300	—	$440
Word and Finance	$250	—	$450	$560
Word, Spread, and Finance	$250	$300	$450	$760

The unit manufacturing costs of each software product are WordMaster, $36; SpreadMaster, $40; and FinanceMaster, $50.

The two main classes of revenue allocation methods are the stand-alone method and the incremental method. We now discuss each in turn. Both methods have analogues for cost allocation as discussed in Chapter 14.

Stand-Alone Revenue Allocation Methods

The **stand-alone revenue allocation method** uses product-specific information pertaining to products in the bundle to determine the weights used to allocate the bundled revenues to those individual products. The term *stand-alone* refers to the product as a separate (non-suite) item. Consider the Word and Finance suite, which sells for $560. Four stand-alone sources of weights are as follows.

1. **Selling prices.** The individual selling prices are $250 for WordMaster and $450 for FinanceMaster. The weights for allocating the $560 between the two products are:

$$\text{Word:} \quad \frac{\$250}{\$250 + 450} \times \$560 = 0.36 \times \$560 = \$202$$

$$\text{Finance:} \quad \frac{\$450}{\$250 + 450} \times \$560 = 0.64 \times \$560 = \$358$$

2. **Unit costs.** This method uses costs of individual products to determine the weights to allocate revenues. Assume unit manufacturing costs are used to determine the weights to allocate the $560 and Word and Finance suite revenues.

$$\text{Word:} \quad \frac{\$36}{\$36 + \$50} \times \$560 = 0.42 \times \$560 = \$235$$

$$\text{Finance:} \quad \frac{\$50}{\$36 + \$50} \times \$560 = 0.58 \times \$560 = \$325$$

This method does not recognize differences across products in the willingness of customers to purchase individual products.

3. **Physical units.** This method gives each product unit in the suite the same weight when allocating suite revenue to individual products. Thus, with two products in the Word plus Finance suite, each product gets 50% of the suite revenues allocated to it.

$$\text{Word:} \quad \frac{1}{1 + 1} \times \$560 = 0.50 \times \$560 = \$280$$

$$\text{Finance:} \quad \frac{1}{1 + 1} \times \$560 = 0.50 \times \$560 = \$280$$

Stand-alone revenue allocation method. Revenue allocation method that uses product-specific information pertaining to products in the bundle to determine the weights used to allocate the bundled revenues to those individual products.

4. **Stand-alone product revenues.** Stand-alone product revenues will capture the quantity of each product sold as well as their selling prices. Assume that the stand-alone revenues are WordMaster $56 million, SpreadMaster $30 million, and FinanceMaster $14 million. The weights for the Word and Finances suite would be:

Word: $\dfrac{\$56 \text{ million}}{\$56 \text{ million} + \$14 \text{ million}} \times \$560 = 0.80 \times \$560 = \$448$

Finance: $\dfrac{\$14 \text{ million}}{\$56 \text{ million} + \$14 \text{ million}} \times \$560 = 0.20 \times \$560 = \$112$

The lower revenue allocation to FinanceMaster is, in part, due to it only being released partway through the year.

These four approaches to determining weights with the stand-alone method yield the following revenue allocations to individual products:

Revenue Allocation Weights	WordMaster	FinanceMaster
Selling prices	$202	$358
Unit manufacturing costs	235	325
Physical units	280	280
Stand-alone product revenues	448	112

The unit selling price weights are advantageous in that they frequently are the best available external indicator of the benefits companies receive from selling products. Market-based weighting schemes that are closer to the customer better capture a benefits-received notion in a bundled product allocation setting than do cost-based or unit-based weights. Unit-based revenue allocation is typically rationalized on the basis of ease of use or limitations of alternative methods (such as: unit selling prices are unstable; or unit manufacturing costs are difficult to calculate at the individual-product level).

Incremental Revenue Allocation Method

Incremental revenue allocation method. Revenue allocation method that ranks the individual products in a bundle and then uses this ranking to allocate the bundled revenues to these individual products.

The **incremental revenue allocation method** ranks the individual products in a bundle and then uses this ranking to allocate the bundled revenues to these individual products. The first-ranked product is termed the *primary product* in the bundle. The second-ranked product is termed the *first incremental product*, the third-ranked product in the *second incremental product*, and so on.

Who decides on the ranking of products in the incremental revenue allocation method? One approach is to survey customers on the relative importance of individual products in their decision to purchase the bundled products. A second approach is to use data on recent stand-alone performance of the individual products in the bundle. A third approach is for top management to decide the rankings based on their knowledge or intuition.

Consider again the Word and Finance suite of Superhighway. Assume Finance-Master is designated as the primary product. If the suite revenue exceeds the stand-alone revenue of the primary product, the primary product is allocated 100% of its stand-alone revenue. This is the case for the Word and Finance suite. The suite revenue of $560 exceeds the stand-alone revenue of $450 for Finance. Thus, Finance is allocated $450 revenues and the $110 ($560 – $450) remaining revenue is allocated to Word:

Product	Revenue Allocated	Revenue Remaining to Be Allocated to Other Products
Finance	$450	$110 ($560 – $450)
Word	110	0

If the suite revenue is less than or equal to the stand-alone revenue of the primary product, the primary product is allocated 100% of the suite revenue. All other products in the suite would receive zero allocation of revenues.

Where there are more than two products in the suite, the suite revenue is allocated sequentially. Consider the Word, Spread, and Finance suite, which sells for $760. Assume Superhighway ranks Finance as the primary product, Spread as the first incremental product, and Word as the second incremental product. The allocation of the $760 suite revenue proceeds as follows:

Product	Revenue Allocated	Revenue Remaining to Be Allocated to Other Products
Finance	$450	$310 ($760 – $450)
Spread	300	10 ($760 – $450 – $300)
Word	10	0

Clearly, the ranking of the individual products in the suite is a key factor in determining the revenues allocated to individual products.

Product managers at Superhighway would likely differ on how they believe their individual products contribute to sales of the suite products. It is possible that each individual product manager would claim to be responsible for the primary product in the Word + Spread + Finance suite! The stand-alone revenue allocation method does not require rankings of individual products in the suite. It is therefore less likely to involve product managers in highly acrimonious debates.

Other Revenue Allocation Methods

Management judgment not explicitly based on a specific formula is an alternative method of revenue allocation. In one case, the President of a software company decided to issue a set of revenue allocation weights after the managers of the three products in the bundled suite could not themselves agree on a set of weights. The weights chosen by the President for the three products were 45% for Product A, 45% for Product B, and 10% for Product C. The factors the President considered included stand-alone selling prices (all three were very similar), stand-alone unit sales (A and B were over 10 times more than C), product ratings by independent experts, and consumer awareness. The Product C manager complained that his 10% weighting dramatically short-changed the contribution of Product C to suite revenues. The President responded that its inclusion in the suite greatly increased consumer exposure to Product C with the result that Product C's total revenues would be far larger (even with only 10% of suite revenues) than had it not been included in the suite.

Part One of this chapter has discussed revenue allocation. Part Two discusses sales variances.

PROBLEM FOR SELF-STUDY

PROBLEM

Business Horizons (BH) produces and markets videos for sale to the business community. It hires well-known business speakers to present new developments in their area of expertise in video format. The compensation paid to each speaker is individually negotiated. It always has a component based on the percentage of revenues from the sale of the video, but that percentage is not uniform across speakers. Moreover, some speakers negotiate separate fixed-dollar payments or multiple-video deals.

BH sells most videos as separate items. However, there is a growing trend for videos also to be sold as part of bundled packages. BH offered bundled packages of its three best-selling videos in 2000. Individual and bundled sales of these three videos for 2000 are:

Individual Sales

Speaker	Title	Units Sold	Selling Price	Speaker Royalty
Jeannett Smith	Negotiating for Win-Win	25,000	$150	24%
Mark Coyne	Marketing for the Internet	17,000	$120	16%
Laurie Daley	Electronic Commerce	8,000	$130	19%

Bundled Product Sales

Titles in Bundle	Units Sold	Selling Price
Negotiating for Win-Win + Marketing for the Internet	12,000	$210
Negotiating for Win-Win + Electronic Commerce	5,000	$220
Marketing for the Internet + Electronic Commerce	4,000	$190
Negotiating + Marketing + Electronic	11,000	$280

REQUIRED

1. Allocate the bundled product revenues to the individual videos using the stand-alone revenue-allocation method (using selling prices as the weights).
2. Describe (without computations) an alternative method of allocating the bundled product revenues to that in requirement 1.

SOLUTION

1. The weights in the stand-alone method are based on the stand-alone selling prices of the videos in the bundled package. The following table details these weights, which are then used to allocate the revenues of each bundled package to the three individual videos.

	Allocation Formula	Negotiating	Marketing	Electronic
N + M:	($150/$270) × $210 × 12,000	$1,400,000		
N + E:	($150/$280) × $220 × 5,000	589,286		
N + M + E:	($150/$400) × $280 × 11,000	1,155,000		
Total		$3,144,286		
M + N:	($120/$270) × $210 × 12,000		$1,120,000	
M + E:	($120/$250) × $190 × 4,000		364,800	
M + N + E:	($120/$400) × $280 × 11,000		924,000	
Total			$2,408,800	
E + N:	($130/$280) × $220 × 5,000			$ 510,714
E + M:	($130/$250) × $190 × 4,000			395,200
E + N + M:	($130/$400) × $280 × 11,000			1,001,000
Total				$1,906,914

2. An alternative approach to allocating the bundled product revenues is the incremental revenue-allocation method. Here the individual videos in the bundle are ranked in order of importance, and the revenues are allocated to each product using stand-alone selling prices until all the bundled revenue has been fully allocated. Use of this approach would likely create some friction among the three business speakers. It would be in each speaker's interest to claim to be the primary speaker driving sales of the bundle. The actual 2000 units sold figures would enable Business Horizons to give a market-success-based ranking of individual business speakers if it used the incremental revenue-allocation method.

◆ PART TWO: SALES VARIANCES

SALES-VOLUME VARIANCE COMPONENTS

Part One of this chapter highlighted several issues in obtaining reliable information on the revenues of individual products or services. In this Part we examine how variances that use revenue information as a key output can be computed. Special attention is paid to companies with multiple products or services and to companies selling the same product or service in multiple countries.

Customer Profitability Analysis at PHH

PHH is a vehicle management company. It leases vehicles to its customers (both corporations and individuals) and also offers them a broad range of related services. These services include a vehicle maintenance program and accident-related support. PHH has over 750,000 vehicles under contract with its 5,200 plus customers.

PHH has adopted an activity-based costing approach to assist in cost management and the pricing of new business. One key part of its ABC system examines customer profitability. PHH has a menu of the activities it undertakes with respect to its customers. Some activities, such as account maintenance occur for every customer (but often with varying degrees of detail). Other activities, such as vehicle maintenance and accident assistance, are purchased by a subset of its customers.

PHH
www.phh.com

PHH Customer Case Studies
www.phh.com/3afacs.htm

When its ABC-based customer-profitability system was first implemented, PHH found higher variability in customer profitability than they had thought. The previous price bidding system did not adequately recognize differences in the complexity of different customers. For example, some customers wanted quick vehicle deliveries of vehicles while others gave PHH relatively long lead times. Orders with short delivery times were more likely to be purchased at a higher cost from a dealer rather than a manufacturer. Customers differed sizably in their accident rates, and in the extent to which vehicle repairs and maintenance were done by PHH or at the customer-site. Customers also differed in the level of detail requested in their vehicle reports from PHH. While PHH had a standardized set of reports, some customers wanted their own customized reports. Fleet vehicle diversity per customer was sizable. Several large customers had a small range of vehicles under lease while some smaller customers had a far more diverse set of vehicles being leased. The ABC system highlighted the extra costs of this fleet vehicle diversity and many other types of diversity when determining customer profitability.

PHH's price quoting group now uses the ABC information to price different vehicle/service combinations for existing and new customers. It has also established a pricing committee that must review now contracts that are below profitability thresholds. The committee was charged with creating a "more consistent and disciplined approach to pricing."

Source: Conversations with PHH management and with D. Swenson of University of Idaho.

The levels approach introduced in Chapter 7 shows how the variances we now discuss are linked to each other:

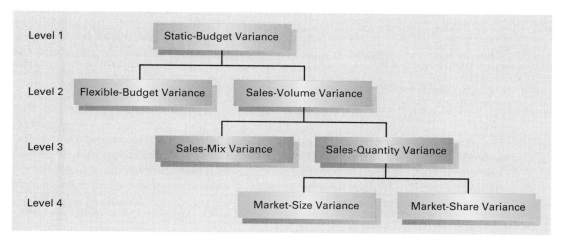

We continue to use the Superhighway Group in our analysis. This time we examine Superhighway's Computer Division which manufactures and sells three related products:

1. Plum—is sold mostly to college students and for the home market.
2. Portable Plum—is a portable version of the Plum, with an organizer and internet capabilities.
3. Super Plum—has a larger memory and more capabilities than the Plum and is targeted at the business market.

Budgeted and actual operating data for 2000 follow:

Budget for 2000

	Selling Price per Unit	Variable Costs per Unit	Contribution Margin per Unit	Sales Volume in Units	Sales Mix	Contribution Margin
Plum	$1,200	$ 700	$ 500	700	70%	$350,000
Portable Plum	800	500	300	100	10	30,000
Super Plum	5,000	3,000	2,000	200	20	400,000
				1,000	100%	$780,000

Actual Results for 2000

	Selling Price per Unit	Variable Costs per Unit	Contribution Margin per Unit	Sales Volume in Units	Sales Mix	Contribution Margin
Plum	$1,100	$ 500	$ 600	825	75%	$495,000
Portable Plum	650	400	250	165	15	41,250
Super Plum	3,500	2,500	1,000	110	10	110,000
				1,100	100%	$646,250

The analysis in Part Two emphasizes variance analysis of Superhighway's contribution margin. The basic framework we present can also be used to analyze revenues or individual variable costs.

Static-Budget Variance

The *static-budget variance* is the difference between actual result and a budgeted amount in the static budget.

$$\text{Static-budget variance} = \text{Actual results} - \text{Static budget amount}$$

Plum	$495,000	−	$350,000	=	$145,000	F
Portable Plum	41,250	−	30,000	=	11,250	F
Super Plum	110,000	−	400,000	=	290,000	U
Total	$646,250	−	$780,000	=	$133,750	U

Superhighway has favourable static-budget variances for the Plum and Portable Plum and an unfavourable one for the Super Plum. More information about the $133,750 unfavourable total static-budget variance can be gained by examining the flexible-budget variance and the sales-volume variance.

Flexible-Budget and Sales-Volume Variances

The *flexible-budget variance* is the difference between an actual result and the flexible-budget amount based on the level of output actually achieved in the budget period. The actual result is equal to the actual contribution margin times the actual unit volume. The flexible-budget amount is equal to the budgeted contribution margin times the actual unit volume.

Flexible-budget variance = Actual results − Flexible budget amount

Plum	= $(600 × 825)	− ($500 × 825)	
	= $495,000	− $412,500	= $82,500 F
Portable Plum	= $(250 × 165)	− ($300 ×165)	
	= $41,250	− $49,500	= 8,250 U
Super Plum	= $(1,000 × 110)	− ($2,000 × 110)	
	= $110,000	− $220,000	= 110,000 U
Total			$ 35,750 U

The $35,750 unfavourable total flexible-budget variance is heavily influenced by the actual contribution margin on the Super Plum being only $1,000 per unit compared to the budgeted $2,000 per unit.

The sales-volume variance shows the effect of the difference between the actual and budgeted quantity of the variable used to "flex" the flexible budget. For the contribution margin of Superhighway, this variable is units sold. This variance can be computed for each computer product as follows:

$$\text{Sales-volume variance} = \left(\begin{array}{c} \text{Actual sales} \\ \text{quantity in units} \end{array} - \begin{array}{c} \text{Static budget sales} \\ \text{quantity in units} \end{array} \right) \times \begin{array}{c} \text{Budgeted contribution} \\ \text{margin per unit} \end{array}$$

Plum	= (825 − 700) × $500	
	= 125 × $500	= $62,500 F
Portable Plum	= (165 − 100) × $300	
	= 65 × $300	= 19,500 F
Super Plum	= (110 − 200) × $2,000	
	= −90 × $2000	= 180,000 U
Total		$98,000 U

While the total sales-volume variance is $98,000 unfavourable, there is a combination of favourable variances for Plum and Portable Plum and an unfavourable variance for Super Plum. Managers can gain additional insight into sales volume changes by separating the sales-volume variance into a sales-mix variance and a sales-quantity variance.

SALES-MIX AND SALES-QUANTITY VARIANCES

Exhibit 16-1 shows how both the sales-mix and sales-quantity variances can be computed using the columnar approach introduced in Chapter 7. Refer to this exhibit when reading the following discussion of these two variances.

Sales-Mix Variance

The **sales-mix variance** is the difference between two amounts: (1) the budgeted amount for the actual sales mix and (2) the budgeted amount for the budgeted sales mix. The formula for computing the sales-mix variance in terms of the contribution margin for Superhighway is:

$$\text{Sales-mix variance} = \begin{array}{c} \text{Actual units of} \\ \text{all products sold} \end{array} \times \left(\begin{array}{c} \text{Actual sales} \\ \text{mix percentage} \end{array} - \begin{array}{c} \text{Budgeted sales} \\ \text{mix percentage} \end{array} \right) \times \begin{array}{c} \text{Budgeted contribution} \\ \text{margin per unit} \end{array}$$

Plum	= 1,100 × (0.75 − 0.70) × $500	= $27,500 F
Portable Plum	= 1,100 × (0.15 − 0.10) × $300	= 16,500 F
Super Plum	= 1,100 × (0.10 − 0.20) × $2,000	= 220,000 U
Total		$176,000 U

A favourable sales-mix variance arises for individual products when the actual sales-mix percentage exceeds the budgeted sales mix percentage. A favourable sales-mix variance arises for both Plum (75% actual versus 70% budgeted) and Portable Plum

OBJECTIVE 3

Provide additional information about the sales-volume variance by calculating the sales-mix and sales-quantity variances

Sales-mix variance. The difference between (1) the budgeted amount for the actual sales mix and (2) the budgeted amount if the budgeted sales mix had been unchanged.

EXHIBIT 16-1

Sales-Mix and Sales-Quantity Variance Analysis of the Contribution Margin of Superhighway's Group's Computer Division for 2000

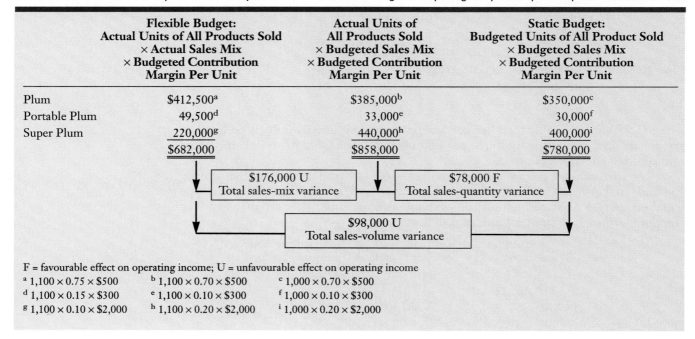

	Flexible Budget: Actual Units of All Products Sold × Actual Sales Mix × Budgeted Contribution Margin Per Unit	Actual Units of All Products Sold × Budgeted Sales Mix × Budgeted Contribution Margin Per Unit	Static Budget: Budgeted Units of All Product Sold × Budgeted Sales Mix × Budgeted Contribution Margin Per Unit
Plum	$412,500[a]	$385,000[b]	$350,000[c]
Portable Plum	49,500[d]	33,000[e]	30,000[f]
Super Plum	220,000[g]	440,000[h]	400,000[i]
	$682,000	$858,000	$780,000

$176,000 U
Total sales-mix variance

$78,000 F
Total sales-quantity variance

$98,000 U
Total sales-volume variance

F = favourable effect on operating income; U = unfavourable effect on operating income
[a] $1,100 \times 0.75 \times \$500$ [b] $1,100 \times 0.70 \times \$500$ [c] $1,000 \times 0.70 \times \$500$
[d] $1,100 \times 0.15 \times \$300$ [e] $1,100 \times 0.10 \times \$300$ [f] $1,000 \times 0.10 \times \$300$
[g] $1,100 \times 0.10 \times \$2,000$ [h] $1,100 \times 0.20 \times \$2,000$ [i] $1,000 \times 0.20 \times \$2,000$

(15% actual versus 10% budgeted). In contrast, Super Plum has an unfavourable variance because the actual sales mix percentage (10%) is less than the budgeted sales mix percentage (20%).

    The concept underlying the sales-mix variance is best explained in terms of the budgeted contribution margin per composite unit of the sales mix. A *composite product unit* is a hypothetical unit with weights based on the mix of individual products. In the following analysis, the weights for the variances are computed in column 3 for the actual mix and column 5 for the budgeted mix:

	Budgeted Contribution Margin Per Unit (1)	Actual Sales- Mix Percentage (2)	Budgeted Selling Price Per Composite Unit For Actual Mix (3) = (1) × (2)	Budgeted Sales- Mix Percentage (4)	Budgeted Selling Price Per Composite Unit For Budgeted Mix (5) = (1) × (4)
Plum	$ 500	0.75	$375	0.70	$350
Portable Plum	300	0.15	45	0.10	30
Super Plum	2,000	0.10	200	0.20	400
			$620		$780

The actual sales mix has a budgeted contribution margin per composite unit of $620. The budgeted sales mix has a budgeted contribution margin per composite unit of $780. Thus, the effect of the sales-mix shift for Superhighway is to decrease the budgeted contribution margin per composite unit by $160 ($780 – $620). For the 1,100 units actually sold, this decrease translates to an unfavourable sales-mix variance of $176,000 (1,100 × $160).

    Managers should probe why the unfavourable sales-mix variance of $176,000 occurred in 2000. Is the major shift in Superhighway's sales-mix due to the Plum and Portable Plum having better product performance vis-à-vis the Super Plum? Is it due to a major competitor in Super Plum's end of the market launching a technologically superior product that is lower priced? Is this sales-mix shift due to the initial sales volume estimates being made without adequate analysis of the potential market in 2000? These and other possible explanations should be examined.

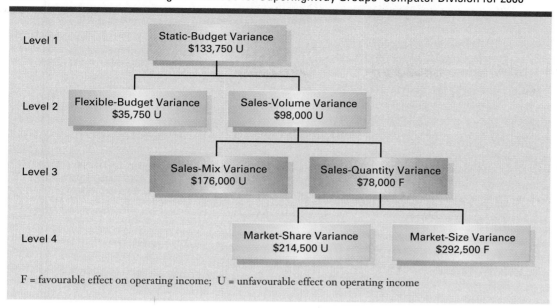

Level 1 — Static-Budget Variance $133,750 U

Level 2 — Flexible-Budget Variance $35,750 U; Sales-Volume Variance $98,000 U

Level 3 — Sales-Mix Variance $176,000 U; Sales-Quantity Variance $78,000 F

Level 4 — Market-Share Variance $214,500 U; Market-Size Variance $292,500 F

F = favourable effect on operating income; U = unfavourable effect on operating income

key to success in the computer industry. Consider also the favourable market-size variance of $292,500 in Exhibit 16–3. Is this market-size increase expected to continue in 2001, 2002, and beyond? If yes, the upside to Superhighway getting back to its budgeted 20% market share is very high.

Parts One and Two of this chapter have discussed revenue allocation and sales variances. Part Three discusses customer profitability analysis.

PROBLEM FOR SELF-STUDY

PROBLEM

Assume the same information for Superhighway as underlies Exhibits 16-1 and 16-2 with one change. This change is that at the end of 2000, Micro-Information reports actual industry sales of 4,000 units.

REQUIRED

1. Compute the market-share and market-size variances assuming actual industry sales of 4,000 units.
2. What insights do the variances in requirement 1 provide about Superhighway's performance in 2000?

SOLUTION

1. Superhighway's actual market share is 0.275 (1,100 ÷ 4,000) compared to a budgeted 0.2000 (1,000 ÷ 5,000).

$$\text{Market-share variance} = \text{Actual market size in units} \times \left(\text{Actual market share} - \text{Budgeted market share} \right) \times \begin{array}{l}\text{Budgeted contribution}\\ \text{margin per composite}\\ \text{unit for budgeted mix}\end{array}$$

$$= 4,000 \times (0.275 - 0.200) \times \$780$$

$$= \$234,000 \ F$$

$$\text{Market-share variance} = \left(\text{Actual market size in units} - \text{Budgeted market size} \right) \times \text{Budgeted market share} \times \begin{array}{l}\text{Budgeted contribution}\\ \text{margin per composite}\\ \text{unit for budgeted mix}\end{array}$$

$$= (4,000 - 5,000) \times 0.20 \times \$780$$

$$= \$156,000 \ U$$

2. There is both good news and bad news in the variances from requirement 1. The good news is the $234,000 favourable market-share variance. Superhighway has gained 7.5 market-share points in 2000 above its budgeted share (from the budgeted 20% to 27.5%). Explanations for this outcome include superb product quality and service at Superhighway and production delays or service problems at its competitors. The bad news is the decline in total market size, which resulted in an unfavourable market-size variance of $156,000. Managers at Superhighway likely will claim they have less control over market size than market share. Both factors, however, affect Superhighway's profitability. An important challenge for its managers is anticipating which markets are growing, and then positioning Superhighway to have an increasing portion of its business in growing market areas.

◆ PART THREE: CUSTOMER PROFITABILITY ANALYSIS

Customer profitability analysis.
Examines how individual customers, or groupings of customers, differ in their profitability.

Companies that prosper have a strong customer focus in their decisions. Management accountants are giving increased attention to **customer profitability analysis**, which is the reporting and analysis of customer revenues and customer costs. Armed with this information, managers can ensure that customers contributing sizably to the profitability of an organization receive a comparable level of attention from the organization.

CUSTOMER REVENUES AND CUSTOMER COSTS

OBJECTIVE 6

Discuss why revenues can differ across customers purchasing the same product

ARC Business Solutions—
Customer Profitability Optimiser
Model
www.arc-solutions.com/
optimiser_model.htm

An analysis of customer differences on both revenues and costs can provide important insight into why differences in customer profitability exist. Consider Spring Distribution Company which sells bottled water. It has two distribution channels— (a) a retail distribution channel of over 1,000 business and residential customers, and (b) a wholesale distribution channel that covers sales to supermarkets, drugstores, and other stores. We will focus mainly on customer profitability analysis in Spring's retail distribution channel. The list selling price in this channel is $0.60 per bottle while the purchase cost to Spring is $0.50 per bottle. If every bottle is sold at its list price in this distribution channel, Spring would earn a gross margin of $0.10 per bottle.

Customer Revenue Analysis

Let us first consider customer revenues. Data for four of Spring's customers in June 2000 are:

	Customer			
	A	**B**	**G**	**J**
1. Bottles sold	1,000,000	800,000	70,000	60,000
2. List selling price	$0.60	$0.60	$0.60	$0.60
3. Invoice price	$0.56	$0.59	$0.55	$0.60
4. Revenues (1 × 3)	$560,000	$472,000	$38,500	$36,000

Price discounting. The reduction of selling prices below listed levels in order to encourage an increase in purchases by customers.

Customer revenue analysis is enhanced by tracking as much detail as possible about why customers differ in their revenues. Two variables explain revenue differences across these four customers: (a) the volume of bottles purchased, and (b) the magnitude of price discounting. **Price discounting** is the reduction of selling prices below listed levels in order to encourage an increase in purchases by customers. Companies that record only the invoice price in their information system would not be able to readily track the magnitude of their price discounting (except in the extreme case of a single product company with a constant list price in the accounting period).[1]

Limiting the magnitude of price discounting can be essential to maintaining customer profitability. Price discounts may be due to multiple factors, including the volume of product purchased (higher volume customers get higher discounts) and whether having the customer brings marketing benefits (name recognition) that helps promote other sales. Discounts could also be due to poor negotiating by a salesperson or the dysfunctional effect of an incentive plan that is based only on revenues.

Tracking discounts by customer, and by salesperson, can provide valuable information about ways to improve customer profitability. For example, Spring Distribution may institute a corporate policy to ensure that any volume-based price discounting policy is enforced for customers with decreasing volume as well as those with increasing volume. It may also require its salespeople to obtain approval before giving large discounts to customers not normally qualifying for them. In addition, it could track the future sales of customers that its salespeople argue warrant a sizable price discount due to their predicted "high growth potential." Salespeople who have a poor track record in predicting the future growth of customers may be given additional training in sales forecasting (or may even be encouraged to seek employment elsewhere).

Customer revenues are one element customer profitability. We now consider the other element, customer costs.

Customer Cost Analysis

Chapter 5 and 14 discussed the *cost hierarchy* concept in which costs are categorized into different cost pools on the basis of different types of cost drivers (or cost-allocation bases) or different degrees of difficulty in determining cause-and-effect (or benefits received) relationships. Spring Distribution has an activity-based costing system that classifies its costs into four categories:

◆ *Customer specific costs.* These are costs that are traceable or allocated to individual customers. Examples are cost of goods sold and selling-related costs for individual customers.

◆ *Distribution channel costs.* Costs that are traceable or allocated to a customer distribution channel but not to individual customers. An example is the cost of a booth at a trade fair that customers in its wholesale distribution channel attend.

◆ *Customer support costs.* Costs that are traceable or allocated to customer support but not to individual customers or distribution channels. An example is the cost of a 24 hour hot-line that handles consumer complaints about the bottled waters Spring distributes in both its distribution channels.

◆ *Corporate sustaining costs.* These include the President's salary, interest on corporate debt, and corporate donation to charities.

Spring uses its customer-cost hierarchy to assist managers in decisions made at different levels in this hierarchy. We will now consider decisions made at the individual customer level.

Customer Specific Costs

Spring includes cost of goods sold and selling-related costs for individual customers in this category. The five activity areas used to collect costs for selling-related costs and their cost drivers are:

---

[1] Further analysis of customer revenues could distinguish between gross revenues and net revenues. This approach would highlight differences across customers in sales returns. Additional discussion of ways to analyze revenue differences across customers is in R. S. Kaplan and R. Cooper, *Cost and Effect* (Boston, Mass.: Harvard Business School Press, 1998), Chapter 10.

Activity Area	Cost Driver and Rate
Order taking	$ 100 per purchase order
Sales visits	$ 80 per sales visit
Delivery vehicles	$ 2 per delivery mile travelled
Product handling	$0.02 per bottle sold
Expedited deliveries	$ 300 per expedited delivery

Exhibit 16-4 shows a customer profitability analysis for the four representative customers whose revenues were previously presented (p. 566). Exhibit 16-4 includes information on customer revenues and customer-specific costs using its ABC system. Data underlying the activity-area costs for each customer are:

	Customer			
	A	**B**	**G**	**J**
Number of purchase orders	30	25	15	10
Number of sales visits	6	5	4	3
Number of deliveries	60	30	20	15
Miles travelled per delivery	5	12	20	6
Number of expedited deliveries	1	0	2	0

Spring Distribution can use the information underlying Exhibit 16-4 to assist its customers in reducing usage of the cost drivers. For example, consider Customer G which is only 7% the size of Customer A (in terms of bottles purchased—G purchased 70,000 while A purchased 1,000,000). Yet, G uses 50% the number of purchase orders, $66\frac{2}{3}$% the number of sales visits, $33\frac{1}{3}$% the number of deliveries, and twice the number of expedited deliveries. Spring Distribution could seek to have Customer G make fewer purchase orders, require less sales visits, have fewer deliveries,

EXHIBIT 16-4
Customer-Profitability Analysis for Four Customers of Spring Distribution for June 2000

	Customer			
	A	**B**	**G**	**J**
Revenues at list prices[a]	$600,000	$480,000	$42,000	$36,000
Discount[b]	40,000	8,000	3,500	0
Net revenues	560,000	472,000	38,500	36,000
Cost of goods sold[c]	500,000	400,000	35,000	30,000
Gross margin	60,000	72,000	3,500	6,000
Customer-specific operating costs				
Order taking[d]	3,000	2,500	1,500	1,000
Sales visits[e]	480	400	320	240
Delivery vehicles[f]	600	720	800	180
Product handling[g]	20,000	16,000	1,400	1,200
Expedited deliveries[h]	300	0	600	0
Total	24,380	19,620	4,620	2,620
Customer-specific contribution	$35,620	$52,380	$(1,120)	$3,380

[a]$0.60 × 1,000,000; $0.60 × 800,000; $0.60 × 70,000; $0.60 × 60,000
[b]$0.04 × 1,000,000; $0.01 × 800,000; $0.05 × 70,000; $0 × 60,000
[c]$0.50 × 1,000,000; $0.50 × 800,000; $0.50 × 70,000; $0.50 × 60,000
[d]$100 × 30; $100 × 25; $100 × 15; $100 × 10
[e]$80 × 6; $80 × 5; $80 × 4; $80 × 3
[f]$2 × (5 × 60); $2 × (12 × 30); $2 × (20 × 20); $2 × (6 × 15)
[g]$0.02 × 1,000,000; $0.02 × 800,000; $0.02 × 70,000; $0.02 × 60,000
[h]$300 × 1; $300 × 0; $300 × 2; $300 × 0

EXHIBIT 16-5
Income Statement of Spring Distribution for June 2000

	Total (1)	Customer Distribution Channels									
		Wholesale Customers					Retail Customers				
		Total (2)	A1 (3)	A2 (4)	● (5)	● (6)	Total (7)	Customer A[a] (8)	Customer B[a] (9)	● (10)	● (11)
Net revenues	$12,470,000	$9,230,000	$1,946,000	$1,476,000			$3,240,000	$560,000	$472,000		
Customer-specific costs	11,939,000	8,861,000	1,868,000	1,416,000			3,078,000	524,380	419,620		
Customer-specific contribution	531,000	369,000	$ 78,000	$ 60,000			162,000	$35,620	$52,380		
Customer-distn channel costs	190,000	104,000					86,000				
Customer-distn. channel contribution	341,000	$ 265,000					$76,000				
Customer-support costs	102,000										
Customer contribution	239,000										
Corporate sustaining costs	161,000										
Operating income	$ 78,000										

[a]Full details in Exhibit 16-4

and reduce expedited deliveries. The ABC system underlying Exhibit 16-4 provides a road-map to facilitate less use of cost drivers by a customer in order to promote cost reduction. Another advantage of ABC is that it highlights a second way cost reduction can be promoted by Spring Distribution. Spring can take actions to reduce the costs in each of its own activity areas. For example, order taking currently is estimated to cost $100 per purchase order. By making its own ordering process more efficient (such as having its customers order electronically), Spring can reduce its costs even if its customers make the same number of orders.

Exhibit 16-5 above reports the monthly operating income for Spring Distribution. The customer-specific contributions of customers A and B in Exhibit 16-4 are shown in columns (8) and (9) of Exhibit 16-5. The format of Exhibit 16-5 is structured on Spring Distribution's cost hierarchy. This format dovetails with the different levels at which Spring Distribution makes decisions.

CUSTOMER-PROFITABILITY PROFILES

Managers find customer profitability analysis useful for several reasons. First, it frequently highlights how vital a small set of customers is to total profitability. Managers need to ensure that the interests of these customers receive high priority. Microsoft uses the phrase "not all revenue dollars are endowed equally in profitability" to stress this key point. Second, when a customer is ranked in the "loss category," managers can focus on ways to make future business with this customer more profitable.

Exhibit 16-6 shows two approaches to presenting customer-profitability profiles. For simplicity, we use data on the customer-specific contribution of ten of Spring Distribution's customers, (four of which are already analyzed in Exhibit 16-4). Panel A ranks customers on customer-specific contribution. Column 4 shows the cumulative customer-specific contribution for these customers. This column is computed by cumulatively adding up the individual amounts in Column 2. For example, row three for customer C has a cumulative income of $108,650 in column 4. This is the sum of $52,380 for customer B, $35,620 for customer A, and $20,650 for customer C. Column 5 shows what percentage this $108,650 amount is of the total customer-specific contribution of $134,000 for these ten customers. Thus, the three

OBJECTIVE 7

Prepare a customer-profitability report

EXHIBIT 16-6
Customer-Profitability Analysis for Spring Distribution in 2000

PANEL A: CUSTOMERS RANKED ON CUSTOMER-SPECIFIC CONTRIBUTION

Customer Code (1)	Customer Specific Contribution (2)	Customer Revenue (3)	Cumulative Customer Specific Contribution (4)	Customer Specific Contribution as a % of Total Customer Specific Contribution (5)
B	$ 52,380	$ 480,000	$ 52,380	39%
A	35,620	600,000	88,000	66
C	20,650	247,000	108,650	81
D	16,840	227,000	125,490	94
F	6,994	99,000	132,484	99
J	3,380	36,000	135,864	101
E	3,176	193,000	139,040	104
G	–1,120	42,000	137,920	103
H	–1,760	39,000	136,160	102
I	–2,160	37,000	134,000	100
	$134,000	$2,000,000		

PANEL B: CUSTOMERS RANKED ON REVENUES

Customer Code (1)	Customer Revenue (2)	Customer Specific Contribution (3)	Customer Specific Contribution as a % of Revenues (4)	Cumulative Customer Revenue (5)	Cumulative Customer Revenue as a % of Total Revenues (6)
A	$600,000	$35,620	0.059	$600,000	30%
B	480,000	52,380	0.109	1,080,000	54
C	247,000	20,650	0.084	1,327,000	66
D	227,000	16,840	0.074	1,554,000	78
E	193,000	3,176	0.016	1,747,000	87
F	99,000	6,994	0.071	1,846,000	92
G	42,000	–1,120	(0.027)	1,888,000	94
H	39,000	–1,760	(0.045)	1,927,000	96
I	37,000	–2,160	(0.058)	1,964,000	98
J	36,000	3,380	0.094	2,000,000	100
	$2,000,000	$134,000			

most profitable customers contribute 81% of total customer-specific contribution. This high percentage contribution by a small number of customers is a common finding in many studies. It highlights the importance of Spring Distribution maintaining good relations with this pivotal set of customers.

Exhibit 16-6, Panel B, ranks customers on revenue (before price discounts). Three of the four smallest customers (based on revenue) are unprofitable. Moreover, customer E, with revenues of $193,000, is only marginally profitable. Further analysis revealed that a former sales representative gave customer E an excessively high price discounts in an attempt to meet a monthly sales-volume target.

Managers often find the bar chart presentation in Exhibit 16-7 to be the most intuitive way to analyze customer profitability. The highly profitable customers clearly stand out. Moreover, the number of loss-customers and the magnitude of their losses are apparent.

EXHIBIT 16-7
Bar Chart Presentation of Customer Profitability for Spring Distribution

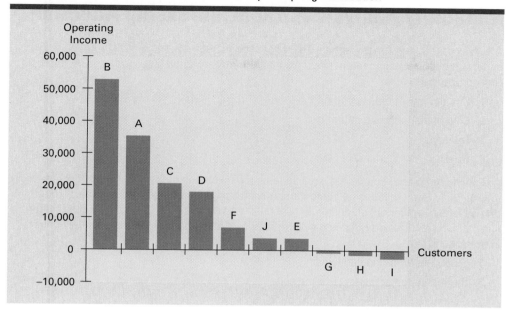

Assessing Customer Value

The information in Exhibits 16-4 and 16-7 relates to customer profitability in a single accounting period. This is one of several factors that managers should consider in deciding how to allocate resources across customers. These factors include:

1. **Short-run and long-run customer profitability.** This factor will be influenced by factors 2 and 3 below as well as by the level of resources likely to be required to retain the accounts.

2. **Customer retention likelihood.** The more likely a customer is to continue doing business with a company, the more valuable the customer. Customers can differ in their loyalty and their willingness to "shop their business" on a frequent basis.

3. **Customer growth potential.** This factor will be influenced by the likely growth of the industry of the customer and the likely growth of the customer (due to, say, its ability to develop new products). This factor will also be influenced by cross-selling opportunities, that is, when a customer of one of the company's products becomes a customer of one or more of the company's other products.

4. **Increases in overall demand from having well-known customers.** Some customers are highly valuable because they have established reputations that make them very useful to mention in sales visits. Other customers are valuable because of their willingness to provide product endorsements.

5. **Ability to learn from a customer.** Customers can be an important source of ideas about new products or ways to improve existing products. Customers willing to provide such input can be especially valuable.

Managers should be particularly cautious when deciding to drop customers. Short-run profitability reports may provide misleading signals about their long-run profitability. Moreover, as discussed next, not all costs assigned to a customer may be variable with respect to short-run reductions in purchases by customers. It is typically not the case that a policy of dropping any customer currently unprofitable (sometimes called "revenue shedding") will eliminate in the short-run all the costs assigned to that customer.

SURVEYS OF COMPANY PRACTICE

Customer Profitability Analysis Attracts Increasing Attention

A survey of U.S. and Australian managers[a] asked respondents about "the three most important general management priorities that your organization faces today." The top ranked priorities were:

1. Customer profitability/satisfaction
2. Cost management/cost control
3. Quality
4. Growth

A growing number of companies are now developing customer profitability systems to reinforce this strategic focus on customers. A survey of United Kingdom companies[b] found that 50% had "embarked on customer profitability analysis... A further 12% planned to pursue it in future." The uses of customer profitability analysis were ranked as follows (most important = 1)

1. Guidance for pricing policies
2. Renegotiation of customer contracts
3. Guidance for customer relations policies
4. Influence cost control in respect of customers.

"The 80/20 rule applied (that is, 20% of their customers were generating 80% of the profits)" to 60% of those who had examined cumulative contributions of customers to total profits.

[a]Foster, G. and S. M. Young, "Frontiers of Management Accounting Research," *Journal of Management Accounting Research* (1997)

[b]Innes, J., and F. Mitchell, "A Survey of Activity-Based Costing in the U.K.'s Largest Companies," *Management Accounting Research* (June 1995)

PROBLEM FOR SELF-STUDY

PROBLEM

Spring Distribution is concerned with the level of its profitability. Its June 2000 operating income of $78,000 is less than 1% of sales ($78,000 ÷ $12,470,000 = 0.63%). Suppose that July 2000 is identical to June 2000 with one exception. In July 2000, Spring conducts an extensive efficiency analysis of its activity areas and is able to reduce their costs to the levels shown below:

Activity Area	Cost Driver Rate
Order taking	$60 per purchase order
Sales visits	$50 per visit
Delivery vehicles	$1.50 per delivery mile travelled
Product handling	$0.015 per bottle sold
Expedited deliveries	$200 per expedited delivery

REQUIRED

1. What is the effect of these activity-area-cost reductions on the July 2000 profitability (customer-specific contribution) of customers A, B, G, and J in Exhibit 16-4?
2. What are additional ways Spring could seek to improve the profitability of customers A, B, G and J?

SOLUTION

1. The July 2000 activity-area cost rate reductions affect only the customer-specific operating costs in Exhibit 16-4. The revised customer-specific contributions to operating income are:

	Customer			
	A	B	G	J
Gross margin	$60,000	$72,000	$3,500	$6,000
Customer-specific Operating costs				
Order taking[a]	1,800	1,500	900	600
Sales visits[b]	300	250	200	150
Delivery vehicles[c]	450	540	600	135
Product handling[d]	15,000	12,000	1,050	900
Expedited deliveries[e]	200	0	400	0
Total	17,750	14,290	3,150	1,785
Customer-specific contribution	$42,250	$57,710	$ 350	$4,215

[a]$60 × 30; $60 × 25; $60 × 15; $60 × 10
[b]$50 × 6; $50 × 5; $50 × 4; $50 × 3
[c]$1.50 × (5 × 60); $1.50 × (12 × 30); $1.50 × (20 × 20); $1.50 × (6 × 15)
[d]$0.015 × 1,000,000; $0.015 × 800,000; $0.015 × 70,000; $0.015 × 60,000
[e]$200 × 1; $200 × 0; $200 × 2; $200 × 0

The customer-specific contribution has increased for each customer. The total contribution from these four customers is $104,525 in July 2000 compared to $90,260 in June 2000, an increase of 15.8%.

2. Spring could also seek to improve the profitability of its customers by reducing its cost of goods sold through better negotiating with its supplier. It could also explore the effect of a list price increase, a reduction in price discounts, or encouraging customers to use fewer service units from its five activity areas. The challenge here is to retain, or possibly increase, the customer's willingness to purchase from Spring given the new pricing and cost parameters.

SUMMARY

The following points are linked to the chapter's learning objectives.

1. Bundling occurs when a package of two or more products is sold for a single price. Where product managers of the individual components in the bundle seek information on product revenues, revenue allocation of the bundled price is required.

2. Revenue allocation for a bundled product can be done using the stand-alone method, the incremental method, or by management judgement.

3. Further information on the sales-volume variance can be gained by examining the effect of (a) a change in the actual sales mix from the budgeted sales mix (a sales-mix variance), and (b) a change in the actual unit sales from the budgeted unit sales (a sales-quantity variance).

4. Two key explanations for a sales-quantity variance are (a) a change in the actual share of the market attained compared to its budgeted share (the market-share variance), and (b) a change in the actual market size in units compared to the budgeted market size (the market-size variance).

5. Obtaining reliable information on the total market size and the relative market shares of products is essential to the reliability of the market-share and market-size variances.

6. The revenues of customers purchasing the same product can differ due to differences in the quantity of units purchased and in discounts given from the list price.

7. Customer profitability reports, shown in a cumulative form, often reveal that a small percentage of customers contributes a large percentage of profits. It is important that companies devote sufficient resources to maintaining and expanding relationships with these key contributors to profitability.

CONCEPTS IN ACTION

Hewlett-Packard Adopts Customer Profitability Analysis

Hewlett-Packard's North American Distribution Organization (HP-NADO) is one of four HP distribution organizations worldwide. NADO is the contact point between HP and its customers. It is always the information node between HP's production plants and its reseller

channels. In many cases, their product also physically passes through the distribution depot, where any specific customization (such as product combinations and packaging) is undertaken.

The previous costing system at HP-NADO was typical of many existing systems. It focussed on costs at a single function (distribution) and concentrated on the costs of distributing products. The most telling criticism of the system was that it did not assist managers in making many of their key decisions—for example, what channels to push and what individual customers to emphasize.

HP decided to use activity-based costing to develop a "data warehouse." This data warehouse is based on the activities undertaken by HP in linking a product from its manufacturing to its delivery to customers. Each activity is assigned a cost. Then the cost of a chosen focal object (be it a reseller channel, customer, or product) is determined by examining how that focal object uses the activities of the organization. Different focal objects are costed by slicing and dicing data in the warehouse in different ways. A key aspect here is the flexibility that the data warehouse concept

Hewlett-Packard
www.canada.hp.com

provides to managers. What occurs at NADO can always be expressed in terms of its usage of one or more activity areas.

The customer-based profitability reports facilitate decisions in key areas. From a strategic perspective, the customer profile reveals the importance of a small set of customers. Less than 25% of customers account for over 85% of all HP revenues. By cutting across the diverse product lines, the NADO data base facilitates a customer focus that was not previously possible. The database profiles the specific mix of revenue and cost activities that individual customers utilize. This information can be very insightful in explaining differences in customer profitability. Customer price discounting policies are an important concern here. Customers with relatively low revenues or relatively low profitability but relatively frequent and large price discounting are highlighted. The onus is on marketing personnel to reduce these price discounts unless compelling reasons exist for keeping them.

Source: Based on discussions with management.

---

8. Customer cost hierarchies are being used by companies such as General Motors and Hewlett-Packard to determine how some costs can be reliably assigned to individual customers while others can only be reliably assigned to distribution channels or to general corporatewide efforts. The result is that not all costs are "fully loaded" onto each individual customer.

APPENDIX: MIX AND YIELD VARIANCES FOR SUBSTITUTABLE INPUTS

Part Two of this chapter analyzed sales-mix and sales-quantity variances for a company with multiple products. This analysis extended the Chapter 7 coverage of the sales-volume variance. The sales-mix and sales-quantity framework outlined in Part Two can also be applied to the analysis of production-input variances. The prior discussion of these variances in Chapter 7 is easiest to interpret when the inputs into a production process are *nonsubstitutable*, which is often the case. Consider a company assembling voyager satellites for NASA's space program. Once a product design for a satellite is approved, there is a mandate that it be adhered to. The contractor cannot substitute a different combination of doors and door locks, irrespective of price movements of alternative doors and locks. In other cases, however, managers have some leeway in combining inputs. For example, Del Monte can combine material inputs (such as pineapples, cherries, and grapes) in varying proportions for its cans of fruit salad. Within limits, these individual fruits are *substitutable* inputs in making a fruit salad.

This Appendix presents mix and yield variances that highlight the financial implications of mix and yield decisions by managers. These variances divide the efficiency variance that was discussed in Chapter 7. To illustrate mix and yield variances, we examine Delpino Corporation which makes tomato ketchup. Our example focuses on direct material inputs and substitution among three of these inputs. The same approach can also be used to examine substitutable direct labour inputs.

To produce ketchup of the desired consistency, colour, and taste, Delpino mixes three types of tomatoes grown in three different regions–Latin American tomatoes (Latoms), California tomatoes (Caltoms), and Florida tomatoes (Flotoms). Delpino's production standards require 1.60 tonnes of tomatoes to produce 1 tonne of ketchup, with 50% of the tomatoes being Latoms, 30% Caltoms, and 20% Flotoms. The direct materials input standards to produce 1 tonne of ketchup are

0.80 (50% of 1.6) tonne of Latoms at $70 per tonne	$ 56.00
0.48 (30% of 1.6) tonne of Caltoms at $80 per tonne	38.40
0.32 (20% of 1.6) tonne of Flotoms at $90 per tonne	28.80
Total standard cost of 1.6 tonnes of tomatoes	$123.20

Budgeted average cost per tonne of tomatoes is $123.20 ÷ 1.60 tonnes = $77.

Because Delpino uses fresh tomatoes to make ketchup, no inventories of tomatoes are kept. Purchases are made as needed, so all price variances relate to tomatoes purchased and used. Actual results for June 2000 show that a total of 6,500 tonnes of tomatoes were used to produce 4,000 tonnes of ketchup:

3,250	tonnes of Latoms at actual cost of $70 per tonne	$227,500
2,275	tonnes of Caltoms at actual cost of $82 per tonne	186,550
975	tonnes of Flotoms at actual cost of $96 per tonne	93,600
6,500	tonnes of tomatoes	507,650
	Standard cost of 4,000 tonnes of ketchup at $123.20 per tonne	492,800
	Total variance to be explained	$ 14,850 U

Given the standard ratio of 1.60 tonnes of tomatoes to 1 tonne of ketchup, 6,400 tonnes of tomatoes should be used to produce 4,000 tonnes of ketchup. At the standard mix, the quantities of each type of tomato required are

Latoms	0.50 × 6,400 =	3,200 tonnes
Caltoms	0.30 × 6,400 =	1,920 tonnes
Flotoms	0.20 × 6,400 =	1,280 tonnes

Direct Materials Price and Efficiency Variances

Exhibit 16-8 presents the columnar analysis of the flexible-budget variance for direct materials discussed in Chapter 7. The direct materials price and efficiency variances are calculated separately for each input material and then added together. The variance analysis prompts Delpino to investigate the unfavourable price and efficiency variances—why did they pay more for the tomatoes and use greater quantities than they should have? Were the market prices of tomatoes higher, in general, or could the Purchasing Department have negotiated lower prices? Did the inefficiencies result from inferior tomatoes or from problems in processing?

Direct Materials Mix and Direct Materials Yield Variances

Managers sometimes do have discretion to substitute one material for another. For example, the manager of Delpino's ketchup plant has some leeway in combining

EXHIBIT 16-8
Direct Materials Price and Efficiency Variances for the Delpino Corporation for June 2000*

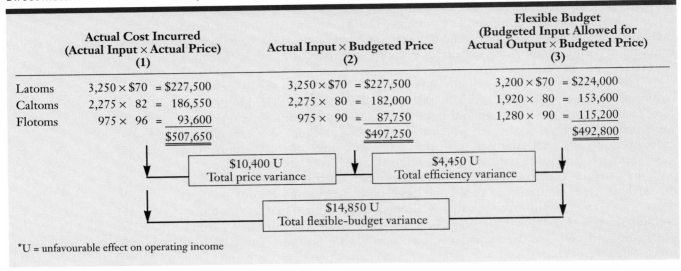

	Actual Cost Incurred (Actual Input × Actual Price) (1)	Actual Input × Budgeted Price (2)	Flexible Budget (Budgeted Input Allowed for Actual Output × Budgeted Price) (3)
Latoms	3,250 × $70 = $227,500	3,250 × $70 = $227,500	3,200 × $70 = $224,000
Caltoms	2,275 × 82 = 186,550	2,275 × 80 = 182,000	1,920 × 80 = 153,600
Flotoms	975 × 96 = 93,600	975 × 90 = 87,750	1,280 × 90 = 115,200
	$507,650	$497,250	$492,800

$10,400 U
Total price variance

$4,450 U
Total efficiency variance

$14,850 U
Total flexible-budget variance

*U = unfavourable effect on operating income

Latoms, Caltoms, and Flotoms without affecting quality. We will assume that to maintain quality, the mix percentages of each type of tomato can only vary up to 5% from the standard mix:. For example, the percentage of Caltoms in the mix can vary between 25% and 35% (30% ± 5%). When inputs are substitutable, direct materials efficiency improvement relative to budgeted costs can come from two sources: (1) using a cheaper mix to produce a given quantity of output, and (2) using less input to achieve a given quantity of output. The direct materials yield and mix variances divide the efficiency variance into two variances: the mix variance focuses on how the multiple types of substitutable materials or labour are combined and the yield variance focuses on how much of those inputs are used.

Holding the actual total quantity of all direct materials inputs used constant, the total **direct materials mix variance** is the difference between two amounts: (1) the budgeted cost for the actual mix of the total quantity of direct materials used, and (2) the budgeted cost of the budgeted mix of the actual total quantity of direct materials used. Holding the budgeted input mix constant, the **direct materials yield variance** is the difference between two amounts: (1) the budgeted cost of direct materials based on the actual total quantity of all direct materials inputs used, and (2) the flexible-budget cost of direct materials based on the budgeted total quantity of direct materials inputs for the actual output.

Exhibit 16-9 presents the total direct materials mix and yield variances for the Delpino Corporation.

Direct Materials Mix Variance. Compare columns I and 2 in Exhibit 16-9. Both columns calculate cost using the actual total quantity of all inputs used (6,500 tonnes) and budgeted input prices (Latoms, $70; Caltoms, $80; and Flotoms, $90). The *only* difference is that column 1 uses *actual input mix* (Latoms, 50%; Caltoms, 35%; Flotoms, 15%), and column 2 uses *budgeted input mix* (Latoms, 50%; Caltoms, 30%; and Flotoms, 20%). The difference in costs between the two columns is the total direct materials mix variance, attributable solely to differences in the mix of inputs used. The total direct materials mix variance is the sum of the direct materials mix variances for each input.

Direct materials mix variance is the difference between two amounts: (1) the budgeted cost for the actual mix of the total quantity of direct materials used, and (2) the budgeted cost of the budgeted mix of the actual total quantity of direct materials used.

Direct materials yield variance is the difference between (1) the budgeted cost of direct materials based on the actual total quantity of all direct materials inputs used and (2) the flexible-budget cost of direct materials based on the budgeted total quantity of direct materials inputs for the actual output.

$$\begin{array}{c} \text{Direct} \\ \text{materials mix} \\ \text{variance for} \\ \text{each input} \end{array} = \left(\begin{array}{c} \text{Actual direct} \\ \text{materials} \\ \text{input mix} \\ \text{percentage} \end{array} - \begin{array}{c} \text{Budgeted} \\ \text{direct materials} \\ \text{input mix} \\ \text{percentage} \end{array} \right) \times \begin{array}{c} \text{Actual total} \\ \text{quantity of all} \\ \text{direct materials} \\ \text{inputs used} \end{array} \times \begin{array}{c} \text{Budgeted} \\ \text{price of direct} \\ \text{materials} \\ \text{input} \end{array}$$

EXHIBIT 16-9
Total Direct Materials Yield and Mix Variances for the Delpino Corporation for June 2000*

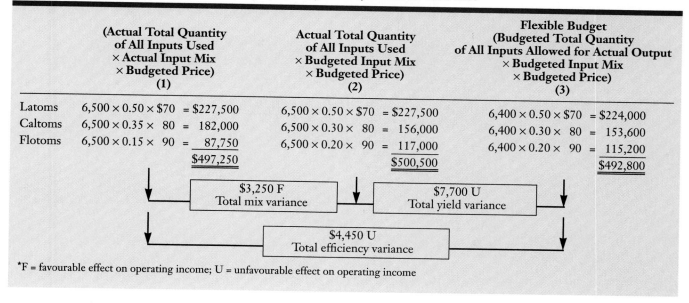

	(Actual Total Quantity of All Inputs Used × Actual Input Mix × Budgeted Price) (1)	Actual Total Quantity of All Inputs Used × Budgeted Input Mix × Budgeted Price) (2)	Flexible Budget (Budgeted Total Quantity of All Inputs Allowed for Actual Output × Budgeted Input Mix × Budgeted Price) (3)
Latoms	$6,500 \times 0.50 \times \$70 = \$227,500$	$6,500 \times 0.50 \times \$70 = \$227,500$	$6,400 \times 0.50 \times \$70 = \$224,000$
Caltoms	$6,500 \times 0.35 \times 80 = 182,000$	$6,500 \times 0.30 \times 80 = 156,000$	$6,400 \times 0.30 \times 80 = 153,600$
Flotoms	$6,500 \times 0.15 \times 90 = \underline{87,750}$	$6,500 \times 0.20 \times 90 = \underline{117,000}$	$6,400 \times 0.20 \times 90 = \underline{115,200}$
	$\$497,250$	$\$500,500$	$\$492,800$

$3,250 F
Total mix variance

$7,700 U
Total yield variance

$4,450 U
Total efficiency variance

*F = favourable effect on operating income; U = unfavourable effect on operating income

The direct materials mix variances are

Latoms	$(0.50 - 0.50) \times 6,500 \times \$70 = 0.00 \times 6,500 \times \$70$	$= \$ \quad 0$
Caltoms	$(0.35 - 0.30) \times 6,500 \times \$80 = 0.05 \times 6,500 \times \$80$	$= 26,000\ U$
Flotoms	$(0.15 - 0.20) \times 6,500 \times \$90 = (0.05) \times 6,500 \times \$90$	$= \underline{29,250}\ F$
Total direct materials mix variance		$\underline{\$ 3,250}\ F$

Total Direct Materials Yield Variance. Compare columns 2 and 3 of Exhibit 16–9. Column 2 calculates costs using the budgeted input mix and the budgeted prices. Column 3 calculates the flexible-budget cost based on the budgeted cost of the budgeted total quantity of all inputs used (6,400 tonnes of tomatoes) for the actual output achieved (4,000 tonnes of ketchup) times the budgeted input mix (Latoms, 50%; Caltoms, 30%; Flotoms, 20%). The only difference in the two columns is that column 2 uses the actual total quantity of all inputs used (6,500 tonnes), while column 3 uses the budgeted total quantity of all inputs used (6,400 tonnes). Hence, the difference in costs between the two columns is the total direct materials yield variance, due solely to differences in actual and budgeted total input quantity used. The total direct materials yield variance is the sum of the direct materials yield variances for each input.

$$\begin{array}{c} \text{Direct} \\ \text{materials} \\ \text{yield} \\ \text{variance for} \\ \text{each input} \end{array} = \left(\begin{array}{c} \text{Actual total} \\ \text{quantity of} \\ \text{all direct} \\ \text{materials} \\ \text{inputs used} \end{array} - \begin{array}{c} \text{Budgeted total} \\ \text{quantity of all} \\ \text{direct materials} \\ \text{inputs allowed for} \\ \text{actual output} \end{array} \right) \times \begin{array}{c} \text{Budgeted} \\ \text{direct} \\ \text{materials} \\ \text{input mix} \\ \text{percentage} \end{array} \times \begin{array}{c} \text{Budgeted} \\ \text{price of} \\ \text{direct} \\ \text{materials} \\ \text{input} \end{array}$$

The direct materials yield variances are

Latoms	$(6,500 - 6,400) \times 0.50 \times \$70 = 100 \times 0.50 \times \$70 =$	$\$3,500\ U$
Caltoms	$(6,500 - 6,400) \times 0.30 \times \$80 = 100 \times 0.30 \times \$80 =$	$2,400\ U$
Flotoms	$(6,500 - 6,400) \times 0.20 \times \$90 = 100 \times 0.20 \times \$90 =$	$\underline{1,800}\ U$
Total direct materials yield variance		$\underline{\$7,700}\ U$

The total direct materials yield variance is unfavourable because Delpino used 6,500 tonnes of tomatoes rather than the 6,400 tonnes that it should have used to produce 4,000 tonnes of ketchup. Holding the budgeted mix and budgeted prices of tomatoes constant, the budgeted cost per tonne of tomatoes in the budgeted mix is $77 per tonne. The unfavourable yield variance represents the budgeted cost of using 100 more tonnes of tomatoes, $(6{,}500 - 6{,}400) \times \$77 = \$7{,}700$ U.

The direct materials variances computed in Exhibits 16-8 and 16-9 can be summarized as follows:

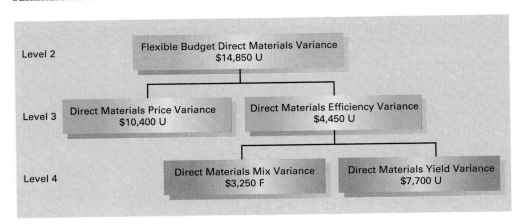

This chapter contains definitions of the following important terms:

bundled product (p. 554)
customer profitability analysis (p. 566)
direct materials mix variance (p. 576)
direct materials yield variance (p. 576)
incremental revenue allocation method (p. 556)
market-share variance (p. 563)

market-size variance (p. 564)
price discounting (p. 566)
revenue allocation (p. 554)
sales-mix variance (p. 561)
sales-quantity variance (p. 563)
stand-alone revenue allocation method (p. 555)

ASSIGNMENT MATERIAL

QUESTIONS

16-1 Describe how companies are increasingly facing revenue allocation decisions.

16-2 Distinguish between the stand-alone revenue allocation method and the incremental revenue allocation method.

16-3 Identify and discuss arguments individual product managers may put forward to support their preferred revenue allocation method.

16-4 How might a dispute over the allocation of revenues of a bundled product be resolved?

16-5 Show how managers can gain insight into the causes of a sales-volume variance by drilling down into the components of this variance.

16-6 How can the concept of a composite unit be used to explain why an unfavourable total sales-mix variance for revenues occurs?

16-7 Explain why a favourable sales-quantity variance occurs.

16-8 Distinguish between a market-size variance and a market-share variance.

16-9 Why might some companies not compute market-size and market-share variances?

16-10 Why is customer profitability analysis a vitally important topic to managers?

16-11 How can the extent of price discounting be tracked on a customer-by-customer basis?

16-12 "A customer profitability profile highlights those customers that should be dropped to improve profitability." Do you agree?

16-13 Give an example of three types of different levels of costs in a customer cost hierarchy.

16-14 Distinguish between processes where the inputs are nonsubstitutable and where they are substitutable.

16-15 Explain how the direct materials mix and yield variances provide additional information about the direct materials efficiency variance.

EXERCISES

16-16 Revenue allocation, speaking fees. Geoff Carr is a leading public relations expert. He recently convinced three well-known sports personalities to jointly appear on a one-day seminar.

◆ Linda Young is a leading soccer coach. She gave six speeches last year, each at $10,000 per appearance. Young refuses most invitations, preferring to focus on ways to win matches or relax at home.

◆ Vince Rock is an olympic gold medallist. Rock gave 50 speeches last year, each at $4,000 per appearance. He loves publicity and rarely says no to invitations.

◆ Juan Malvido is a television sports commentator. Malvido charged $2,000 for each of the 40 appearances he made last year. His television network actively solicits venues at which Malvido talks.

In the past, each speaker has been the only presenter at events at which they appear. Young, Rock, and Malvido will each speak for 2 hours at Carr's one-day seminar.

The first seminar draws 500 people at $200 per head. Carr promised his three speakers he would give them in aggregate 30% of the total revenues. Without discussing it with each speaker, Carr assumes this 30% would be split equally–10% of total revenues to Young, 10% to Rock, and 10% to Malvido.

REQUIRED

1. Describe two alternative ways (other than equal splitting) to allocate the 30% of total revenues among the three speakers.

2. Discuss possible reactions of each speaker to Carr's proposed equal splitting of the 30% of revenues allotted for speaking fees.

16-17 Revenue allocation, bundled products. Pebble Resorts operates a five-star hotel with a world-recognized championship golf course. It has a decentralized management structure. There are three divisions:

◆ Lodging (rooms, conference facilities)

◆ Food (restaurants and in-room service)

◆ Recreation (the golf course, tennis courts, and so on)

Starting next month, Pebble will offer a two-day, two-person "getaway package" deal for $700. This deal includes:

◆ Two nights' stay for two in an ocean view room—separately priced at $640 ($320 per night for two).

◆ Two rounds of golf separately priced at $300 ($150 per round). One person can do two rounds, or two can do one round each.

◆ Candlelight dinner for two at the exclusive Pebble Pacific Restaurant—separately priced at $80 per person.

Samantha Lee, president of the Recreation Division, recently asked the CEO of Pebble Resorts how her division would share in the $700 revenue from the package. The golf course was operating at 100% capacity (and then some). Under the "getaway package" rules, participants who booked one week in advance were guaranteed access to the golf course. Lee noted that every "getaway" booking would displace a $150 booking. She stressed that the high demand reflected the devotion of her team to keeping the golf course rated in the "Best 10 Courses in the World" listings in *Golf Monthly*. As an aside she also noted that the Lodging and Food divisions only had to turn away customers on "peak-season events such as the New Year's period."

REQUIRED

1. Allocate the $700 "getaway package" revenue to the three divisions using:
   a. The stand-alone revenue allocation method
   b. The incremental revenue allocation method (with recreation first, then lodging, and then food)
   Use unit selling prices as the weights in (a) and (b).

2. What are the pros and cons of (a) and (b) in requirement 1?

16-18 Revenue allocation, bundled products, additional complexities (continuation of 16-17). The individual items in the "getaway package" deal at Pebble Resorts are not fully used by each guest. Assume that 10% of the "getaway package" users in its first month do not use the golfing option, while 5% do not use the food option. The lodging option has a 100% usage rate.

REQUIRED

How should Pebble Resorts recognize this nonuse factor in its revenue sharing of the $700 package across the Lodging, Food, and Recreation divisions?

16-19 Variance analysis of revenues, multiple products. The Penguins play in the North American Ice Hockey League. The Penguins play in the Downtown Arena, which has a capacity of 30,000 seats (10,000 lower-tier seats and 20,000 upper-tier seats). The Downtown Arena charges the Penguins a per-ticket charge for use of their facility. All tickets are sold by the Reservation Network, which charges the Penguins a reservation fee per ticket. The Penguins budgeted net revenue for each type of ticket in 2000 is computed as follows:

	Lower-Tier Tickets	Upper-Tier Tickets
Selling price	$35	$14
Downtown Arena fee	10	6
Reservation Network fee	5	3
Contribution margin	$20	$ 5

The budgeted and actual average attendance figures per game in the 2000 season are:

	Budgeted Seats Sold	Actual Seats Sold
Lower-tier	8,000	6,600
Upper-tier	12,000	15,400
Total	20,000	22,000

There was no difference between the budgeted and actual net revenue for lower-tier or upper-tier seats.

The manager of the Penguins was delighted that actual attendance was 10% above budgeted attendance per game, especially given the depressed state of the local economy in the past six months.

REQUIRED

1. Compute the sales volume variance for individual "product" net revenues and total net revenues for the Penguins in 2000.
2. Compute the sales quantity and sales mix variances for individual "product" net revenues and total net revenues in 2000.
3. Present a summary of the variances in requirements 1 and 2. Comment on the results.

16-20 7 Up Using Variances to Read the Market. The following is an excerpt from an article that appeared in a recent issues of a trade magazine:

Remember about 30 years back, when 7 Up began describing itself as the Uncola and ran those great commercials celebrating the "uncola nut"? And remember those cool upside-down 7 Up glasses?

This, paradoxically, is part of 7 Up's problem. As John Sicher, editor of *Beverage Digest* explains, "7 Up is perceived today as something that appeals to an older generation, not as a hip, with-it brand." Indeed, 7 Up's own research shows that while the soft drink continues to be popular with boomers who grew up on the Uncola campaign, its brand identity is barely a blip on the cultural radar of today's 12- to 24-year-olds, the demographic segment that consumes the most soda. As a result, 7 Up's market share has deteriorated throughout the '90s, even though the share of the citrus-flavoured soda category—which includes 7 Up's primary competitor, Sprite—has increased during the same period.

In the ten years prior to the article, 7 Up's market share had declined from 3.2% to 2.4%. Five years prior to the article, 7 Up held a 2.8% market share compared to Sprite's 4.9%. (Sprite is the category leader in the lemon-lime segment of the soft drink market.) 7 Up's slide has been steady and consistent over the last ten years.

1. In light of these comments, what variances should 7 Up management have been tracking over the past decade? What story would those variances have told?
2. What factors should you consider in evaluating 7 Up's strategy in the last decade?

16-21 Variance analysis of contribution margin, multiple products; working backward. The Jinwa Corporation sells two brands of wine glasses—Plain and Chic. Jinwa provides the following information for sales in the month of June 2000:

Static budget total contribution margin	$5,600
Budgeted units to be sold of all glasses in June 2000	2,000 units
Budgeted contribution margin per unit of Plain	$2 per unit
Budgeted contribution margin per unit of Chic	$6 per unit
Total sales quantity variance	$1,400 U
Actual sales mix percentage of Plain	60%

All variances are to be computed in contribution margin terms.

REQUIRED

1. Calculate the sales quantity variances for each product for June 2000.
2. Calculate the individual product and total sales mix variances for June 2000. Calculate the individual product and total sales volume variances for June 2000.
3. Briefly describe the conclusions you would draw from the variances.

16-22 Variance analysis of revenues, multiple countries. Cola-King manufactures and sells cola soft drinks in three countries—Canada, Mexico, and the United States. The same product is sold in each market. Budgeted and actual results for 2000 (all in Canadian dollars) are as follows:

	Budget for 2000			Actual for 2000		
Country	Selling Price per Carton	Variable Cost per Carton	Units Sold (cartons in thousands)	Selling Price per Carton	Variable Cost per Carton	Units Sold (cartons in thousands)
Canada	$6.00	$4.00	400,000	$6.20	$4.50	480,000
Mexico	$4.00	$2.80	600,000	$4.25	$2.75	900,000
United States	$7.00	$4.50	1,500,000	$6.80	$4.60	1,620,000

REQUIRED

1. Compute the flexible-budget variance, the sales-volume variance, sales-mix variance, and sales-mix variance, and sales-quantity variance. Show results for each country in your computations.
2. What inferences do you make from the variances computed in requirement 1?

16-23 Customer profitability, service company. Instant Service (IS) is a repair service company specializing in the rapid repair of photocopying machines. Each of its ten clients pays a fixed monthly service fee (based on the type of photocopying machines owned by that client and the number of employees at that site). IS keeps records of the time technicians spend at each client as well as the cost of the equipment used to repair each photocopying machine. IS recently decided to compute the profitability of each customer. The following data (in thousands) pertain to May 2000:

	Customer Revenues	Customer Costs
Avery Group	$260	$182
Duran Systems	180	184
Retail Systems	163	178
Wizard Partners	322	225
Santa Clara College	235	308
Grainger Services	80	74
Software Partners	174	100
Problem Solvers	76	108
Business Systems	137	110
Okie Enterprises	373	231

1. Compute the operating income of each customer. Prepare exhibits for Instant Service that are similar to Exhibits 16-6 and 16-7. Comment on the results.
2. What options regarding individual customers should Instant Service consider in light of your customer profitability analysis in requirement 1?
3. What problems might Instant Service encounter in accurately estimating the operating cost of each customer?

 16-24 Customer profitability, distribution. Figure Four is a distributor of pharmaceutical products. Its activity-based costing system has five activity areas:

Activity Area	Cost Driver and 2000 Rate
1. Order processing	$40 per order
2. Line item ordering	$ 3 per line item
3. Store deliveries	$50 per store delivery
4. Carton deliveries	$ 1 per carton
5. Shelf stocking	$16 per stocking-hour

Rick Flair, the controller of Figure Four, wants to use this activity-based costing system to examine individual customer profitability within each distribution market. He focuses first on the "mom and pop" single-store distribution market. Two customers are used to exemplify the insights available with the activity-based costing approach. Data pertaining to these two customers in August 2000 are as follows:

	Maple Pharmacy	Oak Hill Pharmacy
Total orders	12	10
Average line items per order	10	18
Total store deliveries	6	10
Average cartons shipped per store delivery	24	20
Average hours of shelf stocking per store delivery	0	0.5
Average revenue per delivery	$2,400	$1,800
Average cost of goods sold per delivery	$2,100	$1,650

REQUIRED

1. Use the activity-based costing information to compute the operating income of each customer in August 2000. Comment on the results.
2. Flair ranks the individual customers in the "mom and pop" single-store distribution market on the basis of operating income. The cumulative operating income of the top 20% of customers is $55,680. Figure Four reports negative operating income of $21,247 for the bottom 40% of its customers. Make four recommendations that you think Figure Four should consider in light of this new customer profitability information.

16-25 Direct materials efficiency, mix and yield variances. (Chapter Appendix, CMA adapted) The Energy Products Company produces a gasoline additive, Gas Gain, that increases engine efficiency and improves gasoline mileage. The actual and budgeted quantities (in litres) of materials required to produce Gas Gain and the budgeted prices of materials in August 2000 are as follows:

Chemical	Actual Quantity	Budgeted Quantity	Budgeted Price
Echol	24,080	25,200	$0.20
Protex	15,480	16,800	0.45
Benz	36,120	33,600	0.15
CT-40	10,320	8,400	0.30

REQUIRED

1. Calculate the total direct materials efficiency variance for August 2000.
2. Calculate the total direct materials mix and yield variances for August 2000.
3. What conclusions would you draw from the variance analysis?

16-26 Direct materials price, efficiency, mix and yield variances. (Chapter Appendix) Greenwood, Inc., manufactures apple products such as apple jelly and applesauce. It makes applesauce by blending Tolman, Golden Delicious, and Ribston apples. Budgeted costs to produce 100,000 kilograms of applesauce in November 2000 are as follows:

45,000 kilograms of Tolman apples at $0.30 per kilogram	$13,500
180,000 kilograms of Golden Delicious apples at $0.26 per kilogram	46,800
75,000 kilograms of Ribston apples at $0.22 per kilogram	16,500

Actual costs in November 2000 are:

62,000 kilograms of Tolman apples at $0.28 per kilogram	$17,360
155,000 kilograms of Golden Delicious applies at $0.26 per kilogram	40,300
93,000 kilograms of Ribston apples at $0.20 per kilogram	18,600

REQUIRED

1. Calculate the total direct materials price and efficiency variances for November 2000.
2. Calculate the total direct materials mix and yield variances for November 2000.
3. Comment on your results in requirements 1 and 2.

PROBLEMS

16-27 Revenue allocation, bundled products. Athletic Programs (AP) sells exercise videos through television infomercials. It uses a well-known sporting celebrity in each video. Each celebrity receives a share (typically varying between 10% and 25%) of the revenues from sale of that video.

In recent months, AP has started selling its exercise videos in bundled form as well as in individual form. Typically, the bundled products are offered to people who telephone for a specific video after watching an infomercial. Each infomercial is for a specific exercise tape. As a marketing experiment, AP has begun advertising the bundled product at the end of some infomercials in a select set of markets.

Sales in 2000 of three products that have been sold individually, as well as in bundled form, are as follows:

	Average Retail Price	Net Units Sold	Royalty Paid to Celebrity
Individual sales:			
SuperAbs	$40	27,000	15%
SuperArms	$35	53,000	25%
SuperLegs	$25	20,000	18%
Bundled product sales:			
SuperAbs + SuperArms	$60	18,000	?
SuperAbs + SuperLegs	$52	6,000	?
SuperArms + SuperLegs	$42	11,000	?
SuperAbs + SuperArms + SuperLegs	$65	22,000	?

The AP infomercials have received widespread recognition.

REQUIRED

1. What royalty would be paid to the celebrity on each tape for the individual sales in 2000?
2. What royalty would be paid to each celebrity for the bundled product sales in 2000 using:
   a. The stand-alone revenue allocation method (with average retail price as the weight)?
   b. The incremental revenue allocation method (with SuperArms ranked 1, SuperAbs 2, and SuperLegs 3)?
3. Discuss the relative merits of the two revenue allocation methods in requirement 2.

4. Assume the incremental revenue allocation method is used. What alternative approaches could be used to determine the sequence in which the bundled revenue could be allocated to individual products?

16-28 Variance analysis, sales-mix and sales quantity variances. Aussie Infonautics, Inc., produces handheld Windows™ compatible organizers. Aussie Infonautics markets three different handheld models. PalmPro is a souped-up version for the executive on the go; PalmCE is a consumer-oriented version; PalmKid is a stripped down version for the young adult market. You are Aussie Infonautics Senior Vice-President of Marketing. The CEO has discovered that the total contribution margin came in lower than budget, and it is your responsibility to explain to him why actual results are different than the budget. Budgeted and actual operating data for Aussie Infonautics, Inc.'s third quarter (2000) are as follows:

Budgeted Operating Data, Third Quarter 2000

	Selling Price	Variable Costs per Unit	Contribution Margin per Unit	Sales Volume in Units
PalmPro	$379	$182	$197	12,500
PalmCE	269	98	171	37,500
PalmKid	149	65	84	50,000
				100,000

Actual Operating Data, Third Quarter 2000

	Selling Price	Variable Costs per Unit	Contribution Margin per Unit	Sales Volume in Units
PalmPro	$349	$178	$171	11,000
PalmCE	285	92	193	44,000
PalmKid	102	73	29	55,000
				110,000

REQUIRED
1. Compute the actual and budgeted contribution margins in dollars and in percentage terms.
2. Calculate the actual and budgeted gales mix for the three products.
3. Calculate the individual product flexible-budget, sales-volume, sales-mix and sales-quantity variances for the third quarter of 2000.
4. Calculate total sales-volume, sales-mix and sales-quantity variances for the third quarter of 2000.
5. Given that your CEO is known to have temper tantrums, you want to be well prepared for this meeting. In order to prepare, write a paragraph or two explaining why actual results were not as good as the budgeted amounts.

16-29 Market-share and market-size variance (continuation of 16-28). Aussie Infonautics, Inc. SVP of Marketing prepared his budget at the beginning of the third quarter assuming a 25% market share. The total handheld organizer market was estimated by Foolinstead Research to reach sales of 400,000 units worldwide in the third quarter. However, actual sales were 500,000 units.

REQUIRED
1. Calculate the market-share and market-size variances for Aussie Infonautics in the third quarter of 2000 (report all variances in terms of contribution margins).
2. Explain what happened based on the market-share and market-size variances.
3. Calculate the actual market-size, in units, that would have led to no market-size variance (again using budgeted average contribution margin per unit). Use this market size figure to find the actual market share that would have led to a zero market-share variance.

16-30 Variance analysis of contribution margin, multiple products. Debbie's Delight, Inc. operates a chain of cookie stores. Budgeted and actual operating data of its three Calgary stores for August 2000 are as follows:

Budget for August

	Selling Price per Kilogram	Variable Costs per Kilogram	Contribution Margin per Kilogram	Sales Volume in Kilograms
Chocolate chip	$4.50	$2.50	$2.00	45,000
Oatmeal raisin	5.00	2.70	2.30	25,000
Coconut	5.50	2.90	2.60	10,000
White chocolate	6.00	3.00	3.00	5,000
Macadamia nut	6.50	3.40	3.10	15,000
				100,000

Actual for August

	Selling Price per Kilogram	Variable Costs per Kilogram	Contribution Margin per Kilogram	Sales Volume in Kilograms
Chocolate chip	$4.50	$2.60	$1.90	57,600
Oatmeal raisin	5.20	2.90	2.30	18,000
Coconut	5.50	2.80	2.70	9,600
White chocolate	6.00	3.40	2.60	13,200
Macadamia nut	7.00	4.00	3.00	21,600
				120,000

Debbie's Delight focuses on contribution margin in its variance analysis.

REQUIRED
1. Compute the individual product and total sales volume variances for August 2000.
2. Compute the individual product and total sales quantity variances for August 2000.
3. Compute the individual product and total sales mix variances for August 2000.
4. Comment on your results in requirements 1, 2, and 3.

16-31 Market size and market share variances (continuation of 16-30). Debbie's Delight assumes a 10% market share of the Calgary market and a budgeted total Calgary market for August 2000 of 1,000,000 sales volume in pounds. The actual total Calgary market for August 2000 was 960,000 sales volume in kilograms.

REQUIRED
Compute the market size and market share variances for Debbie's Delight in August 2000. Report all variances in contribution margin terms. Comment on the results.

16-32 Customer profitability analysis. Zoot's Suits is a ready-to-wear suit manufacturer with headquarters in Toronto. Zoot's has three customers:
◆ April Department Stores, a large department store chain that uses Zoot's to manufacture its own private-label brand;
◆ Brothers Stores, a chain of mall-based men's clothing stores; and
◆ Suitors, a company that sells suits to students on campus through a network of salespersons who travel across the country visiting college campuses.

Zoot's owner and CEO, Al Sims, has developed the following activity-based costing system:

Activity Area	Cost Driver	Rate in 2001
1. Order Processing	Purchase Order	$ 245
2. Sales Visits	Sales Visit	$1,430
3. Delivery - Regular	Regular Delivery	$ 300
4. Delivery - Rushed	Rushed Delivery	$ 850
5. Returns Processing	Return	$ 185

Each suit returned also incurs a $5 stocking fee. In addition, Zoot's credits the customer's account for the full purchase price of all suits returned. Sims wants to evaluate the profitability of each of the three customers in 2000 in order to explore opportunities for increasing the profitability of his company in 2001. Use the following data to answer the questions that follow:

Item	April	Brothers	Suitors
Total number of orders	44	62	212
Total number of sales visits	8	12	22
Regular deliveries	41	48	166
Rush deliveries	3	14	46
Number of returns	4	6	16
Average number of suits per order	400	200	30
List selling price	$200	$200	$200
Average selling price	$140	$160	$170
Average cost	$110	$110	$110
Average number of suits returned	220	160	80

REQUIRED

1. Calculate the operating income per customer. Who is the most profitable customer? Who is the least profitable customer? What contributes to each customer's profitability (or lack thereof)?
2. Provide some recommendations for Al Sims to ponder as he considers his options for increasing the company's profitability in 2001.

16-33 **Customer profitability, distribution.** Spring Distribution has decided to analyze the profitability of another five customers (see pp. 566–571). It buys bottled water at $0.50 per bottle and sells to wholesale customers at a list price of $0.60 per bottle. Data pertaining to five customers are:

	Customer				
	P	Q	R	S	T
Bottles sold	50,000	210,000	1,460,000	764,000	94,000
List selling price	$0.60	$0.60	$0.60	$0.60	$0.60
Actual selling price	$0.60	$0.59	$0.55	$0.58	$0.54
Number of purchase orders	15	25	30	25	30
Number of sales visits	2	4	6	2	3
Number of deliveries	10	30	60	40	20
Kilometres travelled per delivery	14	4	3	8	40
Number of hot-hot runs	0	0	0	0	1

Its five activity areas and their cost drivers are:

Activity Area	Cost Driver and Rate
Order taking	$100 per purchase order
Sales visits	$80 per sales visit
Delivery vehicles	$2 per delivery kilometre travelled
Product handling	$0.02 per bottle sold
Hot-hot runs	$300 per hot-hot run

REQUIRED

1. Compute the operating income of each of the five customers now being examined (P, Q, R, S, and T). Comment on the results.
2. What insights are gained by reporting both the list selling price and the actual selling price for each customer?
3. What factors should Spring Distribution consider in deciding whether to drop one or more of customers P, Q, R, S, or T?

16-34 **Customer loyalty clubs and profitability analysis.** The Sherriton Hotels chain embarked on a new customer loyalty program in 2000. The 2000 year-end data have been collected, and it is now time for you to determine whether the loyalty program should be continued, discontinued or perhaps altered to improve loyalty and profitability levels at Sherriton.

Sherriton's loyalty program consists of three different customer loyalty levels. All new customers can sign up for the Sherriton Bronze Card–this card provides guests with a complimentary bottle of wine (cost to the chain is $5 per bottle) and

$20 in restaurant coupons each night (cost to the chain is $10). Bronze customers also receive a 10% discount off the nightly rate. The program enables the chain to track a member's stays and activities. Once a customer has stayed and paid for 20 nights at any of the chain's locations worldwide they are upgraded to Silver Customer status. Silver benefits include the bottle of wine (cost to the chain is $5 per bottle), $30 in restaurant coupons (cost to the chain is $15) and a 20% off every night from the 21st night on. A customer that reaches the 50-night level is upgraded to Gold Customer status. Gold status increases the nightly discount to 30% and replaces the $5 bottle of wine with a bottle of champagne (cost to the chain is $20 per bottle). As well, $40 in restaurant coupons are granted (cost to the chain is $20). The restaurant at each hotel is operated by a company not owned by Sherriton.

The average full price for one night's stay is $200. The chain incurs variable costs of $65 per night, exclusive of loyalty program costs. Total fixed costs for the chain are $140,580,000. Sherriton operates ten hotels with, on average, 500 rooms each. All hotels are open for business 365 days a year, and approximate average occupancy rates are around 80%. Following are some loyalty program characteristics:

Loyalty Program	Number of Customers	Average Number of Nights per Customer
Gold	2,430	60
Silver	8,340	35
Bronze	80,300	10
No program	219,000	1

Note that a Gold Customer would have received the 10% discount for his or her first 20 stays, received the 20% discount for the next 30 stays, and the 30% discount only for the last ten nights. Assume that all program members signed on to the program the first time they stayed with one of the chain's hotels. Also, assume the restaurants are managed by a 100% owned subsidiary of Sherriton.

REQUIRED

1. Calculate the program contribution, margin for each of the three programs, as well as for the group of customers not subscribing to the loyalty program. Which of the programs is the most profitable? Which is the least profitable? Do not allocate fixed costs to individual rooms or specific loyalty programs.
2. Develop an income statement for Sherriton for the year ended December 31, 2000.
3. What is the average room rate per night? What are average variable costs per night inclusive of the loyalty program?
4. Explain what drives the profitability (or lack thereof) of the most and least profitable loyalty program (again, one of these may be the "no program" option).

16-35 Direct materials price and efficiency variances, direct materials mix and yield variances. Tropical Fruits, Inc., processes tropical fruit into fruit salad mix, which it sells to a food-service company. Tropical Fruits has in its budget the following standards for the direct materials inputs to produce a batch of 80 kilograms of tropical fruit salad.

Note that 100 kilograms of input quantities are required to produce 80 kilograms of fruit salad. No inventories of direct materials are kept. Purchases are made as needed, so all price variances are related to direct materials used. The actual direct materials inputs used to produce 54,000 kilograms of tropical fruit salad for the month of October were:

36,400 kilograms of pineapple at $0.90 per kilogram	$32,760
18,200 kilograms of watermelon at $0.60 per kilogram	10,920
15,400 kilograms of strawberries at $0.70 per kilogram	10,780
70,000	$54,460

REQUIRED

1. Compute the total direct materials price and efficiency variances in October.
2. Compute the total direct materials mix and yield variances for October.
3. Comment on your results in requirements 1 and 2.
4. How might the management of Tropical Fruits, Inc., use information about the direct materials mix and yield variances?

16-36 Customer profitability, responsibility for environmental cleanup, ethics. Industrial Fluids, Inc. (IF) manufactures and sells fluids used by metal-cutting plants.

These fluids enable metal-cutting to be done more accurately and more safely.

IF has over 1,000 customers. It is currently undertaking a customer profitability analysis. Ariana Papandopolis, a newly hired MBA, is put in charge of the project. One issue in this analysis is IF's liability for its customers' fluid disposal.

Papandopolis discovers that IF may have a responsibility under Canadian environmental legislation for the disposal of toxic waste by its customers. Moreover, she visits ten customer sites and finds dramatic differences in their toxic-waste-handling procedures. She describes one site owned by Acme Metal as an "environmental nightmare about to become a reality." She tells the IF Controller that even if they have only one-half of the responsibility for the cleanup at Acme's site, they will still be facing very high damages. He is displeased at the news. Acme Metal has not paid its account to IF for the past three months and has formally announced bankruptcy. He cautions Papandopolis to be careful in her written report. He notes that, "IF does not want any smoking guns in its files in the case of subsequent litigation."

REQUIRED

1. As Papandopolis prepares IF's customer profitability analysis, how should she handle any estimates of litigation and cleanup costs that IF may be held responsible for?
2. How should Papandopolis handle the Acme Metal situation when she prepares a profitability report for that customer?

COLLABORATIVE LEARNING PROBLEM

16-37 Customer profitability, credit card operations. The Freedom Card is a credit card that competes with national credit cards such as VISA and MasterCard. Freedom Card is marketed by the Bay Bank. Mario Verdolini is manager of the Freedom Card division. He is seeking to develop a customer profitability reporting system. He collects the following information on four users of the Freedom Card:

	Customer			
	A	**B**	**C**	**D**
Annual purchases at retail merchants	$80,000	$26,000	$34,000	$8,000
Customer transactions at retail merchants	800	520	272	200
Membership fee paid	$50	$0	$50	$0
Average annual outstanding balance on credit card on which interest is paid to Bay Bank	$6,000	0	$2,000	$100
Inquiries to Bay Bank	6	12	8	2
Credit card replacement due to loss or theft	0	2	1	0

Customer B pays no membership fee as his card was issued under a special "lifetime promotion program" in which annual fees are waived as long as the card is used at least once a year. Customer D is a student. Bay Bank does not charge a membership fee to student credit card holders at select universities.

Bay Bank has an activity-based costing system that Verdolini can use in his analysis. The following data apply to 2000:

a. Each customer transaction with a retail merchant costs Bay Bank $0.50 to process.
b. Each customer inquiry to Bay Bank costs $5.
c. Replacing a lost card costs $120.
d. Annual cost to Bay Bank of maintaining a credit card account is $108 (includes sending out monthly statements).

Bay Bank receives 2.0% of the purchase amount from retail merchants when the Freedom Card is used. Bad debts of the Freedom Card in 2000 were 0.5% of the purchase amounts. Thus, Bay Bank nets 1.5% revenue when its credit card holders use the Freedom Card at retail merchants.

Bay Bank had an interest spread of 9% in 2000 on the average outstanding balances on which interest is paid by its credit card holders. An interest spread is the difference between what Bay Bank receives from card holders on outstanding balances and what it pays to obtain the funds so used. Thus, on a $500 average annual outstanding balance in 2000, Bay Bank would receive $45 in interest payment revenues (9% × $500).

Form groups of two or more students to complete the following requirements.

REQUIRED

1. Compute the 2000 customer profitability of the four representative credit card users of The Freedom Card.

2. Develop profiles of (a) profitable card holders and (b) unprofitable card holders for Bay Bank.

3. Should Bay Bank charge its card holders for making inquiries (such as outstanding balances) or for replacing lost or stolen cards? At present, no such charges are made.

4. Verdolini has an internal proposal that Bay Bank discontinue a sizable number of the low-volume credit card customers. What factors should he consider in evaluating and responding to this proposal?

5. Verdolini seeks your group's advice on an ethical issue he is facing. A chain of gambling casinos (Lucky Roller) has offered to provide Freedom Card holders with money advances of up to $500 at its casinos. Verdolini observes that from a strict financial perspective, providing money advances to its customers was highly profitable in 2000. Should Freedom Card holders be able to obtain money advances at Lucky Roller gambling casinos?

17

PROCESS COSTING

Milk is processed in a series of standard production steps, and like or similar bottles of milk are mass-produced. To compute the cost per bottle of milk, Dean Foods Company uses process-costing systems at its various production plants. Manufacturing costs are averaged over the bottles of milk produced.

LEARNING OBJECTIVES

After studying this chapter, you should be able to:

1. Determine when process-costing systems are appropriate
2. Describe five key steps in process costing
3. Calculate and use equivalent units
4. Prepare journal entries for process-costing systems
5. Demonstrate the weighted-average method of process costing
6. Demonstrate the first-in, first-out (FIFO) method of process costing
7. Incorporate standard costs into a process-costing system
8. Apply process costing to cases with transferred-in costs

OBJECTIVE 1

Determine when process-costing systems are appropriate

Process Costing Systems—
University of Canberra
management.canberra.edu.au/
lectures/accounting/sem981/
unit4827/lcr11.htm

Global Defence Review 1999
www.global-defence.com/
default.htm

A *process-costing system* is a costing system in which the cost of a product or service is obtained by assigning costs to masses of like or similar units. Process-costing systems are used in industries that cost like or similar units of products, which are often mass-produced. In these industries, relatively homogeneous products are processed in a very similar manner and are hence assumed to receive the same amount of direct materials, direct manufacturing labour costs, and manufacturing overhead costs. Industries using process costing in their manufacturing area include chemical processing, oil refining, pharmaceuticals, plastics, brick and tile manufacturing, semiconductor chips, beverages, and breakfast cereals.

The principal difference between process costing and job costing is the extent of averaging used to compute unit costs of products or services. The cost object in a job-costing system is a job that constitutes a distinctly identifiable product or service. Individual jobs use different quantities of manufacturing resources, so it would be incorrect to cost each job at the same average manufacturing cost. In contrast, when like or similar units are mass-produced, and not processed as individual jobs, process costing averages manufacturing costs over all units produced.

ILLUSTRATING PROCESS COSTING

The easiest way to learn process costing is by example. Let us consider the following illustration.

Example: Global Defence, Inc. manufactures thousands of components for missiles and military equipment. We will focus on the production of one of these components, DG-19. The product-costing system for DG-19 has a single direct cost category (direct materials) and a single indirect cost category (conversion costs). Each DG-19 unit passes through two departments—the Assembly Department and the Testing Department. Every effort is made to ensure that all DG-19 units are identical and meet a set of demanding performance specifications. Direct materials are added at the beginning of the process in Assembly. Additional direct materials are added at the end of processing in the Testing Department where final assembly of the DG-19 component occurs. Conversion costs are added evenly during both processes. *Conversion costs* are all manufacturing costs other than direct materials costs. Conversion costs include manufacturing labour, indirect materials, energy, plant amortization, and so on. When the Testing Department finishes work on each DG-19 component, it is immediately transferred to Finished Goods. The following graphic summarizes these facts:

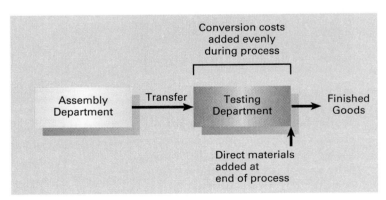

We will use the manufacture of the DG-19 component to illustrate three cases:

◆ **Case 1** Process costing with no beginning or ending work-in-process inventory of DG-19—that is, all units are started and fully completed by the end of the accounting period. *This case illustrates the basic averaging of costs idea that is a key feature of process-costing systems.*

◆ **Case 2** Process-costing with no beginning work-in-process inventory but an ending work-in-process inventory of DG-19—that is, some units of DG-19

Process Costing in Different Industries

A survey of cost accounting practices in Australian manufacturing companies indicates the widespread use of process-costing systems for product costing across a variety of industries. The reported percentages exceed 100% because several companies surveyed use more than one product-costing system.

	Food	Textiles	Primary Metals	Chemicals	Refining
Process costing	96%	91%	92%	75%	100%
Job order costing	4	18	25	25	25
Other	—	—	8	12	—

	Printing and Publishing	Furniture and Fixtures	Machinery and Computers	Electronics
Process costing	20%	38%	43%	55%
Job order costing	73	63	65	58
Other	13	—	9	10

The survey data indicate that the use of process costing varies considerably among industries. Process costing is widely used in mass-production industries that manufacture homogeneous products—food, textiles, primary metals, chemicals, and refining. In contrast, as we move across the spectrum to industries that produce many distinct and different products, job order costing is favoured over process costing, as in industries like printing and publishing, furniture and fixtures, machinery and computers, and electronics.

Source: Joye, M., and P. Blayney, "Cost Management Accounting Practices in Australian Manufacturing Companies: Survey Results," (Accounting Research Centre, The University of Sydney, 1991)

started during the accounting period are incomplete at the end of the period. *This case introduces the concept of equivalent units.*

◆ **Case 3**   Process costing with both beginning and ending work-in-process inventory of DG-19. *This case describes the effect of weighted-average and first-in, first-out (FIFO) cost flow assumptions on cost of units completed and cost of work-in-process inventory.*

CASE 1: PROCESS COSTING WITH NO BEGINNING OR ENDING WORK-IN-PROCESS INVENTORY

On January 1, 2000, there was no beginning inventory of DG-19 units. During January 2000, Global Defence started, completed assembly of, and transferred out to the Testing Department 400 DG-19 units.

Data for the Assembly Department for January 2000 are:

Physical Units for January 2000

Work in process, beginning inventory (January 1)	0 units
Started during January	400 units
Completed and transferred out during January	400 units
Work in process, ending inventory (January 31)	0 units

Total Costs for January 2000

Direct materials costs added during January	$32,000
Conversion costs added during January	24,000
Total Assembly Department costs added during January	$56,000

Global Defence records direct materials and conversion costs in the Assembly Department as these costs are incurred. By averaging, the assembly cost per unit of DG-19 would simply be $56,000 ÷ 400 units = $140, itemized as follows:

Direct materials ($32,000 ÷ 400) cost per unit	$ 80
Conversion costs ($24,000 ÷ 400) per unit	60
Assembly Department cost per unit	$140

This case shows that in a process-costing system, unit costs can be averaged by dividing total costs in a given accounting period by total units produced in that period. Because each unit is identical, we assume that all units receive the same amount of direct materials and conversion costs. This approach can be used by organizations that mass-produce standard units and have no incomplete units when each accounting period ends. This situation frequently occurs in service sector organizations. For example, banks can adopt this process costing approach to compute the unit cost of 100,000 similar customer deposits made in a month.

CASE 2: PROCESS COSTING WITH NO BEGINNING BUT AN ENDING WORK-IN-PROCESS INVENTORY

OBJECTIVE 2

Describe five key steps in process costing

In February 2000, Global Defence places another 400 units of DG-19 into production. Since the assembly of all units placed into production in January 2000 had been fully completed, there is no beginning inventory of partially completed units in the Assembly Department on February 1, 2000. Customer delays in placing orders for DG-19 prevented the complete assembly of all units started in February. Only 175 units were completed and transferred out to the Testing Department.

Data for the Assembly Department for February 2000 are:

Physical Units for February 2000

Work in process, beginning inventory (February 1)	0 units
Started during February	400 units
Completed and transferred out	175 units
Work in process, ending inventory (February 28)	225 units

The 225 partially assembled units as of February 28, 2000 were fully processed with respect to direct materials. Why? Because all direct materials in the Assembly Department are added at the beginning of the assembly process. Conversion costs are added evenly during the assembly process. On the basis of work completed relative to the total work required to be done, an Assembly Department supervisor estimates that the partially assembled units were, on average, 60% complete as to conversion costs.

The accuracy of the completion percentages depends on the care and skill of the estimator and the nature of the process. Estimating the degree of completion is usually easier for direct materials than for conversion costs. The conversion sequence usually consists of a number of basic operations or a specified number of hours, days, weeks, or months for various steps in machining, assembling, testing, and so forth. Thus, the degree of completion for conversion costs depends on what proportion of the total effort needed to complete one unit or one batch has been devoted to units still in process. In industries where no exact estimate is possible or, as in the textile industry, where vast quantities in process prohibit making costly physical estimates, all work in process in every department is assumed to be complete to some reasonable degree (for example, one-third, one-half, or two-thirds complete).

Total Costs for February 2000

Direct materials costs added during February	$32,000
Conversion costs added during February	18,600
Total Assembly Department costs added during February	$50,600

The key point in this example is that a partially assembled unit is not the same as a fully assembled unit. Faced with some fully assembled and some partially assembled units, how should Global Defence calculate (1) the cost of fully assembled units in February 2000 and (2) the cost of the partially assembled units still in process at the end of February 2000?

We can find the answers to these two questions using a process-costing system and the following five steps:

◆ **Step 1**. Summarize the flow of physical units of output.
◆ **Step 2**. Compute output in terms of equivalent units.
◆ **Step 3**. Compute equivalent unit costs.
◆ **Step 4**. Summarize total costs to account for.
◆ **Step 5**. Assign these costs to units completed and to units in ending work in process.

Physical Units and Equivalent Units (Steps 1 and 2)

Step 1 tracks the physical units of output. Where did the units come from and how many units are there to account for? Where did they go and how are they accounted for? The physical units column of Exhibit 17-1 tracks where the physical units went—175 units completed and transferred out, and 225 units in ending inventory, and where they came from—400 units started.

In step 2, how should the output for February be measured? The output was 175 fully assembled units plus 225 partially assembled units. Since all physical units of output are not uniformly completed, output in step 2 is stated in *equivalent units*, not in physical units.

Equivalent units measure output in terms of the physical quantities of each of the inputs (factors of production) that have been consumed when producing the units. For example, each equivalent unit of DG-19 comprises the physical quantities of direct materials and the conversion costs inputs necessary to produce output of one fully complete unit of DG-19.

Process-costing systems separate costs into cost categories according to the timing of when costs are introduced into the process. Often, only two cost classifications, direct materials and conversion costs, are necessary to assign costs to products, since all conversion costs are generally added to the process at about the same time. If, however, manufacturing labour is added to the process at different times than other conversion costs, an additional cost category (direct manufacturing labour costs) would be used for separately assigning these costs to products. Equivalent units are calculated separately for each cost category. Instead of thinking of output in terms of physical units, think of output in terms of the quantities of completed units

Equivalent units. Measure of the output in terms of the physical quantities of each of the inputs (factors of production) that have been consumed when producing the units; it is the physical quantities of inputs necessary to produce output of one fully complete unit.

EXHIBIT 17-1

Steps 1 and 2: Summarize Output in Physical Units and Compute Equivalent Units, Assembly Department of Global Defence, Inc., for February 2000

Flow of Production	(Step 1) Physical Units	(Step 2) Equivalent Units	
		Direct Materials	Conversion Costs
Completed and transferred out during current period	175	175	175
Add: Work in process, ending*	225		
225 × 100%; 225 × 60%		225	135
Total accounted for	400	400	310
Deduct: Work in process, beginning	0	0	0
Started during current period			
Work done in current period only	400	400	310

*Degree of completion in this department: direct materials, 100%; conversion costs, 60%.

that can be made from inputs of direct materials and conversion costs. *Disregard dollar amounts until equivalent units are computed.*

All 400 units, the 175 fully assembled ones and the 225 partially assembled ones, are complete in terms of equivalent units of direct materials. Why? Because all direct materials are added in the Assembly Department at the initial stage of the process. Exhibit 17-1 shows output as 400 *equivalent* units of direct materials because all 400 units are fully complete with respect to materials.

The 175 fully assembled units are completely processed with respect to conversion costs. The partially assembled units in ending work in process are 60% complete (on average). Therefore, the conversion costs in the 225 partially assembled units is *equivalent* to conversion costs in 135 (60% of 225) fully assembled units. Hence, Exhibit 17-1 shows output as 310 *equivalent* units of conversion costs—175 equivalent units assembled and transferred out and 135 equivalent units in ending work-in-process inventory.

Calculation of Product Costs (Steps 3, 4, and 5)

Exhibit 17-2 shows step 3: computing equivalent unit costs. Step 3 calculates equivalent unit costs by dividing direct materials and conversion costs added during February by the related quantity of equivalent units of work done in February calculated in Exhibit 17-1.

We can see the importance of using equivalent units in unit cost calculations by comparing conversion costs for the months of January and February 2000. Observe that the total conversion costs of $18,600 for the 400 units worked on during February are less than the conversion costs of $24,000 for the 400 units worked on in January. However, the conversion costs to fully assemble a unit are $60 in both January and February. Total conversion costs are lower in February because fewer equivalent units of conversion costs work were completed in February (310) than in January (400). If, however, we had used physical units instead of equivalent units in the per-unit calculation, we would have erroneously concluded that conversion costs per unit declined from $60 in January to $46.50 ($18,600 ÷ 400) in February. This incorrect costing might have prompted Global Defence, for example, to inappropriately lower the price of DG-19.

Step 4 in Exhibit 17-2 summarizes total costs to account for. Because the beginning balance of the work-in-process inventory is zero, total costs to account for

EXHIBIT 17-2

Steps 3, 4, and 5: Compute Equivalent Unit Costs, Summarize Total Costs to Account For, and Assign Costs to Units Completed and to Units in Ending Work in Process, Assembly Department of Global Defence Inc. for February 2000

	Total Production Costs	Direct Materials	Conversion Costs
(Step 3) Cost added during February	$50,600	$32,000	$18,600
Divided by equivalent units of work done in current period (Exhibit 17–1)		÷ 400	÷ 310
Cost per equivalent unit		$ 80	$ 60
(Step 4) Total costs to account for	$50,600		
(Step 5) Assignment of costs:			
Completed and transferred out (175 units)	$24,500	$175^* × 80 + 175^* × 60	
Work in process ending (225 units):			
Direct materials	18,000	$225^† × 80	
Conversion costs	8,100		$135^† × 60
Total work in process	26,100		
Total cost account for	$50,600		

*Equivalent units completed and transferred out from Exhibit 17–1, Step 2.
†Equivalent units in work in process, ending from Exhibit 17–1, Step 2.

consist of the costs added during February: direct materials, $32,000 and conversion costs, $18,600, for a total of $50,600.

Step 5 in Exhibit 17-2 assigns these costs to units completed and transferred out and to units in ending inventory. For example, the 225 physical units in work in process are completely processed with respect to direct materials. Therefore, direct materials costs are 225 equivalent units times $80, which equals $18,000. In contrast, the 225 physical units are 60% complete with respect to conversion costs. Therefore, the conversion costs are 135 equivalent units (60% of 225 physical units) times $60, which equals $8,100. The total cost of ending work in process equals $26,100 ($18,000 + $8,100).

Journal Entries

Process costing journal entries are basically like those made in the job-costing system. That is, direct materials and conversion costs are accounted for as in job-costing systems. The main difference is that, in process costing, there is often more than one work-in-process account—in our example, Work in Process—Assembly and Work in Process—Testing. Global Defence purchases direct materials as needed. These materials are delivered directly to the Assembly Department. Using dollar amounts from Exhibit 17-2, summary journal entries for the month of February at Global Defence, Inc. are:

OBJECTIVE 4

Prepare journal entries for process-costing systems

1. Work in Process—Assembly	32,000	
Accounts Payable		32,000
To record direct materials purchased and		
used in production during February.		
2. Work in Process—Assembly	18,600	
[Various accounts]		18,600
To record Assembly Department conversion costs		
for February; examples include energy,		
manufacturing supplies, all manufacturing		
labour, and plant amortization.		
3. Work in Process—Testing	24,500	
Work in Process—Assembly		24,500
To record cost of goods completed and transferred from		
Assembly to Testing during February.		

Exhibit 17-3 shows a general sketch of the flow of costs through the T-accounts. The key T-account, Work in Process—Assembly, shows an ending balance of $26,100.

EXHIBIT 17-3
Flow of Costs in a Process-Costing System, Assembly Department of Global Defence, Inc., for February 2000

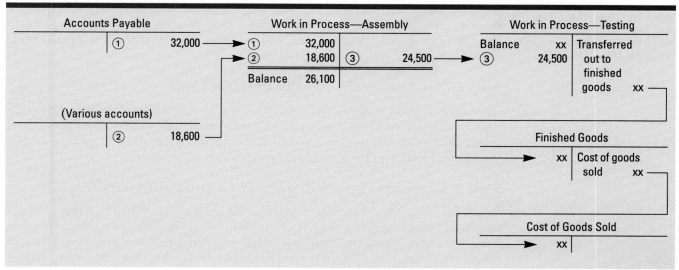

CASE 3: PROCESS COSTING WITH BOTH BEGINNING AND ENDING WORK-IN-PROCESS INVENTORY

At the beginning of March 2000, Global Defence had 225 partially assembled DG-19 units in the Assembly Department. During March 2000, Global Defence placed another 275 units into production. Data for the Assembly Department for March 2000 are:

Physical Units for March 2000

Work in process, beginning inventory (March 1)	225 units
Direct materials (100% complete)	
Conversion costs (60% complete)	
Started during March	275 units
Completed and transferred out during March	400 units
Work in process, ending inventory (March 31)	100 units
Direct materials (100% complete)	
Conversion costs (50% complete)	

Total Costs for March 2000

Work in process, beginning inventory:		
Direct materials	$18,000	
Conversion costs	8,100	$26,100
Direct materials costs added during March		19,800
Conversion costs added during March		16,380
Total costs to account for		$62,280

We now have incomplete units in both beginning and ending work-in-process inventory to account for. Our goal is to use the five steps we described earlier to calculate (1) the cost of units completed and transferred out, and (2) the cost of ending work in process. To assign costs to each of these categories, however, we need to specify assumptions regarding the flow of costs. We next describe the five-step approach to process costing using two alternative cost-flow assumptions–the weighted-average method and the first-in, first-out method. The different assumptions will produce different numbers of cost of units completed and for ending work in process.

WEIGHTED-AVERAGE METHOD

Weighted-average process-costing method. Method of process costing that assigns the average equivalent unit cost of all work done to date (regardless of when it was done) to equivalent units completed and transferred out, and to equivalent units in ending inventory.

The **weighted-average process-costing method** calculates the average equivalent unit cost of the work done to date (regardless of the period in which it was done) and assigns it to equivalent units completed and transferred out and to equivalent units in ending work-in-process inventory. The weighted-average cost is the total of all costs entering the Work in Process account (regardless of whether it is from beginning work in process or from work started during the period) divided by total equivalent units of work done to date. We now describe the five-step procedure introduced in Case 2 using the weighted-average method.

Step 1: Summarize the Flow of Physical Units

The physical units column of Exhibit 17-4 shows where the units came from–225 units from beginning inventory and 275 units started during the current period, and where they went–400 units completed and transferred out and 100 units in ending inventory. These data for March were given above on this page.

Step 2: Compute Output in Terms of Equivalent Units

As we saw in Case 2, even partially assembled units are complete in terms of direct materials because direct materials are introduced at the beginning of the process. For conversion costs, the fully assembled physical units transferred out are, of course, fully completed. The Assembly Department supervisor estimates the partially assembled physical units in March 31 work in process to be 50% complete (on average).

The equivalent units columns in Exhibit 17-4 show the equivalent units of work done to date–equivalent units completed and transferred out and equivalent units in ending work in process (500 equivalent units of direct materials and 450 equivalent units of conversion costs). Notice that the equivalent units of work done to date *also* equal the sum of the equivalent units in beginning inventory (work done in the previous period) and the equivalent units of work done in the current period, because

$$
\begin{array}{c}
\text{Equivalent units} \\
\text{in beginning} \\
\text{work in process}
\end{array}
+
\begin{array}{c}
\text{Equivalent units} \\
\text{of work done in} \\
\text{current period}
\end{array}
=
\begin{array}{c}
\text{Equivalent units completed} \\
\text{and transferred out} \\
\text{in current period}
\end{array}
+
\begin{array}{c}
\text{Equivalent} \\
\text{units in ending} \\
\text{work in process}
\end{array}
$$

The equivalent unit calculation in the weighted-average method is only concerned with total equivalent units of *work done to date* regardless of (a) whether the work was done during the preceding period and is part of beginning work in process or (b) whether it was done during the current period. That is, the weighted-average method *merges* equivalent units in beginning inventory (work done before March) with equivalent units of work done in the current period. Thus, the stage of completion of the current period beginning work in process is *irrelevant* and *not* used in the computation.

Step 3: Compute Equivalent Unit Costs

Exhibit 17-5, step 3 shows the computation of equivalent unit costs separately for direct materials and conversion costs. The weighted-average cost per equivalent unit is obtained by dividing the sum of costs for beginning work in process and costs for work done in the current period by total equivalent units of work done to date. When calculating the weighted-average conversion cost per equivalent unit in Exhibit 17-5, for example, we divide total conversion costs, $24,480 (beginning work in process, $8,100, plus work done in current period, $16,380) by total equivalent units, 450 (equivalent units of conversion costs in beginning work in process and in work done in current period), to get a weighted-average cost of $54.40.

Step 4: Summarize Total Costs to Account For

The total costs to account for in March 2000 are described in the example data: beginning work in process, $26,100 (direct materials, $18,000 and conversion costs,

EXHIBIT 17-4
Steps 1 and 2: Summarize Output in Physical Units and Compute Equivalent Units
Weighted-Average Method of Process Costing, Assembly Department of Global Defence Inc.
for March 2000

Flow of Production	(Step 1) Physical Units	(Step 2) Equivalent Units	
		Direct Materials	Conversion Costs
Work in process, beginning	225		
Started during current period	275		
To account for	500		
Completed and transferred out during current period	400	400	400
Work in process, ending*	100		
100 × 100%; 100 × 50%		100	50
Accounted for	500		
Work done to date		500	450

*Degree of completion in this department: direct materials, 100%; conversion costs, 50%.

EXHIBIT 17-5

Steps 3, 4, and 5: Compute Equivalent Unit Costs, Summarize Total Costs to Account For, and Assign Costs to Units Completed and to Units in Ending Work in Process
Weighted-Average Method of Process Costing, Assembly Department of Global Defence Inc. for March 2000

	Total Production Costs	Direct Materials	Conversion Costs
(Step 3) Work in process, beginning (given, p. 598)	$26,100	$18,000	$8,100
Costs added in current period (given, p. 598)	36,180	19,800	16,380
Costs incurred to date		$37,800	$24,480
Divide by equivalent units of work done to date (Exhibit 17-4)		÷ 500	÷ 450
Cost per equivalent unit of work done to date		$ 75.60	$ 54.40
(Step 4) Total costs to account for	$62,280		
(Step 5) Assignment of costs:			
Completed and transferred out (400 units)	52,000	400* × $75.60 + 400* × $54.40	
Work in process ending (100 units):			
Direct materials	7,560	100† × $75.60	
Conversion costs	2,720		50† × $54.40
Total work in process	10,280		
Total costs accounted for	$62,280		

*Equivalent units completed and transferred out from Exhibit 17-4, Step 2.
†Equivalent units in work in process, ending from Exhibit 17-4, Step 2.

$8,100) plus $36,180 (direct material costs added during March $19,800 and conversion costs, $16,380). The total of these costs is $62,280.

Step 5: Assign Costs to Units Completed and to Units in Ending Work in Process

The key point in this step is to cost all work done to date: (1) the cost of units completed and transferred out, and (2) the cost of ending work in process. Step 5 in Exhibit 17-5 takes the equivalent units completed and transferred out and equivalent units in ending work in process calculated in Exhibit 17-4, Step 2, and attaches dollar amounts to them. These dollar amounts are the weighted-average costs per equivalent unit for direct materials and conversion costs calculated in Step 3. For example, note that the total cost of the 100 physical units in ending work in process consists of

Direct materials:
    100 equivalent units × weighted-average cost per equivalent unit of $75.60 $7,560
Conversion costs:
    50 equivalent units × weighted-average cost per equivalent unit of $54.40   2,720
    Total costs of ending work in process $10,280

The following table summarized the total costs to account for and the $62,280 accounted for in Exhibit 17-5. The arrows indicate that costs of units completed and transferred out and in ending work in process are calculated using average total costs obtained after merging costs of beginning work in process and costs added in the current period.

Costs to Account For		Costs Accounted For Calculated at Weighted-Average Cost	
Beginning work in process	$26,100	Completed and transferred out	$52,000
Costs added in current period	36,180	Ending work in process	10,280
Total costs to account for	$62,280	Total costs accounted for	$62,280

Before proceeding, please pause and review Exhibits 17-4 and 17-5 carefully to check your understanding of the weighted-average method. Note that Exhibit 17-4 deals only with physical and equivalent units but not costs. Exhibit 17-5 shows the cost amounts.

Using dollar amounts from Exhibit 17-5, summary journal entries for the month of March at Global Defence, Inc. are:

1.	Work in Process—Assembly	19,800	
	Accounts Payable		19,800
	To record direct materials purchased and used in production during March.		
2.	Work in Process—Assembly	16,380	
	[Various accounts]		16,380
	To record Assembly Department conversion costs for March; examples include energy, manufacturing supplies, all manufacturing labour, and plant amortization.		
3.	Work in Process—Testing	52,000	
	Work in Process—Assembly		52,000
	To record cost of goods completed and transferred from Assembly to Testing during March.		

The key T-account, Work in Process—Assembly, would show the following:

Work in Process—Assembly

Beginning inventory, March 1	26,100	③	Transferred out to Work in	
① Direct materials	19,800		Process—Testing	52,000
② Conversion costs	16,380			
Ending inventory, March 31	10,280			

FIRST-IN, FIRST-OUT METHOD

In contrast to the weighted-average method, the **first-in, first-out (FIFO) process-costing method** assigns the cost of the prior accounting period's equivalent units in beginning work-in-process inventory to the first units completed and transferred out, and assigns the cost of equivalent units worked on during the current period first to complete beginning inventory, then to start and complete new units and finally to units in ending work-in-process inventory. This method assumes that the earliest equivalent units in the Work in Process-Assembly account are completed first.

A distinctive feature of the FIFO process costing method is that work done on beginning inventory before the current period is kept separate from work done in the current period. Costs incurred in the current period and units produced in the current period are used to calculate costs per equivalent unit of work done in the current period. In contrast, equivalent-unit and cost-per-equivalent-unit calculations in the weighted average method merge the units and costs in beginning inventory with units and costs of work done in the current period.

We now describe the five-step procedure introduced in Case 2 using the FIFO method.

OBJECTIVE 6

Demonstrate the first-in, first-out (FIFO) method of process costing

First-in, first-out (FIFO) process-costing method. Method of process costing that assigns the cost of the earliest equivalent units available (starting with the equivalent units in beginning work-in-process inventory) to units completed and transferred out, and the cost of the most recent equivalent units worked on during the period to ending work-in-process inventory.

Step 1: Summarize the Flow of Physical Units

Exhibit 17-6, Step 1 traces the flow of physical units of production. The following observations help explain the physical units calculations.

◆ The first physical units assumed to be completed and transferred out during the period are the 225 units from the beginning work-in-process inventory.

Of the 275 physical units started, 175 are assumed to be completed. Recall from the March data given on p. 598 that 400 physical units were completed during March. The FIFO method assumes that the first 225 of these units were from beginning inventory; thus 175 physical units (400–225) must have been started and completed during March.

EXHIBIT 17-6
Steps 1 and 2: Summarize Output in Physical Units and Compute Equivalent Units
FIFO Method of Process Costing, Assembly Department of Global Defence Inc. for March 2000

Flow of Production	(Step 1) Physical Units	(Step 2) Equivalent Units Direct Materials	Conversion Costs
Work in process, beginning	225	(work done before current period)	
Started during current period	275		
To account for	500		
Completed and transferred out during current period:			
From beginning work in process§	225		
225 × (100% − 100%); 225 × (100% − 60%)		0	90
Started and completed	175†		
175 × 100%, 175 × 100%		175	175
Work in process, ending*	100		
100 × 100%; 100 × 50%		100	50
Accounted for	500		
Work done in current period only		275	315

§Degree of completion in this department: direct materials, 100%; conversion costs, 60%.

†400 physical units completed and transferred out minus 225 physical units completed and transferred out from beginning work-in-process inventory.

*Degree of completion in this department: direct materials, 100%; conversion costs, 50%.

◆ Ending work-in-process inventory consists of 100 physical units—the 275 physical units started minus the 175 of these physical units completed.

◆ Note that the physical units "to account for" equal the physical units "accounted for" (500 units).

Step 2: Compute Output in Terms of Equivalent Units

Exhibit 17-6 also presents the computations for Step 2 under the FIFO method. *The equivalent unit calculations focus on the equivalent units of work done in the current period (March) only.*

Under the FIFO method, the work done in the current period is assumed to first complete the 225 units in beginning work in process. The equivalent units of work done in March on the beginning work-in-process inventory are computed by multiplying the 225 physical units *by the percentage of work remaining to be done to complete these units:* 0% for direct materials, because the beginning work in process is 100% complete with respect to direct materials, and 40% for conversion costs, because the beginning work in process is 60% complete with respect to conversion costs. The results are 0 (0% × 225) equivalent units of work for direct materials and 90 (40% × 225) equivalent units of work for conversion costs.

Next, the work done in the current period is assumed to start and complete the next 175 units. The equivalent units of work done on the 175 physical units started and completed are computed by multiplying 175 units by 100% for both direct materials and conversion costs, because all work on these units is done in the current period.

Finally, the work done in the current period is assumed to start but leave incomplete the final 100 units as ending work in process. The equivalent units of work done on the 100 units of ending work in process are calculated by multiplying 100 physical units by 100% for direct materials (because all direct materials have been added for these units in the current period) and 50% for conversion costs (because 50% of conversion costs work has been done on these units in the current period).

Step 3: Compute Equivalent Unit Costs

Exhibit 17-7 shows the Step 3 computation of equivalent units costs *for work done in the current period only* for direct materials and conversion costs. For example, we divide current period conversion costs of $16,380 by current period equivalent units for conversion costs of 315 to obtain cost per equivalent unit of $52.

Step 4: Summarize Total Costs to Account For

The total production costs column in Exhibit 17-7 presents Step 4 and summarizes the total costs to account for in March 2001 (beginning work in process and costs added in the current period) of $62,280, as described in the example data (p. 598).

Step 5: Assign Costs to Units Completed and to Units in Ending Work in Process

Finally, Exhibit 17-7 shows the Step 5 assignment of costs under the FIFO method. The costs of work done in the current period are first assigned to the additional work done to complete the beginning work in process, then to the work done on units started and completed during the current period, and finally to the ending work in process. The easiest way to follow Step 5 is to take each of the equivalent units calculated in Exhibit 17-6, step 2, and attach dollar amounts to them (using the cost per equivalent unit calculations in step 3). The goal is to determine the total cost of all units completed from beginning inventory and from work started and completed in the current period, and the costs of ending work in process done in the current period.

EXHIBIT 17-7

Steps 3, 4, and 5: Compute Equivalent Unit Costs, Summarize Total Costs to Account For, and Assign Costs to Units Completed and to Units in Ending Work in Process

FIFO Method of Process Costing, Assembly Department of Global Defence Inc. for March 2000

	Total Production Costs	Direct Materials	Conversion Costs
Work in process, beginning	$26,100	(costs of work done before current period)	
(Step 3) Costs added in current period	36,180	$19,800	$16,380
Divide by equivalent units of work done in current period (Exhibit 17-6)		÷ 275	÷ 315
Cost per equivalent unit of work done in current period		$ 72	$ 52
(Step 4) Total costs to account for	$62,280		
(Step 5) Assignment of costs:			
Completed and transferred out (400 units):			
Work in process, beginning (225 units)	$26,100		
Direct materials added in current period	0	0* × $72	
Conversion costs added in current period	4,680		90* × $52
Total from beginning inventory	30,780		
Started and completed (175 units)	21,700	175† × $72 + 175† × $52	
Total costs of units completed and transferred out	52,480		
Work in process, ending (100 units)			
Direct materials	7,200	100# × $72	
Conversion costs	2,600		50# × $52
Total work in process, ending	9,800		
Total costs accounted for	$62,280		

*Equivalent units used to complete beginning work in process from Exhibit 17-6, Step 2.
†Equivalent units started and completed from Exhibit 17-6, Step 2.
#Equivalent units in work in process, ending from Exhibit 17-6, Step 2.

Notice that the 400 completed units are of two types: 225 units come from beginning inventory, and 175 units are started and completed during March. The FIFO method starts by assigning the costs of the beginning work-in-process inventory of $26,100 to the first units completed and transferred out. This $26,100 is the cost of the 225 equivalent units of direct materials and 135 equivalent units of conversion costs that comprise beginning inventory. The work that generated these costs was done in February, so these units are costed (see data on p. 598) at the February prices of $80 for direct materials and $60 for conversion costs ($225 \times \$80 + 135 \times \$60 = \$26,100$). As we saw in Step 2, an additional 90 equivalent units of conversion costs are needed to complete these units in the current period. The current period conversion costs per equivalent unit is $52, so $4,680 ($90 \times \$52$) of additional costs are needed to complete the beginning inventory. The total production cost for the units in beginning inventory is $26,100 + $4,680 = $30,780. The 175 units started and completed in the current period consist of 175 equivalent units of direct materials and 175 equivalent units of conversion costs. These units are costed at the cost per equivalent unit in the current period (direct materials, $72 and conversion costs, $52) for a total production cost of $21,700.

Under FIFO, the ending work-in-process inventory comes from units that were started but not fully completed during the current period. The total cost of the 100 partially assembled physical units in ending work in process consists of

Direct materials:	
100 equivalent units × cost per equivalent unit in March of $72	$7,200
Conversion costs:	
50 equivalent units × cost per equivalent unit in March of $52	2,600
Total costs of work in process on March 31	$9,800

The following table summarizes the total costs to account for and the costs accounted for of $62,280 in Exhibit 17-7. Notice how under the FIFO method, the layers of beginning work in process and costs added in the current period are kept separate. The arrows indicate where the costs in each layer go (that is, to units completed and transferred out or to ending work in process). Be sure to include the costs of beginning work in process ($26,100) when calculating the costs of units completed from beginning inventory.

Costs to Account For		Costs Accounted For Calculated on a FIFO Basis	
Beginning work in process		Completed and transferred out:	
Costs added in current period	$26,100	Beginning work in process	$26,100
	36,180	Used to complete beginning work in process	4,680
		Started and completed	21,700
		Completed and transferred out	52,480
		Ending work in process	9,800
Total costs to account for	$62,280	Total costs accounted for	$62,280

Before proceeding, please pause and review Exhibits 17-6 and 17-7 carefully to check your understanding of the FIFO method. Note that Exhibit 17-6 deals only with physical and equivalent units but no costs. Exhibit 17-7 shows the cost amounts.

The journal entries under the FIFO method parallel the journal entries under the weighted-average method. The only difference is that the entry to record the cost of goods completed and transferred out would be for $52,480 under the FIFO method instead of for $52,000 under the weighted-average method.

Only rarely is an application of pure FIFO ever encountered in process costing. As a result it should really be called a *modified* or *departmental* FIFO method. Why? Because FIFO is applied within a department to compile the cost of units transferred *out*, but the units transferred *in* during a given period usually are carried at a single average unit cost as a matter of convenience. For example, the average cost of units transferred out of the Assembly Department is $52,480 ÷ 400 units = $131.20 per

DG-19 unit. The Assembly Department uses FIFO to distinguish between monthly batches of production. The succeeding department, Testing, however, costs these units (that consist of costs incurred in February and March) at one average unit cost ($131.20 in this illustration). If this averaging were not done, the attempt to track costs on a pure FIFO basis throughout a series of processes would be unduly cumbersome.

COMPARISON OF WEIGHTED-AVERAGE AND FIFO METHOD

The following table summarizes the costs assigned to units completed and those still in process under the weighted-average and FIFO process-costing methods for our example:

	Weighted Average (from Exhibit 17-5)	FIFO (from Exhibit 17-7)	Difference
Cost of units completed and transferred out	$52,000	$52,480	+$480
Work in process, ending	10,280	9,800	−$480
Total costs accounted for	$62,280	$62,280	

The weighted-average ending inventory is higher than the FIFO ending inventory by $480, or 4.9% ($480 ÷ $9,800). This is a significant difference when aggregated over the many thousands of components that Global Defence makes. The weighted-average method in our example also results in lower cost of goods sold and hence higher operating income and higher tax payments than the FIFO method. Differences in equivalent unit costs of beginning inventory and work done during the current period account for the differences in weighted-average and FIFO costs. Recall that the cost per equivalent unit of beginning work in process was greater than the cost per equivalent unit of work done during the period.

For the Assembly Department, FIFO assumes that all the higher-cost prior-period units in beginning work in process are the first to be completed and transferred out while ending work in process consists of only the lower-cost current-period units. The weighted-average method, however, smoothes out cost per equivalent unit by assuming that more of the lower-cost units are completed and transferred out, while some of the higher-cost units are placed in ending work in process. Hence, in this example, the weighted-average method results in a lower cost of units completed and transferred out and a higher ending work-in-process inventory relative to FIFO.

Unit costs can differ materially between the weighted-average and FIFO methods when (1) the direct materials or conversion costs per unit vary from period to period and (2) the physical inventory levels of work in process are large in relation to the total number of units transferred out.

Managers need feedback about their most recent performance (March in this illustration) in order to plan and improve their future performance. A major advantage of FIFO is that it gives managers information from which they can judge their performance in the current period independently from that in the preceding period. Work done during the current period is vital information for these planning and control purposes.

STANDARD COSTS AND PROCESS COSTING

This section assumes that you have already studied Chapters 7 and 8. If you have not, proceed to the next major section, Transferred-In Costs in Process Costing.

As we have mentioned, companies that use process-costing systems produce numerous like or similar units of output. Setting standard quantities for inputs is often relatively straightforward in such companies. Standard costs per input unit may then be assigned to the physical standards to develop standard costs.

OBJECTIVE 7

Incorporate standard costs into a process-costing system

Weighted-average and FIFO methods become very complicated when used in industries that produce a variety of products. For example, a steel rolling mill uses various steel alloys and produces sheets of various sizes and of various finishes. The items of direct materials are not numerous; neither are the operations performed. But used in various combinations, they yield so great a variety of products that inaccurate costs for each product result if the broad averaging procedure of historical process costing is used. Similarly complex conditions are frequently found, for example, in plants that manufacture rubber products, textiles, ceramics, paints, and packaged food products. As we shall see, standard costing is especially useful in these situations. The intricacies of weighted-average and FIFO historical costing methods and the conflicts between them are also eliminated by using standard costs.

Computations Under Standard Costing

We again use the Assembly Department of Global Defence, Inc. as an example, except this time we assign standard costs to the process. The same standard costs apply in February and March of 2000:

Direct materials	$ 74 per unit
Conversion costs	54 per unit
Total standard manufacturing costs	$128 per unit

Data for the Assembly Department are:

Physical Units for March 2000

Work in process, beginning inventory (March 1)	225 units
Direct materials (100% complete)	
Conversion costs (60% complete)	
Started during March	275 units
Completed and transferred out during March	400 units
Work in process, ending inventory (March 31)	100 units
Direct materials (100% complete)	
Conversion costs (50% complete)	

Total Costs for March 2000

Work in process, beginning inventory at standard costs:		
Direct materials: 225 equivalent units × $74 per unit	$16,650	
Conversion costs: 135 equivalent units × $54 per unit	7,290	$23,940
Actual direct materials costs added during March		19,800
Actual conversion costs added during March		16,380

We follow the five steps introduced earlier. Exhibit 17-8 presents steps 1 and 2. Steps 1 and 2 for standard costing are identical to the steps described for the weighted-average and FIFO methods in Exhibit 17-6. Work done in the current period equals direct materials, 275 equivalent units, and conversion costs, 315 equivalent units.

Exhibit 17-9 shows the step 3 computation of equivalent units. Step 3 is easier under standard costing than under the weighted-average and FIFO methods. Why? Because the cost per equivalent unit does not have to be computed, as was done for the weighted-average and FIFO methods. Instead, the costs per equivalent unit are the standard costs: direct materials, $74, and conversion costs, $54. Using standard costs simplifies the computations for assigning total costs to account for, costs completed and transferred out, and ending work-in-process inventory.

Exhibit 17-9 summarizes the total costs to account for step 4, that is, the total debits in Work in Process. The debits differ from the debits to Work in Process—Assembly under the actual cost-based weighted-average and FIFO methods explained earlier in the chapter. Why? Because *in standard-costing systems* the debits to the Work in Process account are at standard costs rather than actual costs. These standard costs total $61,300.

Exhibit 17-9 assigns total costs to units completed and to units in ending work-in-process inventory (step 5). All equivalent units are costed at standard costs. Note

EXHIBIT 17-8

Steps 1 and 2: Summarize Output in Physical Units and Compute Equivalent Units
Use of Standard Costs in Process Costing, Assembly Department of Global Defence Inc. for March 2000

	(Step 1)	(Step 2) Equivalent Units	
Flow of Production	Physical Units	Direct Materials	Conversion Costs
Work in process, beginning	225		
Started during current period	275		
To account for	500		
Completed and transferred out during current period:			
From beginning work in process§			
225 × (100% – 100%); 225 × (100% – 60%)	225	0	90
Started and completed	175$^\#$		
175 × 100%, 175 × 100%		175	175
Work in process, ending*	100		
100 × 100%; 100 × 50%		100	50
Accounted for	500		
Work done in current period only		275	315

§Degree of completion in this department: direct materials, 100%; conversions, 60%.

$^\#$400 physical units completed and transferred out minus 225 physical units completed and transferred out from beginning work-in-process inventory.

*Degree of completion in this department: direct materials, 100%; conversion costs, 50%.

how the total costs accounted for in step 5 of Exhibit 17-9, $61,300, equal the total costs to account for.

Accounting for Variances

Process-costing systems using standard costs usually accumulate actual costs separately from the inventory accounts. The following is an example. The actual data are recorded in the first two entries. Recall that Global Defence purchases direct materials as needed and that these materials are delivered directly to the Assembly Department. The total variances are recorded in the next two entries. The final entry transfers out the completed goods at standard costs.

1. Assembly Department Direct Materials Control (at actual)   19,800
       Accounts Payable   19,800
   To record direct materials purchased and used in production during March.
       This cost control account is debited with actual costs and credited later
       with standard costs assigned to the units worked on.

2. Assembly Department Conversion Costs Control (at actual)   16,380
       [Various accounts]   16,380
   To record Assembly Department conversion costs for March.

(*Entries 3, 4, and 5 use standard cost dollar amounts from Exhibit 17-9:*)

3. Work in Process—Assembly (at standard costs)   20,350
       Direct Materials Variances   550
       Assembly Department Direct Materials Control   19,800
   To record actual direct materials used and total direct materials variances.

4. Work in Process—Assembly (at standard costs)   17,010
       Conversion Costs Variances   630
       Assembly Department Conversion Costs Control   16,380
   To record actual conversion costs and total conversion costs variances.

5. Work in Process—Testing (at standard costs)   51,200
       Work in Process—Assembly (at standard costs)   51,200
   To record cost of units completed and transferred
       at standard cost from Assembly to Testing.

EXHIBIT 17-9

Steps 3, 4 and 5: Compute Equivalent Unit Costs, Summarize Total Costs to Account For, and Assign Costs to Units Completed and to Units in Ending Work in Process

Use of Standard Costs in Process Costing, Assembly Department of Global Defence Inc. for March 2000

	Total Production Costs	Direct Materials	Conversion Costs
(Step 3) Standard cost per equivalent unit		$ 74	$ 54
Work in process, beginning			
Direct materials, 225 × $74; Conversion costs, 135 × $54	$23,940		
Costs added in current period at standard costs	———		
Direct materials, 275 × $74; Conversion costs, 315 × $54	37,360	20,350	17,010
(Step 4) Costs to account for	$61,300		
(Step 5) Assignment of costs at standard costs:			
Completed and transferred out (400 units):			
Work in process, beginning (225 units)	$23,940		
Direct materials added in current period	0	0* × $74	
Conversion costs added in current period	4,860		90* × $54
Total from beginning inventory	28,800		
Started and completed (175 units)	22,400	175† × $74 + 175† × $54	
Total costs of units transferred out	51,200		
Work in process, ending (100 units)			
Direct materials	7,400	100# × $74	
Conversion costs	2,700		50# × $54
Total work in process, ending	10,100		
Total costs accounted for	$61,300		
Summary of variances for current performance			
Costs added in current period at standard prices (see step 3 above)		$20,350	$17,010
Actual costs incurred		19,800	16,380
Variance		$ 550 F	$ 630 F

*Equivalent units to complete beginning work in process from Exhibit 17-8, Step 2.
†Equivalent units started and completed from Exhibit 17-8, Step 2.
#Equivalent units in work in process, ending from Exhibit 17-8, Step 2.

Variances arise under the standard-costing method, as in entries 3 and 4 above, because the standard costs assigned to products on the basis of work done in the current period do not usually equal the actual costs incurred in the current period. Variances can be measured and analyzed in little or great detail for feedback, control, and decision-making purposes, in the same manner as described in Chapters 7 and 8. Exhibit 17-10 on p. 609 shows how the costs flow through the accounts.

TRANSFERRED-IN COSTS IN PROCESS COSTING

OBJECTIVE 8

Apply process costing to cases with transferred-in costs

Many process-costing systems have two or more departments or processes in the production cycle. Ordinarily, as units move from department to department, related costs are also transferred by monthly journal entries. If standard costs are used, the accounting for such transfers is relatively simple. However, if weighted average or FIFO is used, the accounting can become more complex. To illustrate, we now extend our Global Defence, Inc. example to encompass the Testing Department.

Recall that the Assembly Department of Global Defence transfers DG-19 units to its Testing Department. Here the units receive additional direct materials, such as crating and other packing materials to prepare the units for shipment, at the *end* of the process. Conversion costs are added evenly during the Testing Depart-

EXHIBIT 17-10
Flow of Standard Costs in a Process-Costing System, Assembly Department of Global Defence, Inc., for March 2000

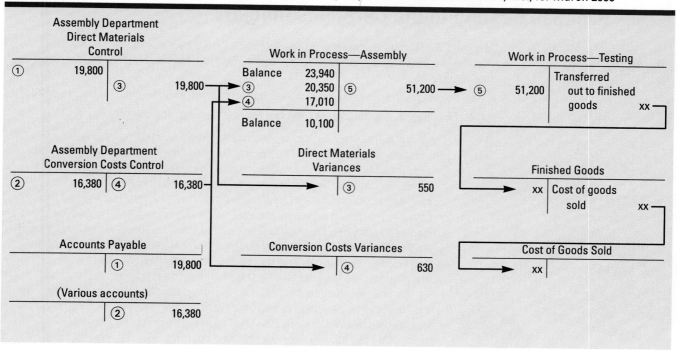

ment's process. As the process in Assembly is completed, units are immediately transferred to Testing; as units are completed in Testing, they are immediately transferred to Finished Goods.

The following graphic summarizes these facts:

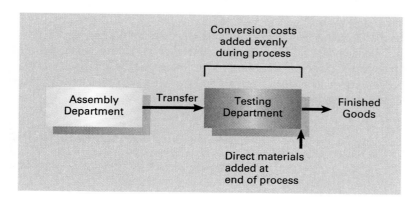

Data for the Testing Department for the month of March 2000 are:

Physical Units for March 2000

Work in process, beginning inventory (March 1)	240 units
Transferred-in costs (100% complete)	
Direct materials (0% complete)	
Conversion costs (⅝ or 62.5% complete)	
Transferred in during March	400 units
Completed during March	440 units
Work in process, ending inventory (March 31)	200 units
Transferred-in costs (100% complete)	
Direct materials (0% complete)	
Conversion costs (80% complete)	

Process Costing in the Ceramics Industry

Ceramics, Inc. produces ceramic products (such as multilayer packages for integrated circuits) in a batch-flow manufacturing process. Forming and finishing are the two major production stages.

◆ **Forming.** Ceramic material is mixed, forced through an extruder, and sent to a dryer.

◆ **Finishing.** The products are fired in a kiln, cut, ground, and packaged.

For many years Ceramics, Inc. has manufactured like or similar products in large production runs for industrial customers (termed "original equipment manufacturers," or OEMs) such as computer companies and defence companies.

Ceramics, Inc. costs individual products using standard costs in a process-costing system. Cost data are accumulated and tracked for the forming and finishing operations. Conversion costs are allocated to departments using standard (scheduled) hours of production time in each department. Amortization on plant and equipment is included in this conversion cost. The controller at Ceramics believes that this system "accurately measures the cost of manufacturing OEM products." These products are manufactured in large batches in a highly standardized way.

Ceramics, Inc. recently added a "custom production line" at its plant. This line manufactures ceramic products that vary greatly in production volume and frequently are tailored to each individual customer's needs. For example, custom-designed nozzles used for pollution control are being manufactured for one customer who needs to rid its flue gas of sulfur.

The controller is skeptical about the accuracy of product costs for these custom products based on the existing process-costing system. She believes that the costs of these products are driven by more variables than standard hours in production at each department. For example, many custom jobs require specialized finishing steps that are undertaken in a job shop adjoining the main production area. Currently she is keeping a separate, largely manual job-costing system that uses some data from the main system and some separately maintained cost data.

The controller is now exploring ways to adapt the formal process-costing system to incorporate some elements of a job-costing system. Her point is that custom jobs put different demands on the resources of Ceramics, Inc. than does the average large production run job. For these custom jobs, a hybrid-costing system with elements of both process costing and job costing may be appropriate.

Source: Adapted from U. Karmarkar, P. Lederer, and J. Zimmerman, "Choosing Manufacturing Production Control and Cost Accounting Systems," in R. Kaplan, *Measures For Manufacturing Excellence* (Boston, Mass.: Harvard Business School Press, 1990). Ceramics, Inc. is a fictitious name for the actual company.

Costs of Testing Department for March 2000

Work in process, beginning inventory[1]		
Transferred-in costs	$33,600	
Direct materials	0	
Conversion costs	18,000	$51,600
Transferred in during March		
Weighted average (from Exhibit 17-7)		52,000
FIFO (from Exhibit 17-8)		52,480
Direct materials costs added during March		13,200
Conversion costs added during March		48,600

[1]The work-in-process beginning inventory is the same under both the weighted-average and the FIFO inventory method because we assumed costs per equivalent unit to be the same in both January and February. If the cost per equivalent unit had been different in February compared to January, the work-in-process inventory at the end of February (beginning of March) would be costed differently under the weighted-average and FIFO methods. If this were the case, the basic approach to process costing with transferred-in costs would still be the same as what we describe in this section. Only the beginning balances of work in process would be different.

EXHIBIT 17-11

Steps 1 and 2: Summarize Output in Physical Units and Compute Equivalent
Units Weighted-Average Method of Process Costing, Testing Department of Global Defence Inc. for March 2000

Flow of Production	(Step 1) Physical Units	(Step 2) Equivalent Units		
		Transferred in Costs	Direct Materials	Conversion Costs
Work in process, beginning	240			
Transferred in during current period	400			
To account for	640			
Completed and transferred out during current period	440	440	440	440
Work in process, ending*	200			
200 × 100%; 200 × 0%; 200 × 80%		200	0	160
Accounted for	640			
Work done to date		640	440	600

*Degree of completion in this department: transferred-in costs, 100%; direct materials, 0%; conversion costs, 80%.

Transferred-in costs (or **previous department costs**) are costs incurred in a previous department that are carried forward as part of the product's cost as it moves to a subsequent department for processing. That is, as the units move from one department to the next, their costs move with them. Thus, computations of Testing costs must include transferred-in costs, as well as any additional direct materials costs and conversion costs added in Testing.

Transferred-in costs are treated as if they are a separate direct material added at the beginning of the process. In other words, when successive departments are involved, transferred units from one department become all or a part of the direct materials of the next department; however, they are called transferred-in costs, not direct materials costs.

Transferred-in costs (previous department costs). Costs incurred in a previous department that are carried forward as part of the product's cost as it moves to a subsequent department for processing.

Transferred-In Costs and the Weighted Average Method

To examine the weighted-average process-costing method with transferred-in costs, we use the five-step procedure described earlier to assign costs of the Testing Department to units completed and transferred out and to units in ending work in process. Exhibit 17-11 above shows steps 1 and 2. The computations are basically the same as the calculations of equivalent units under the weighted-average method for the Assembly Department in Exhibit 17-4, except for the addition of transferred-in costs. The units are fully completed as to transferred-in costs because these costs are simply carried forward from the previous process. Note, however, that direct material costs have a zero degree of completion in both the beginning and ending work in process inventories because, in Testing, direct materials are introduced at the *end* of the process.

Exhibit 17-12 describes steps 3, 4, and 5 for the weighted-average method. Note that beginning work in process and work done in the current period are combined for purposes of computing equivalent unit costs for transferred-in costs, direct materials, and conversion costs.

Using the dollar amount from Exhibit 17-12, the journal entry for the transfer out of Testing to finished goods inventory is:

Finished Goods	120,890	
Work in Process—Testing		120,890
To transfer units to finished goods.		

Entries to the key T-account, Work in Process—Testing follow, using information from Exhibit 17-13.

EXHIBIT 17-12
Steps 3, 4, and 5: Compute Equivalent Unit Costs, Summarize Total Costs to Account For, and Assign Costs to Units Completed and to Units in Ending Work in Process
Weighted-Average Method of Process Costing, Testing Department of Global Defence Inc. for March 2000

	Total Production Costs	Transferred-in Costs	Direct Materials	Conversion Costs
(Step 3) Work in process, beginning	$ 51,600	$33,600	$ 0	$18,000
Costs added in current period	113,800	52,000	13,200	48,600
Costs incurred to date		$85,600	$13,200	$66,600
Divided by equivalent units of work done to date (Exhibit 17-11)		÷ 640	÷ 440	÷ 600
Equivalent unit costs of work done to date		$133.75	$ 30	$ 111
(Step 4) Total costs to account for	$165,400			
(Step 5) Assignment of costs:				
Completed and transferred out (440 units)	$120,890	440* × $133.75 + 400* × $30 + 400* × $111		
Work in process, ending (200 units)				
Transferred-in costs	26,750	200† × $133.75		
Direct materials	0		0† × $30	
Conversion costs	17,760			160† × $111
Total work in process	44,510			
Total costs accounted for	$165,400			

*Equivalent units completed and transferred out from Exhibit 17-11, Step 2.
†Equivalent units in work in process, ending from Exhibit 17-11, Step 2.

Work in Process—Testing			
Beginning inventory, March 1	51,600	Transferred out	120,890
Transferred-in costs	52,000		
Direct materials	13,200		
Conversion costs	48,600		
Ending inventory, March 31	44,510		

Transferred-In Costs and the FIFO Method

To examine the FIFO process-costing process-costing method with transferred-in costs, we again use the five-step procedure. Exhibit 17-13 shows steps 1 and 2. Other than considering transferred-in costs, the computations of equivalent units are basically the same as those under the FIFO method for the Assembly Department shown in Exhibit 17-6.

Exhibit 17-14 describes steps 3, 4 and 5. Note that the costs per equivalent unit for the current period in step 3 are only calculated on the basis of costs transferred in and work done in the current period. In steps 4 and 5, the total costs to account for and accounted for of $165,880 under the FIFO method differ from the corresponding amounts under the weighted-average method of $165,400. Why? Because of the different costs of completed units transferred in from the Assembly Department under the two methods ($52,480 under FIFO and $52,000 under weighted average).

Using the dollar amount from Exhibit 17-14, the journal entry for the transfer out to finished goods inventory is:

Finished Goods	122,360	
Work in Process—Testing		122,360
To transfer units to finished goods.		

EXHIBIT 17-13

Steps 1 and 2: Summarize Output in Physical Units and Compute Equivalent Units
FIFO Method of Process Costing
Testing Department of Global Defence Inc. for March 2000

Flow of Production	(Step 1) Physical Units	(Step 2) Equivalent Units Transferred-in Costs	Direct Materials	Conversion Costs
Work in process, beginning	240	(work done before current period)		
Transferred-in during current period	400			
To account for	640			
Completed and transferred out during current period:				
From beginning work in process$	240			
240 × (100% – 100%); 240 × (100% – 0%); 240 × (100% – 62.5%)		0	240	90
Started and completed	200†			
200 × 100%; 200 × 100%; 200 × 100%		200	200	200
Work in process, ending*	200			
200 × 100%; 200 × 0%; 200 × 80%		200	0	160
Accounted for	640			
Work done in current period only		400	440	450

$Degree of completion in this department. Transferred-in costs, 100%; direct materials, 0%; conversion costs, 62.5%

†440 physical units completed and transferred out minus 240 physical units completed and transferred out from beginning work-in process inventory.

*Degree of completion in this department: transferred-in costs, 100%; direct materials, 0%; conversion costs, 80%.

EXHIBIT 17-14

Steps 3, 4, and 5: Compute Equivalent Unit Costs, Summarize Total Costs to Account For, and Assign Costs to Units Completed and to Units in Ending Work in Process
FIFO Method of Process Costing, Testing Department of Global Defence Inc. for March 2000

		Total Production Costs	Transferred-in Costs	Direct Materials	Conversion Costs
	Work in process, beginning	$ 51,600	(Costs of work done before current period)		
(Step 3)	Costs added in current period	114,280	$52,480	$13,200	$48,600
	Divided by equivalent units of work done in current period (Exhibit 17-12)		÷ 400	÷ 440	÷ 450
	Cost per equiv. unit of work done in current period		$131.20	$ 30	$ 108
(Step 4)	Total costs to account for	$165,880			
(Step 5)	Assignment of costs:				
	Completed and transferred out (440 units):				
	Work in process, beginning (240 units)	$ 51,600			
	Transferred-in costs added in current period	0	0* × $131.20		
	Direct materials added in current period	7,200		240* × $30	
	Conversion costs added in current period	9,720			90* × $108
	Total from beginning inventory	68,520			
	Started and completed (200 units)	53,840	200† × $131.20 + 200† × $30 +200† × $108		
	Total costs of units completed and transferred out	122,360			
	Work in process, ending (200 units)				
	Transferred-in costs	26,240	200# × $131.20		
	Direct materials	0		0# × $30	
	Conversion costs	17,280			160# × $108
	Total work in process, ending	43,520			
	Total costs accounted for	$165,880			

*Equivalent units used to complete beginning work in process from Exhibit 17-13, Step 2.
†Equivalent units started and completed from Exhibit 17-13, Step 2.
#Equivalent units in work in process, ending from Exhibit 17-13, Step 2.

Entries to the key T-account, Work in Process—Testing follow, using information from Exhibit 17-14.

Work in Process—Testing			
Beginning inventory, March 1	51,600	Transferred out	120,890
Transferred-in costs	52,480		
Direct materials	13,200		
Conversion costs	48,600		
Ending inventory, March 31	43,520		

Remember that in a series of interdepartmental transfers, each department is regarded as being separate and distinct for accounting purposes. All costs transferred in during a given accounting period are carried at one unit cost figure regardless of whether previous departments used the weighted-average or the FIFO method.

Common Mistakes with Transferred-In Costs

Here are some common pitfalls to avoid when accounting for transferred-in costs:

1. Remember to include transferred-in costs from previous departments in your calculations.

2. In calculating costs to be transferred on a FIFO basis, do not overlook the costs assigned at the beginning of the period to units that were in process but are now included in the units transferred. For example, do not overlook the $51,600 in Exhibit 17-14.

3. Unit costs may fluctuate between periods. Therefore, transferred units may contain batches accumulated at different unit costs. For example, the 400 units transferred in at $52,480 in Exhibit 17-14 using the FIFO method consist of units that have different unit costs for direct materials and conversion costs when these units were worked on in the Assembly Department (see Exhibit 17-7). Remember, however, that when these units are transferred in to the Testing Department, they are costed at *one* average unit cost of $131.20 ($52,480 ÷ 400) as in Exhibit 17-14.

4. Units may be measured in different terms in different departments. Consider each department separately. Unit costs could be based on kilograms in the first department and litres in the second, so as units are received by the second department, their measurements must be converted to litres.

HYBRID-COSTING SYSTEMS

Hybrid-costing system. Blends of characteristics from both job-costing systems and process-costing systems.

Product-costing systems do not always fall neatly into the categories of job costing or process costing. A **hybrid-costing system** blends characteristics from both job-costing systems and process-costing systems. Job-costing and process-costing systems are best viewed as ends of a continuum:

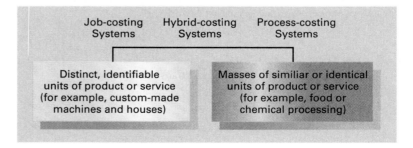

Product-costing systems must often be designed to fit the particular characteristics of different production systems. Many production systems are a hybrid—they have some features of custom-order manufacturing and other features of mass-production manufacturing. Manufacturers of a relatively wide variety of closely related standardized products tend to use a hybrid system. Consider Ford Motor Company. Automobiles may be manufactured in a continuous flow, but each may be customized with a special combination of engine size, transmission, music system, and so on. Companies develop hybrid-costing systems to meet these individual needs. The concepts in action box describes the evolution of a hybrid-costing system. The chapter appendix presents *operating costing*, a type of hybrid-costing system frequently found in practice.

PROBLEM

Allied Chemicals operates a thermoassembly process as the second of three processes at its plastics plant. Direct materials in thermoassembly are added at the end of the process. The following data pertain to the Thermoassembly Department for June 2000:

Work in process, beginning inventory	50,000 units
Transferred-in costs (100% complete)	
Direct materials (0% complete)	
Conversion costs (80% complete)	
Transferred in during current period	200,000 units
Completed and transferred out during current period	210,000 units
Work in process, ending inventory	? units
Transferred-in costs (100% complete)	
Direct materials (0% complete)	
Conversion costs (40% complete)	

REQUIRED

Compute the equivalent units under (1) the weighted-average method and (2) the FIFO method.

SOLUTION

1. The weighted-average method uses equivalent units of work done to date to compute equivalent unit costs. The calculations follow:

Flow of Production	(Step 1) Physical Units (given)	(Step 2) Equivalent Units		
		Transferred-in Costs	Direct Materials	Conversion Costs
Work in process, beginning	50,000			
Transferred in during current period	200,000			
To account for	250,000			
Completed and transferred out during current period	210,000	210,000	210,000	210,000
Work in process, ending*	40,000			
40,000 × 100%; 40,000 × 0%; 40,000 × 40%		40,000	0	16,000
Accounted for	250,000			
Work done to date		250,000	210,000	226,000

*Degree of completion in this department: transferred-in costs, 100%; direct materials, 0%; conversion costs, 40%.

2. The FIFO method uses equivalent units of work done in current period only when computing equivalent unit costs. The calculations follow:

Flow of Production	(Step 1) Physical Units (given)	(Step 2) Equivalent Units		
		Transferred-in Costs	Direct Materials	Conversion Costs
Work in process, beginning (given)	50,000			
Transferred-in during current period (given)	200,000			
To account for	250,000			
Completed and transferred out during current period	50,000			
From beginning work in process§				
50,000 × (100% – 100%); 50,000 × (100% – 0%); 50,000 × (100% – 80%)		0	50,000	10,000
Started and completed	160,000†			
160,000 × 100%; 160,000 × 100%; 160,000 × 100%		160,000	160,000	160,000
Work in process, ending* (given)	40,000			
40,000 × 100%; 40,000 × 0%; 40,000 × 40%		40,000	0	16,000
Accounted for	250,000			
Work done in current period only		200,000	210,000	186,000

§Degree of completion in this department: Transferred-in costs, 100%; direct materials, 0%; conversion costs, 80%.

†210,000 physical units completed and transferred out minus 50,000 physical units completed and transferred out from beginning work-in process inventory.

*Degree of completion in this department: transferred-in costs, 100%; direct materials, 0%; conversion costs, 40%.

SUMMARY

The following points are linked to the chapter's learning objectives.

1. Process-costing systems are used in industries such as chemical processing, oil refining, and breakfast cereals to cost like or similar products or services. The key feature of process costing is the averaging of costs over a quantity (often large) of these like or similar units.

2. The five key steps in a process-costing system using equivalent units are (a) summarize flow of physical units of output, (b) compute output in terms of equivalent units, (c) compute equivalent unit costs, (d) summarize total costs to account for, and (e) assign these costs to units completed and to units in ending work in process.

3. An equivalent unit measures output in terms of the physical quantities of inputs necessary to produce one fully complete unit of the product or service. Equivalent unit calculations are necessary when all physical units of output are not uniformly completed.

4. Journal entries in a process-costing system are similar to entries in a job-costing system. The main difference is that in a process-costing system, there is a separate work-in-process account for each department rather than for each job.

5. The weighted-average method of process costing computes unit costs by focusing on the total costs and the total equivalent units completed to date and assigns this average cost to units completed and to units in ending work-in-process inventory.

6. The first-in, first-out (FIFO) method of process costing assigns unit costs of the earliest equivalent units available to units completed, and the unit costs of the most

order 424) are $11.60 \times 100 = \$1,160$. If work order 424 had contained 75 units, its total costs in operation 1 would be $870 ($11.60 \times 75$). If equivalent units have been used to calculate the conversion cost rate, costs are allocated to work orders by multiplying the conversion cost per equivalent unit by the number of equivalent units in the work order. Direct materials costs of $6,000 for the 50 wool blazers (work order 423) and $3,000 for the 100 polyester blazers (work order 424) are specifically identified with each order as in a job-costing system. Note that operation unit costs are assumed to be the same regardless of the work order but direct materials costs vary across orders as the materials themselves vary.

Journal Entries

Actual conversion costs for operation 1 in March 2000 (assumed to be $24,400, of which $580 are on work order 423 and $1,160 are on work order 424) are entered into a Conversion Costs Control account:

1. Conversion Costs Control	24,400	
Various accounts (such as Wages Payable and Accumulated Depreciation)		24,400

Summary journal entries for assigning costs to the polyester blazers (work order 424) follow. Entries for the wool blazers would be similar.

Of the $3,000 of direct materials for work order 424, $2,975 are used in Operation 1. The journal entry for the use of direct materials, which are traced directly to particular batches, for the 100 polyester blazers is:

2. Work in Process, Operation 1	2,975	
Materials Inventory Control		2,975

The allocation of conversion costs to products in operation costing uses the budgeted rate $11.60 times the 100 units processed, or $1,160.

3. Work in Process, Operation 1	1,160	
Conversion Costs Allocated		1,160

The transfer of the polyester blazers from operation 1 to operation 3 (recall that the polyester blazers do not go through operation 2) would be journalized as follows:

4. Work in Process, Operation 3	4,135	
Work in Process, Operation 1		4,135

After posting, Work in Process, Operation 1 account, appears as follows:

Work in Process, Operation 1

2. Direct materials	2,975	4. Transferred to Operation 3	4,135
3. Conversion costs allocated	1,160		

The costs of the blazers are transferred through the pertinent operations and then to finished goods in the usual manner. Costs are added throughout the year in the accounts, Conversion Costs Control and Conversion Costs Allocated. Any overallocation or underallocation of conversion costs is disposed of in the same way as overallocated or underallocated manufacturing overhead in a job-costing system.

TERMS TO LEARN

This chapter contains definitions of the following important terms:

equivalent units (p. 595)
first-in, first-out (FIFO) process-costing method (p. 601)
hybrid-costing system (p. 614)
operation (p. 617)

operation-costing system (p. 617)
previous department costs (p. 611)
transferred-in costs (p. 611)
weighted-average process-costing method (p. 598)

QUESTIONS

17-1 Give three examples of industries that often use process-costing systems.

17-2 In process costing, why are costs often divided into two main classifications?

17-3 What problems might arise in estimating the degree of completion of an aircraft blade in a machining shop?

17-4 Name the five key steps in process costing when equivalent units are computed.

17-5 State two conditions under which computing equivalent units will make a material difference to reported inventory amounts.

17-6 Name the three inventory methods commonly associated with process costing.

17-7 Describe the distinctive characteristic of weighted-average computations in assigning costs to units completed and ending work in process.

17-8 Describe the distinctive characteristic of FIFO computations in assigning costs to units completed and ending work in process.

17-9 Why should the FIFO method be called the *modified* or *departmental* FIFO method?

17-10 Identify a major advantage of the FIFO method for purposes of planning and control.

17-11 Identify the main difference between journal entries in process costing and the ones in job costing.

17-12 "Standard cost procedures are particularly applicable to process costing situations." Do you agree? Why?

17-13 Why should the accountant distinguish between transferred-in costs and additional direct materials costs for a particular department?

17-14 "Transferred-in costs are those incurred in the preceding accounting period." Do you agree? Explain.

17-15 "There's no reason for me to get excited about the choice between the weighted-average and FIFO methods in my process-costing system. I have long-term contracts with my materials suppliers at fixed prices." State the conditions under which you would (a) agree and (b) disagree with this statement, made by a plant controller. Explain.

EXERCISES

17-16 **Equivalent units: No beginning inventory.** International Electronics manufactures microchips in large quantities. Each microchip undergoes assembly and testing. The total assembly costs during January 2000 were:

Direct materials used	$ 720,000
Coversion costs	760,000
Total manufacturing costs	$1,480,000

REQUIRED

1. Assume there was no beginning inventory on January 1, 2000. During January, 10,000 microchips were placed into production and all 10,000 microchips were fully completed at the end of January. What is the unit cost of an assembled microchip in January 2000?

2. Assume that during February 10,000 microchips were placed into production. Further assume the same total assembly costs for January are also incurred in February 2000, but only 9,000 microchips are fully completed at the end of February. All direct materials had been added to the remaining 1,000 microchips. However, on average, these remaining 1,000 microchips were only 50% complete as to conversion costs. (a) What are the equivalent units for direct materials and conversion costs and their respective equivalent unit costs for February? (b) What is the unit cost of an assembled microchip in February 2000?

3. Explain the difference in your answers to requirements 1 and 2.

17-17 **Journal entries (continuation of 17-16).** Refer to requirement 2 of Exercise 17-16.

REQUIRED

Prepare summary journal entries for the use of direct materials and conversion costs. Also prepare a journal entry to transfer out the cost of goods completed. Show the postings to the Work in Process account.

17-18 No beginning inventory, materials introduced in middle of process. Vaasa Chemicals has a mixing department and a refining department. Its process costing system in the mixing department has two direct materials cost categories (chemical P and chemical Q) and one conversion costs pool. The following data pertain to the mixing department for July 2000:

Units:		
Work in process, July 1		0
Units started		50,000
Completed and transferred to refining department		35,000
Costs:		
Chemical P	$250,000	
Chemical Q	70,000	
Conversion costs	135,000	

Chemical P is introduced at the start of operations in the mixing department, and chemical Q is added when the product is three-fourths completed in the mixing department. Conversion costs are added uniformly during the process. The ending work in process in the mixing department is two-thirds completed.

REQUIRED
1. Compute the equivalent units in the mixing department for July 2000 for each cost element.
2. Compute (a) the cost of goods completed and transferred to the refining department during July and (b) the cost of work in process as of July 31, 2000.

17-19 Weighted-average method. The Chatham Company makes chemical compounds in a single processing department. The following information about equivalent units and actual costs for July 2000 is available.

	Direct Materials		**Conversion Costs**	
	Equivalent Units	**Total Costs**	**Equivalent Units**	**Total Costs**
Work in process, July 1*	20,000	$120,000	14,000	$140,000
Work done during July 2000	30,000	210,000	28,000	301,000
To account for	50,000	$330,000	42,000	$441,000
Completed during July 2000	34,000	?	34,000	?
Work in process, July 31†	16,000	?	8,000	?

*Degree of completion: direct materials, 100%; conversion costs, 70%.
†Degree of completion: direct materials, 100%; conversion costs, 50%.

REQUIRED
1. Calculate the cost per equivalent unit for direct materials and conversion costs.
2. Summarize total costs to account for, and assign these costs to units completed (and transferred out) and to units in ending work in process using the weighted-average method.

17-20 FIFO method. Refer to the information in Exercise 17-19.

REQUIRED
Do Exercise 17-19 using the FIFO method.

Note that you first need to calculate the equivalent units of work done in the current period (for direct materials and conversion costs) to complete beginning work in process, to start and complete new units, and to produce ending work in process.

17-21 Standard-costing method, assigning costs. Refer to the information in Exercise 17-19. Suppose Chatham determines standard costs of $6.10 per (equivalent) unit for direct materials and $10.20 per (equivalent) unit for conversion costs for both beginning work in process and work done in the current period.

REQUIRED
1. Do Exercise 17-19 using the standard-costing method. Note that you first need to calculate the equivalent units of work done in the current period (for direct

materials and conversion costs) to complete beginning work in process, to start and complete new units, and to produce ending work in process.

2. Compute the total direct materials and conversion costs variances for July 2000.

17-22 Weighted-average method, equivalent units and unit costs. Consider the following data for the Satellite Assembly Division of Aerospatiale:

	Physical Units (Satellites)	Direct Materials	Conversion Costs
Beginning work in process, (May 1)*	8	$ 4,933,600	$ 910,400
Started in May 2000	50		
Completed during May 2000	46		
Ending work in process (May 31)†	12		
Costs added during May 2000		$32,200,000	$13,920,000

*Degree of completion: direct materials, 90%; conversion costs, 40%.
†Degree of completion: direct materials, 60%; conversion costs, 30%.

The Satellite Assembly Division uses the weighted-average method of process costing.

REQUIRED

1. Compute equivalent units for direct materials and conversion costs. Show physical units in the first column of your schedule.
2. Calculate cost per equivalent unit for direct materials and conversion costs.

17-23 Weighted-average method, assigning costs (continuation of 17-22).

REQUIRED

For the data in Exercise 17-22, summarize total costs to account for, and assign these costs to units completed (and transferred out) and to units in ending work in process.

17-24 FIFO method, equivalent units and unit costs. Refer to the information in Exercise 17-22. Suppose the Satellite Assembly Division uses the FIFO method of process costing instead of the weighted-average method.

REQUIRED

1. Compute equivalent units for direct materials and conversion costs. Show physical units in the first column of your schedule.
2. Calculate cost per equivalent unit for direct materials and conversion costs.

17-25 FIFO method, assigning costs (continuation of 17-24).

REQUIRED

For the data in Exercise 17-22, use the FIFO method to summarize total costs to account for, and assign these costs to units completed and transferred out, and to units in ending work in process.

17-26 Standard-costing method, assigning costs. Refer to the information in Exercise 17-22. Suppose the Satellite Assembly Division uses the standard-costing method of process costing. Suppose further that the Satellite Assembly Division determines standard costs of $695,000 per (equivalent) unit for direct materials and $295,000 per (equivalent) unit for conversion costs for both beginning work in process and work done in the current period.

REQUIRED

1. Compute equivalent units for direct materials and conversion costs. Show physical units in the first column of your schedule.
2. Summarize total costs to account for, and assign these costs to units completed and transferred out, and to units in ending work in process.
3. Compute the total direct material and conversion cost variances for May 2000.

17-27 Transferred-in costs, weighted-average method. Hideo Chemicals manufactures an industrial solvent in two departments—mixing and cooking. This question focuses on the Cooking Department. During June 2000, 90 tonnes of solvent were completed and transferred out from the Cooking Department. Direct materials are added at one point in time during the process. Conversion costs are added uniformly during the process. Hideo Chemicals uses the weighted-average process costing method. The following information about the actual costs for June 2000 is available.

	Transferred-In Costs		Direct Materials		Conversion Costs	
	Equivalent Tonnes	Total Costs	Equivalent Tonnes	Total Costs	Equivalent Tonnes	Total Costs
Work in process, June 1	40	$40,000	0	$ 0	30	$18,000
Work done in June 2000	80	$87,200	90	$36,000	75	$49,725
Completed in June 2000	?	?	?	?	?	?
Work in process, June 30	?	?	?	?	?	?

REQUIRED

1. Calculate the equivalent tonnes of solvent completed and transferred out, and in ending work in process for each cost element.
2. Compute cost per equivalent unit for beginning work in process and work done in current period.
3. Summarize total costs to account for, and assign these costs to units completed (and transferred out) and to units in ending work in process using the weighted-average method.

17-28 Transferred-in costs, FIFO method. Refer to the information in Exercise 17-27. Suppose that Hideo uses the FIFO method instead of the weighted-average method in all its departments. The only changes under the FIFO method are that the total transferred-in cost of beginning work in process is $39,200 and that the cost of work done in the current period is $85,600.

REQUIRED

Do Exercise 17-27 using the FIFO method.

17-29 Operation costing. (Chapter Appendix) The Gabriel Corporation produces a standard-sized window in four operations—framing, assembly, staining, and painting. The windows differ in the type of wood (pine, oak) and glass (regular, tempered) used. The framing and assembly operations are common to all windows, but thereafter they are either stained or painted but not both. The total conversion costs for the month of June are

	Framing	Assembly	Staining	Painting
Total conversion costs	$75,000	$105,000	$36,000	$54,000

There is no beginning or ending inventory of windows in the month of June. A total of 3,000 windows are produced in June, half of which are stained and half of which are painted. The conversion cost for each unit passing through a given operation is the same.

Details of two work orders processed in June are as follows:

	Work Order 626	Work Order 750
Number of windows	50	100
Direct materials costs	$5,500	$9,800
Finishing operation	Painting	Staining

REQUIRED

1. Tabulate the conversion costs of each operation, the total units produced, and the conversion cost per unit.
2. Calculate the total costs and the total cost per window of work order 626 and work order 750.

PROBLEMS

17-30 Weighted-average method. Global Defence, Inc. is a manufacturer of military equipment. Its Halifax plant manufactures the Interceptor missile under contract to the Canadian government and friendly countries. All Interceptors go through an identical manufacturing process. Every effort is made to ensure that all Interceptors are identical and meet many demanding performance specifications. The product-costing system at the Halifax plant has a single direct cost category (direct materials) and a single indirect cost category (conversion costs). Each Interceptor passes through two departments—the Assembly Department and the Testing Department. Direct materials are added at the beginning of the process in Assembly. Conversion costs are added evenly throughout the two departments. When the Assembly Department finishes work on each Interceptor, it is immediately transferred to Testing.

Global Defence uses the weighted-average method of process costing. Data for the Assembly Department for October 2000 are:

	Physical Units (missiles)	Direct Materials	Conversion Costs
Work in process, October 1*	20	$ 460,000	$120,000
Started during October 2000	80		
Completed during October 2000	90		
Work in process, October 31†	10		
Costs added during October 2000		$2,000,000	$935,000

*Degree of completion: direct materials, ?%; conversion costs, 60%.
†Degree of completion: direct materials, ?%; conversion costs, 70%.

REQUIRED

1. For each cost element, compute equivalent units of work done in October 2000 in the Assembly Department. Show physical units in the first column.
2. For each cost element, calculate cost per equivalent unit of beginning work in process and of work done in October 2000.
3. Summarize the total Assembly Department costs for October 2000, and assign these costs to units completed (and transferred out) and to units in ending work in process using the weighted-average method.

17-31 **Journal entries (continuation of 17-30).**

REQUIRED

Prepare a set of summarized journal entries for all October 2000 transactions affecting Work in Process—Assembly. Set up a T-account for Work in Process—Assembly, and post the entries to it.

 17-32 **FIFO method (continuation of 17-30 and 17-31).**

REQUIRED

Do Problem 17-30 using the FIFO method of process costing. Explain any difference between the cost of work completed and transferred out and cost of ending work in process in the Assembly Department under the weighted-average method and the FIFO method.

17-33 **Transferred-in costs, weighted average (related to 17-30 to 17-32).** Global Defence, Inc., as you know, manufactures the Interceptor missile at its Halifax plant. It has two departments—Assembly Department and Testing Department. This problem focuses on the Testing Department. (Problems 17-30 to 17-32 focused on the Assembly Department.) Direct materials are added at the end of the Testing Department. Conversion costs are added evenly during the Testing Department's process. As work in Assembly is completed, each unit is immediately transferred to Testing. As each unit is completed in Testing, it is immediately transferred to Finished Goods.

Global Defence uses the weighted-average method of process costing. Data for the Testing Department for October 2000 are:

	Physical Units (missiles)	Transferred-In Costs	Direct Materials	Conversion Costs
Work in process, October 1*	30	$ 985,800	$ 0	$ 331,800
Transferred in during October 2000	?			
Completed during October 2000	105			
Work in process, October 31†	15			
Costs added during October 2000		$3,192,866	$3,885,000	$1,581,000

*Degree of completion: transferred-in costs, ?%; direct materials, ?%; conversion costs, 70%.
†Degree of completion: transferred-in costs, ?%; direct materials, ?%; conversion costs, 60%.

1. What is the percentage of completion for (a) transferred-in costs and direct materials in beginning work-in-process inventory and (b) transferred-in costs and direct materials in ending work-in-process inventory?
2. For each cost element, compute equivalent units of work done in October 2000 in the Testing Department. Show physical units in the first column.
3. For each cost element, calculate the cost per equivalent unit of beginning work in process and of work done in October 2000.
4. Summarize total Testing Department costs for October 2000, and assign these costs to units completed (and transferred out) and to units in ending work in process using the weighted-average method.
5. Prepare journal entries for October transfers from the Assembly Department to the Testing Department and from Testing to Finished Goods.

17-34 Transferred-in costs, FIFO costing (continuation of 17-33).

REQUIRED

Using the FIFO process costing method, do the requirements of Problem 17-33. The transferred-in costs from the Assembly Department for the beginning work in process on October 1 are $980,060. During October, costs transferred in to the Testing Department are $3,188,000. All other data are unchanged.

17-35 Weighted-average method. Star Toys manufactures one type of wooden toy figure. It buys wood as its direct material for the Forming Department of its Fredericton plant. The toys are transferred to the Finishing Department, where they are hand-shaped and metal is added to them.

Star Toys uses the weighted-average method of process costing. Consider the following data for the Forming Department in April 2000:

	Physical Units (toys)	Direct Materials	Conversion Costs
Work in process, April 1*	300	$ 7,500	$ 2,125
Started during April 2000	2,200		
Completed during April 2000	2,000		
Work in process, April 30†	500		
Costs added during April 2000		$70,000	$42,500

*Degree of completion: direct materials, 100%; conversion costs, 40%.
†Degree of completion: direct materials, 100%; conversion costs, 25%.

REQUIRED

Summarize the total Forming Department costs for April 2000, and assign these costs to units completed (and transferred out) and to units in ending work in process using the weighted-average method.

17-36 Journal entries (continuation of 17-35).

REQUIRED

Prepare a set of summarized journal entries for all April transactions affecting Work in Process—Forming. Set up a T-account for Work in Process—Forming, and post the entries to it.

17-37 FIFO computations (continuation of 17-35 and 17-36).

REQUIRED

Do Problem 17-35, using FIFO and four decimal places for unit costs. Explain any difference between the cost of work completed and transferred out and cost of ending work in process in the Forming Department under the weighted-average method and the FIFO method.

17-38 Transferred-in costs, weighted-average (related to 17-35 through 17-37). Star Toys manufactures wooden toy figures at its Fredericton plant. It has two departments—the Forming Department and the Finishing Department. Problems 17-35 to 17-37 focused on the Forming Department. Consider now the Finishing Department, which processes the formed toys through hand-shaping and the addition of metal. For simplicity here, suppose all additional direct materials are added at the end of the process. Conversion costs are added evenly during Finishing operations.

Star Toys uses the weighted-average method of process costing. The following is a summary of the April 2000 operations in the Finishing Department:

	Physical Units (toys)	Transferred-In Costs	Direct Materials	Conversion Costs
Work in process, April 1*	500	$ 17,750	$ 0	$ 7,250
Transferred in during April 2000	2,000			
Completed during April 2000	2,100			
Work in process, April 30†	400			
Costs added during April 2000		$104,000	$23,100	$38,400

*Degree of completion: transferred-in costs, 100%; direct materials, 0%; conversion costs, 60%.
†Degree of completion: transferred-in costs, 100%; direct materials, 0%; conversion costs, 30%.

REQUIRED

1. Summarize the total Finishing Department costs for April 2000, and assign these costs to units completed (and transferred out) and to units in ending work in process using the weighted-average method.
2. Prepare journal entries for April transfers from the Forming Department to the Finishing Department and from the Finishing Department to Finished Goods.

17-39 Transferred-in costs, FIFO costing (continuation of 17-38).

REQUIRED

1. Using the FIFO process costing method, do the requirements of Problem 17-38. The transferred-in costs from the Forming Department for the April beginning work in process are $17,520. During April, the costs transferred in are $103,566. All other data are unchanged.
2. Explain any difference between the cost of work completed and transferred out and cost of ending work in process in the Finishing Department under the weighted-average method and the FIFO method.

17-40 Transferred-in costs, weighted-average and FIFO. Frito-Lay, Inc. manufactures convenience foods, including potato chips and corn chips. Production of corn chips occurs in four departments: cleaning, mixing, cooking, and drying and packaging. Consider the Drying and Packaging Department, where direct materials (packaging) is added at the end of the process. Conversion costs are added evenly during the process. Suppose the accounting records of a Frito-Lay plant provided the following information for corn chips in its Drying and Packaging Department during a weekly period (week 37):

	Physical Units (cases)	Transferred-In Costs	Direct Materials	Conversion Costs
Beginning work in process, week 37*	1,250	$29,000	$ 0	$ 9,060
Transferred in during week 37 from Cooking Department	5,000			
Completed during week 37	5,250			
Ending work in process, week 37†	1,000			
Costs added during week 37		$96,000	$25,200	$38,400

*Degree of completion: transferred-in costs, 100%; direct materials, ?%; conversion costs, 80%.
†Degree of completion: transferred-in costs, ?%; direct materials, ?%; conversion costs, 40%.

REQUIRED

1. For each cost element, compute equivalent units of work done in week 37 in the Drying and Packaging Department. Show physical units in the first column.
2. Summarize the total Drying and Packaging Department costs for week 37, and assign these costs to units completed (and transferred out) and to units in ending work in process using the weighted-average method.
3. Assume that the FIFO method is used for the Drying and Packaging Department. The transferred-in costs for work-in-process beginning inventory are $28,920. The transferred-in costs during the week from the Cooking Department are $94,000. All other data are unchanged. Summarize the total Drying and Packaging Department costs for week 37 and assign these costs to units completed (and transferred out) and to units in ending work in process using the FIFO method.

17-41 Standard costing with beginning and ending work in process. The Victoria Corporation uses a standard costing system for its manufacturing operations. Standard costs for the cooking process are $6 per unit for direct materials and $3 per unit for conversion costs. All direct materials are introduced at the beginning of the process, but conversion costs are added uniformly during the process. The operating summary for May 2000 included the following data for the cooking process:

Work-in-process inventories:
> May 1: 3,000 units*
> (direct materials $18,000; conversion costs $5,400)
> May 31: 5,000 units†
> Units started in May: 20,000
> Units completed and transferred out of cooking in May: 18,000
> Additional actual costs incurred for cooking during May:
> > Direct materials: $125,000
> > Conversion cost: $57,000

*Degree of completion: direct materials, 100%; conversion costs, 60%.
†Degree of completion: direct materials, 100%; conversion costs, 50%.

REQUIRED
1. Compute the total standard costs of units transferred out in May and the total standard costs of the May 31 inventory of work in process.
2. Compute the total May variances for direct materials and conversion costs.

17-42 **Operation costing, equivalent units.** (Chapter Appendix, CMA, adapted) Gregg Industries manufactures a variety of plastic products, including a series of molded chairs. The three models of molded chairs, which are all variations of the same design, are Standard (can be stacked), Deluxe (with arms), and Executive (with arms and padding). The company uses batch manufacturing and has an operation-costing system.

Gregg has an extrusion operation and subsequent operations to form, trim, and finish the chairs. Plastic sheets are produced by the extrusion operation, some of which are sold directly to other manufacturers. During the forming operation, the remaining plastic sheets are molded into chair seats and the legs are added. The Standard model is sold after this operation. During the trim operation, the arms are added to the Deluxe and Executive models and the chair edges are smoothed. Only the Executive model enters the finish operation, where the padding is added. All of the units produced receive the same steps within each operation.

The May production run had a total manufacturing cost of $898,000. The units of production and direct materials costs incurred are as follows:

	Units Produced	Extrusion Materials	Form Materials	Trim Materials	Finished Materials
Plastic sheets	5,000	$ 60,000	$ 0	$ 0	$ 0
Standard model	6,000	72,000	24,000	0	0
Deluxe model	3,000	36,000	12,000	9,000	0
Executive model	2,000	24,000	8,000	6,000	12,000
	16,000	$192,000	$44,000	$15,000	$12,000

Manufacturing costs of production assigned during the month of May were:

	Extrusion Operation	Form Operation	Trim Operation	Finish Operation
Direct manufacturing labour	$152,000	$60,000	$30,000	$18,000
Manufacturing overhead	240,000	72,000	39,000	24,000

REQUIRED
1. For each product produced by Gregg Industries during the month of May, determine (a) the unit cost, and (b) the total cost. Be sure to account for all costs incurred during the month, and support your answer with appropriate calculations.
2. Without considering your answer in requirement 1, assume that 1,000 units of the Deluxe model produced during May remained in work in process at the end of the month. These units were 100% complete as to materials costs and 60% complete in the trim operation. Determine the cost of the 1,000 units of the Deluxe model in the work-in-process inventory at the end of May.

17-43 Equivalent unit computations, benchmarking, ethics. Margaret Major is the corporate controller of Leisure Suits. Leisure Suits has 20 plants worldwide that manufacture basic suits for retail stores. Each plant uses a process-costing system. At the end of each month, each plant manager submits a production report and a production cost report. The production report includes the plant manager's estimate of the percentage of completion of the ending work in process as to direct materials and conversion costs. Major uses these estimates to compute the equivalent units of work done in each plant and the cost per equivalent unit of work done for both direct materials and conversion costs in each month. Plants are ranked from 1 to 20 in terms of (a) cost per equivalent unit of direct materials and (b) cost per equivalent unit of conversion costs. Each month Major publishes a report that she calls "Benchmarking for Efficiency Gains at Leisure Suits." The three top-ranked plants on each category receive a bonus and are written up as the best in their class in the company newsletter.

Major has been pleased with the success of her benchmarking program. However, she has heard some disturbing news. She has received some unsigned letters stating that two plant managers have been manipulating their monthly estimates of percentage of completion in an attempt to obtain "best in class" status.

REQUIRED

1. How and why might plant managers "manipulate" their monthly estimates of percentage of completion?
2. Major's first reaction is to contact each plant controller and discuss the problem raised by the unsigned letters. Is that a good idea?
3. Assume that the plant controller's primary reporting responsibility is to the plant manager and that each plant controller receives the phone call from Major mentioned in requirement 2. What is the ethical responsibility of each plant controller (a) to Margaret Major and (b) to Leisure Suits in relation to the equivalent unit information each plant provides for the "Benchmarking for Efficiency" report?
4. How might Major gain some insight into whether the equivalent unit figures provided by particular plants are being manipulated?

COLLABORATIVE LEARNING PROBLEM

17-44 Transferred-in costs, equivalent unit costs, working backwards. Lennox Plastics has two processes–extrusion and thermo-assembly. Consider the June 2000 data for physical units in the thermo-assembly process: beginning work in process, 15,000 units: transferred in from the Extruding Department during September, 9,000; ending work in process, 5,000. Direct materials are added when the process in the Thermo-assembly Department is 80% complete. Conversion costs are added evenly during the process. Lennox Plastics uses the FIFO method of process costing. The following information is available.

	Transferred-in Costs	Direct Materials	Conversion Costs
Beginning work in process	$90,000		$45,000
Percentage completion of beginning work in process	100%	—	60%
Costs added in current period	$58,500	$57,000	$57,200
Cost per equivalent unit of work done in current period	$ 6.50	$ 3	$ 5.20

INSTRUCTIONS

Form pairs of students to complete the following requirements.

REQUIRED

1. For each cost category, compute equivalent units of work done in the current period.
2. For each cost category, compute equivalent units of work done to complete beginning work-in-process inventory, to start and complete new units and to produce ending work in process.
3. For each cost category, calculate the percentage of completion of ending work-in-process inventory.
4. Summarize total costs to account for, and assign these costs to units completed (and transferred out) and to units in ending work in process.

PART FIVE

18

SPOILAGE, REWORK, AND SCRAP

Reducing spoilage, reworked units, and scrap is an important aspect of cost management. Motorola monitors both financial and nonfinancial variables in its efforts to minimize reworked units and scrap and to improve quality. Motorola estimates that these initiatives have resulted in billions of dollars of cost savings.

LEARNING OBJECTIVES

After studying this chapter, you should be able to:

1. Distinguish between spoilage, reworked units, and scrap
2. Describe the general accounting procedures for normal and abnormal spoilage
3. Account for spoilage in process costing using the weighted-average method
4. Account for spoilage in process costing using the first-in, first-out method
5. Account for spoilage in process costing using the standard costs method
6. Account for spoilage in job costing
7. Account for reworked units
8. Account for scrap

Motorola Canada
www.motorola.ca

Managers are focusing increasingly on improving quality and reducing defects. Executives have learned that a rate of defects regarded as normal in the past is no longer tolerable. Many managers believe that reducing defects reduces costs and makes their company more competitive. Consider these words from a speech by George Fisher when he was chief executive officer of Motorola, an electronics manufacturer:

> We want to improve our quality in everything we do by ten times in two years, by a hundred times in four years, and in six years . . . three and a half defects for every million operations, whether typing, manufacturing, or serving a customer.

Recording and highlighting the costs of defects in a timely way helps managers make more informed decisions about managing these costs. Using this information, managers have taken steps to reduce defects and costs by designing better products and processes, investing in production systems such as just-in-time (JIT) and computer-integrated manufacturing (CIM), training and motivating workers, and properly maintaining machines.

This chapter concentrates on three types of costs that arise as a result of defects–spoilage, rework and scrap–and ways to account for them. The focus is on determining the cost of products and on valuing inventory and cost of goods sold. Chapter 19 discusses other aspects of quality with greater emphasis on cost management and control.

TERMINOLOGY

OBJECTIVE 1

Distinguish between spoilage, reworked units, and scrap

Spoilage. Unacceptable units of production that are discarded or sold for net disposal proceeds.

Reworked units. Unacceptable units of production that are subsequently reworked and sold as acceptable finished goods.

We start by defining key terms used in the chapter.

Spoilage refers to unacceptable units of production that are discarded or are sold for net disposal proceeds. Partially completed or fully completed units of output may be spoiled. Examples are defective shirts, jeans, shoes, and carpets sold as "seconds," and defective aluminum cans sold to aluminum manufacturers for remelting and production of aluminum foils. **Reworked units** are unacceptable units of production that are subsequently reworked and sold as acceptable finished goods. For example, defective units of products such as pagers, computer disk drives, computers, and telephones can sometimes be repaired and sold as good products. Scrap is material left over when making a main or joint product. *Scrap* is defined in Chapter 15 as a product that has minimal (frequently zero) sales value compared with the sales value of the main or joint product(s). Examples are shavings and short lengths from woodworking operations, steel edges left over from stamping operations, and frayed cloth and end cuts from suit-making operations.

Some amount of spoilage, rework, or scrap appears to be an inherent part of many production processes. One example is semiconductor manufacturing, where the products are so complex and delicate that some spoiled units are invariably produced. In this case, the spoiled units cannot be reworked. An example involving spoilage and rework occurs in the manufacture of high-precision machine tools that must be built to very demanding tolerances. In this case, spoiled units can be reworked to meet standards but only at a considerable cost. And in the mining industry, companies process ore that contains varying amounts of valuable metals and rock. Some amount of rock, which is scrap, is inevitable, but its volume can often be decreased. We first focus on spoilage.

OBJECTIVE 2

Describe the general accounting procedures for normal and abnormal spoilage

DIFFERENT TYPES OF SPOILAGE

Normal spoilage. Spoilage that arises under efficient operating conditions; it is an inherent result of the particular production process.

Two key objectives when accounting for spoilage are determining the magnitude of the costs of spoilage and distinguishing between the costs of normal and abnormal spoilage. Managers use this information both to cost products and to control and reduce costs by improving the quality of the product and process.

Normal Spoilage

Normal spoilage is spoilage that arises under efficient operating conditions; it is an inherent result of the particular production process. For a given production process, management must decide the rate of spoilage it is willing to accept as normal. Costs of normal spoilage are typically viewed as a part of the costs of good units manufactured, when good units cannot be made without the simultaneous appearance of spoiled units.

Normal spoilage rates should be computed using the total *good* units completed as the base, not the total *actual* units started. Why? Because total actual units started also include any abnormal spoilage in addition to normal spoilage.

Abnormal Spoilage

Abnormal spoilage is spoilage that is not expected to arise under efficient operating conditions; it is not an inherent part of the chosen production process. Most abnormal spoilage is usually regarded as avoidable and controllable. Line operators and other plant personnel can generally decrease abnormal spoilage by minimizing machine breakdowns, accidents, and the like. Abnormal spoilage costs are written off as losses of the accounting period in which detection of the spoiled units occurs. For the most informative feedback, the Loss from Abnormal Spoilage account should appear in a detailed income statement as a separate line item and not be buried as an indistinguishable part of the cost of goods manufactured.

Many companies such as the Toyota Motor Corporation adhere to a perfection standard as a part of their emphasis on total quality control. Their ideal goal is zero defects. Hence, all spoilage would be treated as abnormal.

Issues about accounting for spoilage arise in both process-costing and job-costing systems. We first present the accounting for spoilage in process-costing systems because it is an extension of the discussion of process costing introduced in Chapter 17.

Abnormal spoilage. Spoilage not expected to arise under efficient operating conditions; it is not an inherent part of the chosen production process.

PROCESS COSTING AND SPOILAGE

A key issue in accounting for spoilage in process-costing systems is how to count spoiled units. As we have already discussed, units of abnormal spoilage should be counted and recorded separately. But what about units of normal spoilage? These units can either be recognized (approach A) or not counted (approach B) when computing output units—actual or equivalent—in a process-costing system. Approach A makes visible the costs associated with spoilage. Approach B spreads the spoilage costs over good units, potentially resulting in less accurate product costs.

Spoilage is typically assumed to occur at the stage of completion where inspection takes place. Why? Because spoilage is not detected until that point.

Example 1: Chipmakers, Inc. manufactures computer chips for television sets. All direct materials are added at the beginning of the chip-making process. To highlight issues that arise with spoilage, we assume no beginning inventory. In May 2000, $270,000 in direct materials were introduced. Production data for May indicate that 10,000 units were started, 5,000 good units were completed, 1,000 units were spoiled (all normal spoilage). Ending work in process had 4,000 units (each 100% complete as to direct materials costs). Spoilage is detected upon completion of the process.

The direct materials unit costs are computed and assigned using approaches A and B as shown in Exhibit 18-1. Not counting the equivalent units for spoilage decreases equivalent units, resulting in a higher cost of each good unit. A $30 equivalent unit cost (instead of a $27 equivalent unit cost) is assigned to work in process that has not reached the inspection point. Simultaneously, the direct materials costs assigned to good units completed, which include the cost of normal spoilage, are too low ($150,000 instead of $162,000). Consequently, the 4,000 units in ending work in process contain costs of spoilage of $12,000 ($120,000 – $108,000) that do not pertain to those units and that, in fact, belong with the good units completed and transferred out. The 4,000 units in ending work in process undoubtedly include some units that will be detected as spoiled in the subsequent accounting period. In effect, under approach B, these units will bear two charges for spoilage. The ending

EXHIBIT 18-1
Effect of Recognizing Equivalent Units in Spoilage for Direct Materials Costs,
Chip-Makers, Inc., for May 2000

	Approach A: Recognizing Spoiled Units When Computing Output in Equivalent Units	Approach B: Not Counting Spoiled Units When Computing Output in Equivalent Units
Costs to account for	$270,000	$270,000
Divide by: Equivalent units	÷ 10,000	÷ 9,000
Cost per equivalent unit	$ 27	$ 30
Assigned to:		
Good units transferred out:		
Good units completed:		
5,000 × $27; 5,000 × $30	$135,000	$150,000
Add: Normal spoilage: 1,000 × $27	27,000	0
Good units transferred out	162,000	150,000
Work in process, ending:		
4,000 × $27; 4,000 × $30	108,000	120,000
Costs accounted for	$270,000	$270,000

work in process is being charged for spoilage in the current period, and it will be charged again when inspection occurs as the units are completed. Such cost distortions do not occur when spoiled units are recognized in the computation of equivalent units. Approach A has a further advantage. It highlights the cost of normal spoilage to management and thereby focuses management's attention on reducing spoilage. Therefore, we will use approach A to present process costing with spoilage.

The Five-Step Procedure for Process Costing with Spoilage

We illustrate process costing with spoilage using the following example.

Example 2: The Anzio Company manufactures a wooden recycling container in its Processing Department. Direct materials for this product are introduced at the beginning of the production cycle. At the start of production, all direct materials required to make one output unit are bundled together in a single kit. Conversion costs are added evenly during the cycle. Some units of this product are spoiled as a result of defects only detectable at inspection of finished units. Normally, the spoiled units are 10% of the good output. Summary data for July 2000 are:

Physical Units for July 2000

Work in process, beginning inventory (July 1)	1,500 units
Direct materials (100% complete)	
Conversion costs (60% complete)	
Started during July	8,500 units
Completed and transferred out in July (good units)	7,000 units
Work in process, ending inventory (July 31)	2,000 units
Direct materials (100% complete)	
Conversion costs (50% complete)	

Total Costs for July 2000

Work in process, beginning inventory:		
Direct materials	$12,000	
Conversion costs	9,000	$ 21,000
Direct materials costs added during July		76,500
Conversion costs added during July		89,100
Total costs to account for		$186,600

The five-step approach used in Chapter 17 needs only slight modification to accommodate spoilage. The key change is in calculating the number of spoiled units in Step 1.

◆ **Step 1:** *Summarize the flow of physical units of output.* Identify both normal and abnormal spoilage.

The number of total spoiled units is computed as follows:

$$\text{Total spoiled units} = \left(\begin{array}{c} \text{Beginning} \\ \text{units} \end{array} + \begin{array}{c} \text{Units} \\ \text{started} \end{array} \right) - \left(\begin{array}{c} \text{Good units} \\ \text{transferred out} \end{array} + \begin{array}{c} \text{Ending} \\ \text{units} \end{array} \right)$$

$$= (1{,}500 + 8{,}500) - (7{,}000 + 2{,}000)$$

$$= 10{,}000 - 9{,}000$$

$$= 1{,}000 \text{ units}$$

Normal spoilage at Anzio's Processing Department is 10% of the 7,000 units of good output, or 700 units. Thus:

$$\text{Abnormal spoilage} = \text{Total spoilage} - \text{Normal spoilage}$$

$$= 1{,}000 - 700$$

$$= 300 \text{ units}$$

◆ **Step 2:** *Compute output in terms of equivalent units.* Compute equivalent units for spoilage in the same way as for good units. Because Anzio inspects at the completion point, the same amount of work will be done on each spoiled unit and each completed good unit.

◆ **Step 3:** *Compute equivalent unit costs.* The details of this step do not differ from those in Chapter 17. We assume that spoiled units are included in the computation of output units.

◆ **Step 4:** *Summarize total costs to account for.* These are all the costs debited to Work in Process. The details of this step do not differ from those in Chapter 17.

◆ **Step 5:** *Assign these costs to units completed, spoiled units, and units in ending work in process.* This step now includes computation of the cost of spoiled units and the cost of good units.

To proceed through the five steps, we first need to specify the inventory costing method—weighted-average, FIFO, or standard costing. We illustrate process costing under each of these inventory methods and show how the computations incorporate normal and abnormal spoilage.

Weighted-Average Method and Spoilage

Exhibit 18-2 Panel A presents Steps 1 and 2 to calculate equivalent units of work done to date and includes calculations of equivalent units of normal and abnormal spoilage. Exhibit 18-2, Panel B presents Steps 3, 4 and 5 (together called the production cost worksheet). Step 3 presents the equivalent unit cost calculations using the weighted-average method. Note how, for each cost category, the costs of beginning work in process and costs of work done in the current period are totalled and divided by the equivalent units of all work done to date to calculate the weighted-average cost. Step 4 summarizes the total costs to account for. Step 5 assigns costs to completed units, spoiled units, and ending inventory by multiplying the equivalent units calculated in Step 2 by the cost per equivalent unit calculated in Step 3. Note how the costs of normal spoilage, $13,825, are added to the costs of their related good units. Hence, the cost per good unit completed and transferred out equals the total costs transferred out (including the costs of normal spoilage) divided by the number of good units produced, $152,075 \div 7,000 = \$21,725$. It is not equal to $19.75, the sum of the costs per equivalent unit of direct materials, $8.85 and conversion costs, $10.90. Instead, the cost per good unit is equal to the total cost of direct materials and conversion costs per equivalent unit, $19.75, *plus* a share of the normal spoilage, $1.975 ($13,825 \div 7,000) = \$21.725$. The $5,925 costs of abnormal spoilage are

EXHIBIT 18-2
Weighted-Average Method of Process Costing with Spoilage Forming Department of the Anzio Company for July 2000

PANEL A: STEPS 1 AND 2—SUMMARIZE OUTPUT IN PHYSICAL UNITS AND COMPUTE EQUIVALENT UNITS

Flow of Production	(Step 1) Physical Units (given, p. 632)	(Step 2) Equivalent Units	
		Direct Materials	Conversion Costs
Work in process, beginning	1,500		
Started during current period	8,500		
To account for	10,000		
Good units completed and transferred out during current period:	7,000	7,000	7,000
Normal spoilage*	700		
700 × 100%; 700 × 100%		700	700
Abnormal spoilage†	300		
300 × 100%; 300 × 100%		300	300
Work in process, ending‡	2,000		
2,000 × 100%; 2,000 × 50%		2,000	1,000
Accounted for	10,000		
Work done to date		10,000	9,000

*Normal spoilage is 10% of good units transferred out: 10% × 7,000 = 700 units. Degree of completion of normal spoilage in this department: direct materials, 100%; conversion costs, 100%.
†Abnormal spoilage = Actual spoilage –Normal spoilage = 1,000 – 700 = 300 units. Degree of completion of abnormal spoilage in this department: direct materials, 100%; conversion costs, 100%.
‡Degree of completion in this department: direct materials, 100%; conversion costs, 50%.

PANEL B: STEPS 3, 4 AND 5—COMPUTE EQUIVALENT UNIT COSTS, SUMMARIZE TOTAL COSTS TO ACCOUNT FOR, AND ASSIGN COSTS TO UNITS COMPLETED, TO SPOILAGE UNITS, AND TO UNITS IN ENDING WORK IN PROCESS

		Total Production Costs	Direct Materials	Conversion Costs
(Step 3)	Work in process, beginning	$ 21,000	$ 12,000	$9,000
	Costs added in current period	165,600	76,500	89,100
			88,500	98,100
	Divided by equivalent units of work done to date		÷ 10,000	÷ 119,000
	Equivalent unit costs of work done to date		$ 8.85	$ 10.90
(Step 4)	Total costs to account for	$186,600		
(Step 5)	Assignment of costs			
	Good units completed and transferred out (7,000 units)	—		
	Costs before adding normal spoilage	$138,250	7,000# × $8.85 + 7,000# × $10.90	
	Normal spoilage (700 units)	13,825	700# × $8.85 + 700# × $10.90	
(A)	Total cost of good units completed & transf. out	152,075		
(B)	Abnormal spoilage (300 units)	5,925	300# × $8.85 + 300# × $10.90	
	Work in process, ending (2,000 units)			
	Direct materials	17,700	2,000# × $8.85	
	Conversion costs	10,900		1,000# × $10.90
(C)	Total work in process, ending	28,600		
(A)+(B)+(C)	Total costs accounted for	$186,600		

#Equivalent units of direct materials and conversion costs calculated in Step 2 in Panel A above.

EXHIBIT 18-3
First-in, First-out (FIFO) Method of Process Costing with Spoilage Forming Department of the Anzio Company for July 2000

PANEL A: UNITS STEPS 1 AND 2—SUMMARIZE OUTPUT IN PHYSICAL UNITS AND COMPUTE EQUIVALENT UNITS

| | | (Step 2) Equivalent Units | |
| | (Step 1) | | |
Flow of Production	Physical Units	Direct Materials	Conversion Costs
Work in process, beginning	1,500		
Started during current period	8,500		
To account for	10,000		
Good units completed and transferred out during current period:			
From beginning work in process[§]	1,500		
$1,500 \times (100\% - 100\%)$: $1,500 \times (100\% - 60\%)$		0	600
Started and completed	5,500[#]		
$5,500 \times 100\%$; $5,500 \times 100\%$		5,500	5,500
Normal spoilage*	700		
$700 \times 100\%$; $700\% \times 100\%$		700	700
Abnormal spoilage[†]	300		
$300 \times 100\%$; $300 \times 100\%$		300	300
Work in process, ending[‡]	2,000		
$2,000 \times 100\%$; $2,000 \times 50\%$		2,000	1,000
Accounted for	10,000		
Work done in current period only		8,500	8,100

[§]Degree of completion in this department: direct materials, 100%; conversion costs, 60%.
[#]7,000 physical units completed and transferred out minus 1,500 physical units completed and transferred out from beginning work in process inventory.
*Normal spoilage is 10% of good units transferred out: $10\% \times 7,000 = 700$ units. Degree of completion of normal spoilage in this department: direct materials, 100%; conversion costs, 100%.
[†]Abnormal spoilage = Actual spoilage – Normal spoilage = 1,000 – 700 = 300 units. Degree of completion of abnormal spoilage in this department: direct materials, 100%; conversion costs, 100%.
[‡]Degree of completion in this department: direct materials, 100%; conversion costs, 50%.

PANEL B: STEPS 3, 4 AND 5—COMPUTE EQUIVALENT UNIT COSTS, SUMMARIZE TOTAL COSTS TO ACCOUNT FOR, AND ASSIGN COSTS TO UNITS COMPLETED, TO SPOILAGE UNITS, AND TO UNITS IN ENDING WORK IN PROCESS

		Total Production Costs	Direct Materials	Conversion Costs
(Step 3)	Work in process, beginning	$ 21,000		
	Costs added in current period	165,600	$76,500	$89,100
	Divided by equivalent units of work done in current period		$\div$ 8,500	$\div$ 8,100
	Equivalent unit costs of work done in current period		$ 9	$ 11
(Step 4)	Total costs to account for	$186,600		
(Step 5)	Assignment of costs:			
	Good units completed and transferred out (7,000 units)			
	Work in process, beginning (1,500 units)	$ 21,000		
	Direct materials added in current period	0	0[§] $\times$ $9	
	Conversion costs added in current period	6,600		600[§] $\times$ $11
	Total from beginning inventory before normal spoilage	27,600		
	Started and completed before normal spoilage (5,500 units)	110,000	5,500[§] $\times$ $9 + 5,500[§] $\times$ $11	
	Normal spoilage (700 units)	14,00	700[§] $\times$ $9 + 700[§] $\times$ $11	
(A)	Total cost of good units transferred out	151,600		
(B)	Abnormal spoilage (300 units)	6,000		
	Work in process, ending (2,000 units)		300[§] $\times$ $9 + 300 $\times$ $11	
	Direct materials	18,000		
	Conversion costs	11,000	2,000[§] $\times$ $9	
(C)	Total work in process, ending	29,000		1,000[§] $\times$ $11
(A)+(B)+(C)	Total costs accounted for	$186,600		

[§]Equivalent units of direct materials and conversion costs calculated in Step 2 in Panel A above.

assigned to the Loss from Abnormal Spoilage account and do not appear in the good-unit costs.[1]

OBJECTIVE 4

Account for spoilage in process costing using the first-in, first-out method

FIFO Method and Spoilage

Exhibit 18-3 on page 635, Panel A presents Steps 1 and 2 using the FIFO method that focuses on equivalent units of work done in the current period. Exhibit 18-3, Panel B presents Steps 3, 4 and 5. Note how the FIFO method keeps the costs of the beginning work-in-process inventory separate and distinct from the costs of work done in the current period when assigning costs. All spoilage costs are assumed to be related to units completed during this period, using the unit costs of the current period.[2] With the exception of accounting for spoilage, the FIFO method is the same as presented in Chapter 17.

OBJECTIVE 5

Account for spoilage in process costing using the standard costs method

Standard Costs and Spoilage

This section assumes you have studied Chapters 7 and 8 and the standard costs method in Chapter 17. Otherwise, omit this section.

Standard costing methods can also be used to account for normal and abnormal spoilage. We illustrate how much simpler the calculations become by continuing our Anzio Company example.

Suppose the Anzio Company develops standard costs for the Processing Department. Assume the same standard costs apply to the beginning inventory and to work done in July 2000.

Standard Costs for Processing Department for July 2000

Direct materials	$ 8.50 per unit
Conversion costs	10.50 per unit
Total production costs	$19.00 per unit

Hence the beginning inventory at standard costs is:

Direct materials	1,500 × $8.50	$12,750
Conversion costs	900 × $10.50	9,450
Total costs		$22,200

Exhibit 18-4, Panel A, presents Steps 1 and 2. These steps are the same as for the FIFO methods described in Exhibit 18-3. In Step 3, the cost per equivalent unit is simply the standard cost: direct materials $8.50, and conversion costs, $10.50. Standard costing makes calculating equivalent unit costs unnecessary and so simplifies process costing. The costs to account for in Step 4 are at *standard* costs and hence differ from the costs to account for under the weighted-average and FIFO methods, which are at *actual* costs. Step 5 uses standard costs to assign costs to units completed, to normal and abnormal spoilage, and to ending work-in-process inventory. Variances can be measured and analyzed in the manner described in Chapters 7 and 8.

Journal Entries

The information from Panel B in Exhibits 18-2, 18-3, and 18-4 supports the following journal entries:

---

[1] The actual costs of spoilage (and rework) are often greater than the costs recorded in the accounting system because opportunity costs of disruption of the production line, storage, and lost contribution margins are not recorded in accounting systems. Chapter 19 discusses these opportunity costs from a cost management viewpoint.

[2] If the FIFO method were used in its purest form, normal spoilage costs would be split between the goods started and completed during the current period and those completed from beginning work in process—using the appropriate unit costs of the period in which the units were worked on. The simpler, modified FIFO method, as illustrated in Exhibit 18-3, in effect uses the unit costs of the current period for assigning normal spoilage costs to the goods completed from beginning work in process. This modified FIFO method assumes that all normal spoilage traceable to the beginning work in process was started and completed during the current period.

EXHIBIT 18-4
Use of Standard Costs in Process Costing with Spoilage Forming Department of the Anzio Company for July 2000

PANEL A: STEPS 1 AND 2—SUMMARIZE OUTPUT IN PHYSICAL UNITS AND COMPUTE EQUIVALENT UNITS

		(Step 2) Equivalent Units	
Flow of Production	(Step 1) Physical Units	Direct Materials	Conversion Costs
Work in process, beginning	1,500		
Started during current period	8,500		
To account for	10,000		
Good units completed and transferred out during current period:			
From beginning work in process§	1,500		
1,500 × (100% − 100%); 1,500 × (100% − 60%)		0	600
Started and completed	5,500$^\#$		
5,500 × 100%; 5,500 × 100%		5,500	5,500
Normal spoilage*	700		
700 × 100%; 700 × 100%		700	700
Abnormal spoilage†	300		
300 × 100%; 300 × 100%		300	300
Work in process, ending‡	2,000		
2,000 × 100%; 2,000 × 50%		2,000	1,000
Accounted for	10,000		
Work done in current period only		8,500	8,100

§Degree of completion in this department: direct materials, 100%; conversion costs, 60%.
$^\#$7,000 physical units completed and transferred out minus 1,500 physical units completed and transferred out from beginning work in process inventory.
*Normal spoilage is 10% of good units transferred out: 10% × 7,000 = 700 units. Degree of completion of normal spoilage in this department: direct materials, 100%; conversion costs, 100%.
†Abnormal spoilage = Actual spoilage − Normal spoilage = 1,000 − 700 = 300 units. Degree of completion of abnormal spoilage in this department: direct materials, 100%, conversion costs, 100%.
‡Degree of completion in this department: direct materials, 100%; conversion costs, 50%.

PANEL B: STEPS 3, 4 AND 5—COMPUTE EQUIVALENT UNIT COSTS, SUMMARIZE TOTAL COSTS TO ACCOUNT FOR, AND ASSIGN COSTS TO UNITS COMPLETED, TO SPOILAGE UNITS, AND TO UNITS IN ENDING WORK IN PROCESS

		Total Production Costs	Direct Materials	Conversion Costs
(Step 3)	Standard cost per equivalent unit	$ 19.00	$ 8.50	$10.50
	Work in process, beginning	$ 22,000		
	Costs added in current period at standard prices			
	Direct materials, 8,500 × $8.50; conversion costs, 8,100 × $10.50	157,300	72,250	85,050
(Step 4)	Costs to account for			
(Step 5)	Assignment of costs at standard costs:	$179,500		
	Good units completed and transferred out (7,000 units)			
	Work in process, beginning (1,500 units)	$ 22,200		
	Direct materials added in current period	0	0§ × $8.50	
	Conversion costs added in current period	6,300		600§ × $10.50
	Total from beginning inventory before normal spoilage	28,500		
	Started and completed before normal spoilage (5,500 units)	104,500	5,500§ × $8.50 + 5,500§ × $10.50	
	Normal spoilage (700 units)	13,300	700§ × $8.50 + 700§ × $10.50	
(A)	Total cost of good units transferred out	146,300		
(B)	Abnormal spoilage (300 units)	5,700	300§ × $18.50 + 300§ × $10.50	
	Work in process, ending (2,000 units)			
	Direct materials	17,000	2,000§ × $8.50	
	Conversion costs	10,500		1,000§ × $10.50
(C)	Total work in process, ending	27,500		
(A)+(B)+(C)	Total costs accounted for	$179,500		

§Equivalent units of direct materials and conversion costs calculated in Step 2 in Panel A above.

	Weighted Average		FIFO	
1. Finished Goods	152,075		151,600	
Work in Process—Processing		152,075		151,600
To transfer good units completed in July.				
2. Loss from Abnormal Spoilage	5,925		6,000	
Work in Process—Processing		5,925		6,000
To recognize abnormal spoilage detected in July.				

Allocating Costs of Normal Spoilage

Spoilage might actually occur at various points or stages of the production cycle, but spoilage is typically not detected until one or more specific points of inspection. The cost of spoiled units is assumed to be all costs incurred by spoiled units prior to inspection. When spoiled goods have a disposal value, the net cost of spoilage is computed by deducting disposal value from the costs of the spoiled goods accumulated to the point of inspection. The unit costs of abnormal and normal spoilage are the same when the two are detected simultaneously. However, situations might arise when abnormal spoilage is detected at a different point than normal spoilage. In such cases, the unit cost of abnormal spoilage would differ from the unit cost of normal spoilage.

Costs of abnormal spoilage are separately accounted for as losses for the period. Recall, however, that normal spoilage costs are added to costs of good units. Accounting for normal spoilage, therefore, raises an additional issue: Should normal spoilage costs be allocated between completed units and ending work-in-process inventory? One approach is to presume that normal spoilage occurs at the inspection point in the production cycle and to allocate its cost over all units that have passed that point. In the Anzio Company example, spoilage is assumed to occur when finished units are inspected, so no cost of normal spoilage is allocated to ending work in process.

Whether the cost of normal spoilage is allocated to the units in ending work-in-process inventory, in addition to completed units, depends strictly on whether they have passed the point of inspection. For example, if the inspection point is presumed to be the halfway stage of the production cycle, work in process that is more than 50% completed would be allocated a full measure of normal spoilage costs, calculated on the basis of all costs incurred prior to the point of inspection. But work in process that is under 50% completed would not be allocated any normal spoilage costs. The appendix to this chapter contains additional discussion concerning various assumptions about spoilage.

JOB COSTING AND SPOILAGE

OBJECTIVE 6

Account for spoilage in job costing

The concepts of normal and abnormal spoilage also apply to job costing systems. Abnormal spoilage is usually regarded as controllable by the manager. It is separately identified with the goal of eliminating it altogether. Costs of abnormal spoilage are not considered as product manufacturing costs and are written off as costs of the period in which detection occurs. Normal or planned spoilage in job costing systems, however, are considered part of normal manufacturing costs, although increasingly, managements are tolerating only small amounts of spoilage as normal. The costs are then assigned to individually distinct jobs, a step unnecessary in process costing since masses of similar units are manufactured.

We illustrate the accounting for spoilage in job costing using the following example.

Example 3: In the Hull Machine Shop, 5 aircraft parts out of a job lot of 50 aircraft parts are spoiled. Costs assigned up to the point of inspection are $100 per unit. Hull calculates these costs on the basis of its inventory costing assumptions—weighted average, FIFO, or standard costs. We do not, however, emphasize cost flow assumptions in our presentation here or in subsequent sections. The current disposal price of the spoiled parts is estimated to be $30 per part. When the spoilage is detected, the spoiled goods are inventoried at $30 per unit.

Normal Spoilage Attributable to a Specific Job   When normal spoilage occurs because of the specifications of a specific job, that job bears the cost of the spoilage reduced by the current disposal value of that spoilage. The journal entry to recognize the disposal value of the salvage (items in parentheses indicate subsidiary postings) is as follows:

Materials Control (spoiled goods at current disposal value): 5 × $30	150	
Work-in-Process Control (specific job): 5 × $30		150

The effect of this accounting is that the net cost of the normal spoilage, $350 ($500 − $150) becomes a direct cost of the 45 (50 − 5) good units produced.

Normal Spoilage Common to All Jobs   In some cases, spoilage may be considered a normal characteristic of a given production cycle. The spoilage inherent in the process only coincidentally occurs when a specific job is being worked on. The spoilage then is not attributable, and hence is not charged, to the specific job. Instead, it is costed as manufacturing overhead. The budgeted manufacturing overhead allocation rate includes a provision for normal spoilage cost. Therefore, normal spoilage cost is spread, through overhead allocation, over all jobs rather than loaded on particular jobs only.[3]

Materials Control (spoiled goods at current disposal value): 5 × $30	150	
Manufacturing Department Overhead Control (normal spoilage): 5 × $70	350	
Work-in-Process Control (specific job): 5 × $100		500

Abnormal Spoilage   If the spoilage is abnormal, the net loss is highlighted to management by charging the loss to an abnormal loss account:

Materials Control (spoiled goods at current disposal value): 5 × $30	150	
Loss from Abnormal Spoilage: 5 × $70	350	
Work-in-Process Control (specific job): 5 × $100		500

REWORKED UNITS

Reworked units are unacceptable units of production that are subsequently reworked into good units and sold.

   Consider the Hull Machine Shop data (Example 3). Assume that the five spoiled parts used in our Hull Machine Shop illustration are reworked. The journal entry for the $500 of total costs (details of costs assumed) assigned to the five spoiled units before considering rework costs are as follows:

OBJECTIVE 7

Account for reworked units

Work-in-Process Control	500	
Materials Control		200
Wages Payable		200
Manufacturing Overhead Allocated		100

Assume that rework costs equal $190 (direct materials, $40; direct labour, $100; manufacturing overhead, $50).

Normal Rework Attributable to a Specific Job   If the rework is normal but occurs because of the requirements of a specific job, the rework costs are charged to that job. The journal entry is as follows:

[3]Note that costs *already assigned to products* are being charged back to Manufacturing Overhead Control, which generally accumulates only *costs incurred*, not both costs incurred and costs already assigned.

Work-in-Process Control (specific job)	190	
Materials Control		40
Wages Payable		100
Manufacturing Overhead Allocated		50

Normal Rework Common to All Jobs   When rework is normal and not attributable to any specific job, the costs of rework are charged to manufacturing overhead and spread, through overhead allocation, over all jobs.

Manufacturing Department Overhead Control (rework)	190	
Materials Control		40
Wages Payable		100
Manufacturing Overhead Allocated		50

Abnormal Rework   If the rework is abnormal, it is highlighted to management by charging abnormal rework to a separate loss account.

Loss from Abnormal Rework	190	
Materials Control		40
Wages Payable		100
Manufacturing Overhead Allocated		50

Accounting for rework in process costing only requires abnormal rework to be distinguished from normal rework. Abnormal rework is accounted for as in job costing. Since masses of similar units are manufactured, accounting for normal rework follows the accounting described for normal rework common to all jobs.

Costing rework highlights the resources wasted on activities that would not have to be undertaken if the product were made correctly. It prompts management to seek ways to reduce rework, for example, by designing new products or processes, training workers, or investing in new machines. Calculating rework costs helps management perform cost-benefit analyses for various alternatives. To emphasize the importance of eliminating rework and to simplify the accounting, some companies expense all rework, including the costs of normal rework, as an expense of the current period.

ACCOUNTING FOR SCRAP

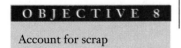

OBJECTIVE 8

Account for scrap

Scrap is a product that has minimal (frequently zero) sales value compared with the sales value of the main or joint product(s).

There are two major aspects of accounting for scrap:

1. Planning and control, including physical tracking
2. Inventory costing, including when and how to affect operating income

Initial entries to scrap records are most often in physical or nonfinancial terms such as in kilograms or units. In various industries, items such as stamped-out metal sheets are quantified by weighing, counting, or some other expedient means. Scrap records not only help measure efficiency, but also often focus on a tempting source for theft. Scrap reports are prepared as source documents for periodic summaries of the amount of actual scrap compared with budgeted norms or standards. Scrap is either sold or disposed of quickly, or stored in some routine way for later sale, disposal, or reuse.

The tracking of scrap often extends into the financial records. For example, in one survey, 60% of the companies maintained a distinct cost for scrap somewhere in their cost accounting system.[4] The issues here are similar to those discussed in Chapter 15 regarding the accounting for byproducts:

[4]Price Waterhouse, *Survey of the Cost Management Practices of Selected Midwest Manufacturers* (Cleveland: Price Waterhouse, 1989), p. 10.

Rejection in the Electronics Industry

From country to country and from industry to industry, the rates of rejected and reworked units vary tremendously. The data in the following table focus on different segments of the U.S. electronics industry. The data reported are median numbers drawn from companies that are members of the American Electronics Association. The reject rate is the rejects as a percentage of items checked by quality control. The rework rate is reworked items as a percentage of rejects and returns. The scrap rate reports scrap as a percentage of all materials and products purchased. Also reported is the operating income to net sales figure for each segment of the electronics industry.

Segment of Electronics Industry	Reject Rate (% rejects)	Rework Rate (% rework)	Scrap Rate (% scrap)	Operating Income to Net Sales
1. Computers and office equipment (includes mainframes, minicomputers, microcomputers, printers, and point-of-sale equipment)	2.55%	6.50%	0.62%	5.33%
2. Electronic components and accessories (includes printed circuit boards and semiconductors)	1.55	2.00	1.63	4.53
3. Specialized production equipment (includes semiconductor production equipment)	7.50	10.00	0.43	5.67
4. Telecommunications equipment (includes telephone, radio, and TV apparatus)	1.00	2.00	1.29	4.73
5. Aerospace, nautical, and military equipment (includes aircraft manufacture and guided missiles)	—	1.50	0.52	6.52
6. Laboratory and measurement devices (includes optical instruments and process control equipment)	4.90	3.30	0.66	3.89
7. Prepackaged software	1.00	0.80	0.06	4.02
8. Computer-related services (includes data processing and computer systems design)	5.00	N/A	N/A	7.78

The reject rate for specialized production equipment is five times as great as that for electronic components and semiconductors. Electronic components and semiconductors show a low percentage of rework (in part because rework is not always possible when defects arise). Scrap rates are reasonably small across all industry segments. The operating income to net sales ratio ranges from 3.89% for laboratory and measurement devices to 6.52% for aerospace, nautical, and military equipment. Given these profitability percentages, reductions in reject and rework rates can markedly increase the profitability of many companies in the electronics industry.

Source: American Electronics Association, *Operating Ratios Survey* 1993-94, (Santa Clara, CA: American Electronics Association, 1993)

1. When should any value of scrap be recognized in the accounting records: at the time of production of scrap or at the time of sale of scrap?
2. How should revenue from scrap be accounted for?

To illustrate, we extend our Hull Machine Shop example by assuming that the manufacture of aircraft parts generates scrap. We further assume that the normal scrap from a job lot has a total sales value of $45.

Recognizing Scrap at the Time of Sale of Scrap

When scrap is sold, the simplest accounting is to regard scrap sales as a separate line item of other revenues. The journal entry is:

Sale of scrap:	Cash or Accounts Receivable	45	
	Sales of Scrap		45

Scrap Attributable to a Specific Job Job costing systems sometimes trace the sales of scrap to the jobs that yielded the scrap. This method is used only when the tracing can be done in an economically feasible way. For example, the Hull Machine Shop and particular customers may reach an agreement that provides for charging specific jobs with all rework or spoilage costs and for crediting these jobs with all scrap sales that arise from them. The journal entry is:

Scrap returned to storeroom:	[No journal entry. Memo of quantity received and related job is entered in the inventory record.]		
Sale of scrap:	Cash or Accounts Receivable	45	
	Work in Process Control		45
	Posting made to specific job record.		

Unlike spoilage and rework, there is no cost attached to the scrap, and hence no normal or abnormal scrap. All scrap sales, whatever the amount, are credited to the specific job. Scrap sales reduce the materials' costs of the job.

Scrap Common to All Jobs In this case:

Scrap returned to storeroom:	[No journal entry. Memo of quantity received and related job is entered in the inventory record.]	

This method does not link scrap with any particular physical product. Instead, all products bear regular production costs without any credit for scrap sales except in an indirect manner: The sales of scrap are considered when setting budgeted manufacturing overhead rates. Thus, the budgeted overhead rate is lower than it would be if no credit for scrap sales were allowed in the overhead budget. This accounting for scrap is used in both process-costing and job-costing systems.

Recognizing Scrap at the Time of Production of Scrap

Our preceding illustrations assume that scrap returned to the storeroom is sold or disposed of quickly and hence not assigned an inventory cost figure. Scrap, however, sometimes has a significant market value, and the time between storing it and selling or reusing it can be quite long. Under these conditions, the company is justified in inventorying scrap at a conservative estimate of net realizable value so that production costs and related scrap recovery may be recognized in the same accounting period. Some companies tend to delay sales of scrap until the market price is most attractive. Volatile price fluctuations are typical for scrap metal. If scrap inventory becomes significant, it should be inventoried at some "reasonable value"—a difficult task in the face of volatile market prices.

Scrap Attributable to a Specific Job The journal entry in the Hull Machine Shop example is:

Scrap returned to storeroom:	Materials Control	45	
	Work in Process Control		45

Scrap Common to All Jobs The journal entry in this case is:

Scrap returned to storeroom:	Materials Control	45	
	Manufacturing Department Overhead Control		45

Observe that Materials Control account is debited in place of Cash or Accounts Receivable.

Managing Waste and Environmental Costs at the DuPont Corporation

The DuPont Corporation manufactures a wide range of chemicals and chemical products. DuPont classifies the spoilage and scrap it generates as waste. Besides the cost of lost materials, chemical waste is a particular problem because of its impact on the environment. Strict environmental laws require that chemical waste be disposed of in an environmentally safe way, further adding to the cost of generating waste.

DuPont calculates the full cost of waste to include (1) the costs of materials lost in the chemical process minus their scrap value; (2) the full costs of semifinished and finished products spoiled; (3) the full cost of disposing of or treating the waste, such as site charges for hazardous waste, or costs of scrubbers and biotreatment plants to treat the waste; and (4) the cost of any solvents used to clean plant and equipment as a result of generating waste.

DuPont believes that calculating the total costs of waste helps businesses understand the operational and environmental costs of waste. This motivates individual plants to take actions such as redesigning products, reconfiguring processes, or investing in capital equipment to reduce these costs.

DuPont's acrylonitrile process at Beaumont, Texas is a good example of how DuPont reduces waste costs. This plant generated more than 110 million pounds of ammonium sulfate waste, which was disposed of by injecting the waste in deep wells. While DuPont considered the disposal of the waste environmentally safe, the U.S. Environmental Protection Agency included ammonium sulfate in its figures of the toxic releases generated by DuPont. To improve its environmental performance and to reduce its waste costs, a team of DuPont engineers began modifying the reactor operating conditions for producing acrylonitrile. By changing the process, the team improved the yields of acrylonitrile and reduced ammonium sulfate waste by 70 million pounds. By altering its acrylonitrile process, DuPont saved a million dollars a year in lower waste and waste disposal costs.

Dupont Canada
www.dupont.ca

Source: Adapted from 1990 Environmental Respect Awards, DuPont Corporation, and based on discussions with Dale Martin, Manager, Environmental Effectiveness.

When this scrap is sold, the journal entry is:

Sale of scrap:	Cash or Accounts Receivable	45	
	Materials Control		45

Scrap is sometimes reused as direct materials rather than sold as scrap. Then it should be debited to Materials Control as a class of direct materials and carried at its estimated net realizable value. For example, the entries when the scrap generated is common to all jobs are:

Scrap returned to storeroom:	Materials Control	45	
	Manufacturing Department Overhead Control		45
Reuse of scrap:	Work in Process Control	45	
	Materials Control		45

The accounting for scrap under process costing follows the accounting for jobs when scrap is common to all jobs since process costing is used to cost the mass manufacture of similar units. The high cost of scrap focuses management's attention on ways to reduce scrap and to use it more profitably. For example, General Motors has redesigned its plastic injection molding processes to reduce the scrap plastic that must be broken away from its molded products. General Motors also regrinds and reuses the plastic scrap as direct materials, saving substantial input costs.

PROBLEM

Burlington Textiles has some spoiled goods that had an assigned cost of $4,000 and zero net disposal value.

REQUIRED

Prepare a journal entry for each of the following conditions under both (a) process costing (Department A) and (b) job costing:

1. Abnormal spoilage of $4,000
2. Normal spoilage of $4,000 related to general plant operations
3. Normal spoilage of $4,000 related to specifications of a particular job

SOLUTION

(a) Process Costing			(b) Job Costing		
1. Loss from Abnormal Spoilage	4,000		Loss from Abnormal Spoilage	4,000	
Work in Process—Dept. A		4,000	Work in Process Control (job)		4,000
2. [No entry until units are transferred. Then the normal spoilage costs are transferred along with the other costs:]			Manufacturing Dept. Overhead Control	4,000	
			Work in Process Control (job)		4,000
Work in Process—Dept. B	4,000				
Work in Process—Dept. A		4,000			
3. [Not applicable]			[No entry. Spoilage cost remains in Work in Process Control (job)]		

SUMMARY

The following points are linked to the chapter's learning objectives.

1. Spoilage is unacceptable units of production that are discarded or are sold for net disposal proceeds. Reworked units are unacceptable units that are subsequently reworked and sold as acceptable finished goods. Scrap is a product that has minimal sales value compared with the sales value of the main or joint product(s).

2. Normal spoilage is spoilage that arises under efficient operating conditions. Abnormal spoilage is spoilage that is not expected to arise under efficient operating conditions. Many accounting systems explicitly recognize both forms of spoilage when computing output units. Normal spoilage is typically included in the cost of good output units, while abnormal spoilage is recorded as a loss for the period.

3. The weighted-average method of process costing combines costs in beginning inventory with costs in the current period when determining the costs of good units (which includes a normal spoilage amount) and the costs of abnormal spoilage.

4. The FIFO method of process costing keeps costs in beginning inventory separate from the costs in the current period when determining the cost of good units (which includes a normal spoilage amount). The cost of abnormal spoilage is kept separate from the cost of good units.

5. The standard costing method of process costing uses standard costs to determine the cost of good units (which includes a normal spoilage amount) and the costs of abnormal spoilage.

6. With a job-costing system, companies can decide to assign spoilage to specific jobs. Alternatively, they can allocate spoilage to all jobs as part of manufacturing overhead. Loss from abnormal spoilage is recorded as a period cost.

7. Reworked units should be indistinguishable from nonreworked good units when completed, and hence the two are assigned the same costs. Normal rework can be assigned to a specific job, or if common, to all jobs as part of manufacturing overhead. Abnormal rework is written off as a period cost.

8. Scrap is recognized in the accounting records either at the time of its sale or at the time of its production.

APPENDIX: INSPECTION AND SPOILAGE AT INTERMEDIATE STAGES OF COMPLETION IN PROCESS COSTING

Consider how the timing of inspection at various stages of completion affects the amount of normal and abnormal spoilage. Assume that normal spoilage is 10% of the good units passing inspection in the Forging Department of the Dana Corporation, a manufacturer of automobile parts. Direct materials are added at the start of production in the Forging Department. Conversion costs are allocated evenly during the process.

Dana Corporation
www.dana.com

Suppose inspection had occurred at the 20%, 50%, or 100% completion stage. A total of 8,000 units are spoiled in all cases. Note how the number of units of normal spoilage and abnormal spoilage change. Normal spoilage is computed on the number of *good units* that pass the inspection point *in the current period*. The following data are for October.

Flow of Production	Physical Units Inspection at Stage of Completion		
	At 20%	At 50%	At 100%
Work in process, beginning (25%)*	11,000	11,000	11,000
Started during October	74,000	74,000	74,000
To account for	85,000	85,000	85,000
Good units completed and transferred out (85,000 − 8,000 spoiled − 16,000 ending)	61,000	61,000	61,000
Normal spoilage	6,600†	7,700‡	6,100§
Abnormal spoilage (8,000 − normal spoilage)	1,400	300	1,900
Work in process, ending (75%)*	16,000	16,000	16,000
Accounted for	85,000	85,000	85,000

*Degree of completion for conversion costs of this department at the dates of the work-in-process inventories.
†10% × (74,000 units started − 8,000 units spoiled), since only the units started passed the 20% completion inspection point in the current period. Beginning work in process is excluded from this calculation since it is 25% complete.
‡10% × (85,000 units − 8,000 units spoiled), since *all* units passed the 50% completion inspection point in the current period.
§10% × 61,000, since 61,000 units were fully completed and inspected in the current period.

The following diagram shows the flow of physical units for January and illustrates the preceding normal spoilage numbers. Note that 61,000 good units are completed and transferred out (11,000 from beginning work in process and 50,000 started and completed during the period), and 16,000 units are in ending work in process.

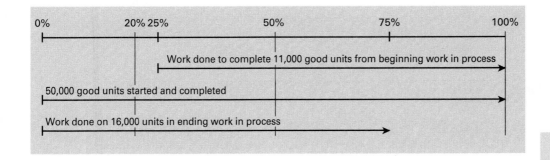

EXHIBIT 18-5
Steps 1 and 2: Computing Equivalent Units with Spoilage, Forging Department of the Dana
Corporation for October 2000

Flow of Production	(Step 1) Physical Units	(Step 2) Equivalent Units	
		Direct Materials	Conversion Costs
Good units completed and transferred out during current period	61,000	61,000	61,000
Normal spoilage	7,700	7,700	3,850
Abnormal spoilage	300	300	150
Work in process, ending*	16,000	16,000	12,000
Total	85,000	85,000	77,000
Deduct work in process, beginning†	11,000	11,000	2,250
Started during current period	74,000		
Work done in current period only		74,000	74,750

*Degree of completion: direct materials, 100%; conversion costs, 75%.
†Degree of completion: direct materials, 100%; conversion costs, 25%.

To see the number of units passing each inspection point, draw vertical lines at the 20%, 50% and 100% inspection points. Note that the vertical line at 20% cuts two horizontal lines, 50,000 good units started and completed and 16,000 units in ending work in process for a total of 66,000 good units. (It does not cut the line representing work done on the 11,000 good units completed from beginning work in process because these units were already 25% complete at the start of the period and hence were not inspected this period.) Normal spoilage equals 10% × 66,000 = 6,600 units. Similarly, the vertical line at the 50% point cuts all three horizontal lines indicating that 11,000 + 50,000 + 16,000 = 77,000 good units pass this point. Normal spoilage in this case is 10% × 77,000 = 7,700 units. At the 100% point, normal spoilage = 10% × (11,000 + 50,000) = 6,100 units.

Exhibit 18-5 above shows the computation of equivalent units assuming inspection at the 50% completion stage. The calculations depend on how much direct materials and conversion costs were incurred to get the units to the point of inspection. In Exhibit 18-5 the spoiled units have a full measure of direct materials and a 50% measure of conversion costs. The computations of equivalent unit costs and the assignments of total costs to units completed and in ending work in process would be similar to those in previous illustrations. Since ending work in process has passed the inspection point in this example, these units would bear normal spoilage costs, just like the units that have been completed and transferred out.

TERMS TO LEARN

This chapter contains definitions of the following important terms:
abnormal spoilage (p. 631)   reworked units (p. 630)
normal spoilage (p. 630)   spoilage (p. 630)

ASSIGNMENT MATERIAL

QUESTIONS

18-1 Why is there an unmistakable trend in manufacturing to improve quality?

18-2 Distinguish between spoilage, reworked units, and scrap.

18-3 "Normal spoilage is planned spoilage." Discuss.

18-4 "Costs of abnormal spoilage are lost costs." Explain.

18-5 "What has been regarded as normal spoilage in the past is not necessarily acceptable as normal in the present or future." Explain.

18-6 "Abnormal units are inferred rather than identified." Explain.

18-7 "In accounting for spoiled goods, we are dealing with cost assignment rather than cost incurrence." Explain.

18-8 "Total input includes abnormal as well as normal spoilage and is therefore irrational as a basis for computing normal spoilage." Do you agree? Why?

18-9 "The point of inspection is the key to the allocation of spoilage costs." Do you agree? Explain.

18-10 "The unit cost of normal spoilage is the same as the unit cost of abnormal spoilage." Do you agree? Explain.

18-11 "In job order costing, the costs of specific normal spoilage are charged to specific jobs." Do you agree? Explain.

18-12 "The costs of reworking defective units are always charged to the specific jobs where the defects were originally discovered." Do you agree? Explain.

18-13 "Abnormal rework costs should be charged to a loss account, not to manufacturing overhead." Do you agree? Explain.

18-14 When is a company justified in inventorying scrap?

18-15 How do company managements use information about scrap?

EXERCISES

18-16 Normal and abnormal spoilage in units. The following data, in physical units, describe a grinding process for January:

Work process, beginning	19,000
Started during current period	150,000
To account for	169,000
Spoiled units	12,000
Good units completed and transferred out	132,000
Work in process, ending	25,000
Accounted for	169,000

Inspection occurs at the 100% conversion stage. Normal spoilage is 5% of the good units passing inspection.

REQUIRED
1. Compute the normal and abnormal spoilage in units.
2. Assume that the equivalent unit cost of a spoiled unit is $10. Compute the amount of potential savings if all spoilage were eliminated, assuming that all other costs would be unaffected. Comment on your answer.

18-17 Weighted-average method, spoilage. Anderson Plastics makes plastic rear lamps for cars using an injection molding process. Spoiled units are detected upon inspection at the end of the process and are disposed of at zero net disposal price. Assume normal spoilage is 15% of the good output produced. Anderson Plastics uses the weighted-average method of process costing. The following information about actual costs for April 2000 is available.

	Direct Materials		Conversion Costs	
	Equivalent Units	**Total Costs**	**Equivalent Units**	**Total Costs**
Work in process, April 1 (15,000 units)	15,000	$120,000	14,000	$140,000
Work done during April 2000	25,000	210,000	28,000	301,000
To account for	40,000	$330,000	42,000	$441,000
Good units completed and transferred out during April 2000	20,000	?	20,000	?
Normal and abnormal spoilage	4,000		4,000	
Work in process, April 30 (20,000 units)	16,000	?	18,000	?

REQUIRED

1. Calculate the cost per equivalent unit of beginning work in process and of work done in the current period for direct materials and conversion costs.
2. Summarize total costs to account for, and assign these costs to units completed (and transferred out), normal spoilage, abnormal spoilage, and ending work in process using the weighted-average method.
3. What is the cost of a good unit completed and transferred out under the weighted-average method?

18-18 FIFO method. Refer to the information in Exercise 18-17.

REQUIRED
Do Exercise 18-17 using the FIFO method.

18-19 Standard costing method. Refer to the information in Exercise 18-17. Suppose Anderson determines standard costs of $8.20 per (equivalent) unit for direct materials and $10.20 per (equivalent) unit for conversion costs for both beginning work in process and work done in the current period.

REQUIRED
Do Exercise 18-17 using the standard costing method.

18-20 Equivalent units, equivalent unit costs, spoilage. (CMA, adapted) Consider the following data for November 2000 from the Gray Manufacturing Company, which makes silk pennants and operates a process-costing system. All direct materials are added at the beginning of the process and conversion costs are added evenly during the process. Spoilage is detected upon inspection at the completion of the process. Spoiled units are disposed of at zero net disposal price.

	Physical Units (pennants)	Direct Materials	Conversion Costs
Work in process, November 1*	1,000	$ 1,300	$ 1,250
Started in November 2000	?		
Good units completed and transferred out during November 2000	9,000		
Normal spoilage	100		
Abnormal spoilage	50		
Work in process, November 30†	2,000		
Costs added during November 2000		$12,180	$27,750

*Degree of completion: direct materials, 100%; conversion costs, 50%.
†Degree of completion: direct materials, 100%; conversion costs, 30%.

REQUIRED

1. Compute the equivalent units of work done in the current period for direct materials and conversion costs. Show physical units in the first column.
2. Calculate the cost per equivalent unit for direct materials and conversion costs.

18-21 Weighted-average method, assigning costs (continuation of 18-20).

REQUIRED
For the data in Exercise 18-20, summarize total costs to account for, and assign these costs to units completed (and transferred out), normal spoilage, abnormal spoilage, and to units in ending work in process.

18-22 FIFO method, spoilage, equivalent units and unit costs. Refer to the information in Exercise 18-20. Suppose Gray Manufacturing Company uses the FIFO method of process costing instead of the weighted-average method.

REQUIRED

1. Compute equivalent units for direct materials and conversion costs. Show physical units in the first column of your schedule.
2. Calculate cost per equivalent unit for direct materials and conversion costs.

18-23 FIFO method, assigning costs (continuation of 18-22).

REQUIRED
For the data in Exercise 18-20, use the FIFO method to summarize total costs to account for, and assign these costs to units completed and transferred out, normal spoilage, abnormal spoilage, and to units in ending work in process.

18-24 Weighted-average method, spoilage. Superchip specializes in the manufacture of microchips for aircraft. Direct materials are added at the start of the production process. Conversion costs are added evenly during the process. Some units of this product are spoiled as a result of defects not detectable before inspection of finished goods. Normally, the spoiled units are 15% of the good units transferred out. Spoiled units are disposed of at zero net disposal price.

Superchip uses the weighted-average method of process costing. Summary data for September 2000 are:

	Physical Units (microchips)	Direct Materials	Conversion Costs
Work in process, September 1*	400	$ 64,000	$ 10,200
Started in September 2000	1,700		
Good units completed and transferred out during September 2000	1,400		
Work in process, September 30†	300		
Costs added during September 2000		$378,000	$153,600

*Degree of completion: direct materials, 100%; conversion costs, 30%.
†Degree of completion: direct materials, 100%; conversion costs, 40%.

REQUIRED

1. For each cost element, compute the equivalent units. Show physical units in the first column.
2. For each cost element, calculate the cost per equivalent unit.
3. Summarize the total costs to account for, and assign these costs to units completed (and transferred out), normal spoilage, abnormal spoilage, and ending work in process.

18-25 FIFO method, spoilage. Refer to the information in Exercise 18-24.

REQUIRED

Do Exercise 18-24 using the FIFO method of process costing.

18-26 Standard costing method, spoilage. Refer to the information in Exercise 18-24. Suppose Superchip determines standard costs of $205 per (equivalent) unit for direct materials and $80 per (equivalent) unit for conversion costs for both beginning work in process and work done in the current period.

REQUIRED

Do Exercise 18-24 using standard costs.

18-27 Spoilage and job costing. (L. Bamber) Bamber Kitchens produces a variety of items in accordance with special job orders from hospitals, plant cafeterias, and university dormitories. An order for 2,500 cases of mixed vegetables costs $6 per case: direct materials, $3; direct manufacturing labour, $2; and manufacturing overhead allocated, $1. The manufacturing overhead rate includes a provision for normal spoilage. Consider each requirement independently.

REQUIRED

1. Assume that a labourer dropped 200 cases. Suppose that part of the 200 cases could be sold to a nearby prison for $200 cash. Prepare a journal entry to record this event. Calculate and explain briefly the unit cost of the remaining 2,300 cases.
2. Refer to the original data. Tasters at the company reject 200 of the 2,500 cases. The 200 cases are disposed of for $400. Assume that this rejection rate is considered normal. Prepare a journal entry to record this event, and calculate the unit cost if:
   a. The rejection is attributable to exacting specifications of this particular job.
   b. The rejection is characteristic of the production process and is not attributable to this specific job.
   Are unit costs the same in requirements 2(a) and 2(b)? Explain your reasoning briefly.
3. Refer to the original data. Tasters rejected 200 cases that had insufficient salt. The product can be placed in a vat, salt added, and reprocessed into jars. This operation, which is considered normal, will cost $200. Prepare a journal entry to record this event, and calculate the unit cost of all the cases if:
   a. This additional cost was incurred because of the exacting specifications of this particular job.
   b. This additional cost occurs regularly because of difficulty in seasoning.

Are unit costs the same in requirements 3(a) and 3(b)? Explain your reasoning briefly.

18-28 Reworked units, costs of rework. White Goods assembles washing machines at its Cambridge plant. In February 2000, 60 tumbler units that cost $44 each from a new supplier were defective and had to be disposed of at zero disposal price. White Goods was able to rework all 60 washing machines by substituting new tumbler units purchased from one of its existing suppliers. Each replacement tumbler cost $50.

REQUIRED

1. What alternative approaches are there to account for the materials costs of reworked units?
2. Should White Goods use the $44 or $50 amount as the costs of materials reworked? Explain.
3. What other costs might White Goods include in its analysis of the total costs of rework due to the tumbler units purchased from the (now) bankrupt supplier?

18-29 Scrap, job order costing. The Mendoza Company has an extensive job costing facility that uses a variety of metals. Consider each requirement independently.

REQUIRED

1. Job 372 uses a particular metal alloy that is not used for any other job. Assume that scrap is accounted for at the time of sale of scrap. The scrap is sold for $490. Prepare the journal entry.
2. The scrap from Job 372 consists of a metal used by many other jobs. No record is maintained of the scrap generated by individual jobs. Assume that scrap is accounted for at the time of its sale. Scrap totalling $4,000 is sold. Prepare two journal entries that could be used to account for the sale of scrap.
3. Suppose the scrap generated in requirement 2 is returned to the storeroom for future use and a journal entry is made to record the scrap. A month later, the scrap is reused as direct material on a subsequent job. Prepare the journal entries to record these transactions.

PROBLEMS

18-30 Weighted-average method, spoilage. The Alston Company operates under a weighted-average method of process costing. It has two departments, Cleaning and Milling. For both departments, conversion costs are added uniformly throughout the processes. However, direct materials are added at the beginning of the process in the Cleaning Department, and additional direct materials are added at the end of the milling process. The costs and unit production statistics for May follow. All unfinished work at the end of May is 25% completed as to conversion costs. The beginning inventory (May 1) was 80% completed as to conversion costs as of May 1. All completed work is transferred to the next department.

	Cleaning	Milling
Beginning Inventories		
Cleaning: $1,000 direct materials, $800 conversion costs	$1,800	
Milling: $6,450 previous department cost (transferred-in cost) and $2,450 conversion costs		$8,900
Costs Added During Current Period		
Direct materials	$9,000	$ 640
Conversion costs	$8,000	$4,950
Physical Units		
Units in beginning inventory	1,000	3,000
Units started this month	9,000	7,400
Good units completed and transferred out	7,400	6,000
Normal spoilage	740*	300[†]
Abnormal spoilage	260	100

*Normal spoilage in the Cleaning Department is 10% of good units completed and transferred out.
[†]Normal spoilage in the Milling Department is 5% of good units completed and transferred out.

ADDITIONAL INFORMATION

1. Spoilage is assumed to occur at the end of each of the two processes when the units are inspected. Spoiled units are disposed of at zero net disposal price.
2. Assume that there is no shrinkage, evaporation, or abnormal spoilage other than that indicated in the information given.
3. Carry unit cost calculations to three decimal places where necessary. Calculate final totals to the nearest dollar.

REQUIRED

Using the weighted-average method, summarize total costs to account for, and assign these costs to units completed (and transferred out), normal spoilage, abnormal spoilage, and ending work in process for the Cleaning Department. (Problem 18-32 explores additional facets of this problem.)

18-31 FIFO method, spoilage. Refer to the information in Problem 18-30.

REQUIRED

Do Problem 18-30 using the FIFO method of process costing. (Problem 18-33 explores additional facets of this problem.)

18-32 Weighted-average method, Milling Department (continuation of 18-30). Refer to the information in Problem 18-30.

REQUIRED

Summarize total costs to account for, and assign these costs to units completed (and transferred out), normal spoilage, abnormal spoilage, and ending work in process for the Milling Department.

18-33 FIFO method, Milling Department (continuation of 18-31). Refer to the information in Problem 18-30.

REQUIRED

Use the FIFO method to summarize total costs to account for, and assign these costs to units completed (and transferred out), normal spoilage, abnormal spoilage, and ending work in process for the Milling Department.

18-34 Job cost spoilage and scrap. (F. Mayne) Canadian Metal Fabricators, Ltd. has a large job, No. 2734, that calls for producing various ore bins, chutes, and metal boxes for enlarging a copper concentrator. The following charges were made to the job in November 2000:

Direct materials	$26,951
Direct manufacturing labour	15,076
Manufacturing overhead	7,538

The contract with the customer called for the total price to be based on a cost-plus approach. The contract defined cost to include direct materials, direct manufacturing labour costs, and manufacturing overhead to be allocated at 50% of direct manufacturing labour costs. The contract also provided that the total costs of all work spoiled were to be removed from the billable cost of the job and that the benefits from scrap sales were to reduce the billable cost of the job.

REQUIRED

1. In accordance with the stated terms of the contract, prepare journal entries for the following two items:
   a. A cutting error was made in production. The up-to-date job cost record for the batch of work involved showed materials of $650, direct manufacturing labour of $500, and allocated overhead of $250. Because fairly large pieces of metal were recoverable, the company believed that the scrap value was $600 and that the materials recovered could be used on other jobs. The spoiled work was sent to the warehouse.
   b. Small pieces of metal cuttings and scrap in November 2000 amounted to $1,250, which was the price quoted by a scrap dealer. No journal entries have been made with regard to the scrap until the price was quoted by the scrap dealer. The scrap dealer's offer was immediately accepted.
2. Consider normal and abnormal spoilage. Suppose the contract described above had contained the clause "a normal spoilage allowance of 1% of the job costs will be included in the billable costs of the job."
   a. Is this clause specific enough to define exactly how much spoilage is normal and how much is abnormal? Explain.

b. Repeat requirement 1(a) with this "normal spoilage of 1%" clause in mind. You should be able to provide two slightly different journal entries.

18-35 Job costing, rework. The Bristol Corporation manufactures two brands of motors, SM-5 and RW-8. The costs of manufacturing each SM-5 motor, excluding rework costs, are direct materials, $300; direct manufacturing labour, $60; and manufacturing overhead, $190. Defective units are sent to a separate rework area. Rework costs per SM-5 motor are direct materials, $60; direct manufacturing labour, $45; and manufacturing overhead, $75.

In February 2000, Bristol manufactured 1,000 SM-5 and 500 RW-8 motors, and 80 of the SM-5 motors required rework. Bristol classifies 50 of these motors as normal rework for SM-5 and RW-8, and not specifically attributable to SM-5. None of the RW-8 motors required rework. Bristol allocates manufacturing overhead on the basis of machine-hours required to manufacture SM-5 and RW-8. Each SM-5 and RW-8 motor requires the same number of machine-hours.

REQUIRED
1. Prepare journal entries to record the accounting for rework.
2. What were the total rework costs for SM-5 motors in February 2000?

18-36 Job costing, scrap. The Wong Corporation makes two different types of hubcaps for cars—models HM3 and JB4. Circular pieces of metal are stamped out of steel sheets (leaving the edges as scrap), formed, and finished. The stamping operation is identical for both types of hubcaps. During March, Wong manufactured 20,000 units of HM3 and 10,000 units of JB4. In March, manufacturing costs per unit of HM3 and JB4 before accounting for the scrap are as follows:

	HM3	JB4
Direct materials	$10	$15
Direct manufacturing labour	3	4
Materials-related manufacturing overhead (materials-handling, storage, etc.)	2	3
Other manufacturing overhead	6	8
Unit manufacturing costs	$21	$30

Materials-related manufacturing costs are allocated to products at 20% of direct materials costs. Other manufacturing overhead is allocated to products at 200% of direct manufacturing labour costs. Since the same metal sheets are used to make both types of hubcaps, Wong maintains no records of the scrap generated by the individual products. Scrap generated during manufacturing is accounted for at the time it is returned to the storeroom as an offset to materials-related manufacturing overhead. The value of scrap generated during March and returned to the storeroom was $7,000.

REQUIRED
1. Prepare a journal entry to summarize the accounting for scrap during March.
2. Suppose the scrap generated in March was sold in April for $7,000. Prepare a journal entry to account for this transaction.
3. What adjustments, if any, would you make for scrap when calculating the manufacturing cost per unit for HM3 and JB4 in March? Explain.

18-37 Physical units, inspection at various stages of completion. (Chapter Appendix) Normal spoilage is 6% of the good units passing inspection in a forging process. In March, a total of 10,000 units were spoiled. Other data include units started during March, 120,000; work in process, beginning, 14,000 units (20% completed for conversion costs); work in process, ending, 11,000 units (70% completed for conversion costs).

REQUIRED
In columnar form, compute the normal and abnormal spoilage in units, assuming inspection at 15%, 40%, and 100% stages of completion.

18-38 Weighted-average, inspection at 80% completion. (A. Atkinson) (Chapter Appendix) Ottawa Manufacturing produces a plastic toy in a two-stage manufacturing operation. The company uses a weighted-average process costing system. During the month of June, the following data were recorded for the Finishing Department:

Units of beginning inventory	10,000
Percentage of beginning units completed	25%
Cost of direct materials in beginning work in process	$0
Units started	70,000
Units completed	50,000
Units in ending inventory	20,000
Percentage of ending units completed	95%
Spoiled units	10,000
Costs added during current period:	
Direct materials	$655,200
Direct manufacturing labour	$635,600
Manufacturing overhead	$616,000
Work in process, beginning:	
Conversion costs	$ 42,000
Transferred-in costs	$ 82,900
Cost of units transferred in during current period	$647,500

Conversion costs are incurred evenly throughout the process. Direct materials costs are incurred when production is 90% complete. Inspection occurs when production is 80% complete. Normal spoilage is 10% of all good units that pass inspection. Spoiled units are disposed of at zero net disposal price.

REQUIRED

For the month of June, summarize total costs to account for, and assign these costs to units completed (and transferred out), normal spoilage, abnormal spoilage, and ending work in process.

18-39 **Job costing, spoilage.** (CMA, adapted) The Richport Company manufactures products that often require specification changes or modifications to meet its customers' needs. Still, Richport has been able to establish a normal spoilage rate of 2.5% of *normal input.* Normal spoilage is recognized during the budgeting process and classified as a component of manufacturing overhead when determining the overhead rate.

Rose Duncan, one of Richport's inspection managers, obtains the following information for Job No. N1192-122 that was recently completed. A total of 122,000 units were started, and 5,000 units were rejected at final inspection yielding 117,000 good units. Duncan noted that 900 of the first units produced were rejected because of a design defect that was considered very unusual; this defect was corrected immediately, and no further units were rejected for this reason. These units were disposed of after incurring an additional cost of $1,200. Duncan was unable to identify a rejection pattern for the remaining 4,100 rejected units. These units can be sold at $7 per unit.

The total costs for all 122,000 units of Job No. N1192-122 are presented here. The job has been completed, but the costs have yet to be transferred to finished goods.

Direct materials	$2,196,000
Direct manufacturing labour	1,830,000
Manufacturing overhead	2,928,000
Total manufacturing costs	$6,954,000

REQUIRED

1. Calculate the unit quantities of normal and abnormal spoilage.
2. Prepare the appropriate journal entry (or entries) to properly account for Job No. N1192-122 including spoilage, disposal, and transfer of costs to finished goods control.
3. Richport Company has small profit margins and is anticipating very low operating income for the year. The controller, Thomas Rutherford, tells Martha Gonzales, the management accountant responsible for Job No. N1192–122, the following, "This was an unusual job. I think all 5,000 spoiled units should be considered normal." Martha knows that similar jobs had been done in the past and that the spoilage levels for Job N1192–122 were much greater than in the past. She feels Thomas made these comments because he wants to show higher operating income for the year.

a. Prepare the journal entry (or entries), similar to the journal entry (or entries) prepared in requirement 2, to account for Job No. N1192–122 if all spoilage were considered normal. By how much will Richport's operating income be affected if all spoilage is considered normal?

b. What should Martha Gonzales do?

COLLABORATIVE LEARNING PROBLEM

18–40 Weighted-average method, spoilage, working backwards. The Cooking Department of Spicer Inc. uses a process-costing system. Direct materials are added at the beginning of the cooking process. Conversion costs are added evenly during the cooking process. Consider the following data for the Cooking Department of Spicer Inc. for the month of January:

	Physical Units	Direct Materials	Conversion Costs
Work in process, January 1[*]	10,000	$220,000	$30,000
Started in January	74,000		
Good units completed and transferred out during January	61,00		
Spoiled units	8,000		
Work in process, January 31	15,000		
Costs added during January		$1,480,000	$942,000
Cost per equivalent unit of work done in January		$20	$12

[*]Degree of completion: direct materials, 100%; conversion costs, 25%.

Spicer uses the FIFO method of process costing. Inspection occurs when production is 100% completed. Normal spoilage is 11% of good units completed and transferred out during the current period.

INSTRUCTION

Form pairs of students to complete the following requirements.

REQUIRED

1. For each cost category, compute equivalent units of work done in the current period (January).
2. For each cost category, compute equivalent units of work done to complete beginning work-in-process inventory, to start and complete new units, for normal and abnormal spoilage units, and to produce ending work-in-process inventory.
3. For each cost category, calculate the percentage of completion of ending work-in-process inventory.
4. Summarize total costs to account for, and assign these costs to units completed (and transferred out), normal spoilage, abnormal spoilage, and ending work in process.

COST MANAGEMENT: QUALITY, TIME, AND THE THEORY OF CONSTRAINTS

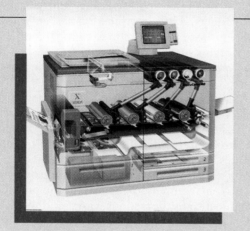

Quality and time are important elements to cost management, as this chapter's Photon Corporation example illustrates for a copy-machine manufacturer. The costs related to poor quality and late deliveries can be significant. In today's competitive technology industries, these elements can make the difference between successful and unsuccessful companies.

LEARNING OBJECTIVES

After studying this chapter, you should be able to:

1. Explain four cost categories in a cost of quality program
2. Describe three methods that companies use to identify quality problems
3. Identify the relevant costs and benefits of quality improvements
4. Provide examples of nonfinancial quality measures of customer satisfaction and internal performance
5. Use both financial and nonfinancial measures of quality
6. Describe customer response time, and explain the reasons for and the cost of lines and delays
7. Define three main measurements in the theory of constraints
8. Describe four steps in managing bottlenecks

As we stated in Chapter 1, global competition and demanding customers have forced managers to improve the quality of their products and to deliver them to customers faster. But achieving higher quality and faster delivery requires managers to identify and overcome a variety of organizational constraints. This chapter examines how management accounting can assist managers in taking initiatives in the quality and time areas, and in making decisions under many constraints.

QUALITY AS A COMPETITIVE WEAPON

British Telecom
www.bt.com

Samsung
www.samsung.com

Many companies throughout the world—for example, Hewlett-Packard and Ford Motor Company in Canada and the United States; British Telecom in the United Kingdom; Fujitsu and Toyota in Japan; Crysel in Mexico; and Samsung in Korea—view total quality management as one of the most important success factors, because it reduces costs and increases customer satisfaction. Several prestigious, high-profile awards—for example, the Malcolm Baldrige Quality Award in the United States, the Deming Prize in Japan, and the Premio Nacional de Calidad in Mexico—have been instituted to recognize exceptional quality.

International quality standards have emerged. For example, ISO 9000, developed by the International Organization for Standardization, is a set of five international standards for quality management adopted by more than 85 countries. ISO 9000 series was created to enable companies to effectively document and certify their quality system elements. Some companies, such as DuPont and General Electric, are increasingly requiring their suppliers to obtain ISO 9000 certification. Why? To reduce their own costs by evaluating, assessing, and working to improve the quality of their suppliers' products. Thus, certification and an emphasis on quality are rapidly becoming conditions for competing in the global market.

Quality improvement programs often result in substantial savings and higher revenues. At Dell Computer, quality initiatives, which have increased customer satisfaction, have also fueled its 3,077% increase in revenues, 18,780% increase in profits, and 29,600% increase in stock price over the past 8 years. (For details, see Concepts in Action Box, p. 657.) Sometimes, the benefit of better quality is preserving revenues, not generating higher revenues. If competitors are improving quality, then a company that does not invest in quality improvement will likely suffer a decline in its market share, revenues, and profits.

As corporations' responsibilities toward the environment grow, many managers are paying increasing attention to environmental quality and the problems of air pollution, waste water, oil and chemical spills, hazardous waste, and waste management. The costs of environmental damage (failure costs) can be extremely high to corporations under environmental legislation. Companies can be charged multimillion-dollar fines. For example, Exxon paid $125 million in fines and restitution on top of $1 billion in civil payments for the *Exxon Valdez* oil spill, which harmed the Alaskan coast. In 1994, the International Organization for Standardization announced ISO 14000, an environmental management standard. The standard's goal is to nudge organizations to pursue environmental goals vigorously by developing (1) environmental management systems to improve the environmental impact of an organization's activities, products, and services and (2) environmental auditing and performance evaluation systems to review and provide feedback on how well an organization has achieved its environmental goals.

Official Exxon Valdez Oil
Spill Restoration Site
www.oilspill.state.ak.us

The term *quality* refers to a wide variety of factors—fitness for use, the degree to which a product satisfies the needs of a customer, and the degree to which a product conforms to design specification and engineering requirements. We discuss two basic aspects of quality—*quality of design* and *conformance quality.*[1]

---

[1]The American Society for Quality Control defines *quality* as the totality of features and characteristics of a product made or a service performed according to specifications, to satisfy customers at the time of purchase and during use. ANSI/ASQC A3-1978, *Quality Systems Terminology* (Milwaukee, Wis.: American Society for Quality Control, 1978). See also R. DeVor, T. Chang, and J. Sutherland, *Statistical Quality Design and Control* (New York: Macmillan, 1992); and J. Evans and W. Lindsay, *The Management and Control of Quality* (St. Paul: West, 1993).

Quality of design measures how closely the characteristics of products or services match the needs and wants of customers. Suppose customers of photocopying machines want copiers that combine copying, faxing, scanning, and electronic printing. Photocopying machines that fail to meet these customer needs fail in the quality of their design. Similarly, if customers of a bank want an automated payment system for their monthly bills, not providing this facility would be a quality of design failure.

Conformance quality is the performance of a product or service according to design and production specifications. For example, if a photocopying machine mishandles paper or breaks down, it will have failed to satisfy conformance quality. Products not conforming to specifications must be repaired, reworked, or scrapped at an additional cost to the organization. If nonconformance errors are not corrected within the plant and the product breaks down at the customer site, even greater repair costs as well as the loss of customer goodwill—often the highest quality cost of all—may result. In the banking industry, depositing a customer's cheque into the wrong bank account is an example of conformance quality failure.

CONCEPTS IN ACTION

Dell Computer's Quest

What has been behind Dell Computer's phenomenal 29,600% increase in stock price, 3,077% growth in revenue, and 18,780% increase in profits over the last 8 years? Certainly not a high gross margin–Dell's is a modest 22% of revenues. In a word, it is QUEST–Quality Underlies Every Single Task–an employee-oriented initiative of total quality management. QUEST is the bedrock of Dell's execution and innovation, leading to a superb product quality, speedy manufacturing, and responsive post-sales customer service.

Under the QUEST approach, workers are organized into teams of salespersons, assemblers, testers, technicians, shippers, and maintenance personnel. The QUEST team starts to work on manufacturing a computer only after a salesperson has received a firm order. Only one person, the assembler, builds the system from start to finish. Testers rigorously test the product for reliability and performance, often for over 24 hours. Technicians then install customized and proprietary software, and shippers ship the product directly to customers. Dell does not sell its computers through retailers.

Dell Computer
www.dell.com

Dells success is built around customer satisfaction. *Fortune* magazine ranked Dell as one of the top two computer manufacturers in customer satisfaction in 1998. Customers cited hardware quality and reliability, performance and speed, and service and support as the reasons for their satisfaction. How does Dell achieve such high customer satisfaction ratings?

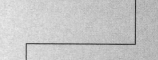

◆ *By helping customers to configure their products to meet customers' own requirements and specifications.* As a result, all hardware and software are designed to be compatible with and seamlessly integrated into existing systems.

◆ *By manufacturing a high-quality product.* During the manufacturing process, operators receive immediate feedback about the product. If the product fails a test, operators troubleshoot to correct the problem. Dell takes no chances with respect to performance in its testing procedures. Its notebooks, for example, must survive intense shaking on a vibrating table, exposure to extreme temperatures, and a series of drop tests. In 1997, Dell won the top spot in *PC Computing* magazine's "notebook torture test."

◆ *By providing excellent technical support after delivering products to its customers.* When customers call with questions, the technical support staff responds promptly with high-quality advice.

Source: Adapted from K. Chambers, "Inside the Cell," *Dell Insider,* May-June 1997: Dell Computer Annual Report 1997.

The following diagram illustrates our framework:

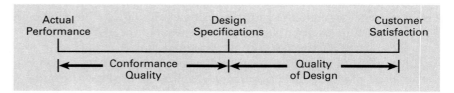

To travel the road from actual performance to customer satisfaction, companies must meet design specifications through conformance quality, but they must also design products to satisfy customers through quality of design.

COSTS OF QUALITY

OBJECTIVE 1

Explain four cost categories in a cost of quality program

Costs of quality (COQ). Costs incurred to prevent or rectify the production of a low-quality product.

Prevention costs. Costs incurred in precluding the production of products that do not conform to specifications.

Appraisal costs. Costs incurred in detecting which of the individual units or products do not conform to specifications.

Internal failure costs. Costs incurred when a nonconforming product is detected before it is shipped to customers.

External failure costs. Costs incurred when a nonconforming product is detected after it is shipped to customers.

The **costs of quality (COQ)** are costs incurred to prevent or rectify the production of a low-quality product. These costs focus on conformance quality and are incurred in all areas of the value chain. They are classified into four categories:

1. **Prevention costs.** Costs incurred in precluding the production of products that do not conform to specifications

2. **Appraisal costs.** Costs incurred in detecting which of the individual units of products do not conform to specifications

3. **Internal failure costs.** Costs incurred when a nonconforming product is detected before it is shipped to customers

4. **External failure costs.** Costs incurred when a nonconforming product is detected after it is shipped to customers

Exhibit 19-1 presents examples of individual cost of quality items in each of these four categories reported on COQ reports. Note that the items included in Exhibit 19-1 come from all value-chain business functions and are broader than the internal failure costs of spoilage, rework, and scrap in manufacturing considered in Chapter 18.

We illustrate the various issues in managing quality—from computing the costs of quality, to identifying quality problems, to taking actions to improve quality—using the Photon Corporation as example. Photon makes many products. Our presentation focuses on Photon's photocopying machines, which earned an operating income of $24 million on sales of $300 million (20,000 copiers) in 2000. Photon determines the costs of quality of its photocopying machines using the 7-step activity-based costing approach described in Chapter 5.

◆ **Step 1:** *Identify the Chosen Cost Object(s).* The cost object is the 20,000 photocopying machines that Photon makes. Photon's goal is to calculate the total costs of quality of these machines.

EXHIBIT 19-1
Items Pertaining to Costs of Quality Reports

Prevention Costs	Appraisal Costs	Internal Failure Costs	External Failure Costs
Design engineering	Inspection	Spoilage	Customer support
Process engineering	On-line product manufacturing and process inspection	Rework	Transportation costs
Quality engineering		Scrap	Manufacturing/ process engineering
Supplier evaluations	Product testing	Breakdown maintenance	Warranty repair costs
Preventive equipment maintenance		Manufacturing/ process engineering on internal failure	Liability claims
Quality training			
New materials used to manufacture products			

- ◆ **Step 2:** *Identify the Direct Costs of Quality of the Product.* The photocopying machines have no direct costs of quality.
- ◆ **Step 3:** *Select the Cost-Allocation Bases to Use for Allocating Indirect Costs of Quality to the Product.* Column 1 of Exhibit 19-2, Panel A, classifies activities that result in prevention, appraisal, internal failure, and external failure costs and indicates the value-chain business functions in which the costs occur. For example, the inspection activity results in appraisal costs and occurs in the manufacturing function. Photon chooses the number of inspection hours rather than the number of inspections as the cost-allocation base for the inspection activity

EXHIBIT 19-2
Activity-Based COQ Analysis for the Photon Corporation

PANEL A: COQ REPORT

Costs of Quality and Value-Chain Category (1)	Allocation Base or Cost Driver		Total Costs (4) = (2) × (3)	Percentage of Sales (5) = (4) ÷ $300,000,000
	Quantity (2)	Rate (number assumed) (3)		
Prevention Costs				
Design engineering (R&D/design)	40,000* hours	$80 per hour	$ 3,200,000	1.07%
Process engineering (R&D/design)	45,000* hours	$60 per hour	2,700,000	0.90
Total prevention costs			5,900,000	1.97
Appraisal Costs				
Inspection (manufacturing)	240,000† hours	$40 per hour	9,600,000	3.20
Total appraisal costs			9,600,000	3.20
Internal Failure Costs				
Rework (manufacturing)	2,500‡ copiers reworked	$4,000 per copier reworked	10,000,000	3.33
Total internal failure costs			10,000,000	3.33
External Failure Costs				
Customer support (marketing)	3,000$ copiers repaired	$200 per copier repaired	600,000	0.20
Transportation costs (distribution)	3,000 copiers repaired	$240 per copier repaired	720,000	0.24
Warranty repair (customer service)	3,000 copiers repaired	$4,400 per copier repaired	13,200,000	4.40
Total external failure costs			14,520,000	4.84
Total costs of quality			$40,020,000	13.34%

PANEL B: OPPORTUNITY COST ANALYSIS

Costs of Quality Category (1)	Quantity of Lost Sales (2)	Contribution Margin per Copier (number assumed) (3)	Total Estimated Contribution Margin Lost (4) = (2) × (3)	Percentage of Sales (5) = (4) ÷ $300,000,000
External Failure Costs				
Estimated forgone contribution margin and income on lost sales	2,000# copiers	$6,000	$12,000,000	4.00%
Total costs of quality			$12,000,000	4.00%

*Based on special studies.
†12 hours per copier × 20,000 copiers.
‡12.5% of 20,000 copiers manufactured required rework.
$15% of 20,000 copiers manufactured required warranty repair service.
#Estimated by Photon's Market Research Department.

because inspection-hours has a better cause-and-effect relationship with inspection costs. To avoid details, we do not provide information on the total quantities of each of these cost-allocation bases used in all of Photon's operations and businesses.

◆ **Step 4:** *Identify the Indirect Costs of Quality Associated with Each Cost-Allocation Base.* These are the total costs (fixed and variable) incurred on each of the costs of quality activities, such as inspections, in all of Photon's operations. To avoid details, we do not provide information about these total costs.

◆ **Step 5:** *Compute the Rate per Unit of Each Cost-Allocation Base Used to Allocate Indirect Costs of Quality to Products.* For each activity, the total costs calculated in Step 4 is divided by the total quantity of the cost-allocation base calculated in Step 3 to compute the rate per unit for each cost-allocation base. Column 2 of Exhibit 19-2, Panel A shows these rates (without supporting calculations). For example, Photon calculates the rate of $40 per hour for the inspection activity by dividing the total costs of inspection incurred in all of Photon's operations by the total quantity of inspection-hours for all of Photon's operations.

◆ **Step 6:** *Compute the Indirect Costs of Quality Allocated to the Product.* Photon first determines the quantities of each of the cost-allocation bases used by the photocopying machines. These quantities are shown in Column 3 of Exhibit 19-2, Panel A. For example, Photon determines that photocopying machines use 240,000 inspection-hours. Column 4 of Exhibit 19-2, Panel A shows the indirect costs of quality of the photocopying machines. To calculate these costs, the total quantity of the cost-allocation base used by the photocopying machines for each activity is multiplied by the cost-allocation rate calculated in Step 5 (Exhibit 19-2, Panel A, column 2). For example, quality-related inspection costs for the photocopying machines are $9,600,000 ($40 per hour × 240,000 inspection-hours).

◆ **Step 7:** *Compute the Total Costs of Quality by Adding all Direct and Indirect Costs of all Quality Assigned to It.* Exhibit 19-2, Panel A, shows Photon's total costs of quality reported on the COQ report for photocopying machines at $40.02 million, of which the largest categories are $14.52 million in total external failure costs and $10 million in total internal failure costs—a sum of $24.52 million. Total reported costs of quality are 13.34% of current sales.

Do not assume, however, that costs reported on COQ reports represent the total costs of quality for a company. COQ reports typically exclude opportunity costs, such as forgone contribution margins and income from lost sales, lost production, or lower prices, that result from poor quality. Why? Because opportunity costs are difficult to estimate and generally not recorded in accounting systems. Nevertheless, opportunity costs can be substantial and important driving forces in quality improvement programs. Exhibit 19-2, Panel B, presents the analysis of the opportunity costs of poor quality at Photon. Photon Corporation's Market Research Department estimates lost sales of 2,000 photocopying machines because of external failures. The forgone contribution and operating income of $12 million measures the financial costs from dissatisfied customers who have returned machines to Photon and from sales lost because of quality problems. Total costs of quality (including opportunity costs) equal $52.02 million (Panel A, $40.02 million + Panel B, $12 million), or 17.34% of current sales. Opportunity costs account for 23% ($12 million ÷ $52.02 million) of Photon's total costs of quality.

The COQ report and the opportunity cost analysis highlight Photon's high internal and external failure costs. To reduce costs of quality, Photon must identify and reduce failures caused by quality problems.

METHODS USED TO ANALYZE QUALITY PROBLEMS

Control Charts

Statistical quality control (SQC) or statistical process control (SPC) is a formal means of distinguishing between random variation and nonrandom variation in an operating process. A key tool in SQC is a control chart. A **control chart** is a graph of a series of successive observations of a particular step, procedure, or operation taken at regular intervals of time. Each observation is plotted relative to specified ranges that represent the expected distribution. Only those observations outside the specified limits are ordinarily regarded as nonrandom and worth investigating.

Exhibit 19-3 presents control charts for the daily defect rates observed at Photon's three production lines. Defect rates in the prior 60 days for each plant were assumed to provide a good basis from which to calculate the distribution of daily defect rates. The arithmetic mean (μ, read "mu") and standard deviation (σ, read "sigma") are the two parameters of the distribution that are used in the control charts in Exhibit 19-3. On the basis of experience, the company decides that any observation outside the $\mu \pm 2\sigma$ range should be investigated.

For production line A in Exhibit 19-3, all observations are within the range of $\pm 2\sigma$ from the mean. Management, then, believes no investigation is necessary. For production line B, the last two observations signal that an out-of-control occurrence is highly likely. Given the $\pm 2\sigma$ rule, both observations would lead to an investigation. Production line C illustrates a process that would not prompt an investigation under the $\pm 2\sigma$ rule but may well be out of control. Note that the last eight observations show a clear direction and that the direction by day 5 (the third point in the last eight) is away from the mean. Statistical procedures have been developed using the trend as well as the level of the variable in question to evaluate whether a process is out of control.

Pareto Diagrams

Observations outside control limits serve as inputs to *Pareto diagrams*. A **Pareto diagram** or Frequency Chart indicates how frequently each type of failure (defect) occurs. Exhibit 19-4 presents a Pareto diagram for Photon's quality problems. Fuzzy and unclear copies are the most frequently recurring problem.

The fuzzy-copy problem results in high rework costs, because, in many cases, Photon discovers the fuzzy image problem only after the copier has been built. Sometimes fuzzy images occur at customer sites, resulting in high warranty and repair costs.

Cause-and-Effect Diagrams

The most frequently occurring problems identified by the Pareto diagram are analyzed using *cause-and-effect diagrams*. A **cause-and-effect diagram** identifies potential causes of failures or defects. As a first step, Photon analyzes the causes of the most frequently occurring failure, fuzzy and unclear copies. Exhibit 19-5 presents the cause-and-effect diagram for this problem. The exhibit identifies four major

OBJECTIVE 2

Describe three methods that companies use to identify quality problems

Control chart. Graph of a series of successive observations of a particular step, procedure, or operation taken at regular intervals of time. Each observation is plotted relative to specified ranges that represent the expected distribution.

Pareto diagram. Diagram that indicates how frequently each type of failure (defect) occurs.

Cause-and-effect diagram (fishbone diagram). Diagram that identifies the potential causes of failures or defects. Four major categories of potential causes of failure are identified: human factors, methods and design factors, machine-related factors, and materials and components factors.

EXHIBIT 19-3
Statistical Quality Control Charts: Daily Defect Rate at the Photon Corporation

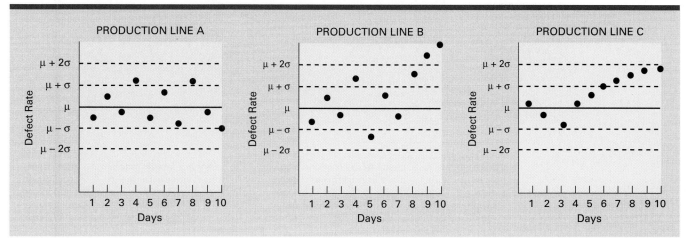

EXHIBIT 19-4
Pareto Diagram for the Photon Corporation

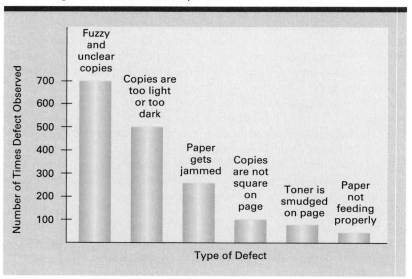

categories of potential causes of failure—human factors, methods and design factors, machine-related factors, and materials and components factors. As additional arrows are added for each cause, the general appearance of the diagram begins to resemble a fishbone (hence, cause-and-effect diagrams are also called *fishbone diagrams*).[2]

EXHIBIT 19-5
Cause-and-Effect Diagram for Fuzzy and Unclear Copies at the Photon Corporation

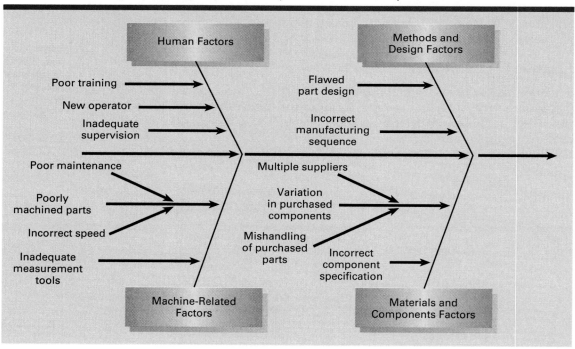

[2]Managers in U.S. electronics companies consider the following factors (ranked in order of importance with 1 = most important) as contributing to improvements in quality: 1. Better product design 2. Improved process design 3. Improved training of operators 4. Improved products from suppliers 5. Investments in technology and equipment. See G. Foster and L. Sjoblom, "Survey of Quality Practices in the U.S. Electronics Industry," *Journal of Management Accounting Research*, Vol. 8, 1996, pp. 55-86.

RELEVANT COSTS AND BENEFITS OF QUALITY IMPROVEMENT

Careful analysis of the cause-and-effect diagram reveals that the steel frame (or chassis) of the copier is often mishandled as it travels from the suppliers' warehouses to Photon's plant. The frame must satisfy very precise specifications and tolerances; otherwise, various copier components (such as drums, mirrors, and lenses) attached to the frame will be improperly aligned. Mishandling causes the dimensions of the frame to vary from specifications, resulting in fuzzy images.

OBJECTIVE 3

Identify the relevant costs and benefits of quality improvements

The team of engineers working to solve the fuzzy-image problem offers two alternative solutions: (1) to improve the inspection of the frame immediately upon delivery or (2) to redesign and strengthen the frame and the containers used to transport them to better withstand mishandling during transportation.

Should Photon inspect incoming frames more carefully or redesign them and their containers? Exhibit 19-6 shows the costs and benefits of each choice. Management estimates that additional inspection will cost $400,000 ($40 per hour × 10,000 hours). Redesign will cost an additional $460,000 (design engineering, $80 per hour × 2,000 hours; process engineering, $60 per hour × 5,000 hours). The potential benefits of incurring these costs are lower internal and external failure costs. The key question here is: What are the relevant cost savings and other relevant benefits? Photon considers only a one-year time horizon for analyzing this decision, because Photon plans to introduce a completely new line of copiers at the end of the year. Photon believes that even as it improves quality, it will not be able to save any of the fixed costs of internal and external failure. To identify the relevant cost savings, Photon divides each category of failure costs into its fixed and variable components.

Consider first the internal failure costs of rework. Fixed and variable costs for each reworked copier are:

Variable costs (including direct materials, direct rework labour, and supplies)	$1,600
Allocated fixed costs (equipment, space, and allocated overhead)	2,400
Total costs (Exhibit 19-2, Panel A, column 3)	$4,000

If Photon chooses to inspect the frame more carefully, it expects to eliminate rework on 600 copiers and save variable costs of $960,000 ($1,600 × 600) in rework. See Exhibit 19-6, column 1. Photon believes that fixed rework costs will be unaffected. If Photon chooses the redesign alternative, it expects to eliminate rework on 800 copiers, saving $1,280,000 ($1,600 × 800). See Exhibit 19-6, column 2.

Next consider external failure costs. Photon currently repairs 3,000 copiers at customer sites. If incoming frames are inspected more carefully, Photon estimates that 500 fewer copiers will require warranty repair and that it will be able to sell 250 additional copiers. If the frame is redesigned, Photon estimates that 700 fewer copiers will require warranty repair and that it will be able to sell 300 additional copiers.

Variable and fixed costs per copier repaired of individual external failure COQ items described in Exhibit 19-2 (Panel A, column 4) are as follows:

	Variable Costs	Fixed Costs	Total Costs
Customer support costs	$ 80	$ 120	$ 200
Transportation costs	180	60	240
Warranty repair costs	1,800	2,600	4,400

As Photon eliminates repair work on copiers, it expects to save only the variable costs of customer support, transportation, and warranty repair.

Note that the savings per copier in rework costs, customer support costs, transportation costs, and warranty repair costs in Exhibit 19-6 differ from the costs per copier for each of these items in Exhibit 19-2. Why? Because Exhibit 19-6 shows only the variable costs that Photon expects to save. Exhibit 19-2 shows the *total* (fixed and variable) costs of each of these items. Also note that Exhibit 19-6 includes the incremental contribution margin from the estimated increases in sales due to the improved quality and performance of Photon's copiers.

Photon's management chooses to redesign the frame since Exhibit 19-6 indicates that the net estimated cost savings are $972,000 greater under this alternative.

EXHIBIT 19-6
Estimated Effect of Quality Improvement Actions on Costs of Quality for the Photon Corporation

Description	Incremental Costs and Benefits Of:	
	Further Inspecting Incoming Frame (1)	Redesigning Frame (2)
Costs of Quality Items		
Additional design engineering costs:		
$80 × 2,000 hours	—	$ 160,000
Additional process engineering costs:		
$60 × 5,000 hours	—	300,000
Additional inspection and testing costs:		
$40 × 10,000 hours	$ 400,000	—
Savings in rework costs:		
$1,600 × 600 fewer copiers reworked	(960,000)	
$1,600 × 800 fewer copiers reworked		(1,280,000)
Savings in customer support costs:		
$80 × 500 fewer copiers repaired	(40,000)	
$80 × 700 fewer copiers repaired		(56,000)
Savings in transportation costs for repair parts:		
$180 × 500 fewer copiers repaired	(90,000)	
$180 × 700 fewer copiers repaired		(126,000)
Savings in warranty repair costs:		
$1,800 × 500 fewer copiers repaired	(900,000)	
$1,800 × 700 fewer copiers repaired		(1,260,000)
Opportunity Costs		
Contribution margin from increased sales:		
$6,000 × 250 additional copiers sold	(1,500,000)	
$6,000 × 300 additional copiers sold	—	(1,800,000)
Net Cost Savings and Additional Contribution Margin	$(3,090,000)	$(4,062,000)
Difference in favour of redesigning frame	$972,000	

The costs of a poorly designed frame appear in the form of higher manufacturing, marketing, distribution, and customer service costs, as internal and external failures begin to mount. But these costs are locked in when the frame is designed. Thus, it is not surprising that redesign will yield significant savings.

In the Photon example, lost contribution margin occurs because Photon's repeated external failures damage its reputation for quality, resulting in lost sales. Lost contribution margin can also occur as a result of internal failures. Suppose Photon's manufacturing capacity is fully used. In this case, rework uses up valuable manufacturing capacity and causes the company to forgo contribution margin from producing and selling additional copiers. Suppose Photon could produce and (subsequently) sell an additional 600 copiers by improving quality and reducing rework. The costs of internal failure would then include lost contribution margin of $3,600,000 ($6,000 contribution margin per copier × 600 copiers). This $3,600,000 is the opportunity cost of poor quality.

Photon can use its COQ report to examine interdependencies across the four categories of quality-related costs. In our example, redesigning the frame increases costs of prevention activities (design and process engineering), decreases costs of internal failure (rework), and decreases costs of external failure (warranty repairs). Costs

Crysel Wins Premio Nacional de Calidad—Mexico's Premier Quality Award

Crysel, a member of the Mexican industrial group CYDSA *(Celulosa y Derivados Society Anonimos)*, is the largest producer of acrylic fibre in Latin America and among the top ten producers of acrylic fibre in the world. In 1991, Crysel was awarded the Premio Nacional de Calidad, Mexico's equivalent of the Malcolm Baldrige quality award.

One element of the Premio Nacional de Calidad's evaluation criteria is a company's costs of quality reporting. Companies vary as to which items they include in their COQ reports, choosing those cost categories that management feels warrant the greatest emphasis. Crysel classifies its costs of failure into six main classes:

1. **Consumption factors.** Excess or wasted direct materials, steam, or energy
2. **Maintenance.** Costs of repairing machines that break down
3. **Human resources.** Costs of extra workers and staff, such as a re-work crew employed to correct quality problems
4. **Accounts receivable.** Finance costs of not receiving money from customers on time
5. **Substandard quality.** Contribution margin lost from selling inferior-grade rather than top-grade fibre
6. **Sales volume.** Contribution margin lost from selling less than the available plant capacity because of quality problems

The first three classes appear in the COQ reports that most companies prepare. Crysel's innovation in quality reporting is to include the last three classes: accounts receivable, substandard quality, and sales volume. Each of these three classes measures an opportunity cost of poor quality, a cost not generally found in COQ reports. The following table indicates that these opportunity costs are a significant percentage of Crysel's total costs of failure. Including them in the COQ reports signals to all employees that top management believes these classes deserve close attention.

Costs of Quality as a Percentage of Sales

	1985	1989	1992
Items Generally Recorded in COQ Reports			
Consumption factors	3.8%	4.1%	2.6%
Maintenance	0.8	0.9	0.8
Human resources	0.6	0.5	0.4
Total	5.2%	5.5%	3.8%
Opportunity Cost Items Generally Not Recorded in COQ Reports			
Accounts receivable	3.7%	0.9%	0.5%
Substandard quality	1.0	0.4	0.8
Sales volume	8.5	2.4	1.6
Total	13.2	3.7	2.9
Total costs of quality as a percentage of sales	18.4%	9.2%	6.7%

An important component of the Premio Nacional de Calidad is a company's safety record. Crysel's safety index, measured by the number of accidents per million labour-hours, declined from 6.3 in 1986 to 3.0 in 1992. Crysel eliminated accidents by re-designing machines, training operators in safety practices, and implementing safe operating procedures.

Source: Based on a presentation by Raul Gil Dufoo, Director General of Crysel, and discussions with company management.

of quality give more insight when managers compare trends over time. In successful quality programs, the costs of quality as a percentage of sales and the costs of internal and external failure as a percentage of total costs of quality should decrease over time. Many companies, for example, Digital Equipment Corporation, Solectron, and Toyota, believe they should eliminate all failure costs and have zero defects.

COSTS OF DESIGN QUALITY

Costs of design quality. Costs incurred to prevent, or arising as a result of, low quality of design.

Our discussion so far has focused on measuring the cost of conformance quality and the methods that companies use to reduce these costs. In addition to conformance quality, companies must also pay attention to quality of design by designing products that satisfy customer needs. The **costs of design quality** refer to costs incurred to prevent, or costs arising as a result of, low quality of design. These costs include the costs of designing a product, and the production, marketing, distribution, and customer-service costs wasted on supporting a poorly designed product. A significant component of these costs is the opportunity cost of sales lost from not producing a product that customers want. Many of these costs are very difficult to measure precisely. For this reason, most companies do no measure the financial costs of design quality.

NONFINANCIAL MEASURES OF QUALITY AND CUSTOMER SATISFACTION

Even if products and services are defect-free and fully satisfy conformance quality, they will not be effective or sell well unless they also have design quality—that is, unless they satisfy customer needs. Yet there is more to customer satisfaction than just design quality. Motorola describes its program of total customer satisfaction as:

◆ Giving the customer product performance features that are perceived by the customer as providing fair value

◆ Delivering the product when promised

◆ Delivering the product with no defects

◆ Ensuring that the product will not experience early failure

◆ Ensuring that the product will not fail excessively in service

To evaluate how well they are doing, Motorola and other companies track customer satisfaction trends over time. Customer satisfaction is difficult to measure precisely, but companies can choose among many indicators in their search for answers.

OBJECTIVE 4

Provide examples of non-financial quality measures of customer satisfaction and internal performance

Nonfinancial Measures of Customer Satisfaction

Nonfinancial measures of customer satisfaction include:

◆ The number of defective units shipped to customers as a percentage of total units of products shipped

◆ The number of customer complaints (companies estimate that for every customer who actually complains, there are ten to twenty others who have had bad experiences with the product but have not complained)

◆ Customer response time (the difference between scheduled delivery date and date requested by the customer)

◆ Timeliness of delivery (percentage of shipments made on or before the scheduled delivery date)

Federal Express tracks similar measures for customer satisfaction in its overnight delivery business. Management steps in and investigates if these numbers deteriorate over time.

In addition to these routine nonfinancial measures, many companies such as Xerox conduct surveys to measure customer satisfaction. Surveys serve two objectives. First, they provide a deeper perspective into customer experiences and preferences. Second, they provide a glimpse into features that customers would like future products to have.

Nonfinancial Measures of Internal Performance

Prevention costs, appraisal costs, and internal failure costs are examples of financial measures of quality performance inside the company. Most companies monitor both financial and nonfinancial measures of internal quality.

What nonfinancial measures might a business use? Analog Devices, a semiconductor manufacturer, follows trends in these gauges of quality:

- ◆ The number of defects for each product line
- ◆ Process yield (ratio of good output to total output)
- ◆ Manufacturing lead time (the time taken to convert direct materials into finished output)
- ◆ Employee turnover (ratio of the number of employees who left the company to the total number of employees)

By themselves, nonfinancial measures of quality have limited meaning. They are more informative when management examines trends over time. To prepare this report, the management accountant must review the numbers to ensure that nonfinancial measures are calculated accurately and consistently, and must then present the information to help management evaluate internal quality performance. Management accountants help companies improve quality in multiple ways—they compute the costs of quality, assist in developing cost-effective solutions to quality problems, and provide feedback about quality improvement.

EVALUATING QUALITY PERFORMANCE

Measuring the financial costs of quality and measuring the nonfinancial aspects of quality have distinctly different advantages.

The advantages of the costs of quality (COQ) measures are:

OBJECTIVE 5

Use both financial and nonfinancial measures of quality

1. COQ focuses attention on how costly poor quality can be.
2. Financial COQ measures are a useful way of comparing different quality improvement programs and setting priorities for achieving maximum cost reduction.
3. Financial COQ measures serve as a common denominator for evaluating tradeoffs among prevention and failure costs. COQ provides a single, summary measure of quality performance.

The advantages of nonfinancial measures of quality:

1. Nonfinancial measures of quality are often easy to quantify and easy to understand.
2. Nonfinancial measures direct attention to physical processes and hence focus attention on the precise problem areas that need improvement.
3. Nonfinancial measures provide immediate short-run feedback on whether quality improvement efforts have, in fact, succeeded in improving quality.
4. Nonfinancial measures are useful indicators of long-run performance.

Most organizations use both financial and nonfinancial quality measures to measure quality performance.

TIME AS A COMPETITIVE WEAPON

Companies increasingly view time as a key variable in competition.[3] Doing things faster helps to increase revenues and decrease costs. For example, a moving company

[3]See G. Stalk and T. Hout, *Competing Against Time* (New York: Free Press, 1990).

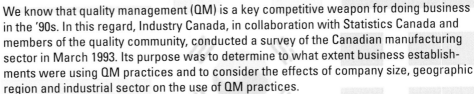

Quality Management in Canadian Manufacturers

We know that quality management (QM) is a key competitive weapon for doing business in the '90s. In this regard, Industry Canada, in collaboration with Statistics Canada and members of the quality community, conducted a survey of the Canadian manufacturing sector in March 1993. Its purpose was to determine to what extent business establishments were using QM practices and to consider the effects of company size, geographic region and industrial sector on the use of QM practices.

Almost 800 businesses representing all parts of the manufacturing sector across Canada completed the 10-minute telephone interview. Respondents were primarily plant managers, company presidents and quality managers. The survey sought information on respondents' use, not opinions, of 27 specific quality management practices, in four important areas: leadership; employee involvement; process improvement; and customer focus.

The practices included such elements as mission statements, quality improvement plans, management involvement, benchmarking, and customer service standards.

Twenty-one per cent of Canadian manufacturers have adopted an integrated approach to quality management, dubbed "high-balanced"—the use of over 80 per cent of the QM practices in each of the four categories. An equal number (20 per cent) made very little use of these management practices. The other 60 per cent of the establishments fell somewhere in between. Some practices, such as having a quality support group and tracking cycle times, were widely used (78 per cent and 71 per cent respectively). Others, like conducting customer satisfaction surveys, were used surprisingly little (34 per cent).

Source: Victoria Kohse, "Quality Management and Competitiveness in Canadian Manufacturers," *CMA Magazine,* July/August 1994. Reprinted with permission from The Society of Management Accountants of Canada.

United Van Lines
www.uvl.com

Customer response time. Amount of time from when a customer places an order for a product or requests a service to when the product or service is delivered to the customer.

OBJECTIVE 6

Describe customer response time, and explain the reasons for and the cost of lines and delays

Manufacturing lead time. (manufacturing cycle time) Time from when an order is ready to start on the production line (ready to be set up) to when it becomes a finished good.

such as United Van Lines will be able to generate more revenues if it can move goods from one place to another faster and on time. Companies such as AT&T and Texas Instruments also report lower costs from their emphasis on time. They cite, for example, the need to carry less inventory because of their ability to respond rapidly to customer demands.

In this chapter, we focus on *operational measures of time*, which reveal how quickly companies respond to customers' demands for their products and services and the reliability with which these companies meet scheduled delivery dates.

Companies need to measure time in order to manage it properly. Two common operational measures of time are customer response time and on-time performance.

Customer Response Time

Customer response time is the amount of time from when a customer places an order for a product or requests a service to when the product or service is delivered to the customer. A timely response to customer requests is a key competitive factor in many industries. Consider a manufacturer of custom machine tools such as Yamazaki Mazak. Yamazaki's customers value faster delivery because it enables them to produce and sell products made using the new machine tools sooner. Customer response time is critical in many other industries, especially service industries such as banking, car rental, and fast food.

Exhibit 19-7 describes components of customer response time.

In the Yamazaki Mazak example, *order receipt time* is the time it takes Mazak's marketing department to describe the customer's exact specifications and to place an order with manufacturing. **Manufacturing lead** (or **cycle**) **time** is the time when the order is ready to start on the production line (ready to be set up) to when it becomes a finished good. Manufacturing lead time includes waiting time plus manufac-

EXHIBIT 19-7
Components of Customer-Response Time

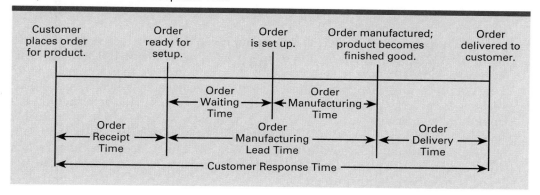

turing time for the order. An order for machine tools, in the Mazak example, may need to wait and be delayed because the equipment the order requires is busy processing orders that arrived earlier. *Order delivery time* is the time it takes distribution to pick up the order from manufacturing and deliver it to the customer.

Several companies have adopted manufacturing lead time as the base for allocating indirect manufacturing costs to products. The Zytec Corporation, a manufacturer of computer equipment, believes that using manufacturing lead time motivates managers to reduce the time taken to manufacture products. In turn, total overhead costs decrease and operating income rises.

On-Time Performance

On-time performance refers to situations in which the product or service is actually delivered at the time it is scheduled to be delivered. Consider Federal Express, which specifies a price per package and a next-day delivery time of 10:30 a.m. for its overnight courier service. Federal Express measures on-time performance by how often it meets its stated delivery time of 10:30 a.m. On-time performance is an important element of customer satisfaction because customers want and expect on-time deliveries. Commercial airlines, for example, gain loyal passengers from consistent on-time service. Note that there is a trade-off between customer-response time and on-time performance. Simply scheduling longer customer-response times, such as Federal Express scheduling deliveries at 1 p.m. instead of 10:30 a.m., or airlines lengthening scheduled arrival times, eases the achieving of on-time performance (although this tactic could displease customers).

On-time performance. Situations in which the product or service is actually delivered at the time it is scheduled to be delivered.

TIME DRIVERS AND COSTS OF TIME

Managing customer-response time and on-time performance in manufacturing, merchandising and service companies requires an understanding of the causes of delays and the resulting costs. Delays can occur, for example, in front of a machine in a manufacturing operation, in front of a teller at a bank, or in front of a check-out counter in a store. We focus first on the reasons for delays.

Mazak Production Facilities
www.mazakusa.com/prodfac.htm

Federal Express
www.fedex.ca

Time driver. Any factor where change in the factor causes a change in the speed with which an activity is undertaken.

Bottleneck. An operation wherein the work required approaches or exceeds the available capacity.

Uncertainty and Bottlenecks as Drivers of Time

A **time driver** is any factor where change in the factor causes a change in the speed with which an activity is undertaken. What are the drivers of time? We consider two of the most important: (1) Uncertainty about when customers will order products or services. For example, the more randomly Mazak receives orders for its machine tools, the more likely that queues will form and delays will occur. (2) Limited capacity and bottlenecks. A **bottleneck** is an operation where the work required to be performed approaches or exceeds the available capacity. For example, a bottleneck is created when products that need to be processed at a particular machine arrive while the machine is busy processing other products.

Falcon Works (FW) uses one turning machine to convert steel bars into one specialty component, A22. FW makes this component only after FW's customers order the component. To focus on manufacturing lead time, we assume that FW's order receipt time and order delivery time are minimal.

FW expects it will receive 30 orders, but it could actually receive 10, 20, or 50 orders of A22. Each order is for 1,000 units. Each order will take 100 hours of manufacturing time (8 hours of setup time to clean and prepare the machine, and 92 hours of processing time). The annual capacity of the machine is 4,000 hours. If FW receives the number of orders it expects, the total amount of manufacturing time required on the machine will be 3,000 (100×30) hours, which is within the available machine capacity of 4,000 hours. Even though expected capacity utilization is not strained, queues and delays will still occur. Why? Because uncertainty about when FW's customers will place an order may cause the order to be received while the machine is processing another order.

Average waiting time. The average amount of time that an order will wait in line before it is set up and processed.

In the single-product case, under certain assumptions about the pattern of customer orders and how orders will be processed,[4] the **average waiting time,** the average amount of time that an order will wait in line before it is set up and processed, equals:

$$\frac{\text{Average number} \atop \text{of orders of A22} \times \left(\text{Manufacturing} \atop \text{time for A22}\right)^2}{2 \times \left[\text{Annual machine} \atop \text{capacity} - \left(\text{Average number} \atop \text{of orders of A22} \times \text{Manufacturing} \atop \text{time for A22}\right)\right]}$$

$$= \frac{30 \times (100)^2}{2 \times [4,000 - (30 \times 100)]} = \frac{30 \times 10,000}{2 \times (4,000 - 3,000)} = \frac{300,000}{2 \times 1,000} = \frac{300,000}{2,000} = 150 \text{ hours}$$

The denominator in this formula measures excess capacity or cushion. The smaller the cushion, the greater the delays. Manufacturing time enters the numerator in the formula as a squared term. The longer the manufacturing time, the greater the chance that the machine will be busy when an order arrives, and the longer the delays.

Our formula describes only the average waiting time. A particular order may happen to arrive when the machine is free, in which case manufacturing will start immediately. In other situations, FW may receive an order while two other orders are waiting to be processed. In this case, the delay will be longer than 150 hours. The average manufacturing lead time for an order of A22 is 250 hours (150 hours of average waiting time + 100 hours of manufacturing time). Throughout this section, we use manufacturing lead time to refer to manufacturing lead time for an order.

FW is considering whether to introduce a new product, C33. FW expects to receive ten orders of C33 (each order for 800 units) in the coming year. Each order will take 50 hours of manufacturing time (4 hours of setup time and 46 hours of processing time). The expected demand for A22 will be unaffected whether or not FW introduces C33.

The average waiting time *before* an order is set up and processed is given by the following formula, which is an extension of the formula described earlier for the single-product case.

$$\frac{\left[\text{Average number} \atop \text{of orders of A22} \times \left(\text{Manufacturing} \atop \text{time for A22}\right)^2\right] + \left[\text{Average number} \atop \text{of orders of C33} \times \left(\text{Manufacturing} \atop \text{time for C33}\right)^2\right]}{2 \times \left[\text{Annual machine} \atop \text{capacity} - \left(\text{Average number} \atop \text{of orders of A22} \times \text{Manufacturing} \atop \text{time for A22}\right) - \left(\text{Average number} \atop \text{of orders of C33} \times \text{Manufacturing} \atop \text{time for C33}\right)\right]}$$

$$= \frac{[30 \times (100)^2] + [10 \times (50)^2]}{2 \times [4,000 - (30 \times 100) - (10 \times 50)]} = \frac{(30 \times 10,000) + (10 \times 2,500)}{2 \times (4,000 - 3,000 - 500)}$$

$$= \frac{300,000 + 25,000}{2 \times 500} = \frac{325,000}{1,000} = 325 \text{ hours}$$

---

[4] The precise technical assumptions are (a) that customer orders for the product follow a Poisson distribution with a mean equal to the expected number of orders (30 in our example) and (b) that orders are processed on a first-in first-out (FIFO) basis. The Poisson arrival pattern for customer orders has been found to be reasonable in many real-world settings. The FIFO assumption can be modified. Under the modified assumptions, the basic queuing and delay effects will still occur, but the precise formulas will be different.

Introducing C33 causes average waiting time to more than double from 150 hours to 325 hours. To understand why, think of excess capacity as a cushion for absorbing the shocks of variability and uncertainty in the arrival of customer orders. Introducing C33 causes excess capacity to shrink, increasing the chance that at any point in time, new orders will arrive while existing orders are being manufactured.

Average manufacturing lead time for A22 is 425 hours (325 hours of average waiting time + 100 hours of manufacturing time), and for C33 it is 375 hours (325 hours of average waiting time + 50 hours of manufacturing time). Note that C33 spends 86.67% (325 ÷ 375) of its manufacturing lead time just waiting for manufacturing to start!

Relevant Revenues and Relevant Costs

Should FW introduce product C33? Consider the following information:

Product	Average Number of Orders	Average Selling Price per Order If Average Manufacturing Lead Time Is:		Direct Material Costs per Order	Inventory Carrying Costs per Order per Hour
		Less Than 300 Hours	More Than 300 Hours		
A22	30	$22,000	$21,500	$16,000	$1.00
C33	10	10,000	9,600	8,000	0.50

Note that manufacturing lead times affect both revenues and costs in our example. Revenues are affected because customers are willing to pay a slightly higher price for faster delivery. Direct materials costs and inventory carrying costs are the only costs affected by the decision to introduce C33. Inventory carrying costs usually consist of the opportunity costs of investment tied up in inventory (see Chapter 11) and the relevant costs of storage such as space rental, spoilage, deterioration, and materials-handling. Companies usually calculate inventory carrying costs on a per-order-per-year basis. To simplify computations, we express inventory carrying costs on a per-order-per-hour basis. FW incurs inventory carrying costs for the duration of the wait time and manufacturing time.

Exhibit 19-8 presents relevant revenues and relevant costs that the management accountant would calculate for this decision. The preferred alternative is not to introduce C33. Note that C33 is rejected despite having a positive contribution margin of at least $1,600 ($9,600 – $8,000) per order. Recall, too, that FW's machine

EXHIBIT 19-8
Determining Expected Relevant Revenues and Expected Relevant Costs for Falcon Works' Decision to Introduce C33

Relevant Items	Alternative 1: Introduce C33 (1)	Alternative 2: Do Not Introduce C33 (2)	Difference (3) = (1) – (2)
Expected revenues	$741,000*	$660,000†	$81,000
Expected variable costs	560,000‡	480,000§	80,000
Expected inventory carrying costs	14,625#	7,500‖	7,125
Expected costs	574,625	487,500	87,125
Expected revenues minus expected costs	$166,375	$172,500	$ (6,125)

*($21,500 × 30) + ($9,600 × 10) = $741,000; average manufacturing lead times will be more than 300 hours.
†$22,000 × 30 = $660,000; average manufacturing lead times will be less than 300 hours.
‡($16,000 × 30) + ($8,000 × 10) = $560,000.
§$16,000 × 30 = $480,000.
#(A22's average manufacturing lead time × A22's unit carrying costs per order × A22's expected number of orders) + (C33's average manufacturing lead time × C33's unit carrying costs per order × C33's expected number of orders) = (425 × $1 × 30) + (375 × $0.50 × 10) = $12,750 + 1,875 = $14,625.
‖A22's average manufacturing lead time hours × A22's unit carrying costs per order × A22's expected number of orders = 250 × $1 × 30 = $7,500.

has the capacity to process C33 because the machine will, on average, use only 3,500 of the available 4,000 hours. Why is C33 rejected? *The key is to recognize the negative effects of C33 on the existing product A22.* The following table presents the expected loss in revenues and expected increase in costs of using up extra capacity on the turning machine to manufacture C33.

	Effect of Increasing Average Manufacturing Lead Times		Expected Loss in Revenues Plus Expected Increase in Costs of Introducing C33
Product	Expected Loss in Revenues for A22 (1)	Expected Increase in Carrying Costs for All Products (2)	(3) = (1) + (2)
A22	$15,000*	$5,250†	$20,250
C33	—	1,875‡	1,875
Total	$15,000	$7,125	$22,125

*($22,000 − $21,500) × 30 expected orders = $15,000.
†(425 hours − 250 hours) × $1 × 30 expected orders = $5,250.
‡(375 hours − 0) × $0.50 × 10 expected orders = $1,875.

Introducing C33 causes the average manufacturing lead time of A22 to increase from 250 hours to 425 hours. This increases inventory carrying costs. Introducing C33 also causes A22's revenues to decrease because it would, on average, take more than 300 hours to manufacture A22. The expected costs of introducing C33 equal $22,125, which exceeds C33's expected contribution margin of $16,000 ($1,600 per order × 10 expected orders). FW should choose not to produce C33.

We have described a simple setting to explain the effects of uncertainty and capacity constraints and the relevant revenues and relevant costs of time.[5] How can delays be reduced? Increasing the capacity of the bottleneck resource can reduce lines, delays, and inventories. When demand uncertainty is high, *some* excess capacity is desirable. Companies can increase capacity in several ways. One way, for example, is to reduce the time required for setups and processing by doing these activities more efficiently. Another is to invest in new equipment. Many companies are investing in flexible manufacturing systems that can be programmed to quickly switch from producing one product to producing another. Delays can also be reduced through careful scheduling of orders on machines—for example, by batching similar jobs together for processing.

THEORY OF CONSTRAINTS AND THROUGHPUT CONTRIBUTION ANALYSIS

OBJECTIVE 7

Define three main measurements in the theory of constraints

Theory of constraints (TOC). Describes methods to maximize operating income when faced with some bottleneck and some nonbottleneck operations.

Throughput contribution. Revenues minus all variable direct materials costs.

We now expand the discussion of the previous section by considering products that are made from multiple parts and processed on different machines. With multiple parts and multiple machines, dependencies arise among operations; some operations cannot be started until parts from a previous operation are available. Some operations are bottlenecks; others are not.

The **theory of constraints (TOC)** describes methods to maximize operating income when faced with some bottleneck and some nonbottleneck operations.[6] It defines three measurements:

1. **Throughput contribution,** equal to sales revenue minus direct materials costs
2. **Investments (inventory),** equal to the sum of materials costs of direct materials inventory, work-in-process inventory, and finished goods inventory; R&D costs; and costs of equipment and buildings

[5] Other complexities such as analyzing a network of machines, priority scheduling, and allowing for uncertainty in processing times are beyond the scope of this book. In these cases, the basic queuing and delay effects persist, but the precise formulas are more complex.
[6] See E. Goldratt and J. Cox, *The Goal* (New York: North River Press, 1986); E. Goldratt, *The Theory of Constraints* (New York: North River Press, 1990); E. Noreen, D. Smith, and J. Mackey, *The Theory of Constraints and Its Implications for Management Accounting* (New York: North River Press, 1995).

3. Operating costs, equal to all operating costs (other than direct materials) incurred to earn throughput contribution; include salaries and wages, rent, utilities, and amortization

The objective of TOC is to increase throughput contribution while decreasing investments and operating costs. *The theory of constraints considers short-run time horizons and assumes other current operating costs to be fixed costs.* The key steps in managing bottleneck resources are as follows:

◆ **Step 1:** Recognize that the bottleneck resource determines throughput contribution of the plant as a whole.

◆ **Step 2:** Search and find the bottleneck resource by identifying resources with large quantities of inventory waiting to be worked on.

◆ **Step 3:** Keep the bottleneck operation busy and subordinate all nonbottleneck resources to the bottleneck resource. That is, the needs of the bottleneck resource determine the production schedule of nonbottleneck resources.

Step 3 represents a key notion described in Chapter 11: To maximize overall contribution margin, the plant must maximize contribution margin (in this case, throughput contribution) of the constrained or bottleneck resource. For this reason, Step 3 suggests that the bottleneck machine always be kept running, not waiting for jobs. To achieve this, companies often maintain a small buffer inventory of jobs waiting for the bottleneck machine. The bottleneck machine sets the pace for all nonbottleneck machines. That is, the output at the nonbottleneck operations are tied or linked to the needs of the bottleneck machine. For example, workers at nonbottleneck machines are not motivated to improve their productivity if the additional output cannot be processed by the bottleneck machine. Producing more nonbottleneck output only creates excess inventory; it does not increase throughput contribution.

◆ **Step 4:** Take actions to increase bottleneck efficiency and capacity—the objective is to increase throughput contribution minus the incremental costs of taking such actions. The management accountant plays a key role in Step 4 by calculating throughput contribution, identifying relevant and irrelevant costs, and doing a cost-benefit analysis of alternative actions to increase bottleneck efficiency and capacity.

We illustrate Step 4 using the example of Cardinal Industries (CI). CI manufactures car doors in two operations—stamping and pressing. Additional information is as follows:

	Stamping	Pressing
Capacity per hour	20 units	15 units
Annual capacity (6,000 hours of capacity available in each of stamping and pressing)	120,000 units	90,000 units
Annual production	90,000 units	90,000 units
Fixed operating costs (excluding direct materials)	$720,000	$1,080,000
Fixed operating costs per unit produced ($720,000 ÷ 90,000; $1,080,000 ÷ 90,000)	$8 per unit	$12 per unit

Each door sells for $100 and has direct materials costs of $40. Variable costs in other functions of the value chain—R&D, design of products and processes, marketing, distribution, and customer service—are negligible. CI's output is constrained by the capacity of 90,000 units at the pressing operation. What can CI do to relieve the bottleneck constraint at the pressing operation?

a. *Eliminate idle time (time when the pressing machine is neither being set up to process products nor actually processing products) at the bottleneck operation.* CI is considering permanently positioning two workers at the pressing operation. Their sole responsibility would be to unload finished units as soon as one batch of units is processed and to set up the machine to process the next batch. Suppose the annual cost of this action is $48,000 and the effect of this action is to increase bottleneck output by 1,000 units per year. Should CI incur the additional

OBJECTIVE 8

Describe four steps in managing bottlenecks

"Corporate Rightsizing and the Theory of Constraints" by Tony Rizzo
www.rogo.com/cac/rizzo1.html

Goldratt's Theory of Constraints: Online Simulation
www.ganesha.org/leading/toc.html

Theory of Constraints—Promodel Corp.
www.promodel.com/aspire/theory_of_constraints.html

Theory of Constraints— CIRAS
www.ciras.iastate.edu/toc/index.html

Throughput Accounting at Allied-Signal in Skelmersdale, U.K.

Allied-Signal in Skelmersdale, U.K. manufactures turbochargers for the automotive industry. In the late 1980s and early 1990s, the Skelmersdale plant was forced to change from producing few products in large quantities to producing many products in small quantities in a very competitive market. The plant also had to cope with frequent changes in its sales mix. The plant often missed delivery dates and incurred high transportation costs to ship via air those parts urgently needed by its automotive customers. John Darlington, the controller of the Skelmersdale plant, recognized the important role finance and accounting could play in this environment, but "we were just not supporting, communicating with, and complementing shop floor management—not until we began emphasizing throughput contributions."

The format designed by the Allied-Signal accountants for the throughput-contribution-based operating income statement is as follows:

Throughput Operating Income Statement
(in thousands)

Sales revenues		£50,000
Direct materials costs		28,500
Throughput contribution		21,500
Operating costs:		
Direct manufacturing labour	£ 4,275	
Engineering costs	1,767	
Other manufacturing costs	11,585	
Marketing costs	1,873	
Total operating costs		19,500
Operating income		£ 2,000

The Skelmersdale management viewed operating costs, other than direct materials costs, as fixed in the short run. The key to improving profitability was maximizing throughput contribution by identifying and optimizing the use of bottleneck resources. Management reduced the load on the bottleneck machines by shifting operations performed there onto other machines. New investments to improve efficiency at nonbottleneck machines were turned down because greater efficiency at nonbottleneck machines did nothing to improve throughput contribution. Instead, Allied-Signal made additional investments to increase bottleneck capacity.

To motivate workers to improve throughput, Allied-Signal managers designed new performance measures. Instead of measuring localized efficiency such as direct labour efficiency at various operations, management introduced "adherence to schedule" as the key performance measure. Workers at nonbottleneck operations were asked not to produce more than what was required according to the bottleneck schedule. In the surplus time available to these workers, they received training in TQM practices and in improving operator skills. The Skelmersdale plant also introduced four other performance measures—costs of quality, customer due date delivery, days inventory on hand, and manufacturing lead time—all with the objective of satisfying customers and maximizing throughput contribution. Over a four-year period, the Skelmersdale plant showed dramatic increases in each of these measures and in profitability, cash flow, and return on investment.

Source: Adapted from Darlington, J., J. Innes, F. Mitchell, and J. Woodward, "Throughput Accounting: The Garrett Automotive Experience," *Management Accounting,* April 1992; Coughlan P., and J. Darlington, "As Fast as the Slowest Operation: The Theory of Constraints," *Management Accounting,* June 1993; and discussions with Skelmersdale management.

costs? Yes, because CI's relevant throughput contribution increases by $60,000 [1,000 units × (selling price, $100 – direct materials costs, $40)], which exceeds the additional cost of $48,000. All other costs are irrelevant.

b. *Process only those parts or products that increase sales and throughput contribution, not parts or products that remain in finished goods or spare parts inventory.* Manufacturing products that sit in inventory does not increase throughput contribution.

c. *Shift products that do not have to be made on the bottleneck machine to nonbottleneck machines or to outside facilities.* Suppose the Spartan Corporation, an outside contractor, offers to press 1,500 doors at $15 per door from direct materials that CI supplies. Spartan's quoted price is greater than CI's own operating costs in the Pressing Department of $12 per door. Should CI accept the offer? Yes, because pressing is the bottleneck operation. Getting additional doors pressed from outside increases throughput contribution by $90,000 [($100 – $40) × 1,500 doors], while relevant costs increase by $22,500 ($15 × 1,500). The fact that CI's unit cost is less than Spartan's quoted price is irrelevant.

Suppose Gemini Industries, another outside contractor, offers to stamp 2,000 doors from direct materials that CI supplies at $6 per door. Gemini's price is lower than CI's operating cost of $8 per door in the Stamping Department. Should CI accept the offer? Since other operating costs are fixed costs, CI will not save any costs by subcontracting the stamping operations. Total costs will be greater by $12,000 ($6 × 2,000) under the subcontracting alternative. Stamping more doors will not increase throughput contribution, which is constrained by pressing capacity. CI should not accept Gemini's offer.

d. *Reduce setup time and processing time at bottleneck operations (for example, by simplifying the design or reducing the number of parts in the product).* Suppose CI can reduce setup time at the pressing operation by incurring additional costs of $55,000 a year. Suppose further that reducing setup time enables CI to press 2,500 more doors a year. Should CI incur the costs to reduce setup time? Yes, because throughput contribution increases by $150,000 [($100 – $40) × 2,500], which exceeds the additional costs incurred of $55,000. Will CI find it worthwhile to incur costs to reduce machining time at the stamping operation? No. Other operating costs will increase, but throughput contribution will remain unaffected. Throughput contribution increases only by increasing bottleneck output; increasing nonbottleneck output has no effect.

e. *Improve the quality of parts or products manufactured at the bottleneck operation.* Poor quality is often more costly at a bottleneck operation than it is at a nonbottleneck operation. The cost of poor quality at a nonbottleneck operation is the cost of materials wasted. If CI produces 1,000 defective doors at the stamping operation, the cost of poor quality is $40,000 (direct materials cost per unit, $40 × 1,000 doors). No throughput contribution is forgone because stamping has excess capacity. Despite the defective production, stamping can produce and transfer 90,000 doors to the pressing operation. At a bottleneck operation, the cost of poor quality is the cost of materials wasted *plus* the opportunity cost of lost throughput contribution. Bottleneck capacity not wasted in producing defective units could be used to generate additional sales and throughput contribution. If CI produces 1,000 defective units at the pressing operation, the cost of poor quality is $100,000: direct materials cost of $40,000 (direct materials cost per unit, $40 × 1,000 units) plus forgone throughput contribution of $60,000 [($100 – $40) × 1,000 doors].

The high costs of poor quality at the bottleneck operation mean that bottleneck time should not be wasted processing units that are defective. That is, inspection should be done before processing parts at the bottleneck to ensure that only good-quality units are transferred to the bottleneck operation. Also, quality improvement programs should focus on ensuring that bottlenecks produce minimal defects.

If the action in Step 4 are successful, the capacity of the pressing operation will increase and eventually exceed the capacity of the stamping operation. The bottleneck will then shift to the stamping operation. CI should then focus continuous-improvement actions on increasing stamping efficiency and capacity. For example, the contract with Gemini Industries to stamp 2,000 doors at $6 per door from direct materials supplied by CI become attractive now. Why? Because throughput contribution increases by ($100 – $40) × 2,000 = $120,000, while costs increase by $12,000 ($6 × 2,000).

The theory of constraints emphasizes the management of bottlenecks as the key to improving the performance of the system as a whole. It focuses on the short-run maximization of throughput contribution—revenues minus materials costs. It is less useful for the long-run management of costs, because it does not model the behaviour of costs or identify individual activities and cost drivers. Instead, it regards operating costs as given and fixed.

PROBLEM FOR SELF-STUDY

PROBLEM

The Sloan Corporation is a moving company that transports household goods from one city to another within North America. It measures quality of service in terms of (a) time required to transport goods, (b) on-time delivery (within two days of agreed-upon delivery date), and (c) number of lost or damaged shipments. Sloan is considering investing in a new scheduling and tracking system costing $160,000 per year, which should help it improve performance with respect to items (b) and (c). The following information describes Sloan's current performance and the expected performance if the new system is implemented:

	Current Performance	Expected Future Performance
On-time delivery performance	85%	95%
Variable costs per carton lost or damaged	$60	$60
Fixed cost per carton lost or damaged	$40	$40
Number of cartons lost or damaged per year	3,000 cartons	1,000 cartons

Sloan expects that each percentage point increase in on-time performance will result in revenue increases of $20,000 per year. Sloan's contribution margin percentage is 45%.

REQUIRED
1. Should Sloan acquire the new system?
2. What is the minimum amount of revenue increase that needs to occur for the benefits from the new system to exceed the costs?

SOLUTION
1. Additional costs of the new scheduling and tracking system are $160,000 per year.

Additional annual benefits of the new scheduling and tracking system are:

Additional annual sales from improving on-time performance $20,000 (95% – 85%)	$200,000
Contribution margin from additional annual revenues 45% × $200,000	$ 90,000
Because in costs per year from fewer cartons lost or damaged (only variable costs are relevant) $60 (3,000 – 1,000)	120,000
Total additional benefits	$210,000

Because the expected benefits of $210,000 exceed the costs of $160,000, Sloan should invest in the new system.
2. As long as Sloan earns a contribution margin of $40,000 (to cover incremental costs of $160,000 – relevant variable cost savings of $120,000) from additional annual sales, investing in the new system is beneficial. This contribution margin corresponds to additional sales of $40,000 ÷ 0.45 = $88,889.

The following points are linked to the chapter's learning objectives.

1. Four cost categories in a costs of quality program are *prevention costs* (costs incurred in precluding the manufacture of products that do not conform to specifications), *appraisal costs* (costs incurred in detecting which of the individual products produced do not conform to specifications), *internal failure costs* (costs incurred when a nonconforming product is detected before its shipment to customers), and *external failure costs* (costs incurred when a nonconforming product is detected after its shipment to customers).

2. Three methods that companies use to improve quality are *control charts*, to distinguish random variations from other sources of variation in an operating process; *Pareto diagrams*, which indicate how frequently each type of failure occurs; and *cause-and-effect diagrams*, which identify potential factors or causes of failure.

3. The relevant costs of quality improvement are the incremental costs incurred to implement the quality program. The relevant benefits are the savings in total costs and the estimated increase in contribution margin from the higher sales that will result from the quality improvements.

4. Nonfinancial measures of customer satisfaction include the number of customer complaints, the on-time delivery rate, and the customer response time. Nonfinancial measures of internal performance include product defect levels, process yields, and manufacturing lead times.

5. Financial measures are helpful to evaluate tradeoffs among prevention and failure costs. They focus attention on how costly poor quality can be. Nonfinancial measures help focus attention on the precise problem areas that need attention.

6. *Customer response time* is the amount of time from when a customer places an order for a product or requests service to when the product or service is delivered to the customer. Lines and delays occur because of (a) uncertainty about when customers will order products or services and (b) limited capacity and bottlenecks. Bottlenecks are operations at which the work to be performed approaches or exceeds the available capacity. The costs of lines and delays include lower revenues and increased inventory carrying costs.

7. The three main measurements in the theory of constraints are throughput contribution (equal to sales dollars minus direct materials costs); investments or inventory (equal to the sum of materials costs of direct materials inventory, work-in-process inventory and finished goods inventory; R&D costs; and costs of equipment and buildings); and operating costs (equal to all operating costs other than direct materials costs incurred to earn throughput contribution).

8. The four steps in managing bottlenecks are (a) recognize that the bottleneck operation determines throughput contribution, (b) search for and find the bottleneck, (c) keep the bottleneck busy and subordinate all nonbottleneck operations to the bottleneck operation, and (d) increase bottleneck efficiency and capacity.

TERMS TO LEARN

This chapter contains definitions of the following important terms:

ASSIGNMENT MATERIAL

QUESTIONS

19-1 Describe two benefits of improving quality.

19-2 How does conformance quality differ from quality of design? Explain.

19-3 Name two items classified as prevention costs.

19-4 Distinguish between internal failure costs and external failure costs.

19-5 Describe three methods that companies use to identify quality problems.

19-6 "Companies should focus on financial measures of quality because these are the only measures of quality that can be linked to bottom-line performance." Do you agree? Explain.

19-7 Give two examples of nonfinancial measures of customer satisfaction.

19-8 Give two examples of nonfinancial measures of internal performance.

19-9 Distinguish between customer response time and manufacturing lead time.

19-10 "There is no tradeoff between customer response time and on-time performance." Do you agree? Explain.

19-11 Give two reasons why delays occur.

19-12 "Companies should always make and sell all products whose selling prices exceed variable costs." Do you agree? Explain.

19-13 Describe the three main measures used in the theory of constraints.

19-14 Describe the four key steps in managing bottleneck resources.

19-15 Describe three ways to improve the performance of a bottleneck operation.

EXERCISES

19-16 Costs of quality. (CMA, adapted) Bergen Inc. produces telephone equipment at its London plant. In recent years, the company's market share has been eroded by stiff competition from Asian and European competitors. Price and product quality are the two key areas in which companies compete in this market.

Jerry Holman, Bergen's president, decided to devote more resources to the improvement of product quality after learning that his company's products had been ranked fourth in product quality in a 1999 survey of telephone equipment users. He believed that Bergen could no longer afford to ignore the importance of product quality.

Bergen's quality improvement program has now been in operation for two years, and the cost report shown below has recently been issued.

As they were reviewing the report, Sheila Haynes, manager of sales, asked Tony Reese, production manager, what he thought of the quality program. "The work is really moving through the Production Department," replied Reese. "We used to spend time helping the Customer Service Department solve their problems but they are leaving us alone these days."

Semi-Annual Costs of Quality Report, Bergen Inc.
(in thousands)

	6/30/2000	12/30/2000	6/30/2001	12/30/2001
Prevention costs				
Machine maintenance	$ 215	$ 215	$ 190	$ 160
Training suppliers	5	45	20	15
Design reviews	20	102	100	95
Total prevention costs	240	362	310	270
Appraisal costs				
Incoming inspection	45	53	36	22
Final testing	160	160	140	94
Total appraisal costs	205	213	176	116

Internal failure costs				
Rework	120	106	88	62
Scrap	68	64	42	40
Total internal failure costs	188	170	130	102
External failure costs				
Warranty repairs	69	31	25	23
Customer returns	262	251	116	80
Total external failure costs	331	282	141	103
Total quality costs	$ 964	$1,027	$ 757	$ 591
Total production and sales	$4,120	$4,540	$4,650	$4,510

REQUIRED

1. By analyzing the Cost of Quality Report presented, determine if Bergen Inc.'s quality improvement program has been successful. List specific evidence to support your answer.
2. Jerry Holman believed that the quality improvement program was essential and that Bergen Inc. could no longer afford to ignore the importance of product quality. Discuss how Bergen could measure the opportunity cost of not implementing the quality improvement program.

19-17 Costs of quality analysis, nonfinancial quality measures. The Hartono Corporation manufactures and sells industrial grinders. The following table presents financial information pertaining to quality in 2000 and 2001 (in thousands):

	2001	2000
Sales	$12,500	$10,000
Line inspection	85	110
Scrap	200	250
Design engineering	240	100
Cost of returned goods	145	60
Product-testing equipment	50	50
Customer support	30	40
Rework costs	135	160
Preventive equipment maintenance	90	35
Product liability claims	100	200
Incoming materials inspection	40	20
Breakdown maintenance	40	90
Product-testing labour	75	220
Training	120	45
Warranty repair	200	300
Supplier evaluation	50	20

REQUIRED

1. Classify the cost items in the table into prevention, appraisal, internal failure, or external failure categories.
2. Calculate the ratio of each COQ category to sales in 2000 and 2001. Comment on the trends in costs of quality between 2000 and 2001.
3. Give two examples of nonfinancial quality measures that Hartono Corporation could monitor as part of a total quality control effort.

19-18 Costs of quality analysis, nonfinancial quality measures. Ontario Industries manufactures two types of refrigerators, Olivia and Solta. Information on each refrigerator is as follows:

	Olivia	Solta
Units manufactured and sold	10,000 units	5,000 units
Selling price	$2,000	$1,500
Variable costs per unit	$1,200	$800
Hours spent on design	6,000	1,000
Testing and inspection hours per unit	1	0.5
Percentage of units reworked in plant	5%	10%
Rework costs per refrigerator	$500	$400
Percentage of units repaired at customer site	4%	8%
Repair costs per refrigerator	$600	$450
Estimated lost sales from poor quality	—	300 units

The labour rates per hour for various activities are as follows:

Design	$75 per hour
Testing and inspection	$40 per hour

REQUIRED

1. Calculate the costs of quality for Olivia and Solta classified into prevention, appraisal, internal failure, and external failure categories.
2. For each type of refrigerator, calculate the ratio of each COQ item as a percentage of sales. Compare and comment on the costs of quality for Olivia and Solta.
3. Give two examples of nonfinancial quality measures that Ontario Industries could monitor as part of a total quality control effort.

19-19 Nonfinancial measures of quality and time. (CMA, adapted) Eastern Switching Co. (ESC) produces telecommunications equipment. Charles Laurant, ESC's president believes that product quality is the key to gaining competitive advantage. Laurant implemented a total quality management (TQM) program with an emphasis on customer satisfaction. The following information is available for the first year (2001) of the TQM program compared to the previous year.

	2000	2001
Total number of units produced and sold	10,000	11,000
Units delivered before scheduled delivery date	8,500	9,900
Number of defective units shipped	400	330
Number of customer complaints other than for defective units	500	517
Average time from when customer places order for a unit to when unit is delivered to the customer	30 days	25 days
Number of units reworked during production	600	627
Manufacturing lead time	20 days	16 days
Direct and indirect manufacturing labour hours	80,000	110,000

REQUIRED

1. For each of the years 2000 and 2001, calculate
   a. Percentage of defective units shipped
   b. Customer complaints as a percentage of units shipped
   c. On-time delivery
   d. Percentage of units reworked
2. On the basis of your calculations in requirement 1, has ESC's performance on quality and timeliness improved?
3. Philip Larkin, a member of ESC's Board of Directors, comments that regardless of the effect that the program has had on quality, the output per labour-hour has declined between 2000 and 2001. Larkin believes that lower output per labour-hour will lead to an increase in costs and lower operating income.

   a. How did Larkin conclude that output per labour-hour declined in 2001 relative to 2000?
   b. Why might output per labour-hour decline in 2001?
   c. Do you think that a lower output per labour-hour will decrease operating income in 2001? Explain briefly.

19-20 Quality improvement, relevant costs, and relevant revenues. The Photon Corporation manufactures and sells 20,000 copiers each year. The variable and fixed costs of reworking and repairing copiers are as follows:

	Variable Costs	Fixed Costs	Total Costs
Rework costs per copier	$1,600	$2,400	$4,000
Repair costs per copier:			
Customer support costs	80	120	200
Transportation costs for repair parts	180	60	240
Warranty repair costs	1,800	2,600	4,400

Photon's engineers are currently working to solve the problem of copies being too light or too dark. They propose changing the lens of the copier. The new lens will cost $50 more then the old lens. Each copier uses one lens. Photon uses a one-year time horizon for this decision, since it plans to introduce a new copier at the end of the year. Photon believes that even as it improves quality, it will not be able to save any of the fixed costs of rework or repair.

By changing the lens, Photon expects that it will (1) rework 300 fewer copiers, (2) repair 200 fewer copiers, and (3) sell 100 additional copiers. Photon's unit contribution margin on its existing copier is $6,000.

REQUIRED

1. What are the additional costs of choosing the new lens?
2. What are the additional financial benefits of choosing the new lens?
3. Should Photon use the new lens?

19-21 Customer-response time, on-time delivery. Pizzafest Inc makes and delivers pizzas to homes and offices in the Vancouver area. Fast, on-time delivery is one of Pizzafest's key strategies. Pizzafest provides the following information for the year 2001 about its customer-response time—the amount of time from when a customer calls to place an order to when the pizza is delivered to the customer.

	January-June	July-December
1. Pizzas delivered in 30 minutes or less	100,000	150,000
2. Pizzas delivered in between 31 and 45 minutes	200,000	260,000
3. Pizzas delivered in between 46 and 60 minutes	80,000	70,000
4. Pizzas delivered in between 61 and 75 minutes	20,000	20,000
Total pizzas delivered	400,000	500,000

REQUIRED

1. For January-June, 2001, and July-December, 2001, calculate the percentage of pizzas delivered in each of the four time intervals (less than 30 minutes, 31 to 45 minutes, 46 to 60 minutes, and 61 to 75 minutes). On the basis of these calculations, has customer-response time improved in July-December, 2001 compared to January-June, 2001?
2. When customers call Pizzafest, they often ask how long it will take for the pizza to be delivered to their home or offices. If Pizzafest quotes a long time interval, customers will often not place the order. If Pizzafest quotes too short a time interval and the pizza is not delivered on time, customers get upset and Pizzafest will lose repeat business. Based on the January-June, 2001, data, what *maximum* customer-response time should Pizzafest quote to its customers if (a) it wants to have an on-time delivery performance of at least 75%? (b) it wants to have an on-time delivery performance of at least 95%?
3. If Pizzafest had quoted the maximum customer-response times you calculated in requirements 2a and 2b, would it have met its on-time delivery performance targets for the period July-December, 2001?
4. Pizzafest is considering giving an on-time guarantee for January-June, 2002. If the pizza is not delivered within 60 minutes of placing the order, the customer gets the pizza free. Pizzafest estimates that it will make additional sales of 20,000 pizzas as a result of giving this guarantee. It estimates that it will fail to deliver a total of 15,000 pizzas on time. The average price of a pizza is $13, and the variable cost of a pizza is $7.
   a. What is the effect on Pizzafest's operating income of making this offer?
   b. What other factors should Pizzafest consider before making this offer?
   c. What actions can Pizzafest take to reduce customer-response time?

19-22 Waiting time, banks. Regal Bank has a small branch in Orillia, Ontario. The counter is staffed by one teller. The counter is open for five hours (300 minutes) each day (the operational capacity). It takes five minutes to serve a customer (service time). The Orillia branch expects to receive 40 customers each day. (Note that the number of customers corresponds to the number of orders in the chapter discussion.)

REQUIRED

1. Using the formula on p. 670, calculate how long, on average, a customer will wait in line before being served.
2. How long, on average, will a customer wait in line if the branch expects 50 customers each day?
3. The bank is considering ways to reduce waiting time. How long will customers have to wait on average, if the time to serve a customer is reduced to four minutes and the bank expects to serve 50 customers each day?

19-23 Waiting time, relevant costs, and relevant revenues. The Orillia branch of Regal Bank is thinking of offering additional services to its customers. Its counter is open for five hours (300 minutes) each day (the operational capacity). If it introduces the new services, the bank expects to serve an average of 60 customers each day instead of the 40 customers it currently averages. It will take four minutes to serve each customer (service time) regardless of whether or not the new services are offered. (Note that the number of customers corresponds to the number of orders in the chapter discussion.)

REQUIRED
1. Using the formula on p. 670, calculate how long, on average, a customer will wait in line before being served.
2. Regal Bank's policy is that the average waiting time in the line should not exceed five minutes. The bank cannot reduce the time to serve a customer below four minutes without significantly affecting quality. To reduce average waiting time for the 60 customers it expects to serve each day, the bank decides to keep the counter open for 336 minutes each day. Verify that by keeping the counter open for a longer time, the bank will be able to achieve its goal of an average waiting time of five minutes or less.
3. The bank expects to generate, on average, $30 in additional operating income each day as a result of offering the new services. The teller is paid $10 per hour and is employed in increments of an hour (that is, the teller can be employed for five, six, seven hours, and so on, but not for a fraction of an hour). If the bank wants average waiting time to be no more than five minutes, should the bank offer the new services?

19-24 Theory of constraints, throughput contribution, relevant costs. The Mayfield Corporation manufactures filing cabinets in two operations—machining and finishing. Additional information is as follows.

	Machining	Finishing
Annual capacity	100,000 units	80,000 units
Annual production	80,000 units	80,000 units
Fixed operating costs (excluding direct materials)	$640,000	$400,000
Fixed operating costs per unit produced ($640,000 ÷ 80,000; $400,000 ÷ 80,000)	$8 per unit	$5 per unit

Each cabinet sells for $72 and has direct materials costs of $32 incurred at the start of the machining operation. Mayfield has no other variable costs. Mayfield can sell whatever output it produces. The following requirements refer only to the preceding data; there is *no connection* between the situations.

REQUIRED
1. Mayfield is considering using some modern jigs and tools in the finishing operation that would increase annual finishing output by 1,000 units. The annual cost of these jigs and tools is $30,000. Should Mayfield acquire these tools?
2. The production manager of the Machining Department has submitted a proposal to do faster setups that would increase the annual capacity of the Machining Department by 10,000 units and cost $5,000 per year. Should Mayfield implement the change?

19-25 Theory of constraints, throughput contribution, relevant costs. Refer to the information in Exercise 19-24 in answering the following requirements; there is no connection between the situations.

REQUIRED
1. An outside contractor offers to do the finishing operation for 12,000 units at $10 per unit, double the $5 per unit that it costs Mayfield to do the finishing in-house. Should Mayfield accept the subcontractor's offer?
2. The Hunt Corporation offers to machine 4,000 units at $4 per unit, half the $8 per unit that it costs Mayfield to do the machining in-house. Should Mayfield accept the subcontractor's offer?

19-26 Theory of constraints, throughput contribution, quality. Refer to the information in Exercise 19-24 in answering the following requirements; there is no connection between the situations.

REQUIRED

1. Mayfield produces 2,000 defective units at the machining operation. What is the cost to Mayfield of the defective items produced? Explain your answer briefly.
2. Mayfield produces 2,000 defective units at the finishing operation. What is the cost to Mayfield of the defective items produced? Explain your answer briefly.

PROBLEMS

19-27 Quality improvement, relevant costs, and relevant revenues. The Thomas Corporation sells 300,000 V262 valves to the automobile and truck industry. Thomas has a capacity of 110,000 machine-hours and can produce 3 valves per machine-hour. V262's contribution margin per unit is $8. Thomas sells only 300,000 valves because 30,000 valves (10% of the good valves) need to be reworked. It takes one machine-hour to rework 3 valves so that 10,000 hours of capacity are lost in the rework process. Thomas's rework costs are $210,000. Rework costs consist of:

Direct materials and direct rework labour (variable costs)	$3 per unit
Fixed costs of equipment, rent, and overhead allocation	$4 per unit

Thomas' process designers have come up with a modification that would maintain the speed of the process and would ensure 100% quality and no rework. The new process would cost $315,000 per year. The following additional information is available:

◆ The demand for Thomas' V262 valves is 370,000 per year.
◆ The Jackson Corporation has asked Thomas to supply 22,000 T971 valves if Thomas implements the new design. The contribution margin per T971 valve is $10. Thomas can make two T971 valves per machine-hour on the existing machine with 100% quality and no rework.

REQUIRED

1. Suppose Thomas' designers implemented the new design. Should Thomas accept Jackson's order for 22,000 T971 valves? Explain.
2. Should Thomas implement the new design?
3. What nonfinancial and qualitative factors should Thomas consider in deciding whether to implement the new design?

19-28 Quality improvement, relevant costs, and relevant revenues. The Tan Corporation makes multicolour plastic lamps in two operations, molding and welding. The molding operation has a capacity of 200,000 units per year; welding has a capacity of 300,000 units per year. Annual costs of quality information recorded by Tan is as follows:

◆ Design of product and process costs $240,000
◆ Inspection and testing costs   170,000
◆ Scrap costs (all in the molding department)   750,000

The demand for lamps is very strong. Tan will be able to sell whatever output quantities it can produce at $40 per lamp.

Tan can start only 200,000 units into production in the Molding Department because of capacity constraints on the molding machines. If a defective unit is produced at the molding operation, it must be scrapped, and the scrap yields no revenue. Of the 200,000 units started at the molding operation, 30,000 units (15%) are scrapped. Scrap costs, based on total (fixed and variable) manufacturing costs incurred up to the molding operation, equal $25 per unit as follows:

Direct materials (variable)	$16 per unit
Direct manufacturing labour, setup labour, and materials-handling labour (variable)	3 per unit
Equipment, rent, and other allocated overhead including inspection and testing costs on scrapped parts (fixed)	6 per unit
	$25 per unit

The good units from the Molding Department are sent to the Welding Department. Variable manufacturing costs at the Welding Department are $2.50 per unit. There is no scrap in the Welding Department. Therefore, Tan's total sales quantity equals the Molding Department's output. Tan incurs no other variable costs.

Tan's designers have determined that adding a different type of material to the existing direct materials would reduce scrap to zero, but it would increase the variable costs per unit in the Molding Department by $3. Recall that only 200,000 units can be started each year.

REQUIRED

1. What is the additional direct materials cost of implementing the new method?
2. What is the additional benefit to Tan from using the new material and improving quality?
3. Should Tan use the new material?
4. What other nonfinancial and qualitative factors should Tan consider in making a decision?

19-29 Statistical quality control, airline operations. Peoples Skyway operates daily round-trip flights on the London-Vancouver route using a fleet of three 747s, the *Spirit of Birmingham*, the *Spirit of Glasgow*, and the *Spirit of Manchester*. The budgeted quantity of fuel for each round-trip flight is the mean (average) fuel usage. Over the last 12 months, the average fuel usage per round trip is 100 gallon-units with a standard deviation of 10 gallon-units. A gallon-unit is 1,000 gallons.

Cilla Black, the operations manager of Peoples Skyway, uses a statistical quality control (SQC) approach in deciding whether to investigate fuel usage per round-trip flight. She investigates those flights with fuel usage greater than two standard deviations from the mean.

In October, Black receives the following report for round-trip fuel usage by the three planes operating on the London-Vancouver route:

Flight	Spirit of Birmingham (gallon-units)	Spirit of Glasgow (gallon-units)	Spirit of Manchester (gallon-units)
1	104	103	97
2	94	94	104
3	97	96	111
4	101	107	104
5	105	92	122
6	107	113	118
7	111	99	126
8	112	106	114
9	115	101	117
10	119	93	123

REQUIRED

1. Using the ±2σ rule, what variance investigation decisions would be made?
2. Present SQC charts for round-trip fuel usage for each of the three 747s in October. What inferences can you draw from them?
3. Some managers propose that Peoples Skyway present its SQC charts in monetary terms rather than in physical quantity terms (gallon-units). What are the advantages and disadvantages of using monetary fuel costs rather than gallon-units in the SQC charts?

19-30 Compensation linked with profitability, on-time delivery, and external quality performance measures; balanced scorecard. Pacific-Dunlop supplies tires to major automotive companies. It has two tire plants in North America, in Detroit and Los Angeles. The quarterly bonus plan for each plant manager has three components:

a. **Profitability performance.** Add 2% of operating income.
b. **On-time delivery performance.** Add $10,000 if on-time delivery performance to the ten most important customers is 98% or better. If on-time performance is below 98%, add nothing.
c. **Product quality performance.** Deduct 50% of cost of sales returns from the ten most important customers.

Quarterly data for 2001 on the Detroit and Los Angeles plants are as follows:

	January–March	April–June	July–September	October–December
Detroit				
Operating income	$800,000	$850,000	$700,000	$900,000
On-time delivery*	98.4%	98.6%	97.1%	97.9%
Cost of sales returns*	$18,000	$26,000	$10,000	$25,000
Los Angeles				
Operating income	$1,600,000	$1,500,000	$1,800,000	$1,900,000
On-time delivery*	95.6%	97.1%	97.9%	98.4%
Cost of sales returns*	$35,000	$34,000	$28,000	$22,000

* For the 10 most important customers.

REQUIRED

1. Compute the bonuses paid each quarter of 2001 to the plant managers of the Detroit and Los Angeles plants.
2. Discuss the three components of the bonus plan as measures of profitability, on-time delivery, and product quality.
3. Why would you want to evaluate plant managers on the basis of both operating income and on-time delivery?
4. Give one example of what might happen if on-time delivery were dropped as a performance evaluation measure.

19-31 Waiting times, manufacturing lead times. The SRG Corporation uses an injection molding machine to make a plastic product, Z39. SRG makes products only after receiving firm orders from its customers. SRG estimates that it will receive 50 orders for Z39 (each order is for 1,000 units) during the coming year. Each order of Z39 will take 80 hours of machine time (4 hours to clean and prepare the machine, called setup, and 76 hours to process the order). The annual capacity of the machine is 5,000 hours.

REQUIRED

1. What percentage of the total available machine capacity does SRG expect to use during the coming year?
2. Calculate the average amount of time that an order for Z39 will wait in line before it is processed and the average manufacturing lead time per order for Z39.
3. SRG is considering introducing a new product, Y28. SRG estimates that, on average, it will receive 25 orders of Y28 (each order for 200 units) in the coming year. Each order of Y28 will take 20 hours of machine time (2 hours to clean and prepare the machine, and 18 hours to process the order). The average demand for Z39 will be unaffected by the introduction of Y28. Calculate the average waiting time for an order received and the average manufacturing lead time per order for each product, if SRG introduces Y28.
4. If SRG introduces Y28, on average what fraction of the total manufacturing lead time will each order of Y28 spend just waiting to be processed?
5. Briefly describe why delays occur in the processing of Z39 and Y28.

19-32 Waiting times, relevant revenues and relevant costs (continuation of 19-31). SRG is still deciding whether or not it should introduce and sell Y28. The following table provides information on selling prices, variable costs, and inventory carrying costs for Z39 and Y28. SRG will incur additional variable costs and inventory carrying costs for Y28 only if it introduces Y28. Fixed costs equal to 40% of variable costs are allocated to all products produced and sold during the year.

Product	Average Number of Orders	Average Selling Price per Order If Average Manufacturing Lead Time Is:		Variable Costs per Order	Inventory Carrying Costs per Order per Hour
		Less Than 320 Hours	More Than 320 Hours		
Z39	50	$27,000	$26,500	$15,000	$0.75
Y28	25	8,400	8,000	5,000	0.25

REQUIRED
1. Should SRG manufacture and sell Y28? Show all your computations.
2. What is the cutoff price per order above which SRG should manufacture and sell Y28 and below which SRG should choose not to manufacture and sell Y28?

19-33 **Manufacturing lead times, relevant revenues, and relevant costs.** The Brandt Corporation makes wire harnesses for the aircraft industry. Brandt is uncertain about when and how many customer orders will be received. Brandt makes harnesses only after receiving firm orders from its customers. Brandt has recently purchased a new machine to make wire harnesses, one for Boeing airplanes (B7) and the other for Airbus Industries airplanes (A3). The annual capacity of the new machine is 6,000 hours. The following information is available for next year:

| Product | Average Number of Orders | Equipment Time Required | Average Selling Price per Order If Average Manufacturing Lead Time Is: | | Variable Costs per Order | Inventory Carrying Costs per Order per Hour |
			Less Than 200 Hours	More Than 200 Hours		
B7	125	40 hours	$15,000	$14,400	$10,000	$0.50
A3	10	50 hours	13,500	12,960	9,000	0.45

REQUIRED
1. Calculate the average manufacturing lead times per order (a) if Brandt manufactures only B7 and (b) if Brandt manufactures both B7 and A3.
2. Even though A3 has a positive contribution margin, Brandt's managers are evaluating whether Brandt should (a) make and sell only B7 or (b) make and sell both B7 and A3. Which alternative will maximize Brandt's operating income? Show all calculations.
3. What other factors should Brandt consider in choosing between the alternatives in requirement 2?

19-34 **Theory of constraints, throughput contribution, relevant costs.** Columbia Industries manufactures electronic testing equipment. Columbia also installs the equipment at the customer's site and ensures that it functions smoothly. Additional information on the Manufacturing and Installation Departments is as follows (capacities are expressed in terms of the number of units of equipment):

	Equipment Manufactured	Equipment Installed
Annual capacity	400 units per year	300 units per year
Equipment manufactured and installed	300 units per year	300 units per year

Columbia manufactures only 300 units per year because the Installation Department has only enough capacity to install 300 units. The equipment sells for $40,000 per unit (installed) and has direct materials costs of $15,000. All costs other than direct materials costs are fixed. The following requirements refer only to the preceding data; there is no connection between the situations.

REQUIRED
1. Columbia's engineers have found a way to reduce equipment manufacturing time. The new method would cost an additional $50 per unit and would allow Colorado to manufacture 20 additional units a year. Should Columbia implement the new method?
2. Columbia's designers have proposed a change in the direct materials that would increase direct materials costs by $2,000 per unit. This change would enable Columbia to install 320 units of equipment each year. If Columbia makes the change, it will implement the new design on all equipment sold. Should Columbia use the new design?
3. A new installation technique has been developed that will enable Columbia's engineers to install 10 additional units of equipment a year. The new method will increase installation costs by $50,000 each year. Should Columbia implement the new technique?
4. Columbia is considering how to motivate workers to improve their productivity (output per hour). One proposal is to evaluate and compensate workers in the Manufacturing and Installation Departments on the basis of their productivities. Do you think the new proposal is a good idea? Explain briefly.

19-35 Theory of constraints, throughput contribution, quality, relevant costs. Aardee Industries manufactures pharmaceutical products in two departments—Mixing and Tablet-Making. Additional information on the two departments follows. Each tablet contains 0.5 gram of direct materials.

	Mixing	Tablet-Making
Capacity per hour	150 grams	200 tablets
Monthly capacity (2,000 hours available in each of mixing and tablet-making)	300,000 grams	400,000 tablets
Monthly production	200,000 grams	390,000 tablets
Fixed operating costs (excluding direct materials)	$16,000	$39,000
Fixed operating costs per tablet ($16,000 ÷ 200,000; $39,000 ÷ 390,000)	$0.08 per gram	$0.10 per tablet

The Mixing Department makes 200,000 grams of direct materials mixture (enough to make 400,000 tablets) because the Tablet-Making Department has only enough capacity to process 400,000 tablets. All direct materials costs are incurred in the Mixing Department. Aardee incurs $156,000 in direct materials costs. The Tablet-Making Department manufactures only 390,000 tablets from the 200,000 grams of mixture processed; 2.5% of the direct materials mixture is lost in the tablet-making process. Each tablet sells for $1. All costs other than direct materials costs are fixed costs. The following requirements refer only to the preceding data; there is no connection between the situations.

REQUIRED

1. An outside contractor makes the following offer: if Aardee will supply the contractor with 10,000 grams of mixture, the contractor will manufacture 19,500 tablets for Aardee (allowing for the normal 2.5% loss during the tablet-making process) at $0.12 per tablet. Should Aardee accept the contractor's offer?
2. Another firm offers to prepare 20,000 grams of mixture a month from direct materials Aardee supplies. The company will charge $0.07 per gram of mixture. Should Aardee accept the company's offer?
3. Aardee's engineers have devised a method that would improve quality in the tablet-making operation. They estimate that the 10,000 tablets currently being lost would be saved. The modification would cost $7,000 a month. Should Aardee implement the new method?
4. Suppose that Aardee also loses 10,000 grams of mixture in its mixing operation. These losses can be reduced to zero if the company is willing to spend $9,000 per month in quality improvement methods. Should Aardee adopt the quality improvement method?
5. What are the benefits of improving quality at the mixing operation compared with the benefits of improving quality at the tablet-making operation?

19-36 Quality improvement, Pareto charts, fishbone diagrams. The Murray Corporation manufactures, sells, and installs photocopying machines. Murray has placed heavy emphasis on reducing defects and failures in its production operations. Murray wants to apply the same total quality management (TQM) principles to managing its accounts receivables.

REQUIRED

1. On the basis of your knowledge and experience, what would you classify as failures in accounts receivables?
2. Give examples of prevention activities that could reduce failures in accounts receivables.
3. Draw a Pareto diagram of the types of failures in accounts receivables and a fishbone diagram of possible causes of one type of failure in accounts receivables.

19-37 Ethics and quality. Information from a quality report for 2001 prepared by Lindsey Williams, assistant controller of Citocell, a manufacturer of electric motors follow:

Revenues	$10,000,000
On-line inspection	90,000
Warranty liability	260,000
Product testing	210,000
Scrap	230,000
Design engineering	200,000
Percentage of customer complaints	5%
On-time delivery	90%

Davey Evans, the plant manager of Citocell, is eligible for a bonus if the total cost of quality as a percentage of revenues is less than 10%, percentage of customer complaints is less than 4% and on-time delivery exceeds 92%. Evans is unhappy because, when preparing her report, Williams actually contacted customers to inquire if they had any complaints and if deliveries had been made on time. Evans would have preferred Williams to be less proactive and wait for customers to complain. Evans's concern with Williams's approach is that it introduces subjectivity into the numbers and also fails to capture the seriousness of customers' concerns. "When you wait for a customer to complain, you know they are complaining because it is something important. When you do customer surveys, customers mention whatever is on their mind, even if it is not terribly important."

John Roche, the controller, asks Williams to see him. He tells her about Evans's concerns. "I think Davey has a point. See what you can do." Williams is very confident that the customer complaints are genuine and that customers are concerned about late deliveries. She believes it is important for Citocell to be proactive and obtain systematic and quick customer feedback, and then to use this information to make future improvements. She is also well aware that Citocell had not done customer surveys in the past, and that but for her surveys, Evans would probably be eligible for the bonus. She is confused about how to handle Roche's request.

REQUIRED
1. Calculate the ratio of each cost of quality category (prevention, appraisal, internal failure, and external failure) to revenues in 2001. Are the total costs of quality as a percentage of revenues less than 10%?
2. Is John Roche's suggestion to Williams to reconsider her numbers unethical? Would it be unethical for Williams to modify her analysis? What steps should Williams take to resolve this situation?

COLLABORATIVE LEARNING PROBLEM

19-38 Quality improvement, relevant costs, and relevant revenues. The Wellesley Corporation makes printed cloth in two operations, weaving and printing. Direct materials costs are Wellesley's only variable costs. The demand for Wellesley's cloth is very strong. Wellesley can sell whatever output quantities it produces at $1,250 per roll to a distributor who then markets, distributes, and provides customer service for the product.

	Weaving	Printing
Monthly capacity	10,000 rolls	15,000 rolls
Monthly production	9,500 rolls	8,550 rolls
Direct material variable costs per roll of cloth processed at each operation	$500	$100
Fixed operating costs	$2,850,000	$427,500
Fixed operating costs per roll ($2,850,000 ÷ 9,500; $427,500 ÷ 8,550)	$300 per roll	$50 per roll

Monthly costs of quality information recorded by Wellesley are as follows:
◆ Product and process design costs $300,000
◆ Scrap costs in Weaving Department   392,500
◆ Scrap costs in Printing Department   883,500

Wellesley can start only 10,000 rolls of cloth in the Weaving Department because of capacity constraints at the weaving machines. If the weaving operation produces defective cloth, the cloth must be scrapped and yields zero net revenue. Of the 10,000 rolls of cloth started at the weaving operation, 500 rolls (5%) are scrapped. Scrap costs per roll, based on total (fixed and variable) manufacturing costs per roll incurred up to the end of the weaving operation, equal $785 per roll as follows:

Direct materials costs per roll (variable)	$500
Fixed operating costs per roll ($2,850,000 ÷ 10,000 rolls)	285
Total manufacturing costs per roll in Weaving Department	$785

The good rolls from the Weaving Department (called gray cloth) are sent to the Printing Department. Of the 9,500 good rolls started at the printing operation,

950 rolls (10%) are scrapped and yield zero net revenue. Scrap costs based on total (fixed and variable) manufacturing costs per unit incurred up to the end of the printing operation equal $930 per roll calculated as follows:

Total manufacturing costs per roll in Weaving Department		$785
Printing Department manufacturing costs:		
Direct materials costs per roll (variable)	$100	
Fixed operating costs per roll		
($427,500 ÷ 9,500 rolls)	45	
Total manufacturing costs per roll in Printing Department		145
Total manufacturing costs per roll		$930

The Wellesley Corporation's total monthly sales of printed cloth equals the Printing Department's output. The following requirements refer only to the preceding data; there is no connection between the situations.

INSTRUCTIONS

Form groups of three students to complete the following requirements.

REQUIRED

1. The Printing Department is considering buying 5,000 rolls of gray cloth from an outside supplier at $900 per roll. The Printing Department manager is concerned that the cost of purchasing the gray cloth is much higher than Wellesley's cost of manufacturing the gray cloth. The quality of the gray cloth acquired from outside is very similar to that manufactured in-house. The Printing Department expects that 10% of the rolls obtained from the outside supplier will be scrapped. Should the Printing Department buy the gray cloth from the outside supplier?

2. How much does Wellesley lose if a defective roll is produced in the Printing Department?

3. What is the expected loss to Wellesley if a defective roll is produced in the Weaving Department? Use the expected monetary value criterion described in the appendix to Chapter 3.

4. Wellesley's engineers have developed a method that would lower the Printing Department's scrap rate to 6% at the printing operation. Implementing the new method would cost $350,000 per month. Should Wellesley implement the change?

5. The design engineering team has proposed a modification that would lower the Weaving Department's scrap rate to 3%. The modification would cost the company $175,000 per month. Should Wellesley implement the change?

6. From your answers to requirements 1 to 5, what general conclusions can you draw about implementing TQM programs?

CHAPTER 20

INVENTORY MANAGEMENT, JUST-IN-TIME, AND BACKFLUSH COSTING

Manufacturers are demanding more frequent deliveries with shorter purchase order lead times from their suppliers. To better service the companies who use their automotive products, Challenger Freight has invested in new information systems and technology. Better coordination and faster response times are helping Challenger Freight and its customers to reduce inventory levels.

LEARNING OBJECTIVES

After studying this chapter, you should be able to:

1. Identify five categories of costs associated with goods for sale
2. Balance ordering costs and carrying costs using the economic-order-quantity (EOQ) decision model
3. Identify and reduce conflicts that can arise between EOQ decision models and models used for performance evaluation
4. Use a supply-chain approach to inventory management
5. Differentiate materials requirements planning (MRP) systems from just-in-time (JIT) systems for manufacturing
6. Identify the major features of a just-in-time production system
7. Use backflush costing
8. Describe different ways backflush costing can simplify traditional job-costing systems

Inventory management is a pivotal part of profit planning for manufacturing and merchandising companies. Materials costs often account for more than 50% of total costs in manufacturing companies and over 70% of total costs in retail companies. Accounting information can play a key role in inventory management. We first consider retail organizations and then manufacturing companies.

INVENTORY MANAGEMENT IN RETAIL ORGANIZATIONS

Inventory management is the planning, coordinating, and control activities related to the flow of inventory into, through, and from the organization. Consider retailers where cost of goods sold constitutes the largest single cost item. The following breakdown of operations for two major retailers is illustrative:

	Loblaw Companies Limited	Oshawa Group Limited
Sales	100%	100%
Cost of sales and other expenses	96%	97%
Depreciation and amortization	1%	1%
Interest and taxes and other	1.5%	1%
Net income	1.5%	1%

These low percentages of net income to revenues mean that better decisions regarding the purchasing and managing of goods for sale can cause dramatic percentage increases in net income.

Costs Associated with Goods for Sale

The following cost categories are important when managing inventories and goods for sale.

1. **Purchasing costs. Purchasing costs** consist of the costs of goods acquired from suppliers including incoming freight or transportation costs. These costs usually make up the largest single cost category of goods for sale. Discounts for different purchase order sizes and supplier credit terms affect purchasing costs.

2. **Ordering costs. Ordering costs** consist of the costs of preparing and issuing a purchase order. Related to the number of purchase orders processed are special processing, receiving, inspection, and payment costs.

3. **Carrying costs. Carrying costs** arise when a business holds inventories of goods for sale. These costs include the opportunity cost of the investment tied up in inventory (see Chapter 11) and the costs associated with storage, such as storage space rental and insurance, obsolescence, and spoilage.

4. **Stockout costs. A stockout** occurs when a company runs out of an item for which there is customer demand. A company may respond to the shortfall or stockout by expediting an order from a supplier. Expediting costs of a stockout include the additional ordering costs plus any associated transportation costs. Alternatively, the company may lose a sale due to the stockout. In this case, stockout costs include the lost contribution margin on the sale plus any contribution margin lost on future sales hurt by customer ill-will caused by the stockout.

5. **Quality costs.** The *quality* of a product or service is its conformance with a preannounced or prespecified standard. As described in Chapter 19, four categories of costs of quality are often distinguished: (a) prevention costs, (b) appraisal costs, (c) internal failure costs, and (d) external failure costs.

The descriptions of the cost categories indicate that some of the relevant costs for making inventory decisions and managing goods for sale are not available in existing accounting systems. Opportunity costs, which are not typically recorded in accounting systems, are an important component in several of these cost categories.

Inventory management. The planning, organizing, and control of activities focused on the flow of materials into, through, and from the organization.

Effective Inventory Management Home Page
www.effectiveinventory.com/

OBJECTIVE 1

Identify five categories of costs associated with goods for sale

Purchasing costs. Cost of goods acquired from suppliers, including freight and transportation costs.

Ordering costs. Costs of preparing and issuing a purchase order.

Carrying costs. Costs that arise when a business holds inventories of goods for sale.

Stockout. Arises when a supplier runs out of a particular item for which there is customer demand.

Advances in information-gathering technology, however, are attempting to increase the reliability and timeliness of inventory data and reduce costs in these five categories. For example, bar coding technology allows a scanner to capture purchases and sales of individual units. This creates an instantaneous record of inventory movements and helps in the management of purchasing, carrying, and stockout costs.

OBJECTIVE 2

Balance ordering costs and carrying costs using the economic-order-quantity (EOQ) decision model

Economic order quantity (EOQ). Decision model that calculates the optimal quantity of inventory to order. Simplest model incorporates only ordering costs and carrying costs.

Purchase order lead time. Amount of time between the placement of an order and its delivery.

Economic Order Quantity Decision Model

The first major decision in managing goods for sale is deciding how much of a given product to order. The **economic order quantity (EOQ)** decision model calculates the optimal quantity of inventory to order. The simplest version of this model incorporates only ordering costs and carrying costs into the calculation. It assumes the following:

1. The same fixed quantity is ordered at each reorder point.
2. Demand, ordering costs, and carrying costs are certain. The **purchase order lead time**—the time between the placement of an order and its delivery—is also certain.
3. Purchasing costs per unit are unaffected by the quantity ordered. This assumption makes purchasing costs irrelevant to determining EOQ, because purchasing costs of all units acquired will be the same, whatever the order size in which the units are ordered.
4. No stockouts occur. One justification for this assumption is that the costs of a stockout are prohibitively high. We assume that to avoid these potential costs, management always maintains adequate inventory so that no stockout can occur.
5. In deciding the size of the purchase order, management considers the costs of quality only to the extent that these costs affect ordering costs or carrying costs.

Given these assumptions, EOQ analysis ignores purchasing costs, stockout costs, and quality costs. To determine EOQ, we minimize the relevant ordering and carrying costs (those ordering and carrying costs that are affected by the quantity of inventory ordered):

Total relevant costs = Total relevant ordering costs + Total relevant carrying costs

Example: Video Galore sells packages of blank videotapes to its customers; it also rents out tapes of movies and sporting events. It purchases packages of videotapes from Sontek at $14 a package. Sontek pays all incoming freight. No incoming inspection is necessary, as Sontek has a superb reputation for delivering quality merchandise. Annual demand is 13,000 packages, at a rate of 250 packages per week. Video Galore requires a 15% annual return on investment. The purchase order lead time is two weeks. The following cost data are available:

Relevant ordering costs per purchase order		$200.00
Relevant carrying costs per package per year:		
Required annual return on investment, $15\% \times \$14$	$2.10	
Relevant insurance, materials-handling, breakage, etc. per year	3.10	5.20

What is the economic order quantity of packages of videotapes?

The formula underlying the EOQ model is:

$$EOQ = \sqrt{\frac{2DP}{C}}$$

where:

EOQ = Economic order quantity
D = Demand in units for a specified time period (one year in this example)
P = Relevant ordering costs per purchase order
C = Relevant carrying costs of one unit in stock for the time period used for D (one year in this example)

The formula indicates that EOQ increases with demand and ordering costs and decreases with carrying costs.

We can use this formula to determine the EOQ for Video Galore as follows:

$$EOQ = \sqrt{\frac{2 \times 13{,}000 \times \$200}{\$5.20}} = \sqrt{1{,}000{,}000} = 1{,}000 \text{ packages}$$

Therefore, Video Galore should order 1,000 tape packages each time to minimize total ordering and carrying costs.

The total annual relevant costs (TRC) for any order quantity Q can be calculated using the following formula:

$$TRC = \frac{\text{Total annual relevant}}{\text{ordering costs}} + \frac{\text{Total annual relevant}}{\text{carrying costs}}$$

$$= \frac{\text{Number of}}{\text{purchase orders}} \times \frac{\text{Relevant}}{\text{ordering costs per}} + \frac{\text{Average inventory}}{\text{in units}} \times \frac{\text{Annual relevant}}{\text{carrying costs of 1}}$$
$$\text{per year} \qquad \text{purchase order} \qquad \qquad \text{unit for a year}$$

$$= \left(\frac{D}{Q}\right) \times P + \left(\frac{Q}{2}\right) \times C = \frac{DP}{Q} + \frac{QC}{2}$$

(Note that in this formula, Q can be any order quantity, not just the EOQ.)

When $Q = 1,000$ units:

$$TRC = \frac{13{,}000 \times \$200}{1{,}000} + \frac{1{,}000 \times \$5.20}{2}$$

$$= \$2{,}600 + \$2{,}600 = \$5{,}200$$

The number of deliveries each time period (in our example, one year) is:

$$\frac{D}{EOQ} = \frac{13{,}000}{1{,}000} = 13 \text{ deliveries}$$

Exhibit 20-1 shows a graph analysis of the total annual relevant costs of ordering (DP/Q) and carrying inventory ($QC/2$) under various order sizes (Q), and illustrates the tradeoff between the two types of costs. The larger the order quantity, the higher the annual relevant carrying costs, but the lower the annual relevant ordering costs. *The total annual relevant costs are at a minimum where total relevant ordering costs and total relevant carrying costs are equal* (in the Video Galore example, each equals $2,600).

EXHIBIT 20-1
Ordering Costs and Carrying Costs for Video Galore

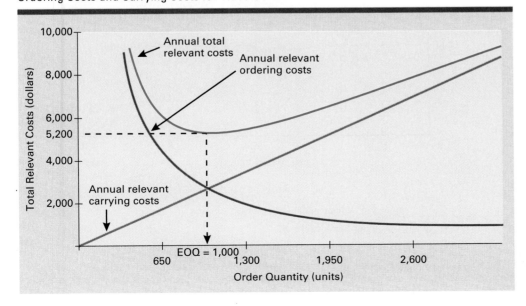

When to Order, Assuming Certainty

Reorder point. The quantity level of the inventory on hand that triggers a new order.

The second major decision in dealing with cost of goods for sale is when to order. The **reorder point** is the quantity level of the inventory on hand that triggers a new order. The reorder point is simplest to compute when both demand and lead time are certain:

$$\text{Reorder point} = \frac{\text{Number of units sold}}{\text{per unit of time}} \times \text{Purchase order lead time}$$

Consider our Video Galore example. We choose a week as the unit of time:

Economic order quantity	1,000 packages
Number of units sold per week	250 packages
Purchase order lead time	2 weeks

Thus:

$$\text{Reorder point} = \frac{\text{Number of units sold}}{\text{per unit of time}} \times \text{Purchase order lead time}$$

$$= 250 \times 2 = 500 \text{ packages}$$

So, Video Galore will order 1,000 packages of tapes each time its inventory stock falls to 500 packages.

The graph in Exhibit 20-2 presents the behaviour of the inventory level of tape packages, assuming demand occurs uniformly throughout each week.[1] If the purchase order lead time is two weeks, a new order will be placed when the inventory level reaches 500 tape packages so that the 1,000 packages ordered are received at the time inventory reaches zero.

Safety Stock

Safety stock. Inventory held at all times regardless of inventory ordered using EOQ. It is a buffer against unexpected increases in demand or lead time and unexpected unavailability of stock from suppliers.

So far, we have assumed that demand and purchase order lead time are certain. When retailers are uncertain about the demand, the lead time, or the quantity that suppliers can provide, they often hold safety stock. **Safety stock** is inventory held at all times regardless of inventory ordered using EOQ. It is used as a buffer against unexpected increases in demand or lead time and unavailability of stock from suppli-

EXHIBIT 20-2
Inventory Level of Tape Packages for Video Galore*

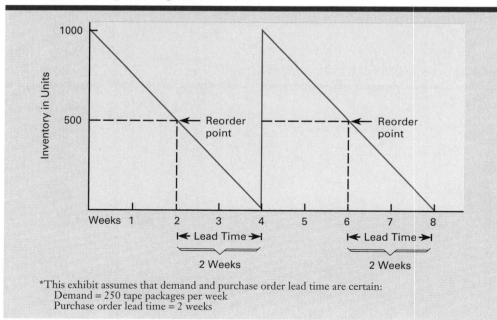

*This exhibit assumes that demand and purchase order lead time are certain:
Demand = 250 tape packages per week
Purchase order lead time = 2 weeks

[1]This handy but special formula does not apply when the receipt of the order fails to increase inventory to the reorder-point quantity (for example, when the lead time is three weeks and the order is a one-week supply). In these cases, orders will overlap.

ers. In our Video Galore example, expected demand is 250 packages per week, but the company's managers feel that a maximum demand of 400 packages per week may occur. If Video Galore's managers decide that the costs of stockout are prohibitive, they may decide to hold safety stock of 300 packages. This amount is the maximum excess demand of 150 packages per week for the two weeks of purchase order lead time. The computation of safety stock hinges on demand forecasts. Managers will have some notion—usually based on experience—of the range of weekly demand.

A frequency distribution based on prior daily or weekly levels of demand provides data for computing the associated costs of maintaining safety stock. Assume that one of seven different levels of demand will occur over the two-week purchase order lead time at Video Galore.

Total Demand for Two Weeks	Units						
	200	300	400	500	600	700	800
Probability (sums to 1.00)	0.06	0.09	0.20	0.30	0.20	0.09	0.06

We see that 500 is the most likely level of demand for two weeks, because it is assigned the highest probability of occurrence. We also see that there is a 0.35 probability that demand will be between 600, 700, or 800 packages $(0.20 + 0.09 + 0.06 = 0.35)$.

If a customer calls Video Galore to buy videotapes, and the store has none in stock, it can "rush" them to the customer at a cost to Video Galore of $4 per package. The relevant stockout costs in this case are $4 per package. The optimal safety stock level is the quantity of safety stock that minimizes the sum of the relevant annual stockout and carrying costs. Recall that the relevant carrying costs for Video Galore are $5.20 per unit per year.

Exhibit 20-3 presents the total annual relevant stockout and carrying costs when the reorder point is 500 units. We need only consider safety stock levels of 0,

EXHIBIT 20-3
Computation of Safety Stock for Video Galore When Reorder Point Is 500 Units

Safety Stock Level in Units (1)	Demand Realizations Resulting in Stockouts (2)	Stockout in Units* (3) = (2) − 500 − (1)	Probability of Stockout (4)	Relevant Stockout Costs[†] (5) = (3) × $4	Number of Orders per Year[‡] (6)	Expected Stockout Costs[§] (7) = (4) × (5) × (6)	Relevant Carrying Costs[#] (8) = (1) × $5.20	Total Relevant Costs (9) = (7) + (8)
0	600	100	0.20	$ 400	13	$1,040		
	700	200	0.09	800	13	936		
	800	300	0.06	1,200	13	936		
						$2,912	$ 0	$2,912
100	700	100	0.09	400	13	$ 468		
	800	200	0.06	800	13	624		
						$1,092	$ 520	$1,612
200	800	100	0.06	400	13	$ 312	$1,040	$1,352
300	—	—	—	—	—	$ 0[‖]	$1,560	$1,560

*Realized demand − inventory available during lead time (excluding safety stock), 500 units − safety stock.
[†]Stockout units × relevant stockout costs of $4 per unit.
[‡]Annual demand 13,000 ÷ 1,000 EOQ = 13 orders per year.
[§]Probability of stockout × relevant stockout costs × number of orders per year.
[#]Safety stock × annual relevant carrying costs of $5.20 per unit (assumes that safety stock is on hand at all times and that there is no overstocking caused by decreases in expected usage).
[‖]At a safety stock level of 300 units, no stockouts will occur and hence expected stockout costs = $0.

100, 200 and 300 units, since demand will exceed the 500 units of stock available at reordering by 0 if demand is 500, by 100 if demand is 600, by 200 if demand is 700, and by 300 if demand is 800. The total annual relevant stockout and carrying costs would be minimized at $1,352, when a safety stock of 200 packages is maintained. Think of the 200 units of safety stock as extra stock that Video Galore maintains. For example, Video Galore's total inventory of tapes at the time of reordering its EOQ of 1,000 units would be 700 units (the reorder point of 500 units plus the safety stock of 200 units).

CHALLENGES IN ESTIMATING INVENTORY-RELATED COSTS AND THEIR EFFECTS

Considerations in Obtaining Estimates of Relevant Costs

Obtaining accurate estimates of the cost parameters used in the EOQ decision model is a challenging task. For example, the relevant annual carrying costs of inventory consist of *incremental* or *outlay costs* plus the *opportunity cost of capital*.

What are the relevant incremental costs of carrying inventory? Only those costs that vary with the quantity of inventory held—for example, insurance, property taxes, costs of obsolescence, and costs of breakage. Consider the salaries paid to clerks, storekeepers, and materials-handlers. These costs are irrelevant if they are unaffected by changes in inventory levels. Suppose, however, that as inventories decrease, these salary costs also decrease as the clerks, storekeepers, and materials-handlers are transferred to other activities or laid off. In this case, the salaries paid to these persons are relevant incremental costs of carrying inventory. Similarly, the costs of storage space owned that cannot be used for other profitable purposes as inventories decrease are irrelevant. But if the space has other profitable uses, or if rental cost is tied to the amount of space occupied, storage costs are relevant incremental costs of carrying inventory.

What is the relevant opportunity cost of capital? It is the return forgone by investing capital in inventory rather than elsewhere. It is calculated as the required rate of return multiplied by those costs per unit that vary with the number of units purchased and that are incurred at the time the units are received. (Examples of these costs per unit are purchase price, incoming freight, and incoming inspection.) Opportunity costs are not computed on investments, say, in buildings, if these investments are unaffected by changes in inventory levels. In the case of stockouts, calculating the relevant opportunity costs requires an estimate of the lost contribution margin on that sale as well as on future sales hurt by customer ill-will resulting from the stockout.

Cost of a Prediction Error

Our discussion suggests that predicting relevant costs requires care and is difficult. Managers understand that their projections will seldom be flawless. This leads to the question: What is the cost of an incorrect prediction when actual relevant costs are different from the relevant predicted costs used for decision-making?

Continuing our example, suppose Video Galore's relevant ordering costs per purchase order are $242 instead of the predicted $200. We can calculate the cost of this prediction error with a three-step approach.

◆ **Step 1:** *Compute the monetary outcome from the best action that could have been taken, given the actual amount of the cost input.* The appropriate inputs are $D = 13,000$ units, $P = \$242$, and $C = \$5.20$. The economic order quantity size is:

$$EOQ = \sqrt{\frac{2DP}{C}}$$

$$= \sqrt{\frac{2 \times 13,000 \times \$242}{\$5.20}} = \sqrt{1,210,000}$$

$$= 1,100 \text{ packages}$$

The total annual relevant costs when EOQ = 1,100 is:

$$TRC = \frac{DP}{Q} + \frac{QC}{2}$$

$$= \frac{13,000 \times \$242}{1,100} + \frac{1,100 \times \$5.20}{2}$$

$$= \$2,860 + \$2,860 = \$5,720$$

◆ **Step 2:** *Compute the monetary outcome from the best action based on the basis of the incorrect amount of the predicted cost input.* The planned action when the relevant ordering costs per purchase order are predicted to be $200 is to purchase 1,000 packages in each order. The total annual relevant costs using this order quantity when $D = 13,000$ units, $P = \$242$, and $C = \$5.20$ are:

$$TRC = \frac{13,000 \times \$242}{1,000} + \frac{1,000 \times \$5.20}{2}$$

$$= \$3,146 + \$2,600 = \$5,746$$

◆ **Step 3:** *Compute the difference between the monetary outcomes from Steps 1 and 2.*

	Monetary Outcome
Step 1	$5,720
Step 2	5,746
Difference	$ (26)

The cost of the prediction error is only $26. Why? Because the total annual relevant costs curve in Exhibit 20-1 is relatively flat over the range of order quantities from 650 to 1,300. *An important feature of the EOQ model is that the total relevant costs are rarely sensitive to minor variations in cost predictions. The square root in the EOQ model reduces the sensitivity of the decision to errors in predicting its inputs.*

Goal-Congruence Issues

Goal-congruence issues can arise when there is an inconsistency between the decision model and the model used to evaluate the performance of the person implementing the decision. For example, the absence of recorded opportunity costs in conventional accounting systems raises the possibility of a conflict between the EOQ model's optimal order quantity and the order quantity that the purchasing manager, evaluated on conventional accounting numbers, regards as optimal.

OBJECTIVE 3

Identify and reduce conflicts that can arise between EOQ decision models and models used for performance evaluation

If annual carrying costs are excluded when evaluating the performance of managers, the managers may favour purchasing a larger order quantity than the EOQ decision model indicates is optimal. Companies such as Coca-Cola and Wal-Mart resolve this conflict by designing the performance evaluation system so that the carrying costs, including a required return on investment, are charged to the appropriate manager.

The opportunity cost of the investment tied up in inventory can be reduced by reducing inventory levels. We now discuss just-in-time purchasing, an approach that has led to dramatic reductions in inventories being held by some companies.

JUST-IN-TIME PURCHASING

Just-in-time (JIT) purchasing is the purchase of goods or materials such that a delivery immediately precedes demand or use. JIT purchasing requires organizations to restructure their relationships with suppliers and place smaller and more frequent purchase orders. JIT purchasing can be implemented in both the retail and manufacturing sectors of the economy. Consider JIT purchasing for Hewlett-Packard's (HP's) manufacture of the Kayak work-station product line. HP has long-term agreements with suppliers who provide the major components for this product line. Each supplier is required to deliver components such that HP's final assembly plants meet their own production schedules and yet have minimal inventories on hand of the various components. Delivery to the production floor rather than to a store warehouse is the

Just-in-time (JIT) purchasing. The purchase of goods or materials such that delivery immediately precedes demand or use.

norm under JIT purchasing. A supplier who does not deliver components on time, or delivers components that fail to meet agreed-upon quality standards, can cause a HP assembly plant to not meet its own scheduled deliveries for Kayak work-stations. Companies adopting JIT purchasing do not have large amounts of material inventories on hand that can enable a production line to continue operating even when some deliveries do not occur on time or where defective materials are delivered. HP shares its planned production schedule with each supplier. JIT purchasing for HP requires a high level of information sharing with suppliers who commit to deliver components in narrow time-windows. We now explore the relationship between JIT purchasing and the EOQ decision model already discussed in this chapter.

JIT Purchasing and EOQ Model Parameters

Information About Just-In-Time
www.clubpom.com/Student_
Wing/Public/JITtutorial.html

"Just In Time at Empire West
Plastics"—Press Release
www.empirewest.com/news/
justintime.html

Companies moving toward JIT purchasing argue that the cost of carrying inventories (parameter C in the EOQ model) has been dramatically underestimated in the past. This cost includes storage costs, spoilage, obsolescence, and opportunity costs such as investment tied up in inventory. The cost of placing a purchase order (parameter P in the EOQ model) is also being re-evaluated. Three factors are causing sizable reductions in P:

◆ Companies increasingly are establishing long-run purchasing arrangements in which price and quality dimensions that apply over an extended period are agreed to by both parties. Individual purchase orders occur without any additional negotiation over price or quality in this period.

◆ Companies are using electronic links, such as the internet, to place purchase orders. Electronic commerce is one of the fastest growing areas of the internet. The cost of placing some orders on the internet is estimated to be less than one-tenth (even less than one-hundredth) the cost of placing orders by telephone or by mail.

◆ Companies are increasing the use of purchase order cards (similar to consumer credit cards like VISA and MasterCard). Purchasing personnel are given total dollar limits or individual transaction dollar limits. As long as personnel stay within these limits, the traditional labour-intensive procurement approval mechanisms are not required.

Both increases in the carrying cost (C) and decreases in the ordering cost per purchase order (P) result in smaller EOQ amounts.

Exhibit 20-4 analyzes the sensitivity of Video Galore's EOQ to illustrate the economics of smaller and more frequent purchase orders. The analysis presented in Exhibit 20-4 supports JIT purchasing—that is, having a smaller EOQ and placing more frequent orders—as relevant carrying costs increase and relevant ordering costs per purchase order decrease.

Relevant Benefits and Relevant Costs of JIT Purchasing

JIT purchasing model is not guided solely by the EOQ model. As discussed earlier (p. 692), the EOQ model is designed to emphasize only the tradeoff between carry-

EXHIBIT 20-4
Sensitivity of EOQ to Variations in Relevant Ordering and Carrying Costs for Video Galore*

Relevant Carrying Costs per Package per Year	Relevant Ordering Costs per Purchase Order			
	$200	$150	$100	$30
$ 5.20	EOQ = 1,000	EOQ = 866	EOQ = 707	EOQ = 387
$ 7.00	862	746	609	334
$10.00	721	624	510	279
$15.00	589	510	416	228

*Assuming annual demand is always 13,000 packages.

Porsche's Just-in-Time Revival

In 1993, Porsche was reeling. It had posted losses for three consecutive years and its sales in the United States had declined to 4,000 cars from 30,000 cars in 1986. But two short years later, Porsche is looking leaner and healthier as a result of slashing costs and revamping production and marketing. Wendelin Wiedeking, Porsche's CEO, credits the production turnaround to two former Toyota production engineers, Yoshiki Iwata and Chihiro Nakao, who introduced Porsche to JIT systems. When they first arrived at Porsche, Mr. Iwata remarked that Porsche looked like a shipping company, not a car factory, because workers spent less time assembling cars, and more time climbing up and down rows of inventory to find the parts they needed.

Porsche
www.porsche.com

As a result of implementing JIT, Porsche freed up 100 million Deutschmarks that had been tied up in inventory; slashed production time on its popular Carrera 911 model from 120 hours to 80; and reduced defects, scrap, and rework. By next year, production time is expected to be halved. Porsche also redesigned its cars to have 36% of parts common to its Boxster and 911 product lines. This reduced production, development, and inventory costs.

To get its JIT purchasing efforts on the road, Porsche has sharply reduced the number of suppliers. Porsche is working closely with its suppliers to have parts and components delivered just as they are needed, resulting in substantially lower direct materials inventories.

Source: Adapted from A. Choi, "Porsche, Once Near Collapse, Now Purrs; Automaker Cut Costs, Reduced Dependency on U.S.," *The Wall Street Journal,* December 15, 1994, and Porsche's 1993/94 annual report.

---

ing and ordering costs. Inventory management extends beyond ordering and carrying costs to include purchasing costs, stockout costs, and quality costs. The quality of materials and goods and timely deliveries are important motivations for using JIT purchasing, and stockout costs are an important concern. We add these features as we move from the EOQ decision model to the JIT purchasing model.

Let us revisit the Video Galore example, and consider the following information. Video Galore has recently established an EDI hookup to Sontek. Video Galore triggers a purchase order for tapes by a single computer entry. Computer programs match receiving documents with purchase orders. Payments are made electronically for batches of deliveries rather than for each individual delivery. These changes make ordering costs negligible. Video Galore is negotiating to have Sontek deliver 100 packages of videotapes 130 times each year (five times every two weeks) instead of delivering 1,000 packages 13 times each year as calculated in Exhibit 20-1. Sontek is willing to make these frequent deliveries, but it will tack a small additional amount of $0.02 onto the price per package. Video Galore's required return on investment remains 15%. Assume that relevant annual carrying costs of insurance, materials-handling, breakage, and so on remain at $3.10 per package per year.

Suppose that Video Galore incurs no stockout costs under its current purchasing policy because demand and purchase order lead times over each four-week period are certain. Video Galore's major concern is that lower inventory levels from implementing JIT purchasing will lead to more stockouts because demand variations and delays in supplying tapes are more likely to occur in the short time intervals between supplies under JIT purchasing. Sontek assures Video Galore that its new manufacturing processes enable it to respond rapidly to changing demand patterns. Consequently, stockouts may not be a serious problem. Video Galore expects to incur stockout costs on 50 tape packages each year under a JIT purchasing policy. In the event of a stockout, Video Galore will have to rush-order tape packages at a cost of $4 per package. Should Video Galore implement JIT purchasing?

Exhibit 20-5 compares (1) the incremental costs Video Galore incurs when it purchases videotapes from Sontek under its current purchasing policy with (2) the incremental costs Video Galore would incur if Sontek supplied videotapes under a JIT policy. The difference in the two incremental costs is the relevant savings of JIT purchasing. In other methods of comparing the two purchasing policies, the analysis would include only the relevant costs—those costs that differ between the two alternatives. Exhibit 20-5 shows a net cost savings of $1,879.85 per year from shifting to a JIT purchasing policy.

Supplier Evaluation and Relevant Costs of Quality and Timely Deliveries

The timely delivery of quality products is particularly crucial in JIT purchasing environments. Defective materials and late deliveries often bring the whole plant to a halt, resulting in forgone contribution margin on lost sales. Companies that implement JIT purchasing choose their suppliers carefully and pay special attention to developing long-run supplier partnerships. Some suppliers are very cooperative with a business's attempts to adopt JIT purchasing. For example, Frito-Lay, which has a large market share in potato chips and other snack foods, makes more frequent deliveries to retail outlets than many of its competitors. The company's corporate strategy emphasizes service to retailers and consistency, freshness, and quality of the delivered product.

What are the relevant costs when choosing suppliers? Consider again our Video Galore example. The Denton Corporation also supplies videotapes. It offers to supply all of Video Galore's videotape needs at a price of $13.60 per package (less than Sontek's price of $14.02) under the same JIT delivery terms as those that Sontek offers. Denton proposes an electronic hookup identical to Sontek's that would make Video Galore's ordering costs negligible. Video Galore's relevant outlay carry-

Frito-Lay, Inc.
www.fritolay.com

EXHIBIT 20-5
Annual Relevant Costs of Current Purchasing Policy and JIT Purchasing Policy for Video Galore

Relevant Item	Incremental Costs Under Current Purchasing Relevant Item	Incremental Costs Under JIT Purchasing Policy
Purchasing costs:		
$14 per unit × 13,000 units per year	$182,000.00	
$14.02 per unit × 13,000 units per year		$182,260.00
Required return on investment:		
15% per year × $14 cost per unit × 500* units of average inventory per year	1,050.00	
15% per year × $14.02 cost per unit × 50† units of average inventory per year		105.15
Outlay carrying costs (insurance, materials-handling, breakage, and so on):		
$3.10 per unit per year × 500* units of average inventory per year	1,550.00	
$3.10 per unit per year × 50† units of average inventory per year		155.00
Stockout costs:		
No stockouts	0	
$4 per unit × 50 units per year		200.00
Total annual relevant costs	$184,600.00	$182,720.15
Annual difference in favour of JIT purchasing	$1,879.85	

*Order quantity ÷ 2 = 1,000 ÷ 2 = 500.
†Order quantity ÷ 2 = 100 ÷ 2 = 50.

ing costs of insurance, materials-handling, breakage, and so on per package per year is $3.10 if it purchases videotapes from Sontek and $3.00 if it purchases from Denton. Should Video Galore buy from Denton? Not before considering the relevant costs of quality and also the relevant costs of failing to deliver on time.

Video Galore has used Sontek in the past and knows that Sontek fully deserves its reputation for delivering quality merchandise on time. Video Galore does not, for example, find it necessary to inspect the tape packages that Sontek supplies. Denton, however, does not enjoy so sterling a reputation for quality. Video Galore anticipates the following negative aspects of using Denton:

◆ Video Galore would incur additional inspection costs of $0.05 per package.

◆ Average stockouts of 360 tape packages each year would occur, largely resulting from late deliveries. Denton cannot rush-order tape packages to Video Galore on short notice. Video Galore anticipates lost contribution margin per unit of $8 from stockouts.

◆ Customers would likely return 2% of all packages sold owing to poor quality of the tapes. Video Galore estimates its additional costs to handle each returned package is $25.

Exhibit 20-6 presents the relevant costs of purchasing from Sontek and from Denton. Even though Denton is offering a lower price per package, the total relevant costs of purchasing goods from Sontek are lower by $4,361.85 per year. Selling

EXHIBIT 20-6
Annual Relevant Costs of Purchasing from Sontek and Denton

Relevant Item	Incremental Costs of Purchasing from Sontek	Incremental Costs of Purchasing from Denton
Purchasing costs:		
$14.02 per unit × 13,000 units per year	$182,260.00	
$13.60 per unit × 13,000 units per year		$176,800.00
Inspection costs:		
No inspection necessary	0	
$0.05 per unit × 13,000 units		650.00
Required return on investment:		
15% per year × $14.02 × 50* units of average inventory per year	105.15	
15% per year × $13.60 × 50* units of average inventory per year		102.00
Outlay carrying costs: (insurance, materials-handling, breakage, and so on):		
$3.10 per unit per year × 50* units of average inventory per year	155.00	
$3 per unit per year × 50* units of average inventory per year		150.00
Stockout costs:		
$4 per unit × 50 units per year	200.00	
$8 per unit × 360 units per year		2,880.00
Customer returns costs:		
No customer returns	0	
$25 per unit returned × 2% × 13,000 units returned		6,500.00
Total annual relevant costs	$182,720.15	$187,082.00
Annual difference in favour of Sontek	$4,361.85	

*Order quantity ÷ 2 = 100 ÷ 2 = 50.

high-quality merchandise also has nonfinancial and qualitative benefits. For example, offering Sontek's high-quality tapes enhances Video Galore's reputation and increases customer goodwill, which may lead to higher future profitability.

INVENTORY MANAGEMENT AND SUPPLY-CHAIN ANALYSIS

OBJECTIVE 4

Use a supply-chain approach to inventory management

The level of inventories held by retailers is influenced by demand patterns of their customers and supply relationships with their distributors, manufacturers, and their suppliers, and so on. The term *supply chain* describes the flow of goods, services, and information from cradle to grave (womb to tomb), regardless of whether those activities occur same organizations or other organizations. Chapter 1 introduced this concept using the example of a supply chain in the beverage industry. One point well-documented in supply-chain analysis is that there are significant total gains to companies in this supply chain from coordinating their activities and sharing information.

Proctor and Gamble's (P&G) experience with their Pampers product illustrates the gains from supply chain coordination. Retailers selling Pampers encounter some

---

SURVEYS OF COMPANY PRACTICE

Challenges in Obtaining the Benefits from a Supply-Chain Analysis

Supply-chain studies reported in the business press frequently cite a wide-range of benefits to both manufacturers and retailers. These benefits include fewer stockouts, reduced manufacture of items not subsequently demanded at the retail level, a reduction in rushed manufacturing orders, and lower inventory levels. A survey of 220 retailers and manufacturers highlights some key issues that companies adopting a supply-chain approach to inventory management must address in order to achieve the full extent of these benefits.

One issue is deciding the information to exchange among companies in the supply chain. Manufacturers gave the following rankings (in terms of importance) of information to receive from retailers stocking their products:

1. Retail sales forecasts for the products
2. Sales data on the products (such as daily sales at each retail outlet)
3. Pricing and advertising strategies by the retailer
4. Inventory levels at each retail outlet.

A second issue is reducing the obstacles to manufacturers and retailers achieving the benefits of a supply-chain approach. Respondents cited the following obstacles:

1. Communication obstacles—includes the unwillingness of some parties to share information.
2. Trust obstacles—includes the concern that all parties will not meet their agreed-upon commitments.
3. Information system obstacles—includes problems due to the information systems of different parties not being technically compatible.
4. Limited resources—includes problems due to the people and financial resources given to support a supply chain initiative not being adequate.

Adopting a supply-chain approach requires diverse organizations to cooperate and communicate on a broad set of issues. Respondents emphasized this challenge was not always successfully met. Not surprisingly, not all supply-chain initiatives have delivered the initial financial and operating projected benefits.

Source: Research Incorporated, "Synchronizing the Supply Chain Through Collaborative Design," (Alpharetta, Georgia, 1998)

variability in weekly demand, despite babies consuming diapers at a relatively steady rate. However, there was pronounced variability in retailers' orders to the manufacturer (P&G), and even more variability in orders by P&G to its own suppliers. This higher level of variability at suppliers than at manufacturers, and at manufacturers than at retailers, is called the "bullwhip effect" or the "whiplash effect." It is a widely observed phenomenon.[2] One consequence of the bullwhip effect is that high levels of inventory are often held at various stages in the supply chain.

There are multiple gains to companies in a supply chain by coordinating their activities and sharing information. Suppose all retailers share daily sales information about Pampers with P&G, P&G's distributors, and P&G's suppliers. This updated sales information reduces the level of uncertainty that manufacturers and suppliers to manufacturers have about retail demand for Pampers. This reduction in demand uncertainty can lead to fewer stockouts at the retail level, reduced manufacture of Pampers not subsequently demanded by retailers, a reduction in expedited manufacturing orders, and lower inventories being held by each company in the supply chain.

A supply chain is one way for manufacturers to start managing their own inventory better. Of course, the need to produce high-quality products at competitive cost levels leads managers at manufacturing companies to also seek out additional ways to manage their inventories. Numerous systems have been developed to help managers plan and implement production and inventory activities. We now consider two widely used types of systems—materials requirements planning (MRP) and just-in-time (JIT) production.

INVENTORY MANAGEMENT AND MRP

Materials requirements planning (MRP) is a push-through system that manufactures finished goods for inventory on the basis of demand forecasts. MRP uses (a) demand forecasts for the final products; (b) a bill of materials outlining the materials, components, and subassemblies for each final product; and (c) the quantities of materials, components, finished products, and product inventories to predetermine the necessary outputs at each stage of production. Taking into account the lead time required to purchase materials and to manufacture components and finished products, a master production schedule specifies the quantity and timing of each item to be produced. Once scheduled production starts, the output of each department is pushed through the production line whether it is needed or not. The result is often an accumulation of inventory at workstations that receive work they are not yet ready to process.

Inventory management is a key challenge in an MRP system. The management accountant can play several important roles in meeting this challenge. A key role is maintaining accurate and timely information pertaining to materials, work in process and finished goods inventories. A major cause of unsuccessful attempts to implement MRP systems has been the problem of collecting and updating inventory records. Calculating the full cost of carrying finished goods inventory motivates other actions. For example, instead of storing product at multiple (and geographically dispersed) warehouses, National Semiconductor contracted with Federal Express to airfreight its microchips from a central location in Singapore to customer sites worldwide. The change enabled National to move products from plant to customer in 4 days rather than 45, and to reduce distribution costs from 2.6% to 1.9% of revenues. These benefits subsequently led National to outsource all its logistics to Federal Express, including shipments between its own plants in the U.S., Scotland and Malaysia.

A second role of the management accountant is providing estimates of the setup costs for each production run at a plant, the downtime costs, and carrying costs of inventory. Costs of setting up a production run are analogous to ordering costs in the EOQ model. When the costs of setting up machines or sections of the production line are high (for example, as with a blast furnace in an integrated steel mill), processing larger batches of materials and incurring larger inventory carrying costs

OBJECTIVE 5

Differentiate materials requirements planning (MRP) systems from just-in-time (JIT) systems for manufacturing

Materials requirements planning (MRP). A push-through system that manufactures finished goods for inventory on the basis of demand forecasts.

---

[2]See H. Lee, V. Padmanabhan, and S. Whang, "The Bullwhip Effect in Supply Chains," *Sloan Management Review* (Spring 1997).

is the optimal approach, because it reduces the number set ups that must be made. When setup costs are small, processing smaller batches is optimal because it reduces carrying costs. Similarly, when the costs of downtime are high, there can be sizable benefits from maintaining continuous production.

A key feature of MRP is its push-through approach. We now consider JIT production, which has a demand-pull approach.

INVENTORY MANAGEMENT AND JIT PRODUCTION

Just-in-time (JIT) production (lean production). Production system in which each component on a production line is produced immediately as needed by the next step in the production line.

Just-in-time (JIT) production (also called **lean production**) is a "demand-pull" system in which each component in a production line is produced immediately as needed by the next step in the production line. In a JIT production line, manufacturing activity at any particular workstation is prompted by the need for that station's output at the following station. Demand triggers each step of the production process, starting with customer demand for a finished product at the end of the process and working all the way back to the demand for direct materials at the beginning of the process. In this way, demand pulls an order through the production line.

SURVEYS OF COMPANY PRACTICE

JIT Performance Measures Around the Globe

What performance measures do companies around the globe use to evaluate their JIT systems? The following table ranks in order of importance (1 = most important) the performance measures that companies in four countries apply. The rankings also indicate the relative importance of the different reasons that motivated the companies to implement JIT in the first place.

	Canada*	United States[†]	Ireland[‡]	United Kingdom*
Inventory investment	1	1	3	1
Delivery performance	4	2	1	2
Quality measures	2	3	4	3
Manufacturing lead time	3	4	2	5
Labour productivity	—	5	—	4
Space utilization	5	6	—	6

A pattern emerges. The most important reasons for JIT implementation are reducing inventory investment, getting deliveries on time, and improving quality. To a lesser extent, companies also view reducing manufacturing lead time as important.

A survey of Italian companies[§] also reveals extensive use of these performance measures. The survey, however, provides no information on the relative importance of individual measures.

One survey* also found distinct differences between management control systems in JIT and non-JIT companies. JIT companies are characterized by greater decentralization, more frequent and timely reporting, and increased worker responsibility and autonomy for starting and stopping production to ensure quality.

Adapted from: [†]Billesbach, T., A. Harrison, and S. Croom-Morgan, "Just-in-Time: A United States United Kingdom Comparison, " *International Journal of Operations & Production Management* (Vol. 11, No. 10, 1991); [‡]Clarke, P., and T. O'Dea, "Management Accounting Systems: Some Field Evidence from Sixteen Multinational Companies in Ireland," (Working Paper, Trinity College, Dublin, Ireland, 1993); [§]Bartezzaghi, E., F. Turco, and G. Spina, "The Impact of the Just-in-Time Approach on Production System Performance: A Survey of Italian Industry," *International Journal of Operations & Production Management* (Vol. 12, No. 1, 1992); *Lindsay, R., and S. Kalagnanam, *The Adoption of Just-in-Time Production Systems in Canada and Their Association with Management Control Practices*, (Hamilton, Canada: Society of Management Accountants of Canada, 1993)

The demand-pull feature of JIT production systems achieves close coordination among workstations. It smooths the flow of goods, despite low quantities of inventory. JIT production systems aim to simultaneously (a) meet customer demand in a timely way, (b) with high quality products, and (c) at the lowest possible total cost.

Companies implementing JIT production systems manage inventories by eliminating (or at least minimizing) them. There are five main features in a JIT production system:

OBJECTIVE 6

Identify the major features of a just-in-time production system

Manufacturing cells. Grouping of all the different types of equipment used to manufacture a given product.

- ◆ Organize production in **manufacturing cells**, a grouping of all the different types of equipment used to make a given product. Materials move from one machine to another where various operations are preformed in sequence. Materials handling costs are minimized.

- ◆ Hire and retain workers who are multi-skilled so that they are capable of performing a variety of operations and tasks. These tasks include minor repairs and routine maintenance of equipment. This training adds greatly to the flexibility of the plant.

- ◆ Aggressively pursue total quality management (TQM) to eliminate defects. Because of the tight links between stages in the production line, and the minimal inventories at each stage, defects arising at one stage quickly affect other stages in the line. JIT creates an urgency for solving problems immediately and eliminating the root causes of defects as quickly as possible. TQM is an essential component of any JIT production system.

- ◆ Place emphasis on reducing *setup time*, which is the time required to get equipment, tools, and materials ready to start the production of a component or product, and *manufacturing lead time*, which is the amount of time from when an order is ready to start on the production line (ready to be set up) to when it becomes a finished good. Reducing setup time makes production in smaller batches economical, which in turn reduces inventory levels. Reducing manufacturing lead time enables a company to respond faster to changes in customer demand.

- ◆ Carefully select suppliers who are capable of delivering quality materials in a timely manner. Most companies implementing *JIT production* also implement the *JIT purchasing* methods described earlier in this chapter. JIT plants expect JIT suppliers to provide high-quality goods and make frequent deliveries of the exact quantities specified on a timely basis. Suppliers often deliver materials directly to the plant floor to be immediately placed into production.

Financial Benefits of JIT and Relevant Costs

Early advocates of JIT production emphasized the benefits of lower carrying costs of inventory. *An important benefit of lower inventories, however, is the heightened emphasis on eliminating the root causes of rework, scrap, and waste and on reducing the manufacturing lead time of their products.* In computing the relevant benefits and relevant costs of reducing inventories in JIT production systems, the cost analyst must consider all benefits.

Consider the Emco Corporation, a manufacturer of brass fittings. Emco is considering implementing a JIT production system. Suppose that to implement JIT production, Emco must incur $100,000 in annual tooling costs to reduce setup times. Suppose further that JIT will reduce average inventory by $500,000. Also, relevant costs of insurance, space, materials-handling, and setup will decline by $30,000 per year. The company's required rate of return on inventory investments is 10% per year. Should Emco implement JIT? On the basis of the numbers provided, we would be tempted to say no. Why? Because annual relevant cost savings in carrying costs amount to $80,000 [(10% of $500,000) + $30,000], which is less than the additional annual tooling costs of $100,000.

Our analysis, however, has not considered other benefits of lower inventories in JIT production. For example, Emco estimates that implementing JIT will reduce rework on 500 units each year, resulting in savings of $50 per unit. Also, better quality and faster delivery will allow Emco to charge $2 more per unit on the 20,000 units that it sells each year. The annual relevant quality and delivery benefits from JIT and lower inventory levels equal $65,000 (rework savings, $50 × 500 + additional contribution margin, $2 × 20,000). Total annual relevant benefits and cost savings equal $145,000 ($80,000 + $65,000), which exceeds annual JIT implementation costs of $100,000. Therefore, Emco should implement a JIT production system.

Performance Measures and Control in JIT Production

To manage and reduce inventories, the management accountant must also design performance measures to evaluate and control JIT production. Examples of information the management accountant may use are:

- Personal observation by production line workers and team leaders
- Financial performance measures (such as inventory turnover ratios) and variances based on standard materials costs and conversion costs
- Nonfinancial performance measures of time, inventory, and quality, such as manufacturing lead time, units produced per hour, and days inventory is on hand
- $$\frac{\text{Total setup time for machines}}{\text{Total manufacturing time}}$$
- $$\frac{\text{Number of units requiring rework or scrap}}{\text{Total number of units started and completed}}$$

Personal observation and nonfinancial performance measures are the dominant methods of control. Why? Because they are the most timely, intuitive, and easy-to-comprehend measures of plant performance. Rapid, meaningful feedback is critical because the lack of buffer inventories in a demand-pull system creates added urgency to detect and solve problems quickly.

JIT's Effect on Costing Systems

In reducing the need for materials handling, warehousing, and incoming inspection, JIT systems reduce overhead costs. JIT systems also facilitate the direct tracing of some costs that were formerly classified as overhead. For example, the use of manufacturing cells makes it easy to trace material handling and machine operating costs to specific products or product families made in specific cells. These costs then become direct costs of those products. Also, the use of multi-skilled workers in these cells allows the costs of setup, minor maintenance and quality inspection to become easily traced direct costs.

The next section discusses *backflush costing*, which is a job-costing system that dovetails with JIT production and is less costly to operate than most traditional costing systems described in Chapter 4, 7, 8 and 9.

BACKFLUSH COSTING

OBJECTIVE 7

Use backflush costing

Sequential tracking (synchronous tracking). Product costing method in which the accounting system entries occur in the same order as actual purchases and production.

A unique production system such as JIT leads to its own unique costing system. Organizing manufacturing in cells, reducing defects and manufacturing lead time, and ensuring timely delivery of materials enables purchasing, production, and sales to occur in quick succession with minimal inventories. The absence of inventories makes choices about cost flow assumptions (such as weighted-average or first-in, first-out) or inventory costing methods (such as absorption or variable costing) unimportant—all manufacturing costs of a period flow directly into cost of goods sold. The rapid conversion of direct materials to finished goods that are immediately sold simplifies job costing.

Simplified Budgeted or Standard Job Costing

Traditional and standard costing systems (discussed in Chapters 4, 7, and 8) use **sequential tracking** (also called *synchronous tracking*), which is any product costing method in which the accounting system entries occur in the same order as actual purchases and production. These traditional systems track costs sequentially as products pass from direct materials, to work in process, to finished goods, and finally to sales.

OBJECTIVE 8

Describe different ways backflush costing can simplify traditional job-costing systems

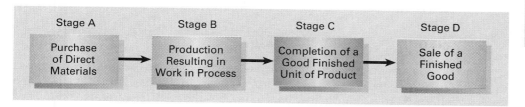

A sequential tracking costing system would have four trigger points, corresponding to separate journal entries being made at Stages A, B, C and D. The term **trigger point** refers to a stage in the cycle going from purchase of direct materials (Stage A) to sale of finished goods (Stage D) at which journal entries are made in the accounting system.

An alternative approach to sequential tracking is backflush costing. **Backflush costing** is a costing system that omits recording some or all of the journal entries relating to the cycle from purchase of direct materials to the sale of finished goods. Where journal entries for one or more stages in the cycle are omitted., the journal entries for a subsequent stage use normal or standard costs to work backward to flush out the costs in the cycle for which journal entries were not made.

The following three examples illustrate backflush costing. To underscore basic concepts, we assume no direct materials variances in any of the examples. The three examples differ in the number and placement of trigger points at which journal entries are made in the accounting system:

Trigger point. A stage in the cycle going from purchase of direct materials (Stage A) to sale of finished goods (Stage D) at which journal entries are made in the accounting system.

Backflush costing. Costing system that delays recording changes in the status of a product being produced until good finished units appear; it then uses budgeted or standard costs to work backward to flush out manufacturing costs for the units produced.

	Number of Journal Entry Trigger Points	Location in Cycle Where Journal Entries Made
Example 1	3	Stage A. Purchase of direct materials (called "raw materials")
		Stage C. Completion of good finished units of product
		Stage D. Sale of finished goods.
Example 2	2	Stage A. Purchase of direct materials (called "raw materials")
		Stage D. Sale of finished goods.
Example 3	2	Stage C. Completion of good finished units of product
		Stage D. Sale of finished goods.

In all three examples, there are no journal entries in the accounting system for work in process (Stage C). These three examples of backflush costing are typically used where the amounts of work in process are small. With just-in-time production, sizable reductions in work in process have occurred.

Example 1: Trigger Points Are Purchase of Direct Materials (Stage A), Completion of Good Finished Units of Product (Stage C), and Sale of Finished Goods (Stage D)

This example uses three trigger points to illustrate how backflushing can eliminate the need for a separate Work in Process account. A hypothetical company, Silicon Valley Computer (SVC), produces keyboards for personal computers. For April, there were no beginning inventories of raw materials. Moreover, there is zero beginning and ending work in process.

SVC has only one direct manufacturing cost category (direct or raw materials) and one indirect manufacturing cost category (conversion costs). All labour costs at the manufacturing facility are included in conversion costs. From its bill of materials (description of the types and quantities of materials) and an operations list (description of operations to be undergone), SVC determines the April standard direct materials costs per keyboard unit of $19 and the standard conversion costs of $12. SVC has two inventory accounts:

Type	Account Title
Combined direct materials and any direct materials in work in process	Inventory: Raw and In-Process Control
Finished goods	Finished Goods Control

Trigger point 1 occurs when materials are purchased. These costs are charged to Inventory: Raw and In-Process Control.

Actual conversion costs are recorded as incurred under backflush costing, just as in other costing systems, and charged to Conversion Costs Control. Conversion costs are allocated to products at trigger point 2—the transfer of units to Finished Goods. This example assumes that under- or overallocated conversion costs are written off to cost of goods sold monthly.

SVC takes the following steps when assigning costs to units sold and to inventories.

◆ **Step 1:** *Record the direct materials purchased during the accounting period.* Assume April purchases of $1,950,000:

Entry (a)	Inventory: Raw and In-Process Control	1,950,000	
	Accounts Payable Control		1,950,000

◆ **Step 2:** *Record the incurrence of conversion costs during the accounting period.* Assume that conversion costs are $1,260,000:

Entry (b)	Conversion Costs Control	1,260,000	
	[Various accounts (such as Accounts Payable Control and Wages Payable)]		1,260,000

◆ **Step 3:** *Determine the number of finished units manufactured during the accounting period.* Assume that 100,000 keyboard units were manufactured in April.

◆ **Step 4:** *Compute the budgeted or standard costs of each finished unit.* The standard cost is $31 ($19 direct materials + $12 conversion costs) per unit.

◆ **Step 5:** *Record the cost of finished goods completed during the accounting period.* In this case, 100,000 units × $31 = $3,100,000. This step gives backflush costing its name. Up to this point in the operations, the costs have not been recorded sequentially with the flow of product along its production route. Instead, the output trigger reaches back and pulls the standard costs of direct materials from Inventory: Raw and In-Process and the standard conversion costs for manufacturing the finished goods.

Entry (c)	Finished Goods Control	3,100,000	
	Inventory: Raw and In-Process Control		1,900,000
	Conversion Costs Allocated		1,200,000

◆ **Step 6:** *Record the cost of goods sold during the accounting period.* Assume that 99,000 units were sold in April (99,000 units × $31 = $3,069,000).

Entry (d)	Cost of Goods Sold	3,069,000	
	Finished Goods Control		3,069,000

◆ **Step 7:** *Record under- or overallocated conversion costs.* Actual conversion costs may be under- or overallocated in any given accounting period. Chapter 4 discussed various ways to account for under- or overallocated manufacturing overhead costs. Many companies write off underallocations or overallocations to cost of goods sold only at year-end; other companies, like SVC, do so monthly. Companies that use backflush costing typically have low inventories, so proration of under- or overallocated costs between finished goods and cost of goods sold is less often necessary. The journal entry for the $60,000 difference between actual conversion costs incurred and standard conversion costs allocated would be:

Entry (e)	Conversion Costs Allocated	1,200,000	
	Cost of Goods Sold	60,000	
	Conversion Costs Control		1,260,000

The April ending inventory balances are:

Inventory: Raw and In-Process	$50,000	
Finished Goods, 1,000 units × $31	31,000	
Total inventories	$81,000	

Exhibit 20-7, Panel A summarizes the journal entries for this example. Exhibit 20-8 provides an overview of this version of backflush costing. The elimination of the typical Work in Process account reduces the amount of detail in the accounting system. Units on the production line may still be tracked in physical terms, but there is "no attaching of costs" to specific work orders as they flow along the production cycle. In fact, there are no work orders or labour time tickets in the accounting system. Champion International uses a method similar to Example 1 in its specialty papers plant.

The use of three triggers to make journal entries in Example 1 will result in SVC's backflush costing system reporting costs similar to sequential tracking when SVC has minimal work in process inventory. In Example 1, any inventories of raw materials or finished goods are recognized in SVC's backflush costing system when they first appear (as would be done in a costing system using sequential tracking).

Accounting for Variances   The accounting for variances between actual costs incurred and standard costs allowed and the disposition of variances is basically the same under all standard costing systems. The procedures are described in Chapters 7 and 8. In Example 1, suppose the direct materials purchased had an unfavourable price variance of $42,000. Entry (a) would then be:

Inventory: Raw and In-Process Control	1,950,000	
Raw Materials Price Variance	42,000	
Accounts Payable Control		1,992,000

Direct materials are often a large proportion of total manufacturing costs, sometimes over 60%. Consequently, many companies will at least measure the direct materials efficiency variance in total by physically comparing what remains in direct materials inventory against what should be remaining, given the output of finished goods for the accounting period. In our example, suppose that such a comparison showed an unfavourable materials efficiency variance of $90,000. The journal entry would be:

Raw Materials Efficiency Variance	90,000	
Inventory: Raw and In-Process Control		90,000

The under- or overallocated manufacturing overhead costs may be split into various overhead variances (spending variance, efficiency variance, and production volume variance) as explained in Chapters 7 and 8.

Example 2: Trigger Points Are Materials Purchases of Direct Materials (Stage A) and Sale of Finished Goods (Stage D)

This example, also based on SVC and using the same data, presents a backflush costing system that, relative to Example 1, is a more dramatic departure from a sequential tracking inventory costing system. The first trigger point in this example is the same as the first trigger point in Example 1 (the purchase of direct materials), but the second trigger point is the sale—not the completed manufacture—of finished units. Toyota's cost accounting at its Kentucky plant is similar to this type of costing system. There are two justifications for this accounting system:

◆ To remove the incentive for managers to produce for inventory. If the value of finished goods inventory includes conversion costs, managers can bolster

EXHIBIT 20-7
Journal Entries in Backflush Costing

PANEL A, EXAMPLE 1: THREE TRIGGER POINTS: PURCHASES OF RAW MATERIALS AND FINISHED UNITS PRODUCED

Transactions

a. Purchases of raw materials	Inventory: Raw and In-Process Control	1,950,000	
	Accounts Payable Control		1,950,000
b. Incur conversion costs	Conversion Costs Control	1,260,000	
	Various Accounts		1,260,000
c. Finished units produced	Finished Goods Control	3,100,000	
	Inventory: Raw and In-Process Control		1,900,000
	Conversion Costs Allocated		1,200,000
d. Finished units sold	Cost of Goods Sold	3,069,000	
	Finished Goods Control		3,069,000
e. Under- or overallocated conversion costs	Conversion Costs Allocated	1,200,000	
	Cost of Goods Sold	60,000	
	Conversion Costs Control		1,260,000

PANEL B, EXAMPLE 2: TWO TRIGGER POINTS: PURCHASES OF RAW MATERIALS AND FINISHED UNITS SOLD

Transactions

a. Purchases of raw materials	Inventory Control	1,950,000	
	Accounts Payable Control		1,950,000
b. Incur conversion costs	Conversion Costs Control	1,260,000	
	Various Accounts		1,260,000
c. Finished units produced	(No entry)		
d. Finished units sold	Cost of Goods Sold	3,069,000	
	Inventory Control		1,881,000
	Conversion Costs Allocated		1,188,000
e. Under- or overallocated conversion costs	Conversion Costs Allocated	1,188,000	
	Cost of Goods Sold	72,000	
	Conversion Costs Control		1,260,000

PANEL C, EXAMPLE 3: ONE TRIGGER POINT: FINISHED UNITS PRODUCED

Transactions

a. Purchases of raw materials	(No entry)		
b. Incur conversion costs	Conversion Costs Control	1,260,000	
	Various Accounts		1,260,000
c. Finished units produced	Finished Goods Control	3,100,000	
	Accounts Payable Control		1,900,000
	Conversion Costs Allocated		1,200,000
d. Finished units sold	Cost of Goods Sold	3,069,000	
	Finished Goods Control		3,069,000
e. Under- or overallocated conversion costs	Conversion Costs Allocated	1,200,000	
	Cost of Goods Sold	60,000	
	Conversion Costs Control		1,260,000

operating income by producing more units than are sold. Having trigger point 2 as the sale instead of the completion of production, however, reduces the attractiveness of producing for inventory by recording conversion costs as period costs instead of capitalizing them as inventoriable costs.

◆ To increase managers' focus on selling units.

This variation of backflush costing treats all conversion costs as period costs.

EXHIBIT 20-8
General-Ledger Overview of Backflush Costing

PANEL A, EXAMPLE 1: THREE TRIGGER POINTS—PURCHASE OF RAW MATERIALS, COMPLETION OF FINISHED GOODS, AND SALE OF FINISHED GOODS

PANEL B, EXAMPLE 2: TWO TRIGGER POINTS—PURCHASE OF RAW MATERIALS AND SALE OF FINISHED GOODS

PANEL C, EXAMPLE 3: TWO TRIGGER POINTS—COMPLETION OF FINISHED GOODS AND SALE OF FINISHED GOODS

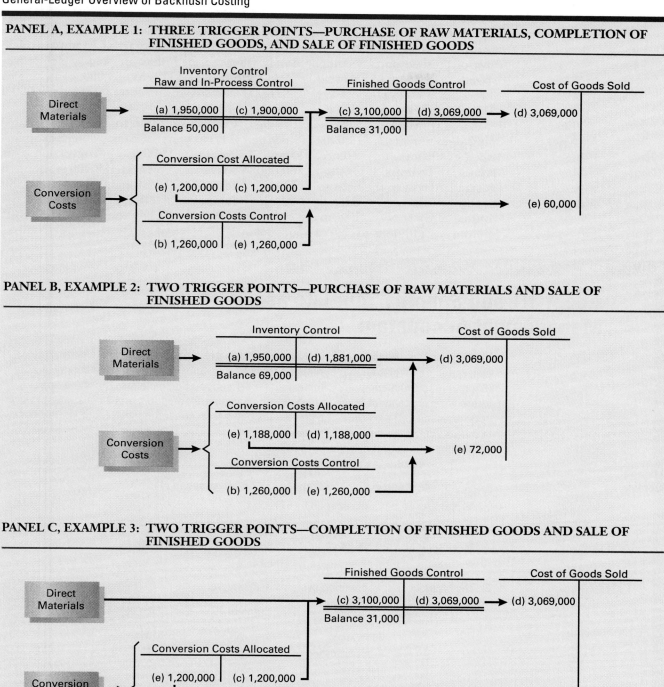

The inventory account in this example is confined solely to direct materials (whether they are in storerooms, in process, or in finished goods). There is only one inventory account:

Type	Account Title
Combined direct materials inventory and any direct materials in work in process and finished goods	Inventory Control

Exhibit 20-7, Panel B presents the journal entries in this case. Entry (a) is prompted by the same trigger point 1 as in Example 1, the purchase of direct materials. Entry (b) for the conversion costs incurred is recorded in an identical manner as in Example 1. Trigger point 2 is the sale of good finished units (not their production, as in Example 1), so there is no entry corresponding to entry (c) of Example 1. The cost of finished units is computed only when finished units are sold (which corresponds to entry (d) of Example 1): 99,000 units sold × $31 = $3,069,000, consisting of direct materials (99,000 × $19 = $1,881,000) and conversion costs allocated (99,000 × $12 = $1,188,000).

No conversion costs are inventoried. That is, compared to Example 1, Example 2 does not attach $12,000 ($12 per unit × 1,000 units) of conversion costs to finished goods inventory. Hence, Example 2 allocates $12,000 less in conversion costs relative to Example 1. Of the $1,260,000 in conversion costs, $1,188,000 is allocated at standard cost to the units sold. The remaining $72,000 ($1,260,000 − $1,188,000) of conversion costs is underallocated. Entry (e) in Exhibit 20-7, Panel B presents the journal entry if SVC, like many companies, writes off these underallocated costs monthly as additions to cost of goods sold.

SURVEYS OF COMPANY PRACTICE

Adopt JIT and Simplify Your Life as a Management Accountant

Many companies adopting JIT production systems are reporting reductions in the complexity and detail of their management accounting systems. The results of a survey of 22 U.S. manufacturing companies implementing JIT support these claims. These manufacturers were made up of 11 machinery, 7 transportation, 2 computer, and 2 consumer products companies. On average, the companies had begun converting to JIT four years prior to the survey. At the time of the survey, they had converted an average 63% of their plant operations and inventory systems to JIT.

These are the key results from the survey:

1. Mean reductions in four key areas following JIT adoption were:
   ◆ Number of vendors reduced by 67%
   ◆ Quantity of rework and scrap reduced by 44%
   ◆ Setup time for product changes on machines reduced by 47%
   ◆ Quantity in total inventory reduced by 46%

2. The types of cost accounting systems in use were:

Type	Before JIT	After JIT
Job costing	70%	30%
Process costing	20	60
Hybrid costing	10	10

3. Cost accounting systems following implementation of JIT were:
   ◆ Less complex: 72.7%
   ◆ More complex: 27.3%

4. Eight of the 22 companies adopted backflush costing after implementing JIT, eliminating accounting transactions for the movement of materials to work in process.

5. Performance measurement systems following implementation of JIT were:
   ◆ Less complex: 77.3%
   ◆ More complex: 22.7%

Source: Adapted from Swenson, D., and J. Cassidy, "The Effect of JIT on Management Accounting," *Journal of Cost Management* (Spring 1993)

The April ending balance of Inventory Control is $69,000 ($50,000 direct materials still on hand + $19,000 direct materials embodied in the 1,000 units manufactured but not sold during the period). Exhibit 20-6 provides an overview of this version of backflush costing. Entries are keyed to Exhibit 20-7, Panel B. The approach described in Example 2 closely approximates the costs computed using sequential tracking when a company holds minimal work in process and finished goods inventories.

Example 3: Trigger Points Are Completion of Good Finished Units of Product (Stage C) and Sale of Finished Goods (Stage D)

This example presents an extreme and simpler version of backflush costing. It has only one trigger point for making journal entries to inventory. The trigger point is SVC's completion of finished units. Exhibit 20-7, Panel C presents the journal entries in this case, using the same data as in Examples 1 and 2. Note that since the purchase of direct materials is not a trigger point, there is no entry corresponding to entry (a)—purchases of direct materials. Exhibit 20-8 provides an overview of this version of backflush costing. Entries are keyed to Exhibit 20-7, Panel C.

Compare entry (c) in Exhibit 20-7, Panel C with entries (a) and (c) in Exhibit 20-7, Panel A. The simpler version in Example 3 ignores the $1,950,000 purchases of direct materials (entry (a) of Example 1). At the end of April, $50,000 of direct materials purchased has not yet been placed into production ($1,950,000 − $1,900,000 = $50,000), nor has it been entered into the inventory costing system.

Extending Example 3, backflush costing systems could also use the sale of finished goods (instead of the production of finished goods) as the only trigger point. This version of backflush costing would be most suitable for a JIT production system with minimal direct materials, work-in-process, and finished goods inventories. Why? Because this backflush costing system would maintain no inventory accounts.

Special Considerations in Backflush Costing

The accounting illustrated in Examples 1, 2, and 3 does not strictly adhere to generally accepted accounting principles of external reporting. For example, work in process (an asset) exists but is not recognized in the accounting system. Advocates of backflush costing, however, cite the materiality concept in support of these versions of backflushing. They claim that if inventories are low or their total costs are not subject to significant change from one accounting period to the next, operating income and inventory costs developed in a backflush costing system will not differ materially from the results generated by a system that adheres to generally accepted accounting principles.

Suppose material differences in operating income and inventories do exist between the results of a backflush costing system and those of a conventional standard costing system. An adjustment can be recorded to make the backflush numbers satisfy external reporting requirements. For example, the backflush entries in Example 2 would result in expensing all conversion costs as a part of Cost of Goods Sold ($1,188,000 at standard costs + $72,000 writeoff of under-allocated conversion costs = $1,260,000). But suppose conversion costs were re-garded as sufficiently material in amount to be included in Inventory Control. Then entry (d), closing the Conversion Costs accounts, would change as shown below:

Original entry (d)	Conversion Costs Allocated	1,188,000	
	Cost of Goods Sold	72,000	
	Conversion Costs Control		1,260,000
Revised entry (d)	Conversion Costs Allocated	1,188,000	
	Inventory Control (1,000 units × $12)	12,000	
	Cost of Goods Sold	60,000	
	Conversion Costs Control		1,260,000

Criticisms of backflush costing focus mainly on the absence of audit trails—the ability of the accounting system to pinpoint the uses of resources at each step of the production process. The absence of large amounts of materials and work in process inventory means that managers can keep track of operations by personal observations, computer monitoring, and nonfinancial measures.

What are the implications of JIT and backflush costing systems for activity-based costing (ABC) systems? Simplifying the production process, as in a JIT system, makes more of the costs direct and so reduces the extent of overhead cost allocations. Simplified ABC systems are often adequate for companies implementing JIT. But even these simpler ABC systems can enhance backflush costing. Costs from ABC systems give relatively more accurate budgeted conversion costs per unit for different products, which are then used in the backflush costing system. The activity-based cost data are also useful for product costing, decision-making, and cost management.

PROBLEMS FOR SELF-STUDY

PROBLEM 1

The Lee Company has a Singapore plant that manufactures transistor radios. One key component is a XT transistor. Expected demand for radio production in March 2000 is 5,200 transistors. Lee purchases the XT transistor from Singapore Electronics. Lee estimates the ordering cost per purchase order to be $250. The carrying cost for one unit of XT in stock is $5.00.

REQUIRED

1. Compute the EOQ for the XT transistor.
2. Compute the number of deliveries of XT that Singapore Electronics will make in April 2000.

SOLUTION 1

1.
$$EOQ = \sqrt{\frac{2\ (5,200)\ \$250}{\$5}}$$

$$= 721 \text{ transistors (approximate)}$$

2.
$$\text{Number of deliveries} = \frac{5,200}{721}$$

$$= 7.2$$

Singapore will make approximately 7 deliveries (rounded down) in March 2000.

PROBLEM 2

The Lee Company (from Problem 1) seeks to streamline the costing system at its Singapore plant. It will use a backflush costing system with three trigger points:

◆ Purchase of raw materials

◆ Completion of good finished units of product

◆ Sale of finished goods

There are no beginning inventories. The following data pertain to April 2000 manufacturing:

Raw materials purchased	$ 880,000
Raw materials used	850,000
Conversion costs incurred	422,000
Conversion costs allocated	400,000
Costs transferred to finished goods	1,250,000
Cost of goods sold	1,190,000

REQUIRED

1. Prepare summary journal entries for April (without disposing of underallocated or overallocated conversion costs). Assume no direct materials variances.

2. Under an ideal JIT production system, how would the amounts in your journal entries differ from those in requirement 1?

SOLUTION 2

1. Journal entries for April are as follows:

Entry (a)	Inventory: Raw and In-Process Control	880,000	
	Accounts Payable Control		880,000
	(raw materials purchased)		
Entry (b)	Conversion Costs Control	422,000	
	Various Accounts (such as Wages Payable Control)		422,000
	(conversion costs incurred)		
Entry (c)	Finished Goods Control	1,250,000	
	Inventory: Raw and In-Process Control		850,000
	Conversion Costs Allocated		400,000
	(standard cost of finished goods completed)		
Entry (d)	Cost of Goods Sold	1,190,000	
	Finished Goods Control		1,190,000
	(standard costs of finished goods sold)		

2. Under an ideal JIT production system, if the manufacturing lead time per unit is very short, there conceivably would be zero inventories at the end of each day. Entry (c) would be $1,190,000 finished goods production, not $1,250,000. If the marketing department could only sell goods costing $1,190,000, the JIT production system would call for direct material purchases and conversion costs of lower than $880,000 and $422,000, respectively, in Entries (a) and (b).

SUMMARY

The following points are linked to the chapter's learning objectives.

1. Five categories of costs associated with goods for sale are purchasing costs, ordering costs (costs of preparing a purchase order and receiving goods), carrying costs (costs of holding inventory of goods for sale), stockout costs (costs arising when a customer demands a unit of product and that unit is not on hand), and quality costs (prevention costs, appraisal costs, internal failure costs, and external failure costs).

2. The economic-order-quantity (EOQ) decision model calculates the optimal quantity of inventory to order by balancing ordering costs and carrying costs. The larger the order quantity, the higher the annual carrying costs and the lower the annual ordering costs. The EOQ model includes both costs routinely recorded in the accounting system and opportunity costs not routinely recorded in the accounting system.

3. The opportunity cost of investment tied up in inventory is a key input in the EOQ decision model. Some companies now include opportunity costs as well as actual costs when evaluating managers so that there is goal congruence between managers and the company.

4. Supply-chain analysis describes the flow of goods, services, and information from cradle to grave (womb to tomb), regardless of whether those activities occur in the same organization or other organizations.

5. Materials requirements planning (MRP) systems take a "push-through" approach that manufactures finished goods for inventory on the basis of demand forecasts. Just-in-time (JIT) production systems take a "demand-pull" approach in which goods are only manufactured to satisfy customer orders.

6. The five major features of a JIT production system are (a) organizing production in manufacturing cells, (b) hiring and retaining multi-skilled workers, (c) emphasizing total quality management, (d) reducing manufacturing lead time and setup time, and (e) building strong supplier relationships.

7. Backflush costing describes a costing system that delays recording some or all of the journal entries relating to the cycle from purchase of direct materials to the sale of finished goods.

8. Traditional job-costing systems use sequential tracking where recording of the journal entries occurs in the same order as actual purchases and progress in production. Most backflush costing systems do not record journal entries for the work in process stage of production. Some backflush costing systems also do not record entries for either the purchase of direct materials or the completion of finished goods.

▼ TERMS TO LEARN

This chapter contains definitions of the following important terms:

backflush costing (p. 707)
carrying costs (p. 691)
economic order quantity (EOQ) (p. 692)
inventory management (p. 691)
just-in-time (JIT) production (p. 704)
just-in-time (JIT) purchasing (p. 697)
lean production (p. 704)
manufacturing cells (p. 705)
materials requirements planning (MRP) (p. 703)

ordering costs (p. 691)
purchasing costs (p. 691)
purchase order lead time (p. 692)
reorder point (p. 694)
safety stock (p. 694)
sequential tracking (p. 706)
stockout (p. 691)
trigger point (p. 707)

▼ ASSIGNMENT MATERIAL

QUESTIONS

20-1 Why do better decisions regarding the purchasing and managing of goods for sale frequently cause dramatic percentage increases in net income?

20-2 Name five cost categories that are important in managing goods for sale in a retail organization.

20-3 What assumptions are made when using the simplest version of the economic order quantity (EOQ) decision model?

20-4 Give examples of costs included in annual carrying costs of inventory when using the EOQ decision model.

20-5 Give three examples of opportunity costs that typically are not recorded in accounting systems, although they are relevant to the EOQ model.

20-6 What are the steps in computing the cost of a prediction error when using the EOQ decision model?

20-7 Why might goal-congruence issues arise when an EOQ model is used to guide decisions on how much to order?

20-8 Describe just-in-time (JIT) purchasing and its benefits.

20-9 What are three factors causing reductions in the cost to place purchase orders of materials?

20-10 Describe how the internet can be used to reduce the costs of placing purchase orders.

20-11 What is supply-chain analysis and how can it benefit manufacturers and retailers?

20-12 What are some obstacles to companies adopting a supply-chain approach?

20-13 What are the main features in a JIT production system?

20-14 Distinguish job-costing systems using sequential tracking from backflush costing.

20-15 Describe three different versions of backflush costing.

EXERCISES

20-16 Economic order quantity for retailer. Football World (FW) operates a megastore featuring sports merchandise. It uses an EOQ decision model to make inventory decisions. It is now considering inventory decisions for its Toronto Argo's jerseys product line. This is a highly popular item. Data for 2001 are:

Expected annual demand for jerseys	10,000
Ordering costs for purchase order	$225
Carrying costs per year	$ 10 per jersey

Each jersey costs FW $40 and sells for $75. The $10 carrying cost per jersey comprises the required annual return on investments of $3.20 (12% x $40 purchase price) plus $6.80 relevant insurance, handling costs, and theft-related costs. The purchasing lead time is one week.

REQUIRED
1. Calculate the EOQ.
2. Calculate the number of orders that will be placed each year.
3. Calculate the reorder point.

20-17 Economic order quantity, effect of parameter changes (continuation of 20-16). Athletic Products (AP) manufactures the Argo's jerseys that Football World (FW) sells to its customers. AP has recently installed computer software that enables its customers to conduct "one-stop" purchasing using state-of-the-art website technology developed by Cisco Systems. FW's ordering cost per purchase order will be $20 using this new technology.

REQUIRED
1. Calculate the EOQ for the Argo's jerseys using the revised ordering cost of $20 per purchase order. Assume all other data from Exercise 20-16 is the same. Comment on the result.
2. Suppose AP proposes to "assist" FW. AP will allow FW's customers to directly order from the AP website. AP would directly ship to these customers. AP would pay $10 to FW for every Argo's jersey purchased by one of FW's customers. How would this offer affect inventory management at FW? Should FW accept AP's proposal? Explain.

20-18 EOQ for a retailer. The Cloth Centre buys and sells fabrics to a wide range of industrial and consumer users. One of the products it carries is denim cloth, used in the manufacture of jeans and carrying bags. The supplier for the denim cloth pays all incoming freight. No incoming inspection of the denim is necessary, because the supplier has a track record of delivering high-quality merchandise. The purchasing officer of the Cloth Centre has collected the following information:

Annual demand for denim cloth	20,000 metres
Ordering costs per purchase order	$160
Carrying costs per year	20% of purchase cost
Safety stock requirements	None
Cost of denim cloth	$8 per metre

The purchasing lead time is two weeks. The Cloth Centre is open 250 days a year (50 weeks for five days a week).

REQUIRED
1. Calculate the EOQ for denim cloth.
2. Calculate the number of orders that will be placed each year.
3. Calculate the reorder point for denim cloth.

20-19 EOQ for manufacturer. Beaumont Corporation makes air conditioners. It purchases 12,000 units of a particular type of compressor part, CU29, each year at a cost of $50 per unit. Beaumont requires a 12% annual return on investment. In addition, relevant carrying costs (for insurance, materials-handling, breakage, and so on) are $2 per unit per year. Relevant costs per purchase order are $120.

1. Calculate Beaumont's EOQ for CU29.
2. Calculate Beaumont's total ordering and carrying costs using EOQ.
3. Assume that demand is uniform throughout the year and is known with certainty. The purchasing lead time is half a month. Calculate Beaumont's reorder point for CU29.

20-20 Economic order quantity for retailer, ordering and carrying costs. Office Emporium (OE) is deciding the purchase order quantity for a new modem product. Annual demand is 20,000 units. Ordering costs per purchase order are $120. Carrying costs per modem unit are $10 per year. OE uses an economic-order-quantity model in its purchasing decisions. OE is open 360 days a year.

REQUIRED
1. Calculate OE's EOQ for modems.
2. Calculate OE's total ordering and carrying costs.
3. Assume that demand is known with certainty and the purchasing lead time is five days. Calculate OE's reorder point for modems.

20-21 Purchase order size for retailer, EOQ, just-in-time purchasing. The 24-Hour Mart operates a chain of supermarkets. Its best-selling soft drink is Fruitslice. Demand in April for Fruitslice at its Regina supermarket is estimated to be 6,000 cases (24 cans in each case). In March, the Regina supermarket estimated the ordering costs per purchase order (P) for Fruitslice to be $30. The carrying costs (C) of each case of Fruitslice in inventory for a month were estimated to be $1. At the end of March, the Regina 24-Hour Mart reestimated its carrying costs to be $1.50 per case per month to take into account an increase in warehouse-related costs.

During March, 24-Hour Mart restructured its relationship with suppliers. It reduced the number of suppliers from 600 to 180. Long-term contracts were signed only with those suppliers that agreed to make product quality checks before shipping. Each purchase order would be made by linking into the suppliers' computer network. The Regina 24-Hour Mart estimated that these changes would reduce the ordering costs per purchase order to $5. The 24-Hour Mart is open 30 days in April.

REQUIRED
1. Calculate the economic order quantity in April for Fruitslice. Use the EOQ model, and assume in turn that:
   a. $D = 6,000$; $P = 30; $C = 1
   b. $D = 6,000$; $P = 30; $C = 1.50
   c. $D = 6,000$; $P = 5; $C = 1.50
2. How does your answer to requirement 1 give insight into the retailer's movement toward JIT purchasing policies?

20-22 JIT production, relevant benefits, relevant costs. The Evans Corporation manufactures cordless telephones. Evans is planning to implement a JIT production system, which requires annual tooling costs of $150,000. Evans estimates that the following annual benefits would arise from JIT production.
   a. Average inventory will decline by $700,000, from $900,000 to $200,000.
   b. Insurance, space, materials-handling, and setup costs, which currently total $200,000, would decline by 30%.
   c. The emphasis on quality inherent in JIT systems would reduce rework costs by 20%. Evans currently incurs $350,000 on rework.
   d. Better quality would enable Evans to raise the prices of its products by $3 per unit. Evans sells 30,000 units each year.

Evans's required rate of return on inventory investment is 12% per year.

REQUIRED
1. Calculate the net benefit or cost to the Evans Corporation from implementing a JIT production system.
2. What other nonfinancial and qualitative factors should Evans consider before deciding on whether it should implement a JIT system?

20-23 Backflush costing and JIT production. Road Warrior Corp. assembles hand-held computers that have scaled-down capabilities of laptop computers. Each hand-held computer takes 6 hours to assemble. Road Warrior uses a just-in-time production system and a backflush costing system with three trigger points:
   ◆ Purchase of direct (raw) materials
   ◆ Completion of good finished units of product
   ◆ Sale of finished goods

There are no beginning inventories of materials or finished goods. The following data are for August 2000:

Direct (raw) materials purchased	$2,754,000
Direct (raw) materials used	2,733,600
Conversion cost incurred	723,600
Conversion costs allocated	750,400

Road Warrior records direct materials purchased and conversion costs incurred at actual costs. When finished goods are sold, the backflush costing system "pulls through" standard direct materials costs ($102 per unit) and standard conversion costs ($28 per unit). It produced 26,800 finished goods units in August 2000 and sold 26,400 units. The actual direct materials cost per unit in August 2000 was $102 while the actual conversion cost per unit was $27.

REQUIRED

1. Prepare summary journal entries for August 2000 (without disposing of underallocated or overallocated conversion costs).
2. Post the entries in requirement 1 to T-accounts for applicable Inventory: Raw and In-Process, Conversion Costs Control, Conversion Costs Allocated, and Cost of Goods Sold.
3. Under an ideal JIT production system, how would the amounts in your journal entries differ from those in requirement 1?

20-24 Backflush costing, two trigger points, materials purchase and sale (continuation of 20-23). Assume the same facts in Exercise 20-23, except for the following change. Road Warrior Corp. now uses a backflush costing system with the following two trigger points:

◆ Purchase of direct (raw) materials
◆ Sale of finished goods

The Inventory Control account here will include direct materials purchased but not yet in production, materials in work in process, and materials in finished goods but not sold. No conversion costs are inventoried. Any underallocated or overallocated conversion costs are written off monthly to Cost of Goods Sold.

REQUIRED

1. Prepare summary journal entries for August, including the disposition of underallocated or overallocated conversion costs.
2. Post the entries in requirement 1 to T-accounts for Inventory Control, Conversion Costs Control, Conversion Costs Allocated, and Cost of Goods Sold.

20-25 Backflush costing, two trigger points, production completion and sale (continuation of 20-23). Assume the same facts as in Exercise 20-23 except now Road Warrior uses only two trigger points, the completion of a good finished unit of product and the sale of finished goods. Any under- or overallocated conversion costs are written off monthly to cost of goods sold.

REQUIRED

1. Prepare summary journal entries for August, including the disposition of under or overallocated conversion costs.
2. Post the entries in requirement 1 to T-accounts for Finished Goods Control, Conversion Cost Control, Conversion Costs Allocated, and Costs of Goods Sold.

PROBLEMS

20-26 Effect of different order quantities on ordering costs and carrying costs, EOQ. Koala Blue retails a broad line of Australian merchandise at its London store. It sells 26,000 Ken Done linen bedroom packages (two sheets and two pillowcases) each year. Koala Blue pays Ken Done Merchandise, Inc., $104 per package. Its ordering costs per purchase order are $72. The carrying costs per package are $10.40 per year.

Liv Carrol, manager of the London store, seeks your advice on how ordering costs and carrying costs vary with different order quantities. Ken Done Merchandise, Inc. guarantees the $104 purchase cost per package for the 26,000 units budgeted to be purchased in the coming year.

1. Compute the annual ordering costs, the annual carrying costs, and their sum for purchase order quantities of 300, 500, 600, 700, and 900, using the formulas described in this chapter. What is the economic order quantity? Comment on your results.
2. Assume that Ken Done Merchandise, Inc. introduces a computerized ordering network for its customers. Liv Carrol estimates that Koala Blue's ordering costs will be reduced to $40 per purchase order. How will this reduction in ordering costs affect the EOQ for Koala Blue on their linen bedroom packages?

20-27 EOQ, uncertainty, safety stock, reorder point. (CMA, adapted) The Starr Company distributes a wide range of electrical products. One of its best-selling items is a standard electric motor. The management of the Starr Company uses the EOQ decision model to determine the optimal number of motors to order. Management now wants to determine how much safety stock to hold.

The Starr Company estimates annual demand (300 working days) to be 30,000 electric motors. Using the EOQ decision model, the company orders 3,000 motors at a time. The lead time for an order is five days. The annual carrying costs of one motor in safety stock are $10. Management has also estimated that the stockout costs are $20 for each motor they are short.

The Starr Company has analyzed the demand during 200 past reorder periods. The records indicate the following patterns:

Demand During Lead Time	Number of Times Quantity Was Demanded
440	6
460	12
480	16
500	130
520	20
540	10
560	6
	200

REQUIRED

1. Determine the level of safety stock for electric motors that the Starr Company should maintain in order to minimize expected stockout costs and carrying costs. When computing carrying costs, assume that the safety stock is on hand at all times and that there is no overstocking caused by decreases in expected demand. (Consider safety stock levels of 0, 20, 40, and 60 units.)
2. What would be the Starr Company's new reorder point?
3. What factors should the Starr Company have considered in estimating the stockout costs?

20-28 EOQ, cost of prediction error. Ralph Menard is the owner of a truck repair shop. He uses an EOQ model for each of his truck parts. He initially predicts the annual demand for heavy-duty tires to be 2,000. Each tire has a purchase price of $50. The incremental ordering costs per purchase order are $40. The incremental carrying costs per year are $4 per unit plus 10% of the supplier's purchase price.

REQUIRED

1. Calculate the EOQ for heavy-duty tires, along with the sum of annual relevant ordering costs and carrying costs.
2. Suppose Menard is correct in all his predictions except the purchase price. (He ignored a new law that abolished tariff duties on imported heavy-duty tires, which led to lower prices from foreign competitors.) If he had been a faultless predictor, he would have foreseen that the purchase price would drop to $30 at the beginning of the year and would be unchanged throughout the year. What is the cost of the prediction error?

20-29 JIT purchasing, relevant benefits, relevant costs. (CMA, adapted) The Margro Corporation is an automotive supplier that uses automatic turning machines to manufacture precision parts from steel bars. Margro's inventory of raw steel averages $600,000. John Oates, President of Margro, and Helen Gorman, Margro's controller, are concerned about the costs of carrying inventory. The steel supplier is willing to supply steel in smaller lots at no additional charge. Helen Gorman identified the following effects of adopting a JIT inventory program to virtually eliminate steel inventory.

♦ Without scheduling any overtime, lost sales due to stockouts would increase by 35,000 units per year. However, by incurring overtime premiums of $40,000 per year, the increase in lost sales could be reduced to 20,000 units. This would be the maximum amount of overtime that would be feasible for Margro.

♦ Two warehouses presently used for steel bar storage would no longer be needed. Margro rents one warehouse from another company under a cancellable leasing arrangement at an annual cost of $60,000. The other warehouse is owned by Margro and contains 12,000 square metres. Three-quarters of the space in the owned warehouse could be rented for $1.50 per square metre per year.

♦ Insurance and property tax costs totalling $14,000 per year would be eliminated.

Margro's projected operating results for the 2000 calendar year follow. Long-term capital investments by Margro are expected to produce a rate of return of 20%.

Margro Corporation Budgeted Income Statement
For the Year Ending December 31, 2000
(in thousands)

Revenues (900,000 units)		$10,800
Cost of goods sold:		
Variable costs	$4,050	
Fixed costs	1,450	
Total costs of goods sold:		5,500
Gross margin		5,300
Marketing and distribution costs:		
Variable costs	$ 900	
Fixed costs	1,500	
Total marketing and distribution costs		2,400
Operating income		$ 2,900

REQUIRED

1. Calculate the estimated dollar savings (loss) for the Margro Corporation that would result in 2000 from the adoption of the JIT inventory control method.
2. Identify and explain other factors that Margro should consider before deciding whether to install a JIT system.

20-30 Supply-chain analysis, company viewpoints. Manufacturing companies participating in a supply-chain initiative linking manufacturers and retailers recently made the following comments on the benefits of the initiative:

♦ "receiving better information has allowed for us to forecast and reduce inventory levels..."

♦ "You only produce what you need and that keeps the product and floor cost down"

♦ "There is more accuracy with the retailer's needs so that we can fine tune our production schedule"

♦ "The inventory levels are lower and we have less waste by not overstocking the warehouses"

Manufacturing companies highlighted the following information from retailers as most valuable to them:

♦ "We would like to see [the retailers] forward planning expectation of their sales."

♦ "We could use retail store level data on a daily basis and better scanner information"

♦ "Better forecasts, decisions about shelving and shelf allocations by retailers would help"

♦ "I wish we had access to each retailer's sales forecasts and the advertisements that they will be running next"

REQUIRED

1. What are the major benefits from adopting a supply-chain approach? Use the above comments as a prompt to a more detailed discussion. Explain how these benefits can lead to increased operating income.
2. What are the key obstacles to a manufacturer adopting a supply-chain approach?

20-31 Backflush costing and JIT production. The Acton Corporation manufactures electrical meters. For August, there were no beginning inventories of direct (raw) materials and no beginning and ending work in process. Acton uses a JIT production system and backflush costing with two trigger points for making entries in the accounting system:

◆ Purchase of direct materials debited to Inventory: Raw and In-Process Control
◆ Completion of good finished units of product debited to Finished Goods Control at standard costs

Acton's August standard costs per unit are direct materials, $25; conversion costs, $20. The following data apply to August manufacturing:

Direct (raw) materials purchased	$550,000
Conversion costs incurred	$440,000
Number of finished units manufactured	21,000
Number of finished units sold	20,000

REQUIRED

1. Prepare summary journal entries for August (without disposing of under- or overallocated conversion costs). Assume no direct materials variances.
2. Post the entries in requirement 1 to T-accounts for applicable Inventory Control, Conversion Costs Control, Conversion Costs Allocated, and Cost of Goods Sold.

20-32 Backflush, two trigger points, materials purchase and sale. Assume the same facts as in 20-31. Assume that the second trigger point for the Acton Corporation is the sale—rather than the production—of finished units. Also, the Inventory Control account is confined solely to direct materials, whether these materials are in a storeroom, in work in process, or in finished goods. No conversion costs are inventoried. They are allocated at standard cost to the units sold. Any under- or overallocated conversion costs are written off monthly to Cost of Goods Sold.

REQUIRED

1. Prepare summary journal entries for August, including the disposition of under- or overallocated conversion costs. Assume no direct materials variances.
2. Post the entries in requirement 1 to T-accounts for applicable Inventory Control, Conversion Costs Control, Conversion Costs Allocated, and Cost of Goods Sold.

20-33 Backflush, two trigger points, production completion and sale (continuation of 20-31). Assume the same facts as in Problem 20-31 except now there are only two trigger points, the completion of good finished units of product and the sale of finished goods.

REQUIRED

1. Prepare summary journal entries for August, including the disposition of under- or overallocated conversion costs. Assume no direct materials variances.
2. Post the entries in requirement 1 to T-accounts for applicable Inventory Control, Conversion Costs Control, Conversion Costs Allocated, and Cost of Goods Sold.

PROBLEMS

20-34 Backflush costing and JIT production. The Ronowski Company produces telephones. For June, there were no beginning inventories of raw materials and no beginning and ending work in process. Ronowski uses a JIT production system and backflush costing with three trigger points for making entries in its accounting system:

◆ Purchase of direct (raw) materials
◆ Completion of good finished units of product
◆ Sale of finished goods

Ronowski's June standard cost per unit of telephone product is direct materials, $26; conversion costs, $15. There are three inventory accounts:

◆ Inventory: Raw and In-Process Control
◆ Finished Goods Control

The following data apply to June manufacturing:

Raw materials purchased	$5,300,000
Conversion costs incurred	$3,080,000
Number of finished units manufactured	200,000
Number of finished units sold	192,000

REQUIRED

1. Prepare summary journal entries for June (without disposing of under- or overallocated conversion costs). Assume no direct materials variances.
2. Post the entries in requirement 1 to T-accounts for applicable Inventory Control, Conversion Costs Control, Conversion Costs Allocated, and Cost of Goods Sold.

20-35 Backflush, two trigger points, materials purchase and sale. Assume the same facts as in Problem 20-34. Assume that the second trigger point for the Ronowski Company is the sale—rather than the production—of finished units. Also, the inventory account is confined solely to direct materials, whether they would be in a storeroom, in work in process, or in finished goods.

No conversion costs are inventoried. They are allocated at standard cost to the units sold. Any under- or overallocated conversion costs are written off monthly to Cost of Goods Sold.

REQUIRED

1. Prepare summary journal entries for June, including the disposition of under- or overallocated conversion costs. Assume no direct materials variances.
2. Post the entries in requirement 1 to T-accounts for applicable Inventory Control, Conversion Costs Control, Conversion Costs Allocated, and Cost of Goods Sold. Explain the composition of the ending balance of Inventory Control.
3. Suppose conversion costs were sufficiently material in amount to be included in Inventory Control. Using a backflush system, show how your journal entries would be changed in requirement 1. Explain briefly.

20-36 Backflush, two trigger points, production completion and sale (continuation of 20-34). Assume the same facts as in Problem 20-34 except now there are trigger points at the completion of good finished units of product (which are debited to Finished Goods Control at standard costs) and at the sale of finished goods. Any underallocated or overallocated conversion costs are written off monthly to Cost of Goods Sold.

REQUIRED

1. Prepare summary journal entries for June, including the disposition of under- or overallocated conversion costs. Assume no direct materials variances.
2. Post the entries in requirement 1 to T-accounts for applicable Inventory Control, Conversion Costs Control, Conversion Costs Allocated, and Cost of Goods Sold. Explain the composition of the ending balance of Inventory Control.
3. If you did Problem 20-34, compare and explain any differences between the results here and those in Problem 20-34.

20-37 Backflush costing, income manipulation, ethics. Carol Brown, the Chief Financial Officer of Silicon Valley Computer, is an enthusiastic advocate of just-in-time production. The SVC Keyboard Division that produces keyboards for personal computers has made dramatic improvements in its operations by a highly successful JIT implementation. The Keyboard Division president now wants to adopt backflush costing.

Brown discusses the backflush costing proposal with Ralph Strong, the Controller of SVC. Strong is totally opposed to backflush costing. He argues that it will open up "Pandora's box" as regards allowing division managers to manipulate reported division operating income. A member of Strong's group outlines the three possible variations of backflush costing shown in Exhibit 20-8. Strong notes that none of these three methods track work in process. He asserts that this omission would allow managers to "artificially change" reported operating income by manipulating work in process levels. He is especially scathing about the backflush costing where no entries are made until a sale occurs. He comments:

> Suppose the Division has already met its target operating income and wants to shift some of this year's income to next year. Under backflush costing with sale of finished goods as the trigger point, the Division will have an incentive to not make sales this year of goods produced this year. This is a bizarre incentive. I rest my case about why we should stay with a job-costing system using sequential tracking.

Strong concludes that as long as reported accounting numbers are central to SVC's performance and bonus reviews, backflush costing should never be adopted.

1. What factors should SVC consider in deciding whether to adopt a version of backflush costing?
2. Are Strong's concerns about income manipulation sufficiently important for SVC to not adopt backflush costing?
3. What other ways has SVC to motivate managers to not "artificially change" reported income?

COLLABORATIVE LEARNING PROBLEM

20-38 **Backflushing.** The following conversation occurred between Brian Richardson, plant manager at Glendale Engineering, and Charles Cheng, plant controller. Glendale manufactures automotive component parts such as gears and crankshafts for automobile manufacturers. Richardson has been very enthusiastic about implementing JIT and about simplifying and streamlining the production and other business processes.

Richardson: Charles, I would like to substantially simplify our accounting in the new JIT environment. Can't we just record one accounting entry at the time we ship products to our customers? I don't want to have our staff spending time tracking inventory from one stage to the next, when we have as little inventory as we do.

Cheng: Brian, I think you are right about simplifying the accounting, but we still have a fair amount of raw material and finished goods inventory that varies from period to period depending on the demand for specific products. Doing away with all inventory accounting may be a problem.

Richardson: Well, you know my desire to simplify, simplify, simplify. I know that there are some costs of oversimplifying, but I believe that, in the long run, simplification pays big dividends. Why don't you and your staff study the issues involved, and I will put it on the agenda for our next senior plant management meeting.

INSTRUCTIONS

Form groups of two or more students to complete the following requirements.

REQUIRED

1. What backflush costing method would you recommend that Cheng adopt? Remember Richardson's desire to simplify the accounting as much as possible. Develop support for your recommendation.
2. Think about the three examples of backflush costing described in this chapter. These examples differ with respect to the number and types of trigger points used. Suppose your goal of implementing backflush costing is to simplify the accounting, but only if it closely matches the sequential tracking approach. Which backflush costing method would you propose if:
   a. Glendale had no raw materials or work-in-process inventories but did have finished goods inventory?
   b. Glendale had no work-in-process or finished goods inventories but did have raw material inventory?
   c. Glendale had no raw material, work-in-process, or finished goods inventories?
3. Backflush costing has its critics. In an article in the magazine *Management Accounting*, entitled "Beware the New Accounting Myths," R. Calvasina, E. Calvasina, and G. Calvasina state:

   The periodic (backflush) system has never been reflective of the reporting needs of a manufacturing system. In the highly standardized operating environments of the present JIT era, the appropriate system to be used is a perpetual accounting system based on an up-to-date, realistic set of standard costs. For management accountants to backflush on an actual cost basis is to return to the days of the outdoor privy.

   Comment on this statement.

PART SIX

21
CHAPTER
CAPITAL BUDGETING
AND COST ANALYSIS

Budgets are major long-term investments that have significant financial and non-financial impacts. In addition to discounted cash flow analysis, issues such as the environment and tourism were assesed when building the Confederation Bridge which connects Prince Edward Island to New Brunswick.

LEARNING OBJECTIVES

After studying this chapter, you should be able to:

1. Differentiate between project-by-project orientation of capital budgeting and period-by-period orientation of accrual accounting
2. Explain the time value of money and opportunity costs
3. Identify the six stages of capital budgeting for a project and its predicted outcomes
4. Use and evaluate the two main discounted cash flow (DCF) methods, the net present value (NPV) method, and the internal rate-of-return (IRR) method
5. Use and evaluate how the two main discounted cash flow methods (NPV and IRR) differ
6. Identify relevant cash inflows and outflows for capital budgeting decisions that use DCF methods
7. Use and evaluate the payback method
8. Use and evaluate the accrual accounting rate-of-return (AARR) method
9. Recognize the impact of nonfinancial and qualitative factors in capital budgeting decisions
10. Identify and reduce conflicts in using DCF for capital budgeting and accrual accounting for performance evaluation

Air Canada
www.aircanada.ca

Investment projects (investment programs). Investments and outcomes from those investments (which generally cover a number of years).

Capital budgeting. The process of making long-term planning decisions for investments.

Organizations are often required to make decisions whose consequences are felt over many future years. Such decisions frequently involve large investments of money and have uncertain actual outcomes that have long-lasting effects on the organization. For example, General Motors must decide whether it should spend billions of dollars developing a new minivan. Air Canada must decide whether it should invest millions of dollars in new Boeing 777 airplanes. The investments and the outcomes from those investments (which generally cover a number of years) are collectively referred to as **investment projects** or **investment programs.** Poor long-term investment decisions can affect the future stability of an organization, because it is often difficult for organizations to recover money tied up in bad investments. Managers need a long-range planning tool or process to analyze and control investments with long-term consequences.

Capital budgeting is the process of making those long-term planning decisions for investments. Income determination and the planning and control of routine operations focus primarily on the current time period. Capital budgeting is a decision-making and control tool that focuses primarily on projects or programs whose effects span multiple time periods.

TWO FOCUSES OF COST ANALYSIS

O B J E C T I V E   1

Differentiate between project-by-project orientation of capital budgeting and period-by-period orientation of accrual accounting

Capital Investment Appraisal—lecture notes by Steve Fong, University of Hong Kong www.cityu.edu.hk/afdragon/teach/capbud.html

"Capital Budgeting for a New Dairy Facility"—C.V. Thomas, M.A. DeLorenzo, D.R. Bray—University of Florida hammock.ifas.ufl.edu/txt/fairs/55932

Recall a central theme of this book: different costs for different purposes. Capital budgeting decisions focus on the project, which spans multiple time periods. There is a great danger in basing capital budgeting decisions on the current accounting period's income statement, ignoring the future implications of investing in a project. Investment in a project might depress the current period's reported income, but it may still be a worthwhile investment because of the high future cash inflows that it is expected to generate.

Exhibit 21-1 illustrates two different dimensions of cost analysis: (1) the project dimension and (2) the time dimension. Each project is represented in Exhibit 21-1 as a distinct horizontal rectangle. The life of each project is longer than one accounting period. Capital budgeting focusses on the entire life of the project in order to consider *all* cash inflows or cash savings from the investment. The white area in Exhibit 21-1 illustrates the accounting-period focus on income determination and routine planning and control. This cross-section emphasizes the company's performance for the 2000 accounting period. Accounting income is of particular interest to the manager because bonuses are frequently based on reported income. Income reported in an accounting period is also important to a company because of its impact on the company's stock price. Excessive focus on short-run accounting income, however, can cause a company to forgo long-term profitability. Successful managers balance

EXHIBIT 21-1
The Project and Time Dimensions of Capital Budgeting

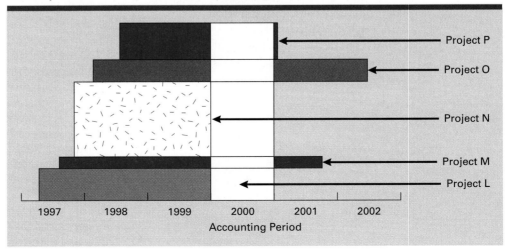

short-term accounting-period considerations and longer-term project considerations in their decision process.

The accounting system that corresponds to the project dimension in Exhibit 21-1 is termed *life cycle costing*. This system, described in Chapter 12, accumulates revenues and costs on a project-by-project basis. For example, a life cycle costing statement for a new car project at the Ford Motor Company could encompass a four-year period and would accumulate costs for all business functions in the value chain, from R&D to customer service. This accumulation expands the accrual accounting system, which measures income on a period-by-period basis, to a system that computes income over the entire project covering many accounting periods.

Any system that focuses on the life span of a project must cover several years and thus must consider the time value of money. The *time value of money* takes into account the fact that a dollar (or any other monetary unit) received today is worth more than a dollar received tomorrow. The reason is that a $1 received today can be invested to start earning a return of 15% per year (say) so that it grows to $1.15 at the end of the year. The time value of money is the opportunity cost (the return of $0.15 forgone) from not having the money today.

Capital budgeting focuses on projects that can be accounted for using life cycle costing and that must be evaluated taking into consideration the time value of money.

OBJECTIVE 2

Explain the time value of money and opportunity costs

STAGES OF CAPITAL BUDGETING

We describe six stages in capital budgeting.

OBJECTIVE 3

Identify the six stages of capital budgeting for a project and its predicted outcomes

- ◆ **Stage 1—Identification stage.** *To distinguish which types of capital expenditure projects are necessary to accomplish organization objectives.* Capital expenditure initiatives are closely tied to the strategies of an organization or an organizational subunit. For example, an organization's strategy could be to increase revenues by targeting new products, customers, or markets, or to reduce costs by improving productivity and efficiency. Identifying which types of capital investment projects to invest in is largely the responsibility of line management.

- ◆ **Stage 2—Search stage.** *To explore several alternative capital expenditure investments that will achieve organization strategies and goals.* Employee teams from all parts of the value chain evaluate alternative technologies, machines, and project specifications. Some alternatives are rejected early. Others are evaluated more thoroughly in the information-acquisition stage.

- ◆ **Stage 3—Information-acquisition stage.** *To consider the predicted costs and predicted consequences of alternative capital investments.* These consequences can be quantitative and qualitative. Capital budgeting emphasizes financial quantitative factors, but nonfinancial quantitative and qualitative factors are also very important. Management accountants help identify these factors.

- ◆ **Stage 4—Selection stage.** *To choose projects for implementation.* Organizations choose those projects whose predicted outcomes (benefits) exceed predicted costs by the greatest amount. The formal analysis includes only predicted outcomes quantified in financial terms. Managers reevaluate the conclusions reached on the basis of the formal analysis, using managerial judgement to take into account nonfinancial and qualitative considerations. Evaluating costs and benefits is often the responsibility of the management accountant.

- ◆ **Stage 5—Financing stage.** *To obtain project funding.* Sources of financing include internally (within the organization) generated cash and the capital market (equity and debt securities). Financing is often the responsibility of the treasury function of an organization.

- ◆ **Stage 6—Implementation and control stage.** *To put the project in motion and monitor performance.* As the project is implemented, the company must evaluate whether capital investments are being made as scheduled and within the budget. As the project generates cash inflows, monitoring and control may include a postinvestment audit, in which the predictions made at the time the project was selected are compared with the actual results.

This chapter emphasizes the information-acquisition, selection, and implementation and control stages of capital budgeting because these are the stages in which the management accountant is most involved. Beyond the numbers, however, the ability of individual managers to "sell" their own projects to senior management is often pivotal in the acceptance or rejection of projects.

We use information from Lifetime Care Hospital to illustrate capital budgeting. Lifetime Care is a not-for-profit organization that is not subject to taxes. Chapter 22 introduces tax considerations in capital budgeting.

One of Lifetime Care's goals is to improve the productivity of its X-ray Department. To achieve this goal, the manager of Lifetime Care *identifies* a need to purchase a new state-of-the-art X-ray machine to replace an existing machine. The *search* stage yields several alternative models, but the hospital's technical staff focusses on one machine, XCAM8, as being particularly suitable. They next begin to *acquire information* for a more detailed evaluation. Quantitative financial information for the formal analysis follows:

> Regardless of whether the new X-ray machine is acquired or not, revenue will not change. Lifetime Care charges a fixed rate for a particular diagnosis, regardless of the number of X-rays taken. The only relevant financial benefit in evaluating Lifetime's decision to purchase the X-ray machine is the cash savings in operating costs. The existing X-ray machine can operate for another five years and will have a disposal price of zero at the end of five years. The required net initial investment for the new machine is $379,100. The initial investment consists of the cost of the new machine—$372,890—plus an additional cash investment in working capital (supplies and spare parts for the new machine) of $10,000 minus cash of $3,790 obtained from the disposal of the existing machine ($372,890 + $10,000 − $3,790 = $379,100).

> The manager expects the new machine to have a five-year useful life and a disposal price of zero at the end of five years. The new machine is faster and easier to operate and has the ability to X-ray a larger area. This will decrease labour costs and will reduce the average number of X-rays taken per patient. The manager expects the investment to result in annual cash inflows of $100,000. These cash flows will generally occur throughout the year; however, to simplify computations, we assume that operating cash flows occur at the end of each year. The cash inflows are expected to come from cash savings in operating costs of $100,000 for each of the first four years and $90,000 in year 5 plus recovery of working capital investment of $10,000 in year 5.

Managers at Lifetime Care also identify the following nonfinancial quantitative and qualitative benefits of investing in the new X-ray equipment:

1. **The quality of X-rays.** Higher-quality X-rays will lead to improved diagnoses and better patient treatment.

2. **The safety of technicians and patients.** The greater efficiency of the new machine would mean that X-ray technicians and patients are less exposed to the possibly harmful effects of X-rays.

These benefits are not considered in the formal financial analysis.

In the *selection* stage, managers must decide whether Lifetime Care should purchase the new X-ray machine. They start with financial information. This chapter discusses the following methods that they can use:

◆ Discounted cash flow methods: net present value (NPV) and internal rate-of-return (IRR)

◆ Payback method

◆ Accrual accounting rate-of-return method

Discounted cash flow (DCF) measures the cash inflows and outflows of a project as if they occurred at a single point in time so that they can be compared in an appropriate way. The discounted cash flow methods recognize that the use of money has an opportunity cost—return forgone. Because the DCF methods explicitly and routinely weight cash flows by the time value of money, they are usually the best (most comprehensive) methods to use for long-run decisions.

DCF focuses on *cash* inflows and outflows rather than on *operating income* as used in conventional accrual accounting. Cash is invested now with the expectation of receiving a greater amount of cash in the future. Try to avoid injecting accrual concepts of accounting into DCF analysis. For example, amortization is deducted as an accrual expense when calculating operating income under accrual accounting. It is not deducted in DCF analysis because such expense entails no cash outflow.

The compound interest tables and formulas used in DCF analysis are included in Appendix B. (Appendix B will be used frequently in Chapters 21 and 22.)

There are two main DCF methods:

1. Net present value (NPV)
2. Internal rate of return (IRR)

NPV is calculated using the **required rate of return (RRR),** which is the minimum acceptable rate of return on an investment. It is the return that the organization could expect to receive elsewhere for an investment of comparable risk. This rate is also called the **discount rate, hurdle rate,** or **(opportunity) cost of capital.** When working with IRR, the RRR is used as a point of comparison. Chapter 22 discusses issues encountered in estimating this rate.

Assume that the required rate of return, or discount rate, for the Lifetime Care X-ray machine project is 8%.

Net Present Value Method

The **net present value (NPV) method** calculates the expected net monetary gain or loss from a project by discounting all expected future cash inflows and outflows to the present point in time, using the required rate of return. Only projects with a positive net present value are acceptable. Why? Because the return from these projects exceeds the cost of capital (the return available by investing the capital elsewhere). Managers prefer projects with higher NPVs to projects with lower NPVs, if all other things are equal. Using the NPV method entails the following steps:

◆ **Step 1:** *Sketch the relevant cash inflows and outflows.* The right side of Exhibit 21-2 shows how these cash flows are portrayed. Outflows appear in parentheses. The sketch helps the decision-maker organize the data in a systematic way. Note that Exhibit 21-2 includes the outflow for the new machine at year 0, the time of the acquisition. The NPV method focuses only on cash flows. NPV analysis is indifferent to where the cash flows come from (operations, purchase or sale of equipment, or investment or recovery of working capital) and to the accrual accounting treatments of individual cash flow items (for example, amortization costs on equipment purchases).

◆ **Step 2:** *Choose the correct compound interest table from Appendix B.* In our example, we can discount each year's cash flow separately using Table 2 (Appendix B), or we can compute the present value of an annuity using Table 4 (Appendix B). If we use Table 2, we find the discount factors for periods 1–5 under the 8% column. Approach 1 in Exhibit 21-2 presents the five discount factors. Because the investment produces an annuity, a series of equal cash flows at equal intervals, we may use Table 4. We find the discount factor for five periods under the 8% column. Approach 2 in Exhibit 21-2 shows that this discount factor is 3.993 (3.993 is the sum of the five discount factors used in approach 1). To obtain the present value figures, multiply the discount factors by the appropriate cash amounts in the sketch in Exhibit 21-2.

OBJECTIVE 4

Use and evaluate the two main discounted cash flow (DCF) methods, the net present value (NPV) method, and the internal rate-of-return (IRR) method

Discounted cash flow (DCF). Capital budgeting method that measures the cash inflows and outflows of a project as if they occurred at a single point in time so that they can be compared in an appropriate way.

Required rate of return (RRR) (discount rate, hurdle rate, opportunity cost of capital). The minimum acceptable rate of return on an investment; the return that the organization could expect to receive elsewhere for an investment of comparable risk.

Net present value (NPV) method. Discounted cash flow method that calculates the expected net monetary gain or loss from a project by discounting all expected future cash inflows and outflows to the present point in time, using the required rate of return.

EXHIBIT 21-2
Net Present Value Method: Lifetime Care Hospital

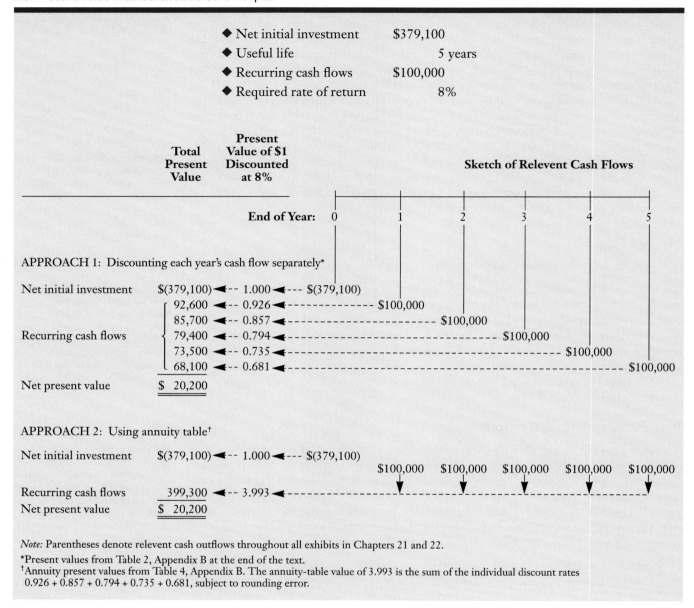

◆ Net initial investment $379,100
◆ Useful life 5 years
◆ Recurring cash flows $100,000
◆ Required rate of return 8%

Note: Parentheses denote relevent cash outflows throughout all exhibits in Chapters 21 and 22.

*Present values from Table 2, Appendix B at the end of the text.

†Annuity present values from Table 4, Appendix B. The annuity-table value of 3.993 is the sum of the individual discount rates 0.926 + 0.857 + 0.794 + 0.735 + 0.681, subject to rounding error.

◆ **Step 3:** *Sum the present value figures to determine the net present value.* If the sum is zero or positive, the NPV model indicates that the project should be accepted. That is, its expected rate of return equals or exceeds the required rate of return. If the total is negative, the project is undesirable. Its expected rate of return is below the required rate of return.

Exhibit 21-2 indicates an NPV of $20,200 at the required rate of return of 8%; the expected return from the project exceeds the 8% required rate of return. Therefore, the project is desirable. The cash flows from the project are adequate to (1) recover the net initial investment in the project and (2) earn a return greater than 8% on the investment tied up in the project from period to period. Had the NPV been negative, the project would be undesirable on the basis of financial considerations.

Of course, the manager of the hospital must also weigh nonfinancial factors. Consider the reduction in the average number of individual X-rays taken per patient with the new machine. This reduction is a qualitative benefit of the new machine given the health risks to patients and technicians. Other qualitative benefits of the new machine are the better diagnoses and treatments that patients receive. Had the

NPV been negative, the manager would need to judge whether the nonfinancial benefits outweigh the negative NPV.

It is important that you not proceed until you thoroughly understand Exhibit 21-2. Compare approach 1 with approach 2 in Exhibit 21-2 to see how Table 4 in Appendix B merely aggregates the present value factors of Table 2. That is, the fundamental table is Table 2; Table 4 reduces calculations when there is an annuity—a series of equal cash flows at equal intervals.

Internal Rate-of-Return Method

The **internal rate of return (IRR)** is the discount rate at which the present value of expected cash inflows from a project equals the present value of expected cash outflows of the project. That is, the IRR is the discount rate that makes NPV = $0. IRR is sometimes called the *time-adjusted rate of return*. As in the NPV method, the sources of cash flows and the accrual accounting treatment of individual cash flows are irrelevant to the IRR calculations. We illustrate the computation of the IRR using the X-ray machine project of Lifetime Care. Exhibit 21-3 presents the cash flows and shows the calculation of the NPV using a 10% discount rate. At a 10% discount rate, the NPV of the project is zero. Therefore, the IRR for the project is 10%.

How do we determine the 10% discount rate that yields NPV = $0? In most cases, analysts solving capital budgeting problems have a calculator or computer programmed to provide the internal rate of return. Without a calculator or computer program, a trial-and-error approach can provide the answer.

◆ **Step 1:** Try a discount rate and calculate the NPV of the project using that discount rate.

◆ **Step 2:** If the NPV is less than zero, try a lower discount rate. (A lower discount rate will increase the NPV; remember, we are trying to find a discount rate for which NPV = $0.) If the NPV is greater than zero, try a higher discount rate to lower the NPV. Keep adjusting the discount rate until NPV = $0. In the Lifetime Care example, a discount rate of 8% yields NPV of +$20,200 (see Exhibit 21-2). A discount rate of 12% yields NPV of –$18,600 (3.605, the present value annuity factor from Table 4, × $100,000 – $379,100). Therefore, the discount rate that makes NPV = $0 must lie between 8% and 12%. We happen to try 10% and get NPV = $0. Hence, the IRR is 10%.

The step-by-step computations of an internal rate of return are easier when the cash inflows are equal, as in our example. Information from Exhibit 21-3 can be expressed in the following equation:

$$\$379{,}100 = \text{Present value of annuity of } \$100{,}000 \text{ at } x\% \text{ for 5 years}$$

Or, using Table 4 (Appendix B) what factor F will satisfy the following equation?

$$\$379{,}100 = \$100{,}000F$$
$$F = 3.791$$

On the five-period line of Table 4, find the percentage column that is closest to 3.791. It is exactly 10%. If the factor F falls between the factors in two columns, straight-line interpolation is used to approximate the IRR. (For an illustration of interpolation, see requirement 1 of the Problem for Self-Study.)

A project is accepted only if the internal rate of return exceeds the required rate of return (the opportunity cost of capital). In the Lifetime Care example, the X-ray machine has an IRR of 10%, which is greater than the required rate of return of 8%. On the basis of financial factors, Lifetime Care should invest in the new machine. If the IRR exceeds the RRR, then the project has a positive NPV when project cash flows are discounted at the RRR. If the IRR equals the RRR, NPV = $0. If the IRR is less than the RRR, NPV is negative. Obviously, managers prefer projects with higher IRRs to projects with lower IRRs, if all other things are equal. The IRR of 10% means that the cash inflows from the project are adequate to (1) recover the net initial investment in the project and (2) earn a return of exactly 10% on investment tied up in the project over its useful life.

Internal rate of return (IRR) (time-adjusted rate of return). Discount rate at which the present value of expected cash inflows from a project equals the present value of expected cash outflows of the project. The IRR is the discount rate that makes NPV = $0.

EXHIBIT 21-3
Internal Rate-of-Return Method: Lifetime Care Hospital

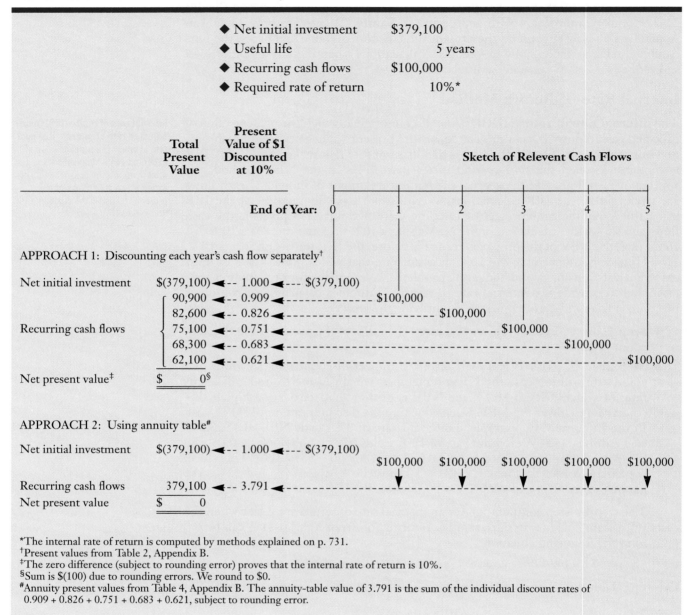

- ◆ Net initial investment $379,100
- ◆ Useful life   5 years
- ◆ Recurring cash flows $100,000
- ◆ Required rate of return   10%*

*The internal rate of return is computed by methods explained on p. 731.
†Present values from Table 2, Appendix B.
‡The zero difference (subject to rounding error) proves that the internal rate of return is 10%.
§Sum is $(100) due to rounding errors. We round to $0.
#Annuity present values from Table 4, Appendix B. The annuity-table value of 3.791 is the sum of the individual discount rates of
 0.909 + 0.826 + 0.751 + 0.683 + 0.621, subject to rounding error.

OBJECTIVE 5

Use and evaluate how the two main discounted cash flow methods (NPV and IRR) differ

Comparison of Net Present Value and Internal Rate-of-Return Method

This text emphasizes the NPV method, which has the important advantage that the end result of the computations is dollars, not a percentage. We can therefore add the NPVs of individual independent projects to estimate the effect of accepting a combination of projects. In contrast, the IRRs of individual projects cannot be added or averaged to derive the IRR of the combination of projects.

A second advantage of the NPV method is that we can use it in situations where the required rate of return varies over the life of the project. For example, suppose in the X-ray machine example, Lifetime Care has a required rate of return of 8% in years 1, 2, and 3 and 12% in years 4 and 5. The total present value of the cash inflows is as follows:

Year	Cash Inflows	Required Rate of Return	Present Value of $1 Discounted at Required Rate	Total Present Value of Cash Inflows
1	$100,000	8%	0.926	$ 92,600
2	100,000	8	0.857	85,700
3	100,000	8	0.794	79,400
4	100,000	12	0.636	63,600
5	100,000	12	0.567	56,700
				$378,000

Given the net initial investment of $379,100, NPV calculations indicate that the project is unattractive: it has a negative NPV of −$1,100 ($378,000 − $379,100). However, it is not possible to use the IRR method to infer that the project should be rejected. The existence of different required rates of return in different years (8% for years 1, 2, and 3 versus 12% for years 4 and 5) means there is not a single RRR that the IRR (a single figure) must exceed for the project to be acceptable.

SENSITIVITY ANALYSIS

To highlight the basic differences between the NPV and IRR methods, we have assumed that the expected values of cash flows will occur for certain. Obviously, managers know that their predictions are imperfect and thus uncertain. To examine how a result will change if the predicted financial outcomes are not achieved or if an underlying assumption changes, managers can use sensitivity analysis, a what-if technique first introduced in Chapter 3.

Sensitivity analysis can take various forms. For example, suppose Lifetime Care management believes forecasted savings are uncertain and difficult to predict. Management could then ask: What is the minimum annual cash savings that will cause us to invest in the new X-ray machine (that is, for NPV = $0)? For the data in Exhibit 21-2, let ACI = annual cash inflows and let NPV = $0. The net initial investment is $379,100, and the present-value factor at the 8% required rate of return for a five-year annuity of $1 is 3.993. Then:

$$\text{NPV} = \$0$$
$$3.993 \times \text{ACI} - \$379,100 = \$0$$
$$3.993 \times \text{ACI} = \$379,100$$
$$\text{ACI} = \$94,941$$

Thus, at the discount rate of 8%, annual cash inflows can decrease to $94,941 (a decline of $100,000 − $94,941 = $5,059) before NPV falls below zero. If management believes it can attain annual cash savings of at least $94,941, it could justify investing in the new X-ray machine on financial grounds alone.

Computer spreadsheets enable managers to conduct systematic, efficient sensitivity analysis. Exhibit 21-4 shows how the net present value of the X-ray machine

EXHIBIT 21-4

Net Present Value Calculations for Lifetime Care Hospital Under Different Assumptions of Annual Cash Inflows and Required Rates of Return

Required Rate of Return	Annual Cash Inflows*				
	$80,000	$90,000	$100,000	$110,000	$120,000
6%	$(42,140)	$ (22)	$42,100	$84,220	$126,340
8%	(59,660)	(19,730)	22,200	60,130	100,060
10%	(75,820)	(37,910)	0	37,910	75,820

*All entries in cells assume a useful project life of five years.

project is affected by variations in (1) the annual cash inflows and (2) the required rate of return. NPVs can also vary with the useful life of a project. Sensitivity analysis helps a manager focus on those decisions that are most sensitive, and it eases the manager's mind about those decisions that are not so sensitive. For the X-ray machine project, Exhibit 21-4 shows that variations in either the annual cash inflows or the required rate of return have sizable effects on NPV.

RELEVANT CASH FLOWS IN DISCOUNTED CASH FLOW ANALYSIS

OBJECTIVE 6

Identify relevant cash inflows and outflows for capital budgeting decisions that use DCF methods

The key point of discounted cash flow methods is to focus exclusively on differences in expected future cash flows that result from implementing a project. All cash flows are treated the same, whether they arise from operations, purchase or sale of equipment, or investment in or recovery of working capital. The opportunity cost and the time value of money are tied to the cash flowing in or out of the organization, not to the source of the cash.

One of the biggest challenges in DCF analysis is determining those cash flows that are relevant to making the decision. Relevant cash flows are expected future cash flows that differ between the alternatives. At Lifetime Care, the alternatives are either to continue to use the old X-ray machine or to replace it with the new machine. The relevant cash flows are the *differences* in cash flows between continuing to use the old machine and purchasing the new one. *When reading this section, focus on identifying future expected cash flows of each alternative and differences in cash flows between alternatives.*

Capital investment projects (for example, purchasing a new machine) typically have five major categories of cash flows: (1) initial investment in machine and working capital, (2) cash flow from current disposal of the old machine, (3) recurring operating cash flows, (4) cash flow from terminal disposal of machine and recovery of working capital, and (5) income tax impacts on cash flows. We discuss the first four categories here, using Lifetime Care's purchase decision of the X-ray machine as an illustration. Income tax impacts are described in Chapter 22.

1. **Initial investment.** Two components of investment cash flows are (a) the cash outflow to purchase the machine and (b) the working capital cash outflows.
   a. *Initial machine investment.* These outflows, made for purchasing plant, equipment, and machines, occur in the early periods of the project's life and include cash outflows for transporting and installing the item. In the Lifetime Care example, the $372,890 cost (including transportation and installation costs) of the X-ray machine is an outflow in year 0. These cash flows are relevant to the capital budgeting decision because they will be incurred only if Lifetime decides to purchase the new machine.
   b. *Initial working capital investment.* Investments in plant, equipment, and machines and in the sales promotions for product lines are invariably accompanied by incremental investments in working capital. These investments take the form of current assets, such as receivables and inventories (supplies and spare parts for the new machine in the Lifetime Care example), minus current liabilities, such as accounts payable. Working capital investments are similar to machine investments. In each case, available cash is tied up.
      The Lifetime Care example assumes a $10,000 incremental investment in working capital (supplies and spare parts inventory) if the new machine is acquired. The incremental working capital investment is the difference between the working capital required to operate the new machine (say $15,000) and the working capital required to operate the old machine (say $5,000). The $10,000 additional investment in working capital is a cash outflow in year 0.

2. **Current disposal price of old machine.** Any cash received from disposal of the old machine is a relevant cash inflow (in year 0) because it is an expected future cash flow that differs between the alternatives of investing and not investing in the new project. If Lifetime Care invests in the new X-ray machine, it

will be able to dispose of its old machine for $3,790. These proceeds are included as cash inflow in year 0.

Recall from Chapter 11 that the book value (original cost minus accumulated amortization) of the old equipment is irrelevant. It is a past cost. Nothing can change what has already been spent or what has already happened.

The net initial investment for the new X-ray machine, $379,100, is the initial machine investment plus the initial working capital investment minus current disposal price of the old machine: $372,890 + $10,000 − $3,790 = $379,100.

3. **Recurring operating cash flows.** This category includes all recurring operating cash flows that differ among the alternatives. Organizations make capital investments to generate cash inflows in the future. These inflows may result from producing and selling additional goods or services, or, as in the Lifetime Care example, from savings in operating cash costs. Recurring operating cash flows can be net outflows in some periods. For example, oil production may require large expenditures every five years (say) to improve oil extraction rates. Focus on operating cash flows, not on accrued revenues and costs.

To underscore this point, consider the following additional facts about the Lifetime Care X-ray machine example:

◆ Total X-Ray Department overhead costs will not change whether the new machine is purchased or the old machine is kept. The X-Ray Department overhead costs are allocated to individual X-ray machines—Lifetime has several—on the basis of the labour costs for operating each machine. Because the new X-ray machine will have lower labour costs, overhead allocated to it will be $30,000 less than the amount allocated to the machine it is replacing.

◆ Amortization on the new X-ray machine using the straight-line method is $74,578 [(original cost, $372,890 − expected terminal disposal price, $0) ÷ useful life, 5 years].

The savings in operating cash flows (labour and materials) of $100,000 in each of the first four years and $90,000 in the fifth year are clearly relevant because they are expected future cash flows that will differ between the alternatives of investing and not investing in the new machine. But what about the decrease in allocated overhead costs of $30,000? What about amortization of $74,578?

a. *Overhead costs.* The key question is: Do total overhead cash flows decrease as a result of acquiring the new machine? In our example, they do not. Total X-Ray Department overhead costs remain the same whether or not the new machine is acquired. Only the overhead allocated to individual machines changes. The overhead costs allocated to the new machine are $30,000 less. This $30,000 will be allocated to *other* machines in the department. No cash flow savings in total overhead occur. Therefore, the $30,000 should not be included as part of recurring operating cash inflows.

b. *Amortization.* Amortization is irrelevant. It is a noncash allocation of costs, whereas DCF is based on inflows and outflows of *cash*. In DCF methods, the initial cost of equipment is regarded as a *lump sum* outflow of cash at year 0. Deducting amortization from operating cash inflows would be counting the lump sum amount twice.

4. **Terminal disposal price of investment.** The disposal of the investment at the date of termination of a project generally increases cash inflow in the year of disposal. Errors in forecasting the terminal disposal price are seldom critical on long-duration projects, because the present value of amounts to be received in the distant future is usually small. Two components of the terminal disposal price of an investment are (a) the terminal disposal price of the machine and (b) the recovery of working capital.

a. *Terminal disposal price of machine.* At the end of the useful life of the project, the initial machine investment may not be recovered at all, or it may be only partially recovered in the amount of the terminal disposal price.

The relevant cash inflow is the difference in expected terminal disposal prices at the end of five years under the two alternatives—the terminal

EXHIBIT 21-5
Relevant Cash Inflows and Outflows for Lifetime Care Hospital

		Sketch of Relevant Cash Flows					
End of Year:	0	1	2	3	4	5	
1. a. Initial machine investment	$ (372,890)						
b. Initial working capital investment	(10,000)						
2. Current disposal price of old machine	3,790						
Net initial investment	(379,100)						
3. Recurring operating cash flows		$100,000	$100,000	$100,000	$100,000	$ 90,000	
4. a. Terminal disposal price of machine						0	
b. Recovery of working capital						10,000	
Total relevant cash inflows and outflows as shown in Exhibits 21-2 and 21-3	$ (379,100)	$100,000	$100,000	$100,000	$100,000	$100,000	

disposal price of the new machine (zero in the case of Lifetime Care) minus the terminal disposal price of the old machine (also zero in the Lifetime Care example).[1]

b. *Recovery of working capital.* The initial investment in working capital is usually fully recouped when the project is terminated. At that time, inventories and receivables necessary to support the project are no longer needed. The relevant cash inflow is the difference in the expected working capital recovered under the two alternatives. If the new X-ray machine is purchased, Lifetime Care will recover $15,000 of working capital in year 5. If the new machine is not acquired, Lifetime will recover $5,000 of working capital in year 5, at the end of the useful life of the old machine. The relevant cash inflow in year 5 if Lifetime invests in the new machine is $10,000 ($15,000 – $5,000).

Some capital investments *reduce* working capital. Assume that a computer-integrated manufacturing project with a seven-year life will reduce inventories and hence working capital by $20 million from, say, $50 million to $30 million. This reduction will be represented as a $20 million cash inflow for the project at year 0. At the end of seven years, the recovery of working capital will show a relevant cash *outflow* of $20 million. Why? Because the company recovers only $30 million of working capital under CIM rather than the $50 million of working capital it would have recovered had it not implemented CIM.

Exhibit 21-5 above presents the relevant cash inflows and outflows for Lifetime Care's decision to purchase the new machine as described in items 1–4 in the preceding list. The total relevant cash flows for each year are the same as the relevant cash flows used in Exhibits 21-2 and 21-3 to illustrate the NPV and IRR methods.

PAYBACK METHOD

OBJECTIVE 7

Use and evaluate the payback method

Payback method. Capital budgeting method that measures the time it will take to recoup, in the form of net cash inflows, the net initial investment in a project.

Uniform Cash Flows

We now consider a third method for analyzing the financial aspects of projects. The **payback method** measures the time it will take to recoup, in the form of net cash inflows, the net initial investment in a project. Like NPV and IRR, the payback method does not distinguish the sources of cash inflows (operations, disposal of equipment, or recovery of working capital). In the Lifetime Care example, the X-ray

[1]The Lifetime Care example assumes that both the new and the old machine have a future useful life of five years. If instead the old machine only had a useful life of four years, management could choose to evaluate the investment decision over a four-year horizon. In this case, Lifetime's management would need to predict the terminal disposal price of the new machine at the end of four years.

machine costs $379,100, has a five-year expected useful life, and generates a $100,000 uniform cash inflow each year. The payback calculations[2] are as follows:

$$\text{Payback} = \frac{\text{Net initial investment}}{\text{Uniform increase in annual cash flows}}$$

$$= \frac{\$379,100}{100,000} = 3.791 \text{ years}$$

Under the payback method, organizations often choose a cutoff period for a project. The greater the risks of a project, the smaller the cutoff period. Why? Because faced with higher risks, managers would like to more quickly recover the investments they have made. For example, the Tesoro Petroleum Corporation uses a payback period of three to four years for investment decisions at its Kenai, Alaska oil refinery. Projects with a payback period less than the cutoff period are acceptable. Those with a payback period greater than the cutoff period are rejected. If Lifetime's cutoff period under the payback method is three years, Lifetime will reject the new machine. If Lifetime uses a cutoff period of four years, Lifetime will consider the new machine to be acceptable.

The payback method highlights liquidity, which is often an important factor in capital budgeting decisions. Managers prefer projects with shorter paybacks (more liquid) to projects with longer paybacks, if all other things are equal. Projects with shorter payback periods give the organization more flexibility because funds for other projects become available sooner. Also, managers are less confident about cash flow predictions that stretch far into the future. The shorter the payback, the more confident managers can feel that their forecasts are on target.

The major strength of the payback method is that it is easy to understand. Like the DCF methods described previously, the payback method is not affected by accrual accounting conventions such as amortization. Advocates of the payback method argue that it is a handy measure when (1) estimates of profitability are not crucial and preliminary screening of many proposals is necessary and (2) the predicted cash flows in later years of the project are highly uncertain.

Two major weaknesses of the payback method are (1) it neglects the time value of money and (2) it neglects to consider project cash flows after the net initial investment is recovered. Consider an alternative to the $379,100 X-ray machine mentioned earlier. Assume that another X-ray machine, with a three-year useful life and zero terminal disposal price, requires only a $300,000 net initial investment and will also result in cash inflows of $100,000 per year. First, compare the two payback periods:

$$\text{Payback period for machine 1:} = \frac{\$379,100}{100,000} = 3.791 \text{ years}$$

$$\text{Payback period for machine 2:} = \frac{\$300,000}{100,000} = 3.000 \text{ years}$$

The payback criterion would favour buying the $300,000 machine, because it has a shorter payback. In fact, if the cutoff period is three years, then Lifetime Care would not acquire machine 1, because it fails to meet the payback criterion. Consider next the NPV of the two investment options using Lifetime Care's 8% required rate of return for the X-ray machine investment. At a discount rate of 8%, the NPV of machine 2 is –$42,300 (2.577, the present value annuity factor for three years at 8% from Table 4 × $100,000 = $257,700 – the net initial investment of $300,000). Machine 1, as we know, has a positive NPV of $20,200 (from Exhibit 21-2). The NPV criterion suggests that Lifetime Care should acquire machine 1. Machine 2, with a negative NPV, would fail to meet the NPV criterion. The payback method gives a

[2]Cash savings from the new X-ray machine occur *throughout* the year, but for simplicity in calculating NPV and IRR, we assume they occur at the *end* of each year. A literal interpretation of this assumption would imply a payback of four years because Lifetime Care will only recover its investment when cash inflows occur at the end of the fourth year. The calculations shown in this chapter, however, better approximate Lifetime Care's payback on the basis of uniform cash flows throughout the year.

different answer from the NPV method because the payback method (1) does not consider cash flows after the payback period and (2) does not discount cash flows.

An added problem with the payback method is that choosing too short a cutoff period for project acceptance may promote the selection of only short-lived projects. The organization will tend to reject long-term, positive-NPV projects.

Nonuniform Cash Flows

The payback formula on the preceding page is designed for uniform annual cash inflows. When annual cash inflows are not uniform, the payback computation takes a cumulative form. The years' net cash inflows are accumulated until the amount of the net initial investment has been recovered. Assume that Venture Fund Group is considering purchase of a $1,500 fax machine for electronically transmitting documents to its clients. This machine is expected to produce a total cash savings of $3,200 over the next five years (primarily due to a reduction in the use of express mail services). The cash savings occur evenly throughout each year but nonuniformly across five years, the life of the machine. Payback occurs during the third year:

Year	Cash Savings	Cumulative Cash Savings	Net Initial Investment Yet to Be Recovered at End of Year
0	—	—	$1,500
1	$500	$ 500	1,000
2	600	1,100	400
3	800	1,900	—
4	700	2,600	—
5	600	3,200	—

Straight-line interpolation within the third year, which has cash savings of $800, reveals that the final $400 needed to recover the $1,500 investment (that is, $1,500 − $1,100 recovered by the end of year 2) will be achieved halfway through year 3 (in which $800 of cash savings occur):

$$\text{Payback} = 2 \text{ years} + \left(\frac{\$400}{\$800} \times 1 \text{ year} \right) = 2.5 \text{ years}$$

The fax machine example has a single cash outflow of $1,500 at year 0. Where a project has multiple cash outflows occurring at different points in time, these outflows are added to derive a total cash outflow figure for the project. No adjustment is made for the time value of money when adding these cash outflows in computing the payback period.

ACCRUAL ACCOUNTING RATE-OF-RETURN METHOD

OBJECTIVE 8

Use and evaluate the accrual accounting rate-of-return (AARR) method

Accrual accounting rate of return (AARR) (accounting rate of return, return on investment, ROI). Accounting measure of income divided by an accounting measure of investment.

We now consider a fourth method for analyzing the financial aspects of capital-budgeting projects. The **accrual accounting rate of return (AARR)** is an accounting measure of income divided by an accounting measure of investment. It is also called **accounting rate of return** or *return on investment (ROI)*. We illustrate AARR for the Lifetime Care example using the project's net initial investment as the denominator.

$$\text{AARR} = \frac{\text{Increase in expected average annual operating income}}{\text{Net initial investment}}$$

If Lifetime Care purchases the new X-ray machine, the increase in expected average annual savings in operating costs will be $98,000: This amount is the total operating savings of $490,000 ($100,000 for four years and $90,000 in year 5) ÷ 5. The new machine has a zero terminal disposal price. Straight-line amortization on the new machine is $372,890 ÷ 5 = $74,578. The net initial investment is $379,100. The accrual accounting rate of return is equal to:

International Comparison of Capital Budgeting Methods

What methods do companies around the world use for analyzing capital investment decisions? The percentages in the following table indicate how frequently particular capital budgeting methods are used in eight countries. The reported percentages exceed 100% because many companies surveyed use more than one capital budgeting method.

	Canada*	United States[†]	Australia[‡]	Ireland[§]	Japan[‡]	Scotland[#]	Korea[‖]	South Kingdom[‡]	United Poland**
Payback	50%	59%	61%	84%	52%	78%	75%	76%	48%
IRR	62%	52%	37%	↑ 84% ↓	4%	58%	75%	39%	8%
NPV	41%	28%	45%		6%	48%	60%	38%	23%
AARR	17%	13%	24%	24%	36%	31%	68%	28%	11%
Other	8%	44%	7%	—	5%	—	—	7%	13%

Adapted from: *Jog, V., and A. Srivastava, "Corporate Financial Decision Making in Canada," *Canadian Journal of Administrative Sciences* (June 1994); [†]Smith, K., and C. Sullivan, "Survey of Cost Management Systems in Manufacturing," (Working Paper, Purdue University, West Lafayette, Indiana, 1990); [‡]Blayney, P., and I. Yokoyama, "Comparative Analysis of Japanese and Australian Cost Accounting and Management Practices, " (Working Paper, The University of Sydney, Sydney, Australia, 1991); [§]Clarke, P., "Management Accounting Practices and Techniques in Irish Manufacturing Firms, " (Working Paper, Trinity College, Dublin, Ireland, 1995); [#]Sangster, A., "Capital Investment Appraisal Techniques: A Survey of Current Usage," *Journal of Business Finance & Accounting* (April 1993); [‖]Kim, I., and J. Song, "U.S., Korea, and Japan: Accounting Practices in Three Countries," *Management Accounting* (August 1990); **Zarzecki, D., and T. Wisniewski, "Investment Appraisal Practice in Poland," (Working Paper, Szcecin University, Szcecin, Poland, 1995)

We make several observations:

1. Companies in Canada, the United States, Australia, Ireland, Scotland, South Korea, and the United Kingdom tend to use two methods to evaluate capital investments. (The sum of the capital budgeting percentages in the columns for each of these countries is approximately 200%.)

2. Japanese and Polish companies tend to use only one method. (The sum of the capital budgeting percentages for Japan and Poland is approximately 100%.)

3. The payback method is a very popular method among companies in all countries. Japanese companies and (to a lesser extent) Polish companies use the payback method as the primary method of analysis in their capital budgeting decisions. Companies in Canada, the United States, Australia, Ireland, Scotland, South Korea, and the United Kingdom use the discounted cash flow (DCF) methods, internal rate of return (IRR) and net present value (NPV), extensively.

4. The accrual accounting rate-of-return (AARR) method lags behind DCF methods in Canada, the United States, Australia, Ireland, Scotland, the United Kingdom, and Poland. It is on a par with DCF methods in South Korea, and it is very much preferred to DCF methods in Japan.

$$\text{AARR} = \frac{\$98,000 - \$74,578}{\$379,100} = \frac{\$23,422}{\$379,100} = 6.18\%$$

The AARR method focuses on how investment decisions affect operating income numbers routinely reported by organizations. The AARR of 6.18% indicates the rate at which a dollar of investment generates operating income. Projects whose AARR exceeds an accrual accounting return required for the project are considered desirable. Managers using this method prefer projects with higher, rather than lower, AARR, if all other things are equal.

The AARR method is similar in spirit to the IRR method—both methods calculate a rate-of-return percentage. Whereas the AARR computation calculates return using operating income numbers after considering accruals, the IRR method calculates return on the basis of cash flows and the time value of money. For capital-budgeting decisions, the IRR method is conceptually superior to the AARR method described previously.[3]

The AARR computations are simple and easy to understand, and use routinely maintained accounting numbers. Unlike the payback method, the AARR method considers profitability. Unlike the NPV and IRR methods, however, the AARR focuses on operating income effects and hence considers accruals. It does not track cash flows and ignores the time value of money. Critics cite these arguments as major drawbacks of the AARR computations.

COMPLEXITIES IN CAPITAL BUDGETING APPLICATIONS

In this section, we consider some challenging aspects of predicting outcomes in the information-acquisition stage and of choosing projects in the selection stage.

Consider a firm deciding whether to invest in computer-integrated manufacturing (CIM) technology. In CIM plants, computers give instructions that automatically set up and run equipment. Computers monitor the product and directly control the process to ensure defect-free, high-quality output. Applying CIM to its full extent can result in a highly automated plant, where the role of manufacturing labour is largely restricted to computer programming, engineering support, and maintenance of the robotic machinery. The amounts at stake in CIM decisions can be huge—in the billions of dollars for such companies as General Motors and Toyota. Two important factors when evaluating CIM investments are (1) predicting the full set of benefits and costs and (2) recognizing the full time horizon of the project.

OBJECTIVE 9

Recognize the impact of nonfinancial and qualitative factors in capital budgeting decisions

Predicting the Full Set of Benefits and Costs

The factors that companies consider in making CIM decisions are far broader than costs alone. For example, the reasons for introducing CIM technology—faster response time, higher product quality, and greater flexibility in meeting changes in customer preferences—are often to increase revenues and contribution margins. Ignoring the revenue effects underestimates the financial benefits of CIM investments. As we describe below, however, the revenue benefits of technology investments are often difficult to quantify in financial terms. Nevertheless, competitive and revenue advantages are important managerial considerations when introducing CIM.

Exhibit 21-6 presents examples of the broader set of factors that companies in the United States, Australia, Japan, and the United Kingdom weigh in evaluating CIM technology. The benefits include:

1. **Faster response to market changes.** An automated plant can, for example, make major design modifications (such as switching from a two-door to a four-door car) relatively quickly. To quantify this benefit requires some notion of consumer demand changes that may occur many years in the future and of the manufacturing technology choices made by competitors.

2. **Increased worker knowledge of automation.** If workers have a positive experience with CIM, the company can implement other automation projects more quickly and more successfully. Quantifying this benefit requires a prediction of the company's subsequent automation plans. Survey evidence emphasizes the importance of linking CIM decisions to a company's overall competitive strategies.

---

[3]Note that if amortization is calculated as economic amortization (the decline in the present value of future cash flows) under the AARR method, and if operating income and investment are adjusted each year for this amortization, the AARR each year will equal the project's IRR. In practice, however, the book amortization and investment value used in AARR computations are not calculated in this way.

EXHIBIT 21-6
Factors Considered in Making Capital Budgeting Decisions for CIM Projects

Examples of Financial Outcomes	Examples of Nonfinancial and Qualitative Outcomes
Lower direct labour costs	Reduction in manufacturing cycle time
Lower hourly support labour costs	Increase in manufacturing flexibility
Less scrap and rework	Increase in business risk due to higher fixed cost structure
Lower inventory costs	Improved product delivery and service
Increase in software and related costs	Reduction in product development time
Costs of retraining personnel	Faster response to market changes
	Increased learning by workers about automation
	Improved competitive position in the industry

Predicting the full set of costs also presents problems. Three classes of costs are difficult to measure and are often underestimated:

1. Costs associated with a reduced competitive position in the industry. If other companies in the industry are investing in CIM, a company not investing in CIM will probably suffer a decline in market share because of its inferior quality and slower delivery performance. Several companies in the machine tool industry that continued to use a conventional manufacturing approach experienced rapid drops in market share after their competitors introduced CIM.

2. Costs of retraining the operating and maintenance personnel to handle the automated facilities.

3. Costs of developing and maintaining the software and maintenance programs to operate the automated manufacturing activities.

Recognizing the Full Time Horizon of the Project

The time horizon of CIM projects can stretch well beyond ten years. Many of the costs are incurred and are highly visible in the early years of adopting CIM. In contrast, important benefits may not be realized until many years after the adoption of CIM. A long time horizon should be considered when evaluating CIM investments.

Difficulties in predicting the full set of benefits and costs and long time horizons also arise in other investment decisions—for example, R&D projects and oil exploration.

Performance Evaluation and the Selection of Projects

The use of the accrual accounting rate of return for evaluating performance can often deter a manager from using DCF methods for capital budgeting decisions. Consider Peter Costner, the manager of the X-Ray Department at Lifetime Care Hospital. The NPV method for capital budgeting indicates that Peter should purchase the new X-ray machine, since it has a positive NPV of $20,200.

Suppose top management of Lifetime Care uses the AARR for judging the X-Ray Department's performance. Peter Costner may consider not purchasing the new X-ray machine if the AARR of 6.18% on the investment reduces his overall AARR and so negatively affects his department's performance. The AARR on the new X-ray machine is low because the investment increases the denominator and, as a result of amortization, also reduces the numerator (operating income) in the AARR computation.

Obviously, there is an inconsistency between citing DCF methods as being best for capital budgeting decisions and then using a different method to evaluate subsequent performance. As long as such practice continues, managers will be tempted to make capital budgeting choices on the basis of accrual accounting rates of return, even though such choices are not in the best interests of the organization. Such temptations become more pronounced if managers are frequently transferred (or

OBJECTIVE 10

Identify and reduce conflicts in using DCF for capital budgeting and accrual accounting for performance evaluation

Integrating Environmental Costs and Capital Budgeting at Niagara Mohawk and Ontario Hydro

Ontario Hydro
www.hydro.on.ca

Niagara Mohawk
www.nimo.com

Environmental laws seek to reduce the quantity and toxicity of pollution and impose penalties and fines for violating environmental standards. Capital investment decisions can significantly impact pollution and the environment. The key question is how the environmental effects of alternative pieces of equipment should be factored into capital budgeting choices.

Some environmental costs are easy to determine—for example, *prevention* or *compliance costs,* the costs incurred to install, operate, and maintain equipment and to train personnel to prevent pollution from occurring, and *appraisal costs,* the costs incurred to monitor and test for pollution and to report emission levels to government agencies. Other costs such as *failure costs* (the costs of environmental damage) are difficult to assess beyond the obvious penalties and fines for failing to comply with environmental laws. For example, what are the costs that a company should consider for human health problems, animal herd losses, crop damage, and customer backlash from toxic air and water emissions?

Niagara Mohawk and Ontario Hydro have taken two different, equally innovative approaches to integrating environmental costs and capital budgeting. Niagara Mohawk considers environmental costs to equal the costs that need to be incurred to prevent any pollution from occurring. Niagara Mohawk thereby avoids the problem of determining the difficult-to-compute costs of environmental damage. The logic of this argument is that the costs of completely preventing pollution are a reasonable substitute for damage costs.

Ontario Hydro focusses on developing realistic estimates of the costs of environmental damage despite the associated uncertainties. Ontario Hydro uses innovative methods that consider (1) the decline in market prices of crops that have been damaged or lost due to toxic emissions, (2) estimates of differences in real estate values or wage rates resulting from environmental pollution, and (3) survey responses about willingness-to-pay from "perpetrators" and willingness-to-accept from "victims" of environmental damage. Ontario Hydro requires capital budgeting proposals to consider expected damage to ecosystems, communities, and human health, and not just the fact that it meets existing or proposed environmental regulations.

The Niagara Mohawk and Ontario Hydro examples highlight the importance and difficulties of acquiring information that would allow companies to integrate environmental impacts into capital budgeting decisions more thoroughly. Without these approaches, companies cannot include environmental impacts as part of the formal analysis. They would then have to consider environmental pollution as a qualitative factor outside the financial analysis, making it more difficult to understand financial and environmental tradeoffs.

Source: Adapted from M. Epstein, *Measures for Corporate Environmental Performance* (Chicago: Irwin, 1995).

promoted), or if annual operating income is important in their evaluations and their compensation plans. Why? Because the manager's performance is being evaluated over short time horizons. The manager has no motivation to use a DCF model to take into account cash flows that will occur in the distant future. Those cash flows will not influence the manager's performance evaluation.

MANAGING THE PROJECT

This section discusses stage 6 of capital budgeting, which deals with implementation and control. Two different aspects of management control are discussed—management control of the investment activity itself and management control of the project as a whole.

Management Control of the Investment Activity

Some initial investments such as purchasing an X-ray or fax machine are relatively easy to implement. Other initial investments such as building shopping malls or new manufacturing plants are more complex and take more time. In the latter case, monitoring and controlling the investment schedules and budgets is critical to the success of the overall project. The appendix to this chapter describes methods used to control the investment activity itself.

Management Control of the Project—Postinvestment Audit

A postinvestment audit compares the predictions of investment costs and outcomes made at the time a project was selected to the actual results. It provides management with feedback about their performance. Suppose, for example, that actual outcomes (operating cash savings from the new X-ray machine in the Lifetime Care example) are much lower than predicted outcomes. Management must then investigate whether this occurred because the original estimates were overly optimistic or because there were problems in implementing the project. Both types of problems are a concern.

Optimistic estimates are a concern because they may result in the acceptance of a project that would otherwise have been rejected. To discourage optimistic estimates, companies such as DuPont maintain records comparing actual performance to the estimates made by individual managers when seeking approval for capital investments. DuPont believes that postinvestment audits discourage managers from making unrealistic forecasts. Problems in implementing a project are an obvious concern because the returns from the project will not meet expectations. Postinvestment audits can point to areas requiring corrective action.

Care should be exercised when performing a postinvestment audit. It should be done only after project outcomes have stabilized. Doing the audit early may give a misleading picture. Obtaining actual data to compare against estimates is often not easy. For example, actual labour cost savings from the new X-ray machine may not be comparable to the estimated savings, because the actual number and types of X-rays taken may be different from the quantities assumed during the capital budgeting process. Other benefits, such as the impact on patient treatment, may be difficult to quantify.

PROBLEM FOR SELF-STUDY

PROBLEM

Let us revisit the Lifetime Care X-ray machine project. Assume that the expected annual cash inflows are $130,000 instead of $100,000. All other facts are unchanged: a $379,100 net initial investment, a five-year useful life, a zero terminal disposal price, and an 8% required rate of return. Year 5 cash inflows include $10,000 recovery of working capital. When calculating breakeven time, assume that the investment in the X-ray machine will occur immediately after management approves the project. Compute the following:

1. Discounted cash flow
   a. Net present value
   b. Internal rate of return
2. Payback period
3. Accrual accounting rate of return on net initial investment
4. Breakeven time

Assume (for calculation purposes) that cash outflows and cash inflows occur at the end of each period.

SOLUTION

1. a. $NPV = (\$130,000 \times 3.993) - \$379,100$
$= \$519,090 - \$379,100 = \$139,990$

b. There are several approaches to computing the IRR. One is to use a calculator with an IRR function; this gives an IRR of 21.18%. An alternative approach is to use Table 4 in Appendix B:

$$\$379,100 = \$130,000F$$

$$F = \frac{\$379,100}{130,000} = 2.916$$

On the five-period line of Table 4, the column closest to 2.916 is 22%. To obtain a more accurate number, straight-line interpolation can be used:

	Present Value	Factors
20%	2.991	2.991
IRR	—	2.916
22%	2.864	—
Difference	0.127	0.075

$$IRR = 20\% + \frac{0.075}{0.127}(2\%) = 21.18\%$$

2. $\text{Payback} = \dfrac{\text{Net initial investment}}{\text{Uniform increase in annual cash flows}}$

$$= \$379,100 \div \$130,000 = 2.92 \text{ years}$$

3. $\qquad AARR = \dfrac{\text{Increase in expected average annual operating income}}{\text{Net initial investment}}$

$\text{Increase in expected average annual operating savings} = [(\$130,000 \times 4) + \$120,000] \div 5$

$$= \$128,000$$

$\text{Average annual amortization} = \$372,890 \div 5 = \$74,578$

$\text{Increase in expected average annual operating income} = \$128,000 - \$74,578 = \$53,422$

$$AARR = \frac{\$53,422}{\$379,100} = 14.09\%$$

4. Breakeven time computations are as follows:

Year	PV Discount Factor at 14% (1)	Investment Cash Outflows (2)	PV of Investment Cash Outflows* (3) = (1) × (2)	Cumulative PV of Investment Cash Outflows* (4)	Cash Inflows (5)	PV of Cash Inflows* (6) = (1) × (5)	Cumulative PV of Cash Inflows* (7)
0	1.000	\$379,100	\$379,100	\$379,100			
1	0.926				\$130,000	\$120,380	\$120,380
2	0.857				130,000	111,410	231,790
3	0.794				130,000	103,220	335,010
4	0.735				130,000	95,550	430,560
5	0.681				130,000	88,530	519,090

*At year 0.

$$BET = 3 \text{ years} + \frac{\$379,100 - \$335,010}{95,550}$$

$$= 3 \text{ years} + \frac{44,090}{95,550} = 3.46 \text{ years}$$

The following points are linked to the chapter's learning objectives.

1. Capital budgeting is long-term planning for proposed capital projects. The life of a project is usually longer than one year, so capital budgeting decisions consider revenues and costs over relatively long periods. In contrast, accrual accounting measures income on a year-by-year basis.

2. The time value of money takes into account this fact: a dollar received today can be invested to start earning a return (for example, interest), so it is worth more than a dollar received tomorrow. The time value of money is the opportunity cost (return forgone) from not having the money today.

3. Capital budgeting is a six-stage process: (a) the identification stage, (b) the search stage, (c) the information-acquisition stage, (d) the selection stage, (e) the financing stage, and (f) the implementation and control stage.

4. Discounted cash flow (DCF) methods explicitly include all project cash flows and the time value of money in capital budgeting decisions. Two DCF methods are the net present value (NPV) method and the internal rate-of-return (IRR) method. The NPV method calculates the expected net monetary gain or loss from a project by discounting all expected future cash inflows and outflows to the present point in time, using the required rate of return. A project is acceptable if it has a positive NPV. The IRR method computes the rate of return (discount rate) at which the present value of expected cash inflows from a project equals the present value of expected cash outflows from a project. A project is acceptable if its IRR exceeds the required rate of return.

5. The NPV method has two advantages over the IRR method: (a) NPVs of individual projects can be added together to obtain a valid estimate of accepting a combination of projects and (b) the NPV method accommodates different required rates of return across different years of the project.

6. Relevant cash inflows and outflows are expected future cash flows that differ between the alternatives. Only cash inflows and outflows matter. Accrual accounting concepts such as accrued revenues and accrued expenses are irrelevant for the discounted cash flow methods.

7. The payback method measures the time it will take to recoup, in the form of cash inflows, the total amount invested in a project. The payback method neglects profitability and the time value of money.

8. The accrual accounting rate of return (AARR) is operating income divided by a measure of investment. The AARR considers profitability but ignores the time value of money.

9. Nonfinancial and qualitative factors, such as the effects of investment decisions on employee learning and on the company's ability to respond faster to market changes, are often not explicitly considered in capital budgeting decisions. However, nonfinancial and qualitative factors can be extremely important. In making decisions, managers must at times give more weight to nonfinancial and qualitative factors than to financial factors.

10. The widespread use of accrual accounting for evaluating the performance of a manager or division impedes the adoption of DCF methods in capital budgeting. Frequently, the optimal decision made using a DCF method will not report good "operating income" results in the project's early years on the basis of accrual accounting methods, so managers are tempted to ignore DCF methods even though the decisions that stem from them would be optimal for the company over the long run.

This chapter contains definitions of the following important terms:

accounting rate of return (p. 738)

accrual accounting rate of return (AARR) (p. 738)

capital budgeting (p. 726)

discount rate (p. 729)

discounted cash flow (DCF) (p. 729)

hurdle rate (p. 729)

internal rate of return (IRR) (p. 731)

investment projects (p. 726)

investment programs (p. 726)

net present value (NPV) method (p. 729)

opportunity cost of capital (p. 729)

payback method (p. 736)

required rate of return (RRR) (p. 729)

time-adjusted rate of return (p. 731)

QUESTIONS

21-1 "Capital budgeting has the same focus as accrual accounting." Do you agree? Explain.

21-2 List and briefly describe each of the six stages in capital budgeting.

21-3 What is the essence of the discounted cash flow method?

21-4 "Only quantitative outcomes are relevant in capital budgeting analyses." Do you agree? Explain.

21-5 How can sensitivity analysis be incorporated in DCF analysis?

21-6 What is the payback method? What are its main strengths and weaknesses?

21-7 Describe the accrual accounting rate-of-return method. What are its main strengths and weaknesses?

21-8 "The trouble with discounted cash flow techniques is that they ignore amortization costs." Do you agree? Explain.

21-9 "Let's be more practical. DCF is not the gospel. Managers should not become so enchanted with DCF that strategic considerations are overlooked." Do you agree? Explain.

21-10 "The net present value method is the preferred method for capital budgeting decisions. Therefore, managers will always use it." Do you agree? Explain.

21-11 "All overhead costs are relevant in NPV analysis." Do you agree? Explain.

21-12 "Managers' control of job projects generally focuses on four critical success factors." Identify those factors.

21-13 Bill Watts, president of Western Publications, accepts a capital-budgeting project advocated by Division X. This is the division in which the president spent his first 10 years with the company. On the same day, the president rejects a capital-budgeting project proposal from Division Y. The manger of Division Y is incensed. She believes that the Division Y project has an internal rate of return at least 10 percentage points above the Division X project. She comments, "What is the point of all our detailed DCF analysis? If Watts is panting over a project, he can arrange to have the proponents of that project massage the numbers so that it looks like a winner." What advice would you give the manager of Division Y?

EXERCISES

Throughout the assignment material, ignore the effects of income taxes.

21-14 **Exercises in compound interest.** To be sure that you understand how to use the tables in Appendix B at the end of this book, solve the following exercises. Ignore income tax considerations. (The correct answers, rounded to the nearest dollar, appear on pp. 757–758.)

1. You have just won $5,000. How much money will you have at the end of ten years if you invest it at 6% compounded annually? At 14%?
2. Ten years from now, the unpaid principal of the mortgage on your house will be $89,550. How much do you have to invest today at 6% interest compounded annually to accumulate the $89,550 in ten years?
3. If the unpaid mortgage on your house in ten years will be $89,550, how much money do you have to invest annually at 6% to have exactly this amount on hand at the end of the tenth year?
4. You plan to save $5,000 of your earnings at the end of each year for the next ten years. How much money will you have at the end of the tenth year if you invest your savings compounded at 12% per year?
5. You have just turned 65, and an endowment insurance policy has paid you a lump sum of $200,000. If you invest the sum at 6%, how much money can you withdraw from your account in equal amounts each year so that at the end of ten years (age 75) there will be nothing left?
6. You have estimated that for the first ten years after you retire you will need an annual cash inflow of $50,000. How much money must you invest at 6% at your retirement age to obtain this annual cash inflow? At 20%?
7. The following table shows two schedules of prospective operating cash inflows, each of which requires the same net initial investment of $10,000 now:

| | Annual Cash Inflows | |
Year	Plan A	Plan B
1	$ 1,000	$ 5,000
2	2,000	4,000
3	3,000	3,000
4	4,000	2,000
5	5,000	1,000
Total	$15,000	$15,000

The required rate of return is 6% compounded annually. All cash inflows occur at the end of each year. In terms of net present value, which plan is more desirable? Show your computations.

21-15 Comparison of approaches to capital budgeting. The Building Distributors Group is thinking of buying, at a cost of $220,000, some new packaging equipment that is expected to save $50,000 in cash operating costs per year. Its estimated useful life is ten years, and it will have zero terminal disposal price. The required rate of return is 16%.

REQUIRED
1. Compute the payback period.
2. Compute the net present value.
3. Compute the internal rate of return.
4. Compute the accrual accounting rate of return based on net initial investment. Assume straight-line amortization.

21-16 Comparison of approaches to capital budgeting. City Hospital, a nontaxable institution, estimates that it can save $28,000 a year in cash operating costs for the next ten years if it buys a special-purpose machine at a cost of $110,000. A zero terminal disposal price is expected. City Hospital's required rate of return is 14%.

REQUIRED
1. Compute the payback period.
2. Compute the net present value.
3. Compute the internal rate of return.
4. Compute the accrual accounting rate of return based on net initial investment. Assume straight-line amortization.

21-17 Capital budgeting with uneven cash flows. Eastern Cola is considering the purchase of a special-purpose bottling machine for $28,000. It is expected to have a useful life of seven years with a zero terminal disposal price. The plant manager estimates the following savings in cash operating costs:

Year	Amount
1	$10,000
2	8,000
3	6,000
4	5,000
5	4,000
6	3,000
7	3,000
Total	$39,000

Eastern Cola uses a required rate of return of 16% in its capital budgeting decisions.

REQUIRED

1. Compute the payback period.
2. Compute the net present value.
3. Compute the internal rate of return.
4. Compute the accrual accounting rate of return based on net initial investment. Assume straight-line amortization. Use the average annual savings in cash operating costs when computing the numerator of the accrual accounting rate of return.

21-18 Net present value, internal rate of return, sensitivity analysis. The Johnson Corporation is planning to buy equipment costing $120,000 to improve its materials-handling system. The equipment is expected to save $40,000 in cash operating costs per year. Its estimated useful life is six years, and it will have zero terminal disposal price. The required rate of return is 14%.

REQUIRED

1. Compute the net present value. Compute the internal rate of return.
2. What is the minimum annual cash savings that will make the equipment desirable on a net present value basis?
3. When might a manager calculate the minimum annual cash savings described in requirement 2 rather than use the $40,000 savings in cash operating costs per year to calculate the net present value or internal rate of return?

21-19 Comparison of projects, no income taxes. (CMA adapted) Fox Valley Healthcare Inc. is a not-for-profit organization that operates eight nursing homes and ten assisted living facilities. The company has grown considerably over the last three years and expects to continue to expand in the years ahead, particularly in the area of assisted living facilities for seniors.

Jim Ruffalo, president of Fox Valley, has developed a plan to add a new building for top management and the administrative staff. He has selected a building contractor. Vukacek Construction Co., and has reached agreement on the building and its construction. Vukacek is ready to start as soon as the contrast is signed and will complete the work in two years.

The building contractor has offered Fox Valley a choice of three payment plans as follows:

Plan I
Payment of $200,000 on the signing of the contract and $3,000,000 at the time of completion.

Plan II
Payment of $1,000,000 on the signing of the contract and $1,000,000 at the end of each of the two succeeding years. The end of the second year is the completion date.

Plan III
Payment of $100,000 on the signing of the contract and $1,000,000 at the end of each of the three succeeding years.

Ruffalo is not sure which payment plan he should accept. He has asked the treasurer, Lisa Monroe, for her assessment and advice. Fox Valley will finance the construction with a long-term loan and has a borrowing rate of 12%.

REQUIRED

1. Using the net present value method, calculate the comparative cost of each of the three payment plans being considered by Fox Valley Healthcare Inc.
2. Which payment plan should the treasurer recommend? Explain.

3. Discuss the financial factors, other than the cost of the plan, that should be considered in selecting an appropriate payment plan.

21-20 Payback and NPV methods, no income taxes. (CMA adapted) Cording Manufacturing is a small company that is currently analyzing capital expenditure proposals for the purchase of equipment. The capital budget is limited to $500,000, which Cording believes is the maximum capital it can raise.

Richard King, an outside financial advisor, is preparing an analysis of four projects that Walter Minden, Cording's president, is considering. King has projected the future cash flows for each potential purchase. The information concerning the four projects is given below.

	Project A	Project B	Project C	Project D
Projected cash outflow				
Net initial investment	$200,000	$190,000	$250,000	$210,000
Projected cash inflows				
Year 1	$50,000	$40,000	$75,000	$75,000
2	50,000	50,000	75,000	75,000
3	50,000	70,000	60,000	60,000
4	50,000	75,000	80,000	40,000
5	50,000	75,000	100,000	20,000

REQUIRED

1. Since Cording Manufacturing's cash is limited, Walter Minden thinks that the payback method of calculating investments would be the best method for choosing capital-budgeting projects.
  a. Explain what the payback method measures and how it is used. Include in your explanation several benefits and limitations of the payback method.
  b. Calculate the payback period for each of the four projects. Ignore income tax considerations.
2. King would like to compare the projects using the net present value method. The required rate of return for Cording is 12%. All cash flows occur at the end of the year. Calculate the net present value for each project. Ignore income tax considerations.
3. Which projects, if any would you recommend funding? Briefly state your reasons why.

21-21 Equipment replacement, net present value, relevant costs, payback. Monterey Corporation is a distributor of electronic measurement instruments. It is considering replacing one of its distribution trucks that it had purchased for $54,000 two years ago. The truck has a current book value of $38,000 and a remaining useful life of four years. Its current disposal price is $26,000; in four years its terminal disposal price is expected to be $6,000. The annual cash operating costs of the truck are expected to be $35,000 for each of the next three years and $40,000 in year 4.

Monterey is considering the purchase of a new truck for $56,000. Annual cash operating costs for the new truck are expected to be $25,000. The new truck has a useful life of four years and a terminal disposal price of $8,000.

Monterey Corporation amortizes all its trucks using straight-line amortization calculated on the difference between the initial cost and the terminal disposal price divided by the estimated useful life. Monterey uses a rate of return of 14% in its capital budgeting decisions.

REQUIRED

1. Using a net present value criterion, should Monterey Corporation purchase the new truck?
2. Compute the payback period for Monterey Corporation if it purchases the new truck.

21-22 DCF, accrual accounting rate of return, working capital, evaluation of performance. The Hammerlink Company has been offered a special-purpose metal-cutting machine for $110,000. The machine is expected to have a useful life of eight years with a terminal disposal price of $30,000. Savings in cash operating costs are expected to be $25,000 per year. However, additional working capital is needed to keep the machine running efficiently and without stoppages. Working capital includes such items as filters, lubricants, bearings, abrasives, flexible exhaust pipes, and belts. These items must continually be replaced so that an investment of $8,000 must be maintained in them at all times, but this investment is fully recoverable (will be "cashed in") at the end of the useful life. Hammerlink's required rate of return is 14%.

REQUIRED

1. **a.** Compute the net present value.
   b. Compute the internal rate of return.
2. Compute the accrual accounting rate of return based on the net initial investment. Assume straight-line amortization.
3. You have the authority to make the purchase decision. Why might you be reluctant to base your decision on the DCF model?

PROBLEMS

21-23 Equipment replacement, relevant costs, sensitivity analysis. A toy manufacturer that specializes in making fad items has just developed a $50,000 molding machine for producing a special toy. The machine has been used to produce only one unit so far. The company will amortize the $50,000 initial machine investment evenly over four years, after which production of the toy will be stopped. The company's expected annual costs will be direct materials, $10,000; direct manufacturing labour, $20,000; and variable manufacturing overhead, $15,000. Variable manufacturing overhead varies with direct manufacturing labour costs. Fixed manufacturing overhead, exclusive of amortization, is $7,500 annually, and fixed marketing and administrative costs are $12,000 annually.

Suddenly a machine salesperson appears. He has a new machine that is ideally suited for producing this toy. His automatic machine is distinctly superior. It reduces the cost of direct materials by 10% and produces twice as many units per hour. It will cost $44,000 and will have a zero terminal disposal price at the end of four years.

Production and sales of 25,000 units per year (sales of $100,000) will be the same whether the company uses the old machine or the new machine. The current disposal price of the toy company's molding machine is $5,000. Its terminal disposal price in four years will be $2,600.

REQUIRED

1. Assume that the required rate of return is 18%. Using the net present value method, show whether the new machine should be purchased. What is the role of the book value of the old machine in the analysis?
2. What is the payback period for the new machine?
3. As the manager who developed the $50,000 old molding machine, you are trying to justify not buying the new $44,000 machine. You question the accuracy of the expected cash operating savings. By how much must these cash savings fall before the point of indifference—the point where the net present value of investing in the new machine—reaches zero?

21-24 Payback, net present value, relevant costs, sensitivity analysis. The city of Edmonton has been operating a cafeteria for its employees, but it is considering converting to a completely automated set of vending machines. If the change is made, the old equipment would be sold now for whatever cash it might bring.

The vending machines would be purchased immediately for cash. A catering firm would take complete responsibility for servicing and replenishing the vending machines and would pay the city a predetermined percentage of the gross vending receipts.

The present cafeteria equipment has ten years of remaining useful life. The new vending machines have a ten-year useful life. The following data are available (in thousands):

Cafeteria cash revenues per year	$120
Cafeteria cash costs per year	$124
Present cafeteria equipment:	
Net book value	$84
Annual amortization cost	$6
Current disposal price	$4
Terminal disposal price (10 years from now)	$0

New vending machines:

Initial machine investment	$64
Terminal disposal price	$5
Expected annual gross receipts	$80
City's percentage share of receipts	10%
Expected annual cash costs (negligible)	

Present values at 14%:

$1 due in 10 years	$0.27
Annuity of $1 a year for 10 years	$5.20

The city of Edmonton has a 14% required rate of return.

REQUIRED

Compute the following for the vending machine investment:

1. Expected increase in net annual operating cash inflows as a result of investing in the vending machines
2. Payback period
3. Net present value
4. Point of indifference (zero NPV) in terms of annual gross vending machine receipts

21-25 DCF, sensitivity analysis, no income taxes. (CMA adapted) Bristol Engineering Inc. manufacturing electronic components for the automotive and computer industries, as well as producing a variety of small electronic appliances and computer industries, as well as producing a variety of small electronic appliances that are distributed through wholesalers. The company's Research and Development Department has developed an electronic device that management believes could be modified and marketed as an electronic game.

The following information for the new product was developed from the best estimates for the marketing and production managers.

Annual sales volume	1,000,000 units
Selling price	$10 per unit
Cash variable costs	$4 per unit
Cash fixed costs	$2,000,000 per year
Investment required	$12,000,000
Project life	5 years

At the end of the five-year useful life there will be a zero terminal disposal price.

Bristol Engineering uses discounted cash-flow analysis in its decision making. Its required rate of return on this project is 14%.

The toy and game industry is a new market for Bristol Engineering, and management is concerned about the reliability of the estimates. The controller has proposed applying sensitivity analysis to selected factors, and is investigating some alternatives. Ignore income taxes in your calculations.

REQUIRED

1. What is the net present value of this investment proposal?
2. What is the effect on the net present value of the following three changes in assumptions? Treat each item independently of the others.
   a. 10% reduction in the selling price.
   b. 10% reduction in annual sales in units.
   c. 10% reduction in the variable cost per unit.
3. Discuss how management would use the data developed in requirements 1 and 2 in its consideration of the proposed capital investment.

21-26 NPV and Customer profitability, no income taxes. Christen Granite sells granite counter tops to the construction industry. Christen Granite has three customers— Homebuilders, a small construction company that builds private luxury homes; Kitchen Constructors, a company that designs and builds kitchens for hospitals and hotels; and Subdivision Erectors, a construction company that builds large subdivisions in major metro suburbs. Following are Christen Granite's revenue and cost data by customer for the year ended December 31, 2000.

	Homebuilders	Kitchen Constructors	Subdivision Erectors
Revenues	$45,000	$325,000	$860,000
Cost of goods sold	22,000	180,000	550,000
Operating costs	10,000	75,000	235,000

Operating costs include order processing, sales visits, delivery and special delivery costs. Christen estimates that revenue and costs will increase as follows on an annual basis:

	Homebuilders	Kitchen Constructors	Subdivision Erectors
Revenues	5%	15%	8%
Cost of goods sold	4%	4%	4%
Operating costs	4%	4%	4%

Christen Granite's required rate of return is 10%. Assume that (a) all transactions occur at end-of-period, (b) all revenues are cash inflows, and (c) all costs are cash outflows. Ignore income tax considerations in your analysis.

REQUIRED

1. Calculate operating income per customer for 2000 and for each year of the 2001–2005 period.
2. Christen estimates the value of each customer by calculating the customer's projected NPV over the next five years (2001–2005). Use the operating incomes calculated above to compute the value of all three customers.
3. Recently, Kitchen Construction (KC), Christen's most valuable customer, has been threatening to leave. Lawson Tops, Christen's fiercest competitor, has offered KC a greater discount. KC demands a 20% discount from Christen if the latter wants to keep his business. Should Christen grant KC the 20% discount. What is the five-year value of KC after incorporating the 20% discount? What other factors should Christen consider before making his final decision?
4. What are the possible adverse effects of caving in to KC's pressure?

21-27 Relevant costs, replacement decisions performance evaluation. George Handley, the general manager of the Coronado Company, is contemplating replacing the existing assembly-line equipment in the Assembly Department with automated assembly equipment. Production output and revenues will be unaffected by the replacement decision. Transactions related to the capital investment are cash transactions that would occur today.

	Existing Assembly Equipment	New Automated Assembly Equipment
Original cost	$1,100,000	$1,200,000
Useful life	11 years	5 years
Current age	6 years	0 years
Useful life remaining	5 years	5 years
Accumulated amortization	$600,000	$0
Book value	$530,000	Not acquired yet
Current disposal price (in cash)	$200,000	Not acquired yet
Terminal disposal price (in cash, in 5 years)	$0	$0
Average working capital needed	$120,000	$70,000

Current annual Assembly Department costs are as follows:

Direct materials	$ 600,000
Direct manufacturing labour	400,000
Amortization	100,000
Maintenance and repairs	150,000
Other operating costs	50,000
Supervision (allocated as 10% of direct manufacturing labour costs)	40,000
Allocated rent (based on space used)	40,000
Allocated corporate overhead (based on direct manufacturing labour costs)	120,000
Total	$1,500,000

ADDITIONAL INFORMATION

a. Coronado uses straight-line amortization calculated on the difference between the initial equipment investment and the terminal disposal price of the equipment.

b. The new equipment will produce output more swiftly. Therefore, the average working capital investment, if the new equipment is purchased, will decrease.

c. Of the total direct materials costs, $120,000 is waste and scrap. The new equipment is expected to reduce scrap costs to $20,000.

d. The new equipment is expected to reduce direct manufacturing labour costs by $150,000 each year.

e. Maintenance and repairs on the old equipment have been excessive. If the new equipment is acquired, maintenance and repair costs are expected to decrease to $100,000.

f. Coronado collects all supervision costs for all manufacturing departments in the plant into one cost pool. These costs are then allocated to departments on the basis of direct manufacturing labour costs. The Assembly Department has only one supervisor currently. The supervisor will continue in her current position if the new equipment is purchased.

g. The new equipment will reduce the space required for assembly operations by 20%, reducing allocated rent by $8,000. The Coronado Company has no alternative uses for this extra space.

h. Corporate overhead costs are allocated to each department at 30% of direct manufacturing labour costs of each department.

Handley estimates a required rate of return of 12% for this project.

REQUIRED

1. On the basis of the net present value method, should Handley replace the existing assembly equipment?

2. Suppose that next year is the last year Coronado will offer the attractive bonus plan currently in place. Handley's bonus hinges on short-run accrual accounting income for that year. Will Handley be inclined to replace the Assembly Department equipment? Provide quantitative support for your answer.

3. What nonfinancial and qualitative factors should Handley consider in coming to a decision?

21-28 Special order, relevant costs, capital budgeting. (A. Spero, adapted) Toys, Inc. sells neon-coated Nightglow cars to several local toy stores. It has the capacity to make 250,000 of these units per year, but during the year ending December 31, 2000, it made and sold 130,000 cars to its existing customers. It makes these cars by dipping its highly unsuccessful Gander model plastic toy cars into a vat of neon paint. It originally purchased 780,000 of the Ganders but has been unable to sell them as Ganders. These plastic cars originally cost $20 per unit, and 650,000 of them remain in inventory.

Toys' accountant has prepared the following cost sheet per Nightglow car:

Selling price per car		$59
Manufacturing costs per car:		
Direct materials:		
Plastic cars	$20	
Neon paint	6	
Boxes	3	29
Direct manufacturing labour		8
Vat amortization		10
Allocated plant manager's salary		5
Manufacturing costs per car		52
Gross margin per car		7
Marketing costs per car ($2 of which is variable)		6
Operating margin per car		$ 1

On December 31, 2000, the Tiny Tot chain asked Toys, Inc. to provide 100,000 Nightglow cars at a special price of $50 per car. Toys, Inc. will not need to incur any marketing cost for the Tiny Tot sale.

Toys, Inc. expected to sell the Nightglow cars to its existing customers for the next four years at the current level of demand of 130,000 units per year and none thereafter. At the end of four years, Toys, Inc. will dispose of the vat and whatever cars remain at zero net disposal price. If Toys accepts the Tiny Tot order, it is certain that its other customers will refuse to pay the current price of $59 and will demand a discount. Toys estimates a required rate of return of 16%.

REQUIRED

1. Should Toys accept the special order if it must also offer the same price of $50 to its existing customers for the next four years?
2. Suppose Toys is uncertain about the discount the existing customers would demand. Determine the price that Toys, Inc. would have to offer its existing customers for the next four years to be indifferent between accepting and rejecting Tiny Tot's special order.

21-29 Relevant costs, outsourcing, capital budgeting. The Strubel Company currently makes as many units of Part No. 789 as it needs. David Lin, general manager of the Strubel Company, has received a bid from the Gabriella Company for making Part No. 789. Current plans call for Gabriella to supply 1,000 units of Part No. 789 per year at $50 a unit. Gabriella can begin supplying on January 1, 2000, and continue for five years, after which time Strubel will not need the part. Gabriella can accommodate any change in Strubel's demand for the part and will supply it for $50 a unit, regardless of quantity.

Jack Tyson, the controller of the Strubel Company, reports the following costs for manufacturing 1,000 units of Part No. 789:

Direct materials	$22,000
Direct manufacturing labour	11,000
Variable manufacturing overhead	7,000
Amortization on machine	10,000
Product and process engineering	4,000
Rent	2,000
Allocation of general plant overhead costs	5,000
Total costs	$61,000

The following additional information is available:

a. Part No. 789 is made on a machine used exclusively for the manufacture of Part No. 789. The machine was acquired on January 1, 1999, at a cost of $60,000. The machine has a useful life of six years and zero terminal disposal price. Amortization is calculated on the straight-line method.

b. The machine could be sold today for $15,000.

c. Product and process engineering costs are incurred to ensure that the manufacturing process for Part No. 789 works smoothly. Although these costs are fixed in the short run, with respect to units of Part No. 789 produced, they can be saved in the long run if this part is no longer produced. If Part No. 789 is outsourced, product and process engineering costs of $4,000 will be incurred for 2000 but not thereafter.

d. Rent costs of $2,000 are allocated to products on the basis of the floor space used for manufacturing the product. If Part No. 789 is discontinued, the space currently used to manufacture it would become available. The company could then use the space for storage purposes and save $1,000 currently paid for outside storage.

e. General plant overhead costs are allocated to each department on the basis of direct manufacturing labour dollars. These costs will not change in total. But no general plant overhead will be allocated to Part No. 789 if the part is outsourced.

Assume that Strubel requires a 12% rate of return for this project.

REQUIRED

1. Should David Lin outsource Part No. 789? Prepare a quantitative analysis.
2. Describe any sensitivity analysis that seems advisable, but you need not perform any sensitivity calculations.
3. What other factors should Lin consider in making a decision?
4. Lin is particularly concerned about his bonus for 2000. The bonus is based on Strubel's accounting income. What decision will Lin make if he wants to maximize his bonus in 2000?

21-30 Capital budgeting, computer-integrated manufacturing, sensitivity. The Dynamo Corporation is planning to replace one of its production lines, which has a remaining useful life of ten years, book value of $9 million, a current disposal price of

$5 million, and a neglible terminal disposal price ten years from now. The average investment in working capital is $6 million.

Dynamo plans to replace the production line with computer-integrated manufacturing (CIM) system at a cost of $45 million. Jeremy Burns, the production manager, estimates the following annual cash flow effects of implementing CIM:

a. Cost of maintaining software programs and CIM equipment, $1.5 million
b. Reduction in lease payments due to reduced floor space requirements, $1 million
c. Fewer product defects and reduced rework, $4.5 million

In addition, Burns estimates the average investment in working capital will decrease to $2 million. The estimated disposal price of the CIM equipment is $14 million at the end of ten years. Dynamo uses a required rate of return of 14%.

REQUIRED

1. Compute the net present value of the CIM proposal. On the basis of this criterion, should Dynamo adopt CIM?
2. Burns argues that the higher quality and faster production resulting from CIM will also increase Dynamo's revenues. He estimates additional cash revenues net of cash-operating costs from CIM of $3 million per year. Compute the net present value of the CIM proposal under this assumption.
3. Management is uncertain if the cash flows from additional revenues will occur. Compute the minimum annual cash flow from additional revenues that will cause Dynamo to invest in CIM on the basis of the net present value criterion.
4. Discuss the effects of reducing the investment horizon for CIM to five years, Dynamo's usual time period for making investment decisions. Assume disposal prices at the end of five years of CIM line, $20 million; old production line, $4 million. Also assume additional cash revenues net of cash operating costs from CIM of $3 million per year.

21-31 Ethics, capital budgeting. (CMA, adapted) The Evans Company must expand its manufacturing capabilities to meet the growing demand for its products. The first alternative is to expand its current manufacturing facility, which is located next to a vacant lot in the heart of the city. The second alternative is to convert a warehouse, already owned by Evans, located 20 kilometres outside the city. Evans' controller, George Watson, assigns Helen Dodge, assistant controller, to use net present value computations to evaluate both proposals.

Dodge obtains the following information. The investment in plant and equipment to expand the current manufacturing facility is $19 million, while a $22 million investment is required to convert the warehouse. At either site, Evans needs to invest $3 million in working capital. Cash revenues from products made in the new facility are expected to equal $13 million each year. If the warehouse is converted, cash operating costs are expected to be $10 million per year. Expanding the current facility will result in some efficiencies: annual cash operating costs, if the current facility is expanded, will be $1 million lower than the cash operating costs if the warehouse is converted. Evans uses a ten-year period and a 14% required rate of return to evaluate manufacturing investments. The estimated terminal disposal price of the new facility (including recovery of working capital of $3 million) at the end of ten years is estimated to be $8 million—regardless of where the plant is located. Evans amortizes the investment in plant and equipment using straight-line amortization over ten years on the difference between the initial investment and terminal disposal price.

Watson is upset at Dodge's conclusions. He returns the proposal to her with the comment, "You must have made an error. The warehouse proposal should look better and have a positive net present value. Work on the projections and estimates."

Dodge suspects that Watson is anxious to have the warehouse proposal selected because the choice of this location would eliminate his long commute into the city. Feeling some pressure, she checks her calculations but finds no errors. Dodge reviews her projections and estimates. These too are quite reasonable. Even so, she replaces some of her original estimates with new estimates that are more favourable to the warehouse proposal, although these new estimates are less likely to occur. The revised proposal still has a negative net present value. Dodge is confused about what she should do.

REQUIRED

1. Calculate the net present value of the proposals to expand the current manufacturing facility and to convert the warehouse. Which project should Evans choose on the basis of the NPV calculations?

2. Was George Watson's conduct unethical when he gave Helen Dodge specific instructions on revising the proposal?
3. Was Helen Dodge's revised proposal for the warehouse conversion unethical?
4. Identify the steps Helen Dodge should take to resolve this situation.

COLLABORATIVE LEARNING PROBLEM

21-32 **Relevant costs, capital budgeting.** (N. Melumad, S. Reichelstein, adapted) The Special Products Division (SPD) of Plastics Unlimited makes specially designed night goggles. Its main production machine broke down on January 1, 2001 and was no longer usable. SPD's manager requested $320,000 to acquire a new machine. Corporate management responded by requesting an analysis of the acquisition as well as an analysis of closing down SPD. SPD's 2000 income statement is as follows:

Special Products Division Income Statement for 2000

Sales (60,000 units)			$1,200,000
Deduct: Costs:			
Variable production costs		$770,000	
Fixed production costs:*			
Machine amortization	$30,000		
Patent amortization	25,000		
Machine maintenance	20,000		
Building space	20,000		
Manager's salary	55,000		
Other fixed costs	15,000		
Total fixed production costs		165,000	
Variable marketing costs		130,000	
Total costs			1,065,000
Operating income			$ 135,000

*That do not vary with units produced and sold.

The externally reported book values of the division assets as of December 31, 2000 are:

Cash	$190,000
Machine	60,000
Patent	125,000
Total	$375,000

All of SPD's transactions are cash transactions, and the division maintains no inventories. The contribution margin is expected to remain the same over the next five years if SPD continues to produce and sell goggles.

To make the goggles, the company had to acquire a patent three years ago for $200,000. The patent is being amortized (that is, written off on the income statement) evenly over its lifetime. If the company were to shut down SPD, the patent could be sold for $235,000 to an external buyer.

SPD purchased the existing machine three years ago for $150,000. It is amortized on a straight-line basis over five years. The current disposal price of the broken machine is $4,000.

The new machine has a useful life of five years and an expected disposal price of $50,000. It would be amortized under the straight-line method. Maintenance of the new machine would require $25,000 per year. Machine maintenance costs would not be incurred if SPD is closed down.

SPD uses 1,000 square metres of building space and is charged $20 per square metre by corporate management. If SPD is eliminated, the space can be rented externally for $30 per square metre.

Plastics Unlimited needs an assistant manager in another larger department. If SPD closes, its manager will take the assistant manager position at an annual salary of $60,000. If SPD continues operations, Plastics Unlimited will have to fill the assistant manager position with an outsider at an annual salary of $65,000.

Other fixed costs consist of miscellaneous items such as insurance and indirect labour that would remain at the same levels if SPD continues to produce the goggles and would not be incurred if SPD is closed down.

The firm uses a required rate of return of 16%. Ignore income taxes.

INSTRUCTIONS

Form groups of three students to complete the following requirements.

REQUIRED

1. On the basis of the net present value criterion, should Plastics Unlimited purchase the new machine or close down SPD?
2. Suppose the manager making the decision is compensated on the basis of operating income earned by all divisions of Plastics Unlimited after gain or loss on disposal of assets. The manager will retire at the end of 2001. Which decision would the manager favour? Explain.

ANSWERS TO EXERCISES IN COMPOUND INTEREST (EXERCISE 21-14)

The general approach to these exercises centres on a key question: Which of the four tables in Appendix B should be used? No computations should be made until after this basic question has been answered with confidence.

1. **From Table 1.** The $5,000 is the present value P of your winnings. Their future value S in ten years will be:

$$S = P(1 + r)^n$$

The conversion factor, $(1 + r)^n$, is on line 10 of Table 1.

> Substituting at 6%: $S = 5,000 \times 1.791 = \$8,955$
>
> Substituting at 14%: $S = 5,000 \times 3.707 = \$18,535$

2. **From Table 2.** The $89,550 is an *amount of future worth*. You want the present value of that amount, which is $P = S \div (1 + r)^n$.

The conversion factor, $1 \div (1 + r)^n$, is on line 10 of Table 2. Substituting:

$$P = \$89,550 \times 0.558 = \$49,969$$

3. **From Table 3.** The $89,550 is *future worth*. You are seeking the uniform amount (annuity) to set aside annually. Note that $1 invested each year for ten years at 6% has a future worth F of $13.181 after ten years, from line 10 of Table 3.

$$S_n = \text{Annual deposit} \times F$$
$$\$89,550 = \text{Annual deposit} \times 13.181$$
$$\text{Annual deposit} = \frac{\$89,550}{13.181} = \$6,794$$

4. **From Table 3.** You are seeking the *amount of future worth* of an annuity of $5,000 per year. Note that $1 invested each year for ten years at 12% has a future worth F of $17.549 after ten years.

$$S_n = \$5,000F \quad \text{where } F \text{ is the conversion factor}$$
$$= \$5,000 \times 17.549 = \$87,745$$

5. **From Table 4.** When you reach age 65, you will get $200,000, a present value at that time. You must find the annuity that will exactly exhaust the invested principal in ten years. To pay yourself $1 each year for ten years when the interest rate is 6% requires you to have $7.360 today, from line 10 of Table 4.

$$P_n = \text{Annual withdrawal} \times F$$
$$\$200,000 = \text{Annual withdrawal} \times 7.360$$
$$\text{Annual withdrawal} = \frac{\$200,000}{7.360} = \$27,174$$

6. **From Table 4.** You need to find the present value of an annuity for ten years. At 6%:

$$P_n = \text{Annual withdrawal} \times F$$
$$= \$50,000 \times 7.360$$
$$= \$368,000$$

At 20%:

$$P_n = \$50,000 \times 4.192$$
$$= \$209,600, \text{ a much lower figure}$$

7. Plan B is preferable. The net present value of plan B exceeds that of plan A by $980 ($3,126 − $2,146):

Year	PV Factor at 6%	Plan A Cash Inflows	Plan A PV of Cash Inflows	Plan B Cash Inflows	Plan B PV of Cash Inflows
0	1.000	$(10,000)	$(10,000)	$(10,000)	$(10,000)
1	0.943	1,000	943	5,000	4,715
2	0.890	2,000	1,780	4,000	3,560
3	0.840	3,000	2,520	3,000	2,520
4	0.792	4,000	3,168	2,000	1,584
5	0.747	5,000	3,735	1,000	747
			$ 2,146		$ 3,126

Even though plan B and plan A have the same total cash inflows over the five years, plan B is preferred to plan A because it has greater cash inflows occurring earlier.

22

CAPITAL BUDGETING: A CLOSER LOOK

Capital budgeting, for projects like this Canadian communications satellite, reflects a company's long-term strategic plans. A company needs to look to the future to try to assess the ways in which the world is changing. Managers can then assess how their company should make investments to best prepare for the future.

LEARNING OBJECTIVES

After studying this chapter, you should be able to:

1. Analyze the impact of income taxes on operating cash flows
2. Analyze the effect of income taxes on capital cash flows and compute the after-tax net present values of projects
3. Explain the after-tax effect on cash of tradeins and disposals of assets
4. Distinguish between the total project approach and the differential approach in capital budgeting decisions
5. Understand the categories of cash flows considered in capital budgeting analyses
6. Distinguish between the real rate of return and the nominal rate of return
7. Describe two internally consistent ways to account for inflation in capital budgeting
8. Describe alternative approaches used to recognize the degree of risk in capital budgeting projects
9. Explain the excess present value index and its usefulness in capital budgeting
10. Explain why the internal rate-of-return and the net present value decision rules may rank projects differently

$\mathbf{B}$enjamin Franklin said that two things in life are certain: death and taxes. We might add a third: changing prices. This chapter examines how managers analyze income taxes and changing prices in capital budgeting. (We also recognize death in this chapter, although only of projects, not of the individuals who select them!) We also cover risk and uncertainty in capital budgeting in this chapter, as well as capital budgeting in nonprofit organizations, and issues in implementing the net present value and the internal rate-of-return decision methods.

INCOME TAXES AND CAPITAL BUDGETING

General Characteristics

Income taxes are cash disbursements. Income taxes can influence the amount and/or the timing of cash flows. Their basic role in capital budgeting is no different from that of any other cash disbursement. However, taxes tend to narrow the cash differences between projects.

The Canadian and provincial governments raise money through corporate income taxes. Income tax rates differ considerably, and thus, overall corporate income tax rates can vary widely.

Income tax rates also depend on the amount of pretax income. Larger income is taxed at higher rates. In capital budgeting, the relevant rate is the **marginal income tax rate**, that is, the tax rate paid on additional amounts of pretax income. Suppose corporations pay income taxes of 15% on the first $50,000 of pretax income and 30% on pretax income over $50,000. What is the *marginal income tax rate* of a company with $75,000 of pretax income? It is 30%, because 30% of any *additional* income will be paid in taxes. In contrast, the company's *average income tax rate* is only 20% (i.e., 15 % × $50,000 + 30% × $25,000 = $15,000 of taxes on $75,000 of pretax income). When we assess tax effects of capital budgeting decisions, we will always use the *marginal* tax rate. Why? Because that is the rate applied to the additional cash flows generated by a proposed project.

Organizations that pay income taxes generally report two net incomes—one for reporting to the public and one for reporting to the tax authorities. This is not illegal or immoral; in fact, it is necessary. Tax reporting must follow detailed rules designed to achieve certain social goals. These rules do not lead to financial statements that best measure an organization's financial results and position, so it is more informative to financial statement users if a separate set of rules is used for financial reporting. In this chapter we are concerned with effects on the cash outflows for taxes. Therefore we focus on the *tax reporting* rules, not those for public financial reporting.

Marginal income tax rate. The tax rate paid on any additional amounts of pretax income.

Canadian Tax Foundation
ctf.ca/

Tax Resources on the Internet
www.taxresources.com

Tax and Accounting Sites
Directory
www.taxsites.com

CanTax Income Tax Preparation
Software
www.cantax.com

TAX IMPACT ON OPERATING CASH FLOWS

OBJECTIVE 1

Analyze the impact of income taxes on operating cash flows

Recognizing the impact of income taxes on operating cash flows is straightforward. If a capital proposal results in annual savings of $60,000 and the company has a marginal tax rate of 40%, then the company's income taxes will increase by $24,000 ($60,000 × 0.40). A net annual after-tax savings of $36,000 results. This can be computed by deducting the $24,000 of extra income taxes from the pretax annual savings of $60,000. Conversely the $36,000 can be computed by multiplying the $60,000 by (1 minus the tax rate of 40%) or 60%.

If operating expenses increase by $250,000, and if the company has a 40% marginal tax rate, then a net after-tax cost of $150,000 results. The $150,000 is the net of the $100,000 in tax savings of $250,000 multiplied by 40%, and the $250,000. The $150,000 can also be computed by multiplying $250,000 by (1 minus the tax rate of 40%) or 60%.

Thus, to incorporate the impact of income taxes on operating cash flows poses no real difficulty. The difficulty occurs in the recognition of the tax effects of investment expenditures in capital equipment.

In financial reporting, the expenditure on capital equipment results in the recording of the asset and the related amortization expense over the asset's useful economic life. Amortization rates and policies are determined by the company's management and vary from company to company even for the same asset.

To apply a consistent set of regulations and to provide a means to implement government initiatives, the federal government has implemented its own system of **capital cost allowance** (CCA). The Income Tax Act (ITA) does not permit a company to deduct amortization expense in determining taxable income but rather a company is allowed to deduct CCA. If you like, CCA is the income tax counterpart to financial reporting amortization.

OBJECTIVE 2

Analyze the effect of income taxes on capital cash flows and compute the after-tax net present values of projects

Capital cost allowance (CCA).
The income tax counterpart to financial reporting amoritzation.

Capital Cost Allowance—Declining Balance Classes

The ITA assigns all capital purchases to a CCA class. (The appendix to this chapter provides a list of some of the more commonly used CCA classes.) For example, a desk would qualify as a Class 8 asset that includes all furniture and fixtures. Class 8 has a predetermined rate of 20% declining balance capital cost allowance. Exhibit 22-1 depicts the calculation of CCA for a desk that costs $10,000.

A number of years ago, a company could deduct a full year's worth of CCA on any asset acquired during the year, as long as the company had been in business the entire year. Thus, companies with a December 31 year-end would buy assets on or about

EXHIBIT 22-1
Capital Cost Allowance Illustration

CCA — Class 8 Rate — 20% Declining Balance (rounded to the nearest dollar)			
Year 1 (Day 1) Addition	$10,000	Year 13 — UCC	$ 618
CCA — year 1 (10%)	1,000	CCA — year 14	124
Year (end) — UCC	9,000	Year 14 — UCC	494
CCA — year 2 (20%)	1,800	CCA — year 15	99
Year 2 — UCC	7,200	Year 15 — UCC	395
CCA — year 3 (20%)	1,440	CCA — year 16	79
Year 3 — UCC	5,760	Year 16 — UCC	316
CCA — year 4	1,152	CCA — year 17	63
Year 4 — UCC	4,608	Year 17 — UCC	253
CCA — year 5	922	CCA — year 18	51
Year 5 — UCC	3,686	Year 18 — UCC	202
CCA — year 6	737	CCA — year 19	40
Year 6 — UCC	2,949	Year 19 — UCC	162
CCA — year 7	590	CCA — year 20	32
Year 7 — UCC	2,359	Year 20 — UCC	130
CCA — year 8	472	CCA — year 21	26
Year 8 — UCC	1,887	Year 21 — UCC	104
CCA — year 9	377	CCA — year 22	21
Year 9 — UCC	1,510	Year 22 — UCC	83
CCA — year 10	302	CCA — year 23	17
Year 10 — UCC	1,208	Year 23 — UCC	66
CCA — year 11	242	CCA — year 24	13
Year 11 — UCC	966	Year 24 — UCC	53
CCA — year 12	193	CCA — year 25	11
Year 12 — UCC	773	Year 25 — UCC	42
CCA — year 13	155		

December 31 and claim a full year's deduction even though the asset had not really been used to generate the income. To minimize this problem, the government implemented the so-called "half-year rule."

Half-year rule. The assumption, in calculating capital cost allowance, that all net additions to a company's assets are purchased in the middle of the year, so that only half of the applicable capital cost allowance rate is allowed in the first year.

Unamortized capital cost (UCC). The result of subtracting the capital cost allowance from the capital expenditure or its amortized balance.

The **half-year rule** assumes that all net additions are purchased in the middle of the year, and thus only one-half of the stated CCA rate is allowed in the first year. Thus in year 1 of the example in Exhibit 22-1, the CCA is $1,000 or 1/2 times 20% multiplied by the $10,000 capital expenditure. This leaves a balance of $9,000 ($10,000 − $1,000), which is known as the **unamortized capital cost** (UCC).

In year 2 and all succeeding years, the rate of 20% is applied to the UCC of the previous year. This results in a declining amount of capital cost allowance for each year. Even after the 25 years shown in Exhibit 22-1, a UCC of $42 remains and will require 15 more years to get to a zero balance (which in practice can only be obtained by rounding to the nearest dollar).

The CCA of each year is deducted in the calculation of a company's taxable income. Thus the CCA is not a cash flow. Rather we must multiply the CCA of each year by the company's marginal tax rate to calculate the actual tax savings in each year. In Chapter 21, we recognized the time value of money. Thus, to determine the present value of the tax savings, we would need to multiply the tax savings of each year by the present value factor from Appendix D for each year at the company's required rate of return (say 10%).

Tax shield formula. A formula for calculating the tax savings from deducting capital cost allowance.

This, as you could well imagine, would be a long and laborious task to perform for each capital proposal. An efficient way to calculate the present value of the tax savings is to use the following **tax shield formula**:

$$\text{Present value of tax savings} = \left(\text{Investment} \times \text{Marginal tax rate} \right) \left(\frac{\text{CCA rate}}{\text{CCA rate} + \text{required rate of return}} \right) \frac{(2 + \text{required rate of return})}{2\ (1 + \text{required rate of return})}$$

In the case of the $10,000 desk, the present value of the tax savings from deducting CCA, commonly referred to as the tax shield, is $2,548, computed as follows assuming a 10% required rate of return.

$$\text{Tax shield} = (\ \$10,000 \times 40\%) \left(\frac{20\%}{20\% + 10\%} \right) \left(\frac{2 + 10\%}{2(1 + 10\%)} \right)$$
$$= \$4,000 \times 0.667 \times 0.955$$
$$= \$2,668 \times 0.955$$
$$= \$2,548$$

Therefore, the net after-tax cost of the desk is $7,452, or $10,000 less $2,548.

A detailed proof of the tax shield formula is not necessary for our purposes, but some explanation will be useful.

The first component of the formula, investment times the marginal tax rate, computes the total tax savings over the life of the asset from the CCA deduction. The $4,000, however, does not incorporate any time value of money considerations.

The second component, the CCA rate divided by the sum of the CCA rate plus the required rate of return, calculates the present values of all the annual tax savings assuming the half-year rule did not exist. This is important to note when residual values are discussed later in the chapter.

The third component incorporates an adjustment for the half-year rule. For example, in the above scenario, the tax shield was reduced to 95.5% of the benefit that existed prior to the introduction of the half-year rule.

Capital Cost Allowance—Other Classes

Most CCA classes use the declining balance method. However, occasionally the straight-line method is used in which the CCA is the same for each year, except for the first and last years, which have one-half of the CCA due to the half-year rule. For example, for patents, the CCA is computed on a straight-line basis over the legal life of the patent.

Another exception occurs where the CCA rate is varied year by year. For example, Class 39 upon its introduction allowed 40% in 1988 (subject to the half-year rule), 35% 1989, and 30% in the remaining years. Thus, the first two years need to be computed separately and then the tax shield formula could be applied to the UCC at the end of 1989.

Tradeins and Disposals of Capital Assets

OBJECTIVE 3

Explain the after-tax effect on cash of tradeins and disposals of assets

In the case when a capital asset is traded in on another asset or is sold, we do not need to concern ourselves with the net tax book value of the asset.

Assume that a company's Class 8 UCC for all of its furniture and fixtures is $50,000, as shown in Exhibit 22-2, at the end of year 3. Let us also assume that included in the $50,000 is the remaining UCC on the desk of $5,760.

If in year 4 the desk was traded in on a new desk, where the price of the new desk is $12,000 and $4,000 was allowed as a tradein, the Class 8 UCC would increase by $8,000. Note that the CCA system works on a pool basis, in that we are not concerned with the UCC of the specific desk being sold. Rather we are only concerned with the net cash flows. The UCC of the class that existed prior to the disposal is only reduced by the amount of the cash received. Thus, the actual amount of the UCC of the specific asset is irrelevant to the decision. In this example, the net capital expenditure of $8,000 is the relevant cash flow.

Continuing with the example in Exhibit 22-2, the CCA for year 4 is $10,800. This is a combination of the CCA at the rate of 20% on the opening UCC of $50,000 ($10,000) and the CCA at the half-year rule rate of 10% on the net addition of $8,000 ($800).

Thus, as shown in Exhibit 22-3, the net after-tax present value of the cost of the new desk is $5,962. This amount recognizes the fact that the tax shield of $2,038 on the net addition of $8,000 must recognize the half-year rule.

If in the above scenario a new desk had not been purchased, but rather the old desk was sold for $4,000, the CCA would be 20% of $46,000 or $9,200. Note the half-year rule does not apply to net disposals, that is where the amount of disposals exceeds the amount of additions during a given year.

From Exhibit 22-3, note that the sale of $4,000 reduces the future CCA and results in a lost tax shield of $1,067. Thus, the net after-tax present value of the sale is $2,933.

Simplifying Assumptions

It is useful to note that a number of simplifying assumptions have been made when using the tax shield formula.

1. We have assumed that the company's marginal tax rate will remain the same (at 40% in the above examples). Further, the above examples also assume that the company will have a taxable income each year.

EXHIBIT 22-2
Tradein of a Capital Asset

CCA — Class 8	
Ending UCC — year 3	$50,000
Purchase	12,000
Less: Tradein	(4,000)
	8,000
Revised UCC	58,000
Year 4 — CCA:	
20% × $50,000	10,000
10% × $8,000	800
	10,800
UCC — year 4	$47,200

EXHIBIT 22-3
Net Capital Cash Flow of Tradeins and Disposals

Tradein:	Purchase price	$12,000
	Tradein	(4,000)
	Net cash payment	8,000
	Tax shield[1]	(2,038)
	NPV cash outflow	$ 5,962
Sale:	Selling price	$ 4,000
	Lost tax shield[2]	(1,067)
	NPV cash inflow	$ 2,933

[1]Includes the half-year adjustment:

$$(\$8,000 \times 40\%) \times \left(\frac{20\%}{20\% + 10\%}\right) \times \left(\frac{2 + 10\%}{2(1 + 10\%)}\right) = \$2,038$$

[2]Excludes the half-year adjustment:

$$(\$4,000 \times 40\%) \times \left(\frac{20\%}{20\% + 10\%}\right) = \$1,067$$

2. While it is uncommon, governments can change the CCA rates that we have assumed to be constant.

3. We have also assumed that all CCA tax savings occur at the year-end. In reality, companies make monthly installments. However, the additional cost of attempting to be more precise is not warranted, given the degree of uncertainty that already exists in the estimation of the cash flows.

INCOME TAX COMPLICATIONS

Taxation of Canadian Corporations: Doing Business in Canada (1997)—Arthur Andersen Inc. strategis.ic.gc.ca/SSG/mi04887e.html

In the foregoing illustrations, we deliberately avoided many possible income tax complications. As all taxpaying citizens know, income taxes are affected by many intricacies, including progressive tax rates, loss carrybacks and carryforwards, varying provincial income taxes, capital gains, distinctions between capital assets and other assets, offsets of losses against related gains, exchanges of property of like kind, exempt income, and so forth.

Keep in mind that changes in the tax law occur each year. Always check the current tax law before calculating the tax consequences of a decision.

CONFUSION ABOUT AMORTIZATION

The meaning of amortization and book value is widely misunderstood. Pause and consider their role in decisions. Suppose a bank has some printing equipment with a book value of $30,000, an expected terminal disposal value of zero, a current disposal value of $12,000, and a remaining useful life of three years. For simplicity, assume that straight-line amortization of $10,000 yearly will be taken.

In particular, note that the inputs to the decision model are the predicted income tax effects on cash. The book loss of $18,000 or the amortization of $10,000 may be necessary for making *predictions*. By themselves, however, they are not inputs to DCF decision models.

The following points summarize the role of amortization regarding the replacement of equipment:

1. **Initial investment**. The amount paid for (and hence amortization on) old equipment is irrelevant except for its effect on tax cash flows. In contrast, the amount paid for new equipment is relevant, because it is an expected future cost that will not be incurred if replacement is rejected.

2. **Do not double-count.** The investment in equipment is a one-time outlay at time zero, so it should not be double-counted as an outlay in the form of amortization. Amortization by itself is irrelevant; it is not a cash outlay.

3. **Relation to income tax cash flows.** Relevant quantities were defined in Chapter 4, as expected future data that will differ among alternatives. Given this definition, book values and past amortization are irrelevant in all capital budgeting decision models. The relevant item is the *income tax cash effect*, not the book value or the amortization.

ALTERNATIVE APPROACHES TO CAPITAL BUDGETING

We turn now to a fuller discussion of how income taxes can affect cash inflows and outflows and also how they influence manager's decisions. We focus on the information-acquisition and selection stages of capital budgeting, highlight the effect of income taxes, and use the net present value method for the formal financial analysis.

Example: Potato Supreme produces potato products for sale to supermarkets and other retail outlets. It is considering replacing an old packaging machine (purchased three years ago) with a new, more efficient packaging machine that has recently been introduced. The new machine is less labour-intensive and has lower operating costs than the old machine. For simplicity, we assume that:

1. All cash outflows or inflows occur at the end of the year (even though cash operating costs generally occur throughout the year).

2. The tax effects of cash inflows and outflows occur at the same time that the inflows and outflows occur.

3. The income tax rate is 30% each year.

4. The packaging machine qualifies for CCA Class 8, which has a rate of 20% declining balance.

5. Both the old and the new machine have the same working capital requirements.

6. Potato Supreme is a profitable company.

Summary data for the two machines are as follows:

	Old Machine	New Machine
Original cost	$87,500	$200,000
Accumulated amortization	$37,500	—
Current book value	$50,000	—
Current disposal price	$26,000	—
Terminal disposal price, 4 years from now	$6,000	$20,000
Annual cash operating costs	$250,000	$150,000
Remaining useful life	4 years	4 years
After-tax required rate of return	10%	10%
Capital cost allowance rate	20% (declining balance)	20% (declining balance)

Potato Supreme uses the net present value method to evaluate whether it should replace the old packaging machine with the new packaging machine. As in the Lifetime Care example of Chapter 21, the key point in net present value analysis is to identify the relevant cash flows. To emphasize the ideas of relevance, Chapter 21 used the **differential approach**, which analyzes only relevant cash flows—those future cash outflows and inflows that differ between alternatives. The differential approach is generally faster when there are only two alternatives.

When the number of alternatives is more than two, the differential approach becomes unwieldy. Why? Because it forces the analyst into difficult calculations of differences among multiple alternatives. Companies then use the *total-project approach*. The **total-project approach** calculates the present value of *all* future cash inflows and outflows under each alternative separately. It does not require the identification

Differential approach. Approach to decision-making and capital budgeting that analyzes only those future cash outflows and inflows that differ among alternatives.

Total-project approach. Approach to decision-making that incorporates all relevant revenues and relevant costs under each alternative. In capital budgeting decisions, calculates the present value of all future cash inflows and outflows under each alternative separately.

OBJECTIVE 4

Distinguish between the total-project approach and the differential approach in capital budgeting decisions of cash flows that differ among alternatives. The total-project approach has two steps:

◆ **Step 1.** Calculate the present value of all cash inflows and outflows under the status quo alternative.

◆ **Step 2.** Separately calculate the present value of all cash inflows and outflows under another alternative.

We use the Potato Supreme example to illustrate the two steps of the total-project approach. We then use the differential approach to show that both approaches give the same net present value. The categories of cash flows are considered in both approaches:

a. Initial machine investment

b. Tax shield on the initial investment

c. Cash flow from current disposal of old machine

d. Lost tax shield from current disposal of machine

e. Recurring after-tax cash operating flows

f. Cash flow from terminal (at the end of the project) disposal of machine

g. Lost tax shield from terminal disposal of machine

OBJECTIVE 5

Identify the categories of cash flows considered in capital budgeting analyses

Total-Project Approach

◆ **Step 1:** *Calculate the present value of total cash flows of keeping the old packaging machine.* Under this alternative, cash flow categories that specifically pertain to the new machine are not relevant.

a. *Initial machine investment.* No new investment is necessary if Potato Supreme keeps the old packaging machine. Exhibit 22-4, item 1, shows an initial machine investment of $0 in year 0.

b. Tax shield on initial investment. As there is no new investment, there is then no additional tax shield.

c. *Cash flow from current disposal of old machine.* Since the old machine is kept and not disposed of, Exhibit 22-4, item 2, shows after-tax cash flow from current disposal of old machine of $0 in year 0.

d. Lost tax shield from current disposal of machine. As the old machine is not sold, no tax shield adjustments are required.

e. *Recurring after-tax cash operating flows.*

Recurring cash operating flows (costs) for the old machine	$(250,000)
Deduct: Income tax savings at 30% of $250,000	75,000
Recurring after-tax cash operating flows	$(175,000)

After-tax cash operating flows of $(175,000) in years 1–4 appear as relevant cash outflows in Exhibit 22-4, item 3. Our example assumes that Potato Supreme's income tax rate is 30% each year. When future tax rates are uncertain, analysts must predict the tax rate applicable for each year of a project.

f. *Cash flow from terminal disposal of old machine.*

Terminal disposal price of old machine at end of year 4)	$6,000

The cash flow of $6,000 from the terminal disposal of the old machine appears as a cash inflow in year 4 of Exhibit 22-4, item 4.

g. *Lost tax shield.* The terminal disposal of $6,000 would reduce the CCA pool by $6,000, and thus reduce the future cash savings from capital cost allowance deductions by $1,145.

$$(\$6,000 \times 0.30) \times \frac{0.20}{(0.20 + 0.10)} \times \frac{2 + 0.10}{2(1 + 0.10)}$$

$$= \$1,800 \times 2/3 \times 0.954 = \$1,145$$

EXHIBIT 22-4
Total-Project Approach for Potato Supreme: After-Tax Analysis of Keeping Old Machine

	Total Present Value	Present Value Discount Factors at 10%		Sketch of Relevant After-Tax Cash Flows			
		End of Year: 0		1	2	3	4
Explanations for the after-tax cash flow amounts are given on pp. 766–767.							
a. Initial machine investment	$ 0	◄ 1.000 ◄	$0				
c. After-tax cash flow from current disposal of old machine	0	◄ 1.000 ◄	0				
e. Recurring after-tax cash operating flows	(554,750)	◄ 3.170 ◄-------		$(175,000)	$(175,000)	$(175,000)	$(175,000)
f. Cash flow from terminal disposal of old machine	4,098	◄ 0.683 ◄------------------------------					6,000
g. Lost tax shield from the terminal disposal of machine	(782)	◄ 0.683 ◄------------------------------					($1,145)
Total present value of all cash flows if Potato Supreme keeps machine	$(551,434)						

Note: Parentheses denote relevant cash outflows throughout all exhibits in this chapter.

While this is a disposal, the half-year rule and thus the third component of the tax shield formula does apply, as we are assuming that the disposal will be accompanied by an addition. The half-year rule applies to net additions.

Exhibit 22-4 presents all after-tax cash flows that would arise if Potato Supreme continued to use the old packaging machine. Each cash flow is multiplied by its corresponding present value discount factor to give its present value. The total present value is $(551,434).

◆ **Step 2:** *Calculate the present value of total cash flows of replacing the old packaging machine.*

a. *Initial machine investment.* The original cost of the new packaging machine is $200,000. This amount appears as a cash outflow in year 0 in Exhibit 22-5, item 1.

b. *Tax shield.* The original cost of $200,000 will generate a cash savings from capital cost allowance of $38,160. This amount is determined by using the tax shield formula.

$$(\$200,000 \times 0.30) \times \frac{0.20}{(0.20 + 0.10)} \times \frac{2 + 0.10}{2(1 + 0.10)}$$

$$= \$60,000 \times 2/3 \times 2.1/2.2$$

$$= \$40,000 \times 0.954 = \$38,160$$

Recall that the tax shield formula calculate the present value of the cash flows.

c. *Cash flow from current disposal of old machine.*

Current disposal price of old machine $26,000

Review what is included in the present value analysis. It is the *cash inflow* from asset disposal. The book value of the old machine and the loss on disposal do not themselves affect cash flow. The book value, however, enters into the calculation of the loss on disposal of the asset, which in turn affects the accounting net income.

d. *Lost tax shield from current disposal of machine.* The current disposal of $26,000 would reduce the cash savings from future capital cost allowance by $4,961.

$$(\$26,000 \times 0.30) \times \frac{0.20}{0.20 + 0.10} \times \frac{2 + 0.10}{2(1 + 0.10)}$$

$$= \$7,800 \times 2/3 \times 0.954$$

$$= \$4,961$$

In this case the entire tax shield formula is used, including the third component for the half-year rule, as this disposal would be offset by the addition of $200,000. The half-year rule applies to net additions, that is, additions less disposals in any one-year period.

e. *Recurring after-tax cash operating flows.*

Recurring cash operating flows (costs) for the new machine	$(150,000)
Deduct: Income tax savings (30% × $150,000)	45,000
Recurring after-tax cash operating flows	$(105,000)

The after-tax cash operating flows of $(105,000) in years 1–4 appear as relevant cash outflows in Exhibit 22-5, item 5.

f. *Cash flow from terminal disposal of new machine.*

Terminal disposal of new machine is	$20,000

g. *Lost tax shield from terminal disposal of machine.* The disposal of the new machine in four years for $20,000 would reduce the future cash savings from capital cost allowance by $2,732.

$$(\$20,000 \times 0.30) \times \frac{0.20}{(0.20 + 0.10)}$$

$$= \$6,000 \times 2/3 = \$4,000.$$

Note the half-year adjustment does not apply as we have not assumed any additions in new equipment in four years time.

Exhibit 22-5 summarizes the relevant after-tax cash flows that would occur if Potato Supreme replaced its old packaging machine. Present values are derived by multiplying cash flows by the corresponding present value discount factors. The total present value of cash flows equals $(462,723). Recall from Exhibit 22-4 that the present value of after-tax cash flows of keeping the old packaging machine is $(551,434). The decision to replace the old machine with the new machine has a net present value of $88,711 ($551,434 − $462,723) and is therefore preferred.

Differential Approach

Unlike the two-step total-project approach, the differential approach is a one-step method that includes only those cash inflows and outflows that *differ* between the two alternatives. The differential approach compares the cash outflows arising from replacing the old machine with the *savings* in future cash outflows resulting from using the new machine rather than the old machine. We will now examine the differences in cash flows between the keep and replace alternatives in the Potato Supreme example using the categories of cash flows that we described earlier.

a. *Initial machine investment* of $200,000 for the new machine (see Exhibit 22-5) appears as a cash outflow in year 0 in Exhibit 22-6, item 1.

c. *Cash flow from current disposal of old machine* of $26,000 (see Exhibit 22-5) appears as a cash inflow in year 0 in Exhibit 22-6, item 2. The initial machine investment, $200,000, minus the cash flow from current disposal of the old machine, $126,000, is the net initial investment of $174,000, shown as a cash outflow in year 0 in Exhibit 22-6.

b. & d. *Tax shield.* The net initial investment of $174,000 would increase the CCA pool by this amount and thus would generate cash savings from CCA from

EXHIBIT 22-5
Total-Project Approach for Potato Supreme: After-Tax Analysis of Purchasing New Machine

	Total Present Value	Present Value Discount Factors at 10%	Sketch of Relevant After-Tax Cash Flows				
End of Year:			0	1	2	3	4
Explanations for the after-tax cash flow amounts are given on pp. 767 and 769.							
a. Initial machine investment	$(200,000) ← 1.000 ←	$(200,000)					
b. Tax shield	38,160 ← 1.000 ←	$ 38,160					
	$(161,840)						
c. Cash flow from current disposal of old machine	26,000 ← 1.000 ←	$ 26,000					
d. Lost tax shield from current disposal of machine	$ (4,961) ← 1.000 ←	$ (4,961)					
Net investment	$(140,801)						
e. Recurring after-tax cash operating flows	(332,850) ← 3.170 ←	---------	$(105,000)	$(105,000)	$(105,000)	$(105,000)
f. Cash flow from terminal disposal of new machine	13,660 ← 0.683 ←	--				$20,000
g. Lost tax shield from the terminal disposal of machine	(2,732) ← 0.683 ←	--				(4.000)
Total present value of all cash flows if Potato Supreme purchases new machine	$(462,723)						

now to infinity. The cash savings would be $33,199, a figure determined by using the tax shield formula.

$$(\$174,000 \times 0.30) \times \frac{0.20}{(0.20 + 0.10)} \times \frac{(2 + 0.10)}{2(1 + 0.10)}$$

$$= \$52,200 \times 2/3 \times 0.954$$

$$= \$33,199$$

e. *Recurring after-tax cash operating flows.* Replacing the old machine results in lower after-tax cash operating costs, as follows:

Recurring after-tax cash operating costs if old machine kept (Exhibit 22-4, item 3)	$175,000
Deduct: Recurring after-tax cash operating costs if machine replaced (Exhibit 22-5, item 3)	105,000
Savings in recurring after-tax cash operating costs if machine replaced	$ 70,000

f. & g. *Cash flow from terminal disposal of old machine.* While we are examining the current replacement of the old machine, we are giving up the potential sale at the end of four years. Exhibit 22-4 indicates that this opportunity cost is $3,316 ($4,098 – $782).

In Exhibit 22-5, the terminal disposal of the new machine for $20,000 will result in a lost tax shield of $2,732, the net of which is $10,828.

Exhibit 22-6, item 3, shows this $70,000 increase in recurring after-tax cash operating flows in years 1–4.

Both the total-project approach (Exhibits 22-4 and 22-5) and the differential approach (Exhibit 22-6) result in a net present value of $88,711 in favour of replacing the old packaging machine with the new one. When comparing alternatives, these two approaches will always give the same net present value.

EXHIBIT 22-6
Differential Approach for Potato Supreme: After-Tax Analysis of Replacing Old Machine

	Total Present Value	Present Value Discount Factors at 10%	Sketch of Relevant After-Tax Cash Flows				
End of Year:			0	1	2	3	4
Explanations for the after-tax inflow amounts are given on pp. 768 and 769.							
a. Initial machine investment	$(200,000) ← 1.000 ←		$(200,000)				
c. Cash flow from current disposal of old machine	26,000 ← 1.000 ←		26,000				
Net initial investment	(174,000)		(174,000)				
b. & d. Tax shield	33,199 ← 1.000 ←		33,199				
	(140,801)						
e. Recurring after-tax cash operating flows	221,900	3.170		$70,000	$70,000	$70,000	$70,000
f. Cash flow from terminal disposal of old machine	(4,098) ← 0.683						$(6,000)
g. Lost tax shield from disposal	782 ← 0.683						$(1,145)
	(3,316)						
f. Cash flow from terminal disposal of new machine	13,660 ← 0.683						$20,000
g. Lost tax shield from the terminal disposal of machine	(2,732) ← 0.683						(4.000)
	10,828						
Net present value if new machine is purchased	$ 88,711						

CAPITAL BUDGETING AND INFLATION

OBJECTIVE 6

Distinguish between the real rate of return and the nominal rate of return

Inflation. The decline in the general purchasing power of the monetary unit.

Real rate of return. The rate of return required to cover only investment risk.

Nominal rate of return. Rate of return required to cover investment risk and the anticipated decline due to inflation, in the general purchasing power of the cash that the investment generates.

Inflation can be defined as the decline in the general purchasing power of the monetary unit (for example, the dollar in Canada or the yen in Japan). An inflation rate of 10% in one year means that what you could buy with $100 (say) at the start of the year will cost you $110 [$100 + (10% × $100)] at the end of the year. Prices increase as more money chases fewer goods. Some countries—for example, Brazil, Israel, Mexico, and Russia—have experienced annual inflation rates of 15% to over 100%. Even an annual inflation rate of 5% over, say, a five-year period can result in sizable declines in the general purchasing power of the monetary unit over that time.

Why is it important to account for inflation in capital budgeting? Because declines in the general purchasing power of the monetary unit (say dollars) will inflate future cash flows above what they would have been had there been no inflation. These inflated cash flows will cause the project to look better than it is, unless the analyst recognizes that the inflated cash flows are measured in dollars that have lesser value than the dollars that were initially invested. We now examine how inflation can be explicitly recognized in capital budgeting analysis.

Real and Nominal Rates of Return

When analyzing inflation, distinguish between the real rate of return and the nominal rate of return:

◆ **Real rate of return** is the rate of return required to cover only investment risk.

◆ **Nominal rate of return** is the rate of return required to cover investment risk and the anticipated decline, due to inflation, in the general purchasing power of the cash that the investment generates. The rates of return (or interest) earned on the financial markets are nominal rates, because they compensate investors for both risk and inflation.

We next describe the relationship between real and nominal rates of return. Assume that the real rate of return for investments in high-risk cellular data transmission equipment at Network Communications is 20% and that the expected inflation rate is 10%. The nominal rate of return[1] is:

$$\text{Nominal rate} = (1 + \text{Real rate})(1 + \text{Inflation rate}) - 1$$
$$= (1 + 0.20)(1 + 0.10) - 1$$
$$= [(1.20)(1.10)] - 1 = 1.32 - 1 = 0.32$$

The nominal rate of return is also related to the real rate of return and the inflation rate as follows:

Real rate of return	0.20
Inflation rate	0.10
Combination (0.20×0.10)	0.02
Nominal rate of return	0.32

Note that the nominal rate is slightly higher than the real rate (0.20) plus the inflation rate (0.10). Why? Because the nominal rate recognizes that inflation also decreases the purchasing power of the real rate of return earned during the year.

Net Present Value Method and Inflation

The watchword when incorporating inflation into the net present value (NPV) method is *internal consistency*. There are two internally consistent approaches:

◆ **Nominal approach.** Predict cash inflows and outflows in nominal monetary units and use a nominal rate as the required rate of return.

◆ **Real approach.** Predict cash inflows and outflows in real monetary units *and* use a real rate as the required rate of return.

Consider an investment that is expected to generate sales of 100 units and a net cash inflow of $1,000 ($10 per unit) each year for two years *absent inflation*. If inflation of 10% is expected each year, net cash inflows from the sale of each unit would be $11 ($10 × 1.10) in year 1 and $12.10 [$11 × 1.10 or $10 × $(1.10)^2$] in year 2 resulting in net cash inflows of $1,100 in year 1 and $1,210 in year 2. The net cash inflows of $1,100 and $1,210 are nominal cash inflows because they include the impact of inflation. *These are the cash flows recorded by the accounting system.* The cash inflow of $1,000 each year are real cash flows because they exclude inflationary effects. Note that the real cash flows equal the nominal cash flows discounted for inflation, $1,000 = $1,100 ÷ 1.10 = $1,210 ÷ $(1.10)^2$. Many managers find the nominal approach easier to understand and use, because they observe nominal cash flows in their accounting systems and the nominal rates of return on financial markets.

Let's revisit Network Communications, which is deciding whether to invest in equipment to make and sell a cellular data transmission product. The equipment would cost $750,000 immediately. It is expected to have a four-year useful life with a zero terminal disposal price. An annual inflation rate of 10% is expected over this four-year period. Network Communications requires an after-tax real rate of return of 20% from this project or an after-tax nominal rate of return of 32% (see above).

The following table presents the predicted amounts of real (assuming no inflation) and nominal (after considering cumulative inflation) net cash inflows from the equipment over the next four years (excluding the $750,000 investment in the equipment and before any income tax payments):

[1]The real rate of return can be expressed in terms of the nominal rate of return as follows:

$$\text{Real rate} = \frac{(1 + \text{Nominal rate})}{(1 + \text{Inflation rate})} - 1 = \frac{(1 + 0.32)}{(1 + 0.10)} - 1 = 0.20$$

Year	Before-Tax Cash Inflows in Real Dollars (1)	Cumulative Inflation Rate Factor* (2)	Before-Tax Cash Inflows in Nominal Dollars (3) = (1) × (2)
1	$500,000	$(1.10)^1 = 1.1000$	$550,000
2	600,000	$(1.10)^2 = 1.2100$	726,000
3	600,000	$(1.10)^3 = 1.3310$	798,600
4	300,000	$(1.10)^4 = 1.4641$	439,230

*1.10 = 1.00 + 0.10 inflation rate.

The income tax rate is 40%. For tax purposes, the equipment will be amortized using a capital cost allowance rate of 30%, declining balance method.

Exhibit 22-7 presents the capital budgeting approach for predicting cash flows in nominal dollars and using a nominal discount rate.[2] The calculations in Exhibit

EXHIBIT 22-7

Nominal Approach to Inflation for Network Communications: Predict Cash Inflows and Outflows in Nominal Dollars and Use a Nominal Discount Rate*

1. Initial equipment investment:

Year	Investment: Outflows
0	$(750,000)

2. Cash savings from tax shield: $(750,000) ◄ 1,000000 ◄ $(750,000)

3. Recurring after-tax cash operating flows: $ 127,631‡ ◄ 1,000000 ◄ $ 127,631

$(622,369)

Year (1)	Recurring Nominal Cash Operating Inflows (2)	Income Tax Outflows (3) = 0.40 × (2)	Recurring Nominal After-Tax Cash Operating Inflows (4) = (2) − (3)
1	$550,000	$220,000	$330,000
2	726,000	290,400	435,600
3	798,600	319,440	479,160
4	439,230	175,692	263,538

250,000 ◄ 0.757576 ◄ --------$330,000	
250,000 ◄ 0.573921 ◄ --------------$435,600	
208,333 ◄ 0.434789 ◄ ------------------------$479,160	
86,805 ◄ 0.329385 ◄ ------------------------------$263,538	
795,138	

Net present value: $ 172,769

*The nominal discount rate of 32% is made up of the real rate of interest of 20% and the inflation rate of 10%: $[(1 + 0.20)(1 + 0.10)] − 1 = 0.32$.
†Present value discount factors are shown to six decimal digits to emphasize that the approaches to inflation in Exhibits 22-7 and 22-8 are equivalent. The formula on Table 2 of Appendix B is used to compute the present value discount factor.

‡$\$(750,000 \times 0.40) \frac{0.30}{0.30 + 0.32} \times \frac{2 + 0.32}{2(1 + 0.32)}$

$= \$300,000 \times 0.484 \times 0.879$

$= \$127,631.$

[2]The present value discount factors in the example are calculated using six decimal digits to eliminate doubt about the equivalence of the two approaches. In practice, the present value discount factors (to three decimal digits) can be obtained using Table 2 (present value of $1) of Appendix B at the end of the text. The Problem for Self-Study at the end of this chapter uses Table 2.

EXHIBIT 22-8

Real Approach to Inflation for Network Communications: Predict Cash Inflows and Outflows in Real Dollars and Use a Real Discount Rate

				Total Present Value	Present Value Discount Factors at 20%*	Sketch of Relevant After-Tax Cash Flows

End of Year: 0 1 2 3 4

1. Initial equipment investment:

Year	Investment Outflows
0	$(750,000)

$(750,000) ◄── 1.000000 ◄── $(750,000)

2. Cash savings from tax shield‡

127,631‡ ◄── 1.000000 ◄── 127,631

3. Recurring after-tax cash operating flows:

$(622,369)

Year (1)	Recurring Real Cash Operating Inflows (2)	Income Tax Outflows (3) = 0.40 × (2)	Recurring Real After-Tax Cash Operating Inflows (4) = (2) – (3)
1	$500,000	$200,000	$300,000
2	600,000	240,000	360,000
3	600,000	240,000	360,000
4	300,000	120,000	180,000

250,000 ◄── 0.833333 ◄──────── $300,000
250,000 ◄── 0.694444 ◄────────── $360,000
208,333 ◄── 0.578704 ◄──────────────── $360,000
86,805 ◄── 0.482253 ◄──────────────────── $180,000
795,138

Net present value $ 172,769

*Present value factors are shown to six decimal digits and the present value calculations rounded to emphasize that the approaches to inflation in Exhibits 22-7 and 22-8 are equivalent. The formula on Table 2 of Appendix B is used to compute the present value discount factor.
†The computation of these inflation factors is explained in footnote 3 below.
‡The tax shield formula has used the nominal rate of 32%, for demonstration purposes. It is common for companies to use a nominal rate, even though capital cost allowance amounts are not inflated.

22-7 exactly follow the calculations used in the Potato Supreme example for initial machine investment, tax shields, and recurring after-tax cash operating flows.

Exhibit 22-8 presents the approach of predicting cash flows in real terms and using a real discount rate. The calculations for item 3, recurring after-tax cash operating flows, are basically the same as before except that the cash inflows are measured in real terms and discounted at real rates.

Both approaches show that the project has a net present value of $172,769 and should therefore be accepted. Why do the two approaches give the same answer? Because, for example, in going from the real approach to the nominal approach, the cash flows are multiplied by and the discount rates are divided by the same cumulative inflation factor.[3]

The most frequently encountered error when accounting for inflation in capital budgeting is stating cash inflows and outflows in real monetary units and using a nominal discount rate. This error understates the discounted present value of cash flows that occur in the future and therefore creates a bias against the acceptance of many worthwhile capital investment projects.

[3]For example, recurring after-tax *real* cash operating flow in year 2 of $360,000 in Exhibit 22-8 is multiplied by $(1.10)^2$ to give $435,600 in after-tax *nominal* cash operating flows in year 2 in Exhibit 22-7. The *real* discount rate of 0.694444 in year 2 in Exhibit 22-8 is divided by $(1.10)^2$ to give the nominal discount rate of 0.573921 in year 2 in Exhibit 22-7.

PROJECT RISK AND REQUIRED RATE OF RETURN

OBJECTIVE 8

Describe alternative approaches used to recognize the degree of risk in capital budgeting projects

The *required rate of return* (RRR), which we discussed in Chapter 21, is a critical variable in discounted cash flow analysis. It is the rate of return that the organization forgoes by investing in a particular project rather than in an alternative project of comparable risk. *Risk* here refers to the business risk of the project, *independent* of the specific manner in which the project is financed—whether with debt or with equity. Here is a safe generalization: The higher the risk, the higher the required rate of return and the faster management would want to recover the net initial investment. Why? Because higher risk means a greater chance that the project may lose money. Management would only be willing to take this added risk if it was compensated with a higher expected return.

The RRR used in discounted cash flow analysis should be internally consistent with the approach applied to predict cash inflows and outflows. The options include various combinations of (1) the real rate and the nominal rate and (2) the pretax and the after-tax rate. The differences among these rates can be sizable, given estimates of inflation that may exceed 10% and corporate tax rates of 30% or more.

Organizations typically use at least one of the following approaches in dealing with the risk factor of projects:

1. **Varying the required payback time.** Companies such as Nissan that use payback as a project selection criterion vary the required payback to reflect differences in project risk. The higher the risk, the shorter the required payback time. When faced with higher risk, companies also evaluate their downside protection if the project is disbanded.[4]

2. **Adjusting the required rate of return.** Companies such as DuPont and Shell Oil use a higher required rate of return when the risk is higher. Estimating a precise risk factor for each project is difficult. Some organizations simplify the task by having three or four general-risk categories (for example, very high, high, average, and low). Each project under consideration is assigned to a specific category. Management uses a predetermined discount rate, assigned to each category, as the required rate of return for projects in that category.

3. **Adjusting the estimated future cash inflows.** Some companies, such as Dow Chemical, reduce the estimated future cash inflows of riskier projects. For example, they may systematically reduce the predicted cash inflows of very-high-risk projects by 30%, high-risk projects by 20%, and average-risk projects by 10%, and make no change to the projected cash inflows of low-risk projects. This approach is called the *certainty equivalent approach*. Since the cash flows for higher-risk projects have already been adjusted downward for their increased riskiness, the RRR used to evaluate those projects is the same as the RRR for low-risk projects. Note how this approach contrasts to adjusting the required rate of return. In that approach, the cash flows are not adjusted for risk, but the RRR is. In the certainty equivalent approach, the cash flows are adjusted for risk, but the RRR is not. Both adjusting the cash flows for risk and then using risk-adjusted RRRs would double-count the risk adjustment.

4. **Sensitivity (what-if) analysis.** Companies such as Consumers Power use this approach to examine the consequences of changing key assumptions underlying a capital budgeting project.

5. **Estimating the probability distribution of future cash inflows and outflows for each project.** Companies such as Niagara Mohawk use the approach to uncertainty that was discussed in the appendix to Chapter 3. The approach gives due weight to all possible cash flow outcomes to arrive at an expected cash flow and then discounts this amount at the risk-adjusted required rate of return for the investment. Estimating these probability distributions is difficult, but a practical guideline is to limit the number of outcomes under consideration to a small, manageable set. Consider another benefit of estimating the probability distribution of future cash inflows and outflows. Suppose a project has a 60%

Shell Oil
www.shell.com

Dow Chemical
www.dow.com

Consumers Power Company
www.cpco.com

[4]See J. Grinyer and N. Daing, "The Use of Abandonment Values in Capital Budgeting—A Research Note," *Management Accounting Research*, 4 (1993).

Risk Analysis in Capital Budgeting Decisions at Consumers Power

Consumers Power Co. (CP) owns pipelines to distribute natural gas to its customers. About 1,609 of the 32,186 kilometres of Consumers Power's main pipelines are made of cast iron. Most of CP's pipelines are made of cathodically protected coated and wrapped steel or of plastic. Gas leaks from cast-iron pipes are almost ten times more than for the other materials. An important capital budgeting decision for CP is how much of the cast-iron pipes it should replace and when. The benefits of replacing the pipes are lower repairs and maintenance costs and fewer claims following gas leaks, but the precise benefits are far from certain.

To incorporate uncertainty, Consumers Power estimates a range of values for key parameters—the number of times the pipeline might leak, the quantity of gas that may leak, the dollar claims that may have to be paid, and repairs and maintenance costs that may be incurred—under each replacement alternative. CP uses sensitivity analysis to identify the parameters and parameter values that most affect the decision and those that do not. It then develops probability distributions for the key parameters on the basis of structured interviews with experts in different subject areas. CP calculates net present values for the different alternatives by discounting the expected returns by a risk-adjusted required rate of return. CP computes net present values on an after-tax basis, using nominal cash flows and nominal discount rates to consistently consider the effects of inflation.

CP's analysis indicated that the optimal program was to replace the worst cast-iron pipes first and all cast-iron pipes over a 40-year period. In the absence of this detailed and thorough risk-based analysis, CP's managers would have favoured replacing the cast-iron pipes sooner.

Source: Adapted from Elenbars, K. L. and D. O'Neill, "Formal Decision Analysis Process Guides Maintenance Budgeting," *Pipeline Industry,* October 1994.

likelihood of very high cash inflows and a 40% likelihood of minimal cash inflows in its early years. This 40% probability may prompt managers to establish lines of credit with a bank. If the low outcome occurs, these lines of credit would enable the company to avoid a short-run cash flow crisis.

APPLICABILITY TO NONPROFIT ORGANIZATIONS

Discounted cash flow analysis applies to both profit-seeking and nonprofit organizations. Almost all organizations must decide which investments in long-term assets will accomplish various tasks at the least cost.

Studies of the capital budgeting practices of government agencies at various levels (federal, provincial, and local) and in several countries report that, as in the profit-oriented sector, the following prevails:

1. Urgency is an important factor when allocating funds. For example, capital budgeting for roads is often motivated by physical deficiencies in an existing highway rather than a systematic analysis of alternative road construction projects.

2. Project estimates are sometimes systematically biased. For example, studies report overestimates of the benefits, underestimates of the costs, and underestimates of the time it takes to construct dams and other irrigation infrastructures.

3. There is a tendency to cut capital-budget projects first when there is a strong push to balance a budget or reduce a deficit. Consider the effect of efforts to contain health care costs in Canada. As a result of these changes and the increased emphasis on controlling hospital charges through competition and regulation, hospitals are increasingly using analytical capital budgeting methods

(such as discounted cash flow methods) and are also more carefully auditing the benefits of capital expenditures.

IMPLEMENTING THE NET PRESENT VALUE DECISION RULE

OBJECTIVE 9

Explain the excess present value index and its usefulness in capital budgeting

Excess present value index.
Capital budgeting measure in which the total present value of future net cash inflows of a project is divided by the total present value of the net initial investment.

Executives in both profit-seeking and nonprofit organizations must frequently work within an overall capital budget limit. This section discusses problems in using the net present value method when there is a restriction on the total funds available for capital spending.

The **excess present value index** (sometimes called the *profitability index*) is the total present value of future net cash inflows of a project divided by the total present value of the net initial investment. The following table illustrates this index for two software graphics packages—Superdraw and Masterdraw—that Business Systems is evaluating:

Project	Present Value at 10% RRR (1)	Net Initial Investment (2)	Excess Present Value Index (3) = (1) ÷ (2)	Net Present Value (4) = (1) - (2)
Superdraw	$1,400,000	$1,000,000	140%	$400,000
Masterdraw	3,900,000	3,000,000	130%	900,000

The excess present value index or profitability index measures the cash flow return per dollar invested. The index is viewed as particularly helpful in choosing between projects when investment funds are limited. Why? Because profitability indexes can identify the projects that will generate the most money from the limited capital available.

Suppose that the developers of each package require that Business Systems market only one software graphics package, so accepting one software package automatically means rejecting the other—that is, the packages are mutually exclusive. Which package should Business Systems choose?

Using the profitability index, Superdraw will be preferred over Masterdraw, because it has a profitability index of 140%, which is higher than the 130% for Masterdraw. But the profitability index analysis assumes that all other things, such as risk and alternative use of funds, are equal. For example, it assumes that choosing between Superdraw and Masterdraw has no effect on the other projects that Business Systems plans to implement. If "all other things" are not "equal," which is often the case, the profitability index may not result in the optimal choice of investment projects.

Continuing the Business Systems example, assume that Business Systems has a total capital budget limit of $5,000,000 for the coming year. It is considering investing in Superdraw or Masterdraw and in any one or more of eight other projects (coded B, C, . . . , H, I). Exhibit 22-9 presents two alternative combinations of these projects. Note that the project portfolio in alternative 2 is superior to alternative 1, despite the greater cash flow return per dollar invested in Superdraw compared with Masterdraw. Why? Because the $2,000,000 incremental investment in Masterdraw increases net present value (NPV) by $500,000. The $2,000,000 would otherwise be invested in projects E and B, which have a lower combined NPV of $256,000:

	Present Value	Net Initial Investment	Increase in Net Present Value
Masterdraw	$3,900,000	$3,000,000	
Superdraw	1,400,000	1,000,000	
Increment	$2,500,000	$2,000,000	$500,000
Project E	$ 912,000	$ 800,000	
Project B	1,344,000	1,200,000	
Total	$2,256,000	$2,000,000	$256,000

Note that other than Superdraw, alternative 2 includes projects with the highest excess present value indexes and excludes those with the lowest excess present value indexes. The excess present value index is a useful guide for identifying and choosing projects that will offer the best return on limited capital and that will thereby maximize

Risk Adjustment Methods in Capital Budgeting

How do companies around the globe adjust for risk when evaluating capital investments? The percentages in the following table indicate how frequently particular risk adjustment methods are used in capital budgeting in four countries. The reported percentages exceed 100% because some companies use more than one risk adjustment method. Dashes indicate information was not disclosed in survey.

	Canada*	United States[†]	Australia*	United Kingdom[§]	Taiwan[#]	Poland[**]
Sensitivity analysis	59%	29%	57%	63%	—	10%
Increase the required rate of return	31%	18%—	—	42%	61%	13%
Shorten payback period	24%	17%	—	34%	72%	25%
Estimate probability distribution of future cash flows	18%	12%	11%	15%	—	13%
Compare optimistic and pessimistic forecasts	—	—	63%	—	—	—
Make subjective, nonquantitative assessment	29%	54%	37%	22%	69%	4%
Make no adjustments	10%	37%	—	—	—	—

The surveys indicate that the specific methods managers use vary between countries. A common feature, however, is that managers appear to favour simpler methods (for example, sensitivity analysis, shortening the payback period, increasing the required rate of return, and subjective, nonquantitative assessments) rather than more sophisticated techniques (for example, estimating the probability distribution of future cash flows).

*Adapted from: *Jog, V., and A. Srivastava, "Corporate Financial Decision Making in Canada," *Canadian Journal of Administrative Sciences* (June 1994); [†]Sullivan, C., and K. Smith, "Capital Investment Justification for U.S. Factory Automation Projects," *Journal of the Midwest Finance Association* (1994); [‡]Freeman, M., and G. Hobbes, "Capital Budgeting: Theory versus Practice," *Australian Accountant* (September 1991); [§]Ho, S. and R. Pike, "Risk Analysis in Capital Budgeting Contexts: Simple or Sophisticated ?" *Accounting and Business Research* (Vol. 21, No. 83, 1991) [#]Ho, S., and L. Yang, "Managerial Risk Taking and Handling in Corporate Investment: An Exploratory Study in Taiwan," *Proceedings of the Second International Conference on Asian-Pacific Financial Markets*, (September 1991); [**]Zarzecki, D., and T. Wisniewski, "Investment Appraisal Practice in Poland," (Working Paper, Szcecin University, Szcecin, Poland, 1995)

EXHIBIT 22-9

Allocation of $5,000,000 Capital Budget: Comparison of Two Alternatives for Business Systems

	Alternative 1				Alternative 2		
Project	Net Initial Investment	Excess Present Value Index	Total Present Value at 10%	Project	Net Initial Investment	Excess Present Value Index	Total Present Value at 10%
C	$ 600,000	167%	$1,002,000	C	$ 600,000	167%	$1,002,000
Superdraw	1,000,000	140%	1,400,000				
D	400,000	132%	528,000	D	400,000	132%	528,000
				Masterdraw	3,000,000	130%	3,900,000
F	1,000,000	115%	1,150,000	F	1,000,000	115%	1,150,000
					$5,000,000*		$6,580,000[‡]
E	800,000	114%	912,000	E	$ 800,000	114%	Reject
B	1,200,000	112%	1,344,000	B	1,200,000	112%	Reject
	$5,000,000*		$6,336,000[†]				
H	$ 550,000	105%	Reject	H	550,000	105%	Reject
G	450,000	101%	Reject	G	450,000	101%	Reject
I	1,000,000	90%	Reject	I	1,000,000	90%	Reject

*Total budget constraint.
[†]Net present value = $6,336,000 − $5,000,000 = $1,336,000.
[‡]Net present value = $6,580,000 − 5,000,000 = $1,580,000.

net present value. But managers cannot base decisions involving mutually exclusive investments of different sizes solely on the excess present value index. The net present value method is the best general guide.

IMPLEMENTING THE INTERNAL RATE-OF-RETURN DECISION RULE

OBJECTIVE 10

Explain why the internal rate-of-return and the net present value decision rules may rank projects differently

The NPV method always indicates the project (or set of projects) that maximizes the NPV of future cash flows. However, surveys of practice report widespread use of the internal rate-of-return (IRR) method. Why? Probably because managers find this method easier to understand and because, in most instances, their decisions would be unaffected by using one method or the other. In some cases, however, the two methods will not indicate the same decision.

Where mutually exclusive projects have unequal lives or unequal investments, the IRR method can rank projects differently from the NPV method. Consider Exhibit 22-10.[5] The ranking by the IRR method favours project X, while the ranking by the NPV method favours project Z. The projects ranked in Exhibit 22-10 differ in both life (5, 10, and 15 years) and net initial investment ($286,400, $419,200, and $509,200).

Managers using the IRR method implicitly assume that the reinvestment rate is equal to the indicated rate of return for the shortest-lived project. Managers using the NPV method implicitly assume that the funds obtainable from competing projects can be reinvested at the company's required rate of return. The NPV method is generally regarded as conceptually superior. Students should refer to corporate finance texts for more details on these issues, and on the problems of ranking projects with unequal lives or unequal investments.

EXHIBIT 22-10
Ranking of Projects Using Internal Rate of Return and Net Present Value

				IRR Method		NPV Method		
Project	Life	Net Initial Investment	Annual Cash Flow from Operations, Net of Income Taxes	IRR	Ranking	PV of Annual Cash Flow from Operations, Net of Income Taxes	NPV	Ranking
X	5	$286,400	$100,000	22%	1	$379,100	$ 92,700	3
Y	10	419,200	100,000	20	2	614,500	195,300	2
Z	15	509,200	100,000	18	3	760,600	251,400	1

PROBLEM FOR SELF-STUDY

This is a comprehensive review problem. It illustrates both income tax factors and capital budgeting with inflation.

PROBLEM

Stone Aggregates (SA) operates 92 plants producing a crushed stone that is used in many construction projects. Transportation is a major cost item. A scale clerk weighs the products and on a delivery ticket, records details of the product shipped: its weight, its freight charges, and whether or not it is taxed.

SA is considering a proposal to use computerized delivery ticket-writing equipment at each of its 92 plants. One plant has used the equipment as a pilot site for the past 12 months, generating cash operating cost savings (before taxes) of $300,000 by improving productivity, and by reducing plant operating costs and excess shipments to customers. The cost analyst estimates that if the equipment had been in use at all of the company's plants for the past year, net cost savings would have been $25 million (expressed in today's dollars).

[5]Exhibit 22-10 concentrates on differences in project lives. Similar conflicting results can occur when the terminal dates are the same but the sizes of the net initial investments differ.

The cost of the equipment for all 92 plants is $45 million, which would be payable immediately. This equipment has an expected useful life of four years and a terminal disposal price of $10 million (expressed in today's dollars). The equipment qualifies for a capital cost allowance rate of 25% declining balance. Stone Aggregates expects a 30% income tax rate in each of the next four years.

REQUIRED
1. Does the proposal for the computerized delivery ticket-writing equipment meet SA's 16% after-tax required rate-of-return criterion? This rate of return includes an 8% inflation component. (The real rate of return is 7.4%; recall that nominal rate of return = $[(1 + 0.074)(1 + 0.08)] - 1 = 0.16$.) This 8% inflation prediction applies to both the cost savings and the terminal disposal price of the equipment. Compute the NPV using nominal dollars and a nominal required rate of return.
2. What other factors would you recommend that SA consider when evaluating the computerized delivery ticket-writing equipment?

SOLUTION
1. Exhibit 22-11 shows the NPV computations. To illustrate an alternative presentation found in practice, the format of Exhibit 22-11 differs from that of Exhibits 22-4, 22-5, and 22-6. The proposal for computerized delivery ticket-writing equipment has an NPV of $29,562 million, indicating that—on the basis of financial factors—it is an attractive investment.
2. The analysis in Exhibit 22-11 assumes that net cash savings are $25 million each year. However, operating and implementation costs in the year of changeover to the computerized equipment are often 200% higher than in subsequent years. Consequently, net cash savings may be lower in the first year.

EXHIBIT 22-11
Net Present Value Analysis of Computerized Ticket-Writing System for Stone Aggregates (in thousands; n.d. = nominal dollars)

	Total Present Value	End of Year 1	End of Year 2	End of Year 3	End of Year 4
Recurring After-Tax Cash Operating Flows					
1. Recurring cash operating savings (real dollars)	—	$25,000	$25,000	$25,000	$25,000
2. Cumulative inflation factor (from Table 1, Appendix B for 8%)	—	1.080	1.166	1.260	1.360
3. Cash operating savings (n.d.): 1×2	—	$27,000	$29,150	$31,500	$34,000
4. Tax payments: $30\% \times 3$	—	$ 8,100	$ 8,745	$ 9,450	$10,200
5. Recurring after-tax cash operating savings (n.d.): $3 - 4$	—	$ 8,900	$20,405	$22,050	$23,800
6. Present value discount factor (16% nominal)	—	0.862	0.743	0.641	0.552
7. PV of recurring after-tax cash operating savings (n.d.): 5×6	$ 58,725	$16,292	$15,161	$14,134	$13,138
Initial Equipment Investment					
New equipment	$(45,000)				
Tax shield	7,667*				
	(37,333)				
Terminal disposal	10,000				
Lost tax shield	(1,830)†				
	8,170				
	(29,163)				
Net present value	$ 29,562				

$*(\$45,000 \times 0.30) \times \dfrac{0.25}{0.25 + 0.16} \times \dfrac{(2 + 0.16)}{2(1 + 0.16)} = \$13,500 \times 0.610 \times 0.931$
$= \$7,667.$

$†(\$10,000 \times 0.30) \times \dfrac{0.25}{0.25 + 0.16} = \$3,000 \times 0.610 = \$1,830.$

(Half-year rule does not apply to disposals.)

SUMMARY

The following points are linked to the chapter's learning objectives.

1. Operating cash flows need to be adjusted for the income tax effect.

2. Amortization is a noncash cost. But capital cost allowance is a deductible cost for calculating tax outflows. The taxes saved as a result of capital cost allowance deductions increase cash flows in discounted cash flow (DCF) computations.

3. The total-project approach calculates the present value of all cash inflows and outflows under each alternative. The differential approach includes only those cash inflows and outflows that differ across the alternatives.

4. Five categories of cash flows considered in capital budgeting analyses involving a machine are (a) initial machine investment, (b) cash flow from the current disposal of the old machine, (c) recurring after-tax cash operating flows, (d) income tax cash savings from capital cost allowance deductions, and (e) cash flow from the terminal disposal of the machine.

5. The real rate of return is the rate of return required to cover only investment risk. The nominal rate of return is the rate of return required to cover investment risk and the anticipated decline, due to inflation, in the general purchasing power of the cash that the investment generates.

6. Two internally consistent ways to account for inflation in capital budgeting are (a) to predict cash flows and outflows in nominal terms and to use a nominal discount rate and (b) to predict cash inflows and outflows in real terms and to use a real discount rate. The nominal and real approaches are equivalent: they yield the same net present value, but many managers find the nominal approach easier to work with.

7. The higher the risk, the higher the required rate of return on an investment. Alternative approaches to recognizing project risk in capital budgeting decisions are (a) reducing the required payback time, (b) increasing the required rate of return, (c) reducing estimated future cash inflows, (d) performing sensitivity analysis, and (e) estimating the probability distribution of future cash inflows and outflows.

8. The excess present value index (profitability index) is the total present value of future net cash inflows of a project divided by the total present value of the net initial investment. It is a useful guide when allocating limited finds among projects, but it cannot be used as the sole criterion.

9. The net present value and internal rate-of-return methods make different assumptions about the rate at which project cash inflows are reinvested. Consequently, the two methods may rank projects differently.

APPENDIX: SELECTED CCA CLASSES AND RATES

Class 1	(4%)	Buildings or other structures, including component parts acquired after 1987
Class 3	(5%)	Buildings or other structures, including component parts acquired before 1988
Class 8	(20%)	Miscellaneous tangible capital property and machinery or equipment not included in another class
Class 9	(25%)	Electrical generating equipment, radar and radio equipment, acquired before 1976
Class 10	(30%)	Automotive equipment and general-purpose electronic data processing equipment with its systems software
Class 12	(100%)	Tools or utensils costing less than $200, videotape, certified feature films, computer software
Class 14		Patent, franchise, concession, or licence for a limited period (straight-line over legal life)

Class 29   Property used in manufacturing or processing acquired before 1988 (2 years straight-line)

Class 39   Property used in manufacturing or processing acquired after 1987 (1988—40%; 1989—35%; 1990—30%; after 1990—25%)

▼ TERMS TO LEARN

This chapter contains definitions of the following important terms:

capital cost allowance (p. 761)	nominal rate of return (p. 770)
differential approach (p. 765)	real rate of return (p. 770)
excess present value index (p. 776)	tax shield formula (p. 762)
half-year rule (p. 762)	total-project approach (p. 765)
inflation (p. 770)	unamortized capital cost (p. 762)
marginal income tax rate (p. 760)	

▼ ASSIGNMENT MATERIAL

QUESTIONS

22-1 Describe three types of cash flows impacted by income taxes.

22-2 "It doesn't matter what accounting amortization method is used. The total dollar tax bills are the same." Do you agree? Explain.

22-3 Give examples of four categories of cash flows considered in capital budgeting analyses.

22-4 Distinguish between the total-project approach and the differential approach to choosing between two capital budgeting projects.

22-5 "Accounting amortization is an irrelevant factor in deciding whether to replace an existing delivery vehicle with a more energy-efficient vehicle." Do you agree? Explain.

22-6 "Income taxes only play a role in capital budgeting because of capital cost allowance tax savings." Do you agree? Explain.

22-7 What are the two basic types of capital cost allowance classes?

22-8 Distinguish between the *nominal* rate of return and the *real* rate of return.

22-9 What are the two internally consistent approaches to incorporating inflation into DCF analysis?

22-10 What approaches might be used to recognize risk in capital budgeting?

22-11 "In practice there is no single rate that a given company can use as a guide for sifting among all projects." Do you agree? Explain.

22-12 "Discounted cash flow techniques are relevant only to profit-seeking organizations." Do you agree? Explain.

22-13 "The excess present value index or profitability index is a useful guide when allocating limited funds among projects." Do you agree? Explain.

22-14 "The net present value method and the internal rate-of-return method always rank different projects identically." Do you agree? Explain.

EXERCISES

22-15 New equipment purchase. Presentation Graphics prepares slides and other aids for individuals making presentations. It estimates it can save $35,000 a year in cash operating costs for the next five years if it buys a special-purpose colour-slide workstation at a cost of $75,000. The workstation qualifies for a capital cost allowance rate of 25%, declining balance, and will have a zero terminal disposal price at the end of year 5. Presentation Graphics has a 12% after-tax required rate of return. Its income tax rate is 40% each year for the next five years.

Compute (a) net present value, (b) payback period, and (c) internal rate of return.

22-16 Multiple choice. (CPA, adapted) The Apex Company is evaluating a capital budgeting proposal for the current year. The relevant data are as follows:

Year	Present Value of an Annuity of $1 in Arrears at 15%
1	$0.870
2	1.626
3	2.284
4	2.856
5	3.353
6	3.785

The initial equipment investment would be $30,000. Apex would amortize the equipment for accounting purposes on a straight-line basis over six years with a zero terminal disposal price. The before-tax annual cash inflow arising from this investment is $10,000. The income tax rate is 40%, and income tax is paid the same year as incurred. The capital investment qualifies for a capital cost allowance rate of 20%, declining balance. The after-tax required rate of return is 15%. Choose the best answer for each question and show your computations.

1. What is the after-tax accrual accounting rate of return on Apex's initial equipment investment?
   (a) 10%, (b) 16⅔%, (c) 26⅔%, (d) 33⅓%.
2. What is the after-tax payback period (in years) for Apex's capital budgeting proposal?
   (a) 5, (b) 2.6, (c) 3, (d) 2.
3. What is the net present value of Apex's capital budgeting proposal?
   (a) $(7,290), (b) $(885), (c) $7,850, (d) $11,760.
4. How much would Apex have had to invest five years ago at 15% compounded annually to have $30,000 now?
   (a) $12,960, (b) $14,910, (c) $17,160, (d) cannot be determined from the information given.

22-17 Automated materials-handling capital project, income taxes, sensitivity analysis. Ontime Distributors operates a large distribution network for health-related products. It is considering an automated materials-handling (AMH) proposal for its major warehouse to reduce storage space, labour costs, and product damage. The before-tax net cash operating savings from the automation are estimated to be $2.5 million a year. The AMH equipment will cost $6 million, payable immediately. The equipment has a useful life of four years and a zero terminal disposal price. The lease on the warehouse expires in four years and is not expected to be renewed. The company has an income tax rate of 40% and an after-tax required rate of return of 12%. Under existing tax laws, the $6 million equipment cost qualifies for a capital cost allowance rate of 30%, declining balance.

REQUIRED
1. Compute (a) the net present value and (b) the payback period on the automated materials-handling project.
2. Calculate the minimum annual before-tax net cash operating savings that will make the AMH equipment desirable from a net present value standpoint.
3. What other factors should Ontime Distributors consider in its decision?

22-18 Total project versus differential approach, income taxes. A manufacturer of automobile parts acquired a special-purpose shaping machine for automatically producing a particular part. The machine has been used for one year. It will have no useful economic life after three more years. It cost $88,000, has a current disposal price of $29,000, and has a terminal disposal price of $6,000.

A new machine has become available and is far more efficient than the present machine. It would cost $63,000, would cut annual cash operating costs from $60,000 to $40,000, and would have zero terminal disposal price at the end of its useful life of three years. The applicable income tax rate is 30%. The after-tax required rate of return is 14%.

These machines qualify for a capital cost allowance rate of 20%, declining balance.

REQUIRED

Using the net present value method, show whether the new machine should be purchased (a) under a total project approach and (b) under a differential approach.

22-19 Selling plant, income taxes. (CMA, adapted) Waterford Specialties Corporation, a clothing manufacturer, has a plant that will become idle on December 31, 2000. John Landry, corporate controller, has been asked to look at three options regarding the disposition of the plant.

◆ **Option 1.** The plant, which has been fully amortized for financial reporting, can be sold immediately for $9 million.

◆ **Option 2.** The plant can be leased to Auburn Mills, one of Waterford's suppliers, for four years. Under the terms of the lease, Auburn would pay Waterford $200,000 per month in rent and would grant Waterford a special 10% discount off the normal price of $2 per metre on 2.37 million metres of fabric purchased by another Waterford plant. Auburn would cover all of the plant's ownership costs including property taxes. Waterford expects to sell this plant for $2 million at the end of the four-year lease.

◆ **Option 3.** The plant could be used for four years to make souvenir jackets for the 2004 Olympics. Fixed overhead, before any equipment upgrades, is estimated to be $200,000 annually for the four-year period. The jackets are expected to sell for $42 each. Unit variable costs are expected to be as follows: direct materials, $20.80; direct manufacturing, marketing, and distribution labour, $6.40; variable manufacturing, marketing, and distribution overhead, $5.80.

The following production and sales of jackets are expected: 2001, 200,000 units; 2002, 300,000 units; 2003, 400,000 units; 2004 100,000 units. In order to manufacture the souvenir jackets, some of the plant equipment would have to be upgraded at an immediate cost of $1.5 million to be amortized for financial reporting purposes using straight-line amortization over the four years it will be in use. Because of the modernization of the equipment, Waterford could sell the plant for $3 million at the end of four years. The equipment qualifies for a 25% declining balance capital cost allowance rate.

Waterford treats all cash flows as if they occur at the end of the year, and uses an after-tax cost of capital of 12%. Waterford is subject to a 40% tax rate.

REQUIRED

1. Would you use the total project approach or the differential approach to choose among the three options? Why?
2. Calculate the net present value of each of the options available to Waterford and determine which option Waterford should select using the net present value criterion.
3. What nonfinancial and qualitative factors should Waterford consider before making its choice?

22-20 Project risk, required rate of return. Esso Petroleum is considering two investment projects. The first project, viewed as a high-risk investment, is drilling equipment for oil exploration activities. Esso expects the drilling equipment to cost $1 million and result in operating cash flows before taxes of $370,000 per year for five years. The equipment has a five-year life and a terminal disposal price of zero.

The second project, viewed as a low-risk investment, is production equipment that will improve the yield in Esso's refinery. Esso expects the production equipment to cost $800,000 and result in operating cash flows before taxes of $300,000 per year for four years. The equipment has a four-year life and a terminal disposal price of zero. Esso's income tax rate is 30%. The production and drilling equipment capital cost allowance rate is 25%, declining balance.

REQUIRED

1. Which project has the higher net present value if Esso uses an after-tax required rate of return (RRR) of 12% for both projects?
2. A manager at Esso objects to the calculations in requirement 1 arguing that riskier investments should have a higher RRR. Suppose Esso requires an 18% after-tax RRR for high-risk investments and a 12% after-tax RRR for low-risk investments. Which project has the higher net present value?
3. Which project do you favour? Why?

22-21 Income taxes, inflation. James Delusio, plant manager of Peoria Metal Works, is considering an investment in special tools of $200,000 on December 31, 2000. The tools have an estimated useful life of four years and a $20,000 terminal disposal price. The tools will enable Peoria to manufacture drill bits to very high tolerances without incurring any incremental costs, and to earn additional cash flows of $2 per unit in 2001, $2.12 in 2002, $2.25 in 2003, and $2.38 in 2004. Peoria expects to sell 35,000 units each year for the next four years. Peoria is subject to a 40% tax rate. The after-tax required rate of return is 18%. The tools qualify for a capital cost allowance rate of 35%, declining balance.

REQUIRED

1. Compute the net present value of the project.
2. Delusio feels that inflation will persist for the next four years at the rate of 6% per year. However, the 18% minimum desired rate of return already includes a return required to cover the effects of anticipated inflation. Repeat requirement 1, to take inflationary effects into consideration.
3. Could you have taken inflation into account in a way different from what you did in requirement 2? Broadly describe how without actually performing any calculations.

22-22 **Inflation and nonprofit institution, no tax aspects.** Eastern University is considering the purchase of a photocopying machine for $3,500 on December 31, 2000. It has a useful life of five years, has a zero terminal disposal price, and is amortized on a straight-line basis. The cash operating savings are expected to be $1,000 annually, measured in December 31, 2000 dollars. The required rate of return is 18.8%, which includes a return required to cover the effects of anticipated inflation of 10%. The university pays no taxes. The present values of $1 discounted at 18.8% received at the end of 1, 2, 3, 4, and 5 periods are 0.842, 0.709, 0.596, 0.502, and 0.423.

REQUIRED

1. A university official computed the net present value of the project using an 18.8% discount rate without adjusting the cash operating savings for inflation. What net present value figure did he compute? Is this approach correct? If not, how would you redo the analysis?
2. (a) What is the real rate of return required by Eastern University for investing in the photocopying machine? (b) Calculate the net present value using the real rate of return approach to incorporating inflation.
3. Compare your analyses in requirements 1 and 2. Present generalizations that seem applicable about the analysis of inflation in capital budgeting.

22-23 **Excess present value index.** The Bristol Company is a design engineering firm that specializes in designing different types of application-specific chips for the semiconductor industry. It is considering buying new design equipment and has identified two mutually exclusive options, Design Pro and Easychip. It is also considering other capital investments (coded C and D). The following table describes the financial characteristics of these projects.

Project	Present Value of Cash Inflows at 14% Required Rate of Return	Net Initial Investment
Design Pro	$ 750,000	$500,000
Easychip	1,050,000	750,000
Project C	585,000	450,000
Project D	320,000	200,000

REQUIRED

1. For each project, calculate (a) the net present value and (b) the excess present value index. On the basis of the excess present value index only, should Bristol choose Design Pro or Easychip?
2. Suppose Bristol must choose one of Design Pro or Easychip, and suppose Bristol has a capital investment budget of $950,000, which projects should Bristol choose?
3. Comment on your answers to requirements 1 and 2.

22-24 **Comparison of projects with unequal lives.** The manager of the Robin Hood Company is considering two investment projects that are mutually exclusive. The after-tax required rate of return of this company is 10%, and the anticipated cash flows are as follows:

Project No.	Investment Required Now	Cash Inflows			
		Year 1	Year 2	Year 3	Year 4
1	$10,000	$12,000	$0	$0	$ 0
2	10,000	0	0	0	17,500

REQUIRED

1. Compute the internal rate of return of both projects. Which project is preferable?
2. Compute the net present value of both projects. Which project is preferable?
3. Comment briefly on the results in requirements 1 and 2. Be specific in your comparisons.

PROBLEMS

22-25 Equipment replacement, income taxes. (CMA, adapted) VacuTech manufactures testing instruments for microcircuits. These instruments sell for $3,500 each. VacuTech incurs cash operating costs of $2,450 to manufacture these instruments. On January 1, 2001, VacuTech bought a vacuum pump for $400,000. VacuTech is considering the purchase of a new, more efficient pump on January 1, 2005 (4 years later). The new pump costs $620,000. The pump qualifies for a capital cost allowance rate of 25%, declining balance. The new pump is expected to have a terminal disposal price of $80,000 at the end of four years. At current rates of production, the new pump's greater efficiency will result in annual cash savings of $125,000.

The old pump will be fully amortized for accounting purposes by December 31, 2004, but it can still be used for another four years. It has a current disposal price of $50,000. If it is used for another four years, the pump's terminal disposal price will be zero.

VacuTech is able to sell all the testing instruments it produces. Because of the increased speed of the new pump, output is expected to increase by 30 units in 2005, 50 units in 2006 and 2007, and 70 units in 2008. Over and above the annual cash savings at current production levels, VacuTech's cash manufacturing costs will decrease by $150 per unit on all *additional* units produced.

VacuTech is subject to a 40% tax rate. VacuTech's after-tax required rate of return is 16%.

REQUIRED

1. Determine whether VacuTech should purchase the new pump by calculating the net present value at January 1, 2005, of the estimated after-tax cash flows that would result from the acquisition.
2. Describe the nonfinancial and qualitative factors that VacuTech should consider before making the pump replacement decision.

22-26 Replacement of a machine, income taxes, sensitivity. (CMA, adapted) The WRL Company operates a snack food centre at the Hartsfield Airport. On January 2, 2000, WRL purchased a special cookie-cutting machine, which has been used for three years. WRL is considering purchasing a newer, more efficient machine. If purchased, the new machine would be acquired today on January 2, 2003. WRL expects to sell 300,000 cookies in each of the next four years. The selling price of each cookie is expected to average $0.50.

WRL has two options: (1) continue to operate the old machine or (2) sell the old machine and purchase the new machine. The seller of the new machine offered no tradein. The following information has been assembled to help management decide which option is more desirable:

	Old Machine	New Machine
Initial machine investment	$80,000	$120,000
Terminal disposal price at the end of useful life assumed for amortization purposes	$10,000	$ 20,000
Useful life from date of acquisition	7 years	4 years
Expected annual cash operating costs:		
Variable cost per cookie	$0.20	$0.14
Total fixed costs	$15,000	$ 14,000
Amortization method used for accounting purposes	Straight-line	Straight-line
Estimated disposal prices of machines:		
January 2, 2000	$40,000	$120,000
December 31, 2003	$ 7,000	$ 20,000
Capital cost allowance rate (declining balance)	25%	25%

WRL has a 40% income tax rate and an after-tax required rate of return of 16%.

REQUIRED

1. Use the net present value method to determine whether WRL should retain the old machine or acquire the new machine.

2. How much more or less would the recurring after-tax variable cash operating savings have to be for WRL to exactly earn the 16% after-tax required rate of return? Assume all other data about the investment does not change.

3. Assume that the financial differences between the net present values of the two options are so slight that WRL is indifferent between the two proposals. Identify and discuss the nonfinancial and qualitative factors that WRL should consider.

22-27 Capital budgeting, make versus buy, income taxes, relevant costs. (CMA, adapted) The Jonfran Company manufactures three different models of paper shredders. Each has a waste container. Jonfran estimates the following number of waste containers needed over the next five years: 2000, 50,000; 2001, 50,000; 2002, 52,000; 2003, 55,000; 2004, 55,000.

The equipment used to manufacture waste containers must be replaced because it has broken. The old equipment has a current disposal price of $1,500. The new equipment would cost $960,000. The equipment would go into service on January 1, 2000, and would have a five-year useful life. Under the prevailing tax laws, capital cost allowance is calculated on the double-declining-balance method at a rate of 25%. The terminal disposal at the end of five years is estimated at $12,000.

Jonfran's current manufacturing costs for waste containers are as follows:

Direct materials		$10
Direct manufacturing labour		8
Variable manufacturing overhead		4
Fixed manufacturing overhead:		
Supervision	$2	
Amortization on old equipment	3	
General administrative overhead	6	11
Total manufacturing cost per unit		$33

An outside supplier has offered to supply all the containers that Jon-fran needs over the next five years at a fixed price of $29 per container. If the supplier's offer is accepted, Jonfran would not need to replace the equipment.

If the waste containers are purchased outside, the salary and benefits of one supervisor, included in the fixed overhead at $45,000, would be eliminated. There would, however, be no change in general administrative overhead. Jonfran has no alternative use for the extra space that would become available if the containers were purchased from outside. Working capital requirements are approximately the same whether the containers are made or purchased.

Jonfran has a 40% income tax rate. Its after-tax required rate of return on new equipment is 12%.

REQUIRED

1. Use a net present value analysis to determine whether Jonfran should purchase the waste containers from the outside supplier or purchase the new equipment.

2. What nonfinancial and qualitative factors should Jonfran consider before coming to a decision?

22-28 Capital budgeting, inventory changes. (M. Wolfson, J. Harris, adapted) Total Fitness is a small company that makes products for physical fitness. The company is considering whether to add a new line of running shoes to be sold to retail stores. To produce these shoes, special machines costing a total of $109,200 must be acquired. The machines have a useful life of four years, with a combined terminal disposal price of $18,000. The new line of shoes would be dropped at the end of four years. The estimates for the new product line are as follows:

Year	Units Produced	Units Sold	Selling Price	Variable Manufacturing Costs per Unit
1	7,000	6,000	$25	$12
2	6,500	6,200	25	13
3	6,500	7,700	24	14
4	3,000	3,100	22	15
	23,000	23,000		

Variable marketing, distribution, and customer service costs are estimated at $3 per unit and are not expected to change over the four-year period. The selling price data and all cost estimates are expressed in nominal dollars. Accounts receivable and current liabilities are expected to be minimal.

For tax purposes, the machines qualifies for a capital cost allowance rate of 25%, declining balance. Manufacturing costs are deductible for tax purposes in the year when the related goods are sold. The company uses the first-in, first-out inventory method for its tax return. Marketing, distribution, and customer service costs are deduct-ible for tax purposes in the year when they are incurred. Assume a 40% tax rate. Also, assume that all operating cash flows and income tax payments occur at the end of the year. The after-tax nominal required rate of return is 16%.

Absorption costing must be used for tax purposes. Amortization is allocated on the basis of the estimates of the units produced each year.

REQUIRED
1. Prepare a schedule of relevant cash flows, including income taxes, for each year.
2. Compute the net present value of adding the new line of running shoes.

22-29 Capital budgeting, inflation, taxation. (J. Fellingham, adapted) Abbie Young is manager of the customer service division of an electrical appliance store. Abbie is considering buying a repairing machine that costs $10,000 on December 31, 2000. The machine will last five years. Abbie estimates that the incremental pretax cash savings from using the machine will be $3,000 annually. The $3,000 is measured at current prices and will be received at the end of each year. For tax purposes, the machinery qualifies for a capital cost allowance rate of 25%, declining balance. Abbie requires a 10% after-tax real rate of return (that is, the rate of return is 10% when all cash flows are denominated in December 31, 2000 dollars). Use the 10% after-tax real rate of return when answering all four requirements.

REQUIRED
Treat each of the following cases independently.
1. Abbie lives in a world without income taxes and without inflation. What is the net present value of the machine in this world?
2. Abbie lives in a world without inflation, but there is an income tax rate of 40%. What is the net present value of the machine in this world?
3. There are no income taxes, but the annual inflation rate is 20%. What is the net present value of the machine? The cash savings each year will be increased by a factor equal to the cumulative inflation rate.
4. The annual inflation rate is 20%, and the income tax rate is 40%. What is the net present value of the machine?

22-30 Mining, income taxes, inflation, sensitivity analysis. (CMA, adapted) VanDyk Enterprises has been operating a large gold mine for many years. The company wants to acquire equipment that will allow it to extract gold ore from a currently inaccessible area of this mine. Rich Salzman, VanDyk's controller, has gathered the following data to analyze the investment.

The initial cost of acquiring and installing the equipment is $3 million. The useful life of the specialized equipment is five years with no salvage value at the end of this period. VanDyk uses the straight-line amortization method for this equipment for financial reporting purposes.

Using the equipment, VanDyk estimates that an additional 300 pounds of gold (16 ounces per pound) will be extracted annually for the next five years. Salzman plans to use an estimated market price of $350 per ounce of gold in his analysis based on expert information. The price of gold is determined by many factors and represents a significant risk factor in this analysis.

The out-of-pocket variable costs to extract, sort, and pack the gold is $100 per ounce. Allocated fixed overhead costs are $40 per ounce.

Two skilled technicians will be hired to operate the new equipment. The total salary and fringe benefit costs for these two employees will be $110,000 annually over the next five years. Periodic maintenance on the equipment is expected to cost $50,000 per year in out-of-pocket costs.

When analyzing projects of this kind, VanDyk uses a 12% after-tax required rate of return and a 40% tax rate. The equipment qualifies for a 30% declining balance capital cost allowance rate.

REQUIRED
1. Determine the payback period.

2. Calculate the after-tax net present value for VanDyk's proposed acquisition of the extraction equipment.
3. Determine the revenue per ounce of gold at which VanDyk's acquisition of the extraction equipment will break even from a net present value perspective where VanDyk earns the 12% after-tax required rate of return.
4. Salzman feels that inflation will occur and persist for the next five years at the rate of 2% per year. Assume all the data given in the problem are already in nominal dollars and that the 12% minimum desired rate of return already includes an element attributable to anticipated inflation. Repeat requirement 2, to take inflationary effects into consideration.

22-31 Robotics capital project, inflation, income taxes. Rustbelt, Inc. purchases second-hand pipeline equipment and "rehabilitates" it for resale. Rustbelt has experienced many industrial accidents involving workers at the spot-welding activity and is looking to invest in robots. The investment will cost $10 million payable immediately and will reduce labour costs, worker insurance costs, and materials usage costs by a total of $7 million (in January 1, 2001 dollars) a year. The robots require an addition to annual cash operating costs of $3 million (in January 1, 2001 dollars) a year. Hence the net cash operating savings from using the robots will be $4 million annually (in January 1, 2001 dollars). Rustbelt believes that using the robots will eliminate industrial accidents involving workers at the spot-welding activity.

The robots have a four-year useful life with a terminal disposal price of $1 million (in January 1, 2001 dollars). The robots qualify for a 25% declining balance capital cost allowance rate. Rustbelt anticipates inflation in its operating costs and in the terminal disposal price of the robots of 20% per year. It uses a 10% after-tax required rate of return for investments expressed in real dollars. Rustbelt's income tax rate is 40%.

REQUIRED
1. What is the nominal after-tax required rate of return of Rustbelt for investments expressed in nominal dollars?
2. What is the net present value of the $10 million investment in robots? Use the approach of predicting cash inflows and outflows in nominal dollars and using a nominal discount rate.
3. What are the advantages of the approach to capital budgeting for inflation in requirement 2 relative to the approach of predicting real cash inflows and outflows and using a real discount rate?
4. What factors other than the net present value figure in requirement 2 should Rustbelt consider in deciding whether or not to invest in robots?

22-32 Ranking projects. (Adapted from NAA Research Report No. 35, pp. 83–85) Assume that six projects, A–F in the table that follows, have been submitted for inclusion in the coming year's budget for capital expenditures:

Project Cash Flows

	Year	A	B	C	D	E	F
Investment	0	$(100,000)	$(100,000)	$(200,000)	$(200,000)	$(200,000)	$(50,000)
	1	0	20,000	70,000	0	5,000	23,000
	2	10,000	20,000	70,000	0	15,000	20,000
	3	20,000	20,000	70,000	0	30,000	10,000
	4	20,000	20,000	70,000	0	50,000	10,000
	5	20,000	20,000	70,000	0	50,000	
Per year	6–9	20,000	20,000		200,000	50,000	
	10	20,000	20,000			50,000	
Per year	11–15	20,000					
Internal rate of return		14%	?	?	?	12.6%	12.0%

REQUIRED
1. Compute the internal rates of return (to the nearest half-percent) for projects B, C, and D. Rank all projects in descending order in terms of the internal rate of return. Show your computations.
2. On the basis of your answer in requirement 1, state which projects you would select, assuming a 10% required rate of return (a) if $500,000 is the limit to be spent, (b) if $550,000 is the limit, and (c) if $650,000 is the limit.

3. Assuming a 16% required rate of return and using the net present value method, compute the net present values and rank all the projects. Which project is more desirable, C or D? Compare your answer with your ranking in requirement 1.

4. What factors other than those considered in requirements 1–3 would influence your project rankings? Be specific.

22-33 Ranking of capital budgeting projects, alternative selection methods, capital rationing. (CMA, adapted) Brendan Rogers, division president of Wildwood Manufacturing, is preparing the 2001 capital budget for submission to corporate headquarters at AmiBrands, Inc. AmiBrands has not yet told Rogers what the total amount of funds available for capital projects at Wildwood will be, but the after-tax required rate of return is 12%.

Each project is considered to have the same degree of risk. Projects A and D are mutually exclusive. If project A is chosen, project D cannot be chosen. If project D is chosen, project A cannot be chosen.

When analyzing projects, Wildwood assumes that any budgeted amount not spent on the identified projects will be invested at the after-tax required rate of return, and funds released at the end of a project can be reinvested at the hurdle rate. Further information about each of these projects is presented in the following schedule:

Wildwood Manufacturing Proposed Capital Projects

	Project A	Project B	Project C	Project D	Project E	Project F
Capital investment	$106,000	$200,000	$140,000	$160,000	$144,000	$130,000
Net present value at 12%	$ 69,683	$ 23,773	$ (10,228)	$ 74,374	$ 6,027	$ 69,513
Excess present value index (profitability index)	1.66	1.12	0.93	1.46	1.04	1.53
Internal rate of return	35%	15%	9%	22%	14%	26%
Payback period	2.2 years	4.5 years	3.9 years	4.3 years	2.9 years	3.3 years
Economic life	6 years	8 years	5 years	8 years	6 years	8 years

REQUIRED

1. Assume that Wildwood Manufacturing has no budget restrictions for capital expenditures and wants to maximize its value to AmiBrands. Identify the capital investment projects that Wildwood should include in the capital budget it submits to AmiBrands, Inc. Explain the basis for your selection.

2. Ignore your response to requirement 1. Assume that AmiBrands, Inc. has specified that Wildwood Manufacturing will have a restricted budget for capital expenditures, and that Wildwood should select the projects that maximize the company's value. Identify the capital investment projects Wildwood should include in its capital expenditures budget, and explain the basis for your selections, if the budget is (a) $450,000 and (b) $500,000.

22-34 Ethics, discounted cash flow analysis. Eric Griffey, manager of the Household Products Division of the Dudley Company, is trying to decide whether to launch a new model of food blender, BF97. Griffey is particularly excited about this proposal, because it calls for producing the product in the company's old plant at Beaverton, Griffey's home town. During the last recession, Dudley had to shut down this plant and lay off its workers, many of whom had grown up with Griffey and were his friends. Griffey had been very upset when the plant was closed down. If BF97 were produced in the new plant, most of the laid-off workers would be rehired.

Griffey asks Andrew Chen, the management accountant of the Household Products Division, to analyze the BF97 proposal. Through the years the company has found that its products have a useful life of six years, after which the product is dropped and replaced by another new product. Chen gathers the following data.

a. BF97 will require new special-purpose equipment costing $900,000. The useful life of the equipment is six years, with a $140,000 estimated terminal disposal price at that time. The equipment qualifies for a capital cost allowance rate of 25%, declining balance.

b. The old plant has a book value of $250,000 and is being amortized for accounting purposes on a straight-line basis at $25,000 annually. The plant is currently being leased to another company. This lease has six years remaining at an annual rental of $45,000. The lease contains a cancellation clause whereby the landlord can obtain immediate possession of the premises upon payment of $30,000 cash (fully deductible for income tax purposes).

c. Certain nonrecurring market research studies and sales promotion activities will amount to a cost of $300,000 at the end of year 1. The entire amount is deductible in full for income tax purposes in the year of expenditure.

d. Additions to working capital will require $200,000 at the outset and an additional $200,000 at the end of two years. This total is fully recoverable at the end of six years.

e. Net cash inflow from operations before amortization and income taxes are expected to be $400,000 in years 1 and 2, $600,000 in years 3–5, and $100,000 in year 6.

The after-tax required rate of return is 12%. The income tax rate is 36%.

REQUIRED

1. Use a net present value analysis to determine whether Chen should recommend launching BF97.

2. Chen learns that the new special-purpose equipment required to make BF97 may only be available at a cost of $1.15 million. All other data remain unchanged. He revises his analysis and presents it to Griffey. Griffey is very unhappy with what he sees. He tells Chen, "Try different assumptions and redo your analysis. I have no doubt that this project should be worth pursuing on financial grounds." Chen is aware of Griffey's interest in supporting his home-town community. There is also the possibility that Griffey may be hired as a consultant by the new plant management after he retires next year. Why is Griffey unhappy with Chen's revised analysis? How should Chen respond to Griffey's suggestions? Identify the specific steps that Chen should take to resolve this situation.

22-35 Introduction of new product, income taxes. (W. Bruns) In December 2000, R.E. Torgler was trying to decide whether to add a new line of injection molded plastic products to those already manufactured and distributed by Reto S.A. In order to do so, the company would have to buy new injection molding equipment; none of the existing equipment could be adapted to perform the necessary operation, and Torgler was anxious to retain control of manufacturing. Actually, new injection molding equipment has been postponed because the product concept was judged to need additional development. But now the product seemed ready.

Sales of the new product were forecast at SFr. 2,000,000 per year, from which a sales commission of 15% would be paid to Reto's sales agents. Actual sales were made in several different currencies but, for simplicity here, all money measurements are stated in their Swiss franc equivalent.

Direct manufacturing costs were budgeted at SFr. 600,000 for materials and SFr. 900,000 for labour, leaving an annual cash flow before tax of SFr. 200,000. The new equipment would cost SFr. 600,000 delivered and installed, and was expected to have a useful life of 10 years, with a zero terminal disposal value.

Reto was able to borrow money at 8%.

REQUIRED

1. Ignoring the effect of taxes, what is the internal rate of return (IRR) on the proposed investment. Assume the new equipment would be installed by January 1, 2001, and begin producing on that date.

2. The cost of the equipment can be deduced from annual cash flows before they are subjected to tax. Assuming that the equipment will last 10 years, and that an equal amount of the cost of SFr. 600,000 will be deducted each year, and that the tax rate is expected to be 45%, what is the IRR on an after-tax basis?

3. Torgler has stated that Reto should be willing to purchase this machine as long as it yielded a return of 12% after taxation. Should he make the investment? Show your calculations.

4. Actually, to stimulate industrial development, the tax rules allow for depreciation deductions up to one third of the cost of any such investment to be deducted from reported earnings in the first year after the investment, and up to one fifth of the remainder of the undepreciated investment amount can be deduced in the second year. Thereafter, annual deductions are computed on a straight-line basis such that no more than the original cost of the equipment is depreciated over its useful life. How, if at all, does this affect the attractiveness of the investment?

5. Reto has learned that investment in working capital (receivables and inventories, less payables) amounts to approximately 15% of revenues. With the additional SFr. 300,000 investment for the new line decrease the rate of return on investment to less than the 12% criterion Torgler has been using?

6. In late December 2000, Reto purchased the equipment, and the operating results turned out as forecast. A year later, Torgler learned that the manufacturer of the new equipment had introduced new models that were more automated. The new equipment cost SFr. 1,000,000 and would permit labour savings of SFr. 200,000 per year, thus doubling the net operating cash flow on the product. As a result of the technological advance, Torgler expected the one-year-old machine could be sold for only SFr. 200,000 despite the fact that its book value was SFr. 400,000. If Reto buys the new machine and depreciates it using allowed tax depreciation over 10 years, would the investment meet the 12% after-tax criterion? Show your calculations.

7. If the one-year-old machine has a zero disposal price, would replacing it with the new machine still be desirable? Show your calculations.

8. Torgler was loathe to throw away a nearly new machine and thought he might be better off to keep it one more year and then replace it. Would he be better off? How would you go about addressing this issue? Explain.

9. During 2001, the rate of inflation remained low, and it was expected that it would average about 4% for the year. Torgler wondered how Reto's analysis should reflect this rate of inflation, which he expected might continue for several years. Should an assumed inflation rate change his decision? Explain.

COLLABORATIVE LEARNING PROBLEM

22-36 **Equipment replacement, income taxes, unequal project lives.** (CMA, adapted) Instant Dinners, Inc. (IDI) makes microwaveable frozen foods. The company is considering purchasing an automated materials-movement system (AMMS) for its Western Plant. Bill Rolland, IDI's chief financial officer, has asked Lealand Forrest, assistant controller, to prepare a net present value analysis for the proposal.

Rolland was instrumental in convincing the board of directors to open the Western Plant. Now, unless significant improvements in cost control and production efficiency are achieved, the Western Plant may be sold. Rolland is anxious to have the Western Plant continue to operate to maintain his credibility with the board and also to help Western's production manager, a longtime friend of Rolland.

The AMMS would replace a number of forklift trucks, eliminate the need for a number of materials-handlers, and increase the output capacity of the Western plant.

Rolland has given Forrest the following information regarding the AMMS investment for the net present value analysis:

Projected useful life	10 years
Purchase/installation	$4,400,000
Increased working capital needed	1,000,000
Increased annual operating costs (excluding amortization) over current costs	200,000
Reduction in annual manufacturing costs over current costs	400,000
Reduction in annual maintenance costs over current costs	300,000
Increase in cash flow from higher sales revenue	700,000
Estimated disposal price at end of useful life	850,000
Estimated recovery of working capital at end of useful life	1,000,000

IDI uses straight-line amortization for financial reporting purposes for all its equipment assuming a zero terminal disposal price. The forklift trucks have a net book value of $480,000 with a remaining useful life of eight years and a zero terminal disposal price. If IDI purchases AMMS now, it can sell the forklift trucks for $100,000. To make the ten-year project life of AMMS comparable to that of the forklift alternative, Forrest estimates that if IDI does not buy the AMMS, the company will lease new forklift trucks for the Western Plant for years 9 and 10 at a cost of $80,000 each year.

IDI has a 40% tax rate and requires a 12% after-tax rate of return on this project. Assume that tax effects and cash flows from equipment acquisition and disposal occur at the time of the transaction and that tax effects and cash flows from operations occur at the end of each year. The equipment qualifies for a 30% declining balance capital cost allowance rate.

Roland was pleased with Forrest's initial analysis. After the initial analysis was completed, Forrest discovered that the estimated terminal disposal price of the AMMS should be $100,000, not $850,000, and that the useful life of the system was expected to be eight years, not ten years. Forrest prepared a revised, second analysis based on this new information. On seeing the second analysis, Rolland told Forrest to discard the revised analysis and not to discuss it with anyone at IDI or with the board of directors.

INSTRUCTIONS

Form groups of three students to complete the following requirements.

REQUIRED

1. What is the net present value of the decision to replace forklifts with the AMMS based on the *original estimates* Rolland gave to Forrest?
2. Using net present value analysis, determine whether IDI should purchase and install the AMMS on the basis of the *revised estimates* that Forrest obtained.
3. Explain how Forrest, a management accountant, should evaluate Rolland's directives to conceal the revised analysis.
4. Identify the specific steps Forrest should take to resolve this situation.

23

PART SEVEN

MANAGEMENT CONTROL SYSTEMS, TRANSFER PRICING, AND MULTINATIONAL CONSIDERATIONS

Choosing transfer prices is an important aspect of transactions between internal divisions based in different countries. Companies consider tax as well as other factors— such as goal congruence, incentives, and autonomy—when determining transfer pricing policy. Transfer prices affect the profits reported in each division and are therefore of interest to division managers and tax officials in the different countries.

LEARNING OBJECTIVES

After studying this chapter, you should be able to:

1. Describe a management control system and its three key properties
2. Describe the benefits and costs of decentralization
3. Identify three general methods for determining transfer prices
4. Illustrate how market-based transfer prices generally promote goal-congruence in perfectly competitive markets
5. Recognize why a transfer price based on full cost plus a markup may lead to suboptimal decisions
6. Understand the range over which two divisions generally negotiate the transfer price when there is excess capacity
7. Present a general guideline for determining a minimum transfer price in transfer pricing situations
8. Recognize income tax considerations in multinational transfer pricing

Michelin
www.michelin.com

Pirelli
www.pirelli.com

Which company has the better management control system: the Ford Motor Company or the Toyota Motor Company? Michelin or Pirelli? Beyond the technical aspects, it is essential to consider how the system will influence the behaviour of the people who use it. What role can accounting information play in management control systems? For example, how does cost and budget information help in planning and coordinating the actions of multiple divisions within these companies? This chapter develops the link between strategy, organization structure, management control systems, and accounting information. It examines the benefits and costs of centralized and decentralized organizational structures and looks at the pricing of products or services transferred between subunits of the same organization.

MANAGEMENT CONTROL SYSTEMS

OBJECTIVE 1

Describe a management control system and its three key properties

Management control system. Means of gathering and using information to aid and coordinate the process of making planning and control decisions throughout the organization and to guide employee behaviour.

Performance Management Homepage
www.dutch.nl/bart/index.htm

Managing Performance software—Xebec Inc.
www.xebec-online.com/us/manage/perform.htm

A **management control system** is a means of gathering and using information to aid and coordinate the process of making planning and control decisions throughout the organization and to guide employee behaviour. The goal of the system is to improve the collective decisions within an organization.

Consider General Electric (GE). GE's management control system gathers and reports information for management control at various levels:

1. **Customer/market level.** For example, customer satisfaction, time taken to respond to customer requests for products, and cost of competitors' products

2. **Total organization level.** For example, stock price, net income, return on investment, cash flow from operations, total employment, pollution control, and contributions to the community

3. **Individual facility level.** For example, materials costs, labour costs, absenteeism, and accidents in various divisions or business functions (such as R&D, manufacturing, and distribution)

4. **Individual activity level.** For example, the time taken and costs incurred for receiving, storing, assembling, and dispatching goods in a warehouse; scrap rates, defects, and units reworked on a manufacturing line; the number of sales transactions and sales dollars per salesperson; and the number of shipments per employee at distribution centres

As the preceding examples indicate, management control systems collect both financial data (for example, net income, materials costs, and storage costs) and nonfinancial data (for example, the time taken to respond to customer requests for products, absenteeism, and accidents). Some of the information is obtained from within the company (such as net income and number of shipments per employee); other information is obtained from outside the company (such as stock price and cost of competitors' products).

The levels indicate the different kinds of information that are needed by managers performing different tasks. For example, stock price information is important at the total organization level but not at the individual activity level in the warehouse, where information about the time taken for receiving and storing is more relevant. At the individual activity level, management control reports focus on internal financial and nonfinancial data. At higher levels, management control reports also emphasize external financial and nonfinancial data.

Management control systems have both formal and informal components. The formal management control system of an organization includes those explicit rules, procedures, performance measures, and incentive plans that guide the behaviour of its managers and employees. The formal control system itself consists of several systems. The management accounting system is a formal accounting system that provides information on costs, revenues, and income. Examples of other formal control systems are human resource systems (providing information on recruiting, training, absenteeism, and accidents), and quality systems (providing information on scrap, defects, rework, and late deliveries to customers).

The informal part of the management control system includes such aspects as shared values, loyalties, and mutual commitments among members of the organization and the unwritten norms about acceptable behaviour for promotion that also influence employee behaviour. Examples of slogans that reinforce values and loyalties are "At Ford, Quality Is Job 1," and "At Home Depot, low prices are just the beginning."

EVALUATING MANAGEMENT CONTROL SYSTEMS

To be effective, management control systems should be closely aligned to an organization's strategies and goals. Examples of strategies are doubling net income in four years, increasing market share by 50% in two years, or maximizing short-run income. Suppose management decides, wisely or unwisely, to emphasize maximizing short-run income as a strategy. Then the management control system must reinforce this strategy. It should provide managers with information that will help them make short-run decisions—for example, contribution margins on individual products. It should tie manager's incentives to short-run net income numbers.

A second important feature of management control systems is that they should be designed to fit the organization's structure and the decision-making responsibility of individual managers. For example, the management control information for the R&D manager at Glaxo Laboratories, a pharmaceutical company, should focus on the R&D activities required for different drug projects, the number of scientists needed, the scheduled dates for completing different projects, and the preparation of reports comparing actual and budgeted performance. On the other hand, consider a product line manager responsible for the manufacture, sale, and distribution of ketchup at Heinz, a food products company. The management control system to support this manager should focus on information about customer satisfaction, market share, manufacturing costs and product line profitability that helps the manager better plan and control the business. The manager of the Heinz ketchup product line requires very different information than the R&D manager at Glaxo Laboratories.

Finally, effective management control systems motivate managers and employees. **Motivation** is the desire to attain a selected goal (the goal-congruence aspect) combined with the resulting drive or pursuit toward that goal (the effort aspect).

Goal-congruence exists when individuals and groups work toward the organization goals that top management desires—that is, managers working in their own best interest take actions that further the overall goals of top management. Goal-congruence issues have arisen in earlier chapters. For example, in capital budgeting decisions, making decisions by discounting long-run cash flows at the required rate of return best achieves organization goals. But if the management control system evaluates managers on the basis of short-run accrual accounting income, managers will be tempted to make decisions to maximize accrual accounting income that may not be in the best interests of the organization.

Effort is defined as exertion toward a goal. Effort goes beyond physical exertion, such as a worker producing at a faster rate, to include all conscientious actions (physical and mental).

Management control systems motivate employees to exert effort toward attaining organization goals through a variety of incentives tied to the achievement of those goals. These incentives can be monetary (cash, stock, use of a company car, and membership of a club) or nonmonetary (power, self-esteem, and pride in working for a successful company).

To summarize, the primary criterion for evaluating a system is how it promotes the attainment of top management's goals in a cost-effective manner. Central to applying this criterion is how well the management control system fits the organization structure and the decision-making responsibility of individual managers, as well as how well it motivates individuals within the organization.

ORGANIZATIONAL STRUCTURE AND DECENTRALIZATION

As we have just seen, management control systems must fit an organization's structure. Many organizations have decentralized structures that give rise to an additional set of management control issues.

Glaxo Wellcome
www.glaxowellcome.co.uk/home.html

Heinz Gateway
www.heinz.com

Motivation. The desire to attain a selected goal (the goal-congruence aspect) combined with the resulting drive or pursuit toward that goal (the effort aspect).

Goal-congruence. Exists when individuals and groups work toward the organization goals that top management desires.

Effort. Exertion toward a goal.

Decentralization. The freedom of managers at lower levels (subunits) of the organization to make decisions.

Top management makes decisions about decentralization that affect day-to-day operations at all levels of the organization. The essence of **decentralization** is the freedom for managers at lower levels of the organization to make decisions.

As we discuss the issues of decentralization, we use the term *subunit* to refer to any part of an organization. In practice, a subunit may be a large division (the Chevrolet Division of General Motors) or a small group (the two-person advertising department of a local clothing boutique).

Total decentralization *means minimum constraints and maximum freedom for managers to make decisions at the lowest levels of an organization.* Total centralization *means maximum constraints and minimum freedom for managers at the lowest levels.* Most companies' structures fall somewhere in between these two extremes.

Benefits of Decentralization

How should top managers decide how much decentralization is optimal? Conceptually, they try to choose the degree of decentralization that maximizes the excess of benefits over costs. From a practical standpoint, top managers can seldom quantify either the benefits or the costs. Still, the cost-benefit approach helps them focus on the central issues.

Advocates of decentralizing decision-making and granting responsibilities to managers of subunits claim the following benefits:

1. **Creates greater responsiveness to local needs.** Information is the key to intelligent decisions. Compared with top managers, subunit managers are better informed about their customers, competitors, suppliers, and employees, as well as about factors that affect the performance of their jobs such as ways to decrease costs and improve quality. Eastman Kodak reports that one advantage of decentralization is an "increase in the company's knowledge of the marketplace and improved service to customers."

2. **Leads to quicker decision-making.** An organization that gives lower-level managers the responsibility for making decisions can make decisions quickly, creating a competitive advantage over organizations that are slower, because they send the decision-making responsibility upward through layer after layer of management. Interlake, a manufacturer of materials-handling equipment, notes this important benefit of increased decentralization: "We have distributed decision-making powers more broadly to the cutting edge of product and market opportunity." Interlake's materials-handling equipment must often be customized to fit individual customers' needs. Delegating decision-making to the sales force allows Interlake to respond quickly to changing customer requirements.

3. **Increases motivation.** Subunit managers are usually more highly motivated when they can exercise greater individual initiative. Johnson & Johnson, a highly decentralized company, maintains that "Decentralization = Creativity = Productivity."

4. **Aids management development and learning**. Giving managers more responsibility promotes the development of an experienced pool of management talent—a pool that the organization can draw from to fill higher-level management positions. The organization also learns which people are not management material. Tektronix, an electronics instruments company, expressed this benefit as follows: "Decentralized units provide a training ground for general managers, and a visible field of combat where product champions may fight for their ideas."

5. **Sharpens the focus of managers.** In a decentralized setting, the manager of a small subunit has a concentrated focus. A small subunit is more flexible and nimble than a larger subunit and better able to adapt itself quickly to a fast-opening market opportunity. Also, top management, relieved of the burden of day-to-day operating decisions, can spend more time and energy on strategic planning for the entire organization.

Tektronix
www.tektronix.com

Costs of Decentralization

Advocates of more centralized decision-making point out the following costs of decentralizing decision-making:

1. **Leads to suboptimal decision-making. Suboptimal** (also called **goal-incongruent) decision-making** arises when a decision's benefit to one subunit is more than offset by the costs or loss of benefits to the organization as a whole. This cost arises because top management has given up some control over decision-making.

   Suboptimal decision-making may occur (1) when there is a lack of harmony or congruence among the overall organization goals, the subunit goals, and the individual goals of decision-makers or (2) when no guidance is given to subunit managers concerning the effects of their decisions on other parts of the organization. Suboptimal decision-making is most likely to occur when the subunits in the organization are highly interdependent, such as when the end product of one subunit is the direct material of another subunit.

2. **Results in duplication of activities.** Several individual subunits of the organization may undertake the same activity separately. For example, there may be a duplication of staff functions (accounting, employee relations, and legal) if an organization is highly decentralized. Centralizing these functions helps to consolidate, streamline, and downsize these activities.

3. **Decreases loyalty toward the organization as a whole.** Individual subunit managers may regard the managers of other subunits in the same organization as external parties. Consequently, managers may be unwilling to share significant information or to assist when another subunit faces an emergency.

4. **Increases costs of gathering information.** Managers may spend too much time negotiating the prices for internal products or services transferred among subunits.

Suboptimal decision-making (goal-incongruent decision-making). Decisions in which the benefit to one subunit is more than offset by the costs or loss of benefits to the organization as a whole.

Comparison of Benefits and Costs

To choose an appropriate organization structure, top managers must compare the benefits and costs of decentralization, often on a function-by-function basis. For example, the controller's function may be highly decentralized for many attention-directing and problem-solving purposes (such as preparing operating budgets and performance reports) but highly centralized for other purposes (such as processing accounts receivable and developing income tax strategies). Decentralizing budgeting and cost reporting enables the marketing manager of a subunit, for example, to influence the design of product line profitability reports for the subunit. Tailoring the report to the specific information that the manager may need helps the manager make better decisions and hence increases profits. Centralizing income tax strategies, on the other hand, allows the organization to trade off profits in some subunit with losses in others to evaluate the impact on the organization as a whole.

Surveys of North American and European companies report that the decisions made most frequently at the decentralized level and least frequently at the corporate level are related to sources of supplies, products to manufacture, and product advertising. Decisions related to the type and source of long-term financing are made least frequently at the decentralized level and most frequently at the corporate level.[1] Decentralized companies are generally large and unregulated, face great uncertainties in their environments, require detailed local knowledge for performing various jobs, and have few interdependencies among divisions.[2]

---

[1]*Evaluating the Performance of International Operations* (New York: Business International, 1989), p. 4; and *Managing the Global Finance Function* (London: Business International, 1992), p. 31.
[2]See Christie, A., M. Joye, and R. Watts, "Decentralization of the Firm: Theory and Evidence," working paper (University of Rochester, April 1991).

Decentralization in Multinational Companies

Multinational corporations are often decentralized. Language, customs, cultures, business practices, rules, laws, and regulations vary significantly across countries. Decentralization enables country managers to make decisions that exploit their knowledge of local business and political conditions and to deal with uncertainties in their individual environments. Philips, a Dutch conglomerate, delegates marketing and pricing decisions for its television business in the Indian and Singaporean markets to its respective country managers. Multinational corporations often rotate managers between foreign locations and the home office. Job rotation combined with decentralization helps develop managers' abilities to operate in global environments.

Of course, there are several drawbacks to decentralizing multinational companies. One of the most important is the lack of control. Barings PLC, a British investment banking firm, went bankrupt and had to be sold when one of its traders in Singapore caused the firm to lose over £1 billion on unauthorized trades. Multinational corporations that implement decentralized decision-making usually also design their management control systems to measure and monitor division performance. Information and communications technology eases the flow of data for reporting and control.

Barings PLC
www.liquidity.com

CHOICES ABOUT RESPONSIBILITY CENTRES

To measure the performance of subunits in centralized or decentralized organizations, the management control system uses one or a mix of the four types of responsibility centres presented in Chapter 6:

◆ **Cost centre.** Manager accountable for costs only
◆ **Revenue centre.** Manager accountable for revenues only
◆ **Profit centre.** Manager accountable for revenues and costs
◆ **Investment centre.** Manager accountable for investments, revenues, and costs

Centralization or decentralization is not mentioned in these descriptions. Why? Because each of these responsibility units can be found in either of the extremes of centralized and decentralized organizations.

A common misconception is that the term *profit centre* (and, in some cases, *investment centre*) is a synonym for a decentralized subunit and that *cost centre* is a synonym for a centralized subunit. *Profit centres can be coupled with a highly centralized organization, and cost centres can be coupled with a highly decentralized organization.* For example, managers in a division organized as a profit centre may have little leeway in making decisions. They may need to obtain approval from corporate headquarters for every expenditure over, say, $10,000 and may be forced to accept central staff "advice." In another company, divisions may be organized as cost centres, but their managers may have great latitude on capital expenditures and on where to purchase materials and services. In short, the labels "profit centre" and "cost centre" are independent of the degree of decentralization in an organization.

TRANSFER PRICING

Intermediate product. Product transferred from one subunit to another subunit of the organization. This product may be processed further and sold to an external customer.

Transfer price. Price one subunit (segment, department, division, etc.) of an organization charges for a product or service supplied to another subunit of the same organization.

In decentralized organizations, individual subunits of an organization act as separate units. In these settings, the management control system often uses transfer prices to coordinate actions and to evaluate performance of the subunits.

An **intermediate product** is a product transferred from one subunit to another subunit of the same organization. This product may be processed further and sold to an external customer. A **transfer price** is the price one subunit (segment, department, division, and so on) of an organization charges for a product or service supplied to another subunit of the same organization. The transfer price creates revenue for the selling subunit and a purchase cost for the buying subunit, affecting operating income numbers for both subunits. The operating incomes can be used to evaluate the performance of each subunit and to motivate managers.

Shop Floor Scholars

What happens when you put a University of Waterloo professor and a graduate student to work in your plant? If you're Northern Telecom, you get some useful insights on making just-in-time and other management techniques work.

For the past several years, Frank Safayeni, a UoW management sciences professor, along with Ph.D. student Rob Duimering, have been working at Northern Telecom's manufacturing and distribution plants in Bramalea, Milton, and other Ontario communities.

The initial idea was to have the academics look at how Northern Telcom staff was responding to the implementation of JIT.

The key difficulty, Safayeni and Duimering say, has to do with the traditional structure of large North American enterprises—their functional units are simply not designed to accommodate the degree of communication and coordination that JIT requires.

"It's often hard to get different departments to coordinate with one another," says Safayeni. "For example, the purchasing department may be told to keep inventory levels down, but doing so leads to stoppages on the assembly line."

To help find ways to improve communication, the two interviewed workers on the shop floor, focussing on relationships between teams. This work has almost invariably resulted "in immediate spinoffs, "reports Bob Robinson, Northern Telecom's engineering manager." Almost every idea they have collected through their interviews has been implemented . . . and is showing benefits.

The scholars are now working on a videotape, which Northern Telecom will use as a training tool for teamwork and problem-solving.

Nortel
www.nortelnetworks.com/
index.html

Source: Dena Brooker, "Shop Floor Scholar," *Materials Management & Distribution,* June 1994.

Alternative Transfer Pricing Methods

There are three general methods for determining transfer prices:

1. **Market-based transfer prices.** Upper management may choose to use the price of a similar product or service publicly listed in, say, a trade journal. Also, upper management may select, for the internal price, the external price that a subunit charges to outside customers.

2. **Cost-based transfer prices.** Upper management may choose a transfer price based on the costs of producing the product in question. Examples include variable manufacturing costs, manufacturing (absorption) costs, and full product costs. "Full product costs" include all production costs as well as costs from other business functions (R&D, design, marketing, distribution, and customer service). The costs used in cost-based transfer prices can be actual costs or budgeted costs.

3. **Negotiated transfer prices.** In some cases, the subunits of a company are free to negotiate the transfer price between themselves and then to decide whether to buy and sell internally or deal with outside parties. Subunits may use information about costs and market prices in these negotiations, but there is no requirement that the chosen transfer price bear any specific relationship to either cost or market price data. Negotiated transfer prices are often employed when market prices are volatile and change occurs constantly. The negotiated transfer price is the outcome of a bargaining process between the selling and the buying divisions.

OBJECTIVE 3

Identify three general methods for determining transfer prices

Ideally, the chosen transfer pricing method should lead each subunit manager to make optimal decisions for the organization as a whole. As in all management control systems, transfer prices should help achieve an organization's strategies and goals, and fit its structure. In particular, it should promote *goal-congruence* and a sustained high level of *management effort*. Sellers should be motivated to hold down costs of supplying a product or service, and buyers should be motivated to acquire and use inputs efficiently. If top management favours a high degree of decentralization, transfer prices should also promote a high level of subunit *autonomy* in decision-making. **Autonomy** is the degree of freedom to make decisions.

Autonomy. The degree of freedom to make decisions.

AN ILLUSTRATION OF TRANSFER PRICING

Northern Petroleum has three divisions. Each operates as a profit centre. The Production Division manages the production of crude oil from a petroleum field near Calgary, Alberta. The Transportation Division manages the operation of a pipeline that transports crude oil from the Calgary area to Sarnia, Ontario. The Refining Division manages a refinery at Sarnia that processes crude oil into gasoline. (For simplicity, assume that gasoline is the only salable product the refinery makes and that it takes two barrels of crude oil to yield one barrel of gasoline.)

Variable costs in each division are assumed to be variable with respect to a single cost driver in each division: barrels of crude oil produced by the Production Division, barrels of crude oil transported by the Transportation Division, and barrels of gasoline produced by the Refining Division. The fixed costs per unit are based on the budgeted annual output of crude oil to be produced and transported and the amount of gasoline to be produced. Northern Petroleum reports all costs and revenues of its non-Canadian operations in Canadian dollars using the prevailing exchange rate.

♦ The Production Division can sell crude oil to outside parties in the Calgary area at $13 per barrel.

♦ The Transportation Division "buys" crude oil from the Production Division, transports it to Sarnia, and then "sells" it to the Refining Division. The pipeline from Calgary to Sarnia has the capacity to carry 40,000 barrels of crude oil per day.

♦ The Refining Division has been operating at capacity, 30,000 barrels of crude oil a day, using oil from Northern's Production Division (an average of 10,000 barrels per day) and oil bought from other producers and delivered to the Sarnia Refinery (an average of 20,000 barrels per day, at $18 per barrel).

♦ The Refining Division sells the gasoline it produces at $52 per barrel.

Exhibit 23-1 summarizes Northern Petroleum's variable and fixed costs per unit of the cost driver in each division, the external market prices of buying and selling crude oil, and the external market prices of selling gasoline. Consider the division operating income resulting from three transfer pricing methods applied to a series of transactions involving 100 barrels of crude oil produced by Northern's Production Division.

♦ **Method A.** Market-based transfer prices

♦ **Method B.** Cost-based transfer prices at 110% of full costs, where full costs are the cost of the transferred-in product plus the division's own variable and fixed costs

♦ **Method C.** Negotiated transfer prices

The transfer prices per barrel of crude oil under each method are as follows. The transferred-in cost component in method B is denoted by an asterisk (*).

♦ **Method A: Market-Based Transfer Prices**
From Production Division to Transportation Division = $13
From Transportation Division to Refining Division = $18

♦ **Method B: Cost-Based Transfer Prices at 110% of Full Costs**
From Production Division to Transportation Division = 1.10($2 + $6)
$$= \$8.80$$

EXHIBIT 23-1
Operating Data for Northern Petroleum

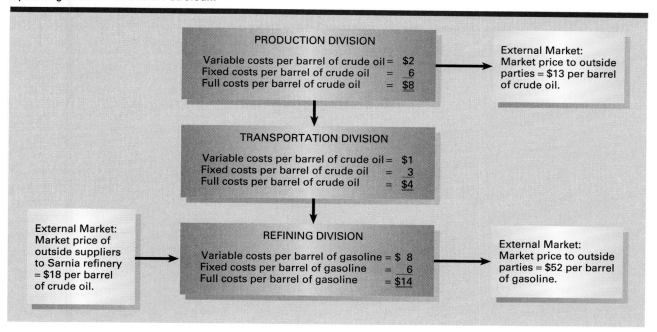

From Transportation Division to Refining Division = 1.10($8.80* + $1 + $3)
= $14.08

◆ **Method C: Transfer Prices Negotiated by Divisions to Be Between Market-Based and Cost-Based Transfer Prices**
From Production Division to Transportation Division = $10
From Transportation Division to Refining Division = $16.75

Exhibit 23-2 presents division operating incomes per 100 barrels of crude oil reported under each transfer pricing method. Transfer prices create income for the "selling" division and corresponding costs for the "buying" division that cancel out when divisional results are consolidated. The exhibit assumes that the different transfer pricing methods have no effect on the decisions made and actions taken by the Production, Transportation, and Refining Division managers. Northern Petroleum's total operating income from producing, transporting, and refining the 100 barrels of crude oil is therefore the same, $700 (revenues of $2,600 minus costs of $800 in production, $400 in transportation, and $700 in refining), regardless of internal transfer prices used. Keeping total operating income the same focusses attention on the effects of different transfer pricing methods on division operating incomes. These incomes differ under the three methods. The operating income amounts span a $420 range ($80–$500) in the Production Division; a $175 range ($100–$275) in the Transportation Division; and a $392 range ($100–$492) in the Refining Division. Note that each division would choose a different transfer pricing method if its sole criterion were to maximize its own division operating income: the Production Division would choose market prices, the Transportation Division would favour negotiated prices, and the Refining Division would choose 110% of full costs. Little wonder that division managers take considerable interest in the setting of transfer prices, especially those managers whose compensation or promotion directly depends on division operating income.

Exhibit 23-2 maintains companywide operating income at $700 and illustrates how the choice of a transfer pricing method divides the companywide operating income pie among individual divisions. Subsequent sections of this chapter illustrate that the choice of a transfer pricing method can also affect the decisions that individual division managers make and hence the size of the operating income pie itself. We consider this effect as we expand our discussion of market-based, cost-based, and negotiated transfer prices.

EXHIBIT 23-2
Division Operating Income of Northern Petroleum for 100 Barrels of Crude Oil Under
Alternative Transfer Pricing Methods

	Method A	Method B	Method C
	Internal Transfers at Market Prices	Internal Transfers at 110% of Full Costs	Internal Transfers at Negotiated Prices
1. Production Division:			
Revenues:			
$13, $8.80, $10, × 100 barrels crude oil	$1,300	$ 880	$1,000
Deduct:			
Division variable costs, $2 × 100 barrels crude oil	200	200	200
Division fixed costs, $6 × 100 barrels crude oil	600	600	600
Division operating income	$ 500	$ 80	$ 200
2. Transportation Division:			
Revenues:			
$18, $14.08, $16.75, × 100 barrels crude oil	$1,800	$1,408	$1,675
Deduct:			
Transferred-in costs, $13, $8.80, $10, × 100 barrels crude oil	1,300	880	1,000
Division variable costs, $1 × 100 barrels crude oil	100	100	100
Division fixed costs, $3 × 100 barrels crude oil	300	300	300
Division operating income	$ 100	$ 128	$ 275
3. Refining Division:			
Revenues:			
$52 × 50 barrels gasoline	$2,600	$2,600	$2,600
Deduct:			
Transferred-in costs, $18, $14.08, $16.75, × 100 barrels crude oil	1,800	1,408	1,675
Division variable costs, $8 × 50 barrels gasoline	400	400	400
Division fixed costs, $6 × 50 barrels gasoline	300	300	300
Division operating income	$ 100	$ 492	$ 225

MARKET-BASED TRANSFER PRICES

Perfectly Competitive Market Case

OBJECTIVE 4

Illustrate how market-based transfer prices generally promote goal-congruence in perfectly competitive markets

Transferring products or services at market prices generally leads to optimal decisions when three conditions are satisfied: (1) the intermediate market is perfectly competitive, (2) interdependencies of subunits are minimal, and (3) there are no additional costs or benefits to the corporation as a whole in using the market instead of transacting internally. A **perfectly competitive market** exists when there is a homogeneous product with equivalent buying and selling prices and no individual buyers or sellers can affect those prices by their own actions. By using market-based transfer prices in perfectly competitive markets, a company can meet the criteria of goal-congruence, management effort, and (if desired) subunit autonomy.

Reconsider the Northern Petroleum example, assuming that there is a perfectly competitive market for crude oil in the Calgary area. As a result, the Production Division can sell and the Transportation Division can buy as much crude oil as each wants at $13 per barrel. Northern would like its managers to buy or sell crude oil internally. Think about the decisions that Northern's division managers would make if each had the option to sell or buy crude oil externally. If the transfer price between Northern's Production Division and Transportation Division is set below $13, the manager of the Production Division will be motivated to sell all production to outside buyers at $13 per barrel. If the transfer price is set above $13, the manager of the Transportation Division will be motivated to purchase all its crude oil requirements from outside suppliers. A transfer price of $13 will motivate the Production Division and the Transportation Division to buy and sell internally.

Suppose each division manager is motivated to maximize his or her own division operating income. The Production Division will sell (either internally or externally) as much crude oil as it can profitably sell, and the Transportation Division will buy (either internally or externally) as much crude oil as it can profitably transport. At a transfer price of $13, the actions that maximize division operating income are also the actions that maximize operating income of Northern Petroleum as a whole. Market prices also serve to evaluate the economic performance and profitability of each division individually.

Distress Prices

When supply outstrips demand, market prices may drop well below their historical average. If the drop in prices is expected to be temporary, these low market prices are sometimes called "distress prices." Deciding whether a current market price is a distress price is often difficult. The market prices of several agricultural commodities, such as wheat and oats, have stayed for many years at what observers initially believed were temporary distress levels.

Which transfer pricing method should be used for judging performance if distress prices prevail? Some companies use the distress prices themselves, but others use long-run average prices, or "normal" market prices. In the short run, the manager of the supplier division should meet the distress price as long as it exceeds the incremental costs of supplying the product or service; if not, the supplying division should stop producing and the buying division should buy the product or service from an outside supplier. These actions would increase overall companywide operating income. If the long-run average market price is used, forcing the manager to buy internally at a price above the current market price will hurt the buying division's short-run performance and understate its profitability. If, however, prices remain low in the long run, the manager of the supplying division must decide whether to dispose of some manufacturing facilities or shut down and have the buying division purchase the product from outside.

COST-BASED TRANSFER PRICES

Cost-based transfer prices are helpful when market prices are unavailable, inappropriate, or too costly to obtain. For example, the product may be specialized or unique, price lists may not be widely available, or the internal product may be different from the products available externally in terms of quality and service.

Full-Cost Bases

In practice, many companies use transfer prices based on full costs. These prices, however, can lead to suboptimal decisions. Assume that Northern Petroleum makes internal transfers at 110% of full cost. The Sarnia Refining Division purchases, on average, 20,000 barrels of crude oil per day from a local Sarnia supplier, who delivers the crude oil to the refinery. Purchase and delivery cost $18 per barrel. To reduce crude oil costs, the Refining Division has located an independent producer in Calgary who is willing to sell 20,000 barrels of crude oil per day at $13 per barrel, delivered to Northern's pipeline in Calgary. Given Northern's organization structure, the

Perfectly competitive market.
Exists when there is a homogeneous product with equivalent buying and selling prices and no individual buyers or sellers can affect those prices by their own actions.

OBJECTIVE 5

Recognize why a transfer price based on full cost plus a markup may lead to suboptimal decisions

Transportation Division would purchase the 20,000 barrels of crude oil in Calgary, transport it to Sarnia, and then sell it to the Refining Division. The pipeline has excess capacity and can ship the 20,000 barrels at its variable costs of $1 per barrel without affecting the shipment of crude oil from Northern's own Production Division. Will Northern Petroleum incur lower costs by purchasing crude oil from the independent producer in Calgary or by purchasing crude oil from the Sarnia supplier? Will the Refining Division show lower crude oil purchasing costs by using oil from the Calgary producer or by using its current Sarnia supplier?

The following analysis shows that operating income of Northern Petroleum as a whole would be maximized by purchasing oil from the independent Calgary producer. The analysis compares the incremental costs in all divisions under the two alternatives.

- ◆ **Alternative 1.** Buy 20,000 barrels from Sarnia supplier at $18 per barrel. Total costs to Horizon Petroleum = 20,000 × $18 = $360,000.
- ◆ **Alternative 2.** Buy 20,000 barrels in Calgary at $13 per barrel and transport it to Sarnia at $1 per barrel variable costs. Total costs to Northern Petroleum = 20,000 × ($13 + $1) = $280,000.

There is a reduction in total costs to Northern Petroleum of $80,000 by using the independent producer in Calgary.

In turn, suppose the Transportation Division's transfer price to the Refining Division is 110% of full cost. The Refining Division will see its reported division costs increase if the crude oil is purchased from the independent producer in Calgary:

$$\frac{\text{Transfer}}{\text{price}} = 1.10 \times \left(\begin{array}{c} \text{Purchase price} \\ \text{from Calgary} \\ \text{producer} \end{array} + \begin{array}{c} \text{Unit variable cost} \\ \text{of Transportation} \\ \text{Division} \end{array} + \begin{array}{c} \text{Unit fixed cost} \\ \text{of Transportation} \\ \text{Division} \end{array} \right)$$

$$= 1.10 \times (\$13 + \$1 + \$3) = 1.10 \times \$17 = \$18.70$$

- ◆ **Alternative 1.** Buy 20,000 barrels from Sarnia supplier at $18 per barrel. Total costs to Refining Division = 20,000 × $18 = $360,000.
- ◆ **Alternative 2.** Buy 20,000 barrels from the Transportation Division of Northern Petroleum that are purchased from the independent producer in Calgary. Total costs to Refining Division = 20,000 × $18.70 = $374,000.

As a profit centre, the Refining Division can maximize its short-run division operating income by purchasing from the Sarnia supplier ($360,000 versus $374,000).

The transfer pricing method has led the Refining Division to regard the fixed cost (and the 10% markup) of the Transportation Division as a variable cost. Why? Because the Refining Division looks at each barrel that it obtains from the Transportation Division as a variable cost of $18.70—if 10 barrels are transferred, it costs the Refining Division $187; if 100 barrels are transferred, it costs $1,870. From the point of view of Northern Petroleum as a whole, its variable costs per barrel are $14 ($13 to purchase the oil from the independent producer and $1 to transport it to Sarnia). The remaining $4.70 ($18.70 – $14) per barrel are fixed costs and markups of the Transportation Division. Buying crude oil in Sarnia costs Northern Petroleum an additional $18 per barrel. For the company, it is cheaper to buy from Calgary. But the Refining Division sees the problem differently. From its standpoint, it prefers buying from the Sarnia supplier at a cost of $360,000 (20,000 barrels × $18 per barrel), because buying from Calgary costs the division $374,000 (20,000 barrels × $18.70). Goal-incongruence is induced by the transfer price based on full cost plus a markup.

What transfer price will promote goal-congruence for both the Transportation Division and the Refining Division? The minimum transfer price is $14 per barrel; a transfer price below $14 does not provide the Transportation Division with an incentive to purchase crude oil from the independent producer in Calgary while a transfer price above $14 generates contribution margin to cover fixed costs. The maximum transfer price is $18 per barrel; a transfer price above $18 will cause the Refining Division to purchase crude oil from the external market rather than from the Transportation Division. A transfer price between the minimum and maximum transfer prices of $14 and $18 respectively will promote goal-congruence—both divisions will increase their own reported division operating income by purchasing crude oil from the independent producer in Calgary. In particular, a transfer price based on the full costs of $17 without a markup will achieve goal-congruence. The Transportation Division will show no operating income and will be evaluated as a cost centre. Surveys indicate that managers prefer to use full-cost transfer pricing because it yields relevant costs for long-run decisions. and because it facilitates pricing on the basis of full product costs.

Using full-cost transfer prices that include an allocation of fixed overhead costs raises other issues. How are indirect costs allocated to products? Have the correct activities, cost pools, and cost drivers been identified? Are the chosen overhead rates actual or budgeted rates? The issues here are similar to the issues that arise in allocating fixed costs (Chapter 14). Full-cost-based transfer prices calculated using activity-based cost drivers can provide more refined allocation bases for allocating costs to products. Using budgeted costs and budgeted rates lets both divisions know the transfer price in advance. Also variations in the quantity of units produced by the selling division do not affect the transfer price.

Prorating the Difference Between Minimum and Maximum Transfer Prices

An alternative cost-based approach is for Northern Petroleum to choose a transfer price that splits the $4 difference between the maximum transfer price the Refining Division is willing to pay and the minimum transfer price the Transportation Division wants on some equitable basis. Suppose Northern Petroleum allocates the $4 difference on the basis of the budgeted variable costs incurred by the Transportation Division and the Refining Division for a given quantity of crude oil. Using the data in Exhibit 23-2 the variable costs are as follows:

Transportation Division to transport 100 barrels of crude oil	$100
Refining Division to refine 100 barrels of crude oil	400
	$500

The Transportation Division gets to keep $\frac{\$100}{\$500} \times \$4 = \$0.80$, and the Refining Division gets to keep $\frac{\$400}{\$500} \times \$4 = \$3.20$ of the $4 difference. That is, the transfer price between the Transportation Division and the Refining Division would be $14.80 per barrel of crude oil ($13 purchase cost + $1 variable costs + $0.80 that the Transportation Division gets to keep). Essentially, this approach is a budgeted variable cost plus transfer price; the "plus" indicates the setting of a transfer price above variable costs.

To decide on the $0.80 and $3.20 allocation of the $4 contribution to total corporate operating income per barrel, the divisions must share information about their variable costs. In effect, each division does not operate (at least for this transaction) in a totally decentralized manner. Because most organizations are hybrids of centralization and decentralization anyway, this approach deserves serious consideration when transfers are significant. Note, however, that each division has an incentive to overstate its variable costs in order to receive a more favourable transfer price.

Dual Pricing

There is seldom a *single* transfer price that simultaneously meets the criteria of goal-congruence, management effort, and subunit autonomy. Some companies turn to **dual pricing,** using two separate transfer pricing methods to price each interdivision transaction. An example of dual pricing arises when the selling division receives a full cost plus markup–based price and the buying division pays the market price for the internally transferred products. Assume that Northern Petroleum purchases crude oil from the independent producer in Calgary at $13 per barrel. One way of recording

Dual pricing. Approach to transfer pricing using two separate transfer pricing methods to price each inter-division transaction.

Domestic and Multinational Transfer Pricing Practices

What transfer pricing practices are used around the world? The following tables indicate how frequently particular transfer pricing methods are used in different countries.

TRANSFER PRICING METHODS

A. Domestic

Method	Canada*	United States[†]	Australia[‡]	Japan[†]	India[§]	United Kingdom[#]	New Zealand[||]
1. Market-price-based	34%	37%	13%	34%	47%	26%	18%
2. Cost-based:							
Variable costs	6	4	—	2	6	10	10
Absorption or full costs	37	41	—	44	47	38	61
Other	3	1	—	—	—	1	—
Total	46	46	65	46	53	49	71
3. Negotiated	18	16	11	19	—	24	11
4. Other	2	1	11	1	—	1	—
	100%	100%	100%	100%	100%	100%	100%

B. Multinational

Method	Canada*	United States[†]	Australia[‡]	Japan[†]	India[§]	United Kingdom**	New Zealand[||]
1. Market-price-based	37%	46%	—	37%	—	31%	—
2. Cost-based:							
Variable costs	5	3	—	3	—	5	—
Absorption or full costs	26	37	—	38	—	28	—
Other	2	1	—	—	—	5	—
Total	33	41	—	41	—	38	—
3. Negotiated	26	13	—	22	—	20	—
4. Other	4	0	—	—	—	11	—
	100%	100%	—	100%	—	100%	—

The surveys indicate that managers in all countries use cost-based transfer prices more frequently than market-price-based transfer prices for domestic transfer pricing. For multinational transfer pricing, managers use market-price-based and cost-based methods equally frequently.

What factors do executives consider important in decisions on domestic transfer pricing? Survey evidence indicates the following (in order of importance): (1) performance evaluation, (2) management motivation, (3) pricing and product emphasis, and (4) external market recognition.[‡]

Factors cited as important in decisions on multinational transfer pricing policy are (in order of importance) (1) overall income of the company, (2) income tax rate and other tax differences among countries, (3) income or dividend repatriation restrictions, and (4) competitive position of subsidiaries in their respective markets.[‡]

Note: Dashes indicate information was not disclosed in survey.
*Tang, R., "Canadian Transfer Pricing in the 1990s," *Management Accounting* (February 1992); [†]adapted from Tang, R., C. Walter, and R. Raymond, "Transfer Pricing—Japanese vs. American Style," *Management Accounting* (January 1979); [‡]Joye, M., and P. Blayney, "Cost and Management Accounting Practices in Australian Manufacturing Companies: Survey Results," (Accounting Research Centre, The University of Sydney, 1991); [§]Govindarajan, V., and B. Ramamurthy, "Transfer Pricing Policies in Indian Companies: A Survey," *Chartered Accountant* (November 1983); [#]Drury, C., S. Braund, P. Osborne, and M. Tayles, *A Survey of Management Accounting Practices in UK Manufacturing Companies*, (London, U.K.: Chartered Association of Certified Accountants, 1993); [||]Hoque, Z., and M. Alam, "Organization Size, Business Objectives, Managerial Autonomy, Industry Conditions, and Management's Choice of Transfer Pricing Methods: A Contextual Analysis of New Zealand Companies," (Working Paper, Victoria University of Wellington, Wellington, New Zealand); **Mostafa, A., J. Sharp, and K. Howard, "Transfer Pricing—A Survey Using Discriminant Analysis," *Omega*, (Vol. 12, No. 5, 1984)
[‡]Price Waterhouse, *Transfer Pricing Practices of American Industry* (New York: Price Waterhouse, 1984)

the journal entry for the transfer between the Transportation Division and the Refining Division is:

1. Credit the Transportation Division (the selling division) with the 110%-of-full-cost transfer price of $18.70 per barrel of crude oil.
2. Debit the Refining Division (the buying division) with the market-based transfer price of $18 per barrel of crude oil.
3. Debit a corporate cost account for the $0.70 ($18.70 − $18) difference between the two transfer prices for the cost of crude oil borne by corporate rather than the Refining Division.

The dual-price method promotes goal-congruence because it makes the Refining Division no worse off if it purchases the crude oil from the Transportation Division rather than from the outside supplier. In either case, the Refining Division's cost is $18 per barrel of crude oil. This dual-price system essentially gives the Transportation Division a corporate subsidy. The results of dual pricing? The operating income for Northern Petroleum as a whole is less than the sum of the operating incomes of the divisions.

Dual pricing is not widely used in practice even though it reduces the goal-congruence problems associated with a pure cost-plus-based transfer pricing method. One concern of top management is that the manager of the supplying division does not have sufficient incentive to control costs with a dual-price system. A second concern is that the dual-price system confuses division managers about the level of decentralization top management seeks. Above all, dual pricing tends to insulate managers from the frictions of the marketplace. Managers should know as much as possible about their subunits' buying and selling markets, and dual pricing reduces the incentive to gain this knowledge.

NEGOTIATED TRANSFER PRICES

OBJECTIVE 6

Understand the range over which two divisions generally negotiate the transfer price when there is excess capacity

Negotiated transfer prices arise as the outcome of a bargaining process between selling and buying divisions. Consider again the choice of a transfer price between the Transportation and Refining Divisions of Northern Petroleum. The Transportation Division has excess capacity that it can use to transport oil from Calgary to Sarnia. The Transportation Division will only be willing to "sell" oil to the Refining Division if the transfer price equals or exceeds $14 per barrel of crude oil (its variable costs). The Refining Division will only be willing to "buy" crude oil from the Transportation Division if the cost equals or is below $18 per barrel (the price at which the Refining Division can buy crude oil in Sarnia).

From the viewpoint of Northern Petroleum as a whole, operating income would be maximized if the Refining Division purchased from the Transportation Division rather than from the Sarnia market (incremental costs of $14 per barrel versus incremental costs of $18 per barrel). Both divisions would be interested in transacting with each other if the transfer price is set between $14 and $18. For example, a transfer price of $16.75 per barrel will increase the Transportation Division's operating income by $16.75 − $14 = $2.75 per barrel. It will increase the Refining Division's operating income by $18 − $16.75 = $1.25 per barrel because Refining can now "buy" the oil for $16.75 inside rather than for $18 outside.

The key question is where between the $14 and $18 the transfer price will be. The answer depends on the bargaining strengths of the two divisions. Negotiations become particularly sensitive if Northern evaluates each division's performance on the basis of divisional operating income. The price negotiated by the two divisions will, in general, have no specific relationship to either costs or market price. But cost and price information are often useful starting points in the negotiation process.

A GENERAL GUIDELINE FOR TRANSFER PRICING SITUATIONS

Is there an all-pervasive rule for transfer pricing that leads toward optimal decisions for the organization as a whole? No. Why? Because the three criteria of goal-congruence, management effort, and subunit autonomy must all be considered simultaneously. The following general guideline, however, has proven to be a helpful first step in setting a minimum transfer price in many specific situations:

$$\text{Minimum transfer price} = \text{Additional } \textit{incremental} \text{ or } \textit{outlay costs} \text{ per unit incurred up to the point of transfer} + \textit{Opportunity costs} \text{ per unit to the supplying division}$$

The term *incremental* or *outlay costs* in this context represents the additional costs that are directly associated with the production and transfer of the products or services. *Opportunity costs* are defined here as the maximum contribution forgone by the supplying division if the products or services are transferred internally. For example, if the supplying division is operating at capacity, the opportunity cost of transferring a unit internally rather than selling it externally is equal to the market price minus variable costs. We distinguish incremental costs from opportunity costs because the accounting system typically records incremental costs but not opportunity costs. We illustrate the general guideline in some specific situations using data from the Production and Transportation Divisions of Northern Petroleum.

1. **A perfectly competitive market for the intermediate product exists, and the supplying division has no idle capacity.** If the market for crude oil is perfectly competitive, the Production Division can sell all the crude oil it produces to the external market at $13 per barrel, and it will have no idle capacity. The Production Division's incremental costs (see Exhibit 23-1) are $2 per barrel of crude oil. The Production Division's opportunity cost per barrel of transferring the oil internally is the contribution margin per barrel of $11 (market price, $13 – variable cost, $2) forgone by not selling the crude oil in the external market. In this case:

$$\text{Minimum transfer price per barrel} = \text{Incremental costs per barrel} + \text{Opportunity costs per barrel}$$

$$= \$2 + \$11 = \$13 = \text{Market price per barrel}$$

Market-based transfer prices are ideal in perfectly competitive markets when there is no idle capacity.

2. **An intermediate market exists that is not perfectly competitive, and the supplying division has idle capacity.** In markets that are not perfectly competitive, capacity utilization can only be increased by decreasing prices. Idle capacity exists because decreasing prices is often not worthwhile—it decreases operating income.

If the Production Division has idle capacity, its opportunity cost of transferring the oil internally is zero because the division does not forgo any external sales and hence does not forgo any contribution margin from internal transfers. In this case:

$$\text{Minimum transfer price per barrel} = \text{Incremental costs per barrel} = \$2 \text{ per barrel}$$

Note that any transfer price between $2 and $13 (the price at which the Transportation Division can buy crude oil in Calgary) motivates the Production Division to produce and sell crude oil to the Transportation Division and the Transportation Division to buy crude oil from the Production Division. In this situation, the company could either use a cost-based transfer price or allow the two divisions to negotiate a transfer price between themselves.

In general, though, in markets that are not perfectly competitive, the potential to influence demand and operating income through prices makes measuring opportunity costs more complicated. The transfer price depends on constantly changing levels of supply and demand. There is not just one transfer price; rather, a transfer pricing schedule yields the transfer price for various quantities supplied and demanded, depending on the incremental costs and opportunity costs of the units transferred.

3. **No market exists for the intermediate product.** This would occur, for example, in the Northern Petroleum case if oil from the production well flows directly into the pipeline and cannot be sold to outside parties. Here,

the opportunity cost of supplying crude oil internally is zero because the inability to sell crude oil externally means no contribution margin is forgone. At the Production Division of Northern Petroleum, the minimum transfer price under the general guideline would be the incremental costs per barrel of $2. As in the previous case, any transfer price between $2 and $13 will achieve goal-congruence. If the transfer price is set at $2, of course, the Production Division would never record positive operating income and would show poor performance. One approach to overcoming this problem is to have the Transportation Division make a lump sum payment to cover fixed costs and generate some operating income for the Production Division while the Production Division continues to make transfers at incremental costs of $2 per barrel.

MULTINATIONAL TRANSFER PRICING AND TAX CONSIDERATIONS

Transfer prices often have tax implications. Tax factors include not only income taxes, but also payroll taxes, customs duties, tariffs, sales taxes, value-added taxes, environment-related taxes, and other government levies on organizations. Full consideration of tax aspects of transfer pricing decisions is beyond the scope of this book. Our aim here is to highlight tax factors and, in particular, income taxes as an important consideration in transfer pricing decisions.

OBJECTIVE 8

Recognize income tax considerations in multinational transfer pricing

Consider the Northern Petroleum data in Exhibit 23-2. Assume that the Production Division also has an operation in Mexico which pays Mexican income taxes at 30% of operating income and that both the Transportation and Refining Divisions based in Canada pay income taxes at 20% of operating income. Northern Petroleum would minimize its total income tax payments with the 110%-of-full-costs transfer pricing method, as shown in the following table:

Transfer Pricing Method	Operating Income for 100 Barrels of Crude Oil			Income Tax on 100 Barrels of Crude Oil		
	Mexican Production Division (1)	Canadian Transportation and Refining Division (2)	Total (3) = (1) + (2)	Mexican Production Division (4) = 0.30 × (1)	Canadian Transportation and Refining Divisions (5) = 0.20 × (2)	Total (6) = (4) + (5)
A. Market price	$500	$200	$700	$150	$ 40	$190
B. 110% of full costs	80	620	700	24	124	148
C. Negotiated price	200	500	700	60	100	160

Tax considerations raise additional issues that may conflict with other objectives of transfer pricing. Suppose that the market for crude oil in Mexico is perfectly competitive. In this case, the market-based transfer price achieves goal-congruence and provides effort incentives. It also helps Northern to evaluate the economic profitability of the Production Division. But it is costly from an income tax standpoint.

Northern Petroleum would favour using 110% of full costs for tax reporting. Tax laws in Canada and Mexico constrain this option. In particular, the Mexican tax authorities are fully aware of Northern Petroleum's incentives to minimize income taxes by reducing the income reported in Mexico. They would challenge any attempts to shift income to the Transportation and Refining Divisions through a low transfer price.

In Canada, Information Circular 87-2 provides guidance to Canadian companies about Revenue Canada's approach to tax issues concerning international transfer prices.

In basic terms the taxpayer in Canada is expected to report taxable income on the basis of having charged a fair price for goods and services provided to non-resident affiliates, and of having paid no more than a fair price for goods and services received from non-resident affiliates. In this latter connection, it must be emphasized that the taxpayer should not absorb any duplication in the intercompany prices and other charges that are incurred.

U.S. Internal Revenue Service, Japanese National Tax Agency, and Transfer Pricing Games

Ciba-Geigy
www.ciba.com

Roche
www.roche.com

Hoechst
www.hoechst.com

Tax authorities and government officials all over the world pay close attention to taxes paid by foreign corporations operating within their boundaries. In the United States, the huge federal budget deficit has heightened interest in whether foreign corporations pay their fair share of U.S. taxes. At the heart of the issue: the transfer prices that companies use to transfer products from one country to another.

In 1993, the U.S. Internal Revenue Service (IRS) investigated and concluded that Nissan Motor Company had minimized U.S. taxes by setting transfer prices on passenger cars and trucks imported from Japan at "unrealistically" high levels. Nissan argued that it had maintained low margins in the United States to increase long-run market share in a very competitive market. Eventually, Nissan agreed to pay the IRS $170 million. But Nissan suffered no loss. The Japanese National Tax Agency (NTA), Japan's tax authority, refunded Nissan the full amount of the IRS payment.

In May 1994, Japan's NTA alleged that Coca-Cola Corporation had deliberately underrecorded profits earned in Japan both by charging "excessive" transfer prices to its local subsidiary for materials and concentrate imported from the parent company and by levying "excessive" royalty payments on its Japanese subsidiary. The NTA imposed taxes and penalties of $150 million. The NTA also took similar action against three European pharmaceutical companies, Ciba-Geigy, Roche, and Hoechst.

The dispute over what is a "fair" transfer price arises in each of these cases because of the absence of an easily observable market price for the transferred product. Multinational transfer pricing disputes are likely to remain a significant issue given the substantial and increasing amounts of multinational investments.

Source: Adapted from Pass, C. "Transfer Pricing in Multinational Companies," *Management Accounting,* September 1994.

In effect, companies should use transfer prices that are comparable to those that would exist in uncontrolled transactions.

The perfectly competitive market for crude oil in Mexico would probably force Northern Petroleum to use the market price for transfers from the Production Division to the Transportation Division. Northern Petroleum might successfully argue that the transfer price should be set below the market price because the Production Division incurs no marketing and distribution costs when "selling" crude oil to the Transportation Division. Northern Petroleum could obtain advanced approval of the transfer pricing arrangements from the appropriate tax authorities.

Consider another example of a Canadian company that manufactures and sells products from Ireland. Tax and other incentives offered by Ireland result in the Irish division paying lower taxes on its income in Ireland. Therefore, the company has an incentive to set the transfer price for transfers into Canada as high as possible. Why? To maximize income reported in Ireland where tax rates are lower and reduce income reported in Canada that is taxed at rates as high as 40%.

To meet multiple transfer pricing objectives, a company may choose to keep one set of accounting records for tax reporting and a second set for internal management reporting. The difficulty here is that tax authorities may interpret two sets of books as suggestive of the company manipulating its reported taxable income to avoid tax payments.[3]

Additional factors that arise in multinational transfer pricing include tariffs and customs duties levied on imports of products into a country. The issues here are simi-

---

[3]To minimize some of the uncertainty concerning international transfer prices, companies can request an advance pricing agreement from Revenue Canada. See Alexander Gelardi and Sophia Wong, "New Solution to Transfer Pricing Problems," *CGA Magazine,* January 1996.

lar to the income tax considerations discussed earlier—companies will have incentives to lower transfer prices for products imported into a country to reduce the tariffs and customs duties that those products will attract.

In addition to the various motivations for choosing transfer prices described so far, multinational transfer prices are sometimes influenced by restrictions that some countries place on the payment of income or dividends to parties outside their national borders. By increasing the prices of goods or services transferred into divisions in these countries, companies can increase the funds paid out of these countries without appearing to violate income or dividend restrictions.

PROBLEM

The Pillercat Corporation is a highly decentralized company. Each division manager has full authority for sourcing decisions and selling decisions. The Machining Division of Pillercat has been the major supplier of the 2,000 crankshafts that the Tractor Division needs each year.

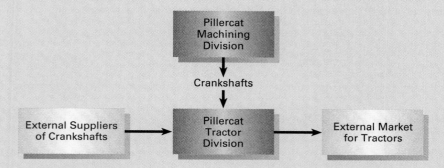

The Tractor Division, however, has just announced that it plans to purchase all its crankshafts in the forthcoming year from two external suppliers at $200 per crankshaft. The Machining Division of Pillercat recently increased its price for the forthcoming year to $220 per unit (from $200 per unit in the current year).

Juan Gomez, manager of the Machining Division, feels that the 10% price increase is fully justified. It results from a higher amortization charge on some new specialized equipment used to manufacture crankshafts and an increase in labour costs. Gomez wants the president of Pillercat Corporation to direct the Tractor Division to buy all its crankshafts from the Machining Division at the price of $220. The additional incremental costs per unit that Pillercat incurs to produce each crankshaft is the Machining Division's variable costs of $190. Fixed costs per crankshaft in the Machining Division equals $20.

REQUIRED

1. Compute the advantage or disadvantage (in terms of monthly operating income) to the Pillercat Corporation as a whole if the Tractor Division buys crankshafts internally from the Machining Division under each of the following cases.
   a. The Machining Division has no alternative use for the facilities used to manufacture crankshafts.
   b. The Machining Division can use the facilities for other production operations, which will result in monthly cash operating savings of $29,000.
   c. The Machining Division has no alternative use for the facilities, and the external supplier drops its price to $185 per crankshaft.
2. As the president of Pillercat, how would you respond to Juan Gomez's request to order the Tractor Division to purchase all of its crankshafts from the Machining Division? Would your response differ according to the scenarios described in parts (a), (b), and (c) of requirement 1? Why?

SOLUTION

1. Computations for the Tractor Division buying crankshafts internally:

	Case		
	(a)	**(b)**	**(c)**
Total purchase costs if buying from an external supplier (2,000 × $200, $200, $185)	$400,000	$400,000	$370,000
Total incremental costs if buying from the Machining Division (2,000 × $190)	380,000	380,000	380,000
Total opportunity costs of the Machining Division	—	29,000	—
Total relevant costs	380,000	409,000	380,000
Monthly operating income advantage (disadvantage) to the Pillercat Corporation of buying from the Machining Division	$ 20,000	$ (9,000)	$ (10,000)

The general guideline that was introduced in the chapter as a first step in setting a transfer price can be used to highlight the alternatives:

Case	Additional Incremental Costs per Unit Incurred to Point of Transfer	+	Opportunity Costs per Unit to the Supplying Division	=	Transfer Price	External Market Price
(a)	$190	+	$0	=	$190	$200
(b)	$190	+	$14.50 ($29,000 ÷ 2,000)	=	$204.50	$200
(c)	$190	+	$0	=	$190	$185

The Tractor Division will maximize monthly operating income of Pillercat Corporation as a whole by purchasing from the Machining Division in Case (a) and by purchasing from the external supplier in Cases (b) and (c).

2. Pillercat Corporation is a highly decentralized company. If no forced transfer were made, the Tractor Division would use an external supplier, resulting in an optimal decision for the company as a whole in Cases (b) and (c) of requirement 1 but not in Case (a).

Suppose that in Case 1(a), the Machining Division refuses to meet the price of $200. This decision means that the company will be $20,000 worse off in the short run. Should top management interfere and force a transfer at $200? This interference would undercut the philosophy of decentralization. Many top managements would not interfere because they would view the $20,000 as an inevitable cost of a suboptimal decision that occasionally occurs under decentralization. But how high must this cost be before the temptation to interfere would be irresistible? $30,000? $40,000?

Any top management interference with lower-level decision-making weakens decentralization. Of course, such interference may occasionally be necessary to prevent costly blunders. But recurring interference and constraints simply transform a decentralized organization into a centralized organization.

SUMMARY

The following points are linked to the chapter's learning objectives.

1. A management control system is a means of gathering and using information to aid and coordinate the process of making planning and control decisions throughout the organization, and to guide employee behaviour. Effective management control systems are closely aligned to the organization's strategy, fit the organization's structure, and motivate managers and employees to give effort to achieve the organization's goals.

2. The benefits of decentralization include (a) greater responsiveness to local needs, (b) gains from quicker decision-making, (c) increased motivation of subunit managers, (d) greater management development and learning, and (e) sharper management focus. The costs of decentralization include (a) dysfunctional decision making (control loss), (b) duplication of activities, (c) decreased loyalty toward the organization, and (d) increased costs of information gathering.

3. Transfer prices can be (a) market-based, (b) cost-based, or (c) negotiated. Different transfer pricing methods produce different revenues and costs for individual subunits, and hence different operating incomes for them.

4. In perfectly competitive markets, there is no idle capacity, and division managers can buy and sell as much as they want at the market price. Setting the transfer price at the market price motivates division managers to deal internally and to take exactly the same actions as they would if they were dealing in the external market.

5. A transfer price based on full cost plus a markup may lead to suboptimal decisions, because it leads the "buying" division to regard the fixed costs and the markup of the selling division as variable costs.

6. When there is excess capacity, the transfer price range for negotiations generally lies between the minimum price at which the selling division is willing to sell (its variable costs) and the maximum price the buying division is willing to pay (the price at which the product is available from outside suppliers).

7. The general guideline for transfer pricing states that the minimum transfer price equals the incremental costs per unit incurred up to the point of transfer plus the opportunity costs per unit to the supplying division resulting from transferring products or services internally.

8. Transfer prices can reduce income tax payments by recognizing more income in low tax rate countries and lower income in high tax rate countries.

▼ TERMS TO LEARN

This chapter contains definitions of the following important terms:

autonomy (p. 800)
decentralization (p. 796)
dual pricing (p. 805)
effort (p. 795)
goal-congruence (p. 795)
goal-incongruent decision-making (p. 797)

intermediate product (p. 798)
management control system (p. 794)
motivation (p. 795)
perfectly competitive market (p. 803)
suboptimal decision-making (p. 797)
transfer price (p. 798)

▼ ASSIGNMENT MATERIAL

QUESTIONS

23-1 What is a management control system?

23-2 Describe three criteria you would use to evaluate whether a management control system is effective.

23-3 What is the relationship among motivation, goal-congruence, and effort?

23-4 Name three benefits and two costs of decentralization.

23-5 "Organizations typically adopt a consistent decentralization or centralization philosophy across all their business functions." Do you agree? Explain.

23-6 "Transfer pricing is confined to profit centres." Do you agree? Why?

23-7 What are the three general methods for determining transfer prices?

23-8 What properties should transfer pricing systems have?

23-9 "All transfer pricing methods give the same division operating income." Do you agree? Explain.

23-10 Under what conditions is a market-based transfer price optimal?

23-11 What is one potential limitation of full-cost-based transfer prices?

23-12 Give two reasons why a dual-price approach to transfer pricing is not widely used.

23-13 "Cost and price information play no role in negotiated transfer prices." Do you agree? Explain.

23-14 "Under the general transfer pricing guideline, the minimum transfer price will vary depending on whether the supplying division has idle capacity or not." Do you agree? Explain.

23-15 Why should managers consider income tax issues when choosing a transfer pricing method?

EXERCISES

23-16 Decentralization, responsibility centres. Quinn Corporation manufactures and sells lighting products. Quinn's sales and marketing divisions are organized along product lines—wall sconces, recessed lights, track lights, and so on. The manufacturing division produces lighting products for all the divisions.

During the planning process, each sales and marketing division specifies the quantity of each style of lights to be manufactured. Senior management then assigns the task of manufacturing the lights to different plants in the manufacturing division. Because manufacturing capacity is limited, some of the production is also outsourced. Senior management determines the manufacturing schedule on the basis of detailed studies that have been done to measure the time and cost of manufacturing different types of lighting products. Manufacturing managers are evaluated based on achieving target output within budgeted costs.

REQUIRED
1. Are the manufacturing plants in the Manufacturing Division cost centres or profit centres? Explain.
2. Quinn Corporation is considering decentralizing its marketing and manufacturing decisions by letting manufacturing and marketing managers directly negotiate the prices for manufacturing various products.
   a. How should Quinn evaluate manufacturing plant managers under this proposal?
   b. Would you recommend that Quinn Corporation decentralized its marketing and manufacturing decisions? Explain.

23-17 Decentralization, goal-congruence, responsibility centres. Hexton Chemicals consists of seven operating divisions that each operate independently. The operating divisions are supported by a number of support divisions such as R&D, labour relations, and environmental management. The environmental management group consists of 20 environmental engineers. These engineers must seek out business from the operating divisions—that is, the projects they work on must be mutually agreed to and paid for by one of the operating divisions. Under Hexton's rules, the environmental group is required to charge the operating divisions for environmental services at cost.

REQUIRED
1. Is the environmental management organization centralized or decentralized?
2. What type of responsibility centre is the environmental management group?
3. What benefits and problems do you see in structuring the environmental management group the way Hexton has? Does it lead to goal-congruence and motivation?

23-18 Multinational transfer pricing, effect of alternative transfer pricing methods, global income tax minimization. User Friendly Computer, Inc., with headquarters in Regina, manufactures and sells desktop computers. User Friendly has three divisions, each of which is located in a different country:
   a. China Division—manufactures memory devices and keyboards

CHAPTER 23

b. South Korea Division—assembles desktop computers, using internally manufactured parts and memory devices and keyboards from the China Division

c. Canadian Division—packages and distributes desktop computers

Each division is run as a profit centre. The costs for the work done in each division that is associated with a single desktop computer unit are as follows:

China Division:

    Variable costs = 1,000 yuan
    Fixed costs   = 1,800 yuan

South Korea Division:

    Variable costs = 240,000 won
    Fixed costs   = 320,000 won

Canadian Division:

    Variable costs = $100
    Fixed costs   = $200

Chinese income tax rate on China Division's operating income	40%
South Korean income tax rate in South Korea Division's operating income	20%
Canadian income tax rate on Canadian Division's operating income	30%

Each desktop computer is sold to retail outlets in Canada for $3,200. Assume that the current foreign exchange rates are:

$$8 \text{ yuan} = \$1 \text{ Cdn.}$$
$$800 \text{ won} = \$1 \text{ Cdn.}$$

Both the China and the South Korea Division sell part of their production under a private label. The China Division sells the comparable memory/keyboard package used in each User Friendly desktop computer to a Chinese manufacturer for 3,600 yuan. The South Korea division sells the comparable desktop computer to a South Korean distributor for 1,040,000 won.

REQUIRED

1. Calculate the after-tax operating income per unit earned by each division under each of the following transfer pricing methods: (a) market price, (b) 200% of full costs, and (c) 300% of variable costs. (Income taxes are *not* included in the computation of the cost-based transfer prices.)
2. Which transfer pricing method(s) will maximize the net income per unit of User Friendly Computer, Inc.?

23-19 Transfer pricing methods, goal-congruence. British Columbia Lumber has a Raw Lumber Division and Finished Lumber Division. The variable costs are:

◆ Raw Lumber Division: $100 per 100 board-feet of raw lumber (a board-foot is about 2,360 cubic centimetres).

◆ Finished Lumber Division: $125 per 100 board-feet of finished lumber

Assume that there is no board-feet loss in processing raw lumber into finished lumber. Raw lumber can be sold at $200 per 100 board-feet. Finished lumber can be sold at $275 per 100 board-feet.

REQUIRED

1. Should British Columbia Lumber process raw lumber into its finished form?
2. Assume that internal transfers are made at 110% of variable costs. Will each division maximize its division operating income contribution by adopting the action that is in the best interests of British Columbia Lumber?
3. Assume that internal transfers are made at market prices. Will each division maximize its division operating income contribution by adopting the action that is in the best interests of British Columbia Lumber?

23-20 Effect of alternative transfer pricing methods on division operating income. (CMA, adapted) Ajax Corporation has two divisions. The Mining Division makes toldine, which is then transferred to the Metals Division. The toldine is further processed by the Metals Division and is sold to customers at a price of $150 per unit. The Mining Division is currently required by Ajax to transfer its total yearly output of 400,000 units of toldine to the Metals Division at 110% of full manufacturing cost. Unlimited quantities of toldine can be purchased and sold on the outside market at $90 per unit. To sell the toldine it produces at $90 per unit on the outside market, the Mining Division would have to incur variable marketing and distribution costs of $5 per unit. Similarly, if the Metals Division purchased toldine from the outside market, it would have to incur variable purchasing costs of $3 per unit.

The following table gives the manufacturing costs per unit in the Mining and Metals Divisions for the year 2000:

	Mining Division	Metals Division
Direct materials	$12	$ 6
Direct manufacturing labour costs	16	20
Manufacturing overhead costs	32*	25†
Manufacturing costs per unit	$60	$51

*Manufacturing overhead costs in the Mining Division are 25% fixed and 75% variable.
†Manufacturing overhead costs in the Metals Division are 60% fixed and 40% variable.

REQUIRED
1. Calculate the operating incomes for the Mining and Metals Divisions for the 400,000 units of toldine transferred under each of the following transfer pricing methods: (a) market price and (b) 110% of full manufacturing costs.
2. Suppose Ajax rewards each division manager with a bonus, calculated as 1% of division operating income (if positive). What is the amount of bonus that will be paid to each division manager under each of the transfer pricing methods in requirement 1? Which transfer pricing method will each division manager prefer to use?
3. What arguments would Brian Jones, manager of the Mining Division, make to support the transfer pricing method that he prefers?

23-21 Decentralization, general guideline, goal congruence. (CMA, adapted) The Igo Division of Nogo Motors, Inc. purchases most of its airbags from the Airbag Division. The Airbag Division's incremental costs for manufacturing the airbags are $110 per unit. The Airbag Division is currently working at 80% of capacity. The current market price of the airbags is $140 per unit.

REQUIRED
1. Using the general guideline presented in the chapter, what is the minimum price at which the Airbag Division would sell airbags to the Igo Division?
2. Suppose that Nogo Motors Inc. requires that whenever divisions with idle capacity sell products internally, they must do so at incremental costs. Evaluate this transfer pricing policy using the criteria of goal congruence, evaluating division performance, motivating management effort, and preserving division autonomy.
3. If the two divisions were to negotiate a transfer price, what is the range of possible transfer prices? Evaluate this negotiated transfer pricing policy using the criteria of goal congruence, evaluating division performance, motivating management effort, and preserving division autonomy.
4. Do you prefer the transfer pricing policy in requirement 2 or requirement 3? Explain your answer briefly.

23-22 General guideline, transfer price range. The Shamrock Company manufactures and sells television sets. The Assembly Division assembles the television sets. It buys the screens for the television sets from the Screen Division. The Screen Division is operating at capacity. The incremental cost of manufacturing the screens is $70 per unit. The Screen Division can sell as many screens as it wants in the outside market at a price of $110 per screen. If it sells screens in the outside market, the Screen Division will incur variable sales and distribution cost of $4 per unit. Similarly, if the Assembly Division purchases screens from the outside market, it will incur variable purchasing costs of $2 per unit.

REQUIRED
1. Using the general guideline presented in the chapter, what is the minimum transfer price at which the Screen Division will sell screens to the Assembly Division?
2. Suppose division managers act autonomously to maximize their division's operating income either by transacting internally or buying and selling in the market. If the two division managers were to negotiate a transfer price, what is the range of acceptable transfer prices?

23-23 Multinational transfer pricing, global tax minimization. The Mornay Company manufactures telecommunications equipment at its Winnipeg factory. The company has marketing divisions throughout the world. A Mornay marketing division in Vienna, Austria imports 1,000 units of a piece of equipment called Product 4A36 from Canada. The following information is available:

Canadian income tax rate on the Canadian division's operating income	40%
Austrian income tax rate on the Austrian division's operating income	44%
Austrian import duty	10%
Variable manufacturing cost per unit of Product 4A36	$350
Full manufacturing cost per unit of Product 4A36	$500
Selling price (net of marketing and distribution costs) in Austria	$750

Suppose the Canadian and Austrian tax authorities only allow transfer prices that are between the full manufacturing cost per unit and a market price of $650 based on comparable imports into Austria. The Austrian import duty is charged on the price at which the product is transferred into Austria. Any import duty paid to the Austrian authorities is a deductible expense for calculating Austrian income taxes due.

REQUIRED

1. Calculate the after-tax operating income earned by the Canadian and Austrian divisions from transferring 1,000 units of Product 4A36 at (a) full manufacturing cost per unit and (b) market price of comparable imports. (Income taxes are *not* included in the computation of the cost-based transfer prices.)
2. Which transfer price should the Mornay Company select to minimize the total of company import duties and income taxes? Recall that the transfer price must be between the full manufacturing cost per unit of $500 and the market price of of $650 comparable imports into Austria. Explain your reasoning.

23-24 Multinational transfer pricing, goal-congruence (continuation of 23-23). Suppose that the Canadian division could sell as many units of Product 4A36 as it makes at $600 per unit in the Canadian market, net of all marketing and distribution costs.

REQUIRED

1. From the viewpoint of the Mornay Company as a whole, would after-tax operating income be maximized if it sold the 1,000 units of Product 4A36 in Canada or in Austria?
2. Suppose each division manager acts autonomously to maximize his or her division's after-tax operating income. Will the transfer price calculated in requirement 2 of Exercise 23-23 result in the Canadian division manager taking the actions determined to be optimal in requirement 1 of this exercise? Explain.
3. What is the minimum transfer price that the Canadian division manager would agree to? Does this transfer price result in the Mornay Company as a whole paying more import duty and taxes than the answer to requirement 2 of Exercise 23-23? If so, by how much?

23-25 Transfer pricing dispute. The Allison-Chambers Corporation, manufacturer of tractors and other heavy farm equipment, is organized along decentralized lines, with each manufacturing division operating as a separate profit centre. Each division manager has been delegated full authority on all decisions involving the sale of that division's output both to outsiders and to other divisions of Allison-Chambers. Division C has in the past always purchased its requirement of a particular tractor-engine component from Division A. However, when informed that Division A is increasing its selling price to $150, Division C's manager decides to purchase the engine component from outside suppliers.

Division C can purchase the component for $135 on the open market. Division A insists that, because of the recent installation of some highly specialized equipment and the resulting high amortization charges, it will not be able to earn an adequate return on its investment unless it raises its price. Division A's manager appeals to top management of Allison-Chambers for support in the dispute with Division C and supplies the following operating data:

C's annual purchases of tractor-engine component	1,000 units
A's variable costs per unit of tractor-engine component	$120
A's fixed costs per unit of tractor-engine component	$20

REQUIRED

1. Assume that there are no alternative uses for internal facilities. Determine whether the company as a whole will benefit if Division C purchases the component from outside suppliers for $135 per unit.
2. Assume that internal facilities of Division A would not otherwise be idle. By not producing the 1,000 units for Division C, Division A's equipment and other facilities would be used for other production operations that would result in annual

cash operating savings of $18,000. Should Division C purchase from outside suppliers?

3. Assume that there are no alternative uses for Division A's internal facilities and that the price from outsiders drops $20. Should Division C purchase from outside suppliers?

23-26 Transfer pricing problem (continuation of 23-25). Refer to Exercise 23-25. Assume that Division A can sell the 1,000 units to other customers at $155 per unit with variable marketing costs 5 per unit.

REQUIRED

Determine whether Allison-Chambers will benefit if Division C purchases the 1,000 components from outside suppliers at $135 per unit.

PROBLEMS

23-27 Pertinent transfer price. Europa, Inc. has two divisions, A and B, which manufacture expensive bicycles. Division A produces the bicycle frame, and Division B assembles the rest of the bicycle onto the frame. There is a market for both the subassembly and the final product. Each division has been designated as a profit centre. The transfer price for the subassembly has been set at the long-run average market price. The following data are available to each division:

Estimated selling price for final product	$300
Long-run average selling price for intermediate product	200
Incremental costs for completion in Division B	150
Incremental costs in Division A	120

The manager of Division B has made the following calculation:

Selling price for final product		$300
Transferred-in costs (market)	$200	
Incremental costs for completion	150	350
Contribution (loss) on product		$ (50)

REQUIRED

1. Should transfers be made to Division B if there is no excess capacity in Division A? Is the market price the correct transfer price?
2. Assume that Division A's maximum capacity for this product is 1,000 units per month and sales to the intermediate market are now 800 units. Should 200 units be transferred to Division B? At what transfer price? Assume that for a variety of reasons, A will maintain the $200 selling price indefinitely; that is, A is not considering lowering the price to outsiders even if idle capacity exists.
3. Suppose Division A quoted a transfer price of $150 for up to 200 units. What would be the contribution to the company as a whole if the transfer were made? As manager of Division B, would you be inclined to buy at $150?

23-28 Pricing in imperfect markets (continuation of 23-27). Refer to Problem 23-27.

REQUIRED

1. Suppose the manager of Division A has the option of (a) cutting the external price to $195 with the certainty that sales will rise to 1,000 units or (b) maintaining the outside price of $200 for the 800 units and transferring the 200 units to Division B at some price that would produce the same operating income for Division A. What transfer price would produce the same operating income for Division A? Does that price coincide with that produced by the general guideline in the chapter so that the desirable decision for the company as a whole would result?
2. Suppose that if the selling price for the intermediate product is dropped to $195, outside sales can be increased to 900 units. Division B wants to acquire as many as 200 units if the transfer price is acceptable. For simplicity, assume that there is no outside market for the final 100 units of Division A's capacity.
   a. Using the general guideline, what is (are) the minimum transfer price(s) that should lead to the correct economic decision? Ignore performance evaluation considerations.
   b. Compare the total contributions under the alternatives to show why the transfer price(s) recommended lead(s) to the optimal economic decision.

23-29 Effect of alternative transfer pricing methods on division operating income. Oceanic Products is a tuna fishing company based in St. John's. It has three divisions:
   a. Tuna Harvesting—operates a fleet of 20 trawling vessels.
   b. Tuna Processing—processes the raw tuna into tuna fillets.
   c. Tuna Marketing—packages tuna fillets in two-kilogram packets that are sold to wholesale distributors at $12 each.

The Tuna Processing Division has a yield of 500 kilograms of processed tuna fillets from 1,000 kilograms of raw tuna provided by the Tuna Harvesting Division. The Tuna Marketing Division has a yield of 300 two-kilogram packets from every 500 kilograms of processed tuna fillets provided by the Tuna Processing Division. (The weight of the packaging material is included in the two-kilogram weight.) Cost data for each division are as follows:

Tuna Harvesting Division	
Variable costs per kilogram of raw tuna	$0.20
Fixed costs per kilogram of raw tuna	$0.40
Tuna Processing Division	
Variable costs per kilogram of processed tuna	$0.80
Fixed costs per kilogram of processed tuna	$0.60
Tuna Marketing Division	
Variable costs per two-kilogram packet	$0.30
Fixed costs per two-kilogram packet	$0.70

Fixed costs per unit are based on the estimated quantity of raw tuna, processed tuna, and two-kilogram packets to be produced during the current fishing season.

Oceanic Products has chosen to process internally all raw tuna brought in by the Tuna Harvesting Division. Other tuna processors in St. John's purchase raw tuna from boat operators at $1 per kilogram. Oceanic Products has also chosen to process internally all tuna fillets into the two-kilogram packets sold by the Tuna Marketing Division. Several fish marketing companies in St. John's purchase tuna fillets at $5 per kilogram.

REQUIRED
1. Compute the overall operating income to Oceanic Products of harvesting 1,000 kilograms of raw tuna, processing it into tuna fillets, and then selling it in two-kilogram packets.
2. Compute the transfer prices that will be used for internal transfers (i) from the Tuna Harvesting Division to the Tuna Processing Division and (ii) from the Tuna Processing Division to the Tuna Marketing Division under each of the following transfer pricing methods:
   a. 200% of variable costs. Variable costs are the costs of the transferred-in product (if any) plus the division's own variable costs.
   b. 150% of full costs. Full costs are the costs of the transferred-in product (if any) plus the division's own variable and fixed costs.
   c. Market price.
3. Oceanic rewards each division manager with a bonus, calculated as 10% of division operating income (if positive). What is the amount of the bonus that will be paid to each division manager under each of the three transfer pricing methods in requirement 2? Which transfer pricing method will each division manager prefer to use?

23-30 Goal-congruence problems with cost-plus transfer pricing methods, dual-price method (continuation of 23-29). Assume that Oceanic Products uses a transfer price of 150% of full cost. Pat Forgione, the company president, attends a seminar on the virtues of decentralization. Forgione decides to implement decentralization at Oceanic Products. A memorandum is sent to all division managers: "Starting immediately, each division of Oceanic Products is free to make its own decisions regarding the purchase of its direct materials and the sale of its finished product."

REQUIRED
1. Give two examples of goal-congruence problems that may arise if Oceanic continues to use the 150%-of-full-costs transfer pricing method and a policy of decentralization is adopted.
2. Forgione is investigating whether a dual transfer pricing policy will reduce goal-congruence problems at Oceanic Products. Transfers out of each selling division

will be made at 150% of full cost; transfers into each buying division will be made at market price. Using this dual transfer-pricing policy, compute the operating income of each division for a harvest of 1,000 kilograms of raw tuna that is further processed and marketed by Oceanic Products.

3. Compute the sum of the division operating incomes in requirement 2. Why might this sum not equal the overall corporate operating income from the harvesting of 1,000 kilograms of raw tuna and its further processing and marketing?

4. What problems may arise if Oceanic Products uses the dual transfer-pricing system described in requirement 2?

23-31 Multinational transfer pricing, global tax minimization. Industrial Diamonds, Inc., based in Vancouver, has two divisions:

    a. Philippine Mining Division. Operates a mine in the Philippines containing a rich body of raw diamonds.

    b. Canadian Processing Division. Processes the raw diamonds into polished diamonds used in industrial applications.

The costs of the Philippine Mining Division are:

◆ Variable costs, 2,500 pesos per kilogram of raw industrial diamonds

◆ Fixed costs, 5,000 pesos per kilogram of raw industrial diamonds

    Industrial Diamonds has a corporate policy of further processing diamonds in Vancouver. Several diamond polishing companies in the Philippines buy raw diamonds from other local mining companies at 10,000 pesos per kilogram. Assume that the current foreign exchange rate is 25 pesos = $1 Cdn.

    The costs of the Canadian Processing Division are:

◆ Variable costs, $200 per kilogram of polished industrial diamonds

◆ Fixed costs, $600 per kilogram of polished industrial diamonds

Assume that it takes two kilograms of raw industrial diamonds to yield one kilogram of polished industrial diamonds. Polished diamonds sell for $4,000 per kilogram.

REQUIRED

1. Compute the transfer price (in $Cdn.) for one kilogram of raw industrial diamonds transferred from the Philippine Mining Division to the Canadian Processing Division under two methods: (a) 300% of full costs and (b) market price.

2. Assume a world of no income taxes. One thousand pounds of raw industrial diamonds are mined by the Philippine Division and then processed and sold by the Canadian Processing Division. Compute the operating income (in $Cdn.) for each division of Industrial Diamonds, Inc. under each transfer pricing method in requirement 1.

3. Assume that the corporate income tax rate is 20% in the Philippines and 35% in Canada. Compute the after-tax operating income (in $Cdn.) for each division under each transfer pricing method in requirement 1. (Income taxes are not included in the computation of the cost-based transfer price. Industrial Diamonds does not pay Canadian taxes on income already taxed in the Philippines.)

4. Which transfer pricing method in requirement 1 will maximize the total after-tax operating income of Industrial Diamonds?

5. What factors, in addition to global tax minimization, might Industrial Diamonds consider in choosing a transfer pricing method for transfers between its two divisions?

23-32 Multinational transfer pricing and taxation. (Richard Lambert, adapted) Anita Corporation, headquartered in Canada, manufactures state-of-the-art milling machines. It has two marketing subsidiaries, one in Brazil and one in Switzerland, that sell its products. Anita is building one new machine, at a cost of $500,000. There is no market for the equipment in Canada. The equipment can be sold in Brazil for $1,000,000, but the Brazilian subsidiary would incur transportation and modification costs of $200,000. Alternatively, the equipment can be sold in Switzerland for $950,000, but the Swiss subsidiary would incur transportation and modification costs of $250,000. The Canadian company can sell the equipment to either its Brazilian subsidiary or its Swiss subsidiary but not to both. The Anita Corporation and its subsidiaries operate in a very decentralized manner. Managers in each company have considerable autonomy, with each manager interested in maximizing company income.

REQUIRED

1. From the viewpoint of Anita and its subsidiaries taken together, should the Anita Corporation manufacture the equipment? If it does, where should it sell the equipment to maximize corporate operating income? What would the oper-

ating income for Anita and its subsidiaries be from the sale? Ignore any income tax effects.

2. What range of transfer prices will result in achieving the actions determined to be optimal in requirement 1? Explain your answer.

3. The effective income tax rates for this transaction are as follows: 40% in Canada, 60% in Brazil, and 15% in Switzerland. The tax authorities in the three countries are uncertain about the cost of the intermediate product and will allow any transfer price between $500,000 and $700,000. If Anita and its subsidiaries want to maximize after-tax operating income, (a) should the equipment be manufactured and (b) where and at what price should it be transferred?

4. Now suppose managers act autonomously to maximize their own company's after-tax operating income. The tax authorities will allow transfer prices only between $500,000 and $700,000. Which subsidiary will get the product and at what price? Is your answer the same as your answer in requirement 3? Explain why or why not.

23-33 Transfer pricing, goal congruence. The Sather Corporation manufactures and sells 10,000 boom boxes. It buys the cassette deck for the boom box from the Cassette Deck Division. The Cassette Deck Division is operating at capacity and producing 12,000 cassette decks. The demand for cassette decks is strong. Any cassette deck not sold to the Assembly Division can be sold in the outside market for $35 per unit. The Cassette Deck Division currently sells 10,000 cassette decks to the Assembly Division and 2,000 cassette decks in the outside market. The incremental cost of manufacturing the cassette deck is $25 per unit.

A crucial component for producing high-quality cassette decks is the (cassette) head mechanism. The Cassette Deck Division manufactures the head mechanism for its cassette decks. Many outside suppliers have offered to supply cassette decks to Sather. To ensure quality, Sather requires that any outside supplier wanting to supply cassette decks to Sather must purchase the head mechanism from the Cassette Deck Division. The Cassette Deck Division's incremental cost of manufacturing the head mechanism is $12 per unit. The Cassette Deck Division will charge $18 per unit for the head mechanism. The Cassette Deck Division has excess manufacturing capacity for manufacturing the head mechanism. That is, even if the Cassette Deck Division manufactures the head mechanism for outside suppliers, it will still be able to manufacture and sell 12,000 cassette decks for sale in the outside market at $35 per unit.

Johnson Corporation, an outside supplier, is currently negotiating to supply 10,000 cassette decks to the Assembly Division for a price in the range of $37 to $43. If Johnson gets the business it will buy the head mechanism from the Cassette Deck Division for $18 per unit.

REQUIRED

1. From the standpoint of Sather Corporation as a whole, should the Assembly Division accept Johnson Corporation's offer at (a) a price of $37 per cassette deck? (b) at a price of $43 per cassette deck? Show all calculations.

2. What transfer price for cassette decks will result in the Cassette Deck Division and the Assembly Division taking actions that are optimal for Sather Corporation as a whole? Explain your answer.

23-34 Utilization of capacity. (J. Patell, adapted) The California Instrument Company (CIC) consists of the Semiconductor Division and the Process-Control Division, each of which operates as an independent profit centre. The Semiconductor Division employs craftsmen who produce two different electronic components, the new high-performance Super-chip and an older product called Okay-chip. These two products have the following cost characteristics:

	Super-Chip	Okay-Chip
Direct materials	$ 2	$ 1
Direct manufacturing labour		
2 hours × $14; 0.5 hours × $14	28	7

Annual overhead in the Semiconductor Division totals $400,000, all fixed. Owing to the high skill level necessary for the craftsmen, the semiconductor division's capacity is set at 50,000 hours per year.

One customer orders a maximum of 15,000 Super-chips per year, at a price of $60 per chip. If CIC cannot meet this entire demand, the customer curtails its own production. The rest of the Semiconductor's Division's capacity is devoted to the Okay-chip, for which there is unlimited demand at $12 per chip.

The Process-Control Division provides only one product, a process-control unit, with the following cost structure:

Direct materials (circuit board)	$60
Direct manufacturing labour (5 hours x $10)	50

Fixed overhead costs of the Process-Control Division are $80,000 per year. The current market price of the control unit is $132 per unit.

A joint research project has just revealed that a single Super-chip could be substituted for the circuit board currently used to make the process-control unit. Using Super-chip would require an extra hour of labour per control unit for a new total of 6 hours per control unit.

REQUIRED

1. Calculate the contribution margin per hour of selling Super-chip and Okay-chip. If no transfers of Super-chip were made to the Process-Control Division, how many Super-chips and Okay-chips should the Semiconductor Division sell?
2. The Process-Control Division expects to sell 5,000 control units this year. From the viewpoint of California Instruments as a whole, should 5,000 Super-chips be transferred to the Process-Control Division to replace circuit boards? Show all calculations.
3. If demand for the control unit is sure to be 5,000 units, but its *price* is uncertain, what should the transfer price of Super-chip be to ensure that the division managers' actions maximize operating income for CIC as a whole? (All other data are unchanged.)
4. If demand for the control unit is sure to be 12,000 units, but its *price* is uncertain, what should the transfer price of Super-chip be to ensure that the division managers' actions maximize operating income for CIC as a whole? (All other data are unchanged.)

23-35 **Ethics, transfer pricing.** The Belmont Division of Durham Industries manufactures components R47, which it transfers to the Alston Division at 200% of variable costs. The variable costs of R47 are $14 per unit. Joe Lasker, the management accountant of the Belmont Division calls Hal Tanner, his assistant, into his office. Lasker says, "I am not sure about the fixed and variable cost distinctions you are making. I think the variable costs are higher than $14 per unit."

Tanner knows that showing higher variable costs will increase the Belmont Division's profits and lead to higher bonuses for the division employees. However, Tanner is uncomfortable about making any changes because he has used the same method over the last few years. But Tanner knows that fixed and variable cost distinctions are not always clearcut.

REQUIRED

1. Calculate Belmont Division's contribution margin from transferring 10,000 units of R47 in 2001 if (a) variable costs are $14 per unit, and (b) if variable costs are $16 per unit.
2. Evaluate whether Lasker's suggestion to Tanner regarding variable costs is ethical. Would it be ethical for Tanner to revise the variable cost per unit? What steps should Tanner take to resolve this situation?

COLLABORATIVE LEARNING PROBLEM

23-36 **Goal-congruence, taxes, different market conditions.** The Saskatchewan Corporation makes water pumps. The Engine Division makes the engines and supplies them to the Assembly Division where the pumps are assembled. Saskatchewan is a successful and profitable corporation that attributes much of its success to its decentralized operating style. Each division manager is compensated on the basis of division operating income.

The Assembly Division currently acquires all its engines from the Engine Division. The Assembly Division manager could purchase similar engines in the market for $400.

The Engine Division is currently operating at 80% of its capacity of 4,000 units and has the following particulars:

Direct materials ($125 per unit × 3,200 units)	$400,000
Direct manufacturing labour ($50 per unit × 3,200 units)	160,000
Variable manufacturing overhead costs ($25 per unit × 3,200 units)	80,000
Fixed manufacturing overhead costs	520,000

All the Engine Division's 3,200 units are currently transferred to the Assembly Division. No engines are sold in the outside market.

The Engine Division has just received an order for 2,000 units at $375 per engine that would utilize half the capacity of the plant. The order has either to be taken in full or rejected totally. The order is for a slightly different engine than what the Engine Division currently makes but takes the same amount of manufacturing time. To produce the new engine would require direct materials per unit of $100, direct manufacturing labour per unit of $40, and variable manufacturing overhead costs per unit of $25.

INSTRUCTIONS

Form groups of two or three students to complete the following requirements.

REQUIRED

1. From the viewpoint of the Saskatchewan Corporation as a whole, should the Engine Division accept the order for the 2,000 units?
2. What range of transfer prices result in achieving the actions determined to be optimal in requirement 1, if division managers act in a decentralized manner?
3. The manager of the Assembly Division has proposed a transfer price for the engines equal to the full cost of the engines including an allocation of overhead costs. The Engine Division allocates overhead costs to engines on the basis of the total capacity of the plant used to manufacture the engines.
   a. Calculate the transfer price for the engines transferred to the Assembly Division under this arrangement.
   b. Do you think that the transfer price calculated in requirement 3(a) will result in achieving the actions determined to be optimal in requirement 1, if division managers act in a decentralized manner?
   c. Comment in general on one advantage and one disadvantage of using full costs of the producing division as the basis for setting transfer prices.
4. Now consider the effect of taxes.
   a. Suppose the Assembly Division is located in a country that imposes a 10% tax on income earned within its boundaries, while the Engine Division is located in a country that imposes no tax on income earned within its boundaries. What transfer price would be chosen by the Saskatchewan Corporation to minimize tax payments for the corporation as a whole? Assume that only transfer prices that are greater than or equal to full manufacturing costs and less than or equal to the market price of "substantially similar" engines are acceptable to the taxing authorities.
   b. Suppose that the Saskatchewan Corporation announces the transfer price computed in requirement 4(a) to price all transfers between the Engine and Assembly Divisions. Each division manager then acts autonomously to maximize division operating income. Will division managers acting in a decentralized manner achieve the actions determined to be optimal in requirement 1?
5. Consider your responses to requirements 1–4 and assume the Engine Division will continue to have opportunities for outside business as described in requirement 1. What transfer pricing policy would you recommend Saskatchewan use and why? Would you continue to evaluate division performance on the basis of division operating incomes?

24

PERFORMANCE MEASUREMENT, COMPENSATION, AND MULTINATIONAL CONSIDERATIONS

Hotels, such as the Sheraton in Tasmania, aim to maximize return on investment by increasing the income earned on each dollar of revenue and by increasing revenue per dollar of investment. Hotel managers' performance measures generally include both financial performance measures such as return on investment and nonfinancial performance measures such as occupancy levels.

LEARNING OBJECTIVES

After studying this chapter, you should be able to:

1. Measure performance from a financial and nonfinancial perspective
2. Design an accounting-based performance measure
3. Analyze profitability using the DuPont method
4. Use the residual-income measure and recognize its advantages
5. Describe the economic value added method
6. Distinguish between current cost and historical cost asset measurement methods
7. Indicate the difficulties that arise when comparing the performance of divisions operating in different countries
8. Recognize the role of salaries and incentives in compensation arrangements
9. Describe the management accountant's role in helping organizations provide better incentives

We have discussed performance measurement in many of the earlier chapters, each time within a specific accounting context. Chapter 11, for example, described situations where the correct decision based on a relevant cost analysis (buying new equipment, say) may not be implemented because the performance measurement system induced the manager to act differently. This chapter discusses the design, implementation, and uses of performance measures more generally.

Performance measures are a central component of a management control system. Making good planning and control decisions requires information about how different subunits of the organization have performed. To be effective, management control systems must also motivate managers and employees to strive to achieve organization goals. Performance evaluation and rewards are key elements for motivating employees.

Performance measurement of an organization's subunits should be a prerequisite for allocating resources within that organization. When a subunit undertakes new activities, it forecasts revenues, costs, and investments. Periodic comparisons of the actual revenues, costs, and investments with the budgeted amounts can help guide top management's decisions about future allocations.

Performance measurement of managers is used in decisions about their salaries, bonuses, future assignments, and career advancement. Moreover, the very act of measuring their performance can motivate managers to strive for the goals used in their evaluation.

This chapter examines issues in designing performance measures for different levels of an organization and for managers at these different levels. We discuss both financial and nonfinancial performance measures.

Performance Appraisal Links—
Zigon Performance Group
www.zigonperf.com/Links.htm

FINANCIAL AND NONFINANCIAL PERFORMANCE MEASURES

Chapter 23 noted how the information used in a management control system can be financial or nonfinancial. Many common performance measures such as operating income rely on internal financial and accounting information. Increasingly, companies are supplementing internal financial measures with measures based on external financial information (for example, stock prices), internal nonfinancial information (such as manufacturing lead time), and external nonfinancial information (such as customer satisfaction). In addition, companies are benchmarking their financial and nonfinancial measures against other companies that are regarded as the "best performers." To compete effectively in the global market, companies need to perform at or near the "best of the breed."

Some organizations present financial and nonfinancial performance measures for various organization subunits in a single report called the *balanced scorecard* (see Chapter 13). Different companies stress various elements in their scorecards, but most scorecards include (1) profitability measures; (2) customer satisfaction measures; (3) internal measures of efficiency, quality, and time; and (4) innovation measures.[1]

Some performance measures, such as the number of new patents developed, have a long-run time horizon. Other measures, such as direct materials efficiency variances, overhead spending variances, and yield, have a short-run time horizon. We focus on the most widely used performance measures covering an intermediate to long-run time horizon. These are internal financial measures based on accounting numbers routinely maintained by organizations.

OBJECTIVE 1

Measure performance from a financial and nonfinancial perspective

"Accounting for the Environment"—George Harte, University of Glasgow—Linda Lewis, David Owen, University of Sheffield
les.man.ac.uk/cpa96/txt/harte.txt

DESIGNING AN ACCOUNTING-BASED PERFORMANCE MEASURE

Designing an accounting-based performance measure requires the following steps:

◆ **Step 1:** *Choosing the variable(s) that represent(s) top management's financial goal(s).* Does operating income, net income, return on assets, or revenues, for example, best measure a division's financial performance?

[1]See Kaplan, R. and D. Norton, *The Balanced Scorecard* (Boston: Harvard Business School Press, 1996); Hronec, S. *Vital Signs* (New York: American Management Association, 1993).

Nonfinancial Measures of Performance

Companies around the world supplement financial performance measures with nonfinancial information. The following table ranks nonfinancial measures used in five countries in order of importance (1 = most important):

	United States*	Australia[†]	Ireland[‡]	Japan[†]	United Kingdom[†]
Product quality and defects	1	1	3	1	1
Delivery performance	2	2	4	2	2
Schedule attainment	3	—	—	—	—
Output per hour	4	—	1	—	—
Absenteeism	—	3	—	4	3
New product time	—	4	—	3	4
Plant utilization	—	—	2	—	—

Adapted from: *Smith, K., and C. Sullivan, "Survey of Cost Management Systems in Manufacturing," (Working Paper, Purdue University, West Lafayette, Indiana, 1990); [†]Blayney, P., and I. Yokoyama, "Comparative Analysis of Japanese and Australian Cost Accounting and Management Practices, " (Working Paper, The University of Sydney, Sydney, Australia, 1991); [‡]Clarke, P., "Management Accounting Practices and Techniques in Irish Manufacturing Firms, " (Working Paper, Trinity College, Dublin, Ireland, 1995)

The surveys indicate that these nonfinancial performance measures are used extensively. Product quality is the most important nonfinancial/internal performance measure over all. Delivery performance is the most important nonfinancial/external measure of performance.

OBJECTIVE 2

Design an accounting-based performance measure

◆ **Step 2:** *Choosing definitions of the items included in the variables in step 1.* For example, should assets be defined as total assets or net assets (total assets minus total liabilities)?

◆ **Step 3:** *Choosing measures for the items included in the variables in step 1.* For example, should assets be measured at historical cost, current cost, or present value?

◆ **Step 4:** *Choosing a target against which to gauge performance.* For example, should all divisions have as a target the same required rate of return on assets?

◆ **Step 5:** *Choosing the timing of feedback.* For example, should manufacturing performance reports be sent to top management daily, weekly, or monthly?

These five steps need not be done sequentially. The issues considered in each step are interdependent, and a decision-maker will often proceed through these steps several times before deciding on an accounting-based performance measure. The answers to the questions raised at each step depend on top management's beliefs about how cost-effectively and how well each alternative fulfills the behavioural criteria of goal-congruence, employee effort, and subunit autonomy discussed in Chapter 23.

DIFFERENT PERFORMANCE MEASURES

This section presents step 1 by describing four measures commonly used to evaluate the economic performance of organization subunits. Good performance measures promote goal-congruence with the organization's objectives and facilitate comparisons across different subunits. We illustrate these measures using the example of Hospitality Inns.

Hospitality Inns owns and operates three motels, located in Saskatoon, Brandon, and Hull. Exhibit 24-1 summarizes data for each of the three motels for the

EXHIBIT 24-1
Annual Financial Data for Hospitality Inns for 2000

	Saskatoon Motel (1)	Brandon Motel (2)	Hull Motel (3)	Total (4) = (1) + (2) + (3)
Motel revenues (sales)	$1,200,000	$1,400,000	$3,185,000	$5,785,000
Motel variable costs	310,000	375,000	995,000	1,680,000
Motel fixed costs	650,000	725,000	1,680,000	3,055,000
Motel operating income	$ 240,000	$ 300,000	$ 510,000	1,050,000
Interest costs on long-term debt at 10%	—	—	—	450,000
Income before income taxes	—	—	—	600,000
Income taxes at 30%	—	—	—	180,000
Net income	—	—	—	$ 420,000
Average book values for 2000:				
Current assets	$ 400,000	$ 500,000	$ 600,000	$1,500,000
Long-term assets	600,000	1,500,000	2,400,000	4,500,000
Total assets	$1,000,000	$2,000,000	$3,000,000	$6,000,000
Current liabilities	$ 50,000	$ 150,000	$ 300,000	$ 500,000
Long-term debt	—	—	—	4,500,000
Stockholders' equity	—	—	—	1,000,000
Total liabilities and stockholders' equity				$6,000,000

most recent year (2000). At present, Hospitality Inns does not allocate to the three separate motels the total long-term debt of the company. Exhibit 24-1 indicates that the Hull motel generates the highest operating income, $510,000. The Brandon motel generates $300,000; the Saskatoon motel, $240,000. But is this comparison appropriate? Is the Hull motel the most "successful"? Actually, the comparison of operating income ignores potential differences in the *size* of the investments in the different motels. **Investment** refers to the resources or assets used to generate income. The question then is not how large operating income is per se, but how large it is given the resources that were used to earn it.

> **Investment.** Resources or assets used to generate income.

Three approaches include investment in performance measures: return on investment (ROI), residual income (RI), and economic value added (EVA®). A fourth approach measures return on sales (ROS).

Return on Investment

Return on investment (ROI) is an accounting measure of income divided by an accounting measure of investment.

$$\text{Return on investment (ROI)} = \frac{\text{Income}}{\text{Investment}}$$

ROI is the most popular approach to incorporating the investment base into a performance measure. ROI appeals conceptually because it blends all the major ingredients of profitability (revenues, costs, and investment) into a single number. ROI can be compared with the rate of return on opportunities elsewhere, inside or outside the company. Like any single performance measure, however, ROI should be used cautiously and in conjunction with other performance measures.

ROI is also called the accounting rate of return or the accrual accounting rate of return (see Chapter 21). Managers usually use the term ROI in the context of evaluating the performance of a division or subunit, and accrual accounting rate of return when evaluating a project. Companies vary in the way they define both the numerator and the denominator of the ROI. For example, some firms use operating income for the numerator. Other firms use net income. Some firms use total assets in the denominator. Others use total assets minus current liabilities.

> **OBJECTIVE 3**
> Analyze profitability using the DuPont method

> **Return on investment (ROI).** An accounting measure of income divided by an accounting measure of investment.

Hospitality Inns can increase ROI by increasing revenues or decreasing costs (both these actions increase the numerator), or by decreasing investments (decreases the denominator). ROI can often provide more insight into performance when it is divided into the following components:

$$\frac{\text{Revenues}}{\text{Investment}} \times \frac{\text{Income}}{\text{Revenues}} = \frac{\text{Income}}{\text{Investment}}$$

This approach is widely known as the *DuPont method of profitability analysis.* The DuPont approach recognizes that there are two basic ingredients in profit-making: using assets to generate more revenue and increasing income per dollar of revenue. An improvement in either ingredient without changing the other increases return on investment.

Consider the ROI of each of the three Hospitality motels in Exhibit 24-1. For our calculations, we are using the operating income of each motel for the numerator and total assets of each motel for the denominator.

Motel	Operating Income	÷	Total Assets	=	ROI
Saskatoon	$240,000	÷	$1,000,000	=	24%
Brandon	$300,000	÷	$2,000,000	=	15%
Hull	$510,000	÷	$3,000,000	=	17%

Using these ROI figures, the Saskatoon motel appears to make the best use of its total assets.

Assume that the top management at Hospitality Inns adopts a 30% target ROI for the Saskatoon motel. How can this return be attained? The DuPont method illustrates the present situation and three alternatives:

	$\dfrac{\text{Revenues}}{\text{Total Assets}}$	×	$\dfrac{\text{Operating Income}}{\text{Revenues}}$			=	$\dfrac{\text{Operating Income}}{\text{Total Assets}}$
Present Situation	$\dfrac{\$1,200,000}{\$1,000,000}$	×	$\dfrac{\$240,000}{\$1,200,000}$	=	1.20×0.20	=	0.24 or 24%
Alternatives							
A. Decrease assets (for example, receivables), keeping revenues and operating income per dollar of revenue constant.	$\dfrac{\$1,200,000}{\$800,000}$	×	$\dfrac{\$240,000}{\$1,200,000}$	=	1.50×0.20	=	0.30 or 30%
B. Increase revenues (by selling more rooms), keeping assets and operating income per dollar of revenue constant.	$\dfrac{\$1,500,000}{\$1,000,000}$	×	$\dfrac{\$300,000}{\$1,500,000}$	=	1.50×0.20	=	0.30 or 30%
C. Decrease costs (for example, via efficient maintenance) to increase operating income per dollar of revenue, keeping revenues and assets constant.	$\dfrac{\$1,200,000}{\$1,000,000}$	×	$\dfrac{\$300,000}{\$1,200,000}$	=	1.20×0.25	=	0.30 or 30%

Other alternatives, such as increasing the selling price per room, could increase both the revenue per dollar of total assets and the operating income per dollar of revenue.

ROI highlights the benefits that managers can obtain by reducing their investments in current or fixed assets. Some managers are conscious of the need to boost revenues or to control costs but pay less attention to reducing their investment base. Reducing investments means decreasing idle cash, managing credit judiciously, determining proper inventory levels, and spending carefully on fixed assets.

Residual Income

Residual income. Income minus a required dollar return on the investment.

Residual income is income minus a required dollar return on the investment.[2]

Residual income = Income − (Required rate of return × Investment)

[2]Just as in the case of ROI, companies using RI vary in the way they define income (for example, operating income or net income) and investment (for example, total assets or total assets minus current liabilities).

The required rate of return multiplied by investment is also called the *imputed cost* of the investment. **Imputed costs** are costs recognized in particular situations that are not regularly recognized by accrual accounting procedures. An imputed cost is not recognized in accounting records because it is not an incremental cost but instead represents the return forgone by Hospitality Inns as a result of tying up cash in various investments of similar risk. Assume that each motel faces similar risks. Hospitality Inns defines residual income for each motel as motel operating income minus a required rate of return of 12% of the total assets of the motel:

Imputed costs. Costs recognized in particular situations that are not regularly recognized by accrual accounting procedures.

Motel	Operating Income	−	Required Rate of Return × Investment	=	Income
Saskatoon	$240,000	−	$120,000 (12% × $1,000,000)	=	$120,000
Brandon	$300,000	−	$240,000 (12% × $2,000,000)	=	$ 60,000
Hull	$510,000	−	$360,000 (12% × $3,000,000)	=	$150,000

Given the 12% required rate of return, the Hull motel is performing best in terms of residual income.

Some firms favour the residual-income approach because managers will concentrate on maximizing an absolute amount (dollars of residual income) rather than a percentage (return on investment). The objective of maximizing residual income assumes that as long as a division earns a rate in excess of the required return for investments, that division should expand.

The objective of maximizing ROI may induce managers of highly profitable divisions to reject projects that, from the viewpoint of the organization as a whole, should be accepted. To illustrate, assume that Hospitality's required rate of return on investment is 12%. Assume also that an expansion of the Saskatoon motel will increase its operating income by $160,000 and increase its total assets by $800,000. The ROI for the expansion is 20% ($160,000 ÷ $800,000), which makes it attractive to Hospitality Inns as a whole. By making this expansion, however, the Saskatoon manager will see the motel's ROI decrease:

$$\text{Preexpansion ROI} = \frac{\$240,000}{1,000,000} = 24\%$$

$$\text{Postexpansion ROI} = \frac{(\$240,000 + \$160,000)}{(\$1,000,000 + \$800,000)} = \frac{\$400,000}{1,800,000} = 22.2\%$$

The annual bonus paid to the Saskatoon manager may decrease if ROI is a key component in the bonus calculation and the expansion option is selected. In contrast, if the annual bonus is a function of residual income, the Saskatoon manager will view the expansion favourably:

Preexpansion residual income = $240,000 − (12% × $1,000,000) = $120,000

Postexpansion residual income = $400,000 − (12% × $1,800,000) = $184,000

Goal-congruence is more likely to be promoted by using residual income rather than ROI as a measure of the division manager's performance.

Both ROI and residual income represent the results for a single time period (such as a year). Managers could take actions that cause short-run increases in ROI or residual income but are in conflict with the long-run interests of the organization. For example, managers may curtail R&D and plant maintenance in the past three months of a fiscal year to achieve a target level of annual operating income. For this reason, some companies evaluate subunits on the basis of ROI and residual income over multiple years.

Economic Value Added (EVA®)

Economic value added (EVA®)[3] is a specific type of residual income calculation that has recently attracted considerable attention. **Economic value added (EVA®)** equals

[3]G. B. Stewart III, "EVA: Fact and Fantasy," *Journal of Applied Corporate Finance*, (Summer, 1994); B. Birchard, "Measuring the New Metrics," *CFO*, (October 1994); "A New Way to Find Bargains, *Fortune*, December 9, 1996.

after-tax operating income *minus* the (after-tax) weighted-average cost of capital *multiplied* by total assets minus current liabilities.[4]

$$\text{Economic value added (EVA®)} = \text{After-tax operating income} - \left[\text{Weighted-average cost of capital} \times \left(\text{Total assets} - \text{Current liabilities} \right) \right]$$

EVA® substitutes the following numbers in the residual-income calculations: (1) income equal to after-tax operating income (2) a required rate of return equal to the weighted-average cost of capital, and (3) investment equal to total assets minus current liabilities. We use the Hospitality Inns data in Exhibit 24-1 to illustrate EVA®.

The key calculation is the weighted-average cost of capital (WACC), which equals *after-tax* average cost of all the long-term funds used by Hospitality Inns. The company has two sources of long-term funds—long-term debt with a market and book value of $4.5 million issued at an interest rate of 10%, and equity capital that has a market value of $3 million (and a book value of $1 million).[5] Since interest costs are tax-deductible, the after-tax cost of debt financing equals $0.10 \times (1 - \text{tax rate}) = 0.10 \times (1 - 0.30) = 0.10 \times 0.70 = 0.07$, or 7%. The cost of equity capital is the opportunity cost to investors of not investing their capital in another investment that is similar in risk to Hospitality Inns. Suppose that Hospitality's cost of equity capital is 15%. The WACC computation, which uses market values of debt and equity, is as follows:

$$\text{WACC} = \frac{(0.07 \times \$4,500,00) + (0.15 \times \$3,000,000)}{\$4,500,000 + \$3,000,000}$$

$$= \frac{\$315,000 + \$450,000}{\$7,500,000} = \frac{\$765,000}{\$7,500,000}$$

$$= 0.102 \text{ or } 10.2\%$$

The company applies the same WACC to all its motels, since each motel faces similar risks.

Long-term assets minus current liabilities (see Exhibit 24-1) can also be computed as:

$$\text{Total assets} - \text{Current liabilities} = \text{Long-term assets} + \text{Current assets} - \text{Current liabilities}$$
$$= \text{Long-term assets} + \text{Working capital}$$

where working capital = current assets − current liabilities. After-tax motel operating income is:

$$\text{Motel operating income} \times (1 - \text{Tax rate}) = \text{Motel operating income} \times (1 - 0.30) = \text{Motel operating income} \times 0.70$$

EVA® calculations for Hospitality Inns are as follows:

Motel	After-Tax Operating Income	−	[Weighted-Average Cost of Capital × (Total Assets − Current Liabilities)]		=	Economic Value Added (EVA®)
Saskatoon	$240,000 × 0.7	−	[10.2% × ($1,000,000 − $50,000)]	= $168,000 − $96,900	=	$71,100
Brandon	$300,000 × 0.7	−	[10.2% × ($2,000,000 − $150,000)]	= $210,000 − $188,700	=	$21,300
Hull	$510,000 × 0.7	−	[10.2% × ($3,000,000 − $300,000)]	= $357,000 − $275,400	=	$81,600

The Hull motel has the highest EVA®. EVA®, like residual income, charges managers for the cost of their investments in long-term assets and working capital.

[4]When implementing EVA®, companies make several adjustments to the operating income and asset numbers reported under generally accepted accounting principles (GAAP). For example, when calculating EVA®, costs such as R&D, restructuring costs and leases that have long-run benefits are recorded as assets (which are then amortized), rather than as current operating costs. The goal of these adjustments is to obtain a better representation of the economic assets, particularly intangible assets, used to earn income. Naturally, the specific adjustments applicable to a company will depend on its individual circumstances.

[5]The market value of Hospitality Inns equity exceeds book value because book values, based on historical costs, do not measure the current values of the company's assets and because various intangible assets, such as the company's brand name, are not shown at current value in the balance sheet under GAAP.

Value is created only if after-tax operating income exceeds the cost of investing the capital. To improve EVA®, managers must earn more operating income with the same capital, use less capital, or invest capital in high-return projects. After implementing EVA®, CSX, a railroad company, began running trains with three locomotives instead of four by scheduling arrivals just in time for unloading, rather than having trains arrive at their destination several hours in advance. The result? Higher profits because of lower fuel costs, and less capital invested in locomotives. Chief executive officers of companies such as AT&T, Briggs & Stratton, Coca-Cola, CSX, Equifax, FMC, and Quaker Oats credit the EVA® concept with motivating decisions that have increased shareholder value.

Quaker Oats
www.quakeroats.com

Return on Sales

The income-to-revenue (sales) ratio—often called return on sales (ROS)—is a frequently used financial performance measure. ROS is one component of ROI in the

CONCEPTS IN ACTION

Equifax, AT&T and EVA®

A recent *Fortune* magazine article described EVA as "Today's hottest financial idea and getting hotter." Equifax, the company that provides credit histories and other transaction-processing information to banks, auto dealerships retailers, and other clients, agrees.

Equifax believes that EVA® streamlines decision making, enhances accountability, and strengthens incentives. Thus EVA® analysis is now central to Equifax's investment decisions. So far, EVA® has helped Equifax (a) earn more operating income without adding capital, (b) reduce capital investments needed to earn operating income, and (c) invest in and retain only those projects and businesses for which operating income exceeds the cost of capital.

To earn more operating income, Equifax took strategic initiatives to cut operating costs by, for example, centralizing its payables, payroll, and travel management departments. The move reduced equipment and space costs and increased Equifax's bargaining power to lower its costs of supplies, travel, and hotels. Equifax also generated profitable revenue by finding new markets or customers for its products and by providing better customer service.

To reduce capital invested in its businesses, Equifax outsourced its computer operations and disposed of its data processing equipment. Also, after reviewing operating income and cost of capital figures, Equifax decided to sell Elrick and Lavidge and Quick Test, two of its marketing companies.

How does Equifax get its managers to think in terms of EVA®? First, the company carefully explains EVA® concepts to them. Second, Equifax budgets the EVA® and then link a significant portion of incentive compensation to achieving the EVA® projections. Equifax's management credits EVA®, in part, as contributing to the almost 200% increase in market capitalization from $1.6 billion in 1992 when it first implemented EVA® to $4.6 billion in 1998.

EVA®, however, has not worked for everyone. AT&T began using EVA® in 1992, but found the measure to be incomplete. Within two years the company supplemented EVA® with two non-financial measures—Customer Value Added and People Value Added. Furthermore, AT&T found that although internal EVA® results from 1992 to 1996 increased, total shareholder return was −6.46%, substantially lower than that of its competitors. In 1997, following AT&T's replacement of CEO Robert Allen with Mike Armstrong, the company dropped EVA® in favor of traditional accounting measures. The company considered EVA® too complex, noting that despite extensive training, employees outside of corporate headquarters had difficulty understanding how their actions affected EVA® results.

EVA® Information
www.sternstewart.com

AT&T Canada
www.attcanada.com

Equifax Canada
www.equifax.ca

Adapted from Equifax brochure on EVA® and C. Ittner and D. Larcker, "Innovations in Performance Measurement: Trends and Research Implications," Working Paper, (University of Pennsylvania, June 1998).

DuPont method of profitability analysis. To calculate the ROS of each of Hospitality's motels, we use operating income divided by revenues. The ROS for each motel is:

Motel	Operating Income	÷	Revenues (Sales)	=	ROS
Saskatoon	$240,000	÷	$1,200,000	=	20.0%
Brandon	$300,000	÷	$1,400,000	=	21.4%
Hull	$510,000	÷	$3,185,000	=	16.0%

The Brandon hotel has the highest ROS, whereas its performance is rated worse than the other hotels using performance measures such as ROI, RI, and EVA®. We compare performance measures in the next section.

The following table summarizes the performance and ranking of each motel under each of the four performance measures:

Motel	ROI (rank)	Residual Income (rank)	EVA® (rank)	ROS (rank)
Saskatoon	24% (1)	$120,000 (2)	$71,100 (2)	20.0% (2)
Brandon	15% (3)	$60,000 (3)	$21,300 (3)	21.4% (1)
Hull	17% (2)	$150,000 (1)	$81,600 (1)	16.0% (3)

The residual-income and EVA® rankings differ from the ROI and ROS rankings. Consider the ROI and residual-income rankings for the Saskatoon and Hull motels. The Hull motel has a smaller ROI. Although its operating income is only slightly more than twice that of the Saskatoon motel ($510,000 versus $240,000), its total assets are three times as large ($3 million versus $1 million). The return on assets invested in the Hull motel is not as high as the return on assets invested in the Saskatoon motel. The Hull motel has a higher residual income because it earns a higher operating income after covering the 12% required return on investment. The Brandon motel has the highest ROS but the lowest ROI. Why? Because although it earns very high income per dollar of revenue, it generates very low revenues per dollar of assets invested. Is any one method superior to the others? No, because each evaluates a slightly different aspect of performance. For example, in markets where revenue growth is limited, return on sales is the most meaningful indicator of a subunit's performance.

To evaluate overall aggregate performance, ROI or residual-income-based measures are more appropriate, since they consider both income earned and investments made. Residual-income and EVA® measures overcome some of the goal-congruence problems that ROI measures might introduce. Some managers favour EVA®, because it explicitly considers tax effects while pre tax residual-income measures do not. Other managers favour pre-tax residual-income, because it is easier to compute and because it often leads to the same conclusions as EVA®.

Surveys of North American and Japanese companies indicate extensive use of net income as a performance measure. After net income measures, North American companies favour ROI over ROS, while Japanese companies use ROS more than ROI. More recently, many large North American companies have begun using EVA®, which also focuses on income and investment. These differences are also consistent with differences in pricing practices in the two countries. Japanese companies emphasize sales margins, while North American companies emphasize return on investment.[6] Some researchers speculate that Japanese managers favour ROS because it is easier to calculate and because achieving a sufficient sales margin will be likely to benefit ROI sooner or later. Deemphasizing ROI has other advantages. Managers are not induced to delay investment in facilities or equipment because of the negative effects it might have on ROI in the short run. Exhibit 24-2 presents the key financial performance measures used by eleven companies. Note the diversity in the use of income-based measures, ROS, ROI, and EVA®.

[6]See Smith, K. and C. Sullivan, "Survey of Cost Management Systems in Manufacturing," working paper, Purdue University, 1990; and Scarbrough, P. A., Nanni, and M. Sakurai, "Japanese Management Accounting Practices and the Effects of Assembly and Process Automation," *Management Accounting Research*, Vol. 2 (1991).

EXHIBIT 24-2
Company Examples of Key Financial Performance Measures

Company	Country Headquarters	Product/Business	Key Financial Performance Measures
Dow Chemical	U.S.	Chemicals	Income
Xerox	U.S.	Photocopiers	ROS and ROI
Ford Motor	U.S.	Automotive	ROS and ROI
Quaker Oats	U.S.	Food products	EVA®
AT&T	U.S.	Telecommunications/computers	EVA®
Guinness	U.K.	Consumer products	Income and ROS
Krones	Germany	Machinery/equipment	Sales and income
Mayne Nickless	Australia	Security/transportation	ROI and ROS
Mitsui	Japan	Trading	Sales and income
Pirelli	Italy	Tires/manufacturing	Income and cash flow
Swedish Match	Sweden	Consumer products	ROI

Source: Business International Corporation, *Evaluating the Performance of International Operations* (New York, 1989); Business International Corporation, *101 More Checklists for Global Financial Management* (New York, 1992); and G. B. Stewart, "EVA®: Fact and Fantasy," *Journal of Applied Corporate Finance,* Summer 1994.

CHOOSING THE TIME HORIZON OF THE PERFORMANCE MEASURES

Another consideration in designing accounting-based performance measures is choosing the time horizon of the performance measures. The ROI, RI, EVA®, and ROS calculations represent the results for a single time period, a year in our example. Managers could take actions that cause short-run increases in these measures but are in conflict with the long-run interests of the organization. For example, managers may curtail R&D and plant maintenance in the last three months of a fiscal year to achieve a target level of annual operating income. For this reason, many companies evaluate subunits on the basis of ROI, RI, EVA®, and ROS over multiple years.

Another reason for evaluating subunits over a multi-year time horizon is that the benefits of actions taken in the current period may not show up in short-run performance metrics such as the current year's ROI or RI. For example, the investment in a new hotel may adversely affect ROI and RI in the short run but benefit ROIs and RIs in the long run.

A multi-year analysis highlights another advantage of the RI measure. The net present value of all the cash flows over the life of an investment equals the net present value of RIs.[7] This means that if managers use net present value analysis to make investment decisions (as prescribed in Chapter 21), using multi-year RI to evaluate managers' performances achieves goal congruence.

[7] We are grateful to S. Reichelstein for pointing this out. To see this equivalence, suppose the $400,000 investment in the Saskatoon hotel increases operating income by $70,000 per year as follows: Increase in operating cash flows of $150,000 each year for five years minus depreciation of $80,000 per year ($400,000 ÷ 5), assuming straight-line depreciation and zero terminal disposal price. Depreciation reduces the investment amount by $80,000 each year. Assuming a required rate of return of 12%, net present values of cash flows and residual incomes are as follows:

Year	0	1	2	3	4	5	Net Present Value
(1) Cash flow	–$400,000	$150,000	$150,000	$150,000	$150,000	$150,000	
(2) Present value of $1 discounted at 12%	1	0.89286	0.79719	0.71178	0.63552	0.56743	
(3) Present value: (1) × (2)	–$400,000	$133,929	$119,578	$106,767	$ 95,328	$ 85,115	$140,717
(4) Operating income		$ 70,000	$ 70,000	$ 70,000	$ 70,000	$ 70,000	
(5) Assets at start of year		$400,000	$320,000	$240,000	$160,000	$ 80,000	
(6) Capital charge: (5) × 12%		$ 48,000	$ 38,400	$ 28,800	$ 19,200	$ 9,600	
(7) Residual income: (4) – (6)		$ 22,000	$ 31,600	$ 41,200	$ 50,800	$ 60,400	
(8) Present value of RI: (7) × (2)		$ 19,643	$ 25,191	$ 29,325	$ 32,284	$ 34,272	$140,717

Another way that companies motivate managers to take a long-run perspective is by compensating them on changes in the market price of the company's stock (in addition to using multi-year accounting-based performance measures). Why does this approach help to extend managers' time horizons? Because stock prices more rapidly incorporate, the expected future period effects of current decisions.

ALTERNATIVE DEFINITIONS OF INVESTMENT

We use the different definitions of investment that companies use to illustrate step 2 when designing accounting-based performance measures. Definitions include the following:

1. **Total assets available.** Includes all business assets, regardless of their particular purpose.
2. **Total assets employed.** Defined as total assets available minus idle assets and minus assets purchased for future expansion. For example, if the Hull motel in Exhibit 24-1 has unused land set aside for potential expansion, the total assets employed by the motel would exclude the cost of that land.
3. **Working capital (current assets minus current liabilities) plus long-term assets.** This definition excludes that portion of current assets financed by short-term creditors.
4. **Stockholders' equity.** Use of this definition for each individual motel in Exhibit 24-1 requires allocation of the long-term liabilities of Hospitality Inns to the three motels, which would then be deducted from the total assets of each motel.

Most companies that employ ROI, residual income, or EVA® for performance measurement use either total assets available or working capital plus long-term assets as the definition of investment. However, when top management directs a division manager to carry extra assets, total assets employed can be more informative than total assets available. The most common rationale for using working capital plus long-term assets is that the division manager often influences decisions on the short-term debt of the division.

CHOOSING MEASUREMENT ALTERNATIVES FOR PERFORMANCE MEASURES

OBJECTIVE 6

Distinguish between current cost and historical cost asset measurement methods

To illustrate step 3 in the design of accounting-based performance measures consider different ways to measure assets included in the investment calculations. Should they be measured at historical cost, present value, current cost, or current disposal price? Should gross book value or net book value be used for depreciable assets? We now examine these issues.

Current Cost

Current cost. Asset measure based on the cost of purchasing an asset today identical to the one currently held. It is the cost of purchasing the services provided by that asset if an identical asset cannot currently be purchased.

Current cost is the cost of purchasing an asset today identical to the one currently held. It is the cost of purchasing the services provided by that asset if an identical asset cannot currently be purchased. Of course, measuring assets at current costs will result in different ROIs compared to the ROIs calculated based on historical costs.

We illustrate the current-cost ROI calculations using the Hospitality Inns example (see Exhibit 24-1) and then compare current- and historical-cost-based ROIs. Assume the following information about the long-term assets of each motel:

	Saskatoon	Brandon	Hull
Age of facility (at end of 2000)	8 years	4 years	2 years
Gross book value	$1,400,000	$2,100,000	$2,800,000
Accumulated amortization	$800,000	$600,000	$400,000
Net book value (at end of 2000)	$600,000	$1,500,000	$2,400,000
Amortization for 2000	$100,000	$150,000	$200,000

Hospitality Inns assumes a 14-year estimated useful life, assumes no terminal disposal price for the physical facilities, and calculates amortization on a straight-line basis.

An index of construction costs for the eight-year period that Hospitality Inns has been operating (year 0 = 100) is as follows:

Year	1	2	3	4	5	6	7	8
Construction cost index	110	122	136	144	152	160	174	180

Earlier in this chapter, we computed an ROI of 24% for Saskatoon, 15% for Brandon, and 17% for Hull (see p. 828). One possible explanation of the high ROI for Saskatoon is that this motel's long-term assets are expressed in terms of year 0 construction price levels (eight years ago) and that the long-term assets for the Brandon and Hull motels are expressed in terms of the higher, more recent construction price levels, which depress ROIs for these motels.

Exhibit 24-3 illustrates a step-by-step approach for incorporating current-cost estimates for long-term assets and amortization into the ROI calculation. The aim is to approximate what it would cost today to obtain assets that would produce the same expected operating income that the subunits currently earn. (Similar adjustments to represent current costs of capital employed and amortization can also be made in the residual income and EVA® calculations.) The current-cost adjustment dramatically reduces the ROI of the Saskatoon motel.

	Historical-Cost ROI	Current-Cost ROI
Saskatoon	24%	10.81%
Brandon	15%	11.05%
Hull	17%	14.70%

Adjusting for current costs negates differences in the investment base caused solely by differences in construction price levels. Consequently, compared to historical-cost ROI, current-cost ROI is a better measure of the current economic returns from the investment. For example, current-cost ROI indicates that taking into account current construction price levels, investing in a new motel in Saskatoon will result in an ROI closer to 10.81% rather than 24%. If Hospitality Inns were to invest in a new motel today, investing in one like the Hull motel offers the best ROI.

A drawback of the current-cost method is that obtaining current-cost estimates for some assets can be difficult.[8] Why? Because the estimate requires a company to consider technological advances when determining the current cost of assets needed to earn today's operating income.

Long-Term Assets: Gross or Net Book Value?

Because historical-cost investment measures are used often in practice, there has been much discussion about the relative merits of using gross book value (original cost) or net book value (original cost minus accumulated amortization). Using the data in Exhibit 24-1 and page 827, the ROI calculations using net book values and gross book values of plant and equipment are as follows:

	Saskatoon	Brandon	Hull
ROI for Year 8 using net book value of total assets given in Exhibit 24-1 and calculated earlier	$\frac{\$240,000}{\$1,000,000} = 24\%$	$\frac{\$300,000}{\$2,000,000} = 15\%$	$\frac{\$510,000}{\$3,000,000} = 17\%$
ROI for Year 8 using gross book value of total assets obtained by adding accumulated amortization to net book value of total assets in Exhibit 24-1	$\frac{\$240,000}{\$1,800,000} = 13.33\%$	$\frac{\$300,000}{\$2,600,000} = 11.54\%$	$\frac{\$510,000}{\$3,400,000} = 15\%$

[8]When a specific cost index (such as the construction cost index) is not available, companies use a general index (such as the consumer price index) to approximate current costs.

Step 1: Restate long-term assets from gross book value at historical cost to gross book value at current cost as of the end of Year 8.

$$\begin{array}{l}\text{Gross book value of long-term assets} \\ \text{at current cost at the end of Year 8}\end{array} = \begin{array}{l}\text{Gross book value of long-} \\ \text{term assets at historical cost}\end{array} \times \frac{\text{Construction cost index in Year 8}}{\text{Construction cost index in year of construction}}$$

Saskatoon	$1,400,000 \times (180 \div 100) = \$2,520,000$
Brandon	$2,100,000 \times (180 \div 144) = \$2,625,000$
Hull	$2,800,000 \times (180 \div 160) = \$3,150,000$

Step 2: Derive the net book value of long-term assets at current cost as of the end of Year 8. (The estimated useful life of each motel is 14 years.)

$$\begin{array}{l}\text{Net book value of long-term assets at} \\ \text{current cost at the end of Year 8}\end{array} = \begin{array}{l}\text{Gross book value of long-term assets} \\ \text{at current cost at the end of Year 8}\end{array} \times \frac{\text{Estimated useful life remaining}}{\text{Estimated total useful life}}$$

Saskatoon	$2,520,000 \times (6 \div 14) = \$1,080,000$
Brandon	$2,625,000 \times (10 \div 14) = \$1,875,000$
Hull	$3,150,000 \times (12 \div 14) = \$2,700,000$

Step 3: Compute the current cost of total assets at the end of Year 8. (Assume that the current assets of each motel are expressed in Year 8 dollars.)

$$\begin{array}{l}\text{Current cost of total assets} \\ \text{at the end of Year 8}\end{array} = \begin{array}{l}\text{Current assets at the end of} \\ \text{Year 8 (from Exhibit 24-1)}\end{array} + \begin{array}{l}\text{Net book value of long-term assets at current} \\ \text{cost at the end of Year 8 (from step 2)}\end{array}$$

Saskatoon	$400,000 + \$1,080,000 = \$1,480,000$
Brandon	$500,000 + \$1,875,000 = \$2,375,000$
Hull	$600,000 + \$2,700,000 = \$3,300,000$

Step 4: Compute the current-cost amortization expense in Year 8 dollars.

$$\begin{array}{l}\text{Current-cost amortization} \\ \text{expense in Year 8 dollars}\end{array} = \begin{array}{l}\text{Gross book value of long-term assets at current} \\ \text{cost at the end of Year 8 (from step 1)}\end{array} \times \frac{1}{\text{Estimated total useful life}}$$

Saskatoon	$2,520,000 \times (1 \div 14) = \$180,000$
Brandon	$2,625,000 \times (1 \div 14) = \$187,500$
Hull	$3,150,000 \times (1 \div 14) = \$225,000$

Step 5: Compute Year 8 operating income using Year 8 current-cost amortization.

$$\begin{array}{l}\text{Operating income for Year 8 using} \\ \text{Year 8 current-cost amortization}\end{array} = \begin{array}{l}\text{Historical-cost} \\ \text{operating income}\end{array} - \left(\begin{array}{l}\text{Current-cost amortization expense} \\ \text{in Year 8 dollars (from step 4)}\end{array} - \begin{array}{l}\text{Historical-cost} \\ \text{amortization}\end{array} \right)$$

Saskatoon	$240,000 - (\$180,000 - \$100,000) = \$160,000$
Brandon	$300,000 - (\$187,500 - \$150,000) = \$262,500$
Hull	$510,000 - (\$225,000 - \$200,000) = \$485,000$

Step 6: Compute the ROI using current-cost estimates for long-term assets and amortization.

$$\begin{array}{l}\text{ROI using current-} \\ \text{cost estimates}\end{array} = \frac{\text{Operating income for Year 8 using Year 8 current-cost amortization (from step 5)}}{\text{Current cost of total assets at the end of Year 8 (from step 3)}}$$

Saskatoon	$160,000 \div \$1,480,000 = 10.81\%$
Brandon	$262,500 \div \$2,375,000 = 11.05\%$
Hull	$485,000 \div \$3,300,000 = 14.70\%$

Using the gross book value, the ROI of the older Saskatoon motel (13.33%) is lower than that of the newer Hull motel (15%). Those who favour using gross book value claim that it enables more accurate comparisons across subunits. For example, using gross book value calculations, the return on the original plant and equipment investment is higher for the newer Hull motel than for the older Saskatoon motel. This probably reflects the decline in earning power of the Saskatoon motel. In contrast, using the net book value masks this decline in earning power, because the constantly decreasing base results in a higher ROI (24%); this higher rate may mislead decision-makers into thinking that the earning power of the Saskatoon motel has not decreased.

The proponents of using net book value as a base maintain that it is less confusing because (1) it is consistent with the total assets shown on the conventional balance sheet and (2) it is consistent with net income computations that include deductions for amortization. Surveys of company practice report net book value to be the dominant asset measure used by companies in their internal performance evaluations.

CHOOSING TARGETED LEVELS OF PERFORMANCE AND TIMING OF FEEDBACK

Choosing Targets to Compare Performance

We next consider step 4 and the setting of targets to compare actual performance against. Recall that historical-cost-based accounting measures are often inadequate for evaluating economic returns on new investments and sometimes create disincentives for new expansion. Despite these problems, historical-cost ROIs *can* be used to evaluate current performance by adjusting target ROIs. Consider our Hospitality Inns example. The key is to recognize that the motels were built at different times, which in turn means they were built at different levels of the construction cost index. Top management could adjust the target historical cost ROIs accordingly, perhaps setting Saskatoon's ROI at 26%, Brandon's at 18%, and Hull's at 19%.

Nevertheless, the alternative of comparing actual to target performance is frequently overlooked in the literature. Critics of historical cost have indicated how high rates of return on old assets may erroneously induce a manager not to replace assets. Regardless, the manager's mandate is often "Go forth and attain the budgeted results." The budget, then, should be carefully negotiated with full knowledge of historical-cost accounting pitfalls. *The desirability of tailoring a budget to a particular subunit and a particular accounting system cannot be overemphasized.* For example, many problems of asset valuation and income measurement (whether based on historical cost or current cost) can be satisfactorily solved if top management gets everybody to focus on what is attainable in the forthcoming budget period—regardless of whether the financial measures are based on historical costs or some other measure, such as current costs.

Top management often sets continuous improvement targets. Consider companies implementing EVA®. These companies have generally found it cost-effective to use historical-cost net assets rather than estimates of market or replacement values. Why? Because top management evaluates operations on year-to-year changes in EVA®, not on absolute measures of EVA®. Evaluating performance on the basis of *improvements* in EVA® makes the initial method of calculating EVA® less important.

Timing of Feedback

The fifth and final step in designing accounting-based performance measures is the timing of feedback. Timing of feedback depends largely on how critical the information is for the success of the organization, the specific level of management that is receiving the feedback, and on the sophistication of the organization's information technology. For example, motel managers responsible for room sales will want information on the number of rooms sold each day on a daily or, at most, weekly basis. Why? Because a large percentage of motel costs are fixed costs, so that achieving high room sales and taking quick action to reverse any declining sales trends are critical to the financial success of each motel. Supplying managers with daily information about room sales would be much easier if Hospitality Inns had a computerized room reservation and check-in system. Senior management, on the other hand, in their oversight role may look at information about daily room sales only on a monthly basis. In some instances, for example, because of concern about the low sales to total assets ratio of the Brandon motel, they may want the information weekly.

PERFORMANCE MEASUREMENT IN MULTINATIONAL COMPANIES

OBJECTIVE 7

Indicate the difficulties that arise when comparing the performance of divisions operating in different countries

Comparing the performance of divisions of a multinational company operating in different countries creates additional difficulties.[9]

◆ The economic, legal, political, social, and cultural environments differ significantly across countries.

◆ Governments in some countries may impose controls and limit selling prices of a company's products. For example, developing countries in Asia, Latin America, and Eastern Europe impose tariffs and duties to restrict the import of certain goods.

◆ Availability of materials and skilled labour, as well as costs of materials, labour, and infrastructure (power, transportation, and communication) may also differ significantly across countries.

◆ Divisions operating in different countries keep score of their performance in different currencies. Issues of inflation and fluctuations in foreign currency exchange rates then become important.

We focus on the last of these issues next.

Calculating the Foreign Division's ROI in the Foreign Currency

Suppose Hospitality Inns invests in a motel in Mexico City. The investment consists mainly of the costs of buildings and furnishings. The following information is available:

◆ The exchange rate at the time of Hospitality's investment on December 31, 1999 is 3 pesos = $1.

◆ During 2000, the Mexican peso suffers a steady and steep decline in its value.

◆ The exchange rate on December 31, 2000 is 6 pesos = $1.

◆ The average exchange rate during 2000 is $[(3 + 6) \div 2] = 4.5$ pesos = $1.

◆ The investment (total assets) in the Mexico City motel = 9,000,000 pesos.

◆ The operating income of the Mexico City motel in 2000 = 1,800,000 pesos.

What is the historical-cost-based ROI for the Mexico City motel in 2000?

Some specific questions arise. Should we calculate the ROI in pesos or in dollars? If we calculate the ROI in dollars, what exchange rate should we use? How does the ROI of Hospitality Inns Mexico City (HIMC) compare with the ROI of Hospitality Inns Hull (HIH), which is also a relatively new motel of roughly the same size? Hospitality Inns may be interested in this information for making future investment decisions.

$$\text{HIMC's ROI (calculated using pesos)} = \frac{\text{Operating income}}{\text{Total assets}} = \frac{1,800,000 \text{ pesos}}{9,000,000 \text{ pesos}} = 20\%$$

HIMC's ROI of 20% is higher than HIH's ROI of 17% (computed on p. 828). Does this mean that HIMC outperformed HIH on the ROI criterion? Not necessarily. Why? Because HIMC operates in a very different economic environment than does HIH.

---

[9]M. Z. Iqbal, T. Melcher, and A. Elmallah, *International Accounting—A Global Perspective* (Cincinatti: Southwestern ITP, 1996).

The peso has declined steeply in value relative to the dollar in 2000. Research studies show that the peso's decline is correlated with correspondingly higher inflation in Mexico relative to Canada.[10] A consequence of the higher inflation in Mexico is that HIMC will charge higher prices for its motel rooms, which will increase HIMC's operating income and lead to a higher ROI. Inflation clouds the real economic returns on an asset and makes ROI calculated on historical cost of assets unrealistically high. Why? Because had there been no inflation, HIMC's room rates and hence operating income would have been much lower. Differences in inflation rates between the two countries make a direct comparison of HIMC's peso-denominated ROI with HIH's dollar-denominated ROI misleading.

Calculating the Foreign Division's ROI in Canadian Dollars

One way to achieve greater comparability of historical-cost-based ROIs is to restate HIMC's performance in dollars. But what exchange rate(s) should we use to make the comparison meaningful? Assume operating income was earned evenly throughout 2000. We use the average exchange rate of 4.5 pesos = $1 to convert the operating income from pesos to dollars: 1,800,000 pesos ÷ 4.5 = $400,000. The effect of dividing the operating income in pesos by the higher pesos-to-dollars exchange rate is that any increase in operating income in pesos as a result of inflation is undone when converting back to dollars.

At what rate should we convert HIMC's total assets of 9,000,000 pesos? At the exchange rate prevailing when the assets were acquired on December 31, 1999, namely 3 pesos = $1. Why? Because HIMC's book value of assets is recorded at the December 31, 1999 cost, and is not revalued as a result of inflation in Mexico in 2000. Since the book value of assets is unaffected by subsequent inflation, so should the exchange rate used to convert it into dollars. Using exchange rates after December 31, 1999 would be incorrect, because these rates incorporate the higher inflation in Mexico in 2000. Total assets would be converted to 9,000,000 pesos ÷ 3 = $3,000,000. Then:

$$\text{HIMC's ROI (calculated using dollars)} = \frac{\text{Operating income}}{\text{Total assets}} = \frac{\$400,000}{\$3,000,000} = 13.33\%$$

These adjustments make the historical-cost-based ROIs of the two motels comparable because they negate the effects of any differences in inflation rates between the two countries. HIMC's ROI of 13.33% is less than HIH's ROI of 17%.

Residual income calculated in pesos suffers from the same problems as ROI calculated using pesos. Instead, calculating HIMC's residual income in dollars adjusts for changes in exchange rates and facilitates comparisons with Hospitality's other motels:

$$\text{HIMC's residual income} = \$400,000 - (12\% \times \$3,000,000)$$
$$= \$400,000 - \$360,000 = \$40,000$$

which is also less than HIH's residual income of $150,000. In interpreting HIMC's and HIH's ROI and residual income, note that they are historical-cost-based calculations. They do, however, pertain to relatively new motels.

DISTINCTION BETWEEN MANAGERS AND ORGANIZATIONAL UNITS[11]

As noted before in this and several earlier chapters, the performance evaluation of a manager should be distinguished from the performance evaluation of an organization subunit, such as a division of a company. For example, historical-cost-based ROIs for a particular division can be used to evaluate a manager's performance relative

---

[10]Beaver, W. and M. Wolfson, "Foreign Currency Translation Gains and Losses: What Effect Do They Have and What Do They Mean?" *Financial Analysts Journal*, March–April 1984; F.D.S. Choi, "Resolving the Inflation/Currency Translation Dilemma," *Management International Review*, Vol. 34, Special Issue, 1994.

[11]The presentations here draw (in part) on teaching notes prepared by S. Huddart, N. Melumad, and S. Reichelstein.

to a budget or over time, even though historical-cost ROIs may be unsatisfactory for evaluating economic returns earned by the subunit. But using historical-cost ROIs to compare the performance of managers of different subunits can be misleading. In the Hospitality Inns example, Hospitality Inns Hull's (HIH's) ROI of 17% exceeds Hospitality Inns Mexico City's (HIMC's) ROI of 13.33% after adjusting for the higher inflation in Mexico. The ROIs may give some indication of the economic returns from each motel but do not mean that the manager of HIH performed better than the manager of HIMC. Why? Because among other factors, HIMC's ROI may have been adversely affected relative to HIN's ROI because of legal, political, and government regulations as well as economic conditions in Mexico over which the HIMC manager has no control.

Consider another example. Companies often put the most skillful division manager in charge of the weakest division in an attempt to change its fortunes. Such an effort may take years to bear fruit. Furthermore, the manager's efforts may result merely in bringing the division up to a minimum acceptable ROI. The division may continue to be a poor profit performer in comparison with other divisions, but it would be a mistake to conclude from the poor performance of the division that the manager is necessarily performing poorly.

This section focuses on developing basic principles for evaluating the performance of a division manager of an individual subunit. The concepts we discuss apply, however, to all organization levels. Later sections consider specific examples at the individual-activity level and the total-organization level. For specificity, we use the residual income (RI) performance measure throughout.

OBJECTIVE 8

Recognize the role of salaries and incentives in compensation arrangements

The Basic Tradeoff: Creating Incentives Versus Imposing Risk

The performance evaluation of managers and employees often affects their compensation. Compensation arrangements run the range from a flat salary with no direct performance-based bonus (as in the case of some government officials) to rewards based only on performance (as in the case of employees of real estate agencies). Most often, however, a manager's total compensation includes some combination of salary and a performance-based bonus. An important consideration in designing compensation arrangements is the tradeoff between creating incentives and imposing risk. We illustrate this tradeoff in the context of our Hospitality Inns example.

Sally Fonda owns the Hospitality Inns chain of motels. Roger Brett manages the Hospitality Inns Saskatoon (HIS) motel. Assume that Fonda uses RI to measure performance. To achieve good results as measured by RI, Fonda would like Brett to control costs, provide prompt and courteous service, and reduce receivables. But even if Brett did all those things, good results are by no means guaranteed. HIS's RI is affected by many factors outside Fonda's and Brett's control, such as a recession in the Saskatoon economy, or weather that might negatively affect HIS. Alternatively, noncontrollable factors might have a positive influence on HIS's RI. Noncontrollable factors make HIS's profitability uncertain and risky.

Fonda is an entrepreneur and does not mind bearing risk, but Brett does not like being subject to risk. One way of insuring Brett against risk is to pay Brett a flat salary, regardless of the actual amount of residual income attained. All the risk would then be borne by Fonda. There is a problem here, however, because the effort that Brett puts in is difficult to monitor, and the absence of performance-based compensation will provide Brett with no incentive to work harder or undertake extra physical and mental effort beyond what is necessary to retain his job or to uphold his own personal values.

Moral hazard[12] describes contexts in which an employee prefers to exert less effort (or report distorted information) than the effort (or information) desired by the owner because the employee's effort (or information) cannot be accurately monitored and enforced. In some repetitive jobs—for example, in electronic assembly—a

Moral hazard. Describes contexts in which an employee prefers to exert less effort (or report distorted information) than the effort (or information) desired by the owner because the employee's effort (or information) cannot be accurately monitored and enforced.

---

[12]The term *moral hazard* originated in insurance contracts to represent situations where insurance coverage caused insured parties to take less care of their properties than they might otherwise. One response to moral hazard in insurance contracts is the system of deductibles (that is, the insured pays for damages below a specified amount).

supervisor can monitor the workers' actions, and the moral hazard problem may not arise. However, the manager's job is often to gather information and exercise judgement on the basis of the information obtained, and monitoring a manager's effort is thus considerably more difficult.

Paying no salary and rewarding Brett *only* on the basis of some performance measure—RI, in our example—raises different concerns. Brett would now be motivated to strive to increase RI because his rewards would increase with increases in RI. But compensating Brett on RI also subjects Brett to risk. Why? Because HIS's RI depends not only on Brett's effort, but also on random factors such as the local economy over which Brett has no control.

To compensate Brett (who does not like being subject to risk) for taking on uncontrollable risk, Fonda must pay Brett some extra compensation within the structure of the RI-based arrangement. Thus, using performance-based incentives will cost Fonda more money, *on average*, than paying Brett a flat salary. Why "on average"? Because Fonda's compensation payment to Brett will vary with RI outcomes. When averaged over these outcomes, the RI-based compensation will cost Fonda more than would paying Brett a flat salary. The motivation for having some salary and some performance-based bonus in compensation arrangements is to balance the benefits of incentives against the extra costs of imposing uncontrollable risk on the manager.

Intensity of Incentives and Financial and Nonfinancial Measurements

O B J E C T I V E   9

Describe the management accountant's role in helping organizations provide better incentives

What dictates the intensity of the incentives? That is, how large should the incentive component be relative to salary? A key question is: How well does the performance measure capture the manager's ability to influence the desired results?

Measures of performance that are superior change significantly with the manager's performance and not very much with changes in factors that are beyond the manager's control. Consequently, superior performance measures motivate the manager but limit the manager's exposure to uncontrollable risk and hence reduce the cost of providing incentives to get the manager to accept the incentive program. On the other hand, measures of performance are inferior if they fail to capture the manager's performance and fail to induce managers to improve. When owners have superior performance measures available to them, they place greater reliance on incentive compensation.

Suppose Brett has no authority to determine investments. Further suppose revenue is determined largely by external factors such as the local economy. Brett's actions influence only costs. Using RI as a performance measure in these circumstances subjects Brett's bonus to excessive risk, because two components of the performance measure (investments and revenues) are unrelated to his actions. The management accountant might suggest that, to create stronger incentives, Fonda consider using a different performance measure for Brett—perhaps HIS's costs—that more closely captures Brett's effort. Note that in this case, RI may be a perfectly good measure of the economic viability of HIS, but it is not a good measure of Brett's performance.

The benefits of tying performance measures more closely to a manager's efforts encourage the use of nonfinancial measures. Consider two possible measures for evaluating the manager of the Housekeeping Department at one of Hospitality's motels—the costs of the Housekeeping Department and the average time taken by the housekeeping staff to clean a room. Suppose housekeeping costs are affected by factors such as wage rates, which the housekeeping manager does not determine. In this case, the average time taken to clean a room may more precisely capture the manager's performance.

The salary component of compensation dominates in the absence of good measures of performance (as in the case of some corporate staff and government officials). This is not to say, however, that incentives are completely absent; promotions and salary increases do depend on some overall measure of performance, but the incentives are less direct. Employers give stronger incentives when superior measures of performance are available to them and when monitoring the employee's effort is

Kidder Peabody's Paper Profits and High Compensations

Incentives based on superior performance measures motivate managers and employees to work hard, because these measures change significantly with actions that the senior management wants managers and employees to take. At no time should employees be able to manipulate performance measures to make their performance look better than what it is. Besides being unethical, such measures fail to achieve the objectives of the company.

In April 1994, Kidder Peabody, a Wall Street investment banking firm and a subsidiary of General Electric, made a dramatic announcement. It dismissed its chief government bond trader alleging fraudulent trading apparently intended to inflate profits and the trader's performance bonus in 1993. Kidder Peabody said $350 million in profits it recorded in 1993 never existed. The trader alleged that his superiors had suggested and were aware of the scheme, and that they also benefited from big bonuses resulting from it.

The problems arose with respect to trades in government bonds (debt issued by the U.S. government) and zero-coupon bonds (bonds that accumulate and pay interest only when the bond is finally paid off). Kidder alleged that the trades took advantage of the difference in the accounting for government bonds and zero-coupon bonds in Kidder's system. For zero-coupon bonds, Kidder's accounting recognized future interest yet to be earned as paper profits today, boosting income. "Creating" profits increased employee bonuses based on those profits when the firm itself earned no cash or real economic profit. The trades had another effect. They shrank Kidder's assets by $73 billion making the firm's return on assets look better to its parent company, General Electric.

Kidder stated that as the profits of the government trading division grew, it started its own internal examination and uncovered the phony trades. It responded by strengthening its accounting controls for trading in government and zero-coupon bonds. Kidder also began reexamining its incentive compensation and goal-setting programs to ensure that performance measures could not be manipulated in the future.

Source: Adapted from Hansell, S., "Kidder Reports Fraud and Ousts a Top Trader," *New York Times,* April 18, 1994; Spiro, L., L. Himelstein, and M. Schroeder, "They Said, He Said at Kidder Peabody," *Business Week,* August 8, 1994.

---

very difficult (real estate agencies, for example, reward employees mainly on commissions on houses sold).

Surveys show that division managers' compensation plans include a mix of salary, bonus, and long-term compensation tied to earnings and stock price of the company. The goal is to balance division and companywide, as well as short-term and long-term incentives. One survey of companies reports average annual contingent compensation as follows: (1) bonuses based on short-run performance equal to 40% of current salary and (2) average annual cash and stock compensation based on long-run performance equal to 57% of current salary. These percentages, however, vary widely over the sample—some companies use much stronger performance incentives than others.[13]

Benchmarks and Relative Performance Evaluation

Owners can use benchmarks to evaluate performance. Benchmarks representing best practice may be available inside or outside the overall organization. In our Hospitality Inns example, benchmarks could be other similar motels, either within or outside the Hospitality Inns chain. Suppose Brett has authority over revenues, costs, and in-

---

[13]Bushman, R., R. Indjejikian and A. Smith, "Aggregate Performance Measures in Business Unit Manager Compensation: The Role of Intrafirm Interdependencies," *Journal of Accounting Research* (Vol. 33 Supplement 1995).

vestments. In evaluating Brett's performance, Fonda would want to use as a benchmark, a motel of a similar size that is influenced by the same uncontrollable factors—for example, location, demographic trends, and economic conditions—that affect HIS. *Differences* in performances of the two motels occur only because of differences in the two managers' performances, not because of random factors. Thus, benchmarking, also called *relative performance evaluation*, "filters out" the effects of the common noncontrollable factors.

Can the performance of two managers responsible for running similar operations within a company be benchmarked against one another? Yes, but one problem is that the use of these benchmarks may reduce incentives for these managers to help one another. That is, a manager's performance evaluation measure improves either by doing a better job or by making the other manager look bad. Not working together as a team is not in the best interests of the organization as a whole. In this case, using benchmarks for performance evaluation can lead to goal-incongruence.

PERFORMANCE MEASURES AT THE INDIVIDUAL ACTIVITY LEVEL

This section focuses on incentive issues that arise in the context of individual activities. The principles described here, however, can be applied at all levels of the organization.

Performing Multiple Tasks

Most employees perform more than one task as part of their jobs. Marketing representatives sell products, provide customer support, and gather market information. Other jobs have multiple aspects to them. Manufacturing workers, for example, are responsible for both the quantity and the quality of their products. Employers want employees to allocate their time and effort intelligently among various tasks or aspects of their jobs.

Consider, for example, mechanics at an auto repair shop. Their jobs have at least two distinct and important aspects. The first aspect is the repair work. Performing more repair work would generate more revenues for the shop. The second aspect is customer satisfaction. The higher the quality of the job, the more likely the customer will be pleased. If the employer wants an employee to focus on both these aspects, then the employer must measure and compensate performance on both.

Suppose the employer can easily measure the quantity of auto repairs but not their quality. If the employer rewards workers on a piece-rate system—which pays workers only on the basis of the number of repairs actually performed—mechanics will likely increase the number of repairs they make at the expense of quality. Sears experienced this problem when they introduced by-the-job rates for its mechanics. Sears's management responded by taking the following steps to motivate workers to balance both quantity and quality: (1) Management dropped the piece-rate system and paid mechanics an hourly salary, a step that deemphasized the quantity of repair. Mechanics' promotions and pay increases were determined on the basis of management's assessment of each mechanic's overall performance regarding quantity and quality of repairs. (2) Management began evaluating employees, in part, using data such as customer satisfaction surveys, the number of dissatisfied customers, or the number of customer complaints. (3) Management also employed independent staff to randomly monitor whether the repairs performed were of high quality.

Note that nonfinancial measures (such as customer satisfaction measures) play a central role in motivating mechanics to emphasize both quantity and quality. The goal is to measure both aspects of the mechanics' jobs and to balance incentives so that both aspects are properly emphasized.

Team-Based Compensation Arrangements

Many manufacturing, marketing, and design problems require employees with multiple skills, experiences, and judgments to pool their talents. In these situations, a team of employees achieves better results than employees acting on their own.[14]

[14]Katzenbach, J., and D. Smith, *The Wisdom of Teams* (Boston: The Harvard Business School Press, 1993).

Companies give incentives and bonuses to individuals on the basis of team performance. Team incentives encourage cooperation, with individuals helping one another as they strive toward a common goal. The blend of knowledge and skills needed to change methods and improve efficiency puts a team in a better position than a lone individual to respond to incentives. Eaton, TRW, Whirlpool, Monsanto, Dana, and Analog Devices in the United States and Nissan Motors and Nippon Steel in Japan are examples of companies that use some form of team-based incentives.

Whether team-based compensation is desirable depends, to a great extent, on the culture and management style of a particular organization. One criticism of teams is that individual incentives to excel are dampened, harming overall performance.

Whirlpool Corporation
www.whirlpool.com

Nippon Steel
www.ei.nsc.co.jp

EXECUTIVE PERFORMANCE MEASURES AND COMPENSATION

"The Impact of Culture on Compensation Design"—Gary L. Parker, Alan Chesters—*International HR Journal* Spring, 1997
www.windhamint.com/article/html/al_comp_articles_2.html

The principles of performance evaluation described in the previous sections also apply to executive compensation plans at the total-organization level. Executive compensation plans are based on both financial and nonfinancial performance measures and consist of a mix of (1) base salary; (2) annual incentives (for example, cash bonus based on yearly net income); (3) long-term incentives (for example, stock options [described later in this section] based on achieving a specified return by the end of a five-year period); and (4) fringe benefits (for example, life insurance, an office with a view, or a personal secretary). Designers of executive compensation plans emphasize three factors: achievement of organization goals, administrative ease, and the likelihood that affected managers will perceive the plan as fair.

Well-designed plans use a compensation mix that carefully balances risk and short- and long-term incentives. For example, evaluating performance on the basis of annual ROI would sharpen an executive's short-term focus. Using ROI and stock option plans over, say, five years would motivate the executive to take a long-term view as well.

ENVIRONMENTAL AND ETHICAL RESPONSIBILITIES

Lockheed
www.lockheed.com

Duke Power Company
www.dukepower.com

Managers in all organizations shoulder environmental and ethical responsibilities. Environmental violations (such as water and air pollution) and unethical and illegal practices (such as bribery and corruption) carry heavy fines and are prison offences under the laws of Canada, the United States, and other countries. But environmental responsibilities and ethical conduct extend beyond legal requirements.

Socially responsible companies set aggressive environmental targets and measure and report their performance against them. German, Swiss, Dutch, and Scandinavian companies report on environmental performance as part of a larger set of social responsibility disclosures (which include employee welfare and community development information). Some companies, such as DuPont and Lockheed, make environmental performance a line item on every employee's salary appraisal sheet. The Duke Power Company appraises employees on reducing solid waste, cutting emissions and discharges, and implementing environmental plans. The result: Duke Power has met all its environmental goals.

Ethical behaviour on the part of managers is paramount. In particular, the numbers that subunit managers report should not be tainted by "cooking the books"—they should be uncontaminated by, for example, padded assets, understated liabilities, fictitious sales, and understated costs.

Codes of business conduct are circulated in some organizations to signal appropriate and inappropriate individual behaviour. The following is a quote from Caterpillar Tractor's "Code of Worldwide Business Conduct and Operating Principles":

> The law is a floor. Ethical business conduct should normally exist at a level well above the minimum required by law. . . . Caterpillar employees shall not accept costly entertainment or gifts (excepting mementos and novelties of nominal value) from dealers, suppliers and others with whom we do business. And we won't tolerate circumstances that produce, or reasonably appear to produce, conflict between personal interests of an employee and interests of the company.

Division managers often cite enormous top-management pressures "to make the budget" as excuses or rationalizations for not adhering to ethical accounting policies and procedures. A healthy amount of motivational pressure is not bad—as long as the "tone from the top" simultaneously communicates the absolute need for all managers to behave ethically at all times. Management should promptly and severely reprimand unethical conduct irrespective of the benefits that accrue to the company from such actions. Some companies such as Lockheed emphasize ethical behaviour by routinely evaluating employees against a business code of ethics.

PROBLEM FOR SELF-STUDY

PROBLEM

Budgeted data of the baseball manufacturing division of Home Run Sports for February 2000 are as follows:

Current assets	$ 400,000
Long-term assets	600,000
Total assets	$1,000,000
Production output	200,000 baseballs per month
Target ROI (operating income ÷ total assets)	30%
Fixed costs	$400,000 per month
Variable costs	$4 per baseball

REQUIRED

1. Compute the minimum unit selling price necessary to achieve the 30% target ROI, assuming ROI is based on total assets.
2. Using the selling price from requirement 1, separate the target ROI into its two components using the DuPont method.
3. Pamela Stephenson, division manager, receives 5% of the monthly residual income of the baseball manufacturing division as a bonus. Compute her bonus for February 2000, using the selling price from requirement 1. Home Run Sports uses a 12% required rate of return on total division assets when computing division residual income.

SOLUTION

1.
$$\text{Target operating income} = 30\% \text{ of } \$1,000,000$$
$$= \$300,000$$
$$\text{Let } P = \text{Selling price}$$
$$\text{Sales} - \text{Variable costs} - \text{Fixed costs} = \text{Operating income}$$
$$200,000P - (200,000 \times \$4) - \$400,000 = \$300,000$$
$$200,000P = \$300,000 + \$800,000 + \$400,000 = \$1,500,000$$
$$P = \$7.50$$

Proof:		
	Sales, 200,000 × $7.50	$1,500,000
	Variable costs, 200,000 × $4	800,000
	Contribution margin	700,000
	Fixed costs	400,000
	Operating income	$ 300,000

2.
$$\frac{\text{Revenues}}{\text{Investment}} \times \frac{\text{Income}}{\text{Revenues}} = \frac{\text{Income}}{\text{Investment}}$$

$$\frac{\$1,500,000}{\$1,000,000} \times \frac{\$300,000}{\$1,500,000} = \frac{\$300,000}{\$1,000,000}$$

$$1.5 \quad \times \quad 0.2 \quad = 0.30 \text{ or } 30\%$$

3. Residual income = Operating income − Required return on investment
$$= \$300,000 \quad - (0.12 \times \$1,000,000)$$
$$= \$300,000 \quad - \$120,000$$
$$= \$180,000$$

Stephenson's bonus is $9,000 (5% of $180,000).

SUMMARY

The following points are linked to the chapter's learning objectives.

1. Financial measures such as return on investment and residual income can capture important aspects of both manager performance and organization-subunit performance. In many cases, however, financial measures are supplemented with nonfinancial measures of performance, such as those relating to customer service time, number of defects, and productivity.

2. The steps in designing an accounting-based performance measure are (a) choosing variables to include in the performance measure, (b) defining the terms, (c) measuring the items included in the variables, (d) choosing a target for performance, and (e) choosing the timing of feedback.

3. The DuPont method describes return on investment (ROI) as the product of two components: revenues divided by investment and income divided by revenues. ROI can be increased in three ways—increase revenues, decrease costs, and decrease investment.

4. Residual income is income minus a required dollar return on the investment. Residual income was designed to overcome some of the limitations of ROI. For example, residual income is more likely than ROI to promote goal-congruence. That is, actions that are in the best interests of the organization maximize residual income. The objective of maximizing ROI, conversely, may induce managers of highly profitable divisions to reject projects that, from the viewpoint of the organization as a whole, should be accepted.

5. Economic value added (EVA®) is a specific type of residual income calculation. It equals the after-tax operating income minus the after-tax weighted-average cost of capital multiplied by total assets minus current liabilities.

6. The current cost of an asset is the cost now of purchasing an asset identical to the one currently held. Historical-cost asset measurement methods consider the original cost of the asset net of accumulated amortization.

7. Comparing the performance of divisions operating in different countries is difficult because of legal, political, social, economic, and currency differences. ROI calculations for subunits operating in different countries need to be adjusted for differences in inflation between the two countries and changes in exchange rates.

8. Organizations create incentives by rewarding managers on the basis of performance. But managers may face risks because random factors beyond the managers' control may also affect performance. Owners choose a mix of salary and incentive compensation to trade off the incentive benefit against the cost of imposing risk.

9. Obtaining measures of employee performance that are superior is critical for implementing strong incentives. Many management accounting practices, such as the design of responsibility centres and the establishment of financial and nonfinancial measures, have as their goal better performance evaluation.

▼ TERMS TO LEARN

This chapter contains definitions of the following important terms:

current cost (p. 834)
economic value added (EVA®) (p. 829)
imputed costs (p. 829)
investment (p. 827)

moral hazard (p. 840)
residual income (p. 828)
return on investment (ROI) (p. 827)

QUESTIONS

24-1 Give two examples of financial performance measures and two examples of nonfinancial performance measures.

24-2 What are the five steps in designing an accounting-based performance measure?

24-3 What factors affecting ROI does the DuPont method highlight?

24-4 "Residual income is not identical to ROI although both measures incorporate income and investment into their computations." Do you agree? Explain.

24-5 Describe economic value added.

24-6 Give three definitions of investment used in practice when computing ROI.

24-7 Distinguish between measuring assets based on present value, current cost, and historical cost.

24-8 What special problems arise when evaluating performance in multinational companies?

24-9 Why is it important to distinguish between the performance of a manager and the performance of the organization subunit for which the manager is responsible? Give examples.

24-10 Describe moral hazard.

24-11 "Managers should be rewarded only on the basis of their performance measures. They should be paid no salary." Do you agree? Explain.

24-12 Explain the management accountant's role in helping organizations design stronger incentive systems for their employees.

24-13 Explain the role of benchmarking in evaluating managers.

24-14 Explain the incentive problems that can arise when employees have to perform multiple tasks as part of their jobs.

24-15 List four components of executive compensation plans.

EXERCISES

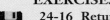

24-16 Return on investment; comparisons of three companies. (CMA, adapted) Return on investment is often expressed as follows:

$$\frac{\text{Income}}{\text{Investment}} = \frac{\text{Revenues}}{\text{Investment}} \times \frac{\text{Income}}{\text{Revenues}}$$

REQUIRED

1. What advantages are there in the breakdown of the computation into two separate components?

2. Fill in the following blanks:

	Companies in Same Industry		
	A	**B**	**C**
Revenue	$1,000,000	$500,000	?
Income	$ 100,000	$ 50,000	?
Investment	$ 500,000	?	$5,000,000
Income as a percentage of revenue	?	?	0.5%
Investment turnover	?	?	2
Return on investment	?	1%	?

After filling in the blanks, comment on the relative performance of these companies as thoroughly as the data permit.

24-17 Analysis of return on invested assets, comparison of three divisions. Quality Products, Inc. is a soft drink and food products company. It has three divisions: soft drinks, snack foods, and family restaurants. Results for the past three years are as follows (in millions):

	Soft Drink Division	Snack Foods Division	Restaurant Division	Quality Products, Inc.
Operating Revenues				
2000	$2,800	$2,000	$1,050	$5,850
2001	3,000	2,400	1,250	6,650
2002	3,600	2,600	1,530	7,730
Operating Income				
2000	120	360	105	585
2001	160	400	114	674
2002	240	420	100	760
Total Assets				
2000	1,200	1,240	800	3,240
2001	1,250	1,400	1,000	3,650
2002	1,400	1,430	1,300	4,130

REQUIRED

Use the DuPont method to explain changes in the operating income to total assets ratio over the 2000 to 2002 period for each division. Comment on the results.

24-18 ROI and RI. (D. Kleespie) The Gaul Company produces and distributes a wide variety of recreational products. One of its divisions, the Goscinny Division, manufactures and sells "menhirs," which are very popular with cross-country skiers. The demand for these menhirs is relatively insensitive to price changes. The Goscinny Division is considered to be an investment centre and in recent years has averaged a return on investment of 20%. The following data are available for the Goscinny Division and its product:

Total annual fixed costs	$1,000,000
Variable costs per menhir	$300
Average number of menhirs sold each year	10,000
Average operating assets invested in the division	$1,600,000

REQUIRED

1. What is the minimum selling price per unit that the Goscinny Division could charge in order for Mary Obelix, the division manager, to get a favourable performance rating? Management considers an ROI below 20% to be unfavourable.
2. Assume that the Gaul Company judges the performance of its investment centre managers on the basis of residual income rather than ROI, as was assumed in requirement 1. The company's required rate of return is considered to be 15%. What is the minimum selling price per unit that the Goscinny Division should charge for Obelix to receive a favourable performance rating?

24-19 Pricing and return on investment. Hardy, Inc. assembles motorcycles and uses long-run (defined as three to five years) average demand to set the budgeted production level and costs for pricing. Prices are then adjusted only for large changes in assembly wage rates or direct materials prices. You are given the following data:

Direct materials, assembly wages, and other variable costs	$1,320 per unit
Fixed costs	$300,000,000 per year
Target return on investment	20%
Normal utilization of capacity (average output)	1,000,000 units
Investment (total assets)	$900,000,000

REQUIRED

1. What operating income percentage on revenues is needed to attain the target return on investment of 20%? What is the selling price per unit?
2. Using the selling price per unit calculated in requirement 1, what rate of return on investment will be earned if Hardy assembles and sells 1,500,000 units? 500,000 units?
3. The company has a management bonus plan based on yearly division performance. Assume that Hardy assembled and sold 1,000,000, 1,500,000, and 500,000 units in three successive years. Each of three people served as division manager for one year before being killed in an automobile accident. As the principal heir of the third manager, comment on the bonus plan.

24-20 Financial and nonfinancial performance measures, goal-congruence. (CMA, adapted) Summit Equipment specializes in the manufacture of medical equipment, a field that has become increasingly competitive. Approximately two years ago, Ben Harrington, president of Summit, decided to revise the bonus plan (based, at the time, entirely on operating income) to encourage division managers to focus on areas that were important to customers and that added value without increasing cost. In addition to a profitability incentive, the revised plan also includes incentives for reduced rework costs, reduced sales returns, and on-time deliveries. Bonuses are calculated and awarded semiannually on the following basis. A base bonus is calculated at 2% of operating income. The bonus amount is then adjusted by the following amounts:

a. i. Reduced by excess of rework costs over 2% of operating income.
   ii. No adjustment if rework costs are less than or equal to 2% of operating income.
b. Increased by $5,000 if over 98% of deliveries are on time, by $2,000 if 96–98% of deliveries are on time, and by $0 if on-time deliveries are below 96%.
c. i. Increased by $3,000 if sales returns are less than or equal to 1.5% of sales.
   ii. Decreased by 50% of excess of sales returns over 1.5% of sales.

Note: If the calculation of the bonus results in a negative amount for a particular period, the manager simply receives no bonus, and the negative amount is *not* carried forward to the next period.

Results for Summit's Charter and Mesa Divisions for the year 2000, the first year under the new bonus plan, follow. In the previous year, 1999, under the old bonus plan, the Charter Division manager earned a bonus of $27,060 and the Mesa Division manager a bonus of $22,440.

	Charter Division		Mesa Division	
	January 1, 2000 to June 30, 2000	July 1, 2000 to December 31, 2000	January 1, 2000 to June 30, 2000	July 1, 2000 to December 31, 2000
Sales	$4,200,000	$4,400,000	$2,850,000	$2,900,000
Operating income	$ 462,000	$ 440,000	$ 342,000	$ 406,000
On-time delivery	95.4%	97.3%	98.2%	94.6%
Rework costs	$ 11,500	$ 11,000	$ 6,000	$ 8,000
Sales returns	$ 84,000	$ 70,000	$ 44,750	$ 42,500

REQUIRED
1. Why did Harrington need to introduce these new performance measures? That is, why does Harrington need to use these performance measures over and above the operating income numbers for the period?
2. Calculate the bonus earned by each manager for each six-month period and for the year 2000.
3. What effect did the change in the bonus plan have on each manager's behaviour? Did the new bonus plan achieve what Harrington desired? What changes, if any, would you make to the new bonus plan?

24-21 RI, EVA®. (D. Solomons, adapted) Consider the following data for the two geographical divisions of the Potomac Electric Company that operate as profit centres:

	Atlantic Division	Pacific Division
Total assets	$1,000,000	$5,000,000
Current liabilities	250,000	1,500,000
Operating income	200,000	750,000

REQUIRED
1. Calculate the return on investment (ROI) using operating income as the measure of income and using total assets as the measure of investment.
2. Potomac Electric has used residual income as a measure of management success, the variable it wants a manager to maximize. Using this criterion, what is the residual income for each division using operating income and total assets if the required rate of return on investment is 12%?
3. Potomac Electric has two sources of funds: long-term debt with a market value of $3,500,000 and an interest rate of 10%, and equity capital with a market value

24-22 RI, EVA®. The Burlingame Transport Company operates two divisions, a Truck Rental Division that rents to individuals, and a Transportation Division that transports goods from one city to another. Results reported for the last year are as follows:

	Truck Rental Division	Transportation Division
Total assets	$650,000	$950,000
Current liabilities	120,000	200,000
Operating income before tax	75,000	160,000

REQUIRED

1. Calculate the residual income for each division using operating income before tax and investment equal to total assets minus current liabilities. The required rate of return on investments is 12%.
2. The company has two sources of funds: long-term debt with a market value of $900,000 at an interest rate of 10% and equity capital with a market value of $600,000 at a cost of equity of 15%. Burlingame's income tax rate is 40%. Burlingame applies the same weighted-average cost of capital to both divisions, since each division faces similar risks. Calculate the economic value added (EVA®) for each division.
3. Using your answers to requirements 1 and 2, what would you conclude about the performance of each division? Explain briefly.

24-23 Various measures of profitability. When the Coronet Company formed three divisions a year ago, the president told the division managers that an annual bonus would be paid to the most profitable division. However, absolute division operating income as conventionally computed would not be used. Instead, the ranking would be affected by the relative investments in the three divisions. Options available include ROI and residual income. Investment can be measured using gross book value or net book value. Each manager has now written a memorandum claiming entitlement to the bonus. The following data are available:

Division	Gross Book Value of Division Assets	Division Operating Income
Mastex	$400,000	$47,500
Banjo	380,000	46,000
Randal	250,000	30,800

All the assets are fixed assets that were purchased ten years ago and have ten years of useful life remaining. A zero terminal disposal price is predicted. Coronet's required rate of return used for computing residual income is 10% of investment.

REQUIRED

Which method for computing profitability did each manager choose? Make your description specific and brief. Show supporting computations. Where applicable, assume straight-line amortization.

24-24 Multinational performance measurement. The Sandvik Corporation manufactures electric motors in Canada and Sweden. The Canadian and Swedish operations are organized as decentralized divisions. The following information is available for 2000:

	Canadian Division	Swedish Division
Operating income	$1,200,000	6,552,000 kronor
Total assets	$8,000,000	42,000,000 kronor

The exchange rate at the time of Sandvik's investment in Sweden on December 31, 1999 was 6 kronor = $1. During 2000, the Swedish krona declined steadily in value so that the exchange rate on December 31, 2000 is 7 kronor = $1. The average exchange rate during 2000 is [(6 + 7) ÷ 2] = 6.5 kronor = $1.

REQUIRED

1. Calculate the Canadian Division's return on investment for 2000.
2. Calculate the Swedish Division's return on investment for 2000 in kronor.
3. Senior management at Sandvik wants to know which division earned a better return on investment in 2000. What would you tell them? Explain your answer.

24-25 Multinational performance measurement, ROI, RI. Loren Press operates two printing presses that operate as separate divisions, one located in Dundas, Ontario and the other in Lyon, France. The following information is available for 2001. The required rate of return on investments is 15%.

	Dundas Division	Lyon Division
Operating income	$765,000	3,600,000 francs
Total assets	$4,500,000	20,000,000 francs

Both investments were made on December 31, 2000. The exchange rate at the time of Loren's investment in France on December 31, 2000 was 4 francs = $1. During 2001, the French franc declined steadily in value reaching an exchange rate on December 31, 2001 of 5 francs = $1. The average exchange rate during 2001 is [(4 + 5) ÷ 2] = 4.5 francs = $1.

REQUIRED

1. a. Calculate Dundas Division's return on investment for 2001.
   b. Calculate Lyon Division's return on investment for 2001 in French francs.
   c. Which division earned a better return on investment in 2001? Explain.
2. Senior management wants to compare the performance of the two divisions using residual income. Which division do you think had the better residual income performance? Explain your answer.
3. On the basis of your answers to requirements 1 and 2, which division is performing better? If you had to promote one of the division managers to vice-president, which would you choose? Explain.

24-26 Risk-sharing, incentives, benchmarking, multiple tasks. The Dexter Division of AMCO sells car batteries. AMCO's corporate management gives Dexter management considerable operating and investment autonomy in running the division. AMCO is considering how it should compensate Jim Marks, the general manager of the Dexter Division. Proposal 1 calls for paying Marks a fixed salary. Proposal 2 calls for paying Marks no salary and compensating him only on the basis of the division's ROI (calculated on the basis of operating income before any bonus payments). Proposal 3 calls for paying Marks some salary and some bonus based on ROI. Assume that Marks does not like bearing risk.

REQUIRED

1. a. Evaluate each of the three proposals, specifying the advantages and disadvantages of each.
   b. Suppose that AMCO competes against Tiara Industries in the car battery business. Tiara is roughly the same size and operates in a business environment that is very similar to Dexter's. The senior management of AMCO is considering evaluating Marks on the basis of Dexter's ROI minus Tiara's ROI. Marks complains that this approach is unfair because the performance of another firm, over which he has no control, is included in his performance evaluation measure. Is Marks's complaint valid? Why or why not?
2. Now suppose that Marks has no authority for making capital investment decisions. Corporate management makes these decisions. Is return on investment a good performance measure to use to evaluate Marks? Is return on investment a good measure to evaluate the economic viability of the Dexter Division? Explain.
3. Dexter's salespersons are responsible for selling and providing customer service and support. Sales are easy to measure. Although customer service is very important to Dexter in the long run, it has not yet implemented customer service measures. Marks wants to compensate his sales force only on the basis of sales commissions paid for each unit of product sold. He cites two advantages to this plan: (a) it creates very strong incentives for the sales force to work hard and (b) the company pays salespersons only when the company itself is earning revenues and has cash. Do you like his plan? Why or why not?

PROBLEMS

24-27 Relevant costs, performance evaluation, goal-congruence. Pike Enterprises has three operating divisions. The managers of these divisions are evaluated on their divisional operating income, a figure that includes an allocation of corporate overhead *proportional to the revenues of each division.* The operating income statement (in thousands) for the first quarter of 2001 is as follows:

	Andorian Division	Orion Division	Tribble Division	Total
Revenues	$2,000	$1,200	$1,600	$4,800
Cost of goods sold	1,050	540	640	2,230
Gross margin	950	660	960	2,570
Division overhead	250	125	160	535
Corporate overhead	400	240	320	960
Division operating income	$ 300	$ 295	$ 480	$1,075

The manager of the Andorian Division is unhappy that his profitability is about the same as the Orion Division's and is much less than the Tribble Division's, even though his revenues are much higher than either of these other two divisions. The manager knows that he is carrying one line of products with very low profitability. He was going to replace this line of business as soon as more profitable product opportunities became available, but he has kept it because the line is marginally profitable and uses facilities that would otherwise be idle. That manager now realizes, however, that the sales from this product line are attracting a fair amount of corporate overhead because of the allocation procedure, and maybe the line is already unprofitable for him. This low-margin line of products had the following characteristics for the most recent quarter (in thousands):

Revenues	$800
Cost of goods sold	600
Avoidable division overhead	100

REQUIRED

1. Prepare the operating income statement for Pike Enterprises for the second quarter of 2001. Assume that revenues and operating results are identical to those of the first quarter except that the manager of the Andorian Division has dropped the low-margin product line from his product group.
2. Is Pike Enterprises better off from this action?
3. Is the Andorian Division manager better off from this action?
4. Suggest changes for Pike's system of division reporting and evaluation that will motivate division managers to make decisions that are in the best interests of Pike Enterprises as a whole. Discuss any potential disadvantages of your proposal.

24-28 Historical cost and current cost ROI measures. Nobillo Corporation owns and manages convenience stores. The following information on three stores is collected for the year 2000.

	City Plaza	South Station	Central Park
Operating income	$ 90,000	$120,000	$ 60,000
Historical cost of investment	$300,000	$500,00	$240,000
Current cost of investment	$600,000	$700,000	$450,000
Age of store	10 years	5 years	8 years

REQUIRED

1. Compute the ROI for each store where investment is measured at (a) historical cost and (b) current cost.
2. How would you judge the performance of each store?

24-29 ROI performance measures based on historical cost and current cost. Mineral Waters Ltd. operates three divisions that process and bottle sparkling mineral water. The historical-cost accounting system reports the following data for 2001:

	Calistoga Division	Alpine Springs Division	Rocky Mountains Division
Revenues	$500,000	$700,000	$1,100,000
Operating costs (excluding amortization)	300,000	380,000	600,000
Plant amortization	70,000	100,000	120,000
Operating income	$130,000	$220,000	$380,000
Current assets	$200,000	$250,000	$300,000
Fixed assets—plant	140,000	900,000	1,320,000
Total assets	$340,000	$1,150,000	$1,620,000

Mineral Waters estimates the useful life of each plant to be twelve years with a zero terminal disposal price. The straight-line amortization method is used. At the end of 2001, the Calistoga plant is ten years old, Alpine Springs plant is three years old, and Rocky Mountains plant is one year old.

An index of construction costs of plants for mineral water production for the ten-year period that Mineral Waters has been operating (1991 year-end = 100) is:

1991	1998	2000	2001
100	136	160	170

Given the high turnover of current assets, management believes that the historical-cost and current-cost measures of current assets are approximately the same.

REQUIRED

1. Compute the ROI (operating income to total assets) ratio of each division using historical-cost measures. Comment on the results.
2. Use the approach in Exhibit 24-3 to compute the ROI of each division, incorporating current-cost estimates as of 2001 for amortization and fixed assets. Comment on the results.
3. What advantages might arise from using current-cost asset measures as compared with historical-cost measures for evaluating the performance of the managers of the three divisions?

24-30 Evaluating managers, ROI, value-chain analysis of cost structure. User Friendly Computer is one of the largest personal computer companies in the world. The board of directors was recently (March 2001) informed that User Friendly's president, Brian Clay, was resigning to "pursue other interests." An executive search firm recommends that the board consider appointing Peter Diamond (current president of Computer Power) or Norma Provan (current president of Peach Computer). You collect the following financial information on Computer Power and Peach Computer for 1999 and 2000 (in millions):

	Computer Power		Peach Computer	
	1999	**2000**	**1999**	**2000**
Total assets	$360.0	$340.0	$160.0	$240.0
Revenues	$400.0	$320.0	$200.0	$350.0
Costs:				
R&D	36.0	16.8	18.0	43.5
Design	15.0	8.4	3.6	11.6
Production	102.0	112.0	82.8	98.6
Marketing	75.0	92.4	36.0	66.7
Distribution	27.0	22.4	18.0	23.2
Customer service	45.0	28.0	21.6	46.4
Total costs	280.0	280.0	180.0	290.0
Operating income	$100.0	$40.0	$20.0	$60.0

In early 2001, a computer magazine gave Peach Computer's main product five stars (its highest rating on a five-point scale). Computer Power's main product was given three stars, down from five stars a year ago because of customer service problems. The computer magazine also ran an article on new product introductions in the personal computer industry. Peach Computer received high marks for new products in

2000. Computer Power's performance was called "mediocre." One "unnamed in-sider" of Computer Power commented: "Our new product cupboard is empty."

REQUIRED

1. Use the DuPont method to analyze the ROI of Computer Power and Peach Computer in 1999 and 2000. Comment on the results.
2. Compute the percentage of costs in each of the six business-function cost categories for Computer Power and Peach Computer in 1999 and 2000. Comment on the results.
3. Rank Diamond and Provan as potential candidates for president of User Friendly Computer.

24-31 ROI, RI, ROS, management incentives. (CMA, adapted) The Jump-Start Division (JSD) of Mason Industries manufactures go-carts and other recreational vehicles. JSD is considering building a new plant in 2001. The investment will cost $2.5 million. The expected revenues and costs for the new plant in 2001 are:

Revenues	$2,400,000
Variable costs	800,000
Fixed costs	1,120,000
Operating income	$ 480,000

JSD's ROI in 2000 is 24% and its return on sales (ROS) is 20%. ROI is defined as operating income divided by total assets. The bonuses of Maureen Grieco, the division manager of JSD and other JSD division managers are based on division ROI.

REQUIRED

1. If Mason Industries uses ROI to evaluate division managers, explain why JSD would be reluctant to build the new plant. Show all calculations.
2. Suppose Mason Industries uses RI as the basis for awarding bonuses to JSD's managers. Suppose further that the required rate of return on investment is 15%. Would JSD be more willing to build the new plant? Explain.
3. Calculate the ROS for the new plant. What are the advantages and disadvantages of using this measure to determine the bonuses paid to JSD's managers?

24-32 Division manager's compensation, risk sharing, incentives (continuation of 23-31). The management of Mason Industries is considering the following alternative compensation arrangements for Maureen Grieco, the division manager of JSD.

◆ Make Grieco's compensation a fixed salary without any bonuses. Mason's management believes that one advantage of this arrangement is that Grieco will be less inclined to reject future investments just because of their impact on ROI or RI.
◆ Make all of Grieco's compensation depend on the division's RI. The benefit of this arrangement is that it creates incentives for Grieco to aggressively seek and accept all proposals that increase JSD's RI.
◆ Evaluate Grieco's performance using benchmarking by comparing JSD's RI against the RI achieved by managers of other companies that also manufacture and sell go-carts and recreational vehicles and have comparable levels of investment. Mason's management believes that the advantage of benchmarking is that it focuses attention on Grieco's performance relative to peers rather than on the division's absolute performance.

REQUIRED

1. Assume Grieco is risk adverse and does not like bearing risk. Using concepts of performance evaluation described in this chapter evaluate each of the three proposals that Mason's management is considering. Indicate the positive and negative features of each proposal.
2. What compensation arrangement would you recommend? Explain briefly.

24-33 ROI, RI, investment decisions. The Media Group has three major divisions:

a. Newspapers—owns leading newspapers on four continents
b. Television—owns major television networks on three continents
c. Film studios—owns one of the five largest film studios in the world

Summary financial data for 1999 and 2000 are as follows (in millions):

	Operating Income		Revenues		Total Assets	
	1999	2000	1999	2000	1999	2000
Newspapers	$900	$1,100	$4,500	$4,600	$4,400	$4,900
Television	130	160	6,000	6,400	2,700	3,000
Film studios	220	200	1,600	1,650	2,500	2,600

The manager of each division has an annual bonus plan based on division return on investment (ROI). ROI is defined as operating income divided by total assets. Senior executives from divisions reporting increases in ROI from the prior year are automatically eligible for a bonus. Senior executives of divisions reporting a decline in the division ROI have to provide persuasive explanations for the decline to be eligible for a limited bonus.

Ken Kearney, manager of the Newspapers Division, is considering a proposal to invest $200 million in high-speed printing presses with colour-print options. The estimated increment to 2001 operating income would be $30 million. The Media Group has a 12% required rate of return for investments in all three divisions.

REQUIRED
1. Use the DuPont method to explain differences among the three divisions in their 2000 division ROI. Use 2000 total assets as the denominator.
2. Why might Kearney be less than enthusiastic about the high-speed printing press investment proposal?
3. Rupert Prince, chairman of the Media Group, receives a proposal to base senior executive compensation at each division on division residual income. Compute the residual income of each division in 2000.
4. Would adoption of a residual income measure reduce Kearney's reluctance to adopt the high-speed printing press investment proposal?

24-34 Division managers' compensation (continuation of 24-33). Rupert Prince seeks your advice on revising the existing bonus plan for division managers of the Media Group. Assume division managers do not like bearing risk. He is considering three ideas:
◆ Make all of each division manager's compensation depend on division ROI.
◆ Make all of each division manager's compensation depend on companywide ROI.
◆ Use benchmarking, and compensate each division manager on the basis of his or her own division's ROI minus the average ROI of the other two divisions.

REQUIRED
Evaluate each of the three ideas Prince has put forth using performance evaluation concepts described in this chapter. Indicate the positive and negative features of each proposal.

24-35 Ethics, manager's performance evaluation. (A. Spero, adapted) Hamilton Semiconductors manufactures specialized chips that sell for $20 each. Hamilton's manufacturing costs consist of variable costs of $2 per chip and fixed costs of $900,000. Hamilton also incurs $400,000 in fixed marketing costs each year.

Hamilton calculates operating income using absorption costing—that is, Hamilton calculates manufacturing costs per unit by dividing total manufacturing costs by actual production. Hamilton costs all units in inventory at this rate and expenses the costs in the income statement only when the units in inventory are sold. The next year, 2001, appears to be a difficult year for Hamilton. It expects to sell only 500,000 units. The demand for these chips fluctuate considerably so Hamilton usually holds minimal inventory.

REQUIRED
1. Calculate Hamilton's operating income in 2001 if Hamilton manufactures (a) 500,000 units and (b) 600,000 units.
2. Would it be unethical for Randy Jones, the general manager of Hamilton Semiconductors, to produce more units than can be sold in order to show better operating results? Jones's compensation has a bonus component based on operating income. Explain your answer.
3. Would it be unethical for Jones to ask distributors to buy more product than they need? Hamilton follows the industry practice of booking sales when products are shipped to distributors. Explain your answer.

COLLABORATIVE LEARNING PROBLEM

24-36 ROI, RI division manager's compensation, nonfinancial measures. Key information for the Peoria Division (PD) of Barrington Industries for 2000 follows.

Revenues	$15,000,000
Operating income	1,800,000
Total assets	10,000,000

PD's managers are evaluated and rewarded on the basis of ROI defined as operating income divided by total assets. Barrington Industries expects its divisions to increase ROI each year.

The year 2001 appears to be a difficult year for PD. PD had planned new investments to improve quality but, in view of poor economic conditions, has postponed the investment. ROI for 2001 was certain to decrease had PD made the investment.

Management is now considering ways to meet its target ROI of 20% for next year. It anticipates revenues to be steady at $15,000,000 in 2001.

INSTRUCTIONS

Form groups of two or more students to complete the following requirements.

1. Calculate PD's return on sales (ROS) and ROI for 2000.
    a. By how much would PD have to cut costs in 2001 to achieve its target ROI of 20% in 2001, assuming no change in total assets between 2000 and 2001?
    b. By how much would PD have to decrease total assets in 2001 to achieve its target ROI of 20% in 2001, assuming no change in operating income between 2000 and 2001?
2. Calculate PD's RI in 2000 assuming a required rate of return on investment of 15%.
3. PD wants to increase RI by 50% in 2001. Assuming it could cut costs by $45,000 in 2001, by how much would PD have to decrease total assets in 2001?
4. Barrington Industries is concerned that the focus on cost cutting and asset sales will have an adverse long-run effect on PD's customers. Yet Barrington wants PD to meet its financial goals. What other measurements, if any, do you recommend that Barrington use? Explain briefly.

APPENDIX A

CASES

CASE 1: PRICING (SMAC)

Canadian Product Corporation Limited (CPCL) is a manufacturer of small household appliances. The company has only one manufacturing facility which services all of Canada. CPCL is well established and sells its products directly to department stores.

CPCL wishes to begin manufacturing and marketing its newly developed cordless steam iron. In order to properly evaluate the performance of this new product, management has decided to create a new division for its production and distribution.

Two of CPCL's competitors have recently introduced their own brands of cordless steam irons at a price of $28 each. CPCL's usual pricing strategy for new products is full absorption cost plus a 100% markup. For the new iron, at a production and sales volume of 350,000 units per year, this strategy would imply a price of $31.50. CPCL's president, Mr. T. C. Leopard, is not sure whether this pricing strategy would be appropriate for the new iron and is considering other proposals as follows:

1. Variable product cost plus a 200% markup

2. A price of $27 to undercut the competition

Mr. Leopard hired a market research firm to study the likely demand for CPCL's cordless steam iron at the three proposed prices. The research firm conducted an extensive market test resulting in projected annual sales volumes over the next five years at these prices. These sales projections are summarized in Exhibit A1-1. The research firm, however, made it clear that there were no guarantees that the market would respond according to the projections.

Mr. Leopard was not happy with the probabilities that the market research firm assigned to the various price/volume levels. He therefore used his own knowledge and past experience to assign different probabilities (see Exhibit A1-2). Mr. Leopard then called Joan Helm, the chief financial officer, to analyze the situation and recommend a five-year pricing strategy for the new cordless steam iron. As a first step, Joan assembled some relevant data which is presented in Exhibit A1-3.

REQUIRED

As Joan Helm, comply with Mr. Leopard's request. Include in your analysis consideration of both quantitative and qualitative factors in determining a five-year pricing strategy for the new iron.

CASE 2: BIDDING (SMAC)

The sales manager of Teak Plastics Limited (Teak), Naomi Moir, was concerned about the company's record in winning bids. Teak was a small manufacturer of high-pressure injection-molded plastic parts, supplied mainly to the automotive industry. Over the past few years, Teak's success in winning large contracts had steadily declined, forcing Teak to pursue greater numbers of small contracts. This has become a serious problem; the company's total business has dropped to such an extent that it is currently operating at only 70% of capacity.

Naomi realized that there was something wrong with her method of preparing bids. In the past year, Naomi found that the rate of success in winning bids increased as the total size of the contract decreased. In her attempt to increase the total amount of sales for Teak during the past year, she had submitted almost double the number of bids compared to previous years. This resulted in two people from the accounting department spending most of their time preparing the cost data for Naomi's bids.

Teak used a standard full-cost accounting system, and bids were prepared with the objective of earning a 20% markup on total costs. Standard hourly operating rates were developed using regression analysis of monthly prior-period costs for each machine and process. These costs included all labour, job setup, and mold development costs as well as fixed and variable processing overhead costs. The job setup and mold development costs were fairly constant from job to job. The coefficients from the regression analysis were used as the rates for variable-cost items and

---

EXHIBIT A1-1
CPCL
Market Research Data for Cordless
Steam Iron

Selling Price	Volume	Probability
$24.00	500,000	20%
	400,000	50
	300,000	30
27.00	400,000	25
	350,000	45
	250,000	30
31.50	300,000	30
	250,000	50
	200,000	20

EXHIBIT A1-2
CPCL
President's Probability Data for
Cordless Steam Iron

Selling Price	Volume	Probability
$24.00	500,000	10%
	400,000	50
	300,000	40
27.00	400,000	20
	350,000	40
	250,000	40
31.50	300,000	40
	250,000	50
	200,000	10

EXHIBIT A1-3
CPCL
Other Relevant Data for Cordless Steam Iron

Expected costs based on annual production of 350,000 units:

Total variable costs $2,800,000

Total fixed overhead 2,712,500

Plant and equipment:
No additional machinery or plant space will be required to produce the cordless steam iron. The plant has capacity available to produce 500,000 units per year.

Inventory levels:
Just-in-time inventory management will result in virtually no inventory being stored at any particular time.

the intercept values were divided by full capacity processing hours to determine the rates for fixed-cost items.

At a recent business luncheon seminar, Naomi had been impressed by the speaker's model for preparing bids. This model involved using contributions, proba-bilities, and expected values. Accordingly, she decided to test the approach in preparing her next bid for a fairly small contract for instrument panel components. She started with her usual bidding method based on the cost estimate prepared by the accounting department (Exhibit A2-1), and made a mental note that she would normally have submitted a bid of $141,000. She then made her best estimates of the probabilities of winning the contract at various bids (Exhibit A2-2).

EXHIBIT A2-1

TEAK

Cost Estimates for Contract to Supply 100,000 Automobile Instrument Panel Components

	Standard Hours	Standard Rate/Hour	Cost per Unit
Processing on machine 5:			
Variable	500	$51.50	$ 2.575
Fixed	500	35.50	1.775
Total machine processing costs			4.350
Material			4.463
Finishing:			
Variable	100	23.50	0.235
Fixed	100	28.50	0.285
Total manufacturing costs before rejects			9.333
Rejects[1]			0.933
Total manufacturing costs			10.266
Selling and administration[2]			0.337
Total cost before royalty			10.603
Markup (20%)			2.121
			12.724
Royalty of 10% of sales[3]			1.414
Standard price per unit			$ 14.138
Standard bid for 10,000 units[4]			$141,380

[1]A 10% standard allowance was added for defective units which would be rejected during final inspection. This reflected a normal spoilage rate.

[2]Selling and administration costs were all treated as fixed.

[3]A royalty of 10% of sales was payable to the inventor of machine 5, a very specialized machine.

[4]This contract would utilize 2% of Teak's total capacity.

EXHIBIT A2-2

TEAK

Probability Estimates Regarding the Potential Contract to Supply 10,000 Automobile Instrument Panel Components

Bid Amount	Probability of Winning Contract
$136,000	95%
141,000	85
146,000	80
151,000	75
156,000	65

CASE 3: VARIANCE ANALYSIS (SMAC)

Harry Adams is the production manager of the Zap Co. Ltd., which produces and sells a molded product called Zap. To produce this product, three raw materials are mixed in a special blender and then poured into large molds. The proportion of raw materials required may vary depending on the quality of each material. Since testing the quality of the materials requires a lengthy procedure and the use of expensive chemicals, the production supervisor uses his judgement as to the mix of the three materials to add to a blended batch. The production supervisor's judgement has proven to be accurate 80% of the time. A single batch of blended material is enough to fill 40 molds. Each mold yields 12,000 units of Zap. After the units of Zap are removed from the molds, they are inspected for defects. The standard rejection rate for units of Zap produced is 2%.

The standard material costs and standard input quantities for a single blended batch are as follows:

Input	Standard Cost per Kilogram	Standard Amount per Blended Batch
A	$100	600 kilograms
B	5	1,600 kilograms
C	20	200 kilograms

The company carries raw material inventory at actual cost, but values work in process at standard cost.

In order to take advantage of price decreases for inputs A and C, the production supervisor substituted more of these inputs for less of input B in the most recent batch. He felt the change in mix would not affect the quality or yield of Zaps produced, since this new mix was consistent with his judgement of the quality of input materials. Actual quantities and costs of materials used in the most recent batch of blended material were as follows:

Input	Actual Quantity	Actual Cost
A	610 kilograms	$60,000
B	1,550 kilograms	8,000
C	240 kilograms	4,200

Of the units of Zap produced from this batch, 458,640 passed inspection and were sold for $0.50 each. The higher than normal rejection rate for this batch has caused Harry to be concerned about the production process.

REQUIRED

1. Assume that the change in raw material input mix caused the higher than normal rejection rate. Calculate the raw material production variances in as much detail as the data permit for the most recent batch of Zap, and evaluate the production supervisor's actions with respect to this batch.

2. Assume that the company saves $1,000 of variable costs per batch (i.e., actual variable costs are $1,000 less than standard variable costs for each batch) by changing the mix of raw material inputs from the standard proportions to those proportions used in the most recent batch. The variable cost savings occur regardless of the batch rejection rate.

   Harry does not know whether the higher than standard rejection rate was a result of the change in mix of raw materials, a malfunction in the machinery, or normal random factors. He estimates that there is only a 20% chance that it was caused by the change in mix, a 70% chance that it was caused by a malfunction in the machinery, and a 10% chance that it was caused by random factors.

   An investigation would reveal the cause of the variation with certainty and would cost $15,000. If it is found that the cause was machinery malfunction, it would cost $10,000 to stop the production process to make repairs. (The production process will be stopped after six more batches are processed in order to service, repair, and clean the machinery; this will be done regardless of any earlier stoppage of the process or machinery repair.) If an investigation is not conducted, the mix of materials will not be changed for the next six batches.

   Should the process be investigated now, or should Harry wait until six more batches are processed?

CASE 4: CAPITAL BUDGETING (SMAC)

Galaxy Science Centre (GSC) is a nonprofit organization which was founded in late 19_7 as the first science museum to serve the city of Britannia. GSC's initial construction and startup costs were provided by provincial and municipal government grants and private sector contributions. In return for its initial support, the provincial government expects GSC to operate an annual science fair that is expected to become one of the premier science fairs in the country within ten years.

GSC's board of trustees reports directly to the municipal government which provided GSC with the following mandate: (1) to educate the general public, (2) to support the science programs of local schools, (3) to provide a science resource centre for the municipality, and (4) to operate on a breakeven basis without the need for further government funding. The local university, which has been experiencing declining enrollment in its science programs, especially welcomes the opening of GSC.

The grand opening of GSC is scheduled for the fall of 19_9. Initially, GSC's services will include various scientific exhibits and educational films. The annual science fair will include a contest where science projects entered by students are to be judged and the best three exhibited at GSC. Future plans include adding a gift shop featuring souvenirs of both the science centre and the city. With the grand opening quickly approaching, the board decided to hire an independent consultant to resolve the following issues:

REQUIRED

1. Board members questioned how budgeting for operations should be applied to GSC, what performance measures are possible, and what should be considered in selecting output measures.

2. Two options are available for financing the computer and related software needed to assist in the operations of GSC—either buy or lease (see Exhibit A4-1). The board requested a complete quantitative analysis of these two options and a recommendation.

3. Given GSC's mandate, the only source of funding to cover the first year's operating expenses would be through admission charges and a one-time subsidy granted by the municipality. The board requested that data resulting from an initial market study and cost analysis (see Exhibit A4-2) be analyzed and an admission price for the first year of operations be recommended.

EXHIBIT A4-1
GSC
Computer Equipment Financing Options

Analysis had indicated that GSC should obtain a model XTZ computer and related software for its operations. This equipment has an expected useful life of five years with no estimated salvage value. The two financing options identified by the board of trustees are described below. The appropriate discount rate to evaluate these options was stipulated to be 11%.

Option One
The XTZ computer and related software could be purchased for $40,500. Since GSC has only $20,000 available for this acquisition, the balance would be financed by a five-year bank loan at an annual interest rate of 11%. Equal annual payments would be due at the end of each year.

Option Two
The XTZ computer and related software could be leased from Acme Computers Ltd. The lease agreement would be for a five-year period requiring equal payments of $10,000 at the beginning of each year.

EXHIBIT A4-2
GSC
Expected Admission Levels and Operating Cost Data

At the request of the municipality, GSC has agreed to admit senior citizens and preschool children free of charge during the first year of operations. To compensate GSC, the municipality reluctantly granted a one-time subsidy of $1,000,000 for GSC's first year of operations. GSC must find an admission price for the first year which would be sufficient to cover operating costs in excess of the subsidy. GSC would be paid full adult admission up to $6 per person by the board of education and the university for students who attend the science centre.

A market study confirmed that demand for admissions to GSC would be relatively inelastic at prices at or below $6.50 per admission. The study also produced the following probability distribution for total admissions (adults, students, senior citizens, and preschool children) for the first year of operations assuming an admission price of zero up to $6.50:

Total Number of Admissions	Probability
950,000 to 1,050,000	0.10
1,050,001 to 1,150,000	0.25
1,150,001 to 1,250,000	0.40
1,250,001 to 1,350,000	0.15
1,350,001 to 1,450,000	0.10

It was estimated that 20% of the admissions would be senior citizens and preschool children, 60% students, and 20% other adults.

Initial cost analysis at various total admission volume levels resulted in the following expected total operating costs for the first year of operations (excluding the XTZ computer and related software costs by including all science fair costs):

Total Number of Admissions	Total Operating Costs
500,000	$6,080,000
1,000,000	6,390,000
1,500,000	6,700,000

(This analysis assumes linear cost behaviour within the relevant range.)

4. Without a subsidy from the municipality after the first year, the board wondered whether it could continue admitting senior citizens and preschool children free of charge and still break even. Three options (see Exhibit A4-3) were put forward by the board for analysis.

5. A general pricing policy for items to be sold in the gift shop was needed.

GSC
Admission Pricing Policy for Second and Subsequent Years

Three admission pricing policy options were identified as follows:

1. Admit senior citizens and preschool children free of charge and promote GSC more vigorously. It was estimated, for example, that a $200,000 increase in annual promotion and advertising expenditures would generate a 10% increase in total number of admissions.
2. Charge a discounted admission price for senior citizens and preschool children.
3. Admit senior citizens and preschool children free of charge and convince the municipality to continue the subsidy.

REQUIRED

As Edyth Plum, the independent consultant hired by GSC's board of trustees, analyze the five issues and prepare a report, complete with recommendations, to GSC's board of trustees.

CASE 5: LINEAR PROGRAMMING (SMAC)

You have recently been hired as Executive Assistant to the Board of Directors of Dyna Tech Inc. The financial statements of the company for the year ended December 31, 19_6 have just been released and they are disappointing. After years of success as a "high-tech wonder company," it appears that Dyna Tech has fallen on hard times.

The Executive Committee of the Board of Directors has taken the position that the company's financial difficulties have come about largely because of two projects—the Series 3000 and Zeus. Some of the other directors are not so sure. They feel that, with some guidance from the Board, the company's management can "work things out," since they are essentially on the right track. The Board of Directors was determined to make some decisions at their March 31, 19_7 meeting. In the meantime, they would consider two outside reports on the projects (see Exhibit A5-1 and Exhibit A5-2). The Executive Assistant would also be asked to comment at that time.

The Company

Dyna Tech Inc. was launched over 20 years ago in Calgary by James Cousins, an engineer. The company began by manufacturing touch-tone telephone converters and, later, telephone switchboards and other communications switching equipment for small and medium-sized businesses. As the company grew, more communications equipment was added to round out a Private Branch Exchange (PBX) line of products directed to the same market segment. It did not take long for Dyna Tech Inc. to acquire an image as a high-technology wonder company. Sales grew from $12,000 in its first year to almost $350,000,000 ten years later. This sales success was based largely on the company's ability to supply reliable, state-of-the-art communications products to the middle portion of the market.

As the company grew in size, it expanded geographically. While the head office, including sales management personnel, remained in Calgary, production was shifted to facilities in Toronto and Montreal. Manufacturing was later undertaken in Britain, France, and the United States. Sales offices were located around the world as well.

Over the years, the most popular Dyna Tech products have been the Series 100 and Series 200 analogue solid state switches. Dyna Tech has a worldwide installed base of over 100,000 of its PBX switches, mainly in the low to medium segment of the market. (This market segment is broadly defined as one having an installed cost of $100,000 or less per unit.) Of these switches, more than half are Series 100 or Series 200 products. It has been company policy to "keep the customer happy" by supplying whatever Dyna Tech expertise and equipment might be relevant to the

EXHIBIT A5-1
DYNA TECH INC.
Executive Summary of Findings re: Zeus Project

By: I.M.A. Consultant
Principal Findings

1. My tests indicate that the Zeus MC is entirely compatible with the IBM PC for all commonly available software. All other functions of the Zeus MC performed within specification.

2. In my opinion, the Zeus MC can be produced equally well at either the Toronto or the Montreal assembly facility.

3. No additional money is available to the Zeus project, either for increased levels of R&D or for advertising.

4. The following information is related to the financial aspects of the production and sale of the Zeus MC in 19_7:

   a. The unit selling price to the dealer network should be $2,800.

   b. For internal purposes, assembly functions for the Zeus MC have been broken down into Equivalent Work Units (EWUs).

   c. 30 EWUs are needed to assemble one Zeus MC at the Montreal assembly facility. 20 EWUs are needed to assemble the same machine at the Toronto assembly facility. However, because the Toronto assembly plant is more automated, the cost of one EWU is $49.05 in Toronto while the cost of one EWU in Montreal is $8.50.

   d. Due to various constraints, a total of only 120,000 EWUs is available in the two locations combined.

   e. Target production of the Zeus MC in 19_7 is 5,000 units, 1,000 units to be produced in Montreal and 4,000 units to be produced in Toronto. It is conceivable, however, that a more desirable combination may be possible.

   f. The cost of material is $851 per unit in either facility.

   g. The Accounting Department expects to be able to recover the following costs from each Zeus MC that is sold:

Zeus MC development costs	$500
Faulty monitor correction costs	$200

   h. Overhead allocations per unit are:

Variable overhead (based on estimated EWUs)	$100
Fixed overhead (based on allocation formula)	$350

   i. Using the figures from the 19_7 production schedules, the average contribution margin per unit will be $1,113.

   j. For purposes of planning, it is the Total Contribution Margin (TCM) that should be maximized.

changing needs of the customer. This policy has been instrumental in allowing Dyna Tech to dominate its segment of the market.

Dyna Tech Inc. began as, and continues to be, a company run by engineers, for engineers. To a large extent, its success can be attributed to the technology developed in its research laboratories. In fact, spending on research and development has approached 20% of sales in recent years. Much of the current research is directed to communications networks, intelligent workstations, and generally the technology necessary to make the "office of the future" a reality.

The Founder

The entrepreneurial spirit and drive of Dyna Tech Inc. originated with its founder. James Cousins is a brilliant engineer and salesman. It was he who insisted that the latest semiconductor technology be used in all Dyna Tech products, even the most inexpensive ones, and he spearheaded the worldwide sales effort that earned the company an Export Canada award from the government. In spite of the company's difficulties, Mr. Cousins remains unshaken in his belief that remaining at the forefront of technology is the path that Dyna Tech Inc. must continue to pursue.

EXHIBIT A5-2

DYNA TECH INC.
Summary Report on Series 3000 Project

By: I. C. Yu

Three of the most important aspects to be considered in assessing the management control of a project are generally thought to be (1) time, (2) cost, and (3) quality.

This summary will consider each in turn for the Series 3000 project.

Time

Series 3000: Implementation Plan and Status Report:

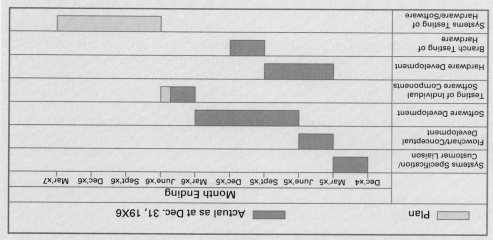

Comments:

a. Following the anticipated completion of the systems testing of hardware/software, it is now estimated that at least a further six months of preparation will be necessary before production can commence.

b. As at December 31, 19_6, the systems testing of hardware/software was exactly six months behind schedule.

c. As at December 31, 19_6, the testing of individual software components was only two-thirds complete.

d. According to the original schedule, production of the new equipment is scheduled to begin in June 19_7.

e. The Series 3000 project was first made public in June 19_5.

Cost *Table of Accumulated Direct Costs as at December 31, 19_6 (millions)*

	Budgeted	Actual	Variance f(U)
Systems Specification/Customer Liaison	$ 0.50	$ 2.10	$ (1.60)
Flowchart/Conceptual Development	2.75	4.15	(1.40)
Software Development	5.50	18.40	(12.90)
Testing of Individual Software Components (only 2/3 complete)	3.00	3.15	(0.15)
Hardware Development	6.25	5.90	0.35
Bench Testing of Hardware	3.00	3.85	(0.85)
Systems Testing of Hardware/Software	4.00	—	4.00
	$25.00	$37.55	$(12.55)

Quality

Excellence in technology does not in and of itself equal quality. Other factors such as reliability, serviceability, and availability should also be considered.

The Zeus Project

The impetus for the development of a microcomputer compatible with the IBM PC came from development work that had already been carried out by Dyna Tech Inc. In 19_4, the company introduced a telephone/computer workstation to work in conjunction with its Series 100 and 200 PBX products. It seemed only logical, therefore, to make the technology compatible with products being offered by the world's largest manufacturer of computers.

It would, the reasoning went, allow Dyna Tech into the mainstream of the office automation market more quickly. The particular attraction of this approach was that the microcomputer, code-named the Zeus, would be a Canadian product designed for world markets. After all, Dyna Tech already had a worldwide marketing network for its other products. In other words, the development, manufacture, and sale of the Zeus MC microcomputer would be immediately profitable while at the same time advance the relevant technology for expansion into the office automation market.

The Dyna Tech Zeus MC was introduced in 19_6. With its special monitor, built-in software, communications, high-tech design, and IBM compatibility, it looked like a sure winner. Almost immediately, however, buyers began reporting that the special monitor, provided by an outside supplier, malfunctioned under sustained use. True to its code of customer satisfaction above all, Dyna Tech resolved the problem, but at a cost of approximately $1,000 to repair each of the more than 2,000 units that had already been sold.

Actual sales of the Zeus MC in 19_6 were less than the sales forecast. Nevertheless, since the monitor problems have been corrected, Dyna Tech plans to manufacture and sell 5,000 Zeus computers in 19_7.

The Series 3000 Project

The Series 3000 was a personal project of James Cousins. He could see the trend toward large-scale integrated transmission and switching of voice (analogue) and computer (digital) information. He also recognized that Dyna Tech Inc. had, by choice, confined itself to the low-medium end of the market for communications products (as defined earlier). And, finally, he felt a personal thrill at the prospect of having his name associated with the development of new, state-of-the-art technology that would lead the world.

The result was an announcement, in June 19_5, that Dyna Tech Inc. had begun development of the integrated communications centre of the future. Using the latest digital technology, the Dyna Tech equipment would be at the centre of an all-encompassing information network, directing everything from telephone calls to the computer mainframe. The project was code-named Series 3000.

The proposed installations would be expensive, probably selling for approximately $1 million per installation. Only the very largest corporations and, perhaps, governments and major universities would have use for equipment of such sophistication. James Cousins saw this as an opportunity. After all, this was the very segment of the communications market in which Dyna Tech Inc. was not active. If the company was to continue its significant growth into the future, it must have products to offer in this market.

Mr. Cousins recognized that competition in this market would be more intense. Dyna Tech would have to compete not only against the major computer manufacturers but also against all of the companies that supplied equipment to the telephone utilities throughout the world. He felt, however, that inasmuch as it was Dyna Tech that had initiated the development, the company had about two years as a "window of opportunity" between the time the Series 3000 project became common knowledge and the time the other companies became serious competition. The true extent of the competitive position of Dyna Tech would, however, not be known until all of the competing products were available and actually being sold in the marketplace. The decision was made to proceed, and a development budget of $25 million, exclusive of any capital costs, was allocated to the project.

REQUIRED

Write a report for your discussion at the next board meeting, including quantitative and qualitative analyses and recommendations with respect to the two projects and the management of the company as a whole.

CASE 6: COMPENSATION PLAN (CGAC)

Riverside Mining and Manufacturing is a vertically integrated company that mines, processes, and finishes various non-precious metals and minerals. Riverside has decentralized both on a geographical and on an operational basis. For example, Exploration and Development, which includes all mining operations, has been designated a strategic business unit (SBU). There are multiple divisions within this SBU, such as North American Exploration and Development, South American Exploration and Development, and other divisions. Similarly, Refining, which has often been located near the mines, is another strategic business unit and is divisionalized by geographical region.

Riverside has a clearly stated management control system that includes long-standing policies on transfer pricing, performance evaluation, and management compensation. Transfers are made at full cost plus a markup to approximate net realizable value. Riverside's primary operating divisions (such as mining) are required to fill internal orders before servicing outside orders. Each division has full responsibility over setting prices and sales targets as well as monitoring costs. Also, divisional managers have decision-making authority over fixed investments (capital equipment) up to $0.5 million as long as the investments can be internally financed. For any investment exceeding $0.5 million, final approval must be given by the SBU and head office.

For performance evaluation purposes, Riverside uses two basic measures to evaluate managers. First, it uses budgeted income, and second, return on investment (ROI). Divisional managers develop their budgets in line with goals set centrally for the organization. All budgets must be approved by the SBU and central executive before final acceptance. Net income includes headquarters' allocations based on a percentage of divisional sales. ROI is calculated as net income divided by total assets. As with the budget target, the ROI target has to be approved. Although the weighted average cost of capital for the company is 12%, each division negotiates its target ROI according to past performance and perceived risks and uncertainty in the environment. Progress toward the budgeted income and ROI targets are evaluated on a quarterly basis.

Riverside's bonus compensation scheme was extended to its divisional managers last year. The bonus consists of a "50/50 cash plus deferred payment" scheme that is measured each quarter. For example, if a division manager exceeds budgeted income and ROI targets for the division, then the manager is awarded a bonus, 50% of which is paid immediately in cash and 50% of which is invested in "phantom shares" that can be redeemed three years hence, given continued good performance. The total value of the bonuses range from 10 to 100% of regular salary, depending on how well managers did and their level in the organization. Actual amounts of bonuses earned in any given year depend on the centrally calculated bonus pool, which is defined as a percentage of overall company income.

Some of the divisional managers have been unhappy with the bonus compensation scheme. They felt they were at a disadvantage because of their lack of control over their prices (due to the nature of the external market), and their inability to achieve the growth in the ROI required by central headquarters. The division managers believed that a shift to residual income would help, but Riverside's CEO rejected this, feeling that residual income would not allow comparison of divisional results. The results of three of these divisions are shown in Exhibit 8A-1.

As well, the managers of the Primary Operating Divisions wanted the restrictions on the internal versus external sales lifted so that they could achieve better results than they were currently experiencing.

REQUIRED

1. **a.** Calculate the residual income figure for each of the three divisions.

   b. In point form, list the advantages and disadvantages that residual income might have over the use of ROI at Riverside.

2. Evaluate the management control system currently in place at Riverside, outlining its strengths and weaknesses, and make recommendations for any changes you feel are necessary.

EXHIBIT A6-1
RIVERSIDE
Selected Divisional Results for the Most Recent Quarter (in thousands)

	Division A	Division B	Division C
Budgeted net income	$ 185	$1,964	$ 895
Actual net income	$48	$1,968	$1,020
Budgeted total assets	$1,310	$8,755	$6,978
Actual total assets	$1,109	$8,811	$6,955
Target ROI	14.12%	22.4%	12.8%
Actual ROI	13.3%	22.3%	14.7%

CASE 7: RELEVANT COST ANALYSIS (CICA)

Fence Company Ltd. (FC) was incorporated in March 19_5, and is equally owned by Robert and Morris Wood. The company constructs residential wood fences. FC's first year was a difficult one. It is now late March 19_6, and the Wood brothers are making plans to improve FC's performance. Having decided that they need outside advice, they asked you to meet with them.

At the meeting, you asked the brothers to describe their operations and to highlight their major concerns. The following paragraphs are your notes from the meeting.

◆ FC lost business last year because it could not meet its promised installation dates during the peak period. The owners consider, however, that their biggest problem last year was caused by the need to repair fences. They guarantee their work, and they had to go back and change broken boards and clean up work sites, which cost them money and did nothing for their reputation.

◆ The owners project that FC will construct 50,000 linear metres of fence this year. To achieve this target, they think that one work team will be needed during the 12 weeks of April, October, and November, and three teams during the 20 weeks from May through September. Their projection assumes an eight-hour day and a regular five-day week. Last year they found that a good work team consisting of three people could build a 100-linear-metre fence in an eight-hour day.

◆ The average labour cost including benefits last year was $5 per hour. Labour and material costs are expected to increase 10% in 19_6. Last year there was little control over the amount of wood used on projects; the owners want to change this situation.

◆ The brothers recognize that fence building is not a year-round activity and are willing to cover any cash deficiency as long as there are prospects of profitability.

◆ The owners need to take out at least $15,000 each per year. In addition, they intend to hire a full-time receptionist to start on April 1 and to employ this person year-round. They expect that the salary will be about $12,000 a year but think that the cost will be worth it to ensure continuity and maintain the company's image.

◆ A truck will have to be rented for each work team, at $500 per month. Robert Wood thinks that they should keep two of the trucks from December to March for snow removal. He and Morris could do the work and lay off everyone except the receptionist.

◆ FC will also need to rent a machine for $600 a month to dig holes. In addition, it will cost approximately $120 to move the machine from one work site to another.

◆ The company spent $8,000 on gas and maintenance and $1,200 on telephone last year. The owners expect to hold the line on these costs this year.

◆ Morris Wood estimates that their costs last year were approximately $6 per linear metre for wood and $1 for nails and stain.

◆ The standard selling price last year was $11 per linear metre. Robert Wood thinks that they should try for $13 this year. FC's salesperson complained last year because he could not discount the price. The brothers think that it might be a good idea to allow the salesperson to go down to $12 if forced to do so in order not to lose the sale. They are considering offering a special in April—perhaps 4% off—to get things rolling. They may also offer a 10% discount on group orders for fences for four or more houses. This discount offer worked well last year.

◆ According to the owners, a good incentive for their salesperson is crucial to increased sales. Last year, they paid the salesperson 5% of gross revenue for a basic one-house order for a fence of about 100 linear metres. For a two- or three-house order, they paid 6%, and for a four-house order, which is about 400 linear metres, they paid 8%. They believe that the incentive was responsible for the fact that FC had a lot of two-house orders last year.

◆ Starting in April, FC will pay $2,500 a month to rent a warehouse for storing wood and equipment for the year. The landlord wants a security deposit of one month's rent. The company also has to buy new tools that cost at least $3,000, since the work teams either stole or broke all the tools used last year.

REQUIRED

Draft a report to the Wood brothers that presents your analysis of the issues and your recommendations.

CASE 8: REGRESSION ANALYSIS (CGAC)

Berengar Ltd. is a small manufacturing company that produces a variety of products using a number of different processes in different-sized job lots. For example, some products will be ordered in lots of 10 or less, while others are produced in batches of up to 1,000 units.

Berengar will modify products as required by customer order and, thus, there is little product standardization. Despite the high level of product differentiation, Berengar has, up until now, used a single factorywide overhead rate based upon direct labour-hours. The company president, J. P. Blomer, believes that this oversimplified way of applying overhead has led to the loss of several contracts for long production runs (that is, large job lots) of two of Berengar's most popular products.

Blomer has consulted with the operations staff in the machining department to see whether they have any suggestions for alternative overhead bases (other than direct labour-hours for their department). Because of the recent addition of five numerically controlled machines, the supervisor of scheduling has noticed that direct labour-hours in the department have declined considerably. The chief production engineer for machining believes that, with the new machine environment, production overhead probably varies more with machine-hours per batch and setup time than it does with the current overhead application base, direct labour-hours.

Blomer asked the controller to run four regressions to assist in predicting overhead cost in the machining department. The four regressions were based on:

1. Direct labour-hours
2. Machine-hours
3. Setup hours
4. Machine-hours and setup hours

One problem that the controller had to deal with was that approximately 35% of departmental overhead consisted of various lump sum monthly charges for central services such as personnel and power. The controller decided that these charges were justifiably an expense of running the machining department and left them in for the regression analyses.

Berengar Ltd.
Machine Department
Data for Regression Analysis
(most recent 24 weeks)

	Overhead Cost	Direct Labour-Hours	Machine-Hours	Set-up Hours
Week 1	$72,892	2,036	379	98
2	76,451	2,125	385	101
3	75,930	2,012	378	110
4	78,591	1,900	390	112
5	77,870	1,934	401	108
6	75,420	2,095	376	110
7	73,529	1,966	365	95
8	78,210	1,924	387	103
9	85,620	1,865	464	130
10	84,322	1,912	451	110
11	89,621	1,901	496	125
12	79,739	1,864	401	101
13	81,221	1,850	425	95
14	85,130	1,812	456	102
17	87,870	1,718	485	135
18	90,565	1,741	502	129
19	89,032	1,622	491	142
20	87,979	1,639	487	110
21	86,646	1,641	479	124
22	90,772	1,628	516	99
23	85,542	1,598	472	125
24	90,159	1,597	508	160

The results of the regressions (using the most recent 24 weeks of data) are given in Exhibit A11-1.

REQUIRED

1. From the results of the regression output of overhead cost with machine-hours and setup hours (Exhibit A11-1, regression 4), identify the following:
   a) The independent variables
   b) The marginal cost of an additional setup hour
   c) The regression equation
2. Using the information provided in Exhibit A11-1, evaluate the results of the regressions, using the coefficient of determination (R^2).

Regression 1

Regression output: overhead cost with direct labour-hours:

Constant		135479.2
Std. err. of Y est.		3523.623
R^2		0.642200
No. of observations		24
Degrees of freedom		22
X coefficient(s)	–28.8174	
Std. err. of coeff.	4.585940	
t-statistic	–6.28387	

Regression 2

Regression output: overhead cost with machine-hours:

Constant		33310.56
Std. err. of Y est.		1010.593

R^2		0.970568
No. of observations		24
Degrees of freedom		22
X coefficient(s)	112.6582	
Std. err. of coeff.	4.182588	
t-statistic	26.93505	

Regression 3

Regression output: overhead cost with setup hours:

Constant		56802.56
Std. err. of Y est.		4524.324
R^2		0.410114
No. of observations		24
Degrees of freedom		22
X coefficient(s)	226.8502	
Std. err. of coeff.	58.00416	
t-statistic	3.910930	

Regression 4

Regression output: overhead cost with machine-hours and setup hours:

Constant		33060.920	
Std. err. of Y est.		1025.838	
R^2		0.971052	
No. of observations		24	
Degrees of freedom		21	
X coefficient		110.6029	10.06200
Std. err. of coeff.	machine hours }	5.482857	16.98414 { setup hours
t-statistic		20.17249	0.592435

APPENDIX B

NOTES ON COMPOUND INTEREST AND INTEREST TABLES

Interest is the cost of using money. It is the rental charge for funds, just as renting a building and equipment entails a rental charge. When the funds are used for a period of time, it is necessary to recognize interest as a cost of using the borrowed ("rented") funds. This requirement applies even if the funds represent ownership capital and if interest does not entail an outlay of cash. Why must interest be considered? Because the selection of one alternative automatically commits a given amount of funds that could otherwise be invested in some other alternative.

Interest is generally important, even when short-term projects are under consideration. Interest looms correspondingly larger when long-run plans are studied. The rate of interest has significant enough impact to influence decisions regarding borrowing and investing funds. For example, $100,000 invested now and compounded annually for 10 years at 8% will accumulate to $215,900; at 20%, the $100,000 will accumulate to $619,200.

INTEREST TABLES

Many computer programs and pocket calculators are available that handle computations involving the time value of money. You may also turn to the following four basic tables to compute interest.

Table 1—Future Amount of $1

Table 1 shows how much $1 invested now will accumulate in a given number of periods at a given compounded interest rate per period. Consider investing $1,000 now for three years at 8% compound interest. A tabular presentation of how this $1,000 would accumulate to $1,259.70 follows:

Year	Interest per Year	Cumulative Interest Called Compound Interest	Total at End of Year
0	$ —	$ —	$1,000.00
1	80.00	80.00	1,080.00
2	86.40	166.40	1,166.40
3	93.30	259.70	1,259.70

This tabular presentation is a series of computations that could appear as follows:

$$S_1 = \$1,000(1.08)^1$$
$$S_2 = \$1,000(1.08)^2$$
$$S_3 = \$1,000(1.08)^3$$

The formula for the "amount of 1," often called the "future value of $1" or "future amount of $1," can be written

$$S = P(1 + r)^n$$
$$S = \$1,000(1 + .08)^3 = \$1,259.70$$

S is the future value amount; P is the present value, $1,000 in this case; r is the rate of interest; and n is the number of time periods.

Fortunately, tables make key computations readily available. A facility in selecting the *proper* table will minimize computations. Check the accuracy of the preceding answer using Table 1.

Table 2—Present Value of $1

In the previous example, if $1,000 compounded at 8% per year will accumulate to $1,259.70 in 3 years, then $1,000 must be the present value of $1,259.70 due at the end of 3 years. The formula for the present value can be derived by reversing the process of *accumulation* (finding the future amount) that we just finished.

$$S = P(1 + r)^n$$

If
$$P = \frac{S}{(1 + r)^n}$$

then
$$P = \frac{\$1,259.70}{(1.08)^3} = \$1,000$$

Use Table 2 to check this calculation.

When accumulating, we advance or roll forward in time. The difference between our original amount and our accumulated amount is called *compound interest*. When discounting, we retreat or roll back in time. The difference between the future amount and the present value is called *compound discount*. Note the following formulas (where $P = \$1,000$):

$$\text{Compound interest} = P[(1 + r)^n - 1] = \$259.70$$

$$\text{Compound discount} = S\left[1 - \frac{1}{(1 + r)^n}\right] = \$259.70$$

Table 3—Amount of Annuity of $1

An (ordinary) *annuity* is a series of equal payments (receipts) to be paid (or received) at the *end* of successive periods of equal length. Assume that $1,000 is invested at the end of each of 3 years at 8%:

```
0        1        2        3
|_____|_____|_____|
```

End of Year	Amount
1st payment	$1,000.00 → $1,080.00 → $1,166.40, which is $1,000(1.08)^2$
2nd payment	$1,000.00 → 1,080.00, which is $1,000(1.08)^1$
3rd payment	1,000.00
Accumulation (future amount)	$3,246.40

The preceding arithmetic may be expressed algebraically as the amount of an ordinary annuity of $1,000 for 3 years = $1,000(1 + r)^2 + $1,000(1 + r)^1 + $1,000.

We can develop the general formula for S_n, the amount of an ordinary annuity of $1, by using the example above as a basis:

1. $S_n = 1 + (1 + r)^1 + (1 + r)^2$

2. Substitute: $S_n = 1 + (1.08)^1 + (1.08)^2$

3. Multiply (2) by (1 + r): $(1.08)S_n = (1.08)^1 + (1.08)^2 + (1.08)^3$

4. Subtract (2) from (3): $1.08 S_n - S_n = (1.08)^3 - 1$
   Note that all terms on the right-hand side are removed except $(1.08)^3$ in equation (3) and 1 in equation (2).

5. Factor (4): $S_n(1.08 - 1) = (1.08)^3 - 1$

6. Divide (5) by (1.08 − 1): $S_n = \dfrac{(1.08)^3 - 1}{1.08 - 1} = \dfrac{(1.08)^3 - 1}{.08}$

7. The general formula for the amount of an ordinary annuity of $1 becomes: $S_n = \dfrac{(1 + r)^n - 1}{r}$ or $\dfrac{\text{Compound interest}}{\text{Rate}}$

This formula is the basis for Table 3. Look at Table 3 or use the formula itself to check the calculations.

Table 4—Present Value of an Ordinary Annuity of $1

Using the same example as for Table 3, we can show how the formula of P_n, *the present value of an ordinary annuity*, is developed.

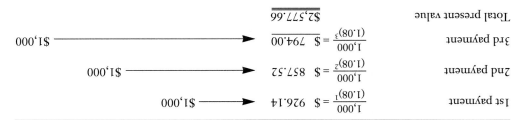

0	1	2	3

End of Year

1st payment $= \$ 926.14 \quad \dfrac{1,000}{(1.08)^1}$ $\$1,000$

2nd payment $= \$ 857.52 \quad \dfrac{1,000}{(1.08)^2}$ $\$1,000$

3rd payment $= \$ 794.00 \quad \dfrac{1,000}{(1.08)^3}$ $\$1,000$

Total present value $\overline{\$2,577.66}$

For the general case, the present value of an ordinary annuity of $1 may be expressed:

1. $P_n = \dfrac{1}{} + \dfrac{1}{} + \dfrac{1}{}$

2. Substitute: $P_n = \dfrac{1}{1.08} + \dfrac{1}{(1.08)^2} + \dfrac{1}{(1.08)^3}$

3. Multiply by $\dfrac{1}{1.08}$: $P_n = \dfrac{1}{(1.08)^2} + \dfrac{1}{(1.08)^3} + \dfrac{1}{(1.08)^4}$

4. Subtract (3) from (2): $P_n - \dfrac{1}{1.08}P_n = \dfrac{1}{1.08} - \dfrac{1}{(1.08)^4}$

5. Factor: $P_n\left(1 - \dfrac{1}{(1.08)}\right) = \dfrac{1}{1.08}\left[1 - \dfrac{1}{(1.08)^3}\right]$

6. or $P_n\left(\dfrac{.08}{1.08}\right) = \dfrac{1}{1.08}\left[1 - \dfrac{1}{(1.08)^3}\right]$

7. Multiple by $\frac{1.08}{.08}$:
$$P_n = \frac{1}{.08}\left[1 - \frac{1}{(1.08)^3}\right]$$

The general formula for the present value of an annuity of $1.00 is:

$$P_n = \frac{1}{r}\left[1 - \frac{1}{(1+r)^n}\right] = \frac{\text{Compound discount}}{\text{Rate}}$$

Solving,

$$P_n = \frac{.2062}{.08} = 2.577$$

The formula is the basis for Table 4. Check the answer in the table. The present value tables, Tables 2 and 4, are used most frequently in capital budgeting.

The tables for annuities are not essential. With Tables 1 and 2, compound interest and compound discount can readily be computed. It is simply a matter of dividing either of these by the rate to get values equivalent to those shown in Tables 3 and 4.

TABLE 1
Compound Amount of $1.00 (The Future Value of $1.00)

$S = P(1 + r)^n$. In this table $P = \$1.00$

Periods	2%	4%	6%	8%	10%	12%	14%	16%	18%	20%	22%	24%	26%	28%	30%	32%	40%	Periods
1	1.020	1.040	1.060	1.080	1.100	1.120	1.140	1.160	1.180	1.200	1.220	1.240	1.260	1.280	1.300	1.320	1.400	1
2	1.040	1.082	1.124	1.166	1.210	1.254	1.300	1.346	1.392	1.440	1.488	1.538	1.588	1.638	1.690	1.742	1.960	2
3	1.061	1.125	1.191	1.260	1.331	1.405	1.482	1.561	1.643	1.728	1.816	1.907	2.000	2.097	2.197	2.300	2.744	3
4	1.082	1.170	1.262	1.360	1.464	1.574	1.689	1.811	1.939	2.074	2.215	2.364	2.520	2.684	2.856	3.036	3.842	4
5	1.104	1.217	1.338	1.469	1.611	1.762	1.925	2.100	2.288	2.488	2.703	2.932	3.176	3.436	3.713	4.007	5.378	5
6	1.126	1.265	1.419	1.587	1.772	1.974	2.195	2.436	2.700	2.986	3.297	3.635	4.002	4.398	4.827	5.290	7.530	6
7	1.149	1.316	1.504	1.714	1.949	2.211	2.502	2.826	3.185	3.583	4.023	4.508	5.042	5.629	6.275	6.983	10.541	7
8	1.172	1.369	1.594	1.851	2.144	2.476	2.853	3.278	3.759	4.300	4.908	5.590	6.353	7.206	8.157	9.217	14.758	8
9	1.195	1.423	1.689	1.999	2.358	2.773	3.252	3.803	4.435	5.160	5.987	6.931	8.005	9.223	10.604	12.166	20.661	9
10	1.219	1.480	1.791	2.159	2.594	3.106	3.707	4.411	5.234	6.192	7.305	8.594	10.086	11.806	13.786	16.060	28.925	10
11	1.243	1.539	1.898	2.332	2.853	3.479	4.226	5.117	6.176	7.430	8.912	10.657	12.708	15.112	17.922	21.199	40.496	11
12	1.268	1.601	2.012	2.518	3.138	3.896	4.818	5.936	7.288	8.916	10.872	13.215	16.012	19.343	23.298	27.983	56.694	12
13	1.294	1.665	2.133	2.720	3.452	4.363	5.492	6.886	8.599	10.699	13.264	16.386	20.175	24.759	30.288	36.937	79.371	13
14	1.319	1.732	2.261	2.937	3.797	4.887	6.261	7.988	10.147	12.839	16.182	20.319	25.421	31.691	39.374	48.757	111.120	14
15	1.346	1.801	2.397	3.172	4.177	5.474	7.138	9.266	11.974	15.407	19.742	25.196	32.030	40.565	51.186	64.359	155.568	15
16	1.373	1.873	2.540	3.426	4.595	6.130	8.137	10.748	14.129	18.488	24.086	31.243	40.358	51.923	66.542	84.954	217.795	16
17	1.400	1.948	2.693	3.700	5.054	6.866	9.276	12.468	16.672	22.186	29.384	38.741	50.851	66.461	86.504	112.139	304.913	17
18	1.428	2.026	2.854	3.996	5.560	7.690	10.575	14.463	19.673	26.623	35.849	48.039	64.072	85.071	112.455	148.024	426.879	18
19	1.457	2.107	3.026	4.316	6.116	8.613	12.056	16.777	23.214	31.948	43.736	59.568	80.731	108.890	146.192	195.391	597.630	19
20	1.486	2.191	3.207	4.661	6.727	9.646	13.743	19.461	27.393	38.338	53.358	73.864	101.721	139.380	190.050	257.916	836.683	20
21	1.516	2.279	3.400	5.034	7.400	10.804	15.668	22.574	32.324	46.005	65.096	91.592	128.169	178.406	247.065	340.449	1171.356	21
22	1.546	2.370	3.604	5.437	8.140	12.100	17.861	26.186	38.142	55.206	79.418	113.574	161.492	228.360	321.184	449.393	1639.898	22
23	1.577	2.465	3.820	5.871	8.954	13.552	20.362	30.376	45.008	66.247	96.889	140.831	203.480	292.300	417.539	593.199	2295.857	23
24	1.608	2.563	4.049	6.341	9.850	15.179	23.212	35.236	53.109	79.497	118.205	174.631	256.385	374.144	542.801	783.023	3214.200	24
25	1.641	2.666	4.292	6.848	10.835	17.000	26.462	40.874	62.669	95.396	144.210	216.542	323.045	478.905	705.641	1033.590	4499.880	25
26	1.673	2.772	4.549	7.396	11.918	19.040	30.167	47.414	73.949	114.475	175.936	268.512	407.037	612.998	917.333	1364.339	6299.831	26
27	1.707	2.883	4.822	7.988	13.110	21.325	34.390	55.000	87.260	137.371	214.642	332.955	512.867	784.638	1192.533	1800.927	8819.764	27
28	1.741	2.999	5.112	8.627	14.421	23.884	39.204	63.800	102.967	164.845	261.864	412.864	646.212	1004.336	1550.293	2377.224	12347.670	28
29	1.776	3.119	5.418	9.317	15.863	26.750	44.693	74.009	121.501	197.814	319.474	511.952	814.228	1285.550	2015.381	3137.935	17286.737	29
30	1.811	3.243	5.743	10.063	17.449	29.960	50.950	85.850	143.371	237.376	389.758	634.820	1025.927	1645.505	2619.996	4142.075	24201.432	30
35	2.000	3.946	7.686	14.785	28.102	52.800	98.100	180.314	327.997	590.668	1053.402	1861.054	3258.135	5653.911	9727.860	16599.217	130161.112	35
40	2.208	4.801	10.286	21.725	45.259	93.051	188.884	378.721	750.378	1469.772	2847.038	5455.913	10347.175	19426.689	36118.865	66520.767	70037.697	40

TABLE 2 (*Place a clip on this page for easy reference.*)
Present Value of $1.00.

$$P = \frac{S}{(1+r)^n} \text{. In this table } S = \$1.00.$$

Periods	2%	4%	6%	8%	10%	12%	14%	16%	18%	20%	22%	24%	26%	28%	30%	32%	40%	Periods
1	0.980	0.962	0.943	0.926	0.909	0.893	0.877	0.862	0.847	0.833	0.820	0.806	0.794	0.781	0.769	0.758	0.714	1
2	0.961	0.925	0.890	0.857	0.826	0.797	0.769	0.743	0.718	0.694	0.672	0.650	0.630	0.610	0.592	0.574	0.510	2
3	0.942	0.889	0.840	0.794	0.751	0.712	0.675	0.641	0.609	0.579	0.551	0.524	0.500	0.477	0.455	0.435	0.364	3
4	0.924	0.855	0.792	0.735	0.683	0.636	0.592	0.552	0.516	0.482	0.451	0.423	0.397	0.373	0.350	0.329	0.260	4
5	0.906	0.822	0.747	0.681	0.621	0.567	0.519	0.476	0.437	0.402	0.370	0.341	0.315	0.291	0.269	0.250	0.186	5
6	0.888	0.790	0.705	0.630	0.564	0.507	0.456	0.410	0.370	0.335	0.303	0.275	0.250	0.227	0.207	0.189	0.133	6
7	0.871	0.760	0.665	0.583	0.513	0.452	0.400	0.354	0.314	0.279	0.249	0.222	0.198	0.178	0.159	0.143	0.095	7
8	0.853	0.731	0.627	0.540	0.467	0.404	0.351	0.305	0.266	0.233	0.204	0.179	0.157	0.139	0.123	0.108	0.068	8
9	0.837	0.703	0.592	0.500	0.424	0.361	0.308	0.263	0.225	0.194	0.167	0.144	0.125	0.108	0.094	0.082	0.048	9
10	0.820	0.676	0.558	0.463	0.386	0.322	0.270	0.227	0.191	0.162	0.137	0.116	0.099	0.085	0.073	0.062	0.035	10
11	0.804	0.650	0.527	0.429	0.350	0.287	0.237	0.195	0.162	0.135	0.112	0.094	0.079	0.066	0.056	0.047	0.025	11
12	0.788	0.625	0.497	0.397	0.319	0.257	0.208	0.168	0.137	0.112	0.092	0.076	0.062	0.052	0.043	0.036	0.018	12
13	0.773	0.601	0.469	0.368	0.290	0.229	0.182	0.145	0.116	0.093	0.075	0.061	0.050	0.040	0.033	0.027	0.013	13
14	0.758	0.577	0.442	0.340	0.263	0.205	0.160	0.125	0.099	0.078	0.062	0.049	0.039	0.032	0.025	0.021	0.009	14
15	0.743	0.555	0.417	0.315	0.239	0.183	0.140	0.108	0.084	0.065	0.051	0.040	0.031	0.025	0.020	0.016	0.006	15
16	0.728	0.534	0.394	0.292	0.218	0.163	0.123	0.093	0.071	0.054	0.042	0.032	0.025	0.019	0.015	0.012	0.005	16
17	0.714	0.513	0.371	0.270	0.198	0.146	0.108	0.080	0.060	0.045	0.034	0.026	0.020	0.015	0.012	0.009	0.003	17
18	0.700	0.494	0.350	0.250	0.180	0.130	0.095	0.069	0.051	0.038	0.028	0.021	0.016	0.012	0.009	0.007	0.002	18
19	0.686	0.475	0.331	0.232	0.164	0.116	0.083	0.060	0.043	0.031	0.023	0.017	0.012	0.009	0.007	0.005	0.002	19
20	0.673	0.456	0.312	0.215	0.149	0.104	0.073	0.051	0.037	0.026	0.019	0.014	0.010	0.007	0.005	0.004	0.001	20
21	0.660	0.439	0.294	0.199	0.135	0.093	0.064	0.044	0.031	0.022	0.015	0.011	0.008	0.006	0.004	0.003	0.001	21
22	0.647	0.422	0.278	0.184	0.123	0.083	0.056	0.038	0.026	0.018	0.013	0.009	0.006	0.004	0.003	0.002	0.001	22
23	0.634	0.406	0.262	0.170	0.112	0.074	0.049	0.033	0.022	0.015	0.010	0.007	0.005	0.003	0.002	0.002	0.000	23
24	0.622	0.390	0.247	0.158	0.102	0.066	0.043	0.028	0.019	0.013	0.008	0.006	0.004	0.003	0.002	0.001	0.000	24
25	0.610	0.375	0.233	0.146	0.092	0.059	0.038	0.024	0.016	0.010	0.007	0.005	0.003	0.002	0.001	0.001	0.000	25
26	0.598	0.361	0.220	0.135	0.084	0.053	0.033	0.021	0.014	0.009	0.006	0.004	0.002	0.002	0.001	0.001	0.000	26
27	0.586	0.347	0.207	0.125	0.076	0.047	0.029	0.018	0.011	0.007	0.005	0.003	0.002	0.001	0.001	0.001	0.000	27
28	0.574	0.333	0.196	0.116	0.069	0.042	0.026	0.016	0.010	0.006	0.004	0.002	0.002	0.001	0.001	0.000	0.000	28
29	0.563	0.321	0.185	0.107	0.063	0.037	0.022	0.014	0.008	0.005	0.003	0.002	0.001	0.001	0.000	0.000	0.000	29
30	0.552	0.308	0.174	0.099	0.057	0.033	0.020	0.012	0.007	0.004	0.003	0.002	0.001	0.001	0.000	0.000	0.000	30
35	0.500	0.253	0.130	0.068	0.036	0.019	0.010	0.006	0.003	0.002	0.001	0.001	0.000	0.000	0.000	0.000	0.000	35
40	0.453	0.208	0.097	0.046	0.022	0.011	0.005	0.003	0.001	0.001	0.000	0.000	0.000	0.000	0.000	0.000	0.000	40

TABLE 3

Compound Amount of Annuity of $1.00 in Arrears* (Future Value of Annuity)

$$S_n = \frac{(1+r)^n - 1}{r}$$

Periods	2%	4%	6%	8%	10%	12%	14%	16%	18%	20%	22%	24%	26%	28%	30%	32%	40%	Periods
1	1.000	1.000	1.000	1.000	1.000	1.000	1.000	1.000	1.000	1.000	1.000	1.000	1.000	1.000	1.000	1.000	1.000	1
2	2.020	2.040	2.060	2.080	2.100	2.120	2.140	2.160	2.180	2.200	2.220	2.240	2.260	2.280	2.300	2.320	2.400	2
3	3.060	3.122	3.184	3.246	3.310	3.374	3.440	3.506	3.572	3.640	3.708	3.778	3.848	3.918	3.990	4.062	4.360	3
4	4.122	4.246	4.375	4.506	4.641	4.779	4.921	5.066	5.215	5.368	5.524	5.684	5.848	6.016	6.187	6.362	7.104	4
5	5.204	5.416	5.637	5.867	6.105	6.353	6.610	6.877	7.154	7.442	7.740	8.048	8.368	8.700	9.043	9.398	10.946	5
6	6.308	6.633	6.975	7.336	7.716	8.115	8.536	8.977	9.442	9.930	10.442	10.980	11.544	12.136	12.756	13.406	16.324	6
7	7.434	7.898	8.394	8.923	9.487	10.089	10.730	11.414	12.142	12.916	13.740	14.615	15.546	16.534	17.583	18.696	23.853	7
8	8.583	9.214	9.897	10.637	11.436	12.300	13.233	14.240	15.327	16.499	17.762	19.123	20.588	22.163	23.858	25.678	34.395	8
9	9.755	10.583	11.491	12.488	13.579	14.776	16.085	17.519	19.086	20.799	22.670	24.712	26.940	29.369	32.015	34.895	49.153	9
10	10.950	12.006	13.181	14.487	15.937	17.549	19.337	21.321	23.521	25.959	28.657	31.643	34.945	38.593	42.619	47.062	69.814	10
11	12.169	13.486	14.972	16.645	18.531	20.655	23.045	25.733	28.755	32.150	35.962	40.238	45.031	50.398	56.405	63.122	98.739	11
12	13.412	15.026	16.870	18.977	21.384	24.133	27.271	30.850	34.931	39.581	44.874	50.895	57.739	65.510	74.327	84.320	139.235	12
13	14.680	16.627	18.882	21.495	24.523	28.029	32.089	36.786	42.219	48.497	55.746	64.110	73.751	84.853	97.625	112.303	195.929	13
14	15.974	18.292	21.015	24.215	27.975	32.393	37.581	43.672	50.818	59.196	69.010	80.496	93.926	109.612	127.913	149.240	275.300	14
15	17.293	20.024	23.276	27.152	31.772	37.280	43.842	51.660	60.965	72.035	85.192	100.815	119.347	141.303	167.286	197.997	386.420	15
16	18.639	21.825	25.673	30.324	35.950	42.753	50.980	60.925	72.939	87.442	104.935	126.011	151.377	181.868	218.472	262.356	541.988	16
17	20.012	23.698	28.213	33.750	40.545	48.884	59.118	71.673	87.068	105.931	129.020	157.253	191.735	233.791	285.014	347.309	759.784	17
18	21.412	25.645	30.906	37.450	45.599	55.750	68.394	84.141	103.740	128.117	158.405	195.994	242.585	300.252	371.518	459.449	1064.697	18
19	22.841	27.671	33.760	41.446	51.159	63.440	78.969	98.603	123.414	154.740	194.254	244.033	306.658	385.323	483.973	607.472	1491.576	19
20	24.297	29.778	36.786	45.762	57.275	72.052	91.025	115.380	146.628	186.688	237.989	303.601	387.389	494.213	630.165	802.863	2089.206	20
21	25.783	31.969	39.993	50.423	64.002	81.699	104.768	134.841	174.021	225.026	291.347	377.465	489.110	633.593	820.215	1060.779	2925.889	21
22	27.299	34.248	43.392	55.457	71.403	92.503	120.436	157.415	206.345	271.031	356.443	469.056	617.278	811.999	1067.280	1401.229	4097.245	22
23	28.845	36.618	46.996	60.893	79.543	104.603	138.297	183.601	244.487	326.237	435.861	582.630	778.771	1040.358	1388.464	1850.622	5737.142	23
24	30.422	39.083	50.816	66.765	88.497	118.155	158.659	213.978	289.494	392.484	532.750	723.461	982.251	1332.659	1806.003	2443.821	8032.999	24
25	32.030	41.646	54.865	73.106	98.347	133.334	181.871	249.214	342.603	471.981	650.955	898.092	1238.636	1706.803	2348.803	3226.844	11247.199	25
26	33.671	44.312	59.156	79.954	109.182	150.334	208.333	290.088	405.272	567.377	795.165	1114.634	1561.682	2185.708	3054.444	4260.434	15747.079	26
27	35.344	47.084	63.706	87.351	121.100	169.374	238.499	337.502	479.221	681.853	971.102	1383.146	1968.719	2798.706	3971.778	5624.772	22046.910	27
28	37.051	49.968	68.528	95.339	134.210	190.699	272.889	392.503	566.481	819.223	1185.744	1716.101	2481.586	3583.344	5164.311	7425.699	30866.674	28
29	38.792	52.966	73.640	103.966	148.631	214.583	312.094	456.303	669.447	984.068	1447.608	2128.965	3127.798	4587.680	6714.604	9802.923	43214.343	29
30	40.568	56.085	79.058	113.263	164.494	241.333	356.787	530.312	790.948	1181.882	1767.081	2640.916	3942.026	5873.231	8729.985	12940.859	60501.081	30
35	49.994	73.652	111.435	172.317	271.024	431.663	693.573	1120.713	1816.652	2948.341	4783.645	7750.225	12527.442	20188.966	32422.868	51869.427	325400.279	35
40	60.402	95.026	154.762	259.057	442.593	767.091	1342.025	2360.757	4163.213	7343.858	12936.535	22728.803	39792.982	69377.460	120392.883	207874.272	1750091.741	40

*Payments (or receipts) at the end of each period.

TABLE 4 (Place a clip on this page for easy reference.)
Present Value of Annuity $1.00 in Arrears*.

$$P_n = \frac{1}{r}\left[1 - \frac{1}{(1+r)^n}\right]$$

Periods	2%	4%	6%	8%	10%	12%	14%	16%	18%	20%	22%	24%	26%	28%	30%	32%	40%	Periods
1	0.980	0.962	0.943	0.926	0.909	0.893	0.877	0.862	0.847	0.833	0.820	0.806	0.794	0.781	0.769	0.758	0.714	1
2	1.942	1.886	1.833	1.783	1.736	1.690	1.647	1.605	1.566	1.528	1.492	1.457	1.424	1.392	1.361	1.331	1.224	2
3	2.884	2.775	2.673	2.577	2.487	2.402	2.322	2.246	2.174	2.106	2.042	1.981	1.923	1.868	1.816	1.766	1.589	3
4	3.808	3.630	3.465	3.312	3.170	3.037	2.914	2.798	2.690	2.589	2.494	2.404	2.320	2.241	2.166	2.096	1.849	4
5	4.713	4.452	4.212	3.993	3.791	3.605	3.433	3.274	3.127	2.991	2.864	2.745	2.635	2.532	2.436	2.345	2.035	5
6	5.601	5.242	4.917	4.623	4.355	4.111	3.889	3.685	3.498	3.326	3.167	3.020	2.885	2.759	2.643	2.534	2.168	6
7	6.472	6.002	5.582	5.206	4.868	4.564	4.288	4.039	3.812	3.605	3.416	3.242	3.083	2.937	2.802	2.677	2.263	7
8	7.325	6.733	6.210	5.747	5.335	4.968	4.639	4.344	4.078	3.837	3.619	3.421	3.241	3.076	2.925	2.786	2.331	8
9	8.162	7.435	6.802	6.247	5.759	5.328	4.946	4.607	4.303	4.031	3.786	3.566	3.366	3.184	3.019	2.868	2.379	9
10	8.983	8.111	7.360	6.710	6.145	5.650	5.216	4.833	4.494	4.192	3.923	3.682	3.465	3.269	3.092	2.930	2.414	10
11	9.787	8.760	7.887	7.139	6.495	5.938	5.453	5.029	4.656	4.327	4.035	3.776	3.543	3.335	3.147	2.978	2.438	11
12	10.575	9.385	8.384	7.536	6.814	6.194	5.660	5.197	4.793	4.439	4.127	3.851	3.606	3.387	3.190	3.013	2.456	12
13	11.348	9.986	8.853	7.904	7.103	6.424	5.842	5.342	4.910	4.533	4.203	3.912	3.656	3.427	3.223	3.040	2.469	13
14	12.106	10.563	9.295	8.244	7.367	6.628	6.002	5.468	5.008	4.611	4.265	3.962	3.695	3.459	3.249	3.061	2.478	14
15	12.849	11.118	9.712	8.559	7.606	6.811	6.142	5.575	5.092	4.675	4.315	4.001	3.726	3.483	3.268	3.076	2.484	15
16	13.578	11.652	10.106	8.851	7.824	6.974	6.265	5.668	5.162	4.730	4.357	4.033	3.751	3.503	3.283	3.088	2.489	16
17	14.292	12.166	10.477	9.122	8.022	7.120	6.373	5.749	5.222	4.775	4.391	4.059	3.771	3.518	3.295	3.097	2.492	17
18	14.992	12.659	10.828	9.372	8.201	7.250	6.467	5.818	5.273	4.812	4.419	4.080	3.786	3.529	3.304	3.104	2.494	18
19	15.678	13.134	11.158	9.604	8.365	7.366	6.550	5.877	5.316	4.843	4.442	4.097	3.799	3.539	3.311	3.109	2.496	19
20	16.351	13.590	11.470	9.818	8.514	7.469	6.623	5.929	5.353	4.870	4.460	4.110	3.808	3.546	3.316	3.113	2.497	20
21	17.011	14.029	11.764	10.017	8.649	7.562	6.687	5.973	5.384	4.891	4.476	4.121	3.816	3.551	3.320	3.116	2.498	21
22	17.658	14.451	12.042	10.201	8.772	7.645	6.743	6.011	5.410	4.909	4.488	4.130	3.822	3.556	3.323	3.118	2.498	22
23	18.292	14.857	12.303	10.371	8.883	7.718	6.792	6.044	5.432	4.925	4.499	4.137	3.827	3.559	3.325	3.120	2.499	23
24	18.914	15.247	12.550	10.529	8.985	7.784	6.835	6.073	5.451	4.937	4.507	4.143	3.831	3.562	3.327	3.121	2.499	24
25	19.523	15.622	12.783	10.675	9.077	7.843	6.873	6.097	5.467	4.948	4.514	4.147	3.834	3.564	3.329	3.122	2.499	25
26	20.121	15.983	13.003	10.810	9.161	7.896	6.906	6.118	5.480	4.956	4.520	4.151	3.837	3.566	3.330	3.123	2.500	26
27	20.707	16.330	13.211	10.935	9.237	7.943	6.935	6.136	5.492	4.964	4.524	4.154	3.839	3.567	3.331	3.123	2.500	27
28	21.281	16.663	13.406	11.051	9.307	7.984	6.961	6.152	5.502	4.970	4.528	4.157	3.840	3.568	3.331	3.124	2.500	28
29	21.844	16.984	13.591	11.158	9.370	8.022	6.983	6.166	5.510	4.975	4.531	4.159	3.841	3.569	3.332	3.124	2.500	29
30	22.396	17.292	13.765	11.258	9.427	8.055	7.003	6.177	5.517	4.979	4.534	4.160	3.842	3.569	3.332	3.124	2.500	30
35	24.999	18.665	14.498	11.655	9.644	8.176	7.070	6.215	5.539	4.992	4.541	4.164	3.845	3.571	3.333	3.125	2.500	35
40	27.355	19.793	15.046	11.925	9.779	8.244	7.105	6.233	5.548	4.997	4.544	4.166	3.846	3.571	3.333	3.125	2.500	40

*Payments (or receipts) at the end of each period.

APPENDIX C

COST ACCOUNTING IN PROFESSIONAL EXAMINATIONS

This appendix describes the role of cost accounting in professional examinations. We use professional examinations in the United States, Canada, Australia, Japan, and the United Kingdom to illustrate the role.[1] A conscientious reader who has solved a representative sample of the problems at the end of the chapters will be well prepared for the professional examination questions dealing with cost accounting. This appendix aims to provide perspective, install confidence, and encourage readers to take the examinations.

CANADIAN PROFESSIONAL EXAMINATIONS

Three professional accounting designations are available in Canada:

Designation	Sponsoring Organization
Certified Management Accountant (CMA)	Society of Management Accountants (SMA)
Certified General Accountant (CGA)	Certified General Accountants' Association (CGA)
Chartered Accountant (CA)	Canadian Institute of Chartered Accountants (CICA)

The SMA represents over 27,000 certified management accountants employed throughout Canadian business, industry, and government.

The CMA Entrance Examination is a two-day examination, divided into three broad categories:

1. Management accounting area   50%–60%
2. Financial accounting area   20%–30%
3. Management studies   15%–25%

Objective questions comprise 40% to 50% and cases 50% to 60% of the exam. Topics covered on recent examinations in the management accounting area include relevant costing, transfer pricing, capital budgeting, performance measures, activity-based costing, cost allocation, and productivity.

The Society of Management Accountants publishes CMA: *The Management Accounting Magazine* monthly. This magazine includes details of courses that assist students in preparing for the CMA examination.

[1] We appreciate help from Bill Langdon (Canada), Tom Craven (United States), John Goodwin (Australia), Michi Sakurai (Japan), and Louise Drysdale and Andrea Jeffries (U.K.).

CPA and CMA Designations

Many American readers may eventually take the Certified Public Accountant (CPA) examination or the Certified Management Accountant (CMA) examination. Certification is important to professional accountants for many reasons, such as:

1. Recognition of achievement and technical competence by fellow accountants and by users of accounting services
2. Increased self-confidence in one's professional abilities
3. Membership in professional organizations offering programs of career-long education
4. Enhancement of career opportunities
5. Personal satisfaction

The CPA certificate is issued by individual states; it is necessary for obtaining a state's licence to practise as a Certified Public Accountant. A prominent feature of public accounting is the use of independent (external) auditors to give assurance about the reliability of the financial statements supplied by managers. These auditors are called Certified Public Accountants in the United States and Chartered Accountants in many other English-speaking nations. The major U.S. professional association in the private sector that regulates the quality of external auditing is the American Institute of Certified Public Accountants (AICPA).

The CMA designation is offered by the Institute of Management Accountants (IMA). The IMA is the largest association of management accountants in the world.[2] The major objective of the CMA certification is to enhance the development of the management accounting profession. In particular, focus is placed on the modern role of the management accountant as an active contributor to and a participant in management. The CMA designation is gaining increased stature in the business community as a credential parallel to the CPA designation.

The CMA examination consists of 4 parts taken during 2 days (16 hours):

◆ **Part 1:** Economics, finance, and management
◆ **Part 2:** Financial accounting and reporting
◆ **Part 3:** Management reporting, analysis, and behavioral issues
◆ **Part 4:** Decision analysis and information systems

Questions regarding ethical issues will appear on any part of the examination. A person who has successfully completed the U.S. CPA examination is exempt from Part 2.

Cost/management accounting questions are prominent in the CMA examination. The CPA examination also includes such questions, although they are less extensive than questions regarding financial accounting, auditing, and business law. On the average, cost/managerial accounting represents 35% to 40% of the CMA examination and 5% of the CPA examination. This book includes many questions and problems used in past CMA and CPA examinations. In addition, a supplement to this book, *Student Guide and Review Manual* [John K. Harris and Dudley W. Curry (Englewood Cliffs, NJ: Prentice Hall, 1997)], contains over one hundred CMA and CPA questions and explanatory answers. Careful study of appropriate topics in this book will give candidates sufficient background for succeeding in the cost accounting portions of the professional examinations.

The IMA publishes *Management Accounting* monthly. Each issue includes advertisements for courses that help students prepare for the CMA examination.[3]

[2] The IMA has a wide range of activities driven by many committees. For example, the Management Accounting Practices Committee issues statements on both financial accounting and management accounting. The IMA also has an extensive continuing-education program.

[3] Other U.S. professional associations also require detailed knowledge of cost accounting. For example, the Certified Cost Estimator/Analyst (CCEA) program is administered by the Society of Cost Estimating and Analysis, 101 South Whiting Street, Suite 313, Alexandria, VA 22304. The society's primary purpose is to improve the effectiveness of cost estimation and price analysis. Special attention is given to contract cost estimation.

AUSTRALIAN PROFESSIONAL EXAMINATIONS

The Australian Society of Certified Practising Accountants is the largest body representing accountants in Australia. Their professional designation is termed a CPA (Certified Practising Accountant). The basic entry requirements for Associate membership of the Society are having an approved Bachelors degree. Associates of the Society can advance to CPA status by passing the CPA program and having the required amount of relevant work experience. There are two compulsory core segments in the program. Core I covers the practical application of the more common accounting standards and ethics, while more technical standards (such as foreign currency translation) are covered in the Core II segment. Candidates are then required to take three segments from seven elective subjects. These subjects are: (1) external reporting, (2) insolvency and reconstruction, (3) management accounting, (4) management of information systems, (5) auditing, (6) treasury, and (7) taxation. Personal Financial Planning and Superannuation is a new elective subject which will soon be added to the electives.

The management accounting segment topics include:

1. Management accounting in the contemporary business environment
2. Accounting for strategic management
3. Long-term project planning and management
4. Costing for decision making
5. Performance measurement and reward systems

The Australian Accountant, published each month (except January), includes advertisements for courses that help students prepare for the CPA examination.

The Institute of Chartered Accountants in Australia (ICAA) has membership requirements that include passing four core modules (Taxation, Accounting I, Accounting II, and Ethics) and one elective module (one of which is Advanced Management Accounting). Management related topics are in both the Accounting 2 and Advanced Management Accounting modules. These include:

◆ purpose and perspective (including strategic and operational management; organizations, goals, ethics; operational environments; cost concepts);
◆ strategic management accounting (including strategic applications, project evaluation and capital budgeting);
◆ operational management accounting (including decision analysis, financial planning and management, product and service costing, control and performance evaluation).

JAPANESE PROFESSIONAL EXAMINATIONS

There are two major management accounting organizations—Japanese Industrial Management and Accounting Association and Enterprise Management Association. The JIMAA is the oldest, largest, and most authoritative accounting organization of its kind in Japan. It directs a School of Cost Control and a School of Corporate Tax Accounting. There are two courses in the School of Cost Control—Preparatory Course and Cost Control Course. These courses are taught by university professors and executives from member corporations. The Enterprise Management Association is the Japanese chapter of the U.S.-based Institute of Management Accountants.

UNITED KINGDOM PROFESSIONAL EXAMINATIONS

The Chartered Institute of Management Accountants (CIMA) is the largest professional management accounting body in the United Kingdom. CIMA provides a wide range of services to members in commerce, education, government, and the accounting profession.

The syllabus for the CIMA examination consists of four stages:

1. Preparation for business and accounting (including "foundation costing")
2. The tools of management accounting (including "operational cost accounting")
3. The rules of a profession (including "management accounting applications")
4. The application of knowledge to business management and finance (including "strategic management accounting," and "management accounting control systems")

Management Accounting, published monthly by CIMA, includes details of courses assisting students in preparing for their examinations.

Management accounting topics are also covered by several other professional bodies. The syllabus for the examinations of the Chartered Association of Certified Accountants (ACCA) has three stages: I (Foundation), II (Certificate), and III (Professional). Skills examined in III include information for control and decision making, management and strategy, and financial strategy. Other accounting bodies include the Institute of Chartered Accountants in England and Wales (ICAEW) and the Institute for Chartered Accountants of Scotland (ICAS). Both institutes have requirements that cover proficiency in "general management" topics as well as professional accounting topics.

NAME INDEX

The names of the companies for which weblinks are provided are printed in boldface, as well as the page number on which the weblink appears.

SUBJECT INDEX

The page on which the key term is defined is printed in boldface.

Composite product unit, 562

Computer-based financial planning models, 191-92

Computer-integrated manufacturing (CIM) technology, 630, 740-41

Conference method, 326

Conformance quality, 657-58

Constant, 322

Constant gross margin percentage NRV method, 531

Constant variance, 346-48

Constraining factor, highest contribution margin per unit of, 382

Constraint, 392

Continuous improvement, 299
    budgeted costs, 234-35

Contracts, and classification of costs, 30, 45

Contribution income statement, 64

Contribution margin, 63-64
    manufacturing sector, 77
    merchandising sector, 76-77
    per unit, 63
    percentage, 64, 77
    ratio, 64
    total, 391

Control, 5-6
    management systems, 794-95
    and technology, 121-22

Control charts, 660-61

Controllability, 196

Controllable cost, 196

Controller, 9

Conversion costs, 43, 592

Coordination, 181, 195

COQ
    See Cost of quality

Cost, 28

Cost accounting, 2

Cost accumulation, 28

Cost allocation, 29
    budgeted cost rates versus cost rates, 496
    for common costs, 503-5
    company practice, 489
    and contracts, 505
    cost pools, 492-94
    cost-benefit, 490
    costing systems, 490-92
    criteria for, 488-90
    direct allocation method, 499
    dual-rate method, 494-96
    incremental method, 504-5
    indirect cost pools, 492-94
    interdepartments, 494-97
    joint costs, 524-39
    purposes, 487-88

single rate method, 494-96
    of spoilage, 638
    stand-alone method, 503
    step-down method, 499-500
    of support department, 497-505

Cost allocation bases, 101, 142, 143, 145-46
    budgeted and actual, 496-97

Cost assignment, 28, 29

Cost behaviour
    direct/indirect, variable/fixed costs, 33-34
    unit costs, 34-36
    variable costs and fixed costs, 31-33

Cost-benefit approach, 7

Cost of capital, 729

Cost centre, 195, 798

Cost drivers, 30, 321-33
    estimation of, 324-25
    evaluation and choice of, 324-25, 332-33
    hierarchy of, 144-46
    multiple, 77-78
    relevant range, 33
    single driver, 321

Cost effect of growth, 463-64

Cost effect of price recovery, 464

Cost estimation, 323, 327-32
    account analysis method, 326-27
    activity-based costing, 334
    approaches, 325-27
    cause-and-effect criterion, 324-25
    conference method, 326
    high-low method, 328-30
    industrial engineering method, 325-26
    quantitative analyses, 327-32
    regression analysis method, 330-32

Cost functions, 321-24
    assumptions, 321-22
    estimation, 327-32
    linear, 321-23
    nonlinear, 333-39
    regression output and, 348
    variations in total costs, 321-22

Cost of goods sold
    budget, 189
    journal entries, 115

Cost hierarchies, 144-46
    multiple regression and, 348-50

Cost incurrence, 423-25

Cost leadership, 454, 467

Cost management, 3, 31

Cost object, 28, 29, 100, 323

Cost pools, 101
    homogeneous, 493-94
    indirect, 142, 492-94

multiple, 494

Cost prediction, 323, 338-39

Cost of quality (COQ), 658-60
    reports, 660, 664-66

Cost reduction decisions, 151

Cost smoothing, 138

Cost tracing, 29, 142

Cost-based transfer prices, 799, 803-5
    full, 802-5
    prorated, 805

Cost-benefit approach, 490

Cost-plus approach, 421, 427-29

Cost-plus target rate of return on investment, 427

Cost-volume-profit (CVP)
    alternative cost structures, 72-73
    assumptions, 62-63
    breakeven point, 64-68
    contribution margin, 63-64
    cost planning and, 72-73
    income taxes, 68-70
    in planning and decision making, 70-71
    revenue mix on income, effect of, 73-75
    in service and nonprofit organizations, 75-76
    time horizon, effect of, 73
    and uncertainty, 71-72

Costing systems, 28, 139-40
    activity-based, 142, 142-54
    building blocks of, 100-1
    comparison of, 150-51
    cost allocation, 490-92
    in manufacturing industry, 109-16
    refined, 142
    single indirect-cost pool, 140-42
    See also Activity-based costing (ABC) systems

Costs, costing, customer, 567

Costs classifications
    by companies, 42, 324
    contracts and, 30, 45
    direct and indirect costs, 29-30
    fringe benefits, 44-43
    labour costs, 43
    manufacturing, 41-42

Costs, costing
    absorption, 39
    activity-based, 142, 152-54
    allowable cost, 505
    appraisal, 658
    artificial, 501
    backflush, 706-14
    batch unit-level, 145-46
    broad average, 138-39
    business function, 374

PHOTO CREDITS

Page 1, Tony Stone Images/Walter Hodges; Page 10, Cummins Enginge Company Inc.; Page 17, Courtesy of Motorola's Semiconductor Products Sector; Page 27, Tony Stone Images/Andy Sacks; Page 42, The Stock Market/Stephen A. Hellerstein; Page 61, ©Flip Chalfant; Page 65, Canapress/AP Photo/Donald Stampfli; Page 74, www.emeryworld.com; Page 99, Courtesy of Papertech; Page 111, Colorscope; Page 137, Copyright General Motors Corp., used with permission; Page 145, Courtesy Oetiker Limited; Page 178, Tony Stone Images/Charles Thatcher; Page 184, Bob Carroll; Page 220, Courtesy Bayer AG, Leverkusen, Germany; Page 235, Courtesy Parker-Hannifin Corporation. Compumotor Division. Photo by Kelley McMannis; Page 257, Courtesy Tomkins, PLC London; Page 272, Indonesia Information Service; Page 288, Matrix/Louis Psihoyos; Page 299, Arriscraft International; Page 320, Courtesy Regal Marine Industries Inc.; Page 334 Courtesy Caterpillar Inc.; Page 368, Superstock; Page 378, Volkswagen AG Hannover; Page 380 Courtesy SHL Systemhouse; Page 414, Gamma Liaison/Lincoln Potter; Page 423 Carrier Corporation; Page 452, Courtesy of Motorola's Semiconductor Products Sector; Page 467, Courtesy Chrysler Corporation; Page 486, Courtesy Pfizer Inc.; Page 491, Courtesy Volkswagen Canada; Page 523, Tony Stone Images/Keith Wood; Page 533, Ontario Ministry of Agriculture & Food; Page 553, Courtesy The Watt Group, Toronto, Canada; Page 559, PhotoDisc; Page 574, Courtesy Hewlett-Packard Company; Page 591, Used by permission of Dean Foods Company; Page 610, Courtesy Coors Ceramics Company; Page 629, Courtesy Motorola; Page 643, Courtesy Dupont Corporation; Page 655, Xerox Corporation ; Page 657, Dell Computer Corporation; Page 665, Courtesy Crysel/CYDSA, Mexico; Page 674, Uniphoto/John Deere; Page 690, Courtesy Challenger Motor Freight; Page 699, PORSCHE and BOXSTER are registered trademarks of Dr. Ing. h.c.F. Porsche AG. The PORSCHE R 911 photograph is used with permission of Porsche Cars North America, Inc.; Page 725, Barrett & Mackay Photo; Page 742, Courtesy Ontario Hydro Corporate Archives, Neg. #004:15748; Page 759, Canadian Space Agency; Page 775, Courtesy Consumers Power Company; Page 793, Superstock; Page 799, Courtesy Northern Telecom; Page 810, Gamma Liaison/Saola; Page 824, Superstock; Page 831, Tony Stone Images/Daniel Bosler; Page 842 Bob Carroll